INVESTIGATIVE CRIMINAL PROCEDURE
A LAW & ORDER CASEBOOK

■ ■ ■

by

Kenneth D. Agran

AMERICAN CASEBOOK SERIES®

WEST
ACADEMIC
PUBLISHING

*For my grandparents—Joe and Lena Friedman and Rube
and Selma Agran—who instilled in our family
the importance of justice*

and

*for my parents—Larry and Phyllis Agran—
who spent a lifetime fighting for it*

and

*for my wife and two terrific kids—Kerrie, Morgan, and Ben—
whose love and support make everything possible.*

PREFACE

Welcome to *Investigative Criminal Procedure*, a comprehensive, multimedia examination of . . . (you've probably guessed it by now) . . . Investigative Criminal Procedure! This casebook—the first in a planned series of *Law & Order* casebooks—includes over 200 U.S. Supreme Court opinions, "black box" explanations of all the key rules and doctrines, links to additional resources and materials available on the Web, a companion website with even more supplementary materials, and 12 complete episodes of *Law & Order* that vividly depict many of the important issues in Investigative Criminal Procedure.

As you might imagine, this book may be a little different from the others you've encountered in your studies, so I wanted to take this opportunity to explain its origins and how to use it, and to invite any comments, questions, or suggestions you might have.

How All of This Started

In 1990, I was a junior at Dartmouth College, majoring in History and Government, with only vague notions of what I might do after graduation. One evening, shortly after the fall term began, I made my way to my dorm's "rec room," turned on the TV, and caught the premiere of *Law & Order*. I tuned in again the next week and the next. In less than a month, I was completely hooked. I couldn't get enough of the "ripped from the headlines" mysteries, explained and resolved in an engaging and satisfying way in just an hour.

What I most enjoyed about the show was its simple but innovative formula. In the first part of each episode, the police investigated a crime, and in the second part, district attorneys prosecuted the offender. Although the police and the prosecutors regularly worked together, their relationship was often filled with tension. In the heat of the moment, the police sometimes cut corners or made mistakes—they might threaten a suspect, or perform a search without a warrant, or begin an interrogation without the benefit of an appropriate *Miranda* warning. These mistakes resulted in the loss of valuable evidence, creating problems for the prosecutors. Conversely, sometimes the prosecutors made poor arguments, bad strategic choices, or failed to adequately defend police tactics, creating additional work and complications for the police.

While *Law & Order* looked superficially like a "cop show," it was actually far more ambitious, providing a glimpse into *all* facets of the criminal justice system, while also managing to tackle, in a thoughtful and entertaining way, many of the "hot button" legal, social, and political controversies that we've confronted as a nation over the past quarter-century—race and gender discrimination, gun control, abortion, hate speech, assisted suicide, drug abuse, domestic violence, terrorism, illegal immigration, gay marriage, and countless others. You name it, and trust me, there's a *Law & Order* episode that addresses it.

With a growing interest in the law—no doubt kindled, in part, by *Law & Order*—I entered Harvard Law School in 1992. The workload was difficult and demanding, but I always made a point of setting aside some time to take in the weekly episodes of my favorite show. I remember watching one night as several of the cases and concepts I was studying in my first-year Criminal Law & Procedure class were depicted in an episode. It began happening with increasing frequency—and with other courses too—almost as if the *Law & Order* writers were working their way through law school along with me. So many of the legal concepts, principles, and rules that were opaque on the dry pages of my textbooks became crystal clear when they were creatively and *accurately* "brought to life" in episodes of *Law & Order*. I found that the show dramatically deepened and enhanced my understanding of the law, and of the role of police, lawyers, and judges in the criminal justice system. Although none of my law school professors ever assigned it, *Law & Order* became an essential component of my legal education.

In January 1994, during my second year of law school, I enrolled in an intensive three-week course in Evidence Law, taught by Professor Charles Nesson. I knew I was in for something a little different when, shortly after the first class began, Professor Nesson picked up a remote control, pushed a button, and images of Los Angeles Police Department officers brutally beating Rodney King flashed across a giant screen in front of the room. When the video ended, Professor Nesson announced that he had recently begun to experiment with computers, and he expected these devices to revolutionize the practice of law. "Very soon," he said, "I believe we will see a new form of legal brief—a multimedia presentation—containing legal arguments, still pictures, and audio and video clips all brought together in a single computer program. I would be derelict in my duties to you if my teaching ignores these technological advances that are already changing the practice of law."

Professor Nesson proceeded to explain that the class of 160 students would be divided into 20 groups, each with eight students, and that each group would be given a Macintosh computer. We would use the computers to test-run a program produced by "Court TV" dealing with the Rodney King beating and the trial of the responsible LAPD officers in California state court. Later, at the end of the course, each group would use its computer to produce its own multimedia presentation dealing with various facets of Evidence Law.

Over next three weeks, Professor Nesson filled each class with dozens of PowerPoint slides quoting the rules of evidence, favorite expressions, random thoughts, and even math concepts. (At one point, he wrote "$e^{\pi i} = -1$" on the blackboard and asked us to admire the beauty of this mathematical equation.) Professor Nesson also played numerous videos throughout the course, including segments from actual trials, documentaries, movies, and television shows, and even some skits from *Saturday Night Live*. Soft music was often playing in the background of each class—hits from Simon & Garfunkel, The Beatles, The Doors, Janis Joplin, Elvis Presley, The Grateful Dead, and many others—even when Professor Nesson was lecturing or students were engaged in discussion. At one point, Professor Nesson put on some weird techno-funk music, then performed his own dance routine in front of the class. He also played a long audiotape of himself delivering a bizarre stream-of-consciousness monologue, weaving together a story about a sailing trip with his wife interspersed with his thoughts about some of the resistance he felt toward his new teaching methods.

Admittedly, I still don't understand the significance of everything Professor Nesson did or said in that course ($e^{\pi i} = -1$ . . . huh?), but to this day, it remains the best and most engaging educational experience I've ever had. It showed me just how good a law school course—or any course—could be with some additional thought, creativity, and effort on the part of the instructor, and with heightened interest and engagement from the students.

Flash forward five years, to 1999. I've been hired to design and teach an Investigative Criminal Procedure course for undergraduates at the University of California, Irvine. Like any first-time teacher, I'm trying to figure out how to convey the complexities of the subject in an interesting, engaging, and memorable way. I remembered Professor Nesson's course and how much I enjoyed it. It occurred to me that just as Professor Nesson had "brought to life" many of the arcane and difficult concepts in Evidence Law, I could do the same with Investigative Criminal Procedure by incorporating in-class exercises and demonstrations, pictures and PowerPoint slides, clips from movies and television shows, and references to current events and popular culture. As I sought out movies and television programs illustrating the important concepts in Investigative Criminal Procedure, I was immediately drawn to *Law & Order*—still my favorite show—that, week after week, did a terrific job depicting police investigative techniques (at their best and worst), along with the legal ramifications.

In 1999, *Law & Order* was already a syndicated global phenomenon, with old episodes running seemingly around-the-clock. With my trusted VCR, I tape-recorded about 60 episodes over a period of several weeks. (I know I must sound like a dinosaur talking reverently about my VCR, but back in the *last century*, DVD players couldn't record, there was no Netflix, no streaming video, no DVRs, no YouTube, and the DVD collections of *Law & Order* were still years away from being released.) From those 60 taped episodes, I found about a dozen favorites that effectively—and accurately—illustrated the most important concepts and doctrines in Investigative Criminal Procedure.

When the time came to actually teach the course, I organized the leading U.S. Supreme Court cases on Investigative Criminal Procedure and some interesting articles from newspapers and journals and assigned it all as reading; I designed several classroom exercises and demonstrations to engage students and provoke classroom discussion; I armed myself with some corny jokes and anecdotes in an effort to inject a little humor into each class; and whenever possible, I showed a *Law & Order* segment that illustrated the cases and doctrines we were covering in class. That original course, alliteratively titled "Cops, Criminals & the Constitution," was a huge hit, provoking intense interest among students, even motivating some who were pursuing degrees in business, engineering, and the sciences to shift gears and attend law school. The course remained a popular draw as I continued to teach it year after year, at both the undergraduate and law school level.

This book is the logical evolution of that original course. I don't know if it will be quite as "far out" as Professor Nesson's 1994 Evidence Law course (I've omitted math equations, and only my wife and kids are permitted to watch my own techno-funk dance routines), but I can promise it will provide a thorough, engaging, and yes—even entertaining—examination of Investigative Criminal Procedure.

A Few Words About My Editing of the Cases

All of the U.S. Supreme Court cases presented in this book have been edited so that students can focus on what I believe to be the most important facts and arguments. Most of the cases are what I refer to as "long form"—shortened versions of the actual Supreme Court opinions, ranging in length from about five to ten pages. But some of the cases— particularly those that are less significant, or that merely emphasize a point considered more fully in another case—are what I refer to as "short form," consisting of just a page or so of my own summary of the basic facts coupled with some brief quotes from the Court's holding. The names of the "long form" cases are all in bold, while the names of the "short form" cases are not in bold so that you can distinguish between the two.

In editing all of the "long form" and "short form" cases, my principal objective was to make them easy to read and follow without sacrificing accuracy. While I've generally maintained the Supreme Court's original words, there are many places where I've omitted large amounts of material, or altered the punctuation, the capitalization, the use of quotation marks, and the system of citations to make this book more "user-friendly." Because I find ellipses distracting, I generally avoid using them to indicate deleted material. I've omitted a lot of the Supreme Court's citations to prior precedents or scholarly works, except where it may be particularly important or useful to know the source. In eliminating most citations, I've also usually removed the quotation marks around the cited material. I've also left out most of the footnotes in the Supreme Court's opinions. When I have left in the footnotes, however, I've retained the original number used by the Court, which is why there may be several footnotes with the same number in any given Chapter. Footnotes that are my own—as opposed to the Supreme Court's—are denoted with letters, rather than numbers. Material that I've added for purposes of clarity is generally indicated by brackets, but in some cases I've omitted the brackets for very minor additions or changes.

The cases presented in this book are good representations of what the Supreme Court actually said. But none of the edited cases in this book presents the material exactly as it appears in the Supreme Court's official opinions. If you need the full official version of a Supreme Court opinion, or are just curious to know how it differs from the edited version in this book, feel free to look it up!

A New Innovation—Black Box Law

When I was in college and law school using casebooks similar to this one, I was always looking for the "black-letter law"—a concise statement of the well-established legal rules governing a particular issue. Later, as an undergraduate instructor and law professor myself, my students also wanted to know the black-letter law so that they could apply the basic rules to the real and hypothetical situations addressed in the classroom and on their exams.

What I've found during my three years as a law student and many more as a teacher is that most legal casebooks don't present the black-letter law in a concise and easy-to-find format. Often it's buried deep in a lengthy excerpt from a case, where the casebook author hopes students and professors will manage to discover it. In some casebooks, the author does make an attempt to more clearly set forth the black-letter law, but it is often stuck in the middle of an essay or wedged into a series of discussion questions.

I've never cared for the term "black-letter law," especially since its meaning is anything but clear. (Haven't almost all laws been written in black letters since the invention of the printing press?) In this book, I've coined a new term for the black-letter law, and, I think, a better way of presenting it. At the end of each heading or sub-heading in every one of the book's 13 Chapters, you'll find a black box containing a summary of the basic legal rules derived from the cases in that section. I hope you'll agree that this modest innovation is helpful in locating and mastering the many discrete rules at the heart of Investigative Criminal Procedure. If it is helpful—and if the students and professors who use and enjoy this book pass along some kind words—perhaps a concise and easily located statement of the "black box law" will become a standard feature in legal casebooks of the future.

More Resources on the Website

Over the years, I've developed an archive of supplemental materials to assist students in understanding the "big picture" and the finer details of Investigative Criminal Procedure. Included in this archive are numerous handouts, sample problems (often with sample answers!), diagrams, and charts of my own creation, along with newspaper clippings, scholarly articles, videos, and the addresses of websites loaded with useful and interesting information. I've integrated some of these supplemental materials into the book itself, but others can be found on a companion website, www.agrancrimpro.com.

When the Supreme Court releases new opinions in the field of Investigative Criminal Procedure, I'll try to post them to the website as soon as possible. And as I come across other interesting materials and create additional content of my own, I plan to post those items too. My hope is that with the casebook, the *Law & Order* episodes, the materials on the website, and, of course, everything you learn in class, you'll have all that you need to understand and appreciate Investigative Criminal Procedure.

Thanks . . . and Please Keep in Touch

This book required a lot of creativity, hard work, and perseverance—not just from me, but from everyone involved. So, before I start naming (and possibly forgetting) any names, let me just issue an all-inclusive "THANKS!" to everyone who contributed, particularly those at NBC Universal, Wolf Films, and West Academic who quickly and enthusiastically embraced this project.

Most of all, thank you—the reader—for your interest in this book and its subject matter. I welcome your questions, comments, and suggestions. Feel free to contact me through the casebook's companion website, www.agrancrimpro.com. I'll try to answer promptly!

KEN AGRAN

May 2015

SUMMARY OF CONTENTS

PART IV. POLICE IDENTIFICATION PROCEDURES

TABLE OF CONTENTS

———————

PART III. LIMITS ON POLICE INTERROGATION AND THE PRIVILEGE AGAINST SELF-INCRIMINATION

PART IV. POLICE IDENTIFICATION PROCEDURES

TABLE OF CASES

The principal cases are in bold type.

INVESTIGATIVE CRIMINAL PROCEDURE

A LAW & ORDER CASEBOOK

PART I

INTRODUCTION

■ ■ ■

These first two Chapters are designed to serve as a brief introduction. Chapter 1 defines a few terms and presents some useful and amusing concepts that will help to focus your studies and frame your understanding of the different arguments and perspectives in Investigative Criminal Procedure. Chapter 2 then introduces some of the constitutional provisions and doctrines relevant to Investigative Criminal Procedure, including the exclusionary rule, the basic remedy for constitutional violations.

CHAPTER 1

USEFUL AND AMUSING
INTRODUCTORY CONCEPTS

■ ■ ■

Welcome to *Investigative Criminal Procedure*, the first in a planned series of *Law & Order* casebooks. If you're a really careful reader, you'll realize that this is actually the second time I've welcomed you to the book. I also welcomed you in the Preface, which you should read now—if you haven't done so already—to learn a little more about the inspiration for this book and how to use it.

This Chapter "gets down to business": It defines some terms and introduces a number of concepts that I've found are helpful to students as they begin to study Investigative Criminal Procedure.

A. WHAT IS CRIMINAL PROCEDURE?

Criminal Procedure encompasses the rules governing the investigation and prosecution of criminal cases. Most of the rules are derived from various provisions of the United States Constitution and from U.S. Supreme Court decisions interpreting those provisions.

There are actually two major branches of Criminal Procedure. Investigative Criminal Procedure—the subject of this book—covers the rules regulating police as they investigate crimes and pursue suspects. In particular, Investigative Criminal Procedure includes the constitutional rules governing search and seizure under the Fourth Amendment; the limitations on police questioning and interrogation under the Fifth Amendment, the Sixth Amendment, and the Due Process Clause of the Fourteenth Amendment; and the doctrines regulating police identification procedures under the Sixth Amendment and the Due Process Clause of the Fourteenth Amendment.

The other branch, Adjudicative Criminal Procedure, examines the rules protecting the rights of a defendant once an investigation is "handed off" by the police to the prosecutor, who—if there is sufficient evidence to pursue it—shepherds the case through the courts and the criminal justice system. Among the topics covered in Adjudicative Criminal Procedure are the Fifth Amendment's prohibition on "double jeopardy"; the defendant's rights under the Sixth Amendment to a speedy public trial before an impartial jury, and with effective assistance of counsel; the Eighth Amendment's prohibitions on excessive bail, excessive fines, and cruel and unusual punishments; and other subjects such as prosecutorial discretion, plea bargaining, and the rules governing the discovery and sharing of evidence between prosecutors and defense attorneys.

Naturally, there is some overlap between the Investigative and Adjudicative components of Criminal Procedure, as events that occur at the investigative stage have a tremendous impact upon a case as it moves into the adjudicative phase. For example, if the police conduct an illegal search in violation of the Fourth Amendment's guarantee against "unreasonable searches and seizures," evidence uncovered as a result of the search may be excluded from a subsequent criminal trial, making the prosecutor's job more difficult. Virtually every episode of *Law & Order* does a superb job of illustrating precisely these kinds of problems, along with the conflicts and tensions that arise when mistakes are made at one stage of a criminal case (whether investigative or adjudicative), with significant consequences for the other. That's why watching episodes of *Law & Order* is actually a terrific (and fun!) way to learn about Criminal Procedure.

B. THE NECKER CUBE

Second reminder: If you haven't yet read the Preface to this book, please take a few minutes to do so now, because in addition to the general idea of a multimedia course, I've borrowed something else from Professor Nesson. In that very first Evidence Law class back in 1994, after a few remarks about the syllabus and his office hours, Professor Nesson put this picture up on the screen:

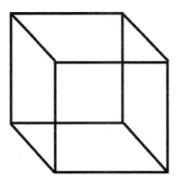

"This is a Necker Cube," Professor Nesson announced. "Stare at it for a few moments and notice how you can't see both orientations at the same time. How you see it depends on how you look at it. The meaning you fasten to something is a function of what you bring to it—context." Whatever he said next was a blur. I was still staring at the Necker Cube, trying to find the second orientation. (If you're interested in learning more about Louis Necker and his famous cube, Google it—but only after you've finished your homework!)

When I started teaching, I began using the Necker Cube diagram at the beginning of my own courses. In fact, I think I've used it in *every* course I've *ever* taught. I use the Necker Cube to illustrate a point somewhat different from Professor Nesson's. There are, in fact, two different ways of viewing the cube. In my experience, most people see the square on the lower right as the front face of the cube, with the rest of the cube extending upward and back toward the left. But by altering your focus, you should be able to see a second orientation, where the square on the upper left is the front of the cube, and the rest of the cube extends slightly downward and to the right.

Take a few moments and see if you can spot the two orientations of the Necker Cube. (Waiting . . . waiting . . . waiting . . . hurry up, the "Final Jeopardy" music is winding down! Waiting . . . waiting . . . done!)

Were you able to see both orientations? If you're unable to see both, you should probably drop this course and enroll in something less abstract—I'm afraid you're just not cut out for Investigative Criminal Procedure. (Ha ha—just kidding!)

In all seriousness, the Necker Cube does illustrate an important point about Investigative Criminal Procedure or any other topic you might choose to study. In order to fully understand and apply what you learn, you have to be able to examine the relevant issues and problems from a variety of different perspectives. How would a police officer or a prosecutor view a particular situation? How would a criminal suspect or a defense attorney view that same scenario? And how might a judge, whose thoughts and reasoning are obviously shaped by his or her own values, experiences, and political ideologies, view the issue?

As I pointed out in the Preface, throughout this book I'll try to summarize the key points and rules in nifty little black boxes. So here's the first:

The Necker Cube Principle

To be good at Investigative Criminal Procedure, like virtually anything else, you must be willing to consider and argue the issues from a variety of different perspectives.

C. GOOD COP/BAD COP

As you may know from scores of movies and television programs—including *Law & Order*—the term "good cop/bad cop" refers to a police interrogation technique. One police officer, the "bad cop," adopts an aggressive, accusatory, and threatening tone with the suspect. This sets the stage for a second police officer, the "good cop," to adopt a more sympathetic posture, appearing supportive and understanding, perhaps even offering to protect the suspect from the bad cop. In some cases, the psychological pressure leads the suspect to confess. (We'll read some actual cases that illustrate this interrogation technique and a number of variants.)

The Good Cop/Bad Cop dichotomy is also a useful framework for discussing and understanding Investigative Criminal Procedure. As you might imagine, people have a range of views about the police, often depending upon their own experiences in dealing with police officers. Many have a distinct Good Cop view of the police. They see police officers as honest, hard-working men and women, selflessly dedicated to ensuring the safety of our communities. There are, of course, plenty of examples of good cops, including the officers who put their lives on the line every day in service to their communities, as well as the officers who have actually given their own lives to save others.

But some people, particularly those who have had bad experiences with police, hold a definitive Bad Cop view. They may see police officers as out-of-control jerks, often racist or sexist or both, less interested in truth and justice than they are in harassing people they don't like. Unfortunately, there are also plenty of examples of bad cops, including officers who have actually been sent to prison for lying, planting evidence, corruption, excessive force, rape, and murder.

It is important to recognize that your view of police—whether Good Cop or Bad Cop or something in between—tends to dictate your views about Investigative Criminal Procedure. If you think that police officers are basically good men and women, selflessly dedicated to the safety and protection of the public, then you likely want to give them broad authority because you know they won't abuse it. If, by contrast, you think of police officers as dishonest, racist, out-of-control jugheads who cannot be trusted, then you likely want to rein in their authority with clear and strict rules governing their conduct. Those who adhere to the Bad Cop view don't want the police to have much discretion because they can't be trusted to use it fairly.

And, of course, just as your own view of the police will influence your thoughts about the rules of Investigative Criminal Procedure, so too the beliefs of judges and attorneys actually working within the criminal justice system are formed, in large measure, by their views and experiences in dealing with the police.

Whether you put yourself in the Good Cop, Bad Cop, or some other camp, don't be afraid to re-examine your assumptions and beliefs. Consistent with the Necker Cube Principle, thoughtfully consider different perspectives!

The Good Cop/Bad Cop Dichotomy

Those with a Good Cop view tend to trust the police and would give them broad authority and discretion because they won't abuse it. Those with a Bad Cop view tend to distrust the police and generally want to limit their authority and discretion.

D. APPLES, JUICE, AND APPLESAUCE: REASONING BY ANALOGY AND DISTINGUISHING CASES

Wouldn't it be cool if you could absorb everything you needed to know about Investigative Criminal Procedure just by watching old episodes of *Law & Order*? Well, don't get too excited, because even though *Law & Order* is a wonderful educational tool, it doesn't capture everything. To fully understand Investigative Criminal Procedure, you've got to put in the hard work of reading the Supreme Court's leading decisions in the area. But even reading all the important decisions isn't enough; you've got to analyze them, break them down, and familiarize yourself with some of the basics of legal reasoning.

As you may already know or soon will learn, the constitutional provisions at the heart of Investigative Criminal Procedure are phrased in general terms that provide little practical guidance in deciding actual cases. The Fourth Amendment bars "unreasonable searches and seizures." What does that mean when an individual is arrested for driving erratically and the police search the car and the arrestee's pockets for drugs or weapons? What about the arrestee's smartphone? May police read through text messages, emails, and the list of calls made and received to see whether the arrestee has had any communications with known drug dealers?

When confronted with precisely these kinds of questions—questions that are not clearly answered by the text of the Constitution itself—the Supreme Court looks to its own prior decisions for guidance. Over the years, the Supreme Court has decided hundreds—perhaps even thousands—of cases involving various facets of Investigative Criminal Procedure, each presenting a slightly different set of facts. By drawing analogies to similar cases it has previously decided, and by distinguishing other cases presenting slightly different facts or legal principles, the Supreme Court arrives at answers to complex questions that the framers of the Constitution never even imagined.

The ability to reason by analogy and the related ability to distinguish one case from another are core skills required for success in Investigative Criminal Procedure and just about any other area of law. Here's a little exercise to help you develop those skills: Imagine a city called Juiceville that has recently enacted two laws designed to protect the interests of its largest employer, MegaJuice Inc. One law, intended to ensure an ample supply of the fruit essential to the production of MegaJuice's juice, declares: "A person *cannot* eat apples." The second law, an effort to boost demand for MegaJuice's only product, declares: "A person *can* drink juice." Neither law has been interpreted by the Juiceville courts.

One day, while strolling down the main street in Juiceville, right in front of the MegaJuice factory, Fran Fruity is arrested for consuming a jar of applesauce. An ambitious prosecutor charges her with violating the first law, while an equally ambitious defense attorney, citing the second law, urges the court to dismiss the charge. The stakes are high: A person convicted of eating an apple must serve two years in prison.

What would the prosecution argue? What would the defense argue? Does it make a difference if Fran was using a fork, a spoon, or a straw to consume the applesauce? Does it make a difference whether Fran was chewing the applesauce or just gulping it down? Does it make a difference whether the applesauce was smooth or chunky? Are there any other facts about Fran's applesauce consumption that you would like to know?

Each of the laws in Fran Fruity's case has two critical words that will ultimately determine her fate. Was Fran *eating* in violation of the first law, or was she permissibly *drinking* under the second law? Does applesauce count as a forbidden *apple* under the first law, or is it an acceptable *juice* under the second law? Additional facts, particularly the answers to some of the questions raised above—Fran's choice of utensil, whether she was gulping or chewing, whether the applesauce was smooth or chunky—may nudge the case closer to one law or the other. Certain facts may even create more ambiguity. Suppose Fran was using a spoon to consume the applesauce. Many people associate a spoon with *eating*, but one can also use a spoon for *drinking* soup, broth, or leftover milk in a bowl of cereal.

Just as the Supreme Court, when confronted with a novel legal question, must grapple with the facts, language, and reasoning in its own prior decisions, so too you should carefully read and analyze each of the assigned cases in this book, noting similarities and differences in prior cases, while searching for the critical facts, arguments, and legal principles that lead the Court in one direction or another.

As you read the Supreme Court decisions in this book, be sure to do so with a critical eye. Although the majority opinion in each case represents the final word on the question before the Court, not every decision is well-reasoned, represents a wise policy choice, or stands the test of time. The Supreme Court Justices themselves are often sharply divided, with just a single vote tipping the result in one direction or the other, and occasionally, as we'll soon see, the Supreme Court simply changes its mind when an earlier decision seems outdated or out-of-touch with constitutional values. To assist you in reading critically, this book frequently presents the opinions of dissenting Justices along with the majority opinions. These dissenting opinions are valuable for calling attention to issues that may have been overlooked by the majority, for exposing flaws or inconsistencies in the majority's reasoning, and for proposing alternative rules that may be more fair, more efficient, and more easily applied. In some cases, arguments made in a dissenting opinion are even persuasive enough to gain the support of a majority when, years later, the Supreme Court revisits the issue and overrules its own prior decision.

The Applesauce Analogy

Most legal questions in Investigative Criminal Procedure aren't apples and aren't juice. Most are, instead, somewhere in the middle, like applesauce. When confronted with an applesauce problem, do what the Supreme Court does—carefully examine the facts, note similarities and differences in prior cases, and determine which rules and arguments seem to provide the best answers.

CHAPTER 2

CORE CONSTITUTIONAL PROVISIONS AND DOCTRINES

■ ■ ■

Now that we've gotten the fuzzy stuff—the Necker Cube, Good Cop/Bad Cop, and applesauce—out of the way, you're ready for some serious "hardcore" law. This Chapter introduces some of the basic constitutional provisions, doctrines, and rules at the heart of Investigative Criminal Procedure.

A. RELEVANT CONSTITUTIONAL PROVISIONS

As noted in Chapter 1, most of the constitutional rules in Investigative Criminal Procedure are derived from just four constitutional amendments: the Fourth, Fifth, Sixth, and Fourteenth Amendments. Even better news: Although the Fourth Amendment, in its entirety, is important in Investigative Criminal Procedure, only certain parts of the Fifth, Sixth, and Fourteenth Amendments—underlined below—are relevant.

Key Constitutional Provisions in Investigative Criminal Procedure

Amendment IV: <u>The right of the people to be secure in their persons, houses, papers, and effects, against unreasonable searches and seizures, shall not be violated, and no Warrants shall issue, but upon probable cause, supported by Oath or affirmation, and particularly describing the place to be searched, and the persons or things to be seized.</u>

Amendment V: No person shall be held to answer for a capital, or otherwise infamous crime, unless on a presentment or indictment of a Grand Jury, except in cases arising in the land or naval forces, or in the Militia, when in actual service in time of War or public danger; <u>nor shall any person</u> be subject for the same offence to be twice put in jeopardy of life or limb; nor shall <u>be compelled in any criminal case to be a witness against himself, nor be deprived of life, liberty, or property, without due process of law</u>; nor shall private property be taken for public use, without just compensation.

Amendment VI: <u>In all criminal prosecutions, the accused shall enjoy the right</u> to a speedy and public trial, by an impartial jury of the State

---

11

and district wherein the crime shall have been committed, which district shall have been previously ascertained by law, and to be informed of the nature and cause of the accusation; to be confronted with the witnesses against him; to have compulsory process for obtaining witnesses in his favor, and <u>to have the Assistance of Counsel for his defence</u>.

Amendment XIV, Section 1: All persons born or naturalized in the United States, and subject to the jurisdiction thereof, are citizens of the United States and of the State wherein they reside. No State shall make or enforce any law which shall abridge the privileges or immunities of citizens of the United States; <u>nor shall any State deprive any person of life, liberty, or property, without due process of law</u>; nor deny to any person within its jurisdiction the equal protection of the laws.

Before we formally delve into the meaning of the constitutional provisions relevant to Investigative Criminal Procedure, a little background is in order. The U.S. Constitution, establishing the framework for the newly-created federal government, and the powers and responsibilities of the legislative, executive, and judicial branches, was adopted in 1787 and ratified by the required two-thirds of the original thirteen states in 1788. To address concerns that the Constitution and the new federal government would fail to adequately protect individual rights, the first United States Congress proposed a series of constitutional amendments, ten of which were ratified in 1791 and are now known as the Bill of Rights. As originally understood, the provisions in the Bill of Rights were intended to limit only the power of the federal government; state constitutions were thought adequate to protect individuals from abuses at the hands of state and local officials.

Following the Civil War, Congress adopted the Thirteenth, Fourteenth, and Fifteenth Amendments, abolishing slavery and guaranteeing basic rights—including voting rights—regardless of race or color. The Fourteenth Amendment was directed explicitly at the states: "No State shall make or enforce any law which shall abridge the privileges or immunities of citizens of the United States; *nor shall any State deprive any person of life, liberty, or property, without due process of law*; nor deny to any person within its jurisdiction the equal protection of the laws." (Note that the italicized portion of the Fourteenth Amendment's Due Process Clause, directed at the states, is virtually identical to the Due Process Clause in the Fifth Amendment, directed at the federal government.)

Beginning in the late nineteenth century, and continuing well into the twentieth century, the U.S. Supreme Court held that various provisions of the Bill of Rights that previously bound only the federal government were now also binding upon state and local governments. The Supreme Court did so by declaring that many of the rights and protections found in the Bill of Rights were part of the "liberty" protected from state interference by the Due Process Clause of the Fourteenth Amendment. Stated differently, the Supreme Court held that the Fourteenth Amendment's Due Process Clause, directed at state and local governments, "incorporates" many of the protections in the Bill of Rights that were previously binding only upon the federal government.

There was a long debate, spanning several decades, among the Justices of the Supreme Court and legal commentators over precisely which liberties in the Bill of Rights were sufficiently important—or "fundamental"—to merit protection from state infringement under the Fourteenth Amendment's Due Process Clause. The "Total Incorporationists," represented by Justices Hugo Black and William O. Douglas, believed that the entirety of the Bill of Rights was incorporated, while the "Selective Incorporationists," represented by Justices Benjamin Cardozo and Felix Frankfurter, believed that only certain provisions of the Bill of Rights were sufficiently fundamental to bind state and local governments. The Selective Incorporationists eventually prevailed, but as a practical matter, the Total Incorporationists won too. Although the Supreme Court has never held that every provision of the Bill of Rights is incorporated, the Court has, over time, incorporated *almost every provision*, including the provisions of the Fourth, Fifth, and Sixth Amendments relevant to Investigative Criminal Procedure.

As a technical matter, the Bill of Rights still applies only to the federal government, so when a case includes an allegation that a state or local police officer has, for example, violated the Fourth Amendment, it is often said that the case involves the Fourth Amendment *as applied to the states through the Due Process Clause of the Fourteenth Amendment.*

So . . . how is all this dense legal history relevant to Investigative Criminal Procedure? A century ago, if a federal agent broke into your home and searched it without a good reason or a valid search warrant, the Fourth Amendment would protect you. If a state agent did the same thing, you would be out of luck under the Fourth Amendment; your only recourse would be a provision—if one existed—in your state constitution or in state law. Today, by contrast, the Fourth Amendment protects individuals against unreasonable searches by federal officials, while the Fourth Amendment, *as applied to the states through the Due Process Clause of the Fourteenth Amendment*, provides the same protection against unreasonable searches by state and local officials.

One additional point worth remembering is that the U.S. Supreme Court cases you'll read in this book declare *constitutional minimums*—the minimum level of protection that must be given to criminal suspects and defendants under the federal Constitution. State and local officials are obliged to honor these minimum constitutional requirements because the "Supremacy Clause" of the Constitution (found in Article VI, Clause 2) declares that the Constitution is the "supreme Law of the Land," superseding anything to the contrary in state law. But the states can—and many do—offer additional legal protections to criminal suspects and defendants beyond the minimum required by the federal Constitution and the U.S. Supreme Court. Most crimes are investigated and prosecuted at the state and local level, so all of the participants in the criminal justice system—the police, the prosecutors, the defense attorneys, and the judges—will typically look first to state law for guidance. The state laws and rules governing Investigative Criminal Procedure often mirror the federal rules announced in the decisions of the U.S. Supreme Court, but in some cases, the state laws and rules are more favorable toward criminal suspects and defendants. State and local laws, rules, and practices that are less favorable toward criminal suspects and defendants than the constitutional minimum prescribed by the U.S. Supreme Court are inevitably challenged—and invalidated—as inconsistent with the federal Constitution and the decisions of the U.S. Supreme Court.

B. THE GOVERNMENT ACTION REQUIREMENT

The constitutional provisions and rules at the heart of Investigative Criminal Procedure apply only to actions taken by *government* officials, whether federal, state, or local officials. In other words, there must be some *government* action in order for an individual to invoke her *constitutional* rights. This basic principle is known as the government action requirement. (It is also sometimes referred to as the *state action requirement*.) The Supreme Court explained this principle in *Skinner v. Railway Labor Executives' Association*, 489 U.S. 602 (1989), a Fourth Amendment case involving drug and alcohol testing of railroad employees:

> The Fourth Amendment provides that "the right of the people to be secure in their persons, houses, papers, and effects, against unreasonable searches and seizures, shall not be violated." The Amendment guarantees the privacy, dignity, and security of persons against certain arbitrary and invasive acts by officers of the Government or those acting at their direction. Before we consider whether the [drug and alcohol] tests in question are reasonable under the Fourth Amendment, we must inquire whether the tests are attributable to the Government or its agents. Although the Fourth Amendment does not apply to a search or seizure, even an arbitrary one, effected by a private party on his own initiative, the Amendment protects against such intrusions if the private party acted as an instrument or agent of the Government.

The government action requirement sometimes becomes an issue in Investigative Criminal Procedure when private citizens—rather than police officers, prosecutors, or other government officials—discover evidence of crime and pass it along to the police. If the private citizen is acting entirely on his own, then there is no government action. If, however, government officials encourage, facilitate, or assist the private citizen, the government action requirement is met and constitutional standards must be satisfied.

A quick example will help to illustrate the principle. Suppose Nora Nosyneighbor suspects that Darrel Druggie, who lives next door, is processing and selling illegal narcotics. One day, when Darrel is away from home, Nora sneaks into his house, rummages through his belongings, and finds cocaine, a measuring scale, and other equipment confirming her suspicions. Nora delivers these items to the police, and Darrel is eventually charged with violating various laws prohibiting the possession and sale of narcotics. At Darrel's criminal trial, the prosecutor seeks to introduce the cocaine, the measuring scale, and other equipment discovered by Nora. Darrel's attorney objects, claiming the evidence was discovered in violation of Darrel's Fourth Amendment right to be free from unreasonable searches and seizures. In particular, the defense attorney would point out that Nora illegally entered and searched Darrel's home, without Darrel's permission and without a search warrant.

While perhaps sympathetic to Darrel's plight, the judge would still permit the prosecutor to introduce the evidence because Nora Nosyneighbor is a private citizen whose actions, while disturbing and illegal, did not violate Darrel's *constitutional* rights under the Fourth Amendment. (Darrel could ask the prosecutor to file criminal charges against Nora for trespassing and burglary. Darrel could also file a civil lawsuit against Nora, seeking monetary damages. But even if successful on both fronts, the evidence Nora uncovered would still be admissible at Darrel's criminal trial.) The result would be different, however, if Nora entered and searched Darrel's home with encouragement or assistance from the police. In that situation, the government action requirement would be met, and Nora's conduct would be evaluated against the constitutional standards of the Fourth Amendment.

The Government Action Requirement

The constitutional rules in Investigative Criminal Procedure provide protection against the actions of government officials or those who act as agents or instruments of the government; the rules provide no protection against private citizens acting without government encouragement or assistance.

LEARN MORE WITH *LAW & ORDER*

In the following episode of *Law & Order* ("Bottomless," Season 18, Episode 4), Mr. Fuller, a former police officer who now works in corporate security for a chain of department stores, discovers evidence in an employee's apartment that links the employee to a murder. Mr. Fuller delivers the evidence to the police and the employee is eventually charged with murder. Initially, the manner in which Mr. Fuller discovered the evidence does not appear to present any problem for the prosecutors because although the police were investigating the murder, they were not involved in the search of the apartment. The case becomes considerably more complex, however, when Mr. Fuller testifies in court that he performed the search at the behest of the police, transforming his private conduct into government action. The government action requirement is the central issue in determining the admissibility of the incriminating evidence and the fate of the prosecution's case.

The segments of the episode that depict the relevant Investigative Criminal Procedure issues appear at:

20:20 to 25:46; 37:58 to 41:51

Law & Order **Episode**

"Bottomless," Season 18, Episode 4

C. THE EXCLUSIONARY RULE

It may seem odd to review the remedy for constitutional violations by the police before examining the police practices that are permitted and prohibited by the Constitution, but I've found that this approach is helpful because it frames one of the most important questions of our time: How do we effectively balance our shared interest in protecting constitutional rights against an equally strong interest in seeing wrongdoers caught, prosecuted, and punished, rendering our streets and communities safer and more secure? This difficult question is at the heart of every case in Investigative Criminal Procedure, and as you'll soon see, the Justices of the Supreme Court are still struggling to answer it.

The exclusionary rule is the basic remedy for police conduct that violates the Constitution. Under the rule, evidence obtained in violation of the Constitution is generally excluded from the defendant's criminal trial and cannot be used to establish guilt. The exclusionary rule is used to exclude many different types of evidence, including tangible items discovered in violation of the Fourth Amendment's prohibition on unreasonable searches and seizures, oral or written confessions obtained in violation of the Fifth Amendment's privilege against self-incrimination, or witness testimony regarding a police lineup or a similar identification technique that did not satisfy the basic standards of fairness required under the Fourteenth Amendment's Due Process Clause.

Where in the Constitution is the exclusionary rule located? Go ahead, take a look. I'll wait. (Cue the "Final Jeopardy" music.) Did you find it? The answer should be no, because the exclusionary rule is *not* in the Constitution. It is, instead, a remedy created by the courts to correct and deter unconstitutional police conduct and to safeguard the constitutional rights of criminal defendants.

As you read the following cases, consider the various arguments for and against the use of the exclusionary rule. What are the rationales for the rule? Does it achieve its objectives? Are there alternatives to the exclusionary rule that work just as well or even better? What are the costs of the exclusionary rule, both for the criminal justice system and for society as a whole?

In *Weeks v. U.S.*, the Supreme Court held—for the first time—that evidence obtained by federal officials in violation of the Fourth Amendment had to be excluded from the defendant's trial.

WEEKS V. U.S.
232 U.S. 383 (1914)

Local police and a federal marshal searched the defendant's home without a warrant, finding documents implicating the defendant in the violation of a federal law prohibiting the mailing of lottery tickets. The Supreme Court held that the documents, obtained in violation of the Fourth Amendment, could not be used as evidence against the defendant:

> If letters and private documents can be [unlawfully] seized and held and used in evidence against a citizen accused of an offense, the protection of the Fourth Amendment, declaring his right to be secure against such searches and seizures, is of no value, and, so far as those thus placed are concerned, might as well be stricken from the Constitution. The efforts of the courts and their officials to bring the guilty to punishment, praiseworthy as they are, are not to be aided by the sacrifice of those great principles established by years of endeavor and suffering which have resulted in their embodiment in the fundamental law of the land. The United States marshal could only have invaded the house of the accused when armed with a warrant issued as required by the Constitution, upon sworn information, and describing with reasonable particularity the thing for which the search was to be made. Instead, he acted without sanction of law, doubtless prompted by the desire to bring further proof to

the aid of the government, and under color of his office undertook to make a seizure of private papers in direct violation of the constitutional prohibition against such action. Under such circumstances, without sworn information and particular description, not even an order of court would have justified such procedure; much less was it within the authority of the United States marshal to thus invade the house and privacy of the accused.

The *Weeks* decision applied only to the conduct of the U.S. marshal and the use of the evidence in federal court. The Supreme Court declined to inquire into any remedies the defendant might have against the local police because, in 1914, the Fourth Amendment had not yet been incorporated and applied to the states through the Due Process Clause of the Fourteenth Amendment.

In *Wolf v. Colorado*, the Supreme Court confronted the questions that it had sidestepped in *Weeks*. First, is the Fourth Amendment a fundamental right, incorporated through the Due Process Clause of the Fourteenth Amendment and binding upon the states? And second, if the Fourth Amendment is binding upon the states, should the federal remedy for a Fourth Amendment violation—the exclusionary rule—be binding upon the states as well?

WOLF V. COLORADO
338 U.S. 25 (1949)

JUSTICE FRANKFURTER delivered the opinion of the Court.

The precise question for consideration is this: Does a conviction by a State court for a State offense deny the "due process of law" required by the Fourteenth Amendment, solely because evidence that was admitted at the trial was obtained under circumstances which would have rendered it inadmissible in a prosecution for violation of a federal law in a court of the United States because there deemed to be an infraction of the Fourth Amendment as applied in *Weeks v. U.S.*, 232 U.S. 383 (1914)? The Supreme Court of Colorado has sustained convictions in which such evidence was admitted, and we brought the cases here.

Unlike the specific requirements and restrictions placed by the Bill of Rights, Amendments I to VIII, upon the administration of criminal justice by federal authority, the Fourteenth Amendment did not subject criminal justice in the States to specific limitations. The notion that the "due process of law" guaranteed by the Fourteenth Amendment is shorthand for the first eight amendments of the Constitution and thereby incorporates them has been rejected by this Court again and again, after impressive consideration.

For purposes of ascertaining the restrictions which the Due Process Clause imposed upon the States in the enforcement of their criminal law, we adhere to the views expressed in *Palko v. Connecticut*, 302 U.S. 319 (1937). That decision speaks to us with the great weight of the authority, particularly in matters of civil liberty, of a court that included Mr. Chief Justice Hughes, Mr. Justice Brandeis, Mr. Justice Stone and Mr. Justice Cardozo, to speak only of the dead. In rejecting the suggestion that the Due Process Clause incorporated the original Bill of Rights, Mr. Justice Cardozo reaffirmed on behalf of that Court a different but deeper and more pervasive conception of the Due Process Clause. This Clause exacts from the States for the lowliest and the most outcast all that is "implicit in the concept of ordered liberty."

Due process of law thus conveys neither formal nor fixed nor narrow requirements. It is the compendious expression for all those rights which the courts must enforce because they are basic to our free society. But basic rights do not become petrified as of any one time, even though, as a matter of human experience, some may not too rhetorically be called eternal verities. It is of the very nature of a free society to advance in its standards of what is deemed reasonable and right. Representing as it does a living principle, due process is not confined within a permanent catalogue of what may at a given time be deemed the limits or the essentials of fundamental rights.

To rely on a tidy formula for the easy determination of what is a fundamental right for purposes of legal enforcement may satisfy a longing for certainty but ignores the movements of a free society. It belittles the scale of the conception of due process. The real clue to the problem confronting the judiciary in the application of the Due Process Clause is not to ask where the line is once and for all to be drawn but to recognize that it is for the Court to draw it by the gradual and empiric process of inclusion and exclusion.

The security of one's privacy against arbitrary intrusion by the police—which is at the core of the Fourth Amendment—is basic to a free society. It is therefore implicit in "the concept of ordered liberty" and as such enforceable against the States through the Due Process Clause. The knock at the door, whether by day or by night, as a prelude to a search, without authority of law but solely on the authority of the police, did not need the commentary of recent history to be condemned as inconsistent with the conception of human rights enshrined in the history and the basic constitutional documents of English-speaking peoples.

Accordingly, we have no hesitation in saying that were a State affirmatively to sanction such police incursion into privacy it would run counter to the guaranty of the Fourteenth Amendment. But the ways of enforcing such a basic right raise questions of a different order. How such arbitrary conduct should be checked, what remedies against it should be afforded, the means by which the right should be made effective, are all questions that are not to be so dogmatically answered as to preclude the varying solutions which spring from an allowable range of judgment on issues not susceptible of quantitative solution.

In *Weeks v. U.S.*, this Court held that in a federal prosecution the Fourth Amendment barred the use of evidence secured through an illegal search and seizure. This ruling was not derived from the explicit requirements of the Fourth Amendment; it was not based on legislation expressing Congressional policy in the enforcement of the Constitution. The decision was a matter of judicial implication. Since then it has been frequently applied and we stoutly adhere to it. But the immediate question is whether the basic right to protection against arbitrary intrusion by the police demands the exclusion of logically relevant evidence obtained by an unreasonable search and seizure because, in a federal prosecution for a federal crime, it would be excluded. As a matter of inherent reason, one would suppose this to be an issue to which men with complete devotion to the protection of the right of privacy might give different answers. When we find that in fact most of the English-speaking world does not regard as vital to such protection the exclusion of evidence thus obtained, we must hesitate to treat this remedy as an essential ingredient of the right. The contrariety of views of the States is particularly impressive in view of the careful reconsideration which they have given the problem in the light of the *Weeks* decision.

I. Before the *Weeks* decision 27 States had passed on the admissibility of evidence obtained by unlawful search and seizure.

 (a) Of these, 26 States opposed the *Weeks* doctrine.

 (b) Of these, 1 State anticipated the *Weeks* doctrine.

II. Since the *Weeks* decision 47 States all told have passed on the *Weeks* doctrine.

 (a) Of these, 20 passed on it for the first time.

  (1) Of the foregoing States, 6 followed the *Weeks* doctrine.

  (2) Of the foregoing States, 14 rejected the *Weeks* doctrine.

 (b) Of these, 26 States reviewed prior decisions contrary to the *Weeks* doctrine.

  (1) Of these, 10 States have followed *Weeks*, overruling or distinguishing their prior decisions.

(2) Of these, 16 States adhered to their prior decisions against *Weeks*.

(c) Of these, 1 State adhered to its prior formulation of the *Weeks* doctrine.

III. As of today 31 States reject the *Weeks* doctrine, 16 States are in agreement with it.

IV. Of 10 jurisdictions within the United Kingdom and the British Commonwealth of Nations which have passed on the question, none has held evidence obtained by illegal search and seizure inadmissible.

The jurisdictions which have rejected the *Weeks* doctrine have not left the right to privacy without other means of protection. Indeed, the exclusion of evidence is a remedy which directly serves only to protect those upon whose person or premises something incriminating has been found. We cannot, therefore, regard it as a departure from basic standards to remand such persons, together with those who emerge scatheless from a search, to the remedies of private action and such protection as the internal discipline of the police, under the eyes of an alert public opinion, may afford. Granting that in practice the exclusion of evidence may be an effective way of deterring unreasonable searches, it is not for this Court to condemn as falling below the minimal standards assured by the Due Process Clause a State's reliance upon other methods which, if consistently enforced, would be equally effective. We cannot brush aside the experience of States which deem the incidence of such conduct by the police too slight to call for a deterrent remedy not by way of disciplinary measures but by overriding the relevant rules of evidence. There are, moreover, reasons for excluding evidence unreasonably obtained by the federal police which are less compelling in the case of police under State or local authority. The public opinion of a community can far more effectively be exerted against oppressive conduct on the part of police directly responsible to the community itself than can local opinion, sporadically aroused, be brought to bear upon remote authority pervasively exerted throughout the country.

We hold, therefore, that in a prosecution in a State court for a State crime the Fourteenth Amendment does not forbid the admission of evidence obtained by an unreasonable search and seizure.

JUSTICE MURPHY, with whom JUSTICE RUTLEDGE joins, dissenting.

It is disheartening to find so much that is right in an opinion which seems to me so fundamentally wrong. Of course I agree with the Court that the Fourteenth Amendment prohibits activities which are proscribed by the search and seizure clause of the Fourth Amendment. Quite apart from the blanket application of the Bill of Rights to the States, a devotee of democracy would ill suit his name were he to suggest that his home's protection against unlicensed governmental invasion was not "of the very essence of a scheme of ordered liberty." It is difficult for me to understand how the Court can go this far and yet be unwilling to make the step which can give some meaning to the pronouncements it utters.

Imagination and zeal may invent a dozen methods to give content to the commands of the Fourth Amendment. But this Court is limited to the remedies currently available. It cannot legislate the ideal system. If we would attempt the enforcement of the search and seizure clause in the ordinary case today, we are limited to three devices: judicial exclusion of the illegally obtained evidence; criminal prosecution of violators; and civil action against violators in the action of trespass.

Alternatives are deceptive. Their very statement conveys the impression that one possibility is as effective as the next. In this case their statement is blinding. For there is but one alternative to the rule of exclusion. That is no sanction at all.

This has been perfectly clear since 1914, when a unanimous Court decided *Weeks v. U.S.*: "If letters and private documents can thus be seized and held and used in evidence against a citizen accused of an offense," we said, "the protection of the Fourth Amendment, declaring his right to be secure against such searches and seizures, is of no value, and, so far as those thus placed are concerned, might as well be stricken from the Constitution."

Today the Court wipes [that statement] from the books with its bland citation of "other remedies." Little need be said concerning the possibilities of criminal prosecution. Self-scrutiny is a lofty ideal, but its exaltation reaches new heights if we expect a District Attorney to prosecute himself or his associates for well-meaning violations of the search and seizure clause during a raid the District Attorney or his associates have ordered. But there is an appealing ring in another alternative. A trespass action for damages is a venerable means of securing reparation for unauthorized invasion of the home. Why not put the old writ to a new use? When the Court cites cases permitting the action, the remedy seems complete.

But what an illusory remedy this is, if by "remedy" we mean a positive deterrent to police and prosecutors tempted to violate the Fourth Amendment. The appealing ring softens when we recall that in a trespass action the measure of damages is simply the extent of the injury to physical property. If the officer searches with care, he can avoid all but nominal damages—a penny, or a dollar. Are punitive damages possible? Perhaps. But a few states permit none, whatever the circumstances. In those that do, the plaintiff must show the real ill will or malice of the defendant, and surely it is not unreasonable to assume that one in honest pursuit of crime bears no malice toward the search victim. If that burden is carried, recovery may yet be defeated by the rule that there must be physical damages before punitive damages may be awarded. In addition, some states limit punitive damages to the actual expenses of litigation. Others demand some arbitrary ratio between actual and punitive damages before a verdict may stand. Even assuming the ill will of the officer, his reasonable grounds for belief that the home he searched harbored evidence of crime is admissible in mitigation of punitive damages. The bad reputation of the plaintiff is likewise admissible. If the evidence seized was actually used at a trial, that fact has been held a complete justification of the search, and a defense against the trespass action. And even if the plaintiff hurdles all these obstacles, and gains a substantial verdict, the individual officer's finances may well make the judgment useless—for the municipality, of course, is not liable without its consent. Is it surprising that there is so little in the books concerning trespass actions for violation of the search and seizure clause?

The conclusion is inescapable that but one remedy exists to deter violations of the search and seizure clause. That is the rule which excludes illegally obtained evidence. Only by exclusion can we impress upon the zealous prosecutor that violation of the Constitution will do him no good. And only when that point is driven home can the prosecutor be expected to emphasize the importance of observing constitutional demands in his instructions to the police.

I cannot believe that we should decide due process questions by simply taking a poll of the rules in various jurisdictions, even if we follow the *Palko* "test." Today's decision will do inestimable harm to the cause of fair police methods in our cities and states. Even more important, perhaps, it must have tragic effect upon public respect for our judiciary. For the Court now allows what is indeed shabby business: lawlessness by officers of the law.

Since the evidence admitted was secured in violation of the Fourth Amendment, the judgment should be reversed.

The Court in *Wolf* held that the Fourth Amendment was a fundamental constitutional right, binding upon the states under the Due Process Clause of the Fourteenth Amendment. But the Court also held that the federal remedy for Fourth Amendment violations—the exclusionary rule—was *not* binding upon the states. In the aftermath of *Wolf*, the states were free to adopt the exclusionary rule if they wanted, but they were not *required* to do so. The *Wolf* majority's decision was rooted in concerns about federalism—the relationship between the states and the federal government. That relationship is strained, in the eyes of the majority, when the Supreme Court—a branch of the federal government—requires the state courts to follow federal rules in the administration of their own criminal justice systems. The *Wolf* majority also believed that states should be free to experiment with alternatives to the exclusionary rule, such as internal police discipline or civil lawsuits against officers who violate the Fourth Amendment.

The dissenting Justices in *Wolf* scoff at these alternatives; they believe that the only effective deterrent to police misconduct is exclusion of the evidence. The dissent concludes with an argument about *judicial integrity*—when the courts tacitly sanction police misconduct by admitting illegally obtained evidence, the courts become complicit in the illegality, undermining "public respect for our judiciary" and the rule of law.

The majority's response to this concern for judicial integrity—although perhaps not clearly stated in *Wolf*—is that public respect for the judiciary is likewise threatened when vital evidence is excluded, criminals go free, and crimes remain unpunished merely because the police have made a mistake. As Judge (later Justice) Benjamin Cardozo famously remarked in *People v. Defore*, 242 N.Y. 13 (1926), criticizing and rejecting the use of the exclusionary rule in New York's courts: "The criminal is to go free because the constable has blundered."

Ultimately, the *Wolf* decision did not stand the test of time. Just twelve years later, the Supreme Court revisited *Wolf* and overruled it in *Mapp v. Ohio*.

MAPP V. OHIO
367 U.S. 643 (1961)

JUSTICE CLARK delivered the opinion of the Court.

Appellant stands convicted of knowingly having had in her possession and under her control certain lewd and lascivious books, pictures, and photographs. The Supreme Court of Ohio found that her conviction was valid though "based primarily upon the introduction in evidence of lewd and lascivious books and pictures unlawfully seized during an unlawful search of defendant's home."

On May 23, 1957, three Cleveland police officers arrived at appellant's residence in that city pursuant to information that "a person was hiding out in the home, who was wanted for questioning in connection with a recent bombing, and that there was a large amount of policy paraphernalia being hidden in the home." Miss Mapp and her daughter by a former marriage lived on the top floor of the two-family dwelling. Upon their arrival at that house, the officers knocked on the door and demanded entrance but appellant, after telephoning her attorney, refused to admit them without a search warrant. They advised their headquarters of the situation and undertook a surveillance of the house.

The officers again sought entrance some three hours later when four or more additional officers arrived on the scene. When Miss Mapp did not come to the door immediately, at least one of the several doors to the house was forcibly opened[2] and the policemen gained admittance. Meanwhile Miss Mapp's attorney arrived, but the officers, having secured their own entry, and continuing in their defiance of the law, would permit him neither to see Miss Mapp nor to enter the house. It appears that Miss Mapp was halfway down the stairs from the upper floor to the front door when the officers, in this highhanded manner, broke into the hall. She demanded to see the search warrant. A paper, claimed to be a warrant, was held up by one of the officers. She grabbed the "warrant" and placed it in her bosom. A struggle ensued in which the officers recovered the piece of paper and as a result of which they handcuffed appellant because she had been "belligerent" in resisting their official rescue of the "warrant" from her person. Running roughshod over appellant, a policeman "grabbed" her, "twisted her hand," and she "yelled and pleaded with him" because "it was hurting." Appellant, in handcuffs, was then forcibly taken upstairs to her bedroom where the officers searched a dresser, a chest of drawers, a closet and some suitcases. They also looked into a photo album and through personal papers belonging to the appellant. The search spread to the rest of the second floor including the child's bedroom, the living room, the kitchen and a dinette. The basement of the building and a trunk found therein were also searched. The obscene materials for possession of which she was ultimately convicted were discovered in the course of that widespread search.

At the trial no search warrant was produced by the prosecution, nor was the failure to produce one explained or accounted for. At best, "There is, in the record, considerable doubt as to whether there ever was any warrant for the search of defendant's home." The Ohio Supreme Court believed a "reasonable argument" could be made that the conviction should be reversed "because the methods employed to obtain the evidence were such as to offend a sense of justice," but the court found determinative the fact that the evidence had not been taken "from defendant's person by the use of brutal or offensive physical force against defendant."

The State says that even if the search were made without authority, or otherwise unreasonably, it is not prevented from using the unconstitutionally seized evidence at trial, citing *Wolf v. Colorado,* 338 U.S. 25 (1949), in which this Court did indeed hold "that in a prosecution in a State court for a State crime the Fourteenth Amendment does not forbid the admission of evidence obtained by an unreasonable search and

---

[2]   A police officer testified that "we did pry the screen door to gain entrance"; the attorney on the scene testified that a policeman "tried to kick in the door" and then "broke the glass in the door and somebody reached in and opened the door and let them in"; the appellant testified that "The back door was broken."

seizure." On this appeal, it is urged once again that we review that holding.

I

In *Weeks v. U.S.*, 232 U.S. 383 (1914), this Court for the first time held that "in a federal prosecution the Fourth Amendment barred the use of evidence secured through an illegal search and seizure." This Court has ever since required of federal law officers a strict adherence to that command which this Court has held to be a clear, specific, and constitutionally required—even if judicially implied—deterrent safeguard without insistence upon which the Fourth Amendment would have been reduced to "a form of words." It meant, quite simply, that conviction by means of unlawful seizures and enforced confessions should find no sanction in the judgments of the courts, and that such evidence shall not be used at all.

There are in the cases of this Court some passing references to the *Weeks* rule as being one of evidence. But the plain and unequivocal language of *Weeks*—and its later paraphrase in *Wolf*—to the effect that the *Weeks* rule is of constitutional origin, remains entirely undisturbed.

II

In 1949, 35 years after *Weeks* was announced, this Court, in *Wolf v. Colorado*, again for the first time, discussed the effect of the Fourth Amendment upon the States through the operation of the Due Process Clause of the Fourteenth Amendment. It said: "We have no hesitation in saying that were a State affirmatively to sanction such police incursion into privacy it would run counter to the guaranty of the Fourteenth Amendment."

Nevertheless, after declaring that the "security of one's privacy against arbitrary intrusion by the police" is "implicit in the concept of ordered liberty and as such enforceable against the States through the Due Process Clause," and announcing that it "stoutly adhered" to the *Weeks* decision, the Court decided that the *Weeks* exclusionary rule would not then be imposed upon the States as "an essential ingredient of the right." The Court's reasons for not considering essential to the right to privacy, as a curb imposed upon the States by the Due Process Clause, that which decades before had been posited as part and parcel of the Fourth Amendment's limitations upon federal encroachment of individual privacy, were bottomed on factual considerations.

While they are not basically relevant to a decision that the exclusionary rule is an essential ingredient of the Fourth Amendment as the right it embodies is vouchsafed against the States by the Due Process Clause, we will consider the current validity of the factual grounds upon which *Wolf* was based.

The Court in *Wolf* first stated that the contrariety of views of the States on the adoption of the exclusionary rule of *Weeks* was "particularly impressive" and, in this connection that it could not "brush aside the experience of States which deem the incidence of such conduct by the police too slight to call for a deterrent remedy by overriding the States' relevant rules of evidence." While in 1949, prior to the *Wolf* case, almost two-thirds of the States were opposed to the use of the exclusionary rule, now, despite the *Wolf* case, more than half of those since passing upon it, by their own legislative or judicial decision, have wholly or partly adopted or adhered to the *Weeks* rule. Significantly, among those now following the rule is California, which, according to its highest court, was "compelled to reach that conclusion because other remedies have completely failed to secure compliance with the constitutional provision." In connection with this California case, we note that the second basis elaborated in *Wolf* in support of its failure to enforce the exclusionary doctrine against the States was that "other means of protection" have been afforded "the right to privacy." The experience of California that such other remedies have been worthless and futile is buttressed by the experience of other States. The obvious futility of relegating the Fourth Amendment to the protection of other remedies has, moreover, been recognized by this Court since *Wolf*.

It, therefore, plainly appears that the factual considerations supporting the failure of the *Wolf* Court to include the *Weeks* exclusionary rule when it recognized the enforceability of the right to privacy against the States in 1949, while not basically relevant to the constitutional consideration, could not, in any analysis, now be deemed controlling.

III

Today we once again examine *Wolf*'s constitutional documentation of the right to privacy free from unreasonable state intrusion, and, after its dozen years on our books, are led by it to close the only courtroom door remaining open to evidence secured by official lawlessness in flagrant abuse of that basic right, reserved to all persons as a specific guarantee against that very same unlawful conduct. We hold that all evidence obtained by searches and seizures in violation of the Constitution is, by that same authority, inadmissible in a state court.

IV

Since the Fourth Amendment's right of privacy has been declared enforceable against the States through the Due Process Clause of the Fourteenth, it is enforceable against them by the same sanction of exclusion as is used against the Federal Government. Were it otherwise, then just as without the *Weeks* rule the assurance against unreasonable federal searches and seizures would be a form of words, valueless and undeserving of mention in a perpetual charter of inestimable human liberties, so too, without that rule the freedom from state invasions of privacy would be so ephemeral and so neatly severed from its conceptual nexus with the freedom from all brutish means of coercing evidence as not to merit this Court's high regard as a freedom "implicit in the concept of ordered liberty." At the time that the Court held in *Wolf* that the Amendment was applicable to the States through the Due Process Clause, the cases of this Court, as we have seen, had steadfastly held that as to federal officers the Fourth Amendment included the exclusion of the evidence seized in violation of its provisions. Even *Wolf* stoutly adhered to that proposition. Therefore, in extending the substantive protections of due process to all constitutionally unreasonable searches—state or federal—it was logically and constitutionally necessary that the exclusion doctrine—an essential part of the right to privacy—be also insisted upon as an essential ingredient of the right newly recognized by the *Wolf* case. In short, the admission of the new constitutional right by *Wolf* could not consistently tolerate denial of its most important constitutional privilege, namely, the exclusion of the evidence which an accused had been forced to give by reason of the unlawful seizure. To hold otherwise is to grant the right but in reality to withhold its privilege and enjoyment.

Indeed, we are aware of no restraint, similar to that rejected today, conditioning the enforcement of any other basic constitutional right. The right to privacy, no less important than any other right carefully and particularly reserved to the people, would stand in marked contrast to all other rights declared as basic to a free society. This Court has not hesitated to enforce as strictly against the States as it does against the Federal Government the rights of free speech and of a free press, the rights to notice and to a fair, public trial, including, as it does, the right not to be convicted by use of a coerced confession, however logically relevant it be, and without regard to its reliability. And nothing could be more certain than that when a coerced confession is involved, the relevant rules of evidence are overridden without regard to the incidence of such conduct by the police, slight or frequent. Why should not the same rule apply to what is tantamount to coerced testimony by way of unconstitutional seizure of goods, papers, effects, documents, etc.? We find that, as to the Federal Government, the Fourth and Fifth Amendments and, as to the States, the freedom from unconscionable invasions of privacy and the freedom from convictions based upon coerced confessions do enjoy an intimate relation in their perpetuation of principles of humanity and civil liberty secured only after years of struggle. They express supplementing phases of the same constitutional purpose—to maintain inviolate large areas of personal privacy. The philosophy of each Amendment and of each freedom is complementary to, although not dependent upon, that of the other in its sphere of influence—the very least that together they assure in either sphere is that no man is to be convicted on unconstitutional evidence.

V

Moreover, our holding that the exclusionary rule is an essential part of both the Fourth and Fourteenth Amendments is not only the logical dictate of prior cases, but it also makes very good sense. There is no war between the Constitution and common sense. Presently, a federal prosecutor may make no use of evidence illegally seized, but a State's attorney across the street may, although he supposedly is operating under the enforceable prohibitions of the same Amendment. Thus the State, by admitting evidence unlawfully seized, serves to encourage disobedience to the Federal Constitution which it is bound to uphold. Moreover, the very essence of a healthy federalism depends upon the avoidance of needless conflict between state and federal courts. In non-exclusionary States, federal officers, being human, were by it invited to and did, as our cases indicate, step across the street to the State's attorney with their unconstitutionally seized evidence. Prosecution on the basis of that evidence was then had in a state court in utter disregard of the enforceable Fourth Amendment. If the fruits of an unconstitutional search had been inadmissible in both state and federal courts, this inducement to evasion would have been sooner eliminated.

Federal-state cooperation in the solution of crime under constitutional standards will be promoted, if only by recognition of their now mutual obligation to respect the same fundamental criteria in their approaches.

There are those who say, as did Justice (then Judge) Cardozo, that under our constitutional exclusionary doctrine "the criminal is to go free because the constable has blundered." In some cases this will undoubtedly be the result. But, there is another consideration—the imperative of judicial integrity. The criminal goes free, if he must, but it is the law that sets him free. Nothing can destroy a government more quickly than its failure to observe its own laws, or worse, its disregard of the charter of its own existence.

The ignoble shortcut to conviction left open to the State tends to destroy the entire system of constitutional restraints on which the liberties of the people rest. Having once recognized that the right to privacy embodied in the Fourth Amendment is enforceable against the States, and that the right to be secure against rude invasions of privacy by state officers is, therefore, constitutional in origin, we can no longer permit that right to remain an empty promise. Because it is enforceable in the same manner and to like effect as other basic rights secured by the Due Process Clause, we can no longer permit it to be revocable at the whim of any police officer who, in the name of law enforcement itself, chooses to suspend its enjoyment. Our decision, founded on reason and truth, gives to the individual no more than that which the Constitution guarantees him, to the police officer no less than that to which honest law enforcement is entitled, and, to the courts, that judicial integrity so necessary in the true administration of justice.

JUSTICE HARLAN, whom JUSTICE FRANKFURTER and JUSTICE WHITTAKER join, dissenting.

What the Court is now doing is to impose upon the States not only federal substantive standards of "search and seizure" but also the basic federal remedy for violation of those standards. For I think it entirely clear that the *Weeks* exclusionary rule is but a remedy which, by penalizing past official misconduct, is aimed at deterring such conduct in the future.

I would not impose upon the States this federal exclusionary remedy. The reasons given by the majority for now suddenly turning its back on *Wolf* seem to me notably unconvincing.

First, it is said that the factual grounds upon which *Wolf* was based have since changed, in that more States now follow the *Weeks* exclusionary rule than was so at the time *Wolf* was decided. While that is true, a recent survey indicates that at present one-half of the States still adhere to the common-law non-exclusionary rule, and one, Maryland, retains the rule as to felonies. But in any case surely all this is beside the point, as the majority itself indeed seems to recognize. Our concern here, as it was in *Wolf*, is not with the desirability of that rule but only with the question whether the States are constitutionally free to follow it or not as they may themselves determine, and the relevance of the disparity of views among the States on this point lies simply in the fact that the judgment involved is a debatable one. Moreover, the very fact on which the majority relies, instead of lending support to what is now being done, points away from the need of replacing voluntary state action with federal compulsion.

The preservation of a proper balance between state and federal responsibility in the administration of criminal justice demands patience on the part of those who might like to see things move faster among the States in this respect. Problems of criminal law enforcement vary widely from State of State. One State, in considering the totality of its legal picture, may conclude that the need for embracing the *Weeks* rule is pressing because other remedies are unavailable or inadequate to secure compliance with the substantive constitutional principle involved. Another, though equally solicitous of constitutional rights, may choose to pursue one purpose at a time, allowing all evidence relevant to guilt to be brought into a criminal trial, and dealing with constitutional infractions by other means. Still another may consider the exclusionary rule too rough-and-ready a remedy, in that it reaches only unconstitutional intrusions which eventuate in criminal prosecution of the victims. Further, a State after experimenting with the *Weeks* rule for a time may, because of unsatisfactory experience with it, decide to revert to a non-exclusionary rule. And so on. For us the question remains, as it has always been, one of state power, not one of passing judgment on the wisdom of one state course or another. In my view this Court should continue to forbear from fettering the States with an adamant rule which may embarrass them in coping with their own peculiar problems in criminal law enforcement.

Further, we are told that imposition of the *Weeks* rule on the States "makes very good sense," in that it will promote recognition by state and federal officials of their "mutual obligation to respect the same fundamental criteria" in their approach to law enforcement, and will avoid "needless conflict between state and federal courts."

An approach which regards the issue as one of achieving procedural symmetry or of serving administrative convenience surely disfigures the boundaries of this Court's functions in relation to the state and federal courts. Our role in promulgating the *Weeks* rule and its extensions was quite a different one than it is here. There, in implementing the Fourth Amendment, we occupied the position of a tribunal having the ultimate responsibility for developing the standards and procedures of judicial administration within the judicial system over which it presides. Here we review state procedures whose measure is to be taken not against the specific substantive commands of the Fourth Amendment but under the flexible contours of the Due Process Clause. I do not believe that the Fourteenth Amendment empowers this Court to mould state remedies effectuating the right to freedom from "arbitrary intrusion by the police" to suit its own notions of how things should be done.

A state conviction comes to us as the complete product of a sovereign judicial system. Typically a case will have been tried in a trial court, tested in some final appellate court, and will go no further. In the comparatively rare instance when a conviction is reviewed by us on due process grounds we deal then with a finished product in the creation of which we are allowed no hand, and our task, far from being one of over-all supervision, is, speaking generally, restricted to a determination of whether the prosecution was constitutionally fair. The specifics of trial procedure, which in every mature legal system will vary greatly in detail, are within the sole competence of the States. I do not see how it can be said that a trial becomes unfair simply because a State determines that evidence may be considered by the trier of fact, regardless of how it was obtained, if it is relevant to the one issue with which the trial is concerned, the guilt or innocence of the accused. Of course, a court may use its procedures as an incidental means of pursuing other ends than the correct resolution of the controversies before it. Such indeed is the *Weeks* rule, but if a State does not choose to use its courts in this way, I do not believe that this Court is empowered to impose this much-debated procedure on local courts, however efficacious we may consider the *Weeks* rule to be as a means of securing constitutional rights.

I regret that I find so unwise in principle and so inexpedient in policy a decision motivated by the high purpose of increasing respect for constitutional rights. But in the last analysis I think this Court can increase respect for the Constitution only if it rigidly respects the limitations which the Constitution places upon it, and respects as well the principles inherent in its own processes. In the present case I think we exceed both, and that our voice becomes only a voice of power, not of reason.

––––––––––––

Most of the arguments made in *Mapp* were essentially the same as those made in *Wolf*, but the result was different. Why? One explanation is that the makeup of the Supreme Court had changed substantially between 1949 and 1961. Chief Justice Fred Vinson and five Associate Justices who took part in the *Wolf* decision had left the Court by the time *Mapp* was decided. Many of their replacements—including Chief Justice Earl Warren and Associate Justice William Brennan—had a more expansive view of the Constitution and were often more sympathetic in evaluating the constitutional claims of criminal defendants. There were, of course, many other significant changes in constitutional interpretation during the years of the Warren Court, between 1953 and 1969. Most notable, perhaps, was the Supreme Court's unanimous decision in *Brown v. Board of Education*, 347 U.S. 483 (1954), holding that segregated public schools are "inherently unequal" and unconstitutional.

Mapp did not end the debate over the exclusionary rule. Far from it. To this day, the Supreme Court and legal commentators continue to grapple with the difficult questions raised in both *Wolf* and *Mapp*. Does the exclusionary rule deter police misconduct and protect constitutional rights? Are there any realistic alternatives? And are the costs of the exclusionary rule—important evidence excluded, convictions lost, crimes left unpunished—justified by the benefits? These and similar questions have led the Supreme Court to carve out a number of important exceptions to the exclusionary rule since *Mapp* was decided. We'll take up those exceptions—and revisit the debate over the costs and benefits of the exclusionary rule—in Chapter 8. For now, just remember the principal justifications for the exclusionary rule set forth in *Mapp* and consider whether you agree with them.

The Exclusionary Rule

Under the exclusionary rule, evidence obtained in violation of the Constitution is generally excluded from the defendant's criminal trial and cannot be used to establish guilt. According to *Mapp v. Ohio*, the exclusionary rule is needed to deter police misconduct, protect constitutional rights, and safeguard judicial integrity.

PART II

SEARCHES AND SEIZURES

▪ ▪ ▪

> **Amendment IV:** The right of the people to be secure in their persons, houses, papers, and effects, against unreasonable searches and seizures, shall not be violated, and no Warrants shall issue, but upon probable cause, supported by Oath or affirmation, and particularly describing the place to be searched, and the persons or things to be seized.

Police solve crimes and prosecutors bring the offenders to justice with evidence. But critical evidence doesn't just materialize—police must search for it, and if they find it, seize it so that it can later be used at trial. The Fourth Amendment, with its prohibition on "unreasonable searches and seizures," both implicitly authorizes and limits two of the most important tools of law enforcement. In their quest for evidence, police may perform searches and seizures, but they must do so *reasonably* in a manner that protects the "right of the people to be secure in their persons, houses, papers, and effects."

What makes a search or seizure reasonable? The Fourth Amendment doesn't explicitly tell us, but it does seem to offer a clue when it requires that warrants be based upon probable cause and particularly describe the place to be searched and the persons or things to be seized. But even in the absence of probable cause or a warrant, there are many circumstances in which a search or seizure might still be considered reasonable. For example, no one seriously suggests that police should wait to obtain a warrant before entering private property to search for an armed gunman or his weapons, hostages, or victims. And long before the horrific events of September 11, 2001, most people readily acknowledged the need for routine searches—without a warrant and without individualized suspicion—of airline passengers and their belongings.

Over time, the Supreme Court has developed many discrete rules and doctrines designed to address the wide variety of contexts in which police perform searches and seizures. The following six Chapters organize and discuss these rules and doctrines. Chapter 3 defines the word "search" in the Fourth Amendment. Chapter 4 discusses the probable cause and warrant requirements. Chapter 5 considers the basic exceptions to the warrant requirement. Chapter 6 reviews seizures of persons and describes the differences between consensual encounters, investigatory stops, and full-scale arrests. Chapter 7 addresses the application of the Fourth Amendment in a number of special contexts. And Chapter 8 brings the Fourth Amendment section of the book full circle by returning to a discussion of the exclusionary rule—first raised in Chapter 2—and exploring its various exceptions.

As you read each of the following Chapters, be sure to consider the Supreme Court's views and your own views with respect to the basic question at the heart of the Fourth Amendment: How do we best balance the privacy rights of individuals against the government's need for efficient and effective law enforcement?

CHAPTER 3

SEARCHES

■ ■ ■

The first part of the Fourth Amendment, sometimes referred to as the Unreasonableness Clause, declares: "The right of the people to be secure in their persons, houses, papers, and effects, against unreasonable searches and seizures, shall not be violated." This Chapter focuses almost exclusively on a single important word—"search"—at the heart of the Fourth Amendment's prohibition on "unreasonable searches and seizures." The Supreme Court's interpretation of that word has changed over time, particularly as technological innovations have altered the way we live, work, and communicate. These new technologies, so many of which have improved and enriched our lives, have also significantly enhanced the investigative tools available to police, placing our privacy at risk. At the core of the legal debate over the meaning of the term "search" in the Fourth Amendment are profound questions about how best to balance the privacy rights of individuals against the needs of law enforcement.

It is sometimes obvious that a search has occurred. If a police officer spots Shannon Shady seated on a park bench, sneaks up behind her, and, in the hope of finding illegal drugs, unzips her purse and rifles through it without her knowledge or permission, everyone—including the Justices of the Supreme Court—would agree that the officer has performed a search.

Now suppose that the same police officer, rather than using his own eyes and hands, directs his specially-trained drug-sniffing dog to determine whether there are any illegal substances in Shannon's purse. Does the use of the drug-sniffing police dog in a public park constitute a search? What if there is no police dog, but instead its technological equivalent, a mechanical device with X-ray vision and chemical sensors capable of revealing to the officer the contents of the purse? These are precisely the kinds of fascinating but difficult questions with which the Supreme Court has grappled in its attempt to define the word "search" in the Fourth Amendment.

A. WHAT IS A SEARCH?

1. THE OLD VIEW: *OLMSTEAD v. U.S.*

Before we dive into the tough questions of today and tomorrow, a little historical perspective is in order, beginning with the Supreme

Court's decision in *Olmstead v. U.S.*, which held that electronic eavesdropping accomplished without a physical trespass on the defendant's property did not amount to a "search" under the Fourth Amendment.

OLMSTEAD V. U.S.

277 U.S. 438 (1928)

CHIEF JUSTICE TAFT delivered the opinion of the Court.

The petitioners were convicted in the District Court for the Western District of Washington of a conspiracy to violate the National Prohibition Act by unlawfully possessing, transporting and importing intoxicating liquors and maintaining nuisances, and by selling intoxicating liquors. Seventy-two others, in addition to the petitioners, were indicted. Some were not apprehended, some were acquitted, and others pleaded guilty.

The evidence in the records discloses a conspiracy of amazing magnitude to import, possess, and sell liquor unlawfully. It involved the employment of not less than 50 persons, of two sea-going vessels for the transportation of liquor to British Columbia, of smaller vessels for coastwise transportation to the state of Washington, the purchase and use of a branch beyond the suburban limits of Seattle, with a large underground cache for storage and a number of smaller caches in that city, the maintenance of a central office manned with operators, and the employment of executives, salesmen, deliverymen dispatchers, scouts, bookkeepers, collectors, and an attorney. In a bad month sales amounted to $176,000; the aggregate for a year must have exceeded $2,000,000.

Olmstead was the leading conspirator and the general manager of the business. He made a contribution of $10,000 to the capital; 11 others contributed $1,000 each. The profits were divided, one-half to Olmstead and the remainder to the other 11. Of the several offices in Seattle, the chief one was in a large office building. In this there were three telephones on three different lines. There were telephones in an office of the manager in his own home, at the homes of his associates, and at other places in the city. Communication was had frequently with Vancouver, British Columbia. Times were fixed for the deliveries of the "stuff" to places along Puget Sound near Seattle, and from there the liquor was removed and deposited in the caches already referred to. One of the chief men was always on duty at the main office to receive orders by the telephones and to direct their filling by a corps of men stationed in another room—the "bull pen." The call numbers of the telephones were given to those known to be likely customers. At times the sales amounted to 200 cases of liquor per day.

The information which led to the discovery of the conspiracy and its nature and extent was largely obtained by intercepting messages on the telephones of the conspirators by four federal prohibition officers. Small wires were inserted along the ordinary telephone wires from the residences of four of the petitioners and those leading from the chief office. The insertions were made without trespass upon any property of the defendants. They were made in the basement of the large office building. The taps from house lines were made in the streets near the houses.

The gathering of evidence continued for many months. Conversations of the conspirators, of which refreshing stenographic notes were currently made, were testified to by the government witnesses. They revealed the large business transactions of the partners and their subordinates. Men at the wires heard the orders given for liquor by customers and the acceptances; they became auditors of the conversations between the partners. All this disclosed the conspiracy charged in the indictment. Many of the intercepted conversations were not merely reports, but parts of the criminal acts. The evidence also disclosed the difficulties to which the conspirators were subjected, the reported news of the capture of vessels, the arrest of their men, and the seizure of cases of liquor in garages and other places. It showed the dealing by Olmstead, the chief conspirator, with members of the Seattle police, the messages to them which secured the release of arrested members of the conspiracy, and also direct promises to officers of payments as soon as opportunity offered.

The well-known historical purpose of the Fourth Amendment, directed against general warrants and writs of assistance, was to prevent the use of governmental force to search a man's house, his person, his papers, and his effects, and to prevent their seizure against his will.

The amendment itself shows that the search is to be of material things—the person, the house, his papers, or his effects. The description of the warrant necessary to make the proceeding lawful is that it must specify the place to be searched and the person or things to be seized.

The Fourth Amendment may have proper application to a sealed letter in the mail. It is plainly within the words of the amendment to say that the unlawful rifling by a government agent of a sealed letter is a search and seizure of the sender's papers of effects. The letter is a paper, an effect, and in the custody of a government that forbids carriage, except under its protection. The United States takes no such care of telegraph or telephone messages as of mailed sealed letters. The amendment does not forbid what was done here. There was no searching. There was no seizure. The evidence was secured by the use of the sense of hearing and that only. There was no entry of the houses or offices of the defendants.

By the invention of the telephone 50 years ago, and its application for the purpose of extending communications, one can talk with another at a far distant place. The language of the amendment cannot be extended and expanded to include telephone wires, reaching to the whole world from the defendant's house or office. The intervening wires are not part of his house or office, any more than are the highways along which they are stretched.

Congress may, of course, protect the secrecy of telephone messages by making them, when intercepted, inadmissible in evidence in federal criminal trials, by direct legislation, and thus depart from the common law of evidence. But the courts may not adopt such a policy by attributing an enlarged and unusual meaning to the Fourth Amendment. The reasonable view is that one who installs in his house a telephone instrument with connecting wires intends to project his voice to those quite outside, and that the wires beyond his house, and messages while passing over them, are not within the protection of the Fourth Amendment. Here those who intercepted the projected voices were not in the house of either party to the conversation.

Neither the cases we have cited nor any of the many federal decisions brought to our attention hold the Fourth Amendment to have been violated as against a defendant, unless there has been an official search and seizure of his person or such a seizure of his papers or his tangible material effects or an actual physical invasion of his house or "curtilage" for the purpose of making a seizure.

We think, therefore, that the wire tapping here disclosed did not amount to a search or seizure within the meaning of the Fourth Amendment.

What has been said disposes of the only question that comes within the terms of our order granting certiorari in these cases. But some of our number, departing from that order, have concluded that there is merit in the twofold objection, overruled in both courts below, that evidence obtained through intercepting of telephone messages by a government agents was inadmissible, because the mode of obtaining it was unethical and a misdemeanor under the law of Washington.

The common-law rule is that the admissibility of evidence is not affected by the illegality of the means by which it was obtained. The common-law rule must apply in the case at bar.

Nor can we, without the sanction of congressional enactment, subscribe to the suggestion that the courts have a discretion to exclude evidence, the admission of which is not unconstitutional, because unethically secured. This would be at variance with the common-law doctrine generally supported by authority. There is no case that sustains, nor any recognized textbook that gives color to, such a view. Our general experience shows that much evidence has always been receivable, although not obtained by conformity to the highest ethics. The history of criminal trials shows numerous cases of prosecutions of oathbound conspiracies for murder, robbery, and other crimes, where officers of the law have distinguished themselves and joined the organizations, taken the oaths, and given themselves every appearance of active members engaged in the promotion of crime for the purpose of securing evidence. Evidence secured by such means has always been received.

A standard which would forbid the reception of evidence, if obtained by other than nice ethical conduct by government officials, would make society suffer and give criminals greater immunity than has been known heretofore. In the absence of controlling legislation by Congress, those who realize the difficulties in bringing offenders to justice may well deem it wise that the exclusion of evidence should be confined to cases where rights under the Constitution would be violated by admitting it.

The statute of Washington, adopted in 1909, provides that: "Every person who shall intercept, read or in any manner interrupt or delay the sending of a message over any telegraph or telephone line shall be guilty of a misdemeanor."

This statute does not declare that evidence obtained by such interception shall be inadmissible, and by the common law, already referred to, it would not be. Whether the state of Washington may prosecute and punish federal officers violating this law, and those whose messages were intercepted may sue them civilly, is not before us. But clearly a statute, passed 20 years after the admission of the state into the Union, cannot affect the rules of evidence applicable in courts of the United States.

JUSTICE BRANDEIS, dissenting.

The defendants were convicted of conspiring to violate the National Prohibition Act. Before any of the persons now charged had been arrested or indicted, the telephones by means of which they habitually communicated with one another and with others had been tapped by federal officers. To this end, a lineman of long experience in wire tapping was employed, on behalf of the government and at its expense. He tapped eight telephones, some in the homes of the persons charged, some in their offices. Acting on behalf of the government and in their official capacity, at least six other prohibition agents listened over the tapped wires and reported the messages taken. Their operations extended over a period of nearly five months. The typewritten record of the notes of conversations overheard occupies 775 typewritten pages. By objections seasonably made and persistently renewed, the defendants objected to the admission of the evidence obtained by wire tapping, on the ground that the government's wire tapping constituted an unreasonable search and seizure, in violation of the Fourth Amendment, and that the use as evidence of the conversations overheard compelled the defendants to be witnesses against themselves, in violation of the Fifth Amendment.

The government makes no attempt to defend the methods employed by its officers. Indeed, it concedes that, if wire tapping can be deemed a search and seizure within the Fourth Amendment, such wire tapping as was practiced in the case at bar was an unreasonable search and seizure, and that the evidence thus obtained was inadmissible. But it relies on the language of the amendment, and it claims that the protection given thereby cannot properly be held to include a telephone conversation.

When the Fourth and Fifth Amendments were adopted, the form that evil had theretofore taken had been necessarily simple. Force and violence were then the only means known to man by which a government could directly effect self-incrimination. It could compel the individual to testify—a compulsion effected, if need be, by torture. It could secure possession of his papers and other articles incident to his private life—a seizure effected, if need be, by breaking and entry. Protection against such invasion of the sanctities of a man's home and the privacies of life was provided in the Fourth and Fifth Amendments by specific language. But time works changes, brings into existence new conditions and purposes. Subtler and more far-reaching means of invading privacy have become available to the government. Discovery and invention have made it possible for the government, by means far more effective than stretching upon the rack, to obtain disclosure in court of what is whispered in the closet.

Moreover, in the application of a Constitution, our contemplation cannot be only of what has been, but of what may be. The progress of science in furnishing the government with means of espionage is not likely to stop with wire tapping. Ways may some day be developed by which the government, without removing papers from secret drawers, can reproduce them in court, and by which it will be enabled to expose to a jury the most intimate occurrences of the home. Advances in the psychic and related sciences may bring means of exploring unexpressed beliefs, thoughts and emotions. Can it be that the Constitution affords no protection against such invasions of individual security?

The evil incident to invasion of the privacy of the telephone is far greater than that involved in tampering with the mails. Whenever a telephone line is tapped, the privacy of the persons at both ends of the line is invaded, and all conversations between them upon any subject, and although proper, confidential, and privileged, may be overheard. Moreover, the tapping of one man's telephone line involves the tapping of the telephone of every other person whom he may call, or who may call him. As a means of espionage, writs of assistance and general warrants are but puny instruments of tyranny and oppression when compared with wire tapping.

The makers of our Constitution undertook to secure conditions favorable to the pursuit of happiness. They recognized the significance of man's spiritual nature, of his feelings and of his intellect. They knew that only a part of the pain, pleasure and satisfactions of life are to be found in material things. They sought to protect Americans in their beliefs, their thoughts, their emotions and their sensations. They conferred, as against the government, the right to be let alone—the most comprehensive of rights and the right most valued by civilized men. To protect that right, every unjustifiable intrusion by the government upon the privacy of the individual, whatever the means employed, must be deemed a violation of the Fourth Amendment. And the use, as evidence in a criminal proceeding, of facts ascertained by such intrusion must be deemed a violation of the Fifth.

Applying to the Fourth and Fifth Amendments the established rule of construction, the defendants' objections to the evidence obtained by wire tapping must, in my opinion, be sustained. It is, of course, immaterial where the physical connection with the telephone wires leading into the defendants' premises was made. And it is also immaterial that the intrusion was in aid of law enforcement. Experience should teach us to be most on our guard to protect liberty when the government's purposes are beneficent. Men born to freedom are naturally alert to repel invasion of their liberty by evil-minded rulers. The greatest dangers to liberty lurk in insidious encroachment by men of zeal, well-meaning but without understanding.

Independently of the constitutional question, I am of opinion that the judgment should be reversed. By the laws of Washington, wire tapping is a crime. To prove its case, the government was obliged to lay bare the crimes committed by its officers on its behalf. A federal court should not permit such a prosecution to continue.

Decency, security, and liberty alike demand that government officials shall be subjected to the same rules of conduct that are commands to the citizen. In a government of laws, existence of the government will be imperiled if it fails to observe the law scrupulously. Our government is the potent, the omnipresent teacher. For good or for ill, it teaches the whole people by its example. Crime is contagious. If the government becomes a lawbreaker, it breeds contempt for law; it invites every man to become a law unto himself; it invites anarchy. To declare that in the administration of the criminal law the end justifies the means—to declare that the government may commit crimes in order to secure the conviction of a private criminal—would bring terrible retribution. Against that pernicious doctrine this court should resolutely set its face.

———————

Chief Justice Taft's majority opinion in *Olmstead* adopts an extremely narrow interpretation of the scope of the Fourth Amendment's protection. First, Taft contends that specific language in the text of the

Fourth Amendment makes it clear that its protection extends only to *material* or *tangible* things, including persons, houses, papers, and effects. A conversation traveling over telephone wires outside the walls of a home does not fall within any of those categories. Second, Taft argues that a search requires a *physical* entry into the defendant's home or property. The government agents didn't make a physical entry since they tapped phone wires *outside* the defendant's home and office, and violated none of the defendant's property interests. Third, Taft implicitly casts aside concerns about judicial integrity. While the wiretapping may have been illegal and unethical under Washington state law, the federal trial court should still admit the evidence rather than apply the exclusionary rule.

In his dissent—one of the most famous and oft-quoted dissents in the entire history of the Supreme Court—Justice Brandeis argues for a more expansive interpretation of the Fourth Amendment. First, Brandeis argues that advances in science and technology require evolution in constitutional interpretation as well, since the specific language in the Fourth Amendment may not adequately address threats to individual liberty that the framers of the Constitution never imagined. Second, Brandeis contends that Fourth Amendment protections should extend beyond strictly physical invasions of particular places, personal effects, and property interests. Instead, the Fourth Amendment is concerned with protecting *privacy*, "the right to be let alone—the most comprehensive of rights and the right most valued by civilized men." Third, Brandeis expresses a profound concern for judicial integrity. When "government becomes a lawbreaker, it breeds contempt for law; it invites every man to become a law unto himself; it invites anarchy."

Note too how both the majority and the dissent use the facts to buttress their arguments. Chief Justice Taft focuses on the defendant's involvement in a massive conspiracy to violate Prohibition. Justice Brandeis pays scant attention to the defendant's conduct and instead focuses on the length and breadth of the government's investigation, the extensive nature of the wiretapping, and the enormous intrusion into the defendant's privacy.

2.   THE MODERN VIEW: *KATZ v. U.S.*

It took nearly 40 years, but the arguments raised by Justice Brandeis in his *Olmstead* dissent eventually prevailed. In *Katz v. U.S.*, the Supreme Court overruled *Olmstead* and announced a new two-part test for determining whether police performed a search within the meaning of the Fourth Amendment.

KATZ V. U.S.
389 U.S. 347 (1967)

JUSTICE STEWART delivered the opinion of the Court.

The petitioner was convicted in the District Court for the Southern District of California under an eight-count indictment charging him with transmitting wagering information by telephone from Los Angeles to Miami and Boston in violation of a federal statute. At trial, the Government was permitted, over the petitioner's objection, to introduce evidence of the petitioner's end of telephone conversations, overheard by FBI agents who had attached an electronic listening and recording device to the outside of the public telephone booth from which he had placed his calls. In affirming his conviction, the Court of Appeals rejected the contention that the recordings had been obtained in violation of the Fourth Amendment, because "there was no physical entrance into the area occupied by (the petitioner)." We granted certiorari in order to consider the constitutional questions thus presented.

The parties have attached great significance to the characterization of the telephone booth from which the petitioner placed his calls. The petitioner has strenuously argued that the booth was a "constitutionally protected area." The Government has maintained with equal vigor that it was not. But this effort to decide whether or not a given "area," viewed in the abstract, is "constitutionally protected" deflects attention from the problem presented by this case. For the Fourth Amendment protects people, not places. What a person knowingly exposes to the public, even in his own home or office, is not a subject of Fourth Amendment protection. But what he seeks to preserve as private, even in an area accessible to the public, may be constitutionally protected.

The Government stresses the fact that the telephone booth from which the petitioner made his calls was constructed partly of glass, so that he was as visible after he entered it as he would have been if he had remained outside. But what he sought to exclude when he entered the booth was not the intruding eye—it was the uninvited ear. He did not shed his right to do so simply because he made his calls from a place where he might be seen. No less than an individual in a business office, in a friend's apartment, or in a taxicab, a person in a telephone booth may rely upon the protection of the Fourth Amendment. One who occupies it, shuts the door behind him, and pays the toll that permits him to place a call is surely entitled to assume that the words he utters into the mouthpiece will not be broadcast to the world. To read the Constitution more narrowly is to ignore the vital role that the public telephone has come to play in private communication.

The Government contends, however, that the activities of its agents in this case should not be tested by Fourth Amendment requirements, for the surveillance technique they employed involved no physical penetration of the telephone booth from which the petitioner placed his calls. It is true that the absence of such penetration was at one time thought to foreclose further Fourth Amendment inquiry, *Olmstead v. U.S.*, 277 U.S. 438 (1928), for that Amendment was thought to limit only searches and seizures of tangible property. But the premise that property interests control the right of the Government to search and seize has been discredited. Thus, although a closely divided Court supposed in *Olmstead* that surveillance without any trespass and without the seizure of any material object fell outside the ambit of the Constitution, we have since departed from the narrow view on which that decision rested. Indeed, we have expressly held that the Fourth Amendment governs not only the seizure of tangible items, but extends as well to the recording of oral statements overheard without any technical trespass under local property law. Once this much is acknowledged, and once it is recognized that the Fourth Amendment protects people—and not simply "areas"—against unreasonable searches and seizures it becomes clear that the reach of that Amendment cannot turn upon the presence or absence of a physical intrusion into any given enclosure.

We conclude that the underpinnings of *Olmstead* have been so eroded by our subsequent decisions that the "trespass" doctrine there enunciated can no longer be regarded as controlling. The Government's activities in electronically listening to and recording the petitioner's words violated the privacy upon which he justifiably relied while using the telephone booth and thus constituted a "search and seizure" within the meaning of the Fourth Amendment. The fact that the electronic device employed to achieve that end did not happen to penetrate the wall of the booth can have no constitutional significance.

The question remaining for decision, then, is whether the search and seizure conducted in this case complied with constitutional standards. In that regard, the Government's position is that its agents acted in an entirely defensible manner: They did not begin their electronic surveillance until investigation of the petitioner's activities had established a strong probability that he was using the telephone in question to transmit gambling information to persons in other States, in violation of federal law. Moreover, the surveillance was limited, both in scope and in duration, to the specific purpose of establishing the contents of the petitioner's unlawful telephonic communications. The agents confined their surveillance to the brief periods during which he used the telephone booth, and they took great care to overhear only the conversations of the petitioner himself.

Accepting this account of the Government's actions as accurate, it is clear that this surveillance was so narrowly circumscribed that a duly authorized magistrate, properly notified of the need for such investigation, specifically informed of the basis on which it was to proceed, and clearly apprised of the precise intrusion it would entail, could constitutionally have authorized, with appropriate safeguards, the very limited search and seizure that the Government asserts in fact took place.

The Government urges that, because its agents relied upon the decision in *Olmstead*, and because they did no more here than they might properly have done with prior judicial sanction, we should retroactively validate their conduct. That we cannot do. It is apparent that the agents in this case acted with restraint. Yet the inescapable fact is that this restraint was imposed by the agents themselves, not by a judicial officer. They were not required, before commencing the search, to present their estimate of probable cause for detached scrutiny by a neutral magistrate. They were not compelled, during the conduct of the search itself, to observe precise limits established in advance by a specific court order. Nor were they directed, after the search had been completed, to notify the authorizing magistrate in detail of all that had been seized. In the absence of such safeguards, this Court has never sustained a search upon the sole ground that officers reasonably expected to find evidence of a particular crime and voluntarily confined their activities to the least intrusive means consistent with that end. Searches conducted without warrants have been held unlawful notwithstanding facts unquestionably showing probable cause, for the Constitution requires that the deliberate, impartial judgment of a judicial officer be interposed between the citizen and the police. Over and again this Court has emphasized that the mandate of the Fourth Amendment requires adherence to judicial processes, and that searches conducted outside the judicial process, without prior approval by judge or magistrate, are *per se* unreasonable under the Fourth Amendment—subject only to a few specifically established and well-delineated exceptions.

It is difficult to imagine how any of those exceptions could ever apply to the sort of search and seizure involved in this case. Even electronic surveillance substantially contemporaneous with an individual's arrest could hardly be deemed an "incident" of that arrest. Nor could the use of electronic surveillance without prior authorization be justified on grounds of "hot pursuit." And, of course, the very nature of electronic surveillance precludes its use pursuant to the suspect's consent.

The Government does not question these basic principles. Rather, it urges the creation of a new exception to cover this case. It argues that surveillance of a telephone booth should be exempted from the usual requirement of advance authorization by a magistrate upon a showing of probable cause. We cannot agree. Omission of such authorization bypasses the safeguards provided by an objective predetermination of probable cause, and substitutes instead the far less reliable procedure of an after-the-event justification for the search, too likely to be subtly influenced by the familiar shortcomings of hindsight judgment. And bypassing a neutral predetermination of the scope of a search leaves individuals secure from Fourth Amendment violations only in the discretion of the police.

These considerations do not vanish when the search in question is transferred from the setting of a home, an office, or a hotel room to that of a telephone booth. Wherever a man may be, he is entitled to know that he will remain free from unreasonable searches and seizures. The government agents here ignored the procedure of antecedent justification that is central to the Fourth Amendment, a procedure that we hold to be a constitutional precondition of the kind of electronic surveillance involved in this case. Because the surveillance here failed to meet that condition, and because it led to the petitioner's conviction, the judgment must be reversed.

JUSTICE HARLAN, concurring.

I join the opinion of the Court, which I read to hold only (a) that an enclosed telephone booth is an area where, like a home, and unlike a field, a person has a constitutionally protected reasonable expectation of privacy; (b) that electronic as well as physical intrusion into a place that is in this sense private may constitute a violation of the Fourth Amendment; and (c) that the invasion of a constitutionally protected area by federal authorities is, as the Court has long held, presumptively unreasonable in the absence of a search warrant.

As the Court's opinion states, "the Fourth Amendment protects people, not places." The question, however, is what protection it affords to those people. Generally, as here, the answer to that question requires reference to a "place." My understanding of the rule that has emerged from prior decisions is that there is a twofold requirement, first that a person have exhibited an actual (subjective) expectation of privacy and, second, that the expectation be one that society is prepared to recognize as "reasonable." Thus a man's home is, for most purposes, a place where he expects privacy, but objects, activities, or statements that he exposes to the "plain view" of outsiders are not "protected" because no intention to keep them to himself has been exhibited. On the other hand, conversations in the open would not be protected against being overheard, for the expectation of privacy under the circumstances would be unreasonable.

The critical fact in this case is that one who occupies a telephone booth shuts the door behind him, and pays the toll that permits him to place a call is surely entitled to assume that his conversation is not being intercepted. The point is not that the booth is accessible to the public at other times, but that it is a temporarily private place whose momentary occupants' expectations of freedom from intrusion are recognized as reasonable.

Finally, I do not read the Court's opinion to declare that no interception of a conversation one-half of which occurs in a public telephone booth can be reasonable in the absence of a warrant. As elsewhere under the Fourth Amendment, warrants are the general rule, to which the legitimate needs of law enforcement may demand specific exceptions. It will be time enough to consider any such exceptions when an appropriate occasion presents itself, and I agree with the Court that this is not one.

JUSTICE WHITE, concurring.

In joining the Court's opinion, I note the Court's acknowledgment that there are circumstances in which it is reasonable to search without a warrant. In this connection, the Court points out that today's decision does not reach national security cases. Wiretapping to protect the security of the Nation has been authorized by successive Presidents. The present Administration would apparently save national security cases from restrictions against wiretapping. We should not require the warrant procedure and the magistrate's judgment if the President of the United States or his chief legal officer, the Attorney General, has considered the requirements of national security and authorized electronic surveillance as reasonable.

JUSTICE DOUGLAS, with whom JUSTICE BRENNAN joins, concurring.

While I join the opinion of the Court, I feel compelled to reply to the separate concurring opinion of my Brother White, which I view as a wholly unwarranted green light for the Executive Branch to resort to electronic eavesdropping without a warrant in cases which the Executive Branch itself labels "national security" matters.

Neither the President nor the Attorney General is a magistrate. In matters where they believe national security may be involved they are not detached, disinterested, and neutral as a court or magistrate must be. Under the separation of powers created by the Constitution, the Executive Branch is not supposed to be neutral and disinterested. Rather it should vigorously investigate and prevent breaches of national security and prosecute those who violate the pertinent federal laws. The President and Attorney General are properly interested parties, cast in the role of adversary, in national security cases. They may even be the intended victims of subversive action. Since spies and saboteurs are as entitled to the protection of the Fourth Amendment as suspected gamblers like petitioner, I cannot agree that where spies and saboteurs are involved adequate protection of Fourth Amendment rights is assured when the President and Attorney General assume both the position of adversary-and-prosecutor and disinterested, neutral magistrate.

JUSTICE BLACK, dissenting.

If I could agree with the Court that eavesdropping carried on by electronic means (equivalent to wiretapping) constitutes a "search" or "seizure," I would be happy to join the Court's opinion.

My basic objection is twofold: (1) I do not believe that the words of the Amendment will bear the meaning given them by today's decision, and (2) I do not believe that it is the proper role of this Court to rewrite the Amendment in order to bring it into harmony with the times and thus reach a result that many people believe to be desirable.

While I realize that an argument based on the meaning of words lacks the scope, and no doubt the appeal, of broad policy discussions and philosophical discourses on such nebulous subjects as privacy, for me the language of the Amendment is the crucial place to look in construing a written document such as our Constitution.

The first clause [of the Fourth Amendment] protects "persons, houses, papers, and effects, against unreasonable searches and seizures." These words connote the idea of tangible things with size, form, and weight, things capable of being searched, seized, or both. The second clause of the Amendment still further establishes its Framers' purpose to limit its protection to tangible things by providing that no warrants shall issue but those "particularly describing the place to be searched, and the persons or things to be seized." A conversation overheard by eavesdropping, whether by plain snooping or wiretapping, is not tangible and, under the normally accepted meanings of the words, can neither be searched nor seized. In addition the language of the second clause indicates that the Amendment refers not only to something tangible so it can be seized but to something already in existence so it can be described. Yet the Court's interpretation would have the Amendment apply to overhearing future conversations which by their very nature are nonexistent until they take place. How can one "describe" a future conversation, and, if one cannot, how can a magistrate issue a warrant to eavesdrop one in the future? It is argued that information showing what is expected to be said is sufficient to limit the boundaries of what later can be admitted into evidence; but does such general information really meet the specific language of the Amendment which says "particularly describing"? Rather than using language in a completely artificial way, I must conclude that the Fourth Amendment simply does not apply to eavesdropping.

Tapping telephone wires, of course, was an unknown possibility at the time the Fourth Amendment was adopted. But eavesdropping (and wiretapping is nothing more than eavesdropping by telephone) was an ancient practice which at common law was condemned as a nuisance. In those days the eavesdropper listened by naked ear under the eaves of houses or their windows, or beyond their walls seeking out private discourse. There can be no doubt that the Framers were aware of this practice, and if they had desired to outlaw or restrict the use of evidence obtained by eavesdropping, I believe that they would have used the appropriate language to do so in the Fourth Amendment. They certainly would not have left such a task to the ingenuity of language-stretching judges. No one, it seems to me, can read the debates on the Bill of Rights without reaching the conclusion that its Framers and critics well knew the meaning of the words they used, what they would be understood to mean by others, their scope and their limitations. Under these circumstances, it strikes me as a charge against their scholarship, their common sense and their candor to give to the Fourth Amendment's language the eavesdropping meaning the Court imputes to it today.

———————

Katz rejects the reasoning and the holding in *Olmstead*. First, Justice Stewart's majority opinion notes that the Fourth Amendment "protects people, not places." What a person "seeks to preserve as private, even in an area accessible to the public, may be constitutionally protected." Second, the majority states that the Fourth Amendment is not limited to physical invasions of tangible places or things in which the defendant holds some property interest, but also extends to "the recording of oral statements overheard without any technical trespass under local property law." It follows from these two points, the majority reasons, that the government's activities "in electronically listening to and recording" Katz's words "violated the privacy upon which he justifiably relied while using the telephone booth," and amounted to a "search and seizure" under the Fourth Amendment.

It is important to remember that the decision in *Katz* does not prohibit wiretapping or any other investigative tool available to the police. *Katz* only holds that the wiretapping of the defendant's calls amounted to a search triggering other protections in the Fourth Amendment, particularly the requirement that police obtain judicial permission in the form of a search warrant based on probable cause.

Although the result in *Katz*—coupled with the abandonment of the old *Olmstead* decision—was undeniably significant, it was Justice Harlan's concurring opinion that most clearly articulated the two-part "*Katz* Test" for determining whether a search has occurred within the meaning of the Fourth Amendment.

What Is a "Search" Under the Fourth Amendment?: The *Katz* Test and Holding

1.   Police perform a "search" within the meaning of the Fourth Amendment when they intrude into an area in which:

> a. The defendant exhibited an actual, subjective expectation of privacy; *and*
>
> b. Society is prepared to recognize that expectation as reasonable.
>
> 2. When police electronically listen to and record an individual's phone calls, it violates the privacy upon which he justifiably relied and constitutes a "search and seizure" within the meaning of the Fourth Amendment.

B. WHICH INVESTIGATIVE TECHNIQUES QUALIFY AS SEARCHES?

While *Katz* is perhaps best known for its two-part definition of "search," the Supreme Court's narrow holding is that electronically listening to and recording an individual's phone calls from a public telephone booth constitutes a search and seizure. Over the years, the Supreme Court has applied the *Katz* Test to many other police investigative techniques beyond the interception of phone calls. Whether the particular technique at issue amounts to a search often depends on the facts and circumstances of each case. The first prong of the *Katz* Test usually presents little difficulty for the Court, since in most cases the defendant will make some attempt to keep his illegal conduct secret, exhibiting an actual, subjective expectation of privacy. The second prong—deciding whether society would recognize that expectation of privacy as reasonable—is much more difficult for the Court to apply, often generating a sharp difference of opinion among the Justices.

1. USE OF A "WIRED" INFORMANT

In *U.S. v. White*, decided just a few years after *Katz*, police had an informant wear a listening device when he met with the defendant. The Supreme Court found that the defendant's reasonable expectations of privacy were substantially lower than those in *Katz*. As a result, the use of a "wired" informant did not constitute a search under the Fourth Amendment.

U.S. v. WHITE
401 U.S. 745 (1971)

JUSTICE WHITE announced the judgment of the Court and an opinion in which CHIEF JUSTICE BURGER, JUSTICE STEWART, and JUSTICE BLACKMUN join.

In 1966, respondent James A. White was tried and convicted under two consolidated indictments charging various illegal transactions in narcotics. He was fined and sentenced as a second offender to 25-year concurrent sentences. The issue before us is whether the Fourth Amendment bars from evidence the testimony of governmental agents who related certain conversations which had occurred between defendant White and a government informant, Harvey Jackson, and which the agents overheard by monitoring the frequency of a radio transmitter carried by Jackson and concealed on his person. On four occasions the conversations took place in Jackson's home; each of these conversations was overheard by an agent concealed in a kitchen closet with Jackson's consent and by a second agent outside the house using a radio receiver. Four other conversations—one in respondent's home, one in a restaurant, and two in Jackson's car—were overheard by the use of radio equipment. The prosecution was unable to locate and produce Jackson at the trial and the trial court overruled objections to the testimony of the agents who conducted the electronic surveillance. The jury returned a guilty verdict and defendant appealed.

Until *Katz v. U.S.*, 389 U.S. 347 (1967), neither wiretapping nor electronic eavesdropping violated a defendant's Fourth Amendment rights unless there has been an official search and seizure of his person, or such a seizure of his papers or his tangible material effects, or an actual physical invasion of his house "or curtilage" for the purpose of making a seizure. *Olmstead v. U.S.*, 277 U.S. 438 (1928). But where eavesdropping was accomplished by means of an unauthorized physical penetration into the premises occupied by the defendant, although falling short of a technical trespass under the local property law, the Fourth Amendment was violated and any evidence of what was seen and heard, as well as tangible objects seized, was considered the inadmissible fruit of an unlawful invasion.

Katz v. U.S., however, finally swept away doctrines that electronic eavesdropping is permissible under the Fourth Amendment unless physical invasion of a constitutionally protected area produced the challenged evidence. In that case government agents, without petitioner's consent or knowledge, attached a listening device to the outside of a public telephone booth and recorded the defendant's end of his telephone conversations. In declaring the recordings inadmissible in evidence in the absence of a warrant authorizing the surveillance, the Court overruled *Olmstead* and held that the absence of physical intrusion into the telephone booth did not justify using electronic devices in listening to and recording Katz's words, thereby violating the privacy on which he justifiably relied while using the telephone in those circumstances.

The Court of Appeals understood *Katz* to render inadmissible against White the agents' testimony concerning conversations that Jackson broadcast to them. We cannot agree. *Katz* involved no revelation to the Government by a party to conversations with the defendant nor did the Court indicate in any way that a defendant has a justifiable and constitutionally protected expectation that a person with whom he is conversing will not then or later reveal the conversation to the police.

Hoffa v. U.S., 385 U.S. 293 (1966), which was left undisturbed by *Katz*, held that however strongly a defendant may trust an apparent colleague, his expectations in this respect are not protected by the Fourth Amendment when it turns out that the colleague is a government agent regularly communicating with the authorities. In these circumstances, no interest legitimately protected by the Fourth Amendment is involved, for that amendment affords no protection to a wrongdoer's misplaced belief that a person to whom he voluntarily confides his wrongdoing will not reveal it. No warrant to "search and seize" is required in such circumstances, nor is it when the Government sends to defendant's home a secret agent who conceals his identity and makes a purchase of narcotics from the accused, or when the same agent, unbeknown to the defendant, carries electronic equipment to record the defendant's words and the evidence so gathered is later offered in evidence.

The Court of Appeals nevertheless read both *Katz* and the Fourth Amendment to require a different result if the agent not only records his conversations with the defendant but instantaneously transmits them electronically to other agents equipped with radio receivers. Where this occurs, the Court of Appeals held, the Fourth Amendment is violated and the testimony of the listening agents must be excluded from evidence.

Concededly a police agent who conceals his police connections may write down for official use his conversations with a defendant and testify concerning them, without a warrant authorizing his encounters with the defendant and without otherwise violating the latter's Fourth Amendment rights. For constitutional purposes, no different result is required if the agent instead of immediately reporting and transcribing his conversations with defendant, either (1) simultaneously records them with electronic equipment which he is carrying on his person; (2) or carries radio equipment which simultaneously transmits the conversations either to recording equipment located elsewhere or to other agents monitoring the transmitting frequency. If the conduct and revelations of an agent operating without electronic equipment do not invade the defendant's constitutionally justifiable expectations of privacy, neither does a simultaneous recording of the same conversations made by the agent or by others from transmissions received from the agent to whom the defendant is talking and whose trustworthiness the defendant necessarily risks.

Inescapably, one contemplating illegal activities must realize and risk that his companions may be reporting to the police. If he sufficiently doubts their trustworthiness, the association will very probably end or never materialize. But if he has no doubts, or allays them, or risks what doubt he has, the risk is his. In terms of what his course will be, what he will or will not do or say, we are unpersuaded that he would distinguish between probable informers on the one hand and probable informers with transmitters on the other. Given the possibility or probability that one of his colleagues is cooperating with the police, it is only speculation to assert that the defendant's utterances would be substantially different or his sense of security any less if he also thought it possible that the suspected colleague is wired for sound. At least there is no persuasive evidence that the difference in this respect between the electronically equipped and the unequipped agent is substantial enough to require discrete constitutional recognition, particularly under the Fourth Amendment which is ruled by fluid concepts of "reasonableness."

Nor should we be too ready to erect constitutional barriers to relevant and probative evidence which is also accurate and reliable. An electronic recording will many times produce a more reliable rendition of what a defendant has said than will the unaided memory of a police agent. It may also be that with the recording in existence it is less likely that the informant will change his mind, less chance that threat or injury will suppress unfavorable evidence and less chance that cross-examination will confound the testimony. Considerations like these obviously do not favor the defendant, but we are not prepared to hold that a defendant who has no constitutional right to exclude the informer's unaided testimony nevertheless has a Fourth Amendment privilege against a more accurate version of the events in question.

It is thus untenable to consider the activities and reports of the police agent himself, though acting without a warrant, to be a "reasonable" investigative effort and lawful under the Fourth Amendment but to view the same agent with a recorder or transmitter as conducting an "unreasonable" and unconstitutional search and seizure.

JUSTICE HARLAN, dissenting.

Before turning to matters of precedent and policy, several preliminary observations should be made. We deal here with the constitutional validity of instantaneous third-party electronic eavesdropping, conducted by federal law enforcement officers, without any prior judicial approval of the technique utilized, but with the consent and cooperation of a participant in the conversation, and where the substance of the matter electronically overheard is related in a federal criminal trial by those who eavesdropped as direct, not merely corroborative, evidence of the guilt of the nonconsenting party. The magnitude of the issue at hand is evidenced not simply by the obvious doctrinal difficulty of weighing such activity in the Fourth Amendment balance, but also, and more importantly, by the prevalence of police utilization of this technique. Numerous devices make technologically feasible the Orwellian Big Brother. "Participant recording," in which one participant in a conversation or meeting, either a police officer or a cooperating party, wears a concealed device that records the conversation or broadcasts it to others nearby is used tens of thousands of times each year throughout the country, particularly in cases involving extortion, conspiracy, narcotics, gambling, prostitution, corruption by police officials and similar crimes.

It is one thing to subject the average citizen to the risk that participants in a conversation with him will subsequently divulge its contents to another, but quite a different matter to foist upon him the risk that unknown third parties may be simultaneously listening in.

Since it is the task of the law to form and project, as well as mirror and reflect, we should not, as judges, merely recite the expectations and risks without examining the desirability of saddling them upon society. The critical question, therefore, is whether under our system of government, as reflected in the Constitution, we should impose on our citizens the risks of the electronic listener or observer without at least the protection of a warrant requirement.

This question must, in my view, be answered by assessing the nature of a particular practice and the likely extent of its impact on the individual's sense of security balanced against the utility of the conduct as a technique of law enforcement. For those more extensive intrusions that significantly jeopardize the sense of security which is the paramount concern of Fourth Amendment liberties, I am of the view that more than self-restraint by law enforcement officials is required and at the least warrants should be necessary.

The impact of the practice of third-party bugging, must, I think, be considered such as to undermine that confidence and sense of security in dealing with one another that is characteristic of individual relationships between citizens in a free society.

Authority is hardly required to support the proposition that words would be measured a good deal more carefully and communication inhibited if one suspected his conversations were being transmitted and transcribed. Were third-party bugging a prevalent practice, it might well smother that spontaneity—reflected in frivolous, impetuous, sacrilegious, and defiant discourse—that liberates daily life. Much offhand exchange is easily forgotten and one may count on the obscurity of his remarks, protected by the very fact of a limited audience, and the likelihood that the listener will either overlook or forget what is said, as well as the listener's inability to reformulate a conversation without having to contend with a documented record. All these values are sacrificed by a rule of law that permits official monitoring of private discourse limited only by the need to locate a willing assistant.

Finally, it is too easy to forget—and, hence, too often forgotten—that the issue here is whether to interpose a search warrant procedure between law enforcement agencies engaging in electronic eavesdropping and the public generally. By casting its "risk analysis" solely in terms of the expectations and risks that "wrongdoers" or "one contemplating illegal activities" ought to bear, the plurality opinion, I think, misses the mark entirely. [My approach] would not end electronic eavesdropping. It would prevent public officials from engaging in that practice unless they first had probable cause to suspect an individual of involvement in illegal activities and had tested their version of the facts before a detached judicial officer. The interest [the plurality] fails to protect is the expectation of the ordinary citizen, who has never engaged in illegal conduct in his life, that he may carry on his private discourse freely, openly, and spontaneously without measuring his every word against the connotations it might carry when instantaneously heard by others unknown to him and unfamiliar with his situation or analyzed in a cold, formal record played days, months, or years after the conversation. Interposition of a warrant requirement is designed not to shield "wrongdoers," but to secure a measure of privacy and a sense of personal security throughout our society.

The Fourth Amendment does, of course, leave room for the employment of modern technology in criminal law enforcement, but in the stream of current developments in Fourth Amendment law I think it must be held that third-party electronic monitoring, subject only to the self-restraint of law enforcement officials, has no place in our society.

Use of a Wired Informant

A criminal suspect has no justifiable and constitutionally protected expectation that a person with whom he is conversing will not then or later reveal the conversation to the police. Accordingly, a search does not occur when police use an informant to electronically record or transmit conversations with a criminal suspect.

---

2. USE OF A PEN REGISTER

In *Smith v. Maryland*, the police used a pen register—a device for recording dialed phone numbers—to trace threatening phone calls made by the defendant. Applying the *Katz* Test, the Supreme Court found that the defendant did not have a reasonable expectation of privacy in the phone numbers he dialed from his home. Accordingly, the use of the pen register did not amount to a search under the Fourth Amendment.

SMITH V. MARYLAND
442 U.S. 735 (1979)

JUSTICE BLACKMUN delivered the opinion of the Court.

This case presents the question whether the installation and use of a pen register[1] constitutes a "search" within the meaning of the Fourth Amendment, made applicable to the States through the Fourteenth Amendment.

On March 5, 1976, in Baltimore, Md., Patricia McDonough was robbed. She gave the police a description of the robber and of a 1975 Monte Carlo automobile she had observed near the scene of the crime. After the robbery, McDonough began receiving threatening and obscene phone calls from a man identifying himself as the robber. On one occasion, the caller asked that she step out on her front porch; she did so, and saw the 1975 Monte Carlo she had earlier described to police moving slowly past her home. On March 16, police spotted a man who met McDonough's description driving a 1975 Monte Carlo in her neighborhood. By tracing the license plate number, police learned that the car was registered in the name of petitioner, Michael Lee Smith.

The next day, the telephone company, at police request, installed a pen register at its central offices to record the numbers dialed from the telephone at petitioner's home. The police did not get a warrant or court order before having the pen register installed. The register revealed that on March 17 a call was placed from petitioner's home to McDonough's phone. On the basis of this and other evidence, the police obtained a warrant to search petitioner's residence. The search revealed that a page in petitioner's phone book was turned down to the name and number of Patricia McDonough; the phone book was seized. Petitioner was arrested, and a six-man lineup was held on March 19. McDonough identified petitioner as the man who had robbed her.

Petitioner was indicted in the Criminal Court of Baltimore for robbery. By pretrial motion, he sought to suppress "all fruits derived from the pen register" on the ground that the police had failed to secure a warrant prior to its installation. The trial court denied the suppression motion, holding that the warrantless installation of the pen register did not violate the Fourth Amendment. The pen register tape (evidencing the fact that a phone call had been made from petitioner's phone to McDonough's phone) and the phone book seized in the search of petitioner's residence were admitted into evidence against him. Petitioner was convicted, and was sentenced to six years.

---

[1] A pen register is a mechanical device that records the numbers dialed on a telephone by monitoring the electrical impulses caused when the dial on the telephone is released. It does not overhear oral communications and does not indicate whether calls are actually completed.

In determining whether a particular form of government-initiated electronic surveillance is a "search" within the meaning of the Fourth Amendment,[4] our lodestar is *Katz v. U.S.*, 389 U.S. 347 (1967). Consistently with *Katz,* this Court uniformly has held that the application of the Fourth Amendment depends on whether the person invoking its protection can claim a "justifiable," a "reasonable," or a "legitimate expectation of privacy" that has been invaded by government action. This inquiry, as Mr. Justice Harlan aptly noted in his *Katz* concurrence, normally embraces two discrete questions. The first is whether the individual, by his conduct, has "exhibited an actual (subjective) expectation of privacy"—whether, in the words of the *Katz* majority, the individual has shown that "he seeks to preserve [something] as private." The second question is whether the individual's subjective expectation of privacy is "one that society is prepared to recognize as reasonable"—whether, in the words of the *Katz* majority, the individual's expectation, viewed objectively, is "justifiable" under the circumstances.

In applying the *Katz* analysis to this case, it is important to begin by specifying precisely the nature of the state activity that is challenged. The activity here took the form of installing and using a pen register. Since the pen register was installed on telephone company property at the telephone company's central offices, petitioner obviously cannot claim that his "property" was invaded or that police intruded into a "constitutionally protected area." Petitioner's claim, rather, is that, notwithstanding the absence of a trespass, the State, as did the Government in *Katz*, infringed a "legitimate expectation of privacy" that petitioner held. Yet a pen register differs significantly from the listening device employed in *Katz,* for pen registers do not acquire the *contents* of communications. Given a pen register's limited capabilities, therefore, petitioner's argument that its installation and use constituted a "search" necessarily rests upon a claim that he had a "legitimate expectation of privacy" regarding the numbers he dialed on his phone.

This claim must be rejected. First, we doubt that people in general entertain any actual expectation of privacy in the numbers they dial. All telephone users realize that they must "convey" phone numbers to the telephone company, since it is through telephone company switching equipment that their calls are completed. All subscribers realize, moreover, that the phone company has facilities for making permanent records of the numbers they dial, for they see a list of their long-distance (toll) calls on their monthly bills. In fact, pen registers and similar devices are routinely used by telephone companies for the purposes of checking

---

[4]   In this case, the pen register was installed, and the numbers dialed were recorded, by the telephone company. The telephone company, however, acted at police request. In view of this, respondent appears to concede that the company is to be deemed an "agent" of the police for purposes of this case, so as to render the installation and use of the pen register "state action" under the Fourth and Fourteenth Amendments. We may assume that "state action" was present here.

billing operations, detecting fraud and preventing violations of law. Electronic equipment is used not only to keep billing records of toll calls, but also to keep a record of all calls dialed from a telephone which is subject to a special rate structure. Pen registers are regularly employed to determine whether a home phone is being used to conduct a business, to check for a defective dial, or to check for overbilling. Although most people may be oblivious to a pen register's esoteric functions, they presumably have some awareness of one common use: to aid in the identification of persons making annoying or obscene calls. Telephone users, in sum, typically know that they must convey numerical information to the phone company; that the phone company has facilities for recording this information; and that the phone company does in fact record this information for a variety of legitimate business purposes. Although subjective expectations cannot be scientifically gauged, it is too much to believe that telephone subscribers, under these circumstances, harbor any general expectation that the numbers they dial will remain secret.

Petitioner argues, however, that, whatever the expectations of telephone users in general, he demonstrated an expectation of privacy by his own conduct here, since he "used the telephone *in his house* to the exclusion of all others." But the site of the call is immaterial for purposes of analysis in this case. Although petitioner's conduct may have been calculated to keep the *contents* of his conversation private, his conduct was not and could not have been calculated to preserve the privacy of the number he dialed. Regardless of his location, petitioner had to convey that number to the telephone company in precisely the same way if he wished to complete his call. The fact that he dialed the number on his home phone rather than on some other phone could make no conceivable difference, nor could any subscriber rationally think that it would.

Second, even if petitioner did harbor some subjective expectation that the phone numbers he dialed would remain private, this expectation is not "one that society is prepared to recognize as reasonable." This Court consistently has held that a person has no legitimate expectation of privacy in information he voluntarily turns over to third parties. When he used his phone, petitioner voluntarily conveyed numerical information to the telephone company and "exposed" that information to its equipment in the ordinary course of business. In so doing, petitioner assumed the risk that the company would reveal to police the numbers he dialed. The switching equipment that processed those numbers is merely the modern counterpart of the operator who, in an earlier day, personally completed calls for the subscriber. Petitioner concedes that if he had placed his calls through an operator, he could claim no legitimate expectation of privacy. We are not inclined to hold that a different constitutional result is required because the telephone company has decided to automate.

Petitioner argues, however, that automatic switching equipment differs from a live operator in one pertinent respect. An operator, in theory at least, is capable of remembering every number that is conveyed to him by callers. Electronic equipment, by contrast can "remember" only those numbers it is programmed to record, and telephone companies, in view of their present billing practices, usually do not record local calls. Since petitioner, in calling McDonough, was making a local call, his expectation of privacy as to her number, on this theory, would be "legitimate."

This argument does not withstand scrutiny. The fortuity of whether or not the phone company in fact elects to make a quasi-permanent record of a particular number dialed does not in our view, make any constitutional difference. Regardless of the phone company's election, petitioner voluntarily conveyed to it information that it had facilities for recording and that it was free to record. In these circumstances, petitioner assumed the risk that the information would be divulged to police. Under petitioner's theory, Fourth Amendment protection would exist, or not, depending on how the telephone company chose to define local-dialing zones, and depending on how it chose to bill its customers for local calls. Calls placed across town, or dialed directly, would be protected; calls placed across the river, or dialed with operator assistance, might not be. We are not inclined to make a crazy quilt of the Fourth Amendment, especially in circumstances where (as here) the pattern of protection would be dictated by billing practices of a private corporation.

We therefore conclude that petitioner in all probability entertained no actual expectation of privacy in the phone numbers he dialed, and that, even if he did, his expectation was not "legitimate." The installation and use of a pen register, consequently, was not a "search," and no warrant was required.

JUSTICE STEWART, with whom JUSTICE BRENNAN joins, dissenting.

I am not persuaded that the numbers dialed from a private telephone fall outside the constitutional protection of the Fourth and Fourteenth Amendments.

In *Katz*, the Court acknowledged the "vital role that the public telephone has come to play in private communications." The role played by a private telephone is even more vital, and since *Katz* it has been abundantly clear that telephone conversations carried on by people in their homes or offices are fully protected by the Fourth and Fourteenth Amendments.

Nevertheless, the Court today says that those safeguards do not extend to the numbers dialed from a private telephone, apparently because when a caller dials a number the digits may be recorded by the telephone company for billing purposes. But that observation no more than describes the basic nature of telephone calls. A telephone call simply cannot be made without the use of telephone company property and without payment to the company for the service. The telephone conversation itself must be electronically transmitted by telephone company equipment, and may be recorded or overheard by the use of other company equipment. Yet we have squarely held that the user of even a public telephone is entitled to assume that the words he utters into the mouthpiece will not be broadcast to the world.

The central question in this case is whether a person who makes telephone calls from his home is entitled to make a similar assumption about the numbers he dials. What the telephone company does or might do with those numbers is no more relevant to this inquiry than it would be in a case involving the conversation itself. It is simply not enough to say, after *Katz,* that there is no legitimate expectation of privacy in the numbers dialed because the caller assumes the risk that the telephone company will disclose them to the police.

I think that the numbers dialed from a private telephone—like the conversations that occur during a call—are within the constitutional protection recognized in *Katz.* It seems clear to me that information obtained by pen register surveillance of a private telephone is information in which the telephone subscriber has a legitimate expectation of privacy. The information captured by such surveillance emanates from private conduct within a person's home or office—locations that without question are entitled to Fourth and Fourteenth Amendment protection. Further, that information is an integral part of the telephonic communication that under *Katz* is entitled to constitutional protection, whether or not it is captured by a trespass into such an area.

The numbers dialed from a private telephone—although certainly more prosaic than the conversation itself—are not without "content." Most private telephone subscribers may have their own numbers listed in a publicly distributed directory, but I doubt there are any who would be happy to have broadcast to the world a list of the local or long distance numbers they have called. This is not because such a list might in some sense be incriminating, but because it easily could reveal the identities of the persons and the places called, and thus reveal the most intimate details of a person's life.

––––––––––––––

The Supreme Court's decision in *Smith v. Maryland* has generated renewed controversy in connection with recent revelations about the nature and extent of the National Security Agency's (NSA) global surveillance programs. In 2013, former NSA contractor Edward Snowden disclosed the existence of these programs by leaking classified documents to several media outlets. One of the NSA's surveillance programs requires telephone companies to collect and transmit to the government bulk telephony metadata—a list of all telephone calls made and received by virtually everyone in the U.S. The metadata does not include any information about the identity of individuals or the content of their calls. The government defended the bulk telephony metadata program by citing the core holding in *Smith v. Maryland*: Government collection of dialed phone numbers is not a search under the Fourth Amendment because individuals have no reasonable expectation of privacy in information voluntarily disclosed to third-party telephone companies.

On December 16, 2013, Judge Richard J. Leon of the U.S. District Court for the District of Columbia ruled in *Klayman v. Obama*, 957 F.Supp.2d 1 (D.D.C. 2013), that the NSA's warrantless collection of bulk telephony metadata was unconstitutional. Citing the enormous scope of the NSA program and the evolving role of telephones and technology in modern society, Judge Leon distinguished *Smith v. Maryland*: "I am convinced that the surveillance program now before me is so different from a simple pen register that *Smith* is of little value in assessing whether the Bulk Telephony Metadata Program constitutes a Fourth Amendment search."

Less than two weeks later, Judge William Pauley III of the U.S. District Court for the Southern District of New York reached the opposite conclusion in *American Civil Liberties Union v. Clapper*, 959 F.Supp.2d 724 (S.D.N.Y. 2013), finding the NSA program constitutional under the "clear precedent" of *Smith v. Maryland*. The federal appellate courts and the U.S. Supreme Court may ultimately have to resolve this conflict.

Use of a Pen Register

The use of a pen register installed on telephone company property to record the numbers dialed from an individual's telephone is not a search. An individual does not generally expect the numbers he dials to remain secret, nor is it reasonable to expect privacy in information voluntarily disclosed to third-party telephone companies whose equipment completes the call.

---

3. SEARCHES OF OPEN FIELDS

In *Hester v. U.S.*, 265 U.S. 57 (1924), decided more than 40 years before *Katz*, the Supreme Court held that the "special protection accorded by the Fourth Amendment to persons, houses, papers, and effects is not extended to open fields." The Court held that the Fourth Amendment applies to a search of the home or the areas immediately surrounding it (the "curtilage"), but it does not apply to a police entry and search of an open field, even if the field is private property. The Court in *Oliver v. U.S.*, decided after *Katz*, reaffirmed the "open fields" doctrine.

OLIVER V. U.S.

466 U.S. 170 (1984)

JUSTICE POWELL delivered the opinion of the Court.

The "open fields" doctrine, first enunciated by this Court in *Hester v. U.S.*, 265 U.S. 57 (1924), permits police officers to enter and search a field without a warrant. We granted certiorari in these cases to clarify confusion that has arisen as to the continued vitality of the doctrine.

I

No. 82–15. Acting on reports that marihuana was being raised on the farm of petitioner Oliver, two narcotics agents of the Kentucky State Police went to the farm to investigate.[1] Arriving at the farm, they drove past petitioner's house to a locked gate with a "No Trespassing" sign. A footpath led around one side of the gate. The agents walked around the gate and along the road for several hundred yards, passing a barn and a parked camper. At that point, someone standing in front of the camper shouted: "No hunting is allowed, come back up here." The officers shouted back that they were Kentucky State Police officers, but found no one when they returned to the camper. The officers resumed their investigation of the farm and found a field of marihuana over a mile from petitioner's home.

After a pretrial hearing, the District Court suppressed evidence of the discovery of the marihuana field. Applying *Katz v. U.S.*, 389 U.S. 347 (1967), the court found that petitioner had a reasonable expectation that the field would remain private because petitioner "had done all that could be expected of him to assert his privacy in the area of farm that was searched." He had posted "No Trespassing" signs at regular intervals and had locked the gate at the entrance to the center of the farm. Further, the court noted that the field itself is highly secluded: it is bounded on all sides by woods, fences, and embankments and cannot be seen from any point of public access. The court concluded that this was not an "open" field that invited casual intrusion.

The Court of Appeals for the Sixth Circuit, sitting en banc, reversed the District Court. We granted certiorari.

No. 82–1273. After receiving an anonymous tip that marihuana was being grown in the woods behind respondent Thornton's residence, two police officers entered the woods by a path between this residence and a neighboring house. They followed a footpath through the woods until they reached two marihuana patches fenced with chicken wire. Later, the officers determined that the patches were on the property of respondent,

---

[1]   It is conceded that the police did not have a warrant authorizing the search, that there was no probable cause for the search, and that no exception to the warrant requirement is applicable.

obtained a warrant to search the property, and seized the marihuana. On the basis of this evidence, respondent was arrested and indicted.

The trial court granted respondent's motion to suppress the fruits of the second search. The warrant for this search was premised on information that the police had obtained during their previous warrantless search, that the court found to be unreasonable. "No Trespassing" signs and the secluded location of the marihuana patches evinced a reasonable expectation of privacy. Therefore, the court held, the open fields doctrine did not apply. The Maine Supreme Judicial Court affirmed. We granted certiorari.

II

The rule announced in *Hester v. U.S.* was founded upon the explicit language of the Fourth Amendment. That Amendment indicates with some precision the places and things encompassed by its protections. As Justice Holmes explained for the Court in his characteristically laconic style: "The special protection accorded by the Fourth Amendment to the people in their persons, houses, papers, and effects is not extended to the open fields. The distinction between the latter and the house is as old as the common law."

Nor are the open fields "effects" within the meaning of the Fourth Amendment. The term "effects" is less inclusive than "property" and cannot be said to encompass open fields.[7] We conclude, as did the Court in deciding *Hester*, that the government's intrusion upon the open fields is not one of those "unreasonable searches" proscribed by the text of the Fourth Amendment.

III

This interpretation of the Fourth Amendment's language is consistent with the understanding of the right to privacy expressed in our Fourth Amendment jurisprudence. Since *Katz v. U.S.*, the touchstone of Amendment analysis has been the question whether a person has a constitutionally protected reasonable expectation of privacy. The Amendment does not protect the merely subjective expectation of privacy, but only those expectations that society is prepared to recognize as "reasonable."

No single factor determines whether an individual legitimately may claim under the Fourth Amendment that a place should be free of government intrusion not authorized by warrant. In assessing the degree to which a search infringes upon individual privacy, the Court has given weight to such factors as the intention of the Framers of the Fourth Amendment, the uses to which the individual has put a location, and our

---

[7]   The Framers would have understood the term "effects" to be limited to personal, rather than real, property.

societal understanding that certain areas deserve the most scrupulous protection from government invasion. These factors are equally relevant to determining whether the government's intrusion upon open fields without a warrant or probable cause violates reasonable expectations of privacy and is therefore a search proscribed by the Amendment.

In this light, the rule of *Hester*, that we reaffirm today, may be understood as providing that an individual may not legitimately demand privacy for activities conducted out of doors in fields, except in the area immediately surrounding the home. This rule is true to the conception of the right to privacy embodied in the Fourth Amendment. The Amendment reflects the recognition of the Framers that certain enclaves should be free from arbitrary government interference. For example, the Court since the enactment of the Fourth Amendment has stressed "the overriding respect for the sanctity of the home that has been embedded in our traditions since the origins of the Republic."

In contrast, open fields do not provide the setting for those intimate activities that the Amendment is intended to shelter from government interference or surveillance. There is no societal interest in protecting the privacy of those activities, such as the cultivation of crops, that occur in open fields. Moreover, as a practical matter these lands usually are accessible to the public and the police in ways that a home, an office, or commercial structure would not be. It is not generally true that fences or "No Trespassing" signs effectively bar the public from viewing open fields in rural areas. And both petitioner Oliver and respondent Thornton concede that the public and police lawfully may survey lands from the air. For these reasons, the asserted expectation of privacy in open fields is not an expectation that "society recognizes as reasonable."[10]

The historical underpinnings of the open fields doctrine also demonstrate that the doctrine is consistent with respect for "reasonable expectations of privacy." As Justice Holmes, writing for the Court, observed in *Hester*, the common law distinguished "open fields" from the "curtilage," the land immediately surrounding and associated with the home. The distinction implies that only the curtilage, not the neighboring open fields, warrants the Fourth Amendment protections that attach to the home. At common law, the curtilage is the area to which extends the intimate activity associated with the "sanctity of a man's home and the

---

[10] The dissent conceives of open fields as bustling with private activity as diverse as lovers' trysts and worship services. But in most instances police will disturb no one when they enter upon open fields. These fields, by their very character as open and unoccupied, are unlikely to provide the setting for activities whose privacy is sought to be protected by the Fourth Amendment. One need think only of the vast expanse of some western ranches or of the undeveloped woods of the Northwest to see the unreality of the dissent's conception. Further, the Fourth Amendment provides ample protection to activities in the open fields that might implicate an individual's privacy. An individual who enters a place defined to be "public" for Fourth Amendment analysis does not lose all claims to privacy or personal security. For example, the Fourth Amendment's protections against unreasonable arrest or unreasonable seizure of effects upon the person remain fully applicable.

privacies of life," and therefore has been considered part of the home itself for Fourth Amendment purposes. Thus, courts have extended Fourth Amendment protection to the curtilage; and they have defined the curtilage, as did the common law, by reference to the factors that determine whether an individual reasonably may expect that an area immediately adjacent to the home will remain private. Conversely, the common law implies, as we reaffirm today, that no expectation of privacy legitimately attaches to open fields.[11]

We conclude, from the text of the Fourth Amendment and from the historical and contemporary understanding of its purposes, that an individual has no legitimate expectation that open fields will remain free from warrantless intrusion by government officers.

Petitioner Oliver and respondent Thornton contend, to the contrary, that the circumstances of a search sometimes may indicate that reasonable expectations of privacy were violated; and that courts therefore should analyze these circumstances on a case-by-case basis. The language of the Fourth Amendment itself answers their contention.

Nor would a case-by-case approach provide a workable accommodation between the needs of law enforcement and the interests protected by the Fourth Amendment. Under this approach, police officers would have to guess before every search whether landowners had erected fences sufficiently high, posted a sufficient number of warning signs, or located contraband in an area sufficiently secluded to establish a right of privacy. This Court repeatedly has acknowledged the difficulties created for courts, police, and citizens by an *ad hoc*, case-by-case definition of Fourth Amendment standards to be applied in differing factual circumstances. The *ad hoc* approach not only makes it difficult for the policeman to discern the scope of his authority; it also creates a danger that constitutional rights will be arbitrarily and inequitably enforced.

IV

In any event, while the factors that petitioner Oliver and respondent Thornton urge the courts to consider may be relevant to Fourth Amendment analysis in some contexts, these factors cannot be decisive on the question whether the search of an open field is subject to the Amendment. Initially, we reject the suggestion that steps taken to protect privacy establish that expectations of privacy in an open field are legitimate. It is true, of course, that petitioner Oliver and respondent

---

[11] Neither petitioner Oliver nor respondent Thornton has contended that the property searched was within the curtilage. Nor is it necessary in these cases to consider the scope of the curtilage exception to the open fields doctrine or the degree of Fourth Amendment protection afforded the curtilage, as opposed to the home itself. It is clear, however, that the term "open fields" may include any unoccupied or undeveloped area outside of the curtilage. An open field need be neither "open" nor a "field" as those terms are used in common speech. For example, contrary to respondent Thornton's suggestion, a thickly wooded area nonetheless may be an open field as that term is used in construing the Fourth Amendment.

Thornton, in order to conceal their criminal activities, planted the marihuana upon secluded land and erected fences and "No Trespassing" signs around the property. And it may be that because of such precautions, few members of the public stumbled upon the marihuana crops seized by the police. Neither of these suppositions demonstrates, however, that the expectation of privacy was legitimate in the sense required by the Fourth Amendment. The test of legitimacy is not whether the individual chooses to conceal assertedly "private" activity. Rather, the correct inquiry is whether the government's intrusion infringes upon the personal and societal values protected by the Fourth Amendment. As we have explained, we find no basis for concluding that a police inspection of open fields accomplishes such an infringement.

Nor is the government's intrusion upon an open field a "search" in the constitutional sense because that intrusion is a trespass at common law. The existence of a property right is but one element in determining whether expectations of privacy are legitimate. The premise that property interests control the right of the Government to search and seize has been discredited.

The common law may guide consideration of what areas are protected by the Fourth Amendment by defining areas whose invasion by others is wrongful. The law of trespass, however, forbids intrusions upon land that the Fourth Amendment would not proscribe. For trespass law extends to instances where the exercise of the right to exclude vindicates no legitimate privacy interest. Thus, in the case of open fields, the general rights of property protected by the common law of trespass have little or no relevance to the applicability of the Fourth Amendment.

We conclude that the open fields doctrine, as enunciated in *Hester*, is consistent with the plain language of the Fourth Amendment and its historical purposes. Moreover, Justice Holmes' interpretation of the Amendment in *Hester* accords with the "reasonable expectation of privacy" analysis developed in subsequent decisions of this Court.

JUSTICE MARSHALL, with whom JUSTICE BRENNAN and JUSTICE STEVENS join, dissenting.

In each of these consolidated cases, police officers, ignoring clearly visible "No Trespassing" signs, entered upon private land in search of evidence of a crime. At a spot that could not be seen from any vantage point accessible to the public, the police discovered contraband, which was subsequently used to incriminate the owner of the land. In neither case did the police have a warrant authorizing their activities.

The Court holds that police conduct of this sort does not constitute an "unreasonable search" within the meaning of the Fourth Amendment. The Court reaches that startling conclusion by two independent analytical routes. First, the Court argues that, because the Fourth

Amendment by its terms renders people secure in their "persons, houses, papers, and effects," it is inapplicable to trespasses upon land not lying within the curtilage of a dwelling. Second, the Court contends that "an individual may not legitimately demand privacy for activities conducted out of doors in fields, except in the area immediately surrounding the home." Because I cannot agree with either of these propositions, I dissent.

I

The first ground on which the Court rests its decision is that the Fourth Amendment "indicates with some precision the places and things encompassed by its protections," and that real property is not included in the list of protected spaces and possessions. This line of argument has several flaws. Most obviously, it is inconsistent with the results of many of our previous decisions, none of which the Court purports to overrule. For example, neither a public telephone booth nor a conversation conducted therein can fairly be described as a person, house, paper, or effect; yet we have held that the Fourth Amendment forbids the police without a warrant to eavesdrop on such a conversation. *Katz v. U.S.*, 389 U.S. 347 (1967). Nor can it plausibly be argued that an office or commercial establishment is covered by the plain language of the Amendment; yet we have held that such premises are entitled to constitutional protection if they are marked in a fashion that alerts the public to the fact that they are private.

Indeed, the Court's reading of the plain language of the Fourth Amendment is incapable of explaining even its own holding in this case. The Court rules that the curtilage, a zone of real property surrounding a dwelling, is entitled to constitutional protection. We are not told, however, whether the curtilage is a "house" or an "effect"—or why, if the curtilage can be incorporated into the list of things and spaces shielded by the Amendment, a field cannot.

The Court's inability to reconcile its parsimonious reading of the phrase "persons, houses, papers, and effects" with our prior decisions or even its own holding is a symptom of a more fundamental infirmity in the Court's reasoning. The Fourth Amendment, like the other central provisions of the Bill of Rights that loom large in our modern jurisprudence, was designed, not to prescribe with "precision" permissible and impermissible activities, but to identify a fundamental human liberty that should be shielded forever from government intrusion. We do not construe constitutional provisions of this sort the way we do statutes, whose drafters can be expected to indicate with some comprehensiveness and exactitude the conduct they wish to forbid or control and to change those prescriptions when they become obsolete. Rather, we strive, when interpreting these seminal constitutional provisions, to effectuate their purposes—to lend them meanings that ensure that the liberties the

Framers sought to protect are not undermined by the changing activities of government officials.

The liberty shielded by the Fourth Amendment, as we have often acknowledged, is freedom from unreasonable government intrusions into legitimate expectations of privacy. That freedom would be incompletely protected if only government conduct that impinged upon a person, house, paper, or effect were subject to constitutional scrutiny. Accordingly, we have repudiated the proposition that the Fourth Amendment applies only to a limited set of locales or kinds of property. In *Katz*, we expressly rejected a proffered locational theory of the coverage of the Amendment, holding that it "protects people, not places." Since that time we have consistently adhered to the view that the applicability of the provision depends solely upon whether the person invoking its protection can claim a "justifiable," a "reasonable," or a "legitimate expectation of privacy" that has been invaded by government action. The Court's contention that, because a field is not a house or effect, it is not covered by the Fourth Amendment is inconsistent with this line of cases and with the understanding of the nature of constitutional adjudication from which it derives.

II

The second ground for the Court's decision is its contention that any interest a landowner might have in the privacy of his woods and fields is not one that society is prepared to recognize as reasonable. The mode of analysis that underlies this assertion is certainly more consistent with our prior decisions than that discussed above. But the Court's conclusion cannot withstand scrutiny.

As the Court acknowledges, we have traditionally looked to a variety of factors in determining whether an expectation of privacy asserted in a physical space is "reasonable." Though those factors do not lend themselves to precise taxonomy, they may be roughly grouped into three categories. First, we consider whether the expectation at issue is rooted in entitlements defined by positive law. Second, we consider the nature of the uses to which spaces of the sort in question can be put. Third, we consider whether the person claiming a privacy interest manifested that interest to the public in a way that most people would understand and respect. When the expectations of privacy asserted by petitioner Oliver and respondent Thornton are examined through these lenses, it becomes clear that those expectations are entitled to constitutional protection.

We have frequently acknowledged that privacy interests are not coterminous with property rights. However, because property rights reflect society's explicit recognition of a person's authority to act as he wishes in certain areas, they should be considered in determining whether an individual's expectations of privacy are reasonable. Indeed, the Court has suggested that, insofar as one of the main rights attaching to property is the right to exclude others, one who owns or lawfully possesses or controls property will in all likelihood have a legitimate expectation of privacy by virtue of this right to exclude.

It is undisputed that Oliver and Thornton each owned the land into which the police intruded. That fact alone provides considerable support for their assertion of legitimate privacy interests in their woods and fields. But even more telling is the nature of the sanctions that Oliver and Thornton could invoke, under local law, for violation of their property rights. In Kentucky, a knowing entry upon fenced or otherwise enclosed land, or upon unenclosed land conspicuously posted with signs excluding the public, constitutes criminal trespass. The law in Maine is similar. Thus, positive law not only recognizes the legitimacy of Oliver's and Thornton's insistence that strangers keep off their land, but subjects those who refuse to respect their wishes to the most severe of penalties— criminal liability. Under these circumstances, it is hard to credit the Court's assertion that Oliver's and Thornton's expectations of privacy were not of a sort that society is prepared to recognize as reasonable.

The uses to which a place is put are highly relevant to the assessment of a privacy interest asserted therein. If, in light of our shared sensibilities, those activities are of a kind in which people should be able to engage without fear of intrusion by private persons or government officials, we extend the protection of the Fourth Amendment to the space in question, even in the absence of any entitlement derived from positive law.

Privately owned woods and fields that are not exposed to public view regularly are employed in a variety of ways that society acknowledges deserve privacy. Many landowners like to take solitary walks on their property, confident that they will not be confronted in their rambles by strangers or policemen. Others conduct agricultural businesses on their property. Some landowners use their secluded spaces to meet lovers, others to gather together with fellow worshippers, still others to engage in sustained creative endeavor. Private land is sometimes used as a refuge for wildlife, where flora and fauna are protected from human intervention of any kind. Our respect for the freedom of landowners to use their posted "open fields" in ways such as these partially explains the seriousness with which the positive law regards deliberate invasions of such spaces, and substantially reinforces the landowners' contention that their expectations of privacy are "reasonable."

Whether a person took normal precautions to maintain his privacy in a given space affects whether his interest is one protected by the Fourth Amendment. The reason why such precautions are relevant is that we do not insist that a person who has a right to exclude others exercise that right. A claim to privacy is therefore strengthened by the fact that the claimant somehow manifested to other people his desire that they keep their distance.

Certain spaces are so presumptively private that signals of this sort are unnecessary; a homeowner need not post a "Do Not Enter" sign on his door in order to deny entrance to uninvited guests. Privacy interests in other spaces are more ambiguous, and the taking of precautions is consequently more important; placing a lock on one's footlocker strengthens one's claim that an examination of its contents is impermissible. Still other spaces are, by positive law and social convention, presumed accessible to members of the public unless the owner manifests his intention to exclude them.

Undeveloped land falls into the last-mentioned category. If a person has not marked the boundaries of his fields or woods in a way that informs passersby that they are not welcome, he cannot object if members of the public enter onto the property. There is no reason why he should have any greater rights as against government officials. Accordingly, we have held that an official may, without a warrant, enter private land from which the public is not excluded and make observations from that vantage point. Fairly read, the case on which the majority so heavily relies, *Hester v. U.S.*, affirms little more than the foregoing unremarkable proposition. From aught that appears in the opinion in that case, the defendants, fleeing from revenue agents who had observed them committing a crime, abandoned incriminating evidence on private land from which the public had not been excluded. Under such circumstances, it is not surprising that the Court was unpersuaded by the defendants' argument that the entry onto their fields by the agents violated the Fourth Amendment.

A very different case is presented when the owner of undeveloped land has taken precautions to exclude the public. As indicated above, a deliberate entry by a private citizen onto private property marked with "No Trespassing" signs will expose him to criminal liability. I see no reason why a government official should not be obliged to respect such unequivocal and universally understood manifestations of a landowner's desire for privacy.

In sum, examination of the three principal criteria we have traditionally used for assessing the reasonableness of a person's expectation that a given space would remain private indicates that interests of the sort asserted by Oliver and Thornton are entitled to constitutional protection. An owner's right to insist that others stay off his posted land is firmly grounded in positive law. Many of the uses to which such land may be put deserve privacy. And, by marking the boundaries of the land with warnings that the public should not intrude, the owner has dispelled any ambiguity as to his desires.

The police in these cases proffered no justification for their invasions of Oliver's and Thornton's privacy interests; in neither case was the entry legitimated by a warrant or by one of the established exceptions to the warrant requirement. I conclude, therefore, that the searches of their land violated the Fourth Amendment, and the evidence obtained in the course of those searches should have been suppressed.

III

A clear, easily administrable rule emerges from the analysis set forth above: Private land marked in a fashion sufficient to render entry thereon a criminal trespass under the law of the State in which the land lies is protected by the Fourth Amendment's proscription of unreasonable searches and seizures. One of the advantages of the foregoing rule is that it draws upon a doctrine already familiar to both citizens and government officials. In each jurisdiction, a substantial body of statutory and case law defines the precautions a landowner must take in order to avail himself of the sanctions of the criminal law. The police know that body of law, because they are entrusted with responsibility for enforcing it against the public; it therefore would not be difficult for the police to abide by it themselves.

By contrast, the doctrine announced by the Court today is incapable of determinate application. Police officers, making warrantless entries upon private land, will be obliged in the future to make on-the-spot judgments as to how far the curtilage extends, and to stay outside that zone. In addition, we may expect to see a spate of litigation over the question of how much improvement is necessary to remove private land from the category of "unoccupied or undeveloped area" to which the "open fields exception" is now deemed applicable.

The Court's holding not only ill serves the need to make constitutional doctrine workable for application by rank-and-file, trained police officers, it withdraws the shield of the Fourth Amendment from privacy interests that clearly deserve protection. By exempting from the coverage of the Amendment large areas of private land, the Court opens the way to investigative activities we would all find repugnant.

The majority in *Oliver v. U.S.* draws a sharp distinction between "curtilage," the area immediately adjacent to a home, and an open field, noting that the Fourth Amendment protects the former, but not the latter. *U.S. v. Dunn* further clarifies this distinction and provides four factors that should be considered in attempting to define the extent of a home's curtilage.

U.S. v. DUNN
480 U.S. 294 (1987)

JUSTICE WHITE delivered the opinion of the Court.

We granted the Government's petition for certiorari to decide whether the area near a barn, located approximately 50 yards from a fence surrounding a ranch house, is, for Fourth Amendment purposes, within the curtilage of the house. The Court of Appeals for the Fifth Circuit held that the barn lay within the house's curtilage, and that the District Court should have suppressed certain evidence obtained as a result of law enforcement officials' intrusion onto the area immediately surrounding the barn. We conclude that the barn and the area around it lay outside the curtilage of the house, and accordingly reverse the judgment of the Court of Appeals.

I

Respondent Ronald Dale Dunn and a codefendant, Robert Lyle Carpenter, were convicted by a jury of conspiring to manufacture phenylacetone and amphetamine, and to possess amphetamine with intent to distribute. Respondent was also convicted of manufacturing these two controlled substances and possessing amphetamine with intent to distribute. The events giving rise to respondent's apprehension and conviction began in 1980 when agents from the Drug Enforcement Administration (DEA) discovered that Carpenter had purchased large quantities of chemicals and equipment used in the manufacture of amphetamine and phenylacetone. DEA agents obtained warrants from a Texas state judge authorizing installation of miniature electronic transmitter tracking devices, or "beepers," in an electric hot plate stirrer, a drum of acetic anhydride, and a container holding phenylacetic acid, a precursor to phenylacetone. All of these items had been ordered by Carpenter. On September 3, 1980, Carpenter took possession of the electric hot plate stirrer, but the agents lost the signal from the "beeper" a few days later. The agents were able to track the "beeper" in the container of chemicals, however, from October 27, 1980, until November 5, 1980, on which date Carpenter's pickup truck, which was carrying the container, arrived at respondent's ranch. Aerial photographs of the ranch property showed Carpenter's truck backed up to a barn behind the ranch house. The agents also began receiving transmission signals from the "beeper" in the hot plate stirrer that they had lost in early September and determined that the stirrer was on respondent's ranch property.

Respondent's ranch comprised approximately 198 acres and was completely encircled by a perimeter fence. The property also contained several interior fences, constructed mainly of posts and multiple strands of barbed wire. The ranch residence was situated 1/2 mile from a public road. A fence encircled the residence and a nearby small greenhouse. Two barns were located approximately 50 yards from this fence. The front of the larger of the two barns was enclosed by a wooden fence and had an open overhang. Locked, waist-high gates barred entry into the barn proper, and netting material stretched from the ceiling to the top of the wooden gates.

On the evening of November 5, 1980, law enforcement officials made a warrantless entry onto respondent's ranch property. A DEA agent accompanied by an officer from the Houston Police Department crossed over the perimeter fence and one interior fence. Standing approximately midway between the residence and the barns, the DEA agent smelled what he believed to be phenylacetic acid, the odor coming from the direction of the barns. The officers approached the smaller of the barns— crossing over a barbed wire fence—and, looking into the barn, observed only empty boxes. The officers then proceeded to the larger barn, crossing another barbed wire fence as well as a wooden fence that enclosed the front portion of the barn. The officers walked under the barn's overhang to the locked wooden gates and, shining a flashlight through the netting on top of the gates, peered into the barn. They observed what the DEA agent thought to be a phenylacetone laboratory. The officers did not enter the barn. At this point the officers departed from respondent's property, but entered it twice more on November 6 to confirm the presence of the phenylacetone laboratory.

On November 6, 1980, at 8:30 p.m., a Federal Magistrate issued a warrant authorizing a search of respondent's ranch. DEA agents and state law enforcement officials executed the warrant on November 8, 1980. The officers arrested respondent and seized chemicals and equipment, as well as bags of amphetamines they discovered in a closet in the ranch house.

II

The curtilage concept originated at common law to extend to the area immediately surrounding a dwelling house the same protection under the law of burglary as was afforded the house itself. The concept plays a part, however, in interpreting the reach of the Fourth Amendment. *Hester v. U.S.*, 265 U.S. 57 (1924), held that the Fourth Amendment's protection accorded "persons, houses, papers, and effects" did not extend to the open fields, the Court observing that the distinction between a person's house and open fields "is as old as the common law."

We reaffirmed the holding of *Hester* in *Oliver v. U.S.*, 466 U.S. 170 (1984). There, we recognized that the Fourth Amendment protects the curtilage of a house and that the extent of the curtilage is determined by factors that bear upon whether an individual reasonably may expect that the area in question should be treated as the home itself. We identified the central component of this inquiry as whether the area harbors the "intimate activity associated with the sanctity of a man's home and the privacies of life."

Drawing upon the Court's own cases and the cumulative experience of the lower courts that have grappled with the task of defining the extent of a home's curtilage, we believe that curtilage questions should be resolved with particular reference to four factors: the proximity of the area claimed to be curtilage to the home, whether the area is included within an enclosure surrounding the home, the nature of the uses to which the area is put, and the steps taken by the resident to protect the area from observation by people passing by. We do not suggest that combining these factors produces a finely tuned formula that, when mechanically applied, yields a "correct" answer to all extent-of-curtilage questions. Rather, these factors are useful analytical tools only to the degree that, in any given case, they bear upon the centrally relevant consideration—whether the area in question is so intimately tied to the home itself that it should be placed under the home's "umbrella" of Fourth Amendment protection. Applying these factors to respondent's barn and to the area immediately surrounding it, we have little difficulty in concluding that this area lay outside the curtilage of the ranch house.

First. The record discloses that the barn was located 50 yards from the fence surrounding the house and 60 yards from the house itself. Standing in isolation, this substantial distance supports no inference that the barn should be treated as an adjunct of the house.

Second. It is also significant that respondent's barn did not lie within the area surrounding the house that was enclosed by a fence. Viewing the physical layout of respondent's ranch in its entirety, it is plain that the fence surrounding the residence serves to demark a specific area of land immediately adjacent to the house that is readily identifiable as part and parcel of the house. Conversely, the barn—the front portion itself enclosed by a fence—and the area immediately surrounding it, stands out as a distinct portion of respondent's ranch, quite separate from the residence.

Third. It is especially significant that the law enforcement officials possessed objective data indicating that the barn was not being used for intimate activities of the home. The aerial photographs showed that the truck Carpenter had been driving that contained the container of phenylacetic acid was backed up to the barn, apparently for the unloading of its contents. When on respondent's property, the officers' suspicion was further directed toward the barn because of a very strong odor of phenylacetic acid. As the DEA agent approached the barn, he could hear a motor running, like a pump motor of some sort. Furthermore, the officers detected an extremely strong odor of phenylacetic acid coming from a small crack in the wall of the barn. Finally, as the officers were standing in front of the barn, immediately prior to looking into its interior through the netting material, "the smell was very, very strong [and the officers] could hear the motor running very loudly." When considered together, the above facts indicated to the officers that the use to which the barn was being put could not fairly be characterized as so associated with the activities and privacies of domestic life that the officers should have deemed the barn as part of respondent's home.

Fourth. Respondent did little to protect the barn area from observation by those standing in the open fields. Nothing in the record suggests that the various interior fences on respondent's property had any function other than that of the typical ranch fence; the fences were designed and constructed to corral livestock, not to prevent persons from observing what lay inside the enclosed areas.

The officers lawfully viewed the interior of respondent's barn, and their observations were properly considered by the Magistrate in issuing a search warrant for respondent's premises.

JUSTICE BRENNAN, with whom JUSTICE MARSHALL joins, dissenting.

The Government agents' intrusions upon Ronald Dunn's privacy and property violated the Fourth Amendment for two reasons. First, the barnyard invaded by the agents lay within the protected curtilage of Dunn's farmhouse. Second, the agents infringed upon Dunn's reasonable expectation of privacy in the barn and its contents. Our society is not so exclusively urban that it is unable to perceive or unwilling to preserve the expectation of farmers and ranchers that barns and their contents are protected from (literally) unwarranted government intrusion.

The overwhelming majority of state courts have consistently held that barns are included within the curtilage of a farmhouse. Federal courts, too, have held that barns, like other rural outbuildings, lie within the curtilage of the farmhouse. Thus, case law demonstrates that a barn is an integral part of a farm home and therefore lies within the curtilage. The Court's opinion provides no justification for its indifference to the weight of state and federal precedent.

The above-[mentioned] authority also reveals the infirmities in the Court's application of its four-part test. First, the distance between the house and the barn does not militate against the barn or barnyard's presence in the curtilage. Many of the [state and federal] cases involve a barn separated from a residence by a distance in excess of 60 yards. Second, the cases make evident that the configuration of fences is not determinative of the status of an outbuilding. Here, where the barn was connected to the house by a "well walked" and a "well driven" path, and was clustered with the farmhouse and other outbuildings in a clearing surrounded by woods, the presence of intervening fences fades into irrelevance.

The third factor in the test—the nature of the uses to which the area is put—has been badly misunderstood and misapplied by the Court. The Court reasons that, because the barn and barnyard were not actually in domestic use, they were not within the curtilage. This reveals a misunderstanding of the level of generality at which the constitutional inquiry must proceed and is flatly inconsistent with the Court's analysis in *Oliver*.

In *Oliver*, the Court held that, as a general matter, the open fields "are unlikely to provide the setting for activities whose privacy is sought to be protected by the Fourth Amendment." The Court expressly refused to do a case-by-case analysis to ascertain whether, on occasion, an individual's expectation of privacy in a certain activity in an open field should be protected. In the instant case, the Court is confronted with the general rule that a barn *is* in domestic use. To be consistent with *Oliver*, the Court should refuse to do a case-by-case analysis of the expectation of privacy in any particular barn and follow the general rule that a barn is in domestic use. What should be relevant here, as in *Oliver*, is the typical use of an area or structure. The Court's willingness to generalize about the absence of a privacy interest in the open fields and unwillingness to generalize about the existence of a privacy interest in a barn near a residence are manifestly inconsistent and reflect a hostility to the purpose of the Fourth Amendment.

Moreover, the discovery that Dunn's barn was actually used as a drug laboratory is irrelevant to the question whether the area is typically in domestic use. No one would contend that, absent exigent circumstances, the police could intrude upon a home without a warrant to search for a drug manufacturing operation. The Fourth Amendment extends that same protection to outbuildings in the curtilage of the home.

Even accepting that courts should do a case-by-case inquiry regarding the use of buildings within the curtilage, the Court's analysis is faulty. The Court finds it significant that, because of the strong odor and the noise of a motor emanating from the barn, the officers knew that the barn was not in domestic use. But these Government agents *were already within the curtilage* when they detected the odor of phenylacetic acid. They were wandering about in the area between the barns and the farmhouse, an area that is itself part of the curtilage. The Court cannot abrogate the general rule that a barn is in the curtilage with evidence gathered after the intrusion has occurred.

Finally, neither the smell of the chemicals nor the sound of the motor running would remove the protection of the Fourth Amendment from an otherwise protected structure. A barn, like a home, may simultaneously be put to domestic and nondomestic uses, even the manufacture of drugs. Dual use does not strip a home or any building within the curtilage of Fourth Amendment protection. What the evidence cited by the Court might suggest is that the DEA agents had probable cause to enter the barn or barnyard *before they made any unconstitutional intrusion*. If so—and I do not concede it—they should have obtained a warrant.

With regard to the fourth factor of the curtilage test, I find astounding the Court's conclusion that "respondent did little to protect the barn area from observation by those standing in the open fields." Initially, I note that the fenced area immediately adjacent to the barn in this case is not part of the open fields, but is instead part of the curtilage and an area in which Dunn had a reasonable expectation of privacy. Second, Dunn, in fact, took elaborate measures to ensure his privacy. He locked his driveway, fenced in his barn, and covered its open end with a locked gate and fishnetting. The Fourth Amendment does not require the posting of a 24-hour guard to preserve an expectation of privacy.

The Fourth Amendment prohibits police activity which, if left unrestricted, would jeopardize individuals' sense of security or would too heavily burden those who wished to guard their privacy. In this case, in order to look inside respondent's barn, the DEA agents traveled one-half mile off a public road over respondent's fenced-in property, crossed over three additional wooden and barbed wire fences, stepped under the eaves of the barn, and then used a flashlight to peer through otherwise opaque fishnetting. For the police habitually to engage in such surveillance—without a warrant—is constitutionally intolerable. Because I believe that farmers' and ranchers' expectations of privacy in their barns and other outbuildings are expectations society would regard as reasonable, and because I believe that sanctioning the police behavior at issue here does violence to the purpose and promise of the Fourth Amendment, I dissent.

Searches of Open Fields

1.   Because open fields are not persons, houses, papers, or effects, a government intrusion upon an open field is not an unreasonable search proscribed by the text of the Fourth Amendment. A government intrusion into a privately owned open field is also not a search because an individual may not legitimately demand privacy for activities conducted outside in fields, except in the curtilage—the area immediately surrounding the home.

2.   In attempting to define the extent of a home's curtilage, the central consideration is whether the area in question is so intimately tied to the home itself that it should be placed under the home's "umbrella" of Fourth Amendment protection. In making that determination, a court should consider the following four factors:

    a.   The proximity of the area claimed to be curtilage to the home.

b.   Whether the area is included within an enclosure surrounding the home.

c.   The nature of the uses to which the area is put.

d.   The steps taken by the resident to protect the area from observation by passersby.

4.   AERIAL OBSERVATION

Although the majority and dissenting opinions in *Oliver v. U.S.* and *U.S. v. Dunn* disagreed on the method for distinguishing an open field from curtilage, all of the Justices appeared to agree that if the police physically enter the curtilage of a home and gather evidence within it, a search has occurred within the meaning of the Fourth Amendment. But what if the police don't actually enter the curtilage of a home and instead simply fly over it? In *California v. Ciraolo*, the Supreme Court concluded that aerial observation of a home's curtilage did not constitute a search under the Fourth Amendment.

CALIFORNIA V. CIRAOLO
476 U.S. 207 (1986)

CHIEF JUSTICE BURGER delivered the opinion of the Court.

We granted certiorari to determine whether the Fourth Amendment is violated by aerial observation without a warrant from an altitude of 1,000 feet of a fenced-in backyard within the curtilage of a home.

I

On September 2, 1982, Santa Clara Police received an anonymous telephone tip that marijuana was growing in respondent's backyard. Police were unable to observe the contents of respondent's yard from ground level because of a 6-foot outer fence and a 10-foot inner fence completely enclosing the yard. Later that day, Officer Shutz, who was assigned to investigate, secured a private plane and flew over respondent's house at an altitude of 1,000 feet, within navigable airspace; he was accompanied by Officer Rodriguez. Both officers were trained in marijuana identification. From the overflight, the officers readily identified marijuana plants 8 feet to 10 feet in height growing in a 15- by 25-foot plot in respondent's yard; they photographed the area with a standard 35mm camera.

On September 8, 1982, Officer Shutz obtained a search warrant on the basis of an affidavit describing the anonymous tip and their observations; a photograph depicting respondent's house, the backyard, and neighboring homes was attached to the affidavit as an exhibit. The warrant was executed the next day and 73 plants were seized; it is not disputed that these were marijuana.

After the trial court denied respondent's motion to suppress the evidence of the search, respondent pleaded guilty to a charge of cultivation of marijuana. The California Court of Appeal reversed, however, on the ground that the warrantless aerial *observation* of respondent's yard which led to the issuance of the warrant violated the Fourth Amendment. That court held first that respondent's backyard marijuana garden was within the "curtilage" of his home, under *Oliver v. U.S.*, 466 U.S. 170 (1984). The court emphasized that the height and existence of the two fences constituted "objective criteria from which we may conclude he manifested a reasonable expectation of privacy by any standard."

Examining the particular method of surveillance undertaken, the court then found it "significant" that the flyover "was not the result of a routine patrol conducted for any other legitimate law enforcement or public safety objective, but was undertaken for the specific purpose of observing this particular enclosure within [respondent's] curtilage." It held this focused observation was "a direct and unauthorized intrusion into the sanctity of the home" which violated respondent's reasonable expectation of privacy. The California Supreme Court denied the State's petition for review. We granted the State's petition for certiorari. We reverse.

The State argues that respondent has "knowingly exposed" his backyard to aerial observation, because all that was seen was visible to the naked eye from any aircraft flying overhead. The State analogizes its mode of observation to a knothole or opening in a fence: if there is an opening, the police may look.

The California Court of Appeal, as we noted earlier, accepted the analysis that unlike the casual observation of a private person flying overhead, this flight was focused specifically on a small suburban yard, and was not the result of any routine patrol overflight. Respondent contends he has done all that can reasonably be expected to tell the world he wishes to maintain the privacy of his garden within the curtilage without covering his yard. Such covering, he argues, would defeat its purpose as an outside living area; he asserts he has not "knowingly" exposed himself to aerial views.

II

The touchstone of Fourth Amendment analysis is whether a person has a "constitutionally protected reasonable expectation of privacy." *Katz v. U.S.*, 389 U.S. 347 (1967), posits a two-part inquiry: first, has the individual manifested a subjective expectation of privacy in the object of the challenged search? Second, is society willing to recognize that expectation as reasonable?

Clearly—and understandably—respondent has met the test of manifesting his own subjective intent and desire to maintain privacy as to his unlawful agricultural pursuits. However, we need not address that issue, for the State has not challenged the finding of the California Court of Appeal that respondent had such an expectation. It can reasonably be assumed that the 10-foot fence was placed to conceal the marijuana crop from at least street-level views. So far as the normal sidewalk traffic was concerned, this fence served that purpose, because respondent took normal precautions to maintain his privacy.

Yet a 10-foot fence might not shield these plants from the eyes of a citizen or a policeman perched on the top of a truck or a two-level bus. Whether respondent therefore manifested a subjective expectation of privacy from *all* observations of his backyard, or whether instead he manifested merely a hope that no one would observe his unlawful gardening pursuits, is not entirely clear in these circumstances. Respondent appears to challenge the authority of government to observe his activity from any vantage point or place if the viewing is motivated by a law enforcement purpose, and not the result of a casual, accidental observation.

We turn, therefore, to the second inquiry under *Katz*, *i.e.*, whether that expectation is reasonable. In pursuing this inquiry, we must keep in mind that "the test of legitimacy is not whether the individual chooses to conceal assertedly private activity," but instead "whether the government's intrusion infringes upon the personal and societal values protected by the Fourth Amendment." *Oliver v. U.S.*, 466 U.S. 170, 181–183 (1984).

Respondent argues that because his yard was in the curtilage of his home, no governmental aerial observation is permissible under the Fourth Amendment without a warrant. The history and genesis of the curtilage doctrine are instructive. At common law, the curtilage is the area to which extends the intimate activity associated with the sanctity of a man's home and the privacies of life. The protection afforded the curtilage is essentially a protection of families and personal privacy in an area intimately linked to the home, both physically and psychologically, where privacy expectations are most heightened. The claimed area here was immediately adjacent to a suburban home, surrounded by high double fences. This close nexus to the home would appear to encompass this small area within the curtilage. Accepting, as the State does, that this yard and its crop fall within the curtilage, the question remains whether naked-eye observation of the curtilage by police from an aircraft lawfully operating at an altitude of 1,000 feet violates an expectation of privacy that is reasonable.

That the area is within the curtilage does not itself bar all police observation. The Fourth Amendment protection of the home has never been extended to require law enforcement officers to shield their eyes when passing by a home on public thoroughfares. Nor does the mere fact that an individual has taken measures to restrict some views of his activities preclude an officer's observations from a public vantage point where he has a right to be and which renders the activities clearly visible. "What a person knowingly exposes to the public, even in his own home or office, is not a subject of Fourth Amendment protection." *Katz v. U.S.*, 389 U.S. 347, 351 (1967).

The observations by Officers Shutz and Rodriguez in this case took place within public navigable airspace in a physically nonintrusive manner; from this point they were able to observe plants readily discernible to the naked eye as marijuana. That the observation from aircraft was directed at identifying the plants and the officers were trained to recognize marijuana is irrelevant. Such observation is precisely what a judicial officer needs to provide a basis for a warrant. Any member of the public flying in this airspace who glanced down could have seen everything that these officers observed. On this record, we readily conclude that respondent's expectation that his garden was protected from such observation is unreasonable and is not an expectation that society is prepared to honor.

The dissent contends that the Court ignores Justice Harlan's warning in his concurrence in *Katz* that the Fourth Amendment should not be limited to proscribing only physical intrusions onto private property. But Justice Harlan's observations about future electronic developments and the potential for electronic interference with private communications were plainly not aimed at simple visual observations from a public place. Indeed, since *Katz* the Court has required warrants for electronic surveillance aimed at intercepting private conversations.

Justice Harlan made it crystal clear that he was resting on the reality that one who enters a telephone booth is entitled to assume that his conversation is not being intercepted. This does not translate readily into a rule of constitutional dimensions that one who grows illicit drugs in his backyard is entitled to assume his unlawful conduct will not be observed by a passing aircraft—or by a power company repair mechanic on a pole overlooking the yard.

One can reasonably doubt that in 1967 Justice Harlan considered an aircraft within the category of future "electronic" developments that could stealthily intrude upon an individual's privacy. In an age where private and commercial flight in the public airways is routine, it is unreasonable for respondent to expect that his marijuana plants were constitutionally protected from being observed with the naked eye from an altitude of 1,000 feet. The Fourth Amendment simply does not require the police traveling in the public airways at this altitude to obtain a warrant in order to observe what is visible to the naked eye.

JUSTICE POWELL, with whom JUSTICE BRENNAN, JUSTICE MARSHALL, and JUSTICE BLACKMUN join, dissenting.

Respondent contends that the police intruded on his constitutionally protected expectation of privacy when they conducted aerial surveillance of his home and photographed his backyard without first obtaining a warrant. The Court rejects that contention, holding that respondent's expectation of privacy in the curtilage of his home, although reasonable as to intrusions on the ground, was unreasonable as to surveillance from the navigable airspace. In my view, the Court's holding rests on only one obvious fact, namely, that the airspace generally is open to all persons for travel in airplanes. The Court does not explain why this single fact deprives citizens of their privacy interest in outdoor activities in an enclosed curtilage.

Katz announced a standard under which the occurrence of a search turned not on the physical position of the police conducting the surveillance, but on whether the surveillance in question had invaded a constitutionally protected reasonable expectation of privacy.

Our decisions following the teaching of *Katz* illustrate that this inquiry normally embraces two discrete questions. The first is whether the individual, by his conduct, has exhibited an actual (subjective) expectation of privacy. The second is whether that subjective expectation is one that society is prepared to recognize as reasonable. While the Court today purports to reaffirm this analytical framework, its conclusory rejection of respondent's expectation of privacy in the yard of his residence as one that is unreasonable represents a turning away from the principles that have guided our Fourth Amendment inquiry.

The second question under *Katz* has been described as asking whether an expectation of privacy is legitimate in the sense required by the Fourth Amendment. The answer turns on whether the government's intrusion infringes upon the personal and societal values protected by the Fourth Amendment. While no single consideration has been regarded as dispositive, the Court has given weight to such factors as the intention of the Framers of the Fourth Amendment, the uses to which the individual has put a location, and our societal understanding that certain areas deserve the most scrupulous protection from government invasion. Our decisions have made clear that this inquiry often must be decided by reference to a place, and that a home is a place in which a subjective expectation of privacy virtually always will be legitimate.

This case involves surveillance of a home, for as we stated in *Oliver v. U.S.*, the curtilage has been considered part of the home itself for Fourth Amendment purposes. In deciding whether an area is within the curtilage, courts have defined the curtilage, as did the common law, by reference to the factors that determine whether an individual reasonably may expect that an area immediately adjacent to the home will remain private. The lower federal courts have agreed that the curtilage is an area of domestic use immediately surrounding a dwelling and usually but not always fenced in with the dwelling. Those courts also have held that whether an area is within the curtilage must be decided by looking at all of the facts. Relevant facts include the proximity between the area claimed to be curtilage and the home, the nature of the uses to which the area is put, and the steps taken by the resident to protect the area from observation by people passing by.

The Court begins its analysis of the Fourth Amendment issue posed here by deciding that respondent had an expectation of privacy in his backyard. I agree with that conclusion because of the close proximity of the yard to the house, the nature of some of the activities respondent conducted there, and because he had taken steps to shield those activities from the view of passersby. The Court then implicitly acknowledges that society is prepared to recognize his expectation as reasonable with respect to ground-level surveillance, holding that the yard was within the curtilage, an area in which privacy interests have been afforded the most heightened protection. As the foregoing discussion of the curtilage doctrine demonstrates, respondent's yard unquestionably was within the curtilage. Since Officer Shutz could not see into this private family area from the street, the Court certainly would agree that he would have conducted an unreasonable search had he climbed over the fence, or used a ladder to peer into the yard without first securing a warrant.

The Court concludes, nevertheless, that Shutz could use an airplane—a product of modern technology—to intrude visually into respondent's yard. The Court argues that respondent had no reasonable expectation of privacy from aerial observation. It notes that Shutz was "within public navigable airspace," when he looked into and photographed respondent's yard. It then relies on the fact that the surveillance was not accompanied by a physical invasion of the curtilage. Reliance on the *manner* of surveillance is directly contrary to the standard of *Katz*, which identifies a constitutionally protected privacy right by focusing on the interests of the individual and of a free society. Since *Katz*, we have consistently held that the presence or absence of physical trespass by police is constitutionally irrelevant to the question whether society is prepared to recognize an asserted privacy interest as reasonable.

The Court's holding, therefore, must rest solely on the fact that members of the public fly in planes and may look down at homes as they fly over them. The Court does not explain why it finds this fact to be significant. One may assume that the Court believes that citizens bear the risk that air travelers will observe activities occurring within backyards that are open to the sun and air. This risk, the Court appears to hold, nullifies expectations of privacy in those yards even as to purposeful police surveillance from the air.

This line of reasoning is flawed. First, the actual risk to privacy from commercial or pleasure aircraft is virtually nonexistent. Travelers on commercial flights, as well as private planes used for business or personal reasons, normally obtain at most a fleeting, anonymous, and nondiscriminating glimpse of the landscape and buildings over which they pass. The risk that a passenger on such a plane might observe private activities, and might connect those activities with particular people, is simply too trivial to protect against. It is no accident that, as a matter of common experience, many people build fences around their residential areas, but few build roofs over their backyards. Therefore, contrary to the Court's suggestion, people do not knowingly expose their residential yards to the public merely by failing to build barriers that prevent aerial surveillance.

Since respondent had a reasonable expectation of privacy in his yard, aerial surveillance undertaken by the police for the purpose of discovering evidence of crime constituted a "search" within the meaning of the Fourth Amendment. Warrantless searches are presumptively unreasonable, though the Court has recognized a few limited exceptions to this general rule. This case presents no such exception. The indiscriminate nature of aerial surveillance, illustrated by Officer Shutz's photograph of respondent's home and enclosed yard as well as those of his neighbors, poses far too serious a threat to privacy interests in the home to escape entirely some sort of Fourth Amendment oversight. Therefore, I would affirm the judgment of the California Court of Appeal ordering suppression of the marijuana plants.

Rapidly advancing technology now permits police to conduct surveillance in the home itself, an area where privacy interests are most cherished in our society, without any physical trespass. While the rule in *Katz* was designed to prevent silent and unseen invasions of Fourth Amendment privacy rights in a variety of settings, we have consistently afforded heightened protection to a person's right to be left alone in the privacy of his house. The Court fails to enforce that right or to give any weight to the longstanding presumption that warrantless intrusions into the home are unreasonable. I dissent.

Aerial Observation

Aerial observation of a home's curtilage is not a search if the curtilage is visible from public navigable airspace. An individual's expectation that his curtilage or garden is protected from such observation is unreasonable and is not an expectation that society is prepared to honor.

---

5.   SEARCHES OF TRASH

In *California v. Greenwood*, the Supreme Court concluded that the defendant had no reasonable expectation of privacy in the garbage he had left out on the curb—outside of his home's curtilage—for collection. Accordingly, the actions of the police in rummaging through the garbage for incriminating evidence did not constitute a search, and no warrant was required.

CALIFORNIA V. GREENWOOD
486 U.S. 35 (1988)

JUSTICE WHITE delivered the opinion of the Court.

The issue here is whether the Fourth Amendment prohibits the warrantless search and seizure of garbage left for collection outside the curtilage of a home. We conclude, in accordance with the vast majority of lower courts that have addressed the issue, that it does not.

I

In early 1984, Investigator Jenny Stracner of the Laguna Beach Police Department received information indicating that respondent Greenwood might be engaged in narcotics trafficking. Stracner learned that a criminal suspect had informed a federal drug enforcement agent in February 1984 that a truck filled with illegal drugs was en route to the Laguna Beach address at which Greenwood resided. In addition, a neighbor complained of heavy vehicular traffic late at night in front of Greenwood's single-family home. The neighbor reported that the vehicles remained at Greenwood's house for only a few minutes.

Stracner sought to investigate this information by conducting a surveillance of Greenwood's home. She observed several vehicles make brief stops at the house during the late-night and early morning hours, and she followed a truck from the house to a residence that had previously been under investigation as a narcotics-trafficking location.

On April 6, 1984, Stracner asked the neighborhood's regular trash collector to pick up the plastic garbage bags that Greenwood had left on the curb in front of his house and to turn the bags over to her without mixing their contents with garbage from other houses. The trash collector cleaned his truck bin of other refuse, collected the garbage bags from the street in front of Greenwood's house, and turned the bags over to Stracner. The officer searched through the rubbish and found items indicative of narcotics use. She recited the information that she had gleaned from the trash search in an affidavit in support of a warrant to search Greenwood's home.

Police officers encountered both respondents at the house later that day when they arrived to execute the warrant. The police discovered quantities of cocaine and hashish during their search of the house. Respondents were arrested on felony narcotics charges. They subsequently posted bail.

The police continued to receive reports of many late-night visitors to the Greenwood house. On May 4, Investigator Robert Rahaeuser obtained Greenwood's garbage from the regular trash collector in the same manner as had Stracner. The garbage again contained evidence of narcotics use.

Rahaeuser secured another search warrant for Greenwood's home based on the information from the second trash search. The police found more narcotics and evidence of narcotics trafficking when they executed the warrant. Greenwood was again arrested.

II

The warrantless search and seizure of the garbage bags left at the curb outside the Greenwood house would violate the Fourth Amendment only if respondents manifested a subjective expectation of privacy in their garbage that society accepts as objectively reasonable. Respondents do not disagree with this standard.

They assert, however, that they had, and exhibited, an expectation of privacy with respect to the trash that was searched by the police: The trash, which was placed on the street for collection at a fixed time, was contained in opaque plastic bags, which the garbage collector was expected to pick up, mingle with the trash of others, and deposit at the garbage dump. The trash was only temporarily on the street, and there was little likelihood that it would be inspected by anyone.

It may well be that respondents did not expect that the contents of their garbage bags would become known to the police or other members of the public. An expectation of privacy does not give rise to Fourth Amendment protection, however, unless society is prepared to accept that expectation as objectively reasonable.

Here, we conclude that respondents exposed their garbage to the public sufficiently to defeat their claim to Fourth Amendment protection. It is common knowledge that plastic garbage bags left on or at the side of a public street are readily accessible to animals, children, scavengers, snoops, and other members of the public. Moreover, respondents placed their refuse at the curb for the express purpose of conveying it to a third party, the trash collector, who might himself have sorted through respondents' trash or permitted others, such as the police, to do so. Accordingly, having deposited their garbage in an area particularly suited for public inspection and, in a manner of speaking, public consumption, for the express purpose of having strangers take it, respondents could have had no reasonable expectation of privacy in the inculpatory items that they discarded.

JUSTICE BRENNAN, with whom JUSTICE MARSHALL joins, dissenting.

Every week for two months, and at least once more a month later, the Laguna Beach police clawed through the trash that respondent Greenwood left in opaque, sealed bags on the curb outside his home. Complete strangers minutely scrutinized their bounty, undoubtedly dredging up intimate details of Greenwood's private life and habits. The intrusions proceeded without a warrant, and no court before or since has concluded that the police acted on probable cause to believe Greenwood was engaged in any criminal activity.

Scrutiny of another's trash is contrary to commonly accepted notions of civilized behavior. I suspect, therefore, that members of our society will be shocked to learn that the Court, the ultimate guarantor of liberty, deems unreasonable our expectation that the aspects of our private lives that are concealed safely in a trash bag will not become public.

Our precedent leaves no room to doubt that had respondents been carrying their personal effects in opaque, sealed plastic bags—identical to the ones they placed on the curb—their privacy would have been protected from warrantless police intrusion.

Respondents deserve no less protection just because Greenwood used the bags to discard rather than to transport his personal effects. Their contents are not inherently any less private, and Greenwood's decision to discard them, at least in the manner in which he did, does not diminish his expectation of privacy.

A single bag of trash testifies eloquently to the eating, reading, and recreational habits of the person who produced it. A search of trash, like a search of the bedroom, can relate intimate details about sexual practices, health, and personal hygiene. Like rifling through desk drawers or intercepting phone calls, rummaging through trash can divulge the target's financial and professional status, political affiliations and inclinations, private thoughts, personal relationships, and romantic interests. It cannot be doubted that a sealed trash bag harbors telling evidence of the intimate activity associated with the sanctity of a man's home and the privacies of life, which the Fourth Amendment is designed to protect.

Had Greenwood flaunted his intimate activity by strewing his trash all over the curb for all to see, or had some nongovernmental intruder invaded his privacy and done the same, I could accept the Court's conclusion that an expectation of privacy would have been unreasonable. Similarly, had police searching the city dump run across incriminating evidence that, despite commingling with the trash of others, still retained its identity as Greenwood's, we would have a different case. But all that Greenwood exposed to the public were the exteriors of several opaque, sealed containers. Faithful application of the warrant requirement does not require police to avert their eyes from evidence of criminal activity that could have been observed by any member of the public. Rather, it only requires them to adhere to norms of privacy that members of the public plainly acknowledge.

The mere *possibility* that unwelcome meddlers *might* open and rummage through the containers does not negate the expectation of privacy in their contents any more than the possibility of a burglary negates an expectation of privacy in the home; or the possibility of a private intrusion negates an expectation of privacy in an unopened package; or the possibility that an operator will listen in on a telephone conversation negates an expectation of privacy in the words spoken on the telephone. "What a person seeks to preserve as private, *even in an area accessible to the public,* may be constitutionally protected." *Katz v. U.S.,* 389 U.S. 347, 351–352 (1967). We have therefore repeatedly rejected attempts to justify a State's invasion of privacy on the ground that the privacy is not absolute.

Nor is it dispositive that respondents placed their refuse at the curb for the express purpose of conveying it to a third party, who might himself have sorted through respondents' trash or permitted others, such as the police, to do so. In the first place, Greenwood can hardly be faulted for leaving trash on his curb when a county ordinance commanded him to do so, and prohibited him from disposing of it in any other way. Unlike in other circumstances where privacy is compromised, Greenwood could not avoid exposing personal belongings by simply leaving them at home. More importantly, even the voluntary relinquishment of possession or control over an effect does not necessarily amount to a relinquishment of a privacy expectation in it. Were it otherwise, a letter or package would lose all Fourth Amendment protection when placed in a mailbox or other depository with the express purpose of entrusting it to the postal officer or a private carrier; those bailees are just as likely as trash collectors (and certainly have greater incentive) to sort through the personal effects entrusted to them, or permit others, such as police to do so. Yet, it has been clear for at least 110 years that the possibility of such an intrusion does not justify a warrantless search by police in the first instance.

In holding that the warrantless search of Greenwood's trash was consistent with the Fourth Amendment, the Court paints a grim picture of our society. It depicts a society in which local authorities may command their citizens to dispose of their personal effects in the manner least protective of the sanctity of the home and the privacies of life, and then monitor them arbitrarily and without judicial oversight—a society that is not prepared to recognize as reasonable an individual's expectation of privacy in the most private of personal effects sealed in an opaque container and disposed of in a manner designed to commingle it imminently and inextricably with the trash of others. The American society with which I am familiar chooses to dwell in reasonable security and freedom from surveillance, and is more dedicated to individual liberty and more sensitive to intrusions on the sanctity of the home than the Court is willing to acknowledge.

————————

The majority and the dissent in *Greenwood* have dramatically different views about society's privacy expectations that yield different answers to the second prong of the *Katz* Test. The Justices in the majority in *Greenwood* have what might be termed a *descriptive* view of privacy: They describe the degree of privacy people *actually have* in a given situation in order to draw conclusions about whether it is reasonable to expect privacy in those situations. So, for example, the *Greenwood* majority points out that we don't actually have much privacy in our discarded trash because anyone—nosy neighbors, scavengers, or even animals—might invade it and expose it to public view. Because people don't *actually have* much privacy in their discarded garbage, it's unreasonable to *expect* that discarded garbage will remain private.

The dissenting Justices in *Greenwood* have what might be termed a *prescriptive* or *aspirational* view of privacy. For these Justices, the degree of privacy that people actually have in a given situation or area is not determinative; instead, the important question is whether we *should*, as a society, be able to *expect* privacy *vis-á-vis the government* in that situation or area. Because discarded trash may contain a great deal of intimate and private information, we should, as a society, expect that our trash will remain private, even if those expectations are occasionally frustrated by nosy neighbors, scavengers, or animals. And simply because nosy neighbors, scavengers, or animals may invade our privacy does not mean that the police or the government should be free to do so.

Those Justices who adhere to the descriptive view generally have a more narrow conception of privacy and are willing to provide the police with greater investigative leeway. Those Justices who adhere to the prescriptive or aspirational view generally have a broader conception of privacy and support tighter limits on police investigative techniques. Which approach best captures your own view of privacy and the Fourth Amendment?

Searches of Trash

A search does not occur when police gather and sort through an individual's trash left for collection outside the curtilage of a home. Because trash left for collection on a public street is readily accessible to others, including the garbage collector, it is not objectively reasonable to expect that its contents will remain private.

6. THERMAL IMAGING OF HOMES

In *Kyllo v. U.S.*, the police used a thermal imaging device to detect heat emanating from a home, confirming their suspicions that the defendant was using special lamps to grow marijuana. The Supreme Court found that the use of the device did amount to a search. The Court was concerned about the fact that the device was not in general public use, and was used to reveal details about a home, an area in which Fourth Amendment protections are traditionally at their zenith.

KYLLO V. U.S.
533 U.S. 27 (2001)

JUSTICE SCALIA delivered the opinion of the Court.

This case presents the question whether the use of a thermal-imaging device aimed at a private home from a public street to detect relative amounts of heat within the home constitutes a "search" within the meaning of the Fourth Amendment.

I

In 1991 Agent William Elliott of the United States Department of the Interior came to suspect that marijuana was being grown in the home belonging to petitioner Danny Kyllo, part of a triplex on Rhododendron Drive in Florence, Oregon. Indoor marijuana growth typically requires high-intensity lamps. In order to determine whether an amount of heat was emanating from petitioner's home consistent with the use of such lamps, at 3:20 a.m. on January 16, 1992, Agent Elliott and Dan Haas used an Agema Thermovision 210 thermal imager to scan the triplex. Thermal imagers detect infrared radiation, which virtually all objects emit but which is not visible to the naked eye. The imager converts radiation into images based on relative warmth—black is cool, white is hot, shades of gray connote relative differences; in that respect, it operates somewhat like a video camera showing heat images. The scan of Kyllo's home took only a few minutes and was performed from the passenger seat of Agent Elliott's vehicle across the street from the front of the house and also from the street in back of the house. The scan showed that the roof over the garage and a side wall of petitioner's home were relatively hot compared to the rest of the home and substantially warmer than neighboring homes in the triplex. Agent Elliott concluded that petitioner was using halide lights to grow marijuana in his house, which indeed he was. Based on tips from informants, utility bills, and the thermal imaging, a Federal Magistrate Judge issued a warrant authorizing a search of petitioner's home, and the agents found an indoor growing operation involving more than 100 plants. Petitioner was indicted on one count of manufacturing marijuana. He unsuccessfully moved to suppress the evidence seized from his home and then entered a conditional guilty plea.

The Court of Appeals for the Ninth Circuit remanded the case for an evidentiary hearing regarding the intrusiveness of thermal imaging. On remand the District Court found that the Agema 210 "is a non-intrusive device which emits no rays or beams and shows a crude visual image of the heat being radiated from the outside of the house"; it "did not show any people or activity within the walls of the structure"; "the device used cannot penetrate walls or windows to reveal conversations or human activities"; and "no intimate details of the home were observed." Based on these findings, the District Court upheld the validity of the warrant that relied in part upon the thermal imaging, and reaffirmed its denial of the motion to suppress. A divided Court of Appeals initially reversed, but that opinion was withdrawn and the panel (after a change in composition) affirmed, with Judge Noonan dissenting. The court held that petitioner had shown no subjective expectation of privacy because he had made no attempt to conceal the heat escaping from his home, and even if he had, there was no objectively reasonable expectation of privacy because the imager "did not expose any intimate details of Kyllo's life," only "amorphous hot spots on the roof and exterior wall." We granted certiorari.

II

The Fourth Amendment provides that "the right of the people to be secure in their persons, houses, papers, and effects, against unreasonable searches and seizures, shall not be violated." At the very core of the Fourth Amendment stands the right of a man to retreat into his own home and there be free from unreasonable governmental intrusion. With few exceptions, the question whether a warrantless search of a home is reasonable and hence constitutional must be answered no.

On the other hand, the antecedent question whether or not a Fourth Amendment "search" has occurred is not so simple under our precedent. The permissibility of ordinary visual surveillance of a home used to be clear because, well into the 20th century, our Fourth Amendment jurisprudence was tied to common-law trespass. Visual surveillance was unquestionably lawful because the eye cannot by the laws of England be guilty of a trespass. We have since decoupled violation of a person's Fourth Amendment rights from trespassory violation of his property, but the lawfulness of warrantless visual surveillance of a home has still been preserved. As we observed in *California v. Ciraolo*, 476 U.S. 207, 213 (1986), "the Fourth Amendment protection of the home has never been extended to require law enforcement officers to shield their eyes when passing by a home on public thoroughfares."

A Fourth Amendment search occurs when the government violates a subjective expectation of privacy that society recognizes as reasonable.

We have subsequently applied this principle to hold that a Fourth Amendment search does *not* occur—even when the explicitly protected location of a *house* is concerned—unless the individual manifested a subjective expectation of privacy in the object of the challenged search, and society is willing to recognize that expectation as reasonable. We have applied this test in holding that it is not a search for the police to use a pen register at the phone company to determine what numbers were dialed in a private home, *Smith v. Maryland*, 442 U.S. 735 (1979), and we have applied the test on two different occasions in holding that aerial surveillance of private homes and surrounding areas does not constitute a search, *California v. Ciraolo*, 476 U.S. 207 (1986); *Florida v. Riley*, 488 U.S. 445 (1989).

The present case involves officers on a public street engaged in more than naked-eye surveillance of a home. We have previously reserved judgment as to how much technological enhancement of ordinary perception from such a vantage point, if any, is too much. While we upheld enhanced aerial photography of an industrial complex in *Dow Chemical Co. v. U.S.*, 476 U.S. 227 (1986), we noted that we found "it important that this is *not* an area immediately adjacent to a private home, where privacy expectations are most heightened."

III

It would be foolish to contend that the degree of privacy secured to citizens by the Fourth Amendment has been entirely unaffected by the advance of technology. For example, as the cases discussed above make clear, the technology enabling human flight has exposed to public view (and hence, we have said, to official observation) uncovered portions of the house and its curtilage that once were private. The question we confront today is what limits there are upon this power of technology to shrink the realm of guaranteed privacy.

The *Katz* test—whether the individual has an expectation of privacy that society is prepared to recognize as reasonable—has often been criticized as circular, and hence subjective and unpredictable. While it may be difficult to refine *Katz* when the search of areas such as telephone booths, automobiles, or even the curtilage and uncovered portions of residences is at issue, in the case of the search of the interior of homes— the prototypical and hence most commonly litigated area of protected privacy—there is a ready criterion, with roots deep in the common law, of the minimal expectation of privacy that *exists*, and that is acknowledged to be *reasonable*. To withdraw protection of this minimum expectation would be to permit police technology to erode the privacy guaranteed by the Fourth Amendment. We think that obtaining by sense-enhancing technology any information regarding the interior of the home that could not otherwise have been obtained without physical intrusion into a constitutionally protected area constitutes a search—at least where (as here) the technology in question is not in general public use. This assures preservation of that degree of privacy against government that existed when the Fourth Amendment was adopted. On the basis of this criterion, the information obtained by the thermal imager in this case was the product of a search.[2]

The Government maintains, however, that the thermal imaging must be upheld because it detected only heat radiating from the external surface of the house. The dissent makes this its leading point, contending that there is a fundamental difference between what it calls "off-the-wall" observations and "through-the-wall surveillance." But just as a thermal imager captures only heat emanating from a house, so also a powerful directional microphone picks up only sound emanating from a house—and a satellite capable of scanning from many miles away would pick up only visible light emanating from a house. We rejected such a mechanical interpretation of the Fourth Amendment in *Katz*, where the eavesdropping device picked up only sound waves that reached the exterior of the phone booth. Reversing that approach would leave the homeowner at the mercy of advancing technology—including imaging technology that could discern all human activity in the home. While the technology used in the present case was relatively crude, the rule we adopt must take account of more sophisticated systems that are already in use or in development. The dissent's reliance on the distinction between "off-the-wall" and "through-the-wall" observation is entirely incompatible with the dissent's belief, which we discuss below, that thermal-imaging observations of the intimate details of a home are impermissible. The most sophisticated thermal-imaging devices continue to measure heat "off-the-wall" rather than "through-the-wall"; the dissent's disapproval of those more sophisticated thermal-imaging devices is an acknowledgement that there is no substance to this distinction. As for the dissent's extraordinary assertion that anything learned through "an inference" cannot be a search, that would validate even the "through-the-wall" technologies that the dissent purports to disapprove. Surely the dissent does not believe that the through-the-wall radar or ultrasound technology produces an 8-by-10 Kodak glossy that needs no analysis (*i.e.*, the making of inferences). And, of course, the novel proposition that

---

[2]   The dissent's repeated assertion that the thermal imaging did not obtain information regarding the interior of the home is simply inaccurate. A thermal imager reveals the relative heat of various rooms in the home. The dissent may not find that information particularly private or important, but there is no basis for saying it is not information regarding the interior of the home. The dissent's comparison of the thermal imaging to various circumstances in which outside observers might be able to perceive, without technology, the heat of the home—for example, by observing snowmelt on the roof—is quite irrelevant. The fact that equivalent information could sometimes be obtained by other means does not make lawful the use of means that violate the Fourth Amendment. The police might, for example, learn how many people are in a particular house by setting up year-round surveillance; but that does not make breaking and entering to find out the same information lawful. In any event, on the night of January 16, 1992, no outside observer could have discerned the relative heat of Kyllo's home without thermal imaging.

inference insulates a search is blatantly contrary to *U.S. v. Karo*, 468 U.S. 705 (1984), where the police "inferred" from the activation of a beeper that a certain can of ether was in the home. The police activity was held to be a search, and the search was held unlawful.

The Government also contends that the thermal imaging was constitutional because it did not detect private activities occurring in private areas. The Fourth Amendment's protection of the home has never been tied to measurement of the quality or quantity of information obtained. In the home, our cases show, *all* details are intimate details, because the entire area is held safe from prying government eyes.

Limiting the prohibition of thermal imaging to "intimate details" would not only be wrong in principle; it would be impractical in application, failing to provide a workable accommodation between the needs of law enforcement and the interests protected by the Fourth Amendment. To begin with, there is no necessary connection between the sophistication of the surveillance equipment and the "intimacy" of the details that it observes—which means that one cannot say (and the police cannot be assured) that use of the relatively crude equipment at issue here will always be lawful. The Agema Thermovision 210 might disclose, for example, at what hour each night the lady of the house takes her daily sauna and bath—a detail that many would consider "intimate"; and a much more sophisticated system might detect nothing more intimate than the fact that someone left a closet light on. We could not, in other words, develop a rule approving only that through-the-wall surveillance which identifies objects no smaller than 36 by 36 inches, but would have to develop a jurisprudence specifying which home activities are "intimate" and which are not. And even when (if ever) that jurisprudence were fully developed, no police officer would be able to know *in advance* whether his through-the-wall surveillance picks up "intimate" details—and thus would be unable to know in advance whether it is constitutional.

The dissent's proposed standard—whether the technology offers the "functional equivalent of actual presence in the area being searched"— would seem quite similar to our own at first blush. The dissent concludes that *Katz* was such a case, but then inexplicably asserts that if the same listening device only revealed the volume of the conversation, the surveillance would be permissible. Yet if, without technology, the police could not discern volume without being actually present in the phone booth, Justice Stevens should conclude a search has occurred. The same should hold for the interior heat of the home if only a person present in the home could discern the heat. Thus the driving force of the dissent, despite its recitation of the above standard, appears to be a distinction among different types of information—whether the "homeowner would even care if anybody noticed." The dissent offers no practical guidance for the application of this standard, and for reasons already discussed, we believe there can be none. The people in their houses, as well as the police, deserve more precision.

We have said that the Fourth Amendment draws a firm line at the entrance to the house. That line, we think, must be not only firm but also bright—which requires clear specification of those methods of surveillance that require a warrant. While it is certainly possible to conclude from the videotape of the thermal imaging that occurred in this case that no "significant" compromise of the homeowner's privacy has occurred, we must take the long view, from the original meaning of the Fourth Amendment forward.

Where, as here, the Government uses a device that is not in general public use, to explore details of the home that would previously have been unknowable without physical intrusion, the surveillance is a "search" and is presumptively unreasonable without a warrant.

Since we hold the Thermovision imaging to have been an unlawful search, it will remain for the District Court to determine whether, without the evidence it provided, the search warrant issued in this case was supported by probable cause—and if not, whether there is any other basis for supporting admission of the evidence that the search pursuant to the warrant produced.

JUSTICE STEVENS, with whom CHIEF JUSTICE REHNQUIST, JUSTICE O'CONNOR, and JUSTICE KENNEDY join, dissenting.

There is, in my judgment, a distinction of constitutional magnitude between "through-the-wall surveillance" that gives the observer or listener direct access to information in a private area, on the one hand, and the thought processes used to draw inferences from information in the public domain, on the other hand. The Court has crafted a rule that purports to deal with direct observations of the inside of the home, but the case before us merely involves indirect deductions from "off-the-wall" surveillance, that is, observations of the exterior of the home. Those observations were made with a fairly primitive thermal imager that gathered data exposed on the outside of petitioner's home but did not invade any constitutionally protected interest in privacy. Moreover, I believe that the supposedly "bright-line" rule the Court has created in response to its concerns about future technological developments is unnecessary, unwise, and inconsistent with the Fourth Amendment.

I

There is no need for the Court to craft a new rule to decide this case, as it is controlled by established principles from our Fourth Amendment jurisprudence. One of those core principles, of course, is that searches and seizures *inside a home* without a warrant are presumptively unreasonable. But it is equally well settled that searches and seizures of property in plain view are presumptively reasonable. Whether that property is residential or commercial, the basic principle is the same: "What a person knowingly exposes to the public, even in his own home or office, is not a subject of Fourth Amendment protection." *Katz v. U.S.*, 389 U.S. 347, 351 (1967). That is the principle implicated here.

While the Court "takes the long view" and decides this case based largely on the potential of yet-to-be-developed technology that might allow "through-the-wall surveillance," this case involves nothing more than off-the-wall surveillance by law enforcement officers to gather information exposed to the general public from the outside of petitioner's home. All that the infrared camera did in this case was passively measure heat emitted from the exterior surfaces of petitioner's home; all that those measurements showed were relative differences in emission levels, vaguely indicating that some areas of the roof and outside walls were warmer than others. As still images from the infrared scans show, no details regarding the interior of petitioner's home were revealed. Unlike an x-ray scan, or other possible "through-the-wall" techniques, the detection of infrared radiation emanating from the home did not accomplish an unauthorized physical penetration into the premises, nor did it obtain information that it could not have obtained by observation from outside the curtilage of the house.

Indeed, the ordinary use of the senses might enable a neighbor or passerby to notice the heat emanating from a building, particularly if it is vented, as was the case here. Additionally, any member of the public might notice that one part of a house is warmer than another part or a nearby building if, for example, rainwater evaporates or snow melts at different rates across its surfaces. Such use of the senses would not convert into an unreasonable search if, instead, an adjoining neighbor allowed an officer onto her property to verify her perceptions with a sensitive thermometer. Nor, in my view, does such observation become an unreasonable search if made from a distance with the aid of a device that merely discloses that the exterior of one house, or one area of the house, is much warmer than another. Nothing more occurred in this case.

Thus, the notion that heat emissions from the outside of a dwelling are a private matter implicating the protections of the Fourth Amendment is not only unprecedented but also quite difficult to take seriously. Heat waves, like aromas that are generated in a kitchen, or in a laboratory or opium den, enter the public domain if and when they leave a building. A subjective expectation that they would remain private is not only implausible but also surely not one that society is prepared to recognize as reasonable.

To be sure, the homeowner has a reasonable expectation of privacy concerning what takes place within the home, and the Fourth Amendment's protection against physical invasions of the home should apply to their functional equivalent. But the equipment in this case did not penetrate the walls of petitioner's home, and while it did pick up details of the home that were exposed to the public, it did not obtain any information regarding the *interior* of the home. In the Court's own words, based on what the thermal imager "showed" regarding the outside of petitioner's home, the officers "concluded" that petitioner was engaging in illegal activity inside the home. It would be quite absurd to characterize their thought processes as "searches," regardless of whether they inferred (rightly) that petitioner was growing marijuana in his house, or (wrongly) that "the lady of the house was taking her daily sauna and bath." In either case, the only conclusions the officers reached concerning the interior of the home were at least as indirect as those that might have been inferred from the contents of discarded garbage, see *California v. Greenwood*, 486 U.S. 35 (1988), or pen register data, see *Smith v. Maryland*, 442 U.S. 735 (1979), or, as in this case, subpoenaed utility records. For the first time in its history, the Court assumes that an inference can amount to a Fourth Amendment violation.

Notwithstanding the implications of today's decision, there is a strong public interest in avoiding constitutional litigation over the monitoring of emissions from homes, and over the inferences drawn from such monitoring. Just as the police cannot reasonably be expected to avert their eyes from evidence of criminal activity that could have been observed by any member of the public, so too public officials should not have to avert their senses or their equipment from detecting emissions in the public domain such as excessive heat, traces of smoke, suspicious odors, odorless gases, airborne particulates, or radioactive emissions, any of which could identify hazards to the community. In my judgment, monitoring such emissions with "sense-enhancing technology" and drawing useful conclusions from such monitoring is an entirely reasonable public service.

On the other hand, the countervailing privacy interest is at best trivial. After all, homes generally are insulated to keep heat in, rather than to prevent the detection of heat going out, and it does not seem to me that society will suffer from a rule requiring the rare homeowner who both intends to engage in uncommon activities that produce extraordinary amounts of heat, and wishes to conceal that production from outsiders, to make sure that the surrounding area is well insulated. The interest in concealing the heat escaping from one's house pales in significance to the chief evil against which the wording of the Fourth Amendment is directed, the physical entry of the home, and it is hard to believe that it is an interest the Framers sought to protect in our Constitution.

Since what was involved in this case was nothing more than drawing inferences from off-the-wall surveillance, rather than any "through-the-wall" surveillance, the officers' conduct did not amount to a search and was perfectly reasonable.

II

Instead of trying to answer the question whether the use of the thermal imager in this case was even arguably unreasonable, the Court has fashioned a rule that is intended to provide essential guidance for the day when "more sophisticated systems" gain the ability to "see" through walls and other opaque barriers. The newly minted rule encompasses "obtaining [1] by sense-enhancing technology [2] any information regarding the interior of the home [3] that could not otherwise have been obtained without physical intrusion into a constitutionally protected area . . . [4] at least where (as here) the technology in question is not in general public use." In my judgment, the Court's new rule is at once too broad and too narrow, and is not justified by the Court's explanation for its adoption. As I have suggested, I would not erect a constitutional impediment to the use of sense-enhancing technology unless it provides its user with the functional equivalent of actual presence in the area being searched.

Despite the Court's attempt to draw a line that is "not only firm but also bright," the contours of its new rule are uncertain because its protection apparently dissipates as soon as the relevant technology is "in general public use." Yet how much use is general public use is not even hinted at by the Court's opinion, which makes the somewhat doubtful assumption that the thermal imager used in this case does not satisfy that criterion. In any event, putting aside its lack of clarity, this criterion is somewhat perverse because it seems likely that the threat to privacy will grow, rather than recede, as the use of intrusive equipment becomes more readily available.

It is clear, however, that the category of "sense-enhancing technology" covered by the new rule is far too broad. It would, for example, embrace potential mechanical substitutes for dogs trained to react when they sniff narcotics. But in *U.S. v. Place*, 462 U.S. 696 (1983), we held that a dog sniff that discloses only the presence or absence of narcotics does not constitute a search within the meaning of the Fourth Amendment, and it must follow that sense-enhancing equipment that identifies nothing but illegal activity is not a search either. Nevertheless, the use of such a device would be unconstitutional under the Court's rule, as would the use of other new devices that might detect the odor of deadly bacteria or chemicals for making a new type of high explosive, even if the devices (like the dog sniffs) are so limited both in the manner in which they obtain information and in the content of the information they reveal. If nothing more than that sort of information could be obtained by using the devices in a public place to monitor emissions from a house, then their use would be no more objectionable than the use of the thermal imager in this case.

The application of the Court's new rule to "any information regarding the interior of the home," is also unnecessarily broad. If it takes sensitive equipment to detect an odor that identifies criminal conduct and nothing else, the fact that the odor emanates from the interior of a home should not provide it with constitutional protection. The criterion, moreover, is too sweeping in that information "regarding" the interior of a home apparently is not just information obtained through its walls, but also information concerning the outside of the building that could lead to (however many) inferences "regarding" what might be inside. Under that expansive view, I suppose, an officer using an infrared camera to observe a man silently entering the side door of a house at night carrying a pizza might conclude that its interior is now occupied by someone who likes pizza, and by doing so the officer would be guilty of conducting an unconstitutional "search" of the home.

Because the new rule applies to information regarding the "interior" of the home, it is too narrow as well as too broad. Clearly, a rule that is designed to protect individuals from the overly intrusive use of sense-enhancing equipment should not be limited to a home. If such equipment did provide its user with the functional equivalent of access to a private place—such as, for example, the telephone booth involved in *Katz*, or an office building—then the rule should apply to such an area as well as to a home.

The final requirement of the Court's new rule, that the information "could not otherwise have been obtained without physical intrusion into a constitutionally protected area," also extends too far as the Court applies it. As noted, the Court effectively treats the mental process of analyzing data obtained from external sources as the equivalent of a physical intrusion into the home. As I have explained, however, the process of drawing inferences from data in the public domain should not be characterized as a search.

The two reasons advanced by the Court as justifications for the adoption of its new rule are both unpersuasive. First, the Court suggests that its rule is compelled by our holding in *Katz*, because in that case, as in this, the surveillance consisted of nothing more than the monitoring of waves emanating from a private area into the public domain. Yet there are critical differences between the cases. In *Katz*, the electronic listening device attached to the outside of the phone booth allowed the officers to pick up the content of the conversation inside the booth, making them the functional equivalent of intruders because they gathered information that was otherwise available only to someone inside the private area; it would be as if, in this case, the thermal imager presented a view of the heat-generating activity inside petitioner's home. By contrast, the thermal imager here disclosed only the relative amounts of heat radiating from the house; it would be as if, in *Katz*, the listening device disclosed only the relative volume of sound leaving the booth, which presumably was discernible in the public domain. Surely, there is a significant difference between the general and well-settled expectation that strangers will not have direct access to the contents of private communications, on the one hand, and the rather theoretical expectation that an occasional homeowner would even care if anybody noticed the relative amounts of heat emanating from the walls of his house, on the other. It is pure hyperbole for the Court to suggest that refusing to extend the holding of *Katz* to this case would leave the homeowner at the mercy of "technology that could discern all human activity in the home."

Second, the Court argues that the permissibility of "through-the-wall surveillance" cannot depend on a distinction between observing "intimate details" such as "the lady of the house taking her daily sauna and bath," and noticing only "the nonintimate rug on the vestibule floor" or "objects no smaller than 36 by 36 inches." This entire argument assumes, of course, that the thermal imager in this case could or did perform "through-the-wall surveillance" that could identify any detail "that would previously have been unknowable without physical intrusion." In fact, the device could not, and did not, enable its user to identify either the lady of the house, the rug on the vestibule floor, or anything else inside the house, whether smaller or larger than 36 by 36 inches. But even if the device could reliably show extraordinary differences in the amounts of heat leaving his home, drawing the inference that there was something suspicious occurring inside the residence—a conclusion that officers far less gifted than Sherlock Holmes would readily draw—does not qualify as "through-the-wall surveillance," much less a Fourth Amendment violation.

III

Although the Court is properly and commendably concerned about the threats to privacy that may flow from advances in the technology available to the law enforcement profession, it has unfortunately failed to heed the tried and true counsel of judicial restraint. Instead of concentrating on the rather mundane issue that is actually presented by the case before it, the Court has endeavored to craft an all-encompassing rule for the future. It would be far wiser to give legislators an unimpeded opportunity to grapple with these emerging issues rather than to shackle them with prematurely devised constitutional constraints.

Can *Kyllo* and *Ciraolo* be reconciled? Why is it a search under the Fourth Amendment when police point a thermal imaging device at a home to detect evidence of indoor marijuana cultivation, but it is not a search when police use an airplane to observe the curtilage of a home for evidence of marijuana cultivation? Both cases involve the same crime occurring within the home and its immediate surroundings. Does the general availability of the investigative technology used by the police account for the different results? Are low-flying airplanes equipped with cameras more common than thermal imaging devices? Should *Kyllo* be reconsidered in light of the fact that thermal imaging devices are now more common, and are even available as an attachment for a smartphone?[a]

Kyllo presents an opportunity to consider an interesting related question: Does the *Katz* Test contain the seeds of its own destruction? Or, as the majority in *Kyllo* suggests, is the *Katz* Test circular? As technology improves, becomes widely available, and grows increasingly intrusive, we have less privacy. When we have less privacy, we begin to expect less privacy, and at a certain point, it becomes unreasonable to expect much privacy at all. And if societal expectations of privacy are low, how can any police investigative technique be regarded as a search under the *Katz* Test?

Thermal Imaging of Homes

When police use a thermal imager or a similar device that is not in general public use to explore details of the home that would previously have been unknowable without physical intrusion, the surveillance is a "search" and is presumptively unreasonable without a warrant.

---

7. TRACKING DEVICES

The Supreme Court has considered police use of tracking devices in three cases: *U.S. v. Knotts*, *U.S. v. Karo*, and *U.S. v. Jones*. The facts regarding the installation and monitoring of the device were somewhat different in each case, leading to different conclusions with respect to whether the police conduct amounted to a search under the Fourth Amendment.

U.S. V. KNOTTS
460 U.S. 276 (1983)

JUSTICE REHNQUIST delivered the opinion of the Court.

A beeper is a radio transmitter, usually battery operated, which emits periodic signals that can be picked up by a radio receiver. In this case, a beeper was placed in a five gallon drum containing chloroform purchased by one of respondent's codefendants. By monitoring the progress of a car carrying the chloroform, Minnesota law enforcement agents were able to trace the can of chloroform from its place of purchase

---

[a] *See* www.flir.com/flirone (advertisement for a thermal imaging attachment for smartphones).

in Minneapolis, Minnesota to respondent's secluded cabin near Shell Lake, Wisconsin. The issue presented by the case is whether such use of a beeper violated respondent's rights secured by the Fourth Amendment to the United States Constitution.

I

Respondent and two codefendants were charged in the United States District Court for the District of Minnesota with conspiracy to manufacture controlled substances, including but not limited to methamphetamine. One of the codefendants, Darryl Petschen, was tried jointly with respondent; the other codefendant, Tristan Armstrong, pleaded guilty and testified for the government at trial.

Suspicion attached to this trio when the 3M Company, which manufactures chemicals in St. Paul, notified a narcotics investigator for the Minnesota Bureau of Criminal Apprehension that Armstrong, a former 3M employee, had been stealing chemicals which could be used in manufacturing illicit drugs. Visual surveillance of Armstrong revealed that after leaving the employ of 3M Company, he had been purchasing similar chemicals from the Hawkins Chemical Company in Minneapolis. The Minnesota narcotics officers observed that after Armstrong had made a purchase, he would deliver the chemicals to codefendant Petschen.

With the consent of the Hawkins Chemical Company, officers installed a beeper inside a five gallon container of chloroform, one of the so-called "precursor" chemicals used to manufacture illicit drugs. Hawkins agreed that when Armstrong next purchased chloroform, the chloroform would be placed in this particular container. When Armstrong made the purchase, officers followed the car in which the chloroform had been placed, maintaining contact by using both visual surveillance and a monitor which received the signals sent from the beeper.

Armstrong proceeded to Petschen's house, where the container was transferred to Petschen's automobile. Officers then followed that vehicle eastward towards the state line, across the St. Croix River, and into Wisconsin. During the latter part of this journey, Petschen began making evasive maneuvers, and the pursuing agents ended their visual surveillance. At about the same time officers lost the signal from the beeper, but with the assistance of a monitoring device located in a helicopter the approximate location of the signal was picked up again about one hour later. The signal now was stationary and the location identified was a cabin occupied by respondent near Shell Lake, Wisconsin. The record before us does not reveal that the beeper was used after the location in the area of the cabin had been initially determined.

Relying on the location of the chloroform derived through the use of the beeper and additional information obtained during three days of intermittent visual surveillance of respondent's cabin, officers secured a search warrant. During execution of the warrant, officers discovered a fully operable, clandestine drug laboratory in the cabin. In the laboratory area, officers found formulas for amphetamine and methamphetamine, over $10,000 worth of laboratory equipment, and chemicals in quantities sufficient to produce 14 pounds of pure amphetamine. Under a barrel outside the cabin, officers located the five gallon container of chloroform.

After his motion to suppress evidence based on the warrantless monitoring of the beeper was denied, respondent was convicted for conspiring to manufacture controlled substances. He was sentenced to five years imprisonment. A divided panel of the United States Court of Appeals for the Eighth Circuit reversed the conviction, finding that the monitoring of the beeper was prohibited by the Fourth Amendment because its use had violated respondent's reasonable expectation of privacy, and that all information derived after the location of the cabin was a fruit of the illegal beeper monitoring. We granted certiorari, and we now reverse the judgment of the Court of Appeals.

II

The governmental surveillance conducted by means of the beeper in this case amounted principally to the following of an automobile on public streets and highways. We have commented more than once on the diminished expectation of privacy in an automobile: One has a lesser expectation of privacy in a motor vehicle because its function is transportation and it seldom serves as one's residence or as the repository of personal effects. A car has little capacity for escaping public scrutiny. It travels public thoroughfares where both its occupants and its contents are in plain view.

A person travelling in an automobile on public thoroughfares has no reasonable expectation of privacy in his movements from one place to another. When Petschen travelled over the public streets he voluntarily conveyed to anyone who wanted to look the fact that he was travelling over particular roads in a particular direction, the fact of whatever stops he made, and the fact of his final destination when he exited from public roads onto private property.

Respondent Knotts, as the owner of the cabin and surrounding premises to which Petschen drove, undoubtedly had the traditional expectation of privacy within a dwelling place insofar as the cabin was concerned. But no such expectation of privacy extended to the visual observation of Petschen's automobile arriving on his premises after leaving a public highway, nor to movements of objects such as the drum of chloroform outside the cabin in the "open fields."

Visual surveillance from public places along Petschen's route or adjoining Knotts' premises would have sufficed to reveal all of these facts to the police. The fact that the officers in this case relied not only on visual surveillance, but on the use of the beeper to signal the presence of Petschen's automobile to the police receiver, does not alter the situation. Nothing in the Fourth Amendment prohibited the police from augmenting the sensory faculties bestowed upon them at birth with such enhancement as science and technology afforded them in this case.

Respondent specifically attacks the use of the beeper insofar as it was used to determine that the can of chloroform had come to rest on his property at Shell Lake, Wisconsin. We think that respondent's contentions to some extent lose sight of the limited use which the government made of the signals from this particular beeper. As we have noted, nothing in this record indicates that the beeper signal was received or relied upon after it had indicated that the drum containing the chloroform had ended its automotive journey at rest on respondent's premises in rural Wisconsin. Admittedly, because of the failure of the visual surveillance, the beeper enabled the law enforcement officials in this case to ascertain the ultimate resting place of the chloroform when they would not have been able to do so had they relied solely on their naked eyes. But scientific enhancement of this sort raises no constitutional issues which visual surveillance would not also raise. A police car following Petschen at a distance throughout his journey could have observed him leaving the public highway and arriving at the cabin owned by respondent, with the drum of chloroform still in the car. This fact, along with others, was used by the government in obtaining a search warrant which led to the discovery of the clandestine drug laboratory. But there is no indication that the beeper was used in any way to reveal information as to the movement of the drum within the cabin, or in any way that would not have been visible to the naked eye from outside the cabin.

We thus return to the question posed at the beginning of our inquiry in discussing *Katz*: did monitoring the beeper signals complained of by respondent invade any legitimate expectation of privacy on his part? For the reasons previously stated, we hold they did not. Since they did not, there was neither a "search" nor a "seizure" within the contemplation of the Fourth Amendment.

JUSTICE STEVENS, with whom JUSTICE BRENNAN, and JUSTICE MARSHALL join, concurring in the judgment.

Since the respondent in this case has never questioned the installation of the radio transmitter in the chloroform drum, I agree that it was entirely reasonable for the police officers to make use of the information received over the airwaves when they were trying to ascertain the ultimate destination of the chloroform. I do not join the Court's opinion, however, because it contains two unnecessarily broad dicta: one distorts the record in this case, and both may prove confusing to courts that must apply this decision in the future.

First, the Court implies that the chloroform drum was parading in "open fields" outside of the cabin, in a manner tantamount to its public display on the highways. The record does not support that implication. This case does not pose any "open fields" issue.

Second, the Court suggests that the Fourth Amendment does not inhibit "the police from augmenting the sensory facilities bestowed upon them at birth with such enhancement as science and technology afforded them." But the Court held to the contrary in *Katz v. U.S.*, 389 U.S. 347 (1967). Although the augmentation in this case was unobjectionable, it by no means follows that the use of electronic detection techniques does not implicate especially sensitive concerns.

———————————

In *Knotts*, the drum of chloroform did not belong to the defendant when the tracking device was planted in it, and the device revealed only what was already evident through ordinary visual surveillance as the defendant drove with the drum from one location to another. Accordingly, the Supreme Court in *Knotts* concluded that the use of the tracking device did not amount to a search under the Fourth Amendment. In *U.S. v. Karo*, the tracking device was installed in a similar fashion, but the monitoring of the device revealed more information than what ordinary visual surveillance would have revealed. This difference was enough for the Court in *Karo* to conclude that the police use of the tracking device did constitute a search.

U.S. v. KARO
468 U.S. 705 (1984)

JUSTICE WHITE delivered the opinion of the Court.

In *U.S. v. Knotts*, 460 U.S. 276 (1983), we held that the warrantless monitoring of an electronic tracking device ("beeper") inside a container of chemicals did not violate the Fourth Amendment when it revealed no information that could not have been obtained through visual surveillance. In this case, we are called upon to address two questions left unresolved in *Knotts*: (1) whether installation of a beeper in a container of chemicals with the consent of the original owner constitutes a search or seizure within the meaning of the Fourth Amendment when the container is delivered to a buyer having no knowledge of the presence of the beeper, and (2) whether monitoring of a beeper falls within the ambit of the Fourth Amendment when it reveals information that could not have been obtained through visual surveillance.

I

In August 1980, Agent Rottinger of the Drug Enforcement Administration (DEA) learned that respondents James Karo, Richard

Horton, and William Harley had ordered 50 gallons of ether from Government informant Carl Muehlenweg of Graphic Photo Design in Albuquerque, N.M. Muehlenweg told Rottinger that the ether was to be used to extract cocaine from clothing that had been imported into the United States. The Government obtained a court order authorizing the installation and monitoring of a beeper in one of the cans of ether. With Muehlenweg's consent, agents substituted their own can containing a beeper for one of the cans in the shipment and then had all 10 cans painted to give them a uniform appearance.

On September 20, 1980, agents saw Karo pick up the ether from Muehlenweg. They then followed Karo to his house using visual and beeper surveillance. At one point later that day, agents determined by using the beeper that the ether was still inside the house, but they later determined that it had been moved undetected to Horton's house, where they located it using the beeper. Agent Rottinger could smell the ether from the public sidewalk near Horton's residence. Two days later, agents discovered that the ether had once again been moved, and, using the beeper, they located it at the residence of Horton's father. The next day, the beeper was no longer transmitting from Horton's father's house, and agents traced the beeper to a commercial storage facility.

Because the beeper equipment was not sensitive enough to allow agents to learn precisely which locker the ether was in, agents obtained a subpoena for the records of the storage company and learned that locker 143 had been rented by Horton. Using the beeper, agents confirmed that the ether was indeed in one of the lockers in the row containing locker 143, and using their noses they detected the odor of ether emanating from locker 143. On October 8, agents obtained an order authorizing installation of an entry tone alarm into the door jamb of the locker so they would be able to tell when the door was opened. While installing the alarm, agents observed that the cans containing ether were still inside. Agents ceased visual and beeper surveillance, relying instead on the entry tone alarm. However, on October 16, Horton retrieved the contents from the locker without sounding the alarm. Agents did not learn of the entry until the manager of the storage facility notified them that Horton had been there.

Using the beeper, agents traced the beeper can to another self-storage facility three days later. Agents detected the smell of ether coming from locker 15 and learned from the manager that Horton and Harley had rented that locker using an alias the same day that the ether had been removed from the first storage facility. The agents obtained an order authorizing the installation of an entry tone alarm in locker 15, but instead of installing that alarm, they obtained consent from the manager of the facility to install a closed-circuit video camera in a locker that had a view of locker 15. On February 6, 1981, agents observed, by means of the video camera, Gene Rhodes and an unidentified woman removing the cans from the locker and loading them onto the rear bed of Horton's pickup truck. Using both visual and beeper surveillance, agents tracked the truck to Rhodes' residence where it was parked in the driveway. Agents then observed Rhodes and a woman bringing boxes and other items from inside the house and loading the items into the trunk of an automobile. Agents did not see any cans being transferred from the pickup.

At about 6 p.m. on February 6, the car and the pickup left the driveway and traveled along public highways to Taos. During the trip, the two vehicles were under both physical and electronic surveillance. When the vehicles arrived at a house in Taos rented by Horton, Harley, and Michael Steele, the agents did not maintain tight surveillance for fear of detection. When the vehicles left the Taos residence, agents determined, using the beeper monitor, that the beeper can was still inside the house. Again on February 7, the beeper revealed that the ether can was still on the premises. At one point, agents noticed that the windows of the house were wide open on a cold windy day, leading them to suspect that the ether was being used. On February 8, the agents applied for and obtained a warrant to search the Taos residence based in part on information derived through use of the beeper. The warrant was executed on February 10, 1981, and Horton, Harley, Steele, and Evan Roth were arrested, and cocaine and laboratory equipment were seized.

II

Because the judgment below in favor of Karo rested in major part on the conclusion that the installation violated his Fourth Amendment rights and that any information obtained from monitoring the beeper was tainted by the initial illegality, we must deal with the legality of the warrantless installation. It is clear that the actual placement of the beeper into the can violated no one's Fourth Amendment rights. The can into which the beeper was placed belonged at the time to the DEA, and by no stretch of the imagination could it be said that respondents then had any legitimate expectation of privacy in it. The ether and the original 10 cans, on the other hand, belonged to, and were in the possession of, Muehlenweg, who had given his consent to any invasion of those items that occurred. Thus, even if there had been no substitution of cans and the agents had placed the beeper into one of the original 10 cans, Muehlenweg's consent was sufficient to validate the placement of the beeper in the can.

The Court of Appeals acknowledged that before Karo took control of the ether "the DEA and Muehlenweg presumably could do with the can and ether whatever they liked without violating Karo's rights." It did not hold that the actual placement of the beeper into the ether can violated the Fourth Amendment. Instead, it held that the violation occurred at the time the beeper-laden can was transferred to Karo. The court stated: "All individuals have a legitimate expectation of privacy that objects coming into their rightful ownership do not have electronic devices attached to them, devices that would give law enforcement agents the opportunity to monitor the location of the objects at all times and in every place that the objects are taken, including inside private residences and other areas where the right to be free from warrantless governmental intrusion is unquestioned."

Not surprisingly, the Court of Appeals did not describe the transfer as either a "search" or a "seizure," for plainly it is neither. A "search" occurs when an expectation of privacy that society is prepared to consider reasonable is infringed. The mere transfer to Karo of a can containing an unmonitored beeper infringed no privacy interest. It conveyed no information that Karo wished to keep private, for it conveyed no information at all. To be sure, it created a potential for an invasion of privacy, but we have never held that potential, as opposed to actual, invasions of privacy constitute searches for purposes of the Fourth Amendment. A holding to that effect would mean that a policeman walking down the street carrying a parabolic microphone capable of picking up conversations in nearby homes would be engaging in a search even if the microphone were not turned on. It is the exploitation of technological advances that implicates the Fourth Amendment, not their mere existence.

We likewise do not believe that the transfer of the container constituted a seizure. A "seizure" of property occurs when there is some meaningful interference with an individual's possessory interests in that property. Although the can may have contained an unknown and unwanted foreign object, it cannot be said that anyone's possessory interest was interfered with in a meaningful way. At most, there was a technical trespass on the space occupied by the beeper. The existence of a physical trespass is only marginally relevant to the question of whether the Fourth Amendment has been violated, however, for an actual trespass is neither necessary nor sufficient to establish a constitutional violation. Of course, if the presence of a beeper in the can constituted a seizure merely because of its occupation of space, it would follow that the presence of any object, regardless of its nature, would violate the Fourth Amendment.

We conclude that no Fourth Amendment interest of Karo or of any other respondent was infringed by the installation of the beeper. Rather, any impairment of their privacy interests that may have occurred was occasioned by the monitoring of the beeper.[3]

---

[3] Despite this holding, warrants for the installation and monitoring of a beeper will obviously be desirable since it may be useful, even critical, to monitor the beeper to determine

III

In *Knotts*, the record did not show that the beeper was monitored while the can containing it was inside the cabin, and we therefore had no occasion to consider whether a constitutional violation would have occurred had the fact been otherwise. Here, there is no gainsaying that the beeper was used to locate the ether in a specific house in Taos, N.M., and that that information was in turn used to secure a warrant for the search of the house. This case thus presents the question whether the monitoring of a beeper in a private residence, a location not open to visual surveillance, violates the Fourth Amendment rights of those who have a justifiable interest in the privacy of the residence. Contrary to the submission of the United States, we think that it does.

At the risk of belaboring the obvious, private residences are places in which the individual normally expects privacy free of governmental intrusion not authorized by a warrant, and that expectation is plainly one that society is prepared to recognize as justifiable. Our cases have not deviated from this basic Fourth Amendment principle. Searches and seizures inside a home without a warrant are presumptively unreasonable absent exigent circumstances. In this case, had a DEA agent thought it useful to enter the Taos residence to verify that the ether was actually in the house and had he done so surreptitiously and without a warrant, there is little doubt that he would have engaged in an unreasonable search within the meaning of the Fourth Amendment. For purposes of the Amendment, the result is the same where, without a warrant, the Government surreptitiously employs an electronic device to obtain information that it could not have obtained by observation from outside the curtilage of the house. The beeper tells the agent that a particular article is actually located at a particular time in the private residence and is in the possession of the person or persons whose residence is being watched. Even if visual surveillance has revealed that the article to which the beeper is attached has entered the house, the later monitoring not only verifies the officers' observations but also establishes that the article remains on the premises. Here, for example, the beeper was monitored for a significant period after the arrival of the ether in Taos and before the application for a warrant to search.

The monitoring of an electronic device such as a beeper is, of course, less intrusive than a full-scale search, but it does reveal a critical fact about the interior of the premises that the Government is extremely interested in knowing and that it could not have otherwise obtained without a warrant. The case is thus not like *Knotts*, for there the beeper told the authorities nothing about the interior of Knotts' cabin. The

---

that it is actually located in a place not open to visual surveillance. As will be evident below, such monitoring without a warrant may violate the Fourth Amendment.

information obtained in *Knotts* was "voluntarily conveyed to anyone who wanted to look"; here, as we have said, the monitoring indicated that the beeper was inside the house, a fact that could not have been visually verified.

We cannot accept the Government's contention that it should be completely free from the constraints of the Fourth Amendment to determine by means of an electronic device, without a warrant and without probable cause or reasonable suspicion, whether a particular article—or a person, for that matter—is in an individual's home at a particular time. Indiscriminate monitoring of property that has been withdrawn from public view would present far too serious a threat to privacy interests in the home to escape entirely some sort of Fourth Amendment oversight.

We also reject the Government's contention that it should be able to monitor beepers in private residences without a warrant if there is the requisite justification in the facts for believing that a crime is being or will be committed and that monitoring the beeper wherever it goes is likely to produce evidence of criminal activity. Warrantless searches are presumptively unreasonable, though the Court has recognized a few limited exceptions to this general rule. The Government's contention that warrantless beeper searches should be deemed reasonable is based upon its deprecation of the benefits and exaggeration of the difficulties associated with procurement of a warrant. The Government argues that the traditional justifications for the warrant requirement are inapplicable in beeper cases, but to a large extent that argument is based upon the contention, rejected above, that the beeper constitutes only a minuscule intrusion on protected privacy interests. The primary reason for the warrant requirement is to interpose a neutral and detached magistrate between the citizen and the officer engaged in the often competitive enterprise of ferreting out crime. Those suspected of drug offenses are no less entitled to that protection than those suspected of nondrug offenses. Requiring a warrant will have the salutary effect of ensuring that use of beepers is not abused, by imposing upon agents the requirement that they demonstrate in advance their justification for the desired search. This is not to say that there are no exceptions to the warrant rule, because if truly exigent circumstances exist no warrant is required under general Fourth Amendment principles.

If agents are required to obtain warrants prior to monitoring a beeper when it has been withdrawn from public view, the Government argues, for all practical purposes they will be forced to obtain warrants in every case in which they seek to use a beeper, because they have no way of knowing in advance whether the beeper will be transmitting its signals from inside private premises. The argument that a warrant requirement would oblige the Government to obtain warrants in a large number of cases is hardly a compelling argument against the requirement. It is worthy of note that, in any event, this is not a particularly attractive case in which to argue that it is impractical to obtain a warrant, since a warrant was in fact obtained in this case, seemingly on probable cause.

We are also unpersuaded by the argument that a warrant should not be required because of the difficulty in satisfying the particularity requirement of the Fourth Amendment. The Government contends that it would be impossible to describe the "place" to be searched, because the location of the place is precisely what is sought to be discovered through the search. However true that may be, it will still be possible to describe the object into which the beeper is to be placed, the circumstances that led agents to wish to install the beeper, and the length of time for which beeper surveillance is requested. In our view, this information will suffice to permit issuance of a warrant authorizing beeper installation and surveillance.

In sum, we discern no reason for deviating from the general rule that a search of a house should be conducted pursuant to a warrant.

JUSTICE O'CONNOR, with whom JUSTICE REHNQUIST joins, concurring in part and concurring in the judgment.

I agree with the Court that the installation of a beeper in a container with the consent of the container's present owner implicates no Fourth Amendment concerns. The subsequent transfer of the container, with the unactivated beeper, to one who is unaware of the beeper's presence is also unobjectionable. It is when the beeper is activated to track the movements of the container that privacy interests are implicated.

In my view, however, these privacy interests are unusually narrow— narrower than is suggested by the Court. If the container is moved on the public highways, or in other places where the container's owner has no reasonable expectation that its movements will not be tracked without his consent, activation of the beeper infringes on no reasonable expectation of privacy. In this situation the location of the container defeats any expectation that its movements will not be tracked.

In addition, one who lacks ownership of the container itself or the power to move the container at will, can have no reasonable expectation that the movements of the container will not be tracked by a beeper within the container, regardless of where the container is moved. In this situation the absence of an appropriate interest in the container itself defeats any expectation of privacy in the movements of the container, even when the container is brought into places where others may have a privacy interest.

As a threshold matter it is clear that the mere presence of electronic equipment inside a home, transmitting information to government agents outside, does not, in and of itself, infringe on legitimate expectations of privacy of all who have an expectation of privacy in the home itself. For example, *U.S. v. White*, 401 U.S. 745 (1971), permitted the use of information obtained from within a home by means of a microphone secreted on a Government agent. We must therefore look for something more before concluding that monitoring of a beeper in a closed container that is brought into a home violates the homeowner's reasonable expectations of privacy.

The Court holds that the crucial additional factor is the container owner's consent, or lack of consent, to the installation of the beeper. If consent is given, movement of the container into the home violates no reasonable expectation of privacy of the homeowner. If the container owner's consent is not obtained, the Court holds that the homeowner's expectations of privacy in the home are violated when the beeper enters and is monitored from inside the home, even if the homeowner has no interest or expectation of privacy in the container itself. In my view this analysis is somewhat flawed.

It is difficult to see how a homeowner's expectations of privacy can depend in any way on an invitee's actual status as a government informant. Expectations are formed on the basis of objective appearances, not on the basis of facts known only to others. Stated another way, the homeowner's expectation that a container does not contain a beeper cannot depend on the container owner's belief that the container is beeper-free. The homeowner's expectation of privacy is either inherently reasonable or it is inherently unreasonable. A guest's undisclosed status as a government informant cannot alter the reasonableness of that expectation.

I would, therefore, use a different and generally narrower test than the one proposed by the Court for determining when an activated beeper in a closed container violates the privacy of a homeowner into whose home the container is moved. I would use as the touchstone the defendant's interest in the container in which the beeper is placed. When a closed container is moved by permission into a home, the homeowner and others with an expectation of privacy in the home itself surrender any expectation of privacy they might otherwise retain in the movements of the container—unless it is their container or under their dominion and control.

The principles for assessing a single person's privacy interests in a particular place, location, or transmission system such as a telephone line, are reasonably well settled. The Court relies on these principles—particularly on the strong presumption of privacy in the home—to analyze the beeper case presented here. But the movement of a guest's closed container into another's home involves overlapping privacy interests. When privacy interests in particular locations are shared by several persons, assessing expectations of privacy requires a more probing analysis. A privacy interest in a home itself need not be coextensive with a privacy interest in the contents or movements of everything situated inside the home.

A more difficult case arises when one person's privacy interests fall within another's, as when a guest in a private home has a private container to which the homeowner has no right of access. The homeowner who permits entry into his home of such a container effectively surrenders a segment of the privacy of his home to the privacy of the owner of the container. Insofar as it may be possible to search the container without searching the home, the homeowner suffers no invasion of his privacy when such a search occurs; the homeowner also lacks the power to give effective consent to the search of the closed container. For example, evidence obtained from an electronic device in the container that transmitted information only about the contents of the container could not be suppressed by the homeowner unless he also had a privacy interest in the container, even if the information were transmitted from inside the home.

The beeper in this case, however, transmitted information about the location, not the contents, of the container. Conceivably, location in a home is an attribute partly of the home and partly of the container itself. But the primary privacy interest is not the homeowner's. By giving consent to another to move a closed container into and out of the home the homeowner has effectively surrendered his privacy insofar as the location of the container may be concerned, or so we should assume absent evidence to the contrary. In other words, one who lacks dominion and control over the object's location has no privacy interest invaded when that information is disclosed. It is simply not his secret that the beeper is disclosing, just as it is not his privacy that would be invaded by a search of the container whose contents he did not control.

In sum, a privacy interest in the location of a closed container that enters a home with the homeowner's permission cannot be inferred mechanically by reference to the more general privacy interests in the home itself. The homeowner's privacy interests are often narrower than those of the owner of the container. A defendant should be allowed to challenge evidence obtained by monitoring a beeper installed in a closed container only if (1) the beeper was monitored when visual tracking of the container was not possible, so that the defendant had a reasonable expectation that the container's movements would remain private, and (2) the defendant had an interest in the container itself sufficient to empower him to give effective consent to a search of the container. A person's right not to have a container tracked by means of a beeper depends both on his power to prevent visual observation of the container and on his power to control its location, a power that can usually be inferred from a privacy interest in the container itself. One who lacks either power has no legitimate expectation of privacy in the movements of the container.

JUSTICE STEVENS, with whom JUSTICE BRENNAN and JUSTICE MARSHALL join, concurring in part and dissenting in part.

The beeper is a species of radio transmitter. Mounted inside a container, it has much in common with a microphone mounted on a person. It reveals the location of the item to which it is attached—the functional equivalent of a radio transmission saying "Now I am at ____."

The threshold question in this case is whether the beeper invaded any interest protected by the Fourth Amendment. In my opinion the surreptitious use of a radio transmitter—whether it contains a microphone or merely a signaling device—on an individual's personal property is both a seizure and a search within the meaning of the Fourth Amendment. Part III of the opinion of the Court correctly concludes that when beeper surveillance reveals the location of property that has been concealed from public view, it constitutes a "search" within the meaning of the Fourth Amendment. I join Part III on that understanding. However, I find it necessary to write separately because I believe the Fourth Amendment's reach is somewhat broader than that which is explicitly acknowledged by the Court, and in particular because my understanding of the Fourth Amendment, as well as my understanding of the issues that have been framed for us by the parties to this case, leads me to a different result than that reached by the Court.

The attachment of the beeper, in my judgment, constituted a "seizure." The owner of property, of course, has a right to exclude from it all the world, including the Government, and a concomitant right to use it exclusively for his own purposes. When the Government attaches an electronic monitoring device to that property, it infringes that exclusionary right; in a fundamental sense it has converted the property to its own use. Surely such an invasion is an "interference" with possessory rights; the right to exclude, which attached as soon as the can respondents purchased was delivered, had been infringed. That interference is also "meaningful"; the character of the property is profoundly different when infected with an electronic bug than when it is entirely germ free.

By attaching a monitoring device to respondents' property, the agents usurped a part of a citizen's property—in this case a part of respondents' exclusionary rights in their tangible personal property. By attaching the beeper and using the container to conceal it, the Government in the most fundamental sense was asserting "dominion and control" over the property—the power to use the property for its own purposes. And asserting dominion and control is a "seizure" in the most basic sense of the term.

The impact of beeper surveillance upon interests protected by the Fourth Amendment leads me to what I regard as the perfectly sensible conclusion that, absent exigent circumstances, Government agents have a constitutional duty to obtain a warrant before they install an electronic device on a private citizen's property.

In *U.S. v. Jones*, police planted a Global Positioning System (GPS) tracking device on the defendant's car, then monitored his movements for a period of four weeks. The Court was unanimous in holding that the police had performed a search under the Fourth Amendment, but there was a difference of opinion as to the reasons. Four Justices (Scalia, Thomas, Kennedy, and Chief Justice Roberts) concluded that there was a search because, by attaching the device to the defendant's car, the police "physically occupied private property for the purpose of obtaining information." These four Justices felt it was unnecessary to apply the *Katz* Test in a case where there was a physical trespass upon the defendant's "effect," his car. Four other Justices (Alito, Ginsburg, Breyer, and Kagan) felt that the physical trespass theory was too similar to the discredited approach in *Olmstead v. U.S.*, and offered no protection against modern surveillance techniques that require no physical intrusion, such as GPS installed in a vehicle or on a smartphone. These four Justices urged application of the *Katz* Test, noting that long-term GPS monitoring constitutes a search because it impinges on reasonable expectations of privacy. Justice Sotomayor agreed with the first four that the physical trespass theory was sufficient to decide the case, but she also agreed with the second four that long-term police monitoring—even without a physical trespass—impinges upon reasonable expectations of privacy.

U.S. V. JONES
132 S.Ct. 945 (2012)

JUSTICE SCALIA delivered the opinion of the Court.

We decide whether the attachment of a Global-Positioning-System (GPS) tracking device to an individual's vehicle, and subsequent use of that device to monitor the vehicle's movements on public streets, constitutes a search or seizure within the meaning of the Fourth Amendment.

I

In 2004 respondent Antoine Jones, owner and operator of a nightclub in the District of Columbia, came under suspicion of trafficking in narcotics and was made the target of an investigation by a joint FBI and Metropolitan Police Department task force. Officers employed various investigative techniques, including visual surveillance of the nightclub, installation of a camera focused on the front door of the club, and a pen register and wiretap covering Jones' cellular phone.

Based in part on information gathered from these sources, in 2005 the Government applied to the United States District Court for the District of Columbia for a warrant authorizing the use of an electronic tracking device on the Jeep Grand Cherokee registered to Jones' wife. A warrant issued, authorizing installation of the device in the District of Columbia and within 10 days.

On the 11th day, and not in the District of Columbia but in Maryland,[1] agents installed a GPS tracking device on the undercarriage of the Jeep while it was parked in a public parking lot. Over the next 28 days, the Government used the device to track the vehicle's movements, and once had to replace the device's battery when the vehicle was parked in a different public lot in Maryland. By means of signals from multiple satellites, the device established the vehicle's location within 50 to 100 feet, and communicated that location by cellular phone to a Government computer. It relayed more than 2,000 pages of data over the 4-week period.

The Government ultimately obtained a multiple-count indictment charging Jones and several alleged co-conspirators with conspiracy to distribute and possess with intent to distribute five kilograms or more of cocaine and 50 grams or more of cocaine base. Before trial, Jones filed a motion to suppress evidence obtained through the GPS device. The District Court granted the motion only in part, suppressing the data obtained while the vehicle was parked in the garage adjoining Jones' residence. It held the remaining data admissible, because "a person traveling in an automobile on public thoroughfares has no reasonable expectation of privacy in his movements from one place to another." Jones' trial in October 2006 produced a hung jury on the conspiracy count.

In March 2007, a grand jury returned another indictment, charging Jones and others with the same conspiracy. The Government introduced at trial the same GPS-derived locational data admitted in the first trial, which connected Jones to the alleged conspirators' stash house that contained $850,000 in cash, 97 kilograms of cocaine, and 1 kilogram of cocaine base. The jury returned a guilty verdict, and the District Court sentenced Jones to life imprisonment.

The United States Court of Appeals for the District of Columbia Circuit reversed the conviction because of admission of the evidence

---

[1]　In this litigation, the Government has conceded noncompliance with the warrant and has argued only that a warrant was not required.

obtained by warrantless use of the GPS device which, it said, violated the Fourth Amendment. We granted certiorari.

II

The Fourth Amendment provides in relevant part that "the right of the people to be secure in their persons, houses, papers, and effects, against unreasonable searches and seizures, shall not be violated." It is beyond dispute that a vehicle is an "effect" as that term is used in the Amendment. We hold that the Government's installation of a GPS device on a target's vehicle,[2] and its use of that device to monitor the vehicle's movements, constitutes a "search."

It is important to be clear about what occurred in this case: The Government physically occupied private property for the purpose of obtaining information. We have no doubt that such a physical intrusion would have been considered a "search" within the meaning of the Fourth Amendment when it was adopted.

The text of the Fourth Amendment reflects its close connection to property, since otherwise it would have referred simply to "the right of the people to be secure against unreasonable searches and seizures"; the phrase "in their persons, houses, papers, and effects" would have been superfluous. Consistent with this understanding, our Fourth Amendment jurisprudence was tied to common-law trespass, at least until the latter half of the 20th century.

Our later cases, of course, have deviated from that exclusively property-based approach. In *Katz v. U.S.*, 389 U.S. 347 (1967), we said that "the Fourth Amendment protects people, not places," and found a violation in attachment of an eavesdropping device to a public telephone booth. Our later cases have applied the analysis of Justice Harlan's concurrence in that case, which said that a violation occurs when government officers violate a person's "reasonable expectation of privacy."

The Government contends that the Harlan standard shows that no search occurred here, since Jones had no "reasonable expectation of privacy" in the area of the Jeep accessed by Government agents (its underbody) and in the locations of the Jeep on the public roads, which were visible to all. But we need not address the Government's contentions, because Jones' Fourth Amendment rights do not rise or fall with the *Katz* formulation. As explained, for most of our history the Fourth Amendment was understood to embody a particular concern for

---

[2] As we have noted, the Jeep was registered to Jones' wife. The Government acknowledged, however, that Jones was "the exclusive driver." If Jones was not the owner he had at least the property rights of a bailee. The Court of Appeals concluded that the vehicle's registration did not affect his ability to make a Fourth Amendment objection, and the Government has not challenged that determination here. We therefore do not consider the Fourth Amendment significance of Jones' status.

government trespass upon the areas ("persons, houses, papers, and effects") it enumerates.[3] *Katz* did not repudiate that understanding.

The Government contends that several of our post-*Katz* cases foreclose the conclusion that what occurred here constituted a search. It relies principally on two cases in which we rejected Fourth Amendment challenges to "beepers," electronic tracking devices that represent another form of electronic monitoring. The first case, *U.S. v. Knotts*, 460 U.S. 276 (1983), upheld against Fourth Amendment challenge the use of a "beeper" that had been placed in a container of chloroform, allowing law enforcement to monitor the location of the container. We said that there had been no infringement of Knotts' reasonable expectation of privacy since the information obtained—the location of the automobile carrying the container on public roads, and the location of the off-loaded container in open fields near Knotts' cabin—had been voluntarily conveyed to the public. But as we have discussed, the *Katz* reasonable-expectation-of-privacy test has been *added to*, not *substituted for*, the common-law trespassory test. The holding in *Knotts* addressed only the former, since the latter was not at issue. The beeper had been placed in the container before it came into Knotts' possession, with the consent of the then-owner. Knotts did not challenge that installation, and we specifically declined to consider its effect on the Fourth Amendment analysis. *Knotts* would be relevant, perhaps, if the Government were making the argument that what would otherwise be an unconstitutional search is not such where it produces only public information. The Government does not make that argument, and we know of no case that would support it.

The second "beeper" case, *U.S. v. Karo*, 468 U.S. 705 (1984), does not suggest a different conclusion. There we addressed the question left open by *Knotts*, whether the installation of a beeper in a container amounted to a search or seizure. As in *Knotts*, at the time the beeper was installed the container belonged to a third party, and it did not come into possession of the defendant until later. Thus, the specific question we considered was whether the installation "with the consent of the original owner constituted a search or seizure when the container is delivered to a buyer having no knowledge of the presence of the beeper." We held not. The Government, we said, came into physical contact with the container only

---

[3]   Justice Alito's concurrence (hereinafter concurrence) doubts the wisdom of our approach because "it is almost impossible to think of late-18th-century situations that are analogous to what took place in this case." But in fact it posits a situation that is not far afield—a constable's concealing himself in the target's coach in order to track its movements. There is no doubt that the information gained by that trespassory activity would be the product of an unlawful search— whether that information consisted of the conversations occurring in the coach, or of the destinations to which the coach traveled. In any case, it is quite irrelevant whether there was an 18th-century analog. Whatever new methods of investigation may be devised, our task, *at a minimum*, is to decide whether the action in question would have constituted a "search" within the original meaning of the Fourth Amendment. Where, as here, the Government obtains information by physically intruding on a constitutionally protected area, such a search has undoubtedly occurred.

before it belonged to the defendant Karo; and the transfer of the container with the unmonitored beeper inside did not convey any information and thus did not invade Karo's privacy. That conclusion is perfectly consistent with the one we reach here. Karo accepted the container as it came to him, beeper and all, and was therefore not entitled to object to the beeper's presence, even though it was used to monitor the container's location. Jones, who possessed the Jeep at the time the Government trespassorily inserted the information-gathering device, is on much different footing.

Finally, the Government's position gains little support from our conclusion in *Oliver v. U.S.*, 466 U.S. 170 (1984), that officers' information-gathering intrusion on an "open field" did not constitute a Fourth Amendment search even though it was a trespass at common law. Quite simply, an open field, unlike the curtilage of a home, is not one of those protected areas enumerated in the Fourth Amendment. The Government's physical intrusion on such an area—unlike its intrusion on the "effect" at issue here—is of no Fourth Amendment significance.

The concurrence faults our approach for "presenting particularly vexing problems" in cases that do not involve physical contact, such as those that involve the transmission of electronic signals. We entirely fail to understand that point. For unlike the concurrence, which would make *Katz* the exclusive test, we do not make trespass the exclusive test. Situations involving merely the transmission of electronic signals without trespass would remain subject to *Katz* analysis.

In fact, it is the concurrence's insistence on the exclusivity of the *Katz* test that needlessly leads us into "particularly vexing problems" in the present case. This Court has to date not deviated from the understanding that mere visual observation does not constitute a search. We accordingly held in *Knotts* that "a person traveling in an automobile on public thoroughfares has no reasonable expectation of privacy in his movements from one place to another." Thus, even assuming that the concurrence is correct to say that "traditional surveillance" of Jones for a 4-week period "would have required a large team of agents, multiple vehicles, and perhaps aerial assistance," our cases suggest that such visual observation is constitutionally permissible. It may be that achieving the same result through electronic means, without an accompanying trespass, is an unconstitutional invasion of privacy, but the present case does not require us to answer that question.

And answering it affirmatively leads us needlessly into additional thorny problems. The concurrence posits that "relatively short-term monitoring of a person's movements on public streets" is okay, but that "the use of longer term GPS monitoring in investigations of most offenses" is no good. That introduces yet another novelty into our jurisprudence. There is no precedent for the proposition that whether a search has occurred depends on the nature of the crime being investigated. And even accepting that novelty, it remains unexplained why a 4-week investigation is "surely" too long and why a drug-trafficking conspiracy involving substantial amounts of cash and narcotics is not an "extraordinary offense" which may permit longer observation. What of a 2-day monitoring of a suspected purveyor of stolen electronics? Or of a 6-month monitoring of a suspected terrorist? We may have to grapple with these "vexing problems" in some future case where a classic trespassory search is not involved and resort must be had to *Katz* analysis; but there is no reason for rushing forward to resolve them here.

JUSTICE SOTOMAYOR, concurring.

I join the Court's opinion because I agree that a search within the meaning of the Fourth Amendment occurs, at a minimum, "where, as here, the Government obtains information by physically intruding on a constitutionally protected area." In this case, the Government installed a Global Positioning System (GPS) tracking device on respondent Antoine Jones' Jeep without a valid warrant and without Jones' consent, then used that device to monitor the Jeep's movements over the course of four weeks. The Government usurped Jones' property for the purpose of conducting surveillance on him, thereby invading privacy interests long afforded, and undoubtedly entitled to, Fourth Amendment protection.

Of course, the Fourth Amendment is not concerned only with trespassory intrusions on property. Rather, even in the absence of a trespass, a Fourth Amendment search occurs when the government violates a subjective expectation of privacy that society recognizes as reasonable. In *Katz*, this Court enlarged its then-prevailing focus on property rights by announcing that the reach of the Fourth Amendment does not turn upon the presence or absence of a physical intrusion. As the majority's opinion makes clear, however, *Katz*'s reasonable-expectation-of-privacy test augmented, but did not displace or diminish, the common-law trespassory test that preceded it. Justice Alito's approach, which discounts altogether the constitutional relevance of the Government's physical intrusion on Jones' Jeep, erodes that longstanding protection for privacy expectations inherent in items of property that people possess or control. By contrast, the trespassory test applied in the majority's opinion reflects an irreducible constitutional minimum: When the Government physically invades personal property to gather information, a search occurs. The reaffirmation of that principle suffices to decide this case.

Nonetheless, as Justice Alito notes, physical intrusion is now unnecessary to many forms of surveillance. With increasing regularity, the Government will be capable of duplicating the monitoring undertaken in this case by enlisting factory- or owner-installed vehicle tracking devices or GPS-enabled smartphones. In cases of electronic or other novel modes of surveillance that do not depend upon a physical invasion on property, the majority opinion's trespassory test may provide little guidance. But "situations involving merely the transmission of electronic signals without trespass would remain subject to *Katz* analysis." As Justice Alito incisively observes, the same technological advances that have made possible nontrespassory surveillance techniques will also affect the *Katz* test by shaping the evolution of societal privacy expectations. Under that rubric, I agree with Justice Alito that, at the very least, "longer term GPS monitoring in investigations of most offenses impinges on expectations of privacy."

In cases involving even short-term monitoring, some unique attributes of GPS surveillance relevant to the *Katz* analysis will require particular attention. GPS monitoring generates a precise, comprehensive record of a person's public movements that reflects a wealth of detail about her familial, political, professional, religious, and sexual associations. The Government can store such records and efficiently mine them for information years into the future. And because GPS monitoring is cheap in comparison to conventional surveillance techniques and, by design, proceeds surreptitiously, it evades the ordinary checks that constrain abusive law enforcement practices: limited police resources and community hostility.

Awareness that the Government may be watching chills associational and expressive freedoms. And the Government's unrestrained power to assemble data that reveal private aspects of identity is susceptible to abuse. The net result is that GPS monitoring—by making available at a relatively low cost such a substantial quantum of intimate information about any person whom the Government, in its unfettered discretion, chooses to track—may alter the relationship between citizen and government in a way that is inimical to democratic society.

I would take these attributes of GPS monitoring into account when considering the existence of a reasonable societal expectation of privacy in the sum of one's public movements. I would ask whether people reasonably expect that their movements will be recorded and aggregated in a manner that enables the Government to ascertain, more or less at will, their political and religious beliefs, sexual habits, and so on. I do not regard as dispositive the fact that the Government might obtain the fruits of GPS monitoring through lawful conventional surveillance techniques. I would also consider the appropriateness of entrusting to the Executive, in the absence of any oversight from a coordinate branch, a tool so amenable to misuse, especially in light of the Fourth Amendment's goal to curb arbitrary exercises of police power to and prevent a too permeating police surveillance.

More fundamentally, it may be necessary to reconsider the premise that an individual has no reasonable expectation of privacy in information voluntarily disclosed to third parties. This approach is ill suited to the digital age, in which people reveal a great deal of information about themselves to third parties in the course of carrying out mundane tasks. People disclose the phone numbers that they dial or text to their cellular providers; the URLs that they visit and the e-mail addresses with which they correspond to their Internet service providers; and the books, groceries, and medications they purchase to online retailers. Perhaps, as Justice Alito notes, some people may find the "tradeoff" of privacy for convenience "worthwhile," or come to accept this "diminution of privacy" as "inevitable," and perhaps not. I for one doubt that people would accept without complaint the warrantless disclosure to the Government of a list of every Web site they had visited in the last week, or month, or year. But whatever the societal expectations, they can attain constitutionally protected status only if our Fourth Amendment jurisprudence ceases to treat secrecy as a prerequisite for privacy. I would not assume that all information voluntarily disclosed to some member of the public for a limited purpose is, for that reason alone, disentitled to Fourth Amendment protection.

Resolution of these difficult questions in this case is unnecessary, however, because the Government's physical intrusion on Jones' Jeep supplies a narrower basis for decision. I therefore join the majority's opinion.

JUSTICE ALITO, with whom JUSTICE GINSBURG, JUSTICE BREYER, and JUSTICE KAGAN join, concurring in the judgment.

This case requires us to apply the Fourth Amendment's prohibition of unreasonable searches and seizures to a 21st-century surveillance technique, the use of a Global Positioning System (GPS) device to monitor a vehicle's movements for an extended period of time. Ironically, the Court has chosen to decide this case based on 18th-century tort law. By attaching a small GPS device to the underside of the vehicle that respondent drove, the law enforcement officers in this case engaged in conduct that might have provided grounds in 1791 for a suit for trespass to chattels. And for this reason, the Court concludes, the installation and use of the GPS device constituted a search.

This holding, in my judgment, is unwise. It strains the language of the Fourth Amendment; it has little if any support in current Fourth Amendment case law; and it is highly artificial. I would analyze the question presented in this case by asking whether respondent's reasonable expectations of privacy were violated by the long-term monitoring of the movements of the vehicle he drove.

The Fourth Amendment prohibits "unreasonable searches and seizures," and the Court makes very little effort to explain how the attachment or use of the GPS device fits within these terms. The Court does not contend that there was a seizure. A seizure of property occurs when there is some meaningful interference with an individual's possessory interests in that property, and here there was none. Indeed, the success of the surveillance technique that the officers employed was dependent on the fact that the GPS did not interfere in any way with the operation of the vehicle, for if any such interference had been detected, the device might have been discovered.

The Court does claim that the installation and use of the GPS constituted a search, but this conclusion is dependent on the questionable proposition that these two procedures cannot be separated for purposes of Fourth Amendment analysis. If these two procedures are analyzed separately, it is not at all clear from the Court's opinion why either should be regarded as a search. It is clear that the attachment of the GPS device was not itself a search; if the device had not functioned or if the officers had not used it, no information would have been obtained. And the Court does not contend that the use of the device constituted a search either. On the contrary, the Court accepts the holding in *Knotts* that the use of a surreptitiously planted electronic device to monitor a vehicle's movements on public roads did not amount to a search.

The Court argues—and I agree—that we must "assure preservation of that degree of privacy against government that existed when the Fourth Amendment was adopted." But it is almost impossible to think of late-18th-century situations that are analogous to what took place in this case. (Is it possible to imagine a case in which a constable secreted himself somewhere in a coach and remained there for a period of time in order to monitor the movements of the coach's owner?) The Court's theory seems to be that the concept of a search, as originally understood, comprehended any technical trespass that led to the gathering of evidence, but we know that this is incorrect. At common law, any unauthorized intrusion on private property was actionable, but a trespass on open fields, as opposed to the "curtilage" of a home, does not fall within the scope of the Fourth Amendment because private property outside the curtilage is not part of a "house" within the meaning of the Fourth Amendment.

The Court's reasoning in this case is very similar to that in the Court's early decisions involving wiretapping and electronic eavesdropping, namely, that a technical trespass followed by the gathering of evidence constitutes a search. By contrast, in cases in which there was no trespass, it was held that there was no search. Thus, in *Olmstead v. U.S.*, 277 U.S. 438 (1928), the Court found that the Fourth Amendment did not apply because "the taps from house lines were made in the streets near the houses." This trespass-based rule was repeatedly criticized. *Katz* finally did away with the old approach, holding that a trespass was not required for a Fourth Amendment violation. In sum, the majority is hard pressed to find support in post-*Katz* cases for its trespass-based theory.

Disharmony with a substantial body of existing case law is only one of the problems with the Court's approach in this case. I will briefly note four others. First, the Court's reasoning largely disregards what is really important (the use of a GPS for the purpose of long-term tracking) and instead attaches great significance to something that most would view as relatively minor (attaching to the bottom of a car a small, light object that does not interfere in any way with the car's operation). Attaching such an object is generally regarded as so trivial that it does not provide a basis for recovery under modern tort law. But under the Court's reasoning, this conduct may violate the Fourth Amendment. By contrast, if long-term monitoring can be accomplished without committing a technical trespass—suppose, for example, that the Federal Government required or persuaded auto manufacturers to include a GPS tracking device in every car—the Court's theory would provide no protection.

Second, the Court's approach leads to incongruous results. If the police attach a GPS device to a car and use the device to follow the car for even a brief time, under the Court's theory, the Fourth Amendment applies. But if the police follow the same car for a much longer period using unmarked cars and aerial assistance, this tracking is not subject to any Fourth Amendment constraints.

In the present case, the Fourth Amendment applies, the Court concludes, because the officers installed the GPS device after respondent's wife, to whom the car was registered, turned it over to respondent for his exclusive use. But if the GPS had been attached prior to that time, the Court's theory would lead to a different result. The Court proceeds on the assumption that respondent "had at least the property rights of a bailee," but a bailee may sue for a trespass to chattel only if the injury occurs during the term of the bailment. So if the GPS device had been installed before respondent's wife gave him the keys, respondent would have no claim for trespass—and, presumably, no Fourth Amendment claim either.

Third, under the Court's theory, the coverage of the Fourth Amendment may vary from State to State. If the events at issue here had occurred in a community property State or a State that has adopted the Uniform Marital Property Act, respondent would likely be an owner of the vehicle, and it would not matter whether the GPS was installed before or after his wife turned over the keys. In non-community-property States, on the other hand, the registration of the vehicle in the name of respondent's wife would generally be regarded as presumptive evidence that she was the sole owner.

Fourth, the Court's reliance on the law of trespass will present particularly vexing problems in cases involving surveillance that is carried out by making electronic, as opposed to physical, contact with the item to be tracked. For example, suppose that the officers in the present case had followed respondent by surreptitiously activating a stolen vehicle detection system that came with the car when it was purchased. Would the sending of a radio signal to activate this system constitute a trespass to chattels? Trespass to chattels has traditionally required a physical touching of the property. In recent years, courts have wrestled with the application of this old tort in cases involving unwanted electronic contact with computer systems, and some have held that even the transmission of electrons that occurs when a communication is sent from one computer to another is enough. But may such decisions be followed in applying the Court's trespass theory? Assuming that what matters under the Court's theory is the law of trespass as it existed at the time of the adoption of the Fourth Amendment, do these recent decisions represent a change in the law or simply the application of the old tort to new situations?

The *Katz* expectation-of-privacy test avoids the problems and complications noted above, but it is not without its own difficulties. It involves a degree of circularity, and judges are apt to confuse their own expectations of privacy with those of the hypothetical reasonable person to which the *Katz* test looks. In addition, the *Katz* test rests on the assumption that this hypothetical reasonable person has a well-developed and stable set of privacy expectations. But technology can change those expectations. Dramatic technological change may lead to periods in which popular expectations are in flux and may ultimately produce significant changes in popular attitudes. New technology may provide increased convenience or security at the expense of privacy, and many people may find the tradeoff worthwhile. And even if the public does not welcome the diminution of privacy that new technology entails, they may eventually reconcile themselves to this development as inevitable.

On the other hand, concern about new intrusions on privacy may spur the enactment of legislation to protect against these intrusions. This is what ultimately happened with respect to wiretapping. After *Katz*, Congress did not leave it to the courts to develop a body of Fourth Amendment case law governing that complex subject. Instead, Congress promptly enacted a comprehensive statute, see 18 U.S.C. §§ 2510–2522 (2006 ed. and Supp. IV), and since that time, the regulation of wiretapping has been governed primarily by statute and not by case law. In an ironic sense, although *Katz* overruled *Olmstead*, Chief Justice Taft's suggestion in the latter case that the regulation of wiretapping was a matter better left for Congress has been borne out.

Recent years have seen the emergence of many new devices that permit the monitoring of a person's movements. In some locales, closed-circuit television video monitoring is becoming ubiquitous. On toll roads, automatic toll collection systems create a precise record of the movements of motorists who choose to make use of that convenience. Many motorists purchase cars that are equipped with devices that permit a central station to ascertain the car's location at any time so that roadside assistance may be provided if needed and the car may be found if it is stolen.

Perhaps most significant, cell phones and other wireless devices now permit wireless carriers to track and record the location of users—and as of June 2011, it has been reported, there were more than 322 million wireless devices in use in the United States. For older phones, the accuracy of the location information depends on the density of the tower network, but new "smart phones," which are equipped with a GPS device, permit more precise tracking. For example, when a user activates the GPS on such a phone, a provider is able to monitor the phone's location and speed of movement and can then report back real-time traffic conditions after combining ("crowdsourcing") the speed of all such phones on any particular road. Similarly, phone-location-tracking services are offered as "social" tools, allowing consumers to find (or to avoid) others who enroll in these services. The availability and use of these and other new devices will continue to shape the average person's expectations about the privacy of his or her daily movements.

In the pre-computer age, the greatest protections of privacy were neither constitutional nor statutory, but practical. Traditional surveillance for any extended period of time was difficult and costly and therefore rarely undertaken. The surveillance at issue in this case—constant monitoring of the location of a vehicle for four weeks—would have required a large team of agents, multiple vehicles, and perhaps aerial assistance. Only an investigation of unusual importance could have justified such an expenditure of law enforcement resources. Devices like the one used in the present case, however, make long-term monitoring relatively easy and cheap. In circumstances involving dramatic technological change, the best solution to privacy concerns may be legislative. A legislative body is well situated to gauge changing public attitudes, to draw detailed lines, and to balance privacy and public safety in a comprehensive way.

To date, however, Congress and most States have not enacted statutes regulating the use of GPS tracking technology for law enforcement purposes. The best that we can do in this case is to apply existing Fourth Amendment doctrine and to ask whether the use of GPS tracking in a particular case involved a degree of intrusion that a reasonable person would not have anticipated.

Under this approach, relatively short-term monitoring of a person's movements on public streets accords with expectations of privacy that our society has recognized as reasonable. But the use of longer term GPS monitoring in investigations of most offenses impinges on expectations of privacy. For such offenses, society's expectation has been that law enforcement agents and others would not—and indeed, in the main, simply could not—secretly monitor and catalogue every single movement of an individual's car for a very long period. In this case, for four weeks, law enforcement agents tracked every movement that respondent made in the vehicle he was driving. We need not identify with precision the point at which the tracking of this vehicle became a search, for the line was surely crossed before the 4-week mark. Other cases may present more difficult questions. But where uncertainty exists with respect to whether a certain period of GPS surveillance is long enough to constitute a Fourth Amendment search, the police may always seek a warrant. We also need not consider whether prolonged GPS monitoring in the context of investigations involving extraordinary offenses would similarly intrude on a constitutionally protected sphere of privacy. In such cases, long-term tracking might have been mounted using previously available techniques.

For these reasons, I conclude that the lengthy monitoring that occurred in this case constituted a search under the Fourth Amendment. I therefore agree with the majority that the decision of the Court of Appeals must be affirmed.

Tracking Devices

1.   A search does not occur when police install an electronic tracking device on property that does not yet belong to the defendant and then use the device, once in the defendant's possession, to reveal information regarding his public movements that could also be obtained through ordinary visual surveillance. A person traveling on public thoroughfares has no reasonable expectation of privacy in his movements from one place to another.

2.   A search occurs when police use an electronic tracking device to obtain information about the interior of a private residence that they could not have obtained by observation from outside the curtilage. Private residences are places in which the individual normally expects privacy free of governmental intrusion not authorized by a warrant, and that expectation is one that society is prepared to recognize as reasonable.

3.   A search occurs when government obtains information by physically intruding on a constitutionally protected area. Accordingly, government installation of a GPS device on an individual's vehicle—an "effect" under the Fourth Amendment—and the use of that device to monitor the vehicle's movements constitutes a search.

Note: Five Justices in *U.S. v. Jones* agreed that "longer term GPS monitoring in investigations of most offenses impinges on expectations of privacy" and therefore constitutes a search under the Fourth Amendment. The five Justices did not define "longer term" with precision, but noted that "the line was surely crossed before the 4-week mark."

8. USE OF DRUG-SNIFFING DOGS

The Supreme Court has considered whether the use of a drug-sniffing dog amounts to a search in a series of three cases—*U.S. v. Place*, *Illinois v. Caballes*, and *Florida v. Jardines*—each presenting a different fact pattern. Perhaps it is not surprising that the Court's ultimate decision as to whether a dog sniff constitutes a search appears to depend on the context in which the dog is used. In the first of the three cases, *U.S. v. Place*, the Supreme Court concluded that subjecting a traveler's luggage to a "sniff test" was not a search.

U.S. V. PLACE
462 U.S. 696 (1983)

Police detained the defendant and his luggage in an airport so that they could subject the bags to a "sniff test" by a trained narcotics detection dog. The dog reacted positively to one of the two bags. Police then obtained a warrant, and upon opening the bag, they discovered cocaine. The Supreme Court concluded that the dog sniff was not a search under the Fourth Amendment:

> The purpose for which respondent's luggage was seized was to arrange its exposure to a narcotics detection dog. Obviously, if this investigative procedure is itself a search requiring probable cause, the initial seizure of respondent's luggage for the purpose of subjecting it to the sniff test—no matter how brief—could not be justified on less than probable cause.

> The Fourth Amendment protects people from unreasonable government intrusions into their legitimate expectations of privacy. We have affirmed that a person possesses a privacy interest in the contents of personal luggage that is protected by the Fourth Amendment. A "canine sniff" by a well-trained narcotics detection dog, however, does not require opening the luggage. It does not expose noncontraband items that otherwise would remain hidden from public view, as does, for example, an officer's rummaging through the contents of the luggage. Thus, the manner in which information is obtained through this investigative technique is much less intrusive than a typical search. Moreover, the sniff discloses only the presence or absence of narcotics, a contraband item. Thus, despite the fact that the sniff tells the authorities something about the contents of the luggage, the information obtained is limited. This limited disclosure also ensures that the owner of the property is not subjected to the embarrassment and inconvenience entailed in less discriminate and more intrusive investigative methods.

In these respects, the canine sniff is *sui generis*. We are aware of no other investigative procedure that is so limited both in the manner in which the information is obtained and in the content of the information revealed by the procedure. Therefore, we conclude that the particular course of investigation that the agents intended to pursue here—exposure of respondent's luggage, which was located in a public place, to a trained canine—did not constitute a "search" within the meaning of the Fourth Amendment.

———————

In the second of the three cases, *Illinois v. Caballes*, the Supreme Court concluded that the use of a drug-sniffing dog around a vehicle that had been stopped for speeding did not constitute a search.

ILLINOIS V. CABALLES
543 U.S. 405 (2005)

The police walked a narcotics detection dog around the defendant's vehicle after he had been stopped for speeding. The dog alerted positively to the car's trunk. The police then searched the trunk and discovered marijuana inside. Relying heavily on *U.S. v. Place*, the Court concluded that the dog sniff was not a search under the Fourth Amendment:

> Official conduct that does not compromise any legitimate interest in privacy is not a search subject to the Fourth Amendment. We have held that any interest in possessing contraband cannot be deemed "legitimate," and thus, governmental conduct that *only* reveals the possession of contraband compromises no legitimate privacy interest. This is because the expectation that certain facts will not come to the attention of the authorities is not the same as an interest in privacy that society is prepared to consider reasonable. In *U.S. v. Place*, 462 U.S. 696 (1983), we treated a canine sniff by a well-trained narcotics-detection dog as "*sui generis*" because it "discloses only the presence or absence of narcotics, a contraband item." Respondent likewise concedes that "drug sniffs are designed, and if properly conducted are generally likely, to reveal only the presence of contraband." Although respondent argues that the error rates, particularly the existence of false positives, call into question the premise that drug-detection dogs alert only to contraband, the record contains no evidence or findings that support his argument. Moreover, respondent does not suggest that an erroneous alert, in and of itself, reveals any legitimate private information, and, in this case, the trial judge

found that the dog sniff was sufficiently reliable to establish probable cause to conduct a full-blown search of the trunk.

Accordingly, the use of a well-trained narcotics-detection dog—one that does not expose noncontraband items that otherwise would remain hidden from public view—during a lawful traffic stop, generally does not implicate legitimate privacy interests. In this case, the dog sniff was performed on the exterior of respondent's car while he was lawfully seized for a traffic violation. Any intrusion on respondent's privacy expectations does not rise to the level of a constitutionally cognizable infringement.

This conclusion is entirely consistent with our recent decision [in *Kyllo v. U.S.*, 533 U.S. 27 (2001)] that the use of a thermal-imaging device to detect the growth of marijuana in a home constituted an unlawful search. Critical to that decision was the fact that the device was capable of detecting lawful activity—in that case, intimate details in a home, such as "at what hour each night the lady of the house takes her daily sauna and bath." The legitimate expectation that information about perfectly lawful activity will remain private is categorically distinguishable from respondent's hopes or expectations concerning the nondetection of contraband in the trunk of his car. A dog sniff conducted during a concededly lawful traffic stop that reveals no information other than the location of a substance that no individual has any right to possess does not violate the Fourth Amendment.

In the last and most recent of the three cases, *Florida v. Jardines*, the Supreme Court concluded that the use of a drug-sniffing dog to investigate a home and its immediate surroundings did amount to a search under the Fourth Amendment.

FLORIDA V. JARDINES
133 S.Ct. 1409 (2013)

JUSTICE SCALIA delivered the opinion of the Court.

We consider whether using a drug-sniffing dog on a homeowner's porch to investigate the contents of the home is a "search" within the meaning of the Fourth Amendment.

I

In 2006, Detective William Pedraja of the Miami-Dade Police Department received an unverified tip that marijuana was being grown in the home of respondent Joelis Jardines. One month later, the Department and the Drug Enforcement Administration sent a joint surveillance team to Jardines' home. Detective Pedraja was part of that team. He watched the home for fifteen minutes and saw no vehicles in the driveway or activity around the home, and could not see inside because the blinds were drawn. Detective Pedraja then approached Jardines' home accompanied by Detective Douglas Bartelt, a trained canine handler who had just arrived at the scene with his drug-sniffing dog. The dog was trained to detect the scent of marijuana, cocaine, heroin, and several other drugs, indicating the presence of any of these substances through particular behavioral changes recognizable by his handler.

Detective Bartelt had the dog on a six-foot leash, owing in part to the dog's "wild" nature and tendency to dart around erratically while searching. As the dog approached Jardines' front porch, he apparently sensed one of the odors he had been trained to detect, and began energetically exploring the area for the strongest point source of that odor. As Detective Bartelt explained, the dog "began tracking that airborne odor by tracking back and forth," engaging in what is called "bracketing," "back and forth, back and forth." Detective Bartelt gave the dog "the full six feet of the leash plus whatever safe distance [he could] give him" to do this—he testified that he needed to give the dog "as much distance as I can." And Detective Pedraja stood back while this was occurring, so that he would not "get knocked over" when the dog was "spinning around trying to find" the source.

After sniffing the base of the front door, the dog sat, which is the trained behavior upon discovering the odor's strongest point. Detective Bartelt then pulled the dog away from the door and returned to his vehicle. He left the scene after informing Detective Pedraja that there had been a positive alert for narcotics.

On the basis of what he had learned at the home, Detective Pedraja applied for and received a warrant to search the residence. When the warrant was executed later that day, Jardines attempted to flee and was arrested; the search revealed marijuana plants, and he was charged with trafficking in cannabis.

At trial, Jardines moved to suppress the marijuana plants on the ground that the canine investigation was an unreasonable search. The Florida Supreme Court approved the trial court's decision to suppress, holding that the use of the trained narcotics dog to investigate Jardines' home was a Fourth Amendment search unsupported by probable cause, rendering invalid the warrant based upon information gathered in that search. We granted certiorari, limited to the question of whether the officers' behavior was a search within the meaning of the Fourth Amendment.

II

The Fourth Amendment provides in relevant part that the "right of the people to be secure in their persons, houses, papers, and effects, against unreasonable searches and seizures, shall not be violated." The Amendment establishes a simple baseline, one that for much of our history formed the exclusive basis for its protections: When "the Government obtains information by physically intruding" on persons, houses, papers, or effects, "a 'search' within the original meaning of the Fourth Amendment" has "undoubtedly occurred." *U.S. v. Jones*, 132 S.Ct. 945, 950–951, n. 3 (2012). By reason of our decision in *Katz v. U.S.*, 389 U.S. 347 (1967), property rights are not the sole measure of Fourth Amendment violations—but though *Katz* may add to the baseline, it does not subtract anything from the Amendment's protections when the Government *does* engage in a physical intrusion of a constitutionally protected area.

That principle renders this case a straightforward one. The officers were gathering information in an area belonging to Jardines and immediately surrounding his house—in the curtilage of the house, which we have held enjoys protection as part of the home itself. And they gathered that information by physically entering and occupying the area to engage in conduct not explicitly or implicitly permitted by the homeowner.

The Fourth Amendment indicates with some precision the places and things encompassed by its protections: persons, houses, papers, and effects. The Fourth Amendment does not, therefore, prevent all investigations conducted on private property; for example, an officer may (subject to *Katz*) gather information in what we have called "open fields"—even if those fields are privately owned—because such fields are not enumerated in the Amendment's text.

But when it comes to the Fourth Amendment, the home is first among equals. At the Amendment's very core stands the right of a man to retreat into his own home and there be free from unreasonable governmental intrusion. This right would be of little practical value if the State's agents could stand in a home's porch or side garden and trawl for evidence with impunity; the right to retreat would be significantly diminished if the police could enter a man's property to observe his repose from just outside the front window.

We therefore regard the area immediately surrounding and associated with the home—what our cases call the curtilage—as part of the home itself for Fourth Amendment purposes. Here there is no doubt that the officers entered [the curtilage]: The front porch is the classic exemplar of an area adjacent to the home and to which the activity of home life extends.

Since the officers' investigation took place in a constitutionally protected area, we turn to the question of whether it was accomplished through an unlicensed physical intrusion. While law enforcement officers need not shield their eyes when passing by the home on public thoroughfares, an officer's leave to gather information is sharply circumscribed when he steps off those thoroughfares and enters the Fourth Amendment's protected areas. In permitting, for example, visual observation of the home from "public navigable airspace" [in *California v. Ciraolo*, 476 U.S. 207 (1986)], we were careful to note that it was done "in a physically nonintrusive manner." As it is undisputed that the detectives had all four of their feet and all four of their companion's firmly planted on the constitutionally protected extension of Jardines' home, the only question is whether he had given his leave (even implicitly) for them to do so. He had not.

We have recognized that the knocker on the front door is treated as an invitation or license to attempt an entry, justifying ingress to the home by solicitors, hawkers and peddlers of all kinds. This implicit license typically permits the visitor to approach the home by the front path, knock promptly, wait briefly to be received, and then (absent invitation to linger longer) leave. Complying with the terms of that traditional invitation does not require fine-grained legal knowledge; it is generally managed without incident by the Nation's Girl Scouts and trick-or-treaters. Thus, a police officer not armed with a warrant may approach a home and knock, precisely because that is no more than any private citizen might do.

But introducing a trained police dog to explore the area around the home in hopes of discovering incriminating evidence is something else. There is no customary invitation to do *that*. An invitation to engage in canine forensic investigation assuredly does not inhere in the very act of hanging a knocker. To find a visitor knocking on the door is routine (even if sometimes unwelcome); to spot that same visitor exploring the front path with a metal detector, or marching his bloodhound into the garden before saying hello and asking permission, would inspire most of us to—well, call the police. The scope of a license—express or implied—is limited not only to a particular area but also to a specific purpose. Consent at a traffic stop to an officer's checking out an anonymous tip that there is a body in the trunk does not permit the officer to rummage through the trunk for narcotics. Here, the background social norms that invite a visitor to the front door do not invite him there to conduct a search.

The State points to our decisions holding that the subjective intent of the officer is irrelevant. But those cases merely hold that a stop or search *that is objectively reasonable* is not vitiated by the fact that the officer's real reason for making the stop or search has nothing to do with the validating reason. Thus, the defendant will not be heard to complain that although he was speeding the officer's real reason for the stop was racial harassment. Here, however, the question before the court is precisely *whether* the officer's conduct was an objectively reasonable search. As we have described, that depends upon whether the officers had an implied license to enter the porch, which in turn depends upon the purpose for which they entered. Here, their behavior objectively reveals a purpose to conduct a search, which is not what anyone would think he had license to do.

III

The State argues that investigation by a forensic narcotics dog by definition cannot implicate any legitimate privacy interest. The State cites for authority our decisions in *U.S. v. Place,* 462 U.S. 696 (1983), and *Illinois v. Caballes,* 543 U.S. 405 (2005), which held, respectively, that canine inspection of luggage in an airport, and canine inspection of an automobile during a lawful traffic stop, do not violate the "reasonable expectation of privacy" described in *Katz.*

Just last Term, we considered an argument much like this. *U.S. v. Jones* held that tracking an automobile's whereabouts using a physically-mounted GPS receiver is a Fourth Amendment search. The Government argued that the *Katz* standard showed that no search occurred, as the defendant had no reasonable expectation of privacy in his whereabouts on the public roads—a proposition with at least as much support in our case law as the one the State marshals here. But because the GPS receiver had been physically mounted on the defendant's automobile (thus intruding on his "effects"), we held that tracking the vehicle's movements was a search: a person's "Fourth Amendment rights do not rise or fall with the *Katz* formulation." The *Katz* reasonable-expectations test "has been *added to,* not *substituted for,*" the traditional property-based understanding of the Fourth Amendment, and so is unnecessary to consider when the government gains evidence by physically intruding on constitutionally protected areas.

Thus, we need not decide whether the officers' investigation of Jardines' home violated his expectation of privacy under *Katz.* One virtue of the Fourth Amendment's property-rights baseline is that it keeps easy cases easy. That the officers learned what they learned only by physically intruding on Jardines' property to gather evidence is enough to establish that a search occurred.

For a related reason we find irrelevant the State's argument (echoed by the dissent) that forensic dogs have been commonly used by police for centuries. This argument is apparently directed to our holding in *Kyllo v. U.S.,* 533 U.S. 27 (2001), that surveillance of the home is a search where "the Government uses a device that is not in general public use" to "explore details of the home that would previously have been unknowable *without physical intrusion.*" But the implication of that statement (*inclusio unius est exclusio alterius*) is that when the government uses a physical intrusion to explore details of the home (including its curtilage), the antiquity of the tools that they bring along is irrelevant.

The government's use of trained police dogs to investigate the home and its immediate surroundings is a "search" within the meaning of the Fourth Amendment.

JUSTICE KAGAN, with whom JUSTICE GINSBURG and JUSTICE SOTOMAYOR join, concurring.

For me, a simple analogy clinches this case—and does so on privacy as well as property grounds. A stranger comes to the front door of your home carrying super-high-powered binoculars. He doesn't knock or say hello. Instead, he stands on the porch and uses the binoculars to peer through your windows, into your home's furthest corners. It doesn't take long (the binoculars are really very fine): In just a couple of minutes, his uncommon behavior allows him to learn details of your life you disclose to no one. Has your "visitor" trespassed on your property, exceeding the license you have granted to members of the public to, say, drop off the mail or distribute campaign flyers? Yes, he has. And has he also invaded your "reasonable expectation of privacy," by nosing into intimacies you sensibly thought protected from disclosure? Yes, of course, he has done that too.

That case is this case in every way that matters. Here, police officers came to Joelis Jardines' door with a super-sensitive instrument, which they deployed to detect things inside that they could not perceive unassisted. The equipment they used was animal, not mineral. But contra the dissent, that is of no significance in determining whether a search occurred. Detective Bartelt's dog was not your neighbor's pet, come to your porch on a leisurely stroll. Drug-detection dogs are highly trained tools of law enforcement, geared to respond in distinctive ways to specific scents so as to convey clear and reliable information to their human partners. They are to the poodle down the street as high-powered binoculars are to a piece of plain glass. Like the binoculars, a drug-detection dog is a specialized device for discovering objects not in plain view (or plain smell). And as in the hypothetical above, that device was aimed here at a home—the most private and inviolate (or so we expect) of all the places and things the Fourth Amendment protects. Was this activity a trespass? Yes, as the Court holds today. Was it also an invasion of privacy? Yes, that as well.

The Court today treats this case under a property rubric; I write separately to note that I could just as happily have decided it by looking to Jardines' privacy interests. A decision along those lines would have looked . . . well, much like this one. It would have talked about the right of a man to retreat into his own home and there be free from unreasonable governmental intrusion. It would have insisted on maintaining the practical value of that right by preventing police officers from standing in an adjacent space and trawling for evidence with impunity. It would have explained that privacy expectations are most heightened in the home and the surrounding area. And it would have determined that police officers invade those shared expectations when they use trained canine assistants to reveal within the confines of a home what they could not otherwise have found there.

It is not surprising that in a case involving a search of a home, property concepts and privacy concepts should so align. The law of property naturally enough influences our shared social expectations of what places should be free from governmental incursions. Jardines' home was his property; it was also his most intimate and familiar space. The analysis proceeding from each of those facts, as today's decision reveals, runs mostly along the same path.

I can think of only one divergence: If we had decided this case on privacy grounds, we would have realized that *Kyllo v. U.S.* already resolved it. The *Kyllo* Court held that police officers conducted a search when they used a thermal-imaging device to detect heat emanating from a private home, even though they committed no trespass. Highlighting our intention to draw both a "firm" and a "bright" line at "the entrance to the house," we announced the following rule: "Where, as here, the Government uses a device that is not in general public use, to explore details of the home that would previously have been unknowable without physical intrusion, the surveillance is a 'search' and is presumptively unreasonable without a warrant."

That rule governs this case: The police officers here conducted a search because they used a "device not in general public use" (a trained drug-detection dog) to "explore details of the home" (the presence of certain substances) that they would not otherwise have discovered without entering the premises.

And again, the dissent's argument that the device is just a dog cannot change the equation. As *Kyllo* made clear, the "sense-enhancing" tool at issue may be "crude" or "sophisticated," may be old or new (drug-detection dogs actually go back not 12,000 years or centuries, but only a few decades), may be either smaller or bigger than a breadbox; still, at least where (as here) the device is not "in general public use," training it on a home violates our "minimal expectation of privacy"—an expectation "that *exists,* and that is acknowledged to be *reasonable.*"[2] That does not

---

[2] The dissent's other principal reason for concluding that no violation of privacy occurred in this case—that police officers themselves might detect an aroma wafting from a house—works no better. If officers can smell drugs coming from a house, they can use that information; a human sniff is not a search, we can all agree. But it does not follow that a person loses his expectation of privacy in the many scents within his home that (his own nose capably tells him) are not usually detectible by humans standing outside. And indeed, *Kyllo* already decided as much.

mean the device is off-limits, as the dissent implies; it just means police officers cannot use it to examine a home without a warrant or exigent circumstance.

With these further thoughts, suggesting that a focus on Jardines' privacy interests would make an "easy case easy" twice over, I join the Court's opinion in full.

JUSTICE ALITO, with whom CHIEF JUSTICE ROBERTS, JUSTICE KENNEDY, and JUSTICE BREYER join, dissenting.

The law of trespass generally gives members of the public a license to use a walkway to approach the front door of a house and to remain there for a brief time. This license is not limited to persons who intend to speak to an occupant or who actually do so. (Mail carriers and persons delivering packages and flyers are examples of individuals who may lawfully approach a front door without intending to converse.) Nor is the license restricted to categories of visitors whom an occupant of the dwelling is likely to welcome; as the Court acknowledges, this license applies even to "solicitors, hawkers and peddlers of all kinds." And the license even extends to police officers who wish to gather evidence against an occupant (by asking potentially incriminating questions).

According to the Court, however, the police officer in this case, Detective Bartelt, committed a trespass because he was accompanied during his otherwise lawful visit to the front door of respondent's house by his dog, Franky. Where is the authority evidencing such a rule? Dogs have been domesticated for about 12,000 years; they were ubiquitous in both this country and Britain at the time of the adoption of the Fourth Amendment; and their acute sense of smell has been used in law enforcement for centuries. Yet the Court has been unable to find a single case—from the United States or any other common-law nation—that supports the rule on which its decision is based. Thus, trespass law provides no support for the Court's holding today.

The Court's decision is also inconsistent with the reasonable-expectations-of-privacy test that the Court adopted in *Katz v. U.S.* A reasonable person understands that odors emanating from a house may be detected from locations that are open to the public, and a reasonable person will not count on the strength of those odors remaining within the range that, while detectible by a dog, cannot be smelled by a human.

Detective Bartelt did not exceed the scope of the license to approach respondent's front door. He adhered to the customary path; he did not approach in the middle of the night; and he remained at the front door for only a very short period (less than a minute or two).

The Court concludes that Detective Bartelt went too far because he had the objective purpose to conduct a search. What this means, I take it, is that anyone aware of what Detective Bartelt did would infer that his subjective purpose was to gather evidence. But if this is the Court's point, then a standard "knock and talk" and most other police visits would likewise constitute searches. With the exception of visits to serve warrants or civil process, police almost always approach homes with a purpose of discovering information. That is certainly the objective of a "knock and talk." The Court offers no meaningful way of distinguishing the "objective purpose" of a "knock and talk" from the "objective purpose" of Detective Bartelt's conduct here.

The Court contends that a "knock and talk" is different because it involves talking, and "all are invited" to do that. But a police officer who approaches the front door of a house in accordance with the limitations already discussed may gather evidence by means other than talking. The officer may observe items in plain view and smell odors coming from the house. So the Court's "objective purpose" argument cannot stand.

What the Court must fall back on, then, is the particular instrument that Detective Bartelt used to detect the odor of marijuana, namely, his dog. But in the entire body of common-law decisions, the Court has not found a single case holding that a visitor to the front door of a home commits a trespass if the visitor is accompanied by a dog on a leash. On the contrary, the common law allowed even unleashed dogs to wander on private property without committing a trespass.

The Court responds that "it is not the dog that is the problem, but the behavior that here involved use of the dog." But where is the support in the law of trespass for *this* proposition? Dogs' keen sense of smell has been used in law enforcement for centuries. If bringing a tracking dog to the front door of a home constituted a trespass, one would expect at least one case to have arisen during the past 800 years. But the Court has found none.

For these reasons, the real law of trespass provides no support for the Court's holding today. The concurring opinion attempts to provide an alternative ground for today's decision, namely, that Detective Bartelt's conduct violated respondent's reasonable expectations of privacy. But we have already rejected a very similar, if not identical argument, [in] *Illinois v. Caballes*, 543 U.S. 405 (2005), and in any event I see no basis for concluding that the occupants of a dwelling have a reasonable expectation of privacy in odors that emanate from the dwelling and reach spots where members of the public may lawfully stand.

It is clear that the occupant of a house has no reasonable expectation of privacy with respect to odors that can be smelled by human beings who are standing in such places. And I would not draw a line between odors that can be smelled by humans and those that are detectible only by dogs.

In an attempt to show that respondent had a reasonable expectation of privacy in the odor of marijuana wafting from his house, the concurrence argues that this case is just like *Kyllo v. U.S.*, which held that police officers conducted a search when they used a thermal imaging device to detect heat emanating from a house. This Court [in *Illinois v. Caballes*] has already rejected the argument that the use of a drug-sniffing dog is the same as the use of a thermal imaging device.

Contrary to the interpretation propounded by the concurrence, *Kyllo* is best understood as a decision about the use of new technology. The *Kyllo* Court focused on the fact that the thermal imaging device was a form of "sense-enhancing technology" that was "not in general public use," and it expressed concern that citizens would be "at the mercy of advancing technology" if its use was not restricted. A dog, however, is not a new form of "technology" or a "device." And, as noted, the use of dogs' acute sense of smell in law enforcement dates back many centuries.

The concurrence suggests that a *Kyllo*-based decision would be much like the actual decision of the Court, but that is simply not so. The holding of the Court is based on what the Court sees as a "physical intrusion of a constitutionally protected area." As a result, it does not apply when a dog alerts while on a public sidewalk or street or in the corridor of a building to which the dog and handler have been lawfully admitted.

The concurrence's *Kyllo*-based approach would have a much wider reach. When the police used the thermal imaging device in *Kyllo*, they were on a public street, and committed no trespass. Therefore, if a dog's nose is just like a thermal imaging device for Fourth Amendment purposes, a search would occur if a dog alerted while on a public sidewalk or in the corridor of an apartment building. And the same would be true if the dog was trained to sniff, not for marijuana, but for more dangerous quarry, such as explosives or for a violent fugitive or kidnapped child. I see no ground for hampering legitimate law enforcement in this way.

The conduct of the police officer in this case did not constitute a trespass and did not violate respondent's reasonable expectations of privacy. I would hold that this conduct was not a search, and I therefore respectfully dissent.

Use of a Drug-Sniffing Dog

1. The use of a narcotics detection dog to sniff a traveler's luggage in a public airport does not constitute a search under the Fourth Amendment.

2. The use of a narcotics detection dog to sniff an individual's vehicle during a lawful traffic stop does not constitute a search under the Fourth Amendment.

3.　The use of a narcotics detection dog to investigate the home and its immediate surroundings is a search within the meaning of the Fourth Amendment. The home and the curtilage are constitutionally protected areas, and bringing a drug-sniffing dog onto the premises is an unlicensed physical intrusion.

C.　A NEW (OR OLD) DEFINITION OF "SEARCH" FOR THE TWENTY-FIRST CENTURY?

Since 1967, when it was first announced, the Supreme Court consistently used the *Katz* Test to determine whether a search had occurred under the Fourth Amendment. But in *U.S. v. Jones*, 132 U.S. 945 (2012), and *Florida v. Jardines*, 133 S.Ct. 1409 (2013), the two most recent Supreme Court cases to consider whether certain police investigative techniques qualified as searches under the Fourth Amendment, a majority of the Justices appeared willing, in appropriate circumstances, to embrace an alternative to the *Katz* Test. As Justice Scalia explained in his opinion in *Jones*:

> Fourth Amendment rights do not rise or fall with the *Katz* formulation. [F]or most of our history the Fourth Amendment was understood to embody a particular concern for government trespass upon the areas ("persons, houses, papers, and effects") it enumerates. *Katz* did not repudiate that understanding.

Later in his *Jones* opinion, Justice Scalia again emphasized the point, noting that "the *Katz* reasonable-expectation-of-privacy test has been *added to*, not *substituted for*, the common-law trespassory test."

In both *Jones* and *Jardines*, a majority of the Justices were willing to use an updated version of what Scalia referred to as the "common-law trespassory test" to determine whether a search had occurred within the meaning of the Fourth Amendment. In *Jones*, a majority of the Court agreed that a search occurs when "the Government obtains information by physically intruding on a constitutionally protected area." And in *Jardines*, a different majority, quoting *Jones*, agreed that "[w]hen the Government obtains information by physically intruding on persons, houses, papers, or effects, a 'search' within the original meaning of the Fourth Amendment has undoubtedly occurred."

Not all of the Justices were comfortable with the "Physical Intrusion Test" used by the majorities in *Jones* and *Jardines*. Much of this discomfort seems to stem from the fact that the Physical Intrusion Test looks a lot like the old—and discredited—approach used in *Olmstead v. U.S.*, 277 U.S. 438 (1928), in which the Court rejected the defendant's claim that the interception of his phone conversations amounted to a search. Adopting a strict textual interpretation of the Fourth Amendment, the Court in *Olmstead* held that a search requires an "actual physical invasion" of "material things—the person, the house, his papers, or his effects." Because Olmstead suffered no "actual physical invasion of his house or curtilage," and because the police intercepted not "material things" but only intangible "projected voices" on telephone wires, there was no search.

At first blush, *Jones* and *Jardines* appeared to resurrect *Olmstead*'s cramped interpretation of the Fourth Amendment. In both cases, the majority held that a search had occurred because the *Olmstead* requirements were met: Police physically intruded on material things explicitly protected by the Fourth Amendment—Jones' vehicle (his "effect") and Jardines' front porch (his "house"). But *Jones* and *Jardines* departed from the *Olmstead* standard in one essential respect: While both cases held that a physical intrusion on a constitutionally protected material thing is *sufficient* to constitute a search, neither case held, as *Olmstead* did, that a physical intrusion on a constitutionally protected material thing is *necessary* to constitute a search. Indeed, both *Jones* and *Jardines* made it clear that the Physical Intrusion Test was intended to complement the *Katz* Test rather than replace it. As Justice Scalia explained in *Jones*, in response to Justice Alito's criticism of his approach: "[U]nlike the concurrence, which would make *Katz* the *exclusive* test, we do not make trespass the exclusive test. Situations involving merely the transmission of electronic signals without trespass would *remain* subject to *Katz* analysis."

Despite the heated debate among the Justices of the Supreme Court, the Physical Intrusion Test may not produce any different results. Indeed, Justice Kagan's concurring opinion in *Jardines*—which was joined by Justices Ginsburg and Sotomayor—suggests that the results in many cases would essentially be the same whether the Court applies the *Jones* Physical Intrusion Test or the *Katz* Reasonable Expectations of Privacy Test because "property concepts and privacy concepts" are "so align[ed]."

While we now have two tests for determining whether a search has occurred under the Fourth Amendment, neither test seems particularly well-suited to deal with the tough questions on the horizon regarding the extent of the government's power to electronically monitor and record—without a warrant—an individual's movements, activities, and contacts. Much of this invasive monitoring can be accomplished with the GPS technology that is pre-installed on smartphones and in many cars, watches, and other devices that people use every day. Extensive monitoring is also possible with satellites and even with drones equipped with powerful cameras and microphones. The Physical Intrusion Test wouldn't bar any of this, since monitoring through a pre-installed GPS system or with a satellite or drone can be achieved without a physical intrusion.

The *Katz* Test doesn't appear to prevent various forms of electronic monitoring either, especially in light of several pre-digital age decisions holding that an individual has no reasonable expectation of privacy in his public movements or in information voluntarily disclosed to third parties. In *Katz* itself, the Supreme Court noted that "[w]hat a person knowingly exposes to the public, even in his own home or office, is not a subject of Fourth Amendment protection." Later, in *Smith v. Maryland*, 442 U.S. 735 (1979), which held that the use of pen register was not a search, the Court explained that even if the defendant "did harbor some subjective expectation that the phone numbers he dialed would remain private, this expectation is not one that society is prepared to recognize as reasonable" because "a person has no legitimate expectation of privacy in information he voluntarily turns over to third parties" like the telephone company. And in *U.S. v. Knotts*, 460 U.S. 276 (1983), which held that electronic monitoring of a person's public movements is not a search, the Court noted that "[a] person travelling in an automobile on public thoroughfares has no reasonable expectation of privacy in his movements from one place to another."

Today, through the use of computers, smartphones, and other devices, individuals knowingly and regularly expose their movements, contacts, activities, and purchases to cellular telephone and Internet providers, to social networks, to web search services, to online retailers, to friends and family, and to many others who are interested in such information for personal, professional, or commercial reasons. But the idea that police or the government can—without a warrant—continuously monitor and record our movements, contacts, activities, and purchases is profoundly disturbing to most people. The problem is that the language in *Katz*, *Smith*, and *Knotts* seems to permit precisely that kind of warrantless electronic monitoring.

The Supreme Court's sentiments appeared to change dramatically in 2012 when five Justices in *U.S. v. Jones*—Justices Alito, Ginsburg, Breyer, Kagan, and Sotomayor—agreed that "longer term GPS monitoring in investigations of most offenses impinges on expectations of privacy." That conclusion does not necessarily follow from an application of the *Katz* Test, nor can that conclusion be easily reconciled with the holdings in *Smith* and *Knotts* that there is no reasonable expectation of privacy in dialed phone numbers or public movements. As Justice Sotomayor explained in her concurring opinion in *Jones*:

> [I]t may be necessary to reconsider the premise that an individual has no reasonable expectation of privacy in information voluntarily disclosed to third parties. This approach is ill suited to the digital age, in which people reveal a great deal of information about themselves to third parties in the course of carrying out mundane tasks. People disclose the phone numbers

that they dial or text to their cellular providers; the URLs that they visit and the e-mail addresses with which they correspond to their Internet service providers; and the books, groceries, and medications they purchase to online retailers. I doubt that people would accept without complaint the warrantless disclosure to the Government of a list of every Web site they had visited in the last week, or month, or year. But whatever the societal expectations, they can attain constitutionally protected status only if our Fourth Amendment jurisprudence ceases to treat secrecy as a prerequisite for privacy. I would not assume that all information voluntarily disclosed to some member of the public for a limited purpose is, for that reason alone, disentitled to Fourth Amendment protection.

What Justice Sotomayor suggests is that our current Fourth Amendment doctrines are inadequate to address a wide array of technological threats to individual privacy in the twenty-first century and beyond. In order to deal with these threats, and fairly balance individual privacy against the needs of law enforcement, the Court may have to limit or overrule decisions like *Smith* and *Knotts*, modify or expand the *Jones* Physical Intrusion Test and the *Katz* Reasonable Expectations of Privacy Test, or perhaps even invent an entirely new test for defining Fourth Amendment searches beyond the two that we have now. Keep an eye on the Supreme Court's Fourth Amendment decisions in the years ahead— we may be in for some dramatic changes!

Two Tests for Determining Whether There Has Been a "Search"

1.   The *Katz* Reasonable Expectations of Privacy Test: Police perform a "search" within the meaning of the Fourth Amendment when they intrude into an area in which:

      a.   The defendant exhibited an actual, subjective expectation of privacy; and

      b.   Society is prepared to recognize that expectation as reasonable.

2.   The *Jones* Physical Intrusion Test: A search occurs when the government obtains information by physically intruding upon persons, houses, papers, or effects.

D. WHO CAN CHALLENGE A SEARCH?

A defendant may challenge a search in court and assert that evidence should be suppressed under the exclusionary rule only if the *defendant's own privacy rights* have been violated. This concept, sometimes referred to as the "standing" requirement, limits the ability of criminal defendants to challenge certain searches.

In the example at the beginning of this Chapter—where a police officer sneaks up behind Shannon Shady seated on a park bench and rummages through her purse in the hope of discovering illegal drugs— only Shannon (with the assistance of her attorney) may challenge the search and urge application of the exclusionary rule if illegal drugs are discovered and she is criminally prosecuted. If Shannon's best friend, Mary Miscreant, saw the officer rummaging through Shannon's purse, Mary may, of course, offer testimony in court, but Mary cannot assert rights on Shannon's behalf; Shannon herself must ask that the court exclude the drugs from her criminal trial.

But what if the drugs discovered in Shannon's purse actually belong to Mary? Suppose Mary had asked Shannon to hold the drugs for her, and Shannon had foolishly agreed. Let's further suppose that Mary Miscreant—and not Shannon Shady—has been criminally charged because only Mary's fingerprints were found on the bag of drugs and the prosecutors believed Shannon when she told them that the drugs didn't belong to her. Will Mary be able to successfully argue that the search was illegal, and that the drugs should be suppressed under the exclusionary rule? Probably not. Under the *Katz* Test, it's unlikely that Mary will be able to show that *she herself* had a reasonable expectation of privacy in Shannon's purse. Similarly, under the *Jones* Physical Intrusion Test, Mary won't be able to demonstrate that the police physically intruded into *her* person, house, papers, or effects.

In reviewing the Supreme Court's pronouncements with regard to the standing requirement, be sure to take note of the general principles as well as the more specific rules limiting the ability of home visitors and car passengers to challenge a search. Beyond the legal doctrines, there is also a practical rule—set forth at the end of this Chapter—that you may wish to remember.

1. GENERAL PRINCIPLES REGARDING STANDING

The Supreme Court broadly defined the standing requirement in an early pre-*Katz* case, *Jones v. U.S.* (Try not to confuse this case, *Jones v. U.S.*, with the 2012 case, *U.S. v. Jones*, that involved GPS monitoring and gave rise to the *Jones* Physical Intrusion Test.)

JONES V. U.S.

362 U.S. 257 (1960)

The defendant was staying at a friend's apartment when police arrived and searched it, discovering narcotics and related paraphernalia belonging to the defendant. When the defendant asked the trial court to suppress the incriminating evidence, the government argued that he lacked standing to challenge the search because he had not claimed ownership of the narcotics, nor had he asserted any significant property interest in the apartment beyond that of an invitee or guest. The Court said that a person "aggrieved by an unlawful search or seizure" had standing to challenge it:

> In order to qualify as a "person aggrieved by an unlawful search and seizure" one must have been a victim of a search or seizure, one against whom the search was directed, as distinguished from one who claims prejudice only through the use of evidence gathered as a consequence of a search or seizure directed at someone else.

The Court concluded that the defendant could, in fact, challenge the search because he was legitimately on the premises where the search occurred:

> Anyone legitimately on premises where a search occurs may challenge its legality by way of a motion to suppress, when its fruits are proposed to be used against him. This would, of course, not avail those who, by virtue of their wrongful presence, cannot invoke the privacy of the premises searched. As [Jones'] testimony established [his friend's] consent to his presence in the apartment, he was entitled to have the merits of his motion to suppress adjudicated.

The broad standard announced in *Jones* would actually seem to provide Mary Miscreant with the requisite standing to challenge the search of Shannon Shady's purse. Using the language in the 1960 *Jones* decision, Mary would argue that the drugs were "legitimately on the premises" of Shannon's purse since they were there with Shannon's permission, just as Jones was "legitimately on the premises" of his friend's apartment, since he was there with his friend's permission. While that argument might have worked shortly after *Jones* was decided in 1960, it is unlikely to prevail today, since the Supreme Court has tightened its approach to standing after *Katz* was decided. In *Rakas v. Illinois*, the Court held that a defendant cannot challenge a search and claim the benefit of the exclusionary rule merely because she is "aggrieved" by an illegal search or legitimately on the searched premises; instead, the defendant must show that *her own* Fourth Amendment rights were violated.

RAKAS V. ILLINOIS
439 U.S. 128 (1978)

JUSTICE REHNQUIST delivered the opinion of the Court.

Petitioners were convicted of armed robbery in the Circuit Court of Kankakee County, Ill., and their convictions were affirmed on appeal. At their trial, the prosecution offered into evidence a sawed-off rifle and rifle shells that had been seized by police during a search of an automobile in which petitioners had been passengers. Neither petitioner is the owner of the automobile and neither has ever asserted that he owned the rifle or shells seized. The Illinois Appellate Court held that petitioners lacked standing to object to the allegedly unlawful search and seizure and denied their motion to suppress the evidence. We granted certiorari in light of the obvious importance of the issues raised to the administration of criminal justice, and now affirm.

I

Because we are not here concerned with the issue of probable cause, a brief description of the events leading to the search of the automobile will suffice. A police officer on a routine patrol received a radio call notifying him of a robbery of a clothing store in Bourbonnais, Ill., and describing the getaway car. Shortly thereafter, the officer spotted an automobile which he thought might be the getaway car. After following the car for some time and after the arrival of assistance, he and several other officers stopped the vehicle. The occupants of the automobile, petitioners and two female companions, were ordered out of the car and, after the occupants had left the car, two officers searched the interior of the vehicle. They discovered a box of rifle shells in the glove compartment, which had been locked, and a sawed-off rifle under the front passenger seat. After discovering the rifle and the shells, the officers took petitioners to the station and placed them under arrest.

Before trial petitioners moved to suppress the rifle and shells seized from the car on the ground that the search violated the Fourth and Fourteenth Amendments. They conceded that they did not own the automobile and were simply passengers; the owner of the car had been the driver of the vehicle at the time of the search. Nor did they assert that they owned the rifle or the shells seized. The prosecutor challenged petitioners' standing to object to the lawfulness of the search of the car because neither the car, the shells nor the rifle belonged to them. The trial court agreed that petitioners lacked standing and denied the motion to suppress the evidence. In view of this holding, the court did not determine whether there was probable cause for the search and seizure. On appeal after petitioners' conviction, the Appellate Court of Illinois, Third Judicial District, affirmed the trial court's denial of petitioners' motion to suppress because it held that "without a proprietary or other similar interest in an automobile, a mere passenger therein lacks standing to challenge the legality of the search of the vehicle." The court stated: "We believe that defendants failed to establish any prejudice to their own constitutional rights because they were not persons aggrieved by the unlawful search and seizure. They wrongly seek to establish prejudice only through the use of evidence gathered as a consequence of a search and seizure directed at someone else and fail to prove an invasion of their own privacy." The Illinois Supreme Court denied petitioners leave to appeal.

II

Petitioners first urge us to relax or broaden the rule of standing enunciated in *Jones v. U.S.*, 362 U.S. 257 (1960), so that any criminal defendant at whom a search was "directed" would have standing to contest the legality of that search and object to the admission at trial of evidence obtained as a result of the search. Alternatively, petitioners argue that they have standing to object to the search under *Jones* because they were "legitimately on the premises" at the time of the search.

The concept of standing discussed in *Jones* focuses on whether the person seeking to challenge the legality of a search as a basis for suppressing evidence was himself the "victim" of the search or seizure. Adoption of the so-called "target" theory advanced by petitioners would in effect permit a defendant to assert that a violation of the Fourth Amendment rights of a third party entitled him to have evidence suppressed at his trial. If we reject petitioners' request for a broadened rule of standing such as this, and reaffirm the holding of *Jones* and other cases that Fourth Amendment rights are personal rights that may not be asserted vicariously, we will have occasion to re-examine the "standing" terminology emphasized in *Jones*. For we are not at all sure that the determination of a motion to suppress is materially aided by labeling the inquiry identified in *Jones* as one of standing, rather than simply recognizing it as one involving the substantive question of whether or not the proponent of the motion to suppress has had his own Fourth Amendment rights infringed by the search and seizure which he seeks to challenge. We shall therefore consider in turn petitioners' target theory, the necessity for continued adherence to the notion of standing discussed in *Jones* as a concept that is theoretically distinct from the merits of a defendant's Fourth Amendment claim, and, finally, the proper disposition of petitioners' ultimate claim in this case.

A

We decline to extend the rule of standing in Fourth Amendment cases in the manner suggested by petitioners. A person who is aggrieved by an illegal search and seizure only through the introduction of damaging evidence secured by a search of a third person's premises or property has not had any of his Fourth Amendment rights infringed. And since the exclusionary rule is an attempt to effectuate the guarantees of the Fourth Amendment, it is proper to permit only defendants whose Fourth Amendment rights have been violated to benefit from the rule's protections. There is no reason to think that a party whose rights have been infringed will not, if evidence is used against him, have ample motivation to move to suppress it. Even if such a person is not a defendant in the action, he may be able to recover damages for the violation of his Fourth Amendment rights, or seek redress under state law for invasion of privacy or trespass.

Each time the exclusionary rule is applied it exacts a substantial social cost for the vindication of Fourth Amendment rights. Relevant and reliable evidence is kept from the trier of fact and the search for truth at trial is deflected. Since our cases generally have held that one whose Fourth Amendment rights are violated may successfully suppress evidence obtained in the course of an illegal search and seizure, misgivings as to the benefit of enlarging the class of persons who may invoke that rule are properly considered when deciding whether to expand standing to assert Fourth Amendment violations.

B

Had we accepted petitioners' request to allow persons other than those whose own Fourth Amendment rights were violated by a challenged search and seizure to suppress evidence obtained in the course of such police activity, it would be appropriate to retain *Jones*' use of standing in Fourth Amendment analysis. Under petitioners' target theory, a court could determine that a defendant had standing to invoke the exclusionary rule without having to inquire into the substantive question of whether the challenged search or seizure violated the Fourth Amendment rights of that particular defendant. However, having rejected petitioners' target theory and reaffirmed the principle that the rights assured by the Fourth Amendment are personal rights, which may be enforced by exclusion of evidence only at the instance of one whose own protection was infringed by the search and seizure, the question necessarily arises whether it serves any useful analytical purpose to consider this principle a matter of standing, distinct from the merits of a defendant's Fourth Amendment claim. We can think of no decided cases of this Court that would have come out differently had we concluded, as we do now, that the type of standing requirement discussed in *Jones* and reaffirmed today is more properly subsumed under substantive Fourth Amendment doctrine. Rigorous application of the principle that the rights secured by this Amendment are personal, in place of a notion of "standing," will produce no additional situations in which evidence must be excluded. The inquiry under either approach is the same. But we think the better analysis forthrightly focuses on the extent of a particular defendant's rights under the Fourth Amendment, rather than on any theoretically separate, but invariably intertwined concept of standing. The Court in *Jones* also may have been aware that there was a certain artificiality in analyzing this question in terms of standing because in at least three separate places in its opinion the Court placed that term within quotation marks.

It should be emphasized that nothing we say here casts the least doubt on cases which recognize that, as a general proposition, the issue of standing involves two inquiries: first, whether the proponent of a particular legal right has alleged "injury in fact," and, second, whether the proponent is asserting his own legal rights and interests rather than basing his claim for relief upon the rights of third parties. But this Court's long history of insistence that Fourth Amendment rights are personal in nature has already answered many of these traditional standing inquiries, and we think that definition of those rights is more properly placed within the purview of substantive Fourth Amendment law than within that of standing.

Analyzed in these terms, the question is whether the challenged search or seizure violated the Fourth Amendment rights of a criminal defendant who seeks to exclude the evidence obtained during it. That inquiry in turn requires a determination of whether the disputed search and seizure has infringed an interest of the defendant which the Fourth Amendment was designed to protect. We are under no illusion that by dispensing with the rubric of standing used in *Jones* we have rendered any simpler the determination of whether the proponent of a motion to suppress is entitled to contest the legality of a search and seizure. But by frankly recognizing that this aspect of the analysis belongs more properly under the heading of substantive Fourth Amendment doctrine than under the heading of standing, we think the decision of this issue will rest on sounder logical footing.

C

Here petitioners, who were passengers occupying a car which they neither owned nor leased, seek to analogize their position to that of the defendant in *Jones v. U.S.* In *Jones,* petitioner was present at the time of the search of an apartment which was owned by a friend. The friend had given Jones permission to use the apartment and a key to it, with which Jones had admitted himself on the day of the search. He had a suit and shirt at the apartment and had slept there "maybe a night," but his home was elsewhere. At the time of the search, Jones was the only occupant of the apartment because the lessee was away for a period of several days. Under these circumstances, this Court stated that while one wrongfully on the premises could not move to suppress evidence obtained as a result of searching them, "anyone legitimately on premises where a search occurs may challenge its legality." Petitioners argue that their occupancy of the automobile in question was comparable to that of Jones in the apartment and that they therefore have standing to contest the legality of the search—or as we have rephrased the inquiry, that they, like Jones, had their Fourth Amendment rights violated by the search.

We do not question the conclusion in *Jones* that the defendant in that case suffered a violation of his personal Fourth Amendment rights if the search in question was unlawful. Nonetheless, we believe that the phrase "legitimately on premises" coined in *Jones* creates too broad a gauge for measurement of Fourth Amendment rights. For example, applied literally, this statement would permit a casual visitor who has never seen, or been permitted to visit, the basement of another's house to object to a search of the basement if the visitor happened to be in the kitchen of the house at the time of the search. Likewise, a casual visitor who walks into a house one minute before a search of the house commences and leaves one minute after the search ends would be able to contest the legality of the search. The first visitor would have absolutely no interest or legitimate expectation of privacy in the basement, the second would have none in the house, and it advances no purpose served by the Fourth Amendment to permit either of them to object to the lawfulness of the search.[11]

We think that *Jones* on its facts merely stands for the unremarkable proposition that a person can have a legally sufficient interest in a place other than his own home so that the Fourth Amendment protects him from unreasonable governmental intrusion into that place. In defining the scope of that interest, we adhere to the view expressed in *Jones* and echoed in later cases that arcane distinctions developed in property and tort law between guests, licensees, invitees, and the like, ought not to control. But the *Jones* statement that a person need only be "legitimately on premises" in order to challenge the validity of the search of a dwelling place cannot be taken in its full sweep beyond the facts of that case.

Katz v. U.S., 389 U.S. 347 (1967), provides guidance in defining the scope of the interest protected by the Fourth Amendment. In the course of repudiating the doctrine derived from *Olmstead v. U.S.*, 277 U.S. 438 (1928), that if police officers had not been guilty of a common-law trespass they were not prohibited by the Fourth Amendment from eavesdropping, the Court in *Katz* held that capacity to claim the protection of the Fourth Amendment depends not upon a property right in the invaded place but upon whether the person who claims the protection of the Amendment has a legitimate expectation of privacy in the invaded place. Viewed in this manner, the holding in *Jones* can best be explained by the fact that Jones had a legitimate expectation of privacy in the premises he was using and therefore could claim the protection of the Fourth Amendment with respect to a governmental invasion of those premises, even though

---

[11] This is not to say that such visitors could not contest the lawfulness of the seizure of evidence or the search if their own property were seized during the search.

his "interest" in those premises might not have been a recognized property interest at common law.

D

Judged by the foregoing analysis, petitioners' claims must fail. They asserted neither a property nor a possessory interest in the automobile, nor an interest in the property seized. And as we have previously indicated, the fact that they were "legitimately on the premises" in the sense that they were in the car with the permission of its owner is not determinative of whether they had a legitimate expectation of privacy in the particular areas of the automobile searched. It is unnecessary for us to decide here whether the same expectations of privacy are warranted in a car as would be justified in a dwelling place in analogous circumstances. We have on numerous occasions pointed out that cars are not to be treated identically with houses or apartments for Fourth Amendment purposes. But here petitioners' claim is one which would fail even in an analogous situation in a dwelling place, since they made no showing that they had any legitimate expectation of privacy in the glove compartment or area under the seat of the car in which they were merely passengers. Like the trunk of an automobile, these are areas in which a passenger *qua* passenger simply would not normally have a legitimate expectation of privacy.

Jones v. U.S. and *Katz v. U.S.* involved significantly different factual circumstances. Jones not only had permission to use the apartment of his friend, but also had a key to the apartment with which he admitted himself on the day of the search and kept possessions in the apartment. Except with respect to his friend, Jones had complete dominion and control over the apartment and could exclude others from it. Likewise in *Katz*, the defendant occupied the telephone booth, shut the door behind him to exclude all others and paid the toll, "which entitled him to assume that the words he uttered into the mouthpiece would not be broadcast to the world." Katz and Jones could legitimately expect privacy in the areas which were the subject of the search and seizure each sought to contest. No such showing was made by these petitioners with respect to those portions of the automobile which were searched and from which incriminating evidence was seized.

JUSTICE WHITE, with whom JUSTICE BRENNAN, JUSTICE MARSHALL, and JUSTICE STEVENS join, dissenting.

The Court today holds that the Fourth Amendment protects property, not people, and specifically that a legitimate occupant of an automobile may not invoke the exclusionary rule and challenge a search of that vehicle unless he happens to own or have a possessory interest in it. Though professing to acknowledge that the primary purpose of the Fourth Amendment's prohibition of unreasonable searches is the protection of privacy—not property—the Court nonetheless effectively ties the application of the Fourth Amendment and the exclusionary rule in this situation to property law concepts. Insofar as passengers are concerned, the Court's opinion today declares an "open season" on automobiles. However unlawful stopping and searching a car may be, absent a possessory or ownership interest, no "mere" passenger may object, regardless of his relationship to the owner. Because the majority's conclusion has no support in the Court's controlling decisions, in the logic of the Fourth Amendment, or in common sense, I must respectfully dissent. If the Court is troubled by the practical impact of the exclusionary rule, it should face the issue of that rule's continued validity squarely instead of distorting other doctrines in an attempt to reach what are perceived as the correct results in specific cases.

It is true that the Court asserts that it is not limiting the Fourth Amendment bar against unreasonable searches to the protection of property rights, but in reality it is doing exactly that. Petitioners were in a private place with the permission of the owner, but the Court states that that is not sufficient to establish entitlement to a legitimate expectation of privacy. But if that is not sufficient, what would be? We are not told, and it is hard to imagine anything short of a property interest that would satisfy the majority. Insofar as the Court's rationale is concerned, no passenger in an automobile, without an ownership or possessory interest and regardless of his relationship to the owner, may claim Fourth Amendment protection against illegal stops and searches of the automobile in which he is rightfully present. The Court approves the result in *Jones*, but it fails to give any explanation why the facts in *Jones* differ, in a fashion material to the Fourth Amendment, from the facts here.[15] More importantly, how is the Court able to avoid answering the question why presence in a private place with the owner's permission is insufficient?

The Court's holding is contrary not only to our past decisions and the logic of the Fourth Amendment but also to the everyday expectations of privacy that we all share. Because of that, it is unworkable in all the various situations that arise in real life. If the owner of the car had not only invited petitioners to join her but had said to them, "I give you a temporary possessory interest in my vehicle so that you will share the right to privacy that the Supreme Court says that I own," then apparently the majority would reverse. But people seldom say such things, though

---

[15] Jones had permission to use the apartment, had slept in it one night, had a key, had left a suit and a shirt there, and was the only occupant at the time of the search. Petitioners here had permission to be in the car and were occupying it at the time of the search. Thus the only distinguishing fact is that Jones could exclude others from the apartment by using his friend's key. But petitioners and their friend the owner had excluded others by entering the automobile and shutting the doors. Petitioners did not need a key because the owner was present. Similarly, the Court attempts to distinguish *Katz* on the theory that Katz had "shut the door behind him to exclude all others," but petitioners here did exactly the same. The car doors remained closed until the police ordered them opened at gunpoint.

they may mean their invitation to encompass them if only they had thought of the problem. If the nonowner were the spouse or child of the owner, would the Court recognize a sufficient interest? If so, would distant relatives somehow have more of an expectation of privacy than close friends? What if the nonowner were driving with the owner's permission? Would nonowning drivers have more of an expectation of privacy than mere passengers? What about a passenger in a taxicab? *Katz* expressly recognized protection for such passengers. Why should Fourth Amendment rights be present when one pays a cabdriver for a ride but be absent when one is given a ride by a friend?

The distinctions the Court would draw are based on relationships between private parties, but the Fourth Amendment is concerned with the relationship of one of those parties to the government. Divorced as it is from the purpose of the Fourth Amendment, the Court's essentially property-based rationale can satisfactorily answer none of the questions posed above. That is reason enough to reject it. The *Jones* rule is relatively easily applied by police and courts; the rule announced today will not provide law enforcement officials with a bright line between the protected and the unprotected. Only rarely will police know whether one private party has or has not been granted a sufficient possessory or other interest by another private party. Surely in this case the officers had no such knowledge. The Court's rule will ensnare defendants and police in needless litigation over factors that should not be determinative of Fourth Amendment rights.

More importantly, the ruling today undercuts the force of the exclusionary rule in the one area in which its use is most certainly justified—the deterrence of bad-faith violations of the Fourth Amendment. This decision invites police to engage in patently unreasonable searches every time an automobile contains more than one occupant. Should something be found, only the owner of the vehicle, or of the item, will have standing to seek suppression, and the evidence will presumably be usable against the other occupants. The danger of such bad faith is especially high in cases such as this one where the officers are only after the passengers and can usually infer accurately that the driver is the owner. The suppression remedy for those owners in whose vehicles something is found and who are charged with crime is small consolation for all those owners *and* occupants whose privacy will be needlessly invaded by officers following mistaken hunches not rising to the level of probable cause but operated on in the knowledge that someone in a crowded car will probably be unprotected if contraband or incriminating evidence happens to be found. After this decision, police will have little to lose by unreasonably searching vehicles occupied by more than one person.

Of course, most police officers will decline the Court's invitation and will continue to do their jobs as best they can in accord with the Fourth Amendment. But the very purpose of the Bill of Rights was to answer the justified fear that governmental agents cannot be left totally to their own devices, and the Bill of Rights is enforceable in the courts because human experience teaches that not all such officials will otherwise adhere to the stated precepts. Some policemen simply do act in bad faith, even if for understandable ends, and some deterrent is needed. In the rush to limit the applicability of the exclusionary rule somewhere, anywhere, the Court ignores precedent, logic, and common sense to exclude the rule's operation from situations in which, paradoxically, it is justified and needed.

Rakas dispenses with a separate inquiry into "standing" to determine whether a defendant can challenge a search and claim the protection of the exclusionary rule. Instead, the proper question is whether the defendant's own Fourth Amendment rights were violated. As *Rakas* notes, that inquiry is already implicit in the *Katz* Test, since the police do not perform a "search" unless they violate the *defendant's* legitimate expectations of privacy.

In *Rawlings v. Kentucky*, the Supreme Court applied the principles announced in *Rakas* in a case involving facts similar to the hypothetical presented earlier, in which Shannon Shady agrees to hold drugs belonging to Mary Miscreant.

RAWLINGS V. KENTUCKY
448 U.S. 98 (1980)

David Rawlings was one of several visitors at a house when it was searched by police. During the search, the police asked one of the visitors, Vanessa Cox, to empty the contents of her purse. The purse contained 1,800 tablets of LSD and various other drugs. Rawlings immediately claimed ownership of the drugs in Cox's purse. The Supreme Court held that Rawlings could not challenge the search of Cox's purse:

> Petitioner bears the burden of proving not only that the search of Cox's purse was illegal, but also that he had a legitimate expectation of privacy in that purse. At the time petitioner dumped thousands of dollars worth of illegal drugs into Cox's purse, he had known her for only a few days. According to Cox's uncontested testimony, petitioner had never sought or received access to her purse prior to that sudden bailment. Nor did petitioner have any right to exclude other persons from access to Cox's purse. The record also contains a frank admission by petitioner that he had no subjective

expectation that Cox's purse would remain free from governmental intrusion.

Petitioner contends nevertheless that, because he claimed ownership of the drugs in Cox's purse, he should be entitled to challenge the search regardless of his expectation of privacy. We disagree. While petitioner's ownership of the drugs is undoubtedly one fact to be considered in this case, *Rakas* emphatically rejected the notion that "arcane" concepts of property law ought to control the ability to claim the protections of the Fourth Amendment. Had petitioner placed his drugs in plain view, he would still have owned them, but he could not claim any legitimate expectation of privacy. Prior to *Rakas*, petitioner might have been given "standing" in such a case to challenge a "search" that netted those drugs but probably would have lost his claim on the merits. After *Rakas*, the two inquiries merge into one: whether governmental officials violated any legitimate expectation of privacy held by petitioner. We find no reason to overturn the lower court's conclusion that petitioner had no legitimate expectation of privacy in Cox's purse at the time of the search.

Who Can Challenge a Search?: General Principles

A criminal defendant cannot challenge a search and claim the protection of the exclusionary rule simply because she was "aggrieved" by the search or legitimately on the searched premises. A criminal defendant can challenge a search and invoke the exclusionary rule only if the police violated *her own* legitimate expectations of privacy under the Fourth Amendment.

---

2. HOME VISITORS

Under what circumstances is a visitor entitled to an expectation of privacy in his host's home? Suppose a pizza delivery man asks a homeowner to use her restroom. The friendly homeowner agrees, and while inside the restroom, the delivery man snorts some cocaine. A police officer, standing just outside the bathroom window but inside the curtilage of the home, observes this conduct and arrests the delivery man when he emerges from the home. When the delivery man is prosecuted for use and possession of drugs, can he move to suppress the officer's testimony about her observations through the restroom window? More specifically, can the pizza delivery man successfully argue that *his own* reasonable expectations of privacy were violated by the officer's actions in entering the curtilage of the home and observing him through the restroom window?

Two Supreme Court decisions help to answer that question. In the first, *Minnesota v. Olson*, the Court held that an overnight social guest may challenge a search of the home he is visiting and claim the protection of the exclusionary rule.

MINNESOTA V. OLSON
495 U.S. 91 (1990)

JUSTICE WHITE delivered the opinion of the Court.

The police in this case made a warrantless, nonconsensual entry into a house where respondent Robert Olson was an overnight guest and arrested him. The issue is whether the arrest violated Olson's Fourth Amendment rights. We hold that it did.

I

Shortly before 6 a.m. on Saturday, July 18, 1987, a lone gunman robbed an Amoco gasoline station in Minneapolis, Minnesota, and fatally shot the station manager. A police officer heard the police dispatcher report and suspected Joseph Ecker. The officer and his partner drove immediately to Ecker's home, arriving at about the same time that an Oldsmobile arrived. The driver of the Oldsmobile took evasive action, and the car spun out of control and came to a stop. Two men fled the car on foot. Ecker, who was later identified as the gunman, was captured shortly thereafter inside his home. The second man escaped.

Inside the abandoned Oldsmobile, police found a sack of money and the murder weapon. They also found a title certificate with the name Rob Olson crossed out as a secured party, a letter addressed to a Roger R. Olson of 3151 Johnson Street, and a videotape rental receipt made out to Rob Olson and dated two days earlier. The police verified that a Robert Olson lived at 3151 Johnson Street.

The next morning, Sunday, July 19, a woman identifying herself as Dianna Murphy called the police and said that a man by the name of Rob drove the car in which the gas station killer left the scene and that Rob was planning to leave town by bus. About noon, the same woman called again, gave her address and phone number, and said that a man named Rob had told a Maria and two other women, Louanne and Julie, that he was the driver in the Amoco robbery. The caller stated that Louanne was Julie's mother and that the two women lived at 2406 Fillmore Northeast. The detective-in-charge who took the second phone call sent police officers to 2406 Fillmore to check out Louanne and Julie. When police arrived they determined that the dwelling was a duplex and that Louanne Bergstrom and her daughter Julie lived in the upper unit but were not home. Police spoke to Louanne's mother, Helen Niederhoffer, who lived in the lower unit. She confirmed that a Rob Olson had been staying upstairs but was not then in the unit. She promised to call the police when Olson returned. At 2 p.m., a pickup order, or "probable cause arrest bulletin," was issued for Olson's arrest. The police were instructed to stay away from the duplex.

At approximately 2:45 p.m., Niederhoffer called police and said Olson had returned. The detective-in-charge instructed police officers to go to the house and surround it. He then telephoned Julie from headquarters and told her Rob should come out of the house. The detective heard a male voice say, "tell them I left." Julie stated that Rob had left, whereupon at 3 p.m. the detective ordered the police to enter the house. Without seeking permission and with weapons drawn, the police entered the upper unit and found respondent hiding in a closet. Less than an hour after his arrest, respondent made an inculpatory statement at police headquarters.

The Hennepin County trial court held a hearing and denied respondent's motion to suppress his statement. The statement was admitted into evidence at Olson's trial, and he was convicted on one count of first-degree murder, three counts of armed robbery, and three counts of second-degree assault. On appeal, the Minnesota Supreme Court reversed. The court ruled that respondent had a sufficient interest in the Bergstrom home to challenge the legality of his warrantless arrest there, that the arrest was illegal because there were no exigent circumstances to justify a warrantless entry, and that respondent's statement was tainted by that illegality and should have been suppressed. Because the admission of the statement was not harmless beyond reasonable doubt, the court reversed Olson's conviction and remanded for a new trial. We granted the State's petition for certiorari, and now affirm.

II

It was held in *Payton v. New York*, 445 U.S. 573 (1980), that a suspect should not be arrested in his house without an arrest warrant, even though there is probable cause to arrest him. The purpose of the decision was not to protect the person of the suspect but to protect his home from entry in the absence of a magistrate's finding of probable cause. In this case, the court below held that Olson's warrantless arrest was illegal because he had a sufficient connection with the premises to be treated like a householder. The State challenges that conclusion.

Since the decision in *Katz v. U.S.*, 389 U.S. 347 (1967), it has been the law that "capacity to claim the protection of the Fourth Amendment depends upon whether the person who claims the protection of the Amendment has a legitimate expectation of privacy in the invaded place." *Rakas v. Illinois*, 439 U.S. 128, 143 (1978). A subjective expectation of privacy is legitimate if it is one that society is prepared to recognize as reasonable.

The State argues that Olson's relationship to the premises does not satisfy the 12 factors which in its view determine whether a dwelling is a "home." Aside from the fact that it is based on the mistaken premise that a place must be one's "home" in order for one to have a legitimate expectation of privacy there, the State's proposed test is needlessly complex. We need go no further than to conclude, as we do, that Olson's status as an overnight guest is alone enough to show that he had an expectation of privacy in the home that society is prepared to recognize as reasonable.

As recognized by the Minnesota Supreme Court, the facts of this case are similar to those in *Jones v. U.S.*, 362 U.S. 257 (1960). In *Jones*, the defendant was arrested in a friend's apartment during the execution of a search warrant and sought to challenge the warrant as not supported by probable cause.

The Court ruled that Jones could challenge the search of the apartment because he was "legitimately on the premises." Although the "legitimately on the premises" standard was rejected in *Rakas* as too broad, the *Rakas* Court explicitly reaffirmed the factual holding in *Jones*. *Rakas* thus recognized that, as an overnight guest, Jones was much more than just legitimately on the premises.

The distinctions relied on by the State between this case and *Jones* are not legally determinative. The State emphasizes that in this case Olson was never left alone in the duplex or given a key, whereas in *Jones* the owner of the apartment was away and Jones had a key with which he could come and go and admit and exclude others. These differences are crucial, it is argued, because in not disturbing the holding in *Jones* the Court in *Rakas* pointed out that while his host was away, Jones had complete dominion and control over the apartment and could exclude others from it. We do not understand *Rakas* however, to hold that an overnight guest can never have a legitimate expectation of privacy except when his host is away and he has a key, or that only when those facts are present may an overnight guest assert the unremarkable proposition that a person may have a sufficient interest in a place other than his home to enable him to be free in that place from unreasonable searches and seizures.

To hold that an overnight guest has a legitimate expectation of privacy in his host's home merely recognizes the everyday expectations of privacy that we all share. Staying overnight in another's home is a longstanding social custom that serves functions recognized as valuable by society. We stay in others' homes when we travel to a strange city for business or pleasure, when we visit our parents, children, or more distant relatives out of town, when we are in between jobs or homes, or when we house-sit for a friend. We will all be hosts and we will all be guests many times in our lives. From either perspective, we think that society recognizes that a houseguest has a legitimate expectation of privacy in his host's home.

From the overnight guest's perspective, he seeks shelter in another's home precisely because it provides him with privacy, a place where he and his possessions will not be disturbed by anyone but his host and those his host allows inside. We are at our most vulnerable when we are asleep because we cannot monitor our own safety or the security of our belongings. It is for this reason that, although we may spend all day in public places, when we cannot sleep in our own home we seek out another private place to sleep, whether it be a hotel room, or the home of a friend. Society expects at least as much privacy in these places as in a telephone booth.

That the guest has a host who has ultimate control of the house is not inconsistent with the guest having a legitimate expectation of privacy. The houseguest is there with the permission of his host, who is willing to share his house and his privacy with his guest. It is unlikely that the guest will be confined to a restricted area of the house; and when the host is away or asleep, the guest will have a measure of control over the premises. The host may admit or exclude from the house as he prefers, but it is unlikely that he will admit someone who wants to see or meet with the guest over the objection of the guest. On the other hand, few houseguests will invite others to visit them while they are guests without consulting their hosts; but the latter, who have the authority to exclude despite the wishes of the guest, will often be accommodating. The point is that hosts will more likely than not respect the privacy interests of their guests, who are entitled to a legitimate expectation of privacy despite the fact that they have no legal interest in the premises and do not have the legal authority to determine who may or may not enter the household. If the untrammeled power to admit and exclude were essential to Fourth Amendment protection, an adult daughter temporarily living in the home of her parents would have no legitimate expectation of privacy because her right to admit or exclude would be subject to her parents' veto.

Because respondent's expectation of privacy in the Bergstrom home was rooted in understandings that are recognized and permitted by society, it was legitimate, and respondent can claim the protection of the Fourth Amendment.

———————

In *Minnesota v. Carter*, the Supreme Court distinguished *Minnesota v. Olson* and held that a short-term business guest may not challenge a search of the home he is visiting and claim the protection of the exclusionary rule.

MINNESOTA V. CARTER
525 U.S. 83 (1998)

CHIEF JUSTICE REHNQUIST delivered the opinion of the Court.

Respondents and the lessee of an apartment were sitting in one of its rooms, bagging cocaine. While so engaged they were observed by a police officer, who looked through a drawn window blind. The Supreme Court of Minnesota held that the officer's viewing was a search that violated respondents' Fourth Amendment rights. We hold that no such violation occurred.

James Thielen, a police officer in the Twin Cities' suburb of Eagan, Minnesota, went to an apartment building to investigate a tip from a confidential informant. The informant said that he had walked by the window of a ground-floor apartment and had seen people putting a white powder into bags. The officer looked in the same window through a gap in the closed blind and observed the bagging operation for several minutes. He then notified headquarters, which began preparing affidavits for a search warrant while he returned to the apartment building. When two men left the building in a previously identified Cadillac, the police stopped the car. Inside were respondents Carter and Johns. As the police opened the door of the car to let Johns out, they observed a black, zippered pouch and a handgun, later determined to be loaded, on the vehicle's floor. Carter and Johns were arrested, and a later police search of the vehicle the next day discovered pagers, a scale, and 47 grams of cocaine in plastic sandwich bags.

After seizing the car, the police returned to Apartment 103 and arrested the occupant, Kimberly Thompson, who is not a party to this appeal. A search of the apartment pursuant to a warrant revealed cocaine residue on the kitchen table and plastic baggies similar to those found in the Cadillac. Thielen identified Carter, Johns, and Thompson as the three people he had observed placing the powder into baggies. The police later learned that while Thompson was the lessee of the apartment, Carter and Johns lived in Chicago and had come to the apartment for the sole purpose of packaging the cocaine. Carter and Johns had never been to the apartment before and were only in the apartment for approximately 2 1/2 hours. In return for the use of the apartment, Carter and Johns had given Thompson one-eighth of an ounce of the cocaine.

Carter and Johns were charged with conspiracy to commit a controlled substance crime in the first degree and aiding and abetting in a controlled substance crime in the first degree. They moved to suppress all evidence obtained from the apartment and the Cadillac, as well as to suppress several postarrest incriminating statements they had made. They argued that Thielen's initial observation of their drug packaging activities was an unreasonable search in violation of the Fourth

Amendment and that all evidence obtained as a result of this unreasonable search was inadmissible as fruit of the poisonous tree. The Minnesota trial court held that since, unlike the defendant in *Minnesota v. Olson*, 495 U.S. 91 (1990), Carter and Johns were not overnight social guests but temporary out-of-state visitors, they were not entitled to claim the protection of the Fourth Amendment against the government intrusion into the apartment. The trial court also concluded that Thielen's observation was not a search within the meaning of the Fourth Amendment. After a trial, Carter and Johns were each convicted of both offenses. The Minnesota Court of Appeals held that respondent Carter did not have "standing" to object to Thielen's actions because his claim that he was predominantly a social guest was "inconsistent with the only evidence concerning his stay in the apartment, which indicates that he used it for a business purpose—to package drugs." In a separate appeal, the Court of Appeals also affirmed Johns' conviction, without addressing what it termed the "standing" issue.

A divided Minnesota Supreme Court reversed, holding that respondents had "standing" to claim the protection of the Fourth Amendment because they had "a legitimate expectation of privacy in the invaded place." The court noted that even though "society does not recognize as valuable the task of bagging cocaine, we conclude that society does recognize as valuable the right of property owners or leaseholders to invite persons into the privacy of their homes to conduct a common task, be it legal or illegal activity. We, therefore, hold that respondents had standing to bring their motion to suppress the evidence gathered as a result of Thielen's observations." Based upon its conclusion that respondents had "standing" to raise their Fourth Amendment claims, the court went on to hold that Thielen's observation constituted a search of the apartment under the Fourth Amendment, and that the search was unreasonable. We granted certiorari, and now reverse.

The Minnesota courts analyzed whether respondents had a legitimate expectation of privacy under the rubric of "standing" doctrine, an analysis that this Court expressly rejected 20 years ago in *Rakas v. Illinois*, 439 U.S. 128 (1978). In that case, we held that automobile passengers could not assert the protection of the Fourth Amendment against the seizure of incriminating evidence from a vehicle where they owned neither the vehicle nor the evidence. Central to our analysis was the idea that in determining whether a defendant is able to show the violation of his (and not someone else's) Fourth Amendment rights, the "definition of those rights is more properly placed within the purview of substantive Fourth Amendment law than within that of standing." Thus, we held that in order to claim the protection of the Fourth Amendment, a defendant must demonstrate that he personally has an expectation of privacy in the place searched, and that his expectation is reasonable; *i.e.,* one that has "a source outside of the Fourth Amendment, either by reference to concepts of real or personal property law or to understandings that are recognized and permitted by society."

The [Fourth] Amendment protects persons against unreasonable searches of "their persons [and] houses" and thus indicates that the Amendment is a personal right that must be invoked by an individual. But the extent to which the Fourth Amendment protects people may depend upon where those people are. We held [in *Rakas*] that "capacity to claim the protection of the Fourth Amendment depends upon whether the person who claims the protection of the Amendment has a legitimate expectation of privacy in the invaded place."

The text of the Amendment suggests that its protections extend only to people in "their" houses. But we have held that in some circumstances a person may have a legitimate expectation of privacy in the house of someone else. In *Minnesota v. Olson*, for example, we decided that an overnight guest in a house had the sort of expectation of privacy that the Fourth Amendment protects.

In *Jones v. U.S.*, 362 U.S. 257 (1960), the defendant seeking to exclude evidence resulting from a search of an apartment had been given the use of the apartment by a friend. He had clothing in the apartment, had slept there "maybe a night," and at the time was the sole occupant of the apartment. But while the holding of *Jones*—that a search of the apartment violated the defendant's Fourth Amendment rights—is still valid, its statement that "anyone legitimately on the premises where a search occurs may challenge its legality," was expressly repudiated in *Rakas v. Illinois*. Thus, an overnight guest in a home may claim the protection of the Fourth Amendment, but one who is merely present with the consent of the householder may not.

Respondents here were obviously not overnight guests, but were essentially present for a business transaction and were only in the home a matter of hours. There is no suggestion that they had a previous relationship with Thompson, or that there was any other purpose to their visit. Nor was there anything similar to the overnight guest relationship in *Olson* to suggest a degree of acceptance into the household. While the apartment was a dwelling place for Thompson, it was for these respondents simply a place to do business.

Property used for commercial purposes is treated differently for Fourth Amendment purposes from residential property. "An expectation of privacy in commercial premises, however, is different from, and indeed less than, a similar expectation in an individual's home." *New York v. Burger*, 482 U.S. 691, 700 (1987). And while it was a "home" in which respondents were present, it was not their home.

If we regard the overnight guest in *Minnesota v. Olson* as typifying those who may claim the protection of the Fourth Amendment in the home of another, and one merely "legitimately on the premises" as typifying those who may not do so, the present case is obviously somewhere in between. But the purely commercial nature of the transaction engaged in here, the relatively short period of time on the premises, and the lack of any previous connection between respondents and the householder, all lead us to conclude that respondents' situation is closer to that of one simply permitted on the premises. We therefore hold that any search which may have occurred did not violate their Fourth Amendment rights.

Because we conclude that respondents had no legitimate expectation of privacy in the apartment, we need not decide whether the police officer's observation constituted a "search." The judgments of the Supreme Court of Minnesota are accordingly reversed, and the cause is remanded for proceedings not inconsistent with this opinion.

JUSTICE SCALIA, with whom JUSTICE THOMAS joins, concurring.

I join the opinion of the Court because I believe it accurately applies our recent case law, including *Minnesota v. Olson*. I write separately to express my view that that case law gives short shrift to the text of the Fourth Amendment, and to the well and long understood meaning of that text. Specifically, it leaps to apply the fuzzy standard of "legitimate expectation of privacy"—a consideration that is often relevant to whether a search or seizure covered by the Fourth Amendment is "unreasonable"—to the threshold question whether a search or seizure covered by the Fourth Amendment *has occurred*. If that latter question is addressed first and analyzed under the text of the Constitution as traditionally understood, the present case is not remotely difficult.

The Fourth Amendment protects "the right of the people to be secure in *their* persons, houses, papers, and effects, against unreasonable searches and seizures." It must be acknowledged that the phrase "their . . . houses" in this provision is, in isolation, ambiguous. It could mean "their respective houses," so that the protection extends to each person only in his *own* house. But it could also mean "their respective and each other's houses," so that each person would be protected even when visiting the house of someone else. As today's opinion for the Court suggests, however, it is not linguistically possible to give the provision the latter, expansive interpretation with respect to "houses" without giving it the same interpretation with respect to the nouns that are parallel to "houses"—"persons, papers, and effects"—which would give me a constitutional right not to have your person unreasonably searched. This is so absurd that it has to my knowledge never been contemplated. The obvious meaning of the provision is that *each* person has the right to be secure against unreasonable searches and seizures in *his own* person, house, papers, and effects.

The founding-era materials that I have examined confirm that this was the understood meaning. Of course this is not to say that the Fourth Amendment protects only the Lord of the Manor who holds his estate in fee simple. People call a house "their" home when legal title is in the bank, when they rent it, and even when they merely occupy it rent free— *so long as they actually live there.*

We went to the absolute limit of what text and tradition permit in *Minnesota v. Olson* when we protected a mere overnight guest against an unreasonable search of his hosts' apartment. But whereas it is plausible to regard a person's overnight lodging as at least his "temporary" residence, it is entirely impossible to give that characterization to an apartment that he uses to package cocaine. Respondents here were not searched in "their . . . house" under any interpretation of the phrase that bears the remotest relationship to the well-understood meaning of the Fourth Amendment.

JUSTICE GINSBURG, with whom JUSTICE STEVENS and JUSTICE SOUTER join, dissenting.

The Court's decision undermines not only the security of short-term guests, but also the security of the home resident herself. In my view, when a homeowner or lessee personally invites a guest into her home to share in a common endeavor, whether it be for conversation, to engage in leisure activities, or for business purposes licit or illicit, that guest should share his host's shelter against unreasonable searches and seizures.

I would here decide only the case of the homeowner who chooses to share the privacy of her home and her company with a guest, and would not reach classroom hypotheticals like the milkman or pizza deliverer.

My concern centers on an individual's choice to share her home and her associations there with persons she selects. Our decisions indicate that people have a reasonable expectation of privacy in their homes in part because they have the prerogative to exclude others. The power to exclude implies the power to include. Our Fourth Amendment decisions should reflect these complementary prerogatives.

A homedweller places her own privacy at risk, the Court's approach indicates, when she opens her home to others, uncertain whether the duration of their stay, their purpose, and their "acceptance into the household" will earn protection. Human frailty suggests that today's decision will tempt police to pry into private dwellings without warrant, to find evidence incriminating guests who do not rest there through the night. *Rakas* tolerates that temptation with respect to automobile searches. I see no impelling reason to extend this risk into the home.

Through the host's invitation, the guest gains a reasonable expectation of privacy in the home. *Minnesota v. Olson* so held with respect to an overnight guest. The logic of that decision extends to shorter term guests as well. Visiting the home of a friend, relative, or business associate, whatever the time of day, serves functions recognized as valuable by society. One need not remain overnight to anticipate privacy in another's home, a place where the guest and his possessions will not be disturbed by anyone but his host and those his host allows inside. In sum, when a homeowner chooses to share the privacy of her home and her company with a short-term guest, the twofold requirement emerging from prior decisions has been satisfied: Both host and guest have exhibited an actual (subjective) expectation of privacy; that expectation is one our society is prepared to recognize as reasonable.

As the Solicitor General acknowledged, the illegality of the host-guest conduct, the fact that they were partners in crime, would not alter the analysis. Indeed, it must be this way. If the illegality of the activity made constitutional an otherwise unconstitutional search, such Fourth Amendment protection, reserved for the innocent only, would have little force in regulating police behavior toward either the innocent or the guilty.

The Court's decision in this case veers sharply from the path marked in *Katz*. I do not agree that we have a more reasonable expectation of privacy when we place a business call to a person's home from a public telephone booth on the side of the street than when we actually enter that person's premises to engage in a common endeavor.

Read together, *Minnesota v. Olson* and *Minnesota v. Carter* make it clear that the ability of a guest to challenge a search of the home depends on the length and purpose of the visit. Under *Olson*, an overnight social guest has a legitimate expectation of privacy in his host's home, but under *Carter*, a short-term business guest does not. While the Supreme Court didn't specifically decide the issue, it seems fairly clear, based on *Olson* and *Carter*, that our hypothetical pizza delivery man—a short-term business guest—would be unable to challenge the illegal search of his customer's home, even though he was using the restroom with her permission.

Although a short-term business visitor cannot challenge a search of his host's home, it is important to remember that he may still object to a search of his *own person or effects* located within the home because he has a legitimate expectation of privacy in his person and personal effects that is entirely independent of any expectation of privacy he may (or may not) have in the host's home itself.

Who Can Challenge a Search?: Home Visitors

1.   An overnight social guest has a legitimate expectation of privacy in his host's home. Accordingly, an overnight social guest can challenge a search of the home he is visiting and may claim the protection of the exclusionary rule.

2.   A short-term business guest does not have a legitimate expectation of privacy in his host's home. Accordingly, a short-term business guest cannot challenge a search of the home he is visiting and may not claim the protection of the exclusionary rule.

3.   Although a short-term business guest cannot challenge a search of his host's home, he may still object to a search of his own person or effects located within the home because he has a legitimate expectation of privacy in his person and personal effects that is independent of any expectation of privacy he may (or may not) have in his host's home itself.

---

3.   CAR PASSENGERS

The *Rakas* decision itself makes it clear that a passenger who has neither a property nor possessory interest in a vehicle cannot challenge a search of the vehicle because the passenger lacks a legitimate expectation of privacy in the vehicle itself or in discrete areas of the vehicle such as the trunk or glove compartment. Thus, if the police stop a vehicle and illegally search it, the owner or driver can challenge the search and seek to have the evidence suppressed under the exclusionary rule, but if the evidence also implicates a passenger (who has neither a property nor possessory interest in the vehicle), the passenger cannot challenge the legality of the search and claim the protection of the exclusionary rule. The passenger may still, however, object to a search of her *own person or property* located within the car (a search of her pockets or purse, for example) because she still has a legitimate expectation of privacy in her person and personal effects that is entirely independent of any expectation of privacy she may (or may not) have in the vehicle itself.

While a passenger may be unable, under *Rakas*, to challenge a search of the vehicle, the passenger may still be able to succeed in suppressing evidence found within the vehicle by challenging the initial traffic stop. If the initial stop was illegal, evidence uncovered during a search of the vehicle may be declared inadmissible as "fruit of the poisonous tree." In *Brendlin v. California*, the Supreme Court held that when police make a traffic stop, any passengers in the car are "seized" along with the driver, and a passenger may therefore challenge the constitutionality of the stop.

BRENDLIN V. CALIFORNIA
551 U.S. 249 (2007)

Two officers pulled over a car with a valid temporary operating permit to verify that the permit matched the vehicle, even though there was nothing unusual about the temporary permit. As one officer asked the driver, Karen Simeroth, for her driver's license, he recognized that the passenger was Bruce Brendlin, a parole violator with an outstanding warrant for his arrest. The officers ordered Brendlin out of the vehicle and arrested him. In a search of Brendlin's person incident to the arrest, the officers found an orange syringe cap. The officers searched Simeroth, finding syringes and a plastic bag of marijuana, and arrested her. The officers then searched the car, finding tubing, a scale, and other items used to produce methamphetamine. Brendlin was charged with possession and manufacture of methamphetamine, and he moved to suppress the evidence obtained in the searches of his person and the car as fruits of an unconstitutional seizure, claiming that the officers lacked probable cause or reasonable suspicion to make the traffic stop.

In a unanimous decision, the Supreme Court held that Brendlin was "seized" from the moment Simeroth's car came to a halt on the side of the road, and he was therefore free to challenge the constitutionality of the initial traffic stop:

> When a police officer makes a traffic stop, the driver of the car is seized within the meaning of the Fourth Amendment. The question in this case is whether the same is true of a passenger. We hold that a passenger is seized as well and so may challenge the constitutionality of the stop.

Who Can Challenge a Search?: Car Passengers

1. A car passenger—one who has neither a property nor possessory interest in the vehicle—does not have a legitimate expectation of privacy in the car or in areas such as the trunk or glove compartment. Accordingly, the passenger cannot challenge a search of the car in which he is riding, nor can he claim the protection of the exclusionary rule.

2. While a car passenger—one who has neither a property nor possessory interest in the vehicle—cannot challenge a search of the car in which he is riding, he may still object to a search of his own person or effects located within the vehicle because he has a legitimate expectation of privacy in his person and personal effects that is independent of any expectation of privacy he may (or may not) have in the vehicle itself.

3. Although a car passenger cannot challenge a search of the vehicle in which he is riding, all occupants of a car are "seized" when the car is stopped by police. Thus, a passenger may challenge the constitutionality of the traffic stop, and if the stop is found to be illegal, evidence that was discovered during a search of the vehicle may be declared inadmissible as "fruit of the poisonous tree."

4. A PRACTICAL RULE

One of the great lessons of all of the Supreme Court's cases describing who may—and may not—challenge a search is that it's far easier to claim the protections of the Fourth Amendment and the exclusionary rule if incriminating evidence is found on your own person or property, rather than on the person or property of your friend or acquaintance. For example, if the police illegally search your home and discover your stash of drugs, you can challenge the search and ask that the evidence be suppressed because you have a legitimate expectation of privacy in your own home. But if your friend has graciously agreed to store your stash in his home or car, which is subsequently searched by the police, it's unlikely that you'll be able to show a legitimate expectation of privacy in your friend's home or car that would allow you to challenge the search. The technical rules that govern this example and that assist in determining whether a criminal defendant can challenge a search have all been set forth above. There is, however, a practical rule that you may wish to remember.

Who Can Challenge a Search?: The Practical Rule

Don't store your stash in your friend's home or car! Unless you're an overnight guest at the home or regularly using the car with your friend's permission, you probably don't enjoy a legitimate expectation of privacy in the home or the car, which means you can't challenge a police search—even if it's an illegal search—of the home or the car!

LEARN MORE WITH *LAW & ORDER*

The following episode of *Law & Order* ("Asylum," Season 2, Episode 4) was inspired by the Connecticut Supreme Court's decision in *Connecticut v. Mooney*, 218 Conn. 85 (1991). In *Mooney*, police learned that the defendant, a murder suspect, was homeless, and had been living under a highway bridge. Proceeding without a search warrant, police searched the area under the bridge and discovered a duffel bag and a closed cardboard box. Both items contained evidence linking Mooney to the murder. The Connecticut Supreme Court held that under the *Katz* Test, Mooney had a reasonable expectation of privacy in the duffel bag and the cardboard box that were found by the police within the area

Mooney considered his home. Because those items were searched without a warrant, the Connecticut Supreme Court ordered the evidence suppressed.

In the *Law & Order* episode, a man is stabbed to death and a diamond engagement ring is stolen from him. As the police investigate, they focus on a potential suspect, Christian "Lemonhead" Tatum. The police locate Tatum's room at a boarding house and search it, finding the diamond ring. After Tatum is apprehended, he tells the police that he assisted another man, James Polesky, in the commission of the crime. Tatum eventually leads the detectives to a clearing in Central Park where Polesky resides. The detectives conduct a search of the area, finding a knife—the weapon used in the murder—beneath a mattress. The knife is introduced into evidence at Polesky's trial, and he is convicted. With assistance from the American Civil Liberties Union, Polesky appeals, contending that the search of his "place of abode" violated the Fourth Amendment because the police lacked a warrant. The Supreme Court's decisions in *Katz v. U.S.*, 389 U.S. 347 (1967), and *Oliver v. U.S.*, 466 U.S. 170 (1984), are featured prominently in the arguments before the appellate court. As you watch the episode, consider two questions:

1.   Are there any other cases or arguments that the prosecution might have used to bolster its contention that Polesky had no reasonable expectation of privacy in the area where he lived in Central Park?

2.   How is the "standing" requirement—the question of whether a defendant can challenge a search and invoke the exclusionary rule—depicted in the episode?

The segments of the episode that depict the relevant Investigative Criminal Procedure issues appear at:

10:19 to 12:49; 15:07 to 17:27; 20:30 to 22:40; 26:34 to 27:24; 29:02 to 31:16; 33:55 to 42:29; 44:24 to 44:37

Law & Order **Episode**

"Asylum," Season 2, Episode 4

---

1.   Are there any other cases or arguments that the prosecution might have used to bolster its contention that Polesky had no reasonable expectation of privacy in the area where he lived in Central Park?

While prosecutor Ben Stone makes a good argument based on *Katz*, *Oliver*, and the public nature of the property where Polesky's belongings were located, his argument might have been even stronger had he cited *California v. Greenwood*, 486 U.S. 35 (1988). As you'll recall, the Supreme

Court held in *Greenwood* that police do not need a warrant to sift through trash left outside the curtilage of a home. The Court noted that it is not reasonable to expect privacy in garbage bags left at the curb because they are accessible to "animals, children, scavengers, snoops, and other members of the public." Although the police in the episode knew that the items in Central Park were Polesky's personal effects and not mere garbage, the items were, like Greenwood's trash, left out in a public location where anyone might have rifled through them.

2.   How is the "standing" requirement—the question of whether a defendant can challenge a search and invoke the exclusionary rule—depicted in the episode?

When the police searched Christian "Lemonhead" Tatum's room, they discovered a ring belonging to the murder victim. Later, when Tatum and James Polesky are charged with murder, the judge orders the ring suppressed in the prosecution's case against Tatum because police had no warrant when they searched his room, an area in which he plainly has a legitimate expectation of privacy. At Polesky's trial, prosecutor Ben Stone offers the ring as evidence against Polesky, but in response to an objection by Polesky's defense attorney, the judge declares it inadmissible. In frustration, Stone refers to the judge as an "idiot." Following Polesky's successful appeal, the prosecutors elect to retry him. This time, the judge recognizes his mistake and says that the prosecution will be able to introduce the ring into evidence against Polesky because he had no "standing" to object to the search of Tatum's room. There was no evidence that Polesky had ever even visited Tatum's room, so Polesky had no legitimate expectation of privacy in the room. Under the technical rules set forth above, Polesky was not an overnight guest in Tatum's room. Accordingly, the police did not violate any of *Polesky's* rights when they searched Tatum's room without a warrant, and Polesky could not, therefore, challenge the search and have the ring excluded. And under the practical rule described above, Polesky can't challenge the search and invoke the exclusionary rule with respect to the ring because he made the mistake of storing his "stash"—the ring—in his friend's room!

CHAPTER 4

PROBABLE CAUSE AND WARRANTS

■ ■ ■

Suppose a court, after analyzing some of the cases in Chapter 3, concludes that the police performed a "search" under the Fourth Amendment. What's next? The Fourth Amendment does not prohibit searches; it only bars "unreasonable" ones. So how does a court determine whether a search is unreasonable? The second part of the Fourth Amendment—known as the Warrant Clause—does appear to provide some guidance: "[N]o Warrants shall issue, but upon probable cause, supported by Oath or affirmation, and particularly describing the place to be searched, and the persons or things to be seized." The Fourth Amendment does *not* explicitly state that a warrant is required prior to a search or seizure, nor does it state that a warrant will render a search or seizure "reasonable." On the other hand, why would the framers of the Constitution put the Warrant Clause in the Fourth Amendment if they hadn't intended to say *something* about the relationship between warrants (or the lack thereof) and unreasonable searches and seizures?

The Supreme Court has long debated the relationship between the first part of the Fourth Amendment (the Unreasonableness Clause), barring "unreasonable searches and seizures," and the second part of the Amendment (the Warrant Clause), describing the requirements for issuance of a warrant. The Court has frequently said that a warrantless search is presumptively unreasonable, meaning the government has the burden of demonstrating its legality. At the same time, the Court has created numerous exceptions to the presumption of unreasonableness (these exceptions are covered primarily in Chapter 5), rendering many warrantless searches reasonable and therefore legal. Justice Clarence Thomas summarized the debate—and the confusion—in his dissenting opinion in *Groh v. Ramirez*, 540 U.S. 551 (2004), a case that is excerpted later in this Chapter:

> The precise relationship between the Amendment's Warrant Clause and Unreasonableness Clause is unclear. But neither Clause explicitly requires a warrant. While it is of course textually possible to consider [a warrant requirement] implicit within the requirement of reasonableness, the text of the Fourth Amendment certainly does not mandate this result. Nor does the Amendment's history, which is clear as to the Amendment's principal target (general warrants), but not as clear with respect to when warrants were required, if ever. Indeed, because of the

very different nature and scope of federal authority and ability to conduct searches and arrests at the founding, it is possible that neither the history of the Fourth Amendment nor the common law provides much guidance. As a result, the Court has vacillated between imposing a categorical warrant requirement and applying a general reasonableness standard. The Court has most frequently held that warrantless searches are presumptively unreasonable, but has also found a plethora of exceptions to presumptive unreasonableness. That is, our cases stand for the illuminating proposition that warrantless searches are *per se* unreasonable, except, of course, when they are not.

While the debate over the precise relationship between the Fourth Amendment's two clauses is not likely to be settled anytime soon, the Supreme Court has often held that a search or seizure supported by probable cause and a warrant creates a presumption that the search or seizure was reasonable. Given this view, it's important to understand the role of probable cause and warrants in police investigations.

A. PROBABLE CAUSE

A full understanding of probable cause requires a basic definition along with an examination of two essential questions. First, what must be shown to satisfy the probable cause requirement? Stated differently, what counts as probable cause? And second, is probable cause an objective or subjective standard? The following two sections address those questions.

1. WHAT COUNTS AS PROBABLE CAUSE?

When the Fourth Amendment states that "no Warrants shall issue, but upon probable cause," the meaning is clear: A judge may issue a search warrant or an arrest warrant only if there is probable cause. But what counts as probable cause? In *Brinegar v. U.S.*, 338 U.S. 160 (1949), the Supreme Court said that probable cause means "more than bare suspicion," but requires "less than evidence which would justify condemnation or conviction."

In *Draper v. U.S.*, the Court elaborated on the meaning of probable cause. Although *Draper* and several other cases in this section deal with the probable cause needed to make an arrest, the Supreme Court has never suggested a that a different degree of probable cause is necessary to support a search.

DRAPER V. U.S.

358 U.S. 307 (1959)

JUSTICE WHITTAKER delivered the opinion of the Court.

Petitioner was convicted of knowingly concealing and transporting narcotic drugs in Denver, Colorado. His conviction was based in part on the use in evidence against him of two "envelopes containing 865 grams of heroin" and a hypodermic syringe that had been taken from his person, following his arrest, by the arresting officer. Before the trial, he moved to suppress that evidence as having been secured through an unlawful search and seizure. After hearing, the District Court found that the arresting officer had probable cause to arrest petitioner without a warrant and that the subsequent search and seizure were therefore incident to a lawful arrest, and overruled the motion to suppress. At the subsequent trial, that evidence was offered and, over petitioner's renewed objection, was received in evidence, and the trial resulted in petitioner's conviction. The Court of Appeals affirmed the conviction, and certiorari was sought on the sole ground that the search and seizure violated the Fourth Amendment and therefore the use of the heroin in evidence vitiated the conviction. We granted the writ to determine that question.

The evidence offered at the hearing on the motion to suppress was not substantially disputed. It established that one Marsh, a federal narcotic agent with 29 years' experience, was stationed at Denver; that one Hereford had been engaged as a "special employee" of the Bureau of Narcotics at Denver for about six months, and from time to time gave information to Marsh regarding violations of the narcotic laws, for which Hereford was paid small sums of money, and that Marsh had always found the information given by Hereford to be accurate and reliable. On September 3, 1956, Hereford told Marsh that James Draper (petitioner) recently had taken up abode at a stated address in Denver and "was peddling narcotics to several addicts" in that city. Four days later, on September 7, Hereford told Marsh "that Draper had gone to Chicago the day before [September 6] by train and that he was going to bring back three ounces of heroin and that he would return to Denver either on the morning of the 8th of September or the morning of the 9th of September also by train." Hereford also gave Marsh a detailed physical description of Draper and of the clothing he was wearing,[2] and said that he would be carrying "a tan zipper bag," and that he habitually "walked real fast."

On the morning of September 8, Marsh and a Denver police officer went to the Denver Union Station and kept watch over all incoming trains from Chicago, but they did not see anyone fitting the description that Hereford had given. Repeating the process on the morning of

---

[2] Hereford told Marsh that Draper was a Negro of light brown complexion, 27 years of age, 5 feet 8 inches tall, weighed about 160 pounds, and that he was wearing a light colored raincoat, brown slacks and black shoes.

September 9, they saw a person, having the exact physical attributes and wearing the precise clothing described by Hereford, alight from an incoming Chicago train and start walking "fast" toward the exit. He was carrying a tan zipper bag in his right hand and the left was thrust in his raincoat pocket. Marsh, accompanied by the police officer, overtook, stopped and arrested him. They then searched him and found the two "envelopes containing heroin" clutched in his left hand in his raincoat pocket, and found the syringe in the tan zipper bag. Marsh then took him (petitioner) into custody. Hereford died four days after the arrest and therefore did not testify at the hearing on the motion.

The Narcotic Control Act of 1956 provides, in pertinent part: "The Commissioner and agents of the Bureau of Narcotics may make arrests without warrant for violations of any law of the United States relating to narcotic drugs where the violation is committed in the presence of the person making the arrest or where such person has reasonable grounds to believe that the person to be arrested has committed or is committing such violation."

The crucial question for us then is whether knowledge of the related facts and circumstances gave Marsh "probable cause" within the meaning of the Fourth Amendment, and "reasonable grounds" within the meaning of the Narcotic Control Act[3] to believe that petitioner had committed or was committing a violation of the narcotic laws. If it did, the arrest, though without a warrant was lawful and the subsequent search of petitioner's person and the seizure of the found heroin were validly made incident to a lawful arrest, and therefore the motion to suppress was properly overruled and the heroin was competently received in evidence at the trial.

Petitioner does not dispute this analysis of the question for decision. Rather, he contends (1) that the information given by Hereford to Marsh was "hearsay" and, because hearsay is not legally competent evidence in a criminal trial, could not legally have been considered, but should have been put out of mind, by Marsh in assessing whether he had "probable cause" and "reasonable grounds" to arrest petitioner without a warrant, and (2) that, even if hearsay could lawfully have been considered, Marsh's information should be held insufficient to show "probable cause" and "reasonable grounds" to believe that petitioner had violated or was violating the narcotic laws and to justify his arrest without a warrant.

Considering the first contention, we find petitioner entirely in error. *Brinegar v. U.S.*, 338 U.S. 160 (1949), has settled the question the other way. There, in a similar situation, the convict contended "that the factors relating to inadmissibility of the evidence for *purposes of proving guilt at the trial*, deprived the evidence as a whole of sufficiency to show probable

---

[3]   The terms "probable cause" as used in the Fourth Amendment and "reasonable grounds" as used in the Narcotic Control Act are substantial equivalents of the same meaning.

cause for the search." But this Court, rejecting that contention, said: "The so-called distinction places a wholly unwarranted emphasis upon the criterion of admissibility in evidence, to prove the accused's guilt, of the facts relied upon to show probable cause. That emphasis, we think, goes much too far in confusing and disregarding the difference between what is required to prove guilt in a criminal case and what is required to show probable cause for arrest or search. It approaches requiring (if it does not in practical effect require) proof sufficient to establish guilt in order to substantiate the existence of probable cause. There is a large difference between the two things to be proved [guilt and probable cause], as well as between the tribunals which determine them, and therefore a like difference in the *quanta* and modes of proof required to establish them."

Nor can we agree with petitioner's second contention that Marsh's information was insufficient to show probable cause and reasonable grounds to believe that petitioner had violated or was violating the narcotic laws and to justify his arrest without a warrant. The information given to narcotic agent Marsh by "special employee" Hereford may have been hearsay to Marsh, but coming from one employed for that purpose and whose information had always been found accurate and reliable, it is clear that Marsh would have been derelict in his duties had he not pursued it. And when, in pursuing that information, he saw a man, having the exact physical attributes and wearing the precise clothing and carrying the tan zipper bag that Hereford had described, alight from one of the very trains from the very place stated by Hereford and start to walk at a "fast" pace toward the station exit, Marsh had personally verified every facet of the information given him by Hereford except whether petitioner had accomplished his mission and had the three ounces of heroin on his person or in his bag. And surely, with every other bit of Hereford's information being thus personally verified, Marsh had "reasonable grounds" to believe that the remaining unverified bit of Hereford's information—that Draper would have the heroin with him— was likewise true.

In dealing with probable cause, as the very name implies, we deal with probabilities. These are not technical; they are the factual and practical considerations of everyday life on which reasonable and prudent men, not legal technicians, act. Probable cause exists where the facts and circumstances within the arresting officers' knowledge and of which they had reasonably trustworthy information are sufficient in themselves to warrant a man of reasonable caution in the belief that an offense has been or is being committed.

We believe that, under the facts and circumstances here, Marsh had probable cause and reasonable grounds to believe that petitioner was committing a violation of the laws of the United States relating to narcotic drugs at the time he arrested him. The arrest was therefore lawful, and the subsequent search and seizure, having been made incident to that lawful arrest, were likewise valid. It follows that petitioner's motion to suppress was properly denied and that the seized heroin was competent evidence lawfully received at the trial.

JUSTICE DOUGLAS, dissenting.

With all due deference, the arrest made here on the mere word of an informer violated the spirit of the Fourth Amendment and the requirement of the law governing arrests in narcotics cases. If an arrest is made without a warrant, the offense must be committed in the presence of the officer or the officer must have "reasonable grounds to believe that the person to be arrested has committed or is committing" a violation of the narcotics law. The arresting officers did not have a bit of evidence, known to them and as to which they could take an oath had they gone to a magistrate for a warrant, that petitioner had committed any crime. The arresting officers did not know the grounds on which the informer based his conclusion; nor did they seek to find out what they were. They acted solely on the informer's word. In my view that was not enough.

So far as I can ascertain the mere word of an informer, not bolstered by some evidence that a crime had been or was being committed, has never been approved by this Court as "reasonable grounds" for making an arrest without a warrant. Whether the act complained of be seizure of goods, search of premises, or the arrest of the citizen, the judicial inquiry has been directed toward the reasonableness of inferences to be drawn from suspicious circumstances attending the action thought to be unlawful. Evidence required to prove guilt is not necessary. But the attendant circumstances must be sufficient to give rise in the mind of the arresting officer at least to inferences of guilt.

Here the officers had no evidence—apart from the mere word of an informer—that petitioner was committing a crime. The fact that petitioner walked fast and carried a tan zipper bag was not evidence of any crime. The officers knew nothing except what they had been told by the informer. If they went to a magistrate to get a warrant of arrest and relied solely on the report of the informer, it is not conceivable to me that one would be granted. For they could not present to the magistrate any of the facts which the informer may have had. They could swear only to the fact that the informer had made the accusation. They could swear to no evidence that lay in their own knowledge. They could present, on information and belief, no facts which the informer disclosed. No magistrate could issue a warrant on the mere word of an officer, without more. We are not justified in lowering the standard when an arrest is made without a warrant and allowing the officers more leeway than we grant the magistrate.

In this case it was only after the arrest and search were made that there was a shred of evidence known to the officers that a crime was in the process of being committed.

———————

Hereford, the informant in *Draper*, provided the police with *detailed information* about Draper's appearance, mannerisms, and travel plans on a particular day. The police then *corroborated* Hereford's information— they found Draper exiting from the specific train Hereford had mentioned, and Draper was wearing certain clothes, carrying a tan zipper bag, and walking quickly, exactly as Hereford had described. But there is nothing illegal or even particularly suspicious about any of that; many people carry bags and walk quickly upon exiting a train. What appears to have tipped the balance for the Supreme Court in its assessment of probable cause was the testimony of Marsh, an experienced federal narcotics agent, who said that Hereford had told him Draper was carrying heroin. Marsh further testified that Hereford's information regarding violations of the narcotics laws had always been *accurate and reliable.* Although *Draper* didn't frame it as such, the Court's probable cause determination appeared to rest on three factors: (1) a reliable source of information; (2) detailed information; and (3) police corroboration of the information.

In the aftermath of *Draper*, in *Aguilar v. Texas*, 378 U.S. 108 (1964), and *Spinelli v. U.S.*, 393 U.S. 410 (1969), the Supreme Court refined the probable cause inquiry to assist courts in evaluating warrant applications based on information provided by informants. These cases gave rise to the two-part *Aguilar-Spinelli* Test, requiring that the judge or magistrate evaluating the warrant application be informed of: (1) facts demonstrating the informant's basis for knowledge; and (2) facts demonstrating that the informant is credible and reliable.

The *Aguilar-Spinelli* Test ultimately proved too rigid for the Supreme Court. In *Illinois v. Gates*, a majority abandoned it in favor of a "totality of the circumstances" approach similar to that in *Draper*.

ILLINOIS V. GATES
462 U.S. 213 (1983)

JUSTICE REHNQUIST delivered the opinion of the Court.

Respondents Lance and Susan Gates were indicted for violation of state drug laws after police officers, executing a search warrant, discovered marijuana and other contraband in their automobile and home. Prior to trial the Gateses moved to suppress evidence seized during this search. The Illinois Supreme Court affirmed the decisions of lower state courts granting the motion. It held that the affidavit submitted in support of the State's application for a warrant to search the Gateses' property was inadequate under this Court's decisions in *Aguilar v. Texas*, 378 U.S. 108 (1964), and *Spinelli v. U.S.*, 393 U.S. 410 (1969).

We granted certiorari to consider the application of the Fourth Amendment to a magistrate's issuance of a search warrant on the basis of a partially corroborated anonymous informant's tip.

II

We turn to the question presented in the State's original petition for certiorari, which requires us to decide whether respondents' rights under the Fourth and Fourteenth Amendments were violated by the search of their car and house. A chronological statement of events usefully introduces the issues at stake. Bloomingdale, Ill., is a suburb of Chicago located in DuPage County. On May 3, 1978, the Bloomingdale Police Department received by mail an anonymous handwritten letter which read as follows:

> This letter is to inform you that you have a couple in your town who strictly make their living on selling drugs. They are Sue and Lance Gates, they live on Greenway, off Bloomingdale Rd. in the condominiums. Most of their buys are done in Florida. Sue his wife drives their car to Florida, where she leaves it to be loaded up with drugs, then Lance flys down and drives it back. Sue flys back after she drops the car off in Florida. May 3 she is driving down there again and Lance will be flying down in a few days to drive it back. At the time Lance drives the car back he has the trunk loaded with over $100,000.00 in drugs. Presently they have over $100,000.00 worth of drugs in their basement. They brag about the fact they never have to work, and make their entire living on pushers. I guarantee if you watch them carefully you will make a big catch. They are friends with some big drugs dealers, who visit their house often.

The letter was referred by the Chief of Police of the Bloomingdale Police Department to Detective Mader, who decided to pursue the tip. Mader learned, from the office of the Illinois Secretary of State, that an Illinois driver's license had been issued to one Lance Gates, residing at a stated address in Bloomingdale. He contacted a confidential informant, whose examination of certain financial records revealed a more recent address for the Gates, and he also learned from a police officer assigned to O'Hare Airport that "L. Gates" had made a reservation on Eastern Airlines flight 245 to West Palm Beach, Fla., scheduled to depart from Chicago on May 5 at 4:15 p.m.

Mader then made arrangements with an agent of the Drug Enforcement Administration for surveillance of the May 5 Eastern Airlines flight. The agent later reported to Mader that Gates had boarded the flight, and that federal agents in Florida had observed him arrive in West Palm Beach and take a taxi to the nearby Holiday Inn. They also reported that Gates went to a room registered to one Susan Gates and that, at 7:00 a.m. the next morning, Gates and an unidentified woman left the motel in a Mercury bearing Illinois license plates and drove northbound on an interstate frequently used by travelers to the Chicago area. In addition, the DEA agent informed Mader that the license plate number on the Mercury was registered to a Hornet station wagon owned by Gates. The agent also advised Mader that the driving time between West Palm Beach and Bloomingdale was approximately 22 to 24 hours.

Mader signed an affidavit setting forth the foregoing facts, and submitted it to a judge of the Circuit Court of DuPage County, together with a copy of the anonymous letter. The judge of that court thereupon issued a search warrant for the Gateses' residence and for their automobile. The judge, in deciding to issue the warrant, could have determined that the *modus operandi* of the Gateses had been substantially corroborated. As the anonymous letter predicted, Lance Gates had flown from Chicago to West Palm Beach late in the afternoon of May 5th, had checked into a hotel room registered in the name of his wife, and, at 7:00 a.m. the following morning, had headed north, accompanied by an unidentified woman, out of West Palm Beach on an interstate highway used by travelers from South Florida to Chicago in an automobile bearing a license plate issued to him.

At 5:15 a.m. on March 7th, only 36 hours after he had flown out of Chicago, Lance Gates, and his wife, returned to their home in Bloomingdale, driving the car in which they had left West Palm Beach some 22 hours earlier. The Bloomingdale police were awaiting them, searched the trunk of the Mercury, and uncovered approximately 350 pounds of marijuana. A search of the Gateses' home revealed marijuana, weapons, and other contraband. The Illinois Circuit Court ordered suppression of all these items, on the ground that the affidavit submitted to the Circuit Judge failed to support the necessary determination of probable cause to believe that the Gateses' automobile and home contained the contraband in question. This decision was affirmed in turn by the Illinois Appellate Court and by a divided vote of the Supreme Court of Illinois.

The Illinois Supreme Court concluded—and we are inclined to agree—that, standing alone, the anonymous letter sent to the Bloomingdale Police Department would not provide the basis for a magistrate's determination that there was probable cause to believe contraband would be found in the Gateses' car and home. The letter provides virtually nothing from which one might conclude that its author is either honest or his information reliable; likewise, the letter gives absolutely no indication of the basis for the writer's predictions regarding the Gateses' criminal activities. Something more was required, then, before a magistrate could conclude that there was probable cause to believe that contraband would be found in the Gateses' home and car.

The Illinois Supreme Court also properly recognized that Detective Mader's affidavit might be capable of supplementing the anonymous letter with information sufficient to permit a determination of probable cause. In holding that the affidavit in fact did not contain sufficient additional information to sustain a determination of probable cause, the Illinois court applied a "two-pronged test," derived from our decision in *Spinelli v. U.S.* The Illinois Supreme Court, like some others, apparently understood *Spinelli* as requiring that the anonymous letter satisfy each of two independent requirements before it could be relied on. According to this view, the letter, as supplemented by Mader's affidavit, first had to adequately reveal the "basis of knowledge" of the letter writer—the particular means by which he came by the information given in his report. Second, it had to provide facts sufficiently establishing either the "veracity" of the affiant's informant, or, alternatively, the "reliability" of the informant's report in this particular case.

The Illinois court, alluding to an elaborate set of legal rules that have developed among various lower courts to enforce the "two-pronged test," found that the test had not been satisfied. First, the "veracity" prong was not satisfied because "there was simply no basis for concluding that the anonymous person [who wrote the letter to the Bloomingdale Police Department] was credible." The court indicated that corroboration by police of details contained in the letter might never satisfy the "veracity" prong, and in any event, could not do so if, as in the present case, only "innocent" details are corroborated. In addition, the letter gave no indication of the basis of its writer's knowledge of the Gateses' activities. The Illinois court understood *Spinelli* as permitting the detail contained in a tip to be used to infer that the informant had a reliable basis for his statements, but it thought that the anonymous letter failed to provide sufficient detail to permit such an inference. Thus, it concluded that no showing of probable cause had been made.

We agree with the Illinois Supreme Court that an informant's "veracity," "reliability," and "basis of knowledge" are all highly relevant in determining the value of his report. We do not agree, however, that these elements should be understood as entirely separate and independent requirements to be rigidly exacted in every case, which the opinion of the Supreme Court of Illinois would imply. Rather, as detailed below, they should be understood simply as closely intertwined issues that may usefully illuminate the commonsense, practical question whether there is "probable cause" to believe that contraband or evidence is located in a particular place.

III

This totality-of-the-circumstances approach is far more consistent with our prior treatment of probable cause than is any rigid demand that specific "tests" be satisfied by every informant's tip. Perhaps the central teaching of our decisions bearing on the probable cause standard is that it is a practical, nontechnical conception. "In dealing with probable cause, as the very name implies, we deal with probabilities. These are not technical; they are the factual and practical considerations of everyday life on which reasonable and prudent men, not legal technicians, act." *Brinegar v. U.S.*, 338 U.S. 160, 175 (1949).

As these comments illustrate, probable cause is a fluid concept—turning on the assessment of probabilities in particular factual contexts—not readily, or even usefully, reduced to a neat set of legal rules. Informants' tips doubtless come in many shapes and sizes from many different types of persons. Rigid legal rules are ill-suited to an area of such diversity.

Moreover, the "two-pronged test" directs analysis into two largely independent channels—the informant's "veracity" or "reliability" and his "basis of knowledge." There are persuasive arguments against according these two elements such independent status. Instead, they are better understood as relevant considerations in the totality-of-the-circumstances analysis that traditionally has guided probable cause determinations: a deficiency in one may be compensated for, in determining the overall reliability of a tip, by a strong showing as to the other, or by some other indicia of reliability.

If, for example, a particular informant is known for the unusual reliability of his predictions of certain types of criminal activities in a locality, his failure, in a particular case, to thoroughly set forth the basis of his knowledge surely should not serve as an absolute bar to a finding of probable cause based on his tip. Likewise, if an unquestionably honest citizen comes forward with a report of criminal activity—which if fabricated would subject him to criminal liability—we have found rigorous scrutiny of the basis of his knowledge unnecessary. Conversely, even if we entertain some doubt as to an informant's motives, his explicit and detailed description of alleged wrongdoing, along with a statement that the event was observed first-hand, entitles his tip to greater weight than might otherwise be the case. Unlike a totality-of-the-circumstances analysis, which permits a balanced assessment of the relative weights of all the various indicia of reliability (and unreliability) attending an informant's tip, the "two-pronged test" has encouraged an excessively technical dissection of informants' tips, with undue attention being focused on isolated issues that cannot sensibly be divorced from the other facts presented to the magistrate.

The rigorous inquiry into the *Spinelli* prongs and the complex superstructure of evidentiary and analytical rules that some have seen implicit in our *Spinelli* decision, cannot be reconciled with the fact that many warrants are—quite properly—issued on the basis of nontechnical, common-sense judgments of laymen applying a standard less demanding than those used in more formal legal proceedings.

If the affidavits submitted by police officers are subjected to the type of scrutiny some courts have deemed appropriate, police might well resort to warrantless searches, with the hope of relying on consent or some other exception to the warrant clause that might develop at the time of the search.

The strictures that inevitably accompany the "two-pronged test" cannot avoid seriously impeding the task of law enforcement. If, as the Illinois Supreme Court apparently thought, that test must be rigorously applied in every case, anonymous tips would be of greatly diminished value in police work. Ordinary citizens, like ordinary witnesses, generally do not provide extensive recitations of the basis of their everyday observations. Likewise, as the Illinois Supreme Court observed in this case, the veracity of persons supplying anonymous tips is by hypothesis largely unknown, and unknowable. As a result, anonymous tips seldom could survive a rigorous application of either of the *Spinelli* prongs. Yet, such tips, particularly when supplemented by independent police investigation, frequently contribute to the solution of otherwise "perfect crimes." While a conscientious assessment of the basis for crediting such tips is required by the Fourth Amendment, a standard that leaves virtually no place for anonymous citizen informants is not.

Our earlier cases illustrate the limits beyond which a magistrate may not venture in issuing a warrant. A sworn statement of an affiant that "he has cause to suspect and does believe that" liquor illegally brought into the United States is located on certain premises will not do. An affidavit must provide the magistrate with a substantial basis for determining the existence of probable cause, and a wholly conclusory statement fails to meet this requirement. An officer's statement that "affiants have received reliable information from a credible person and believe" that heroin is stored in a home, is likewise inadequate. This is a mere conclusory statement that gives the magistrate virtually no basis at all for making a judgment regarding probable cause. Sufficient information must be presented to the magistrate to allow that official to determine probable cause; his action cannot be a mere ratification of the bare conclusions of others. In order to ensure that such an abdication of the magistrate's duty does not occur, courts must continue to conscientiously review the sufficiency of affidavits on which warrants are issued. But when we move beyond the "bare bones" affidavits, this area simply does not lend itself to a prescribed set of rules, like that which had developed from *Spinelli*. Instead, the flexible, common-sense standard better serves the purposes of the Fourth Amendment's probable cause requirement.

For all these reasons, we conclude that it is wiser to abandon the "two-pronged test" established by our decisions in *Aguilar* and *Spinelli*. In its place we reaffirm the totality-of-the-circumstances analysis that traditionally has informed probable cause determinations. The task of the issuing magistrate is simply to make a practical, common-sense decision whether, given all the circumstances set forth in the affidavit before him, including the "veracity" and "basis of knowledge" of persons supplying hearsay information, there is a fair probability that contraband or evidence of a crime will be found in a particular place. And the duty of a reviewing court is simply to ensure that the magistrate had a substantial basis for concluding that probable cause existed. We are convinced that this flexible, easily applied standard will better achieve the accommodation of public and private interests that the Fourth Amendment requires than does the approach that has developed from *Aguilar* and *Spinelli*.

IV

Our decisions applying the totality-of-the-circumstances analysis outlined above have consistently recognized the value of corroboration of details of an informant's tip by independent police work. Likewise, we recognized the probative value of corroborative efforts of police officials.

Our decision in *Draper v. U.S.*, 358 U.S. 307 (1959), is the classic case on the value of corroborative efforts of police officials. There, an informant named Hereford reported that Draper would arrive in Denver on a train from Chicago on one of two days, and that he would be carrying a quantity of heroin. The informant also supplied a fairly detailed physical description of Draper, and predicted that he would be wearing a light colored raincoat, brown slacks and black shoes, and would be walking "real fast." Hereford gave no indication of the basis for his information.

On one of the stated dates police officers observed a man matching this description exit a train arriving from Chicago; his attire and luggage matched Hereford's report and he was walking rapidly. We explained in *Draper* that, by this point in his investigation, the arresting officer "had personally verified every facet of the information given him by Hereford except whether petitioner had accomplished his mission and had the three ounces of heroin on his person or in his bag. And surely, with every other bit of Hereford's information being thus personally verified, the officer had reasonable grounds to believe that the remaining unverified bit of Hereford's information—that Draper would have the heroin with him—was likewise true."

The showing of probable cause in the present case was fully as compelling as that in *Draper*. Even standing alone, the facts obtained through the independent investigation of Mader and the DEA at least suggested that the Gateses were involved in drug trafficking. In addition to being a popular vacation site, Florida is well-known as a source of narcotics and other illegal drugs. Lance Gates' flight to Palm Beach, his brief, overnight stay in a motel, and apparent immediate return north to Chicago in the family car, conveniently awaiting him in West Palm Beach, is as suggestive of a pre-arranged drug run, as it is of an ordinary vacation trip.

In addition, the magistrate could rely on the anonymous letter, which had been corroborated in major part by Mader's efforts—just as had occurred in *Draper*.[13] The Supreme Court of Illinois reasoned that *Draper* involved an informant who had given reliable information on previous occasions, while the honesty and reliability of the anonymous informant in this case were unknown to the Bloomingdale police. While this distinction might be an apt one at the time the police department received the anonymous letter, it became far less significant after Mader's independent investigative work occurred. The corroboration of the letter's predictions that the Gateses' car would be in Florida, that Lance Gates would fly to Florida in the next day or so, and that he would drive the car north toward Bloomingdale all indicated, albeit not with certainty, that the informant's other assertions also were true.

Finally, the anonymous letter contained a range of details relating not just to easily obtained facts and conditions existing at the time of the tip, but to future actions of third parties ordinarily not easily predicted. The letter writer's accurate information as to the travel plans of each of the Gateses was of a character likely obtained only from the Gateses themselves, or from someone familiar with their not entirely ordinary travel plans. If the informant had access to accurate information of this type a magistrate could properly conclude that it was not unlikely that he also had access to reliable information of the Gateses' alleged illegal activities. Of course, the Gateses' travel plans might have been learned

---

[13] The Illinois Supreme Court thought that the verification of details contained in the anonymous letter in this case amounted only to "the corroboration of innocent activity," and that this was insufficient to support a finding of probable cause. We are inclined to agree, however, with the observation of Justice Moran in his dissenting opinion that, "In this case, just as in *Draper*, seemingly innocent activity became suspicious in the light of the initial tip." And it bears noting that *all* of the corroborating detail established in *Draper* was of entirely innocent activity. This is perfectly reasonable. As discussed previously, probable cause requires only a probability or substantial chance of criminal activity, not an actual showing of such activity. By hypothesis, therefore, innocent behavior frequently will provide the basis for a showing of probable cause; to require otherwise would be to *sub silentio* impose a drastically more rigorous definition of probable cause than the security of our citizens demands. We think the Illinois court attempted a too rigid classification of the types of conduct that may be relied upon in seeking to demonstrate probable cause. In making a determination of probable cause the relevant inquiry is not whether particular conduct is "innocent" or "guilty," but the degree of suspicion that attaches to particular types of non-criminal acts.

from a talkative neighbor or travel agent; under the "two-pronged test" developed from *Spinelli*, the character of the details in the anonymous letter might well not permit a sufficiently clear inference regarding the letter writer's "basis of knowledge." But, as discussed previously, probable cause does not demand the certainty we associate with formal trials. It is enough that there was a fair probability that the writer of the anonymous letter had obtained his entire story either from the Gateses or someone they trusted. And corroboration of major portions of the letter's predictions provides just this probability. It is apparent, therefore, that the judge issuing the warrant had a substantial basis for concluding that probable cause to search the Gateses' home and car existed.

JUSTICE BRENNAN, with whom JUSTICE MARSHALL joins, dissenting.

I write separately to dissent from the Court's unjustified and ill-advised rejection of the two-prong test for evaluating the validity of a warrant based on hearsay announced in *Aguilar v. Texas*, 378 U.S. 108 (1964), and refined in *Spinelli v. U.S.*, 393 U.S. 410 (1969).

Spinelli stands for the proposition that corroboration of certain details in a tip may be sufficient to satisfy the veracity, but not the basis of knowledge, prong of *Aguilar*. *Spinelli* also suggests that in some limited circumstances considerable detail in an informant's tip may be adequate to satisfy the basis of knowledge prong of *Aguilar*.

Although the rules drawn from the cases are cast in procedural terms, they advance an important underlying substantive value: Findings of probable cause, and attendant intrusions, should not be authorized unless there is some assurance that the information on which they are based has been obtained in a reliable way by an honest or credible person. As applied to police officers, the rules focus on the way in which the information was acquired. As applied to informants, the rules focus both on the honesty or credibility of the informant and on the reliability of the way in which the information was acquired. Insofar as it is more complicated, an evaluation of affidavits based on hearsay involves a more difficult inquiry. This suggests a need to structure the inquiry in an effort to insure greater accuracy. The standards announced in *Aguilar*, as refined by *Spinelli*, fulfill that need. The standards inform the police of what information they have to provide and magistrates of what information they should demand. The standards also inform magistrates of the subsidiary findings they must make in order to arrive at an ultimate finding of probable cause. *Spinelli*, properly understood, directs the magistrate's attention to the possibility that the presence of self-verifying detail might satisfy *Aguilar*'s basis of knowledge prong and that corroboration of the details of a tip might satisfy *Aguilar*'s veracity prong. By requiring police to provide certain crucial information to magistrates and by structuring magistrates' probable cause inquiries, *Aguilar* and *Spinelli* assure the magistrate's role as an independent arbiter of probable cause, insure greater accuracy in probable cause determinations, and advance the substantive value identified above.

In light of the important purposes served by *Aguilar* and *Spinelli*, I would not reject the standards they establish.

Under the "totality of the circumstances" approach to probable cause, a judge reviewing an application for a warrant should still look for: (1) a reliable source of information, including the source's basis of knowledge; (2) detailed information suggestive of criminal activity; and (3) police corroboration of the information. The Supreme Court makes it clear in *Gates*, however, that these three elements are not rigid independent requirements; instead, they should be considered collectively, and additional information in one area can compensate for a deficit of information in another. In the end, the judge should examine all of the available evidence and make a common-sense determination as to whether probable cause exists.

In *Maryland v. Pringle*, the Supreme Court reaffirmed its common-sense, "totality of the circumstances" approach to probable cause, finding that the presence of unclaimed contraband in a car gives the police probable cause to arrest any one—or all—of the occupants.

MARYLAND V. PRINGLE
540 U.S. 366 (2003)

CHIEF JUSTICE REHNQUIST delivered the opinion of the Court.

In the early morning hours a passenger car occupied by three men was stopped for speeding by a police officer. The officer, upon searching the car, seized $763 of rolled-up cash from the glove compartment and five glassine baggies of cocaine from between the back-seat armrest and the back seat. After all three men denied ownership of the cocaine and money, the officer arrested each of them. We hold that the officer had probable cause to arrest Pringle—one of the three men.

At 3:16 a.m. on August 7, 1999, a Baltimore County Police officer stopped a Nissan Maxima for speeding. There were three occupants in the car: Donte Partlow, the driver and owner, respondent Pringle, the front-seat passenger, and Otis Smith, the back-seat passenger. The officer asked Partlow for his license and registration. When Partlow opened the glove compartment to retrieve the vehicle registration, the officer observed a large amount of rolled-up money in the glove compartment. The officer returned to his patrol car with Partlow's license and registration to check the computer system for outstanding violations. The computer check did not reveal any violations. The officer returned to the stopped car, had Partlow get out, and issued him an oral warning.

After a second patrol car arrived, the officer asked Partlow if he had any weapons or narcotics in the vehicle. Partlow indicated that he did not. Partlow then consented to a search of the vehicle. The search yielded $763 from the glove compartment and five plastic glassine baggies containing cocaine from behind the back-seat armrest. When the officer began the search the armrest was in the upright position flat against the rear seat. The officer pulled down the armrest and found the drugs, which had been placed between the armrest and the back seat of the car.

The officer questioned all three men about the ownership of the drugs and money, and told them that if no one admitted to ownership of the drugs he was going to arrest them all. The men offered no information regarding the ownership of the drugs or money. All three were placed under arrest and transported to the police station.

Later that morning, Pringle waived his rights under *Miranda v. Arizona*, 384 U.S. 436 (1966), and gave an oral and written confession in which he acknowledged that the cocaine belonged to him, that he and his friends were going to a party, and that he intended to sell the cocaine or "use it for sex." Pringle maintained that the other occupants of the car did not know about the drugs, and they were released.

The trial court denied Pringle's motion to suppress his confession as the fruit of an illegal arrest, holding that the officer had probable cause to arrest Pringle. A jury convicted Pringle of possession with intent to distribute cocaine and possession of cocaine. He was sentenced to 10 years' incarceration without the possibility of parole. The Court of Special Appeals of Maryland affirmed.

The Court of Appeals of Maryland, by divided vote, reversed, holding that, absent specific facts tending to show Pringle's knowledge and dominion or control over the drugs, "the mere finding of cocaine in the back armrest when Pringle was a front seat passenger in a car being driven by its owner is insufficient to establish probable cause for an arrest for possession." We granted certiorari, and now reverse.

Maryland law authorizes police officers to execute warrantless arrests for felonies committed in an officer's presence or where an officer has probable cause to believe that a felony has been committed or is being committed in the officer's presence. A warrantless arrest of an individual in a public place for a felony, or a misdemeanor committed in the officer's presence, is consistent with the Fourth Amendment if the arrest is supported by probable cause. *U.S. v. Watson*, 423 U.S. 411 (1976).

It is uncontested in the present case that the officer, upon recovering the five plastic glassine baggies containing suspected cocaine, had probable cause to believe a felony had been committed. The sole question is whether the officer had probable cause to believe that Pringle committed that crime.

The long-prevailing standard of probable cause protects citizens from rash and unreasonable interferences with privacy and from unfounded charges of crime, while giving fair leeway for enforcing the law in the community's protection. On many occasions, we have reiterated that the probable-cause standard is a "practical, nontechnical conception" that deals with "the factual and practical considerations of everyday life on which reasonable and prudent men, not legal technicians, act." *Illinois v. Gates*, 462 U.S. 213, 231 (1983).

The probable-cause standard is incapable of precise definition or quantification into percentages because it deals with probabilities and depends on the totality of the circumstances. We have stated, however, that the substance of all the definitions of probable cause is a reasonable ground for belief of guilt, and that the belief of guilt must be particularized with respect to the person to be searched or seized.

To determine whether an officer had probable cause to arrest an individual, we examine the events leading up to the arrest, and then decide whether these historical facts, viewed from the standpoint of an objectively reasonable police officer, amount to probable cause.

In this case, Pringle was one of three men riding in a Nissan Maxima at 3:16 a.m. There was $763 of rolled-up cash in the glove compartment directly in front of Pringle.[2] Five plastic glassine baggies of cocaine were behind the back-seat armrest and accessible to all three men. Upon questioning, the three men failed to offer any information with respect to the ownership of the cocaine or the money.

We think it an entirely reasonable inference from these facts that any or all three of the occupants had knowledge of, and exercised dominion and control over, the cocaine. Thus, a reasonable officer could conclude that there was probable cause to believe Pringle committed the crime of possession of cocaine, either solely or jointly.

Pringle's attempt to characterize this case as a guilt-by-association case is unavailing. In *Wyoming v. Houghton*, 526 U.S. 295, 304–305 (1999), we noted that "a car passenger will often be engaged in a common enterprise with the driver, and have the same interest in concealing the fruits or the evidence of their wrongdoing." Here we think it was reasonable for the officer to infer a common enterprise among the three men. The quantity of drugs and cash in the car indicated the likelihood of drug dealing, an enterprise to which a dealer would be unlikely to admit an innocent person with the potential to furnish evidence against him.

---

[2]   The Court of Appeals of Maryland dismissed the $763 seized from the glove compartment as a factor in the probable-cause determination, stating that "money, without more, is innocuous." The court's consideration of the money in isolation, rather than as a factor in the totality of the circumstances, is mistaken in light of our precedents. See, *e.g.*, *Illinois v. Gates*, 462 U.S. 213 (1983) (opining that the totality of the circumstances approach is consistent with our prior treatment of probable cause). We think it is abundantly clear from the facts that this case involves more than money alone.

We hold that the officer had probable cause to believe that Pringle had committed the crime of possession of a controlled substance. Pringle's arrest therefore did not contravene the Fourth and Fourteenth Amendments.

In *Florida v. Harris*, the Supreme Court again applied its common-sense, "totality of the circumstances" approach to probable cause, even though the source of the information was a drug-sniffing dog.

FLORIDA V. HARRIS
133 S.Ct. 1050 (2013)

JUSTICE KAGAN delivered the opinion of the Court.

In this case, we consider how a court should determine if the "alert" of a drug-detection dog during a traffic stop provides probable cause to search a vehicle. The Florida Supreme Court held that the State must in every case present an exhaustive set of records, including a log of the dog's performance in the field, to establish the dog's reliability. We think that demand inconsistent with the flexible, common-sense standard of probable cause [announced in *Illinois v. Gates,* 462 U.S. 213 (1983)].

I

William Wheetley is a K-9 Officer in the Liberty County, Florida Sheriff's Office. On June 24, 2006, he was on a routine patrol with Aldo, a German shepherd trained to detect certain narcotics (methamphetamine, marijuana, cocaine, heroin, and ecstasy). Wheetley pulled over respondent Clayton Harris' truck because it had an expired license plate. On approaching the driver's-side door, Wheetley saw that Harris was "visibly nervous," unable to sit still, shaking, and breathing rapidly. Wheetley also noticed an open can of beer in the truck's cup holder. Wheetley asked Harris for consent to search the truck, but Harris refused. At that point, Wheetley retrieved Aldo from the patrol car and walked him around Harris' truck for a "free air sniff." Aldo alerted at the driver's-side door handle—signaling, through a distinctive set of behaviors, that he smelled drugs there.

Wheetley concluded, based principally on Aldo's alert, that he had probable cause to search the truck. His search did not turn up any of the drugs Aldo was trained to detect. But it did reveal 200 loose pseudoephedrine pills, 8,000 matches, a bottle of hydrochloric acid, two containers of antifreeze, and a coffee filter full of iodine crystals—all ingredients for making methamphetamine. Wheetley accordingly arrested Harris, who admitted after proper *Miranda* warnings that he routinely "cooked" methamphetamine at his house and could not go "more than a few days without using" it. The State charged Harris with possessing pseudoephedrine for use in manufacturing methamphetamine.

While out on bail, Harris had another run-in with Wheetley and Aldo. This time, Wheetley pulled Harris over for a broken brake light. Aldo again sniffed the truck's exterior, and again alerted at the driver's-side door handle. Wheetley once more searched the truck, but on this occasion discovered nothing of interest.

Harris moved to suppress the evidence found in his truck on the ground that Aldo's alert had not given Wheetley probable cause for a search. At the hearing on that motion, Wheetley testified about both his and Aldo's training in drug detection. In 2004, Wheetley (and a different dog) completed a 160-hour course in narcotics detection offered by the Dothan, Alabama Police Department, while Aldo (and a different handler) completed a similar, 120-hour course given by the Apopka, Florida Police Department. That same year, Aldo received a one-year certification from Drug Beat, a private company that specializes in testing and certifying K-9 dogs. Wheetley and Aldo teamed up in 2005 and went through another, 40-hour refresher course in Dothan together. They also did four hours of training exercises each week to maintain their skills. Wheetley would hide drugs in certain vehicles or buildings while leaving others "blank" to determine whether Aldo alerted at the right places. According to Wheetley, Aldo's performance in those exercises was "really good." The State introduced "Monthly Canine Detection Training Logs" consistent with that testimony: They showed that Aldo always found hidden drugs and that he performed "satisfactorily" (the higher of two possible assessments) on each day of training.

On cross-examination, Harris' attorney chose not to contest the quality of Aldo's or Wheetley's training. She focused instead on Aldo's certification and his performance in the field, particularly the two stops of Harris' truck. Wheetley conceded that the certification (which, he noted, Florida law did not require) had expired the year before he pulled Harris over. Wheetley also acknowledged that he did not keep complete records of Aldo's performance in traffic stops or other field work; instead, he maintained records only of alerts resulting in arrests. But Wheetley defended Aldo's two alerts to Harris' seemingly narcotics-free truck: According to Wheetley, Harris probably transferred the odor of methamphetamine to the door handle, and Aldo responded to that "residual odor."

The trial court concluded that Wheetley had probable cause to search Harris' truck and so denied the motion to suppress. The Florida Supreme Court reversed, holding that Wheetley lacked probable cause to search Harris' vehicle under the Fourth Amendment. "[W]hen a dog alerts," the court wrote, "the fact that the dog has been trained and certified is simply not enough to establish probable cause." To demonstrate a dog's reliability, the State needed to produce a wider array of evidence: "[T]he State must present the dog's training and certification records, an explanation of the meaning of the particular training and certification, field performance records (including any unverified alerts), and evidence concerning the experience and training of the officer handling the dog, as well as any other objective evidence known to the officer about the dog's reliability."

The court particularly stressed the need for "evidence of the dog's performance history," including records showing "how often the dog has alerted in the field without illegal contraband having been found." That data, the court stated, could help to expose such problems as a handler's tendency (conscious or not) to "cue [a] dog to alert" and "a dog's inability to distinguish between residual odors and actual drugs." Accordingly, an officer like Wheetley who did not keep full records of his dog's field performance could never have the requisite cause to think "that the dog is a reliable indicator of drugs."

II

A police officer has probable cause to conduct a search when the facts available to him would warrant a person of reasonable caution in the belief that contraband or evidence of a crime is present. The test for probable cause is not reducible to precise definition or quantification. Finely tuned standards such as proof beyond a reasonable doubt or by a preponderance of the evidence have no place in the probable-cause decision. All we have required is the kind of fair probability on which reasonable and prudent people, not legal technicians, act.

In evaluating whether the State has met this practical and common-sensical standard, we have consistently looked to the totality of the circumstances. We have rejected rigid rules, bright-line tests, and mechanistic inquiries in favor of a more flexible, all-things-considered approach. In *Gates,* for example, we abandoned our old test for assessing the reliability of informants' tips because it had devolved into a "complex superstructure of evidentiary and analytical rules," any one of which, if not complied with, would derail a finding of probable cause. We lamented the development of a list of "inflexible, independent requirements applicable in every case." Probable cause, we emphasized, is "a fluid concept—turning on the assessment of probabilities in particular factual contexts—not readily, or even usefully, reduced to a neat set of legal rules."

The Florida Supreme Court flouted this established approach to determining probable cause. To assess the reliability of a drug-detection dog, the court created a strict evidentiary checklist, whose every item the State must tick off. Most prominently, an alert cannot establish probable cause under the Florida court's decision unless the State introduces comprehensive documentation of the dog's prior "hits" and "misses" in the field. (One wonders how the court would apply its test to a rookie dog.) No matter how much other proof the State offers of the dog's reliability, the absent field performance records will preclude a finding of probable cause. That is the antithesis of a totality-of-the-circumstances analysis. It is, indeed, the very thing we criticized in *Gates* when we overhauled our method for assessing the trustworthiness of an informant's tip. A gap as to any one matter, we explained, should not sink the State's case; rather, that "deficiency may be compensated for, in determining the overall reliability of a tip, by a strong showing as to other indicia of reliability." So too here, a finding of a drug-detection dog's reliability cannot depend on the State's satisfaction of multiple, independent evidentiary requirements. No more for dogs than for human informants is such an inflexible checklist the way to prove reliability, and thus establish probable cause.

Making matters worse, the decision below treats records of a dog's field performance as the gold standard in evidence, when in most cases they have relatively limited import. Errors may abound in such records. If a dog on patrol fails to alert to a car containing drugs, the mistake usually will go undetected because the officer will not initiate a search. Field data thus may not capture a dog's false negatives. Conversely (and more relevant here), if the dog alerts to a car in which the officer finds no narcotics, the dog may not have made a mistake at all. The dog may have detected substances that were too well hidden or present in quantities too small for the officer to locate. Or the dog may have smelled the residual odor of drugs previously in the vehicle or on the driver's person. Field data thus may markedly overstate a dog's real false positives. By contrast, those inaccuracies—in either direction—do not taint records of a dog's performance in standard training and certification settings. There, the designers of an assessment know where drugs are hidden and where they are not—and so where a dog should alert and where he should not. The better measure of a dog's reliability thus comes away from the field, in controlled testing environments.

For that reason, evidence of a dog's satisfactory performance in a certification or training program can itself provide sufficient reason to trust his alert. If a bona fide organization has certified a dog after testing his reliability in a controlled setting, a court can presume (subject to any conflicting evidence offered) that the dog's alert provides probable cause to search. The same is true, even in the absence of formal certification, if the dog has recently and successfully completed a training program that evaluated his proficiency in locating drugs. After all, law enforcement units have their own strong incentive to use effective training and certification programs, because only accurate drug-detection dogs enable officers to locate contraband without incurring unnecessary risks or wasting limited time and resources.

A defendant, however, must have an opportunity to challenge such evidence of a dog's reliability, whether by cross-examining the testifying officer or by introducing his own fact or expert witnesses. The defendant, for example, may contest the adequacy of a certification or training program, perhaps asserting that its standards are too lax or its methods faulty. So too, the defendant may examine how the dog (or handler) performed in the assessments made in those settings. Indeed, evidence of the dog's (or handler's) history in the field, although susceptible to the kind of misinterpretation we have discussed, may sometimes be relevant. And even assuming a dog is generally reliable, circumstances surrounding a particular alert may undermine the case for probable cause—if, say, the officer cued the dog (consciously or not), or if the team was working under unfamiliar conditions.

In short, a probable-cause hearing focusing on a dog's alert should proceed much like any other. The court should allow the parties to make their best case, consistent with the usual rules of criminal procedure. And the court should then evaluate the proffered evidence to decide what all the circumstances demonstrate. If the State has produced proof from controlled settings that a dog performs reliably in detecting drugs, and the defendant has not contested that showing, then the court should find probable cause. If, in contrast, the defendant has challenged the State's case (by disputing the reliability of the dog overall or of a particular alert), then the court should weigh the competing evidence. In all events, the court should not prescribe, as the Florida Supreme Court did, an inflexible set of evidentiary requirements. The question—similar to every inquiry into probable cause—is whether all the facts surrounding a dog's alert, viewed through the lens of common sense, would make a reasonably prudent person think that a search would reveal contraband or evidence of a crime. A sniff is up to snuff when it meets that test.

III

And here, Aldo's did. The record in this case amply supported the trial court's determination that Aldo's alert gave Wheetley probable cause to search Harris' truck.

The State, as earlier described, introduced substantial evidence of Aldo's training and his proficiency in finding drugs. The State showed that two years before alerting to Harris' truck, Aldo had successfully completed a 120-hour program in narcotics detection, and separately obtained a certification from an independent company. And although the certification expired after a year, the Sheriff's Office required continuing training for Aldo and Wheetley. The two satisfied the requirements of another, 40-hour training program one year prior to the search at issue. And Wheetley worked with Aldo for four hours each week on exercises designed to keep their skills sharp. Wheetley testified, and written records confirmed, that in those settings Aldo always performed at the highest level.

Harris declined to challenge in the trial court any aspect of Aldo's training. To be sure, Harris' briefs in *this* Court raise questions about that training's adequacy—for example, whether the programs simulated sufficiently diverse environments and whether they used enough blind testing (in which the handler does not know the location of drugs and so cannot cue the dog). Similarly, Harris here queries just how well Aldo performed in controlled testing. But Harris never voiced those doubts in the trial court, and cannot do so for the first time here. As the case came to the trial court, Aldo had successfully completed two recent drug-detection courses and maintained his proficiency through weekly training exercises. Viewed alone, that training record—with or without the prior certification—sufficed to establish Aldo's reliability.

And Harris' cross-examination of Wheetley, which focused on Aldo's field performance, failed to rebut the State's case. Harris principally contended in the trial court that because Wheetley did not find any of the substances Aldo was trained to detect, Aldo's two alerts must have been false. But we have already described the hazards of inferring too much from the failure of a dog's alert to lead to drugs; and here we doubt that Harris' logic does justice to Aldo's skills. Harris cooked and used methamphetamine on a regular basis; so as Wheetley later surmised, Aldo likely responded to odors that Harris had transferred to the driver's-side door handle of his truck. A well-trained drug-detection dog *should* alert to such odors; his response to them might appear a mistake, but in fact is not. And still more fundamentally, we do not evaluate probable cause in hindsight, based on what a search does or does not turn up. For the reasons already stated, Wheetley had good cause to view Aldo as a reliable detector of drugs. And no special circumstance here gave Wheetley reason to discount Aldo's usual dependability or distrust his response to Harris' truck.

Because training records established Aldo's reliability in detecting drugs and Harris failed to undermine that showing, we agree with the trial court that Wheetley had probable cause to search Harris' truck. We accordingly reverse the judgment of the Florida Supreme Court.

Defining and Applying Probable Cause

1. Probable cause for a *search* exists where the facts and circumstances within an officer's knowledge and of which she has reasonably trustworthy information are sufficient in themselves to warrant a person of reasonable caution in the belief that an offense has been or is being committed and that evidence bearing on that offense will be found in the place to be searched.

2. Probable cause for an *arrest* exists where the facts and circumstances within an officer's knowledge and of which she has reasonably trustworthy information are sufficient in themselves to warrant a person of reasonable caution in the belief that an offense has been or is being committed by the person whom the officer intends to arrest.

3. Under the common-sense, "totality of the circumstances" approach to probable cause, a court should look for:

a. A reliable source of information, including the source's basis of knowledge.

b. Detailed information suggestive of criminal activity.

c. Verification or corroboration of the information by the police.

These three elements are not rigid independent requirements; instead, they should be considered collectively, and additional information in one area can compensate for a deficit of information in another.

2. IS PROBABLE CAUSE AN OBJECTIVE OR SUBJECTIVE STANDARD?

Although a judge's probable cause determination may require an examination of a particular police officer's knowledge and information, probable cause is an *objective standard* focused on what a hypothetical "reasonable officer" would believe with the same knowledge and information. In *Whren v. U.S.*, the Supreme Court made it clear that the subjective beliefs and motivations of any particular officer are not relevant to the probable cause determination.

WHREN V. U.S.
517 U.S. 806 (1996)

JUSTICE SCALIA delivered the opinion of the Court.

In this case we decide whether the temporary detention of a motorist who the police have probable cause to believe has committed a civil traffic violation is inconsistent with the Fourth Amendment's prohibition against unreasonable seizures unless a reasonable officer would have been motivated to stop the car by a desire to enforce the traffic laws.

I

On the evening of June 10, 1993, plainclothes vice-squad officers of the District of Columbia Metropolitan Police Department were patrolling a "high drug area" of the city in an unmarked car. Their suspicions were aroused when they passed a dark Pathfinder truck with temporary license plates and youthful occupants waiting at a stop sign, the driver looking down into the lap of the passenger at his right. The truck remained stopped at the intersection for what seemed an unusually long time—more than 20 seconds. When the police car executed a U-turn in order to head back toward the truck, the Pathfinder turned suddenly to its right, without signaling, and sped off at an "unreasonable" speed. The policemen followed, and in a short while overtook the Pathfinder when it stopped behind other traffic at a red light. They pulled up alongside, and Officer Ephraim Soto stepped out and approached the driver's door, identifying himself as a police officer and directing the driver, petitioner Brown, to put the vehicle in park. When Soto drew up to the driver's window, he immediately observed two large plastic bags of what appeared to be crack cocaine in petitioner Whren's hands. Petitioners were arrested, and quantities of several types of illegal drugs were retrieved from the vehicle.

Petitioners were charged in a four-count indictment with violating various federal drug laws. At a pretrial suppression hearing, they challenged the legality of the stop and the resulting seizure of the drugs. They argued that the stop had not been justified by probable cause to believe, or even reasonable suspicion, that petitioners were engaged in illegal drug-dealing activity; and that Officer Soto's asserted ground for approaching the vehicle—to give the driver a warning concerning traffic violations—was pretextual. The District Court denied the suppression motion.

Petitioners were convicted of the counts at issue here. The Court of Appeals affirmed the convictions, holding with respect to the suppression issue that, "regardless of whether a police officer subjectively believes that the occupants of an automobile may be engaging in some other illegal behavior, a traffic stop is permissible as long as a reasonable officer in the same circumstances *could have* stopped the car for the suspected traffic violation."

II

The Fourth Amendment guarantees "[t]he right of the people to be secure in their persons, houses, papers, and effects, against unreasonable searches and seizures." Temporary detention of individuals during the stop of an automobile by the police, even if only for a brief period and for a limited purpose, constitutes a "seizure" of "persons" within the meaning of this provision. An automobile stop is thus subject to the constitutional imperative that it not be "unreasonable" under the circumstances. As a general matter, the decision to stop an automobile is reasonable where the police have probable cause to believe that a traffic violation has occurred.

Petitioners accept that Officer Soto had probable cause to believe that various provisions of the District of Columbia traffic code had been violated. They argue, however, that "in the unique context of civil traffic regulations" probable cause is not enough. Since, they contend, the use of automobiles is so heavily and minutely regulated that total compliance with traffic and safety rules is nearly impossible, a police officer will almost invariably be able to catch any given motorist in a technical violation. This creates the temptation to use traffic stops as a means of investigating other law violations, as to which no probable cause or even articulable suspicion exists. Petitioners, who are both black, further contend that police officers might decide which motorists to stop based on decidedly impermissible factors, such as the race of the car's occupants. To avoid this danger, they say, the Fourth Amendment test for traffic stops should be, not the normal one (applied by the Court of Appeals) of whether probable cause existed to justify the stop; but rather, whether a police officer, acting reasonably, would have made the stop for the reason given.

Petitioners contend that the standard they propose is consistent with our past cases' disapproval of police attempts to use valid bases of action against citizens as pretexts for pursuing other investigatory agendas. But only an undiscerning reader would regard these cases as endorsing the principle that ulterior motives can invalidate police conduct that is justifiable on the basis of probable cause to believe that a violation of law has occurred. In each case we were addressing the validity of a search conducted in the *absence* of probable cause.

Not only have we never held, outside the context of inventory search or administrative inspection, that an officer's motive invalidates objectively justifiable behavior under the Fourth Amendment; but we have repeatedly held and asserted the contrary. We think [our prior] cases foreclose any argument that the constitutional reasonableness of traffic stops depends on the actual motivations of the individual officers involved. We of course agree with petitioners that the Constitution prohibits selective enforcement of the law based on considerations such as race. But the constitutional basis for objecting to intentionally discriminatory application of laws is the Equal Protection Clause, not the Fourth Amendment. Subjective intentions play no role in ordinary, probable-cause Fourth Amendment analysis.

Recognizing that we have been unwilling to entertain Fourth Amendment challenges based on the actual motivations of individual officers, petitioners disavow any intention to make the individual officer's subjective good faith the touchstone of "reasonableness." They insist that the standard they have put forward—whether the officer's conduct deviated materially from usual police practices, so that a reasonable officer in the same circumstances would not have made the stop for the reasons given—is an "objective" one.

But although framed in empirical terms, this approach is plainly and indisputably driven by subjective considerations. Its whole purpose is to prevent the police from doing under the guise of enforcing the traffic code what they would like to do for different reasons. Petitioners' proposed standard may not use the word "pretext," but it is designed to combat nothing other than the perceived "danger" of the pretextual stop, albeit only indirectly and over the run of cases. Instead of asking whether the individual officer had the proper state of mind, the petitioners would have us ask, in effect, whether (based on general police practices) it is plausible to believe that the officer had the proper state of mind.

Why one would frame a test designed to combat pretext in such fashion that the court cannot take into account *actual and admitted pretext* is a curiosity that can only be explained by the fact that our cases have foreclosed the more sensible option. If those cases were based only upon the evidentiary difficulty of establishing subjective intent, petitioners' attempt to root out subjective vices through objective means might make sense. But they were not based only upon that, or indeed even principally upon that. Their principal basis—which applies equally to attempts to reach subjective intent through ostensibly objective means—is simply that the Fourth Amendment's concern with "reasonableness" allows certain actions to be taken in certain circumstances, *whatever* the subjective intent. But even if our concern had been only an evidentiary one, petitioners' proposal would by no means assuage it. Indeed, it seems to us somewhat easier to figure out the intent of an individual officer than to plumb the collective consciousness of law enforcement in order to determine whether a "reasonable officer" would have been moved to act upon the traffic violation. While police manuals and standard procedures may sometimes provide objective assistance, ordinarily one would be reduced to speculating about the hypothetical reaction of a hypothetical constable— an exercise that might be called virtual subjectivity.

Moreover, police enforcement practices, even if they could be practicably assessed by a judge, vary from place to place and from time to time. We cannot accept that the search and seizure protections of the Fourth Amendment are so variable, and can be made to turn upon such trivialities. The difficulty is illustrated by petitioners' arguments in this case. Their claim that a reasonable officer would not have made this stop is based largely on District of Columbia police regulations which permit plainclothes officers in unmarked vehicles to enforce traffic laws "only in the case of a violation that is so grave as to pose an *immediate threat* to the safety of others." This basis of invalidation would not apply in jurisdictions that had a different practice. And it would not have applied even in the District of Columbia, if Officer Soto had been wearing a uniform or patrolling in a marked police cruiser.

III

In what would appear to be an elaboration on the "reasonable officer" test, petitioners argue that the balancing inherent in any Fourth Amendment inquiry requires us to weigh the governmental and individual interests implicated in a traffic stop such as we have here. That balancing, petitioners claim, does not support investigation of minor traffic infractions by plainclothes police in unmarked vehicles; such investigation only minimally advances the government's interest in traffic safety, and may indeed retard it by producing motorist confusion and alarm—a view said to be supported by the Metropolitan Police Department's own regulations generally prohibiting this practice. And as for the Fourth Amendment interests of the individuals concerned, petitioners point out that our cases acknowledge that even ordinary traffic stops entail "a possibly unsettling show of authority"; that they at best "interfere with freedom of movement, are inconvenient, and consume time" and at worst "may create substantial anxiety." That anxiety is likely to be even more pronounced when the stop is conducted by plainclothes officers in unmarked cars.

It is of course true that in principle every Fourth Amendment case, since it turns upon a reasonableness determination, involves a balancing of all relevant factors. With rare exceptions not applicable here, however, the result of that balancing is not in doubt where the search or seizure is based upon probable cause.

Where probable cause has existed, the only cases in which we have found it necessary actually to perform the "balancing" analysis involved searches or seizures conducted in an extraordinary manner, unusually harmful to an individual's privacy or even physical interests—such as, for example, seizure by means of deadly force, unannounced entry into a home, entry into a home without a warrant, or physical penetration of the body. The making of a traffic stop out of uniform does not remotely qualify as such an extreme practice, and so is governed by the usual rule that probable cause to believe the law has been broken "outbalances" private interest in avoiding police contact.

Petitioners urge as an extraordinary factor in this case that the "multitude of applicable traffic and equipment regulations" is so large and so difficult to obey perfectly that virtually everyone is guilty of violation, permitting the police to single out almost whomever they wish for a stop. But we are aware of no principle that would allow us to decide at what point a code of law becomes so expansive and so commonly violated that infraction itself can no longer be the ordinary measure of the lawfulness of enforcement. And even if we could identify such exorbitant codes, we do not know by what standard (or what right) we would decide, as petitioners would have us do, which particular provisions are sufficiently important to merit enforcement.

For the run-of-the-mine case, which this surely is, we think there is no realistic alternative to the traditional common-law rule that probable cause justifies a search and seizure.

Here the District Court found that the officers had probable cause to believe that petitioners had violated the traffic code. That rendered the stop reasonable under the Fourth Amendment [and] the evidence thereby discovered admissible.

Probable Cause: An Objective Standard

Probable cause is an objective standard focused on what a "reasonable officer" would believe with the same knowledge and information. The subjective beliefs and motivations of any particular officer are not relevant to the probable cause determination.

B. WARRANTS

America's Founding Fathers—and many ordinary American colonists—were outraged by the British government's use of *general warrants* that failed to specify the person or place to be searched or the person or item to be seized. These general warrants gave British law enforcement officers virtually unfettered discretion to search and arrest. British officers often abused this discretion by targeting those who were perceived to be disloyal to the British government. The Fourth Amendment—and the Warrant Clause in particular—was a reaction to abusive searches and arrests made under the authority of general warrants.

Today, search and arrest warrants serve three principal objectives. First, and perhaps most significant, they check the police by conditioning the authority to search or arrest upon the approval of a neutral judge or magistrate. Second, a warrant limits the scope of a search or an arrest because the warrant must particularly describe the place to be searched and the persons or things to be seized. And third, the procedures for obtaining a warrant create a "paper trail" setting forth the probable cause for the search or the arrest, allowing a court to examine all of the evidence after-the-fact to determine whether all Fourth Amendment requirements have been satisfied.

You can view a sample federal search and seizure warrant at the link below. Note that the blank areas on the sample warrant represent constitutional requirements—a valid warrant must be supported by probable cause, and it must describe the location to be searched and any items to be seized. These constitutional requirements for obtaining and executing search warrants are explained in more detail below.

Sample Federal Search Warrant

http://www.uscourts.gov/uscourts/FormsAndFees/Forms/AO093.pdf

---

1. REQUIREMENTS FOR OBTAINING A WARRANT

The Warrant Clause sets forth a number of requirements that must be satisfied prior to the issuance of a warrant: "[N]o Warrants shall issue, but upon probable cause, supported by Oath or affirmation, and particularly describing the place to be searched and the persons or things to be seized." As noted above, each of these requirements is designed to limit the power and discretion of the police.

a. Neutral and Detached Magistrate

Although it is not explicitly set forth in the Warrant Clause, the Supreme Court has long held that a warrant may only be issued by a *neutral and detached magistrate.* Justice Robert Jackson explained the reasons for this requirement in *Johnson v. U.S.*, 333 U.S. 10 (1948):

> The point of the Fourth Amendment, which often is not grasped by zealous officers, is not that it denies law enforcement the support of the usual inferences which reasonable men draw from evidence. Its protection consists in requiring that those inferences be drawn by a neutral and detached magistrate instead of being judged by the officer engaged in the often competitive enterprise of ferreting out crime. Any assumption that evidence sufficient to support a magistrate's disinterested determination to issue a search warrant will justify the officers in making a search without a warrant would reduce the Amendment to a nullity and leave the people's homes secure only in the discretion of police officers. When the right of privacy must reasonably yield to the right of search is, as a rule, to be decided by a judicial officer, not by a policeman or Government enforcement agent.

The Supreme Court has further clarified the neutral and detached magistrate requirement in several cases excerpted below. In *Coolidge v. New Hampshire*, for example, a search warrant was issued by the same government official who was leading the criminal investigation. The Supreme Court held that the warrant was invalid because it was not issued by a neutral and detached magistrate.

COOLIDGE V. NEW HAMPSHIRE
403 U.S. 443 (1971)

The New Hampshire Attorney General was supervising a police investigation into the brutal murder of Pamela Mason, a 14-year-old girl.

After accumulating evidence implicating Edward Coolidge in the murder, the police sought a warrant authorizing a search of his car. Acting as a justice of the peace, the New Hampshire Attorney General himself issued the warrant. The Supreme Court found the warrant defective because it was not issued by a neutral and detached magistrate:

> In this case, the determination of probable cause was made by the chief "government enforcement agent" of the State—the Attorney General—who was actively in charge of the investigation and later was to be chief prosecutor at the trial. The State argues that the Attorney General, who was unquestionably authorized as a justice of the peace to issue warrants under then existing state law, did in fact act as a "neutral and detached magistrate." Without disrespect to the state law enforcement agent here involved, prosecutors and policemen simply cannot be asked to maintain the requisite neutrality with regard to their own investigations that must rightly engage their single-minded attention.

> We find no escape from the conclusion that the seizure and search of the Pontiac automobile cannot constitutionally rest upon the warrant issued by the state official who was the chief investigator and prosecutor in this case. Since he was not the neutral and detached magistrate required by the Constitution, the search stands on no firmer ground than if there had been no warrant at all.

In *Connally v. Georgia*, a judge received compensation for issuing warrants, but no compensation when an application for a warrant was denied. The Supreme Court held that these financial interests prevented the judge from being neutral and detached.

CONNALLY V. GEORGIA
429 U.S. 245 (1977)

Acting pursuant to a search warrant issued by an unsalaried justice of the peace, police discovered marijuana in the defendant's home. Under state law, a justice of the peace received five dollars for each warrant that was issued, but nothing when a warrant application was reviewed and denied. The Supreme Court found that the financial interests of the justice of the peace prevented him from being neutral and detached:

> The justice is not salaried. He is paid, so far as search warrants are concerned, by receipt of the fee prescribed by statute for his *issuance* of the warrant, and he receives nothing for his *denial* of the warrant. His financial welfare, therefore, is enhanced by

positive action and is not enhanced by negative action. The defendant is subjected to judicial action by an officer of a court who has a direct, personal, substantial, pecuniary interest in his conclusion to issue or to deny the warrant.

In *Lo-Ji Sales, Inc. v. New York*, a judge actually participated in the search conducted pursuant to the warrant he had issued. The Supreme Court held that the judge had failed to act as a neutral and detached magistrate.

LO-JI SALES, INC. V. NEW YORK
442 U.S. 319 (1979)

A town justice issued a warrant allowing the police to search for and seize obscene materials in an adult bookstore. The warrant application requested that the town justice accompany the police during the execution of the warrant to independently determine whether items at the bookstore violated the obscenity laws and were subject to seizure. The town justice agreed and went to the bookstore with the police, where, over the next six hours, he inspected hundreds of adult magazines and films and ordered them seized. Under these circumstances, the Supreme Court held that the town justice was not neutral and detached:

> The Town Justice did not manifest that neutrality and detachment demanded of a judicial officer when presented with a warrant application for a search and seizure. We need not question the subjective belief of the Town Justice in the propriety of his actions, but the objective facts of record manifest an erosion of whatever neutral and detached posture existed at the outset. He allowed himself to become a member, if not the leader, of the search party which was essentially a police operation. Once in the store, he was not acting as a judicial officer but as an adjunct law enforcement officer.

In *Shadwick v. City of Tampa*, the Supreme Court held that a warrant need not be issued by a lawyer or judge, but can instead be issued by a court clerk, provided the clerk is neutral and detached and capable of determining whether probable cause exists.

SHADWICK V. CITY OF TAMPA
407 U.S. 345 (1972)

The city of Tampa authorized municipal court clerks to issue arrest warrants for violations of municipal ordinances. Shadwick was arrested for impaired driving on a warrant issued by a municipal court clerk. He argued that a court clerk did not qualify as a neutral and detached magistrate capable of issuing a warrant under the Fourth Amendment. The Supreme Court held that a person empowered to issue warrants need not be a lawyer or judge, but "must meet two tests. He must be neutral and detached, and he must be capable of determining whether probable cause exists for the requested arrest or search."

The Court held that the municipal court clerk was neutral and detached under the first part of the test:

> Whatever else neutrality and detachment might entail, it is clear that they require severance and disengagement from activities of law enforcement. There has been no showing whatever here of partiality, or affiliation of these clerks with prosecutors or police. The record shows no connection with any law enforcement activity or authority which would distort the independent judgment the Fourth Amendment requires.

The Court also held, under the second part of the test, that municipal court clerks were capable of determining probable cause:

> The clerk's authority extends only to the issuance of arrest warrants for breach of municipal ordinances. We presume from the nature of the clerk's position that he would be able to deduce from the facts on an affidavit before him whether there was probable cause to believe a citizen guilty of impaired driving, breach of peace, drunkenness, trespass, or the multiple other common offenses covered by a municipal code. There has been no showing that this is too difficult a task for a clerk to accomplish.

Neutral and Detached Magistrate Requirement

In order to be a valid, a search or arrest warrant must be issued by a neutral and detached magistrate. The magistrate need not be a lawyer or judge, but he must be capable of determining probable cause and must not have financial interests or connections to law enforcement that would compromise his independence.

---

b. Probable Cause Supported by Oath or Affirmation

In order to obtain a warrant, a police officer must first demonstrate probable cause to a judge or magistrate. The officer can make this showing with oral statements given under oath, or with a sworn written statement known as an *affidavit*. The federal courts and most states also permit police officers to apply for warrants and submit sworn statements electronically or by telephone. Whether the police officer's statement is transmitted orally or in writing, the "Oath or affirmation" requirement means that it must be sworn—submitted under penalty of perjury—impressing upon the officer the importance of providing truthful information.

The police officer's sworn testimony or affidavit must itself establish probable cause. Additional information provided by the officer after a warrant has been issued cannot "cure" an otherwise defective affidavit. *Whiteley v. Warden* illustrates this point.

WHITELEY V. WARDEN, WYOMING STATE PENITENTIARY
401 U.S. 560 (1971)

A local sheriff received a tip that Harold Whiteley and Jack Daley had committed a burglary. The sheriff appeared before a justice of the peace and requested an arrest warrant for the two men by filing a "bare-bones" complaint alleging that Whiteley and Daley did "unlawfully break and enter a locked and sealed building." The Supreme Court found the complaint inadequate to establish probable cause:

> [The] complaint consists of nothing more than the [sheriff's] conclusion that the individuals named therein perpetrated the offense described in the complaint. The actual basis for [the sheriff's] conclusion was an informer's tip, but that fact, as well as every other operative fact, is omitted from the complaint. That document alone could not support the independent judgment of a disinterested magistrate.

The Supreme Court acknowledged that the sheriff had additional information implicating Whiteley and Daley that was never conveyed to the justice of the peace prior to issuance of the warrant, but noted that "an otherwise insufficient affidavit cannot be rehabilitated by testimony concerning information possessed by the affiant when he sought the warrant but not disclosed to the issuing magistrate."

The Oath or Affirmation Requirement

1. Whether submitted in written form, orally, or electronically, statements made by police to a magistrate in support of an application for a warrant must be sworn and must be sufficient to establish probable cause.

2. An insufficient statement or affidavit in support of a warrant cannot be rehabilitated by later sworn testimony concerning information known to the police—but not disclosed to the magistrate—at the time the application for the warrant was under review.

---

c. Particularity

The Fourth Amendment requires that a warrant "particularly describ[e] the place to be searched, and the persons or things to be seized." The "particularity" requirement was a direct reaction to the British government's use of general warrants in the American colonies, and, like the other provisions of the Warrant Clause, it serves to limit the power and discretion of authorities when they perform searches and seizures. As the Supreme Court explained in *Marron v. U.S.*, 275 U.S. 192 (1927):

> The requirement that warrants shall particularly describe the things to be seized makes general searches under them impossible and prevents the seizure of one thing under a warrant describing another. As to what is to be taken, nothing is left to the discretion of the officer executing the warrant.

Because of the particularity requirement, a properly issued warrant will usually contain a precise description of the location to be searched and any items the police are authorized to seize. As the Supreme Court noted in *Steele v. U.S.*, 267 U.S. 498 (1925), the description of the location need not be perfect: "It is enough if the description is such that the officer with a search warrant can with reasonable effort ascertain and identify the place intended."

In some cases, the police may not know ahead of time exactly what they will find when executing a warrant, and the warrant may therefore include some general language allowing the officers to search for and seize evidence related to the crime they are investigating. Does the inclusion of some general language in a warrant violate the particularity requirement? In *Andresen v. Maryland*, the Supreme Court confronted this question and held that on the facts before it, the warrant was still valid.

ANDRESEN V. MARYLAND
427 U.S. 463 (1976)

JUSTICE BLACKMUN delivered the opinion of the Court.

In early 1972, a Bi-County Fraud Unit, acting under the joint auspices of the State's Attorneys' Offices of Montgomery and Prince George's Counties, Md., began an investigation of real estate settlement activities in the Washington, D.C., area. At the time, petitioner Andresen was an attorney who, as a sole practitioner, specialized in real estate settlements in Montgomery County. During the Fraud Unit's investigation, his activities came under scrutiny, particularly in connection with a transaction involving Lot 13T in the Potomac Woods subdivision of Montgomery County. The investigation, which included interviews with the purchaser, the mortgage holder, and other lienholders of Lot 13T, as well as an examination of county land records, disclosed that petitioner, acting as settlement attorney, had defrauded Standard-Young Associates, the purchaser of Lot 13T. Petitioner had represented that the property was free of liens and that, accordingly, no title insurance was necessary, when in fact, he knew that there were two outstanding liens on the property. In addition, investigators learned that the lienholders, by threatening to foreclose their liens, had forced a halt to the purchaser's construction on the property. When Standard-Young had confronted petitioner with this information, he responded by issuing, as an agent of a title insurance company, a title policy guaranteeing clear title to the property. By this action, petitioner also defrauded that insurance company by requiring it to pay the outstanding liens.

The investigators, concluding that there was probable cause to believe that petitioner had committed the state crime of false pretenses against Standard-Young, applied for warrants to search petitioner's law office and the separate office of Mount Vernon Development Corporation, of which petitioner was incorporator, sole shareholder, resident agent, and director. The application sought permission to search for specified documents pertaining to the sale and conveyance of Lot 13T. A judge of the Sixth Judicial Circuit of Montgomery County concluded that there was probable cause and issued the warrants.

The searches of the two offices were conducted simultaneously during daylight hours on October 31, 1972. Petitioner was present during the search of his law office and was free to move about. Counsel for him was present during the latter half of the search. Between 2% and 3% of the files in the office were seized. A single investigator, in the presence of a police officer, conducted the search of Mount Vernon Development Corporation. This search, taking about four hours, resulted in the seizure of less than 5% of the corporation's files.

Petitioner eventually was charged, partly by information and partly by indictment, with the crime of false pretenses, based on his misrepresentation to Standard-Young concerning Lot 13T, and with fraudulent misappropriation by a fiduciary, based on similar false claims made to three home purchasers. Before trial began, petitioner moved to suppress the seized documents. The trial court held a full suppression hearing. At the hearing, the State returned to petitioner 45 of the 52 items taken from the offices of the corporation. The trial court suppressed six other corporation items on the ground that there was no connection between them and the crimes charged. The net result was that the only item seized from the corporation's offices that was not returned by the State or suppressed was a single file labeled "Potomac Woods General." In addition, the State returned to petitioner seven of the 28 items seized from his law office, and the trial court suppressed four other law office items based on its determination that there was no connection between them and the crime charged.

With respect to all the items not suppressed or returned, the trial court ruled that admitting them into evidence would not violate the Fifth and Fourth Amendments. It reasoned that the searches and seizures did not force petitioner to be a witness against himself because he had not been required to produce the seized documents, nor would he be compelled to authenticate them. Moreover, the search warrants were based on probable cause, and the documents not returned or suppressed were either directly related to Lot 13T, and therefore within the express language of the warrants, or properly seized and otherwise admissible to show a pattern of criminal conduct relevant to the charge concerning Lot 13T.

At trial, the State proved its case primarily by public land records and by records provided by the complaining purchasers, lienholders, and the title insurance company. It did introduce into evidence, however, a number of the seized items.

After a trial by jury, petitioner was found guilty upon five counts of false pretenses and three counts of fraudulent misappropriation by a fiduciary. He was sentenced to eight concurrent two-year prison terms.

We turn to petitioner's contention that rights guaranteed him by the Fourth Amendment were violated because the descriptive terms of the search warrants were so broad as to make them impermissible "general" warrants.

Although petitioner concedes that the warrants for the most part were models of particularity, he contends that they were rendered fatally "general" by the addition, in each warrant, to the exhaustive list of particularly described documents, of the phrase "together with other fruits, instrumentalities and evidence of crime at this (time) unknown." The quoted language, it is argued, must be read in isolation and without reference to the rest of the long sentence at the end of which it appears. When read "properly," petitioner contends, it permits the search for and seizure of any evidence of any crime.

General warrants, of course, are prohibited by the Fourth Amendment. The problem posed by the general warrant is not that of intrusion *per se*, but of a general, exploratory rummaging in a person's belongings. The Fourth Amendment addresses the problem by requiring a "particular description" of the things to be seized. This requirement makes general searches impossible and prevents the seizure of one thing under a warrant describing another. As to what is to be taken, nothing is left to the discretion of the officer executing the warrant.

In this case we agree with the determination of the Court of Special Appeals of Maryland that the challenged phrase must be read as authorizing only the search for and seizure of evidence relating to "the crime of false pretenses with respect to Lot 13T." The challenged phrase is not a separate sentence. Instead, it appears in each warrant at the end of a sentence containing a lengthy list of specified and particular items to be seized, all pertaining to Lot 13T.[10] We think it clear from the context that the term "crime" in the warrants refers only to the crime of false pretenses with respect to the sale of Lot 13T. The "other fruits" clause is one of a series that follows the colon after the word "Maryland." All clauses in the series are limited by what precedes that colon, namely, "items pertaining to . . . lot 13, block T." The warrants, accordingly, did not authorize the executing officers to conduct a search for evidence of other crimes but only to search for and seize evidence relevant to the crime of false pretenses and Lot 13T.[11]

JUSTICE BRENNAN, dissenting.

I believe that the warrants under which petitioner's papers were seized were impermissibly general. I therefore dissent. General warrants are especially prohibited by the Fourth Amendment. Thus the requirement plainly appearing on the face of the Fourth Amendment that a warrant specify with particularity the place to be searched and the things to be seized is imposed to the end that unauthorized invasions of "the sanctity of a man's home and the privacies of life" be prevented.

The Court recites these requirements, but their application in this case renders their limitation on unlawful governmental conduct an empty promise. After a lengthy and admittedly detailed listing of items to be seized, the warrants in this case further authorized the seizure of "other fruits, instrumentalities and evidence of crime at this (time) unknown." The Court construes this sweeping authorization to be limited to evidence pertaining to the crime of false pretenses with respect to the sale of Lot 13T. However, neither this Court's construction of the warrants nor the similar construction by the Court of Special Appeals of Maryland was

---

[10] Petitioner also suggests that the specific list of the documents to be seized constitutes a "general" warrant. We disagree. Under investigation was a complex real estate scheme whose existence could be proved only by piecing together many bits of evidence. Like a jigsaw puzzle, the whole "picture" of petitioner's false-pretense scheme with respect to Lot 13T could be shown only by placing in the proper place the many pieces of evidence that, taken singly, would show comparatively little. The complexity of an illegal scheme may not be used as a shield to avoid detection when the State has demonstrated probable cause to believe that a crime has been committed and probable cause to believe that evidence of this crime is in the suspect's possession.

[11] We recognize that there are grave dangers inherent in executing a warrant authorizing a search and seizure of a person's papers that are not necessarily present in executing a warrant to search for physical objects whose relevance is more easily ascertainable. In searches for papers, it is certain that some innocuous documents will be examined, at least cursorily, in order to determine whether they are, in fact, among those papers authorized to be seized. Similar dangers, of course, are present in executing a warrant for the "seizure" of telephone conversations. In both kinds of searches, responsible officials, including judicial officials, must take care to assure that they are conducted in a manner that minimizes unwarranted intrusions upon privacy.

available to the investigators at the time they executed the warrants. The question is not how those warrants are to be viewed in hindsight, but how they were in fact viewed by those executing them. The overwhelming quantity of seized material that was either suppressed or returned to petitioner is irrefutable testimony to the unlawful generality of the warrants. The Court's attempt to cure this defect by *post hoc* judicial construction evades principles settled in this Court's Fourth Amendment decisions. "The scheme of the Fourth Amendment becomes meaningful only when it is assured that at some point the conduct of those charged with enforcing the laws can be subjected to the more detached, neutral scrutiny of a judge." It is not the function of a detached and neutral review to give effect to warrants whose terms unassailably authorize the far-reaching search and seizure of a person's papers especially where that has in fact been the result of executing those warrants.

In *Groh v. Ramirez*, a law enforcement officer's affidavit and warrant application both included a detailed explanation of the items for which the officer planned to search. When the actual search warrant was issued, however, it did not describe the items, nor did the warrant incorporate by reference the information in the warrant application and the affidavit. The Supreme Court held that the warrant violated the particularity requirement.

As you read *Groh*, note the disagreement between the majority and the dissent over the interpretation of the Warrant Clause. Justice Stevens' majority opinion treats the Warrant Clause as an independent requirement under the Fourth Amendment: If the Warrant Clause is violated, the warrant is defective, and the search is warrantless and unreasonable. Justice Thomas' dissenting opinion argues that a search pursuant to a defective warrant is not a warrantless search, and there is no Fourth Amendment violation as long as the search is reasonable.

GROH V. RAMIREZ
540 U.S. 551 (2004)

JUSTICE STEVENS delivered the opinion of the Court.

Petitioner conducted a search of respondents' home pursuant to a warrant that failed to describe the "persons or things to be seized." The question presented is whether the search violated the Fourth Amendment.

I

Respondents, Joseph Ramirez and members of his family, live on a large ranch in Butte-Silver Bow County, Montana. Petitioner, Jeff Groh, has been a Special Agent for the Bureau of Alcohol, Tobacco and Firearms

(ATF) since 1989. In February 1997, a concerned citizen informed petitioner that on a number of visits to respondents' ranch the visitor had seen a large stock of weaponry, including an automatic rifle, grenades, a grenade launcher, and a rocket launcher. Based on that information, petitioner prepared and signed an application for a warrant to search the ranch. The application stated that the search was for "any automatic firearms or parts to automatic weapons, destructive devices to include but not limited to grenades, grenade launchers, rocket launchers, and any and all receipts pertaining to the purchase or manufacture of automatic weapons or explosive devices or launchers." Petitioner supported the application with a detailed affidavit, which he also prepared and executed, that set forth the basis for his belief that the listed items were concealed on the ranch. Petitioner then presented these documents to a Magistrate, along with a warrant form that petitioner also had completed. The Magistrate signed the warrant form.

Although the application particularly described the place to be searched and the contraband petitioner expected to find, the warrant itself was less specific; it failed to identify any of the items that petitioner intended to seize. In the portion of the form that called for a description of the "person or property" to be seized, petitioner typed a description of respondents' two-story blue house rather than the alleged stockpile of firearms. The warrant did not incorporate by reference the itemized list contained in the application. It did, however, recite that the Magistrate was satisfied the affidavit established probable cause to believe that contraband was concealed on the premises, and that sufficient grounds existed for the warrant's issuance.

The day after the Magistrate issued the warrant, petitioner led a team of law enforcement officers, including both federal agents and members of the local sheriff's department, in the search of respondents' premises. Although respondent Joseph Ramirez was not home, his wife and children were. Petitioner states that he orally described the objects of the search to Mrs. Ramirez in person and to Mr. Ramirez by telephone. According to Mrs. Ramirez, however, petitioner explained only that he was searching for "an explosive device in a box." At any rate, the officers' search uncovered no illegal weapons or explosives. When the officers left, petitioner gave Mrs. Ramirez a copy of the search warrant, but not a copy of the application, which had been sealed. The following day, in response to a request from respondents' attorney, petitioner faxed the attorney a copy of the page of the application that listed the items to be seized. No charges were filed against the Ramirezes.

Respondents sued petitioner and the other officers under 42 U.S.C. § 1983, raising eight claims, including violation of the Fourth Amendment. The District Court entered summary judgment for all defendants. The court found no Fourth Amendment violation, because it considered the case comparable to one in which the warrant contained an inaccurate address, and in such a case, the court reasoned, the warrant is sufficiently detailed if the executing officers can locate the correct house.

II

The warrant was plainly invalid. The Fourth Amendment states unambiguously that "no Warrants shall issue, but upon probable cause, supported by Oath or affirmation, and *particularly describing* the place to be searched, and *the persons or things to be seized.*" The warrant in this case complied with the first three of these requirements: It was based on probable cause and supported by a sworn affidavit, and it described particularly the place of the search. On the fourth requirement, however, the warrant failed altogether. Indeed, petitioner concedes that "the warrant was deficient in particularity because it provided no description of the type of evidence sought."

The fact that the *application* adequately described the "things to be seized" does not save the *warrant* from its facial invalidity. The Fourth Amendment by its terms requires particularity in the warrant, not in the supporting documents. And for good reason: "The presence of a search warrant serves a high function," and that high function is not necessarily vindicated when some other document, somewhere, says something about the objects of the search, but the contents of that document are neither known to the person whose home is being searched nor available for her inspection. We do not say that the Fourth Amendment prohibits a warrant from cross-referencing other documents. Indeed, most Courts of Appeals have held that a court may construe a warrant with reference to a supporting application or affidavit if the warrant uses appropriate words of incorporation, and if the supporting document accompanies the warrant. But in this case the warrant did not incorporate other documents by reference, nor did either the affidavit or the application (which had been placed under seal) accompany the warrant. Hence, we need not further explore the matter of incorporation.

Petitioner argues that even though the warrant was invalid, the search nevertheless was "reasonable" within the meaning of the Fourth Amendment. He notes that a Magistrate authorized the search on the basis of adequate evidence of probable cause, that petitioner orally described to respondents the items to be seized, and that the search did not exceed the limits intended by the Magistrate and described by petitioner. Thus, petitioner maintains, his search of respondents' ranch was functionally equivalent to a search authorized by a valid warrant.

We disagree. This warrant did not simply omit a few items from a list of many to be seized, or misdescribe a few of several items. Nor did it make what fairly could be characterized as a mere technical mistake or typographical error. Rather, in the space set aside for a description of the items to be seized, the warrant stated that the items consisted of a "single dwelling residence blue in color." In other words, the warrant did not describe the items to be seized *at all*. In this respect the warrant was so obviously deficient that we must regard the search as "warrantless" within the meaning of our case law. Because the right of a man to retreat into his own home and there be free from unreasonable governmental intrusion stands at the very core of the Fourth Amendment, our cases have firmly established the basic principle of Fourth Amendment law that searches and seizures inside a home without a warrant are presumptively unreasonable. Thus, absent exigent circumstances, a warrantless entry to search for weapons or contraband is unconstitutional even when a felony has been committed and there is probable cause to believe that incriminating evidence will be found within.

We have clearly stated that the presumptive rule against warrantless searches applies with equal force to searches whose only defect is a lack of particularity in the warrant. Petitioner asks us to hold that a search conducted pursuant to a warrant lacking particularity should be exempt from the presumption of unreasonableness if the goals served by the particularity requirement are otherwise satisfied. He maintains that the search in this case satisfied those goals—which he says are "to prevent general searches, to prevent the seizure of one thing under a warrant describing another, and to prevent warrants from being issued on vague or dubious information"—because the scope of the search did not exceed the limits set forth in the application. But unless the particular items described in the affidavit are also set forth in the warrant itself (or at least incorporated by reference, and the affidavit present at the search), there can be no written assurance that the Magistrate actually found probable cause to search for, and to seize, every item mentioned in the affidavit. In this case, for example, it is at least theoretically possible that the Magistrate was satisfied that the search for weapons and explosives was justified by the showing in the affidavit, but not convinced that any evidentiary basis existed for rummaging through respondents' files and papers for receipts pertaining to the purchase or manufacture of such items. Or, conceivably, the Magistrate might have believed that some of the weapons mentioned in the affidavit could have been lawfully possessed and therefore should not be seized. The mere fact that the Magistrate issued a warrant does not necessarily establish that he agreed that the scope of the search should be as broad as the affiant's request. Even though petitioner acted with restraint in conducting the search, the inescapable fact is that this restraint was imposed by the agents themselves, not by a judicial officer.

We have long held, moreover, that the purpose of the particularity requirement is not limited to the prevention of general searches. A particular warrant also "assures the individual whose property is searched or seized of the lawful authority of the executing officer, his need to search, and the limits of his power to search."

It is incumbent on the officer executing a search warrant to ensure the search is lawfully authorized and lawfully conducted. Because petitioner did not have in his possession a warrant particularly describing the things he intended to seize, proceeding with the search was clearly "unreasonable" under the Fourth Amendment.

JUSTICE THOMAS, with whom JUSTICE SCALIA joins, dissenting.

The precise relationship between the [Fourth] Amendment's Warrant Clause and Unreasonableness Clause is unclear. But neither Clause explicitly requires a warrant. While it is of course textually possible to consider a warrant requirement implicit within the requirement of reasonableness, the text of the Fourth Amendment certainly does not mandate this result. Nor does the Amendment's history, which is clear as to the Amendment's principal target (general warrants), but not as clear with respect to when warrants were required, if ever. Indeed, because of the very different nature and scope of federal authority and ability to conduct searches and arrests at the founding, it is possible that neither the history of the Fourth Amendment nor the common law provides much guidance.

As a result, the Court has vacillated between imposing a categorical warrant requirement and applying a general reasonableness standard. The Court has most frequently held that warrantless searches are presumptively unreasonable, but has also found a plethora of exceptions to presumptive unreasonableness. That is, our cases stand for the illuminating proposition that warrantless searches are *per se* unreasonable, except, of course, when they are not.

Today the Court holds that the warrant in this case was "so obviously deficient" that the ensuing search must be regarded as a warrantless search and thus presumptively unreasonable. However, the text of the Fourth Amendment, its history, and the sheer number of exceptions to the Court's categorical warrant requirement seriously undermine the bases upon which the Court today rests its holding. Instead of adding to this confusing jurisprudence, as the Court has done, I would turn to first principles in order to determine the relationship between the Warrant Clause and the Unreasonableness Clause. But even within the Court's current framework, a search conducted pursuant to a defective warrant is constitutionally different from a "warrantless search." Consequently, despite the defective warrant, I would still ask whether this search was unreasonable and would conclude that it was not.

Any Fourth Amendment case may present two separate questions: whether the search was conducted pursuant to a warrant issued in accordance with the second Clause, and, if not, whether it was nevertheless "reasonable" within the meaning of the first. By categorizing the search here to be a "warrantless" one, the Court declines to perform a reasonableness inquiry and ignores the fact that this search is quite different from searches that the Court has considered to be "warrantless" in the past. Our cases involving "warrantless" searches do not generally involve situations in which an officer has obtained a warrant that is later determined to be facially defective, but rather involve situations in which the officers neither sought nor obtained a warrant. By simply treating this case as if no warrant had even been sought or issued, the Court glosses over what should be the key inquiry: whether it is always appropriate to treat a search made pursuant to a warrant that fails to describe particularly the things to be seized as presumptively unreasonable.

The Court also rejects the argument that the details of the warrant application and affidavit save the warrant, because "the presence of a search warrant serves a high function." But it is not only the physical existence of the warrant and its typewritten contents that serve this high function. The Warrant Clause's principal protection lies in the fact that the "Fourth Amendment has interposed a magistrate between the citizen and the police so that an objective mind might weigh the need to invade [the searchee's] privacy in order to enforce the law."

But the actual contents of the warrant are simply manifestations of this protection. Hence, in contrast to the case of a truly warrantless search, where a warrant (due to a mistake) does not specify on its face the particular items to be seized but the warrant application passed on by the magistrate judge contains such details, a searchee still has the benefit of a determination by a neutral magistrate that there is probable cause to search a particular place and to seize particular items. In such a circumstance, the principal justification for applying a rule of presumptive unreasonableness falls away.

In the instant case, the items to be seized were clearly specified in the warrant application and set forth in the affidavit, both of which were given to the Judge (Magistrate). The Magistrate reviewed all of the documents and signed the warrant application and made no adjustment or correction to this application. It is clear that respondents here received the protection of the Warrant Clause. Under these circumstances, I would not hold that any ensuing search constitutes a presumptively unreasonable warrantless search. Instead, I would determine whether, despite the invalid warrant, the resulting search was reasonable and hence constitutional.

Because the search was not unreasonable, I would conclude that it was constitutional. Prior to execution of the warrant, petitioner briefed the search team and provided a copy of the search warrant application, the supporting affidavit, and the warrant for the officers to review. Petitioner orally reviewed the terms of the warrant with the officers, including the specific items for which the officers were authorized to search. Petitioner and his search team then conducted the search entirely within the scope of the warrant application and warrant; that is, within the scope of what the Magistrate had authorized. Finding no illegal weapons or explosives, the search team seized nothing. When petitioner left, he gave respondents a copy of the search warrant. Upon request the next day, petitioner faxed respondents a copy of the more detailed warrant application. Indeed, putting aside the technical defect in the warrant, it is hard to imagine how the actual search could have been carried out any more reasonably.

The Particularly Requirement

1.   A warrant must particularly describe the place to be searched and the persons or things to be seized. The description need not be perfect, but must be such that an officer can reasonably ascertain and identify the location or items intended.

2.   The inclusion of some general language in a warrant does not render the warrant itself impermissibly general as long as the language is construed narrowly and is not used by the police to justify a search for or seizure of items not relevant to the crime under investigation.

3.   A description in a warrant that is insufficiently particular may be saved by an adequate description in the affidavit or application submitted in support of the warrant, but only if the warrant itself uses appropriate words of incorporation and the supporting affidavit or application accompanies the warrant.

---

2.   ANTICIPATORY WARRANTS

An anticipatory warrant grants the police authority to search or seize only if certain events first take place. For example, an officer might request permission to search for and seize illegal drugs in a home after they have been delivered to the premises. The Supreme Court approved anticipatory warrants in *U.S. v. Grubbs.*

U.S. v. GRUBBS
547 U.S. 90 (2006)

Grubbs purchased a videotape containing child pornography from a website operated by an undercover postal inspector. Officers from the Postal Inspection Service arranged a controlled delivery of a package containing the videotape to Grubbs' residence. The affidavit in support of a search warrant stated that the warrant would not be executed until the package was received and taken into the residence. Grubbs argued that the warrant was invalid because, at the time it was issued, there was no probable cause to believe there was contraband at his home. The Supreme Court rejected Grubbs' argument:

When an anticipatory warrant is issued, the fact that the contraband is not presently located at the place described in the warrant is immaterial, so long as there is probable cause to believe that it will be there when the search warrant is executed.

The Supreme Court approved anticipatory warrants, subject to a two-part probable cause standard:

> For a conditioned anticipatory warrant to comply with the Fourth Amendment's requirement of probable cause, two prerequisites of probability must be satisfied. It must be true not only that *if* the triggering condition occurs there is a fair probability that contraband or evidence of a crime will be found in a particular place, but also that there is probable cause to believe the triggering condition *will occur*. The supporting affidavit must provide the magistrate with sufficient information to evaluate both aspects of the probable-cause determination.

Anticipatory Warrants

1. The fact that an item which police are authorized to search for and seize is not currently located at the place described in a warrant is immaterial as long as there is probable cause to believe that it will be there when the search warrant is executed.

2. Two prerequisites of probability must be satisfied for an anticipatory warrant to meet the Fourth Amendment requirement of probable cause, and the supporting affidavit must provide the magistrate with sufficient information to evaluate both aspects of the probable cause determination.

    a. There must be probable cause to believe that a triggering condition—such as the arrival of the contraband—will occur.

    b. There must be probable cause to believe that if the triggering condition occurs, there is a fair probability that contraband or evidence of a crime will be found in a particular place.

---

3. EXECUTING WARRANTS

A number of issues arise concerning the execution of warrants. First, do the police have to knock on the door, announce their presence, and request entry, or does the warrant give them the power to barge right in? Second, how should the police treat persons present on the premises when a warrant is executed? Can they be detained and searched as well? Third, what happens if the police make a mistake while executing a warrant? The Supreme Court has addressed each of these questions in the cases excerpted below.

a.   The "Knock and Announce" Requirement

In *Wilson v. Arkansas*, 514 U.S. 927 (1995), the Supreme Court held that in the absence of exigent circumstances, the police must knock and announce their presence before entering a residence to execute a search warrant. Just two years later, in *Richards v. Wisconsin*, the Supreme Court considered and rejected a blanket exception to the "knock and announce" requirement in drug cases. The Court did, however, announce a standard for determining when officers may enter without first knocking and announcing their presence.

RICHARDS V. WISCONSIN
520 U.S. 385 (1997)

JUSTICE STEVENS delivered the opinion of the Court.

In *Wilson v. Arkansas*, 514 U.S. 927 (1995), we held that the Fourth Amendment incorporates the common law requirement that police officers entering a dwelling must knock on the door and announce their identity and purpose before attempting forcible entry. At the same time, we recognized that the "flexible requirement of reasonableness should not be read to mandate a rigid rule of announcement that ignores countervailing law enforcement interests," and left "to the lower courts the task of determining the circumstances under which an unannounced entry is reasonable under the Fourth Amendment."

In this case, the Wisconsin Supreme Court concluded that police officers are *never* required to knock and announce their presence when executing a search warrant in a felony drug investigation. We disagree with the court's conclusion that the Fourth Amendment permits a blanket exception to the knock-and-announce requirement for this entire category of criminal activity. But because the evidence presented to support the officers' actions in this case establishes that the decision not to knock and announce was a reasonable one under the circumstances, we affirm the judgment of the Wisconsin court.

I

On December 31, 1991, police officers in Madison, Wisconsin, obtained a warrant to search Steiney Richards' motel room for drugs and related paraphernalia. The search warrant was the culmination of an investigation that had uncovered substantial evidence that Richards was one of several individuals dealing drugs out of motel rooms in Madison. The police requested a warrant that would have given advance authorization for a "no-knock" entry into the motel room, but the Magistrate explicitly deleted those portions of the warrant.

The officers arrived at the motel room at 3:40 a.m. Officer Pharo, dressed as a maintenance man, led the team. With him were several plainclothes officers and at least one man in uniform. Officer Pharo knocked on Richards' door and, responding to the query from inside the room, stated that he was a maintenance man. With the chain still on the door, Richards cracked it open. Although there is some dispute as to what occurred next, Richards acknowledges that when he opened the door he saw the man in uniform standing behind Officer Pharo. He quickly slammed the door closed and, after waiting two or three seconds, the officers began kicking and ramming the door to gain entry to the locked room. At trial, the officers testified that they identified themselves as police while they were kicking the door in. When they finally did break into the room, the officers caught Richards trying to escape through the window. They also found cash and cocaine hidden in plastic bags above the bathroom ceiling tiles.

Richards sought to have the evidence from his motel room suppressed on the ground that the officers had failed to knock and announce their presence prior to forcing entry into the room. The trial court denied the motion, concluding that the officers could gather from Richards' strange behavior when they first sought entry that he knew they were police officers and that he might try to destroy evidence or to escape. The judge emphasized that the easily disposable nature of the drugs the police were searching for further justified their decision to identify themselves as they crossed the threshold instead of announcing their presence before seeking entry. Richards appealed the decision to the Wisconsin Supreme Court and that court affirmed.

II·

We recognized in *Wilson* that the knock-and-announce requirement could give way "under circumstances presenting a threat of physical violence," or "where police officers have reason to believe that evidence would likely be destroyed if advance notice were given." It is indisputable that felony drug investigations may frequently involve both of these circumstances. The question we must resolve is whether this fact justifies dispensing with case-by-case evaluation of the manner in which a search was executed.

The Wisconsin court explained its blanket exception as necessitated by the special circumstances of today's drug culture, and the State asserted at oral argument that the blanket exception was reasonable in "felony drug cases because of the convergence in a violent and dangerous form of commerce of weapons and the destruction of drugs." But creating exceptions to the knock-and-announce rule based on the "culture" surrounding a general category of criminal behavior presents at least two serious concerns.

First, the exception contains considerable overgeneralization. For example, while drug investigation frequently does pose special risks to officer safety and the preservation of evidence, not every drug investigation will pose these risks to a substantial degree. For example, a search could be conducted at a time when the only individuals present in a residence have no connection with the drug activity and thus will be unlikely to threaten officers or destroy evidence. Or the police could know that the drugs being searched for were of a type or in a location that made them impossible to destroy quickly. In those situations, the asserted governmental interests in preserving evidence and maintaining safety may not outweigh the individual privacy interests intruded upon by a no-knock entry. Wisconsin's blanket rule impermissibly insulates these cases from judicial review.

A second difficulty with permitting a criminal-category exception to the knock-and-announce requirement is that the reasons for creating an exception in one category can, relatively easily, be applied to others. Armed bank robbers, for example, are, by definition, likely to have weapons, and the fruits of their crime may be destroyed without too much difficulty. If a *per se* exception were allowed for each category of criminal investigation that included a considerable—albeit hypothetical—risk of danger to officers or destruction of evidence, the knock-and-announce element of the Fourth Amendment's reasonableness requirement would be meaningless.

Thus, the fact that felony drug investigations may frequently present circumstances warranting a no-knock entry cannot remove from the neutral scrutiny of a reviewing court the reasonableness of the police decision not to knock and announce in a particular case. Instead, in each case, it is the duty of a court confronted with the question to determine whether the facts and circumstances of the particular entry justified dispensing with the knock-and-announce requirement.

In order to justify a "no-knock" entry, the police must have a reasonable suspicion that knocking and announcing their presence, under the particular circumstances, would be dangerous or futile, or that it would inhibit the effective investigation of the crime by, for example, allowing the destruction of evidence. This standard—as opposed to a probable-cause requirement—strikes the appropriate balance between the legitimate law enforcement concerns at issue in the execution of search warrants and the individual privacy interests affected by no-knock entries. This showing is not high, but the police should be required to make it whenever the reasonableness of a no-knock entry is challenged.

III

Although we reject the Wisconsin court's blanket exception to the knock-and-announce requirement, we conclude that the officers' no-knock entry into Richards' motel room did not violate the Fourth Amendment. We agree with the trial court that the circumstances in this case show that the officers had a reasonable suspicion that Richards might destroy evidence if given further opportunity to do so.

The judge who heard testimony at Richards' suppression hearing concluded that it was reasonable for the officers executing the warrant to believe that Richards knew, after opening the door to his motel room the first time, that the men seeking entry to his room were the police. Once the officers reasonably believed that Richards knew who they were, the court concluded, it was reasonable for them to force entry immediately given the disposable nature of the drugs.

In arguing that the officers' entry was unreasonable, Richards places great emphasis on the fact that the Magistrate who signed the search warrant for his motel room deleted the portions of the proposed warrant that would have given the officers permission to execute a no-knock entry. But this fact does not alter the reasonableness of the officers' decision, which must be evaluated as of the time they entered the motel room. At the time the officers obtained the warrant, they did not have evidence sufficient, in the judgment of the Magistrate, to justify a no-knock warrant. Of course, the Magistrate could not have anticipated in every particular the circumstances that would confront the officers when they arrived at Richards' motel room.[7] These actual circumstances— petitioner's apparent recognition of the officers combined with the easily disposable nature of the drugs—justified the officers' ultimate decision to enter without first announcing their presence and authority.

———————————

Although *Wilson v. Arkansas* and *Richards v. Wisconsin* said that the "knock and announce" requirement was part of the "reasonableness" inquiry under the Fourth Amendment, in *Hudson v. Michigan*, 547 U.S. 586 (2006), the Supreme Court held that the exclusionary rule does not apply to evidence discovered after the police violate the "knock and announce" requirement. (*Hudson v. Michigan* is presented in Chapter 8, which deals with exceptions to the exclusionary rule.) If the Fourth Amendment requires police to knock and announce their presence before executing a warrant, but evidence will not be suppressed if they fail to do so, are there adequate incentives for police to comply with the "knock and announce" requirement?

The "Knock and Announce" Requirement

1. In the absence of exigent circumstances, police must knock and announce their presence before entering a residence to execute a search warrant.

---

[7] The practice of allowing magistrates to issue no-knock warrants seems entirely reasonable when sufficient cause to do so can be demonstrated ahead of time. But, as the facts of this case demonstrate, a magistrate's decision not to authorize a no-knock entry should not be interpreted to remove the officers' authority to exercise independent judgment concerning the wisdom of a no-knock entry at the time the warrant is being executed.

2.   In order to justify a "no-knock" entry, the police must have a reasonable suspicion that knocking and announcing their presence, under the particular circumstances, would be dangerous or futile, or that it would inhibit the effective investigation of the crime by, for example, allowing the destruction of evidence.

3.   Evidence discovered following a "knock and announce" violation will not be suppressed under the exclusionary rule.

b.   Treatment of Persons Present When a Warrant Is Executed

A warrant authorizing the police to perform a search at a certain location does *not* authorize the police to search persons present at the location when the warrant is executed. The Supreme Court explained this principle in *Ybarra v. Illinois*.

YBARRA V. ILLINOIS

444 U.S. 85 (1979)

Based on an informant's tip alleging that a bartender was selling drugs from behind the bar in a tavern, police obtained a warrant to search the tavern and the bartender. While executing the warrant, police officers "frisked" the patrons in the bar, finding several packets of heroin in a cigarette pack in Ventura Ybarra's pocket. The Supreme Court held that the search of Ybarra was illegal:

> It is true that the police possessed a warrant based on probable cause to search the tavern in which Ybarra happened to be at the time the warrant was executed. But, a person's mere propinquity to others independently suspected of criminal activity does not, without more, give rise to probable cause to search that person. Where the standard is probable cause, a search or seizure of a person must be supported by probable cause particularized with respect to that person. This requirement cannot be undercut or avoided by simply pointing to the fact that coincidentally there exists probable cause to search or seize another or to search the premises where the person may happen to be. The Fourth and Fourteenth Amendments protect the legitimate expectations of privacy of persons, not places.

While *Ybarra* makes it clear that a warrant authorizing a search of certain premises does not permit the police to search a person present at the premises when the warrant is executed, the Supreme Court has also held, in *Michigan v. Summers*, that those present may be *detained* while the search takes place.

MICHIGAN V. SUMMERS
452 U.S. 692 (1981)

As Detroit police officers prepared to execute a warrant to search a house for narcotics, they encountered George Summers descending the front steps. Police requested his assistance in gaining entry and detained him while they searched the premises. After finding narcotics in the basement and ascertaining that Summers owned the house, the police arrested him, searched his person, and found an envelope containing heroin in his coat pocket. Summers moved to suppress the heroin, claiming that his initial detention violated his Fourth Amendment right to be secure against an unreasonable seizure of his person.

The Supreme Court identified three law enforcement interests that justify detaining a person who is present when a search warrant is executed:

> Most obvious is the legitimate law enforcement interest in preventing flight in the event that incriminating evidence is found. Less obvious, but sometimes of greater importance, is the interest in minimizing the risk of harm to the officers. Although no special danger to the police is suggested by the evidence in this record, the execution of a warrant to search for narcotics is the kind of transaction that may give rise to sudden violence or frantic efforts to conceal or destroy evidence. The risk of harm to both the police and the occupants is minimized if the officers routinely exercise unquestioned command of the situation. Finally, the orderly completion of the search may be facilitated if the occupants of the premises are present. Their self-interest may induce them to open locked doors or locked containers to avoid the use of force that is not only damaging to property but may also delay the completion of the task at hand.

The Supreme Court ultimately concluded that "a warrant to search for contraband founded on probable cause implicitly carries with it the limited authority to detain the occupants of the premises while a proper search is conducted."

––––––––––––

The Supreme Court applied the *Summers* rule in *Muehler v. Mena*, holding that it was reasonable to detain an occupant for more than two hours in handcuffs while a search warrant for a home was being executed.

MUEHLER V. MENA
544 U.S. 93 (2005)

CHIEF JUSTICE REHNQUIST delivered the opinion of the Court.

Respondent Iris Mena was detained in handcuffs during a search of the premises that she and several others occupied. Petitioners were lead members of a police detachment executing a search warrant of these premises. She sued the officers under 42 U.S.C. § 1983, and the District Court found in her favor. The Court of Appeals affirmed the judgment, holding that the use of handcuffs to detain Mena during the search violated the Fourth Amendment and that the officers' questioning of Mena about her immigration status during the detention constituted an independent Fourth Amendment violation. We hold that Mena's detention in handcuffs for the length of the search was consistent with our opinion in *Michigan v. Summers*, 452 U.S. 692 (1981), and that the officers' questioning during that detention did not violate her Fourth Amendment rights.

Based on information gleaned from the investigation of a gang-related, driveby shooting, petitioners Muehler and Brill had reason to believe at least one member of a gang—the West Side Locos—lived at 1363 Patricia Avenue. They also suspected that the individual was armed and dangerous, since he had recently been involved in the driveby shooting. As a result, Muehler obtained a search warrant for 1363 Patricia Avenue that authorized a broad search of the house and premises for, among other things, deadly weapons and evidence of gang membership. In light of the high degree of risk involved in searching a house suspected of housing at least one, and perhaps multiple, armed gang members, a Special Weapons and Tactics (SWAT) team was used to secure the residence and grounds before the search.

At 7 a.m. on February 3, 1998, petitioners, along with the SWAT team and other officers, executed the warrant. Mena was asleep in her bed when the SWAT team, clad in helmets and black vests adorned with badges and the word "POLICE," entered her bedroom and placed her in handcuffs at gunpoint. The SWAT team also handcuffed three other individuals found on the property. The SWAT team then took those individuals and Mena into a converted garage, which contained several beds and some other bedroom furniture. While the search proceeded, one or two officers guarded the four detainees, who were allowed to move around the garage but remained in handcuffs.

Aware that the West Side Locos gang was composed primarily of illegal immigrants, the officers had notified the Immigration and Naturalization Service (INS) that they would be conducting the search, and an INS officer accompanied the officers executing the warrant. During their detention in the garage, an officer asked for each detainee's name, date of birth, place of birth, and immigration status. The INS officer later asked the detainees for their immigration documentation. Mena's status as a permanent resident was confirmed by her papers.

The search of the premises yielded a .22 caliber handgun with .22 caliber ammunition, a box of .25 caliber ammunition, several baseball bats with gang writing, various additional gang paraphernalia, and a bag of marijuana. Before the officers left the area, Mena was released.

In her § 1983 suit against the officers she alleged that she was detained "for an unreasonable time and in an unreasonable manner" in violation of the Fourth Amendment. In addition, she claimed that the warrant and its execution were overbroad, that the officers failed to comply with the "knock and announce" rule, and that the officers had needlessly destroyed property during the search. After a trial, a jury, pursuant to a special verdict form, found that Officers Muehler and Brill violated Mena's Fourth Amendment right to be free from unreasonable seizures by detaining her both with force greater than that which was reasonable and for a longer period than that which was reasonable. The jury awarded Mena $10,000 in actual damages and $20,000 in punitive damages against each petitioner for a total of $60,000.

The Court of Appeals affirmed the judgment on two grounds. It first held that the officers' detention of Mena violated the Fourth Amendment because it was objectively unreasonable to confine her in the converted garage and keep her in handcuffs during the search. In the Court of Appeals' view, the officers should have released Mena as soon as it became clear that she posed no immediate threat. The court additionally held that the questioning of Mena about her immigration status constituted an independent Fourth Amendment violation.

In *Michigan v. Summers*, we held that officers executing a search warrant for contraband have the authority "to detain the occupants of the premises while a proper search is conducted." Such detentions are appropriate, we explained, because the character of the additional intrusion caused by detention is slight and because the justifications for detention are substantial. We made clear that the detention of an occupant is "surely less intrusive than the search itself," and the presence of a warrant assures that a neutral magistrate has determined that probable cause exists to search the home. Against this incremental intrusion, we posited three legitimate law enforcement interests that provide substantial justification for detaining an occupant: "preventing flight in the event that incriminating evidence is found"; "minimizing the risk of harm to the officers"; and facilitating "the orderly completion of the search," as detainees' "self-interest may induce them to open locked doors or locked containers to avoid the use of force."

Mena's detention was, under *Summers*, plainly permissible. An officer's authority to detain incident to a search is categorical; it does not depend on the "quantum of proof justifying detention or the extent of the intrusion to be imposed by the seizure." Thus, Mena's detention for the duration of the search was reasonable under *Summers* because a warrant existed to search 1363 Patricia Avenue and she was an occupant of that address at the time of the search.

Inherent in *Summers'* authorization to detain an occupant of the place to be searched is the authority to use reasonable force to effectuate the detention. Indeed, *Summers* itself stressed that the risk of harm to officers and occupants is minimized "if the officers routinely exercise unquestioned command of the situation."

The officers' use of force in the form of handcuffs to effectuate Mena's detention in the garage, as well as the detention of the three other occupants, was reasonable because the governmental interests outweigh the marginal intrusion. The imposition of correctly applied handcuffs on Mena, who was already being lawfully detained during a search of the house, was undoubtedly a separate intrusion in addition to detention in the converted garage. The detention was thus more intrusive than that which we upheld in *Summers*.

But this was no ordinary search. The governmental interests in not only detaining, but using handcuffs, are at their maximum when, as here, a warrant authorizes a search for weapons and a wanted gang member resides on the premises. In such inherently dangerous situations, the use of handcuffs minimizes the risk of harm to both officers and occupants. Though this safety risk inherent in executing a search warrant for weapons was sufficient to justify the use of handcuffs, the need to detain multiple occupants made the use of handcuffs all the more reasonable.

Mena argues that, even if the use of handcuffs to detain her in the garage was reasonable as an initial matter, the duration of the use of handcuffs made the detention unreasonable. The duration of a detention can, of course, affect the balance of interests. However, the 2- to 3-hour detention in handcuffs in this case does not outweigh the government's continuing safety interests. As we have noted, this case involved the detention of four detainees by two officers during a search of a gang house for dangerous weapons. We conclude that the detention of Mena in handcuffs during the search was reasonable.

The Court of Appeals also determined that the officers violated Mena's Fourth Amendment rights by questioning her about her immigration status during the detention. This holding, it appears, was premised on the assumption that the officers were required to have independent reasonable suspicion in order to question Mena concerning her immigration status because the questioning constituted a discrete Fourth Amendment event. But the premise is faulty. We have held repeatedly that mere police questioning does not constitute a seizure. "Even when officers have no basis for suspecting a particular individual, they may generally ask questions of that individual; ask to examine the individual's identification; and request consent to search his or her luggage." As the Court of Appeals did not hold that the detention was prolonged by the questioning, there was no additional seizure within the meaning of the Fourth Amendment. Hence, the officers did not need reasonable suspicion to ask Mena for her name, date and place of birth, or immigration status.

In summary, the officers' detention of Mena in handcuffs during the execution of the search warrant was reasonable and did not violate the Fourth Amendment. Additionally, the officers' questioning of Mena did not constitute an independent Fourth Amendment violation. Mena has advanced in this Court, as she did before the Court of Appeals, an alternative argument for affirming the judgment below. She asserts that her detention extended beyond the time the police completed the tasks incident to the search. Because the Court of Appeals did not address this contention, we too decline to address it.

———————

The *Summers* rule, permitting police to detain a person who is present when a search warrant is executed, only applies to those within the immediate vicinity of the premises to be searched. In *Bailey v. U.S.*, the Supreme Court held that the *Summers* rule does *not* permit the apprehension and detention of someone who has left the premises a few minutes before the warrant is executed.

BAILEY V. U.S.
133 S.Ct. 1031 (2013)

While police were preparing to execute a warrant to search an apartment for a handgun, detectives conducting surveillance in an unmarked car saw two men leave the gated area above the apartment, get in a car, and drive away. The detectives followed the car for about a mile before stopping it. During a patdown search of the two men, police found a ring of keys on Chunon Bailey; he initially said he resided at the apartment but later denied it when informed that the search warrant was being executed. Both men were handcuffed and driven back to the apartment, where the search team had already found a gun and illegal drugs. After arresting the men, police discovered that one of Bailey's keys unlocked the apartment's door. Bailey moved to suppress the apartment key and the statements he made to police when he was stopped, but the trial court held that Bailey's detention was justified under *Michigan v. Summers*. The Supreme Court carefully examined the three law enforcement interests that justified the detention in *Summers*— preventing flight if incriminating evidence is found, minimizing the risk of harm to officers, and facilitating the orderly completion of the search—

and concluded that none of those interests justified the detention of anyone beyond the immediate vicinity of the premises to be searched:

> Of the three law enforcement interests identified to justify the detention in *Summers*, none applies with the same or similar force to the detention of recent occupants beyond the immediate vicinity of the premises to be searched. Any of the individual interests is also insufficient, on its own, to justify an expansion of the rule in *Summers* to permit the detention of a former occupant, wherever he may be found away from the scene of the search. This would give officers too much discretion. The categorical authority to detain incident to the execution of a search warrant must be limited to the immediate vicinity of the premises to be searched.

Treatment of Persons Present When a Search Warrant Is Executed

1.   In the absence of individualized suspicion of wrongdoing, police may not search a person present on the premises while executing a warrant authorizing a search of the premises.

2.   Police officers may detain a person present on the premises while executing a search warrant. If necessary for officer safety or other legitimate reasons, such a detention may last for several hours and include the use of handcuffs.

3.   The authority of police to detain a person while executing a search warrant on the premises is limited to those within the immediate vicinity of the premises to be searched.

---

c.   Mistakes in the Execution of Warrants

In *Maryland v. Garrison*, the Supreme Court held that if police make a mistake while executing a warrant, the search is constitutionally valid as long as the police acted reasonably given the information that was available to them at the time.

MARYLAND V. GARRISON
480 U.S. 79 (1987)

JUSTICE STEVENS delivered the opinion of the Court.

Baltimore police officers obtained and executed a warrant to search the person of Lawrence McWebb and "the premises known as 2036 Park Avenue third floor apartment." When the police applied for the warrant and when they conducted the search pursuant to the warrant, they reasonably believed that there was only one apartment on the premises described in the warrant. In fact, the third floor was divided into two apartments, one occupied by McWebb and one by respondent Garrison. Before the officers executing the warrant became aware that they were in a separate apartment occupied by respondent, they had discovered the contraband that provided the basis for respondent's conviction for violating Maryland's Controlled Substances Act. The question presented is whether the seizure of that contraband was prohibited by the Fourth Amendment.

There is no question that the warrant was valid and was supported by probable cause. The trial court found, and the two appellate courts did not dispute, that after making a reasonable investigation, including a verification of information obtained from a reliable informant, an exterior examination of the three-story building at 2036 Park Avenue, and an inquiry of the utility company, the officer who obtained the warrant reasonably concluded that there was only one apartment on the third floor and that it was occupied by McWebb. When six Baltimore police officers executed the warrant, they fortuitously encountered McWebb in front of the building and used his key to gain admittance to the first-floor hallway and to the locked door at the top of the stairs to the third floor. As they entered the vestibule on the third floor, they encountered respondent, who was standing in the hallway area. The police could see into the interior of both McWebb's apartment to the left and respondent's to the right, for the doors to both were open. Only after respondent's apartment had been entered and heroin, cash, and drug paraphernalia had been found did any of the officers realize that the third floor contained two apartments. As soon as they became aware of that fact, the search was discontinued. All of the officers reasonably believed that they were searching McWebb's apartment. No further search of respondent's apartment was made.

The matter on which there is a difference of opinion concerns the proper interpretation of the warrant. A literal reading of its plain language, as well as the language used in the application for the warrant, indicates that it was intended to authorize a search of the entire third floor. This is the construction adopted by the intermediate appellate court, and it also appears to be the construction adopted by the trial judge. One sentence in the trial judge's oral opinion, however, lends support to the construction adopted by the Court of Appeals, namely, that the warrant authorized a search of McWebb's apartment only. Under that interpretation, the Court of Appeals concluded that the warrant did not authorize the search of respondent's apartment and the police had no justification for making a warrantless entry into his premises.

In our view, the case presents two separate constitutional issues, one concerning the validity of the warrant and the other concerning the reasonableness of the manner in which it was executed. We shall discuss the questions separately.

I

The Warrant Clause of the Fourth Amendment categorically prohibits the issuance of any warrant except one "particularly describing the place to be searched and the persons or things to be seized." The manifest purpose of this particularity requirement was to prevent general searches. By limiting the authorization to search to the specific areas and things for which there is probable cause to search, the requirement ensures that the search will be carefully tailored to its justifications, and will not take on the character of the wide-ranging exploratory searches the Framers intended to prohibit. Thus, the scope of a lawful search is "defined by the object of the search and the places in which there is probable cause to believe that it may be found. Just as probable cause to believe that a stolen lawnmower may be found in a garage will not support a warrant to search an upstairs bedroom, probable cause to believe that undocumented aliens are being transported in a van will not justify a warrantless search of a suitcase."

In this case there is no claim that the "persons or things to be seized" were inadequately described or that there was no probable cause to believe that those things might be found in "the place to be searched" as it was described in the warrant. With the benefit of hindsight, however, we now know that the description of that place was broader than appropriate because it was based on the mistaken belief that there was only one apartment on the third floor of the building at 2036 Park Avenue. The question is whether that factual mistake invalidated a warrant that undoubtedly would have been valid if it had reflected a completely accurate understanding of the building's floor plan.

Plainly, if the officers had known, or even if they should have known, that there were two separate dwelling units on the third floor of 2036 Park Avenue, they would have been obligated to exclude respondent's apartment from the scope of the requested warrant. But we must judge the constitutionality of their conduct in light of the information available to them at the time they acted. Those items of evidence that emerge after the warrant is issued have no bearing on whether or not a warrant was validly issued. Just as the discovery of contraband cannot validate a warrant invalid when issued, so is it equally clear that the discovery of facts demonstrating that a valid warrant was unnecessarily broad does not retroactively invalidate the warrant. The validity of the warrant must be assessed on the basis of the information that the officers disclosed, or had a duty to discover and to disclose, to the issuing Magistrate. On the basis of that information, we agree with the conclusion of all three Maryland courts that the warrant, insofar as it authorized a search that turned out to be ambiguous in scope, was valid when it issued.

II

The question whether the execution of the warrant violated respondent's constitutional right to be secure in his home is somewhat less clear. We have no difficulty concluding that the officers' entry into the third-floor common area was legal; they carried a warrant for those premises, and they were accompanied by McWebb, who provided the key that they used to open the door giving access to the third-floor common area. If the officers had known, or should have known, that the third floor contained two apartments before they entered the living quarters on the third floor, and thus had been aware of the error in the warrant, they would have been obligated to limit their search to McWebb's apartment. Moreover, as the officers recognized, they were required to discontinue the search of respondent's apartment as soon as they discovered that there were two separate units on the third floor and therefore were put on notice of the risk that they might be in a unit erroneously included within the terms of the warrant. The officers' conduct and the limits of the search were based on the information available as the search proceeded. While the purposes justifying a police search strictly limit the permissible extent of the search, the Court has also recognized the need to allow some latitude for honest mistakes that are made by officers in the dangerous and difficult process of making arrests and executing search warrants.

The validity of the search of respondent's apartment pursuant to a warrant authorizing the search of the entire third floor depends on whether the officers' failure to realize the overbreadth of the warrant was objectively understandable and reasonable. Here it unquestionably was. The objective facts available to the officers at the time suggested no distinction between McWebb's apartment and the third-floor premises.

For that reason, the officers properly responded to the command contained in a valid warrant even if the warrant is interpreted as authorizing a search limited to McWebb's apartment rather than the entire third floor. Prior to the officers' discovery of the factual mistake, they perceived McWebb's apartment and the third-floor premises as one and the same; therefore their execution of the warrant reasonably included the entire third floor. Under either interpretation of the warrant, the officers' conduct was consistent with a reasonable effort to ascertain and identify the place intended to be searched within the meaning of the Fourth Amendment.

JUSTICE BLACKMUN, with whom JUSTICE BRENNAN and JUSTICE MARSHALL join, dissenting.

Under this Court's precedents, the search of respondent Garrison's apartment violated the Fourth Amendment. While executing a warrant specifically limited to McWebb's residence, the officers expanded their search to include respondent's adjacent apartment, an expansion made without a warrant and in the absence of exigent circumstances. In my view, Maryland's highest court correctly concluded that the trial judge should have granted respondent's motion to suppress the evidence seized as a result of this warrantless search of his apartment. Moreover, even if I were to accept the majority's analysis of this case as one involving a mistake on the part of the police officers, I would find that the officers' error, either in obtaining or in executing the warrant, was not reasonable under the circumstances.

The Fourth Amendment states that "no Warrants shall issue, but upon probable cause, supported by Oath or affirmation, and *particularly describing* the place to be searched, and the persons or things to be seized." The particularity-of-description requirement is satisfied where the description is such that the officer with a search warrant can with reasonable effort ascertain and identify the place intended. In applying this requirement to searches aimed at residences within multiunit buildings, such as the search in the present case, courts have declared invalid those warrants that fail to describe the targeted unit with enough specificity to prevent a search of all the units.

Applying the above principles to this case, I conclude that the search of respondent's apartment was improper. The words of the warrant were plain and distinctive: the warrant directed the officers to seize marijuana and drug paraphernalia on the person of McWebb and in *McWebb's* apartment, *i.e.*, "on the premises known as 2036 Park Avenue third floor apartment." As the Court of Appeals observed, this warrant specifically authorized a search only of McWebb's—not respondent's—residence. In its interpretation of the warrant, the majority suggests that the language of this document, as well as that in the supporting affidavit, permitted a search of the *entire* third floor. It escapes me why the language in question, "third floor apartment," when used with reference to a single unit in a multiple-occupancy building and in the context of one person's residence, plainly has the meaning the majority discerns, rather than its apparent and, indeed, obvious signification—one apartment located *on* the third floor. Accordingly, if, as appears to be the case, the warrant was limited in its description to the third floor apartment of McWebb, then the search of an additional apartment—respondent's—was warrantless and is presumed unreasonable in the absence of some one of a number of well defined exigent circumstances. Because the State has not advanced any such exception to the warrant requirement, the evidence obtained as a result of this search should have been excluded.

Even if one accepts the majority's view that there is no Fourth Amendment violation where the officers' mistake is reasonable, it is questionable whether that standard was met in this case. The officers should have realized the error in the warrant from their initial security sweep. Once on the third floor, the officers first fanned out through the rooms to conduct a preliminary check for other occupants who might pose a danger to them. As the map of the third floor demonstrates, the two apartments were almost a mirror image of each other—each had a bathroom, a kitchen, a living room, and a bedroom. Given the somewhat symmetrical layout of the apartments, it is difficult to imagine that, in the initial security sweep, a reasonable officer would not have discerned that two apartments were on the third floor, realized his mistake, and then confined the ensuing search to McWebb's residence.

Accordingly, even if a reasonable error on the part of police officers prevents a Fourth Amendment violation, the mistakes here, both with respect to obtaining and executing the warrant, are not reasonable and could easily have been avoided.

The Supreme Court has excused even obvious mistakes in the execution of warrants, including mistakes that result in significant embarrassment for those who are innocent of any wrongdoing. The Court's decision in *Los Angeles County v. Rettele* is a good example.

LOS ANGELES COUNTY, CALIFORNIA V. RETTELE
550 U.S. 609 (2007)

PER CURIAM.

Deputies of the Los Angeles County Sheriff's Department obtained a valid warrant to search a house, but they were unaware that the suspects being sought had moved out three months earlier. When the deputies searched the house, they found in a bedroom two residents who were of a different race than the suspects. The deputies ordered these innocent residents, who had been sleeping unclothed, out of bed. The deputies required them to stand for a few minutes before allowing them to dress.

The residents brought suit under 42 U.S.C. § 1983, naming the deputies and other parties and accusing them of violating the Fourth Amendment right to be free from unreasonable searches and seizures. The District Court granted summary judgment to all named defendants. The Court of Appeals for the Ninth Circuit reversed, concluding both that the deputies violated the Fourth Amendment and that they were not entitled to qualified immunity because a reasonable deputy would have stopped the search upon discovering that respondents were of a different race than the suspects and because a reasonable deputy would not have ordered respondents from their bed. We grant the petition for certiorari and reverse the judgment of the Court of Appeals by this summary disposition.

I

From September to December 2001, Los Angeles County Sheriff's Department Deputy Dennis Watters investigated a fraud and identity-theft crime ring. There were four suspects of the investigation. One had registered a 9-millimeter Glock handgun. The four suspects were known to be African-Americans.

On December 11, Watters obtained a search warrant for two houses in Lancaster, California, where he believed he could find the suspects. The warrant authorized him to search the homes and three of the suspects for documents and computer files. In support of the search warrant an affidavit cited various sources showing the suspects resided at respondents' home. The sources included Department of Motor Vehicles reports, mailing address listings, an outstanding warrant, and an Internet telephone directory. In this Court respondents do not dispute the validity of the warrant or the means by which it was obtained.

What Watters did not know was that one of the houses (the first to be searched) had been sold in September to a Max Rettele. He had purchased the home and moved into it three months earlier with his girlfriend Judy Sadler and Sadler's 17-year-old son Chase Hall. All three, respondents here, are Caucasians.

On the morning of December 19, Watters briefed six other deputies in preparation for the search of the houses. Watters informed them they would be searching for three African-American suspects, one of whom owned a registered handgun. The possibility a suspect would be armed caused the deputies concern for their own safety. Watters had not obtained special permission for a night search, so he could not execute the warrant until 7 a.m. Around 7:15 Watters and six other deputies knocked on the door and announced their presence. Chase Hall answered. The deputies entered the house after ordering Hall to lie face down on the ground.

The deputies' announcement awoke Rettele and Sadler. The deputies entered their bedroom with guns drawn and ordered them to get out of their bed and to show their hands. They protested that they were not wearing clothes. Rettele stood up and attempted to put on a pair of sweatpants, but deputies told him not to move. Sadler also stood up and attempted, without success, to cover herself with a sheet. Rettele and Sadler were held at gunpoint for one to two minutes before Rettele was allowed to retrieve a robe for Sadler. He was then permitted to dress. Rettele and Sadler left the bedroom within three to four minutes to sit on the couch in the living room.

By that time the deputies realized they had made a mistake. They apologized to Rettele and Sadler, thanked them for not becoming upset, and left within five minutes. They proceeded to the other house the warrant authorized them to search, where they found three suspects. Those suspects were arrested and convicted.

Rettele and Sadler, individually and as guardians ad litem for Hall, filed this § 1983 suit against Los Angeles County, the Los Angeles County Sheriff's Department, Deputy Watters, and other members of the sheriff's department. Respondents alleged petitioners violated their Fourth Amendment rights by obtaining a warrant in reckless fashion and conducting an unreasonable search and detention. The District Court held that the warrant was obtained by proper procedures and the search was reasonable. A divided panel of the Court of Appeals for the Ninth Circuit reversed in an unpublished opinion.

II

Because respondents were of a different race than the suspects the deputies were seeking, the Court of Appeals held that "[a]fter taking one look at [respondents], the deputies should have realized that [respondents] were not the subjects of the search warrant and did not pose a threat to the deputies' safety." We need not pause long in rejecting this unsound proposition. When the deputies ordered respondents from their bed, they had no way of knowing whether the African-American suspects were elsewhere in the house. The presence of some Caucasians in the residence did not eliminate the possibility that the suspects lived there as well. As the deputies stated in their affidavits, it is not uncommon in our society for people of different races to live together. Just as people of different races live and work together, so too might they engage in joint criminal activity. The deputies, who were searching a house where they believed a suspect might be armed, possessed authority to secure the premises before deciding whether to continue with the search.

In *Michigan v. Summers*, 452 U.S. 692 (1981), this Court held that officers executing a search warrant for contraband may "detain the occupants of the premises while a proper search is conducted." In weighing whether the search in *Summers* was reasonable the Court first found that "detention represents only an incremental intrusion on personal liberty when the search of a home has been authorized by a valid warrant." Against that interest, it balanced "preventing flight in the event that incriminating evidence is found"; "minimizing the risk of harm to the officers"; and facilitating "the orderly completion of the search."

In executing a search warrant officers may take reasonable action to secure the premises and to ensure their own safety and the efficacy of the search. The test of reasonableness under the Fourth Amendment is an objective one. Unreasonable actions include the use of excessive force or restraints that cause unnecessary pain or are imposed for a prolonged and unnecessary period of time.

The orders by the police to the occupants, in the context of this lawful search, were permissible, and perhaps necessary, to protect the safety of the deputies. Blankets and bedding can conceal a weapon, and one of the suspects was known to own a firearm, factors which underscore this point. The Constitution does not require an officer to ignore the possibility that an armed suspect may sleep with a weapon within reach. The reports are replete with accounts of suspects sleeping close to weapons.

The deputies needed a moment to secure the room and ensure that other persons were not close by or did not present a danger. Deputies were not required to turn their backs to allow Rettele and Sadler to retrieve clothing or to cover themselves with the sheets. Rather, "the risk of harm to both the police and the occupants is minimized if the officers routinely exercise unquestioned command of the situation."

This is not to say, of course, that the deputies were free to force Rettele and Sadler to remain motionless and standing for any longer than necessary. We have recognized that "special circumstances, or possibly a prolonged detention," might render a search unreasonable. There is no accusation that the detention here was prolonged. The deputies left the home less than 15 minutes after arriving. The detention was shorter and less restrictive than the 2- to 3-hour handcuff detention upheld in *Muehler v. Mena*, 544 U.S. 93 (2005). And there is no allegation that the deputies prevented Sadler and Rettele from dressing longer than necessary to protect their safety. Sadler was unclothed for no more than two minutes, and Rettele for only slightly more time than that. Sadler testified that once the police were satisfied that no immediate threat was presented, "they wanted us to get dressed and they were pressing us really fast to hurry up and get some clothes on."

The Fourth Amendment allows warrants to issue on probable cause, a standard well short of absolute certainty. Valid warrants will issue to search the innocent, and people like Rettele and Sadler unfortunately bear the cost. Officers executing search warrants on occasion enter a house when residents are engaged in private activity; and the resulting frustration, embarrassment, and humiliation may be real, as was true here. When officers execute a valid warrant and act in a reasonable manner to protect themselves from harm, however, the Fourth Amendment is not violated.

Mistakes in the Execution of Warrants

A mistake in the execution of a valid warrant does not violate the Fourth Amendment and does not require suppression of any evidence discovered if the mistake was objectively reasonable and understandable.

C. SUPPRESSION HEARINGS: CHALLENGING PROBABLE CAUSE AND WARRANTS

When a police officer applies for a search warrant, she appears before the judge or magistrate *ex parte*—outside the presence of the party against whom the search is directed. The purpose, of course, is to avoid "tipping off" the suspect. If a drug dealer learns that police have applied for a warrant to search his home or place of business, he will move or destroy any evidence before the police arrive to execute the warrant.

Because defendants and their attorneys generally have no opportunity to challenge probable cause before a search warrant is issued, such challenges are made after-the-fact in a suppression hearing. A suppression hearing, which typically takes place before a trial begins, provides the defendant with the opportunity to argue that certain items of evidence were obtained illegally and should be suppressed under the exclusionary rule. In *Franks v. Delaware*, the Supreme Court held that a defendant who wishes to challenge a warrant application must make a preliminary showing that the officers who prepared it deliberately falsified information or recklessly disregarded the truth. Even if that preliminary showing is made, a formal suppression hearing may not be appropriate if there is sufficient truthful information in the warrant application to support the issuance of the warrant.

FRANKS V. DELAWARE
438 U.S. 154 (1978)

Acting pursuant to a warrant authorizing a search of Jerome Franks' apartment, police discovered several items of clothing and a knife that implicated Franks in a recent rape. Prior to his trial, Franks sought to suppress the incriminating evidence by challenging the truthfulness of factual statements made in the affidavit supporting the search warrant. The Delaware Supreme Court held that a defendant may not, under any circumstances, challenge the veracity of a sworn statement used by police to secure a search warrant. The Supreme Court reversed:

> There is, of course, a presumption of validity with respect to the affidavit supporting the search warrant. To mandate an evidentiary hearing, the challenger's attack must be more than conclusory and must be supported by more than a mere desire to cross-examine. There must be allegations of deliberate falsehood or of reckless disregard for the truth, and those allegations must be accompanied by an offer of proof. They should point out specifically the portion of the warrant affidavit that is claimed to be false; and they should be accompanied by a statement of supporting reasons. Affidavits or sworn or otherwise reliable statements of witnesses should be furnished, or their absence

satisfactorily explained. Allegations of negligence or innocent mistake are insufficient. The deliberate falsity or reckless disregard whose impeachment is permitted today is only that of the affiant, not of any nongovernmental informant. Finally, if these requirements are met, and if, when material that is the subject of the alleged falsity or reckless disregard is set to one side, there remains sufficient content in the warrant affidavit to support a finding of probable cause, no hearing is required. On the other hand, if the remaining content is insufficient, the defendant is entitled, under the Fourth and Fourteenth Amendments, to his hearing. Whether he will prevail at that hearing is, of course, another issue.

While a suppression hearing provides a mechanism by which a defendant can challenge the admissibility of a disputed item of evidence, there is no guarantee that police officers, defendants, or witnesses will testify truthfully at the hearing. Defendants have strong incentives to lie, and judges are often disinclined to believe the testimony of someone who has been charged with a crime or caught with contraband. On the other hand, police also have incentives to lie—or at least shade the truth—at suppression hearings, lest vital evidence be declared inadmissible. Irving Younger, a noted prosecutor, defense attorney, judge, and law professor described the problem:

> It is a peculiarity of our legal system that the police have unique opportunities (and unique temptations) to give false testimony. When the Supreme Court lays down a rule to govern the conduct of the police, the rule does not enforce itself. Some further proceeding, such as the "probable cause" hearing, is almost always necessary to determine what actually happened.

> Such hearings usually follow a standard pattern. The policemen testify to their version of the circumstances of the search, always reflecting perfect legality. The defendant testifies to his version, always reflecting egregious illegality. The judge must choose between two statements, and, not surprisingly, he almost always accepts the policeman's word.

> The difficulty arises when one stands back from the particular case and looks at a series of cases. It then becomes apparent that policemen are committing perjury at least in some of them, and perhaps in nearly all of them. Narcotics prosecutions in New York City can be so viewed. Before *Mapp* [*v. Ohio*, 367 U.S. 643 (1961)], the policeman typically testified that he stopped the defendant for little or no reason, searched him, and found narcotics on his person. This had the ring of truth. It

was an illegal search (not based upon "probable cause"), but the evidence was admissible because *Mapp* had not yet been decided. Since it made no difference, the policeman testified truthfully. After the decision in *Mapp*, it made a great deal of difference. For the first few months, New York policemen continued to tell the truth about the circumstances of their searches, with the result that evidence was suppressed. Then the police made the great discovery that if the defendant drops the narcotics on the ground, after which the policeman arrests him, then the search is reasonable and the evidence is admissible. Spend a few hours in the New York City Criminal Court nowadays, and you will hear case after case in which a policeman testifies that the defendant dropped the narcotics on the ground, whereupon the policeman arrested him. Usually the very language of the testimony is identical from one case to another.

This is now known among defense lawyers and prosecutors as "dropsy" testimony. The judge has no reason to disbelieve it in any particular case, and of course the judge must decide each case on its own evidence, without regard to the testimony in other cases. Surely, though, not in *every* case was the defendant unlucky enough to drop his narcotics at the feet of a policeman. It follows that at least in some of these cases the police are lying.[a]

While many legal commentators have written extensively about police perjury—sometimes referred to as "testilying"—there is no consensus about the extent of the problem or what should be done to stop it.[b] As a practical matter, defendants confronted with false police testimony have few options other than pointing out the inconsistencies through cross-examination or with testimony from other witnesses, and hoping that the judge or jury will somehow arrive at the truth.

Suppression Hearings

A defendant who wishes to challenge the truthfulness of statements in a warrant application must make a preliminary showing that the officers who prepared it deliberately falsified information or recklessly disregarded the truth. Allegations of negligence or innocent mistake are insufficient. If the defendant makes the required preliminary showing, and if, when material that is the subject of the alleged falsity or reckless disregard is set to one side, there remains sufficient content in the warrant affidavit to support a finding of probable cause, no

---

[a]   Irving Younger, *The Perjury Routine*, 3 CRIMINAL LAW BULLETIN 551 (1967).

[b]   *See, e.g.*, Morgan Cloud, *The Dirty Little Secret*, 43 EMORY LAW JOURNAL 1311 (1994); Christopher Slobogin, *Testilying: Police Perjury and What to Do About It*, 67 COLORADO LAW REVIEW 1037 (1996).

suppression hearing is required. But if the remaining content is insufficient to establish probable cause, the defendant is entitled to a full evidentiary suppression hearing.

LEARN MORE WITH *LAW & ORDER*

In the following episode of *Law & Order* ("Intolerance," Season 2, Episode 20), Tim Chong, a high school student with a promising future in science, is murdered. Police suspect that the family of a rival student, Carl Borland, was involved in Tim's murder. A police ballistics expert examines the bullets that killed Tim and determines that they were fired by a .380 Tanfoglio Titan, the same type of gun registered to Ronald Borland, Carl's father. Police seek a search warrant for Borland's gun, but the judge denies it because the Tanfoglio Titan is a common gun and the police lack probable cause to believe that Ronald Borland was involved in Tim's murder. Later, the police receive an anonymous telephone tip that further implicates the Borland family in Tim's murder; the informant also describes the make and location of the Borland gun. With this new information, police obtain a search warrant and locate the Borland gun, which the police ballistics expert confirms is the murder weapon. Ronald Borland's fingerprints are also found on the gun. Police arrest Ronald Borland, but he denies the murder. In fact, other evidence suggests that Carl Borland's mother, Marian, and his brother, Randy, may have killed Tim Chong.

Prosecutors ultimately charge Randy and Marian Borland with Tim Chong's murder. At a suppression hearing, Judge Thomas Simon declares the Borland gun inadmissible. Applying the two-part *Aguilar-Spinelli* Test (which was the standard for evaluating probable cause based on an informant's tip in New York), Judge Simon finds that the anonymous tip was unreliable and insufficiently specific, and the search warrant was therefore invalid. The lead prosecutor, Ben Stone, is unable to persuade Judge Simon to follow the more flexible probable cause standard adopted by the U.S. Supreme Court in *Illinois v. Gates*, 462 U.S. 213 (1983). The inability of the prosecutor to introduce the murder weapon at trial makes the case much harder to prove, but a key witness offers compelling testimony. Prosecutors and police later discover that the key witness lied.

The episode nicely portrays many of the topics covered in this Chapter, including probable cause, search warrants, suppression hearings, and the problem of witness perjury.

**The segments of the episode that depict the relevant
Investigative Criminal Procedure issues appear at:**

16:37 to 23:39; 29:55 to 32:52

Law & Order Episode

"Intolerance," Season 2, Episode 20

CHAPTER 5

EXCEPTIONS TO THE SEARCH WARRANT REQUIREMENT

■ ■ ■

Although the Supreme Court has generally expressed a preference for warrants by repeatedly holding that warrantless searches are presumptively unreasonable, the Court has also created numerous exceptions to the warrant requirement. This Chapter surveys the most common and well-known exceptions. (Some less conventional exceptions are presented in Chapter 7, which deals with the operation of the Fourth Amendment in special contexts, while the circumstances under which police may seize or arrest a person without a warrant are presented in Chapter 6.) It's important to remember that these exceptions are *not* mutually exclusive; more than one exception may apply in a particular situation. For example, a warrantless search of a vehicle following an arrest might be justified under the search incident to arrest exception, under the automobile exception, or under the inventory search exception.

In deciding whether to create an exception, the Supreme Court engages in *balancing*, comparing the significance of the individual privacy interests at stake and the extent to which compliance with the warrant requirement would hamper effective law enforcement. With respect to each exception, consider whether you believe the Court has struck the right balance. It's also worth asking, given the number and breadth of the exceptions, just how much is left of the search warrant requirement?

A. EXIGENT CIRCUMSTANCES

"Exigent circumstances" is a fancy term for an emergency that justifies dispensing with the warrant requirement. The Supreme Court has considered the exigent circumstances exception in a variety of situations, most of which fall into four categories: hot pursuit, destruction of evidence, emergency aid or assistance, and murder scenes. Exigent circumstances should not be presumed simply because a particular case seems to fit within an established category; the Supreme Court has cautioned that exigency should be evaluated case-by-case based on the totality of the circumstances.

1. HOT PURSUIT

In *Kyllo v. U.S.*, 533 U.S. 27 (2001), and *Florida v. Jardines*, 133 S.Ct. 1409 (2013), both presented in Chapter 3, the Supreme Court strongly disapproved of warrantless intrusions into the home. When police are in "hot pursuit" of a suspected criminal, however, the Supreme Court has been willing to suspend the warrant requirement, both because there is no time for the police to obtain a search warrant, and because the pursuit often presents significant dangers to the police and the general public. *Warden v. Hayden* is a leading example of the Supreme Court's reasoning.

WARDEN, MARYLAND PENITENTIARY V. HAYDEN
387 U.S. 294 (1967)

JUSTICE BRENNAN delivered the opinion of the Court.

About 8 a.m. on March 17, 1962, an armed robber entered the business premises of the Diamond Cab Company in Baltimore, Maryland. He took some $363 and ran. Two cab drivers in the vicinity, attracted by shouts of "Holdup," followed the man to 2111 Cocoa Lane. One driver notified the company dispatcher by radio that the man was a Negro about 5'8" tall, wearing a light cap and dark jacket, and that he had entered the house on Cocoa Lane. The dispatcher relayed the information to police who were proceeding to the scene of the robbery. Within minutes, police arrived at the house in a number of patrol cars. An officer knocked and announced their presence. Mrs. Hayden answered, and the officers told her they believed that a robber had entered the house, and asked to search the house. She offered no objection.

The officers spread out through the first and second floors and the cellar in search of the robber. Hayden was found in an upstairs bedroom feigning sleep. He was arrested when the officers on the first floor and in the cellar reported that no other man was in the house. Meanwhile an officer was attracted to an adjoining bathroom by the noise of running water, and discovered a shotgun and a pistol in a flush tank; another officer who, according to the District Court, "was searching the cellar for a man or the money" found in a washing machine a jacket and trousers of the type the fleeing man was said to have worn. A clip of ammunition for the pistol and a cap were found under the mattress of Hayden's bed, and ammunition for the shotgun was found in a bureau drawer in Hayden's room. All these items of evidence were introduced against respondent at his trial.

We agree with the Court of Appeals that neither the entry without warrant to search for the robber, nor the search for him without warrant was invalid. Under the circumstances of this case, the exigencies of the situation made that course imperative. The police were informed that an armed robbery had taken place, and that the suspect had entered 2111 Cocoa Lane less than five minutes before they reached it. They acted reasonably when they entered the house and began to search for a man of the description they had been given and for weapons which he had used in the robbery or might use against them. The Fourth Amendment does not require police officers to delay in the course of an investigation if to do so would gravely endanger their lives or the lives of others. Speed here was essential, and only a thorough search of the house for persons and weapons could have insured that Hayden was the only man present and that the police had control of all weapons which could be used against them or to effect an escape.

Here, the seizures occurred prior to or immediately contemporaneous with Hayden's arrest, as part of an effort to find a suspected felon, armed, within the house into which he had run only minutes before the police arrived. The permissible scope of search must, therefore, at the least, be as broad as may reasonably be necessary to prevent the dangers that the suspect at large in the house may resist or escape.

It is argued that, while the weapons, ammunition, and cap may have been seized in the course of a search for weapons, the officer who seized the clothing was searching neither for the suspect nor for weapons when he looked into the washing machine in which he found the clothing. But even if we assume, although we do not decide, that the exigent circumstances in this case made lawful a search without warrant only for the suspect or his weapons, it cannot be said on this record that the officer who found the clothes in the washing machine was not searching for weapons. He testified that he was searching for the man or the money, but his failure to state explicitly that he was searching for weapons, in the absence of a specific question to that effect, can hardly be accorded controlling weight. He knew that the robber was armed and he did not know that some weapons had been found at the time he opened the machine. In these circumstances the inference that he was in fact also looking for weapons is fully justified.

As its name suggests, the hot pursuit exception applies only when there is, in fact, some kind of chase or the suspect is attempting to evade the police. In *Payton v. New York*, 445 U.S. 573 (1980), the Supreme Court held that even when the underlying crime is very serious, such as murder or armed robbery, the Fourth Amendment "prohibits the police from making a warrantless and nonconsensual entry into a suspect's home in order to make a routine felony arrest." In other words, an arrest at the home of a suspected felon does not, by itself, create the exigent circumstances or hot pursuit necessary to dispense with the warrant requirement.

In *Welsh v. Wisconsin*, 466 U.S. 740 (1984), police made a warrantless entry into the defendant's home after learning that he had been driving erratically and swerved off the road, abandoning his car in an open field. Police found the defendant lying naked in his bed and arrested him for driving while intoxicated. Noting that "an important factor to be considered when determining whether any exigency exists is the gravity of the underlying offense for which the arrest is being made," the Supreme Court held that the warrantless arrest for what amounted to a nonjailable traffic offense was invalid. The Court found the claim of hot pursuit unconvincing because "there was no immediate or continuous pursuit of the [defendant] from the scene of the crime," and because there was "little remaining threat to public safety" since the defendant had already arrived home after abandoning his car in the field.

The Supreme Court's decision in *Welsh* led many lower federal and state courts to conclude that the hot pursuit exception justifying a warrantless entry into a home applies only when police are trying to apprehend someone who has committed a serious crime. In *Stanton v. Sims*, 134 S.Ct. 3 (2013), however, the Supreme Court made it clear that it had not yet decided whether the hot pursuit exception to the warrant requirement applied in cases where police were attempting to apprehend a suspect who had committed a minor offense:

> *Welsh* [did not involve] hot pursuit. Thus, despite our emphasis in *Welsh* on the fact that the crime at issue was minor—indeed, a mere nonjailable civil offense—nothing in the opinion establishes that the seriousness of the crime is equally important *in cases of hot pursuit*. [O]ur opinion [in *Welsh*] is equivocal: We held not that warrantless entry to arrest a misdemeanant is never justified, but only that such entry should be rare.

Exigent Circumstances: Hot Pursuit

1.   Police may enter and search private property without a warrant if they are in hot pursuit of a suspected felon. The permissible scope of the search is as broad as is reasonably necessary to prevent the dangers that the suspect at large may resist or escape.

2.   Police need a warrant to make a routine felony arrest in a suspect's home, even if the crime for which the arrest is being made is a serious one.

3.   The Supreme Court has not yet decided whether the hot pursuit exception to the warrant requirement applies in cases where police are attempting to apprehend a suspect who has committed only a minor offense.

2.   DESTRUCTION OF EVIDENCE

The imminent loss or destruction of evidence creates exigent circumstances justifying an exception to the warrant requirement. In *Schmerber v. California*, 384 U.S. 757 (1966), the Supreme Court applied this principle to permit a warrantless blood test of an individual arrested on suspicion of driving while intoxicated. More recently, in *Missouri v. McNeely*, the Supreme Court clarified its decision in *Schmerber*, holding that exigency must be determined case-by-case based on the totality of the circumstances.

MISSOURI V. MCNEELY

133 S.Ct. 1552 (2013)

JUSTICE SOTOMAYOR announced the judgment of the Court.

In *Schmerber v. California*, 384 U.S. 757 (1966), this Court upheld a warrantless blood test of an individual arrested for driving under the influence of alcohol because the officer "might reasonably have believed that he was confronted with an emergency, in which the delay necessary to obtain a warrant, under the circumstances, threatened the destruction of evidence." The question presented here is whether the natural metabolization of alcohol in the bloodstream presents a *per se* exigency that justifies an exception to the Fourth Amendment's warrant requirement for nonconsensual blood testing in all drunk-driving cases. We conclude that it does not, and we hold, consistent with general Fourth Amendment principles, that exigency in this context must be determined case by case based on the totality of the circumstances.

I

While on highway patrol at approximately 2:08 a.m., a Missouri police officer stopped Tyler McNeely's truck after observing it exceed the posted speed limit and repeatedly cross the centerline. The officer noticed several signs that McNeely was intoxicated, including McNeely's bloodshot eyes, his slurred speech, and the smell of alcohol on his breath. McNeely acknowledged to the officer that he had consumed "a couple of beers" at a bar, and he appeared unsteady on his feet when he exited the truck. After McNeely performed poorly on a battery of field-sobriety tests and declined to use a portable breath-test device to measure his blood alcohol concentration (BAC), the officer placed him under arrest.

The officer began to transport McNeely to the station house. But when McNeely indicated that he would again refuse to provide a breath sample, the officer changed course and took McNeely to a nearby hospital for blood testing. The officer did not attempt to secure a warrant. Upon arrival at the hospital, the officer asked McNeely whether he would consent to a blood test. Reading from a standard implied consent form, the officer explained to McNeely that under state law refusal to submit voluntarily to the test would lead to the immediate revocation of his driver's license for one year and could be used against him in a future prosecution. McNeely nonetheless refused. The officer then directed a hospital lab technician to take a blood sample, and the sample was secured at approximately 2:35 a.m. Subsequent laboratory testing measured McNeely's BAC at 0.154 percent, which was well above the legal limit of 0.08 percent.

McNeely was charged with driving while intoxicated (DWI). He moved to suppress the results of the blood test, arguing in relevant part that, under the circumstances, taking his blood for chemical testing without first obtaining a search warrant violated his rights under the Fourth Amendment. The trial court agreed. It concluded that the exigency exception to the warrant requirement did not apply because, apart from the fact that "[a]s in all cases involving intoxication, [McNeely's] blood alcohol was being metabolized by his liver," there were no circumstances suggesting the officer faced an emergency in which he could not practicably obtain a warrant.

The Missouri Supreme Court affirmed. Recognizing that this Court's decision in *Schmerber* "provide[d] the backdrop" to its analysis, the Missouri Supreme Court held that "*Schmerber* directs lower courts to engage in a totality of the circumstances analysis when determining whether exigency permits a nonconsensual, warrantless blood draw." The court further concluded that *Schmerber* "requires more than the mere dissipation of blood-alcohol evidence to support a warrantless blood draw in an alcohol-related case." According to the court, exigency depends heavily on the existence of additional "special facts," such as whether an officer was delayed by the need to investigate an accident and transport an injured suspect to the hospital, as had been the case in *Schmerber*. Finding that this was "unquestionably a routine DWI case" in which no factors other than the natural dissipation of blood-alcohol suggested that there was an emergency, the court held that the nonconsensual warrantless blood draw violated McNeely's Fourth Amendment right to be free from unreasonable searches of his person.

We granted certiorari to resolve a split of authority on the question whether the natural dissipation of alcohol in the bloodstream establishes a *per se* exigency that suffices on its own to justify an exception to the warrant requirement for nonconsensual blood testing in drunk-driving investigations. We now affirm.

II

Our cases have held that a warrantless search of the person is reasonable only if it falls within a recognized exception. That principle applies to the type of search at issue in this case, which involved a compelled physical intrusion beneath McNeely's skin and into his veins to obtain a sample of his blood for use as evidence in a criminal investigation. Such an invasion of bodily integrity implicates an individual's most personal and deep-rooted expectations of privacy.

We first considered the Fourth Amendment restrictions on such searches in *Schmerber*, where, as in this case, a blood sample was drawn from a defendant suspected of driving while under the influence of alcohol. Noting that "[s]earch warrants are ordinarily required for searches of dwellings," we reasoned that "absent an emergency, no less could be required where intrusions into the human body are concerned," even when the search was conducted following a lawful arrest. We explained that the importance of requiring authorization by a "neutral and detached magistrate" before allowing a law enforcement officer to "invade another's body in search of evidence of guilt is indisputable and great."

As noted, the warrant requirement is subject to exceptions. One well-recognized exception, and the one at issue in this case, applies when the exigencies of the situation make the needs of law enforcement so compelling that a warrantless search is objectively reasonable under the Fourth Amendment. A variety of circumstances may give rise to an exigency sufficient to justify a warrantless search, including law enforcement's need to provide emergency assistance to an occupant of a home, engage in "hot pursuit" of a fleeing suspect, or enter a burning building to put out a fire and investigate its cause. As is relevant here, we have also recognized that in some circumstances law enforcement officers may conduct a search without a warrant to prevent the imminent destruction of evidence. While these contexts do not necessarily involve equivalent dangers, in each a warrantless search is potentially reasonable because there is compelling need for official action and no time to secure a warrant.

To determine whether a law enforcement officer faced an emergency that justified acting without a warrant, this Court looks to the totality of circumstances. We apply this "finely tuned approach" to Fourth Amendment reasonableness in this context because the police action at issue lacks the traditional justification that a warrant provides. Absent that established justification, the fact-specific nature of the reasonableness inquiry demands that we evaluate each case of alleged exigency based on its own facts and circumstances.

Our decision in *Schmerber* applied this totality of the circumstances approach. In that case, the petitioner had suffered injuries in an automobile accident and was taken to the hospital. While he was there receiving treatment, a police officer arrested the petitioner for driving while under the influence of alcohol and ordered a blood test over his objection. After explaining that the warrant requirement applied generally to searches that intrude into the human body, we concluded that the warrantless blood test "in the present case" was nonetheless permissible because the officer "might reasonably have believed that he was confronted with an emergency, in which the delay necessary to obtain a warrant, under the circumstances, threatened the destruction of evidence."

In support of that conclusion, we observed that evidence could have been lost because "the percentage of alcohol in the blood begins to diminish shortly after drinking stops, as the body functions to eliminate it from the system." We added that "[p]articularly in a case such as this, where time had to be taken to bring the accused to a hospital and to investigate the scene of the accident, there was no time to seek out a magistrate and secure a warrant." "Given these special facts," we found that it was appropriate for the police to act without a warrant. We further held that the blood test at issue was a reasonable way to recover the evidence because it was highly effective, "involve[d] virtually no risk, trauma, or pain," and was conducted in a reasonable fashion "by a physician in a hospital environment according to accepted medical practices." And in conclusion, we noted that our judgment that there had been no Fourth Amendment violation was strictly based "on the facts of the present record."

Thus, our analysis in *Schmerber* fits comfortably within our case law applying the exigent circumstances exception. In finding the warrantless blood test reasonable in *Schmerber*, we considered all of the facts and circumstances of the particular case and carefully based our holding on those specific facts.

The State properly recognizes that the reasonableness of a warrantless search under the exigency exception to the warrant requirement must be evaluated based on the totality of the circumstances. But the State nevertheless seeks a *per se* rule for blood testing in drunk-driving cases. The State contends that whenever an officer has probable cause to believe an individual has been driving under the influence of alcohol, exigent circumstances will necessarily exist because BAC evidence is inherently evanescent. As a result, the State claims that so long as the officer has probable cause and the blood test is conducted in a reasonable manner, it is categorically reasonable for law enforcement to obtain the blood sample without a warrant.

It is true that as a result of the human body's natural metabolic processes, the alcohol level in a person's blood begins to dissipate once the alcohol is fully absorbed and continues to decline until the alcohol is eliminated. Testimony before the trial court in this case indicated that the percentage of alcohol in an individual's blood typically decreases by approximately 0.015 percent to 0.02 percent per hour once the alcohol has been fully absorbed. More precise calculations of the rate at which alcohol dissipates depend on various individual characteristics (such as weight, gender, and alcohol tolerance) and the circumstances in which the alcohol was consumed. Regardless of the exact elimination rate, it is sufficient for our purposes to note that because an individual's alcohol level gradually declines soon after he stops drinking, a significant delay in testing will negatively affect the probative value of the results. This fact was essential to our holding in *Schmerber*, as we recognized that, under the circumstances, further delay in order to secure a warrant after the time spent investigating the scene of the accident and transporting the injured suspect to the hospital to receive treatment would have threatened the destruction of evidence.

But it does not follow that we should depart from careful case-by-case assessment of exigency and adopt the categorical rule proposed by the State. In those drunk-driving investigations where police officers can reasonably obtain a warrant before a blood sample can be drawn without significantly undermining the efficacy of the search, the Fourth Amendment mandates that they do so. We do not doubt that some circumstances will make obtaining a warrant impractical such that the dissipation of alcohol from the bloodstream will support an exigency justifying a properly conducted warrantless blood test. That, however, is a reason to decide each case on its facts, as we did in *Schmerber*, not to accept the considerable overgeneralization that a *per se* rule would reflect.

The context of blood testing is different in critical respects from other destruction-of-evidence cases in which the police are truly confronted with a "now or never" situation. In contrast to, for example, circumstances in which the suspect has control over easily disposable evidence, BAC evidence from a drunk-driving suspect naturally dissipates over time in a gradual and relatively predictable manner. Moreover, because a police officer must typically transport a drunk-driving suspect to a medical facility and obtain the assistance of someone with appropriate medical training before conducting a blood test, some delay between the time of the arrest or accident and the time of the test is inevitable regardless of whether police officers are required to obtain a warrant. This reality undermines the force of the State's contention, endorsed by the dissent, that we should recognize a categorical exception to the warrant requirement because BAC evidence "is actively being destroyed with every minute that passes." Consider, for example, a situation in which the warrant process will not significantly increase the delay before the blood test is conducted because an officer can take steps to secure a warrant while the suspect is being transported to a medical facility by another officer. In such a circumstance, there would be no plausible justification for an exception to the warrant requirement.

The State's proposed *per se* rule also fails to account for advances in the 47 years since *Schmerber* was decided that allow for the more expeditious processing of warrant applications, particularly in contexts like drunk-driving investigations where the evidence offered to establish probable cause is simple. The Federal Rules of Criminal Procedure were amended in 1977 to permit federal magistrate judges to issue a warrant based on sworn testimony communicated by telephone. As amended, the law now allows a federal magistrate judge to consider "information communicated by telephone or other reliable electronic means." States have also innovated. Well over a majority of States allow police officers or prosecutors to apply for search warrants remotely through various means, including telephonic or radio communication, electronic communication such as e-mail, and video conferencing. And in addition to technology-based developments, jurisdictions have found other ways to streamline the warrant process, such as by using standard-form warrant applications for drunk-driving investigations.

We by no means claim that telecommunications innovations have, will, or should eliminate all delay from the warrant-application process. Warrants inevitably take some time for police officers or prosecutors to complete and for magistrate judges to review. Telephonic and electronic warrants may still require officers to follow time-consuming formalities designed to create an adequate record, such as preparing a duplicate warrant before calling the magistrate judge. And improvements in communications technology do not guarantee that a magistrate judge will be available when an officer needs a warrant after making a late-night arrest. But technological developments that enable police officers to secure warrants more quickly, and do so without undermining the neutral magistrate judge's essential role as a check on police discretion, are relevant to an assessment of exigency. That is particularly so in this context, where BAC evidence is lost gradually and relatively predictably.

Of course, there are important countervailing concerns. While experts can work backwards from the BAC at the time the sample was taken to determine the BAC at the time of the alleged offense, longer intervals may raise questions about the accuracy of the calculation. For that reason, exigent circumstances justifying a warrantless blood sample may arise in the regular course of law enforcement due to delays from the warrant application process. But adopting the State's *per se* approach would improperly ignore the current and future technological developments in warrant procedures, and might well diminish the incentive for jurisdictions to pursue progressive approaches to warrant acquisition that preserve the protections afforded by the warrant while meeting the legitimate interests of law enforcement.

In short, while the natural dissipation of alcohol in the blood may support a finding of exigency in a specific case, as it did in *Schmerber*, it does not do so categorically. Whether a warrantless blood test of a drunk-driving suspect is reasonable must be determined case by case based on the totality of the circumstances.

IV

Here and in its own courts the State based its case on an insistence that a driver who declines to submit to testing after being arrested for driving under the influence of alcohol is always subject to a nonconsensual blood test without any precondition for a warrant. That is incorrect.

Because this case was argued on the broad proposition that drunk-driving cases present a *per se* exigency, the arguments and the record do not provide the Court with an adequate analytic framework for a detailed discussion of all the relevant factors that can be taken into account in determining the reasonableness of acting without a warrant. It suffices to say that the metabolization of alcohol in the bloodstream and the ensuing loss of evidence are among the factors that must be considered in deciding whether a warrant is required. No doubt, given the large number of arrests for this offense in different jurisdictions nationwide, cases will arise when anticipated delays in obtaining a warrant will justify a blood test without judicial authorization, for in every case the law must be concerned that evidence is being destroyed. But that inquiry ought not to be pursued here where the question is not properly before this Court.

We hold that in drunk-driving investigations, the natural dissipation of alcohol in the bloodstream does not constitute an exigency in every case sufficient to justify conducting a blood test without a warrant.

CHIEF JUSTICE ROBERTS, with whom JUSTICE BREYER and JUSTICE ALITO join, concurring in part and dissenting in part.

A police officer reading this Court's opinion would have no idea—no idea—what the Fourth Amendment requires of him, once he decides to obtain a blood sample from a drunk driving suspect who has refused a breathalyzer test. I have no quarrel with the Court's "totality of the circumstances" approach as a general matter; that is what our cases require. But the circumstances in drunk driving cases are often typical, and the Court should be able to offer guidance on how police should handle cases like the one before us.

In my view, the proper rule is straightforward. Our cases establish that there is an exigent circumstances exception to the warrant requirement. That exception applies when there is a compelling need to prevent the imminent destruction of important evidence, and there is no time to obtain a warrant. The natural dissipation of alcohol in the bloodstream constitutes not only the imminent but ongoing destruction of critical evidence. That would qualify as an exigent circumstance, except that there may be time to secure a warrant before blood can be drawn. If there is, an officer must seek a warrant. If an officer could reasonably conclude that there is not, the exigent circumstances exception applies by its terms, and the blood may be drawn without a warrant.

In *Cupp v. Murphy*, the Supreme Court permitted police—acting without a search warrant—to take fingernail scrapings from a man suspected of strangling his wife. The man's behavior while being questioned at the police station suggested that he was attempting to destroy the evidence under his fingernails.

CUPP V. MURPHY
412 U.S. 291 (1973)

Daniel Murphy's wife was found strangled in her home, and abrasions and lacerations were found on her throat. There was no sign of a break-in or robbery. Word of the murder was sent to Murphy, who was not then living with his wife; they had had a stormy marriage. Upon receiving the news of his wife's murder, Murphy voluntarily submitted to questioning at the police station. The police noticed a dark spot on Murphy's finger. Suspecting that the spot might be dried blood and knowing that evidence of strangulation is often found under the assailant's fingernails, the police asked Murphy if they could take a sample of scrapings from his fingernails. He refused. Under protest and without a warrant, the police proceeded to take the samples, which turned out to contain traces of skin and blood cells, and fabric from the victim's nightgown. This incriminating evidence was admitted at trial, and Murphy was convicted. Murphy appealed, claiming that the fingernail scrapings were the product of an unconstitutional search under the Fourth Amendment.

The Supreme Court approved the warrantless fingernail scrapings, in part because Murphy was attempting to destroy the evidence:

> At the time Murphy was being detained at the station house, he was obviously aware of the detectives' suspicions. Though he did not have the full warning of official suspicion that a formal arrest provides, Murphy was sufficiently apprised of his suspected role in the crime to motivate him to attempt to destroy what evidence he could without attracting further attention. Testimony at trial indicated that after he refused to consent to the taking of fingernail samples, he put his hands behind his back and appeared to rub them together. He then put his hands in his pockets, and a "metallic sound, such as keys or change rattling" was heard. These circumstances justified the police in subjecting him to the very limited search necessary to preserve the highly evanescent evidence they found under his fingernails.

Suppose the police pound on the front door of a suspected drug dealer and announce their presence, knowing that he is likely to attempt to destroy the drugs in his possession. If the police are responsible for creating a situation in which evidence is likely to be destroyed, can they still rely on the exigent circumstances exception to make a warrantless entry and search? The Supreme Court considered this question in *Kentucky v. King*.

KENTUCKY V. KING
131 S.Ct. 1849 (2011)

JUSTICE ALITO delivered the opinion of the Court.

It is well established that "exigent circumstances," including the need to prevent the destruction of evidence, permit police officers to conduct an otherwise permissible search without first obtaining a warrant. In this case, we consider whether this rule applies when police, by knocking on the door of a residence and announcing their presence, cause the occupants to attempt to destroy evidence. The Kentucky Supreme Court held that the exigent circumstances rule does not apply in the case at hand because the police should have foreseen that their conduct would prompt the occupants to attempt to destroy evidence. We reject this interpretation of the exigent circumstances rule. The conduct of the police prior to their entry into the apartment was entirely lawful. They did not violate the Fourth Amendment or threaten to do so. In such a situation, the exigent circumstances rule applies.

I

This case concerns the search of an apartment in Lexington, Kentucky. Police officers set up a controlled buy of crack cocaine outside an apartment complex. Undercover Officer Gibbons watched the deal take place from an unmarked car in a nearby parking lot. After the deal occurred, Gibbons radioed uniformed officers to move in on the suspect. He told the officers that the suspect was moving quickly toward the breezeway of an apartment building, and he urged them to "hurry up and get there" before the suspect entered an apartment.

In response to the radio alert, the uniformed officers drove into the nearby parking lot, left their vehicles, and ran to the breezeway. Just as they entered the breezeway, they heard a door shut and detected a very strong odor of burnt marijuana. At the end of the breezeway, the officers saw two apartments, one on the left and one on the right, and they did not know which apartment the suspect had entered. Gibbons had radioed that the suspect was running into the apartment on the right, but the officers did not hear this statement because they had already left their vehicles. Because they smelled marijuana smoke emanating from the apartment on the left, they approached the door of that apartment.

Officer Steven Cobb, one of the uniformed officers who approached the door, testified that the officers banged on the left apartment door "as loud as they could" and announced, "This is the police" or "Police, police, police." Cobb said that "as soon as the officers started banging on the door," they "could hear people inside moving," and "it sounded as though things were being moved inside the apartment." These noises, Cobb testified, led the officers to believe that drug-related evidence was about to be destroyed.

At that point, the officers announced that they "were going to make entry inside the apartment." Cobb then kicked in the door, the officers entered the apartment, and they found three people in the front room: respondent Hollis King, respondent's girlfriend, and a guest who was smoking marijuana. The officers performed a protective sweep of the apartment during which they saw marijuana and powder cocaine in plain view. In a subsequent search, they also discovered crack cocaine, cash, and drug paraphernalia.

Police eventually entered the apartment on the right. Inside, they found the suspected drug dealer who was the initial target of their investigation.

In the Fayette County Circuit Court, a grand jury charged respondent with trafficking in marijuana, first-degree trafficking in a controlled substance, and second-degree persistent felony offender status. Respondent filed a motion to suppress the evidence from the warrantless search, but the Circuit Court denied the motion. The Circuit Court concluded that the officers had probable cause to investigate the marijuana odor and that the officers "properly conducted the investigation by initially knocking on the door of the apartment unit and awaiting the response or consensual entry." Exigent circumstances justified the warrantless entry, the court held, because "there was no response at all to the knocking," and because "Officer Cobb heard movement in the apartment which he reasonably concluded were persons in the act of destroying evidence, particularly narcotics because of the smell." Respondent then entered a conditional guilty plea, reserving his right to appeal the denial of his suppression motion. The court sentenced respondent to 11 years' imprisonment.

The Kentucky Court of Appeals affirmed. It held that exigent circumstances justified the warrantless entry because the police reasonably believed that evidence would be destroyed. The police did not impermissibly create the exigency, the court explained, because they did not deliberately evade the warrant requirement.

The Supreme Court of Kentucky reversed. As a preliminary matter, the court observed that there was "certainly some question as to whether the sound of persons moving inside the apartment was sufficient to establish that evidence was being destroyed." But the court did not answer that question. Instead, it "assumed for the purpose of argument that exigent circumstances existed."

To determine whether police impermissibly created the exigency, the Supreme Court of Kentucky announced a two-part test. First, the court held, police cannot "deliberately create the exigent circumstances with the bad faith intent to avoid the warrant requirement." Second, even absent bad faith, the court concluded, police may not rely on exigent circumstances if "it was reasonably foreseeable that the investigative tactics employed by the police would create the exigent circumstances." Although the court found no evidence of bad faith, it held that exigent circumstances could not justify the search because it was reasonably foreseeable that the occupants would destroy evidence when the police knocked on the door and announced their presence.

II

The text of the Fourth Amendment expressly imposes two requirements. First, all searches and seizures must be reasonable. Second, a warrant may not be issued unless probable cause is properly established and the scope of the authorized search is set out with particularity.

Although the text of the Fourth Amendment does not specify when a search warrant must be obtained, this Court has inferred that a warrant must generally be secured. It is a basic principle of Fourth Amendment law, we have often said, that searches and seizures inside a home without a warrant are presumptively unreasonable. But we have also recognized that this presumption may be overcome in some circumstances because the ultimate touchstone of the Fourth Amendment is "reasonableness." Accordingly, the warrant requirement is subject to certain reasonable exceptions.

One well-recognized exception applies when "the exigencies of the situation" make the needs of law enforcement so compelling that a warrantless search is objectively reasonable under the Fourth Amendment. This Court has identified several exigencies that may justify a warrantless search of a home. Under the "emergency aid" exception, for example, officers may enter a home without a warrant to render emergency assistance to an injured occupant or to protect an occupant from imminent injury. Police officers may enter premises without a warrant when they are in hot pursuit of a fleeing suspect. And—what is relevant here—the need to prevent the imminent destruction of evidence has long been recognized as a sufficient justification for a warrantless search.

Over the years, lower courts have developed an exception to the exigent circumstances rule, the so-called "police-created exigency" doctrine. Under this doctrine, police may not rely on the need to prevent destruction of evidence when that exigency was "created" or "manufactured" by the conduct of the police.

In applying this exception for the "creation" or "manufacturing" of an exigency by the police, courts require something more than mere proof that fear of detection by the police caused the destruction of evidence. An additional showing is obviously needed because in some sense the police always create the exigent circumstances. That is to say, in the vast majority of cases in which evidence is destroyed by persons who are engaged in illegal conduct, the reason for the destruction is fear that the evidence will fall into the hands of law enforcement. Destruction of evidence issues probably occur most frequently in drug cases because drugs may be easily destroyed by flushing them down a toilet or rinsing them down a drain. Persons in possession of valuable drugs are unlikely to destroy them unless they fear discovery by the police. Consequently, a rule that precludes the police from making a warrantless entry to prevent the destruction of evidence whenever their conduct causes the exigency would unreasonably shrink the reach of this well-established exception to the warrant requirement.

Presumably for the purpose of avoiding such a result, the lower courts have held that the police-created exigency doctrine requires more than simple causation, but the lower courts have not agreed on the test to be applied. Indeed, the petition in this case maintains that there are currently five different tests being used by the United States Courts of Appeals, and that some state courts have crafted additional tests.

III

Despite the welter of tests devised by the lower courts, the answer to the question presented in this case follows directly and clearly from the principle that permits warrantless searches in the first place. As previously noted, warrantless searches are allowed when the circumstances make it reasonable, within the meaning of the Fourth Amendment, to dispense with the warrant requirement. Therefore, the answer to the question before us is that the exigent circumstances rule justifies a warrantless search when the conduct of the police preceding the exigency is reasonable in the same sense. Where, as here, the police did not create the exigency by engaging or threatening to engage in conduct that violates the Fourth Amendment, warrantless entry to prevent the destruction of evidence is reasonable and thus allowed.[4]

We have taken a similar approach in other cases involving warrantless searches. For example, we have held that law enforcement

---

[4]   There is a strong argument to be made that, at least in most circumstances, the exigent circumstances rule should not apply where the police, without a warrant or any legally sound basis for a warrantless entry, threaten that they will enter without permission unless admitted. In this case, however, no such actual threat was made, and therefore we have no need to reach that question.

officers may seize evidence in plain view, provided that they have not violated the Fourth Amendment in arriving at the spot from which the observation of the evidence is made.

Similarly, officers may seek consent-based encounters if they are lawfully present in the place where the consensual encounter occurs. If consent is freely given, it makes no difference that an officer may have approached the person with the hope or expectation of obtaining consent.

Some lower courts have adopted a rule that is similar to the one that we recognize today. But others, including the Kentucky Supreme Court, have imposed additional requirements that are unsound and that we now reject.

Respondent contends that law enforcement officers impermissibly create an exigency when they "engage in conduct that would cause a reasonable person to believe that entry is imminent and inevitable." In respondent's view, relevant factors include the officers' tone of voice in announcing their presence and the forcefulness of their knocks. But the ability of law enforcement officers to respond to an exigency cannot turn on such subtleties.

Police officers may have a very good reason to announce their presence loudly and to knock on the door with some force. A forceful knock may be necessary to alert the occupants that someone is at the door. Furthermore, unless police officers identify themselves loudly enough, occupants may not know who is at their doorstep. Officers are permitted—indeed, encouraged—to identify themselves to citizens, and in many circumstances this is cause for assurance, not discomfort. Citizens who are startled by an unexpected knock on the door or by the sight of unknown persons in plain clothes on their doorstep may be relieved to learn that these persons are police officers. Others may appreciate the opportunity to make an informed decision about whether to answer the door to the police.

If respondent's test were adopted, it would be extremely difficult for police officers to know how loudly they may announce their presence or how forcefully they may knock on a door without running afoul of the police-created exigency rule. And in most cases, it would be nearly impossible for a court to determine whether that threshold had been passed. The Fourth Amendment does not require the nebulous and impractical test that respondent proposes.

For these reasons, we conclude that the exigent circumstances rule applies when the police do not gain entry to premises by means of an actual or threatened violation of the Fourth Amendment. This holding provides ample protection for the privacy rights that the Amendment protects.

When law enforcement officers who are not armed with a warrant knock on a door, they do no more than any private citizen might do. And whether the person who knocks on the door and requests the opportunity to speak is a police officer or a private citizen, the occupant has no obligation to open the door or to speak. And even if an occupant chooses to open the door and speak with the officers, the occupant need not allow the officers to enter the premises and may refuse to answer any questions at any time.

Occupants who choose not to stand on their constitutional rights but instead elect to attempt to destroy evidence have only themselves to blame for the warrantless exigent-circumstances search that may ensue.

IV

In this case, we see no evidence that the officers either violated the Fourth Amendment or threatened to do so prior to the point when they entered the apartment. Officer Cobb testified without contradiction that the officers "banged on the door as loud as they could" and announced either "Police, police, police" or "This is the police." This conduct was entirely consistent with the Fourth Amendment, and we are aware of no other evidence that might show that the officers either violated the Fourth Amendment or threatened to do so (for example, by announcing that they would break down the door if the occupants did not open the door voluntarily).

Respondent argues that the officers "demanded" entry to the apartment, but he has not pointed to any evidence in the record that supports this assertion.

Finally, respondent claims that the officers "explained to the occupants that the officers were going to make entry inside the apartment," but the record is clear that the officers did not make this statement until after the exigency arose. As Officer Cobb testified, the officers "knew that there was possibly something that was going to be destroyed inside the apartment," and "*[a]t that point*, they explained that they were going to make entry." Given that this announcement was made *after* the exigency arose, it could not have created the exigency.

Like the court below, we assume for purposes of argument that an exigency existed. Because the officers in this case did not violate or threaten to violate the Fourth Amendment prior to the exigency, we hold that the exigency justified the warrantless search of the apartment.

JUSTICE GINSBURG, dissenting.

The Court today arms the police with a way routinely to dishonor the Fourth Amendment's warrant requirement in drug cases. In lieu of presenting their evidence to a neutral magistrate, police officers may now knock, listen, then break the door down, nevermind that they had ample time to obtain a warrant. I dissent from the Court's reduction of the Fourth Amendment's force.

The question presented: May police, who could pause to gain the approval of a neutral magistrate, dispense with the need to get a warrant by themselves creating exigent circumstances? I would answer no, as did the Kentucky Supreme Court. The urgency must exist, I would rule, when the police come on the scene, not subsequent to their arrival, prompted by their own conduct.

There was little risk that drug-related evidence would have been destroyed had the police delayed the search pending a magistrate's authorization. Nothing in the record shows that, prior to the knock at the apartment door, the occupants were apprehensive about police proximity.

Under an appropriately reined-in "emergency" or "exigent circumstances" exception, the result in this case should not be in doubt. The target of the investigation's entry into the building, and the smell of marijuana seeping under the apartment door into the hallway, the Kentucky Supreme Court rightly determined, gave the police "probable cause sufficient to obtain a warrant to search the apartment." As that court observed, nothing made it impracticable for the police to post officers on the premises while proceeding to obtain a warrant authorizing their entry. Before this Court, Kentucky does not urge otherwise.

There is every reason to conclude that securing a warrant was entirely feasible in this case, and no reason to contract the Fourth Amendment's dominion.

The exigent circumstances exception permits police to perform a warrantless search when they reasonably believe that the destruction of evidence is imminent and there is no time to obtain a warrant. As an alternative to a warrantless search, police may temporarily seize or secure the premises to prevent the destruction of evidence and provide time for officers to obtain a search warrant. In *Illinois v. McArthur*, the Supreme Court approved this approach in cases where the police have probable cause to believe evidence of a crime is on the premises.

ILLINOIS V. MCARTHUR

531 U.S. 326 (2001)

JUSTICE BREYER delivered the opinion of the Court.

Police officers, with probable cause to believe that a man had hidden marijuana in his home, prevented that man from entering the home for about two hours while they obtained a search warrant. We must decide whether those officers violated the Fourth Amendment. We conclude that the officers acted reasonably. They did not violate the Amendment's requirements.

I

On April 2, 1997, Tera McArthur asked two police officers to accompany her to the trailer where she lived with her husband, Charles, so that they could keep the peace while she removed her belongings. The two officers, Assistant Chief John Love and Officer Richard Skidis, arrived with Tera at the trailer at about 3:15 p.m. Tera went inside, where Charles was present. The officers remained outside.

When Tera emerged after collecting her possessions, she spoke to Chief Love, who was then on the porch. She suggested he check the trailer because "Chuck had dope in there." She added (in Love's words) that she had seen Chuck "slide some dope underneath the couch."

Love knocked on the trailer door, told Charles what Tera had said, and asked for permission to search the trailer, which Charles denied. Love then sent Officer Skidis with Tera to get a search warrant.

Love told Charles, who by this time was also on the porch, that he could not reenter the trailer unless a police officer accompanied him. Charles subsequently reentered the trailer two or three times (to get cigarettes and to make phone calls), and each time Love stood just inside the door to observe what Charles did.

Officer Skidis obtained the warrant by about 5 p.m. He returned to the trailer and, along with other officers, searched it. The officers found under the sofa a marijuana pipe, a box for marijuana (called a "one-hitter" box), and a small amount of marijuana. They then arrested Charles.

Illinois subsequently charged Charles McArthur with unlawfully possessing drug paraphernalia and marijuana (less than 2.5 grams), both misdemeanors. McArthur moved to suppress the pipe, box, and marijuana on the ground that they were the "fruit" of an unlawful police seizure, namely, the refusal to let him reenter the trailer unaccompanied, which would have permitted him, he said, to "have destroyed the marijuana."

The trial court granted McArthur's suppression motion. We granted certiorari to determine whether the Fourth Amendment prohibits the kind of temporary seizure at issue here.

II

The Fourth Amendment says that the "right of the people to be secure in their persons, houses, papers, and effects, against unreasonable searches and seizures, shall not be violated." Its central requirement is one of reasonableness. In order to enforce that requirement, this Court has interpreted the Amendment as establishing rules and presumptions designed to control conduct of law enforcement officers that may significantly intrude upon privacy interests. Sometimes those rules require warrants. We have said, for example, that in the ordinary case, seizures of personal property are unreasonable within the meaning of the Fourth Amendment, without more, unless accomplished pursuant to a judicial warrant, issued by a neutral magistrate after finding probable cause.

We nonetheless have made it clear that there are exceptions to the warrant requirement. When faced with special law enforcement needs, diminished expectations of privacy, minimal intrusions, or the like, the Court has found that certain general, or individual, circumstances may render a warrantless search or seizure reasonable.

In the circumstances of the case before us, we cannot say that the warrantless seizure was *per se* unreasonable. It involves a plausible claim of specially pressing or urgent law enforcement need, *i.e.*, "exigent circumstances." Moreover, the restraint at issue was tailored to that need, being limited in time and scope, and avoiding significant intrusion into the home itself. Consequently, rather than employing a *per se* rule of unreasonableness, we balance the privacy-related and law enforcement-related concerns to determine if the intrusion was reasonable.

We conclude that the restriction at issue was reasonable, and hence lawful, in light of the following circumstances, which we consider in combination. First, the police had probable cause to believe that McArthur's trailer home contained evidence of a crime and contraband, namely, unlawful drugs. The police had had an opportunity to speak with Tera McArthur and make at least a very rough assessment of her reliability. They knew she had had a firsthand opportunity to observe her husband's behavior, in particular with respect to the drugs at issue. And they thought, with good reason, that her report to them reflected that opportunity.

Second, the police had good reason to fear that, unless restrained, McArthur would destroy the drugs before they could return with a warrant. They reasonably might have thought that McArthur realized that his wife knew about his marijuana stash; observed that she was angry or frightened enough to ask the police to accompany her; saw that after leaving the trailer she had spoken with the police; and noticed that she had walked off with one policeman while leaving the other outside to observe the trailer. They reasonably could have concluded that McArthur, consequently suspecting an imminent search, would, if given the chance, get rid of the drugs fast.

Third, the police made reasonable efforts to reconcile their law enforcement needs with the demands of personal privacy. They neither searched the trailer nor arrested McArthur before obtaining a warrant. Rather, they imposed a significantly less restrictive restraint, preventing McArthur only from entering the trailer unaccompanied. They left his home and his belongings intact—until a neutral Magistrate, finding probable cause, issued a warrant.

Fourth, the police imposed the restraint for a limited period of time, namely, two hours. As far as the record reveals, this time period was no longer than reasonably necessary for the police, acting with diligence, to obtain the warrant. Given the nature of the intrusion and the law enforcement interest at stake, this brief seizure of the premises was permissible.

In various other circumstances, this Court has upheld temporary restraints where needed to preserve evidence until police could obtain a warrant. We have found no case in which this Court has held unlawful a temporary seizure that was supported by probable cause and was designed to prevent the loss of evidence while the police diligently obtained a warrant in a reasonable period of time.

Nor are we persuaded by the countervailing considerations that the parties or lower courts have raised. McArthur argues that the police proceeded without probable cause. But McArthur has waived this argument. And, in any event, it is without merit.

The Appellate Court of Illinois concluded that the police could not order McArthur to stay outside his home because McArthur's porch, where he stood at the time, was part of his home; hence the order "amounted to a constructive eviction" of McArthur from his residence. This Court has held, however, that a person standing in the doorway of a house is in a "public" place, and hence subject to arrest without a warrant permitting entry of the home. Regardless, we do not believe the difference to which the Appellate Court points—porch versus, *e.g.*, front walk—could make a significant difference here as to the reasonableness of the police restraint; and that, from the Fourth Amendment's perspective, is what matters.

The Appellate Court also found negatively significant the fact that Chief Love, with McArthur's consent, stepped inside the trailer's doorway to observe McArthur when McArthur reentered the trailer on two or three occasions. McArthur, however, reentered simply for his own convenience, to make phone calls and to obtain cigarettes. Under these circumstances, the reasonableness of the greater restriction (preventing reentry) implies the reasonableness of the lesser (permitting reentry conditioned on observation).

Finally, McArthur points to a case (and we believe it is the only case) that he believes offers direct support, namely, *Welsh v. Wisconsin*, 466 U.S. 740 (1984). In *Welsh*, this Court held that police could not enter a home without a warrant in order to prevent the loss of evidence (namely, the defendant's blood alcohol level) of the "nonjailable traffic offense" of driving while intoxicated. McArthur notes that his two convictions are for misdemeanors, which, he says, are as minor, and he adds that the restraint, keeping him out of his home, was nearly as serious.

We nonetheless find significant distinctions. The evidence at issue here was of crimes that were "jailable," not "nonjailable." In *Welsh*, we noted that, "given that the classification of state crimes differs widely among the States, the penalty that may attach to any particular offense seems to provide the clearest and most consistent indication of the State's interest in arresting individuals suspected of committing that offense." The same reasoning applies here, where class C misdemeanors include such widely diverse offenses as drag racing, drinking alcohol in a railroad car or on a railroad platform, bribery by a candidate for public office, and assault.

And the restriction at issue here is less serious. Temporarily keeping a person from entering his home, a consequence whenever police stop a person on the street, is considerably less intrusive than police entry into the home itself in order to make a warrantless arrest or conduct a search.

We have explained above why we believe that the need to preserve evidence of a "jailable" offense was sufficiently urgent or pressing to justify the restriction upon entry that the police imposed. We need not decide whether the circumstances before us would have justified a greater restriction for this type of offense or the same restriction were only a "nonjailable" offense at issue.

In sum, the police officers in this case had probable cause to believe that a home contained contraband, which was evidence of a crime. They reasonably believed that the home's resident, if left free of any restraint, would destroy that evidence. And they imposed a restraint that was both limited and tailored reasonably to secure law enforcement needs while protecting privacy interests. In our view, the restraint met the Fourth Amendment's demands.

Exigent Circumstances: Destruction of Evidence

1.   The exigent circumstances exception permits police to perform a search without a warrant if they reasonably believe it is necessary to prevent the imminent destruction of evidence. Exigency is determined case-by-case based on the totality of the circumstances.

2.   The police must not create or "manufacture" the exigency by engaging or threatening to engage in conduct that violates the Fourth Amendment.

3.   As an alternative to a warrantless search, police with probable cause to believe evidence of a crime is on the premises may temporarily seize or secure the premises to prevent the destruction of evidence and provide time for officers to obtain search warrant.

3. EMERGENCY AID OR ASSISTANCE

In *Brigham City, Utah v. Stuart*, 547 U.S. 398 (2006), the Supreme Court held that police may enter a home without a warrant to provide emergency assistance to an injured occupant or to protect an occupant from imminent injury. The Supreme Court reaffirmed its holding three years later in *Michigan v. Fisher*.

MICHIGAN V. FISHER
558 U.S. 45 (2009)

Per Curiam.

Police officers responded to a complaint of a disturbance near Allen Road in Brownstown, Michigan. Officer Christopher Goolsby later testified that, as he and his partner approached the area, a couple directed them to a residence where a man was "going crazy." Upon their arrival, the officers found a household in considerable chaos: a pickup truck in the driveway with its front smashed, damaged fenceposts along the side of the property, and three broken house windows, the glass still on the ground outside. The officers also noticed blood on the hood of the pickup and on clothes inside of it, as well as on one of the doors to the house. (It is disputed whether they noticed this immediately upon reaching the house, but undisputed that they noticed it before the allegedly unconstitutional entry.) Through a window, the officers could see respondent, Jeremy Fisher, inside the house, screaming and throwing things. The back door was locked, and a couch had been placed to block the front door.

The officers knocked, but Fisher refused to answer. They saw that Fisher had a cut on his hand, and they asked him whether he needed medical attention. Fisher ignored these questions and demanded, with accompanying profanity, that the officers go to get a search warrant. Officer Goolsby then pushed the front door partway open and ventured into the house. Through the window of the open door he saw Fisher pointing a long gun at him. Officer Goolsby withdrew.

Fisher was charged under Michigan law with assault with a dangerous weapon and possession of a firearm during the commission of a felony. The trial court concluded that Officer Goolsby violated the Fourth Amendment when he entered Fisher's house, and granted Fisher's motion to suppress the evidence obtained as a result—that is, Officer Goolsby's statement that Fisher pointed a rifle at him. The Michigan Court of Appeals affirmed. Because the decision of the Michigan Court of Appeals is contrary to our Fourth Amendment case law, particularly *Brigham City v. Stuart*, 547 U.S. 398 (2006), we grant the State's petition for certiorari and reverse.

The ultimate touchstone of the Fourth Amendment, we have often said, is "reasonableness." Therefore, although searches and seizures inside a home without a warrant are presumptively unreasonable, that presumption can be overcome. For example, the exigencies of the situation may make the needs of law enforcement so compelling that the warrantless search is objectively reasonable.

Brigham City identified one such exigency: the need to assist persons who are seriously injured or threatened with such injury. Thus, law enforcement officers may enter a home without a warrant to render emergency assistance to an injured occupant or to protect an occupant from imminent injury. This "emergency aid exception" does not depend on the officers' subjective intent or the seriousness of any crime they are investigating when the emergency arises. It requires only an objectively reasonable basis for believing that a person within the house is in need of immediate aid.

Brigham City illustrates the application of this standard. There, police officers responded to a noise complaint in the early hours of the morning. As they approached the house, they could hear from within an altercation occurring, some kind of fight. Following the tumult to the back of the house whence it came, the officers saw juveniles drinking beer in the backyard and a fight unfolding in the kitchen. They watched through the window as a juvenile broke free from the adults restraining him and punched another adult in the face, who recoiled to the sink, spitting blood. Under these circumstances, we found it "plainly reasonable" for the officers to enter the house and quell the violence, for they had "an objectively reasonable basis for believing both that the injured adult might need help and that the violence in the kitchen was just beginning."

A straightforward application of the emergency aid exception, as in *Brigham City*, dictates that the officer's entry was reasonable. Just as in *Brigham City*, the police officers here were responding to a report of a disturbance. Just as in *Brigham City*, when they arrived on the scene they encountered a tumultuous situation in the house—and here they also found signs of a recent injury, perhaps from a car accident, outside. And just as in *Brigham City*, the officers could see violent behavior inside. Although Officer Goolsby and his partner did not see punches thrown, as did the officers in *Brigham City*, they did see Fisher screaming and throwing things. It would be objectively reasonable to believe that Fisher's projectiles might have a human target (perhaps a spouse or a child), or that Fisher would hurt himself in the course of his rage. In short, we find it as plain here as we did in *Brigham City* that the officer's entry was reasonable under the Fourth Amendment.

The Michigan Court of Appeals, however, thought the situation "did not rise to a level of emergency justifying the warrantless intrusion into a residence." Although the Court of Appeals conceded that "there was evidence an injured person was on the premises," it found it significant that "the mere drops of blood did not signal a likely serious, life-threatening injury." The court added that the cut Officer Goolsby observed on Fisher's hand "likely explained the trail of blood" and that Fisher "was very much on his feet and apparently able to see to his own needs."

Even a casual review of *Brigham City* reveals the flaw in this reasoning. Officers do not need ironclad proof of "a likely serious, life-threatening" injury to invoke the emergency aid exception. The only injury police could confirm in *Brigham City* was the bloody lip they saw the juvenile inflict upon the adult. Fisher argues that the officers here could not have been motivated by a perceived need to provide medical assistance, since they never summoned emergency medical personnel. This would have no bearing, of course, upon their need to ensure that Fisher was not endangering someone else in the house. Moreover, even if the failure to summon medical personnel conclusively established that Goolsby did not subjectively believe, when he entered the house, that Fisher or someone else was seriously injured (which is doubtful), the test, as we have said, is not what Goolsby believed, but whether there was an objectively reasonable basis for believing that medical assistance was needed, or persons were in danger.

It was error for the Michigan Court of Appeals to replace that objective inquiry into appearances with its hindsight determination that there was in fact no emergency. It does not meet the needs of law enforcement or the demands of public safety to require officers to walk away from a situation like the one they encountered here. Only when an apparent threat has become an actual harm can officers rule out innocuous explanations for ominous circumstances. But the role of a peace officer includes preventing violence and restoring order, not simply rendering first aid to casualties. It sufficed to invoke the emergency aid exception that it was reasonable to believe that Fisher had hurt himself (albeit nonfatally) and needed treatment that in his rage he was unable to provide, or that Fisher was about to hurt, or had already hurt, someone else. The Michigan Court of Appeals required more than what the Fourth Amendment demands.

Exigent Circumstances: Emergency Aid or Assistance

Police officers may enter a home without a warrant to render emergency assistance to an injured occupant or to protect an occupant from imminent injury. This exception does not depend on the officers' subjective intent or the seriousness of any crime they are investigating when the emergency arises. It requires only an objectively reasonable basis for believing that a person within the house is in need of immediate aid.

4. MURDER SCENES

A violent crime that is in progress or has recently concluded is another obvious emergency that justifies a warrantless entry by police to attend to victims or to search for the perpetrator. But once the immediate emergency has passed, police should obtain a warrant to search the crime scene for additional evidence. In *Mincey v. Arizona*, the Supreme Court made it clear that there is no "murder scene" exception to the warrant requirement after the initial emergency has ended.

MINCEY V. ARIZONA
437 U.S. 385 (1978)

An undercover police officer and nine plainclothes policemen participated in a narcotics raid on Mincey's apartment. Gunfire erupted during the raid. The undercover officer was shot and later died at the hospital. After the shooting, the narcotics agents looked around quickly for other victims; they found that Mincey and two of his guests had been wounded. The agents summoned emergency assistance, then guarded the suspects and the premises. The agents did not search for or seize any evidence because a Tucson Police Department directive instructed officers not to investigate incidents in which they were involved.

About 10 minutes later, homicide detectives arrived and took charge of the investigation. Their search of the apartment lasted four days. Officers opened drawers, closets, cupboards, and inspected their contents; they emptied clothing pockets; they dug bullet fragments out of the walls and floors; they pulled up sections of the carpet and removed them for examination. Every item in the apartment was closely examined and inventoried, and 200 to 300 objects were seized. No warrant was ever obtained.

Much of the evidence introduced against Mincey at trial—including photographs and diagrams, bullets and shell casings, guns, narcotics, and narcotics paraphernalia—was the product of the four-day search of his apartment. The Arizona Supreme Court held that the warrantless search of a homicide scene is constitutionally permissible. The U.S. Supreme Court reversed:

> We do not question the right of the police to respond to emergency situations. Numerous state and federal cases have recognized that the Fourth Amendment does not bar police officers from making warrantless entries and searches when they reasonably believe that a person within is in need of immediate aid. Similarly, when the police come upon the scene of a homicide they may make a prompt warrantless search of the area to see if there are other victims or if a killer is still on the premises. And the police may seize any evidence that is in plain

view during the course of their legitimate emergency activities. But a warrantless search must be strictly circumscribed by the exigencies which justify its initiation, and it simply cannot be contended that this search was justified by any emergency threatening life or limb. All the persons in Mincey's apartment had been located before the investigating homicide officers arrived there and began their search. And a four-day search that included opening dresser drawers and ripping up carpets can hardly be rationalized in terms of the legitimate concerns that justify an emergency search.

The Supreme Court reaffirmed *Mincey*—and confirmed that there is no "murder scene" exception to the warrant requirement—in *Thompson v. Louisiana*, 469 U.S. 17 (1984), and again in *Flippo v. West Virginia*, 528 U.S. 11 (1999). The evidence was suppressed *Mincey*, *Thompson*, and *Flippo* because in each case, the defendant had a reasonable expectation of privacy in the searched premises. In *Mincey*, the police searched the defendant's apartment; in *Thompson*, the police searched the defendant's home; and in *Flippo*, the police searched the defendant's vacation cabin. When police perform a warrantless search of a murder scene in which the defendant has no reasonable expectation of privacy—where, for example, the killer is an intruder—the evidence is admissible against the defendant, not because the warrantless search is permissible, but because the defendant lacks "standing" to object to the search.

Exigent Circumstances: Murder Scenes
When police arrive at the scene of a homicide, they may make a quick warrantless search of the area to see if there are other victims or if a killer is still on the premises, and they may seize any evidence that is in plain view during their legitimate emergency activities. Once the emergency has passed, however, subsequent searches must be authorized by a warrant.

B. SEARCH INCIDENT TO ARREST

Arrests can become chaotic and violent, particularly if the arrestee is caught by surprise or is uncooperative. Accordingly, when police make a lawful arrest, they may search the arrestee and the immediate area of the arrest without a warrant and without probable cause. This "search incident to arrest" exception to the warrant requirement is justified by two considerations: the need to protect the safety of the officers making the arrest, and the need to prevent the destruction of valuable evidence.

The basic rules governing the search incident to arrest exception vary somewhat depending on the location of the arrest and scope of the search that the police perform. Most of the cases involving this exception can be divided into three categories: searches of homes incident to arrest, searches of persons and personal effects incident to arrest, and searches of cars incident to arrest.

1. SEARCHES OF HOMES INCIDENT TO ARREST

In *Chimel v. California*, the Supreme Court sketched the basic parameters of the search incident to arrest exception in the context of an arrest that took place within the defendant's home.

CHIMEL V. CALIFORNIA
395 U.S. 752 (1969)

JUSTICE STEWART delivered the opinion of the Court.

This case raises basic questions concerning the permissible scope under the Fourth Amendment of a search incident to a lawful arrest.

The relevant facts are essentially undisputed. Late in the afternoon of September 13, 1965, three police officers arrived at the Santa Ana, California, home of the petitioner with a warrant authorizing his arrest for the burglary of a coin shop. The officers knocked on the door, identified themselves to the petitioner's wife, and asked if they might come inside. She ushered them into the house, where they waited 10 or 15 minutes until the petitioner returned home from work. When the petitioner entered the house, one of the officers handed him the arrest warrant and asked for permission to "look around." The petitioner objected, but was advised that "on the basis of the lawful arrest," the officers would nonetheless conduct a search. No search warrant had been issued.

Accompanied by the petitioner's wife, the officers then looked through the entire three-bedroom house, including the attic, the garage, and a small workshop. In some rooms the search was relatively cursory. In the master bedroom and sewing room, however, the officers directed the petitioner's wife to open drawers and "to physically move contents of the drawers from side to side so that they might view any items that would have come from the burglary." After completing the search, they seized numerous items—primarily coins, but also several medals, tokens, and a few other objects. The entire search took between 45 minutes and an hour.

At the petitioner's subsequent state trial on two charges of burglary, the items taken from his house were admitted into evidence against him, over his objection that they had been unconstitutionally seized. He was convicted, and the judgments of conviction were affirmed by both the

California Court of Appeal and the California Supreme Court. Both courts accepted the petitioner's contention that the arrest warrant was invalid because the supporting affidavit was set out in conclusory terms, but held that since the arresting officers had procured the warrant "in good faith," and since in any event they had had sufficient information to constitute probable cause for the petitioner's arrest, that arrest had been lawful. From this conclusion the appellate courts went on to hold that the search of the petitioner's home had been justified, despite the absence of a search warrant, on the ground that it had been incident to a valid arrest. We granted certiorari in order to consider the petitioner's substantial constitutional claims.

Without deciding the question, we proceed on the hypothesis that the California courts were correct in holding that the arrest of the petitioner was valid under the Constitution. This brings us directly to the question whether the warrantless search of the petitioner's entire house can be constitutionally justified as incident to that arrest.

When an arrest is made, it is reasonable for the arresting officer to search the person arrested in order to remove any weapons that the latter might seek to use in order to resist arrest or effect his escape. Otherwise, the officer's safety might well be endangered, and the arrest itself frustrated. In addition, it is entirely reasonable for the arresting officer to search for and seize any evidence on the arrestee's person in order to prevent its concealment or destruction. And the area into which an arrestee might reach in order to grab a weapon or evidentiary items must, of course, be governed by a like rule. A gun on a table or in a drawer in front of one who is arrested can be as dangerous to the arresting officer as one concealed in the clothing of the person arrested. There is ample justification, therefore, for a search of the arrestee's person and the area "within his immediate control"—construing that phrase to mean the area from within which he might gain possession of a weapon or destructible evidence.

There is no comparable justification, however, for routinely searching any room other than that in which an arrest occurs—or, for that matter, for searching through all the desk drawers or other closed or concealed areas in that room itself. Such searches, in the absence of well-recognized exceptions, may be made only under the authority of a search warrant.

It is argued in the present case that it is "reasonable" to search a man's house when he is arrested in it. But that argument is founded on little more than a subjective view regarding the acceptability of certain sorts of police conduct, and not on consideration relevant to Fourth Amendment interests. Under such an unconfined analysis, Fourth Amendment protection in this area would approach the evaporation point. It is not easy to explain why, for instance, it is less subjectively "reasonable" to search a man's house when he is arrested on his front lawn—or just down the street—than it is when he happens to be in the house at the time of arrest.

Application of sound Fourth Amendment principles to the facts of this case produces a clear result. The search here went far beyond the petitioner's person and the area from within which he might have obtained either a weapon or something that could have been used as evidence against him. There was no constitutional justification, in the absence of a search warrant, for extending the search beyond that area. The scope of the search was, therefore, "unreasonable" under the Fourth and Fourteenth Amendments and the petitioner's conviction cannot stand.

JUSTICE WHITE, with whom JUSTICE BLACK joins, dissenting.

The rule which has prevailed, but for very brief or doubtful periods of aberration, is that a search incident to an arrest may extend to those areas under the control of the defendant and where items subject to constitutional seizure may be found. The justification for this rule must, under the language of the Fourth Amendment, lie in the reasonableness of the rule.

In terms, then, the Court must decide whether a given search is reasonable. The Amendment does not proscribe "warrantless searches" but instead it proscribes "unreasonable searches" and this Court has never held nor does the majority today assert that warrantless searches are necessarily unreasonable.

Applying this reasonableness test to the area of searches incident to arrests, one thing is clear at the outset. Search of an arrested man and of the items within his immediate reach must in almost every case be reasonable. There is always a danger that the suspect will try to escape, seizing concealed weapons with which to overpower and injure the arresting officers, and there is a danger that he may destroy evidence vital to the prosecution. Circumstances in which these justifications would not apply are sufficiently rare that inquiry is not made into searches of this scope, which have been considered reasonable throughout.

The justifications which make such a search reasonable obviously do not apply to the search of areas to which the accused does not have ready physical access. This is not enough, however, to prove such searches unconstitutional. The Court has always held, and does not today deny, that when there is probable cause to search and it is "impracticable" for one reason or another to get a search warrant, then a warrantless search may be reasonable.

This is not to say that a search can be reasonable without regard to the probable cause to believe that seizable items are on the premises. But when there are exigent circumstances, and probable cause, then the search may be made without a warrant, reasonably. An arrest itself may often create an emergency situation making it impracticable to obtain a warrant before embarking on a related search. Again assuming that there is probable cause to search premises at the spot where a suspect is arrested, it seems to me unreasonable to require the police to leave the scene in order to obtain a search warrant when they are already legally there to make a valid arrest, and when there must almost always be a strong possibility that confederates of the arrested man will in the meanwhile remove the items for which the police have probable cause to search. This must so often be the case that it seems to me as unreasonable to require a warrant for a search of the premises as to require a warrant for search of the person and his very immediate surroundings.

This case provides a good illustration of my point that it is unreasonable to require police to leave the scene of an arrest in order to obtain a search warrant when they already have probable cause to search and there is a clear danger that the items for which they may reasonably search will be removed before they return with a warrant. There was doubtless probable cause not only to arrest petitioner, but also to search his house. He had obliquely admitted, both to a neighbor and to the owner of the burglarized store, that he had committed the burglary. In light of this, and the fact that the neighbor had seen other admittedly stolen property in petitioner's house, there was surely probable cause on which a warrant could have issued to search the house for the stolen coins. Moreover, had the police simply arrested petitioner, taken him off to the station house, and later returned with a warrant, it seems very likely that petitioner's wife, who in view of petitioner's generally garrulous nature must have known of the robbery, would have removed the coins. For the police to search the house while the evidence they had probable cause to search out and seize was still there cannot be considered unreasonable.

If circumstances so often require the warrantless arrest that the law generally permits it, the typical situation will find the arresting officers lawfully on the premises without arrest or search warrant. Like the majority, I would permit the police to search the person of a suspect and the area under his immediate control either to assure the safety of the officers or to prevent the destruction of evidence. And like the majority, I see nothing in the arrest alone furnishing probable cause for a search of any broader scope. However, where as here the existence of probable cause is independently established and would justify a warrant for a broader search for evidence, I would follow past cases and permit such a search to be carried out without a warrant, since the fact of arrest supplies an exigent circumstance justifying police action before the evidence can be removed, and also alerts the suspect to the fact of the search so that he can immediately seek judicial determination of probable cause in an adversary proceeding, and appropriate redress.

An arrested man, by definition conscious of the police interest in him, and provided almost immediately with a lawyer and a judge, is in an excellent position to dispute the reasonableness of his arrest and contemporaneous search in a full adversary proceeding. I would uphold the constitutionality of this search contemporaneous with an arrest since there were probable cause both for the search and for the arrest, exigent circumstances involving the removal or destruction of evidence, and satisfactory opportunity to dispute the issues of probable cause shortly thereafter. In this case, the search was reasonable.

As *Chimel* makes clear, the search incident to arrest exception does not permit police to perform a warrantless search of an entire home when they arrest a suspect within or near her home; the exception is limited to the person of the arrestee and her immediate surroundings, where she might grab a weapon or attempt to destroy evidence. In *Maryland v. Buie*, however, the Supreme Court effectively extended the scope of the search incident to arrest exception in homes by allowing police to perform a "protective sweep" when making an arrest to ensure that there are no other people inside the home who might present a threat.

MARYLAND V. BUIE
494 U.S. 325 (1990)

JUSTICE WHITE delivered the opinion of the Court.

A "protective sweep" is a quick and limited search of premises, incident to an arrest and conducted to protect the safety of police officers or others. It is narrowly confined to a cursory visual inspection of those places in which a person might be hiding. In this case we must decide what level of justification is required by the Fourth and Fourteenth Amendments before police officers, while effecting the arrest of a suspect in his home pursuant to an arrest warrant, may conduct a warrantless protective sweep of all or part of the premises. The Court of Appeals of Maryland held that a running suit seized in plain view during such a protective sweep should have been suppressed at respondent's armed robbery trial because the officer who conducted the sweep did not have probable cause to believe that a serious and demonstrable potentiality for danger existed. We conclude that the Fourth Amendment would permit the protective sweep undertaken here if the searching officer possessed a reasonable belief based on specific and articulable facts which, taken together with the rational inferences from those facts, reasonably warranted the officer in believing that the area swept harbored an individual posing a danger to the officer or others. We accordingly vacate the judgment below and remand for application of this standard.

I

On February 3, 1986, two men committed an armed robbery of a Godfather's Pizza restaurant in Prince George's County, Maryland. One of the robbers was wearing a red running suit. That same day, Prince George's County police obtained arrest warrants for respondent Jerome Edward Buie and his suspected accomplice in the robbery, Lloyd Allen. Buie's house was placed under police surveillance.

On February 5, the police executed the arrest warrant for Buie. They first had a police department secretary telephone Buie's house to verify that he was home. The secretary spoke to a female first, then to Buie himself. Six or seven officers proceeded to Buie's house. Once inside, the officers fanned out through the first and second floors. Corporal James Rozar announced that he would "freeze" the basement so that no one could come up and surprise the officers. With his service revolver drawn, Rozar twice shouted into the basement, ordering anyone down there to come out. When a voice asked who was calling, Rozar announced three times: "this is the police, show me your hands." Eventually, a pair of hands appeared around the bottom of the stairwell and Buie emerged from the basement. He was arrested, searched, and handcuffed by Rozar. Thereafter, Detective Joseph Frolich entered the basement "in case there was someone else" down there. He noticed a red running suit lying in plain view on a stack of clothing and seized it.

The trial court denied Buie's motion to suppress the running suit, stating in part: "The man comes out from a basement, the police don't know how many other people are down there. He is charged with a serious offense." The State introduced the running suit into evidence at Buie's trial. A jury convicted Buie of robbery with a deadly weapon and using a handgun in the commission of a felony.

The Court of Special Appeals of Maryland affirmed the trial court's denial of the suppression motion. The court stated that Detective Frolich did not go into the basement to search for evidence, but to look for the suspected accomplice or anyone else who might pose a threat to the officers on the scene.

The Court of Appeals of Maryland reversed by a 4-to-3 vote. The court acknowledged that "when the intrusion is slight, as in the case of a brief stop and frisk on a public street, and the public interest in prevention of crime is substantial, reasonable articulable suspicion may be enough to pass constitutional muster." The court, however, stated that when the sanctity of the home is involved, the exceptions to the warrant requirement are few, and held: "To justify a protective sweep of a home, the government must show that there is probable cause to believe that a serious and demonstrable potentiality for danger exists." The court went on to find that the State had not satisfied that probable-cause requirement. We granted certiorari.

II

It is not disputed that until the point of Buie's arrest the police had the right, based on the authority of the arrest warrant, to search anywhere in the house that Buie might have been found, including the basement. There is also no dispute that if Detective Frolich's entry into the basement was lawful, the seizure of the red running suit, which was in plain view and which the officer had probable cause to believe was evidence of a crime, was also lawful under the Fourth Amendment. The issue in this case is what level of justification the Fourth Amendment required before Detective Frolich could legally enter the basement to see if someone else was there.

Petitioner, the State of Maryland, argues that, under a general reasonableness balancing test, police should be permitted to conduct a protective sweep whenever they make an in-home arrest for a violent crime. As an alternative to this suggested bright-line rule, the State contends that protective sweeps fall within the ambit of the doctrine announced in *Terry v. Ohio*, 392 U.S. 1 (1968), and that such sweeps may be conducted in conjunction with a valid in-home arrest whenever the police reasonably suspect a risk of danger to the officers or others at the arrest scene. The United States, as *amicus curiae* supporting the State, also argues for a *Terry*-type standard of reasonable, articulable suspicion of risk to the officer, and contends that that standard is met here. Respondent argues that a protective sweep may not be undertaken without a warrant unless the exigencies of the situation render such warrantless search objectively reasonable. According to Buie, because the State has shown neither exigent circumstances to immediately enter Buie's house nor an unforeseen danger that arose once the officers were in the house, there is no excuse for the failure to obtain a search warrant to search for dangerous persons believed to be on the premises. Buie further contends that, even if the warrant requirement is inapplicable, there is no justification for relaxing the probable-cause standard. If something less than probable cause is sufficient, respondent argues that it is no less than individualized suspicion—specific, articulable facts supporting a reasonable belief that there are persons on the premises who are a threat to the officers. According to Buie, there were no such specific, articulable facts to justify the search of his basement.

III

It goes without saying that the Fourth Amendment bars only unreasonable searches and seizures. Our cases show that in determining reasonableness, we have balanced the intrusion on the individual's Fourth Amendment interests against its promotion of legitimate governmental interests. Under this test, a search of the house or office is generally not reasonable without a warrant issued on probable cause. There are other contexts, however, where the public interest is such that neither a warrant nor probable cause is required.

The *Terry* case is most instructive for present purposes. There we held that an on-the-street "frisk" for weapons must be tested by the Fourth Amendment's general proscription against unreasonable searches because such a frisk involves "an entire rubric of police conduct— necessarily swift action predicated upon the on-the-spot observations of the officer on the beat—which historically has not been, and as a practical matter could not be, subjected to the warrant procedure." We stated that there is "no ready test for determining reasonableness other than by balancing the need to search against the invasion which the search entails." Applying that balancing test, it was held that although a frisk for weapons "constitutes a severe, though brief, intrusion upon cherished personal security," such a frisk is reasonable when weighed against the "need for law enforcement officers to protect themselves and other prospective victims of violence in situations where they may lack probable cause for an arrest." We therefore authorized a limited patdown for weapons where a reasonably prudent officer would be warranted in the belief, based on "specific and articulable facts" and not on a mere "inchoate and unparticularized suspicion or 'hunch' that he is dealing with an armed and dangerous individual."

In *Michigan v. Long*, 463 U.S. 1032 (1983), the principles of *Terry* were applied in the context of a roadside encounter: "The search of the passenger compartment of an automobile, limited to those areas in which a weapon may be placed or hidden, is permissible if the police officer possesses a reasonable belief based on specific and articulable facts which, taken together with the rational inferences from those facts, reasonably warrant the officer in believing that the suspect is dangerous and the suspect may gain immediate control of weapons." The *Long* Court expressly rejected the contention that *Terry* restricted preventative searches to the person of a detained suspect. In a sense, *Long* authorized a "frisk" of an automobile for weapons.

The ingredients to apply the balance struck in *Terry* and *Long* are present in this case. Possessing an arrest warrant and probable cause to believe Buie was in his home, the officers were entitled to enter and to search anywhere in the house in which Buie might be found. Once he was found, however, the search for him was over, and there was no longer that particular justification for entering any rooms that had not yet been searched.

That Buie had an expectation of privacy in those remaining areas of his house, however, does not mean such rooms were immune from entry. In *Terry* and *Long* we were concerned with the immediate interest of the police officers in taking steps to assure themselves that the persons with whom they were dealing were not armed with, or able to gain immediate control of, a weapon that could unexpectedly and fatally be used against them. In the instant case, there is an analogous interest of the officers in taking steps to assure themselves that the house in which a suspect is being, or has just been, arrested is not harboring other persons who are dangerous and who could unexpectedly launch an attack. The risk of danger in the context of an arrest in the home is as great as, if not greater than, it is in an on-the-street or roadside investigatory encounter. A *Terry* or *Long* frisk occurs before a police-citizen confrontation has escalated to the point of arrest. A protective sweep, in contrast, occurs as an adjunct to the serious step of taking a person into custody for the purpose of prosecuting him for a crime. Moreover, unlike an encounter on the street or along a highway, an in-home arrest puts the officer at the disadvantage of being on his adversary's "turf." An ambush in a confined setting of unknown configuration is more to be feared than it is in open, more familiar surroundings.

We recognized in *Terry* that "even a limited search of the outer clothing for weapons constitutes a severe, though brief, intrusion upon cherished personal security, and it must surely be an annoying, frightening, and perhaps humiliating experience." But we permitted the intrusion, which was no more than necessary to protect the officer from harm. Nor do we here suggest, as the State does, that entering rooms not examined prior to the arrest is a *de minimis* intrusion that may be disregarded. We are quite sure, however, that the arresting officers are permitted in such circumstances to take reasonable steps to ensure their safety after, and while making, the arrest. That interest is sufficient to outweigh the intrusion such procedures may entail.

We agree with the State, as did the court below, that a warrant was not required. We also hold that as an incident to the arrest the officers could, as a precautionary matter and without probable cause or reasonable suspicion, look in closets and other spaces immediately adjoining the place of arrest from which an attack could be immediately launched. Beyond that, however, we hold that there must be articulable facts which, taken together with the rational inferences from those facts, would warrant a reasonably prudent officer in believing that the area to be swept harbors an individual posing a danger to those on the arrest scene. This is no more and no less than was required in *Terry* and *Long*, and as in those cases, we think this balance is the proper one.

We should emphasize that such a protective sweep, aimed at protecting the arresting officers, if justified by the circumstances, is nevertheless not a full search of the premises, but may extend only to a cursory inspection of those spaces where a person may be found. The sweep lasts no longer than is necessary to dispel the reasonable suspicion of danger and in any event no longer than it takes to complete the arrest and depart the premises.

IV

Affirmance is not required by *Chimel v. California*, 395 U.S. 752 (1969), where it was held that in the absence of a search warrant, the justifiable search incident to an in-home arrest could not extend beyond the arrestee's person and the area from within which the arrestee might have obtained a weapon. First, *Chimel* was concerned with a full-blown search of the entire house for evidence of the crime for which the arrest was made, not the more limited intrusion contemplated by a protective sweep. Second, the justification for the search incident to arrest considered in *Chimel* was the threat posed by the arrestee, not the safety threat posed by the house, or more properly by unseen third parties in the house. To reach our conclusion today, therefore, we need not disagree with the Court's statement in *Chimel* that "the invasion of privacy that results from a top-to-bottom search of a man's house cannot be characterized as minor," nor hold that "simply because some interference with an individual's privacy and freedom of movement has lawfully taken place, further intrusions should automatically be allowed despite the absence of a warrant that the Fourth Amendment would otherwise require." The type of search we authorize today is far removed from the "top-to-bottom" search involved in *Chimel*; moreover, it is decidedly not "automatic," but may be conducted only when justified by a reasonable, articulable suspicion that the house is harboring a person posing a danger to those on the arrest scene.

V

We conclude that by requiring a protective sweep to be justified by probable cause to believe that a serious and demonstrable potentiality for danger existed, the Court of Appeals of Maryland applied an unnecessarily strict Fourth Amendment standard. The Fourth Amendment permits a properly limited protective sweep in conjunction with an in-home arrest when the searching officer possesses a reasonable belief based on specific and articulable facts that the area to be swept harbors an individual posing a danger to those on the arrest scene.

JUSTICE BRENNAN, with whom JUSTICE MARSHALL joins, dissenting.

Today the Court for the first time extends *Terry v. Ohio*, 392 U.S. 1 (1968), into the home, dispensing with the Fourth Amendment's general requirements of a warrant and probable cause and carving a "reasonable suspicion" exception for protective sweeps in private dwellings.

While the Fourth Amendment protects a person's privacy interests in a variety of settings, physical entry of the home is the chief evil against which the wording of the Fourth Amendment is directed. The Court discounts the nature of the intrusion because it believes that the scope of the intrusion is limited. The Court explains that a protective sweep's scope is "narrowly confined to a cursory visual inspection of those places in which a person might be hiding," and confined in duration to a period "no longer than is necessary to dispel the reasonable suspicion of danger and in any event no longer than it takes to complete the arrest and depart the premises." But these spatial and temporal restrictions are not particularly limiting. A protective sweep would bring within police purview virtually all personal possessions within the house not hidden from view in a small enclosed space. Police officers searching for potential ambushers might enter every room including basements and attics; open up closets, lockers, chests, wardrobes, and cars; and peer under beds and behind furniture. The officers will view letters, documents, and personal effects that are on tables or desks or are visible inside open drawers; books, records, tapes, and pictures on shelves; and clothing, medicines, toiletries and other paraphernalia not carefully stored in dresser drawers or bathroom cupboards. While perhaps not a "full-blown" or "top-to-bottom" search, a protective sweep is much closer to it than to a "limited patdown for weapons" or a "frisk" of an automobile. Because the nature and scope of the intrusion sanctioned here are far greater than those upheld in *Terry* and *Long,* the Court's conclusion that "the ingredients to apply the balance struck in *Terry* and *Long* are present in this case" is unwarranted. The "ingredient" of a minimally intrusive search is absent, and the Court's holding today therefore unpalatably deviates from *Terry* and its progeny.

In light of the special sanctity of a private residence and the highly intrusive nature of a protective sweep, I firmly believe that police officers must have probable cause to fear that their personal safety is threatened by a hidden confederate of an arrestee before they may sweep through the entire home. Given the state-court determination that the officers searching Buie's home lacked probable cause to perceive such a danger and therefore were not lawfully present in the basement, I would affirm the state court's decision to suppress the incriminating evidence.

In *Buie*, the Supreme Court describes the protective sweep as a "cursory visual inspection of those places in which a person might be hiding." Under the rule announced by the Court, police may—without probable cause or reasonable suspicion—look in closets and other spaces immediately adjoining the place of an arrest from which an attack could be launched. In order to look in rooms or other spaces beyond the area immediately adjoining the place of an arrest, police need *reasonable suspicion* to believe that the area harbors an individual posing a danger to those on the scene. The reasonable suspicion standard in *Buie*—a standard of suspicion that is lower than probable cause—is borrowed from *Terry v. Ohio*, 392 U.S. 1 (1968), a case presented in Chapter 6.

If police find contraband or evidence of crime in plain view during a legitimate protective sweep, they may seize it and use it as evidence under the plain view exception to the warrant requirement. (The plain view exception is set forth later in this Chapter.) Thus, the protective sweep rule effectively expands the area in which police may search for and seize evidence incident to an arrest at a home.

Searches of Homes Incident to Arrest

1.   When an arrest is made, police may search the arrestee's person and the area into which the arrestee might reach where he could gain possession of a weapon or destructible evidence. The search incident to arrest may be made without a search warrant and without probable cause.

2.   Incident to an arrest, police may also conduct a warrantless protective sweep—a cursory visual inspection of those places in which a person might be hiding.

   a.   As a precautionary measure and without probable cause or reasonable suspicion, police can look in closets and other spaces immediately adjoining the place of arrest from which an attack could be launched.

   b.   Beyond the areas immediately adjoining the place of arrest, police must have reasonable suspicion that the area to be swept harbors an individual posing a danger to those on the arrest scene.

---

2.   SEARCHES OF PERSONS AND PERSONAL EFFECTS INCIDENT TO ARREST

The rule announced in *Chimel* makes it clear that, incident to the arrest, police may search the arrestee's pockets or a purse or backpack she might be carrying, since these are areas into which the arrestee might reach to grab a weapon or destructible evidence. But how thoroughly may the police search persons and personal effects when they make an arrest? May the police search a packet of cigarettes found in the arrestee's pocket? May they search through the contents of her wallet or her cell phone? May they take a sample of her DNA? The Supreme Court has confronted all of these questions in the cases that follow.

U.S. v. ROBINSON
414 U.S. 218 (1973)

JUSTICE REHNQUIST delivered the opinion of the Court.

On April 23, 1968, at approximately 11 p.m., Officer Richard Jenks, a 15-year veteran of the District of Columbia Metropolitan Police

Department, observed the respondent driving a 1965 Cadillac near the intersection of 8th and C Streets, N.E., in the District of Columbia. Jenks, as a result of previous investigation following a check of respondent's operator's permit four days earlier, determined there was reason to believe that respondent was operating a motor vehicle after the revocation of his operator's permit. This is an offense defined by statute in the District of Columbia which carries a mandatory minimum jail term, a mandatory minimum fine, or both.

Jenks signaled respondent to stop the automobile, which respondent did, and all three of the occupants emerged from the car. At that point Jenks informed respondent that he was under arrest for "operating after revocation and obtaining a permit by misrepresentation." It was assumed by the Court of Appeals, and is conceded by the respondent here, that Jenks had probable cause to arrest respondent, and that he effected a full-custody arrest.

In accordance with procedures prescribed in police department instructions, Jenks then began to search respondent. He explained at a subsequent hearing that he was "face-to-face" with the respondent, and "placed (his) hands on (the respondent), my right-hand to his left breast like this (demonstrating) and proceeded to pat him down thus (with the right hand)." During this patdown, Jenks felt an object in the left breast pocket of the heavy coat respondent was wearing, but testified that he "couldn't tell what it was" and also that he "couldn't actually tell the size of it." Jenks then reached into the pocket and pulled out the object, which turned out to be a "crumpled up cigarette package." Jenks testified that at this point he still did not know what was in the package: "As I felt the package I could feel objects in the package but I couldn't tell what they were. I knew they weren't cigarettes."

The officer then opened the cigarette pack and found 14 gelatin capsules of white powder which he thought to be, and which later analysis proved to be, heroin. Jenks then continued his search of respondent to completion, feeling around his waist and trouser legs, and examining the remaining pockets. The heroin seized from the respondent was admitted into evidence at the trial which resulted in his conviction in the District Court.

We conclude that the search conducted by Jenks in this case did not offend the limits imposed by the Fourth Amendment, and we therefore reverse the judgment of the Court of Appeals.

I

It is well settled that a search incident to a lawful arrest is a traditional exception to the warrant requirement of the Fourth Amendment. This general exception has historically been formulated into two distinct propositions. The first is that a search may be made of the person of the arrestee by virtue of the lawful arrest. The second is that a search may be made of the area within the control of the arrestee.

Examination of this Court's decisions shows that these two propositions have been treated quite differently. The validity of the search of a person incident to a lawful arrest has been regarded as settled from its first enunciation, and has remained virtually unchallenged until the present case. The validity of the second proposition, while likewise conceded in principle, has been subject to differing interpretations as to the extent of the area which may be searched.

Throughout the series of cases in which the Court has addressed the second proposition relating to a search incident to a lawful arrest—the permissible area beyond the person of the arrestee which such a search may cover—no doubt has been expressed as to the unqualified authority of the arresting authority to search the person of the arrestee.

Thus the broadly stated rule, and the reasons for it, have been repeatedly affirmed in the decisions of this Court. Since the statements in the cases speak not simply in terms of an exception to the warrant requirement, but in terms of an affirmative authority to search, they clearly imply that such searches also meet the Fourth Amendment's requirement of reasonableness.

II

In its decision of this case, the Court of Appeals decided that even after a police officer lawfully places a suspect under arrest for the purpose of taking him into custody, he may not ordinarily proceed to fully search the prisoner. He must, instead, conduct a limited frisk of the outer clothing and remove such weapons that he may, as a result of that limited frisk, reasonably believe and ascertain that the suspect has in his possession. While recognizing that *Terry v. Ohio*, 392 U.S. 1 (1968), dealt with a permissible "frisk" incident to an investigative stop based on less than probable cause to arrest, the Court of Appeals felt that the principles of that case should be carried over to this probable-cause arrest for driving while one's license is revoked. Since there would be no further evidence of such a crime to be obtained in a search of the arrestee, the court held that only a search for weapons could be justified.

Terry v. Ohio did not involve an arrest for probable cause, and it made quite clear that the "protective frisk" for weapons which it approved might be conducted without probable cause. This Court's opinion explicitly recognized that there is a "distinction in purpose, character, and extent between a search incident to an arrest and a limited search for weapons." *Terry*, therefore, affords no basis to carry over to a probable-cause arrest the limitations this Court placed on a stop-and-frisk search permissible without probable cause.

III

The Court of Appeals in effect determined that the only reason supporting the authority for a full search incident to lawful arrest was the possibility of discovery of evidence or fruits. Concluding that there could be no evidence or fruits in the case of an offense such as that with which respondent was charged (driving with a suspended license), it held that any protective search would have to be limited by the conditions laid down in *Terry* for a search upon less than probable cause to arrest. Quite apart from the fact that *Terry* clearly recognized the distinction between the two types of searches, and that a different rule governed one than governed the other, we find additional reason to disagree with the Court of Appeals.

The justification or reason for the authority to search incident to a lawful arrest rests quite as much on the need to disarm the suspect in order to take him into custody as it does on the need to preserve evidence on his person for later use at trial. The standards traditionally governing a search incident to lawful arrest are not, therefore, commuted to the stricter *Terry* standards by the absence of probable fruits or further evidence of the particular crime for which the arrest is made.

Nor are we inclined, on the basis of what seems to us to be a rather speculative judgment, to qualify the breadth of the general authority to search incident to a lawful custodial arrest on an assumption that persons arrested for the offense of driving while their licenses have been revoked are less likely to possess dangerous weapons than are those arrested for other crimes. It is scarcely open to doubt that the danger to an officer is far greater in the case of the extended exposure which follows the taking of a suspect into custody and transporting him to the police station than in the case of the relatively fleeting contact resulting from the typical *Terry*-type stop. This is an adequate basis for treating all custodial arrests alike for purposes of search justification.

But quite apart from these distinctions, our more fundamental disagreement with the Court of Appeals arises from its suggestion that there must be litigated in each case the issue of whether or not there was present one of the reasons supporting the authority for a search of the person incident to a lawful arrest. We do not think the long line of authorities of this Court, or what we can glean from the history of practice in this country and in England, requires such a case-by-case adjudication. A police officer's determination as to how and where to search the person of a suspect whom he has arrested is necessarily a quick *ad hoc* judgment which the Fourth Amendment does not require to be broken down in each instance into an analysis of each step in the search. The authority to search the person incident to a lawful custodial arrest, while based upon the need to disarm and to discover evidence, does not depend on what a court may later decide was the probability in a particular arrest situation that weapons or evidence would in fact be found upon the person of the suspect. A custodial arrest of a suspect based on probable cause is a reasonable intrusion under the Fourth Amendment; that intrusion being lawful, a search incident to the arrest requires no additional justification. It is the fact of the lawful arrest which establishes the authority to search, and we hold that in the case of a lawful custodial arrest a full search of the person is not only an exception to the warrant requirement of the Fourth Amendment, but is also a "reasonable" search under that Amendment.

IV

The search of respondent's person conducted by Officer Jenks in this case and the seizure from him of the heroin, were permissible under established Fourth Amendment law. Since it is the fact of custodial arrest which gives rise to the authority to search, it is of no moment that Jenks did not indicate any subjective fear of the respondent or that he did not himself suspect that respondent was armed. Having in the course of a lawful search come upon the crumpled package of cigarettes, he was entitled to inspect it; and when his inspection revealed the heroin capsules, he was entitled to seize them as "fruits, instrumentalities, or contraband" probative of criminal conduct.

JUSTICE MARSHALL, with whom JUSTICE DOUGLAS and JUSTICE BRENNAN join, dissenting.

The majority opinion fails to recognize that the search conducted by Officer Jenks did not merely involve a search of respondent's person. It also included a separate search of effects found on his person. And even were we to assume that it was reasonable for Jenks to remove the object he felt in respondent's pocket, clearly there was no justification consistent with the Fourth Amendment which would authorize his opening the package and looking inside.

To begin with, after Jenks had the cigarette package in his hands, there is no indication that he had reason to believe or did in fact believe that the package contained a weapon. More importantly, even if the crumpled-up cigarette package had in fact contained some sort of small weapon, it would have been impossible for respondent to have used it once the package was in the officer's hands. Opening the package, therefore, did not further the protective purpose of the search.

It is suggested, however, that since the custodial arrest itself represents a significant intrusion into the privacy of the person, any additional intrusion by way of opening or examining effects found on the person is not worthy of constitutional protection. But such an approach was expressly rejected by the Court in *Chimel v. California*, 395 U.S. 752 (1969). There it was suggested that since the police had lawfully entered petitioner's house to effect an arrest, the additional invasion of privacy stemming from an accompanying search of the entire house was inconsequential. The Court answered: "We can see no reason why, simply because some interference with an individual's privacy and freedom of movement has lawfully taken place, further intrusions should automatically be allowed despite the absence of a warrant that the Fourth Amendment would otherwise require."

Chimel established the principle that the lawful right of the police to interfere with the security of the person did not, standing alone, automatically confer the right to interfere with the security and privacy of his house. Hence, the mere fact of an arrest should be no justification, in and of itself, for invading the privacy of the individual's personal effects.

The Government argues that it is difficult to see what constitutionally protected "expectation of privacy" a prisoner has in the interior of a cigarette pack. One wonders if the result in this case would have been the same were respondent a businessman who was lawfully taken into custody for driving without a license and whose wallet was taken from him by the police. Would it be reasonable for the police officer, because of the possibility that a razor blade was hidden somewhere in the wallet, to open it, remove all the contents, and examine each item carefully? Or suppose a lawyer lawfully arrested for a traffic offense is found to have a sealed envelope on his person. Would it be permissible for the arresting officer to tear open the envelope in order to make sure that it did not contain a clandestine weapon—perhaps a pin or a razor blade? Would it not be more consonant with the purpose of the Fourth Amendment and the legitimate needs of the police to require the officer, if he has any question whatsoever about what the wallet or letter contains, to hold on to it until the arrestee is brought to the precinct station?

I, for one, cannot characterize any of these intrusions into the privacy of an individual's papers and effects as being negligible incidents to the more serious intrusion into the individual's privacy stemming from the arrest itself. Nor can any principled distinction be drawn between the hypothetical searches I have posed and the search of the cigarette package in this case. The only reasoned distinction is between warrantless searches which serve legitimate protective and evidentiary functions and those that do not.

The search conducted by Officer Jenks in this case went far beyond what was reasonably necessary to protect him from harm or to ensure that respondent would not effect an escape from custody. In my view, it therefore fell outside the scope of a properly drawn "search incident to arrest" exception to the Fourth Amendment's warrant requirement. I would affirm the judgment of the Court of Appeals holding that the fruits of the search should have been suppressed at respondent's trial.

Under *Robinson*, the police do not need probable cause, reasonable suspicion, or any level of suspicion whatsoever to search the person of the arrestee and any containers in his possession incident to the arrest. Moreover, the search may proceed even if the offense for which the person has been arrested is minor, and even if the arrestee is unlikely to have any weapons or destructible evidence in his possession.

A search incident to an arrest, like the search in *Robinson*, is typically *contemporaneous* with the arrest. In *U.S. v. Edwards*, however, the Supreme Court said that a search incident to arrest may be conducted later, when the arrestee arrives at the place of detention. Indeed, the Court in *Edwards* approved a search of the arrestee's clothing that occurred 10 hours after the arrest.

U.S. v. EDWARDS
415 U.S. 800 (1974)

JUSTICE WHITE delivered the opinion of the Court.

The question here is whether the Fourth Amendment should be extended to exclude from evidence certain clothing taken from respondent Edwards while he was in custody at the city jail approximately 10 hours after his arrest.

Shortly after 11 p.m. on May 31, 1970, respondent Edwards was lawfully arrested on the streets of Lebanon, Ohio, and charged with attempting to break into that city's Post Office. He was taken to the local jail and placed in a cell. Contemporaneously or shortly thereafter, investigation at the scene revealed that the attempted entry had been made through a wooden window which apparently had been pried up with a pry bar, leaving paint chips on the window sill and wire mesh screen. The next morning, trousers and a T-shirt were purchased for Edwards to substitute for the clothing which he had been wearing at the time of and since his arrest. His clothing was then taken from him and held as evidence. Examination of the clothing revealed paint chips matching the samples that had been taken from the window. This evidence and his clothing were received at trial over Edwards' objection that neither the clothing nor the results of its examination were admissible because the warrantless seizure of his clothing was invalid under the Fourth Amendment.

The Court of Appeals reversed. Expressly disagreeing with two other Courts of Appeals, it held that although the arrest was lawful and probable cause existed to believe that paint chips would be discovered on respondent's clothing, the warrantless seizure of the clothing carried out "after the administrative process and the mechanics of the arrest have come to a halt" was nevertheless unconstitutional under the Fourth Amendment. We granted certiorari, and now conclude that the Fourth

Amendment should not be extended to invalidate the search and seizure in the circumstances of this case.

The prevailing rule under the Fourth Amendment that searches and seizures may not be made without a warrant is subject to various exceptions. One of them permits warrantless searches incident to custodial arrests, and has traditionally been justified by the reasonableness of searching for weapons, instruments of escape, and evidence of crime when a person is taken into official custody and lawfully detained.

It is also plain that searches and seizures that could be made on the spot at the time of arrest may legally be conducted later when the accused arrives at the place of detention.

The Courts of Appeals have followed this same rule, holding that both the person and the property in his immediate possession may be searched at the station house after the arrest has occurred at another place and if evidence of crime is discovered, it may be seized and admitted in evidence. Nor is there any doubt that clothing or other belongings may be seized upon arrival of the accused at the place of detention and later subjected to laboratory analysis or that the test results are admissible at trial.

Conceding all this, the Court of Appeals in this case nevertheless held that a warrant is required where the search occurs after the administrative mechanics of arrest have been completed and the prisoner is incarcerated. But even on these terms, it seems to us that the normal processes incident to arrest and custody had not been completed when Edwards was placed in his cell on the night of May 31. With or without probable cause, the authorities were entitled at that point not only to search Edwards' clothing but also to take it from him and keep it in official custody. There was testimony that this was the standard practice in this city. The police were also entitled to take from Edwards any evidence of the crime in his immediate possession, including his clothing. And the Court of Appeals acknowledged that contemporaneously with or shortly after the time Edwards went to his cell, the police had probable cause to believe that the articles of clothing he wore were themselves material evidence of the crime for which he had been arrested. But it was late at night; no substitute clothing was then available for Edwards to wear, and it would certainly have been unreasonable for the police to have stripped respondent of his clothing and left him exposed in his cell throughout the night. When the substitutes were purchased the next morning, the clothing he had been wearing at the time of arrest was taken from him and subjected to laboratory analysis. This was no more than taking from respondent the effects in his immediate possession that constituted evidence of crime. This was and is a normal incident of a custodial arrest, and reasonable delay in effectuating it does not change the fact that Edwards was no more imposed upon than he could have been at the time and place of the arrest or immediately upon arrival at the place of detention. The police did no more on June 1 than they were entitled to do incident to the usual custodial arrest and incarceration.

Other closely related considerations sustain the examination of the clothing in this case. It must be remembered that on both May 31 and June 1 the police had lawful custody of Edwards and necessarily of the clothing he wore. When it became apparent that the articles of clothing were evidence of the crime for which Edwards was being held, the police were entitled to take, examine, and preserve them for use as evidence, just as they are normally permitted to seize evidence of crime when it is lawfully encountered. Surely, the clothes could have been brushed down and vacuumed while Edwards had them on in the cell, and it was similarly reasonable to take and examine them as the police did, particularly in view of the existence of probable cause linking the clothes to the crime. Indeed, it is difficult to perceive what is unreasonable about the police's examining and holding as evidence those personal effects of the accused that they already have in their lawful custody as the result of a lawful arrest.

Most cases in the Courts of Appeals have long since concluded that once the accused is lawfully arrested and is in custody, the effects in his possession at the place of detention that were subject to search at the time and place of his arrest may lawfully be searched and seized without a warrant even though a substantial period of time has elapsed between the arrest and subsequent administrative processing, on the one hand, and the taking of the property for use as evidence, on the other. This is true where the clothing or effects are immediately seized upon arrival at the jail, held under the defendant's name in the "property room" of the jail, and at a later time searched and taken for use at the subsequent criminal trial. The result is the same where the property is not physically taken from the defendant until sometime after his incarceration.

In upholding this search and seizure, we do not conclude that the Warrant Clause of the Fourth Amendment is never applicable to post-arrest seizures of the effects of an arrestee. But we do think that while the legal arrest of a person should not destroy the privacy of his premises, it does—for at least a reasonable time and to a reasonable extent—take his own privacy out of the realm of protection from police interest in weapons, means of escape, and evidence.

JUSTICE STEWART, with whom JUSTICE DOUGLAS, JUSTICE BRENNAN, and JUSTICE MARSHALL join, dissenting.

The Court says that the question before us "is whether the Fourth Amendment should be extended" to prohibit the warrantless seizure of Edwards' clothing. I think, on the contrary, that the real question in this case is whether the Fourth Amendment is to be ignored. For in my view the judgment of the Court of Appeals can be reversed only by disregarding established Fourth Amendment principles firmly embodied in many previous decisions of this Court.

Since it is conceded here that the seizure of Edwards' clothing was not made pursuant to a warrant, the question becomes whether the Government has met its burden of showing that the circumstances of this seizure brought it within one of the jealously and carefully drawn exceptions to the warrant requirement.

The Court finds a warrant unnecessary in this case because of the custodial arrest of the respondent. It is, of course, well settled that the Fourth Amendment permits a warrantless search or seizure incident to a constitutionally valid custodial arrest. But the mere fact of an arrest does not allow the police to engage in warrantless searches of unlimited geographic or temporal scope. Rather, the search must be spatially limited to the person of the arrestee and the area within his reach, and must, as to time, be substantially contemporaneous with the arrest.

Under the facts of this case, I am unable to agree with the Court's holding that the search was "incident" to Edwards' custodial arrest. The search here occurred fully 10 hours after he was arrested, at a time when the administrative processing and mechanics of arrest had long since come to an end. His clothes were not seized as part of an "inventory" of a prisoner's effects, nor were they taken pursuant to a routine exchange of civilian clothes for jail garb. And the considerations that typically justify a warrantless search incident to a lawful arrest were wholly absent here.[3]

Accordingly, I see no justification for dispensing with the warrant requirement. The police had ample time to seek a warrant, and no exigent circumstances were present to excuse their failure to do so.

The Court says that the relevant question is "not whether it was reasonable to procure a search warrant, but whether the search itself was reasonable."

The intrusion here was hardly a shocking one, and it cannot be said that the police acted in bad faith. The Fourth Amendment, however, was not designed to apply only to situations where the intrusion is massive and the violation of privacy shockingly flagrant.

In *Maryland v. King*, the Supreme Court upheld a state law that permitted police—without a search warrant—to obtain a DNA sample from anyone arrested for a serious crime. The majority sees DNA sampling as a legitimate means of identifying and booking a suspect

---

[3]   No claim is made that the police feared that Edwards either possessed a weapon or was planning to destroy the paint chips on his clothing. Indeed, the Government has not even suggested that he was aware of the presence of the paint chips on his clothing

incident to arrest, much like fingerprinting. The dissent contends that the DNA sampling has nothing to do with identifying or booking the suspect, but is instead a warrantless and suspicionless fishing expedition for evidence connecting the arrestee to other unsolved crimes. Who makes the better argument?

MARYLAND V. KING
133 S.Ct. 1958 (2013)

JUSTICE KENNEDY delivered the opinion of the Court.

In 2003 a man concealing his face and armed with a gun broke into a woman's home in Salisbury, Maryland. He raped her. The police were unable to identify or apprehend the assailant based on any detailed description or other evidence they then had, but they did obtain from the victim a sample of the perpetrator's DNA.

In 2009 Alonzo King was arrested in Wicomico County, Maryland, and charged with first- and second-degree assault for menacing a group of people with a shotgun. As part of a routine booking procedure for serious offenses, his DNA sample was taken by applying a cotton swab or filter paper—known as a buccal swab—to the inside of his cheeks. The DNA was found to match the DNA taken from the Salisbury rape victim. King was tried and convicted for the rape. Additional DNA samples were taken from him and used in the rape trial, but there seems to be no doubt that it was the DNA from the cheek sample taken at the time he was booked in 2009 that led to his first having been linked to the rape and charged with its commission.

The Court of Appeals of Maryland, on review of King's rape conviction, ruled that the DNA taken when King was booked for the 2009 charge was an unlawful seizure because obtaining and using the cheek swab was an unreasonable search of the person. It set the rape conviction aside. This Court granted certiorari and now reverses the judgment of the Maryland court.

II

The [Maryland DNA Collection] Act authorizes Maryland law enforcement authorities to collect DNA samples from "an individual who is charged with a crime of violence or an attempt to commit a crime of violence; or burglary or an attempt to commit burglary." Maryland law defines a crime of violence to include murder, rape, first-degree assault, kidnapping, arson, sexual assault, and a variety of other serious crimes. Once taken, a DNA sample may not be processed or placed in a database before the individual is arraigned (unless the individual consents). It is at this point that a judicial officer ensures that there is probable cause to detain the arrestee on a qualifying serious offense. If "all qualifying criminal charges are determined to be unsupported by probable cause, the

DNA sample shall be immediately destroyed." DNA samples are also destroyed if "a criminal action begun against the individual does not result in a conviction," "the conviction is finally reversed or vacated and no new trial is permitted," or "the individual is granted an unconditional pardon."

The Act also limits the information added to a DNA database and how it may be used. Specifically, "only DNA records that directly relate to the identification of individuals shall be collected and stored." No purpose other than identification is permissible. Tests for familial matches are also prohibited. The officers involved in taking and analyzing respondent's DNA sample complied with the Act in all respects.

Respondent's DNA was collected in this case using a common procedure known as a "buccal swab." This involves wiping a small piece of filter paper or a cotton swab similar to a Q-tip against the inside cheek of an individual's mouth to collect some skin cells. The procedure is quick and painless. The swab touches inside an arrestee's mouth, but it requires no surgical intrusion beneath the skin, and it poses no threat to the health or safety of arrestees.

Respondent's identification as the rapist resulted in part through the operation of a national project to standardize collection and storage of DNA profiles. Authorized by Congress and supervised by the Federal Bureau of Investigation, the Combined DNA Index System (CODIS) connects DNA laboratories at the local, state, and national level. Since its authorization in 1994, the CODIS system has grown to include all 50 States and a number of federal agencies. CODIS collects DNA profiles provided by local laboratories taken from arrestees, convicted offenders, and forensic evidence found at crime scenes. To participate in CODIS, a local laboratory must sign a memorandum of understanding agreeing to adhere to quality standards and submit to audits to evaluate compliance with the federal standards for scientifically rigorous DNA testing. In short, CODIS sets uniform national standards for DNA matching and then facilitates connections between local law enforcement agencies who can share more specific information about matched profiles.

All 50 States require the collection of DNA from felony convicts, and respondent does not dispute the validity of that practice. Twenty-eight States and the Federal Government have adopted laws similar to the Maryland Act authorizing the collection of DNA from some or all arrestees. Although those statutes vary in their particulars, such as what charges require a DNA sample, their similarity means that this case implicates more than the specific Maryland law. At issue is a standard, expanding technology already in widespread use throughout the Nation.

III

It can be agreed that using a buccal swab on the inner tissues of a person's cheek in order to obtain DNA samples is a search. Virtually any intrusion into the human body will work an invasion of cherished personal security that is subject to constitutional scrutiny. The Court has applied the Fourth Amendment to police efforts to draw blood, scraping an arrestee's fingernails to obtain trace evidence, and even to a breathalyzer test.

A buccal swab is a far more gentle process than a venipuncture to draw blood. It involves but a light touch on the inside of the cheek; and although it can be deemed a search within the body of the arrestee, it requires no surgical intrusions beneath the skin. The fact that an intrusion is negligible is of central relevance to determining reasonableness, although it is still a search as the law defines that term.

As the text of the Fourth Amendment indicates, the ultimate measure of the constitutionality of a governmental search is "reasonableness." In giving content to the inquiry whether an intrusion is reasonable, the Court has preferred some quantum of individualized suspicion as a prerequisite to a constitutional search or seizure. But the Fourth Amendment imposes no irreducible requirement of such suspicion.

In some circumstances, such as when faced with special law enforcement needs, diminished expectations of privacy, minimal intrusions, or the like, the Court has found that certain general, or individual, circumstances may render a warrantless search or seizure reasonable.

The Maryland DNA Collection Act provides that, in order to obtain a DNA sample, all arrestees charged with serious crimes must furnish the sample on a buccal swab applied, as noted, to the inside of the cheeks. The arrestee is already in valid police custody for a serious offense supported by probable cause. The DNA collection is not subject to the judgment of officers whose perspective might be colored by their primary involvement in the often competitive enterprise of ferreting out crime. As noted by this Court in a different but still instructive context involving blood testing, "both the circumstances justifying toxicological testing and the permissible limits of such intrusions are defined narrowly and specifically in the regulations that authorize them. Indeed, in light of the standardized nature of the tests and the minimal discretion vested in those charged with administering the program, there are virtually no facts for a neutral magistrate to evaluate." Here, the search effected by the buccal swab of respondent falls within the category of cases this Court has analyzed by reference to the proposition that the touchstone of the Fourth Amendment is reasonableness, not individualized suspicion.

Even if a warrant is not required, a search is not beyond Fourth Amendment scrutiny; for it must be reasonable in its scope and manner of execution. Urgent government interests are not a license for indiscriminate police behavior. To say that no warrant is required is merely to acknowledge that rather than employing a *per se* rule of unreasonableness, we balance the privacy-related and law enforcement-related concerns to determine if the intrusion was reasonable. This application of traditional standards of reasonableness requires a court to weigh the promotion of legitimate governmental interests against the degree to which the search intrudes upon an individual's privacy. An assessment of reasonableness to determine the lawfulness of requiring this class of arrestees to provide a DNA sample is central to the instant case.

IV

The legitimate government interest served by the Maryland DNA Collection Act is one that is well established: the need for law enforcement officers in a safe and accurate way to process and identify the persons and possessions they must take into custody. It is beyond dispute that probable cause provides legal justification for arresting a person suspected of crime, and for a brief period of detention to take the administrative steps incident to arrest. Also uncontested is the right on the part of the Government to search the person of the accused when legally arrested. The validity of the search of a person incident to a lawful arrest has been regarded as settled from its first enunciation, and has remained virtually unchallenged. Even in that context, the Court has been clear that individual suspicion is not necessary, because the constitutionality of a search incident to an arrest does not depend on whether there is any indication that the person arrested possesses weapons or evidence. The fact of a lawful arrest, standing alone, authorizes a search.

The routine administrative procedures at a police station house incident to booking and jailing the suspect derive from different origins and have different constitutional justifications than, say, the search of a place, for the search of a place not incident to an arrest depends on the fair probability that contraband or evidence of a crime will be found in a particular place. The interests are further different when an individual is formally processed into police custody. Then the law is in the act of subjecting the body of the accused to its physical dominion. When probable cause exists to remove an individual from the normal channels of society and hold him in legal custody, DNA identification plays a critical role in serving those interests.

First, in every criminal case, it is known and must be known who has been arrested and who is being tried. An individual's identity is more than just his name or Social Security number, and the government's interest in identification goes beyond ensuring that the proper name is typed on the indictment. Identity has never been considered limited to the name on the arrestee's birth certificate. In fact, a name is of little value compared to the real interest in identification at stake when an individual is brought into custody.

A suspect's criminal history is a critical part of his identity that officers should know when processing him for detention. It is a common occurrence that people detained for minor offenses can turn out to be the most devious and dangerous criminals. Hours after the Oklahoma City bombing, Timothy McVeigh was stopped by a state trooper who noticed he was driving without a license plate. Police stopped serial killer Joel Rifkin for the same reason. One of the terrorists involved in the September 11 attacks was stopped and ticketed for speeding just two days before hijacking Flight 93. Police already seek this crucial identifying information. They use routine and accepted means as varied as comparing the suspect's booking photograph to sketch artists' depictions of persons of interest, showing his mugshot to potential witnesses, and of course making a computerized comparison of the arrestee's fingerprints against electronic databases of known criminals and unsolved crimes. In this respect the only difference between DNA analysis and the accepted use of fingerprint databases is the unparalleled accuracy DNA provides.

The task of identification necessarily entails searching public and police records based on the identifying information provided by the arrestee to see what is already known about him. The DNA collected from arrestees is an irrefutable identification of the person from whom it was taken. A DNA profile is useful to the police because it gives them a form of identification to search the records already in their valid possession. In this respect the use of DNA for identification is no different than matching an arrestee's face to a wanted poster of a previously unidentified suspect; or matching tattoos to known gang symbols to reveal a criminal affiliation; or matching the arrestee's fingerprints to those recovered from a crime scene. DNA is another metric of identification used to connect the arrestee with his or her public persona, as reflected in records of his or her actions that are available to the police. Those records may be linked to the arrestee by a variety of relevant forms of identification, including name, alias, date and time of previous convictions and the name then used, photograph, Social Security number, or CODIS profile. These data, found in official records, are checked as a routine matter to produce a more comprehensive record of the suspect's complete identity. Finding occurrences of the arrestee's CODIS profile in outstanding cases is consistent with this common practice. It uses a different form of identification than a name or fingerprint, but its function is the same.

Second, law enforcement officers bear a responsibility for ensuring that the custody of an arrestee does not create inordinate risks for facility staff, for the existing detainee population, and for a new detainee. DNA identification can provide untainted information to those charged with detaining suspects and detaining the property of any felon. For these purposes officers must know the type of person whom they are detaining, and DNA allows them to make critical choices about how to proceed. Knowledge of identity may inform an officer that a suspect is wanted for another offense, or has a record of violence or mental disorder. On the other hand, knowing identity may help clear a suspect and allow the police to concentrate their efforts elsewhere. Recognizing that a name alone cannot address this interest in identity, the Court has approved, for example, a visual inspection for certain tattoos and other signs of gang affiliation as part of the intake process, because the identification and isolation of gang members before they are admitted protects everyone.

Third, looking forward to future stages of criminal prosecution, the Government has a substantial interest in ensuring that persons accused of crimes are available for trials. A person who is arrested for one offense but knows that he has yet to answer for some past crime may be more inclined to flee the instant charges, lest continued contact with the criminal justice system expose one or more other serious offenses. For example, a defendant who had committed a prior sexual assault might be inclined to flee on a burglary charge, knowing that in every State a DNA sample would be taken from him after his conviction on the burglary charge that would tie him to the more serious charge of rape. In addition to subverting the administration of justice with respect to the crime of arrest, this ties back to the interest in safety; for a detainee who absconds from custody presents a risk to law enforcement officers, other detainees, victims of previous crimes, witnesses, and society at large.

Fourth, an arrestee's past conduct is essential to an assessment of the danger he poses to the public, and this will inform a court's determination whether the individual should be released on bail. DNA identification of a suspect in a violent crime provides critical information to the police and judicial officials in making a determination of the arrestee's future dangerousness.

Finally, in the interests of justice, the identification of an arrestee as the perpetrator of some heinous crime may have the salutary effect of freeing a person wrongfully imprisoned for the same offense. Prompt DNA testing would speed up apprehension of criminals before they commit additional crimes, and prevent the grotesque detention of innocent people.

Because proper processing of arrestees is so important and has consequences for every stage of the criminal process, the Court has recognized that the governmental interests underlying a station-house search of the arrestee's person and possessions may in some circumstances be even greater than those supporting a search immediately following arrest. Thus, the Court has been reluctant to circumscribe the authority of the police to conduct reasonable booking searches. Nor are these interests in identification served only by a search of the arrestee himself. Inspection of an arrestee's personal property may assist the police in ascertaining or verifying his identity.

Perhaps the most direct historical analogue to the DNA technology used to identify respondent is the familiar practice of fingerprinting arrestees. From the advent of this technique, courts had no trouble determining that fingerprinting was a natural part of the administrative steps incident to arrest. DNA identification is an advanced technique superior to fingerprinting in many ways, so much so that to insist on fingerprints as the norm would make little sense to either the forensic expert or a layperson. The additional intrusion upon the arrestee's privacy beyond that associated with fingerprinting is not significant, and DNA is a markedly more accurate form of identifying arrestees. A suspect who has changed his facial features to evade photographic identification or even one who has undertaken the more arduous task of altering his fingerprints cannot escape the revealing power of his DNA.

The respondent's primary objection to this analogy is that DNA identification is not as fast as fingerprinting, and so it should not be considered to be the 21st-century equivalent. But rapid analysis of fingerprints is itself of recent vintage. The FBI's vaunted Integrated Automated Fingerprint Identification System (IAFIS) was only launched on July 28, 1999. Prior to this time, the processing of fingerprint submissions was largely a manual, labor-intensive process, taking weeks or months to process a single submission. It was not the advent of this technology that rendered fingerprint analysis constitutional in a single moment. The question of how long it takes to process identifying information obtained from a valid search goes only to the efficacy of the search for its purpose of prompt identification, not the constitutionality of the search. Given the importance of DNA in the identification of police records pertaining to arrestees and the need to refine and confirm that identity for its important bearing on the decision to continue release on bail or to impose new conditions, DNA serves an essential purpose despite the existence of delays such as the one that occurred in this case. Even so, the delay in processing DNA from arrestees is being reduced to a substantial degree by rapid technical advances. And the FBI has already begun testing devices that will enable police to process the DNA of arrestees within 90 minutes.

In sum, there can be little reason to question the legitimate interest of the government in knowing for an absolute certainty the identity of the person arrested, in knowing whether he is wanted elsewhere, and in ensuring his identification in the event he flees prosecution. To that end, courts have confirmed that the Fourth Amendment allows police to take certain routine administrative steps incident to arrest—*i.e.*, booking, photographing, and fingerprinting. DNA identification of arrestees, of the type approved by the Maryland statute here at issue, is no more than an extension of methods of identification long used in dealing with persons under arrest. In the balance of reasonableness required by the Fourth Amendment, therefore, the Court must give great weight both to the significant government interest at stake in the identification of arrestees and to the unmatched potential of DNA identification to serve that interest.

V

By comparison to this substantial government interest and the unique effectiveness of DNA identification, the intrusion of a cheek swab to obtain a DNA sample is a minimal one. True, a significant government interest does not alone suffice to justify a search. The government interest must outweigh the degree to which the search invades an individual's legitimate expectations of privacy. In considering those expectations in this case, however, the necessary predicate of a valid arrest for a serious offense is fundamental.

The expectations of privacy of an individual taken into police custody necessarily are of a diminished scope. Both the person and the property in his immediate possession may be searched at the station house. A search of the detainee's person when he is booked into custody may involve a relatively extensive exploration, including requiring at least some detainees to lift their genitals or cough in a squatting position. DNA identification like that at issue here thus does not require consideration of any unique needs that would be required to justify searching the average citizen. Unlike the search of a citizen who has not been suspected of a wrong, a detainee has a reduced expectation of privacy.

This is not to suggest that any search is acceptable solely because a person is in custody. Some searches, such as invasive surgery, or a search of the arrestee's home, involve either greater intrusions or higher expectations of privacy than are present in this case. In those situations, when the Court must balance the privacy-related and law enforcement-related concerns to determine if the intrusion was reasonable, the privacy-related concerns are weighty enough that the search may require a warrant, notwithstanding the diminished expectations of privacy of the arrestee.

Here, by contrast to the approved standard procedures incident to any arrest detailed above, a buccal swab involves an even more brief and still minimal intrusion. A gentle rub along the inside of the cheek does not break the skin, and it involves virtually no risk, trauma, or pain. A crucial factor in analyzing the magnitude of the intrusion is the extent to which the procedure may threaten the safety or health of the individual, and nothing suggests that a buccal swab poses any physical danger whatsoever. A brief intrusion of an arrestee's person is subject to the Fourth Amendment, but a swab of this nature does not increase the indignity already attendant to normal incidents of arrest.

In addition, the processing of respondent's DNA sample's 13 CODIS loci did not intrude on respondent's privacy in a way that would make his DNA identification unconstitutional. The CODIS loci come from noncoding parts of the DNA that do not reveal the genetic traits of the arrestee. It is undisputed that law enforcement officers analyze DNA for the sole purpose of generating a unique identifying number against which future samples may be matched. If in the future police analyze samples to determine, for instance, an arrestee's predisposition for a particular disease or other hereditary factors not relevant to identity, that case would present additional privacy concerns not present here. Finally, the Act provides statutory protections that guard against further invasion of privacy. As noted above, the Act requires that "only DNA records that directly relate to the identification of individuals shall be collected and stored." No purpose other than identification is permissible. In light of the scientific and statutory safeguards, once respondent's DNA was lawfully collected the analysis of respondent's DNA pursuant to CODIS procedures did not amount to a significant invasion of privacy that would render the DNA identification impermissible under the Fourth Amendment.

In light of the context of a valid arrest supported by probable cause respondent's expectations of privacy were not offended by the minor intrusion of a brief swab of his cheeks. By contrast, that same context of arrest gives rise to significant state interests in identifying respondent not only so that the proper name can be attached to his charges but also so that the criminal justice system can make informed decisions concerning pretrial custody. Upon these considerations the Court concludes that DNA identification of arrestees is a reasonable search that can be considered part of a routine booking procedure. When officers make an arrest supported by probable cause to hold for a serious offense and they bring the suspect to the station to be detained in custody, taking and analyzing a cheek swab of the arrestee's DNA is, like fingerprinting and photographing, a legitimate police booking procedure that is reasonable under the Fourth Amendment.

JUSTICE SCALIA, with whom JUSTICE GINSBURG, JUSTICE SOTOMAYOR, and JUSTICE KAGAN join, dissenting.

The Fourth Amendment forbids searching a person for evidence of a crime when there is no basis for believing the person is guilty of the crime or is in possession of incriminating evidence. That prohibition is categorical and without exception; it lies at the very heart of the Fourth

Amendment. Whenever this Court has allowed a suspicionless search, it has insisted upon a justifying motive apart from the investigation of crime.

It is obvious that no such noninvestigative motive exists in this case. The Court's assertion that DNA is being taken, not to solve crimes, but to *identify* those in the State's custody, taxes the credulity of the credulous. And the Court's comparison of Maryland's DNA searches to other techniques, such as fingerprinting, can seem apt only to those who know no more than today's opinion has chosen to tell them about how those DNA searches actually work.

Although there is a closely guarded category of constitutionally permissible suspicionless searches, that has never included searches designed to serve the normal need for law enforcement. Even the common name for suspicionless searches—"special needs" searches—itself reflects that they must be justified, *always*, by concerns other than crime detection. We have approved random drug tests of railroad employees, yes—but only because the Government's need to regulate the conduct of railroad employees to ensure safety is distinct from normal law enforcement. So too we have approved suspicionless searches in public schools—but only because there the government acts in furtherance of its responsibilities as guardian and tutor of children entrusted to its care.

So while the Court is correct to note that there are instances in which we have permitted searches without individualized suspicion, in none of these cases did we indicate approval of a search whose primary purpose was to detect evidence of ordinary criminal wrongdoing. That limitation is crucial. It is only when a governmental purpose aside from crime-solving is at stake that we engage in the free-form "reasonableness" inquiry that the Court indulges at length today. To put it another way, both the legitimacy of the Court's method and the correctness of its outcome hinge entirely on the truth of a single proposition: that the primary purpose of these DNA searches is something other than simply discovering evidence of criminal wrongdoing. As I detail below, that proposition is wrong.

The Court alludes at several points to the fact that King was an arrestee, and arrestees may be validly searched incident to their arrest. But the Court does not really *rest* on this principle, and for good reason: The objects of a search incident to arrest must be either (1) weapons or evidence that might easily be destroyed, or (2) evidence relevant to the crime of arrest. Neither is the object of the search at issue here.

No matter the degree of invasiveness, suspicionless searches are *never* allowed if their principal end is ordinary crime-solving. A search incident to arrest either serves other ends (such as officer safety, in a search for weapons) or is not suspicionless (as when there is reason to believe the arrestee possesses evidence relevant to the crime of arrest).

Sensing (correctly) that it needs more, the Court elaborates at length the ways that the search here served the special purpose of "identifying" King. But that seems to me quite wrong—unless what one means by "identifying" someone is "searching for evidence that he has committed crimes unrelated to the crime of his arrest." At points the Court does appear to use "identifying" in that peculiar sense—claiming, for example, that knowing "an arrestee's past conduct is essential to an assessment of the danger he poses." If identifying someone means finding out what unsolved crimes he has committed, then identification is indistinguishable from the ordinary law-enforcement aims that have never been thought to justify a suspicionless search. Searching every lawfully stopped car, for example, might turn up information about unsolved crimes the driver had committed, but no one would say that such a search was aimed at "identifying" him, and no court would hold such a search lawful.

That taking DNA samples from arrestees has nothing to do with identifying them is confirmed not just by actual practice (which the Court ignores) but by the enabling statute itself (which the Court also ignores). The Maryland Act at issue has a section helpfully entitled "Purpose of collecting and testing DNA samples." That provision lists five purposes for which DNA samples may be tested. By this point, it will not surprise the reader to learn that the Court's imagined purpose is not among them.

Instead, the law provides that DNA samples are collected and tested, as a matter of Maryland law, "as part of an official investigation into a crime." (Or, as our suspicionless-search cases would put it: for ordinary law-enforcement purposes.) That is certainly how everyone has always understood the Maryland Act until today.

So, to review: The Act forbids the Court's purpose (identification), but prescribes as its purpose what our suspicionless-search cases forbid ("official investigation into a crime"). Against all of that, it is safe to say that if the Court's identification theory is not wrong, there is no such thing as error.

The Court also attempts to bolster its identification theory with a series of inapposite analogies. Is not taking DNA samples the same, asks the Court, as taking a person's photograph? No—because that is not a Fourth Amendment search at all. It does not involve a physical intrusion onto the person, and we have never held that merely taking a person's photograph invades any recognized "expectation of privacy."

It is on the fingerprinting of arrestees, however, that the Court relies most heavily. The Court does not actually say whether it believes that taking a person's fingerprints is a Fourth Amendment search, and our cases provide no ready answer to that question. Even assuming so, however, law enforcement's post-arrest use of fingerprints could not be more different from its post-arrest use of DNA. Fingerprints of arrestees are taken primarily to identify them (though that process sometimes solves crimes); the DNA of arrestees is taken to solve crimes (and nothing else).

Today, it can fairly be said that fingerprints really are used to identify people—so well, in fact, that there would be no need for the expense of a separate, wholly redundant DNA confirmation of the same information. What DNA adds—what makes it a valuable weapon in the law-enforcement arsenal—is the ability to solve unsolved crimes, by matching old crime-scene evidence against the profiles of people whose identities are already known. That is what was going on when King's DNA was taken, and we should not disguise the fact. Solving unsolved crimes is a noble objective, but it occupies a lower place in the American pantheon of noble objectives than the protection of our people from suspicionless law-enforcement searches. The Fourth Amendment must prevail.

The Court disguises the vast (and scary) scope of its holding by promising a limitation it cannot deliver. The Court repeatedly says that DNA testing, and entry into a national DNA registry, will not befall thee and me, dear reader, but only those arrested for "serious offenses." I cannot imagine what principle could possibly justify this limitation, and the Court does not attempt to suggest any. If one believes that DNA will "identify" someone arrested for assault, he must believe that it will "identify" someone arrested for a traffic offense. When there comes before us the taking of DNA from an arrestee for a traffic violation, the Court will predictably (and quite rightly) say, "We can find no significant difference between this case and *King*." Make no mistake about it: As an entirely predictable consequence of today's decision, your DNA can be taken and entered into a national DNA database if you are ever arrested, rightly or wrongly, and for whatever reason.

Today's judgment will, to be sure, have the beneficial effect of solving more crimes; then again, so would the taking of DNA samples from anyone who flies on an airplane (surely the Transportation Security Administration needs to know the "identity" of the flying public), applies for a driver's license, or attends a public school. Perhaps the construction of such a genetic panopticon is wise. But I doubt that the proud men who wrote the charter of our liberties would have been so eager to open their mouths for royal inspection.

I therefore dissent, and hope that today's incursion upon the Fourth Amendment will some day be repudiated.

———————————

In *Riley v. California*, the Supreme Court declined to approve a warrantless search of a cell phone under the search incident to arrest exception. The Court unanimously held that in most circumstances, police must obtain a warrant before searching the contents of an arrestee's cell phone.

RILEY V. CALIFORNIA
134 S.Ct. 2473 (2014)

CHIEF JUSTICE ROBERTS delivered the opinion of the Court.

These two cases raise a common question: whether the police may, without a warrant, search digital information on a cell phone seized from an individual who has been arrested.

I

In the first case, petitioner David Riley was stopped by a police officer for driving with expired registration tags. In the course of the stop, the officer also learned that Riley's license had been suspended. The officer impounded Riley's car, pursuant to department policy, and another officer conducted an inventory search of the car. Riley was arrested for possession of concealed and loaded firearms when that search turned up two handguns under the car's hood.

An officer searched Riley incident to the arrest and found items associated with the "Bloods" street gang. He also seized a cell phone from Riley's pants pocket. According to Riley, the phone was a "smart phone," a cell phone with a broad range of other functions based on advanced computing capability, large storage capacity, and Internet connectivity. The officer accessed information on the phone and noticed that some words (presumably in text messages or a contacts list) were preceded by the letters "CK"—a label that, he believed, stood for "Crip Killers," a slang term for members of the Bloods gang.

At the police station about two hours after the arrest, a detective specializing in gangs further examined the contents of the phone. The detective testified that he "went through" Riley's phone "looking for evidence, because gang members will often video themselves with guns or take pictures of themselves with the guns." Although there was "a lot of stuff" on the phone, particular files that "caught [the detective's] eye" included videos of young men sparring while someone yelled encouragement using the moniker "Blood." The police also found photographs of Riley standing in front of a car they suspected had been involved in a shooting a few weeks earlier.

Riley was ultimately charged, in connection with that earlier shooting, with firing at an occupied vehicle, assault with a semiautomatic firearm, and attempted murder. The State alleged that Riley had committed those crimes for the benefit of a criminal street gang, an aggravating factor that carries an enhanced sentence. Prior to trial, Riley moved to suppress all evidence that the police had obtained from his cell phone. He contended that the searches of his phone violated the Fourth Amendment, because they had been performed without a warrant and were not otherwise justified by exigent circumstances. The trial court rejected that argument. At Riley's trial, police officers testified about the photographs and videos found on the phone, and some of the photographs were admitted into evidence. Riley was convicted on all three counts and received an enhanced sentence of 15 years to life in prison.

In the second case, a police officer performing routine surveillance observed respondent Brima Wurie make an apparent drug sale from a car. Officers subsequently arrested Wurie and took him to the police station. At the station, the officers seized two cell phones from Wurie's person. The one at issue here was a "flip phone," a kind of phone that is flipped open for use and that generally has a smaller range of features than a smart phone. Five to ten minutes after arriving at the station, the officers noticed that the phone was repeatedly receiving calls from a source identified as "my house" on the phone's external screen. A few minutes later, they opened the phone and saw a photograph of a woman and a baby set as the phone's wallpaper. They pressed one button on the phone to access its call log, then another button to determine the phone number associated with the "my house" label. They next used an online phone directory to trace that phone number to an apartment building.

When the officers went to the building, they saw Wurie's name on a mailbox and observed through a window a woman who resembled the woman in the photograph on Wurie's phone. They secured the apartment while obtaining a search warrant and, upon later executing the warrant, found and seized 215 grams of crack cocaine, marijuana, drug paraphernalia, a firearm and ammunition, and cash.

Wurie was charged with distributing crack cocaine, possessing crack cocaine with intent to distribute, and being a felon in possession of a firearm and ammunition. He moved to suppress the evidence obtained from the search of the apartment, arguing that it was the fruit of an unconstitutional search of his cell phone. The District Court denied the motion. Wurie was convicted on all three counts and sentenced to 262 months in prison.

II

The ultimate touchstone of the Fourth Amendment is "reasonableness." Our cases have determined that where a search is undertaken by law enforcement officials to discover evidence of criminal wrongdoing, reasonableness generally requires the obtaining of a judicial warrant. In the absence of a warrant, a search is reasonable only if it falls within a specific exception to the warrant requirement.

The two cases before us concern the reasonableness of a warrantless search incident to a lawful arrest. It has been well accepted that such a search constitutes an exception to the warrant requirement. Although the existence of the exception for such searches has been recognized for a century, its scope has been debated for nearly as long. That debate has focused on the extent to which officers may search property found on or near the arrestee. Three related precedents set forth the rules governing such searches:

The first, *Chimel v. California*, 395 U.S. 752 (1969), laid the groundwork for most of the existing search incident to arrest doctrine. Police officers in that case arrested Chimel inside his home and proceeded to search his entire three-bedroom house, including the attic and garage. In particular rooms, they also looked through the contents of drawers.

The Court crafted the following rule for assessing the reasonableness of a search incident to arrest:

> When an arrest is made, it is reasonable for the arresting officer to search the person arrested in order to remove any weapons that the latter might seek to use in order to resist arrest or effect his escape. Otherwise, the officer's safety might well be endangered, and the arrest itself frustrated. In addition, it is entirely reasonable for the arresting officer to search for and seize any evidence on the arrestee's person in order to prevent its concealment or destruction. There is ample justification, therefore, for a search of the arrestee's person and the area "within his immediate control"—construing that phrase to mean the area from within which he might gain possession of a weapon or destructible evidence.

The extensive warrantless search of Chimel's home did not fit within this exception, because it was not needed to protect officer safety or to preserve evidence.

Four years later, in *U.S. v. Robinson*, 414 U. S. 218 (1973), the Court applied the *Chimel* analysis in the context of a search of the arrestee's person. A police officer had arrested Robinson for driving with a revoked license. The officer conducted a patdown search and felt an object that he could not identify in Robinson's coat pocket. He removed the object, which turned out to be a crumpled cigarette package, and opened it. Inside were 14 capsules of heroin.

The Court of Appeals concluded that the search was unreasonable because Robinson was unlikely to have evidence of the crime of arrest on his person, and because it believed that extracting the cigarette package and opening it could not be justified as part of a protective search for weapons. This Court reversed, rejecting the notion that "case-by-case adjudication" was required to determine "whether or not there was present one of the reasons supporting the authority for a search of the person incident to a lawful arrest." As the Court explained, "[t]he authority to search the person incident to a lawful custodial arrest, while based upon the need to disarm and to discover evidence, does not depend on what a court may later decide was the probability in a particular arrest situation that weapons or evidence would in fact be found upon the person of the suspect." Instead, a "custodial arrest of a suspect based on probable cause is a reasonable intrusion under the Fourth Amendment; that intrusion being lawful, a search incident to the arrest requires no additional justification."

The Court thus concluded that the search of Robinson was reasonable even though there was no concern about the loss of evidence, and the arresting officer had no specific concern that Robinson might be armed. In doing so, the Court did not draw a line between a search of Robinson's person and a further examination of the cigarette pack found during that search. It merely noted that, "[h]aving in the course of a lawful search come upon the crumpled package of cigarettes, [the officer] was entitled to inspect it." A few years later, the Court clarified that this exception was limited to "personal property immediately associated with the person of the arrestee."

The search incident to arrest trilogy concludes with *Arizona v. Gant*, 556 U.S. 332 (2009), which analyzed searches of an arrestee's vehicle. *Gant*, like *Robinson*, recognized that the *Chimel* concerns for officer safety and evidence preservation underlie the search incident to arrest exception. As a result, the Court concluded that *Chimel* could authorize police to search a vehicle "only when the arrestee is unsecured and within reaching distance of the passenger compartment at the time of the search." *Gant* added, however, an independent exception for a warrantless search of a vehicle's passenger compartment when it is "reasonable to believe evidence relevant to the crime of arrest might be found in the vehicle." That exception stems not from *Chimel*, the Court explained, but from "circumstances unique to the vehicle context."

III

These cases require us to decide how the search incident to arrest doctrine applies to modern cell phones, which are now such a pervasive and insistent part of daily life that the proverbial visitor from Mars might conclude they were an important feature of human anatomy. A smart phone of the sort taken from Riley was unheard of ten years ago; a significant majority of American adults now own such phones. Even less sophisticated phones like Wurie's, which have already faded in popularity since Wurie was arrested in 2007, have been around for less than 15 years. Both phones are based on technology nearly inconceivable just a few decades ago, when *Chimel* and *Robinson* were decided.

Absent more precise guidance from the founding era, we generally determine whether to exempt a given type of search from the warrant requirement by assessing, on the one hand, the degree to which it intrudes upon an individual's privacy and, on the other, the degree to which it is needed for the promotion of legitimate governmental interests. Such a balancing of interests supported the search incident to arrest exception in *Robinson*, and a mechanical application of *Robinson* might well support the warrantless searches at issue here.

But while *Robinson*'s categorical rule strikes the appropriate balance in the context of physical objects, neither of its rationales has much force with respect to digital content on cell phones. On the government interest side, *Robinson* concluded that the two risks identified in *Chimel*—harm to officers and destruction of evidence—are present in all custodial arrests. There are no comparable risks when the search is of digital data. In addition, *Robinson* regarded any privacy interests retained by an individual after arrest as significantly diminished by the fact of the arrest itself. Cell phones, however, place vast quantities of personal information literally in the hands of individuals. A search of the information on a cell phone bears little resemblance to the type of brief physical search considered in *Robinson*.

We therefore decline to extend *Robinson* to searches of data on cell phones, and hold instead that officers must generally secure a warrant before conducting such a search.

A

We first consider each *Chimel* concern in turn. In doing so, we do not overlook *Robinson*'s admonition that searches of a person incident to arrest, "while based upon the need to disarm and to discover evidence," are reasonable regardless of "the probability in a particular arrest situation that weapons or evidence would in fact be found." Rather than requiring the "case-by-case adjudication" that *Robinson* rejected, we ask instead whether application of the search incident to arrest doctrine to this particular category of effects would untether the rule from the justifications underlying the *Chimel* exception.

Digital data stored on a cell phone cannot itself be used as a weapon to harm an arresting officer or to effectuate the arrestee's escape. Law enforcement officers remain free to examine the physical aspects of a phone to ensure that it will not be used as a weapon—say, to determine whether there is a razor blade hidden between the phone and its case. Once an officer has secured a phone and eliminated any potential physical threats, however, data on the phone can endanger no one.

Perhaps the same might have been said of the cigarette pack seized from Robinson's pocket. Once an officer gained control of the pack, it was unlikely that Robinson could have accessed the pack's contents. But unknown physical objects may always pose risks, no matter how slight, during the tense atmosphere of a custodial arrest. The officer in *Robinson* testified that he could not identify the objects in the cigarette pack but knew they were not cigarettes. Given that, a further search was a reasonable protective measure. No such unknowns exist with respect to digital data.

The United States and California both suggest that a search of cell phone data might help ensure officer safety in more indirect ways, for example by alerting officers that confederates of the arrestee are headed to the scene. There is undoubtedly a strong government interest in warning officers about such possibilities, but neither the United States nor California offers evidence to suggest that their concerns are based on actual experience. The proposed consideration would also represent a broadening of *Chimel's* concern that an *arrestee himself* might grab a weapon and use it against an officer "to resist arrest or effect his escape." And any such threats from outside the arrest scene do not lurk in all custodial arrests. Accordingly, the interest in protecting officer safety does not justify dispensing with the warrant requirement across the board. To the extent dangers to arresting officers may be implicated in a particular way in a particular case, they are better addressed through consideration of case-specific exceptions to the warrant requirement, such as the one for exigent circumstances.

The United States and California focus primarily on the second *Chimel* rationale: preventing the destruction of evidence.

Both Riley and Wurie concede that officers could have seized and secured their cell phones to prevent destruction of evidence while seeking a warrant. That is a sensible concession. See *Illinois v. McArthur*, 531 U.S. 326 (2001). And once law enforcement officers have secured a cell phone, there is no longer any risk that the arrestee himself will be able to delete incriminating data from the phone.

The United States and California argue that information on a cell phone may nevertheless be vulnerable to two types of evidence destruction unique to digital data—remote wiping and data encryption. Remote wiping occurs when a phone, connected to a wireless network, receives a signal that erases stored data. This can happen when a third party sends a remote signal or when a phone is preprogrammed to delete data upon entering or leaving certain geographic areas (so-called "geofencing"). Encryption is a security feature that some modern cell phones use in addition to password protection. When such phones lock, data becomes protected by sophisticated encryption that renders a phone all but "unbreakable" unless police know the password.

As an initial matter, these broader concerns about the loss of evidence are distinct from *Chimel's* focus on a defendant who responds to arrest by trying to conceal or destroy evidence within his reach. With respect to remote wiping, the Government's primary concern turns on the actions of third parties who are not present at the scene of arrest. And data encryption is even further afield. There, the Government focuses on the ordinary operation of a phone's security features, apart from *any* active attempt by a defendant or his associates to conceal or destroy evidence upon arrest.

We have also been given little reason to believe that either problem is prevalent. The briefing reveals only a couple of anecdotal examples of remote wiping triggered by an arrest. Similarly, the opportunities for officers to search a password-protected phone before data becomes encrypted are quite limited. Law enforcement officers are very unlikely to come upon such a phone in an unlocked state because most phones lock at the touch of a button or, as a default, after some very short period of inactivity.

Moreover, in situations in which an arrest might trigger a remote-wipe attempt or an officer discovers an unlocked phone, it is not clear that the ability to conduct a warrantless search would make much of a difference. The need to effect the arrest, secure the scene, and tend to other pressing matters means that law enforcement officers may well not be able to turn their attention to a cell phone right away. Cell phone data would be vulnerable to remote wiping from the time an individual anticipates arrest to the time any eventual search of the phone is completed, which might be at the station house hours later. Likewise, an officer who seizes a phone in an unlocked state might not be able to begin his search in the short time remaining before the phone locks and data becomes encrypted.

In any event, as to remote wiping, law enforcement is not without specific means to address the threat. Remote wiping can be fully prevented by disconnecting a phone from the network. There are at least two simple ways to do this: First, law enforcement officers can turn the phone off or remove its battery. Second, if they are concerned about encryption or other potential problems, they can leave a phone powered on and place it in an enclosure that isolates the phone from radio waves. Such devices are commonly called "Faraday bags," after the English scientist Michael Faraday. They are essentially sandwich bags made of aluminum foil: cheap, lightweight, and easy to use. They may not be a complete answer to the problem, but at least for now they provide a reasonable response. In fact, a number of law enforcement agencies around the country already encourage the use of Faraday bags.

To the extent that law enforcement still has specific concerns about the potential loss of evidence in a particular case, there remain more targeted ways to address those concerns. If the police are truly confronted with a "now or never" situation—for example, circumstances suggesting that a defendant's phone will be the target of an imminent remote-wipe attempt—they may be able to rely on exigent circumstances to search the phone immediately. Or, if officers happen to seize a phone in an unlocked state, they may be able to disable a phone's automatic-lock feature in order to prevent the phone from locking and encrypting data. Such a preventive measure could be analyzed under the principles set forth in our decision in *Illinois v. McArthur*, which approved officers' reasonable steps to secure a scene to preserve evidence while they awaited a warrant.

B

The search incident to arrest exception rests not only on the heightened government interests at stake in a volatile arrest situation, but also on an arrestee's reduced privacy interests upon being taken into police custody. *Robinson* focused primarily on the first of those rationales. Put simply, a patdown of Robinson's clothing and an inspection of the cigarette pack found in his pocket constituted only minor additional intrusions compared to the substantial government authority exercised in taking Robinson into custody.

The fact that an arrestee has diminished privacy interests does not mean that the Fourth Amendment falls out of the picture entirely. To the contrary, when privacy-related concerns are weighty enough a search may require a warrant, notwithstanding the diminished expectations of privacy of the arrestee. One such example, of course, is *Chimel*. Because a search of the arrestee's entire house was a substantial invasion beyond the arrest itself, the Court concluded that a warrant was required.

Robinson is the only decision from this Court applying *Chimel* to a search of the contents of an item found on an arrestee's person. Lower courts applying *Robinson* and *Chimel*, however, have approved searches of a variety of personal items carried by an arrestee.

The United States asserts that a search of all data stored on a cell phone is "materially indistinguishable" from searches of these sorts of physical items. That is like saying a ride on horseback is materially indistinguishable from a flight to the moon. Both are ways of getting from point A to point B, but little else justifies lumping them together. Modern cell phones, as a category, implicate privacy concerns far beyond those implicated by the search of a cigarette pack, a wallet, or a purse. A conclusion that inspecting the contents of an arrestee's pockets works no substantial additional intrusion on privacy beyond the arrest itself may make sense as applied to physical items, but any extension of that reasoning to digital data has to rest on its own bottom.

Cell phones differ in both a quantitative and a qualitative sense from other objects that might be kept on an arrestee's person. The term "cell phone" is itself misleading shorthand; many of these devices are in fact minicomputers that also happen to have the capacity to be used as a telephone. They could just as easily be called cameras, video players, rolodexes, calendars, tape recorders, libraries, diaries, albums, televisions, maps, or newspapers.

One of the most notable distinguishing features of modern cell phones is their immense storage capacity. Before cell phones, a search of a person was limited by physical realities and tended as a general matter to constitute only a narrow intrusion on privacy. Most people cannot lug around every piece of mail they have received for the past several months, every picture they have taken, or every book or article they have read—nor would they have any reason to attempt to do so. And if they did, they would have to drag behind them a trunk, rather than a container the size of the cigarette package in *Robinson*.

But the possible intrusion on privacy is not physically limited in the same way when it comes to cell phones. The current top-selling smart phone has a standard capacity of 16 gigabytes (and is available with up to 64 gigabytes). Sixteen gigabytes translates to millions of pages of text, thousands of pictures, or hundreds of videos. Cell phones couple that capacity with the ability to store many different types of information: Even the most basic phones that sell for less than $20 might hold photographs, picture messages, text messages, Internet browsing history, a calendar, a thousand-entry phone book, and so on. We expect that the gulf between physical practicability and digital capacity will only continue to widen in the future.

The storage capacity of cell phones has several interrelated consequences for privacy. First, a cell phone collects in one place many distinct types of information—an address, a note, a prescription, a bank statement, a video—that reveal much more in combination than any isolated record. Second, a cell phone's capacity allows even just one type of information to convey far more than previously possible. The sum of an individual's private life can be reconstructed through a thousand photographs labeled with dates, locations, and descriptions; the same cannot be said of a photograph or two of loved ones tucked into a wallet. Third, the data on a phone can date back to the purchase of the phone, or even earlier. A person might carry in his pocket a slip of paper reminding him to call Mr. Jones; he would not carry a record of all his communications with Mr. Jones for the past several months, as would routinely be kept on a phone.

Finally, there is an element of pervasiveness that characterizes cell phones but not physical records. Prior to the digital age, people did not typically carry a cache of sensitive personal information with them as they went about their day. Now it is the person who is not carrying a cell phone, with all that it contains, who is the exception. According to one poll, nearly three-quarters of smart phone users report being within five feet of their phones most of the time, with 12% admitting that they even use their phones in the shower. A decade ago police officers searching an arrestee might have occasionally stumbled across a highly personal item such as a diary. But those discoveries were likely to be few and far between. Today, by contrast, it is no exaggeration to say that many of the more than 90% of American adults who own a cell phone keep on their person a digital record of nearly every aspect of their lives—from the mundane to the intimate. Allowing the police to scrutinize such records on a routine basis is quite different from allowing them to search a personal item or two in the occasional case.

Although the data stored on a cell phone is distinguished from physical records by quantity alone, certain types of data are also qualitatively different. An Internet search and browsing history, for example, can be found on an Internet-enabled phone and could reveal an individual's private interests or concerns—perhaps a search for certain symptoms of disease, coupled with frequent visits to WebMD. Data on a cell phone can also reveal where a person has been. Historic location information is a standard feature on many smart phones and can reconstruct someone's specific movements down to the minute, not only around town but also within a particular building.

Mobile application software on a cell phone, or "apps," offer a range of tools for managing detailed information about all aspects of a person's life. There are apps for Democratic Party news and Republican Party news; apps for alcohol, drug, and gambling addictions; apps for sharing prayer requests; apps for tracking pregnancy symptoms; apps for planning your budget; apps for every conceivable hobby or pastime; apps for improving your romantic life. There are popular apps for buying or selling just about anything, and the records of such transactions may be accessible on the phone indefinitely. There are over a million apps available in each of the two major app stores; the phrase "there's an app for that" is now part of the popular lexicon. The average smart phone user has installed 33 apps, which together can form a revealing montage of the user's life.

In 1926, Learned Hand observed (in an opinion later quoted in *Chimel*) that it is "a totally different thing to search a man's pockets and use against him what they contain, from ransacking his house for everything which may incriminate him." If his pockets contain a cell phone, however, that is no longer true. Indeed, a cell phone search would typically expose to the government far *more* than the most exhaustive search of a house: A phone not only contains in digital form many sensitive records previously found in the home; it also contains a broad array of private information never found in a home in any form—unless the phone is.

To further complicate the scope of the privacy interests at stake, the data a user views on many modern cell phones may not in fact be stored on the device itself. Treating a cell phone as a container whose contents may be searched incident to an arrest is a bit strained as an initial matter. But the analogy crumbles entirely when a cell phone is used to access data located elsewhere, at the tap of a screen. That is what cell phones, with increasing frequency, are designed to do by taking advantage of "cloud computing." Cloud computing is the capacity of Internet-connected devices to display data stored on remote servers rather than on the device itself. Cell phone users often may not know whether particular information is stored on the device or in the cloud, and it generally makes little difference. Moreover, the same type of data may be stored locally on the device for one user and in the cloud for another.

The United States concedes that the search incident to arrest exception may not be stretched to cover a search of files accessed remotely—that is, a search of files stored in the cloud. Such a search would be like finding a key in a suspect's pocket and arguing that it allowed law enforcement to unlock and search a house. But officers searching a phone's data would not typically know whether the information they are viewing was stored locally at the time of the arrest or has been pulled from the cloud.

Although the Government recognizes the problem, its proposed solutions are unclear. It suggests that officers could disconnect a phone from the network before searching the device—the very solution whose feasibility it contested with respect to the threat of remote wiping. Alternatively, the Government proposes that law enforcement agencies "develop protocols to address" concerns raised by cloud computing. Probably a good idea, but the Founders did not fight a revolution to gain the right to government agency protocols. The possibility that a search might extend well beyond papers and effects in the physical proximity of an arrestee is yet another reason that the privacy interests here dwarf those in *Robinson*.

C

Apart from their arguments for a direct extension of *Robinson*, the United States and California offer various fallback options for permitting warrantless cell phone searches under certain circumstances. Each of the proposals is flawed and contravenes our general preference to provide clear guidance to law enforcement through categorical rules.

The United States first proposes that the *Gant* standard be imported from the vehicle context, allowing a warrantless search of an arrestee's cell phone whenever it is reasonable to believe that the phone contains evidence of the crime of arrest. But *Gant* relied on "circumstances unique to the vehicle context" to endorse a search solely for the purpose of gathering evidence. Those unique circumstances are "a reduced expectation of privacy" and "heightened law enforcement needs" when it comes to motor vehicles. For reasons that we have explained, cell phone searches bear neither of those characteristics.

At any rate, a *Gant* standard would prove no practical limit at all when it comes to cell phone searches. In the vehicle context, *Gant* generally protects against searches for evidence of past crimes. In the cell phone context, however, it is reasonable to expect that incriminating information will be found on a phone regardless of when the crime occurred. Similarly, in the vehicle context *Gant* restricts broad searches resulting from minor crimes such as traffic violations. That would not necessarily be true for cell phones. It would be a particularly inexperienced or unimaginative law enforcement officer who could not come up with several reasons to suppose evidence of just about any crime could be found on a cell phone. Even an individual pulled over for something as basic as speeding might well have locational data dispositive of guilt on his phone. An individual pulled over for reckless driving might have evidence on the phone that shows whether he was texting while driving. The sources of potential pertinent information are virtually unlimited, so applying the *Gant* standard to cell phones would in effect give police officers unbridled discretion to rummage at will among a person's private effects.

The United States also proposes a rule that would restrict the scope of a cell phone search to those areas of the phone where an officer reasonably believes that information relevant to the crime, the arrestee's identity, or officer safety will be discovered. This approach would again impose few meaningful constraints on officers. The proposed categories would sweep in a great deal of information, and officers would not always be able to discern in advance what information would be found where.

We also reject the United States' final suggestion that officers should always be able to search a phone's call log, as they did in Wurie's case. The Government relies on *Smith v. Maryland*, 442 U.S. 735 (1979), which held that no warrant was required to use a pen register at telephone company premises to identify numbers dialed by a particular caller. The Court in that case, however, concluded that the use of a pen register was not a "search" at all under the Fourth Amendment. There is no dispute here that the officers engaged in a search of Wurie's cell phone. Moreover, call logs typically contain more than just phone numbers; they include any identifying information that an individual might add, such as the label "my house" in Wurie's case.

Finally, at oral argument California suggested a different limiting principle, under which officers could search cell phone data if they could have obtained the same information from a pre-digital counterpart. But the fact that a search in the pre-digital era could have turned up a photograph or two in a wallet does not justify a search of thousands of photos in a digital gallery. The fact that someone could have tucked a paper bank statement in a pocket does not justify a search of every bank statement from the last five years. And to make matters worse, such an analogue test would allow law enforcement to search a range of items contained on a phone, even though people would be unlikely to carry such a variety of information in physical form. In Riley's case, for example, it is implausible that he would have strolled around with video tapes, photo albums, and an address book all crammed into his pockets. But because each of those items has a pre-digital analogue, police under California's proposal would be able to search a phone for all of those items—a significant diminution of privacy.

In addition, an analogue test would launch courts on a difficult line-drawing expedition to determine which digital files are comparable to physical records. Is an e-mail equivalent to a letter? Is a voicemail equivalent to a phone message slip? It is not clear how officers could make these kinds of decisions before conducting a search, or how courts would apply the proposed rule after the fact.

IV

We cannot deny that our decision today will have an impact on the ability of law enforcement to combat crime. Cell phones have become important tools in facilitating coordination and communication among members of criminal enterprises, and can provide valuable incriminating information about dangerous criminals. Privacy comes at a cost.

Our holding, of course, is not that the information on a cell phone is immune from search; it is instead that a warrant is generally required before such a search, even when a cell phone is seized incident to arrest. Our cases have historically recognized that the warrant requirement is an important working part of our machinery of government, not merely an inconvenience to be somehow "weighed" against the claims of police efficiency. Recent technological advances similar to those discussed here have, in addition, made the process of obtaining a warrant itself more efficient.

Moreover, even though the search incident to arrest exception does not apply to cell phones, other case-specific exceptions may still justify a warrantless search of a particular phone. One well-recognized exception applies when "the exigencies of the situation" make the needs of law enforcement so compelling that a warrantless search is objectively reasonable under the Fourth Amendment. Such exigencies could include the need to prevent the imminent destruction of evidence in individual cases, to pursue a fleeing suspect, and to assist persons who are seriously injured or are threatened with imminent injury.

In light of the availability of the exigent circumstances exception, there is no reason to believe that law enforcement officers will not be able to address some of the more extreme hypotheticals that have been suggested: a suspect texting an accomplice who, it is feared, is preparing to detonate a bomb, or a child abductor who may have information about the child's location on his cell phone. The defendants here recognize— indeed, they stress—that such fact-specific threats may justify a warrantless search of cell phone data. The critical point is that, unlike the search incident to arrest exception, the exigent circumstances exception requires a court to examine whether an emergency justified a warrantless search in each particular case.

Modern cell phones are not just another technological convenience. With all they contain and all they may reveal, they hold for many Americans "the privacies of life." The fact that technology now allows an individual to carry such information in his hand does not make the information any less worthy of the protection for which the Founders fought. Our answer to the question of what police must do before searching a cell phone seized incident to an arrest is accordingly simple— get a warrant.

Searches of Persons and Personal Effects Incident to Arrest

1.   When an arrest is made, police may search the arrestee's person, pockets, personal effects, and other areas into which the arrestee might reach where he could gain possession of a weapon or destructible evidence. The search incident to arrest may be made without a search warrant and without probable cause or reasonable suspicion. The search need not take place immediately upon arrest; it can occur upon arrival at the place of detention or, with good reason, even hours later.

2.   When the police make an arrest supported by probable cause to hold for a serious offense and they bring the suspect to the station to be detained in custody, the police may—without a warrant, probable cause, or reasonable suspicion—take and analyze a cheek swab of the arrestee's DNA. Like fingerprinting and photographing, the warrantless taking and analysis of the arrestee's DNA is a legitimate police booking procedure that is reasonable under the Fourth Amendment.

3.   The search incident to arrest exception to the warrant requirement does not permit police to search the contents of an arrestee's cell phone. In most circumstances, police must obtain a warrant before searching the contents of an arrestee's cell phone.

---

3.   SEARCHES OF VEHICLES INCIDENT TO ARREST

In *New York v. Belton*, 453 U.S. 454 (1981), the Supreme Court held that "when a policeman has made a lawful custodial arrest of the occupant of an automobile, he may, as a contemporaneous incident of that arrest, search the passenger compartment of that automobile." As part of that search, *Belton* also permitted the police to examine the contents of any containers within the passenger compartment, including the glove compartment, the console, luggage, boxes, bags, clothing, or any object capable of holding another object; only the trunk of the vehicle was specifically excluded. In *Arizona v. Gant*, the Supreme Court limited *Belton* to its facts and announced a new rule governing searches of vehicles incident to an arrest.

ARIZONA V. GANT

556 U.S. 332 (2009)

JUSTICE STEVENS delivered the opinion of the Court.

After Rodney Gant was arrested for driving with a suspended license, handcuffed, and locked in the back of a patrol car, police officers searched his car and discovered cocaine in the pocket of a jacket on the backseat. Because Gant could not have accessed his car to retrieve weapons or evidence at the time of the search, the Arizona Supreme Court held that the search-incident-to-arrest exception to the Fourth Amendment's warrant requirement, as defined in *Chimel v. California*, 395 U.S. 752 (1969), and applied to vehicle searches in *New York v. Belton*, 453 U.S. 454 (1981), did not justify the search in this case. We agree with that conclusion.

Under *Chimel*, police may search incident to arrest only the space within an arrestee's "immediate control," meaning "the area from within which he might gain possession of a weapon or destructible evidence." The safety and evidentiary justifications underlying *Chimel's* reaching-distance rule determine *Belton's* scope. Accordingly, we hold that *Belton* does not authorize a vehicle search incident to a recent occupant's arrest after the arrestee has been secured and cannot access the interior of the vehicle. Consistent with the holding in *Thornton v. U.S.*, 541 U.S. 615 (2004), and following the suggestion in Justice Scalia's opinion concurring in the judgment in that case, we also conclude that circumstances unique to the automobile context justify a search incident to arrest when it is reasonable to believe that evidence of the offense of arrest might be found in the vehicle.

I

On August 25, 1999, acting on an anonymous tip that the residence at 2524 North Walnut Avenue was being used to sell drugs, Tucson police officers Griffith and Reed knocked on the front door and asked to speak to the owner. Gant answered the door and, after identifying himself, stated that he expected the owner to return later. The officers left the residence and conducted a records check, which revealed that Gant's driver's license had been suspended and there was an outstanding warrant for his arrest for driving with a suspended license.

When the officers returned to the house that evening, they found a man near the back of the house and a woman in a car parked in front of it. After a third officer arrived, they arrested the man for providing a false name and the woman for possessing drug paraphernalia. Both arrestees were handcuffed and secured in separate patrol cars when Gant arrived. The officers recognized his car as it entered the driveway, and Officer Griffith confirmed that Gant was the driver by shining a flashlight into the car as it drove by him. Gant parked at the end of the driveway, got out of his car, and shut the door. Griffith, who was about 30 feet away, called to Gant, and they approached each other, meeting 10-to-12 feet from Gant's car. Griffith immediately arrested Gant and handcuffed him.

Because the other arrestees were secured in the only patrol cars at the scene, Griffith called for backup. When two more officers arrived, they locked Gant in the backseat of their vehicle. After Gant had been handcuffed and placed in the back of a patrol car, two officers searched his car: One of them found a gun, and the other discovered a bag of cocaine in the pocket of a jacket on the backseat.

Gant was charged with two offenses—possession of a narcotic drug for sale and possession of drug paraphernalia (*i.e.*, the plastic bag in which the cocaine was found). He moved to suppress the evidence seized from his car on the ground that the warrantless search violated the Fourth Amendment. Among other things, Gant argued that *Belton* did not authorize the search of his vehicle because he posed no threat to the officers after he was handcuffed in the patrol car and because he was arrested for a traffic offense for which no evidence could be found in his vehicle. When asked at the suppression hearing why the search was conducted, Officer Griffith responded: "Because the law says we can do it."

The trial court rejected the State's contention that the officers had probable cause to search Gant's car for contraband when the search began, but it denied the motion to suppress. Relying on the fact that the police saw Gant commit the crime of driving without a license and apprehended him only shortly after he exited his car, the court held that the search was permissible as a search incident to arrest. A jury found Gant guilty on both drug counts, and he was sentenced to a 3-year term of imprisonment.

After protracted state-court proceedings, the Arizona Supreme Court concluded that the search of Gant's car was unreasonable within the meaning of the Fourth Amendment. The court's opinion discussed at length our decision in *Belton*, which held that police may search the passenger compartment of a vehicle and any containers therein as a contemporaneous incident of an arrest of the vehicle's recent occupant. The court distinguished *Belton* as a case concerning the permissible scope of a vehicle search incident to arrest and concluded that it did not answer "the threshold question whether the police may conduct a search incident to arrest at all once the scene is secure." Relying on our earlier decision in

Chimel, the court observed that the search-incident-to-arrest exception to the warrant requirement is justified by interests in officer safety and evidence preservation. When "the justifications underlying *Chimel* no longer exist because the scene is secure and the arrestee is handcuffed, secured in the back of a patrol car, and under the supervision of an officer," the court concluded, a "warrantless search of the arrestee's car cannot be justified as necessary to protect the officers at the scene or prevent the destruction of evidence." Accordingly, the court held that the search of Gant's car was unreasonable.

The dissenting justices would have upheld the search of Gant's car based on their view that "the validity of a *Belton* search clearly does not depend on the presence of the *Chimel* rationales in a particular case." Although they disagreed with the majority's view of *Belton*, the dissenting justices acknowledged that "the bright-line rule embraced in *Belton* has long been criticized and probably merits reconsideration." They thus "added their voices to the others that have urged the Supreme Court to revisit *Belton*."

The chorus that has called for us to revisit *Belton* includes courts, scholars, and Members of this Court who have questioned that decision's clarity and its fidelity to Fourth Amendment principles. We therefore granted the State's petition for certiorari.

II

Consistent with our precedent, our analysis begins, as it should in every case addressing the reasonableness of a warrantless search, with the basic rule that "searches conducted outside the judicial process, without prior approval by judge or magistrate, are *per se* unreasonable under the Fourth Amendment—subject only to a few specifically established and well-delineated exceptions." *Katz v. U.S.*, 389 U.S. 347, 357 (1967). Among the exceptions to the warrant requirement is a search incident to a lawful arrest. The exception derives from interests in officer safety and evidence preservation that are typically implicated in arrest situations.

In *Chimel*, we held that a search incident to arrest may only include "the arrestee's person and the area 'within his immediate control'— construing that phrase to mean the area from within which he might gain possession of a weapon or destructible evidence." That limitation, which continues to define the boundaries of the exception, ensures that the scope of a search incident to arrest is commensurate with its purposes of protecting arresting officers and safeguarding any evidence of the offense of arrest that an arrestee might conceal or destroy. If there is no possibility that an arrestee could reach into the area that law enforcement officers seek to search, both justifications for the search-incident-to-arrest exception are absent and the rule does not apply.

In *Belton*, we considered *Chimel*'s application to the automobile context. A lone police officer in that case stopped a speeding car in which Belton was one of four occupants. While asking for the driver's license and registration, the officer smelled burnt marijuana and observed an envelope on the car floor marked "Supergold"—a name he associated with marijuana. Thus having probable cause to believe the occupants had committed a drug offense, the officer ordered them out of the vehicle, placed them under arrest, and patted them down. Without handcuffing the arrestees,[1] the officer "split them up into four separate areas of the Thruway so they would not be in physical touching area of each other" and searched the vehicle, including the pocket of a jacket on the backseat, in which he found cocaine.

The New York Court of Appeals found the search unconstitutional, concluding that after the occupants were arrested the vehicle and its contents were "safely within the exclusive custody and control of the police." The State asked this Court to consider whether the exception recognized in *Chimel* permits an officer to search "a jacket found inside an automobile while the automobile's four occupants, all under arrest, are standing unsecured around the vehicle." We granted certiorari because "courts had found no workable definition of 'the area within the immediate control of the arrestee' when that area arguably includes the interior of an automobile."

In its brief, the State argued that the Court of Appeals erred in concluding that the jacket was under the officer's exclusive control. Focusing on the number of arrestees and their proximity to the vehicle, the State asserted that it was reasonable for the officer to believe the arrestees could have accessed the vehicle and its contents, making the search permissible under *Chimel*. The United States, as *amicus curiae* in support of the State, argued for a more permissive standard, but it maintained that any search incident to arrest must be "substantially contemporaneous" with the arrest—a requirement it deemed "satisfied if the search occurs during the period in which the arrest is being consummated and before the situation has so stabilized that it could be said that the arrest was completed." There was no suggestion by the parties or *amici* that *Chimel* authorizes a vehicle search incident to arrest when there is no realistic possibility that an arrestee could access his vehicle.

After considering these arguments, we held that when an officer lawfully arrests "the occupant of an automobile, he may, as a contemporaneous incident of that arrest, search the passenger compartment of the automobile" and any containers therein. That holding was based in large part on our assumption "that articles inside the

---

[1] The officer was unable to handcuff the occupants because he had only one set of handcuffs.

relatively narrow compass of the passenger compartment of an automobile are in fact generally, even if not inevitably, within 'the area into which an arrestee might reach.' "

The Arizona Supreme Court read our decision in *Belton* as merely delineating "the proper scope of a search of the interior of an automobile" incident to an arrest. That is, *when* the passenger compartment is within an arrestee's reaching distance, *Belton* supplies the generalization that the entire compartment and any containers therein may be reached. On that view of *Belton*, the state court concluded that the search of Gant's car was unreasonable because Gant clearly could not have accessed his car at the time of the search. It also found that no other exception to the warrant requirement applied in this case.

Gant now urges us to adopt the reading of *Belton* followed by the Arizona Supreme Court.

III

Despite the textual and evidentiary support for the Arizona Supreme Court's reading of *Belton*, our opinion has been widely understood to allow a vehicle search incident to the arrest of a recent occupant even if there is no possibility the arrestee could gain access to the vehicle at the time of the search. This reading may be attributable to Justice Brennan's dissent in *Belton*, in which he characterized the Court's holding as resting on the "fiction that the interior of a car is *always* within the immediate control of an arrestee who has recently been in the car." Under the majority's approach, he argued, "the result would presumably be the same even if the officer had handcuffed Belton and his companions in the patrol car" before conducting the search.

Since we decided *Belton*, Courts of Appeals have given different answers to the question whether a vehicle must be within an arrestee's reach to justify a vehicle search incident to arrest, but Justice Brennan's reading of the Court's opinion has predominated. As Justice O'Connor observed, "lower court decisions seem now to treat the ability to search a vehicle incident to the arrest of a recent occupant as a police entitlement rather than as an exception justified by the twin rationales of *Chimel*." Justice Scalia has similarly noted that, although it is improbable that an arrestee could gain access to weapons stored in his vehicle after he has been handcuffed and secured in the backseat of a patrol car, cases allowing a search in "this precise factual scenario are legion." Indeed, some courts have upheld searches under *Belton* "even when the handcuffed arrestee has already left the scene."

Under this broad reading of *Belton*, a vehicle search would be authorized incident to every arrest of a recent occupant notwithstanding that in most cases the vehicle's passenger compartment will not be within the arrestee's reach at the time of the search. To read *Belton* as authorizing a vehicle search incident to every recent occupant's arrest would thus untether the rule from the justifications underlying the *Chimel* exception—a result clearly incompatible with our statement in *Belton* that it "in no way alters the fundamental principles established in the *Chimel* case regarding the basic scope of searches incident to lawful custodial arrests." Accordingly, we reject this reading of *Belton* and hold that the *Chimel* rationale authorizes police to search a vehicle incident to a recent occupant's arrest only when the arrestee is unsecured and within reaching distance of the passenger compartment at the time of the search.[4]

Although it does not follow from *Chimel*, we also conclude that circumstances unique to the vehicle context justify a search incident to a lawful arrest when it is "reasonable to believe evidence relevant to the crime of arrest might be found in the vehicle." *Thornton v. U.S.*, 541 U.S. 615, 632 (2004) (Scalia, J., concurring in judgment). In many cases, as when a recent occupant is arrested for a traffic violation, there will be no reasonable basis to believe the vehicle contains relevant evidence. But in others, including *Belton* and *Thornton*, the offense of arrest will supply a basis for searching the passenger compartment of an arrestee's vehicle and any containers therein.

Neither the possibility of access nor the likelihood of discovering offense-related evidence authorized the search in this case. Unlike in *Belton*, which involved a single officer confronted with four unsecured arrestees, the five officers in this case outnumbered the three arrestees, all of whom had been handcuffed and secured in separate patrol cars before the officers searched Gant's car. Under those circumstances, Gant clearly was not within reaching distance of his car at the time of the search. An evidentiary basis for the search was also lacking in this case. Whereas Belton and Thornton were arrested for drug offenses, Gant was arrested for driving with a suspended license—an offense for which police could not expect to find evidence in the passenger compartment of Gant's car. Because police could not reasonably have believed either that Gant could have accessed his car at the time of the search or that evidence of the offense for which he was arrested might have been found therein, the search in this case was unreasonable.

IV

The State does not seriously disagree with the Arizona Supreme Court's conclusion that Gant could not have accessed his vehicle at the time of the search, but it nevertheless asks us to uphold the search of his vehicle under the broad reading of *Belton* discussed above. The State

---

[4] Because officers have many means of ensuring the safe arrest of vehicle occupants, it will be the rare case in which an officer is unable to fully effectuate an arrest so that a real possibility of access to the arrestee's vehicle remains. But in such a case a search incident to arrest is reasonable under the Fourth Amendment.

argues that *Belton* searches are reasonable regardless of the possibility of access in a given case because that expansive rule correctly balances law enforcement interests, including the interest in a bright-line rule, with an arrestee's limited privacy interest in his vehicle.

For several reasons, we reject the State's argument. First, the State seriously undervalues the privacy interests at stake. Although we have recognized that a motorist's privacy interest in his vehicle is less substantial than in his home, the former interest is nevertheless important and deserving of constitutional protection. It is particularly significant that *Belton* searches authorize police officers to search not just the passenger compartment but every purse, briefcase, or other container within that space. A rule that gives police the power to conduct such a search whenever an individual is caught committing a traffic offense, when there is no basis for believing evidence of the offense might be found in the vehicle, creates a serious and recurring threat to the privacy of countless individuals. Indeed, the character of that threat implicates the central concern underlying the Fourth Amendment—the concern about giving police officers unbridled discretion to rummage at will among a person's private effects.

At the same time as it undervalues these privacy concerns, the State exaggerates the clarity that its reading of *Belton* provides. Courts that have read *Belton* expansively are at odds regarding how close in time to the arrest and how proximate to the arrestee's vehicle an officer's first contact with the arrestee must be to bring the encounter within *Belton*'s purview and whether a search is reasonable when it commences or continues after the arrestee has been removed from the scene. The rule has thus generated a great deal of uncertainty, particularly for a rule touted as providing a "bright line."

Contrary to the State's suggestion, a broad reading of *Belton* is also unnecessary to protect law enforcement safety and evidentiary interests. Under our view, *Belton* and *Thornton* permit an officer to conduct a vehicle search when an arrestee is within reaching distance of the vehicle or it is reasonable to believe the vehicle contains evidence of the offense of arrest. Other established exceptions to the warrant requirement authorize a vehicle search under additional circumstances when safety or evidentiary concerns demand. For instance, *Michigan v. Long*, 463 U.S. 1032 (1983), permits an officer to search a vehicle's passenger compartment when he has reasonable suspicion that an individual, whether or not the arrestee, is "dangerous" and might access the vehicle to "gain immediate control of weapons." If there is probable cause to believe a vehicle contains evidence of criminal activity, *U.S. v. Ross*, 456 U.S. 798 (1982), authorizes a search of any area of the vehicle in which the evidence might be found. Unlike the searches permitted by Justice Scalia's opinion concurring in the judgment in *Thornton*, which we conclude today are reasonable for purposes of the Fourth Amendment, *Ross* allows searches for evidence relevant to offenses other than the offense of arrest, and the scope of the search authorized is broader. Finally, there may be still other circumstances in which safety or evidentiary interests would justify a search. Cf. *Maryland v. Buie*, 494 U.S. 325 (1990) (holding that, incident to arrest, an officer may conduct a limited protective sweep of those areas of a house in which he reasonably suspects a dangerous person may be hiding).

These exceptions together ensure that officers may search a vehicle when genuine safety or evidentiary concerns encountered during the arrest of a vehicle's recent occupant justify a search. Construing *Belton* broadly to allow vehicle searches incident to any arrest would serve no purpose except to provide a police entitlement, and it is anathema to the Fourth Amendment to permit a warrantless search on that basis. For these reasons, we are unpersuaded by the State's arguments that a broad reading of *Belton* would meaningfully further law enforcement interests and justify a substantial intrusion on individuals' privacy.

V

Our dissenting colleagues argue that the doctrine of *stare decisis* requires adherence to a broad reading of *Belton* even though the justifications for searching a vehicle incident to arrest are in most cases absent. The doctrine of *stare decisis* is of course essential to the respect accorded to the judgments of the Court and to the stability of the law, but it does not compel us to follow a past decision when its rationale no longer withstands careful analysis.

We have never relied on *stare decisis* to justify the continuance of an unconstitutional police practice. And we would be particularly loath to uphold an unconstitutional result in a case that is so easily distinguished from the decisions that arguably compel it. The safety and evidentiary interests that supported the search in *Belton* simply are not present in this case. Indeed, it is hard to imagine two cases that are factually more distinct, as *Belton* involved one officer confronted by four unsecured arrestees suspected of committing a drug offense and this case involves several officers confronted with a securely detained arrestee apprehended for driving with a suspended license. This case is also distinguishable from *Thornton*, in which the petitioner was arrested for a drug offense. It is thus unsurprising that Members of this Court who concurred in the judgments in *Belton* and *Thornton* also concur in the decision in this case.

We do not agree with the contention in Justice Alito's dissent (hereinafter dissent) that consideration of police reliance interests requires a different result. Although it appears that the State's reading of *Belton* has been widely taught in police academies and that law enforcement officers have relied on the rule in conducting vehicle searches during the past 28 years, many of these searches were not justified by the reasons underlying the *Chimel* exception. Countless individuals guilty of nothing more serious than a traffic violation have had their constitutional right to the security of their private effects violated as a result. The fact that the law enforcement community may view the State's version of the *Belton* rule as an entitlement does not establish the sort of reliance interest that could outweigh the countervailing interest that all individuals share in having their constitutional rights fully protected. If it is clear that a practice is unlawful, individuals' interest in its discontinuance clearly outweighs any law enforcement "entitlement" to its persistence.

The experience of the 28 years since we decided *Belton* has shown that the generalization underpinning the broad reading of that decision is unfounded. We now know that articles inside the passenger compartment are rarely "within the area into which an arrestee might reach," and blind adherence to *Belton*'s faulty assumption would authorize myriad unconstitutional searches. The doctrine of *stare decisis* does not require us to approve routine constitutional violations.

VI

Police may search a vehicle incident to a recent occupant's arrest only if the arrestee is within reaching distance of the passenger compartment at the time of the search or it is reasonable to believe the vehicle contains evidence of the offense of arrest. When these justifications are absent, a search of an arrestee's vehicle will be unreasonable unless police obtain a warrant or show that another exception to the warrant requirement applies.

JUSTICE SCALIA, concurring.

To determine what is an "unreasonable" search within the meaning of the Fourth Amendment, we look first to the historical practices the Framers sought to preserve; if those provide inadequate guidance, we apply traditional standards of reasonableness. Since the historical scope of officers' authority to search vehicles incident to arrest is uncertain, traditional standards of reasonableness govern. It is abundantly clear that those standards do not justify what I take to be the rule set forth in *Belton* and *Thornton*: that arresting officers may always search an arrestee's vehicle in order to protect themselves from hidden weapons. When an arrest is made in connection with a roadside stop, police virtually always have a less intrusive and more effective means of ensuring their safety—and a means that is virtually always employed: ordering the arrestee away from the vehicle, patting him down in the open, handcuffing him, and placing him in the squad car.

Law enforcement officers face a risk of being shot whenever they pull a car over. But that risk is at its height at the time of the initial confrontation; and it is *not at all* reduced by allowing a search of the stopped vehicle after the driver has been arrested and placed in the squad car. I observed in *Thornton* that the government had failed to provide a single instance in which a formerly restrained arrestee escaped to retrieve a weapon from his own vehicle; Arizona and its *amici* have not remedied that significant deficiency in the present case.

It must be borne in mind that we are speaking here only of a rule automatically permitting a search when the driver or an occupant is arrested. Where no arrest is made, we have held that officers may search the car if they reasonably believe "the suspect is dangerous and may gain immediate control of weapons." *Michigan v. Long*, 463 U.S. 1032, 1049 (1983). In the no-arrest case, the possibility of access to weapons in the vehicle always exists, since the driver or passenger will be allowed to return to the vehicle when the interrogation is completed. The rule of *Michigan v. Long* is not at issue here.

Justice Stevens acknowledges that an officer-safety rationale cannot justify all vehicle searches incident to arrest, but asserts that that is not the rule *Belton* and *Thornton* adopted. (As described above, I read those cases differently). Justice Stevens would therefore retain the application of *Chimel* in the car-search context but would apply in the future what he believes our cases held in the past: that officers making a roadside stop may search the vehicle so long as the "arrestee is within reaching distance of the passenger compartment at the time of the search." I believe that this standard fails to provide the needed guidance to arresting officers and also leaves much room for manipulation, inviting officers to leave the scene unsecured (at least where dangerous suspects are not involved) in order to conduct a vehicle search. In my view we should simply abandon the *Belton-Thornton* charade of officer safety and overrule those cases. I would hold that a vehicle search incident to arrest is *ipso facto* "reasonable" only when the object of the search is evidence of the crime for which the arrest was made, or of another crime that the officer has probable cause to believe occurred. Because respondent was arrested for driving without a license (a crime for which no evidence could be expected to be found in the vehicle), I would hold in the present case that the search was unlawful.

Justice Alito insists that the Court must demand a good reason for abandoning prior precedent. That is true enough, but it seems to me ample reason that the precedent was badly reasoned and produces erroneous (in this case unconstitutional) results. We should recognize *Belton*'s fanciful reliance upon officer safety for what it was: a return to the broader sort of evidence-gathering search incident to arrest that we allowed before *Chimel*.

Justice Alito argues that there is no reason to adopt a rule limiting automobile-arrest searches to those cases where the search's object is evidence of the crime of arrest. I disagree. This formulation of officers' authority both preserves the outcomes of our prior cases and tethers the scope and rationale of the doctrine to the triggering event. *Belton*, by contrast, allowed searches precisely when its exigency-based rationale was least applicable: The fact of the arrest in the automobile context makes searches on exigency grounds *less* reasonable, not more. I also disagree with Justice Alito's conclusory assertion that this standard will be difficult to administer in practice; the ease of its application in this case would suggest otherwise.

No other Justice, however, shares my view that application of *Chimel* in this context should be entirely abandoned. It seems to me unacceptable for the Court to come forth with a 4-to-1-to-4 opinion that leaves the governing rule uncertain. I am therefore confronted with the choice of either leaving the current understanding of *Belton* and *Thornton* in effect, or acceding to what seems to me the artificial narrowing of those cases adopted by Justice Stevens. The latter, as I have said, does not provide the degree of certainty I think desirable in this field; but the former opens the field to what I think are plainly unconstitutional searches—which is the greater evil. I therefore join the opinion of the Court.

———————

Under the circumstances set forth in *Arizona v. Gant*, the police may perform a warrantless search of a vehicle incident to the arrest of one of the occupants only if an actual arrest is made. In *Knowles v. Iowa*, the Supreme Court made it clear that the search incident to arrest exception does not apply if the police decide to issue a citation rather than making an arrest.

KNOWLES V. IOWA
525 U.S. 113 (1998)

CHIEF JUSTICE REHNQUIST delivered the opinion of the Court.

An Iowa police officer stopped petitioner Knowles for speeding, but issued him a citation rather than arresting him. The question presented is whether such a procedure authorizes the officer, consistently with the Fourth Amendment, to conduct a full search of the car. We answer this question "no."

Knowles was stopped in Newton, Iowa, after having been clocked driving 43 miles per hour on a road where the speed limit was 25 miles per hour. The police officer issued a citation to Knowles, although under Iowa law he might have arrested him. The officer then conducted a full search of the car, and under the driver's seat he found a bag of marijuana and a "pot pipe." Knowles was then arrested and charged with violation of state laws dealing with controlled substances.

Before trial, Knowles moved to suppress the evidence so obtained. He argued that the search could not be sustained under the "search incident to arrest" exception recognized in *U.S. v. Robinson*, 414 U.S. 218 (1973), because he had not been placed under arrest. At the hearing on the motion to suppress, the police officer conceded that he had neither Knowles' consent nor probable cause to conduct the search. He relied on Iowa law dealing with such searches.

Iowa Code Ann. § 321.485(1)(a) (West 1997) provides that Iowa peace officers having cause to believe that a person has violated any traffic or motor vehicle equipment law may arrest the person and immediately take the person before a magistrate. Iowa law also authorizes the far more usual practice of issuing a citation in lieu of arrest or in lieu of continued custody after an initial arrest. Section 805.1(4) provides that the issuance of a citation in lieu of an arrest "does not affect the officer's authority to conduct an otherwise lawful search." The Iowa Supreme Court has interpreted this provision as providing authority to officers to conduct a full-blown search of an automobile and driver in those cases where police elect not to make a custodial arrest and instead issue a citation—that is, a search incident to citation.

Based on this authority, the trial court denied the motion to suppress and found Knowles guilty. The Iowa Supreme Court upheld the constitutionality of the search under a bright-line "search incident to citation" exception to the Fourth Amendment's warrant requirement, reasoning that so long as the arresting officer had probable cause to make a custodial arrest, there need not in fact have been a custodial arrest. We granted certiorari, and we now reverse.

In *Robinson*, we noted the two historical rationales for the "search incident to arrest" exception: (1) the need to disarm the suspect in order to take him into custody, and (2) the need to preserve evidence for later use at trial. But neither of these underlying rationales for the search incident to arrest exception is sufficient to justify the search in the present case.

We have recognized that the first rationale—officer safety—is both legitimate and weighty. The threat to officer safety from issuing a traffic citation, however, is a good deal less than in the case of a custodial arrest. In *Robinson*, we stated that a custodial arrest involves "danger to an officer" because of "the extended exposure which follows the taking of a suspect into custody and transporting him to the police station." We recognized that "the danger to the police officer flows from the fact of the arrest, and its attendant proximity, stress, and uncertainty, and not from the grounds for arrest." A routine traffic stop, on the other hand, is a relatively brief encounter and is more analogous to a so-called "*Terry-*stop" than to a formal arrest.

This is not to say that the concern for officer safety is absent in the case of a routine traffic stop. It plainly is not. But while the concern for officer safety in this context may justify the "minimal" additional intrusion of ordering a driver and passengers out of the car, it does not by itself justify the often considerably greater intrusion attending a full field-type search. Even without the search authority Iowa urges, officers have other, independent bases to search for weapons and protect themselves from danger. For example, they may order out of a vehicle both the driver and any passengers; perform a "patdown" of a driver and any passengers upon reasonable suspicion that they may be armed and dangerous; conduct a "*Terry* patdown" of the passenger compartment of a vehicle upon reasonable suspicion that an occupant is dangerous and may gain immediate control of a weapon; and even conduct a full search of the passenger compartment, including any containers therein, pursuant to a custodial arrest.[a]

Nor has Iowa shown the second justification for the authority to search incident to arrest—the need to discover and preserve evidence. Once Knowles was stopped for speeding and issued a citation, all the evidence necessary to prosecute that offense had been obtained. No further evidence of excessive speed was going to be found either on the person of the offender or in the passenger compartment of the car.

Iowa nevertheless argues that a "search incident to citation" is justified because a suspect who is subject to a routine traffic stop may attempt to hide or destroy evidence related to his identity (*e.g.*, a driver's license or vehicle registration), or destroy evidence of another, as yet undetected crime. As for the destruction of evidence relating to identity, if a police officer is not satisfied with the identification furnished by the driver, this may be a basis for arresting him rather than merely issuing a citation. As for destroying evidence of other crimes, the possibility that an officer would stumble onto evidence wholly unrelated to the speeding offense seems remote.

In *Robinson*, we held that the authority to conduct a full field search as incident to an arrest was a "bright-line rule," which was based on the concern for officer safety and destruction or loss of evidence, but which did not depend in every case upon the existence of either concern. Here we are asked to extend that "bright-line rule" to a situation where the concern for officer safety is not present to the same extent and the concern for destruction or loss of evidence is not present at all. We decline to do so.

---

[a]   The authority of police to "conduct a full search of the passenger compartment, including any containers therein, pursuant to a custodial arrest" is limited by the Supreme Court's more recent decision in *Arizona v. Gant*, 556 U.S. 332 (2009).

> ### Searches of Vehicles Incident to Arrest
>
> 1.   Police may perform a warrantless search of a vehicle incident to a recent occupant's arrest if the arrestee is within reaching distance of the passenger compartment at the time of the search, or if it is reasonable to believe that the vehicle contains evidence relevant to the crime of arrest.
>
> 2.   The police may perform a warrantless search of a vehicle incident to arrest, under the circumstances set forth in *Arizona v. Gant*, only if police actually arrest one of the occupants. If police decide to issue a citation rather than making an arrest, the search incident to arrest exception does not apply.

C. PLAIN VIEW

Suppose the police have a valid warrant that authorizes them to search for and seize any illegal weapons in an apartment. As one officer conducts the search, she observes a large quantity of narcotics in a plastic bag sitting on the kitchen table. The officer continues the search and finds no illegal weapons, but she does seize the narcotics. If the apartment resident is later charged with drug possession, may the prosecution introduce into evidence the plastic bag containing the narcotics?

The defendant would contend that the police officer had no authority to search for or seize the narcotics because the warrant only authorized the seizure of any illegal weapons. This argument would likely fail, however, under the "plain view" exception to the warrant requirement. Under this exception, if police are legitimately on the premises and observe an item in plain view whose incriminating character is immediately apparent, the police may seize the item and introduce it into evidence against a criminal defendant.

In *Coolidge v. New Hampshire*, the Supreme Court set forth the basic requirements of the plain view exception. You may recall that *Coolidge* was excerpted in Chapter 4 to illustrate the requirement that a warrant be issued by a neutral and detached magistrate. The warrant in *Coolidge* was signed by the New Hampshire Attorney General, who was leading the investigation into Pamela Mason's murder. The Supreme Court concluded that the warrant was invalid because it was not issued by a neutral and detached magistrate. Accordingly, the Court was forced to consider other theories upon which the evidence might be admissible, including the plain view exception.

COOLIDGE V. NEW HAMPSHIRE
403 U.S. 443 (1971)

JUSTICE STEWART delivered the opinion of the Court.

We are called upon in this case to decide issues under the Fourth and Fourteenth Amendments arising in the context of a state criminal trial for the commission of a particularly brutal murder. As in every case, our single duty is to determine the issues presented in accord with the Constitution and the law.

Pamela Mason, a 14-year-old girl, left her home in Manchester, New Hampshire, on the evening of January 13, 1964, during a heavy snowstorm, apparently in response to a man's telephone call for a babysitter. Eight days later, after a thaw, her body was found by the site of a major north-south highway several miles away. She had been murdered. The event created great alarm in the area, and the police immediately began a massive investigation.

On January 28, having learned from a neighbor that the petitioner, Edward Coolidge, had been away from home on the evening of the girl's disappearance, the police went to his house to question him. They asked him, among other things, if he owned any guns, and he produced three, two shotguns and a rifle. They also asked whether he would take a lie-detector test concerning his account of his activities on the night of the disappearance. He agreed to do so on the following Sunday, his day off. The police later described his attitude on the occasion of this visit as fully "cooperative." His wife was in the house throughout the interview.

On the following Sunday, a policeman called Coolidge early in the morning and asked him to come down to the police station for the trip to Concord, New Hampshire, where the lie-detector test was to be administered. That evening, two plainclothes policemen arrived at the Coolidge house, where Mrs. Coolidge was waiting with her mother-in-law for her husband's return. These two policemen were not the two who had visited the house earlier in the week, and they apparently did not know that Coolidge had displayed three guns for inspection during the earlier visit. The plainclothesmen told Mrs. Coolidge that her husband was in "serious trouble" and probably would not be home that night. They asked Coolidge's mother to leave, and proceeded to question Mrs. Coolidge. During the course of the interview they obtained from her four guns belonging to Coolidge, and some clothes that Mrs. Coolidge thought her husband might have been wearing on the evening of Pamela Mason's disappearance.

Coolidge was held in jail on an unrelated charge that night, but he was released the next day. [During the lie-detector test, Coolidge confessed to a theft of money from his employer.] During the ensuing two and a half weeks, the State accumulated a quantity of evidence to support the theory that it was he who had killed Pamela Mason. On February 19, the results of the investigation were presented at a meeting between the police officers working on the case and the State Attorney General, who had personally taken charge of all police activities relating to the murder, and was later to serve as chief prosecutor at the trial. At this meeting, it was decided that there was enough evidence to justify the arrest of Coolidge on the murder charge and a search of his house and two cars. At the conclusion of the meeting, the Manchester police chief made formal application, under oath, for the arrest and search warrants. The complaint supporting the warrant for a search of Coolidge's Pontiac automobile, the only warrant that concerns us here, stated that the affiant "has probable cause to suspect and believe, and does suspect and believe, and herewith offers satisfactory evidence, that there are certain objects and things used in the Commission of said offense, now kept, and concealed in or upon a certain vehicle, to wit: 1951 Pontiac two-door sedan." The warrants were then signed and issued by the Attorney General himself, acting as a justice of the peace. Under New Hampshire law in force at that time, all justices of the peace were authorized to issue search warrants.

The police arrested Coolidge in his house on the day the warrant issued. Mrs. Coolidge asked whether she might remain in the house with her small child, but was told that she must stay elsewhere, apparently in part because the police believed that she would be harassed by reporters if she were accessible to them. When she asked whether she might take her car, she was told that both cars had been "impounded," and that the police would provide transportation for her. Some time later, the police called a towing company, and about two and a half hours after Coolidge had been taken into custody the cars were towed to the police station. It appears that at the time of the arrest the cars were parked in the Coolidge driveway, and that although dark had fallen they were plainly visible both from the street and from inside the house where Coolidge was actually arrested. The 1951 Pontiac was searched and vacuumed on February 21, two days after it was seized, again a year later, in January 1965, and a third time in April 1965.

At Coolidge's subsequent jury trial on the charge of murder, vacuum sweepings, including particles of gun powder, taken from the Pontiac were introduced in evidence against him, as part of an attempt by the State to show by microscopic analysis that it was highly probable that Pamela Mason had been in Coolidge's car. Also introduced in evidence was one of the guns taken by the police on their Sunday evening visit to the Coolidge house—a 22-caliber Mossberg rifle, which the prosecution claimed was the murder weapon. Conflicting ballistics testimony was offered on the question whether the bullets found in Pamela Mason's body had been fired from this rifle. Finally, the prosecution introduced vacuum sweepings of the clothes taken from the Coolidge house that same Sunday evening, and attempted to show through microscopic analysis that there was a high probability that the clothes had been in contact with Pamela Mason's body. Pretrial motions to suppress all this evidence were referred by the trial judge to the New Hampshire Supreme Court, which ruled the evidence admissible. The jury found Coolidge guilty and he was sentenced to life imprisonment. The New Hampshire Supreme Court affirmed the judgment of conviction, and we granted certiorari to consider the constitutional questions raised by the admission of this evidence against Coolidge at his trial.

I

The petitioner's first claim is that the warrant authorizing the seizure and subsequent search of his 1951 Pontiac automobile was invalid because not issued by a "neutral and detached magistrate." We agree with the petitioner that the warrant was invalid for this reason.

In this case, the determination of probable cause was made by the chief "government enforcement agent" of the State—the Attorney General—who was actively in charge of the investigation and later was to be chief prosecutor at the trial. The State argues that the Attorney General, who was unquestionably authorized as a justice of the peace to issue warrants under then existing state law, did in fact act as a "neutral and detached magistrate." Further, the State claims that any magistrate, confronted with the showing of probable cause made by the Manchester chief of police, would have issued the warrant in question. To the first proposition it is enough to answer that there could hardly be a more appropriate setting than this for a *per se* rule of disqualification rather than a case-by-case evaluation of all the circumstances. Without disrespect to the state law enforcement agent here involved, prosecutors and policemen simply cannot be asked to maintain the requisite neutrality with regard to their own investigations.

We find no escape from the conclusion that the seizure and search of the Pontiac automobile cannot constitutionally rest upon the warrant issued by the state official who was the chief investigator and prosecutor in this case. Since he was not the neutral and detached magistrate required by the Constitution, the search stands on no firmer ground than if there had been no warrant at all. If the seizure and search are to be justified, they must, therefore, be justified on some other theory.

II

The State's theory in support of the warrantless seizure and search of the Pontiac car is that the car itself was an "instrumentality of the crime," and as such might be seized by the police on Coolidge's property because it was in plain view. We may assume that the police had probable cause to seize the automobile. But, for the reasons that follow, we hold that the "plain view" exception to the warrant requirement is inapplicable to this case.

It is well established that under certain circumstances the police may seize evidence in plain view without a warrant. But it is important to keep in mind that, in the vast majority of cases, any evidence seized by the police will be in plain view, at least at the moment of seizure. The problem with the "plain view" doctrine has been to identify the circumstances in which plain view has legal significance rather than being simply the normal concomitant of any search, legal or illegal.

An example of the applicability of the "plain view" doctrine is the situation in which the police have a warrant to search a given area for specified objects, and in the course of the search come across some other article of incriminating character. Where the initial intrusion that brings the police within plain view of such an article is supported, not by a warrant, but by one of the recognized exceptions to the warrant requirement, the seizure is also legitimate. Thus the police may inadvertently come across evidence while in "hot pursuit" of a fleeing suspect. And an object that comes into view during a search incident to arrest that is appropriately limited in scope under existing law may be seized without a warrant. Finally, the "plain view" doctrine has been applied where a police officer is not searching for evidence against the accused, but nonetheless inadvertently comes across an incriminating object.

What the "plain view" cases have in common is that the police officer in each of them had a prior justification for an intrusion in the course of which he came inadvertently across a piece of evidence incriminating the accused. The doctrine serves to supplement the prior justification— whether it be a warrant for another object, hot pursuit, search incident to lawful arrest, or some other legitimate reason for being present unconnected with a search directed against the accused—and permits the warrantless seizure. Of course, the extension of the original justification is legitimate only where it is immediately apparent to the police that they have evidence before them; the "plain view" doctrine may not be used to extend a general exploratory search from one object to another until something incriminating at last emerges.

The rationale for the "plain view" exception is evident if we keep in mind the two distinct constitutional protections served by the warrant requirement. First, the magistrate's scrutiny is intended to eliminate altogether searches not based on probable cause. The premise here is that any intrusion in the way of search or seizure is an evil, so that no intrusion at all is justified without a careful prior determination of necessity. The second, distinct objective is that those searches deemed necessary should be as limited as possible. Here, the specific evil is the "general warrant" abhorred by the colonists, and the problem is not that of intrusion *per se*, but of a general, exploratory rummaging in a person's belongings. The warrant accomplishes this second objective by requiring a "particular description" of the things to be seized.

The "plain view" doctrine is not in conflict with the first objective because plain view does not occur until a search is in progress. In each case, this initial intrusion is justified by a warrant or by an exception such as "hot pursuit" or search incident to a lawful arrest, or by an extraneous valid reason for the officer's presence. And, given the initial intrusion, the seizure of an object in plain view is consistent with the second objective, since it does not convert the search into a general or exploratory one. As against the minor peril to Fourth Amendment protections, there is a major gain in effective law enforcement. Where, once an otherwise lawful search is in progress, the police inadvertently come upon a piece of evidence, it would often be a needless inconvenience, and sometimes dangerous—to the evidence or to the police themselves— to require them to ignore it until they have obtained a warrant particularly describing it.

The limits on the doctrine are implicit in the statement of its rationale. The first of these is that plain view alone is never enough to justify the warrantless seizure of evidence. This is simply a corollary of the familiar principle discussed above, that no amount of probable cause can justify a warrantless search or seizure absent "exigent circumstances." Incontrovertible testimony of the senses that an incriminating object is on premises belonging to a criminal suspect may establish the fullest possible measure of probable cause. But even where the object is contraband, this Court has repeatedly stated and enforced the basic rule that the police may not enter and make a warrantless seizure.

The second limitation is that the discovery of evidence in plain view must be inadvertent. The rationale of the exception to the warrant requirement, as just stated, is that a plain-view seizure will not turn an initially valid (and therefore limited) search into a "general" one, while the inconvenience of procuring a warrant to cover an inadvertent discovery is great. But where the discovery is anticipated, where the police know in advance the location of the evidence and intend to seize it, the situation is altogether different. The requirement of a warrant to seize imposes no inconvenience whatever, or at least none which is constitutionally cognizable in a legal system that regards warrantless searches as *"per se* unreasonable" in the absence of "exigent circumstances."

If the initial intrusion is bottomed upon a warrant that fails to mention a particular object, though the police know its location and intend to seize it, then there is a violation of the express constitutional requirement of warrants particularly describing the things to be seized.

The initial intrusion may, of course, be legitimate not by a warrant but by one of the exceptions to the warrant requirement, such as hot pursuit or search incident to lawful arrest. But to extend the scope of such an intrusion to the seizure of objects—not contraband nor stolen nor dangerous in themselves—which the police know in advance they will find in plain view and intend to seize, would fly in the face of the basic rule that no amount of probable cause can justify a warrantless seizure.

In the light of what has been said, it is apparent that the "plain view" exception cannot justify the police seizure of the Pontiac car in this case. The police had ample opportunity to obtain a valid warrant; they knew the automobile's exact description and location well in advance; they intended to seize it when they came upon Coolidge's property. And this is not a case involving contraband or stolen goods or objects dangerous in themselves.

The seizure was therefore unconstitutional, and so was the subsequent search at the station house. Since evidence obtained in the course of the search was admitted at Coolidge's trial, the judgment must be reversed and the case remanded to the New Hampshire Supreme Court.

JUSTICE WHITE, with whom CHIEF JUSTICE BURGER joins, concurring and dissenting.

I would affirm the judgment. In my view, Coolidge's Pontiac was lawfully seized as evidence of the crime in plain sight and thereafter was lawfully searched.

The Court [imposes] a condition that the discovery of the disputed evidence be "inadvertent." If it is "anticipated," that is, if "the police know in advance the location of the evidence and intend to seize it," the seizure is invalid.

I have great difficulty with this approach. Let us suppose officers secure a warrant to search a house for a rifle. While staying well within the range of a rifle search, they discover two photographs of the murder victim, both in plain sight in the bedroom. Assume also that the discovery of the one photograph was inadvertent but finding the other was anticipated. The Court would permit the seizure of only one of the photographs. But in terms of the "minor" peril to Fourth Amendment values there is surely no difference between these two photographs: the interference with possession is the same in each case and the officers' appraisal of the photograph they expected to see is no less reliable than their judgment about the other. And in both situations the actual inconvenience and danger to evidence remain identical if the officers must depart and secure a warrant. The Court, however, states that the State will suffer no constitutionally cognizable inconvenience from invalidating anticipated seizures since it had probable cause to search for the items seized and could have included them in a warrant.

This seems a punitive and extravagant application of the exclusionary rule. If the police have probable cause to search for a photograph as well as a rifle and they proceed to seek a warrant, they could have no possible motive for deliberately including the rifle but omitting the photograph. Quite the contrary is true. Only oversight or careless mistake would explain the omission in the warrant application if the police were convinced they had probable cause to search for the photograph. Of course, they may misjudge the facts and not realize they have probable cause for the picture, or the magistrate may find against them and not issue a warrant for it. In either event the officers may validly seize the photograph for which they had no probable cause to search, but the other photograph is excluded from evidence when the Court subsequently determines that the officers, after all, had probable cause to search for it.

The Court admits that "it would be nonsense to pretend that our decision today reduces Fourth Amendment law to complete order and harmony." But it concludes that logical consistency cannot be attained in constitutional law and ultimately comes to rest upon its belief "that the result reached in this case is correct." It may be that constitutional law cannot be fully coherent and that constitutional principles ought not always be spun out to their logical limits, but this does not mean that we should cease to strive for clarity and consistency of analysis. Here the Court has a ready opportunity, one way or another, to bring clarity and certainty to a body of law that lower courts and law enforcement officials often find confusing. Instead, without apparent reason, it only increases their confusion by clinging to distinctions that are both unexplained and inexplicable.

––––––––––––

Justice Stewart's opinion in *Coolidge* set forth three requirements for the plain view exception: (1) the police must be legitimately or lawfully on the premises; (2) the discovery of the evidence must be inadvertent; and (3) it must be immediately apparent to the police that the items found in plain view are evidence of crime, contraband, or otherwise subject to seizure. Justice Stewart concluded that the plain view exception did not apply primarily because the discovery of Coolidge's Pontiac was not inadvertent—the police knew where the car was located and they had plenty of time to secure a search warrant.

Justice White was troubled by the inadvertence requirement in *Coolidge* and urged the Court to abandon it. In *Horton v. California*, the Supreme Court refined the elements of the plain view exception and, consistent with Justice White's suggestion, dispensed with the inadvertence requirement.

HORTON V. CALIFORNIA
496 U.S. 128 (1990)

JUSTICE STEVENS delivered the opinion of the Court.

In this case we revisit an issue that was considered, but not conclusively resolved, in *Coolidge v. New Hampshire*, 403 U.S. 443 (1971): Whether the warrantless seizure of evidence of crime in plain view is prohibited by the Fourth Amendment if the discovery of the evidence was not inadvertent. We conclude that even though inadvertence is a characteristic of most legitimate "plain-view" seizures, it is not a necessary condition.

I

Petitioner was convicted of the armed robbery of Erwin Wallaker, the treasurer of the San Jose Coin Club. When Wallaker returned to his home after the Club's annual show, he entered his garage and was accosted by two masked men, one armed with a machine gun and the other with an electrical shocking device, sometimes referred to as a "stun gun." The two men shocked Wallaker, bound and handcuffed him, and robbed him of jewelry and cash. During the encounter sufficient conversation took place to enable Wallaker subsequently to identify petitioner's distinctive voice. His identification was partially corroborated by a witness who saw the robbers leaving the scene and by evidence that petitioner had attended the coin show.

Sergeant LaRault, an experienced police officer, investigated the crime and determined that there was probable cause to search petitioner's home for the proceeds of the robbery and for the weapons used by the robbers. His affidavit for a search warrant referred to police reports that described the weapons as well as the proceeds, but the warrant issued by the Magistrate only authorized a search for the proceeds, including three specifically described rings.

Pursuant to the warrant, LaRault searched petitioner's residence, but he did not find the stolen property. During the course of the search, however, he discovered the weapons in plain view and seized them. Specifically, he seized an Uzi machine gun, a .38-caliber revolver, two stun guns, a handcuff key, a San Jose Coin Club advertising brochure, and a few items of clothing identified by the victim. LaRault testified that while he was searching for the rings, he also was interested in finding other evidence connecting petitioner to the robbery. Thus, the seized evidence was not discovered "inadvertently."

The trial court refused to suppress the evidence found in petitioner's home and, after a jury trial, petitioner was found guilty and sentenced to prison. The California Court of Appeal affirmed.

II

The criteria that generally guide "plain-view" seizures were set forth in *Coolidge v. New Hampshire.* [Justice Stewart's opinion in *Coolidge*] described the two limitations on the doctrine that he found implicit in its rationale: First, that "plain view *alone* is never enough to justify the warrantless seizure of evidence," and second, that "the discovery of evidence in plain view must be inadvertent."

It is, of course, an essential predicate to any valid warrantless seizure of incriminating evidence that the officer did not violate the Fourth Amendment in arriving at the place from which the evidence could be plainly viewed. There are, moreover, two additional conditions that must be satisfied to justify the warrantless seizure. First, not only must the item be in plain view; its incriminating character must also be "immediately apparent." Thus, in *Coolidge*, the cars were obviously in plain view, but their probative value remained uncertain until after the interiors were swept and examined microscopically. Second, not only must the officer be lawfully located in a place from which the object can be plainly seen, but he or she must also have a lawful right of access to the object itself.

III

Justice Stewart [in *Coolidge*] concluded that the inadvertence requirement was necessary to avoid a violation of the express constitutional requirement that a valid warrant must particularly describe the things to be seized.

The suggestion that the inadvertence requirement is necessary to prevent the police from conducting general searches, or from converting specific warrants into general warrants, is not persuasive because that interest is already served by the requirements that no warrant issue unless it "particularly describ[es] the place to be searched and the persons or things to be seized," and that a warrantless search be circumscribed by the exigencies which justify its initiation. Scrupulous adherence to these requirements serves the interests in limiting the area and duration of the search that the inadvertence requirement inadequately protects. Once those commands have been satisfied and the officer has a lawful right of access, however, no additional Fourth Amendment interest is furthered by requiring that the discovery of evidence be inadvertent. If the scope of the search exceeds that permitted by the terms of a validly issued warrant or the character of the relevant exception from the warrant requirement, the subsequent seizure is unconstitutional without more.

In this case, the scope of the search was not enlarged in the slightest by the omission of any reference to the weapons in the warrant. Indeed, if the three rings and other items named in the warrant had been found at the outset—or if petitioner had them in his possession and had responded to the warrant by producing them immediately—no search for weapons could have taken place. Again, Justice White's concurring and dissenting opinion in *Coolidge* is instructive: "Police with a warrant for a rifle may search only places where rifles might be and must terminate the search once the rifle is found; the inadvertence rule will in no way reduce the number of places into which they may lawfully look."

In this case the items seized from petitioner's home were discovered during a lawful search authorized by a valid warrant. When they were discovered, it was immediately apparent to the officer that they constituted incriminating evidence. He had probable cause, not only to obtain a warrant to search for the stolen property, but also to believe that the weapons and handguns had been used in the crime he was investigating. The search was authorized by the warrant; the seizure was authorized by the "plain-view" doctrine. The judgment is affirmed.

JUSTICE BRENNAN, with whom JUSTICE MARSHALL joins, dissenting.

I remain convinced that Justice Stewart correctly articulated the plain-view doctrine in *Coolidge v. New Hampshire*. The Fourth Amendment permits law enforcement officers to seize items for which they do not have a warrant when those items are found in plain view and (1) the officers are lawfully in a position to observe the items, (2) the discovery of the items is "inadvertent," and (3) it is immediately apparent to the officers that the items are evidence of a crime, contraband, or otherwise subject to seizure. In eschewing the inadvertent discovery requirement, the majority ignores the Fourth Amendment's express command that warrants particularly describe not only the *places* to be searched, but also the *things* to be seized. I respectfully dissent from this rewriting of the Fourth Amendment.

Fortunately, this decision should have only a limited impact, for the Court is not confronted today with what lower courts have described as a "pretextual" search. For example, if an officer enters a house pursuant to a warrant to search for evidence of one crime when he is really interested only in seizing evidence relating to another crime, for which he does not have a warrant, his search is "pretextual" and the fruits of that search should be suppressed. Similarly, an officer might use an exception to the generally applicable warrant requirement, such as "hot pursuit," as a pretext to enter a home to seize items he knows he will find in plain view. Such conduct would be a deliberate attempt to circumvent the constitutional requirement of a warrant "particularly describing the place to be searched, and the persons or things to be seized," and cannot be condoned.

The discovery of evidence in pretextual searches is not "inadvertent" and should be suppressed for that reason. But even state courts that have rejected the inadvertent discovery requirement have held that the Fourth Amendment prohibits pretextual searches. The Court's opinion today does not address pretextual searches, but I have no doubt that such searches violate the Fourth Amendment.

In *Arizona v. Hicks*, the Supreme Court clarified the last prong of the plain view exception, under which the incriminating character of an item found in plain view must be "immediately apparent." This requirement is satisfied only if the police have probable cause—without any manipulation or further "searching" of the item—to believe that it is connected to a crime; a lower standard, such as reasonable suspicion, will not suffice.

ARIZONA V. HICKS
480 U.S. 321 (1987)

JUSTICE SCALIA delivered the opinion of the Court.

In *Coolidge v. New Hampshire*, 403 U.S. 443 (1971), we said that in certain circumstances a warrantless seizure by police of an item that comes within plain view during their lawful search of a private area may be reasonable under the Fourth Amendment. We granted certiorari in the present case to decide whether this "plain view" doctrine may be invoked when the police have less than probable cause to believe that the item in question is evidence of a crime or is contraband.

I

On April 18, 1984, a bullet was fired through the floor of respondent's apartment, striking and injuring a man in the apartment below. Police officers arrived and entered respondent's apartment to search for the shooter, for other victims, and for weapons. They found and seized three weapons, including a sawed-off rifle, and in the course of their search also discovered a stocking-cap mask.

One of the policemen, Officer Nelson, noticed two sets of expensive stereo components, which seemed out of place in the squalid and otherwise ill-appointed four-room apartment. Suspecting that they were stolen, he read and recorded their serial numbers—moving some of the components, including a Bang and Olufsen turntable, in order to do so— which he then reported by phone to his headquarters. On being advised that the turntable had been taken in an armed robbery, he seized it immediately. It was later determined that some of the other serial numbers matched those on other stereo equipment taken in the same armed robbery, and a warrant was obtained and executed to seize that equipment as well. Respondent was subsequently indicted for the robbery.

The state trial court granted respondent's motion to suppress the evidence that had been seized. The Court of Appeals of Arizona affirmed. It was conceded that the initial entry and search, although warrantless, were justified by the exigent circumstance of the shooting. The Court of Appeals viewed the obtaining of the serial numbers, however, as an additional search, unrelated to that exigency. Both courts rejected the State's contention that Officer Nelson's actions were justified under the "plain view" doctrine of *Coolidge v. New Hampshire.* The Arizona Supreme Court denied review, and the State filed this petition.

II

As an initial matter, the State argues that Officer Nelson's actions constituted neither a "search" nor a "seizure" within the meaning of the Fourth Amendment. We agree that the mere recording of the serial numbers did not constitute a seizure. To be sure, that was the first step in a process by which respondent was eventually deprived of the stereo equipment. In and of itself, however, it did not "meaningfully interfere" with respondent's possessory interest in either the serial numbers or the equipment, and therefore did not amount to a seizure.

Officer Nelson's moving of the equipment, however, did constitute a "search" separate and apart from the search for the shooter, victims, and weapons that was the lawful objective of his entry into the apartment. Merely inspecting those parts of the turntable that came into view during the latter search would not have constituted an independent search, because it would have produced no additional invasion of respondent's privacy interest. But taking action, unrelated to the objectives of the authorized intrusion, which exposed to view concealed portions of the apartment or its contents, did produce a new invasion of respondent's privacy unjustified by the exigent circumstance that validated the entry. It matters not that the search uncovered nothing of any great personal value to respondent—serial numbers rather than (what might conceivably have been hidden behind or under the equipment) letters or photographs. A search is a search, even if it happens to disclose nothing but the bottom of a turntable.

III

The remaining question is whether the search was "reasonable" under the Fourth Amendment. On this aspect of the case we reject, at the outset, the apparent position of the Arizona Court of Appeals that because the officers' action directed to the stereo equipment was unrelated to the justification for their entry into respondent's apartment, it was *ipso facto* unreasonable. That lack of relationship *always* exists with regard to action validated under the "plain view" doctrine; where action is taken for the purpose justifying the entry, invocation of the doctrine is superfluous.

We turn, then, to application of the doctrine to the facts of this case. It is well established that under certain circumstances the police may *seize* evidence in plain view without a warrant. Those circumstances include situations where the initial intrusion that brings the police within plain view of such evidence is supported by one of the recognized exceptions to the warrant requirement, such as the exigent-circumstances intrusion here. It would be absurd to say that an object could lawfully be seized and taken from the premises, but could not be moved for closer examination. It is clear, therefore, that the search here was valid if the "plain view" doctrine would have sustained a seizure of the equipment.

There is no doubt it would have done so if Officer Nelson had probable cause to believe that the equipment was stolen. The State has conceded, however, that he had only a "reasonable suspicion," by which it means something less than probable cause. We have not ruled on the question whether probable cause is required in order to invoke the "plain view" doctrine.

We now hold that probable cause is required. To say otherwise would be to cut the "plain view" doctrine loose from its theoretical and practical moorings. The theory of that doctrine consists of extending to nonpublic places such as the home, where searches and seizures without a warrant are presumptively unreasonable, the police's longstanding authority to make warrantless seizures in public places of such objects as weapons and contraband. And the practical justification for that extension is the desirability of sparing police, whose viewing of the object in the course of a lawful search is as legitimate as it would have been in a public place, the inconvenience and the risk—to themselves or to preservation of the evidence—of going to obtain a warrant. Dispensing with the need for a warrant is worlds apart from permitting a lesser standard of *cause* for the seizure than a warrant would require, *i.e.*, the standard of probable cause. No reason is apparent why an object should routinely be seizable on lesser grounds, during an unrelated search and seizure, than would have been needed to obtain a warrant for that same object if it had been known to be on the premises.

We do not say, of course, that a seizure can never be justified on less than probable cause. We have held that it can—where, for example, the seizure is minimally intrusive and operational necessities render it the only practicable means of detecting certain types of crime. No special operational necessities are relied on here, however—but rather the mere fact that the items in question came lawfully within the officer's plain view. That alone cannot supplant the requirement of probable cause.

The same considerations preclude us from holding that, even though probable cause would have been necessary for a *seizure*, the *search* of objects in plain view that occurred here could be sustained on lesser grounds. A dwelling-place search, no less than a dwelling-place seizure, requires probable cause, and there is no reason in theory or practicality why application of the "plain view" doctrine would supplant that requirement. Although the interest protected by the Fourth Amendment injunction against unreasonable searches is quite different from that protected by its injunction against unreasonable seizures, neither the one nor the other is of inferior worth or necessarily requires only lesser protection. We have not elsewhere drawn a categorical distinction between the two insofar as concerns the degree of justification needed to establish the reasonableness of police action, and we see no reason for a distinction in the particular circumstances before us here. Indeed, to treat searches more liberally would especially erode the plurality's warning in *Coolidge* that "the 'plain view' doctrine may not be used to extend a general exploratory search from one object to another until something incriminating at last emerges." In short, whether legal authority to move the equipment could be found only as an inevitable concomitant of the authority to seize it, or also as a consequence of some independent power to search certain objects in plain view, probable cause to believe the equipment was stolen was required.

Justice O'Connor's dissent suggests that we uphold the action here on the ground that it was a "cursory inspection" rather than a "full-blown search," and could therefore be justified by reasonable suspicion instead of probable cause. As already noted, a truly cursory inspection—one that involves merely looking at what is already exposed to view, without disturbing it—is not a "search" for Fourth Amendment purposes, and therefore does not even require reasonable suspicion. We are unwilling to send police and judges into a new thicket of Fourth Amendment law, to seek a creature of uncertain description that is neither a "plain view" inspection nor yet a "full-blown search." Nothing in the prior opinions of this Court supports such a distinction.

Justice Powell's dissent reasonably asks what it is we would have had Officer Nelson do in these circumstances. The answer depends, of course, upon whether he had probable cause to conduct a search, a question that was not preserved in this case. If he had, then he should have done precisely what he did. If not, then he should have followed up his suspicions, if possible, by means other than a search—just as he would have had to do if, while walking along the street, he had noticed the same suspicious stereo equipment sitting inside a house a few feet away from him, beneath an open window. It may well be that, in such circumstances, no effective means short of a search exist. But there is nothing new in the realization that the Constitution sometimes insulates the criminality of a few in order to protect the privacy of us all. Our disagreement with the dissenters pertains to where the proper balance should be struck; we choose to adhere to the textual and traditional standard of probable cause.

The State contends that, even if Officer Nelson's search violated the Fourth Amendment, the court below should have admitted the evidence thus obtained under the "good faith" exception to the exclusionary rule. That was not the question on which certiorari was granted, and we decline to consider it.

JUSTICE O'CONNOR, with whom CHIEF JUSTICE REHNQUIST and JUSTICE POWELL join, dissenting.

The Court today gives the right answer to the wrong question. The Court asks whether the police must have probable cause before either seizing an object in plain view or conducting a full-blown search of that object, and concludes that they must. I agree. In my view, however, this case presents a different question: whether police must have probable cause before conducting a cursory inspection of an item in plain view. Because I conclude that such an inspection is reasonable if the police are aware of facts or circumstances that justify a reasonable suspicion that the item is evidence of a crime, I would reverse the judgment of the Arizona Court of Appeals, and therefore dissent.

In *Coolidge v. New Hampshire*, Justice Stewart summarized three requirements that the plurality thought must be satisfied for a plain-view search or seizure. First, the police must lawfully make an initial intrusion or otherwise be in a position from which they can view a particular area. Second, the officer must discover incriminating evidence "inadvertently." Third, it must be "immediately apparent" to the police that the items they observe may be evidence of a crime, contraband, or otherwise subject to seizure. These three requirements have never been expressly adopted by a majority of this Court, but as the considered opinion of four Members of this Court the *Coolidge* plurality should obviously be the point of reference for further discussion of the issue. There is no dispute in this case that the first two requirements have been satisfied. The officers were lawfully in the apartment pursuant to exigent circumstances, and the discovery of the stereo was inadvertent. Instead, the dispute in this case focuses on the application of the "immediately apparent" requirement; at issue is whether a police officer's reasonable suspicion is adequate to justify a cursory examination of an item in plain view.

The purpose of the "immediately apparent" requirement is to prevent general, exploratory rummaging in a person's belongings. If an officer could indiscriminately search every item in plain view, a search justified by a limited purpose—such as exigent circumstances—could be used to eviscerate the protections of the Fourth Amendment. In order to prevent such a general search, therefore, we require that the relevance of the item be "immediately apparent."

Thus, I agree with the Court that even under the plain-view doctrine, probable cause is required before the police seize an item, or conduct a full-blown search of evidence in plain view. Such a requirement of probable cause will prevent the plain-view doctrine from authorizing general searches. This is not to say, however, that even a mere inspection of a suspicious item must be supported by probable cause. When a police officer makes a cursory inspection of a suspicious item in plain view in order to determine whether it is indeed evidence of a crime, there is no "exploratory rummaging." Only those items that the police officer "reasonably suspects" as evidence of a crime may be inspected, and perhaps more importantly, the scope of such an inspection is quite limited. In short, if police officers have a reasonable, articulable suspicion that an object they come across during the course of a lawful search is evidence of crime, in my view they may make a cursory examination of the object to verify their suspicion. If the officers wish to go beyond such a cursory examination of the object, however, they must have probable cause.

In my view, the balance of the governmental and privacy interests strongly supports a reasonable-suspicion standard for the cursory examination of items in plain view. The additional intrusion caused by an inspection of an item in plain view for its serial number is miniscule.

Weighed against this minimal additional invasion of privacy are rather major gains in law enforcement. The use of identification numbers in tracing stolen property is a powerful law enforcement tool. Serial numbers are far more helpful and accurate in detecting stolen property than simple police recollection of the evidence. Given the prevalence of mass produced goods in our national economy, a serial number is often the only sure method of detecting stolen property. The balance of governmental and private interests strongly supports the view accepted by a majority of courts that a standard of reasonable suspicion meets the requirements of the Fourth Amendment.

Unfortunately, in its desire to establish a "bright-line" test, the Court has taken a step that ignores a substantial body of precedent and that places serious roadblocks to reasonable law enforcement practices. Indeed, in this case no warrant to search the stereo equipment for its serial number could have been obtained by the officers based on reasonable suspicion alone, and in the Court's view the officers may not even move the stereo turntable to examine its serial number. The theoretical advantages of the "search is a search" approach adopted by the Court today are simply too remote to justify the tangible and severe damage it inflicts on legitimate and effective law enforcement.

Even if probable cause were the appropriate standard, I have little doubt that it was satisfied here. When police officers, during the course of a search inquiring into grievously unlawful activity, discover the tools of a thief (a sawed-off rifle and a stocking mask) and observe in a small apartment *two* sets of stereo equipment that are both inordinately expensive in relation to their surroundings and known to be favored targets of larcenous activity, the flexible, common-sense standard of probable cause has been satisfied.

Because the Court today ignores the existence of probable cause, and in doing so upsets a widely accepted body of precedent on the standard of reasonableness for the cursory examination of evidence in plain view, I respectfully dissent.

———————

Collectively, *Coolidge v. New Hampshire*, *Horton v. California*, and *Arizona v. Hicks* establish the basic requirements of the plain view exception: Police may seize an item in plain view if they are legitimately or lawfully on the premises *and* it is immediately apparent that the item is evidence of a crime, contraband, or otherwise subject to seizure.

The first prong of the plain view exception can be satisfied in several ways. First, police may be legitimately or lawfully on the premises if no warrant is necessary to justify their presence. For example, no warrant is necessary when police enter an area generally open to the public, such as a park or shopping center. Second, police may be legitimately or lawfully on the premises if they have a valid warrant that authorizes their presence. For example, police may enter a home if they have a search warrant that authorizes them to look for evidence, or if they have an arrest warrant that authorizes them to take into custody one of the occupants. Third, police may be legitimately or lawfully on the premises if there is an exception to the warrant requirement that permits their presence. For example, exigent circumstances—such as screams or the sound of a gunshot—permit the police to enter private property without a warrant.

Under the second prong of the plain view exception, the incriminating character of an item found in plain view is "immediately apparent" if the police have probable cause—without any manipulation or further "searching" of the item—to believe it is connected to crime. A strong hunch or even reasonable suspicion that the item is evidence of crime or contraband will not suffice.

The facts in *Arizona v. Hicks* provide an opportunity to apply and analyze both prongs of the plain view exception. The police were legitimately in Hicks' apartment because a gunshot was fired from it, injuring someone on the floor below. Thus, exigent circumstances justified the warrantless entry into Hicks' apartment—the police needed to locate the shooter, the weapon, and other potential victims. Once inside the apartment, the officer saw the expensive stereo equipment in plain view. He suspected it was stolen because it looked out of place in an otherwise "squalid" apartment, and because he also saw guns and a stocking-cap mask in plain view in the apartment. But based on these facts, Arizona conceded that the officer only had a "reasonable suspicion" that the stereo was stolen when he saw it. That suspicion ripened into probable cause only *after* he turned over the stereo, recorded the serial numbers, called the police station, and confirmed that it had recently been reported stolen. Thus, the second prong of the plain view exception was not met—it was not "immediately apparent" to the officer that the stereo equipment was stolen until after he performed an additional search by turning it over to record the serial numbers. (For what it's worth, the discovery of the stereo equipment was also inadvertent because the officer was investigating a gunshot and did not anticipate finding a stolen stereo, but inadvertence is no longer required after *Horton v. California*.)

The plain view exception, as explained and applied in *Arizona v. Hicks*, is also a good example of a point raised at the beginning of this Chapter about how the various exceptions to the warrant requirement are not mutually exclusive. The exigent circumstances exception justified the entry into the apartment, and the plain view exception would have justified the seizure of any items—such as illegal drugs—whose incriminating character was immediately apparent.

Let's return for a moment to the hypothetical presented at the beginning of this section, involving a police officer with a valid warrant to search for and seize any illegal weapons in an apartment. While conducting the search, suppose the officer notices a loose floorboard in the back of a closet. The officer lifts up the floorboard, but she can't get close enough to actually see if anything is hidden in the exposed crevice. Instead, the officer reaches her hand into the crevice, moves it around a bit, and detects a plastic baggie that feels as though it contains some kind of powder. Based on her sense of touch, the officer suspects that the baggie contains cocaine. May the officer pull the baggie out of the crevice under the floorboard for further inspection?

As its name implies, the plain view exception usually involves what an officer can *see* when she is legitimately on the premises. But police are permitted to use all of their senses—including *smell* and *touch*—when they are lawfully present at a particular location. Accordingly, in *Minnesota v. Dickerson*, the Supreme Court suggested that there is a "plain touch" corollary to the plain view exception.

MINNESOTA V. DICKERSON
508 U.S. 366 (1993)

Two police officers spotted the defendant leaving a notorious "crack house." The defendant was walking toward the police, but upon spotting the squad car and making eye contact with one of the officers, he abruptly stopped and began walking in the opposite direction. The officers pursued him and ordered him to stop and submit to a patdown search (a "frisk"). During the frisk of the exterior of the defendant's clothing, the officer felt a small lump in the front jacket pocket. The officer examined the lump with his fingers, squeezing, sliding, and manipulating the pocket until concluding the item was a lump of crack cocaine wrapped in cellophane. The officer then reached into the defendant's pocket and retrieved a small plastic bag containing one-fifth of a gram of crack cocaine. In analyzing the facts, the Supreme Court drew an analogy to the plain view doctrine:

> Under [the plain view] doctrine, if police are lawfully in a position from which they view an object, if its incriminating character is immediately apparent, and if the officers have a lawful right of access to the object, they may seize it without a warrant. If, however, the police lack probable cause to believe that an object in plain view is contraband without conducting some further search of the object—i.e., if its incriminating character is not immediately apparent, the plain-view doctrine cannot justify its seizure.

> We think that this doctrine has an obvious application by analogy to cases in which an officer discovers contraband through the sense of touch during an otherwise lawful search. The rationale of the plain-view doctrine is that if contraband is left in open view and is observed by a police officer from a lawful vantage point, there has been no invasion of a legitimate expectation of privacy and thus no "search" within the meaning of the Fourth Amendment—or at least no search independent of the initial intrusion that gave the officers their vantage point. The warrantless seizure of contraband that presents itself in this manner is deemed justified by the realization that resort to a neutral magistrate under such circumstances would often be impracticable and would do little to promote the objectives of the Fourth Amendment. The same can be said of tactile discoveries of contraband. If a police officer lawfully pats down a suspect's outer clothing and feels an object whose contour or mass makes its identity immediately apparent, there has been no invasion of the suspect's privacy beyond that already authorized by the officer's search for weapons; if the object is contraband, its warrantless seizure would be justified by the same practical considerations that inhere in the plain-view context.

Relying heavily on the facts in *Arizona v. Hicks*, the Court in *Dickerson* held that the crack cocaine was inadmissible at Dickerson's trial for drug possession:

Once again, the analogy to the plain-view doctrine is apt. In *Arizona v. Hicks*, 480 U.S. 321 (1987), this Court held invalid the seizure of stolen stereo equipment found by police while executing a valid search for other evidence. Although the police were lawfully on the premises, they obtained probable cause to believe that the stereo equipment was contraband only after moving the equipment to permit officers to read its serial numbers. The subsequent seizure of the equipment could not be justified by the plain-view doctrine, this Court explained, because the incriminating character of the stereo equipment was not immediately apparent; rather, probable cause to believe that the equipment was stolen arose only as a result of a further search—the moving of the equipment—that was not authorized by a search warrant or by any exception to the warrant requirement. The facts of this case are very similar. Although the officer was lawfully in a position to feel the lump in respondent's pocket, because *Terry v. Ohio*, 392 U.S. 1 (1968), entitled him to place his hands upon respondent's jacket, the court below determined that the incriminating character of the object was not immediately apparent to him. Rather, the officer determined that the item was contraband only after conducting a further search, one not authorized by *Terry* or by any other exception to the warrant requirement. Because this further search of respondent's pocket was constitutionally invalid, the seizure of the cocaine that followed is likewise unconstitutional.

As *Dickerson* suggests, our hypothetical officer who feels the plastic baggie in the crevice beneath the floorboard should probably not pull it out for closer inspection unless the incriminating character of the item is "immediately apparent" based only on her brief touch. If the officer manipulates the baggie with her fingers in order to ascertain its contents and thereby develop probable cause to believe that it contains cocaine, the officer is performing a further "search" for which she has no justification under the original search warrant (authorizing a search for illegal weapons), nor under the "plain touch" corollary to the plain view exception. (We will revisit *Dickerson* in Chapter 6, which covers seizures of persons, including the "stop-and-frisk" doctrine announced in *Terry v. Ohio*.)

The Plain View Exception

1.   Police may seize an item in plain view if they are legitimately or lawfully on the premises *and* it is immediately apparent that the item is evidence of a crime, contraband, or otherwise subject to seizure.

2. A police officer can use all of his senses—including smell and touch—when he is lawfully present at a particular location. Accordingly, there is a "plain touch" corollary to the plain view exception that allows an officer to seize an item if he is legitimately in a position to feel it, and if it is immediately apparent—based only on his quick touch and without any further manipulation or "search"—that the item is evidence of a crime, contraband, or otherwise subject to seizure.

LEARN MORE WITH *LAW & ORDER*

In the following episode of *Law & Order* ("I.D.," Season 7, Episode 2), police detectives have an arrest warrant—but no search warrant—when they enter the apartment of William Dunbar, a suspect in a murder investigation. The detectives do not find Dunbar inside the apartment, but they do find a gun on a shelf in a closet, along with some photographs. Fingerprints connect the gun to Lucy Sullivan, the twin sister of Dunbar's wife. Lucy Sullivan is later charged with the murder of her sister. When prosecutors seek to use the gun against Sullivan, there is a dispute over whether it was found in plain view. As you watch the episode, consider two questions:

1. How does the episode illustrate the elements of the plain view exception?

2. If the plain view exception does not apply, as the judge decides, then why is the gun nonetheless admissible against the defendant, Lucy Sullivan?

The segments of the episode that depict the relevant Investigative Criminal Procedure issues appear at:

17:51 to 24:56

Law & Order **Episode**

"I.D.," Season 7, Episode 2

---

1. How does the episode illustrate the elements of the plain view exception?

The police are legitimately on premises because they have a valid arrest warrant for Dunbar. When he doesn't answer the door, it is appropriate for the police to go inside because he may be hiding in the apartment and, by virtue of the warrant, is subject to arrest. It was also appropriate for Detective Curtis to open the closet door because Dunbar might have been hiding there. Upon opening the closet door, Curtis claims that he saw the gun on the top shelf, in plain view. Because the detectives were investigating a murder in which the victim was shot, Curtis had probable cause to believe the gun in Dunbar's closet was connected to the crime. Or to put it somewhat differently, the incriminating nature of the gun is "immediately apparent."

Note that the judge does not believe that Detective Curtis saw the gun in plain view; he thinks that Detective Curtis conducted an additional search of the closet—one not authorized by a search warrant or probable cause—by feeling around the top shelf with his hand. This is analogous to the officer in *Arizona v. Hicks*, 480 U.S. 321 (1987), turning over the stereo to read the serial number, or the officer in *Minnesota v. Dickerson*, 508 U.S. 366 (1993), manipulating the exterior of Dickerson's pocket to confirm his suspicion that the object inside was a rock of crack cocaine. The judge is likewise skeptical when prosecutor Jamie Ross attempts to invoke the "plain touch" corollary to the plain view exception to justify the admissibility of the photographs. The police had no search warrant for the apartment, only an arrest warrant for Dunbar. As a consequence, Detective Curtis had no authority to search the closet shelf with his fingers once it was apparent that Dunbar wasn't hiding in the closet.

2. If the plain view exception does not apply, as the judge decides, then why is the gun nonetheless admissible against the defendant, Lucy Sullivan?

To answer this question, you must recall the material in Chapter 3 dealing with the *Katz* Test and the rule of "standing" limiting the ability of certain persons to challenge a search. When the judge initially excludes the gun because he believes it was not found in plain view, that only makes the gun inadmissible against William Dunbar, the owner of the apartment, since it was *his* expectation of privacy that was violated when police searched his apartment without a search warrant. Prosecutor Jack McCoy correctly points out that Lucy Sullivan has no legal "standing" to object to the search unless *her* expectation of privacy in the apartment was also violated by the police. Recall that the first prong of the *Katz* Test asks whether the defendant herself had a reasonable expectation of privacy in the place or thing that was searched. Under the New York appellate court decision cited by McCoy, *People v. Ortiz*, 83 N.Y.2d 840 (1994), an overnight guest is entitled to a reasonable expectation of privacy in a home in which she is staying, but a more casual visitor is not. (Two U.S. Supreme Court decisions excerpted in Chapter 3, *Minnesota v. Olson*, 495 U.S. 91 (1990), and *Minnesota v. Carter*, 525 U.S. 83 (1998), reached the same conclusion.) In order to have "standing" to challenge the admissibility of the gun at her trial, Lucy Sullivan would have to admit that she was an overnight guest in Dunbar's apartment on the night immediately preceding the search. Such an admission—that she was, perhaps, having an affair with Dunbar—would provide the prosecutors with powerful evidence of a motive to murder her sister. For this reason, Sullivan's attorney will not permit his client to make what the judge describes as a "naughty confession," and the gun is admissible into evidence against Lucy Sullivan.

D. THE AUTOMOBILE EXCEPTION

The automobile exception allows police who have legitimately stopped a vehicle and have probable cause to believe that items subject to seizure are being carried within it to search the vehicle without a warrant. The Supreme Court first articulated the rule and its rationale in an old Prohibition-era case, *Carroll v. U.S.*

CARROLL V. U.S.
267 U.S. 132 (1925)

In the course of an investigation, federal agents developed probable cause to believe that Carroll was transporting alcohol in his car in violation of the National Prohibition Act. The agents stopped the car and searched it without a warrant, discovering 68 bottles of whiskey and gin hidden behind the upholstery of the seats. Carroll claimed that the search violated the Fourth Amendment because the federal agents had no warrant. The Supreme Court disagreed, declaring that the mobile nature of the vehicle made it impractical for the police to obtain a warrant:

> On reason and authority, the true rule is that, if the search and seizure without a warrant are made upon probable cause, that is, upon a belief, reasonably arising out of circumstances known to the seizing officer, that an automobile or other vehicle contains that which by law is subject to seizure and destruction, the search and seizure are valid.

The Court concluded that the mobile nature of vehicles justified a departure from the warrant requirement:

> [T]he guaranty of freedom from unreasonable searches and seizures by the Fourth Amendment has been construed, practically since the beginning of the Government, as recognizing a necessary difference between a search of a store, dwelling house or other structure in respect of which a proper official warrant readily may be obtained, and a search of a ship, motor boat, wagon or automobile, for contraband goods, where it is not practicable to secure a warrant because the vehicle can be quickly moved out of the locality or jurisdiction in which the warrant must be sought.

In *Chambers v. Maroney*, the Supreme Court expanded the automobile exception, permitting police to perform a search without a warrant after the vehicle had been taken to the police station and was no longer mobile.

CHAMBERS V. MARONEY
399 U.S. 42 (1970)

JUSTICE WHITE delivered the opinion of the Court.

The principal question in this case concerns the admissibility of evidence seized from an automobile, in which petitioner was riding at the time of his arrest, after the automobile was taken to a police station and was there thoroughly searched without a warrant.

I

During the night of May 20, 1963, a Gulf service station in North Braddock, Pennsylvania, was robbed by two men, each of whom carried and displayed a gun. The robbers took the currency from the cash register; the service station attendant, one Stephen Kovacich, was directed to place the coins in his right-hand glove, which was then taken by the robbers. Two teenagers, who had earlier noticed a blue compact station wagon circling the block in the vicinity of the Gulf station, then saw the station wagon speed away from a parking lot close to the Gulf station. About the same time, they learned that the Gulf station had been robbed. They reported to police, who arrived immediately, that four men were in the station wagon and one was wearing a green sweater. Kovacich told the police that one of the men who robbed him was wearing a green sweater and the other was wearing a trench coat. A description of the car and the two robbers was broadcast over the police radio. Within an hour, a light blue compact station wagon answering the description and carrying four men was stopped by the police about two miles from the Gulf station. Petitioner was one of the men in the station wagon. He was wearing a green sweater and there was a trench coat in the car. The occupants were arrested and the car was driven to the police station. In the course of a thorough search of the car at the station, the police found concealed in a compartment under the dashboard two .38-caliber revolvers (one loaded with dumdum bullets), a right-hand glove containing small change, and certain cards bearing the name of Raymond Havicon, the attendant at a Boron service station in McKeesport, Pennsylvania, who had been robbed at gunpoint on May 13, 1963. In the course of a warrant-authorized search of petitioner's home the day after petitioner's arrest, police found and seized certain .38-caliber ammunition, including some dumdum bullets similar to those found in one of the guns taken from the station wagon.

Petitioner was indicted for both robberies. His first trial ended in a mistrial but he was convicted of both robberies at the second trial. Both Kovacich and Havicon identified petitioner as one of the robbers. The materials taken from the station wagon were introduced into evidence, Kovacich identifying his glove and Havicon the cards taken in the May 13 robbery. The bullets seized at petitioner's house were also introduced over objections of petitioner's counsel. Petitioner was sentenced to a term of four to eight years' imprisonment for the May 13 robbery and to a term of two to seven years' imprisonment for the May 20 robbery, the sentences to run consecutively.

II

We pass quickly the claim that the search of the automobile was the fruit of an unlawful arrest. Both the courts below thought the arresting officers had probable cause to make the arrest. We agree. Having talked to the teenage observers and to the victim Kovacich, the police had ample cause to stop a light blue compact station wagon carrying four men and to arrest the occupants, one of whom was wearing a green sweater and one of whom had a trench coat with him in the car.

Even so, the search that produced the incriminating evidence was made at the police station some time after the arrest and cannot be justified as a search incident to an arrest: Once an accused is under arrest and in custody, then a search made at another place, without a warrant, is simply not incident to the arrest; the reasons that have been thought sufficient to justify warrantless searches carried out in connection with an arrest no longer obtain when the accused is safely in custody at the station house.

There are, however alternative grounds arguably justifying the search of the car in this case. The police had probable cause to believe that the robbers, carrying guns and the fruits of the crime, had fled the scene in a light blue compact station wagon which would be carrying four men, one wearing a green sweater and another wearing a trench coat. As the state courts correctly held, there was probable cause to arrest the occupants of the station wagon that the officers stopped; just as obviously was there probable cause to search the car for guns and stolen money.

In terms of the circumstances justifying a warrantless search, the Court has long distinguished between an automobile and a home or office. In *Carroll v. U.S.*, 267 U.S. 132 (1925), the issue was the admissibility in evidence of contraband liquor seized in a warrantless search of a car on the highway. After surveying the law from the time of the adoption of the Fourth Amendment onward, the Court held that automobiles and other conveyances may be searched without a warrant in circumstances that would not justify the search without a warrant of a house or an office, provided that there is probable cause to believe that the car contains articles that the officers are entitled to seize.

The Court [in *Carroll*] also noted that the search of an auto on probable cause proceeds on a theory wholly different from that justifying the search incident to an arrest: "The right to search and the validity of the seizure are not dependent on the right to arrest. They are dependent on the reasonable cause the seizing officer has for belief that the contents of the automobile offend against the law." Finding that there was probable cause for the search and seizure at issue before it, the Court affirmed the convictions.

Neither *Carroll* nor other cases in this Court require or suggest that, in every conceivable circumstance, the search of an auto even with probable cause may be made without the extra protection for privacy that a warrant affords. But the circumstances that furnish probable cause to search a particular auto for particular articles are most often unforeseeable; moreover, the opportunity to search is fleeting since a car is readily movable. Where this is true, as in *Carroll* and the case before us now, if an effective search is to be made at any time, either the search must be made immediately without a warrant or the car itself must be seized and held without a warrant for whatever period is necessary to obtain a warrant for the search.

In enforcing the Fourth Amendment's prohibition against unreasonable searches and seizures, the Court has insisted upon probable cause as a minimum requirement for a reasonable search permitted by the Constitution. As a general rule, it has also required the judgment of a magistrate on the probable-cause issue and the issuance of a warrant before a search is made. Only in exigent circumstances will the judgment of the police as to probable cause serve as a sufficient authorization for a search. *Carroll* holds a search warrant unnecessary where there is probable cause to search an automobile stopped on the highway; the car is movable, the occupants are alerted, and the car's contents may never be found again if a warrant must be obtained. Hence an immediate search is constitutionally permissible.

Arguably, because of the preference for a magistrate's judgment, only the immobilization of the car should be permitted until a search warrant is obtained; arguably, only the "lesser" intrusion is permissible until the magistrate authorizes the "greater." But which is the "greater" and which the "lesser" intrusion is itself a debatable question and the answer may depend on a variety of circumstances. For constitutional purposes, we see no difference between, on the one hand, seizing and holding a car before presenting the probable cause issue to a magistrate and, on the other hand, carrying out an immediate search without a warrant. Given probable cause to search, either course is reasonable under the Fourth Amendment.

On the facts before us, the blue station wagon could have been searched on the spot when it was stopped, since there was probable cause to search and it was a fleeting target for a search. The probable-cause factor still obtained at the station house, and so did the mobility of the car, unless the Fourth Amendment permits a warrantless seizure of the car and the denial of its use to anyone until a warrant is secured. In that event, there is little to choose in terms of practical consequences between an immediate search without a warrant and the car's immobilization until a warrant is obtained.

In *California v. Carney*, the Supreme Court applied the automobile exception to permit the warrantless search of a parked motor home in which the defendant was residing. The Supreme Court made it clear that it was unwilling to distinguish among the different types and sizes of vehicles subject to the automobile exception.

CALIFORNIA V. CARNEY
471 U.S. 386 (1985)

CHIEF JUSTICE BURGER delivered the opinion of the Court.

We granted certiorari to decide whether law enforcement agents violated the Fourth Amendment when they conducted a warrantless search, based on probable cause, of a fully mobile "motor home" located in a public place.

I

On May 31, 1979, Drug Enforcement Agency Agent Robert Williams watched respondent, Charles Carney, approach a youth in downtown San Diego. The youth accompanied Carney to a Dodge Mini Motor Home parked in a nearby lot. Carney and the youth closed the window shades in the motor home, including one across the front window. Agent Williams had previously received uncorroborated information that the same motor home was used by another person who was exchanging marihuana for sex. Williams, with assistance from other agents, kept the motor home under surveillance for the entire one and one-quarter hours that Carney and the youth remained inside. When the youth left the motor home, the agents followed and stopped him. The youth told the agents that he had received marihuana in return for allowing Carney sexual contacts.

At the agents' request, the youth returned to the motor home and knocked on its door; Carney stepped out. The agents identified themselves as law enforcement officers. Without a warrant or consent, one agent entered the motor home and observed marihuana, plastic bags, and a scale of the kind used in weighing drugs on a table. Agent Williams took Carney into custody and took possession of the motor home. A subsequent search of the motor home at the police station revealed additional marihuana in the cupboards and refrigerator.

Respondent was charged with possession of marihuana for sale. At a preliminary hearing, he moved to suppress the evidence discovered in the motor home. The Magistrate denied the motion, upholding the initial search as a justifiable search for other persons, and the subsequent search as a routine inventory search.

Respondent renewed his suppression motion in the Superior Court. The Superior Court also rejected the claim, holding that there was probable cause to arrest respondent, that the search of the motor home was authorized under the automobile exception to the Fourth Amendment's warrant requirement, and that the motor home itself could be seized without a warrant as an instrumentality of the crime. Respondent then pleaded *nolo contendere* to the charges against him, and was placed on probation for three years.

Respondent appealed from the order placing him on probation. The California Court of Appeal affirmed, reasoning that the vehicle exception applied to respondent's motor home.

The California Supreme Court reversed the conviction. The Supreme Court did not disagree with the conclusion of the trial court that the agents had probable cause to arrest respondent and to believe that the vehicle contained evidence of a crime; however, the court held that the search was unreasonable because no warrant was obtained, rejecting the State's argument that the vehicle exception to the warrant requirement should apply. That court reached its decision by concluding that the mobility of a vehicle "is no longer the prime justification for the automobile exception; rather, the answer lies in the diminished expectation of privacy which surrounds the automobile." The California Supreme Court held that the expectations of privacy in a motor home are more like those in a dwelling than in an automobile because the primary function of motor homes is not to provide transportation but to "provide the occupant with living quarters."

We granted certiorari. We reverse.

II

There are, of course, exceptions to the general rule that a warrant must be secured before a search is undertaken; one is the so-called "automobile exception" at issue in this case. This exception to the warrant requirement was first set forth by the Court 60 years ago in *Carroll v. U.S.*, 267 U.S. 132 (1925). There, the Court recognized that the privacy interests in an automobile are constitutionally protected; however, it held that the ready mobility of the automobile justifies a lesser degree of protection of those interests.

[A]lthough ready mobility alone was perhaps the original justification for the vehicle exception, our later cases have made clear that ready mobility is not the only basis for the exception. The reasons for the vehicle exception, we have said, are twofold. Besides the element of mobility, less rigorous warrant requirements govern because the expectation of privacy with respect to one's automobile is significantly less than that relating to one's home or office.

Even in cases where an automobile was not immediately mobile, the lesser expectation of privacy resulting from its use as a readily mobile vehicle justified application of the vehicular exception. In some cases, the configuration of the vehicle contributed to the lower expectations of privacy; for example, we held that, because the passenger compartment of a standard automobile is relatively open to plain view, there are lesser expectations of privacy. But even when enclosed "repository" areas have been involved, we have concluded that the lesser expectations of privacy warrant application of the exception. We have applied the exception in the context of a locked car trunk, a sealed package in a car trunk, a closed compartment under the dashboard, the interior of a vehicle's upholstery, or sealed packages inside a covered pickup truck.

These reduced expectations of privacy derive not from the fact that the area to be searched is in plain view, but from the pervasive regulation of vehicles capable of traveling on the public highways. Automobiles, unlike homes, are subjected to pervasive and continuing governmental regulation and controls, including periodic inspection and licensing requirements. As an everyday occurrence, police stop and examine vehicles when license plates or inspection stickers have expired, or if other violations, such as exhaust fumes or excessive noise, are noted, or if headlights or other safety equipment are not in proper working order.

The public is fully aware that it is accorded less privacy in its automobiles because of this compelling governmental need for regulation. Historically, individuals always have been on notice that movable vessels may be stopped and searched on facts giving rise to probable cause that the vehicle contains contraband, without the protection afforded by a magistrate's prior evaluation of those facts. In short, the pervasive schemes of regulation, which necessarily lead to reduced expectations of privacy, and the exigencies attendant to ready mobility justify searches without prior recourse to the authority of a magistrate so long as the overriding standard of probable cause is met.

When a vehicle is being used on the highways, or if it is readily capable of such use and is found stationary in a place not regularly used for residential purposes—temporary or otherwise—the two justifications for the vehicle exception come into play. First, the vehicle is obviously readily mobile by the turn of an ignition key, if not actually moving. Second, there is a reduced expectation of privacy stemming from its use as a licensed motor vehicle subject to a range of police regulation inapplicable to a fixed dwelling. At least in these circumstances, the overriding societal interests in effective law enforcement justify an immediate search before the vehicle and its occupants become unavailable.

While it is true that respondent's vehicle possessed some, if not many of the attributes of a home, it is equally clear that the vehicle falls clearly within the scope of the exception laid down in *Carroll* and applied in succeeding cases. Like the automobile in *Carroll*, respondent's motor home was readily mobile. Absent the prompt search and seizure, it could readily have been moved beyond the reach of the police. Furthermore, the vehicle was licensed to operate on public streets, was serviced in public places, and was subject to extensive regulation and inspection. And the vehicle was so situated that an objective observer would conclude that it was being used not as a residence, but as a vehicle.

Respondent urges us to distinguish his vehicle from other vehicles within the exception because it was *capable of functioning as a home.* In our increasingly mobile society, many vehicles used for transportation can be and are being used not only for transportation but for shelter, *i.e.,* as a "home" or "residence." To distinguish between respondent's motor home and an ordinary sedan for purposes of the vehicle exception would require that we apply the exception depending upon the size of the vehicle and the quality of its appointments. Moreover, to fail to apply the exception to vehicles such as a motor home ignores the fact that a motor home lends itself easily to use as an instrument of illicit drug traffic and other illegal activity.

Our application of the vehicle exception has never turned on the other uses to which a vehicle might be put. The exception has historically turned on the ready mobility of the vehicle, and on the presence of the vehicle in a setting that objectively indicates that the vehicle is being used for transportation.[3] These two requirements for application of the exception ensure that law enforcement officials are not unnecessarily hamstrung in their efforts to detect and prosecute criminal activity, and that the legitimate privacy interests of the public are protected. Applying the vehicle exception in these circumstances allows the essential purposes served by the exception to be fulfilled, while assuring that the exception will acknowledge legitimate privacy interests.

III

The question remains whether, apart from the lack of a warrant, this search was unreasonable. Under the vehicle exception to the warrant

---

[3] We need not pass on the application of the vehicle exception to a motor home that is situated in a way or place that objectively indicates that it is being used as a residence. Among the factors that might be relevant in determining whether a warrant would be required in such a circumstance is its location, whether the vehicle is readily mobile or instead, for instance, elevated on blocks, whether the vehicle is licensed, whether it is connected to utilities, and whether it has convenient access to a public road.

requirement, only the prior approval of the magistrate is waived; the search otherwise must be such as the magistrate could authorize.

This search was not unreasonable; it was plainly one that the magistrate could authorize if presented with these facts. The DEA agents had fresh, direct, uncontradicted evidence that the respondent was distributing a controlled substance from the vehicle, apart from evidence of other possible offenses. The agents thus had abundant probable cause to enter and search the vehicle for evidence of a crime notwithstanding its possible use as a dwelling place.

JUSTICE STEVENS, with whom JUSTICE BRENNAN and JUSTICE MARSHALL join, dissenting.

Our prior cases teach us that inherent mobility is not a sufficient justification for the fashioning of an exception to the warrant requirement, especially in the face of heightened expectations of privacy in the location searched. Motor homes, by their common use and construction, afford their owners a substantial and legitimate expectation of privacy when they dwell within. When a motor home is parked in a location that is removed from the public highway, I believe that society is prepared to recognize that the expectations of privacy within it are not unlike the expectations one has in a fixed dwelling. As a general rule, such places may only be searched with a warrant based upon probable cause. Warrantless searches of motor homes are only reasonable when the motor home is traveling on the public streets or highways, or when exigent circumstances otherwise require an immediate search without the expenditure of time necessary to obtain a warrant.

In this case, the motor home was parked in an off-the-street lot only a few blocks from the courthouse in downtown San Diego where dozens of magistrates were available to entertain a warrant application. The officers clearly had the element of surprise with them, and with curtains covering the windshield, the motor home offered no indication of any imminent departure. The officers plainly had probable cause to arrest the respondent and search the motor home, and on this record, it is inexplicable why they eschewed the safe harbor of a warrant.

In my opinion, searches of places that regularly accommodate a wide range of private human activity are fundamentally different from searches of automobiles which primarily serve a public transportation function. Although it may not be a castle, a motor home is usually the functional equivalent of a hotel room, a vacation and retirement home, or a hunting and fishing cabin. These places may be as Spartan as a humble cottage when compared to the most majestic mansion, but the highest and most legitimate expectations of privacy associated with these temporary abodes should command the respect of this Court. In my opinion, a warrantless search of living quarters in a motor home is presumptively unreasonable absent exigent circumstances.

In *California v. Acevedo*, the Supreme Court held that if police have probable cause to search a vehicle under the automobile exception, they may also search any containers found within the vehicle.

CALIFORNIA V. ACEVEDO
500 U.S. 565 (1991)

JUSTICE BLACKMUN delivered the opinion of the Court.

This case requires us once again to consider the so-called "automobile exception" to the warrant requirement of the Fourth Amendment and its application to the search of a closed container in the trunk of a car.

I

On October 28, 1987, Officer Coleman of the Santa Ana, Cal., Police Department received a telephone call from a federal drug enforcement agent in Hawaii. The agent informed Coleman that he had seized a package containing marijuana which was to have been delivered to the Federal Express Office in Santa Ana and which was addressed to J.R. Daza at 805 West Stevens Avenue in that city. The agent arranged to send the package to Coleman instead. Coleman then was to take the package to the Federal Express office and arrest the person who arrived to claim it.

Coleman received the package on October 29, verified its contents, and took it to the Senior Operations Manager at the Federal Express office. At about 10:30 a.m. on October 30, a man, who identified himself as Jamie Daza, arrived to claim the package. He accepted it and drove to his apartment on West Stevens. He carried the package into the apartment.

At 11:45 a.m., officers observed Daza leave the apartment and drop the box and paper that had contained the marijuana into a trash bin. Coleman at that point left the scene to get a search warrant. About 12:05 p.m., the officers saw Richard St. George leave the apartment carrying a blue knapsack which appeared to be half full. The officers stopped him as he was driving off, searched the knapsack, and found 1 1/2 pounds of marijuana.

At 12:30 p.m., respondent Charles Steven Acevedo arrived. He entered Daza's apartment, stayed for about 10 minutes, and reappeared carrying a brown paper bag that looked full. The officers noticed that the bag was the size of one of the wrapped marijuana packages sent from Hawaii. Acevedo walked to a silver Honda in the parking lot. He placed the bag in the trunk of the car and started to drive away. Fearing the loss of evidence, officers in a marked police car stopped him. They opened the trunk and the bag, and found marijuana.

Respondent was charged in state court with possession of marijuana for sale. He moved to suppress the marijuana found in the car. The motion was denied. He then pleaded guilty but appealed the denial of the suppression motion.

The California Court of Appeal, Fourth District, concluded that the marijuana found in the paper bag in the car's trunk should have been suppressed. The court concluded that the officers had probable cause to believe that the paper bag contained drugs but lacked probable cause to suspect that Acevedo's car, itself, otherwise contained contraband. Although the court agreed that the officers could seize the paper bag, it held that they could not open the bag without first obtaining a warrant for that purpose.

We granted certiorari to reexamine the law applicable to a closed container in an automobile, a subject that has troubled courts and law enforcement officers since it was first considered.

II

Contemporaneously with the adoption of the Fourth Amendment, the First Congress, and, later, the Second and Fourth Congresses, distinguished between the need for a warrant to search for contraband concealed in "a dwelling house or similar place" and the need for a warrant to search for contraband concealed in a movable vessel. In *Carroll v. U.S.*, 267 U.S. 132 (1925), this Court held that a warrantless search of an automobile, based upon probable cause to believe that the vehicle contained evidence of crime in the light of an exigency arising out of the likely disappearance of the vehicle, did not contravene the Warrant Clause of the Fourth Amendment.

The Court refined the exigency requirement in *Chambers v. Maroney*, 399 U.S. 42 (1970), when it held that the existence of exigent circumstances was to be determined at the time the automobile is seized. The car search at issue in *Chambers* took place at the police station, where the vehicle was immobilized, some time after the driver had been arrested. Given probable cause and exigent circumstances at the time the vehicle was first stopped, the Court held that the later warrantless search at the station passed constitutional muster. The validity of the later search derived from the ruling in *Carroll* that an immediate search without a warrant at the moment of seizure would have been permissible. The Court reasoned in *Chambers* that the police could search later whenever they could have searched earlier, had they so chosen. Following *Chambers*, if the police have probable cause to justify a warrantless seizure of an automobile on a public roadway, they may conduct either an immediate or a delayed search of the vehicle.

In *U.S. v. Ross*, 456 U.S. 798 (1982), we held that a warrantless search of an automobile under the *Carroll* doctrine could include a search of a container or package found inside the car when such a search was supported by probable cause. The warrantless search of Ross' car occurred after an informant told the police that he had seen Ross complete a drug transaction using drugs stored in the trunk of his car. The police stopped the car, searched it, and discovered in the trunk a brown paper bag containing drugs. We decided that the search of Ross' car was not unreasonable under the Fourth Amendment: "The scope of a warrantless search based on probable cause is no narrower—and no broader—than the scope of a search authorized by a warrant supported by probable cause." Thus, "if probable cause justifies the search of a lawfully stopped vehicle, it justifies the search of every part of the vehicle and its contents that may conceal the object of the search." In *Ross*, therefore, we clarified the scope of the *Carroll* doctrine as properly including a "probing search" of compartments and containers within the automobile so long as the search is supported by probable cause.

III

The facts in this case closely resemble the facts in *Ross*. In *Ross*, the police had probable cause to believe that drugs were stored in the trunk of a particular car. Here, the California Court of Appeal concluded that the police had probable cause to believe that respondent was carrying marijuana in a bag in his car's trunk. Furthermore, for what it is worth, in *Ross*, as here, the drugs in the trunk were contained in a brown paper bag.

We now must decide the question deferred in *Ross*: whether the Fourth Amendment requires the police to obtain a warrant to open the sack in a movable vehicle simply because they lack probable cause to search the entire car. We conclude that it does not.

IV

We now agree that a container found after a general search of the automobile and a container found in a car after a limited search for the container are equally easy for the police to store and for the suspect to hide or destroy. In fact, we see no principled distinction in terms of either the privacy expectation or the exigent circumstances between the paper bag found by the police in *Ross* and the paper bag found by the police here. Furthermore, by attempting to distinguish between a container for which the police are specifically searching and a container which they come across in a car, we have provided only minimal protection for privacy and have impeded effective law enforcement.

The line between probable cause to search a vehicle and probable cause to search a package in that vehicle is not always clear, and separate rules that govern the two objects to be searched may enable the police to broaden their power to make warrantless searches and disserve privacy interests. We noted this in *Ross* in the context of a search of an entire vehicle. Recognizing that under *Carroll*, the "entire vehicle itself could be searched without a warrant," we concluded that "prohibiting police from opening immediately a container in which the object of the search is most likely to be found and instead forcing them first to comb the entire vehicle would actually exacerbate the intrusion on privacy interests." At the moment when officers stop an automobile, it may be less than clear whether they suspect with a high degree of certainty that the vehicle contains drugs in a bag or simply contains drugs. If the police know that they may open a bag only if they are actually searching the entire car, they may search more extensively than they otherwise would in order to establish the general probable cause required by *Ross*. We cannot see the benefit of a rule that requires law enforcement officers to conduct a more intrusive search in order to justify a less intrusive one.

Finally, the search of a paper bag intrudes far less on individual privacy than does the incursion sanctioned long ago in *Carroll*. In that case, prohibition agents slashed the upholstery of the automobile. This Court nonetheless found their search to be reasonable under the Fourth Amendment. If destroying the interior of an automobile is not unreasonable, we cannot conclude that looking inside a closed container is. We now hold that the Fourth Amendment does not compel separate treatment for an automobile search that extends only to a container within the vehicle. The interpretation of the *Carroll* doctrine set forth in *Ross* now applies to all searches of containers found in an automobile. In other words, the police may search without a warrant if their search is supported by probable cause.

In the case before us, the police had probable cause to believe that the paper bag in the automobile's trunk contained marijuana. That probable cause now allows a warrantless search of the paper bag. The facts in the record reveal that the police did not have probable cause to believe that contraband was hidden in any other part of the automobile and a search of the entire vehicle would have been without probable cause and unreasonable under the Fourth Amendment.

Until today, this Court has drawn a curious line between the search of an automobile that coincidentally turns up a container and the search of a container that coincidentally turns up in an automobile. The protections of the Fourth Amendment must not turn on such coincidences. We therefore interpret *Carroll* as providing one rule to govern all automobile searches. The police may search an automobile and the containers within it where they have probable cause to believe contraband or evidence is contained.

JUSTICE STEVENS, with whom JUSTICE MARSHALL joins, dissenting.

It is a cardinal principle that searches conducted outside the judicial process, without prior approval by judge or magistrate, are *per se* unreasonable under the Fourth Amendment—subject only to a few specifically established and well-delineated exceptions.

Our decisions have always acknowledged that the warrant requirement imposes a burden on law enforcement. And our cases have not questioned that trained professionals normally make reliable assessments of the existence of probable cause to conduct a search. We have repeatedly held, however, that these factors are outweighed by the individual interest in privacy that is protected by advance judicial approval. The Fourth Amendment dictates that the privacy interest is paramount, no matter how marginal the risk of error might be if the legality of warrantless searches were judged only after the fact.

In its opinion today, the Court recognizes that the police did not have probable cause to search respondent's vehicle and that a search of anything but the paper bag that respondent had carried from Daza's apartment and placed in the trunk of his car would have been unconstitutional. Moreover, as I read the opinion, the Court assumes that the police could not have made a warrantless inspection of the bag before it was placed in the car. Finally, the Court also does not question the fact that, under our prior cases, it would have been lawful for the police to seize the container and detain it (and respondent) until they obtained a search warrant.

The Court does not attempt to identify any exigent circumstances that would justify its refusal to apply the general rule against warrantless searches.

Every citizen clearly has an interest in the privacy of the contents of his or her luggage, briefcase, handbag or any other container that conceals private papers and effects from public scrutiny. That privacy interest has been recognized repeatedly in cases spanning more than a century. Under the Court's holding today, the privacy interest that protects the contents of a suitcase or a briefcase from a warrantless search when it is in public view simply vanishes when its owner climbs into a taxicab. Unquestionably, today's decision will result in a significant loss of individual privacy.

The Court's suggestion that [earlier decisions] have created a significant burden on effective law enforcement is unsupported, inaccurate, and, in any event, an insufficient reason for creating a new exception to the warrant requirement. Even if the warrant requirement does inconvenience the police to some extent, that fact does not distinguish this constitutional requirement from any other procedural protection secured by the Bill of Rights. It is merely a part of the price that our society must pay in order to preserve its freedom.

In *Wyoming v. Houghton*, the Supreme Court held that if the police have probable cause to search a vehicle under the automobile exception, the search may also extend to a passenger's personal effects within the vehicle. The search of the passenger's belongings may proceed even if the police have no reason to suspect criminal activity on the part of the passenger or efforts by the driver to hide contraband in the passenger's effects.

WYOMING V. HOUGHTON
526 U.S. 295 (1999)

A Wyoming Highway Patrol officer stopped an automobile for speeding and driving with a faulty brake light. There were three passengers in the front seat of the car: David Young (the driver), his girlfriend, and Sandra Houghton. The officer noticed a hypodermic syringe in Young's shirt pocket. The officer left the occupants under the supervision of two backup officers as he went to get gloves from his patrol car. Upon his return, he instructed Young to step out of the car and place the syringe on the hood. The officer then asked Young why he had a syringe. Young replied that he used it to take drugs. The backup officers ordered the two female passengers out of the car and asked them for identification. Meanwhile, in light of Young's admission, the officer searched the passenger compartment of the car for contraband. On the back seat, he found a purse, which Houghton claimed as hers. Inside the purse, the officer found a brown pouch and a black container resembling a wallet. There was drug paraphernalia and a syringe containing methamphetamine inside both the brown pouch and the black container.

The Supreme Court held that the search of Houghton's purse did not violate the Fourth Amendment. In particular, the Court noted that under the automobile exception, there is no distinction among packages or containers based on ownership:

> When there is probable cause to search for contraband in a car, it is reasonable for police officers to examine packages and containers without a showing of individualized probable cause for each one. A passenger's personal belongings, just like the driver's belongings or containers attached to the car like a glove compartment, are "in" the car, and the officer has probable cause to search for contraband *in* the car.

The Automobile Exception

1. Police may search a vehicle without a warrant if they have probable cause to believe evidence or contraband is inside the vehicle. The search of the vehicle need not take place immediately; it can be done after the vehicle has been taken to a police station and is no longer mobile.

2. The search may include any containers or personal effects within the vehicle, regardless of whether the containers or personal effects belong to the driver or to a passenger.

3. If the probable cause supporting the search extends only to certain items or containers within the vehicle, the police must confine their search to those items or containers and may not search the entire vehicle.

E. INVENTORY SEARCHES

When the police take custody of private property, they will often inventory the contents to check for dangerous items, to protect the owner's property, and to protect the police against claims that certain items are missing or stolen. The Supreme Court has said that these routine inventory searches may be performed without a warrant and without probable cause. If, as occasionally happens, the police discover contraband in the course of an inventory search, it may be introduced into evidence at a subsequent criminal trial.

In *South Dakota v. Opperman*, the Supreme Court approved an inventory search of a car that had been impounded by the police for a parking violation.

SOUTH DAKOTA V. OPPERMAN
428 U.S. 364 (1976)

CHIEF JUSTICE BURGER delivered the opinion of the Court.

We review the judgment of the Supreme Court of South Dakota, holding that local police violated the Fourth Amendment to the Federal Constitution, as applicable to the States under the Fourteenth Amendment, when they conducted a routine inventory search of an automobile lawfully impounded by police for violations of municipal parking ordinances.

I

Local ordinances prohibit parking in certain areas of downtown Vermillion, S.D., between the hours of 2 a.m. and 6 a.m. During the early morning hours of December 10, 1973, a Vermillion police officer observed respondent's unoccupied vehicle illegally parked in the restricted zone. At approximately 3 a.m., the officer issued an overtime parking ticket and placed it on the car's windshield.

At approximately 10 o'clock on the same morning, another officer issued a second ticket for an overtime parking violation. These circumstances were routinely reported to police headquarters, and after the vehicle was inspected, the car was towed to the city impound lot.

From outside the car at the impound lot, a police officer observed a watch on the dashboard and other items of personal property located on the back seat and back floorboard. At the officer's direction, the car door was then unlocked and, using a standard inventory form pursuant to standard police procedures, the officer inventoried the contents of the car, including the contents of the glove compartment which was unlocked. There he found marihuana contained in a plastic bag. All items, including the contraband, were removed to the police department for safekeeping. During the late afternoon of December 10, respondent appeared at the police department to claim his property. The marihuana was retained by police.

Respondent was subsequently arrested on charges of possession of marihuana. His motion to suppress the evidence yielded by the inventory search was denied; he was convicted after a jury trial and sentenced to a fine of $100 and 14 days' incarceration in the county jail. On appeal, the Supreme Court of South Dakota reversed the conviction. The court concluded that the evidence had been obtained in violation of the Fourth Amendment prohibition against unreasonable searches and seizures. We granted certiorari, and we reverse.

II

This Court has traditionally drawn a distinction between automobiles and homes or offices in relation to the Fourth Amendment. Although automobiles are "effects" and thus within the reach of the Fourth Amendment, warrantless examinations of automobiles have been upheld in circumstances in which a search of a home or office would not.

The reason for this well-settled distinction is twofold. First, the inherent mobility of automobiles creates circumstances of such exigency that, as a practical necessity, rigorous enforcement of the warrant requirement is impossible. But the Court has also upheld warrantless searches where no immediate danger was presented that the car would be removed from the jurisdiction. Besides the element of mobility, less rigorous warrant requirements govern because the expectation of privacy with respect to one's automobile is significantly less than that relating to one's home or office. In discharging their varied responsibilities for ensuring the public safety, law enforcement officials are necessarily brought into frequent contact with automobiles. Most of this contact is distinctly noncriminal in nature. Automobiles, unlike homes, are subjected to pervasive and continuing governmental regulation and controls, including periodic inspection and licensing requirements. As an everyday occurrence, police stop and examine vehicles when license plates or inspection stickers have expired, or if other violations, such as exhaust fumes or excessive noise, are noted, or if headlights or other safety equipment are not in proper working order. The expectation of privacy as to automobiles is further diminished by the obviously public nature of automobile travel.

In the interests of public safety and as part of what the Court has called "community caretaking functions," automobiles are frequently taken into police custody. Vehicle accidents present one such occasion. To permit the uninterrupted flow of traffic and in some circumstances to preserve evidence, disabled or damaged vehicles will often be removed from the highways or streets at the behest of police engaged solely in caretaking and traffic-control activities. Police will also frequently remove and impound automobiles which violate parking ordinances and which thereby jeopardize both the public safety and the efficient movement of vehicular traffic. The authority of police to seize and remove from the streets vehicles impeding traffic or threatening public safety and convenience is beyond challenge.

When vehicles are impounded, local police departments generally follow a routine practice of securing and inventorying the automobiles' contents. These procedures developed in response to three distinct needs: the protection of the owner's property while it remains in police custody; the protection the police against claims or disputes over lost or stolen property; and the protection of the police from potential danger. The practice has been viewed as essential to respond to incidents of theft or vandalism. In addition, police frequently attempt to determine whether a vehicle has been stolen and thereafter abandoned.

These caretaking procedures have almost uniformly been upheld by the state courts, which by virtue of the localized nature of traffic regulation have had considerable occasion to deal with the issue. Applying the Fourth Amendment standard of "reasonableness," the state courts have overwhelmingly concluded that, even if an inventory is characterized as a "search," the intrusion is constitutionally permissible.

The majority of the Federal Courts of Appeals have likewise sustained inventory procedures as reasonable police intrusions. These cases have recognized that standard inventories often include an examination of the glove compartment, since it is a customary place for documents of ownership and registration, as well as a place for the temporary storage of valuables.

III

The decisions of this Court point unmistakably to the conclusion reached by both federal and state courts that inventories pursuant to standard police procedures are reasonable.

In applying the reasonableness standard adopted by the Framers, this Court has consistently sustained police intrusions into automobiles impounded or otherwise in lawful police custody where the process is aimed at securing or protecting the car and its contents.

The Vermillion police were indisputably engaged in a caretaking search of a lawfully impounded automobile. The inventory was conducted only after the car had been impounded for multiple parking violations. The owner, having left his car illegally parked for an extended period, and thus subject to impoundment, was not present to make other arrangements for the safekeeping of his belongings. The inventory itself was prompted by the presence in plain view of a number of valuables inside the car. There is no suggestion whatever that this standard procedure, essentially like that followed throughout the country, was a pretext concealing an investigatory police motive.

On this record we conclude that in following standard police procedures, prevailing throughout the country and approved by the overwhelming majority of courts, the conduct of the police was not "unreasonable" under the Fourth Amendment.

JUSTICE MARSHALL, with whom JUSTICE BRENNAN and JUSTICE STEWART join, dissenting.

The Court today holds that the Fourth Amendment permits a routine police inventory search of the closed glove compartment of a locked automobile impounded for ordinary traffic violations. Under the Court's holding, such a search may be made without attempting to secure the consent of the owner and without any particular reason to believe the impounded automobile contains contraband, evidence, or valuables, or presents any danger to its custodians or the public.[1] Because I believe this holding to be contrary to sound elaboration of established Fourth Amendment principles, I dissent.

The requirement of a warrant aside, resolution of the question whether an inventory search of closed compartments inside a locked automobile can ever be justified as a constitutionally "reasonable" search depends upon a reconciliation of the owner's constitutionally protected privacy interests against governmental intrusion, and legitimate governmental interests furthered by securing the car and its contents. The Court fails clearly to articulate the reasons for its reconciliation of these interests in this case, but it is at least clear to me that the considerations alluded to by the Court are insufficient to justify the Court's result in this case.

To begin with, the Court appears to suggest by reference to a "diminished" expectation of privacy, that a person's constitutional interest in protecting the integrity of closed compartments of his locked automobile may routinely be sacrificed to governmental interests requiring interference with that privacy that are less compelling than would be necessary to justify a search of similar scope of the person's

---

[1] The Court does not consider, however, whether the police might open and search the glove compartment if it is locked, or whether the police might search a locked trunk or other compartment.

home or office. This has never been the law. The Court correctly observes that some prior cases have drawn distinctions between automobiles and homes or offices in Fourth Amendment cases; but even as the Court's discussion makes clear, the reasons for distinction in those cases are not present here.

The Court's opinion appears to suggest that its result may in any event be justified because the inventory search procedure is a "reasonable" response to "three distinct needs: the protection of the owner's property while it remains in police custody; the protection of the police against claims or disputes over lost or stolen property; and the protection of the police from potential danger."

This suggestion is flagrantly misleading, however, because the record of this case explicitly belies any relevance of the last two concerns. In any event, it is my view that none of these "needs," separately or together, can suffice to justify the inventory search procedure approved by the Court.

First, this search cannot be justified in any way as a safety measure, for—though the Court ignores it—the sole purpose given by the State for the Vermillion police's inventory procedure was to secure valuables. Nor is there any indication that the officer's search in this case was tailored in any way to safety concerns, or that ordinarily it is so circumscribed. Even aside from the actual basis for the police practice in this case, however, I do not believe that any blanket safety argument could justify a program of routine searches of the scope permitted here. Ordinarily there is little danger associated with impounding unsearched automobiles. Thus, while the safety rationale may not be entirely discounted when it is actually relied upon, it surely cannot justify the search of every car upon the basis of undifferentiated possibility of harm; on the contrary, such an intrusion could ordinarily be justified only in those individual cases where the officer's inspection was prompted by specific circumstances indicating the possibility of a particular danger.

Second, the Court suggests that the search for valuables in the closed glove compartment might be justified as a measure to protect the police against lost property claims. Again, this suggestion is belied by the record, since—although the Court declines to discuss it—the South Dakota Supreme Court's interpretation of state law explicitly absolves the police, as "gratuitous depositors," from any obligation beyond inventorying objects in plain view and locking the car. Moreover, it may well be doubted that an inventory procedure would, in any event, work significantly to minimize the frustrations of false claims.

Finally, the Court suggests that the public interest in protecting valuables that may be found inside a closed compartment of an impounded car may justify the inventory procedure. I recognize the genuineness of this governmental interest in protecting property from pilferage. But even if I assume that the posting of a guard would be fiscally impossible as an alternative means to the same protective end, I cannot agree with the Court's conclusion. The Court's result authorizes—indeed it appears to require—the routine search of nearly every car impounded. In my view, the Constitution does not permit such searches as a matter of routine; absent specific consent, such a search is permissible only in exceptional circumstances of particular necessity.

The Court's result in this case elevates the conservation of property interests above the privacy and security interests protected by the Fourth Amendment. For this reason I dissent.

In *Illinois v. Lafayette*, the Supreme Court relied on *South Dakota v. Opperman* to sustain a warrantless inventory search of an arrestee's shoulder bag.

ILLINOIS V. LAFAYETTE
462 U.S. 640 (1983)

CHIEF JUSTICE BURGER delivered the opinion of the Court.

The question presented is whether, at the time an arrested person arrives at a police station, the police may, without obtaining a warrant, search a shoulder bag carried by that person.

On September 1, 1980, at about 10 p.m., Officer Maurice Mietzner of the Kankakee City Police arrived at the Town Cinema in Kankakee, Illinois, in response to a call about a disturbance. There he found respondent involved in an altercation with the theatre manager. He arrested respondent for disturbing the peace, handcuffed him, and took him to the police station. Respondent carried a purse-type shoulder bag on the trip to the station.

At the police station respondent was taken to the booking room; there, Officer Mietzner removed the handcuffs from respondent and ordered him to empty his pockets and place the contents on the counter. After doing so, respondent took a package of cigarettes from his shoulder bag and placed the bag on the counter. Mietzner then removed the contents of the bag, and found ten amphetamine pills inside a cigarette case package.

Respondent was subsequently charged with violating the Illinois Controlled Substances Act, on the basis of the controlled substances found in his shoulder bag.

The question here is whether, consistent with the Fourth Amendment, it is reasonable for police to search the personal effects of a person under lawful arrest as part of the routine administrative procedure at a police stationhouse incident to booking and jailing the suspect. The justification for such searches does not rest on probable cause, and hence the absence of a warrant is immaterial to the reasonableness of the search. Indeed, we have previously established that the inventory search constitutes a well-defined exception to the warrant requirement.

A so-called inventory search is not an independent legal concept but rather an incidental administrative step following arrest and preceding incarceration. To determine whether the search of respondent's shoulder bag was unreasonable we must balance its intrusion on the individual's Fourth Amendment interests against its promotion of legitimate governmental interests.

In order to see an inventory search in proper perspective, it is necessary to study the evolution of interests along the continuum from arrest to incarceration. We have held that immediately upon arrest an officer may lawfully search the person of an arrestee; he may also search the area within the arrestee's immediate control.

An arrested person is not invariably taken to a police station or confined; if an arrestee is taken to the police station, that is no more than a continuation of the custody inherent in the arrest status. Nonetheless, the factors justifying a search of the person and personal effects of an arrestee upon reaching a police station but prior to being placed in confinement are somewhat different from the factors justifying an immediate search at the time and place of arrest.

The governmental interests underlying a stationhouse search of the arrestee's person and possessions may in some circumstances be even greater than those supporting a search immediately following arrest. Consequently, the scope of a stationhouse search will often vary from that made at the time of arrest. Police conduct that would be impractical or unreasonable—or embarrassingly intrusive—on the street can more readily—and privately—be performed at the station. For example, the interests supporting a search incident to arrest would hardly justify disrobing an arrestee on the street, but the practical necessities of routine jail administration may even justify taking a prisoner's clothes before confining him, although that step would be rare.

At the stationhouse, it is entirely proper for police to remove and list or inventory property found on the person or in the possession of an arrested person who is to be jailed. A range of governmental interests support an inventory process. It is not unheard of for persons employed in police activities to steal property taken from arrested persons; similarly, arrested persons have been known to make false claims regarding what was taken from their possession at the stationhouse. A standardized procedure for making a list or inventory as soon as reasonable after reaching the stationhouse not only deters false claims but also inhibits theft or careless handling of articles taken from the arrested person.

Arrested persons have also been known to injure themselves—or others—with belts, knives, drugs or other items on their person while being detained. Dangerous instrumentalities—such as razor blades, bombs, or weapons—can be concealed in innocent-looking articles taken from the arrestee's possession. The bare recital of these mundane realities justifies reasonable measures by police to limit these risks—either while the items are in police possession or at the time they are returned to the arrestee upon his release. Examining all the items removed from the arrestee's person or possession and listing or inventorying them is an entirely reasonable administrative procedure. It is immaterial whether the police actually fear any particular package or container; the need to protect against such risks arises independent of a particular officer's subjective concerns. Finally, inspection of an arrestee's personal property may assist the police in ascertaining or verifying his identity. In short, every consideration of orderly police administration benefiting both police and the public points toward the appropriateness of the examination of respondent's shoulder bag prior to his incarceration.

Our prior cases amply support this conclusion. In *South Dakota v. Opperman*, 428 U.S. 364 (1976), we upheld a search of the contents of the glove compartment of an abandoned automobile lawfully impounded by the police. We held that the search was reasonable because it served legitimate governmental interests that outweighed the individual's privacy interests in the contents of his car. Those measures protected the owner's property while it was in the custody of the police and protected police against possible false claims of theft. We found no need to consider the existence of less intrusive means of protecting the police and the property in their custody—such as locking the car and impounding it in safe storage under guard. Similarly, standardized inventory procedures are appropriate to serve legitimate governmental interests at stake here.

The Illinois court held that the search of respondent's shoulder bag was unreasonable because "preservation of the defendant's property and protection of police from claims of lost or stolen property could have been achieved in a less intrusive manner. For example, the defendant's shoulder bag could easily have been secured by sealing it within a plastic bag or box and placing it in a secured locker." Perhaps so, but the real question is not what "could have been achieved," but whether the Fourth Amendment *requires* such steps; it is not our function to write a manual on administering routine, neutral procedures of the stationhouse. Our role is to assure against violations of the Constitution.

The reasonableness of any particular governmental activity does not necessarily or invariably turn on the existence of alternative "less intrusive" means. We are hardly in a position to second-guess police departments as to what practical administrative method will best deter theft by and false claims against its employees and preserve the security of the stationhouse. It is evident that a stationhouse search of every item carried on or by a person who has lawfully been taken into custody by the police will amply serve the important and legitimate governmental interests involved.

Even if less intrusive means existed of protecting some particular types of property, it would be unreasonable to expect police officers in the everyday course of business to make fine and subtle distinctions in deciding which containers or items may be searched and which must be sealed as a unit. Applying these principles, we hold that it is not "unreasonable" for police, as part of the routine procedure incident to incarcerating an arrested person, to search any container or article in his possession, in accordance with established inventory procedures.

Inventory Searches

If police are lawfully in possession of private property—such as an impounded vehicle or a bag or purse belonging to an arrestee—they may inventory the contents without probable cause or a warrant as long the inventory is undertaken as part of a routine police policy or procedure. Any evidence or contraband discovered during the routine inventory is admissible.

F. CONSENT

Police do not need a warrant or even probable cause to perform a search if they have permission—consent—do to so. Consent may actually be the most important exception to the warrant requirement simply because it is used so frequently. Some commentators have suggested that 90% or more of all warrantless police searches are accomplished with consent.[b] And several studies have confirmed that when asked by police, an overwhelming majority of people readily provide consent to a search.[c]

In *Schneckloth v. Bustamonte*, the Supreme Court said that consent must be voluntarily given, as determined by the totality of the circumstances. The Court went on to note, however, that consent may still be deemed voluntary even if a person does not know that he can

---

[b] *See* Ric Simmons, *Not "Voluntary" But Still Reasonable: A New Paradigm for Understanding the Consent Searches Doctrine*, 80 INDIANA LAW JOURNAL 773, 773 & n.1 (2005); Paul Sutton, *The Fourth Amendment in Action: An Empirical View of the Search Warrant Process*, 22 CRIMINAL LAW BULLETIN 405, 415 (1986).

[c] *See* Illya Lichtenberg, *Miranda in Ohio: The Effects of Robinette on the Voluntary Waiver of Fourth Amendment Rights*, 44 HOWARD LAW JOURNAL 349, 365–373 (2001) (survey of thousands of motorists in Ohio and Maryland who had been asked for permission to search their cars following a stop for a traffic violation revealed that approximately 90% consented); *State v. Carty*, 170 N.J. 632, 644–645 (2002) (survey of New Jersey motorists revealed a consent rate of nearly 95%); Molly Totman & Dwight Steward, *Searching for Consent: An Analysis of Racial Profiling Data in Texas* 10 (2006), available at https://www.aclutx.org/reports/2006racialprofiling report.pdf (three-month study conducted by the University of North Texas found that 94% of drivers in a five-city area consented to searches requested by police).

withhold consent. Thus, when police seek permission to search, they are not required to inform a person of his right to refuse consent.

SCHNECKLOTH V. BUSTAMONTE

412 U.S. 218 (1973)

JUSTICE STEWART delivered the opinion of the Court.

It is well settled under the Fourth and Fourteenth Amendments that a search conducted without a warrant issued upon probable cause is "*per se* unreasonable subject only to a few specifically established and well-delineated exceptions." *Katz v. U.S.*, 389 U.S. 347, 357 (1967). It is equally well settled that one of the specifically established exceptions to the requirements of both a warrant and probable cause is a search that is conducted pursuant to consent. The constitutional question in the present case concerns the definition of "consent" in this Fourth and Fourteenth Amendment context.

I

The respondent was brought to trial in a California court upon a charge of possessing a check with intent to defraud. He moved to suppress the introduction of certain material as evidence against him on the ground that the material had been acquired through an unconstitutional search and seizure. In response to the motion, the trial judge conducted an evidentiary hearing where it was established that the material in question had been acquired by the State under the following circumstances:

While on routine patrol in Sunnyvale, California, at approximately 2:40 in the morning, Police Officer James Rand stopped an automobile when he observed that one headlight and its license plate light were burned out. Six men were in the vehicle. Joe Alcala and the respondent, Robert Bustamonte, were in the front seat with Joe Gonzales, the driver. Three older men were seated in the rear. When, in response to the policeman's question, Gonzales could not produce a driver's license, Officer Rand asked if any of the other five had any evidence of identification. Only Alcala produced a license, and he explained that the car was his brother's. After the six occupants had stepped out of the car at the officer's request and after two additional policemen had arrived, Officer Rand asked Alcala if he could search the car. Alcala replied, "Sure, go ahead." Prior to the search no one was threatened with arrest and, according to Officer Rand's uncontradicted testimony, it "was all very congenial at this time." Gonzales testified that Alcala actually helped in the search of the car, by opening the trunk and glove compartment. In Gonzales' words: "The police officer asked Joe (Alcala), he goes, 'Does the trunk open?' And Joe said, 'Yes.' He went to the car and got the keys and opened up the trunk." Wadded up under the left rear seat, the police officers found three checks that had previously been stolen from a car wash.

The trial judge denied the motion to suppress, and the checks in question were admitted in evidence at Bustamonte's trial. On the basis of this and other evidence he was convicted.

II

It is important to make it clear at the outset what is not involved in this case. The respondent concedes that a search conducted pursuant to a valid consent is constitutionally permissible. And similarly, the State concedes that "when a prosecutor seeks to rely upon consent to justify the lawfulness of a search, he has the burden of proving that the consent was, in fact, freely and voluntarily given." *Bumper v. North Carolina*, 391 U.S. 543, 548 (1968).

The precise question in this case, then, is what must the prosecution prove to demonstrate that a consent was "voluntarily" given. And upon that question there is a square conflict of views between the state and federal courts that have reviewed the search involved in the case before us. The Court of Appeals for the Ninth Circuit concluded that it is an essential part of the State's initial burden to prove that a person knows he has a right to refuse consent. The California courts have followed the rule that voluntariness is a question of fact to be determined from the totality of all the circumstances, and that the state of a defendant's knowledge is only one factor to be taken into account in assessing the voluntariness of a consent.

The most extensive judicial exposition of the meaning of "voluntariness" has been developed in those cases in which the Court has had to determine the "voluntariness" of a defendant's confession for purposes of the Fourteenth Amendment.

Those cases yield no talismanic definition of "voluntariness," mechanically applicable to the host of situations where the question has arisen. It cannot be taken literally to mean a "knowing" choice. Except where a person is unconscious or drugged or otherwise lacks capacity for conscious choice, all incriminating statements—even those made under brutal treatment—are "voluntary" in the sense of representing a choice of alternatives. On the other hand, if "voluntariness" incorporates notions of "but-for" cause, the question should be whether the statement would have been made even absent inquiry or other official action. Under such a test, virtually no statement would be voluntary because very few people give incriminating statements in the absence of official action of some kind. It is thus evident that neither linguistics nor epistemology will provide a ready definition of the meaning of "voluntariness."

The Due Process Clause does not mandate that the police forgo all questioning, or that they be given *carte blanche* to extract what they can from a suspect. The ultimate test remains that which has been the only clearly established test in Anglo-American courts for two hundred years: the test of voluntariness. Is the confession the product of an essentially free and unconstrained choice by its maker? If it is, if he has willed to confess, it may be used against him. If it is not, if his will has been overborne and his capacity for self-determination critically impaired, the use of his confession offends due process.

In determining whether a defendant's will was overborne in a particular case, the Court has assessed the totality of all the surrounding circumstances—both the characteristics of the accused and the details of the interrogation. Some of the factors taken into account have included the youth of the accused; his lack of education; or his low intelligence; the lack of any advice to the accused of his constitutional rights; the length of detention; the repeated and prolonged nature of the questioning; and the use of physical punishment such as the deprivation of food or sleep. In all of these cases, the Court determined the factual circumstances surrounding the confession, assessed the psychological impact on the accused, and evaluated the legal significance of how the accused reacted.

The significant fact about all of these decisions is that none of them turned on the presence or absence of a single controlling criterion; each reflected a careful scrutiny of all the surrounding circumstances. In none of them did the Court rule that the Due Process Clause required the prosecution to prove as part of its initial burden that the defendant knew he had a right to refuse to answer the questions that were put. While the state of the accused's mind, and the failure of the police to advise the accused of his rights, were certainly factors to be evaluated in assessing the "voluntariness" of an accused's responses, they were not in and of themselves determinative.

Similar considerations lead us to agree with the courts of California that the question whether a consent to a search was in fact "voluntary" or was the product of duress or coercion, express or implied, is a question of fact to be determined from the totality of all the circumstances. While knowledge of the right to refuse consent is one factor to be taken into account, the government need not establish such knowledge as the *sine qua non* of an effective consent. As with police questioning, two competing concerns must be accommodated in determining the meaning of a "voluntary" consent—the legitimate need for such searches and the equally important requirement of assuring the absence of coercion.

In situations where the police have some evidence of illicit activity, but lack probable cause to arrest or search, a search authorized by a valid consent may be the only means of obtaining important and reliable evidence. In the present case for example, while the police had reason to stop the car for traffic violations, the State does not contend that there was probable cause to search the vehicle or that the search was incident to a valid arrest of any of the occupants. Yet, the search yielded tangible evidence that served as a basis for a prosecution, and provided some assurance that others, wholly innocent of the crime, were not mistakenly brought to trial. And in those cases where there is probable cause to arrest or search, but where the police lack a warrant, a consent search may still be valuable. If the search is conducted and proves fruitless, that in itself may convince the police that an arrest with its possible stigma and embarrassment is unnecessary, or that a far more extensive search pursuant to a warrant is not justified. In short, a search pursuant to consent may result in considerably less inconvenience for the subject of the search, and, properly conducted, is a constitutionally permissible and wholly legitimate aspect of effective police activity.

But the Fourth and Fourteenth Amendments require that a consent not be coerced, by explicit or implicit means, by implied threat or covert force. For, no matter how subtly the coercion was applied, the resulting "consent" would be no more than a pretext for the unjustified police intrusion against which the Fourth Amendment is directed.

The problem of reconciling the recognized legitimacy of consent searches with the requirement that they be free from any aspect of official coercion cannot be resolved by any infallible touchstone. To approve such searches without the most careful scrutiny would sanction the possibility of official coercion; to place artificial restrictions upon such searches would jeopardize their basic validity. Just as was true with confessions, the requirement of a "voluntary" consent reflects a fair accommodation of the constitutional requirements involved. In examining all the surrounding circumstances to determine if in fact the consent to search was coerced, account must be taken of subtly coercive police questions, as well as the possibly vulnerable subjective state of the person who consents. Those searches that are the product of police coercion can thus be filtered out without undermining the continuing validity of consent searches. In sum, there is no reason for us to depart in the area of consent searches, from the traditional definition of "voluntariness."

The approach of the Court of Appeals for the Ninth Circuit finds no support in any of our decisions that have attempted to define the meaning of "voluntariness." Its ruling, that the State must affirmatively prove that the subject of the search knew that he had a right to refuse consent, would, in practice, create serious doubt whether consent searches could continue to be conducted. There might be rare cases where it could be proved from the record that a person in fact affirmatively knew of his right to refuse—such as a case where he announced to the police that if he didn't sign the consent form, "you (police) are going to get a search warrant"; or a case where by prior experience and training a person had clearly and convincingly demonstrated such knowledge. But more commonly where there was no evidence of any coercion, explicit or implicit, the prosecution would nevertheless be unable to demonstrate that the subject of the search in fact had known of his right to refuse consent.

The very object of the inquiry—the nature of a person's subjective understanding—underlines the difficulty of the prosecution's burden under the rule applied by the Court of Appeals in this case. Any defendant who was the subject of a search authorized solely by his consent could effectively frustrate the introduction into evidence of the fruits of that search by simply failing to testify that he in fact knew he could refuse to consent. And the near impossibility of meeting this prosecutorial burden suggests why this Court has never accepted any such litmus-paper test of voluntariness.

One alternative that would go far toward proving that the subject of a search did know he had a right to refuse consent would be to advise him of that right before eliciting his consent. That, however, is a suggestion that has been almost universally repudiated by both federal and state courts, and, we think, rightly so. For it would be thoroughly impractical to impose on the normal consent search the detailed requirements of an effective warning. Consent searches are part of the standard investigatory techniques of law enforcement agencies. They normally occur on the highway, or in a person's home or office, and under informal and unstructured conditions. The circumstances that prompt the initial request to search may develop quickly or be a logical extension of investigative police questioning. The police may seek to investigate further suspicious circumstances or to follow up leads developed in questioning persons at the scene of a crime. These situations are a far cry from the structured atmosphere of a trial where, assisted by counsel if he chooses, a defendant is informed of his trial rights. And, while surely a closer question, these situations are still immeasurably far removed from "custodial interrogation" where, in *Miranda v. Arizona*, 384 U.S. 436 (1966), we found that the Constitution required certain now familiar warnings as a prerequisite to police interrogation.

Consequently, we cannot accept the position of the Court of Appeals in this case that proof of knowledge of the right to refuse consent is a necessary prerequisite to demonstrating a "voluntary" consent. Rather, it is only by analyzing all the circumstances of an individual consent that it can be ascertained whether, in fact, it was voluntary or coerced. It is this careful sifting of the unique facts and circumstances of each case that is evidenced in our prior decisions involving consent searches.

In short, neither this Court's prior cases nor the traditional definition of "voluntariness" requires proof of knowledge of a right to refuse as the *sine qua non* of an effective consent to a search.

It is said, however, that a "consent" is a "waiver" of a person's rights under the Fourth and Fourteenth Amendments. The argument is that by allowing the police to conduct a search, a person "waives" whatever right he had to prevent the police from searching. It is argued that under the doctrine of *Johnson v. Zerbst*, 304 U.S. 458 (1938), to establish such a "waiver" the State must demonstrate "an intentional relinquishment or abandonment of a known right or privilege."

But these standards were enunciated in *Johnson* in the context of the safeguards of a fair criminal trial. Our cases do not reflect an uncritical demand for a knowing and intelligent waiver in every situation where a person has failed to invoke a constitutional protection.

The requirement of a "knowing" and "intelligent" waiver was articulated in a case involving the validity of a defendant's decision to forego a right constitutionally guaranteed to protect a fair trial and the reliability of the truth-determining process. *Johnson v. Zerbst* dealt with the denial of counsel in a federal criminal trial. There the Court held that under the Sixth Amendment a criminal defendant is entitled to the assistance of counsel, and that if he lacks sufficient funds to retain counsel, it is the Government's obligation to furnish him with a lawyer. To preserve the fairness of the trial process the Court established an appropriately heavy burden on the Government before waiver could be found—"an intentional relinquishment or abandonment of a known right or privilege."

Almost without exception, the requirement of a knowing and intelligent waiver has been applied only to those rights which the Constitution guarantees to a criminal defendant in order to preserve a fair trial. Hence, and hardly surprisingly in view of the facts of *Johnson* itself, the standard of a knowing and intelligent waiver has most often been applied to test the validity of a waiver of counsel, either at trial, or upon a guilty plea.

There is a vast difference between those rights that protect a fair criminal trial and the rights guaranteed under the Fourth Amendment. Nothing, either in the purposes behind requiring a "knowing" and "intelligent" waiver of trial rights, or in the practical application of such a requirement suggests that it ought to be extended to the constitutional guarantee against unreasonable searches and seizures.

In short, there is nothing in the purposes or application of the waiver requirements of *Johnson v. Zerbst* that justifies, much less compels, the easy equation of a knowing waiver with a consent search. To make such an equation is to generalize from the broad rhetoric of some of our decisions, and to ignore the substance of the differing constitutional guarantees.

Much of what has already been said disposes of the argument that the Court's decision in the *Miranda* case requires the conclusion that knowledge of a right to refuse is an indispensable element of a valid consent. The considerations that informed the Court's holding in *Miranda* are simply inapplicable in the present case. In *Miranda* the Court found that the techniques of police questioning and the nature of custodial surroundings produce an inherently coercive situation.

In this case, there is no evidence of any inherently coercive tactics—either from the nature of the police questioning or the environment in which it took place. Indeed, since consent searches will normally occur on a person's own familiar territory, the specter of incommunicado police interrogation in some remote station house is simply inapposite. There is no reason to believe, under circumstances such as are present here, that the response to a policeman's question is presumptively coerced; and there is, therefore, no reason to reject the traditional test for determining the voluntariness of a person's response. *Miranda*, of course, did not reach investigative questioning of a person not in custody, which is most directly analogous to the situation of a consent search, and it assuredly did not indicate that such questioning ought to be deemed inherently coercive.

It is also argued that the failure to require the Government to establish knowledge as a prerequisite to a valid consent will relegate the Fourth Amendment to the special province of "the sophisticated, the knowledgeable, and the privileged." We cannot agree. The traditional definition of voluntariness we accept today has always taken into account evidence of minimal schooling, low intelligence, and the lack of any effective warnings to a person of his rights; and the voluntariness of any statement taken under those conditions has been carefully scrutinized to determine whether it was in fact voluntarily given.

Our decision today is a narrow one. We hold only that when the subject of a search is not in custody and the State attempts to justify a search on the basis of his consent, the Fourth and Fourteenth Amendments require that it demonstrate that the consent was in fact voluntarily given, and not the result of duress or coercion, express or implied. Voluntariness is a question of fact to be determined from all the circumstances, and while the subject's knowledge of a right to refuse is a factor to be taken into account, the prosecution is not required to demonstrate such knowledge as a prerequisite to establishing a voluntary consent.

JUSTICE MARSHALL, dissenting.

I would have thought that the capacity to choose necessarily depends upon knowledge that there is a choice to be made. But today the Court reaches the curious result that one can choose to relinquish a constitutional right—the right to be free of unreasonable searches—without knowing that he has the alternative of refusing to accede to a police request to search. I cannot agree, and therefore dissent.

I believe that the Court misstates the true issue in this case. That issue is not, as the Court suggests, whether the police overbore Alcala's will in eliciting his consent, but rather, whether a simple statement of assent to search, without more, should be sufficient to permit the police to search and thus act as a relinquishment of Alcala's constitutional right to exclude the police. This Court has always scrutinized with great care claims that a person has forgone the opportunity to assert constitutional rights. I see no reason to give the claim that a person consented to a search any less rigorous scrutiny. Every case in this Court involving this kind of search has heretofore spoken of consent as a waiver. Perhaps one skilled in linguistics or epistemology can disregard those comments, but I find them hard to ignore.

My approach to the case is straight-forward and, to me, obviously required by the notion of consent as a relinquishment of Fourth Amendment rights. I am at a loss to understand why consent cannot be taken literally to mean a "knowing" choice. In fact, I have difficulty in comprehending how a decision made without knowledge of available alternatives can be treated as a choice at all.

Although the Court says without real elaboration that it "cannot agree," the holding today confines the protection of the Fourth Amendment against searches conducted without probable cause to the sophisticated, the knowledgeable, and, I might add, the few. In the final analysis, the Court now sanctions a game of blindman's bluff, in which the police always have the upper hand, for the sake of nothing more than the convenience of the police. But the guarantees of the Fourth Amendment were never intended to shrink before such an ephemeral and changeable interest. The Framers of the Fourth Amendment struck the balance against this sort of convenience and in favor of certain basic civil rights. It is not for this Court to restrike that balance because of its own views of the needs of law enforcement officers. I fear that that is the effect of the Court's decision today.

———————

When two people live together or otherwise share property, questions sometimes arise concerning the authority of one or the other to consent to a search by the police. This is known as *third-party consent*: What happens when a third party, someone other than the target of the search or the owner of the incriminating evidence, has consented to the search? For example, suppose Carl Clean consents to a search of the apartment he shares with Martin Messy and police discover illegal drugs belonging to Martin, wedged under a cushion on his recliner in the living room. Are the drugs admissible against Martin Messy on the basis of Carl Clean's consent to the search? In *Illinois v. Rodriguez*, the Supreme Court considered a similar set of facts and held that a third party's consent to a search is valid if the police reasonably believe that the third party has *common authority* over the premises.

ILLINOIS V. RODRIGUEZ
497 U.S. 177 (1990)

JUSTICE SCALIA delivered the opinion of the Court.

In *U.S. v. Matlock*, 415 U.S. 164 (1974), this Court reaffirmed that a warrantless entry and search by law enforcement officers does not violate the Fourth Amendment's proscription of unreasonable searches and seizures if the officers have obtained the consent of a third party who possesses common authority over the premises. The present case presents an issue we expressly reserved in *Matlock*: Whether a warrantless entry is valid when based upon the consent of a third party whom the police, at the time of the entry, reasonably believe to possess common authority over the premises, but who in fact does not do so.

I

Respondent Edward Rodriguez was arrested in his apartment by law enforcement officers and charged with possession of illegal drugs. The police gained entry to the apartment with the consent and assistance of Gail Fischer, who had lived there with respondent for several months. The relevant facts leading to the arrest are as follows.

On July 26, 1985, police were summoned to the residence of Dorothy Jackson on South Wolcott in Chicago. They were met by Ms. Jackson's daughter, Gail Fischer, who showed signs of a severe beating. She told the officers that she had been assaulted by respondent Edward Rodriguez earlier that day in an apartment on South California. Fischer stated that Rodriguez was then asleep in the apartment, and she consented to travel there with the police in order to unlock the door with her key so that the officers could enter and arrest him. During this conversation, Fischer several times referred to the apartment on South California as "our" apartment, and said that she had clothes and furniture there. It is unclear whether she indicated that she currently lived at the apartment, or only that she used to live there.

The police officers drove to the apartment on South California, accompanied by Fischer. They did not obtain an arrest warrant for Rodriguez, nor did they seek a search warrant for the apartment. At the apartment, Fischer unlocked the door with her key and gave the officers permission to enter. They moved through the door into the living room, where they observed in plain view drug paraphernalia and containers filled with white powder that they believed (correctly, as later analysis showed) to be cocaine. They proceeded to the bedroom, where they found Rodriguez asleep and discovered additional containers of white powder in two open attaché cases. The officers arrested Rodriguez and seized the drugs and related paraphernalia.

Rodriguez was charged with possession of a controlled substance with intent to deliver. He moved to suppress all evidence seized at the time of his arrest, claiming that Fischer had vacated the apartment several weeks earlier and had no authority to consent to the entry. The Cook County Circuit Court granted the motion, holding that at the time she consented to the entry Fischer did not have common authority over the apartment. The Court concluded that Fischer was not a "usual resident" but rather an "infrequent visitor" at the apartment on South California, based upon its findings that Fischer's name was not on the lease, that she did not contribute to the rent, that she was not allowed to invite others to the apartment on her own, that she did not have access to the apartment when respondent was away, and that she had moved some of her possessions from the apartment. The Circuit Court also rejected the State's contention that, even if Fischer did not possess common authority over the premises, there was no Fourth Amendment violation if the police *reasonably believed* at the time of their entry that Fischer possessed the authority to consent.

The Appellate Court of Illinois affirmed the Circuit Court in all respects. The Illinois Supreme Court denied the State's petition for leave to appeal, and we granted certiorari.

II

The Fourth Amendment generally prohibits the warrantless entry of a person's home, whether to make an arrest or to search for specific objects. The prohibition does not apply, however, to situations in which voluntary consent has been obtained, either from the individual whose property is searched, or from a third party who possesses common authority over the premises. The State of Illinois contends that that exception applies in the present case.

As we stated in *Matlock*, "common authority" rests "on mutual use of the property by persons generally having joint access or control for most purposes." The burden of establishing that common authority rests upon the State. On the basis of this record, it is clear that burden was not sustained. The evidence showed that although Fischer, with her two small children, had lived with Rodriguez beginning in December 1984, she had moved out on July 1, 1985, almost a month before the search at issue here, and had gone to live with her mother. She took her and her children's clothing with her, though leaving behind some furniture and household effects. During the period after July 1 she sometimes spent the night at Rodriguez's apartment, but never invited her friends there, and never went there herself when he was not home. Her name was not on the lease nor did she contribute to the rent. She had a key to the apartment, which she said at trial she had taken without Rodriguez's knowledge (though she testified at the preliminary hearing that Rodriguez had given her the key). On these facts the State has not established that, with respect to the South California apartment, Fischer had "joint access or control for most purposes." To the contrary, the Appellate Court's determination of no common authority over the apartment was obviously correct.

III

The State contends that, even if Fischer did not in fact have authority to give consent, it suffices to validate the entry that the law enforcement officers reasonably believed she did.

On the merits of the issue, respondent asserts that permitting a reasonable belief of common authority to validate an entry would cause a defendant's Fourth Amendment rights to be "vicariously waived." We disagree.

We have been unyielding in our insistence that a defendant's waiver of his trial rights cannot be given effect unless it is "knowing" and "intelligent." We would assuredly not permit, therefore, evidence seized in violation of the Fourth Amendment to be introduced on the basis of a trial court's mere "reasonable belief"—derived from statements by unauthorized persons—that the defendant has waived his objection. But one must make a distinction between, on the one hand, trial rights that *derive* from the violation of constitutional guarantees and, on the other hand, the nature of those constitutional guarantees themselves.

What Rodriguez is assured by the trial right of the exclusionary rule, where it applies, is that no evidence seized in violation of the Fourth Amendment will be introduced at his trial unless he consents. What he is assured by the Fourth Amendment itself, however, is not that no government search of his house will occur unless he consents; but that no such search will occur that is "unreasonable." There are various elements, of course, that can make a search of a person's house "reasonable"—one of which is the consent of the person or his cotenant. The essence of respondent's argument is that we should impose upon this element a requirement that we have not imposed upon other elements that regularly compel government officers to exercise judgment regarding the facts: namely, the requirement that their judgment be not only responsible, but correct.

The fundamental objective that alone validates all unconsented government searches is, of course, the seizure of persons who have committed or are about to commit crimes, or of evidence related to crimes. But "reasonableness," with respect to this necessary element, does not demand that the government be factually correct in its assessment that that is what a search will produce. Warrants need only be supported by "probable cause," which demands no more than a proper assessment of probabilities in particular factual contexts. If a magistrate, based upon seemingly reliable but factually inaccurate information, issues a warrant for the search of a house in which the sought-after felon is not present, has never been present, and was never likely to have been present, the owner of that house suffers one of the inconveniences we all expose ourselves to as the cost of living in a safe society; he does not suffer a violation of the Fourth Amendment.

Another element often, though not invariably, required in order to render an unconsented search "reasonable" is, of course, that the officer be authorized by a valid warrant. Here also we have not held that "reasonableness" precludes error with respect to those factual judgments that law enforcement officials are expected to make.

It is apparent that in order to satisfy the "reasonableness" requirement of the Fourth Amendment, what is generally demanded of the many factual determinations that must regularly be made by agents of the government—whether the magistrate issuing a warrant, the police officer executing a warrant, or the police officer conducting a search or seizure under one of the exceptions to the warrant requirement—is not that they always be correct, but that they always be reasonable.

We see no reason to depart from this general rule with respect to facts bearing upon the authority to consent to a search. Whether the basis for such authority exists is the sort of recurring factual question to which law enforcement officials must be expected to apply their judgment; and all the Fourth Amendment requires is that they answer it reasonably. The Constitution is no more violated when officers enter without a warrant because they reasonably (though erroneously) believe that the person who has consented to their entry is a resident of the premises, than it is violated when they enter without a warrant because they reasonably (though erroneously) believe they are in pursuit of a violent felon who is about to escape.

What is at issue when a claim of apparent consent is raised is not whether the right to be free of searches has been *waived*, but whether the right to be free of *unreasonable* searches has been *violated*.

What we hold today does not suggest that law enforcement officers may always accept a person's invitation to enter premises. Even when the invitation is accompanied by an explicit assertion that the person lives there, the surrounding circumstances could conceivably be such that a reasonable person would doubt its truth and not act upon it without further inquiry. As with other factual determinations bearing upon search and seizure, determination of consent to enter must be judged against an objective standard: would the facts available to the officer at the moment warrant a man of reasonable caution in the belief that the consenting party had authority over the premises? If not, then warrantless entry without further inquiry is unlawful unless authority actually exists. But if so, the search is valid.

In the present case, the Appellate Court found it unnecessary to determine whether the officers reasonably believed that Fischer had the authority to consent, because it ruled as a matter of law that a reasonable belief could not validate the entry. Since we find that ruling to be in error, we remand for consideration of that question.

JUSTICE MARSHALL, with whom JUSTICE BRENNAN and JUSTICE STEVENS join, dissenting.

The majority agrees with the Illinois Appellate Court's determination that Fischer did not have authority to consent to the officers' entry of Rodriguez's apartment. The Court holds that the warrantless entry into Rodriguez's home was nonetheless valid if the officers reasonably believed that Fischer had authority to consent. The majority's defense of this position rests on a misconception of the basis for third-party consent searches. That such searches do not give rise to claims of constitutional violations rests not on the premise that they are "reasonable" under the Fourth Amendment, but on the premise that a person may voluntarily limit his expectation of privacy by allowing others to exercise authority over his possessions. Thus, an individual's decision to permit another "joint access to or control over the property for most purposes" limits that individual's reasonable expectation of privacy and, to that extent, limits his Fourth Amendment protections. If an individual has not so limited his expectation of privacy, the police may not dispense with the safeguards established by the Fourth Amendment.

The baseline for the reasonableness of a search or seizure in the home is the presence of a warrant. Indeed, searches and seizures inside a home without a warrant are presumptively unreasonable. Exceptions to the warrant requirement must therefore serve compelling law enforcement goals. Because the sole law enforcement purpose underlying third-party consent searches is avoiding the inconvenience of securing a warrant, a departure from the warrant requirement is not justified simply because an officer reasonably believes a third party has consented to a search of the defendant's home. In holding otherwise, the majority ignores our longstanding view that the informed and deliberate determinations of magistrates as to what searches and seizures are permissible under the Constitution are to be preferred over the hurried action of officers and others who may happen to make arrests.

In the absence of an exigency, warrantless home searches and seizures are unreasonable under the Fourth Amendment. The weighty constitutional interest in preventing unauthorized intrusions into the home overrides any law enforcement interest in relying on the reasonable but potentially mistaken belief that a third party has authority to consent to such a search or seizure. Indeed, as the present case illustrates, only the minimal interest in avoiding the inconvenience of obtaining a warrant weighs in on the law enforcement side.

Unlike searches conducted pursuant to the recognized exceptions to the warrant requirement, third-party consent searches are not based on an exigency and therefore serve no compelling social goal. Police officers, when faced with the choice of relying on consent by a third party or securing a warrant, should secure a warrant and must therefore accept the risk of error should they instead choose to rely on consent.

Our prior cases discussing searches based on third-party consent have never suggested that such searches are "reasonable." In *U.S. v. Matlock,* this Court upheld a warrantless search conducted pursuant to the consent of a third party who was living with the defendant. The Court rejected the defendant's challenge to the search, stating that a person who permits others to have "joint access or control for most purposes assumes the risk that such persons might permit the common area to be searched." As the Court's assumption-of-risk analysis makes clear, third-party consent limits a person's ability to challenge the reasonableness of the search only because that person voluntarily has relinquished some of his expectation of privacy by sharing access or control over his property with another person.

A search conducted pursuant to an officer's reasonable but mistaken belief that a third party had authority to consent is thus on an entirely different constitutional footing from one based on the consent of a third party who in fact has such authority. Even if the officers reasonably believed that Fischer had authority to consent, she did not, and Rodriguez's expectation of privacy was therefore undiminished. Rodriguez accordingly can challenge the warrantless intrusion into his home as a violation of the Fourth Amendment.

Our cases demonstrate that third-party consent searches are free from constitutional challenge only to the extent that they rest on consent by a party empowered to do so. The majority's conclusion to the contrary ignores the legitimate expectations of privacy on which individuals are entitled to rely. That a person who allows another joint access to his property thereby limits his expectation of privacy does not justify trampling the rights of a person who has not similarly relinquished any of his privacy expectation.

In *Illinois v. Rodriguez,* Gail Fischer did not actually have common authority over the apartment; in fact, she had moved out more than three weeks before the search. But as the Supreme Court made clear, whether Fischer actually had common authority was not determinative. Instead, the relevant question was whether police could reasonably believe she had common authority over the apartment, which rests on "mutual use of the property by persons having joint access or control for most purposes." Fischer had a key to the apartment, she referred to it as "our" apartment, and she said she had clothes and furniture there. Under these circumstances, the Supreme Court concluded that it was reasonable for police to believe she lived there and had common authority over the premises even though she did not.

The situation is somewhat different when two people, who do actually share common authority over the premises, disagree as whether the police may perform a search. To make further use of our earlier example, suppose Carl Clean consents to a search of the apartment, but as the police are about to enter, Martin Messy meets them at the front door and tells them to stay out. Can the police rely on Carl's consent and search the apartment, or must they retreat in the face of Martin's objection? The Supreme Court considered this question in *Georgia v. Randolph* and held that a physically present co-occupant's refusal of consent prevails when the occupants disagree.

GEORGIA V. RANDOLPH
547 U.S. 103 (2006)

JUSTICE SOUTER delivered the opinion of the Court.

The Fourth Amendment recognizes a valid warrantless entry and search of premises when police obtain the voluntary consent of an occupant who shares, or is reasonably believed to share, authority over the area in common with a co-occupant who later objects to the use of evidence so obtained. *Illinois v. Rodriguez*, 497 U.S. 177 (1990); *U.S. v. Matlock*, 415 U.S. 164 (1974). The question here is whether such an evidentiary seizure is likewise lawful with the permission of one occupant when the other, who later seeks to suppress the evidence, is present at the scene and expressly refuses to consent. We hold that, in the circumstances here at issue, a physically present co-occupant's stated refusal to permit entry prevails, rendering the warrantless search unreasonable and invalid as to him.

I

Respondent Scott Randolph and his wife, Janet, separated in late May 2001, when she left the marital residence in Americus, Georgia, and went to stay with her parents in Canada, taking their son and some belongings. In July, she returned to the Americus house with the child, though the record does not reveal whether her object was reconciliation or retrieval of remaining possessions.

On the morning of July 6, she complained to the police that after a domestic dispute her husband took their son away, and when officers reached the house she told them that her husband was a cocaine user whose habit had caused financial troubles. She mentioned the marital problems and said that she and their son had only recently returned after a stay of several weeks with her parents. Shortly after the police arrived, Scott Randolph returned and explained that he had removed the child to a neighbor's house out of concern that his wife might take the boy out of the country again; he denied cocaine use, and countered that it was in fact his wife who abused drugs and alcohol.

One of the officers, Sergeant Murray, went with Janet Randolph to reclaim the child, and when they returned she not only renewed her complaints about her husband's drug use, but also volunteered that there were "items of drug evidence" in the house. Sergeant Murray asked Scott Randolph for permission to search the house, which he unequivocally refused.

The sergeant turned to Janet Randolph for consent to search, which she readily gave. She led the officer upstairs to a bedroom that she identified as Scott's, where the sergeant noticed a section of a drinking straw with a powdery residue he suspected was cocaine. He then left the house to get an evidence bag from his car and to call the district attorney's office, which instructed him to stop the search and apply for a warrant. When Sergeant Murray returned to the house, Janet Randolph withdrew her consent. The police took the straw to the police station, along with the Randolphs. After getting a search warrant, they returned to the house and seized further evidence of drug use, on the basis of which Scott Randolph was indicted for possession of cocaine.

He moved to suppress the evidence, as products of a warrantless search of his house unauthorized by his wife's consent over his express refusal. The trial court denied the motion, ruling that Janet Randolph had common authority to consent to the search.

We granted certiorari to resolve a split of authority on whether one occupant may give law enforcement effective consent to search shared premises, as against a co-tenant who is present and states a refusal to permit the search.

II

To the Fourth Amendment rule ordinarily prohibiting the warrantless entry of a person's house as unreasonable *per se,* one jealously and carefully drawn exception recognizes the validity of searches with the voluntary consent of an individual possessing authority. That person might be the householder against whom evidence is sought, or a fellow occupant who shares common authority over property, when the suspect is absent, and the exception for consent extends even to entries and searches with the permission of a co-occupant whom the police reasonably, but erroneously, believe to possess shared authority as an occupant. None of our co-occupant consent-to-search cases, however, has presented the further fact of a second occupant physically present and refusing permission to search, and later moving to suppress evidence so obtained. The significance of such a refusal turns on the underpinnings of the co-occupant consent rule, as recognized since *Matlock*.

The constant element in assessing Fourth Amendment reasonableness in the consent cases is the great significance given to widely shared social expectations, which are naturally enough influenced by the law of property, but not controlled by its rules. *Matlock* accordingly not only holds that a solitary co-inhabitant may sometimes consent to a search of shared premises, but stands for the proposition that the reasonableness of such a search is in significant part a function of commonly held understanding about the authority that co-inhabitants may exercise in ways that affect each other's interests.

It is easy to imagine facts on which, if known, no common authority could sensibly be suspected. A person on the scene who identifies himself, say, as a landlord or a hotel manager calls up no customary understanding of authority to admit guests without the consent of the current occupant. A tenant in the ordinary course does not take rented premises subject to any formal or informal agreement that the landlord may let visitors into the dwelling, and a hotel guest customarily has no reason to expect the manager to allow anyone but his own employees into his room. In these circumstances, neither state-law property rights, nor common contractual arrangements, nor any other source points to a common understanding of authority to admit third parties generally without the consent of a person occupying the premises. And when it comes to searching through bureau drawers, there will be instances in which even a person clearly belonging on premises as an occupant may lack any perceived authority to consent; a child of eight might well be considered to have the power to consent to the police crossing the threshold into that part of the house where any caller, such as a pollster or salesman, might well be admitted, but no one would reasonably expect such a child to be in a position to authorize anyone to rummage through his parents' bedroom.

It is fair to say that a caller standing at the door of shared premises would have no confidence that one occupant's invitation was a sufficiently good reason to enter when a fellow tenant stood there saying, "stay out." Without some very good reason, no sensible person would go inside under those conditions. Fear for the safety of the occupant issuing the invitation, or of someone else inside, would be thought to justify entry, but the justification then would be the personal risk, the threats to life or limb, not the disputed invitation.

The visitor's reticence without some such good reason would show not timidity but a realization that when people living together disagree over the use of their common quarters, a resolution must come through voluntary accommodation, not by appeals to authority. Unless the people living together fall within some recognized hierarchy, like a household of parent and child or barracks housing military personnel of different grades, there is no societal understanding of superior and inferior, a fact reflected in a standard formulation of domestic property law, that each cotenant has the right to use and enjoy the entire property as if he or she were the sole owner, limited only by the same right in the other cotenants. In sum, there is no common understanding that one co-tenant generally has a right or authority to prevail over the express wishes of another, whether the issue is the color of the curtains or invitations to outsiders.

Since the co-tenant wishing to open the door to a third party has no recognized authority in law or social practice to prevail over a present and objecting co-tenant, his disputed invitation, without more, gives a police officer no better claim to reasonableness in entering than the officer would have in the absence of any consent at all. Accordingly, in the balancing of competing individual and governmental interests entailed by the bar to unreasonable searches, the cooperative occupant's invitation adds nothing to the government's side to counter the force of an objecting individual's claim to security against the government's intrusion into his dwelling place. We have, after all, lived our whole national history with an understanding of the ancient adage that a man's house is his castle to the point that the poorest man may in his cottage bid defiance to all the forces of the Crown.

Disputed permission is thus no match for this central value of the Fourth Amendment, and the State's other countervailing claims do not add up to outweigh it. Yes, we recognize the consenting tenant's interest as a citizen in bringing criminal activity to light. And we understand a co-tenant's legitimate self-interest in siding with the police to deflect suspicion raised by sharing quarters with a criminal.

But society can often have the benefit of these interests without relying on a theory of consent that ignores an inhabitant's refusal to allow a warrantless search. The co-tenant acting on his own initiative may be able to deliver evidence to the police, and can tell the police what he knows, for use before a magistrate in getting a warrant.[6] The reliance on a co-tenant's information instead of disputed consent accords with the law's general partiality toward police action taken under a warrant as against searches and seizures without one.

---

[6]   Sometimes, of course, the very exchange of information like this in front of the objecting inhabitant may render consent irrelevant by creating an exigency that justifies immediate action on the police's part; if the objecting tenant cannot be incapacitated from destroying easily disposable evidence during the time required to get a warrant, see *Illinois v. McArthur*, 531 U.S. 326 (2001) (denying suspect access to his trailer home while police applied for a search warrant), a fairly perceived need to act on the spot to preserve evidence may justify entry and search under the exigent circumstances exception to the warrant requirement.

Nor should this established policy of Fourth Amendment law be undermined by the principal dissent's claim that it shields spousal abusers and other violent co-tenants who will refuse to allow the police to enter a dwelling when their victims ask the police for help. It is not that the dissent exaggerates violence in the home; we recognize that domestic abuse is a serious problem in the United States.

But this case has no bearing on the capacity of the police to protect domestic victims. The dissent's argument rests on the failure to distinguish two different issues: when the police may enter without committing a trespass, and when the police may enter to search for evidence. No question has been raised, or reasonably could be, about the authority of the police to enter a dwelling to protect a resident from domestic violence; so long as they have good reason to believe such a threat exists, it would be silly to suggest that the police would commit a tort by entering, say, to give a complaining tenant the opportunity to collect belongings and get out safely, or to determine whether violence (or threat of violence) has just occurred or is about to (or soon will) occur, however much a spouse or other co-tenant objected. (And since the police would then be lawfully in the premises, there is no question that they could seize any evidence in plain view or take further action supported by any consequent probable cause.) Thus, the question whether the police might lawfully enter over objection in order to provide any protection that might be reasonable is easily answered yes. The undoubted right of the police to enter in order to protect a victim, however, has nothing to do with the question in this case, whether a search with the consent of one co-tenant is good against another, standing at the door and expressly refusing consent.

None of the cases cited by the dissent support its improbable view that recognizing limits on merely evidentiary searches would compromise the capacity to protect a fearful occupant. In the circumstances of those cases, there is no danger that the fearful occupant will be kept behind the closed door of the house simply because the abusive tenant refuses to consent to a search.

The dissent's red herring aside, we know, of course, that alternatives to disputed consent will not always open the door to search for evidence that the police suspect is inside. The consenting tenant may simply not disclose enough information, or information factual enough, to add up to a showing of probable cause, and there may be no exigency to justify fast action. But nothing in social custom or its reflection in private law argues for placing a higher value on delving into private premises to search for evidence in the face of disputed consent, than on requiring clear justification before the government searches private living quarters over a resident's objection. We therefore hold that a warrantless search of a shared dwelling for evidence over the express refusal of consent by a physically present resident cannot be justified as reasonable as to him on the basis of consent given to the police by another resident.

A remaining loose end is the significance of *Matlock* and *Rodriguez* after today's decision. Although the *Matlock* defendant was not present with the opportunity to object, he was in a squad car not far away; the *Rodriguez* defendant was actually asleep in the apartment, and the police might have roused him with a knock on the door before they entered with only the consent of an apparent co-tenant. If those cases are not to be undercut by today's holding, we have to admit that we are drawing a fine line; if a potential defendant with self-interest in objecting is in fact at the door and objects, the co-tenant's permission does not suffice for a reasonable search, whereas the potential objector, nearby but not invited to take part in the threshold colloquy, loses out.

This is the line we draw, and we think the formalism is justified. So long as there is no evidence that the police have removed the potentially objecting tenant from the entrance for the sake of avoiding a possible objection, there is practical value in the simple clarity of complementary rules, one recognizing the co-tenant's permission when there is no fellow occupant on hand, the other according dispositive weight to the fellow occupant's contrary indication when he expresses it. For the very reason that *Rodriguez* held it would be unjustifiably impractical to require the police to take affirmative steps to confirm the actual authority of a consenting individual whose authority was apparent, we think it would needlessly limit the capacity of the police to respond to ostensibly legitimate opportunities in the field if we were to hold that reasonableness required the police to take affirmative steps to find a potentially objecting co-tenant before acting on the permission they had already received. There is no ready reason to believe that efforts to invite a refusal would make a difference in many cases, whereas every co-tenant consent case would turn into a test about the adequacy of the police's efforts to consult with a potential objector. Better to accept the formalism of distinguishing *Matlock* from this case than to impose a requirement, time consuming in the field and in the courtroom, with no apparent systemic justification. The pragmatic decision to accept the simplicity of this line is, moreover, supported by the substantial number of instances in which suspects who are asked for permission to search actually consent, albeit imprudently, a fact that undercuts any argument that the police should try to locate a suspected inhabitant because his denial of consent would be a foregone conclusion.

III

This case invites a straightforward application of the rule that a physically present inhabitant's express refusal of consent to a police search is dispositive as to him, regardless of the consent of a fellow occupant. Scott Randolph's refusal is clear, and nothing in the record justifies the search on grounds independent of Janet Randolph's consent. The State does not argue that she gave any indication to the police of a need for protection inside the house that might have justified entry into the portion of the premises where the police found the powdery straw (which, if lawfully seized, could have been used when attempting to establish probable cause for the warrant issued later). Nor does the State claim that the entry and search should be upheld under the rubric of exigent circumstances, owing to some apprehension by the police officers that Scott Randolph would destroy evidence of drug use before any warrant could be obtained.

CHIEF JUSTICE ROBERTS, with whom JUSTICE SCALIA joins, dissenting.

The Court creates constitutional law by surmising what is typical when a social guest encounters an entirely atypical situation. The rule the majority fashions does not implement the high office of the Fourth Amendment to protect privacy, but instead provides protection on a random and happenstance basis, protecting, for example, a co-occupant who happens to be at the front door when the other occupant consents to a search, but not one napping or watching television in the next room. And the cost of affording such random protection is great, as demonstrated by the recurring cases in which abused spouses seek to authorize police entry into a home they share with a nonconsenting abuser.

The correct approach to the question presented is clearly mapped out in our precedents: The Fourth Amendment protects privacy. If an individual shares information, papers, *or places* with another, he assumes the risk that the other person will in turn share access to that information or those papers *or places* with the government. And just as an individual who has shared illegal plans or incriminating documents with another cannot interpose an objection when that other person turns the information over to the government, just because the individual happens to be present at the time, so too someone who shares a place with another cannot interpose an objection when that person decides to grant access to the police, simply because the objecting individual happens to be present.

A warrantless search is reasonable if police obtain the voluntary consent of a person authorized to give it. Co-occupants have assumed the risk that one of their number might permit a common area to be searched. Just as Mrs. Randolph could walk upstairs, come down, and turn her husband's cocaine straw over to the police, she can consent to police entry and search of what is, after all, her home, too.

———————

Let's return one last time to our cantankerous roommates, Carl Clean and Martin Messy. Suppose Carl consents to a search of the apartment, but Martin tells the police, in no uncertain terms, that they may not enter. The police retreat to their vehicle, run a quick background check on Martin Messy, and discover that there is an outstanding warrant for his arrest for an assault that took place three weeks earlier. The police return to the apartment and arrest Martin just outside the front door. Before being taken away, he again tells police that he does not consent to a search of the apartment. An hour later, the police arrive back at the apartment and request permission from Carl Clean to search the apartment. Carl agrees. The police enter and discover drugs belonging to Martin in a coffee can in the kitchen. Are the drugs admissible against Martin Messy on the basis of Carl Clean's consent to the search?

In *Fernandez v. California*, the Supreme Court confronted a similar set of facts and made it clear that the rule announced in *Georgia v. Randolph*—that one resident's refusal of consent to a search prevails over another resident's permission—applies only when the objecting resident is physically present. Once the objecting resident is no longer present, the police are free to search with the consent of another resident who has common authority over the premises.

FERNANDEZ V. CALIFORNIA

134 S.Ct. 1126 (2014)

JUSTICE ALITO delivered the opinion of the Court.

Our cases firmly establish that police officers may search jointly occupied premises if one of the occupants[1] consents. In *Georgia v. Randolph*, 547 U.S. 103 (2006), we recognized a narrow exception to this rule, holding that the consent of one occupant is insufficient when another occupant is present and objects to the search. In this case, we consider whether *Randolph* applies if the objecting occupant is absent when another occupant consents. Our opinion in *Randolph* took great pains to emphasize that its holding was limited to situations in which the objecting occupant is physically present. We therefore refuse to extend *Randolph* to the very different situation in this case, where consent was provided by an abused woman well after her male partner had been removed from the apartment they shared.

I

The events involved in this case occurred in Los Angeles in October 2009. After observing Abel Lopez cash a check, petitioner Walter Fernandez approached Lopez and asked about the neighborhood in which he lived. When Lopez responded that he was from Mexico, Fernandez laughed and told Lopez that he was in territory ruled by the "D.F.S.," *i.e.*, the "Drifters" gang. Petitioner then pulled out a knife and pointed it at

---

[1] We use the terms "occupant," "resident," and "tenant" interchangeably to refer to persons having "common authority" over premises.

Lopez's chest. Lopez raised his hand in self-defense, and petitioner cut him on the wrist.

Lopez ran from the scene and called 911 for help, but petitioner whistled, and four men emerged from a nearby apartment building and attacked Lopez. After knocking him to the ground, they hit and kicked him and took his cell phone and his wallet, which contained $400 in cash.

A police dispatch reported the incident and mentioned the possibility of gang involvement, and two Los Angeles police officers, Detective Clark and Officer Cirrito, drove to an alley frequented by members of the Drifters. A man who appeared scared walked by the officers and said: "The guy is in the apartment." The officers then observed a man run through the alley and into the building to which the man was pointing. A minute or two later, the officers heard sounds of screaming and fighting coming from that building.

After backup arrived, the officers knocked on the door of the apartment unit from which the screams had been heard. Roxanne Rojas answered the door. She was holding a baby and appeared to be crying. Her face was red, and she had a large bump on her nose. The officers also saw blood on her shirt and hand from what appeared to be a fresh injury. Rojas told the police that she had been in a fight. Officer Cirrito asked if anyone else was in the apartment, and Rojas said that her 4-year-old son was the only other person present.

After Officer Cirrito asked Rojas to step out of the apartment so that he could conduct a protective sweep, petitioner appeared at the door wearing only boxer shorts. Apparently agitated, petitioner stepped forward and said, "You don't have any right to come in here. I know my rights." Suspecting that petitioner had assaulted Rojas, the officers removed him from the apartment and then placed him under arrest. Lopez identified petitioner as his initial attacker, and petitioner was taken to the police station for booking.

Approximately one hour after petitioner's arrest, Detective Clark returned to the apartment and informed Rojas that petitioner had been arrested. Detective Clark requested and received both oral and written consent from Rojas to search the premises. In the apartment, the police found Drifters gang paraphernalia, a butterfly knife, clothing worn by the robbery suspect, and ammunition. Rojas' young son also showed the officers where petitioner had hidden a sawed-off shotgun.

Petitioner was charged with robbery, infliction of corporal injury on a spouse, cohabitant, or child's parent, possession of a firearm by a felon, possession of a short-barreled shotgun, and felony possession of ammunition. Before trial, petitioner moved to suppress the evidence found in the apartment, but after a hearing, the court denied the motion. Petitioner then pleaded *nolo contendere* to the firearms and ammunition charges. On the remaining counts—for robbery and infliction of corporal injury—he went to trial and was found guilty by a jury. The court sentenced him to 14 years of imprisonment.

II

The Fourth Amendment prohibits unreasonable searches and seizures and provides that a warrant may not be issued without probable cause, but the text of the Fourth Amendment does not specify when a search warrant must be obtained. Our cases establish that a warrant is generally required for a search of a home, but the ultimate touchstone of the Fourth Amendment is "reasonableness." And certain categories of permissible warrantless searches have long been recognized.

Consent searches occupy one of these categories. It would be unreasonable—indeed, absurd—to require police officers to obtain a warrant when the sole owner or occupant of a house or apartment voluntarily consents to a search. The owner of a home has a right to allow others to enter and examine the premises, and there is no reason why the owner should not be permitted to extend this same privilege to police officers if that is the owner's choice. Where the owner believes that he or she is under suspicion, the owner may want the police to search the premises so that their suspicions are dispelled. This may be particularly important where the owner has a strong interest in the apprehension of the perpetrator of a crime and believes that the suspicions of the police are deflecting the course of their investigation. An owner may want the police to search even where they lack probable cause, and if a warrant were always required, this could not be done. And even where the police could establish probable cause, requiring a warrant despite the owner's consent would needlessly inconvenience everyone involved—not only the officers and the magistrate but also the occupant of the premises, who would generally either be compelled or would feel a need to stay until the search was completed.

While consent by one resident of jointly occupied premises is generally sufficient to justify a warrantless search, we recognized a narrow exception to this rule in *Georgia v. Randolph*. [We] held that "*a physically present inhabitant's* express refusal of consent to a police search [of his home] is dispositive as to him, regardless of the consent of a fellow occupant." The Court's opinion went to great lengths to make clear that its holding was limited to situations in which the objecting occupant is present. Again and again, the opinion of the Court stressed this controlling factor.

III

In this case, petitioner was not present when Rojas consented, but petitioner still contends that *Randolph* is controlling. He advances two main arguments. First, he claims that his absence should not matter since he was absent only because the police had taken him away. Second, he maintains that it was sufficient that he objected to the search while he was still present. Such an objection, he says, should remain in effect until the objecting party no longer wishes to keep the police out of his home. Neither of these arguments is sound.

We first consider the argument that the presence of the objecting occupant is not necessary when the police are responsible for his absence. In *Randolph*, the Court suggested in dictum that consent by one occupant might not be sufficient if "there is evidence that the police have removed the potentially objecting tenant from the entrance for the sake of avoiding a possible objection." We do not believe the statement should be read to suggest that improper motive may invalidate objectively justified removal. Hence, it does not govern here.

The *Randolph* dictum is best understood not to require an inquiry into the subjective intent of officers who detain or arrest a potential objector but instead to refer to situations in which the removal of the potential objector is not objectively reasonable. Our Fourth Amendment cases have repeatedly rejected a subjective approach.

Petitioner does not claim that the *Randolph* Court meant to break from this consistent practice, and we do not think that it did. And once it is recognized that the test is one of objective reasonableness, petitioner's argument collapses. He does not contest the fact that the police had reasonable grounds for removing him from the apartment so that they could speak with Rojas, an apparent victim of domestic violence, outside of petitioner's potentially intimidating presence. In fact, he does not even contest the existence of probable cause to place him under arrest. We therefore hold that an occupant who is absent due to a lawful detention or arrest stands in the same shoes as an occupant who is absent for any other reason.

The *Randolph* holding unequivocally requires the presence of the objecting occupant in every situation other than the one mentioned in the dictum discussed above.

This brings us to petitioner's second argument, that his objection, made at the threshold of the premises that the police wanted to search, remained effective until he changed his mind and withdrew his objection. This argument is inconsistent with *Randolph*'s reasoning in at least two important ways. First, the argument cannot be squared with the "widely shared social expectations" or "customary social usage" upon which the *Randolph* holding was based. Explaining why consent by one occupant could not override an objection by a physically present occupant, the *Randolph* Court stated:

> It is fair to say that a caller standing at the door of shared
> premises would have no confidence that one occupant's

invitation was a sufficiently good reason to enter when a fellow tenant stood there saying, "stay out." Without some very good reason, no sensible person would go inside under those conditions.

It seems obvious that the calculus of this hypothetical caller would likely be quite different if the objecting tenant was not standing at the door. When the objecting occupant is standing at the threshold saying "stay out," a friend or visitor invited to enter by another occupant can expect at best an uncomfortable scene and at worst violence if he or she tries to brush past the objector. But when the objector is not on the scene (and especially when it is known that the objector will not return during the course of the visit), the friend or visitor is much more likely to accept the invitation to enter. Thus, petitioner's argument is inconsistent with *Randolph*'s reasoning.

Second, petitioner's argument would create the very sort of practical complications that *Randolph* sought to avoid. For one thing, there is the question of duration. Petitioner argues that an objection, once made, should last until it is withdrawn by the objector, but such a rule would be unreasonable. Suppose that a husband and wife owned a house as joint tenants and that the husband, after objecting to a search of the house, was convicted and sentenced to a 15-year prison term. Under petitioner's proposed rule, the wife would be unable to consent to a search of the house 10 years after the date on which her husband objected. We refuse to stretch *Randolph* to such strange lengths.

Nor are we persuaded to hold that an objection lasts for a "reasonable" time. It is certainly unusual for this Court to set forth precise time limits governing police action, and what interval of time would be reasonable in this context? A week? A month? A year? Ten years?

Petitioner's rule would also require the police and ultimately the courts to determine whether, after the passage of time, an objector still had "common authority" over the premises, and this would often be a tricky question. Suppose that an incarcerated objector and a consenting co-occupant were joint tenants on a lease. If the objector, after incarceration, stopped paying rent, would he still have "common authority," and would his objection retain its force? Would it be enough that his name remained on the lease? Would the result be different if the objecting and consenting lessees had an oral month-to-month tenancy?

Another problem concerns the procedure needed to register a continuing objection. Would it be necessary for an occupant to object while police officers are at the door? If presence at the time of consent is not needed, would an occupant have to be present at the premises when the objection was made? Could an objection be made pre-emptively? Could a person like Scott Randolph, suspecting that his estranged wife might invite the police to view his drug stash and paraphernalia, register an objection in advance? Could this be done by posting a sign in front of the house? Could a standing objection be registered by serving notice on the chief of police?

Finally, there is the question of the particular law enforcement officers who would be bound by an objection. Would this set include just the officers who were present when the objection was made? Would it also apply to other officers working on the same investigation? Would it extend to officers who were unaware of the objection? How about officers assigned to different but arguably related cases? Would it be limited by law enforcement agency?

If *Randolph* is taken at its word—that it applies only when the objector is standing in the door saying "stay out" when officers propose to make a consent search—all of these problems disappear.

Petitioner argues strenuously that his expansive interpretation of *Randolph* would not hamper law enforcement because in most cases where officers have probable cause to arrest a physically present objector they also have probable cause to search the premises that the objector does not want them to enter, but this argument misunderstands the constitutional status of consent searches. A warrantless consent search is reasonable and thus consistent with the Fourth Amendment irrespective of the availability of a warrant. Even with modern technological advances, the warrant procedure imposes burdens on the officers who wish to search, the magistrate who must review the warrant application, and the party willing to give consent. When a warrantless search is justified, requiring the police to obtain a warrant may unjustifiably interfere with legitimate law enforcement strategies. Such a requirement may also impose an unmerited burden on the person who consents to an immediate search, since the warrant application procedure entails delay. Putting the exception the Court adopted in *Randolph* to one side, the lawful occupant of a house or apartment should have the right to invite the police to enter the dwelling and conduct a search. Any other rule would trample on the rights of the occupant who is willing to consent. Such an occupant may want the police to search in order to dispel suspicion raised by sharing quarters with a criminal. And an occupant may want the police to conduct a thorough search so that any dangerous contraband can be found and removed. In this case, for example, the search resulted in the discovery and removal of a sawed-off shotgun to which Rojas' 4-year-old son had access.

Denying someone in Rojas' position the right to allow the police to enter *her* home would also show disrespect for her independence. Having beaten Rojas, petitioner would bar her from controlling access to her own home until such time as he chose to relent. The Fourth Amendment does not give him that power.

JUSTICE GINSBURG, with whom JUSTICE SOTOMAYOR and JUSTICE KAGAN join, dissenting.

Instead of adhering to the warrant requirement, today's decision tells the police they may dodge it, nevermind ample time to secure the approval of a neutral magistrate. Suppressing the warrant requirement, the Court shrinks to petite size our holding in *Georgia v. Randolph* that "a physically present inhabitant's express refusal of consent to a police search [of his home] is dispositive as to him, regardless of the consent of a fellow occupant."

Despite marked similarities, the Court removes this case from *Randolph*'s ambit. The Court does so principally by seizing on the fact that Fernandez, unlike Scott Randolph, was no longer present and objecting when the police obtained the co-occupant's consent. But Fernandez *was* present when he stated his objection to the would-be searchers in no uncertain terms. The officers could scarcely have forgotten, one hour later, that Fernandez refused consent while physically present. That express, on-premises objection should have been "dispositive as to him."

The Court tells us that the "widely shared social expectations" and "customary social usage" undergirding *Randolph*'s holding apply only when the objector remains physically present. [But] as the Court comprehended just last Term [in *Florida v. Jardines*, 133 S.Ct. 1409, 1416 (2013)], "the background social norms that invite a visitor to the front door do not invite him there to conduct a search." Similarly here, even if shared tenancy were understood to entail the prospect of visits by unwanted social callers while the objecting resident was gone, that unwelcome visitor's license would hardly include free rein to rummage through the dwelling in search of evidence and contraband.

Next, the Court cautions, applying *Randolph* to these facts would pose "a plethora of practical problems." For instance, the Court asks, must a cotenant's objection, once registered, be respected indefinitely? Yet it blinks reality to suppose that Fernandez, by withholding consent, could stop police in their tracks eternally. To mount the prosecution eventuating in a conviction, of course, the State would first need to obtain incriminating evidence, and could get it easily simply by applying for a warrant. Warrant in police hands, the Court's practical problems disappear.

Indeed, reading *Randolph* to require continuous physical presence poses administrative difficulties of its own. Does an occupant's refusal to consent lose force as soon as she absents herself from the doorstep, even if only for a moment? Are the police free to enter the instant after the objector leaves the door to retire for a nap, answer the phone, use the bathroom, or speak to another officer outside? Hypothesized practical considerations, in short, provide no cause for today's drastic reduction of *Randolph*'s holding and attendant disregard for the warrant requirement.

In its zeal to diminish *Randolph*, today's decision overlooks the warrant requirement's venerable role as the bulwark of Fourth Amendment protection. Reducing *Randolph* to a "narrow exception," the Court declares the main rule to be that "consent by one resident of jointly occupied premises is generally sufficient to justify a warrantless search." That declaration has it backwards, for consent searches themselves are a jealously and carefully drawn exception to the Fourth Amendment rule ordinarily prohibiting the warrantless entry of a person's house as unreasonable *per se*.

In this case, the police could readily have obtained a warrant to search the shared residence. The Court does not dispute this, but instead disparages the warrant requirement as inconvenient, burdensome, entailing delay "even with modern technological advances." Shut from the Court's sight is the ease and speed with which search warrants nowadays can be obtained. With these developments in view, dilution of the warrant requirement should be vigilantly resisted.

Although the police have probable cause and could obtain a warrant with dispatch, if they can gain the consent of someone other than the suspect, why should the law insist on the formality of a warrant? Because the Framers saw the neutral magistrate as an essential part of the criminal process shielding all of us, good or bad, saint or sinner, from unchecked police activity. The Fourth Amendment, the Court has long recognized, reflects the view of those who wrote the Bill of Rights that the privacy of a person's home and property may not be totally sacrificed in the name of maximum simplicity in enforcement of the criminal law.

A final word is in order about the Court's reference to Rojas' autonomy, which, in its view, is best served by allowing her consent to trump an abusive cohabitant's objection. Rojas' situation is not distinguishable from Janet Randolph's in this regard. If a person's health and safety are threatened by a domestic abuser, exigent circumstances would justify immediate removal of the abuser from the premises, as happened here. As the Court understood in *Randolph*, the specter of domestic abuse hardly necessitates the diminution of the Fourth Amendment rights at stake here.

For the reasons stated, I would honor the Fourth Amendment's warrant requirement and hold that Fernandez's objection to the search did not become null upon his arrest and removal from the scene. There is every reason to conclude that securing a warrant was entirely feasible in this case, and no reason to contract the Fourth Amendment's dominion.

Consent Searches

1. Police may perform a search without a warrant and without probable cause if they have valid consent. In order to demonstrate valid consent, the prosecution must show that consent was *voluntarily* given, and is not the result of duress or coercion, express or implied. Voluntariness is a question of fact to be determined from the totality of the circumstances. While knowledge of a right to refuse consent is one factor to be taken into account, the prosecution need not prove such knowledge to establish voluntary consent.

2. A third party's consent to a search is valid if it is voluntary and if the police reasonably believe that the third party has *common authority* over the premises. Common authority rests on mutual use of the property by persons generally having joint access or control for most purposes.

3. A physically present resident's refusal of consent to a search prevails over another resident's permission. But once the objecting resident is no longer physically present, the police may search with the voluntary consent of another resident who has common authority over the premises.

LEARN MORE WITH *LAW & ORDER*

In the following episode of *Law & Order* ("Savages," Season 6, Episode 3), the detectives suspect that Paul Sandig, an accountant, murdered an undercover police officer who had discovered Sandig's involvement in laundering money for a drug dealer. The detectives obtain a warrant to search for evidence in Sandig's office. In the course of the search, Sandig's business partner, Lyndon Whitney, shows the police a storage room in the office and points out a locked container where Sandig kept some of his records. Police use a bolt-cutter to open the container, and inside, they find recordings of Sandig's phone calls, including one in which Sandig was informed that the man he later murdered was, in fact, an undercover police officer. (Sandig's knowledge that the murder victim was a police officer is important because it made him eligible for the death penalty, which was reinstated in New York by Governor George Pataki in 1995.) After Sandig is charged with first degree murder, his defense attorney moves to suppress the recordings. As you watch the episode, try to trace the arguments made by both the prosecution and the defense with respect to the admissibility of the recordings, and consider which cases might have been helpful to the judge in making her decision.

> **The segments of the episode that depict the relevant
> Investigative Criminal Procedure issues appear at:**
>
> 17:09 to 20:58; 26:06 to 27:52

> ***Law & Order* Episode**
> **"Savages," Season 6, Episode 3**

The prosecution initially argues that the tape recordings are admissible because police had a warrant to search Sandig's office. But as you know from Chapter 4—and cases such as *Andresen v. Maryland*, 427 U.S. 463 (1976), and *Groh v. Ramirez*, 540 U.S. 551 (2004)—a warrant must particularly describe the place to be searched. The defense attorney points out that Sandig's office is suite 242, while the recordings were found in the storage room, suite 248. Although we can't read and evaluate the language in the search warrant, prosecutor Jack McCoy seems willing to concede that the search cannot be justified on the basis of the warrant.

In an effort to salvage the search, the prosecution next contends that police had consent from Lyndon Whitney. As Sandig's business partner, Whitney had common authority (or actual authority) over the partnership's property. The defense attorney responds by demonstrating that Sandig and Whitney merely had a space-sharing agreement and were not a legal partnership. Thus, Whitney had no actual authority over Sandig's property located in their shared office space.

The prosecution's last argument is that even if Whitney lacked actual authority to consent to the search, he had *apparent authority* because it appeared to the police that Whitney and Sandig were business partners with common authority over their shared office space. Although McCoy doesn't cite it, *Illinois v. Rodriguez*, 497 U.S. 177 (1990), establishes the rule that allows police to search with a third party's consent when it reasonably appears to the police that the third party has common authority over the premises. The defense attorney responds by noting that the container in which the recordings were found was locked and Whitney did not have a key; the police used a bolt-cutter because it was clear that Whitney did not have common authority over the container. The facts in *Rodriguez* support the defense on this point, since Gail Fischer had a key to the apartment and unlocked the door for the police; unlike Whitney, she had *apparent authority* over the apartment even though she lacked *actual authority*.

The judge is ultimately not persuaded by any of the prosecution's arguments, and she excludes the tapes from Sandig's trial. Because the illegally obtained tapes led to the discovery of additional evidence—in particular, insurance adjuster Marty Prince's testimony that he told

Sandig that the murder victim was an undercover police officer—the defense attorney asks the judge to apply the fruits doctrine (covered in Chapter 8) and exclude Prince's testimony as well. The judge agrees. With no remaining evidence showing that Sandig knew the victim was a police officer, the judge is forced to dismiss the first degree murder charge which made Sandig eligible for the death penalty.

CHAPTER 6

SEIZURES OF PERSONS

■ ■ ■

Most of the cases presented thus far deal with the authority of police to search for and seize items of evidence. But very few of those earlier cases focus in any meaningful way on the actual seizure of evidence because the authority to search usually carries with it the power to seize. For example, a search warrant will typically include language specifically authorizing the executing officer to both search for and seize any items described in the warrant. Thus, if the search is valid, any related seizure will usually be valid too.

This Chapter focuses on seizures of persons, a subject that is doctrinally distinct from other Fourth Amendment topics dealing with the authority of police to search for and seize property or items of evidence. The cases in this Chapter describe three types of interactions of increasing intensity between individuals and law enforcement officers: encounters, stops (which may also include a "patdown search" or "frisk"), and arrests.

In an *encounter*—sometimes described as a *voluntary* or *consensual encounter*—an officer approaches an individual, asks a few questions, and might even request permission to conduct a search of the individual or his belongings. Because the individual is not required to answer the questions or consent to the search, and because he is—at least in theory—free to leave at any time, an encounter does not constitute a seizure under the Fourth Amendment.

Closely related to an encounter, but more intrusive and severe, is a *stop*. In a stop—sometimes described as a *forcible stop*, an *investigatory stop*, a *temporary detention*, or a *Terry stop*, after *Terry v. Ohio*, 392 U.S. 1 (1968)—an officer uses physical force or a show of authority to briefly detain an individual for questioning or further investigation including, in some cases, a frisk for weapons. Because the individual is not free to leave, a stop constitutes a seizure under the Fourth Amendment.

An *arrest* is even more intrusive and prolonged than a stop. In an arrest, law enforcement officers restrict an individual's freedom for an extended period of time. A statement by the police that an individual is under arrest or the use of handcuffs are often the clearest indications of an arrest, but one can occur without any words to that effect or the use of physical restraints. An arrest is the paradigmatic example of a seizure of a person under the Fourth Amendment.

The line between an encounter, a stop, and an arrest is not always clear. Subtle differences in the words or actions of the police can transform an encounter into a stop and a stop into an arrest. For example, imagine Tom Traveler, who is nervously pacing back and forth in an airport lobby a few feet from a security checkpoint. A police officer notices Tom, approaches, and asks, "Do you mind answering a few questions?" Tom agrees and proceeds to answer several polite questions about his name, his destination, and his occupation. The officer then tells Tom: "Due to concerns about dangerous weapons and drugs being brought into airports, I'd appreciate it if I could take a quick look in your backpack to dispel any suspicion." Tom hands over his backpack and the officer quickly searches it. Although the interaction, from Tom's perspective, may have felt somewhat coercive, the Supreme Court would likely view it as a voluntary encounter. If the officer discovers contraband in Tom's backpack, it would be admissible against Tom as the product of a voluntary encounter and a consensual search.

Now suppose that the officer, upon approaching Tom, is a little less polite. He puts a firm hand on Tom's shoulder and says in an authoritative voice: "Don't move. I need to ask you some questions." After posing the same routine questions about Tom's name, destination, and occupation, the officer tells Tom: "I need to search your person and your backpack to make sure you're not carrying any weapons or drugs." Tom holds out his arms as the officer performs a frisk, then Tom hands over his backpack and the officer searches it. Although this interaction appears very similar to the first, the subtle differences in language and tone, coupled with the officer's use of a "firm hand" on Tom's shoulder and the subsequent frisk, convey that Tom is not free to leave or refuse consent to the search. The Supreme Court would likely view the interaction as a forcible stop—a seizure—triggering certain protections for Tom under the Fourth Amendment.

Finally, suppose the interaction between Tom and the officer begins as described in the voluntary encounter scenario. After searching Tom's backpack (with Tom's consent) and finding nothing of interest, the officer asks Tom to accompany him to a back room in the airport to answer some additional questions from a supervisor. Tom is reluctant to do this for fear of missing his plane, but the officer tells Tom that it's important that he cooperate with "airport procedures." Tom is then taken to the back room where a supervisor questions him for 45 minutes. At several points during the questioning when Tom asks to leave to catch his plane, the supervisor replies: "We need to finish our investigation before you board an airplane and leave the jurisdiction." While this interaction might have begun as a voluntary encounter, the Supreme Court could easily conclude that it became an arrest—triggering certain Fourth Amendment protections for Tom above and beyond those in the forcible stop scenario—after Tom was taken to the back room, subjected to further questioning, and detained for an extended period of time despite his repeated requests to leave.

As you read the cases in this Chapter, focus on the critical facts that lead the Supreme Court to classify a particular interaction as an encounter, a stop, or an arrest. Focus too on the rules devised by the Supreme Court to regulate encounters, stops, and arrests, and consider whether those rules strike the right balance between the needs of law enforcement and the Fourth Amendment rights of individuals.

A. WHEN IS A PERSON "SEIZED"?: CONSENSUAL ENCOUNTERS

Tom Traveler's travails are based loosely on the facts in *U.S. v. Mendenhall*, in which the Supreme Court considered the subtle differences between encounters, stops, and arrests. While the Court was divided on many of the key issues, Justice Stewart's opinion offered a standard to determine when a person has been seized.

U.S. v. MENDENHALL
446 U.S. 544 (1980)

JUSTICE STEWART announced the judgment of the Court and delivered an opinion, in which JUSTICE REHNQUIST joined.

The respondent was brought to trial in the United States District Court for the Eastern District of Michigan on a charge of possessing heroin with intent to distribute it. She moved to suppress the introduction at trial of the heroin as evidence against her on the ground that it had been acquired from her through an unconstitutional search and seizure by agents of the Drug Enforcement Administration (DEA). The District Court denied the respondent's motion, and she was convicted after a trial upon stipulated facts. The Court of Appeals reversed, finding the search of the respondent's person to have been unlawful.

I

At the hearing in the trial court on the respondent's motion to suppress, it was established how the heroin she was charged with possessing had been obtained from her. The respondent arrived at the Detroit Metropolitan Airport on a commercial airline flight from Los Angeles early in the morning on February 10, 1976. As she disembarked from the airplane, she was observed by two agents of the DEA, who were present at the airport for the purpose of detecting unlawful traffic in narcotics. After observing the respondent's conduct, which appeared to the agents to be characteristic of persons unlawfully carrying narcotics,[1]

---

[1] The agent testified that the respondent's behavior fit the so-called "drug courier profile"—an informally compiled abstract of characteristics thought typical of persons carrying

the agents approached her as she was walking through the concourse, identified themselves as federal agents, and asked to see her identification and airline ticket. The respondent produced her driver's license, which was in the name of Sylvia Mendenhall, and, in answer to a question of one of the agents, stated that she resided at the address appearing on the license. The airline ticket was issued in the name of "Annette Ford." When asked why the ticket bore a name different from her own, the respondent stated that she "just felt like using that name." In response to a further question, the respondent indicated that she had been in California only two days. Agent Anderson then specifically identified himself as a federal narcotics agent and, according to his testimony, the respondent "became quite shaken, extremely nervous. She had a hard time speaking."

After returning the airline ticket and driver's license to her, Agent Anderson asked the respondent if she would accompany him to the airport DEA office for further questions. She did so, although the record does not indicate a verbal response to the request. The office, which was located up one flight of stairs about 50 feet from where the respondent had first been approached, consisted of a reception area adjoined by three other rooms. At the office the agent asked the respondent if she would allow a search of her person and handbag and told her that she had the right to decline the search if she desired. She responded: "Go ahead." She then handed Agent Anderson her purse, which contained a receipt for an airline ticket that had been issued to "F. Bush" three days earlier for a flight from Pittsburgh through Chicago to Los Angeles. The agent asked whether this was the ticket that she had used for her flight to California, and the respondent stated that it was.

A female police officer then arrived to conduct the search of the respondent's person. She asked the agents if the respondent had consented to be searched. The agents said that she had, and the respondent followed the policewoman into a private room. There the policewoman again asked the respondent if she consented to the search, and the respondent replied that she did. The policewoman explained that the search would require that the respondent remove her clothing. The respondent stated that she had a plane to catch and was assured by the policewoman that if she were carrying no narcotics, there would be no problem. The respondent then began to disrobe without further comment. As the respondent removed her clothing, she took from her undergarments two small packages, one of which appeared to contain

---

illicit drugs. In this case the agents thought it relevant that (1) the respondent was arriving on a flight from Los Angeles, a city believed by the agents to be the place of origin for much of the heroin brought to Detroit; (2) the respondent was the last person to leave the plane, "appeared to be very nervous," and "completely scanned the whole area where [the agents] were standing"; (3) after leaving the plane the respondent proceeded past the baggage area without claiming any luggage; and (4) the respondent changed airlines for her flight out of Detroit.

heroin, and handed both to the policewoman. The agents then arrested the respondent for possessing heroin.

It was on the basis of this evidence that the District Court denied the respondent's motion to suppress. The court concluded that the agents' conduct in initially approaching the respondent and asking to see her ticket and identification was a permissible investigative stop under the standards of *Terry v. Ohio*, 392 U.S. 1 (1968), finding that this conduct was based on specific and articulable facts that justified a suspicion of criminal activity. The court also found that the respondent had not been placed under arrest or otherwise detained when she was asked to accompany the agents to the DEA office, but had accompanied the agents "voluntarily in a spirit of apparent cooperation." It was the court's view that no arrest occurred until after the heroin had been found. Finally, the trial court found that the respondent "gave her consent to the search [in the DEA office] and such consent was freely and voluntarily given."

II

The Government concedes that its agents had neither a warrant nor probable cause to believe that the respondent was carrying narcotics when the agents conducted a search of the respondent's person. It is the Government's position, however, that the search was conducted pursuant to the respondent's consent, and thus was excepted from the requirements of both a warrant and probable cause. Evidently, the Court of Appeals concluded that the respondent's apparent consent to the search was in fact not voluntarily given and was in any event the product of earlier official conduct violative of the Fourth Amendment. We must first consider, therefore, whether such conduct occurred, either on the concourse or in the DEA office at the airport.

A

The Fourth Amendment's requirement that searches and seizures be founded upon an objective justification governs all seizures of the person, including seizures that involve only a brief detention short of traditional arrest. Accordingly, if the respondent was "seized" when the DEA agents approached her on the concourse and asked questions of her, the agents' conduct in doing so was constitutional only if they reasonably suspected the respondent of wrongdoing. But obviously, not all personal intercourse between policemen and citizens involves "seizures" of persons. Only when the officer, by means of physical force or show of authority, has in some way restrained the liberty of a citizen may we conclude that a "seizure" has occurred.

The distinction between an intrusion amounting to a "seizure" of the person and an encounter that intrudes upon no constitutionally protected interest is illustrated by the facts of *Terry v. Ohio*: Officer McFadden approached the three men, identified himself as a police officer and asked for their names. When the men mumbled something in response to his inquiries, Officer McFadden grabbed Terry, spun him around so that they were facing the other two, with Terry between McFadden and the others, and patted down the outside of his clothing. Obviously the officer "seized" Terry and subjected him to a "search" when he took hold of him, spun him around, and patted down the outer surfaces of his clothing. What was not determined in that case, however, was that a seizure had taken place before the officer physically restrained Terry for purposes of searching his person for weapons. The Court assumed that up to that point no intrusion upon constitutionally protected rights had occurred. The Court's assumption appears entirely correct in view of the fact, noted in the concurring opinion of Justice White, that "there is nothing in the Constitution which prevents a policeman from addressing questions to anyone on the streets." Police officers enjoy the liberty (again, possessed by every citizen) to address questions to other persons, although ordinarily the person addressed has an equal right to ignore his interrogator and walk away.

We adhere to the view that a person is "seized" only when, by means of physical force or a show of authority, his freedom of movement is restrained. Only when such restraint is imposed is there any foundation whatever for invoking constitutional safeguards. The purpose of the Fourth Amendment is not to eliminate all contact between the police and the citizenry, but to prevent arbitrary and oppressive interference by enforcement officials with the privacy and personal security of individuals. As long as the person to whom questions are put remains free to disregard the questions and walk away, there has been no intrusion upon that person's liberty or privacy as would under the Constitution require some particularized and objective justification.

Moreover, characterizing every street encounter between a citizen and the police as a "seizure," while not enhancing any interest secured by the Fourth Amendment, would impose wholly unrealistic restrictions upon a wide variety of legitimate law enforcement practices. The Court has on other occasions referred to the acknowledged need for police questioning as a tool in the effective enforcement of the criminal laws. Without such investigation, those who were innocent might be falsely accused, those who were guilty might wholly escape prosecution, and many crimes would go unsolved. In short, the security of all would be diminished.

We conclude that a person has been "seized" within the meaning of the Fourth Amendment only if, in view of all of the circumstances surrounding the incident, a reasonable person would have believed that he was not free to leave.[6] Examples of circumstances that might indicate

---

[6] We agree with the District Court that the subjective intention of the DEA agent in this case to detain the respondent, had she attempted to leave, is irrelevant except insofar as that may have been conveyed to the respondent.

a seizure, even where the person did not attempt to leave, would be the threatening presence of several officers, the display of a weapon by an officer, some physical touching of the person of the citizen, or the use of language or tone of voice indicating that compliance with the officer's request might be compelled. In the absence of some such evidence, otherwise inoffensive contact between a member of the public and the police cannot, as a matter of law, amount to a seizure of that person.

On the facts of this case, no "seizure" of the respondent occurred. The events took place in the public concourse. The agents wore no uniforms and displayed no weapons. They did not summon the respondent to their presence, but instead approached her and identified themselves as federal agents. They requested, but did not demand, to see the respondent's identification and ticket. Such conduct, without more, did not amount to an intrusion upon any constitutionally protected interest. The respondent was not seized simply by reason of the fact that the agents approached her, asked her if she would show them her ticket and identification, and posed to her a few questions. Nor was it enough to establish a seizure that the person asking the questions was a law enforcement official. In short, nothing in the record suggests that the respondent had any objective reason to believe that she was not free to end the conversation in the concourse and proceed on her way, and for that reason we conclude that the agents' initial approach to her was not a seizure.

Our conclusion that no seizure occurred is not affected by the fact that the respondent was not expressly told by the agents that she was free to decline to cooperate with their inquiry, for the voluntariness of her responses does not depend upon her having been so informed. See *Schneckloth v. Bustamonte*, 412 U.S. 218 (1973). We also reject the argument that the only inference to be drawn from the fact that the respondent acted in a manner so contrary to her self-interest is that she was compelled to answer the agents' questions. It may happen that a person makes statements to law enforcement officials that he later regrets, but the issue in such cases is not whether the statement was self-protective, but rather whether it was made voluntarily.

B

Although we have concluded that the initial encounter between the DEA agents and the respondent on the concourse at the Detroit Airport did not constitute an unlawful seizure, it is still arguable that the respondent's Fourth Amendment protections were violated when she went from the concourse to the DEA office. Such a violation might in turn infect the subsequent search of the respondent's person.

The District Court specifically found that the respondent accompanied the agents to the office "voluntarily in a spirit of apparent cooperation." Notwithstanding this determination by the trial court, the Court of Appeals evidently concluded that the agents' request that the respondent accompany them converted the situation into an arrest requiring probable cause in order to be found lawful. But because the trial court's finding was sustained by the record, the Court of Appeals was mistaken in substituting for that finding its view of the evidence.

The question whether the respondent's consent to accompany the agents was in fact voluntary or was the product of duress or coercion, express or implied, is to be determined by the totality of all the circumstances, and is a matter which the Government has the burden of proving. The respondent herself did not testify at the hearing. The Government's evidence showed that the respondent was not told that she had to go to the office, but was simply asked if she would accompany the officers. There were neither threats nor any show of force. The respondent had been questioned only briefly, and her ticket and identification were returned to her before she was asked to accompany the officers.

On the other hand, it is argued that the incident would reasonably have appeared coercive to the respondent, who was 22 years old and had not been graduated from high school. It is additionally suggested that the respondent, a female and a Negro, may have felt unusually threatened by the officers, who were white males. While these factors were not irrelevant, neither were they decisive, and the totality of the evidence in this case was plainly adequate to support the District Court's finding that the respondent voluntarily consented to accompany the officers to the DEA office.

C

Because the search of the respondent's person was not preceded by an impermissible seizure of her person, it cannot be contended that her apparent consent to the subsequent search was infected by an unlawful detention. There remains to be considered whether the respondent's consent to the search was for any other reason invalid. The District Court explicitly credited the officers' testimony and found that the "consent was freely and voluntarily given." There was more than enough evidence in this case to sustain that view. First, we note that the respondent, who was 22 years old and had an 11th-grade education, was plainly capable of a knowing consent. Second, it is especially significant that the respondent was twice expressly told that she was free to decline to consent to the search, and only thereafter explicitly consented to it. Although the Constitution does not require proof of knowledge of a right to refuse as the *sine qua non* of an effective consent to a search, such knowledge was highly relevant to the determination that there had been consent. And, perhaps more important for present purposes, the fact that the officers themselves informed the respondent that she was free to withhold her consent substantially lessened the probability that their conduct could reasonably have appeared to her to be coercive.

Counsel for the respondent has argued that she did in fact resist the search, relying principally on the testimony that when she was told that the search would require the removal of her clothing, she stated to the female police officer that "she had a plane to catch." But the trial court was entitled to view the statement as simply an expression of concern that the search be conducted quickly. The respondent had twice unequivocally indicated her consent to the search, and when assured by the police officer that there would be no problem if nothing were turned up by the search, she began to undress without further comment.

Counsel for the respondent has also argued that because she was within the DEA office when she consented to the search, her consent may have resulted from the inherently coercive nature of those surroundings. But in view of the District Court's finding that the respondent's presence in the office was voluntary, the fact that she was there is little or no evidence that she was in any way coerced. And in response to the argument that the respondent would not voluntarily have consented to a search that was likely to disclose the narcotics that she carried, we repeat that the question is not whether the respondent acted in her ultimate self-interest, but whether she acted voluntarily.

We conclude that the District Court's determination that the respondent consented to the search of her person "freely and voluntarily" was sustained by the evidence and that the Court of Appeals was, therefore, in error in setting it aside.

JUSTICE POWELL, with whom CHIEF JUSTICE BURGER and JUSTICE BLACKMUN join, concurring in part and concurring in the judgment.

In my view, we may assume for present purposes that the stop did constitute a seizure. I would hold—as did the District Court—that the federal agents had reasonable suspicion that the respondent was engaging in criminal activity, and, therefore, that they did not violate the Fourth Amendment by stopping the respondent for routine questioning.

The District Court concluded that the decision to stop the respondent was reasonable. I agree. The public interest in preventing drug traffic is great, and the intrusion upon the respondent's privacy was minimal. The specially trained agents acted pursuant to a well-planned, and effective, federal law enforcement program. They observed respondent engaging in conduct that they reasonably associated with criminal activity. Furthermore, the events occurred in an airport known to be frequented by drug couriers. In light of all of the circumstances, I would hold that the agents possessed reasonable and articulable suspicion of criminal activity when they stopped the respondent in a public place and asked her for identification.

JUSTICE WHITE, with whom JUSTICE BRENNAN, JUSTICE MARSHALL, and JUSTICE STEVENS join, dissenting.

The Court today concludes that agents of the Drug Enforcement Administration (DEA) acted lawfully in stopping a traveler changing planes in an airport terminal and escorting her to a DEA office for a strip-search of her person. Justice Stewart concludes that the DEA agents acted lawfully, regardless of whether there were any reasonable grounds for suspecting Ms. Mendenhall of criminal activity, because he finds that Ms. Mendenhall was not "seized" by the DEA agents, even though throughout the proceedings below the Government never questioned the fact that a seizure had occurred necessitating a showing of antecedent reasonable suspicion. Justice Powell's opinion concludes that even though Ms. Mendenhall may have been "seized," the seizure was lawful because her behavior while changing planes in the airport provided reasonable suspicion that she was engaging in criminal activity. The Court then concludes, based on the absence of evidence that Ms. Mendenhall resisted her detention, that she voluntarily consented to being taken to the DEA office, even though she in fact had no choice in the matter. This conclusion is inconsistent with our recognition that consent cannot be presumed from a showing of acquiescence to authority.

Assuming, as we should, that Ms. Mendenhall was "seized" within the meaning of the Fourth Amendment when she was stopped by the DEA agents, the legality of that stop turns on whether there were reasonable grounds for suspecting her of criminal activity at the time of the stop. To establish that there was reasonable suspicion for the stop, it was necessary for the police at least to "be able to point to specific and articulable facts which, taken together with rational inferences from those facts, reasonably warrant that intrusion." *Terry v. Ohio*, 392 U.S. 1, 21 (1968).

At the time they stopped Ms. Mendenhall, the DEA agents' suspicion that she was engaged in criminal activity was based solely on their brief observations of her conduct at the airport. The officers had no advance information that Ms. Mendenhall, or anyone on her flight, would be carrying drugs. What the agents observed Ms. Mendenhall do in the airport was not "unusual conduct" which would lead an experienced officer reasonably to conclude that criminal activity was afoot, but rather the kind of behavior that could reasonably be expected of anyone changing planes in an airport terminal.

None of the aspects of Ms. Mendenhall's conduct, either alone or in combination, were sufficient to provide reasonable suspicion that she was engaged in criminal activity. Because Agent Anderson's suspicion that Ms. Mendenhall was transporting narcotics could be based only on his inchoate and unparticularized suspicion or "hunch," rather than specific reasonable inferences which he is entitled to draw from the facts in light of his experience, he was not justified in "seizing" Ms. Mendenhall.

Whatever doubt there may be concerning whether Ms. Mendenhall's Fourth Amendment interests were implicated during the initial stages of her confrontation with the DEA agents, she undoubtedly was "seized" within the meaning of the Fourth Amendment when the agents escorted her from the public area of the terminal to the DEA office for questioning and a strip-search of her person. In *Dunaway v. New York*, 442 U.S. 200 (1979), we held that a person who accompanied police officers to a police station for purposes of interrogation undoubtedly was "seized" in the Fourth Amendment sense, even though he was not told he was under arrest. We found it significant that the suspect was taken to a police station, was never informed that he was "free to go," and would have been physically restrained if he had refused to accompany the officers or had tried to escape their custody. Like the "seizure" in *Dunaway*, the nature of the intrusion to which Ms. Mendenhall was subjected when she was escorted by DEA agents to their office and detained there for questioning and a strip-search was so great that it was in important respects indistinguishable from a traditional arrest. Although Ms. Mendenhall was not told that she was under arrest, she in fact was not free to refuse to go to the DEA office and was not told that she was. Furthermore, once inside the office, Ms. Mendenhall would not have been permitted to leave without submitting to a strip-search. Because the intrusion to which Ms. Mendenhall was subjected when she was escorted to the DEA office is of the same character as that involved in *Dunaway*, probable cause, which concededly was absent, was required to support the intrusion.

Because Ms. Mendenhall was being illegally detained at the time of the search of her person, her suppression motion should have been granted in the absence of evidence to dissipate the taint.

Justice Stewart's opinion gave rise to the *Mendenhall* Test for determining whether a seizure has taken place: A person is seized within the meaning of the Fourth Amendment only if, in view of all of the circumstances surrounding the incident, a reasonable person would believe that she is not free to leave. While the other Justices in *Mendenhall* seemed comfortable with this definition, they did not agree on how to apply it. Indeed, the facts actually gave rise to three different views of the interaction between the DEA agents and Sylvia Mendenhall. Justices Stewart and Rehnquist thought the entire interaction was a voluntary encounter for which the DEA agents needed no justification under the Fourth Amendment. Justices Blackmun and Powell and Chief Justice Burger viewed the entire episode as a stop, justified by the DEA agents' reasonable suspicion that Mendenhall was a drug courier. Dissenting Justices White, Brennan, Marshall, and Stevens felt that the interaction began as a stop unsupported by reasonable suspicion, then became an arrest unsupported by probable cause once Mendenhall was taken to the DEA office and subjected to a strip-search.

In *Florida v. Bostick*, the Supreme Court modified the *Mendenhall* Test so that it could be applied more broadly to all encounters, including those that take place inside a bus.

FLORIDA V. BOSTICK
501 U.S. 429 (1991)

As part of a drug interdiction program, Broward County Sheriff's Department officers routinely board buses at scheduled stops and ask passengers for permission to search their luggage. During a stopover in Fort Lauderdale, two officers boarded a bus traveling from Miami to Atlanta. The officers approached Terrance Bostick and asked to inspect his ticket and identification. The ticket matched Bostick's identification, and both were returned to him. The officers persisted, explained that they were on the lookout for illegal drugs, and requested Bostick's consent to search his luggage. The officers advised Bostick that he had the right to refuse consent. One officer carried a gun in a zipper pouch, but he did not remove it from the pouch or otherwise threaten Bostick with it. Bostick consented to the search, and the officers discovered cocaine in one of his suitcases.

Bostick moved to suppress the cocaine as the product of an unconstitutional seizure. The trial court denied Bostick's motion to suppress, but the Florida Supreme Court ruled categorically that "an impermissible seizure results when police mount a drug search on buses during scheduled stops and question boarded passengers without articulable reasons for doing so, thereby obtaining consent to search the passengers' luggage."

In the U.S. Supreme Court, the state conceded that the officers lacked the reasonable suspicion required to justify a seizure and that if a seizure took place, the drugs found in Bostick's suitcase must be suppressed as tainted fruit. Citing *Mendenhall* and several other cases, the Supreme Court noted that if the interaction had taken place outside the bus, Bostick would not have been seized:

> There is no doubt that if this same encounter had taken place before Bostick boarded the bus or in the lobby of the bus terminal, it would not rise to the level of a seizure. The Court has dealt with similar encounters in airports and has found them to be the sort of consensual encounters that implicate no Fourth Amendment interest. We have stated that even when officers have no basis for suspecting a particular individual, they may generally ask questions of that individual, ask to examine

the individual's identification, and request consent to search his or her luggage—as long as the police do not convey a message that compliance with their requests is required.

Bostick argued that in the cramped confines of a bus, with police officers standing over him and little room to move around, he did not feel free to leave; had he disembarked, he risked being stranded and losing luggage locked away in the luggage compartment. The Supreme Court answered by noting that Bostick would not have felt free to leave the bus even if the police had not been present. Bostick's sense of confinement was "the natural result of his decision to take the bus; it says nothing about whether or not the police conduct at issue was coercive."

The Supreme Court remanded the case to the Florida courts to determine whether Bostick had been seized under a legal standard somewhat different from the original *Mendenhall* Test:

> We adhere to the rule that, in order to determine whether a particular encounter constitutes a seizure, a court must consider all the circumstances surrounding the encounter to determine whether the police conduct would have communicated to a reasonable person that the person was not free to decline the officers' requests or otherwise terminate the encounter. That rule applies to encounters that take place on a city street or in an airport lobby, and it applies equally to encounters on a bus.

In *U.S. v. Drayton*, police officers boarded a bus and questioned passengers as part of a drug interdiction effort similar to the one that the Supreme Court considered in *Bostick*. But unlike *Bostick*, the police did not inform the passengers of their right not to cooperate. Despite this omission, the Supreme Court concluded that Drayton and a fellow passenger were not seized, and that each had voluntarily consented to a search that revealed cocaine.

U.S. v. DRAYTON

536 U.S. 194 (2002)

JUSTICE KENNEDY delivered the opinion of the Court.

The Fourth Amendment permits police officers to approach bus passengers at random to ask questions and to request their consent to searches, provided a reasonable person would understand that he or she is free to refuse. *Florida v. Bostick*, 501 U.S. 429 (1991). This case requires us to determine whether officers must advise bus passengers during these encounters of their right not to cooperate.

I

On February 4, 1999, respondents Christopher Drayton and Clifton Brown, Jr., were traveling on a Greyhound bus en route from Ft. Lauderdale, Florida, to Detroit, Michigan. The bus made a scheduled stop in Tallahassee, Florida. The passengers were required to disembark so the bus could be refueled and cleaned. As the passengers reboarded, the driver checked their tickets and then left to complete paperwork inside the terminal. As he left, the driver allowed three members of the Tallahassee Police Department to board the bus as part of a routine drug and weapons interdiction effort. The officers were dressed in plain clothes and carried concealed weapons and visible badges.

Once onboard Officer Hoover knelt on the driver's seat and faced the rear of the bus. He could observe the passengers and ensure the safety of the two other officers without blocking the aisle or otherwise obstructing the bus exit. Officers Lang and Blackburn went to the rear of the bus. Blackburn remained stationed there, facing forward. Lang worked his way toward the front of the bus, speaking with individual passengers as he went. He asked the passengers about their travel plans and sought to match passengers with luggage in the overhead racks. To avoid blocking the aisle, Lang stood next to or just behind each passenger with whom he spoke.

According to Lang's testimony, passengers who declined to cooperate with him or who chose to exit the bus at any time would have been allowed to do so without argument. In Lang's experience, however, most people are willing to cooperate. Some passengers go so far as to commend the police for their efforts to ensure the safety of their travel. Lang could recall five to six instances in the previous year in which passengers had declined to have their luggage searched. It also was common for passengers to leave the bus for a cigarette or a snack while the officers were on board. Lang sometimes informed passengers of their right to refuse to cooperate. On the day in question, however, he did not.

Respondents were seated next to each other on the bus. Drayton was in the aisle seat, Brown in the seat next to the window. Lang approached respondents from the rear and leaned over Drayton's shoulder. He held up his badge long enough for respondents to identify him as a police officer. With his face 12-to-18 inches away from Drayton's, Lang spoke in a voice just loud enough for respondents to hear: "I'm Investigator Lang with the Tallahassee Police Department. We're conducting bus interdiction, attempting to deter drugs and illegal weapons being transported on the bus. Do you have any bags on the bus?"

Both respondents pointed to a single green bag in the overhead luggage rack. Lang asked, "Do you mind if I check it?," and Brown responded, "Go ahead." Lang handed the bag to Officer Blackburn to check. The bag contained no contraband.

Officer Lang noticed that both respondents were wearing heavy jackets and baggy pants despite the warm weather. In Lang's experience drug traffickers often use baggy clothing to conceal weapons or narcotics. The officer thus asked Brown if he had any weapons or drugs in his possession. And he asked Brown: "Do you mind if I check your person?" Brown answered, "Sure," and cooperated by leaning up in his seat, pulling a cell phone out of his pocket, and opening up his jacket. Lang reached across Drayton and patted down Brown's jacket and pockets, including his waist area, sides, and upper thighs. In both thigh areas, Lang detected hard objects similar to drug packages detected on other occasions. Lang arrested and handcuffed Brown. Officer Hoover escorted Brown from the bus.

Lang then asked Drayton, "Mind if I check you?" Drayton responded by lifting his hands about eight inches from his legs. Lang conducted a patdown of Drayton's thighs and detected hard objects similar to those found on Brown. He arrested Drayton and escorted him from the bus. A further search revealed that respondents had duct-taped plastic bundles of powder cocaine between several pairs of their boxer shorts. Brown possessed three bundles containing 483 grams of cocaine. Drayton possessed two bundles containing 295 grams of cocaine.

Respondents were charged with conspiring to distribute cocaine, and with possessing cocaine with intent to distribute it. They moved to suppress the cocaine, arguing that the consent to the patdown search was invalid. Following a hearing at which only Officer Lang testified, the United States District Court for the Northern District of Florida denied their motions to suppress.

The Court of Appeals for the Eleventh Circuit reversed and remanded with instructions to grant respondents' motions to suppress. The court held that this disposition was compelled by its previous decisions which held that bus passengers do not feel free to disregard police officers' requests to search absent "some positive indication that consent could have been refused."

We granted certiorari. The respondents, we conclude, were not seized and their consent to the search was voluntary; and we reverse.

II

Law enforcement officers do not violate the Fourth Amendment's prohibition of unreasonable seizures merely by approaching individuals on the street or in other public places and putting questions to them if they are willing to listen. Even when law enforcement officers have no basis for suspecting a particular individual, they may pose questions, ask for identification, and request consent to search luggage—provided they do not induce cooperation by coercive means. If a reasonable person would feel free to terminate the encounter, then he or she has not been seized.

The Court has addressed on a previous occasion the specific question of drug interdiction efforts on buses. In *Bostick*, two police officers requested a bus passenger's consent to a search of his luggage. The passenger agreed, and the resulting search revealed cocaine in his suitcase. The Florida Supreme Court suppressed the cocaine. In doing so it adopted a *per se* rule that due to the cramped confines onboard a bus the act of questioning would deprive a person of his or her freedom of movement and so constitute a seizure under the Fourth Amendment.

This Court reversed. *Bostick* first made it clear that for the most part *per se* rules are inappropriate in the Fourth Amendment context. The proper inquiry necessitates a consideration of "all the circumstances surrounding the encounter." The Court noted next that the traditional rule, which states that a seizure does not occur so long as a reasonable person would feel free "to disregard the police and go about his business," is not an accurate measure of the coercive effect of a bus encounter. A passenger may not want to get off a bus if there is a risk it will depart before the opportunity to reboard. A bus rider's movements are confined in this sense, but this is the natural result of choosing to take the bus; it says nothing about whether the police conduct is coercive. The proper inquiry "is whether a reasonable person would feel free to decline the officers' requests or otherwise terminate the encounter." Finally, the Court rejected Bostick's argument that he must have been seized because no reasonable person would consent to a search of luggage containing drugs. The reasonable person test, the Court explained, is objective and "presupposes an *innocent* person."

In light of the limited record, *Bostick* refrained from deciding whether a seizure occurred. The Court, however, identified two factors particularly worth noting on remand. First, although it was obvious that an officer was armed, he did not remove the gun from its pouch or use it in a threatening way. Second, the officer advised the passenger that he could refuse consent to the search.

Relying upon this latter factor, the Eleventh Circuit has adopted what is in effect a *per se* rule that evidence obtained during suspicionless drug interdiction efforts aboard buses must be suppressed unless the officers have advised passengers of their right not to cooperate and to refuse consent to a search.

Although the Court of Appeals has disavowed a *per se* requirement, the lack of an explicit warning to passengers is the only element common to all its cases. Under these cases, it appears that the Court of Appeals would suppress any evidence obtained during suspicionless drug interdiction efforts aboard buses in the absence of a warning that passengers may refuse to cooperate. The Court of Appeals erred in adopting this approach.

Applying the *Bostick* framework to the facts of this particular case, we conclude that the police did not seize respondents when they boarded the bus and began questioning passengers. The officers gave the passengers no reason to believe that they were required to answer the officers' questions. When Officer Lang approached respondents, he did not brandish a weapon or make any intimidating movements. He left the aisle free so that respondents could exit. He spoke to passengers one by one and in a polite, quiet voice. Nothing he said would suggest to a reasonable person that he or she was barred from leaving the bus or otherwise terminating the encounter.

There were ample grounds for the District Court to conclude that "everything that took place between Officer Lang and [respondents] suggests that it was cooperative" and that there "was nothing coercive or confrontational" about the encounter. There was no application of force, no intimidating movement, no overwhelming show of force, no brandishing of weapons, no blocking of exits, no threat, no command, not even an authoritative tone of voice. It is beyond question that had this encounter occurred on the street, it would be constitutional. The fact that an encounter takes place on a bus does not on its own transform standard police questioning of citizens into an illegal seizure. Indeed, because many fellow passengers are present to witness officers' conduct, a reasonable person may feel even more secure in his or her decision not to cooperate with police on a bus than in other circumstances.

Respondents make much of the fact that Officer Lang displayed his badge. In *Florida v. Rodriguez*, 469 U.S. 1 (1984), however, the Court rejected the claim that the defendant was seized when an officer approached him in an airport, showed him his badge, and asked him to answer some questions. Likewise, in *INS v. Delgado*, 466 U.S. 210 (1984), the Court held that Immigration and Naturalization Service (INS) agents' wearing badges and questioning workers in a factory did not constitute a seizure. And while neither Lang nor his colleagues were in uniform or visibly armed, those factors should have little weight in the analysis. Officers are often required to wear uniforms and in many circumstances this is cause for assurance, not discomfort. Much the same can be said for wearing sidearms. That most law enforcement officers are armed is a fact well known to the public. The presence of a holstered firearm thus is unlikely to contribute to the coerciveness of the encounter absent active brandishing of the weapon.

Officer Hoover's position at the front of the bus also does not tip the scale in respondents' favor. Hoover did nothing to intimidate passengers, and he said nothing to suggest that people could not exit and indeed he left the aisle clear. In *Delgado*, the Court determined there was no seizure even though several uniformed INS officers were stationed near the exits of the factory.

Finally, the fact that in Officer Lang's experience only a few passengers have refused to cooperate does not suggest that a reasonable person would not feel free to terminate the bus encounter. In Lang's experience it was common for passengers to leave the bus for a cigarette or a snack while the officers were questioning passengers. And of more importance, bus passengers answer officers' questions and otherwise cooperate not because of coercion but because the passengers know that their participation enhances their own safety and the safety of those around them.

Drayton contends that even if Brown's cooperation with the officers was consensual, Drayton was seized because no reasonable person would feel free to terminate the encounter with the officers after Brown had been arrested. The Court of Appeals did not address this claim; and in any event the argument fails. The arrest of one person does not mean that everyone around him has been seized by police. If anything, Brown's arrest should have put Drayton on notice of the consequences of continuing the encounter by answering the officers' questions. Even after arresting Brown, Lang addressed Drayton in a polite manner and provided him with no indication that he was required to answer Lang's questions.

We turn now from the question whether respondents were seized to whether they were subjected to an unreasonable search, *i.e.*, whether their consent to the suspicionless search was involuntary. In circumstances such as these, where the question of voluntariness pervades both the search and seizure inquiries, the respective analyses turn on very similar facts. And, as the facts above suggest, respondents' consent to the search of their luggage and their persons was voluntary. Nothing Officer Lang said indicated a command to consent to the search. Rather, when respondents informed Lang that they had a bag on the bus, he asked for their permission to check it. And when Lang requested to search Brown and Drayton's persons, he asked first if they objected, thus indicating to a reasonable person that he or she was free to refuse. Even after arresting Brown, Lang provided Drayton with no indication that he was required to consent to a search. To the contrary, Lang asked for Drayton's permission to search him ("Mind if I check you?"), and Drayton agreed.

The Court has rejected in specific terms the suggestion that police officers must always inform citizens of their right to refuse when seeking permission to conduct a warrantless consent search. Nor do this Court's decisions suggest that even though there are no *per se* rules, a presumption of invalidity attaches if a citizen consented without explicit notification that he or she was free to refuse to cooperate. Instead, the Court has repeated that the totality of the circumstances must control, without giving extra weight to the absence of this type of warning.

Although Officer Lang did not inform respondents of their right to refuse the search, he did request permission to search, and the totality of the circumstances indicates that their consent was voluntary, so the searches were reasonable.

In a society based on law, the concept of agreement and consent should be given a weight and dignity of its own. Police officers act in full accord with the law when they ask citizens for consent. It reinforces the rule of law for the citizen to advise the police of his or her wishes and for the police to act in reliance on that understanding. When this exchange takes place, it dispels inferences of coercion.

We need not ask the alternative question whether, after the arrest of Brown, there were grounds for a *Terry* stop and frisk of Drayton, though this may have been the case. It was evident that Drayton and Brown were traveling together—Officer Lang observed the pair reboarding the bus together; they were each dressed in heavy, baggy clothes that were ill-suited for the day's warm temperatures; they were seated together on the bus; and they each claimed responsibility for the single piece of green carry-on luggage. Once Lang had identified Brown as carrying what he believed to be narcotics, he may have had reasonable suspicion to conduct a *Terry* stop and frisk on Drayton as well. That question, however, has not been presented to us. The fact the officers may have had reasonable suspicion does not prevent them from relying on a citizen's consent to the search. It would be a paradox, and one most puzzling to law enforcement officials and courts alike, were we to say, after holding that Brown's consent was voluntary, that Drayton's consent was ineffectual simply because the police at that point had more compelling grounds to detain him. After taking Brown into custody, the officers were entitled to continue to proceed on the basis of consent and to ask for Drayton's cooperation.

JUSTICE SOUTER, with whom JUSTICE STEVENS and JUSTICE GINSBURG join, dissenting.

Anyone who travels by air today submits to searches of the person and luggage as a condition of boarding the aircraft. It is universally accepted that such intrusions are necessary to hedge against risks that, nowadays, even small children understand. The commonplace precautions of air travel have not, thus far, been justified for ground transportation, however, and no such conditions have been placed on passengers getting on trains or buses. There is therefore an air of unreality about the Court's explanation that bus passengers consent to searches of their luggage to "enhance their own safety and the safety of those around them." Nor are the other factual assessments underlying the Court's conclusion in favor of the Government more convincing.

The issue we took to review is whether the police's examination of the bus passengers, including respondents, amounted to a suspicionless seizure under the Fourth Amendment. If it did, any consent to search was plainly invalid as a product of the illegal seizure.

Florida v. Bostick established the framework for determining whether the bus passengers were seized in the constitutional sense. In that case, we rejected the position that police questioning of bus passengers was a *per se* seizure, and held instead that the issue of seizure was to be resolved under an objective test considering all circumstances: whether a reasonable passenger would have felt "free to decline the officers' requests or otherwise terminate the encounter."

Before applying the standard in this case, it may be worth getting some perspective from different sets of facts. A perfect example of police conduct that supports no colorable claim of seizure is the act of an officer who simply goes up to a pedestrian on the street and asks him a question. A pair of officers questioning a pedestrian, without more, would presumably support the same conclusion. Now consider three officers, one of whom stands behind the pedestrian, another at his side toward the open sidewalk, with the third addressing questions to the pedestrian a foot or two from his face. Finally, consider the same scene in a narrow alley. On such barebones facts, one may not be able to say a seizure occurred, even in the last case, but one can say without qualification that the atmosphere of the encounters differed significantly from the first to the last examples. In the final instance there is every reason to believe that the pedestrian would have understood, to his considerable discomfort, the threatening presence of several officers. The police not only carry legitimate authority but also exercise power free from immediate check, and when the attention of several officers is brought to bear on one civilian the imbalance of immediate power is unmistakable. We all understand this, as well as we understand that a display of power rising to the "threatening" level may overbear a normal person's ability to act freely, even in the absence of explicit commands or the formalities of detention. As common as this understanding is, however, there is little sign of it in the Court's opinion. My own understanding of the relevant facts and their significance follows.

When the bus in question made its scheduled stop in Tallahassee, the passengers were required to disembark while the vehicle was cleaned and refueled. When the passengers returned, they gave their tickets to the driver, who kept them and then left himself, after giving three police officers permission to board the bus in his absence. Although they were not in uniform, the officers displayed badges and identified themselves as police. One stationed himself in the driver's seat by the door at the front, facing back to observe the passengers. The two others went to the rear, from which they worked their way forward, with one of them speaking to passengers, the other backing him up. They necessarily addressed the passengers at very close range; the aisle was only 15 inches wide, and each seat only 18. The quarters were cramped further by the overhead rack, 19 inches above the top of the passenger seats. The passenger by the window could not have stood up straight, and the face of the nearest officer was only a foot or 18 inches from the face of the nearest passenger being addressed. During the exchanges, the officers looked down, and the passengers had to look up if they were to face the police. The officer asking the questions spoke quietly. He prefaced his requests for permission to search luggage and do a body patdown by identifying himself by name as a police investigator "conducting bus interdiction" and saying, "We would like for your cooperation. Do you have any luggage on the bus?"

Thus, for reasons unexplained, the driver with the tickets entitling the passengers to travel had yielded his custody of the bus and its seated travelers to three police officers, whose authority apparently superseded the driver's own. The officers took control of the entire passenger compartment, one stationed at the door keeping surveillance of all the occupants, the others working forward from the back. With one officer right behind him and the other one forward, a third officer accosted each passenger at quarters extremely close and so cramped that as many as half the passengers could not even have stood to face the speaker. None was asked whether he was willing to converse with the police or to take part in the enquiry. Instead the officer said the police were "conducting bus interdiction," in the course of which they "would like cooperation." The reasonable inference was that the "interdiction" was not a consensual exercise, but one the police would carry out whatever the circumstances; that they would prefer "cooperation" but would not let the lack of it stand in their way. There was no contrary indication that day, since no passenger had refused the cooperation requested, and there was no reason for any passenger to believe that the driver would return and the trip resume until the police were satisfied. The scene was set and an atmosphere of obligatory participation was established by this introduction. Later requests to search prefaced with "Do you mind . . ." would naturally have been understood in the terms with which the encounter began.

It is very hard to imagine that either Brown or Drayton would have believed that he stood to lose nothing if he refused to cooperate with the police, or that he had any free choice to ignore the police altogether. No reasonable passenger could have believed that, only an uncomprehending one. It is neither here nor there that the interdiction was conducted by three officers, not one, as a safety precaution. The fact was that there were three, and when Brown and Drayton were called upon to respond, each one was presumably conscious of an officer in front watching, one at his side questioning him, and one behind for cover, in case he became unruly, perhaps, or "cooperation" was not forthcoming. The situation is much like the one in the alley, with civilians in close quarters, unable to move effectively, being told their cooperation is expected. While I am not prepared to say that no bus interrogation and search can pass the *Bostick* test without a warning that passengers are free to say no, the facts here surely required more from the officers than a quiet tone of voice. A police officer who is certain to get his way has no need to shout.

It is true of course that the police testified that a bus passenger sometimes says no, but that evidence does nothing to cast the facts here in a different light. We have no way of knowing the circumstances in which a passenger elsewhere refused a request; maybe that has happened only when the police have told passengers they had a right to refuse (as the officers sometimes advised them). In this case, Brown and Drayton were seemingly pinned-in by the officers and the customary course of events was stopped flat. The bus was going nowhere, and with one officer in the driver's seat, it was reasonable to suppose no passenger would tend to his own business until the officers were ready to let him.

Bostick's totality of circumstances test asks whether a passenger would reasonably have felt free to end his encounter with the three officers by saying no and ignoring them thereafter. In my view the answer is clear.

In *California v. Hodari D.*, the Supreme Court considered whether a police pursuit of a suspect amounts to a seizure under the Fourth Amendment. The Court concluded that a person being chased by police is not seized until he yields to physical force or a show of authority.

CALIFORNIA V. HODARI D.
499 U.S. 621 (1991)

JUSTICE SCALIA delivered the opinion of the Court.

Late one evening in April 1988, Officers Brian McColgin and Jerry Pertoso were on patrol in a high-crime area of Oakland, California. They were dressed in street clothes but wearing jackets with "Police" embossed on both front and back. Their unmarked car proceeded west on Foothill Boulevard, and turned south onto 63rd Avenue. As they rounded the corner, they saw four or five youths huddled around a small red car parked at the curb. When the youths saw the officers' car approaching they apparently panicked, and took flight. The respondent here, Hodari D., and one companion ran west through an alley; the others fled south. The red car also headed south, at a high rate of speed.

The officers were suspicious and gave chase. McColgin remained in the car and continued south on 63rd Avenue; Pertoso left the car, ran back north along 63rd, then west on Foothill Boulevard, and turned south on 62nd Avenue. Hodari, meanwhile, emerged from the alley onto 62nd and ran north. Looking behind as he ran, he did not turn and see Pertoso until the officer was almost upon him, whereupon he tossed away what appeared to be a small rock. A moment later, Pertoso tackled Hodari, handcuffed him, and radioed for assistance. Hodari was found to be carrying $130 in cash and a pager; and the rock he had discarded was found to be crack cocaine.

In the juvenile proceeding brought against him, Hodari moved to suppress the evidence relating to the cocaine. The court denied the motion without opinion. The California Court of Appeal reversed, holding that Hodari had been "seized" when he saw Officer Pertoso running towards him, that this seizure was unreasonable under the Fourth Amendment, and that the evidence of cocaine had to be suppressed as the fruit of that illegal seizure. The California Supreme Court denied the State's application for review. We granted certiorari.

As this case comes to us, the only issue presented is whether, at the time he dropped the drugs, Hodari had been "seized" within the meaning of the Fourth Amendment.[1] If so, respondent argues, the drugs were the fruit of that seizure and the evidence concerning them was properly excluded. If not, the drugs were abandoned by Hodari and lawfully recovered by the police, and the evidence should have been admitted. (In addition, of course, Pertoso's seeing the rock of cocaine, at least if he recognized it as such, would provide reasonable suspicion for the unquestioned seizure that occurred when he tackled Hodari.)

We have long understood that the Fourth Amendment's protection against unreasonable seizures includes seizure of the person. From the time of the founding to the present, the word "seizure" has meant a "taking possession." For most purposes at common law, the word connoted not merely grasping, or applying physical force to, the animate or inanimate object in question, but actually bringing it within physical control. A ship still fleeing, even though under attack, would not be considered to have been seized as a war prize. To constitute an arrest, however—the quintessential "seizure of the person" under our Fourth Amendment jurisprudence—the mere grasping or application of physical force with lawful authority, whether or not it succeeded in subduing the arrestee, was sufficient.

To say that an arrest is effected by the slightest application of physical force, despite the arrestee's escape, is not to say that for Fourth Amendment purposes there is a *continuing* arrest during the period of fugitivity. If, for example, Pertoso had laid his hands upon Hodari to

---

[1] California conceded below that Officer Pertoso did not have the "reasonable suspicion" required to justify stopping Hodari. See *Terry v. Ohio*, 392 U.S. 1 (1968). That it would be unreasonable to stop, for brief inquiry, young men who scatter in panic upon the mere sighting of the police is not self-evident, and arguably contradicts proverbial common sense. See Proverbs 28:1 ("The wicked flee when no man pursueth"). We do not decide that point here, but rely entirely upon the State's concession.

arrest him, but Hodari had broken away and had *then* cast away the cocaine, it would hardly be realistic to say that that disclosure had been made during the course of an arrest. The present case, however, is even one step further removed. It does not involve the application of any physical force; Hodari was untouched by Officer Pertoso at the time he discarded the cocaine. His defense relies instead upon the proposition that a seizure occurs "when the officer, by means of physical force *or show of authority*, has in some way restrained the liberty of a citizen." Hodari contends (and we accept as true for purposes of this decision) that Pertoso's pursuit qualified as a "show of authority" calling upon Hodari to halt. The narrow question before us is whether, with respect to a show of authority as with respect to application of physical force, a seizure occurs even though the subject does not yield. We hold that it does not.

The language of the Fourth Amendment, of course, cannot sustain respondent's contention. The word "seizure" readily bears the meaning of a laying on of hands or application of physical force to restrain movement, even when it is ultimately unsuccessful. ("She seized the purse-snatcher, but he broke out of her grasp.") It does not remotely apply, however, to the prospect of a policeman yelling "Stop, in the name of the law!" at a fleeing form that continues to flee. That is no seizure. Nor can the result respondent wishes to achieve be produced—indirectly, as it were—by suggesting that Pertoso's uncomplied-with show of authority was a common-law arrest, and then appealing to the principle that all common-law arrests are seizures. An arrest requires *either* physical force (as described above) *or*, where that is absent, *submission* to the assertion of authority.

Respondent contends that his position is sustained by the so-called *Mendenhall* test, formulated by Justice Stewart's opinion in *U.S. v. Mendenhall*, 446 U.S. 544, 554 (1980), and adopted by the Court in later cases: "A person has been 'seized' within the meaning of the Fourth Amendment only if, in view of all the circumstances surrounding the incident, a reasonable person would have believed that he was not free to leave." In seeking to rely upon that test here, respondent fails to read it carefully. It says that a person has been seized "only if," not that he has been seized "whenever"; it states a *necessary*, but not a *sufficient*, condition for seizure—or, more precisely, for seizure effected through a "show of authority." *Mendenhall* establishes that the test for existence of a "show of authority" is an objective one: not whether the citizen perceived that he was being ordered to restrict his movement, but whether the officer's words and actions would have conveyed that to a reasonable person.

In sum, assuming that Pertoso's pursuit in the present case constituted a "show of authority" enjoining Hodari to halt, since Hodari did not comply with that injunction he was not seized until he was tackled. The cocaine abandoned while he was running was in this case not the fruit of a seizure, and his motion to exclude evidence of it was properly denied.

In most of the Fourth Amendment cases presented in other Chapters, a search precedes a seizure of incriminating evidence. When analyzing such cases, the Supreme Court generally focuses on the legitimacy of the search because if the search is valid, the seizure will usually be valid as well. In the cases in this Chapter, by contrast, a critical question is whether there has been a seizure of the person prior to the search. That question is important because, except for certain special situations described in Chapter 7, the Supreme Court usually requires that police have at least a reasonable suspicion of criminal activity in order to seize or detain someone. If, considering all the facts and circumstances, a reasonable person in the position of the individual being questioned would have felt free to refuse the officers' requests, terminate the encounter, or simply leave, no seizure has taken place. The interaction is a voluntary encounter, and the police do not need reasonable suspicion of criminal activity for its initiation. And during the encounter, if the individual gives permission to search his person or his belongings and police discover incriminating evidence, it is admissible in court as the product of a voluntary encounter and a consensual search.

But if, considering all the facts and circumstances, a reasonable person in the position of the individual being questioned would *not* have felt free to refuse the officers' requests, terminate the encounter, or simply leave, then the interaction with the officers is a seizure under the Fourth Amendment for which the police must demonstrate reasonable suspicion of criminal activity. If the police cannot demonstrate reasonable suspicion of criminal activity to justify the seizure, any incriminating evidence found with consent to a search will be inadmissible, either because the evidence is the "fruit" of an unlawful seizure, or because the consent to the search was coerced by an unlawful detention.

Do the Supreme Court's voluntary encounter cases strike the right balance between the needs of law enforcement and the Fourth Amendment rights of individuals? In *Drayton*, Officer Lang and his team conducted bus sweeps on a regular basis, questioning thousands of passengers each year, but he could recall only five or six instances in the past year when passengers refused consent to a search of their bags. Are the bus passengers cooperative because they want to be helpful, or because they feel they have no other choice? If *you* were approached by a police officer, questioned, and asked for consent to a search, would *you* feel free to decline the request, terminate the encounter, and leave?

Voluntary Encounters

1.   Police officers may approach individuals at random on the street, in airports, on buses, and in other public places to ask them questions and to request consent to search their persons or luggage. Even when police have no basis for suspecting a particular individual, they may pose questions, ask for identification, and request consent to search, provided they do not induce cooperation by coercive means.

2.   If a reasonable innocent person, approached and questioned by the police under the same circumstances, would feel free to refuse the officer's request, terminate the encounter, or simply leave, the encounter does not constitute a seizure.

3.   In determining whether a reasonable person would feel free to refuse the officer's request, terminate the encounter, or simply leave, a court should examine the totality of the circumstances, including:

    a.   The location of the questioning. Was it an open area or confined? Are exits blocked? Are there others around to witness the interaction?

    b.   The number of officers. A large number of police officers is generally more intimidating than a smaller number.

    c.   The appearance of the officers. Are they in uniforms or wearing badges? Are they carrying visible weapons?

    d.   The behavior of the officers. Did they make intimidating movements or brandish their weapons? How close were the officers to the individual being questioned?

    e.   The tone and language of the questioning. Was it polite and respectful, or did it seem closer to an order or a command? Did the officers indicate or convey that compliance was required? Did the officers inform the individual that he could refuse to answer or decline consent to a search?

    f.   Physical contact. Was there any physical touching of the person being questioned?

4.   A person is not seized until he actually yields to an officer's physical force or show of authority.

B. STOPS AND FRISKS

Although it may appear similar to an encounter, there is nothing voluntary about a stop, in which a police officer uses physical force or a show of authority to briefly detain an individual for questioning or further investigation. A stop is often coupled with a frisk or "patdown search" for weapons. Because the individual is not free to leave, a stop is a seizure under the Fourth Amendment, but it is not sufficiently long or intrusive to be deemed an arrest. The Supreme Court established the basic constitutional standards for stops and frisks in *Terry v. Ohio*.

TERRY V. OHIO
392 U.S. 1 (1968)

CHIEF JUSTICE WARREN delivered the opinion of the Court.

This case presents serious questions concerning the role of the Fourth Amendment in the confrontation on the street between the citizen and the policeman investigating suspicious circumstances.

Petitioner Terry was convicted of carrying a concealed weapon and sentenced to the statutorily prescribed term of one to three years in the penitentiary. Following the denial of a pretrial motion to suppress, the prosecution introduced in evidence two revolvers and a number of bullets seized from Terry and a codefendant, Richard Chilton, by Cleveland Police Detective Martin McFadden. At the hearing on the motion to suppress this evidence, Officer McFadden testified that, while he was patrolling in plain clothes in downtown Cleveland at approximately 2:30 in the afternoon of October 31, 1963, his attention was attracted by two men, Chilton and Terry, standing on the corner of Huron Road and Euclid Avenue. He had never seen the two men before, and he was unable to say precisely what first drew his eye to them. However, he testified that he had been a policeman for 39 years and a detective for 35, and that he had been assigned to patrol this vicinity of downtown Cleveland for shoplifters and pickpockets for 30 years. He explained that he had developed routine habits of observation over the years, and that he would "stand and watch people or walk and watch people at many intervals of the day." He added: "Now, in this case when I looked over they didn't look right to me at the time."

His interest aroused, Officer McFadden took up a post of observation in the entrance to a store 300 to 400 feet away from the two men. He saw one of the men leave the other one and walk southwest on Huron Road, past some stores. The man paused for a moment and looked in a store window, then walked on a short distance, turned around and walked back toward the corner, pausing once again to look in the same store window. He rejoined his companion at the corner, and the two conferred briefly. Then the second man went through the same series of motions, strolling down Huron Road, looking in the same window, walking on a short distance, turning back, peering in the store window again, and returning to confer with the first man at the corner. The two men repeated this ritual alternately between five and six times apiece—in all, roughly a dozen trips. At one point, while the two were standing together on the corner, a third man approached them and engaged them briefly in conversation. This man then left the two others and walked west on

Euclid Avenue. Chilton and Terry resumed their measured pacing, peering, and conferring. After this had gone on for 10 to 12 minutes, the two men walked off together, heading west on Euclid Avenue, following the path taken earlier by the third man.

By this time, Officer McFadden had become thoroughly suspicious. He testified that, after observing their elaborately casual and oft-repeated reconnaissance of the store window on Huron Road, he suspected the two men of "casing a job, a stick-up," and that he considered it his duty as a police officer to investigate further. He added that he feared "they may have a gun." Thus, Officer McFadden followed Chilton and Terry and saw them stop in front of Zucker's store to talk to the same man who had conferred with them earlier on the street corner. Deciding that the situation was ripe for direct action, Officer McFadden approached the three men, identified himself as a police officer and asked for their names. At this point his knowledge was confined to what he had observed. He was not acquainted with any of the three men by name or by sight, and he had received no information concerning them from any other source. When the men "mumbled something" in response to his inquiries, Officer McFadden grabbed petitioner Terry, spun him around so that they were facing the other two, with Terry between McFadden and the others, and patted down the outside of his clothing. In the left breast pocket of Terry's overcoat, Officer McFadden felt a pistol. He reached inside the overcoat pocket, but was unable to remove the gun. At this point, keeping Terry between himself and the others, the officer ordered all three men to enter Zucker's store. As they went in, he removed Terry's overcoat completely, removed a .38-caliber revolver from the pocket and ordered all three men to face the wall with their hands raised. Officer McFadden proceeded to pat down the outer clothing of Chilton and the third man, Katz. He discovered another revolver in the outer pocket of Chilton's overcoat, but no weapons were found on Katz. The officer testified that he only patted the men down to see whether they had weapons, and that he did not put his hands beneath the outer garments of either Terry or Chilton until he felt their guns. So far as appears from the record, he never placed his hands beneath Katz's outer garments. Officer McFadden seized Chilton's gun, asked the proprietor of the store to call a police wagon, and took all three men to the station, where Chilton and Terry were formally charged with carrying concealed weapons.

On the motion to suppress the guns, the prosecution took the position that they had been seized following a search incident to a lawful arrest. The trial court rejected this theory, stating that it "would be stretching the facts beyond reasonable comprehension" to find that Officer McFadden had had probable cause to arrest the men before he patted them down for weapons. However, the court denied the defendants' motion on the ground that Officer McFadden, on the basis of his experience, "had reasonable cause to believe that the defendants were conducting themselves suspiciously, and some interrogation should be made of their action." Purely for his own protection, the court held, the officer had the right to pat down the outer clothing of these men, who he had reasonable cause to believe might be armed. The court distinguished between an investigatory "stop" and an arrest, and between a "frisk" of the outer clothing for weapons and a full-blown search for evidence of crime. The frisk, it held, was essential to the proper performance of the officer's investigatory duties, for without it "the answer to the police officer may be a bullet, and a loaded pistol discovered during the frisk is admissible."

We granted certiorari to determine whether the admission of the revolvers in evidence violated petitioner's rights under the Fourth Amendment, made applicable to the States by the Fourteenth. We affirm the conviction.

I

Unquestionably petitioner was entitled to the protection of the Fourth Amendment as he walked down the street in Cleveland. The question is whether, in all the circumstances of this on-the-street encounter, his right to personal security was violated by an unreasonable search and seizure.

We would be less than candid if we did not acknowledge that this question thrusts to the fore difficult and troublesome issues regarding a sensitive area of police activity—issues which have never before been squarely presented to this Court. Reflective of the tensions involved are the practical and constitutional arguments pressed with great vigor on both sides of the public debate over the power of the police to "stop and frisk"—as it is sometimes euphemistically termed—suspicious persons.

On the one hand, it is frequently argued that, in dealing with the rapidly unfolding and often dangerous situations on city streets, the police are in need of an escalating set of flexible responses, graduated in relation to the amount of information they possess. For this purpose, it is urged that distinctions should be made between a "stop" and an "arrest" (or a "seizure" of a person), and between a "frisk" and a "search." Thus, it is argued, the police should be allowed to "stop" a person and detain him briefly for questioning upon suspicion that he may be connected with criminal activity. Upon suspicion that the person may be armed, the police should have the power to "frisk" him for weapons. If the "stop" and the "frisk" give rise to probable cause to believe that the suspect has committed a crime, then the police should be empowered to make a formal "arrest," and a full incident "search" of the person. This scheme is justified in part upon the notion that a "stop" and a "frisk" amount to a mere minor inconvenience and petty indignity, which can properly be imposed upon the citizen in the interest of effective law enforcement on the basis of a police officer's suspicion.

On the other side, the argument is made that the authority of the police must be strictly circumscribed by the law of arrest and search as it has developed to date in the traditional jurisprudence of the Fourth Amendment. It is contended with some force that there is not—and cannot be—a variety of police activity which does not depend solely upon the voluntary cooperation of the citizen, and yet which stops short of an arrest based upon probable cause to make such an arrest. The heart of the Fourth Amendment, the argument runs, is a severe requirement of specific justification for any intrusion upon protected personal security, coupled with a highly developed system of judicial controls to enforce upon the agents of the State the commands of the Constitution. Acquiescence by the courts in the compulsion inherent in the field interrogation practices at issue here, it is urged, would constitute an abdication of judicial control over, and indeed an encouragement of, substantial interference with liberty and personal security by police officers whose judgment is necessarily colored by their primary involvement in the often competitive enterprise of ferreting out crime. This, it is argued, can only serve to exacerbate police-community tensions in the crowded centers of our Nation's cities.

In this context, we approach the issues in this case mindful of the limitations of the judicial function in controlling the myriad daily situations in which policemen and citizens confront each other on the street. The State has characterized the issue here as the right of a police officer to make an on-the-street stop, interrogate and pat down for weapons (known in street vernacular as "stop and frisk"). But this is only partly accurate. For the issue is not the abstract propriety of the police conduct, but the admissibility against petitioner of the evidence uncovered by the search and seizure. Ever since its inception, the rule excluding evidence seized in violation of the Fourth Amendment has been recognized as a principal mode of discouraging lawless police conduct. Thus, its major thrust is a deterrent one, and experience has taught that it is the only effective deterrent to police misconduct in the criminal context, and that without it the constitutional guarantee against unreasonable searches and seizures would be a mere form of words. The rule also serves another vital function—the imperative of judicial integrity. Courts which sit under our Constitution cannot and will not be made party to lawless invasions of the constitutional rights of citizens by permitting unhindered governmental use of the fruits of such invasions. Thus, in our system, evidentiary rulings provide the context in which the judicial process of inclusion and exclusion approves some conduct as comporting with constitutional guarantees and disapproves other actions by state agents. A ruling admitting evidence in a criminal trial, we recognize, has the necessary effect of legitimizing the conduct which produced the evidence, while an application of the exclusionary rule withholds the constitutional imprimatur.

The exclusionary rule has its limitations, however, as a tool of judicial control. It cannot properly be invoked to exclude the products of legitimate police investigative techniques on the ground that much conduct which is closely similar involves unwarranted intrusions upon constitutional protections. Moreover, in some contexts, the rule is ineffective as a deterrent. Street encounters between citizens and police officers are incredibly rich in diversity. They range from wholly friendly exchanges of pleasantries or mutually useful information to hostile confrontations of armed men involving arrests, or injuries, or loss of life. Moreover, hostile confrontations are not all of a piece. Some of them begin in a friendly enough manner, only to take a different turn upon the injection of some unexpected element into the conversation. Encounters are initiated by the police for a wide variety of purposes, some of which are wholly unrelated to a desire to prosecute for crime. Doubtless some police "field interrogation" conduct violates the Fourth Amendment. But a stern refusal by this Court to condone such activity does not necessarily render it responsive to the exclusionary rule. Regardless of how effective the rule may be where obtaining convictions is an important objective of the police, it is powerless to deter invasions of constitutionally guaranteed rights where the police either have no interest in prosecuting or are willing to forgo successful prosecution in the interest of serving some other goal.

Proper adjudication of cases in which the exclusionary rule is invoked demands a constant awareness of these limitations. The wholesale harassment by certain elements of the police community, of which minority groups, particularly Negroes, frequently complain, will not be stopped by the exclusion of any evidence from any criminal trial. Yet a rigid and unthinking application of the exclusionary rule, in futile protest against practices which it can never be used effectively to control, may exact a high toll in human injury and frustration of efforts to prevent crime. No judicial opinion can comprehend the protean variety of the street encounter, and we can only judge the facts of the case before us. Nothing we say today is to be taken as indicating approval of police conduct outside the legitimate investigative sphere. Under our decision, courts still retain their traditional responsibility to guard against police conduct which is over-bearing or harassing, or which trenches upon personal security without the objective evidentiary justification which the Constitution requires. When such conduct is identified, it must be condemned by the judiciary and its fruits must be excluded from evidence in criminal trials. And, of course, our approval of legitimate and restrained investigative conduct undertaken on the basis of ample factual justification should in no way discourage the employment of other remedies than the exclusionary rule to curtail abuses for which that sanction may prove inappropriate.

Having thus roughly sketched the perimeters of the constitutional debate over the limits on police investigative conduct in general and the background against which this case presents itself, we turn our attention to the quite narrow question posed by the facts before us: whether it is always unreasonable for a policeman to seize a person and subject him to a limited search for weapons unless there is probable cause for an arrest. Given the narrowness of this question, we have no occasion to canvass in detail the constitutional limitations upon the scope of a policeman's power when he confronts a citizen without probable cause to arrest him.

II

Our first task is to establish at what point in this encounter the Fourth Amendment becomes relevant. That is, we must decide whether and when Officer McFadden "seized" Terry, and whether and when he conducted a "search." There is some suggestion in the use of such terms as "stop" and "frisk" that such police conduct is outside the purview of the Fourth Amendment because neither action rises to the level of a "search" or "seizure" within the meaning of the Constitution. We emphatically reject this notion. It is quite plain that the Fourth Amendment governs "seizures" of the person which do not eventuate in a trip to the station house and prosecution for crime—"arrests" in traditional terminology. It must be recognized that, whenever a police officer accosts an individual and restrains his freedom to walk away, he has "seized" that person. And it is nothing less than sheer torture of the English language to suggest that a careful exploration of the outer surfaces of a person's clothing all over his or her body in an attempt to find weapons is not a "search." Moreover, it is simply fantastic to urge that such a procedure performed in public by a policeman while the citizen stands helpless, perhaps facing a wall with his hands raised, is a "petty indignity." It is a serious intrusion upon the sanctity of the person, which may inflict great indignity and arouse strong resentment, and it is not to be undertaken lightly.

The danger in the logic which proceeds upon distinctions between a "stop" and an "arrest," or "seizure" of the person, and between a "frisk" and a "search," is twofold. It seeks to isolate from constitutional scrutiny the initial stages of the contact between the policeman and the citizen. And, by suggesting a rigid all-or-nothing model of justification and regulation under the Amendment, it obscures the utility of limitations upon the scope, as well as the initiation, of police action as a means of constitutional regulation. This Court has held in the past that a search which is reasonable at its inception may violate the Fourth Amendment by virtue of its intolerable intensity and scope. The scope of the search must be strictly tied to and justified by the circumstances which rendered its initiation permissible.

The distinctions of classical "stop-and-frisk" theory thus serve to divert attention from the central inquiry under the Fourth Amendment— the reasonableness in all the circumstances of the particular governmental invasion of a citizen's personal security. "Search" and "seizure" are not talismans. We therefore reject the notions that the Fourth Amendment does not come into play at all as a limitation upon police conduct if the officers stop short of something called a "technical arrest" or a "full-blown search."

In this case there can be no question, then, that Officer McFadden "seized" petitioner and subjected him to a "search" when he took hold of him and patted down the outer surfaces of his clothing. We must decide whether, at that point, it was reasonable for Officer McFadden to have interfered with petitioner's personal security as he did.[16] And, in determining whether the seizure and search were "unreasonable," our inquiry is a dual one—whether the officer's action was justified at its inception, and whether it was reasonably related in scope to the circumstances which justified the interference in the first place.

III

If this case involved police conduct subject to the Warrant Clause of the Fourth Amendment, we would have to ascertain whether "probable cause" existed to justify the search and seizure which took place. However, that is not the case. We do not retreat from our holdings that the police must, whenever practicable, obtain advance judicial approval of searches and seizures through the warrant procedure, or that in most instances failure to comply with the warrant requirement can only be excused by exigent circumstances. But we deal here with an entire rubric of police conduct—necessarily swift action predicated upon the on-the-spot observations of the officer on the beat—which historically has not been, and as a practical matter could not be, subjected to the warrant procedure. Instead, the conduct involved in this case must be tested by the Fourth Amendment's general proscription against unreasonable searches and seizures.

Nonetheless, the notions which underlie both the warrant procedure and the requirement of probable cause remain fully relevant in this context. In order to assess the reasonableness of Officer McFadden's conduct as a general proposition, it is necessary first to focus upon the governmental interest which allegedly justifies official intrusion upon the constitutionally protected interests of the private citizen, for there is no

---

[16] Obviously, not all personal intercourse between policemen and citizens involves "seizures" of persons. Only when the officer, by means of physical force or show of authority, has in some way restrained the liberty of a citizen may we conclude that a "seizure" has occurred. We cannot tell with any certainty upon this record whether any such "seizure" took place here prior to Officer McFadden's initiation of physical contact for purposes of searching Terry for weapons, and we thus may assume that up to that point no intrusion upon constitutionally protected rights had occurred.

ready test for determining reasonableness other than by balancing the need to search (or seize) against the invasion which the search (or seizure) entails. And, in justifying the particular intrusion, the police officer must be able to point to specific and articulable facts which, taken together with rational inferences from those facts, reasonably warrant that intrusion. The scheme of the Fourth Amendment becomes meaningful only when it is assured that, at some point, the conduct of those charged with enforcing the laws can be subjected to the more detached, neutral scrutiny of a judge who must evaluate the reasonableness of a particular search or seizure in light of the particular circumstances. And, in making that assessment, it is imperative that the facts be judged against an objective standard: would the facts available to the officer at the moment of the seizure or the search warrant a man of reasonable caution in the belief that the action taken was appropriate? Anything less would invite intrusions upon constitutionally guaranteed rights based on nothing more substantial than inarticulate hunches, a result this Court has consistently refused to sanction. And simple good faith on the part of the arresting officer is not enough. If subjective good faith alone were the test, the protections of the Fourth Amendment would evaporate, and the people would be secure in their "persons, houses, papers, and effects" only in the discretion of the police.

Applying these principles to this case, we consider first the nature and extent of the governmental interests involved. One general interest is, of course, that of effective crime prevention and detection; it is this interest which underlies the recognition that a police officer may, in appropriate circumstances and in an appropriate manner, approach a person for purposes of investigating possibly criminal behavior even though there is no probable cause to make an arrest. It was this legitimate investigative function Officer McFadden was discharging when he decided to approach petitioner and his companions. He had observed Terry, Chilton, and Katz go through a series of acts, each of them perhaps innocent in itself, but which, taken together, warranted further investigation. There is nothing unusual in two men standing together on a street corner, perhaps waiting for someone. Nor is there anything suspicious about people in such circumstances strolling up and down the street, singly or in pairs. Store windows, moreover, are made to be looked in. But the story is quite different where, as here, two men hover about a street corner for an extended period of time, at the end of which it becomes apparent that they are not waiting for anyone or anything; where these men pace alternately along an identical route, pausing to stare in the same store window roughly 24 times; where each completion of this route is followed immediately by a conference between the two men on the corner; where they are joined in one of these conferences by a third man who leaves swiftly; and where the two men finally follow the third and rejoin him a couple of blocks away. It would have been poor police work indeed for an officer of 30 years' experience in the detection of thievery from stores in this same neighborhood to have failed to investigate this behavior further.

The crux of this case, however, is not the propriety of Officer McFadden's taking steps to investigate petitioner's suspicious behavior, but rather, whether there was justification for McFadden's invasion of Terry's personal security by searching him for weapons in the course of that investigation. We are now concerned with more than the governmental interest in investigating crime; in addition, there is the more immediate interest of the police officer in taking steps to assure himself that the person with whom he is dealing is not armed with a weapon that could unexpectedly and fatally be used against him. Certainly it would be unreasonable to require that police officers take unnecessary risks in the performance of their duties. American criminals have a long tradition of armed violence, and every year in this country many law enforcement officers are killed in the line of duty, and thousands more are wounded. Virtually all of these deaths and a substantial portion of the injuries are inflicted with guns and knives.

In view of these facts, we cannot blind ourselves to the need for law enforcement officers to protect themselves and other prospective victims of violence in situations where they may lack probable cause for an arrest. When an officer is justified in believing that the individual whose suspicious behavior he is investigating at close range is armed and presently dangerous to the officer or to others, it would appear to be clearly unreasonable to deny the officer the power to take necessary measures to determine whether the person is, in fact, carrying a weapon and to neutralize the threat of physical harm.

We must still consider, however, the nature and quality of the intrusion on individual rights which must be accepted if police officers are to be conceded the right to search for weapons in situations where probable cause to arrest for crime is lacking. Even a limited search of the outer clothing for weapons constitutes a severe, though brief, intrusion upon cherished personal security, and it must surely be an annoying, frightening, and perhaps humiliating experience. Petitioner contends that such an intrusion is permissible only incident to a lawful arrest, either for a crime involving the possession of weapons or for a crime the commission of which led the officer to investigate in the first place. However, this argument must be closely examined.

Petitioner does not argue that a police officer should refrain from making any investigation of suspicious circumstances until such time as he has probable cause to make an arrest; nor does he deny that police officers, in properly discharging their investigative function, may find themselves confronting persons who might well be armed and dangerous. Moreover, he does not say that an officer is always unjustified in searching a suspect to discover weapons. Rather, he says it is unreasonable for the policeman to take that step until such time as the situation evolves to a point where there is probable cause to make an arrest. When that point has been reached, petitioner would concede the officer's right to conduct a search of the suspect for weapons, fruits or instrumentalities of the crime, or "mere" evidence, incident to the arrest.

There are two weaknesses in this line of reasoning, however. First, it fails to take account of traditional limitations upon the scope of searches, and thus recognizes no distinction in purpose, character, and extent between a search incident to an arrest and a limited search for weapons. The former, although justified in part by the acknowledged necessity to protect the arresting officer from assault with a concealed weapon, is also justified on other grounds, and can therefore involve a relatively extensive exploration of the person. A search for weapons in the absence of probable cause to arrest, however, must, like any other search, be strictly circumscribed by the exigencies which justify its initiation. Thus, it must be limited to that which is necessary for the discovery of weapons which might be used to harm the officer or others nearby, and may realistically be characterized as something less than a "full" search, even though it remains a serious intrusion.

A second, and related, objection to petitioner's argument is that it assumes that the law of arrest has already worked out the balance between the particular interests involved here—the neutralization of danger to the policeman in the investigative circumstance and the sanctity of the individual. But this is not so. An arrest is a wholly different kind of intrusion upon individual freedom from a limited search for weapons, and the interests each is designed to serve are likewise quite different. An arrest is the initial stage of a criminal prosecution. It is intended to vindicate society's interest in having its laws obeyed, and it is inevitably accompanied by future interference with the individual's freedom of movement, whether or not trial or conviction ultimately follows. The protective search for weapons, on the other hand, constitutes a brief, though far from inconsiderable, intrusion upon the sanctity of the person. It does not follow that because an officer may lawfully arrest a person only when he is apprised of facts sufficient to warrant a belief that the person has committed or is committing a crime, the officer is equally unjustified, absent that kind of evidence, in making any intrusions short of an arrest. Moreover, a perfectly reasonable apprehension of danger may arise long before the officer is possessed of adequate information to justify taking a person into custody for the purpose of prosecuting him for a crime. Petitioner's reliance on cases which have worked out standards of reasonableness with regard to "seizures" constituting arrests and searches incident thereto is thus misplaced. It assumes that the interests sought to be vindicated and the invasions of personal security may be equated in the two cases, and thereby ignores a vital aspect of the analysis of the reasonableness of particular types of conduct under the Fourth Amendment.

Our evaluation of the proper balance that has to be struck in this type of case leads us to conclude that there must be a narrowly drawn authority to permit a reasonable search for weapons for the protection of the police officer, where he has reason to believe that he is dealing with an armed and dangerous individual, regardless of whether he has probable cause to arrest the individual for a crime. The officer need not be absolutely certain that the individual is armed; the issue is whether a reasonably prudent man, in the circumstances, would be warranted in the belief that his safety or that of others was in danger. And in determining whether the officer acted reasonably in such circumstances, due weight must be given, not to his inchoate and unparticularized suspicion or "hunch," but to the specific reasonable inferences which he is entitled to draw from the facts in light of his experience.

IV

We must now examine the conduct of Officer McFadden in this case to determine whether his search and seizure of petitioner were reasonable, both at their inception and as conducted. He had observed Terry, together with Chilton and another man, acting in a manner he took to be preface to a "stick-up." We think, on the facts and circumstances Officer McFadden detailed before the trial judge, a reasonably prudent man would have been warranted in believing petitioner was armed, and thus presented a threat to the officer's safety while he was investigating his suspicious behavior. The actions of Terry and Chilton were consistent with McFadden's hypothesis that these men were contemplating a daylight robbery—which, it is reasonable to assume, would be likely to involve the use of weapons—and nothing in their conduct from the time he first noticed them until the time he confronted them and identified himself as a police officer gave him sufficient reason to negate that hypothesis. Although the trio had departed the original scene, there was nothing to indicate abandonment of an intent to commit a robbery at some point. Thus, when Officer McFadden approached the three men gathered before the display window at Zucker's store he had observed enough to make it quite reasonable to fear that they were armed; and nothing in their response to his hailing them, identifying himself as a police officer, and asking their names served to dispel that reasonable belief. We cannot say his decision at that point to seize Terry and pat his clothing for weapons was the product of a volatile or inventive imagination, or was undertaken simply as an act of harassment; the record evidences the tempered act of a policeman who, in the course of an investigation, had to make a quick decision as to how to protect himself and others from possible danger, and took limited steps to do so.

The manner in which the seizure and search were conducted is, of course, as vital a part of the inquiry as whether they were warranted at all. The Fourth Amendment proceeds as much by limitations upon the scope of governmental action as by imposing preconditions upon its initiation. The entire deterrent purpose of the rule excluding evidence seized in violation of the Fourth Amendment rests on the assumption that limitations upon the fruit to be gathered tend to limit the quest itself. Thus, evidence may not be introduced if it was discovered by means of a seizure and search which were not reasonably related in scope to the justification for their initiation.

We need not develop at length in this case, however, the limitations which the Fourth Amendment places upon a protective seizure and search for weapons. These limitations will have to be developed in the concrete factual circumstances of individual cases. Suffice it to note that such a search, unlike a search without a warrant incident to a lawful arrest, is not justified by any need to prevent the disappearance or destruction of evidence of crime. The sole justification of the search in the present situation is the protection of the police officer and others nearby, and it must therefore be confined in scope to an intrusion reasonably designed to discover guns, knives, clubs, or other hidden instruments for the assault of the police officer.

The scope of the search in this case presents no serious problem in light of these standards. Officer McFadden patted down the outer clothing of petitioner and his two companions. He did not place his hands in their pockets or under the outer surface of their garments until he had felt weapons, and then he merely reached for and removed the guns. He never did invade Katz's person beyond the outer surfaces of his clothes, since he discovered nothing in his patdown which might have been a weapon. Officer McFadden confined his search strictly to what was minimally necessary to learn whether the men were armed and to disarm them once he discovered the weapons. He did not conduct a general exploratory search for whatever evidence of criminal activity he might find.

V

We conclude that the revolver seized from Terry was properly admitted in evidence against him. At the time he seized petitioner and searched him for weapons, Officer McFadden had reasonable grounds to believe that petitioner was armed and dangerous, and it was necessary for the protection of himself and others to take swift measures to discover the true facts and neutralize the threat of harm if it materialized. The policeman carefully restricted his search to what was appropriate to the discovery of the particular items which he sought. Each case of this sort will, of course, have to be decided on its own facts. We merely hold today that, where a police officer observes unusual conduct which leads him reasonably to conclude in light of his experience that criminal activity may be afoot and that the persons with whom he is dealing may be armed and presently dangerous, where, in the course of investigating this behavior, he identifies himself as a policeman and makes reasonable inquiries, and where nothing in the initial stages of the encounter serves to dispel his reasonable fear for his own or others' safety, he is entitled for the protection of himself and others in the area to conduct a carefully limited search of the outer clothing of such persons in an attempt to discover weapons which might be used to assault him. Such a search is a reasonable search under the Fourth Amendment, and any weapons seized may properly be introduced in evidence against the person from whom they were taken.

JUSTICE DOUGLAS, dissenting.

I agree that petitioner was "seized" within the meaning of the Fourth Amendment. I also agree that frisking petitioner and his companions for guns was a "search." But it is a mystery how that "search" and that "seizure" can be constitutional by Fourth Amendment standards, unless there was "probable cause" to believe that (1) a crime had been committed or (2) a crime was in the process of being committed or (3) a crime was about to be committed.

The opinion of the Court disclaims the existence of "probable cause." If loitering were in issue and that was the offense charged, there would be "probable cause" shown. But the crime here is carrying concealed weapons; and there is no basis for concluding that the officer had "probable cause" for believing that that crime was being committed. Had a warrant been sought, a magistrate would, therefore, have been unauthorized to issue one, for he can act only if there is a showing of "probable cause." We hold today that the police have greater authority to make a "seizure" and conduct a "search" than a judge has to authorize such action. We have said precisely the opposite over and over again.

In other words, police officers up to today have been permitted to effect arrests or searches without warrants only when the facts within their personal knowledge would satisfy the constitutional standard of probable cause. At the time of their "seizure" without a warrant, they must possess facts concerning the person arrested that would have satisfied a magistrate that "probable cause" was indeed present. The term "probable cause" rings a bell of certainty that is not sounded by phrases such as "reasonable suspicion." Moreover, the meaning of "probable cause" is deeply imbedded in our constitutional history.

The infringement on personal liberty of any "seizure" of a person can only be "reasonable" under the Fourth Amendment if we require the police to possess "probable cause" before they seize him. Only that line draws a meaningful distinction between an officer's mere inkling and the presence of facts within the officer's personal knowledge which would convince a reasonable man that the person seized has committed, is committing, or is about to commit a particular crime.

To give the police greater power than a magistrate is to take a long step down the totalitarian path. Perhaps such a step is desirable to cope with modern forms of lawlessness. But if it is taken, it should be the deliberate choice of the people through a constitutional amendment. Until the Fourth Amendment, which is closely allied with the Fifth, is rewritten, the person and the effects of the individual are beyond the reach of all government agencies until there are reasonable grounds to believe (probable cause) that a criminal venture has been launched or is about to be launched.

There have been powerful hydraulic pressures throughout our history that bear heavily on the Court to water down constitutional guarantees and give the police the upper hand. That hydraulic pressure has probably never been greater than it is today.

Yet if the individual is no longer to be sovereign, if the police can pick him up whenever they do not like the cut of his jib, if they can "seize" and "search" him in their discretion, we enter a new regime. The decision to enter it should be made only after a full debate by the people of this country.

––––––––––––

Terry introduced a new legal standard—*reasonable suspicion*—that could be used by police to justify certain searches and seizures. The Supreme Court acknowledges that reasonable suspicion is a lower standard than probable cause, but it is more than an "inchoate and unparticularized suspicion" or an "inarticulate hunch." A police officer must be able to point to "specific and articulable facts which, taken together with rational inferences from those facts," reasonably warrant the intrusion. An officer's subjective good faith is insufficient. As with probable cause, reasonable suspicion is judged by an objective standard: Given the facts available to the officer at the moment of the seizure or the search, would a person of reasonable caution believe that the action taken was appropriate?

In evaluating whether a stop or frisk is unreasonable under the Fourth Amendment, the Supreme Court's inquiry is twofold: Was the officer's action *justified at its inception*, and was it *reasonably related in scope* to the circumstances which justified the action in the first place? A stop is justified at its inception if the officer has *reasonable suspicion of criminal activity*, while a frisk is justified at its inception if the officer has *reasonable suspicion that the person stopped is armed and presently dangerous*. With respect to scope, a stop should be no longer or more intrusive than necessary to confirm or dispel the officer's suspicions of criminal activity, while a frisk should be no more probing or intrusive than necessary to confirm or dispel the officer's suspicions that the person stopped is armed and presently dangerous.

One of the rationales for providing police with the authority to make a *"Terry* stop" is the state's strong interest in crime *prevention.* Indeed, Officer McFadden's quick intervention in *Terry* may have prevented an imminent "stick-up." *Terry* did not specifically indicate, however, whether police were justified in making stops to investigate past crimes. In *U.S. v. Hensley*, the Supreme Court addressed this question and held that police may make a stop upon reasonable suspicion that the person they have encountered was involved in a completed felony.

U.S. V. HENSLEY
469 U.S. 221 (1985)

Following an armed robbery in the Cincinnati suburb of St. Bernard, Ohio, a St. Bernard police officer learned from an informant that Thomas Hensley had driven the getaway car. The officer issued a "wanted flyer" to other police departments in the area requesting that they pick up and hold Hensley for the St. Bernard police. Nearly a week later, officers in Covington, Kentucky—another Cincinnati suburb—stopped a vehicle that Hensley was seen driving. One of the officers recognized a passenger in the car as a convicted felon, and upon noticing a revolver butt protruding from underneath the passenger's seat, arrested the passenger. After a search of the car uncovered other handguns, Hensley was also arrested. He was later indicted on the federal charge of being a convicted felon in possession of firearms.

Hensley moved to suppress the handguns from evidence, claiming that the Covington police had stopped him in violation of the Fourth Amendment and the principles announced in *Terry v. Ohio*, 392 U.S. 1 (1968). The federal district court denied the motion, and he was convicted. The Court of Appeals reversed, holding that the stop of Hensley's car was improper because, among other reasons, the crime being investigated was not imminent or ongoing but was already completed. The U.S. Supreme Court unanimously reversed:

> We do not agree with the Court of Appeals that our prior opinions contemplate an inflexible rule that precludes police from stopping persons they suspect of past criminal activity unless they have probable cause for arrest.

> The precise limits on investigatory stops to investigate past criminal activity are difficult to define. The proper way to identify the limits is to apply the same test already used to identify the proper bounds of intrusions that further investigations of imminent or ongoing crimes. That test, which is grounded in the standard of reasonableness embodied in the

Fourth Amendment, balances the nature and quality of the intrusion on personal security against the importance of the governmental interests alleged to justify the intrusion. When this balancing test is applied to stops to investigate past crimes, we think that probable cause to arrest need not always be required.

The factors in the balance may be somewhat different when a stop to investigate past criminal activity is involved rather than a stop to investigate ongoing criminal conduct. This is because the governmental interests and the nature of the intrusions involved in the two situations may differ. As we noted in *Terry*, one general interest present in the context of ongoing or imminent criminal activity is "that of effective crime prevention and detection." A stop to investigate an already completed crime does not necessarily promote the interest of crime prevention as directly as a stop to investigate suspected ongoing criminal activity. Similarly, the exigent circumstances which require a police officer to step in before a crime is committed or completed are not necessarily as pressing long afterwards. Public safety may be less threatened by a suspect in a past crime who now appears to be going about his lawful business than it is by a suspect who is currently in the process of violating the law. Finally, officers making a stop to investigate past crimes may have a wider range of opportunity to choose the time and circumstances of the stop.

Despite these differences, where police have been unable to locate a person suspected of involvement in a past crime, the ability to briefly stop that person, ask questions, or check identification in the absence of probable cause promotes the strong government interest in solving crimes and bringing offenders to justice. Restraining police action until after probable cause is obtained would not only hinder the investigation, but might also enable the suspect to flee in the interim and to remain at large. Particularly in the context of felonies or crimes involving a threat to public safety, it is in the public interest that the crime be solved and the suspect detained as promptly as possible. The law enforcement interests at stake in these circumstances outweigh the individual's interest to be free of a stop and detention that is no more extensive than permissible in the investigation of imminent or ongoing crimes.

We need not and do not decide today whether *Terry* stops to investigate all past crimes, however serious, are permitted. It is enough to say that, if police have a reasonable suspicion, grounded in specific and articulable facts, that a person they encounter was involved in or is wanted in connection with a completed felony, then a *Terry* stop may be made to investigate that suspicion.

Terry involved a stop of individuals on foot, while *Hensley* involved a stop of a vehicle on the road. The Supreme Court has used the basic framework established in *Terry v. Ohio* to evaluate stops and frisks in both of these situations, as explained more fully in the following two sections.

1.   INDIVIDUALS ON FOOT

In *Terry v. Ohio*, it was Officer McFadden's own observations that gave rise to his reasonable suspicion of criminal activity. In *Adams v. Williams*, the Supreme Court held that just as officers may rely upon an informant's tip in developing probable cause, so too may they rely upon informants in developing the requisite reasonable suspicion to stop and frisk.

ADAMS V. WILLIAMS
407 U.S. 143 (1972)

JUSTICE REHNQUIST delivered the opinion of the Court.

Police Sgt. John Connolly was alone early in the morning on car patrol duty in a high-crime area of Bridgeport, Connecticut. At approximately 2:15 a.m. a person known to Sgt. Connolly approached his cruiser and informed him that an individual seated in a nearby vehicle was carrying narcotics and had a gun at his waist.

After calling for assistance on his car radio, Sgt. Connolly approached the vehicle to investigate the informant's report. Connolly tapped on the car window and asked the occupant, Robert Williams, to open the door. When Williams rolled down the window instead, the sergeant reached into the car and removed a fully loaded revolver from Williams' waistband. The gun had not been visible to Connolly from outside the car, but it was in precisely the place indicated by the informant. Williams was then arrested by Connolly for unlawful possession of the pistol. A search incident to that arrest was conducted after other officers arrived. They found substantial quantities of heroin on Williams' person and in the car, and they found a machete and a second revolver hidden in the automobile.

Respondent contends that the initial seizure of his pistol, upon which rested the later search and seizure of other weapons and narcotics, was not justified by the informant's tip to Sgt. Connolly. He claims that absent a more reliable informant, or some corroboration of the tip, the policeman's actions were unreasonable under the standards set forth in *Terry v. Ohio*, 392 U.S. 1 (1968).

In *Terry* this Court recognized that "a police officer may in appropriate circumstances and in an appropriate manner approach a person for purposes of investigating possibly criminal behavior even though there is no probable cause to make an arrest." The Fourth Amendment does not require a policeman who lacks the precise level of information necessary for probable cause to arrest to simply shrug his shoulders and allow a crime to occur or a criminal to escape. On the contrary, *Terry* recognizes that it may be the essence of good police work to adopt an intermediate response. A brief stop of a suspicious individual, in order to determine his identity or to maintain the status quo momentarily while obtaining more information, may be most reasonable in light of the facts known to the officer at the time.

The Court recognized in *Terry* that the policeman making a reasonable investigatory stop should not be denied the opportunity to protect himself from attack by a hostile suspect. "When an officer is justified in believing that the individual whose suspicious behavior he is investigating at close range is armed and presently dangerous to the officer or to others," he may conduct a limited protective search for concealed weapons. The purpose of this limited search is not to discover evidence of crime, but to allow the officer to pursue his investigation without fear of violence, and thus the frisk for weapons might be equally necessary and reasonable, whether or not carrying a concealed weapon violated any applicable state law. So long as the officer is entitled to make a forcible stop, and has reason to believe that the suspect is armed and dangerous, he may conduct a weapons search limited in scope to this protective purpose.

Applying these principles to the present case, we believe that Sgt. Connolly acted justifiably in responding to his informant's tip. The informant was known to him personally and had provided him with information in the past. This is a stronger case than obtains in the case of an anonymous telephone tip. The informant here came forward personally to give information that was immediately verifiable at the scene. Indeed, under Connecticut law, the informant might have been subject to immediate arrest for making a false complaint had Sgt. Connolly's investigation proved the tip incorrect. Thus, while the Court's decisions indicate that this informant's unverified tip may have been insufficient for a narcotics arrest or search warrant, the information carried enough indicia of reliability to justify the officer's forcible stop of Williams.

In reaching this conclusion, we reject respondent's argument that reasonable cause for a stop and frisk can only be based on the officer's personal observation, rather than on information supplied by another person. Informants' tips, like all other clues and evidence coming to a policeman on the scene, may vary greatly in their value and reliability. One simple rule will not cover every situation. Some tips, completely lacking in indicia of reliability, would either warrant no police response or require further investigation before a forcible stop of a suspect would be authorized. But in some situations—for example, when the victim of a street crime seeks immediate police aid and gives a description of his assailant, or when a credible informant warns of a specific impending crime—the subtleties of the hearsay rule should not thwart an appropriate police response.

While properly investigating the activity of a person who was reported to be carrying narcotics and a concealed weapon and who was sitting alone in a car in a high-crime area at 2:15 in the morning, Sgt. Connolly had ample reason to fear for his safety. When Williams rolled down his window, rather than complying with the policeman's request to step out of the car so that his movements could more easily be seen, the revolver allegedly at Williams' waist became an even greater threat. Under these circumstances the policeman's action in reaching to the spot where the gun was thought to be hidden constituted a limited intrusion designed to insure his safety, and we conclude that it was reasonable. The loaded gun seized as a result of this intrusion was therefore admissible at Williams' trial.

Once Sgt. Connolly had found the gun precisely where the informant had predicted, probable cause existed to arrest Williams for unlawful possession of the weapon. Probable cause to arrest depends upon whether, at the moment the arrest was made, the facts and circumstances within the arresting officers' knowledge and of which they had reasonably trustworthy information were sufficient to warrant a prudent man in believing that the suspect had committed or was committing an offense. In the present case the policeman found Williams in possession of a gun in precisely the place predicted by the informant. This tended to corroborate the reliability of the informant's further report of narcotics and, together with the surrounding circumstances, certainly suggested no lawful explanation for possession of the gun. Probable cause does not require the same type of specific evidence of each element of the offense as would be needed to support a conviction. Rather, the court will evaluate generally the circumstances at the time of the arrest to decide if the officer had probable cause for his action.

Under the circumstances surrounding Williams' possession of the gun seized by Sgt. Connolly, the arrest on the weapons charge was supported by probable cause, and the search of his person and of the car incident to that arrest was lawful. The fruits of the search were therefore properly admitted at Williams' trial, and the Court of Appeals erred in reaching a contrary conclusion.

JUSTICE MARSHALL, with whom JUSTICE DOUGLAS joins, dissenting.

The facts are clear that the officer intended to make the search as soon as he approached the respondent. He asked no questions; he made no investigation; he simply searched. There was nothing apart from the information supplied by the informant to cause the officer to search. Our inquiry must focus, therefore, as it did in *Terry*, on whether the officer had sufficient facts from which he could reasonably infer that respondent was not only engaging in illegal activity, but also that he was armed and dangerous. The focus falls on the informant.

The only information that the informant had previously given the officer involved homosexual conduct in the local railroad station. [The officer investigated, found no substantiating information, and no arrest was made.]

Were we asked to determine whether the information supplied by the informant was sufficient to provide probable cause for an arrest and search, rather than a stop and frisk, there can be no doubt that we would hold that it was insufficient. This Court has squarely held that a search and seizure cannot be justified on the basis of conclusory allegations of an unnamed informant who is allegedly credible. Since the testimony of the arresting officer in the instant case patently fails to demonstrate that the informant was known to be trustworthy, and since it is also clear that the officer had no idea of the source of the informant's "knowledge," a search and seizure would have been illegal.

Assuming, *arguendo*, that this case truly involves, not an arrest and a search incident thereto, but a stop and frisk, we must decide whether or not the information possessed by the officer justified this interference with respondent's liberty. *Terry*, our only case to actually uphold a stop and frisk, is not directly in point, because the police officer in that case acted on the basis of his own personal observations. No informant was involved. But the rationale of *Terry* is still controlling, and it requires that we condemn the conduct of the police officer in encountering the respondent.

Terry did not hold that whenever a policeman has a hunch that a citizen is engaging in criminal activity, he may engage in a stop and frisk. It held that if police officers want to stop and frisk, they must have specific facts from which they can reasonably infer that an individual is engaged in criminal activity and is armed and dangerous. It was central to our decision in *Terry* that the police officer acted on the basis of his own personal observations and that he carefully scrutinized the conduct of his suspects before interfering with them in any way. When we legitimated the conduct of the officer in *Terry*, we did so because of the substantial reliability of the information on which the officer based his decision to act.

If the Court does not ignore the care with which we examined the knowledge possessed by the officer in *Terry* when he acted, then I cannot see how the actions of the officer in this case can be upheld. The Court explains what the officer knew about respondent before accosting him. But what is more significant is what he did not know. With respect to the scene generally, the officer had no idea how long respondent had been in the car, how long the car had been parked, or to whom the car belonged. With respect to the gun, the officer did not know if or when the informant had ever seen the gun, or whether the gun was carried legally, as Connecticut law permitted, or illegally. And with respect to the narcotics, the officer did not know what kind of narcotics respondent allegedly had, whether they were legally or illegally possessed, what the basis of the informant's knowledge was, or even whether the informant was capable of distinguishing narcotics from other substances.

Unable to answer any of these questions, the officer nevertheless determined that it was necessary to intrude on respondent's liberty. I believe that his determination was totally unreasonable. As I read *Terry*, an officer may act on the basis of reliable information short of probable cause to make a stop, and ultimately a frisk, if necessary; but the officer may not use unreliable, unsubstantiated, conclusory hearsay to justify an invasion of liberty. *Terry* never meant to approve the kind of knee-jerk police reaction that we have before us in this case.

In *Florida v. J.L.*, the Supreme Court considered whether an anonymous tip that an individual was carrying a gun provided the police with reasonable suspicion to stop and frisk. The Court held that such a tip must have sufficient indicia of reliability—such as predictive information—that would allow the police to test the informant's knowledge and credibility.

FLORIDA V. J.L.

529 U.S. 266 (2000)

JUSTICE GINSBURG delivered the opinion of the Court.

The question presented in this case is whether an anonymous tip that a person is carrying a gun is, without more, sufficient to justify a police officer's stop and frisk of that person. We hold that it is not.

I

On October 13, 1995, an anonymous caller reported to the Miami-Dade Police that a young black male standing at a particular bus stop and wearing a plaid shirt was carrying a gun. So far as the record reveals, there is no audio recording of the tip, and nothing is known about the informant. Sometime after the police received the tip—the record does not say how long—two officers were instructed to respond. They arrived at the bus stop about six minutes later and saw three black males "just hanging out [there]." One of the three, respondent J.L., was wearing a plaid shirt. Apart from the tip, the officers had no reason to suspect any of the three of illegal conduct. The officers did not see a firearm, and J.L. made no threatening or otherwise unusual movements. One of the officers approached J.L., told him to put his hands up on the bus stop, frisked him, and seized a gun from J.L.'s pocket. The second officer frisked the other two individuals, against whom no allegations had been made, and found nothing.

J.L., who was at the time of the frisk 10 days shy of his 16th birthday, was charged under state law with carrying a concealed firearm without a license and possessing a firearm while under the age of 18. He moved to suppress the gun as the fruit of an unlawful search, and the trial court granted his motion. The intermediate appellate court reversed, but the Supreme Court of Florida quashed that decision and held the search invalid under the Fourth Amendment.

Anonymous tips, the Florida Supreme Court stated, are generally less reliable than tips from known informants and can form the basis for reasonable suspicion only if accompanied by specific indicia of reliability, for example, the correct forecast of a subject's "not easily predicted" movements. The tip leading to the frisk of J.L., the court observed, provided no such predictions, nor did it contain any other qualifying indicia of reliability. Two justices dissented. The safety of the police and the public, they maintained, justifies a "firearm exception" to the general rule barring investigatory stops and frisks on the basis of bare-boned anonymous tips.

We granted certiorari, and now affirm the judgment of the Florida Supreme Court.

II

In the instant case, the officers' suspicion that J.L. was carrying a weapon arose not from any observations of their own but solely from a call made from an unknown location by an unknown caller. Unlike a tip from a known informant whose reputation can be assessed and who can be held responsible if her allegations turn out to be fabricated, "an anonymous tip alone seldom demonstrates the informant's basis of knowledge or veracity." *Alabama v. White*, 496 U.S. 325, 329 (1990). As we have recognized, however, there are situations in which an anonymous tip, suitably corroborated, exhibits sufficient indicia of reliability to provide reasonable suspicion to make the investigatory stop. The question we here confront is whether the tip pointing to J.L. had those indicia of reliability.

In *White*, the police received an anonymous tip asserting that a woman was carrying cocaine and predicting that she would leave an apartment building at a specified time, get into a car matching a particular description, and drive to a named motel. Standing alone, the tip would not have justified a *Terry* stop. Only after police observation showed that the informant had accurately predicted the woman's movements, we explained, did it become reasonable to think the tipster had inside knowledge about the suspect and therefore to credit his assertion about the cocaine. Although the Court held that the suspicion in *White* became reasonable after police surveillance, we regarded the case as borderline. Knowledge about a person's future movements indicates some familiarity with that person's affairs, but having such knowledge does not necessarily imply that the informant knows, in particular, whether that person is carrying hidden contraband. We accordingly classified *White* as a "close case."

The tip in the instant case lacked the moderate indicia of reliability present in *White* and essential to the Court's decision in that case. The anonymous call concerning J.L. provided no predictive information and therefore left the police without means to test the informant's knowledge or credibility. That the allegation about the gun turned out to be correct does not suggest that the officers, prior to the frisks, had a reasonable basis for suspecting J.L. of engaging in unlawful conduct: The reasonableness of official suspicion must be measured by what the officers knew before they conducted their search. All the police had to go on in this case was the bare report of an unknown, unaccountable informant who neither explained how he knew about the gun nor supplied any basis for believing he had inside information about J.L. If *White* was a close case on the reliability of anonymous tips, this one surely falls on the other side of the line.

Florida contends that the tip was reliable because its description of the suspect's visible attributes proved accurate: There really was a young black male wearing a plaid shirt at the bus stop. The United States as *amicus curiae* makes a similar argument, proposing that a stop and frisk should be permitted when (1) an anonymous tip provides a description of a particular person at a particular location illegally carrying a concealed firearm, (2) police promptly verify the pertinent details of the tip except the existence of the firearm, and (3) there are no factors that cast doubt on the reliability of the tip. These contentions misapprehend the reliability needed for a tip to justify a *Terry* stop.

An accurate description of a subject's readily observable location and appearance is of course reliable in this limited sense: It will help the police correctly identify the person whom the tipster means to accuse. Such a tip, however, does not show that the tipster has knowledge of concealed criminal activity. The reasonable suspicion here at issue requires that a tip be reliable in its assertion of illegality, not just in its tendency to identify a determinate person.

A second major argument advanced by Florida and the United States as *amicus* is, in essence, that the standard *Terry* analysis should be modified to license a "firearm exception." Under such an exception, a tip alleging an illegal gun would justify a stop and frisk even if the accusation would fail standard pre-search reliability testing. We decline to adopt this position.

Firearms are dangerous, and extraordinary dangers sometimes justify unusual precautions. Our decisions recognize the serious threat that armed criminals pose to public safety; *Terry*'s rule, which permits protective police searches on the basis of reasonable suspicion rather than demanding that officers meet the higher standard of probable cause, responds to this very concern. But an automatic firearm exception to our established reliability analysis would rove too far. Such an exception would enable any person seeking to harass another to set in motion an intrusive, embarrassing police search of the targeted person simply by placing an anonymous call falsely reporting the target's unlawful carriage of a gun. Nor could one securely confine such an exception to allegations involving firearms. Several Courts of Appeals have held it *per se* foreseeable for people carrying significant amounts of illegal drugs to be carrying guns as well. If police officers may properly conduct *Terry* frisks on the basis of bare-boned tips about guns, it would be reasonable to maintain that the police should similarly have discretion to frisk based on bare-boned tips about narcotics. As we clarified when we made indicia of reliability critical in *Adams* and *White*, the Fourth Amendment is not so easily satisfied.

The facts of this case do not require us to speculate about the circumstances under which the danger alleged in an anonymous tip might be so great as to justify a search even without a showing of reliability. We do not say, for example, that a report of a person carrying a bomb need bear the indicia of reliability we demand for a report of a person carrying a firearm before the police can constitutionally conduct a frisk. Nor do we hold that public safety officials in quarters where the reasonable expectation of Fourth Amendment privacy is diminished, such as airports and schools, cannot conduct protective searches on the basis of information insufficient to justify searches elsewhere.

Finally, the requirement that an anonymous tip bear standard indicia of reliability in order to justify a stop in no way diminishes a police officer's prerogative, in accord with *Terry*, to conduct a protective search of a person who has already been legitimately stopped. We speak in today's decision only of cases in which the officer's authority to make the initial stop is at issue. In that context, we hold that an anonymous tip lacking indicia of reliability of the kind contemplated in *Adams* and *White* does not justify a stop and frisk whenever and however it alleges the illegal possession of a firearm.

What circumstances and behavior suggest reasonable suspicion of criminal activity? In *Brown v. Texas*, police officers observed two men in an alley in an area known to have a high incidence of drug traffic. The officers stopped one of the men because they did not recognize him. The Supreme Court concluded that the police lacked the reasonable suspicion of criminal activity necessary to make a stop.

BROWN V. TEXAS
443 U.S. 47 (1979)

CHIEF JUSTICE BURGER delivered the opinion of the Court.

At 12:45 in the afternoon of December 9, 1977, Officers Venegas and Sotelo of the El Paso Police Department were cruising in a patrol car. They observed appellant and another man walking in opposite directions away from one another in an alley. Although the two men were a few feet apart when they first were seen, Officer Venegas later testified that both officers believed the two had been together or were about to meet until the patrol car appeared.

The car entered the alley, and Officer Venegas got out and asked appellant to identify himself and explain what he was doing there. The other man was not questioned or detained. The officer testified that he stopped appellant because the situation "looked suspicious and we had never seen that subject in that area before." The area of El Paso where appellant was stopped has a high incidence of drug traffic. However, the officers did not claim to suspect appellant of any specific misconduct, nor did they have any reason to believe that he was armed.

Appellant refused to identify himself and angrily asserted that the officers had no right to stop him. Officer Venegas replied that he was in a "high drug problem area"; Officer Sotelo then "frisked" appellant, but found nothing.

When appellant continued to refuse to identify himself, he was arrested for violation of Texas Penal Code Ann. § 38.02(a) (1974), which makes it a criminal act for a person to refuse to give his name and address to an officer "who has lawfully stopped him and requested the information." Following the arrest the officers searched appellant; nothing untoward was found.

Appellant waived a jury, and the court convicted him and imposed a fine of $45 plus court costs. We reverse.

When the officers detained appellant for the purpose of requiring him to identify himself, they performed a seizure of his person subject to the requirements of the Fourth Amendment. In convicting appellant, the County Court necessarily found as a matter of fact that the officers "lawfully stopped" appellant. The Fourth Amendment, of course, applies to all seizures of the person, including seizures that involve only a brief detention short of traditional arrest. Whenever a police officer accosts an individual and restrains his freedom to walk away, he has "seized" that person, and the Fourth Amendment requires that the seizure be "reasonable."

The reasonableness of seizures that are less intrusive than a traditional arrest depends on a balance between the public interest and the individual's right to personal security free from arbitrary interference by law officers. Consideration of the constitutionality of such seizures involves a weighing of the gravity of the public concerns served by the seizure, the degree to which the seizure advances the public interest, and the severity of the interference with individual liberty.

A central concern in balancing these competing considerations in a variety of settings has been to assure that an individual's reasonable expectation of privacy is not subject to arbitrary invasions solely at the unfettered discretion of officers in the field. To this end, the Fourth Amendment requires that a seizure must be based on specific, objective facts indicating that society's legitimate interests require the seizure of the particular individual, or that the seizure must be carried out pursuant to a plan embodying explicit, neutral limitations on the conduct of individual officers.

The State does not contend that appellant was stopped pursuant to a practice embodying neutral criteria, but rather maintains that the officers were justified in stopping appellant because they had a "reasonable, articulable suspicion that a crime had just been, was being, or was about to be committed." We have recognized that in some circumstances an officer may detain a suspect briefly for questioning although he does not have "probable cause" to believe that the suspect is involved in criminal activity, as is required for a traditional arrest. However, we have required the officers to have a reasonable suspicion, based on objective facts, that the individual is involved in criminal activity.

The flaw in the State's case is that none of the circumstances preceding the officers' detention of appellant justified a reasonable suspicion that he was involved in criminal conduct. Officer Venegas testified at appellant's trial that the situation in the alley "looked suspicious," but he was unable to point to any facts supporting that conclusion. There is no indication in the record that it was unusual for people to be in the alley. The fact that appellant was in a neighborhood frequented by drug users, standing alone, is not a basis for concluding that appellant himself was engaged in criminal conduct. In short, the appellant's activity was no different from the activity of other pedestrians in that neighborhood. When pressed, Officer Venegas acknowledged that the only reason he stopped appellant was to ascertain his identity. The record suggests an understandable desire to assert a police presence; however, that purpose does not negate Fourth Amendment guarantees.

In the absence of any basis for suspecting appellant of misconduct, the balance between the public interest and appellant's right to personal security and privacy tilts in favor of freedom from police interference. The Texas statute under which appellant was stopped and required to identify himself is designed to advance a weighty social objective in large metropolitan centers: prevention of crime. But even assuming that purpose is served to some degree by stopping and demanding identification from an individual without any specific basis for believing he is involved in criminal activity, the guarantees of the Fourth Amendment do not allow it. When such a stop is not based on objective criteria, the risk of arbitrary and abusive police practices exceeds tolerable limits.

The application of Texas Penal Code § 38.02 to detain appellant and require him to identify himself violated the Fourth Amendment because the officers lacked any reasonable suspicion to believe appellant was engaged or had engaged in criminal conduct.[3] Accordingly, appellant may not be punished for refusing to identify himself, and the conviction is reversed.

In *Brown v. Texas*, the defendant's presence in an area known for drug activity was insufficient to create reasonable suspicion of criminal activity. In *Illinois v. Wardlow*, the defendant was also in an area known for drug activity, but upon seeing the police, he fled. The Supreme Court concluded that these two factors were sufficient to create the reasonable suspicion of criminal activity necessary to justify a stop.

ILLINOIS V. WARDLOW
528 U.S. 119 (2000)

CHIEF JUSTICE REHNQUIST delivered the opinion of the Court.

Respondent Wardlow fled upon seeing police officers patrolling an area known for heavy narcotics trafficking. Two of the officers caught up with him, stopped him and conducted a protective patdown search for weapons. Discovering a .38-caliber handgun, the officers arrested

---

[3] We need not decide whether an individual may be punished for refusing to identify himself in the context of a lawful investigatory stop which satisfies Fourth Amendment requirements.

Wardlow. We hold that the officers' stop did not violate the Fourth Amendment to the United States Constitution.

On September 9, 1995, Officers Nolan and Harvey were working as uniformed officers in the special operations section of the Chicago Police Department. The officers were driving the last car of a four car caravan converging on an area known for heavy narcotics trafficking in order to investigate drug transactions. The officers were traveling together because they expected to find a crowd of people in the area, including lookouts and customers.

As the caravan passed 4035 West Van Buren, Officer Nolan observed respondent Wardlow standing next to the building holding an opaque bag. Respondent looked in the direction of the officers and fled. Nolan and Harvey turned their car southbound, watched him as he ran through the gangway and an alley, and eventually cornered him on the street. Nolan then exited his car and stopped respondent. He immediately conducted a protective patdown search for weapons because in his experience it was common for there to be weapons in the near vicinity of narcotics transactions. During the frisk, Officer Nolan squeezed the bag respondent was carrying and felt a heavy, hard object similar to the shape of a gun. The officer then opened the bag and discovered a .38-caliber handgun with five live rounds of ammunition. The officers arrested Wardlow.

The Illinois trial court denied respondent's motion to suppress, finding the gun was recovered during a lawful stop and frisk. Following a stipulated bench trial, Wardlow was convicted of unlawful use of a weapon by a felon. The Illinois Appellate Court reversed Wardlow's conviction, concluding that the gun should have been suppressed because Officer Nolan did not have reasonable suspicion sufficient to justify an investigative stop pursuant to *Terry v. Ohio*, 392 U.S. 1 (1968).

The Illinois Supreme Court agreed. While rejecting the Appellate Court's conclusion that Wardlow was not in a high crime area, the Illinois Supreme Court determined that sudden flight in such an area does not create a reasonable suspicion justifying a *Terry* stop.

The Illinois Supreme Court also rejected the argument that flight combined with the fact that it occurred in a high crime area supported a finding of reasonable suspicion because the "high crime area" factor was not sufficient standing alone to justify a *Terry* stop. Finding no independently suspicious circumstances to support an investigatory detention, the court held that the stop and subsequent arrest violated the Fourth Amendment. We granted certiorari, and now reverse.

This case, involving a brief encounter between a citizen and a police officer on a public street, is governed by the analysis we first applied in *Terry*. In *Terry*, we held that an officer may, consistent with the Fourth Amendment, conduct a brief, investigatory stop when the officer has a reasonable, articulable suspicion that criminal activity is afoot. While "reasonable suspicion" is a less demanding standard than probable cause and requires a showing considerably less than preponderance of the evidence, the Fourth Amendment requires at least a minimal level of objective justification for making the stop. The officer must be able to articulate more than an inchoate and unparticularized suspicion or "hunch" of criminal activity.[2]

Nolan and Harvey were among eight officers in a four-car caravan that was converging on an area known for heavy narcotics trafficking, and the officers anticipated encountering a large number of people in the area, including drug customers and individuals serving as lookouts. It was in this context that Officer Nolan decided to investigate Wardlow after observing him flee. An individual's presence in an area of expected criminal activity, standing alone, is not enough to support a reasonable, particularized suspicion that the person is committing a crime. *Brown v. Texas*, 443 U.S. 47 (1979). But officers are not required to ignore the relevant characteristics of a location in determining whether the circumstances are sufficiently suspicious to warrant further investigation. Accordingly, we have previously noted the fact that the stop occurred in a "high crime area" among the relevant contextual considerations in a *Terry* analysis. *Adams v. Williams*, 407 U.S. 143 (1972).

In this case, moreover, it was not merely respondent's presence in an area of heavy narcotics trafficking that aroused the officers' suspicion, but his unprovoked flight upon noticing the police. Our cases have also recognized that nervous, evasive behavior is a pertinent factor in determining reasonable suspicion. Headlong flight—wherever it occurs— is the consummate act of evasion: It is not necessarily indicative of wrongdoing, but it is certainly suggestive of such. In reviewing the propriety of an officer's conduct, courts do not have available empirical studies dealing with inferences drawn from suspicious behavior, and we cannot reasonably demand scientific certainty from judges or law enforcement officers where none exists. Thus, the determination of reasonable suspicion must be based on commonsense judgments and inferences about human behavior. We conclude Officer Nolan was justified in suspecting that Wardlow was involved in criminal activity, and, therefore, in investigating further.

Such a holding is entirely consistent with our decision in *Florida v. Royer*, 460 U.S. 491 (1983), where we held that when an officer, without reasonable suspicion or probable cause, approaches an individual, the individual has a right to ignore the police and go about his business. And any "refusal to cooperate, without more, does not furnish the minimal

---

[2]   We granted certiorari solely on the question whether the initial stop was supported by reasonable suspicion. Therefore, we express no opinion as to the lawfulness of the frisk independently of the stop.

level of objective justification needed for a detention or seizure." *Florida v. Bostick*, 501 U.S. 429, 437 (1991). But unprovoked flight is simply not a mere refusal to cooperate. Flight, by its very nature, is not "going about one's business"; in fact, it is just the opposite. Allowing officers confronted with such flight to stop the fugitive and investigate further is quite consistent with the individual's right to go about his business or to stay put and remain silent in the face of police questioning.

Respondent and *amici* also argue that there are innocent reasons for flight from police and that, therefore, flight is not necessarily indicative of ongoing criminal activity. This fact is undoubtedly true, but does not establish a violation of the Fourth Amendment. Even in *Terry,* the conduct justifying the stop was ambiguous and susceptible of an innocent explanation. The officer observed two individuals pacing back and forth in front of a store, peering into the window and periodically conferring. All of this conduct was by itself lawful, but it also suggested that the individuals were casing the store for a planned robbery. *Terry* recognized that the officers could detain the individuals to resolve the ambiguity.

In allowing such detentions, *Terry* accepts the risk that officers may stop innocent people. Indeed, the Fourth Amendment accepts that risk in connection with more drastic police action; persons arrested and detained on probable cause to believe they have committed a crime may turn out to be innocent. The *Terry* stop is a far more minimal intrusion, simply allowing the officer to briefly investigate further. If the officer does not learn facts rising to the level of probable cause, the individual must be allowed to go on his way. But in this case the officers found respondent in possession of a handgun, and arrested him for violation of an Illinois firearms statute. No question of the propriety of the arrest itself is before us.

JUSTICE STEVENS, with whom JUSTICE SOUTER, JUSTICE GINSBURG, and JUSTICE BREYER join, concurring in part and dissenting in part.

The State of Illinois asks this Court to announce a "bright-line rule" authorizing the temporary detention of anyone who flees at the mere sight of a police officer. Respondent counters by asking us to adopt the opposite *per se* rule—that the fact that a person flees upon seeing the police can never, by itself, be sufficient to justify a temporary investigative stop of the kind authorized by *Terry v. Ohio.*

Although I agree with the Court's rejection of the *per se* rules proffered by the parties, unlike the Court, I am persuaded that in this case the brief testimony of the officer who seized respondent does not justify the conclusion that he had reasonable suspicion to make the stop.

The question in this case concerns the degree of suspicion that attaches to a person's flight—or, more precisely, what commonsense conclusions can be drawn respecting the motives behind that flight. A pedestrian may break into a run for a variety of reasons—to catch up with a friend a block or two away, to seek shelter from an impending storm, to arrive at a bus stop before the bus leaves, to get home in time for dinner, to resume jogging after a pause for rest, to avoid contact with a bore or a bully, or simply to answer the call of nature—any of which might coincide with the arrival of an officer in the vicinity. A pedestrian might also run because he or she has just sighted one or more police officers. In short, there are unquestionably circumstances in which a person's flight is suspicious, and undeniably instances in which a person runs for entirely innocent reasons.

Given the diversity and frequency of possible motivations for flight, it would be profoundly unwise to endorse either *per se* rule. The inference we can reasonably draw about the motivation for a person's flight, rather, will depend on a number of different circumstances. Factors such as the time of day, the number of people in the area, the character of the neighborhood, whether the officer was in uniform, the way the runner was dressed, the direction and speed of the flight, and whether the person's behavior was otherwise unusual might be relevant in specific cases. This number of variables is surely sufficient to preclude either a bright-line rule that always justifies, or that never justifies, an investigative stop based on the sole fact that flight began after a police officer appeared nearby.

In addition to these concerns, a reasonable person may conclude that an officer's sudden appearance indicates nearby criminal activity. And where there is criminal activity there is also a substantial element of danger—either from the criminal or from a confrontation between the criminal and the police. These considerations can lead to an innocent and understandable desire to quit the vicinity with all speed.

Among some citizens, particularly minorities and those residing in high crime areas, there is also the possibility that the fleeing person is entirely innocent, but, with or without justification, believes that contact with the police can itself be dangerous, apart from any criminal activity associated with the officer's sudden presence.

"Unprovoked flight," in short, describes a category of activity too broad and varied to permit a *per se* reasonable inference regarding the motivation for the activity. While the innocent explanations surely do not establish that the Fourth Amendment is always violated whenever someone is stopped solely on the basis of an unprovoked flight, neither do the suspicious motivations establish that the Fourth Amendment is never violated when a *Terry* stop is predicated on that fact alone. For these reasons, the Court is surely correct in refusing to embrace either *per se* rule advocated by the parties. The totality of the circumstances, as always, must dictate the result.

Guided by that totality-of-the-circumstances test, the Court concludes that Officer Nolan had reasonable suspicion to stop respondent. In this respect, my view differs from the Court's. The entire justification for the stop is articulated in the brief testimony of Officer Nolan. Some facts are perfectly clear; others are not. This factual insufficiency leads me to conclude that the Court's judgment is mistaken.

Respondent Wardlow was arrested a few minutes after noon on September 9, 1995. Nolan was part of an eight-officer, four-car caravan patrol team. The officers were headed for "one of the areas in the 11th District [of Chicago] that's high in narcotics traffic." The reason why four cars were in the caravan was that "normally in these different areas there's an enormous amount of people, sometimes lookouts, customers." Officer Nolan testified that he was in uniform on that day, but he did not recall whether he was driving a marked or an unmarked car.

Officer Nolan and his partner were in the last of the four patrol cars that "were all caravaning eastbound down Van Buren." Nolan first observed respondent "in front of 4035 West Van Buren." Wardlow "looked in our direction and began fleeing." Nolan then "began driving southbound down the street observing [respondent] running through the gangway and the alley southbound," and observed that Wardlow was carrying a white, opaque bag under his arm. After the car turned south and intercepted respondent as he "ran right towards us." Officer Nolan stopped him and conducted a "protective search," which revealed that the bag under respondent's arm contained a loaded handgun.

This terse testimony is most noticeable for what it fails to reveal. Though asked whether he was in a marked or unmarked car, Officer Nolan could not recall the answer. He was not asked whether any of the other three cars in the caravan were marked, or whether any of the other seven officers were in uniform. Though he explained that the size of the caravan was because "normally in these different areas there's an enormous amount of people, sometimes lookouts, customers," Officer Nolan did not testify as to whether *anyone* besides Wardlow was nearby 4035 West Van Buren. Nor is it clear that that address was the intended destination of the caravan. As the Appellate Court of Illinois interpreted the record, "it appears that the officers were simply driving by, on their way to some unidentified location, when they noticed defendant standing at 4035 West Van Buren." Officer Nolan's testimony also does not reveal how fast the officers were driving. It does not indicate whether he saw respondent notice the other patrol cars. And it does not say whether the caravan, or any part of it, had already passed Wardlow by before he began to run.

Indeed, the Appellate Court thought the record was even "too vague to support the inference that defendant's flight was related to his expectation of police focus on him." Presumably, respondent did not react to the first three cars, and we cannot even be sure that he recognized the occupants of the fourth as police officers. The adverse inference is based entirely on the officer's statement: "He looked in our direction and began fleeing."

No other factors sufficiently support a finding of reasonable suspicion. Though respondent was carrying a white, opaque bag under his arm, there is nothing at all suspicious about that. Certainly the time of day—shortly after noon—does not support Illinois' argument. Nor were the officers "responding to any call or report of suspicious activity in the area." Officer Nolan did testify that he expected to find "an enormous amount of people," including drug customers or lookouts, and the Court points out that "it was in this context that Officer Nolan decided to investigate Wardlow after observing him flee." This observation, in my view, lends insufficient weight to the reasonable suspicion analysis; indeed, in light of the absence of testimony that anyone else was nearby when respondent began to run, this observation points in the opposite direction.

The State, along with the majority of the Court, relies as well on the assumption that this flight occurred in a high crime area. Even if that assumption is accurate, it is insufficient because even in a high crime neighborhood unprovoked flight does not invariably lead to reasonable suspicion. On the contrary, because many factors providing innocent motivations for unprovoked flight are concentrated in high crime areas, the character of the neighborhood arguably makes an inference of guilt less appropriate, rather than more so. Like unprovoked flight itself, presence in a high crime neighborhood is a fact too generic and susceptible to innocent explanation to satisfy the reasonable suspicion inquiry.

It is the State's burden to articulate facts sufficient to support reasonable suspicion. In my judgment, Illinois has failed to discharge that burden. I am not persuaded that the mere fact that someone standing on a sidewalk looked in the direction of a passing car before starting to run is sufficient to justify a forcible stop and frisk.

In *Brown v. Texas*, the Supreme Court found that the stop was unlawful because the police lacked reasonable suspicion of criminal activity; accordingly, the Court did not have to decide whether an individual may be punished for refusing to identify himself in the context of a lawful stop. In *Hiibel v. Sixth Judicial District Court of Nevada*, the Supreme Court resolved the question left undecided in *Brown*, holding that police may require a person to identify himself after being lawfully stopped. Interestingly, the circumstances that gave rise to the *Hiibel* decision were actually captured on video, which is available for you to view at the link below.

Larry Hiibel Arrest Video

http://www.youtube.com/watch?v=APynGWWqD8Y

HIIBEL V. SIXTH JUDICIAL DISTRICT COURT OF NEVADA
542 U.S. 177 (2004)

JUSTICE KENNEDY delivered the opinion of the Court.

The petitioner was arrested and convicted for refusing to identify himself during a stop allowed by *Terry v. Ohio*, 392 U.S. 1 (1968). He challenges his conviction under the Fourth and Fifth Amendments to the United States Constitution, applicable to the States through the Fourteenth Amendment.

I

The sheriff's department in Humboldt County, Nevada, received an afternoon telephone call reporting an assault. The caller reported seeing a man assault a woman in a red and silver GMC truck on Grass Valley Road. Deputy Sheriff Lee Dove was dispatched to investigate. When the officer arrived at the scene, he found the truck parked on the side of the road. A man was standing by the truck, and a young woman was sitting inside it. The officer observed skid marks in the gravel behind the vehicle, leading him to believe it had come to a sudden stop.

The officer approached the man and explained that he was investigating a report of a fight. The man appeared to be intoxicated. The officer asked him if he had "any identification on [him]," which we understand as a request to produce a driver's license or some other form of written identification. The man refused and asked why the officer wanted to see identification. The officer responded that he was conducting an investigation and needed to see some identification. The unidentified man became agitated and insisted he had done nothing wrong. The officer explained that he wanted to find out who the man was and what he was doing there. After continued refusals to comply with the officer's request for identification, the man began to taunt the officer by placing his hands behind his back and telling the officer to arrest him and take him to jail. This routine kept up for several minutes: The officer asked for identification 11 times and was refused each time. After warning the man that he would be arrested if he continued to refuse to comply, the officer placed him under arrest.

We now know that the man arrested on Grass Valley Road is Larry Dudley Hiibel. Hiibel was charged with "willfully resist[ing], delay[ing] or obstruct[ing] a public officer in discharging or attempting to discharge any legal duty of his office" in violation of Nev. Rev. Stat. (NRS) § 199.280 (2003). The government reasoned that Hiibel had obstructed the officer in carrying out his duties under § 171.123, a Nevada statute that defines the legal rights and duties of a police officer in the context of an investigative stop. Section 171.123 provides in relevant part:

> 1.   Any peace officer may detain any person whom the officer encounters under circumstances which reasonably indicate that the person has committed, is committing or is about to commit a crime.

> 3.   The officer may detain the person pursuant to this section only to ascertain his identity and the suspicious circumstances surrounding his presence abroad. Any person so detained shall identify himself, but may not be compelled to answer any other inquiry of any peace officer.

Hiibel was tried in the Justice Court of Union Township. The court agreed that Hiibel's refusal to identify himself as required by § 171.123 "obstructed and delayed Dove as a public officer in attempting to discharge his duty" in violation of § 199.280. Hiibel was convicted and fined $250. The Sixth Judicial District Court affirmed.

II

Stop and identify statutes often combine elements of traditional vagrancy laws with provisions intended to regulate police behavior in the course of investigatory stops. The statutes vary from State to State, but all permit an officer to ask or require a suspect to disclose his identity. In some States, a suspect's refusal to identify himself is a misdemeanor offense or civil violation; in others, it is a factor to be considered in whether the suspect has violated loitering laws. In other States, a suspect may decline to identify himself without penalty.

The Court has recognized constitutional limitations on the scope and operation of stop and identify statutes. In *Brown v. Texas*, 443 U.S. 47 (1979), the Court invalidated a conviction for violating a Texas stop and identify statute on Fourth Amendment grounds. The Court ruled that the initial stop was not based on specific, objective facts establishing reasonable suspicion to believe the suspect was involved in criminal activity. Absent that factual basis for detaining the defendant, the Court held, the risk of "arbitrary and abusive police practices" was too great and the stop was impermissible.

The present case begins where our prior cases left off. Here there is no question that the initial stop was based on reasonable suspicion, satisfying the Fourth Amendment requirements noted in *Brown*. Further, the petitioner has not alleged that the statute is unconstitutionally vague. The Nevada Supreme Court has interpreted NRS § 171.123(3) to require only that a suspect disclose his name. As we understand it, the statute does not require a suspect to give the officer a driver's license or any other document. Provided that the suspect either states his name or communicates it to the officer by other means—a choice, we assume, that the suspect may make—the statute is satisfied and no violation occurs.

III

Hiibel argues that his conviction cannot stand because the officer's conduct violated his Fourth Amendment rights. We disagree.

Asking questions is an essential part of police investigations. In the ordinary course a police officer is free to ask a person for identification without implicating the Fourth Amendment. Interrogation relating to one's identity or a request for identification by the police does not, by itself, constitute a Fourth Amendment seizure. Beginning with *Terry v. Ohio*, the Court has recognized that a law enforcement officer's reasonable suspicion that a person may be involved in criminal activity permits the officer to stop the person for a brief time and take additional steps to investigate further. To ensure that the resulting seizure is constitutionally reasonable, a *Terry* stop must be limited. The officer's action must be justified at its inception, and reasonably related in scope to the circumstances which justified the interference in the first place. For example, the seizure can not continue for an excessive period of time, or resemble a traditional arrest.

Obtaining a suspect's name in the course of a *Terry* stop serves important government interests. Knowledge of identity may inform an officer that a suspect is wanted for another offense, or has a record of violence or mental disorder. On the other hand, knowing identity may help clear a suspect and allow the police to concentrate their efforts elsewhere. Identity may prove particularly important in cases such as this, where the police are investigating what appears to be a domestic assault. Officers called to investigate domestic disputes need to know whom they are dealing with in order to assess the situation, the threat to their own safety, and possible danger to the potential victim.

Although it is well established that an officer may ask a suspect to identify himself in the course of a *Terry* stop, it has been an open question whether the suspect can be arrested and prosecuted for refusal to answer.

The principles of *Terry* permit a State to require a suspect to disclose his name in the course of a *Terry* stop. The reasonableness of a seizure under the Fourth Amendment is determined by balancing its intrusion on the individual's Fourth Amendment interests against its promotion of legitimate government interests. The Nevada statute satisfies that standard. The request for identity has an immediate relation to the purpose, rationale, and practical demands of a *Terry* stop. The threat of criminal sanction helps ensure that the request for identity does not become a legal nullity. On the other hand, the Nevada statute does not alter the nature of the stop itself: it does not change its duration, or its location. A state law requiring a suspect to disclose his name in the course of a valid *Terry* stop is consistent with Fourth Amendment prohibitions against unreasonable searches and seizures.

Petitioner argues that the Nevada statute circumvents the probable-cause requirement, in effect allowing an officer to arrest a person for being suspicious. According to petitioner, this creates a risk of arbitrary police conduct that the Fourth Amendment does not permit. Petitioner's concerns are met by the requirement that a *Terry* stop must be justified at its inception and reasonably related in scope to the circumstances which justified the initial stop. Under these principles, an officer may not arrest a suspect for failure to identify himself if the request for identification is not reasonably related to the circumstances justifying the stop. It is clear in this case that the request for identification was reasonably related in scope to the circumstances which justified the stop. The officer's request was a commonsense inquiry, not an effort to obtain an arrest for failure to identify after a *Terry* stop yielded insufficient evidence. The stop, the request, and the State's requirement of a response did not contravene the guarantees of the Fourth Amendment.

[In another part of the opinion excerpted in Chapter 12, the Court rejected Hiibel's claim that the Nevada statute requiring him to identify himself violated his Fifth Amendment privilege against self-incrimination.]

JUSTICE BREYER, with whom JUSTICE SOUTER and JUSTICE GINSBURG join, dissenting.

This Court's Fourth Amendment precedents make clear that police may conduct a *Terry* stop only within circumscribed limits. And one of those limits invalidates laws that compel responses to police questioning.

[In *Berkemer v. McCarty*, 468 U.S. 420, 439 (1984),] the Court wrote that an "officer may ask the [*Terry*] detainee a moderate number of questions to determine his identity and to try to obtain information confirming or dispelling the officer's suspicions. But the detainee is not obliged to respond." See also *Illinois v. Wardlow*, 528 U.S. 119, 125 (2000) (stating that allowing officers to stop and question a fleeing person "is quite consistent with the individual's right to go about his business or to stay put and remain silent in the face of police questioning").

[T]he Court's statement in *Berkemer*, while technically dicta, is the kind of strong dicta that the legal community typically takes as a statement of the law. And that law has remained undisturbed for more than 20 years.

There is no good reason now to reject this generation-old statement of the law. There are sound reasons rooted in Fifth Amendment considerations for adhering to this Fourth Amendment legal condition circumscribing police authority to stop an individual against his will. Administrative considerations also militate against change. Can a State, in addition to requiring a stopped individual to answer "What's your name?" also require an answer to "What's your license number?" or "Where do you live?"

The majority presents no evidence that the rule, which for nearly a generation has set forth a settled *Terry* stop condition, has significantly interfered with law enforcement. Nor has the majority presented any other convincing justification for change. I would not begin to erode a clear rule with special exceptions.

In addition to asking an individual who has been stopped to identify himself, a police officer may also perform a frisk for weapons if he has reasonable suspicion that the individual is armed and presently dangerous. But what happens if, during the frisk, the officer feels an object that he cannot clearly identify? What if the officer suspects that the object is drugs rather than a weapon? May the officer manipulate the object inside the individual's pocket or remove it for closer inspection? In *Minnesota v. Dickerson*, excerpted in Chapter 5 in connection with the "plain touch" corollary to the plain view exception, the Supreme Court addressed these questions and established limits on the ability of police to seize non-threatening contraband discovered during a frisk.

MINNESOTA V. DICKERSON
508 U.S. 366 (1993)

JUSTICE WHITE delivered the opinion of the Court.

In this case, we consider whether the Fourth Amendment permits the seizure of contraband detected through a police officer's sense of touch during a protective patdown search.

I

On the evening of November 9, 1989, two Minneapolis police officers were patrolling an area on the city's north side in a marked squad car. At about 8:15 p.m., one of the officers observed respondent leaving a 12-unit apartment building on Morgan Avenue North. The officer, having previously responded to complaints of drug sales in the building's hallways and having executed several search warrants on the premises, considered the building to be a notorious "crack house." According to testimony credited by the trial court, respondent began walking toward the police but, upon spotting the squad car and making eye contact with one of the officers, abruptly halted and began walking in the opposite direction. His suspicion aroused, this officer watched as respondent turned and entered an alley on the other side of the apartment building. Based upon respondent's seemingly evasive actions and the fact that he had just left a building known for cocaine traffic, the officers decided to stop respondent and investigate further.

The officers pulled their squad car into the alley and ordered respondent to stop and submit to a patdown search. The search revealed no weapons, but the officer conducting the search did take an interest in a small lump in respondent's nylon jacket. The officer later testified: "As I pat-searched the front of his body, I felt a lump, a small lump, in the front pocket. I examined it with my fingers and it slid and it felt to be a lump of crack cocaine in cellophane."

The officer then reached into respondent's pocket and retrieved a small plastic bag containing one fifth of one gram of crack cocaine. Respondent was arrested and charged in Hennepin County District Court with possession of a controlled substance.

Before trial, respondent moved to suppress the cocaine. The trial court first concluded that the officers were justified under *Terry v. Ohio*, 392 U.S. 1 (1968), in stopping respondent to investigate whether he might be engaged in criminal activity. The court further found that the officers were justified in frisking respondent to ensure that he was not carrying a weapon. Finally, analogizing to the "plain-view" doctrine, under which officers may make a warrantless seizure of contraband found in plain view during a lawful search for other items, the trial court ruled that the officers' seizure of the cocaine did not violate the Fourth Amendment:

> To this Court there is no distinction as to which sensory perception the officer uses to conclude that the material is contraband. An experienced officer may rely upon his sense of smell in DWI stops or in recognizing the smell of burning marijuana in an automobile. The sound of a shotgun being racked would clearly support certain reactions by an officer. The sense of touch, grounded in experience and training, is as reliable as perceptions drawn from other senses. "Plain feel," therefore, is no different than plain view and will equally support the seizure here.

His suppression motion having failed, respondent proceeded to trial and was found guilty. On appeal, the Minnesota Court of Appeals reversed. The court agreed with the trial court that the investigative stop and protective patdown search of respondent were lawful under *Terry* because the officers had a reasonable belief based on specific and articulable facts that respondent was engaged in criminal behavior and that he might be armed and dangerous. The court concluded, however, that the officers had overstepped the bounds allowed by *Terry* in seizing the cocaine. In doing so, the Court of Appeals "declined to adopt the plain feel exception" to the warrant requirement.

The Minnesota Supreme Court affirmed. Like the Court of Appeals, the State Supreme Court held that both the stop and the frisk of respondent were valid under *Terry*, but found the seizure of the cocaine to be unconstitutional. The court expressly refused "to extend the plain view doctrine to the sense of touch" on the grounds that "the sense of touch is inherently less immediate and less reliable than the sense of sight" and that "the sense of touch is far more intrusive into the personal privacy that is at the core of the Fourth Amendment." The court thus appeared to adopt a categorical rule barring the seizure of any contraband detected by an officer through the sense of touch during a patdown search for weapons. The court further noted that "even if we recognized a 'plain feel' exception, the search in this case would not qualify" because "the pat search of the defendant went far beyond what is permissible under *Terry*." As the State Supreme Court read the record, the officer conducting the search ascertained that the lump in respondent's jacket was contraband only after probing and investigating what he certainly knew was not a weapon.

We granted certiorari to resolve a conflict among the state and federal courts over whether contraband detected through the sense of touch during a patdown search may be admitted into evidence. We now affirm.

II

Terry v. Ohio held that "where a police officer observes unusual conduct which leads him reasonably to conclude in light of his experience that criminal activity may be afoot," the officer may briefly stop the suspicious person and make "reasonable inquiries" aimed at confirming or dispelling his suspicions.

Terry further held that "when an officer is justified in believing that the individual whose suspicious behavior he is investigating at close range is armed and presently dangerous to the officer or to others," the officer may conduct a patdown search "to determine whether the person is in fact carrying a weapon." The purpose of this limited search is not to discover evidence of crime, but to allow the officer to pursue his investigation without fear of violence. If the protective search goes beyond what is necessary to determine if the suspect is armed, it is no longer valid under *Terry* and its fruits will be suppressed.

The question presented today is whether police officers may seize nonthreatening contraband detected during a protective patdown search of the sort permitted by *Terry*. We think the answer is clearly that they may, so long as the officers' search stays within the bounds marked by *Terry*.

We have already held that police officers, at least under certain circumstances, may seize contraband detected during the lawful execution of a *Terry* search. In *Michigan v. Long*, 463 U.S. 1032 (1983), for example, police approached a man who had driven his car into a ditch and who appeared to be under the influence of some intoxicant. As the man moved to reenter the car from the roadside, police spotted a knife on the floorboard. The officers stopped the man, subjected him to a patdown search, and then inspected the interior of the vehicle for other weapons. During the search of the passenger compartment, the police discovered an open pouch containing marijuana and seized it. This Court upheld the validity of the search and seizure under *Terry*. The Court held first that, in the context of a roadside encounter, where police have reasonable suspicion based on specific and articulable facts to believe that a driver may be armed and dangerous, they may conduct a protective search for weapons not only of the driver's person but also of the passenger compartment of the automobile. Of course, the protective search of the vehicle, being justified solely by the danger that weapons stored there could be used against the officers or bystanders, must be "limited to those areas in which a weapon may be placed or hidden." The Court then held: "If, while conducting a legitimate *Terry* search of the interior of the automobile, the officer should, as here, discover contraband other than weapons, he clearly cannot be required to ignore the contraband, and the Fourth Amendment does not require its suppression in such circumstances."

The Court in *Long* justified this latter holding by reference to our cases under the "plain-view" doctrine. Under that doctrine, if police are lawfully in a position from which they view an object, if its incriminating character is immediately apparent, and if the officers have a lawful right of access to the object, they may seize it without a warrant. If, however, the police lack probable cause to believe that an object in plain view is contraband without conducting some further search of the object—*i.e.*, if its incriminating character is not "immediately apparent"—the plain-view doctrine cannot justify its seizure. *Arizona v. Hicks*, 480 U.S. 321 (1987).

We think that this doctrine has an obvious application by analogy to cases in which an officer discovers contraband through the sense of touch during an otherwise lawful search. The rationale of the plain-view doctrine is that if contraband is left in open view and is observed by a police officer from a lawful vantage point, there has been no invasion of a legitimate expectation of privacy and thus no "search" within the meaning of the Fourth Amendment—or at least no search independent of the initial intrusion that gave the officers their vantage point. The warrantless seizure of contraband that presents itself in this manner is deemed justified by the realization that resort to a neutral magistrate under such circumstances would often be impracticable and would do little to promote the objectives of the Fourth Amendment. The same can be said of tactile discoveries of contraband. If a police officer lawfully pats down a suspect's outer clothing and feels an object whose contour or mass makes its identity immediately apparent, there has been no invasion of the suspect's privacy beyond that already authorized by the officer's search for weapons; if the object is contraband, its warrantless seizure would be justified by the same practical considerations that inhere in the plain-view context.

The Minnesota Supreme Court rejected an analogy to the plain-view doctrine on two grounds: first, its belief that "the sense of touch is inherently less immediate and less reliable than the sense of sight," and second, that "the sense of touch is far more intrusive into the personal privacy that is at the core of the Fourth Amendment." We have a somewhat different view. First, *Terry* itself demonstrates that the sense of touch is capable of revealing the nature of an object with sufficient reliability to support a seizure. The very premise of *Terry*, after all, is that officers will be able to detect the presence of weapons through the sense of touch and *Terry* upheld precisely such a seizure. Even if it were true that the sense of touch is generally less reliable than the sense of sight, that only suggests that officers will less often be able to justify seizures of unseen contraband. Regardless of whether the officer detects the contraband by sight or by touch, however, the Fourth Amendment's requirement that the officer have probable cause to believe that the item is contraband before seizing it ensures against excessively speculative seizures. The court's second concern—that touch is more intrusive into privacy than is sight—is inapposite in light of the fact that the intrusion the court fears has already been authorized by the lawful search for weapons. The seizure of an item whose identity is already known occasions no further invasion of privacy. Accordingly, the suspect's privacy interests are not advanced by a categorical rule barring the seizure of contraband plainly detected through the sense of touch.

III

It remains to apply these principles to the facts of this case. Respondent has not challenged the finding made by the trial court and affirmed by both the Court of Appeals and the State Supreme Court that the police were justified under *Terry* in stopping him and frisking him for weapons. Thus, the dispositive question before this Court is whether the officer who conducted the search was acting within the lawful bounds marked by *Terry* at the time he gained probable cause to believe that the lump in respondent's jacket was contraband. The State District Court did not make precise findings on this point, instead finding simply that the officer, after feeling "a small, hard object wrapped in plastic" in respondent's pocket, "formed the opinion that the object was crack cocaine." The District Court also noted that the officer made "no claim that he suspected this object to be a weapon," a finding affirmed on appeal. The Minnesota Supreme Court, after a close examination of the record, held that the officer's own testimony "belies any notion that he immediately" recognized the lump as crack cocaine. Rather, the court concluded, the officer determined that the lump was contraband only after "squeezing, sliding and otherwise manipulating the contents of the defendant's pocket"—a pocket which the officer already knew contained no weapon.

Under the State Supreme Court's interpretation of the record before it, it is clear that the court was correct in holding that the police officer in this case overstepped the bounds of the "strictly circumscribed" search for weapons allowed under *Terry*. Where, as here, "an officer who is executing a valid search for one item" seizes a different item, this Court rightly "has been sensitive to the danger that officers will enlarge a specific authorization, furnished by a warrant or an exigency, into the equivalent of a general warrant to rummage and seize at will." Here, the officer's continued exploration of respondent's pocket after having concluded that it contained no weapon was unrelated to the sole justification of the search under *Terry*: the protection of the police officer and others nearby. It therefore amounted to the sort of evidentiary search that *Terry* expressly refused to authorize, and that we have condemned in subsequent cases.

Once again, the analogy to the plain-view doctrine is apt. In *Arizona v. Hicks*, this Court held invalid the seizure of stolen stereo equipment found by police while executing a valid search for other evidence. Although the police were lawfully on the premises, they obtained probable cause to believe that the stereo equipment was contraband only after moving the equipment to permit officers to read its serial numbers. The subsequent seizure of the equipment could not be justified by the plain-view doctrine, this Court explained, because the incriminating character of the stereo equipment was not immediately apparent; rather, probable cause to believe that the equipment was stolen arose only as a result of a further search—the moving of the equipment—that was not authorized by a search warrant or by any exception to the warrant requirement. The facts of this case are very similar. Although the officer was lawfully in a position to feel the lump in respondent's pocket, because *Terry* entitled him to place his hands upon respondent's jacket, the court below determined that the incriminating character of the object was not immediately apparent to him. Rather, the officer determined that the item was contraband only after conducting a further search, one not authorized by *Terry* or by any other exception to the warrant requirement. Because this further search of respondent's pocket was constitutionally invalid, the seizure of the cocaine that followed is likewise unconstitutional.

Dickerson presents a good opportunity to review the constitutional principles governing the various components of a typical stop-and-frisk.

The police were justified in stopping Dickerson because he was present in an area known for drug activity and, upon making eye contact with the officers, he abruptly turned and began walking in the opposite direction. Under *Illinois v. Wardlow*, Dickerson's presence in a high-crime area coupled with his evasive behavior creates the reasonable suspicion of criminal activity necessary to justify a *Terry* stop.

The Supreme Court's opinion in *Dickerson* did not review the testimony of the officers that led them to conclude that a frisk was appropriate, but the factors that produce reasonable suspicion of criminal activity—presence in an area known for drug activity coupled with evasive behavior—might also create reasonable suspicion that a person is armed and presently dangerous. Indeed, the Supreme Court and other courts appear willing to assume that a person suspected of the possession or sale of narcotics is also likely to be armed and dangerous. In *Wardlow*, for example, the Supreme Court did not question the officer's decision to conduct a patdown search for weapons based on "his experience [that] it was common for there to be weapons in the near vicinity of narcotics transactions." The lower federal courts have made similar findings.[a] An individual's body language and gait might also suggest that he is carrying a weapon, creating the requisite reasonable suspicion to justify a frisk. (See the news graphic reproduced below.)

While the stop and frisk of Dickerson were consistent with the Fourth Amendment standards announced in *Terry*, the Supreme Court held that the last part of the interaction—the "reach in" to seize the drugs—was unconstitutional. Following a frisk of the exterior of a suspect's clothing or handbag, an officer may reach inside if he has reasonable suspicion that the item felt during the frisk is a weapon. In order to reach inside a suspect's clothing or handbag for something that is *not* a weapon, the officer must have probable cause—based on the quick exterior frisk without any further manipulation—that the item felt is drugs or other contraband. Stated somewhat differently, if the identity of the item as drugs or contraband is *immediately apparent* to the officer based on the quick exterior frisk, he may reach in and seize it.

In *Dickerson*, the officer felt no weapon during the frisk, but he did feel a small lump in Dickerson's pocket. The identity of the lump was not, however, *immediately apparent* based on the frisk, so the officer slid it

---

[a]   *See, e.g., U.S. v. Dean*, 59 F.3d 1479, 1490 & n.20 (5th Cir. 1995) ("We have observed repeatedly that firearms are the tools of the trade of those engaged in illegal drug activity."); *U.S. v. Evans*, 994 F.2d 317, 321–22 & n.1 (7th Cir. 1993) (defendant's proximity to a reported drug house increased the risk that defendant was armed; trial court did not improperly take judicial notice of the fact that "drugs and weapons are so interrelated that if there is one, there is bound to be the other"); *U.S. v. Crespo*, 834 F.2d 267, 271 (2d Cir. 1987) ("We have often taken judicial notice that, to substantial dealers in narcotics, firearms are as much tools of the trade as are the commonly recognized articles of narcotics paraphernalia."); *U.S. v. Wiener*, 534 F.2d 15, 18 (2d Cir. 1976) ("Experience on the trial and appellate benches has taught that substantial dealers in narcotics keep firearms on their premises as tools of the trade almost to the same extent as they keep scales, glassine bags, cutting equipment and other narcotics equipment.").

around in Dickerson's pocket and further examined it with his fingers until he determined that it was likely crack cocaine wrapped in cellophane. The Supreme Court concluded that the officer did not have probable cause to believe the lump was drugs until *after* he manipulated it in Dickerson's pocket. The manipulation of the lump in Dickerson's pocket was, in effect, an additional search—without probable cause—that was not justified by the concerns about officer safety that form the basis of the stop-and-frisk framework announced in *Terry v. Ohio*. Once the officer frisked Dickerson and was satisfied that there was no weapon, the stop should have ended and Dickerson should have been permitted to leave.

What kinds of things do police look for when deciding whether to make a stop-and-frisk? The news graphic below, created by artist Megan Jaegerman, was based on an interview with Robert T. Gallagher, a former NYPD detective, who was widely known in police circles "for an uncanny ability to spot people carrying guns on the street."[b] The graphic depicts a variety of subtle clues that can assist police in determining whether an individual is armed.

---

[b] *See* Erik Eckholm, *Who's Got a Gun? Clues Are in the Body Language*, NEW YORK TIMES, May 26, 1992, available at http://www.nytimes.com/1992/05/26/nyregion/who-s-got-a-gun-clues-are-in-the-body-language.html.

Spotting a Hidden Handgun

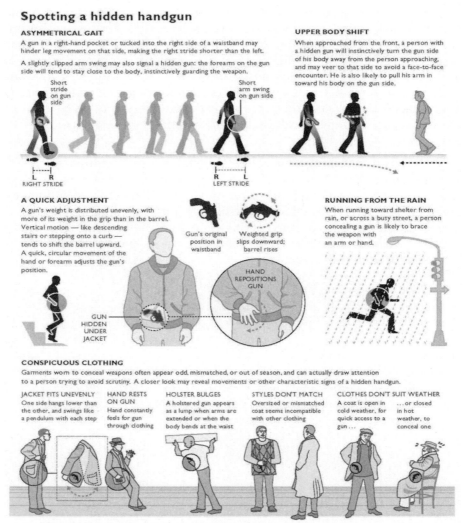

Source: Robert T. Gallagher, former detective, Anti-Robbery Tactical Unit, New York City Police Department   Megan Jaegerman

Reprinted by permission Edward R. Tufte, *Beautiful Evidence*, Graphics Press, Cheshire, CT, 2006.

The following NYPD training video describes additional clues that can signal to an alert officer that an individual is carrying a concealed weapon, justifying a stop-and-frisk.

NYPD Stop-and-Frisk Training Video

http://www.youtube.com/watch?v=zMlt37sVJOs

Critics of police stop-and-frisk practices have long complained that such techniques are often used in a discriminatory manner to target minorities, particularly African-Americans and Hispanics. Chief Justice Warren briefly touched upon these concerns in the first section of his opinion in *Terry v. Ohio*, noting that minority groups had "frequently complain[ed]" of "wholesale harassment by certain elements of the police community." Such conduct, the Chief Justice continued, "must be condemned by the judiciary and its fruits must be excluded from evidence in criminal trials."

Such condemnation recently arrived in the form of a sweeping decision, *Floyd v. City of New York*, 959 F.Supp.2d 540 (S.D.N.Y. 2013), from U.S. District Court Judge Shira Scheindlin, concluding that the stop-and-frisk tactics employed by the New York City Police Department violated the constitutional rights of minorities. Between January 2004 and June 2012, Judge Scheindlin found, New York police made over 4.4 million *Terry* stops; 52% of those stopped were black, 31% were Hispanic, and just 10% were white. At the same time, New York City's resident population was roughly 23% black, 29% Hispanic, and 33% white. A protective frisk for weapons occurred in 52% of all stops, but a weapon was found in only 1.5% of those cases. Judge Scheindlin concluded that the NYPD resorted to a "policy of indirect racial profiling" as it increased the number of stops in minority communities. As a result, officers routinely stopped "blacks and Hispanics who would not have been stopped if they were white."

New York City, led by then-Mayor Michael Bloomberg, appealed Judge Scheindlin's decision. In *Ligon v. City of New York*, 736 F.3d 118 (2d Cir. 2013), the U.S. Court of Appeals for the Second Circuit stayed the remedies imposed by Judge Scheindlin and removed her from the case, finding that she compromised the appearance of impartiality by making certain statements in court and in interviews with the news media while the case was still pending. Shortly after assuming office in January 2014, the new Mayor of New York City, Bill de Blasio, announced that the city would settle the litigation by agreeing to the reforms that Judge Scheindlin originally recommended.[c]

---

[c] *See* Benjamin Weiser and Joseph Goldstein, *Mayor Says New York City Will Settle Suits on Stop-and-Frisk Tactics*, NEW YORK TIMES, January 30, 2014, available at http://www.nytimes.com/2014/01/31/nyregion/de-blasio-stop-and-frisk.html.

Stop-and-Frisk: Individuals on Foot

1.   In a stop, a police officer uses physical force or a show of authority to briefly detain an individual for questioning or further investigation. Because the individual is not free to leave, a stop constitutes a seizure under the Fourth Amendment.

2.   In order to make a stop, police must have reasonable suspicion of imminent or ongoing criminal activity. Police may also stop an individual upon reasonable suspicion that he is involved in or wanted in connection with a completed felony.

   a.   Reasonable suspicion is a lower standard than probable cause, but is more than a mere hunch. A police officer must be able to point to specific and articulable facts, along with rational inferences from those facts, that reasonably warrant the intrusion. As with probable cause, the totality of the circumstances should be considered in the determination of reasonable suspicion.

   b.   Reasonable suspicion is judged by an objective standard, not by the officer's subjective good faith. Given the facts available to the officer, would a person of reasonable caution believe that the action taken was appropriate?

   c.   Reasonable suspicion can be based on an informant's tip, even if the informant is anonymous. Any tip should, however, have sufficient indicia of reliability, such as predictive information, that would allow the police to test the informant's knowledge and credibility.

   d.   A person's presence in a high-crime area coupled with evasive behavior or unprovoked flight creates the reasonable suspicion of criminal activity necessary to justify a stop.

3.   During a lawful stop, police may require an individual to identify himself.

4.   In order to frisk a person who has been stopped, police must have reasonable suspicion that the person is armed and presently dangerous. The officer need not be absolutely certain that the individual is armed; the issue is whether a reasonably prudent person, in the circumstances, would be warranted in the belief that his safety or that of others was in danger. Many of the factors that provide reasonable suspicion of criminal activity will also create reasonable suspicion that a person is armed and presently dangerous.

   a.   In order to "reach in" and seize a weapon, the officer must have reasonable suspicion that the item felt during the frisk is a weapon or could be used as a weapon.

b. In order to "reach in" and seize drugs or contraband, the officer must have probable cause that the item felt during the frisk is drugs or contraband. Or, in slightly different terms, it must be immediately apparent to the officer—based only on the quick exterior frisk, without any manipulation—that the item felt is drugs or contraband.

5. A stop or a frisk must be reasonably related in scope to the circumstances which justified the stop or the frisk in the first place. A stop should be no longer or more intrusive than necessary to confirm or dispel the officer's suspicions of criminal activity, while a frisk should be no more probing or intrusive than necessary to confirm or dispel the officer's suspicions that the person stopped is armed and presently dangerous.

LEARN MORE WITH *LAW & ORDER*

In the following episode of *Law & Order* ("Marathon," Season 10, Episode 6), police are investigating a shooting on a public street. The police identify a suspect, Bobby Sabo, but there is little evidence connecting him to the crime, and police cannot locate his weapon. An acquaintance of Bobby tells the police that Bobby sold his gun to a "Dominican dude" who hangs out in front of a bodega. At the bodega, Detective Briscoe sees a man with what appears to be a heavy object—a gun—in his jacket pocket. The police stop the man (Flaco Ochoa), frisk him, and find a gun that turns out to be the murder weapon. Ochoa tells the police that he bought the gun from Bobby and makes a deal to testify against him. Ochoa later reneges on the deal and moves to suppress the gun and dismiss the indictment for possession of a firearm.

In an exchange in the hallway of the courthouse, prosecutor Abbie Carmichael argues that the stop-and-frisk was lawful because Briscoe, an experienced detective, noticed the heavy object in Ochoa's pocket and an awkward walk indicative of a weapon. Ochoa's defense attorney contends that Briscoe merely had a hunch. The judge ultimately suppresses the gun because there was insufficient evidence of criminal activity to initiate the stop-and-frisk in the first place.

> **The segments of the episode that depict the relevant Investigative Criminal Procedure issues appear at:**
>
> 23:47 to 28:39

> *Law & Order* **Episode**
> **"Marathon," Season 10, Episode 6**

2. VEHICLES ON THE ROAD

Although the *Terry* stop-and-frisk framework was originally developed by the Supreme Court in the context of interactions between police and individuals on foot, the Court has adapted the framework so that it can be used by police to stop and frisk vehicles—and the individuals inside them—traveling on the road.

In *Delaware v. Prouse*, the Supreme Court held that police must have reasonable suspicion of a violation of law in order to make a roving stop of a vehicle.

DELAWARE V. PROUSE
440 U.S. 648 (1979)

A patrolman in a police cruiser stopped William Prouse's car. The patrolman smelled marijuana smoke as he was walking toward the stopped vehicle, and he seized marijuana in plain view on the car floor. Prouse was subsequently indicted for illegal possession of a controlled substance. At a hearing on Prouse's motion to suppress the marijuana seized as a result of the stop, the patrolman testified that prior to stopping the vehicle, he had not observed any traffic or equipment violations, nor any suspicious activity, and that he made the stop only in order to check the driver's license and registration.

The Supreme Court began by noting that "stopping an automobile and detaining its occupants" constitute a "seizure" under the Fourth Amendment, "even though the purpose of the stop is limited and the resulting detention quite brief." A seizure must be "reasonable" under the Fourth Amendment, which is determined by "balancing [the] intrusion on the individual's Fourth Amendment interests against its promotion of legitimate governmental interests."

The State of Delaware argued that patrol officers should be subject to no constraints in deciding which automobiles to stop for a license and registration check because the state's interest in discretionary spot checks as a means of ensuring the safety of its roadways outweighs the resulting intrusion on the privacy and security of the persons detained. The Supreme Court acknowledged Delaware's important interest in ensuring the safety of its roads, but found that the "marginal contribution to roadway safety possibly resulting from a system of spot checks cannot justify subjecting every occupant of every vehicle on the roads to a seizure" at the "unbridled discretion of law enforcement officials."

While reserving judgment on "roadblock-type stops" that do not involve the "unconstrained exercise of discretion," the Court concluded that police must have reasonable suspicion of a driving infraction or some other violation of law in order to stop a vehicle:

We hold that except in those situations in which there is at least articulable and reasonable suspicion that a motorist is unlicensed or that an automobile is not registered, or that either the vehicle or an occupant is otherwise subject to seizure for violation of law, stopping an automobile and detaining the driver in order to check his driver's license and the registration of the automobile are unreasonable under the Fourth Amendment.

In *U.S. v. Arvizu*, the Supreme Court held that the reasonable suspicion necessary to stop a vehicle—like the reasonable suspicion necessary to stop an individual on foot—is based on the totality of the circumstances. Under this approach, conduct which, by itself, may have an innocent explanation can still be given weight in the reasonable suspicion determination when all of the surrounding circumstances are considered.

U.S. V. ARVIZU
534 U.S. 266 (2002)

CHIEF JUSTICE REHNQUIST delivered the opinion of the Court.

Respondent Ralph Arvizu was stopped by a border patrol agent while driving on an unpaved road in a remote area of southeastern Arizona. A search of his vehicle turned up more than 100 pounds of marijuana. The District Court for the District of Arizona denied respondent's motion to suppress, but the Court of Appeals for the Ninth Circuit reversed. In the course of its opinion, it categorized certain factors relied upon by the District Court as simply out of bounds in deciding whether there was "reasonable suspicion" for the stop. We hold that the Court of Appeals' methodology was contrary to our prior decisions and that it reached the wrong result in this case.

On an afternoon in January 1998, Agent Clinton Stoddard was working at a border patrol checkpoint along U.S. Highway 191 approximately 30 miles north of Douglas, Arizona. Douglas has a population of about 13,000 and is situated on the United States-Mexico border in the southeastern part of the State. Only two highways lead north from Douglas. Highway 191 leads north to Interstate 10, which passes through Tucson and Phoenix. State Highway 80 heads northeast through less populated areas toward New Mexico, skirting south and east of the portion of the Coronado National Forest that lies approximately 20 miles northeast of Douglas.

The checkpoint is located at the intersection of 191 and Rucker Canyon Road, an unpaved east-west road that connects 191 and the Coronado National Forest. When the checkpoint is operational, border patrol agents stop the traffic on 191 as part of a coordinated effort to stem the flow of illegal immigration and smuggling across the international border. Agents use roving patrols to apprehend smugglers trying to circumvent the checkpoint by taking the backroads, including those roads through the sparsely populated area between Douglas and the national forest. Magnetic sensors, or "intrusion devices," facilitate agents' efforts in patrolling these areas. Directionally sensitive, the sensors signal the passage of traffic that would be consistent with smuggling activities.

Sensors are located along the only other northbound road from Douglas besides Highways 191 and 80: Leslie Canyon Road. Leslie Canyon Road runs roughly parallel to 191, about halfway between 191 and the border of the Coronado National Forest, and ends when it intersects Rucker Canyon Road. It is unpaved beyond the 10-mile stretch leading out of Douglas and is very rarely traveled except for use by local ranchers and forest service personnel. Smugglers commonly try to avoid the 191 checkpoint by heading west on Rucker Canyon Road from Leslie Canyon Road and thence to Kuykendall Cutoff Road, a primitive dirt road that leads north approximately 12 miles east of 191. From there, they can gain access to Tucson and Phoenix.

Around 2:15 p.m., Stoddard received a report via Douglas radio that a Leslie Canyon Road sensor had been triggered. This was significant to Stoddard for two reasons. First, it suggested to him that a vehicle might be trying to circumvent the checkpoint. Second, the timing coincided with the point when agents begin heading back to the checkpoint for a shift change, which leaves the area unpatrolled. Stoddard knew that alien smugglers did extensive scouting and seemed to be most active when agents were en route back to the checkpoint. Another border patrol agent told Stoddard that the same sensor had gone off several weeks before and that he had apprehended a minivan using the same route and witnessed the occupants throwing bundles of marijuana out the door.

Stoddard drove eastbound on Rucker Canyon Road to investigate. As he did so, he received another radio report of sensor activity. It indicated that the vehicle that had triggered the first sensor was heading westbound on Rucker Canyon Road. He continued east, passing Kuykendall Cutoff Road. He saw the dust trail of an approaching vehicle about a half mile away. Stoddard had not seen any other vehicles and, based on the timing, believed that this was the one that had tripped the sensors. He pulled off to the side of the road at a slight slant so he could get a good look at the oncoming vehicle as it passed by.

It was a minivan, a type of automobile that Stoddard knew smugglers used. As it approached, it slowed dramatically, from about 50–55 to 25–30 miles per hour. He saw five occupants inside. An adult man was driving, an adult woman sat in the front passenger seat, and three children were in the back. The driver appeared stiff and his posture very rigid. He did not look at Stoddard and seemed to be trying to pretend that Stoddard was not there. Stoddard thought this suspicious because in his experience on patrol most persons look over and see what is going on, and in that area most drivers give border patrol agents a friendly wave. Stoddard noticed that the knees of the two children sitting in the very back seat were unusually high, as if their feet were propped up on some cargo on the floor.

At that point, Stoddard decided to get a closer look, so he began to follow the vehicle as it continued westbound on Rucker Canyon Road toward Kuykendall Cutoff Road. Shortly thereafter, all of the children, though still facing forward, put their hands up at the same time and began to wave at Stoddard in an abnormal pattern. It looked to Stoddard as if the children were being instructed. Their odd waving continued on and off for about four to five minutes.

Several hundred feet before the Kuykendall Cutoff Road intersection, the driver signaled that he would turn. At one point, the driver turned the signal off, but just as he approached the intersection he put it back on and abruptly turned north onto Kuykendall. The turn was significant to Stoddard because it was made at the last place that would have allowed the minivan to avoid the checkpoint. Also, Kuykendall, though passable by a sedan or van, is rougher than either Rucker Canyon or Leslie Canyon Roads, and the normal traffic is four-wheel-drive vehicles. Stoddard did not recognize the minivan as part of the local traffic agents encounter on patrol, and he did not think it likely that the minivan was going to or coming from a picnic outing. He was not aware of any picnic grounds on Turkey Creek, which could be reached by following Kuykendall Cutoff all the way up. He knew of picnic grounds and a Boy Scout camp east of the intersection of Rucker Canyon and Leslie Canyon Roads, but the minivan had turned west at that intersection. And he had never seen anyone picnicking or sightseeing near where the first sensor went off.

Stoddard radioed for a registration check and learned that the minivan was registered to an address in Douglas that was four blocks north of the border in an area notorious for alien and narcotics smuggling. After receiving the information, Stoddard decided to make a vehicle stop. He approached the driver and learned that his name was Ralph Arvizu. Stoddard asked if respondent would mind if he looked inside and searched the vehicle. Respondent agreed, and Stoddard discovered marijuana in a black duffel bag under the feet of the two children in the back seat. Another bag containing marijuana was behind the rear seat. In all, the van contained 128.85 pounds of marijuana, worth an estimated $99,080.

Respondent was charged with possession with intent to distribute marijuana. He moved to suppress the marijuana, arguing among other things that Stoddard did not have reasonable suspicion to stop the vehicle as required by the Fourth Amendment. After holding a hearing where Stoddard and respondent testified, the District Court for the District of Arizona ruled otherwise. It pointed to a number of the facts described above and noted particularly that any recreational areas north of Rucker Canyon would have been accessible from Douglas via 191 and another paved road, making it unnecessary to take a 40- to 50-mile trip on dirt roads.

The Court of Appeals for the Ninth Circuit reversed. After characterizing the District Court's analysis as relying on a list of 10 factors, the Court of Appeals proceeded to examine each in turn. It held that seven of the factors, including respondent's slowing down, his failure to acknowledge Stoddard, the raised position of the children's knees, and their odd waving carried little or no weight in the reasonable-suspicion calculus. The remaining factors—the road's use by smugglers, the temporal proximity between respondent's trip and the agents' shift change, and the use of minivans by smugglers—were not enough to render the stop permissible. We granted certiorari to review the decision of the Court of Appeals because of its importance to the enforcement of federal drug and immigration laws.

The Fourth Amendment prohibits "unreasonable searches and seizures" by the Government, and its protections extend to brief investigatory stops of persons or vehicles that fall short of traditional arrest. Because the balance between the public interest and the individual's right to personal security tilts in favor of a standard less than probable cause in such cases, the Fourth Amendment is satisfied if the officer's action is supported by reasonable suspicion to believe that criminal activity may be afoot.

When discussing how reviewing courts should make reasonable-suspicion determinations, we have said repeatedly that they must look at the "totality of the circumstances" of each case to see whether the detaining officer has a "particularized and objective basis" for suspecting legal wrongdoing. This process allows officers to draw on their own experience and specialized training to make inferences from and deductions about the cumulative information available to them that might well elude an untrained person. Although an officer's reliance on a mere "hunch" is insufficient to justify a stop, the likelihood of criminal activity need not rise to the level required for probable cause, and it falls considerably short of satisfying a preponderance of the evidence standard.

Our cases have recognized that the concept of reasonable suspicion is somewhat abstract. But we have deliberately avoided reducing it to a neat set of legal rules. We think that the approach taken by the Court of Appeals here departs sharply from the teachings of these cases. The court's evaluation and rejection of seven of the listed factors in isolation from each other does not take into account the "totality of the circumstances," as our cases have understood that phrase. The court appeared to believe that each observation by Stoddard that was by itself readily susceptible to an innocent explanation was entitled to no weight. *Terry*, however, precludes this sort of divide-and-conquer analysis. The officer in *Terry* observed the petitioner and his companions repeatedly walk back and forth, look into a store window, and confer with one another. Although each of the series of acts was perhaps innocent in itself, we held that, taken together, they "warranted further investigation."

We think it quite reasonable that a driver's slowing down, stiffening of posture, and failure to acknowledge a sighted law enforcement officer might well be unremarkable in one instance (such as a busy San Francisco highway) while quite unusual in another (such as a remote portion of rural southeastern Arizona). Stoddard was entitled to make an assessment of the situation in light of his specialized training and familiarity with the customs of the area's inhabitants.

In another instance, the Court of Appeals chose to dismiss entirely the children's waving on grounds that odd conduct by children was all too common to be probative in a particular case. Yet this case did not involve simply any odd act by children. At the suppression hearing, Stoddard testified about the children's waving several times, and the record suggests that he physically demonstrated it as well. The District Court Judge, who saw and heard Stoddard, then characterized the waving as "methodical," "mechanical," "abnormal," and "certainly a fact that is odd and would lead a reasonable officer to wonder why they are doing this." Though the issue of this case does not turn on the children's idiosyncratic actions, the Court of Appeals should not have casually rejected this factor in light of the District Court's superior access to the evidence and the well-recognized inability of reviewing courts to reconstruct what happened in the courtroom.

Having considered the totality of the circumstances and given due weight to the factual inferences drawn by the law enforcement officer and District Court Judge, we hold that Stoddard had reasonable suspicion to believe that respondent was engaged in illegal activity. It was reasonable for Stoddard to infer from his observations, his registration check, and his experience as a border patrol agent that respondent had set out from Douglas along a little-traveled route used by smugglers to avoid the 191 checkpoint. Stoddard's knowledge further supported a commonsense inference that respondent intended to pass through the area at a time when officers would be leaving their backroads patrols to change shifts. The likelihood that respondent and his family were on a picnic outing was diminished by the fact that the minivan had turned away from the known recreational areas accessible to the east on Rucker Canyon Road.

Corroborating this inference was the fact that recreational areas farther to the north would have been easier to reach by taking 191, as opposed to the 40- to 50-mile trip on unpaved and primitive roads. The children's elevated knees suggested the existence of concealed cargo in the passenger compartment. Finally, for the reasons we have given, Stoddard's assessment of respondent's reactions upon seeing him and the children's mechanical-like waving, which continued for a full four to five minutes, were entitled to some weight.

Respondent argues that we must rule in his favor because the facts suggested a family in a minivan on a holiday outing. A determination that reasonable suspicion exists, however, need not rule out the possibility of innocent conduct. Undoubtedly, each of these factors alone is susceptible of innocent explanation, and some factors are more probative than others. Taken together, we believe they sufficed to form a particularized and objective basis for Stoddard's stopping the vehicle, making the stop reasonable within the meaning of the Fourth Amendment.

In *Navarette v. California*, the Supreme Court held that an anonymous 911 report of reckless driving contained adequate indicia of reliability to provide reasonable suspicion of ongoing criminal activity necessary to stop the vehicle.

NAVARETTE V. CALIFORNIA

134 S.Ct. 1683 (2014)

JUSTICE THOMAS delivered the opinion of the Court.

After a 911 caller reported that a vehicle had run her off the road, a police officer located the vehicle she identified during the call and executed a traffic stop. We hold that the stop complied with the Fourth Amendment because, under the totality of the circumstances, the officer had reasonable suspicion that the driver was intoxicated.

I

On August 23, 2008, a Mendocino County 911 dispatch team for the California Highway Patrol (CHP) received a call from another CHP dispatcher in neighboring Humboldt County. The Humboldt County dispatcher relayed a tip from a 911 caller, which the Mendocino County team recorded as follows: "Showing southbound Highway 1 at mile marker 88, Silver Ford 150 pickup. Plate of 8-David-94925. Ran the reporting party off the roadway and was last seen approximately five [minutes] ago." The Mendocino County team then broadcast that information to CHP officers at 3:47 p.m.

A CHP officer heading northbound toward the reported vehicle responded to the broadcast. At 4:00 p.m., the officer passed the truck near mile marker 69. At about 4:05 p.m., after making a U-turn, he pulled the truck over. A second officer, who had separately responded to the broadcast, also arrived on the scene. As the two officers approached the truck, they smelled marijuana. A search of the truck bed revealed 30 pounds of marijuana. The officers arrested the driver, petitioner Lorenzo Prado Navarette, and the passenger, petitioner José Prado Navarette.

Petitioners moved to suppress the evidence, arguing that the traffic stop violated the Fourth Amendment because the officer lacked reasonable suspicion of criminal activity. Both the magistrate who presided over the suppression hearing and the Superior Court disagreed. Petitioners pleaded guilty to transporting marijuana and were sentenced to 90 days in jail plus three years of probation.

II

The Fourth Amendment permits brief investigative stops—such as the traffic stop in this case—when a law enforcement officer has a particularized and objective basis for suspecting the particular person stopped of criminal activity. The "reasonable suspicion" necessary to justify such a stop is dependent upon both the content of information possessed by police and its degree of reliability. The standard takes into account the totality of the circumstances—the whole picture. Although a mere "hunch" does not create reasonable suspicion, the level of suspicion the standard requires is considerably less than proof of wrongdoing by a preponderance of the evidence, and obviously less than is necessary for probable cause.

These principles apply with full force to investigative stops based on information from anonymous tips. We have firmly rejected the argument that reasonable cause for an investigative stop can only be based on the officer's personal observation, rather than on information supplied by another person. Of course, an anonymous tip *alone* seldom demonstrates the informant's basis of knowledge or veracity. That is because ordinary citizens generally do not provide extensive recitations of the basis of their everyday observations, and an anonymous tipster's veracity is by hypothesis largely unknown, and unknowable. But under appropriate circumstances, an anonymous tip can demonstrate sufficient indicia of reliability to provide reasonable suspicion to make an investigatory stop.

Our decisions in *Alabama v. White*, 496 U.S. 325 (1990), and *Florida v. J.L.*, 529 U.S. 266 (2000), are useful guides. In *White*, an anonymous tipster told the police that a woman would drive from a particular apartment building to a particular motel in a brown Plymouth station wagon with a broken right tail light. The tipster further asserted that the woman would be transporting cocaine. After confirming the innocent details, officers stopped the station wagon as it neared the motel and found cocaine in the vehicle. We held that the officers' corroboration of certain details made the anonymous tip sufficiently reliable to create reasonable suspicion of criminal activity. By accurately predicting future behavior, the tipster demonstrated "a special familiarity with respondent's affairs," which in turn implied that the tipster had "access to reliable information about that individual's illegal activities." We also recognized that an informant who is proved to tell the truth about some things is more likely to tell the truth about other things, "including the claim that the object of the tip is engaged in criminal activity."

In *J.L.*, by contrast, we determined that no reasonable suspicion arose from a bare-bones tip that a young black male in a plaid shirt standing at a bus stop was carrying a gun. The tipster did not explain how he knew about the gun, nor did he suggest that he had any special familiarity with the young man's affairs. As a result, police had no basis for believing "that the tipster ha[d] knowledge of concealed criminal activity." Furthermore, the tip included no predictions of future behavior that could be corroborated to assess the tipster's credibility. We accordingly concluded that the tip was insufficiently reliable to justify a stop and frisk.

The initial question in this case is whether the 911 call was sufficiently reliable to credit the allegation that petitioners' truck "ran the [caller] off the roadway." Even assuming for present purposes that the 911 call was anonymous, we conclude that the call bore adequate indicia of reliability for the officer to credit the caller's account. The officer was therefore justified in proceeding from the premise that the truck had, in fact, caused the caller's car to be dangerously diverted from the highway.

By reporting that she had been run off the road by a specific vehicle—a silver Ford F-150 pickup, license plate 8D94925—the caller necessarily claimed eyewitness knowledge of the alleged dangerous driving. That basis of knowledge lends significant support to the tip's reliability. This is in contrast to *J.L.*, where the tip provided no basis for concluding that the tipster had actually seen the gun. Even in *White*, where we upheld the stop, there was scant evidence that the tipster had actually observed cocaine in the station wagon. We called *White* a "close case" because "[k]nowledge about a person's future movements indicates some familiarity with that person's affairs, but having such knowledge does not necessarily imply that the informant knows, in particular, whether that person is carrying hidden contraband." A driver's claim that another vehicle ran her off the road, however, necessarily implies that the informant knows the other car was driven dangerously.

There is also reason to think that the 911 caller in this case was telling the truth. Police confirmed the truck's location near mile marker 69 (roughly 19 highway miles south of the location reported in the 911 call) at 4:00 p.m. (roughly 18 minutes after the 911 call). That timeline of events suggests that the caller reported the incident soon after she was run off the road. That sort of contemporaneous report has long been treated as especially reliable. In evidence law, we generally credit the proposition that statements about an event and made soon after perceiving that event are especially trustworthy because "substantial contemporaneity of event and statement negate the likelihood of deliberate or conscious misrepresentation." A similar rationale applies to a "statement relating to a startling event"—such as getting run off the road—"made while the declarant was under the stress of excitement that it caused." Unsurprisingly, 911 calls that would otherwise be inadmissible hearsay have often been admitted on those grounds. There was no indication that the tip in *J.L.* (or even in *White*) was contemporaneous with the observation of criminal activity or made under the stress of excitement caused by a startling event, but those considerations weigh in favor of the caller's veracity here.

Another indicator of veracity is the caller's use of the 911 emergency system. A 911 call has some features that allow for identifying and tracing callers, and thus provide some safeguards against making false reports with immunity. As this case illustrates, 911 calls can be recorded, which provides victims with an opportunity to identify the false tipster's voice and subject him to prosecution. The 911 system also permits law enforcement to verify important information about the caller. In 1998, the Federal Communications Commission (FCC) began to require cellular carriers to relay the caller's phone number to 911 dispatchers. Beginning in 2001, carriers have been required to identify the caller's geographic location with increasing specificity. And although callers may ordinarily block call recipients from obtaining their identifying information, FCC regulations exempt 911 calls from that privilege. None of this is to suggest that tips in 911 calls are *per se* reliable. Given the foregoing technological and regulatory developments, however, a reasonable officer could conclude that a false tipster would think twice before using such a system. The caller's use of the 911 system is therefore one of the relevant circumstances that, taken together, justified the officer's reliance on the information reported in the 911 call.

Even a reliable tip will justify an investigative stop only if it creates reasonable suspicion that "criminal activity may be afoot." We must therefore determine whether the 911 caller's report of being run off the roadway created reasonable suspicion of an ongoing crime such as drunk driving as opposed to an isolated episode of past recklessness. We conclude that the behavior alleged by the 911 caller, viewed from the standpoint of an objectively reasonable police officer, amounts to reasonable suspicion of drunk driving. The stop was therefore proper.[2]

---

[2] Because we conclude that the 911 call created reasonable suspicion of an ongoing crime, we need not address under what circumstances a stop is justified by the need to investigate completed criminal activity.

Reasonable suspicion depends on the factual and practical considerations of everyday life on which reasonable and prudent men, not legal technicians, act. Under that commonsense approach, we can appropriately recognize certain driving behaviors as sound indicia of drunk driving. Of course, not all traffic infractions imply intoxication. Unconfirmed reports of driving without a seatbelt or slightly over the speed limit, for example, are so tenuously connected to drunk driving that a stop on those grounds alone would be constitutionally suspect. But a reliable tip alleging the dangerous behaviors discussed above generally would justify a traffic stop on suspicion of drunk driving.

The 911 caller in this case reported more than a minor traffic infraction and more than a conclusory allegation of drunk or reckless driving. Instead, she alleged a specific and dangerous result of the driver's conduct: running another car off the highway. That conduct bears too great a resemblance to paradigmatic manifestations of drunk driving to be dismissed as an isolated example of recklessness. Running another vehicle off the road suggests lane-positioning problems, decreased vigilance, impaired judgment, or some combination of those recognized drunk driving cues. And the experience of many officers suggests that a driver who almost strikes a vehicle or another object is likely intoxicated. As a result, we cannot say that the officer acted unreasonably under these circumstances in stopping a driver whose alleged conduct was a significant indicator of drunk driving.

Petitioners' attempts to second-guess the officer's reasonable suspicion of drunk driving are unavailing. It is true that the reported behavior might also be explained by, for example, a driver responding to "an unruly child or other distraction." But we have consistently recognized that reasonable suspicion "need not rule out the possibility of innocent conduct." *U.S. v. Arvizu*, 534 U.S. 266, 277 (2002).

Nor did the absence of additional suspicious conduct, after the vehicle was first spotted by an officer, dispel the reasonable suspicion of drunk driving. It is hardly surprising that the appearance of a marked police car would inspire more careful driving for a time. Extended observation of an allegedly drunk driver might eventually dispel a reasonable suspicion of intoxication, but the 5-minute period in this case hardly sufficed in that regard. Of course, an officer who already has such a reasonable suspicion need not surveil a vehicle at length in order to personally observe suspicious driving. Once reasonable suspicion of drunk driving arises, the reasonableness of the officer's decision to stop a suspect does not turn on the availability of less intrusive investigatory techniques. This would be a particularly inappropriate context to depart from that settled rule, because allowing a drunk driver a second chance for dangerous conduct could have disastrous consequences.

III

Like *White*, this is a "close case." As in that case, the indicia of the 911 caller's reliability here are stronger than those in *J.L.*, where we held that a bare-bones tip was unreliable. Although the indicia present here are different from those we found sufficient in *White*, there is more than one way to demonstrate a particularized and objective basis for suspecting the particular person stopped of criminal activity. Under the totality of the circumstances, we find the indicia of reliability in this case sufficient to provide the officer with reasonable suspicion that the driver of the reported vehicle had run another vehicle off the road. That made it reasonable under the circumstances for the officer to execute a traffic stop.

JUSTICE SCALIA, with whom JUSTICE GINSBURG, JUSTICE SOTOMAYOR, and JUSTICE KAGAN join, dissenting.

Law enforcement agencies follow closely our judgments on matters such as this, and they will identify at once our new rule: So long as the caller identifies where the car is, anonymous claims of a single instance of possibly careless or reckless driving, called in to 911, will support a traffic stop. This is not my concept, and I am sure would not be the Framers', of a people secure from unreasonable searches and seizures.

The California Highway Patrol in this case knew nothing about the tipster on whose word—and that alone—they seized Lorenzo and José Prado Navarette. They did not know her name. They did not know her phone number or address. They did not even know where she called from.

The tipster said the truck had "[run her] off the roadway," but the police had no reason to credit that charge and many reasons to doubt it, beginning with the peculiar fact that the accusation was anonymous. Anonymity is especially suspicious with respect to the call that is the subject of the present case. When does a victim complain to the police about an arguably criminal act (running the victim off the road) without giving his identity, so that he can accuse and testify when the culprit is caught?

The question before us, the Court agrees, is whether the content of information possessed by police and its degree of reliability gave the officers reasonable suspicion that the driver of the truck (Lorenzo) was committing an ongoing crime. When the only source of the government's information is an informant's tip, we ask whether the tip bears sufficient "indicia of reliability" to establish a particularized and objective basis for suspecting the particular person stopped of criminal activity.

Here the Court makes a big deal of the fact that the tipster was dead right about the fact that a silver Ford F-150 truck (license plate 8D94925) was traveling south on Highway 1 somewhere near mile marker 88. But everyone in the world who saw the car would have that knowledge, and anyone who wanted the car stopped would have to provide that information. Unlike the situation in *White*, that generally available knowledge in no way makes it plausible that the tipster saw the car run someone off the road.

The Court says that "the caller necessarily claimed eyewitness knowledge." So what? The issue is not how she claimed to know, but whether what she claimed to know was true. The claim to "eyewitness knowledge" of being run off the road supports *not at all* its veracity; nor does the amazing, mystifying prediction (so far short of what existed in *White*) that the petitioners' truck *would be heading south on Highway 1*.

The Court finds "reason to think" that the informant "was telling the truth" in the fact that police observation confirmed that the truck had been driving near the spot at which, and at the approximate time at which, the tipster alleged she had been run off the road. According to the Court, the statement therefore qualifies as a "present sense impression" or "excited utterance," kinds of hearsay that the law deems categorically admissible given their low likelihood of reflecting "deliberate or conscious misrepresentation." So, the Court says, we can fairly suppose that the accusation was true.

No, we cannot. It is unsettled whether excited utterances of an unknown declarant are *ever* admissible. A leading treatise reports that "the courts have been reluctant to admit such statements, principally because of uncertainty that foundational requirements, including the impact of the event on the declarant, have been satisfied." In sum, it is unlikely that the law of evidence would deem the mystery caller in this case "especially trustworthy."

Finally, and least tenably, the Court says that another "indicator of veracity" is the anonymous tipster's mere "use of the 911 emergency system." Because, you see, recent "technological and regulatory developments" suggest that the identities of unnamed 911 callers are increasingly less likely to remain unknown. Indeed, the systems are able to identify "the caller's geographic location with increasing specificity." *Amici* disagree with this, and the present case surely suggests that *amici* are right—since we know neither the identity of the tipster nor even the county from which the call was made. But assuming the Court is right about the ease of identifying 911 callers, it proves absolutely nothing in the present case unless the anonymous caller was *aware* of that fact. There is no reason to believe that your average anonymous 911 tipster is aware that 911 callers are readily identifiable.

II

All that has been said up to now assumes that the anonymous caller made, at least in effect, an accusation of drunken driving. But in fact she did not. She said that the petitioners' truck "[r]an [me] off the roadway."

That neither asserts that the driver was drunk nor even raises the *likelihood* that the driver was drunk. The most it conveys is that the truck did some apparently nontypical thing that forced the tipster off the roadway, whether partly or fully, temporarily or permanently. Who really knows what (if anything) happened? The truck might have swerved to avoid an animal, a pothole, or a jaywalking pedestrian.

But let us assume the worst of the many possibilities: that it was a careless, reckless, or even intentional maneuver that forced the tipster off the road. Lorenzo might have been distracted by his use of a hands-free cell phone, or distracted by an intense sports argument with José. Or, indeed, he might have intentionally forced the tipster off the road because of some personal animus, or hostility to her "Make Love, Not War" bumper sticker. I fail to see how reasonable suspicion of a *discrete instance* of irregular or hazardous driving generates a reasonable suspicion of *ongoing intoxicated driving*. What proportion of the hundreds of thousands—perhaps millions—of careless, reckless, or intentional traffic violations committed each day is attributable to drunken drivers? I say 0.1 percent. I have no basis for that except my own guesswork. But unless the Court has some basis in reality to believe that the proportion is many orders of magnitude above that—say 1 in 10 or at least 1 in 20—it has no grounds for its unsupported assertion that the tipster's report in this case gave rise to a *reasonable suspicion* of drunken driving.

Bear in mind that that is the only basis for the stop that has been asserted in this litigation.[3] The stop required suspicion of an ongoing crime, not merely suspicion of having run someone off the road earlier. And driving while being a careless or reckless person, unlike driving while being a drunk person, is not an ongoing crime. In other words, in order to stop the petitioners the officers here not only had to assume without basis the accuracy of the anonymous accusation but also had to posit an unlikely reason (drunkenness) for the accused behavior.

In sum, at the moment the police spotted the truck, it was more than merely *possible* that the petitioners were not committing an ongoing traffic crime. It was overwhelmingly likely that they were not.

III

It gets worse. Not only, it turns out, did the police have no good reason *at first* to believe that Lorenzo was driving drunk, they had very good reason *at last* to know that he was not. The Court concludes that the tip, plus confirmation of the truck's location, produced reasonable suspicion that the truck not only had been *but still was* barreling dangerously and drunkenly down Highway 1. In fact, alas, it was not, and

---

[3] The circumstances that may justify a stop under *Terry v. Ohio*, 392 U.S. 1 (1968), to investigate past criminal activity are far from clear, and have not been discussed in this litigation. This case has been litigated on the assumption that only suspicion of ongoing intoxicated or reckless driving could have supported this stop.

the officers knew it. They followed the truck for five minutes, presumably to see if it was being operated recklessly. And *that* was good police work. While the anonymous tip was not enough to support a stop for drunken driving under *Terry v. Ohio*, it was surely enough to counsel observation of the truck to see if it was driven by a drunken driver. But the pesky little detail left out of the Court's reasonable-suspicion equation is that, for the five minutes that the truck was being followed (five minutes is a *long* time), Lorenzo's driving was irreproachable. Had the officers witnessed the petitioners violate a single traffic law, they would have had cause to stop the truck, and this case would not be before us. And not only was the driving *irreproachable,* but the State offers no evidence to suggest that the petitioners even did anything *suspicious*, such as suddenly slowing down, pulling off to the side of the road, or turning somewhere to see whether they were being followed. Consequently, the tip's suggestion of ongoing drunken driving (if it could be deemed to suggest that) not only went uncorroborated; it was affirmatively undermined.

Resisting this line of reasoning, the Court curiously asserts that, since drunk drivers who see marked squad cars in their rearview mirrors may evade detection simply by driving "more careful[ly]," the "absence of additional suspicious conduct" is "hardly surprising" and thus largely irrelevant. Whether a drunk driver drives drunkenly, the Court seems to think, is up to him. That is not how I understand the influence of alcohol. I subscribe to the more traditional view that the dangers of intoxicated driving are the intoxicant's impairing effects on the body—effects that no mere act of the will can resist. Consistent with this view, I take it as a fundamental premise of our intoxicated-driving laws that a driver soused enough to swerve once can be expected to swerve again—and soon. If he does not, and if the only evidence of his first episode of irregular driving is a mere inference from an uncorroborated, vague, and nameless tip, then the Fourth Amendment requires that he be left alone.

The Court's opinion serves up a freedom-destroying cocktail consisting of two parts patent falsity: (1) that anonymous 911 reports of traffic violations are reliable so long as they correctly identify a car and its location, and (2) that a single instance of careless or reckless driving necessarily supports a reasonable suspicion of drunkenness. All the malevolent 911 caller need do is assert a traffic violation, and the targeted car will be stopped, forcibly if necessary, by the police. If the driver turns out not to be drunk (which will almost always be the case), the caller need fear no consequences, even if 911 knows his identity. After all, he never alleged drunkenness, but merely called in a traffic violation—and on that point his word is as good as his victim's.

Drunken driving is a serious matter, but so is the loss of our freedom to come and go as we please without police interference. To prevent and detect murder we do not allow searches without probable cause or targeted *Terry* stops without reasonable suspicion. We should not do so for drunken driving either. After today's opinion all of us on the road, and not just drug dealers, are at risk of having our freedom of movement curtailed on suspicion of drunkenness, based upon a phone tip, true or false, of a single instance of careless driving. I respectfully dissent.

Is a vehicle stop invalid if the police officer's reasonable suspicion for making the stop is based on a mistake of fact or law? Suppose an officer makes a mistake of fact and stops a motorist for driving alone in the carpool lane, failing to notice a child sleeping in the back seat. Or suppose the officer makes a mistake of law and stops a car under the belief that the vehicle code requires two working brake lights rather than just one? The Supreme Court confronted these questions in *Heien v. North Carolina* and held that a traffic stop is still valid even when based upon a reasonable—but mistaken—interpretation of the law.

HEIEN V. NORTH CAROLINA
134 S.Ct. 1872 (2014)

While in his patrol car observing traffic on the interstate, a police officer noticed a Ford Escort pass by with a driver who appeared very stiff and nervous. The officer began following the Escort. A few miles down the road, the Escort braked as it approached a slower vehicle, and the officer noticed that only the left brake light came on. The officer decided to pull over the vehicle. Two men were in the car: the driver, Maynor Javier Vasquez, and a passenger, Nicholas Brady Heien, who lay across the rear seat. The officer checked Vasquez's license and registration, then gave him a warning ticket for the broken brake light. The officer had become suspicious, however, during the course of the stop—Vasquez appeared nervous, Heien remained lying down the entire time, and the two gave inconsistent answers about their destination. The officer asked Vasquez if he would be willing to answer some questions. Vasquez agreed, and the officer asked whether the men were transporting various types of contraband. Told no, the officer asked whether he could search the Escort. Vasquez said he had no objection, but told the officer to check with Heien, the owner of the car. Heien consented, and the officer—aided by a second officer who had since arrived—began a thorough search of the vehicle. The police found a sandwich bag containing cocaine in the side compartment of a duffel bag, and they arrested both Vasquez and Heien.

Heien was charged with attempted trafficking in cocaine. He moved to suppress the evidence seized from the car, contending that the stop and search violated the Fourth Amendment. The trial court denied the suppression motion, concluding that the faulty brake light had given the officer reasonable suspicion to initiate the stop, and that Heien's subsequent consent to the search was valid.

The North Carolina Court of Appeals reversed, finding that the initial stop was not valid because driving with only one working brake light was not actually a violation of North Carolina law. Citing a portion of North Carolina's vehicle code that refers to the requirement of "a stop lamp," the court concluded that a vehicle is required to have only one working brake light, as Heien's car indisputably did. The court concluded that the justification for the stop was "objectively unreasonable" and therefore violated the Fourth Amendment.

The State appealed, and the North Carolina Supreme Court reversed. The State did not seek review of the Court of Appeals' interpretation of the vehicle code, so the North Carolina Supreme Court assumed for purposes of its decision that the faulty brake light was not a violation. The court concluded, however, that the officer could have reasonably, even if mistakenly, read the vehicle code to require that both brake lights be in good working order. Because the officer's mistaken understanding of the vehicle code was reasonable, the stop was valid.

The U.S. Supreme Court affirmed, concluding that a search or seizure may still be valid if based on a reasonable mistake of fact or law:

> As the text indicates and we have repeatedly affirmed, the ultimate touchstone of the Fourth Amendment is "reasonableness." To be reasonable is not to be perfect, and so the Fourth Amendment allows for some mistakes on the part of government officials, giving them fair leeway for enforcing the law in the community's protection. We have recognized that searches and seizures based on mistakes of fact can be reasonable. The warrantless search of a home, for instance, is reasonable if undertaken with the consent of a resident, and remains lawful when officers obtain the consent of someone who reasonably appears to be but is not in fact a resident. See *Illinois v. Rodriguez*, 497 U.S. 177 (1990). By the same token, if officers with probable cause to arrest a suspect mistakenly arrest an individual matching the suspect's description, neither the seizure nor an accompanying search of the arrestee would be unlawful. See *Hill v. California*, 401 U.S. 797 (1971). The limit is that "the mistakes must be those of reasonable men."

> But reasonable men make mistakes of law, too, and such mistakes are no less compatible with the concept of reasonable suspicion. Reasonable suspicion arises from the combination of an officer's understanding of the facts and his understanding of the relevant law. The officer may be reasonably mistaken on either ground. Whether the facts turn out to be not what was thought, or the law turns out to be not what was thought, the

result is the same: the facts are outside the scope of the law. There is no reason, under the text of the Fourth Amendment or our precedents, why this same result should be acceptable when reached by way of a reasonable mistake of fact, but not when reached by way of a similarly reasonable mistake of law.

In support of his position that the officer's mistake of law rendered the stop unreasonable, Heien cited the well-known maxim, "Ignorance of the law is no excuse," and contended that it is fundamentally unfair to let police officers get away with mistakes of law when citizens are accorded no such leeway. The Supreme Court rejected the analogy:

> Though this argument has a certain rhetorical appeal, it misconceives the implication of the maxim. The true symmetry is this: Just as an individual generally cannot escape criminal liability based on a mistaken understanding of the law, so too the government cannot impose criminal liability based on a mistaken understanding of the law. If the law required two working brake lights, Heien could not escape a ticket by claiming he reasonably thought he needed only one; if the law required only one, [the police officer] could not issue a valid ticket by claiming he reasonably thought drivers needed two. But just because mistakes of law cannot justify either the imposition or the avoidance of criminal liability, it does not follow that they cannot justify an investigatory stop. And Heien is not appealing a brake-light ticket; he is appealing a cocaine-trafficking conviction as to which there is no asserted mistake of fact or law.

The Supreme Court ultimately concluded that the officer's error of law was objectively reasonable by pointing to various provisions of North Carolina's vehicle code, some of which appeared to require just one working brake light, while others appeared to require that all brake lights be functional. Because the officer's mistake of law was objectively reasonable, "there was reasonable suspicion justifying the stop."

After making a lawful traffic stop, police can order the driver and any passengers to exit the vehicle. In *Arizona v. Johnson*, the Supreme Court confirmed that police may frisk the driver and any passengers upon reasonable suspicion that they are armed and presently dangerous.

ARIZONA V. JOHNSON
555 U.S. 323 (2009)

JUSTICE GINSBURG delivered the opinion of the Court.

This case concerns the authority of police officers to "stop and frisk" a passenger in a motor vehicle temporarily seized upon police detection of a traffic infraction. In a pathmarking decision, *Terry v. Ohio*, 392 U.S. 1 (1968), the Court considered whether an investigatory stop (temporary detention) and frisk (patdown for weapons) may be conducted without violating the Fourth Amendment's ban on unreasonable searches and seizures. The Court upheld "stop and frisk" as constitutionally permissible if two conditions are met. First, the investigatory stop must be lawful. That requirement is met in an on-the-street encounter, *Terry* determined, when the police officer reasonably suspects that the person apprehended is committing or has committed a criminal offense. Second, to proceed from a stop to a frisk, the police officer must reasonably suspect that the person stopped is armed and dangerous.

For the duration of a traffic stop, we recently confirmed, a police officer effectively seizes everyone in the vehicle, the driver and all passengers. *Brendlin v. California*, 551 U.S. 249 (2007). Accordingly, we hold that, in a traffic-stop setting, the first *Terry* condition—a lawful investigatory stop—is met whenever it is lawful for police to detain an automobile and its occupants pending inquiry into a vehicular violation. The police need not have, in addition, cause to believe any occupant of the vehicle is involved in criminal activity. To justify a patdown of the driver or a passenger during a traffic stop, however, just as in the case of a pedestrian reasonably suspected of criminal activity, the police must harbor reasonable suspicion that the person subjected to the frisk is armed and dangerous.

I

On April 19, 2002, Officer Maria Trevizo and Detectives Machado and Gittings, all members of Arizona's gang task force, were on patrol in Tucson near a neighborhood associated with the Crips gang. At approximately 9 p.m., the officers pulled over an automobile after a license plate check revealed that the vehicle's registration had been suspended for an insurance-related violation. Under Arizona law, the violation for which the vehicle was stopped constituted a civil infraction warranting a citation. At the time of the stop, the vehicle had three occupants—the driver, a front-seat passenger, and a passenger in the back seat, Lemon Montrea Johnson, the respondent here. In making the stop the officers had no reason to suspect anyone in the vehicle of criminal activity.

The three officers left their patrol car and approached the stopped vehicle. Machado instructed all of the occupants to keep their hands visible. He asked whether there were any weapons in the vehicle; all responded no. Machado then directed the driver to get out of the car. Gittings dealt with the front-seat passenger, who stayed in the vehicle throughout the stop. While Machado was getting the driver's license and information about the vehicle's registration and insurance, Trevizo attended to Johnson.

Trevizo noticed that, as the police approached, Johnson looked back and kept his eyes on the officers. When she drew near, she observed that Johnson was wearing clothing, including a blue bandana, that she considered consistent with Crips membership. She also noticed a scanner in Johnson's jacket pocket, which "struck her as highly unusual and cause for concern," because "most people" would not carry around a scanner that way "unless they're going to be involved in some kind of criminal activity or are going to try to evade the police by listening to the scanner." In response to Trevizo's questions, Johnson provided his name and date of birth but said he had no identification with him. He volunteered that he was from Eloy, Arizona, a place Trevizo knew was home to a Crips gang. Johnson further told Trevizo that he had served time in prison for burglary and had been out for about a year.

Trevizo wanted to question Johnson away from the front-seat passenger to gain "intelligence about the gang Johnson might be in." For that reason, she asked him to get out of the car. Johnson complied. Based on Trevizo's observations and Johnson's answers to her questions while he was still seated in the car, Trevizo suspected that he might have a weapon on him. When he exited the vehicle, she therefore "patted him down for officer safety." During the patdown, Trevizo felt the butt of a gun near Johnson's waist. At that point Johnson began to struggle, and Trevizo placed him in handcuffs.

Johnson was charged in state court with possession of a weapon by a prohibited possessor. He moved to suppress the evidence as the fruit of an unlawful search. The trial court denied the motion, concluding that the stop was lawful and that Trevizo had cause to suspect Johnson was armed and dangerous. A jury convicted Johnson of the gun-possession charge.

A divided panel of the Arizona Court of Appeals reversed Johnson's conviction. Recognizing that "Johnson was lawfully seized when the officers stopped the car," the court nevertheless concluded that prior to the frisk the detention had "evolved into a separate, consensual encounter stemming from an unrelated investigation by Trevizo of Johnson's possible gang affiliation." Absent "reason to believe Johnson was involved in criminal activity," the Arizona appeals court held, Trevizo "had no right to pat him down for weapons, even if she had reason to suspect he was armed and dangerous."

Judge Espinosa dissented. He found it "highly unrealistic to conclude that merely because Trevizo was courteous and Johnson cooperative, the ongoing and virtually simultaneous chain of events had somehow evolved into a consensual encounter in the few short moments involved." Throughout the episode, he stressed, Johnson remained "seized as part of a valid traffic stop." Further, he maintained, Trevizo "had a reasonable basis to consider Johnson dangerous," and could therefore ensure her own safety and that of others at the scene by patting down Johnson for weapons.

The Arizona Supreme Court denied review. We granted certiorari, and now reverse the judgment of the Arizona Court of Appeals.

II

Most traffic stops, this Court has observed, resemble, in duration and atmosphere, the kind of brief detention authorized in *Terry v. Ohio*. Furthermore, the Court has recognized that traffic stops are especially fraught with danger to police officers. The risk of harm to both the police and the occupants of a stopped vehicle is minimized, we have stressed, if the officers routinely exercise unquestioned command of the situation. Three decisions cumulatively portray *Terry*'s application in a traffic-stop setting: *Pennsylvania v. Mimms*, 434 U.S. 106 (1977); *Maryland v. Wilson*, 519 U.S. 408 (1997); and *Brendlin v. California*, 551 U.S. 249 (2007).

In *Mimms*, the Court held that "once a motor vehicle has been lawfully detained for a traffic violation, the police officers may order the driver to get out of the vehicle without violating the Fourth Amendment's proscription of unreasonable searches and seizures." The government's legitimate and weighty interest in officer safety, the Court said, outweighs the *de minimis* additional intrusion of requiring a driver, already lawfully stopped, to exit the vehicle. Citing *Terry* as controlling, the Court further held that a driver, once outside the stopped vehicle, may be patted down for weapons if the officer reasonably concludes that the driver might be armed and presently dangerous.

Wilson held that the *Mimms* rule applied to passengers as well as to drivers. Specifically, the Court instructed that "an officer making a traffic stop may order passengers to get out of the car pending completion of the stop." The same weighty interest in officer safety, the Court observed, is present regardless of whether the occupant of the stopped car is a driver or passenger.

It is true, the Court acknowledged, that in a lawful traffic stop, there is probable cause to believe that the driver has committed a minor vehicular offense, but there is no such reason to stop or detain the passengers. On the other hand, the Court emphasized, the risk of a violent encounter in a traffic-stop setting stems not from the ordinary reaction of a motorist stopped for a speeding violation, but from the fact that evidence of a more serious crime might be uncovered during the stop. The motivation of a passenger to employ violence to prevent apprehension of such a crime, the Court stated, is every bit as great as that of the driver. Moreover, the Court noted, as a practical matter, the passengers are already stopped by virtue of the stop of the vehicle, so the additional intrusion on the passenger is minimal.

Completing the picture, *Brendlin* held that a passenger is seized, just as the driver is, from the moment a car stopped by the police comes to a halt on the side of the road. A passenger therefore has standing to challenge a stop's constitutionality.

After *Wilson* but before *Brendlin*, the Court had stated, in dictum, that officers who conduct routine traffic stops may perform a "patdown" of a driver and any passengers upon reasonable suspicion that they may be armed and dangerous. *Knowles v. Iowa*, 525 U.S. 113, 117–118 (1998). That forecast, we now confirm, accurately captures the combined thrust of the Court's decisions in *Mimms*, *Wilson*, and *Brendlin*.

The Arizona Court of Appeals recognized that, initially, Johnson was lawfully detained incident to the legitimate stop of the vehicle in which he was a passenger. But, that court concluded, once Officer Trevizo undertook to question Johnson on a matter unrelated to the traffic stop, *i.e.*, Johnson's gang affiliation, patdown authority ceased to exist, absent reasonable suspicion that Johnson had engaged, or was about to engage, in criminal activity. In support of the Arizona court's portrayal of Trevizo's interrogation of Johnson as "consensual," Johnson emphasizes Trevizo's testimony at the suppression hearing. Responding to the prosecutor's questions, Trevizo affirmed her belief that Johnson could have "refused to get out of the car" and "to turn around for the pat down."

It is not clear why the prosecutor, in opposing the suppression motion, sought to portray the episode as consensual. In any event, Trevizo also testified that she never advised Johnson he did not have to answer her questions or otherwise cooperate with her. And during cross-examination, Trevizo did not disagree when defense counsel asked "in fact you weren't seeking Johnson's permission?" As the dissenting judge observed, "consensual" is an "unrealistic" characterization of the Trevizo-Johnson interaction. "The encounter took place within minutes of the stop"; the patdown followed "within mere moments" of Johnson's exit from the vehicle; beyond genuine debate, the point at which Johnson could have felt free to leave had not yet occurred.

A lawful roadside stop begins when a vehicle is pulled over for investigation of a traffic violation. The temporary seizure of driver and passengers ordinarily continues, and remains reasonable, for the duration of the stop. Normally, the stop ends when the police have no further need to control the scene, and inform the driver and passengers they are free to leave. An officer's inquiries into matters unrelated to the justification for the traffic stop do not convert the encounter into something other than a lawful seizure, so long as those inquiries do not measurably extend the duration of the stop.

In sum, a traffic stop of a car communicates to a reasonable passenger that he or she is not free to terminate the encounter with the police and move about at will. Nothing occurred in this case that would have conveyed to Johnson that, prior to the frisk, the traffic stop had ended or that he was otherwise free to depart without police permission. Officer Trevizo surely was not constitutionally required to give Johnson an opportunity to depart the scene after he exited the vehicle without first ensuring that, in so doing, she was not permitting a dangerous person to get behind her.

Following a valid traffic stop, in addition to frisking the driver and any passengers upon reasonable suspicion that they are armed and presently dangerous, a police officer may also search the interior of the vehicle if she has reasonable suspicion to believe that any of the occupants is dangerous and may gain immediate control of a weapon inside the vehicle. Any contraband or weapons found in the course of a legitimate *Terry* search of the interior of the vehicle may be seized and admitted into evidence at trial. The Supreme Court explained these principles in *Michigan v. Long*.

MICHIGAN V. LONG
463 U.S. 1032 (1983)

JUSTICE O'CONNOR delivered the opinion of the Court.

In *Terry v. Ohio*, 392 U.S. 1 (1968), we upheld the validity of a protective search for weapons in the absence of probable cause to arrest because it is unreasonable to deny a police officer the right "to neutralize the threat of physical harm," when he possesses an articulable suspicion that an individual is armed and dangerous. We did not, however, expressly address whether such a protective search for weapons could extend to an area beyond the person in the absence of probable cause to arrest. In the present case, respondent David Long was convicted for possession of marijuana found by police in the passenger compartment and trunk of the automobile that he was driving. The police searched the passenger compartment because they had reason to believe that the vehicle contained weapons potentially dangerous to the officers. We hold that the protective search of the passenger compartment was reasonable under the principles articulated in *Terry* and other decisions of this Court.

Deputies Howell and Lewis were on patrol in a rural area one evening when, shortly after midnight, they observed a car traveling erratically and at excessive speed. The officers observed the car turning down a side road, where it swerved off into a shallow ditch. The officers stopped to investigate. Long, the only occupant of the automobile, met the deputies at the rear of the car, which was protruding from the ditch onto the road. The door on the driver's side of the vehicle was left open.

Deputy Howell requested Long to produce his operator's license, but he did not respond. After the request was repeated, Long produced his license. Long again failed to respond when Howell requested him to produce the vehicle registration. After another repeated request, Long, whom Howell thought "appeared to be under the influence of something," turned from the officers and began walking toward the open door of the vehicle. The officers followed Long and both observed a large hunting knife on the floorboard of the driver's side of the car. The officers then stopped Long's progress and subjected him to a *Terry* protective pat-down, which revealed no weapons.

Long and Deputy Lewis then stood by the rear of the vehicle while Deputy Howell shined his flashlight into the interior of the vehicle, but did not actually enter it. The purpose of Howell's action was "to search for other weapons." The officer noticed that something was protruding from under the armrest on the front seat. He knelt in the vehicle and lifted the armrest. He saw an open pouch on the front seat, and upon flashing his light on the pouch, determined that it contained what appeared to be marijuana. After Deputy Howell showed the pouch and its contents to Deputy Lewis, Long was arrested for possession of marijuana. A further search of the interior of the vehicle, including the glovebox, revealed neither more contraband nor the vehicle registration. The officers decided to impound the vehicle. Deputy Howell opened the trunk, which did not have a lock, and discovered inside it approximately 75 pounds of marijuana.

The Barry County Circuit Court denied Long's motion to suppress the marijuana taken from both the interior of the car and its trunk. He was subsequently convicted of possession of marijuana. The Michigan Court of Appeals affirmed Long's conviction, holding that the search of the passenger compartment was valid as a protective search under *Terry*, and that the search of the trunk was valid as an inventory search under *South Dakota v. Opperman*, 428 U.S. 364 (1976). The Michigan Supreme Court reversed. The court held that "the sole justification of the *Terry* search, protection of the police officers and others nearby, cannot justify the search in this case." The marijuana found in Long's trunk was considered by the court below to be the "fruit" of the illegal search of the interior, and was also suppressed.

We granted certiorari in this case to consider the important question of the authority of a police officer to protect himself by conducting a *Terry*-type search of the passenger compartment of a motor vehicle during the lawful investigatory stop of the occupant of the vehicle.

The court below held, and respondent Long contends, that Deputy Howell's entry into the vehicle cannot be justified under the principles set forth in *Terry* because "*Terry* authorized only a limited pat-down search of a *person* suspected of criminal activity" rather than a search of an area.

Although *Terry* did involve the protective frisk of a person, we believe that the police action in this case is justified by the principles that we have already established in *Terry* and other cases.

In *Terry*, the Court examined the validity of a "stop and frisk" in the absence of probable cause and a warrant. The police officer in *Terry* detained several suspects to ascertain their identities after the officer had observed the suspects for a brief period of time and formed the conclusion that they were about to engage in criminal activity. Because the officer feared that the suspects were armed, he patted down the outside of the suspects' clothing and discovered two revolvers.

Although *Terry* itself involved the stop and subsequent pat-down search of a person, we were careful to note that "[w]e need not develop at length in this case, however, the limitations which the Fourth Amendment places upon a protective search and seizure for weapons. These limitations will have to be developed in the concrete factual circumstances of individual cases." Contrary to Long's view, *Terry* need not be read as restricting the preventative search to the person of the detained suspect.

Our past cases indicate that protection of police and others can justify protective searches when police have a reasonable belief that the suspect poses a danger, that roadside encounters between police and suspects are especially hazardous, and that danger may arise from the possible presence of weapons in the area surrounding a suspect. These principles compel our conclusion that the search of the passenger compartment of an automobile, limited to those areas in which a weapon may be placed or hidden, is permissible if the police officer possesses a reasonable belief based on "specific and articulable facts which, taken together with the rational inferences from those facts, reasonably warrant" the officers in believing that the suspect is dangerous and the suspect may gain immediate control of weapons. "The issue is whether a reasonably prudent man in the circumstances would be warranted in the belief that his safety or that of others was in danger." If a suspect is "dangerous," he is no less dangerous simply because he is not arrested. If, while conducting a legitimate *Terry* search of the interior of the automobile, the officer should, as here, discover contraband other than weapons, he clearly cannot be required to ignore the contraband, and the Fourth Amendment does not require its suppression in such circumstances.

The circumstances of this case clearly justified Deputies Howell and Lewis in their reasonable belief that Long posed a danger if he were permitted to reenter his vehicle. The hour was late and the area rural. Long was driving his automobile at excessive speed, and his car swerved into a ditch. The officers had to repeat their questions to Long, who appeared to be under the influence of some intoxicant. Long was not frisked until the officers observed that there was a large knife in the interior of the car into which Long was about to reenter. The subsequent search of the car was restricted to those areas to which Long would generally have immediate control, and that could contain a weapon. The trial court determined that the leather pouch containing marijuana could have contained a weapon.[15] It is clear that the intrusion was strictly circumscribed by the exigencies which justified its initiation.

In evaluating the validity of an officer's investigative or protective conduct under *Terry,* the touchstone of our analysis is always the reasonableness in all circumstances of the particular governmental intrusion of a citizen's personal security. In this case, the officers did not act unreasonably in taking preventive measures to ensure that there were no other weapons within Long's immediate grasp before permitting him to reenter his automobile. Therefore, the balancing required by *Terry* clearly weighs in favor of allowing the police to conduct an area search of the passenger compartment to uncover weapons, as long as they possess an articulable and objectively reasonable belief that the suspect is potentially dangerous.

The Michigan Supreme Court appeared to believe that it was not reasonable for the officers to fear that Long could injure them, because he was effectively under their control during the investigative stop and could not get access to any weapons that might have been located in the automobile. This reasoning is mistaken in several respects. During any investigative detention, the suspect is "in the control" of the officers in the sense that he may be briefly detained against his will. Just as a *Terry* suspect on the street may, despite being under the brief control of a police officer, reach into his clothing and retrieve a weapon, so might a *Terry* suspect in Long's position break away from police control and retrieve a weapon from his automobile. In addition, if the suspect is not placed under arrest, he will be permitted to reenter his automobile, and he will then have access to any weapons inside. Or, as here, the suspect may be permitted to reenter the vehicle before the *Terry* investigation is over, and again, may have access to weapons. In any event, we stress that a *Terry* investigation, such as the one that occurred here, involves a police investigation at close range, when the officer remains particularly vulnerable in part *because* a full custodial arrest has not been effected, and the officer must make a quick decision as to how to protect himself and others from possible danger. In such circumstances, we have not required that officers adopt alternate means to ensure their safety in order to avoid the intrusion involved in a *Terry* encounter.

The trial court and the court of appeals upheld the search of the trunk as a valid inventory search under this Court's decision in *South*

---

[15] Of course, our analysis would apply to justify the search of Long's person that was conducted by the officers after the discovery of the knife.

Dakota v. Opperman. The Michigan Supreme Court did not address this holding, and instead suppressed the marijuana taken from the trunk as a fruit of the illegal search of the interior of the automobile. Our holding that the initial search was justified under *Terry* makes it necessary to determine whether the trunk search was permissible under the Fourth Amendment. However, we decline to address this question because it was not passed upon by the Michigan Supreme Court, whose decision we review in this case. We remand this issue to the court below, to enable it to determine whether the trunk search was permissible under *Opperman* or other decisions of this Court.

———————

In recent years, serious allegations have mounted over discriminatory vehicular stops, mirroring the criticism of conventional *Terry* stops of individuals on foot. There have been many cases of famous African-American athletes, actors, and other celebrities driving fancy cars in largely white neighborhoods, stopped by police for dubious reasons. Scores of less famous individuals have suffered these indignities as well. Many studies—often conducted in conjunction with litigation—document disturbing racial disparities in the frequency of traffic stops. The problem appears so widespread that new terms—"driving while black," or "driving while brown," or even "driving while Asian"—have been coined to describe it.[d]

Stop-and-Frisk: Vehicles on the Road

1. In order to stop a vehicle on the road, police must have reasonable suspicion of a driving infraction or some other violation of law. Reasonable suspicion is based on the totality of the circumstances. Conduct for which there is a possible innocent explanation can still be given weight in the reasonable suspicion determination when all of the surrounding circumstances are considered.

2. An anonymous 911 call reporting reckless or drunk driving can create the reasonable suspicion necessary to make a traffic stop if the call bears adequate indicia of reliability.

3. An officer's objectively reasonable mistake as to the facts or the law is not incompatible with reasonable suspicion. A traffic stop is still valid even when based upon an officer's reasonable—but mistaken—interpretation of the law.

---

[d] *See* David A. Harris, *The Stories, the Statistics, and the Law: Why "Driving While Black" Matters*, 84 MINNESOTA LAW REVIEW 265 (1999); David A. Harris, *Driving While Black: Racial Profiling On Our Nation's Highways*, ACLU Special Report, June 7, 1999, available at https://www.aclu.org/racial-justice/driving-while-black-racial-profiling-our-nations-highways.

4.   During a lawful traffic stop, police may order the driver and any passengers out of the vehicle, and police may frisk the driver and any passengers upon reasonable suspicion that they are armed and presently dangerous.

5.   A police officer may search the interior of a vehicle during a lawful traffic stop if she has reasonable suspicion to believe that any of the occupants is dangerous and may gain immediate control of a weapon inside the vehicle. Any contraband other than weapons found in the course of the search may be seized and admitted into evidence at trial.

Note: The cases and principles governing stops and frisks of individuals on foot are generally applicable to stops and frisks of vehicles (and the persons inside them) on the road. Similarly, the cases and principles governing stops and frisks of vehicles on the road can often be applied to conventional stops and frisks of individuals on foot.

C. THE LINE BETWEEN STOPS AND ARRESTS

As explained earlier, both stops and arrests are regarded as seizures under the Fourth Amendment. They differ, however, in the degree of suspicion required for their initiation. In order to make a stop, police need reasonable suspicion of criminal activity; in order to make an arrest, police need probable cause that a crime has been or is being committed.

An interaction that starts as a consensual encounter can become a stop if the police, through their actions or words, convey that the individual with whom they are dealing is not free to leave. Similarly, a stop can become an arrest if it lasts too long or if the individual is transported to a different location, even if the police never inform the individual that he is under arrest or place him in handcuffs. In *Dunaway v. New York*, for example, the Supreme Court held that the defendant was arrested when officers transported him to the police station for interrogation.

DUNAWAY V. NEW YORK
442 U.S. 200 (1979)

A jail inmate supplied information to the police implicating Irving Dunaway in the murder of the proprietor of a pizza parlor during an attempted robbery. A detective concluded that he lacked sufficient information to get a warrant to arrest Dunaway, but the detective ordered that Dunaway be picked up and brought in for questioning. Although Dunaway was never told he was under arrest, he was picked up, driven to police headquarters, placed in an interrogation room, and questioned by officers after being given the warnings required by *Miranda v. Arizona*, 384 U.S. 436 (1966).

The State argued that the seizure of Dunaway was appropriate because the police had reasonable suspicion to believe that he was involved in the crime. The Supreme Court disagreed, and concluded that Dunaway had been arrested without the requisite probable cause under the Fourth Amendment:

> [T]he detention of petitioner was in important respects indistinguishable from a traditional arrest. Petitioner was not questioned briefly where he was found. Instead, he was taken from a neighbor's home to a police car, transported to a police station, and placed in an interrogation room. He was never informed that he was "free to go"; indeed, he would have been physically restrained if he had refused to accompany the officers or had tried to escape their custody. The application of the Fourth Amendment's requirement of probable cause does not depend on whether an intrusion of this magnitude is termed an "arrest" under state law. The mere facts that petitioner was not told he was under arrest, was not "booked," and would not have had an arrest record if the interrogation had proved fruitless, while not insignificant for all purposes, obviously do not make petitioner's seizure even roughly analogous to the narrowly defined intrusions involved in *Terry* [*v. Ohio*] and its progeny. Indeed, any "exception" that could cover a seizure as intrusive as that in this case would threaten to swallow the general rule that Fourth Amendment seizures are "reasonable" only if based on probable cause.

In *Florida v. Royer*, the police interaction began as a consensual airport encounter similar to the one in *U.S. v. Mendenhall*, but the encounter became an arrest when the defendant was taken to a small room for questioning and a search of his luggage.

FLORIDA V. ROYER
460 U.S. 491 (1983)

Narcotics detectives at the Miami Airport observed Mark Royer and believed his appearance, mannerisms, luggage, and actions fit a "drug courier profile." Royer had purchased a one-way ticket to New York City and checked two suitcases, placing on each bag an identification tag with the name "Holt" and the destination "La Guardia." As Royer walked toward the boarding area, two detectives approached, identified themselves, and asked if Royer had a moment to speak with them. Royer said yes, and upon request, produced his airline ticket and driver's license. The airline ticket bore the name "Holt," while the driver's license had Royer's correct name. Royer explained that a friend had made the reservation under the name "Holt." As Royer became more noticeably nervous, the detectives said that they had reason to suspect him of transporting narcotics. The detectives did not return the airline ticket or identification, but asked Royer to accompany them to a room about 40 feet away. Royer went with the detectives, and without Royer's consent, one of the detectives retrieved his checked luggage. The detectives asked Royer if he would consent to a search of the luggage. Royer did not respond verbally, but he produced a key and unlocked the suitcase, which one detective then opened without seeking further assent from Royer. The detectives found marijuana inside, and more marijuana in the second suitcase. Approximately 15 minutes elapsed from the time the detectives initially approached Royer until his arrest after the discovery of the contraband.

The State initially argued that the entire interaction was a consensual encounter. Justice White, writing for a plurality of the Supreme Court, rejected this argument, finding that Royer was seized when the detectives retained his ticket and driver's license and, without indicating that he was free to leave, informed Royer that he was suspected of transporting narcotics and asked him to accompany them to the private room.

The State next argued that even if Royer had been had been seized, the interaction with the detectives was a stop justified by reasonable suspicion. Justice White explained that a stop must be limited in scope and duration:

> The predicate permitting seizures on suspicion short of probable cause is that law enforcement interests warrant a limited intrusion on the personal security of the suspect. The scope of the intrusion permitted will vary to some extent with the particular facts and circumstances of each case. This much, however, is clear: an investigative detention must be temporary and last no longer than is necessary to effectuate the purpose of the stop. Similarly, the investigative methods employed should be the least intrusive means reasonably available to verify or dispel the officer's suspicion in a short period of time. It is the State's burden to demonstrate that the seizure it seeks to justify on the basis of a reasonable suspicion was sufficiently limited in scope and duration to satisfy the conditions of an investigative seizure.

In the plurality's view, the scope and duration of Royer's detention exceeded the bounds of a permissible stop; he was effectively arrested— without probable cause—even before his luggage had been searched:

> What had begun as a consensual inquiry in a public place had escalated into an investigatory procedure in a police interrogation room, where the police, unsatisfied with previous

explanations, sought to confirm their suspicions. The officers had Royer's ticket, they had his identification, and they had seized his luggage. Royer was never informed that he was free to board his plane if he so chose, and he reasonably believed that he was being detained. At least as of that moment, any consensual aspects of the encounter had evaporated, and we cannot fault the [lower court] for concluding that *Terry v. Ohio* and the cases following it did not justify the restraint to which Royer was then subjected. As a practical matter, Royer was under arrest.

————————————

In *Hayes v. Florida*, the police transported a suspect in a rape investigation to the police station for fingerprinting. The Supreme Court concluded that the police had made an arrest without probable cause. The Court was careful to note, however, that fingerprinting done quickly in the field might be appropriate on the basis of reasonable suspicion of criminal activity.

HAYES V. FLORIDA
470 U.S. 811 (1985)

JUSTICE WHITE delivered the opinion of the Court.

The issue before us in this case is whether the Fourth Amendment to the Constitution of the United States, applicable to the States by virtue of the Fourteenth Amendment, was properly applied by the District Court of Appeal of Florida, Second District, to allow police to transport a suspect to the station house for fingerprinting, without his consent and without probable cause or prior judicial authorization.

A series of burglary-rapes occurred in Punta Gorda, Florida, in 1980. Police found latent fingerprints on the door-knob of the bedroom of one of the victims, fingerprints they believed belonged to the assailant. The police also found a herringbone pattern tennis shoe print near the victim's front porch. Although they had little specific information to tie petitioner Hayes to the crime, after police interviewed him along with 30 to 40 other men who generally fit the description of the assailant, the investigators came to consider petitioner a principal suspect. They decided to visit petitioner's home to obtain his fingerprints or, if he was uncooperative, to arrest him. They did not seek a warrant authorizing this procedure.

Arriving at petitioner's house, the officers spoke to petitioner on his front porch. When he expressed reluctance voluntarily to accompany them to the station for fingerprinting, one of the investigators explained that they would therefore arrest him. Petitioner, in the words of the investigator, then "blurted out" that he would rather go with the officers to the station than be arrested. While the officers were on the front porch, they also seized a pair of herringbone pattern tennis shoes in plain view.

Petitioner was then taken to the station house, where he was fingerprinted. When police determined that his prints matched those left at the scene of the crime, petitioner was placed under formal arrest. Before trial, petitioner moved to suppress the fingerprint evidence, claiming it was the fruit of an illegal detention. The trial court denied the motion and admitted the evidence without expressing a reason. Petitioner was convicted of the burglary and sexual battery committed at the scene where the latent fingerprints were found.

The District Court of Appeal of Florida, Second District, affirmed the conviction. The court declined to find consent, reasoning that in view of the threatened arrest it was, "at best, highly questionable" that Hayes voluntarily accompanied the officers to the station. The court also expressly found that the officers did not have probable cause to arrest petitioner until after they obtained his fingerprints. Nevertheless, although finding neither consent nor probable cause, the court held, analogizing to the stop-and-frisk rule of *Terry v. Ohio*, 392 U.S. 1 (1968), that the officers could transport petitioner to the station house and take his fingerprints on the basis of their reasonable suspicion that he was involved in the crime.

We agree with petitioner that *Davis v. Mississippi*, 394 U.S. 721 (1969), requires reversal of the judgment below. In *Davis,* in the course of investigating a rape, police officers brought petitioner Davis to police headquarters on December 3, 1965. He was fingerprinted and briefly questioned before being released. He was later charged and convicted of the rape. An issue there was whether the fingerprints taken on December 3 were the inadmissible fruits of an illegal detention. Concededly, the police at that time were without probable cause for an arrest, there was no warrant, and Davis had not consented to being taken to the station house. The State nevertheless contended that the Fourth Amendment did not forbid an investigative detention for the purpose of a fingerprinting, even in the absence of probable cause or a warrant. We rejected that submission, holding that Davis' detention for the purpose of fingerprinting was subject to the constraints of the Fourth Amendment and exceeded the permissible limits of those temporary seizures authorized by *Terry v. Ohio.* This was so even though fingerprinting, because it involves neither repeated harassment nor any of the probing into private life and thoughts that often marks interrogation and search, represents a much less serious intrusion upon personal security than other types of searches and detentions. Nor was it a sufficient answer to the Fourth Amendment issue to recognize that fingerprinting is an inherently more reliable and effective crime-solving mechanism than other types of evidence such as lineups and confessions. The Court indicated that perhaps under narrowly confined circumstances, a detention for fingerprinting on less than probable cause might comply with the Fourth Amendment, but found it unnecessary to decide that question since no effort was made to employ the procedures necessary to satisfy the Fourth Amendment. Rather, Davis had been detained at police headquarters without probable cause to arrest and without authorization by a judicial officer.

Here, as in *Davis,* there was no probable cause to arrest, no consent to the journey to the police station, and no judicial authorization for such a detention for fingerprinting purposes. Unless later cases have undermined *Davis* or we now disavow that decision, the judgment below must be reversed.

None of our later cases have undercut the holding in *Davis* that transportation to and investigative detention at the station house without probable cause or judicial authorization together violate the Fourth Amendment. Indeed, some 10 years later, in *Dunaway v. New York,* 442 U.S. 200 (1979), we refused to extend *Terry v. Ohio* to authorize investigative interrogations at police stations on less than probable cause, even though proper warnings under *Miranda v. Arizona,* 384 U.S. 436 (1966), had been given. We relied on and reaffirmed the holding in *Davis* that in the absence of probable cause or a warrant investigative detentions at the police station for fingerprinting purposes could not be squared with the Fourth Amendment, while at the same time repeating the possibility that the Amendment might permit a narrowly circumscribed procedure for fingerprinting detentions on less than probable cause. Since that time, we have several times revisited and explored the reach of *Terry v. Ohio.* But none of these cases have sustained against Fourth Amendment challenge the involuntary removal of a suspect from his home to a police station and his detention there for investigative purposes, whether for interrogation or fingerprinting, absent probable cause or judicial authorization.

Nor are we inclined to forswear *Davis.* There is no doubt that at some point in the investigative process, police procedures can qualitatively and quantitatively be so intrusive with respect to a suspect's freedom of movement and privacy interests as to trigger the full protection of the Fourth and Fourteenth Amendments. And our view continues to be that the line is crossed when the police, without probable cause or a warrant, forcibly remove a person from his home or other place in which he is entitled to be and transport him to the police station, where he is detained, although briefly, for investigative purposes. We adhere to the view that such seizures, at least where not under judicial supervision, are sufficiently like arrests to invoke the traditional rule that arrests may constitutionally be made only on probable cause.

None of the foregoing implies that a brief detention in the field for the purpose of fingerprinting, where there is only reasonable suspicion not amounting to probable cause, is necessarily impermissible under the Fourth Amendment. In addressing the reach of a *Terry* stop in *Adams v. Williams*, 407 U.S. 143 (1972), we observed that "a brief stop of a suspicious individual, in order to determine his identity or to maintain the status quo momentarily while obtaining more information, may be most reasonable in light of the facts known to the officer at the time." Also, just this Term, we concluded that if there are articulable facts supporting a reasonable suspicion that a person has committed a criminal offense, that person may be stopped in order to identify him, to question him briefly, or to detain him briefly while attempting to obtain additional information. *U.S. v. Hensley*, 469 U.S. 221 (1985). There is thus support in our cases for the view that the Fourth Amendment would permit seizures for the purpose of fingerprinting, if there is reasonable suspicion that the suspect has committed a criminal act, if there is a reasonable basis for believing that fingerprinting will establish or negate the suspect's connection with that crime, and if the procedure is carried out with dispatch. Of course, neither reasonable suspicion nor probable cause would suffice to permit the officers to make a warrantless entry into a person's house for the purpose of obtaining fingerprint identification. *Payton v. New York*, 445 U.S. 573 (1980).

We also do not abandon the suggestion in *Davis* and *Dunaway* that under circumscribed procedures, the Fourth Amendment might permit the judiciary to authorize the seizure of a person on less than probable cause and his removal to the police station for the purpose of fingerprinting. We do not, of course, have such a case before us. We do note, however, that some States, in reliance on the suggestion in *Davis,* have enacted procedures for judicially authorized seizures for the purpose of fingerprinting.

As we have said, absent probable cause and a warrant, *Davis v. Mississippi* requires the reversal of the judgment of the Florida District Court of Appeal.

A stop of a motorist, like a stop of a pedestrian, can become an arrest if it is too prolonged. In *U.S. v. Sharpe*, however, the Supreme Court held that a vehicular stop that lasted 20 minutes was not an arrest because the police were diligent and did not detain the defendant any longer than necessary to confirm their suspicions of criminal activity.

U.S. v. SHARPE
470 U.S. 675 (1985)

CHIEF JUSTICE BURGER delivered the opinion of the Court.

We granted certiorari to decide whether an individual reasonably suspected of engaging in criminal activity may be detained for a period of 20 minutes, when the detention is necessary for law enforcement officers to conduct a limited investigation of the suspected criminal activity.

I

On the morning of June 9, 1978, Agent Cooke of the Drug Enforcement Administration (DEA) was on patrol in an unmarked vehicle on a coastal road near Sunset Beach, North Carolina, an area under surveillance for suspected drug trafficking. At approximately 6:30 a.m., Cooke noticed a blue pickup truck with an attached camper shell traveling on the highway in tandem with a blue Pontiac Bonneville. Respondent Savage was driving the pickup, and respondent Sharpe was driving the Pontiac. The Pontiac also carried a passenger, Davis, the charges against whom were later dropped. Observing that the truck was riding low in the rear and that the camper did not bounce or sway appreciably when the truck drove over bumps or around curves, Agent Cooke concluded that it was heavily loaded. A quilted material covered the rear and side windows of the camper.

Cooke's suspicions were sufficiently aroused to follow the two vehicles for approximately 20 miles as they proceeded south into South Carolina. He then decided to make an "investigative stop" and radioed the State Highway Patrol for assistance. Officer Thrasher, driving a marked patrol car, responded to the call. Almost immediately after Thrasher caught up with the procession, the Pontiac and the pickup turned off the highway and onto a campground road. Cooke and Thrasher followed the two vehicles as the latter drove along the road at 55 to 60 miles an hour, exceeding the speed limit of 35 miles an hour. The road eventually looped back to the highway, onto which Savage and Sharpe turned and continued to drive south.

At this point, all four vehicles were in the middle lane of the three right-hand lanes of the highway. Agent Cooke asked Officer Thrasher to signal both vehicles to stop. Thrasher pulled alongside the Pontiac, which was in the lead, turned on his flashing light, and motioned for the driver of the Pontiac to stop. As Sharpe moved the Pontiac into the right lane, the pickup truck cut between the Pontiac and Thrasher's patrol car, nearly hitting the patrol car, and continued down the highway. Thrasher pursued the truck while Cooke pulled up behind the Pontiac.

Cooke approached the Pontiac and identified himself. He requested identification, and Sharpe produced a Georgia driver's license bearing the name of Raymond J. Pavlovich. Cooke then attempted to radio Thrasher to determine whether he had been successful in stopping the pickup truck, but he was unable to make contact for several minutes, apparently because Thrasher was not in his patrol car. Cooke radioed the local police for assistance, and two officers from the Myrtle Beach Police Department arrived about 10 minutes later. Asking the two officers to "maintain the situation," Cooke left to join Thrasher.

In the meantime, Thrasher had stopped the pickup truck about one-half mile down the road. After stopping the truck, Thrasher had approached it with his revolver drawn, ordered the driver, Savage, to get out and assume a "spread eagled" position against the side of the truck, and patted him down. Thrasher then holstered his gun and asked Savage for his driver's license and the truck's vehicle registration. Savage produced his own Florida driver's license and a bill of sale for the truck bearing the name of Pavlovich. In response to questions from Thrasher concerning the ownership of the truck, Savage said that the truck belonged to a friend and that he was taking it to have its shock absorbers repaired. When Thrasher told Savage that he would be held until the arrival of Cooke, whom Thrasher identified as a DEA agent, Savage became nervous, said that he wanted to leave, and requested the return of his driver's license. Thrasher replied that Savage was not free to leave at that time.

Agent Cooke arrived at the scene approximately 15 minutes after the truck had been stopped. Thrasher handed Cooke Savage's license and the bill of sale for the truck; Cooke noted that the bill of sale bore the same name as Sharpe's license. Cooke identified himself to Savage as a DEA agent and said that he thought the truck was loaded with marihuana. Cooke twice sought permission to search the camper, but Savage declined to give it, explaining that he was not the owner of the truck. Cooke then stepped on the rear of the truck and, observing that it did not sink any lower, confirmed his suspicion that it was probably overloaded. He put his nose against the rear window, which was covered from the inside, and reported that he could smell marihuana. Without seeking Savage's permission, Cooke removed the keys from the ignition, opened the rear of the camper, and observed a large number of burlap-wrapped bales resembling bales of marihuana that Cooke had seen in previous investigations. Agent Cooke then placed Savage under arrest and left him with Thrasher.

Cooke returned to the Pontiac and arrested Sharpe and Davis. Approximately 30 to 40 minutes had elapsed between the time Cooke stopped the Pontiac and the time he returned to arrest Sharpe and Davis. Cooke assembled the various parties and vehicles and led them to the Myrtle Beach police station. That evening, DEA agents took the truck to the Federal Building in Charleston, South Carolina. Several days later, Cooke supervised the unloading of the truck, which contained 43 bales weighing a total of 2,629 pounds. Acting without a search warrant, Cooke had eight randomly selected bales opened and sampled. Chemical tests showed that the samples were marihuana.

Sharpe and Savage were charged with possession of a controlled substance with intent to distribute it. The United States District Court for the District of South Carolina denied respondents' motion to suppress the contraband, and respondents were convicted.

A divided panel of the Court of Appeals for the Fourth Circuit reversed the convictions. The majority assumed that Cooke had an articulable and reasonable suspicion that Sharpe and Savage were engaged in marihuana trafficking when he and Thrasher stopped the Pontiac and the truck. But the court held the investigative stops unlawful because they failed to meet the requirement of brevity thought to govern detentions on less than probable cause. Basing its decision solely on the duration of the respondents' detentions, the majority concluded that the length of the detentions effectively transformed them into *de facto* arrests without bases in probable cause, unreasonable seizures under the Fourth Amendment. The majority then determined that the samples of marihuana should have been suppressed as the fruit of respondents' unlawful seizures.

II

In *Terry v. Ohio*, 392 U.S. 1 (1968), we adopted a dual inquiry for evaluating the reasonableness of an investigative stop. Under this approach, we examine "whether the officer's action was justified at its inception, and whether it was reasonably related in scope to the circumstances which justified the interference in the first place."

As to the first part of this inquiry, the Court of Appeals assumed that the police had an articulable and reasonable suspicion that Sharpe and Savage were engaged in marihuana trafficking, given the setting and all the circumstances when the police attempted to stop the Pontiac and the pickup. That assumption is abundantly supported by the record.[3] As to the second part of the inquiry, however, the court concluded that the 30- to 40-minute detention of Sharpe and the 20-minute detention of Savage failed to meet the Fourth Amendment's requirement of brevity.

It is not necessary for us to decide whether the length of Sharpe's detention was unreasonable, because that detention bears no causal

---

[3]   Agent Cooke had observed the vehicles traveling in tandem for 20 miles in an area near the coast known to be frequented by drug traffickers. Cooke testified that pickup trucks with camper shells were often used to transport large quantities of marihuana. Savage's pickup truck appeared to be heavily loaded, and the windows of the camper were covered with a quilted bed-sheet material rather than curtains. Finally, both vehicles took evasive actions and started speeding as soon as Officer Thrasher began following them in his marked car. Perhaps none of these facts, standing alone, would give rise to a reasonable suspicion; but taken together as appraised by an experienced law enforcement officer, they provided clear justification to stop the vehicles and pursue a limited investigation.

relation to Agent Cooke's discovery of the marihuana. The marihuana was in Savage's pickup, not in Sharpe's Pontiac; the contraband introduced at respondents' trial cannot logically be considered the "fruit" of Sharpe's detention. The only issue in this case, then, is whether it was reasonable under the circumstances facing Agent Cooke and Officer Thrasher to detain Savage, whose vehicle contained the challenged evidence, for approximately 20 minutes. We conclude that the detention of Savage clearly meets the Fourth Amendment's standard of reasonableness.

The Court of Appeals did not question the reasonableness of Officer Thrasher's or Agent Cooke's conduct during their detention of Savage. Rather, the court concluded that the length of the detention alone transformed it from a *Terry* stop into a *de facto* arrest. Counsel for respondents, as *amicus curiae*, assert that conclusion as their principal argument before this Court, relying particularly upon our decisions in *Dunaway v. New York*, 442 U.S. 200 (1979); *Florida v. Royer*, 460 U.S. 491 (1983); and *United States v. Place*, 462 U.S. 696 (1983). That reliance is misplaced.

In *Dunaway,* the police picked up a murder suspect from a neighbor's home and brought him to the police station, where, after being interrogated for an hour, he confessed. The State conceded that the police lacked probable cause when they picked up the suspect, but sought to justify the warrantless detention and interrogation as an investigative stop. The Court rejected this argument, concluding that the defendant's detention was "in important respects indistinguishable from a traditional arrest." *Dunaway* is simply inapposite here: the Court was not concerned with the length of the defendant's detention, but with events occurring during the detention.[4]

In *Royer,* government agents stopped the defendant in an airport, seized his luggage, and took him to a small room used for questioning, where a search of the luggage revealed narcotics. The Court held that the defendant's detention constituted an arrest. As in *Dunaway,* though, the focus was primarily on facts other than the duration of the defendant's detention—particularly the fact that the police confined the defendant in a small airport room for questioning.

The plurality in *Royer* did note that an investigative detention must be temporary and last no longer than is necessary to effectuate the purpose of the stop. The Court followed a similar approach in *Place.* In that case, law enforcement agents stopped the defendant after his arrival in an airport and seized his luggage for 90 minutes to take it to a narcotics detection dog for a "sniff test." We decided that an investigative

---

[4]   The pertinent facts relied on by the Court in *Dunaway* were that (1) the defendant was taken from a private dwelling; (2) he was transported unwillingly to the police station; and (3) he there was subjected to custodial interrogation resulting in a confession.

seizure of personal property could be justified under the *Terry* doctrine, but that "the length of the detention of respondent's luggage alone precludes the conclusion that the seizure was reasonable in the absence of probable cause." However, the rationale underlying that conclusion was premised on the fact that the police knew of respondent's arrival time for several hours beforehand, and the Court assumed that the police could have arranged for a trained narcotics dog in advance and thus avoided the necessity of holding respondent's luggage for 90 minutes. "In assessing the effect of the length of the detention, we take into account whether the police diligently pursue their investigation."

Here, the Court of Appeals did not conclude that the police acted less than diligently, or that they *unnecessarily* prolonged Savage's detention. *Place* and *Royer* thus provide no support for the Court of Appeals' analysis.

Admittedly, *Terry, Dunaway, Royer,* and *Place,* considered together, may in some instances create difficult line-drawing problems in distinguishing an investigative stop from a *de facto* arrest. Obviously, if an investigative stop continues indefinitely, at some point it can no longer be justified as an investigative stop. But our cases impose no rigid time limitation on *Terry* stops. While it is clear that the brevity of the invasion of the individual's Fourth Amendment interests is an important factor in determining whether the seizure is so minimally intrusive as to be justifiable on reasonable suspicion, we have emphasized the need to consider the law enforcement purposes to be served by the stop as well as the time reasonably needed to effectuate those purposes. Much as a "bright line" rule would be desirable, in evaluating whether an investigative detention is unreasonable, common sense and ordinary human experience must govern over rigid criteria.

The Court of Appeals' decision would effectively establish a *per se* rule that a 20-minute detention is too long to be justified under the *Terry* doctrine. Such a result is clearly and fundamentally at odds with our approach in this area.

In assessing whether a detention is too long in duration to be justified as an investigative stop, we consider it appropriate to examine whether the police diligently pursued a means of investigation that was likely to confirm or dispel their suspicions quickly, during which time it was necessary to detain the defendant. A court making this assessment should take care to consider whether the police are acting in a swiftly developing situation, and in such cases the court should not indulge in unrealistic second-guessing. A creative judge engaged in *post hoc* evaluation of police conduct can almost always imagine some alternative means by which the objectives of the police might have been accomplished. But the fact that the protection of the public might, in the abstract, have been accomplished by "less intrusive" means does not, itself, render the search unreasonable. The question is not simply whether some other alternative was available, but whether the police acted unreasonably in failing to recognize or to pursue it.

We readily conclude that, given the circumstances facing him, Agent Cooke pursued his investigation in a diligent and reasonable manner. During most of Savage's 20-minute detention, Cooke was attempting to contact Thrasher and enlisting the help of the local police who remained with Sharpe while Cooke left to pursue Officer Thrasher and the pickup. Once Cooke reached Officer Thrasher and Savage,[5] he proceeded expeditiously: within the space of a few minutes, he examined Savage's driver's license and the truck's bill of sale, requested (and was denied) permission to search the truck, stepped on the rear bumper and noted that the truck did not move, confirming his suspicion that it was probably overloaded. He then detected the odor of marihuana.

Clearly this case does not involve any delay unnecessary to the legitimate investigation of the law enforcement officers. Respondents presented no evidence that the officers were dilatory in their investigation. The delay in this case was attributable almost entirely to the evasive actions of Savage, who sought to elude the police as Sharpe moved his Pontiac to the side of the road. Except for Savage's maneuvers, only a short and certainly permissible pre-arrest detention would likely have taken place. The somewhat longer detention was simply the result of a graduated response to the demands of the particular situation.

We reject the contention that a 20-minute stop is unreasonable when the police have acted diligently and a suspect's actions contribute to the added delay about which he complains.

The Line Between Stops and Arrests

The investigative methods used by the police during a stop should not be more intrusive than necessary to confirm or dispel the officer's suspicions within a short period of time. A stop that is prolonged or that involves moving the suspect to a different location for further questioning or investigation may transform a stop into an arrest requiring probable cause, particularly if the police are not reasonably diligent in completing the investigation of the circumstances that inspired the stop in the first place.

---

[5] It was appropriate for Officer Thrasher to hold Savage for the brief period pending Cooke's arrival. Thrasher could not be certain that he was aware of all of the facts that had aroused Cooke's suspicions; and, as a highway patrolman, he lacked Cooke's training and experience in dealing with narcotics investigations. In this situation, it cannot realistically be said that Thrasher, a state patrolman called in to assist a federal agent in making a stop, acted unreasonably because he did not release Savage based solely on his own limited investigation of the situation and without the consent of Agent Cooke.

D. ARRESTS

An arrest—regarded as a seizure of a person under the Fourth Amendment—represents a severe restriction on an individual's freedom and is therefore subject to certain limitations, the most important of which is the requirement of probable cause. As a general matter, it is prudent for police to obtain an arrest warrant prior to making an arrest, but there are situations in which an arrest warrant is not required. The sections below discuss the circumstances in which a warrant is needed for an arrest and the crimes for which a person may be arrested.

You can view a sample federal arrest warrant at the link below. If you want to have a little fun, fill out the form, print it off, show it to your friends, and ask them if they know a good criminal defense attorney!

Sample Federal Arrest Warrant

http://www.uscourts.gov/uscourts/FormsAndFees/Forms/AO442.pdf

---

1. WHEN DO POLICE NEED AN ARREST WARRANT?

In *U.S. v. Watson*, the Supreme Court held that police may make an arrest without a warrant in a public place as long as they have probable cause to believe that the person to be arrested has committed a criminal offense.

U.S. V. WATSON
423 U.S. 411 (1976)

JUSTICE WHITE delivered the opinion of the Court.

This case presents questions under the Fourth Amendment as to the legality of a warrantless arrest and of an ensuing search of the arrestee's automobile carried out with his purported consent.

The relevant events began on August 17, 1972, when an informant, one Khoury, telephoned a postal inspector informing him that respondent Watson was in possession of a stolen credit card and had asked Khoury to cooperate in using the card to their mutual advantage. On five to 10 previous occasions Khoury had provided the inspector with reliable information on postal inspection matters, some involving Watson. Later that day Khoury delivered the card to the inspector. On learning that Watson had agreed to furnish additional cards, the inspector asked Khoury to arrange to meet with Watson. Khoury did so, a meeting being scheduled for August 22.[1] Watson canceled that engagement, but at noon on August 23, Khoury met with Watson at a restaurant designated by the

---

[1]   In the meantime the inspector had verified that the card was stolen.

latter. Khoury had been instructed that if Watson had additional stolen credit cards, Khoury was to give a designated signal. The signal was given, the officers closed in, and Watson was forthwith arrested. He was removed from the restaurant to the street where he was given the warnings required by *Miranda v. Arizona*, 384 U.S. 436 (1966). A search having revealed that Watson had no credit cards on his person, the inspector asked if he could look inside Watson's car, which was standing within view. Watson said, "Go ahead," and repeated these words when the inspector cautioned that "if I find anything, it is going to go against you." Using keys furnished by Watson, the inspector entered the car and found under the floor mat an envelope containing two credit cards in the names of other persons. These cards were the basis for two counts of a four-count indictment charging Watson with possessing stolen mail in violation of 18 U.S.C. § 1708.

Prior to trial, Watson moved to suppress the cards, claiming that his arrest was illegal for want of probable cause and an arrest warrant and that his consent to search the car was involuntary and ineffective because he had not been told that he could withhold consent. The motion was denied, and Watson was convicted of illegally possessing the two cards seized from his car.

A divided panel of the Court of Appeals for the Ninth Circuit reversed, ruling that the admission in evidence of the two credit cards found in the car was prohibited by the Fourth Amendment. In reaching this judgment, the court decided two issues in Watson's favor. First, notwithstanding its agreement with the District Court that Khoury was reliable and that there was probable cause for arresting Watson, the court held the arrest unconstitutional because the postal inspector had failed to secure an arrest warrant although he concededly had time to do so. Second, based on the totality of the circumstances, one of which was the illegality of the arrest, the court held Watson's consent to search had been coerced and hence was not a valid ground for the warrantless search of the automobile. We granted certiorari.

A major part of the Court of Appeals' opinion was its holding that Watson's warrantless arrest violated the Fourth Amendment. Although it did not expressly do so, it may have intended to overturn the conviction on the independent ground that the two credit cards were the inadmissible fruits of an unconstitutional arrest. However that may be, the Court of Appeals treated the illegality of Watson's arrest as an important factor in determining the voluntariness of his consent to search his car. We therefore deal first with the arrest issue.

Contrary to the Court of Appeals' view, Watson's arrest was not invalid because executed without a warrant. Title 18 U.S.C. § 3061(a)(3) expressly empowers the Board of Governors of the Postal Service to authorize Postal Service officers and employees "performing duties related to the inspection of postal matters" to "make arrests without warrant for felonies cognizable under the laws of the United States if they have reasonable grounds to believe that the person to be arrested has committed or is committing such a felony."

The Board of Governors has exercised that power and authorized warrantless arrests. Because there was probable cause in this case to believe that Watson had violated § 1708, the inspector and his subordinates, in arresting Watson, were acting strictly in accordance with the governing statute and regulations. The effect of the judgment of the Court of Appeals was to invalidate the statute as applied in this case and as applied to all the situations where a court fails to find exigent circumstances justifying a warrantless arrest. We reverse that judgment.

Section 3061 represents a judgment by Congress that it is not unreasonable under the Fourth Amendment for postal inspectors to arrest without a warrant provided they have probable cause to do so. This was not an isolated or quixotic judgment of the legislative branch. Other federal law enforcement officers have been expressly authorized by statute for many years to make felony arrests on probable cause but without a warrant. This is true of United States marshals, and of agents of the Federal Bureau of Investigation; the Drug Enforcement Administration; the Secret Service; and the Customs Service.

Because there is a strong presumption of constitutionality due to an Act of Congress, especially when it turns on what is "reasonable," obviously the Court should be reluctant to decide that a search thus authorized by Congress was unreasonable and that the Act was therefore unconstitutional. Moreover, there is nothing in the Court's prior cases indicating that under the Fourth Amendment a warrant is required to make a valid arrest for a felony. Indeed, the relevant prior decisions are uniformly to the contrary.

The cases construing the Fourth Amendment reflect the ancient common-law rule that a peace officer was permitted to arrest without a warrant for a misdemeanor or felony committed in his presence as well as for a felony not committed in his presence if there was reasonable ground for making the arrest. This has also been the prevailing rule under state constitutions and statutes.

The balance struck by the common law in generally authorizing felony arrests on probable cause, but without a warrant, has survived substantially intact. It appears in almost all of the States in the form of express statutory authorization.

This is the rule Congress has long directed its principal law enforcement officers to follow. Congress has plainly decided against conditioning warrantless arrest power on proof of exigent circumstances. Law enforcement officers may find it wise to seek arrest warrants where practicable to do so, and their judgments about probable cause may be more readily accepted where backed by a warrant issued by a magistrate. But we decline to transform this judicial preference into a constitutional rule when the judgment of the Nation and Congress has for so long been to authorize warrantless public arrests on probable cause rather than to encumber criminal prosecutions with endless litigation with respect to the existence of exigent circumstances, whether it was practicable to get a warrant, whether the suspect was about to flee, and the like.

Watson's arrest did not violate the Fourth Amendment, and the Court of Appeals erred in holding to the contrary.

Because our judgment is that Watson's arrest comported with the Fourth Amendment, Watson's consent to the search of his car was not the product of an illegal arrest. To the extent that the issue of the voluntariness of Watson's consent was resolved on the premise that his arrest was illegal, the Court of Appeals was also in error.

While *Watson* permits police to make an arrest in public without a warrant, an arrest in a suspect's home—where privacy rights are historically strongest—is treated differently. In *Payton v. New York*, the Supreme Court held that police need a warrant to make a routine felony arrest in a suspect's home.

PAYTON V. NEW YORK
445 U.S. 573 (1980)

JUSTICE STEVENS delivered the opinion of the Court.

These appeals challenge the constitutionality of New York statutes that authorize police officers to enter a private residence without a warrant and with force, if necessary, to make a routine felony arrest.

We hold that the Fourth Amendment to the United States Constitution, made applicable to the States by the Fourteenth Amendment, prohibits the police from making a warrantless and nonconsensual entry into a suspect's home in order to make a routine felony arrest.

On January 14, 1970, after two days of intensive investigation, New York detectives had assembled evidence sufficient to establish probable cause to believe that Theodore Payton had murdered the manager of a gas station two days earlier. At about 7:30 a.m. on January 15, six officers went to Payton's apartment in the Bronx, intending to arrest him. They had not obtained a warrant. Although light and music emanated from the apartment, there was no response to their knock on the metal door. They summoned emergency assistance and, about 30 minutes later, used crowbars to break open the door and enter the apartment. No one was there. In plain view, however, was a .30-caliber shell casing that was seized and later admitted into evidence at Payton's murder trial.

In due course Payton surrendered to the police, was indicted for murder, and moved to suppress the evidence taken from his apartment. The trial judge held that the warrantless and forcible entry was authorized by the New York Code of Criminal Procedure, and that the evidence in plain view was properly seized. He found that exigent circumstances justified the officers' failure to announce their purpose before entering the apartment as required by the statute. He had no occasion, however, to decide whether those circumstances also would have justified the failure to obtain a warrant, because he concluded that the warrantless entry was adequately supported by the statute without regard to the circumstances. The Appellate Division, First Department, summarily affirmed.

On March 14, 1974, Obie Riddick was arrested for the commission of two armed robberies that had occurred in 1971. He had been identified by the victims in June 1973, and in January 1974 the police had learned his address. They did not obtain a warrant for his arrest. At about noon on March 14, a detective, accompanied by three other officers, knocked on the door of the Queens house where Riddick was living. When his young son opened the door, they could see Riddick sitting in bed covered by a sheet. They entered the house and placed him under arrest. Before permitting him to dress, they opened a chest of drawers two feet from the bed in search of weapons and found narcotics and related paraphernalia. Riddick was subsequently indicted on narcotics charges. At a suppression hearing, the trial judge held that the warrantless entry into his home was authorized by the revised New York statute, and that the search of the immediate area was reasonable under *Chimel v. California*, 395 U.S. 752 (1969). The Appellate Division, Second Department, affirmed the denial of the suppression motion.

The New York Court of Appeals, in a single opinion, affirmed the convictions of both Payton and Riddick.

Before addressing the narrow question presented by these appeals, we put to one side other related problems that are *not* presented today. Although it is arguable that the warrantless entry to effect Payton's arrest might have been justified by exigent circumstances, none of the New York courts relied on any such justification. The Court of Appeals majority treated both Payton's and Riddick's cases as involving routine arrests in which there was ample time to obtain a warrant, and we will do the same. Accordingly, we have no occasion to consider the sort of emergency or dangerous situation, described in our cases as "exigent circumstances," that would justify a warrantless entry into a home for the purpose of either arrest or search.

Nor do these cases raise any question concerning the authority of the police, without either a search or arrest warrant, to enter a third party's home to arrest a suspect. The police broke into Payton's apartment intending to arrest Payton, and they arrested Riddick in his own dwelling. We also note that in neither case is it argued that the police lacked probable cause to believe that the suspect was at home when they entered. Finally, in both cases we are dealing with entries into homes made without the consent of any occupant. In *Payton*, the police used crowbars to break down the door and in *Riddick*, although his 3-year-old son answered the door, the police entered before Riddick had an opportunity either to object or to consent.

It is familiar history that indiscriminate searches and seizures conducted under the authority of "general warrants" were the immediate evils that motivated the framing and adoption of the Fourth Amendment. Indeed, as originally proposed in the House of Representatives, the draft contained only one clause, which directly imposed limitations on the issuance of warrants, but imposed no express restrictions on warrantless searches or seizures. As it was ultimately adopted, however, the Amendment contained two separate clauses, the first protecting the basic right to be free from unreasonable searches and seizures and the second requiring that warrants be particular and supported by probable cause.

It is thus perfectly clear that the evil the Amendment was designed to prevent was broader than the abuse of a general warrant. Unreasonable searches or seizures conducted without any warrant at all are condemned by the plain language of the first clause of the Amendment. Almost a century ago the Court stated in resounding terms that the principles reflected in the Amendment "reached farther than the concrete form" of the specific cases that gave it birth, and "apply to all invasions on the part of the government and its employees of the sanctity of a man's home and the privacies of life." Without pausing to consider whether that broad language may require some qualification, it is sufficient to note that the warrantless arrest of a person is a species of seizure required by the Amendment to be reasonable.

The simple language of the Amendment applies equally to seizures of persons and to seizures of property. Our analysis in this case may therefore properly commence with rules that have been well established in Fourth Amendment litigation involving tangible items. As the Court reiterated just a few years ago, the "physical entry of the home is the chief evil against which the wording of the Fourth Amendment is directed." And we have long adhered to the view that the warrant procedure minimizes the danger of needless intrusions of that sort.

It is a basic principle of Fourth Amendment law that searches and seizures inside a home without a warrant are presumptively unreasonable. Yet it is also well settled that objects such as weapons or contraband found in a public place may be seized by the police without a warrant. The seizure of property in plain view involves no invasion of privacy and is presumptively reasonable, assuming that there is probable cause to associate the property with criminal activity.

The Fourth Amendment protects the individual's privacy in a variety of settings. In none is the zone of privacy more clearly defined than when bounded by the unambiguous physical dimensions of an individual's home—a zone that finds its roots in clear and specific constitutional terms: "The right of the people to be secure in their . . . houses . . . shall not be violated." That language unequivocally establishes the proposition that "at the very core of the Fourth Amendment stands the right of a man to retreat into his own home and there be free from unreasonable governmental intrusion." In terms that apply equally to seizures of property and to seizures of persons, the Fourth Amendment has drawn a firm line at the entrance to the house. Absent exigent circumstances, that threshold may not reasonably be crossed without a warrant.

The parties have argued at some length about the practical consequences of a warrant requirement as a precondition to a felony arrest in the home. In the absence of any evidence that effective law enforcement has suffered in those States that already have such a requirement, we are inclined to view such arguments with skepticism. More fundamentally, however, such arguments of policy must give way to a constitutional command that we consider to be unequivocal.

Finally, we note the State's suggestion that only a search warrant based on probable cause to believe the suspect is at home at a given time can adequately protect the privacy interests at stake, and since such a warrant requirement is manifestly impractical, there need be no warrant of any kind. We find this ingenious argument unpersuasive. It is true that an arrest warrant requirement may afford less protection than a search warrant requirement, but it will suffice to interpose the magistrate's determination of probable cause between the zealous officer and the citizen. If there is sufficient evidence of a citizen's participation in a felony to persuade a judicial officer that his arrest is justified, it is constitutionally reasonable to require him to open his doors to the officers of the law. Thus, for Fourth Amendment purposes, an arrest warrant founded on probable cause implicitly carries with it the limited authority to enter a dwelling in which the suspect lives when there is reason to believe the suspect is within.

Because no arrest warrant was obtained in either of these cases, the judgments must be reversed and the cases remanded to the New York Court of Appeals for further proceedings not inconsistent with this opinion.

JUSTICE WHITE, with whom CHIEF JUSTICE BURGER and JUSTICE REHNQUIST join, dissenting.

The background, text, and legislative history of the Fourth Amendment demonstrate that the purpose was to restrict the abuses that had developed with respect to warrants; the Amendment preserved common-law rules of arrest. Because it was not considered generally unreasonable at common law for officers to break doors to effect a warrantless felony arrest, I do not believe that the Fourth Amendment was intended to outlaw the types of police conduct at issue in the present cases.

Today's decision rests, in large measure, on the premise that warrantless arrest entries constitute a particularly severe invasion of personal privacy. I do not dispute that the home is generally a very private area or that the common law displayed a special reverence for the individual's right of privacy in his house. However, the Fourth Amendment is concerned with protecting people, not places, and no talismanic significance is given to the fact that an arrest occurs in the home rather than elsewhere. It is necessary in each case to assess realistically the actual extent of invasion of constitutionally protected privacy. Further, all arrests involve serious intrusions into an individual's privacy and dignity. Yet we settled in *U.S. v. Watson*, 423 U.S. 411 (1976), that the intrusiveness of a public arrest is not enough to mandate the obtaining of a warrant. The inquiry in the present case, therefore, is whether the incremental intrusiveness that results from an arrest's being made *in the dwelling* is enough to support an inflexible constitutional rule requiring warrants for such arrests whenever exigent circumstances are not present.

Today's decision ignores the carefully crafted restrictions on the common-law power of arrest entry and thereby overestimates the dangers inherent in that practice. At common law, absent exigent circumstances, entries to arrest could be made only for felony. Even in cases of felony, the officers were required to announce their presence, demand admission, and be refused entry before they were entitled to break doors. Further, it seems generally accepted that entries could be made only during daylight hours. And, in my view, the officer entering to arrest must have reasonable grounds to believe, not only that the arrestee has committed a crime, but also that the person suspected is present in the house at the time of the entry.

These four restrictions on home arrests—felony, knock and announce, daytime, and stringent probable cause—constitute powerful and complementary protections for the privacy interests associated with the home. The felony requirement guards against abusive or arbitrary enforcement and ensures that invasions of the home occur only in case of the most serious crimes. The knock-and-announce and daytime requirements protect individuals against the fear, humiliation, and embarrassment of being aroused from their beds in states of partial or complete undress. And these requirements allow the arrestee to surrender at his front door, thereby maintaining his dignity and preventing the officers from entering other rooms of the dwelling. The stringent probable-cause requirement would help ensure against the possibility that the police would enter when the suspect was not home, and, in searching for him, frighten members of the family or ransack parts of the house, seizing items in plain view. In short, these requirements, taken together, permit an individual suspected of a serious crime to surrender at the front door of his dwelling and thereby avoid most of the humiliation and indignity that the Court seems to believe necessarily accompany a house arrest entry. Such a front-door arrest, in my view, is no more intrusive on personal privacy than the public warrantless arrests which we found to pass constitutional muster in *Watson*.

All of these limitations on warrantless arrest entries are satisfied on the facts of the present cases. The arrests here were for serious felonies— murder and armed robbery—and both occurred during daylight hours. The authorizing statutes required that the police announce their business and demand entry; neither Payton nor Riddick makes any contention that these statutory requirements were not fulfilled. And it is not argued that the police had no probable cause to believe that both Payton and Riddick were in their dwellings at the time of the entries. Today's decision, therefore, sweeps away any possibility that warrantless home entries might be permitted in some limited situations other than those in which exigent circumstances are present. The Court substitutes, in one sweeping decision, a rigid constitutional rule in place of the common-law approach, evolved over hundreds of years, which achieved a flexible accommodation between the demands of personal privacy and the legitimate needs of law enforcement.

A rule permitting warrantless arrest entries would not pose a danger that officers would use their entry power as a pretext to justify an otherwise invalid warrantless search. A search pursuant to a warrantless arrest entry will rarely, if ever, be as complete as one under authority of a search warrant. If the suspect surrenders at the door, the officers may not enter other rooms. Of course, the suspect may flee or hide, or may not be at home, but the officers cannot anticipate the first two of these possibilities and the last is unlikely given the requirement of probable cause to believe that the suspect is at home. Even when officers are justified in searching other rooms, they may seize only items within the arrestee's position or immediate control or items in plain view discovered during the course of a search reasonably directed at discovering a hiding suspect. Hence a warrantless home entry is likely to uncover far less evidence than a search conducted under authority of a search warrant.

Furthermore, an arrest entry will inevitably tip off the suspects and likely result in destruction or removal of evidence not uncovered during the arrest. I therefore cannot believe that the police would take the risk of losing valuable evidence through a pretextual arrest entry rather than applying to a magistrate for a search warrant.

While exaggerating the invasion of personal privacy involved in home arrests, the Court fails to account for the danger that its rule will severely hamper effective law enforcement. The policeman on his beat must now make subtle discriminations that perplex even judges in their chambers. Police will sometimes delay making an arrest, even after probable cause is established, in order to be sure that they have enough evidence to convict. Then, if they suddenly have to arrest, they run the risk that the subsequent exigency will not excuse their prior failure to obtain a warrant. This problem cannot effectively be cured by obtaining a warrant as soon as probable cause is established because of the chance that the warrant will go stale before the arrest is made.

Further, police officers will often face the difficult task of deciding whether the circumstances are sufficiently exigent to justify their entry to arrest without a warrant. This is a decision that must be made quickly in the most trying of circumstances. If the officers mistakenly decide that the circumstances are exigent, the arrest will be invalid and any evidence seized incident to the arrest or in plain view will be excluded at trial. On the other hand, if the officers mistakenly determine that exigent circumstances are lacking, they may refrain from making the arrest, thus creating the possibility that a dangerous criminal will escape into the community. The police could reduce the likelihood of escape by staking out all possible exits until the circumstances become clearly exigent or a warrant is obtained. But the costs of such a stakeout seem excessive in an era of rising crime and scarce police resources.

The uncertainty inherent in the exigent-circumstances determination burdens the judicial system as well. In the case of searches, exigent circumstances are sufficiently unusual that this Court has determined that the benefits of a warrant outweigh the burdens imposed, including the burdens on the judicial system. In contrast, arrests recurringly involve exigent circumstances, and this Court has heretofore held that a warrant can be dispensed with without undue sacrifice in Fourth Amendment values. The situation should be no different with respect to arrests in the home. Under today's decision, whenever the police have made a warrantless home arrest there will be the possibility of endless litigation with respect to the existence of exigent circumstances, whether it was practicable to get a warrant, whether the suspect was about to flee, and the like.

Our cases establish that the ultimate test under the Fourth Amendment is one of "reasonableness." I cannot join the Court in declaring unreasonable a practice which has been thought entirely reasonable by so many for so long. It would be far preferable to adopt a clear and simple rule: after knocking and announcing their presence, police may enter the home to make a daytime arrest without a warrant when there is probable cause to believe that the person to be arrested committed a felony and is present in the house. This rule would best comport with the common-law background, with the traditional practice in the States, and with the history and policies of the Fourth Amendment. Accordingly, I respectfully dissent.

———————

The rule in *Payton* applies to *routine*—non-emergency—felony arrests in the suspect's home. *Payton* thus suggests that a warrantless arrest in a suspect's home might still be permissible if there are exigent circumstances. In *Welsh v. Wisconsin*, the Supreme Court considered the kinds of exigent circumstances that would justify a warrantless entry into a home in order to make an arrest. In particular, the Court held that police should consider the gravity of the underlying offense for which the arrest is being made in determining whether a warrantless arrest inside a suspect's home is appropriate.

WELSH V. WISCONSIN
466 U.S. 740 (1984)

JUSTICE BRENNAN delivered the opinion of the Court.

Payton v. New York, 445 U.S. 573 (1980), held that, absent probable cause and exigent circumstances, warrantless arrests in the home are prohibited by the Fourth Amendment. But the Court in that case explicitly refused to consider the sort of emergency or dangerous situation, described in our cases as "exigent circumstances," that would justify a warrantless entry into a home for the purpose of either arrest or search. Certiorari was granted in this case to decide at least one aspect of the unresolved question: whether, and if so under what circumstances, the Fourth Amendment prohibits the police from making a warrantless night entry of a person's home in order to arrest him for a nonjailable traffic offense.

Shortly before 9 o'clock on the rainy night of April 24, 1978, a lone witness, Randy Jablonic, observed a car being driven erratically. After changing speeds and veering from side to side, the car eventually swerved off the road and came to a stop in an open field. No damage to any person or property occurred. Concerned about the driver and fearing that the car would get back on the highway, Jablonic drove his truck up behind the car so as to block it from returning to the road. Another passerby also stopped at the scene, and Jablonic asked her to call the police. Before the police arrived, however, the driver of the car emerged from his vehicle, approached Jablonic's truck, and asked Jablonic for a ride home. Jablonic instead suggested that they wait for assistance in removing or repairing the car. Ignoring Jablonic's suggestion, the driver walked away from the scene.

A few minutes later, the police arrived and questioned Jablonic. He told one officer what he had seen, specifically noting that the driver was either very inebriated or very sick. The officer checked the motor vehicle registration of the abandoned car and learned that it was registered to the petitioner, Edward G. Welsh. In addition, the officer noted that the petitioner's residence was a short distance from the scene, and therefore easily within walking distance.

Without securing any type of warrant, the police proceeded to the petitioner's home, arriving about 9 p.m. When the petitioner's stepdaughter answered the door, the police gained entry into the house. Proceeding upstairs to the petitioner's bedroom, they found him lying naked in bed. At this point, the petitioner was placed under arrest for driving or operating a motor vehicle while under the influence of an intoxicant. The petitioner was taken to the police station, where he refused to submit to a breath-analysis test.

As a result of these events, the petitioner was subjected to two separate but related proceedings: one concerning his refusal to submit to a breath test and the other involving the alleged code violation for driving while intoxicated. Under the Wisconsin Vehicle Code in effect in April 1978, one arrested for driving while intoxicated could be requested by a law enforcement officer to provide breath, blood, or urine samples for the purpose of determining the presence or quantity of alcohol. If such a request was made, the arrestee was required to submit to the appropriate testing or risk a revocation of operating privileges. The arrestee could challenge the officer's request, however, by refusing to undergo testing and then asking for a hearing to determine whether the refusal was justified. If, after the hearing, it was determined that the refusal was not justified, the arrestee's operating privileges would be revoked for 60 days.

The statute also set forth specific criteria to be applied by a court when determining whether an arrestee's refusal to take a breath test was justified. Included among these criteria was a requirement that, before revoking the arrestee's operating privileges, the court determine that "the refusal to submit to a test was unreasonable." It is not disputed by the parties that an arrestee's refusal to take a breath test would be reasonable, and therefore operating privileges could not be revoked, if the underlying arrest was not lawful. Indeed, state law has consistently provided that a valid arrest is a necessary prerequisite to the imposition of a breath test.

It is axiomatic that the physical entry of the home is the chief evil against which the wording of the Fourth Amendment is directed. And a principal protection against unnecessary intrusions into private dwellings is the warrant requirement imposed by the Fourth Amendment on agents of the government who seek to enter the home for purposes of search or arrest. It is not surprising, therefore, that the Court has recognized, as a basic principle of Fourth Amendment law, that searches and seizures inside a home without a warrant are presumptively unreasonable.

Consistently with these long-recognized principles, the Court decided in *Payton v. New York* that warrantless felony arrests in the home are prohibited by the Fourth Amendment, absent probable cause and exigent circumstances. At the same time, the Court declined to consider the scope of any exception for exigent circumstances that might justify warrantless home arrests, thereby leaving to the lower courts the initial application of the exigent-circumstances exception. Prior decisions of this Court, however, have emphasized that exceptions to the warrant requirement are few in number and carefully delineated, and that the police bear a heavy burden when attempting to demonstrate an urgent need that might justify warrantless searches or arrests. Indeed, the Court has recognized only a few such emergency conditions, and has actually applied only the "hot pursuit" doctrine to arrests in the home.

Our hesitation in finding exigent circumstances, especially when warrantless arrests in the home are at issue, is particularly appropriate when the underlying offense for which there is probable cause to arrest is relatively minor. Before agents of the government may invade the sanctity of the home, the burden is on the government to demonstrate exigent circumstances that overcome the presumption of unreasonableness that attaches to all warrantless home entries. When the government's interest is only to arrest for a minor offense, that presumption of unreasonableness is difficult to rebut, and the government usually should be allowed to make such arrests only with a warrant issued upon probable cause by a neutral and detached magistrate.

We therefore conclude that the common-sense approach utilized by most lower courts is required by the Fourth Amendment prohibition on "unreasonable searches and seizures," and hold that an important factor to be considered when determining whether any exigency exists is the gravity of the underlying offense for which the arrest is being made. Moreover, although no exigency is created simply because there is probable cause to believe that a serious crime has been committed, application of the exigent-circumstances exception in the context of a home entry should rarely be sanctioned when there is probable cause to believe that only a minor offense, such as the kind at issue in this case, has been committed.

Application of this principle to the facts of the present case is relatively straightforward. The petitioner was arrested in the privacy of his own bedroom for a noncriminal, traffic offense. The State attempts to justify the arrest by relying on the hot-pursuit doctrine, on the threat to public safety, and on the need to preserve evidence of the petitioner's blood-alcohol level. On the facts of this case, however, the claim of hot pursuit is unconvincing because there was no immediate or continuous pursuit of the petitioner from the scene of a crime. Moreover, because the petitioner had already arrived home, and had abandoned his car at the scene of the accident, there was little remaining threat to the public safety. Hence, the only potential emergency claimed by the State was the need to ascertain the petitioner's blood-alcohol level.

Even assuming, however, that the underlying facts would support a finding of this exigent circumstance, mere similarity to other cases involving the imminent destruction of evidence is not sufficient. The State of Wisconsin has chosen to classify the first offense for driving while intoxicated as a noncriminal, civil forfeiture offense for which no imprisonment is possible. This is the best indication of the State's interest in precipitating an arrest, and is one that can be easily identified both by the courts and by officers faced with a decision to arrest. Given this expression of the State's interest, a warrantless home arrest cannot be upheld simply because evidence of the petitioner's blood-alcohol level might have dissipated while the police obtained a warrant. To allow a warrantless home entry on these facts would be to approve unreasonable police behavior that the principles of the Fourth Amendment will not sanction.

The Supreme Court of Wisconsin let stand a warrantless, nighttime entry into the petitioner's home to arrest him for a civil traffic offense. Such an arrest, however, is clearly prohibited by the special protection afforded the individual in his home by the Fourth Amendment. The petitioner's arrest was therefore invalid.

When Do Police Need an Arrest Warrant?

1. A police officer may make an arrest without a warrant in a public place as long as she has probable cause to believe that the person to be arrested has committed a criminal offense.

2. Police need a warrant to make a routine felony arrest in a suspect's home.

3. Police may make a warrantless arrest at a suspect's home if there are exigent circumstances. The gravity of the underlying offense for which the arrest is being made is an important consideration in determining whether exigent circumstances exist. Application of the exigent circumstances exception in the context of a home entry should rarely be sanctioned when there is probable cause to believe that only a minor offense has been committed.

2. FOR WHAT CRIMES MAY A PERSON BE ARRESTED?

In *Atwater v. City of Lago Vista*, the Supreme Court held that police may make warrantless arrests for minor offenses, including misdemeanor driving violations that carry no jail time and are punishable only by a fine. Four Justices signed a strong dissent.

ATWATER V. CITY OF LAGO VISTA
532 U.S. 318 (2001)

JUSTICE SOUTER delivered the opinion of the Court.

The question is whether the Fourth Amendment forbids a warrantless arrest for a minor criminal offense, such as a misdemeanor seatbelt violation punishable only by a fine. We hold that it does not.

I

In Texas, if a car is equipped with safety belts, a front-seat passenger must wear one, and the driver must secure any small child riding in front. Violation of either provision is "a misdemeanor punishable by a fine not less than $25 or more than $50." Texas law expressly authorizes "any peace officer to arrest without warrant a person found committing a violation" of these seatbelt laws, although it permits police to issue citations in lieu of arrest.

In March 1997, petitioner Gail Atwater was driving her pickup truck in Lago Vista, Texas, with her 3-year-old son and 5-year-old daughter in the front seat. None of them was wearing a seatbelt. Respondent Bart Turek, a Lago Vista police officer at the time, observed the seatbelt violations and pulled Atwater over. According to Atwater's complaint (the allegations of which we assume to be true for present purposes), Turek approached the truck and "yelled" something to the effect of "we've met before" and "you're going to jail." He then called for backup and asked to see Atwater's driver's license and insurance documentation, which state law required her to carry. When Atwater told Turek that she did not have the papers because her purse had been stolen the day before, Turek said that he had "heard that story two-hundred times."

Atwater asked to take her "frightened, upset, and crying" children to a friend's house nearby, but Turek told her, "you're not going anywhere." As it turned out, Atwater's friend learned what was going on and soon arrived to take charge of the children. Turek then handcuffed Atwater, placed her in his squad car, and drove her to the local police station, where booking officers had her remove her shoes, jewelry, and eyeglasses, and empty her pockets. Officers took Atwater's "mug shot" and placed her, alone, in a jail cell for about one hour, after which she was taken before a magistrate and released on $310 bond.

Atwater was charged with driving without her seatbelt fastened, failing to secure her children in seatbelts, driving without a license, and failing to provide proof of insurance. She ultimately pleaded no contest to the misdemeanor seatbelt offenses and paid a $50 fine; the other charges were dismissed.

Atwater and her husband, petitioner Michael Haas, filed suit in a Texas state court under 42 U.S.C. § 1983 against Turek and respondents City of Lago Vista and Chief of Police Frank Miller. So far as concerns us, petitioners (whom we will simply call Atwater) alleged that respondents (for simplicity, the City) had violated Atwater's Fourth Amendment "right to be free from unreasonable seizure," and sought compensatory and punitive damages.

II

The Fourth Amendment safeguards "the right of the people to be secure in their persons, houses, papers, and effects, against unreasonable searches and seizures." In reading the Amendment, we are guided by the traditional protections against unreasonable searches and seizures afforded by the common law at the time of the framing, since an examination of the common-law understanding of an officer's authority to arrest sheds light on the obviously relevant, if not entirely dispositive, consideration of what the Framers of the Amendment might have thought to be reasonable. Thus, the first step here is to assess Atwater's claim that peace officers' authority to make warrantless arrests for misdemeanors was restricted at common law (whether "common law" is understood strictly as law judicially derived or, instead, as the whole body of law extant at the time of the framing). Atwater's specific contention is that "founding-era common-law rules" forbade peace officers to make warrantless misdemeanor arrests except in cases of "breach of the peace," a category she claims was then understood narrowly as covering only those nonfelony offenses "involving or tending toward violence." Although her historical argument is by no means insubstantial, it ultimately fails.

We begin with the state of pre-founding English common law and find that, even after making some allowance for variations in the common-law usage of the term "breach of the peace," the "founding-era common-law rules" were not nearly as clear as Atwater claims; on the contrary, the common-law commentators (as well as the sparsely reported cases) reached divergent conclusions with respect to officers' warrantless misdemeanor arrest power. Moreover, in the years leading up to American independence, Parliament repeatedly extended express warrantless arrest authority to cover misdemeanor-level offenses not amounting to or involving any violent breach of the peace.

An examination of specifically American evidence is to the same effect. Neither the history of the framing era nor subsequent legal development indicates that the Fourth Amendment was originally understood, or has traditionally been read, to embrace Atwater's position.

To begin with, Atwater has cited no particular evidence that those who framed and ratified the Fourth Amendment sought to limit peace officers' warrantless misdemeanor arrest authority to instances of actual breach of the peace, and our own review of the recent and respected compilations of framing-era documentary history has likewise failed to reveal any such design. Nor have we found in any of the modern historical accounts of the Fourth Amendment's adoption any substantial indication that the Framers intended such a restriction. Indeed, to the extent these modern histories address the issue, their conclusions are to the contrary.

The evidence of actual practice also counsels against Atwater's position. During the period leading up to and surrounding the framing of the Bill of Rights, colonial and state legislatures, like Parliament before them, regularly authorized local peace officers to make warrantless misdemeanor arrests without conditioning statutory authority on breach of the peace. We simply cannot conclude that the Fourth Amendment, as originally understood, forbade peace officers to arrest without a warrant for misdemeanors not amounting to or involving breach of the peace.

Nor does Atwater's argument from tradition pick up any steam from the historical record as it has unfolded since the framing, there being no indication that her claimed rule has ever become "woven into the fabric" of American law. The story, on the contrary, is of two centuries of uninterrupted (and largely unchallenged) state and federal practice permitting warrantless arrests for misdemeanors not amounting to or involving breach of the peace.

First, there is no support for Atwater's position in this Court's cases. Although the Court has not had much to say about warrantless misdemeanor arrest authority, what little we have said tends to cut against Atwater's argument. In discussing this authority, we have focused on the circumstance that an offense was committed in an officer's presence, to the omission of any reference to a breach-of-the-peace limitation.[11] See, e.g., *U.S. v. Watson*, 423 U.S. 411, 418 (1976) ("The cases construing the Fourth Amendment thus reflect the ancient common-law rule that a peace officer was permitted to arrest without a warrant for a misdemeanor or felony committed in his presence.").

Second, it is not the case here that early American courts embraced an accepted common-law rule with anything approaching unanimity. To be sure, Atwater has cited several 19th-century decisions that, at least at first glance, might seem to support her contention that "warrantless

---

[11] We need not, and thus do not, speculate whether the Fourth Amendment entails an "in the presence" requirement for purposes of misdemeanor arrests.

misdemeanor arrest was unlawful when not [for] a breach of the peace." But none is ultimately availing.

The reports may well contain early American cases more favorable to Atwater's position than the ones she has herself invoked. But more to the point, we think, are the numerous early- and mid-19th century decisions expressly sustaining (often against constitutional challenge) state and local laws authorizing peace officers to make warrantless arrests for misdemeanors not involving any breach of the peace.

Finally, both the legislative tradition of granting warrantless misdemeanor arrest authority and the judicial tradition of sustaining such statutes against constitutional attack are buttressed by legal commentary that, for more than a century now, has almost uniformly recognized the constitutionality of extending warrantless arrest power to misdemeanors without limitation to breaches of the peace.

Small wonder, then, that today statutes in all 50 States and the District of Columbia permit warrantless misdemeanor arrests by at least some (if not all) peace officers without requiring any breach of the peace, as do a host of congressional enactments.

III

While it is true here that history, if not unequivocal, has expressed a decided, majority view that the police need not obtain an arrest warrant merely because a misdemeanor stopped short of violence or a threat of it, Atwater does not wager all on history. Instead, she asks us to mint a new rule of constitutional law on the understanding that when historical practice fails to speak conclusively to a claim grounded on the Fourth Amendment, courts are left to strike a current balance between individual and societal interests by subjecting particular contemporary circumstances to traditional standards of reasonableness. Atwater accordingly argues for a modern arrest rule, one not necessarily requiring violent breach of the peace, but nonetheless forbidding custodial arrest, even upon probable cause, when conviction could not ultimately carry any jail time and when the government shows no compelling need for immediate detention.

If we were to derive a rule exclusively to address the uncontested facts of this case, Atwater might well prevail. She was a known and established resident of Lago Vista with no place to hide and no incentive to flee, and common sense says she would almost certainly have buckled up as a condition of driving off with a citation. In her case, the physical incidents of arrest were merely gratuitous humiliations imposed by a police officer who was (at best) exercising extremely poor judgment. Atwater's claim to live free of pointless indignity and confinement clearly outweighs anything the City can raise against it specific to her case.

But we have traditionally recognized that a responsible Fourth Amendment balance is not well served by standards requiring sensitive, case-by-case determinations of government need, lest every discretionary judgment in the field be converted into an occasion for constitutional review. Often enough, the Fourth Amendment has to be applied on the spur (and in the heat) of the moment, and the object in implementing its command of reasonableness is to draw standards sufficiently clear and simple to be applied with a fair prospect of surviving judicial second-guessing months and years after an arrest or search is made. Courts attempting to strike a reasonable Fourth Amendment balance thus credit the government's side with an essential interest in readily administrable rules.

At first glance, Atwater's argument may seem to respect the values of clarity and simplicity, so far as she claims that the Fourth Amendment generally forbids warrantless arrests for minor crimes not accompanied by violence or some demonstrable threat of it (whether "minor crime" be defined as a fine-only traffic offense, a fine-only offense more generally, or a misdemeanor). But the claim is not ultimately so simple, nor could it be, for complications arise the moment we begin to think about the possible applications of the several criteria Atwater proposes for drawing a line between minor crimes with limited arrest authority and others not so restricted.

One line, she suggests, might be between "jailable" and "fine-only" offenses, between those for which conviction could result in commitment and those for which it could not. The trouble with this distinction, of course, is that an officer on the street might not be able to tell. It is not merely that we cannot expect every police officer to know the details of frequently complex penalty schemes, but that penalties for ostensibly identical conduct can vary on account of facts difficult (if not impossible) to know at the scene of an arrest. Is this the first offense or is the suspect a repeat offender? Is the weight of the marijuana a gram above or a gram below the fine-only line? Where conduct could implicate more than one criminal prohibition, which one will the district attorney ultimately decide to charge? And so on.

But Atwater's refinements would not end there. She represents that if the line were drawn at nonjailable traffic offenses, her proposed limitation should be qualified by a proviso authorizing warrantless arrests where "necessary for enforcement of the traffic laws or when an offense would otherwise continue and pose a danger to others on the road." The proviso only compounds the difficulties. Would, for instance, either exception apply to speeding? At oral argument, Atwater's counsel said that "it would not be reasonable to arrest a driver for speeding unless the speeding rose to the level of reckless driving." But is it not fair to expect that the chronic speeder will speed again despite a citation in his pocket, and should that not qualify as showing that the "offense would continue" under Atwater's rule? And why, as a constitutional matter, should we assume that only reckless driving will "pose a danger to others on the road" while speeding will not?

There is no need for more examples to show that Atwater's general rule and limiting proviso promise very little in the way of administrability. Atwater's rule therefore would not only place police in an almost impossible spot but would guarantee increased litigation over many of the arrests that would occur. For all these reasons, Atwater's various distinctions between permissible and impermissible arrests for minor crimes strike us as very unsatisfactory lines to require police officers to draw on a moment's notice.

Accordingly, we confirm today what our prior cases have intimated: the standard of probable cause applies to all arrests, without the need to balance the interests and circumstances involved in particular situations. If an officer has probable cause to believe that an individual has committed even a very minor criminal offense in his presence, he may, without violating the Fourth Amendment, arrest the offender.

Atwater's arrest satisfied constitutional requirements. There is no dispute that Officer Turek had probable cause to believe that Atwater had committed a crime in his presence. She admits that neither she nor her children were wearing seatbelts. Turek was accordingly authorized (not required, but authorized) to make a custodial arrest without balancing costs and benefits or determining whether or not Atwater's arrest was in some sense necessary. The arrest and booking were inconvenient and embarrassing to Atwater, but not so extraordinary as to violate the Fourth Amendment.

JUSTICE O'CONNOR, with whom JUSTICE STEVENS, JUSTICE GINSBURG, and JUSTICE BREYER join, dissenting.

A full custodial arrest, such as the one to which Ms. Atwater was subjected, is the quintessential seizure. When a full custodial arrest is effected without a warrant, the plain language of the Fourth Amendment requires that the arrest be reasonable.

We have often looked to the common law in evaluating the reasonableness, for Fourth Amendment purposes, of police activity. But history is just one of the tools we use in conducting the reasonableness inquiry. And when history is inconclusive, as the majority amply demonstrates it is in this case, we will evaluate the search or seizure under traditional standards of reasonableness by assessing, on the one hand, the degree to which it intrudes upon an individual's privacy and, on the other, the degree to which it is needed for the promotion of legitimate governmental interests. In other words, in determining reasonableness, each case is to be decided on its own facts and circumstances.

The majority gives a brief nod to this bedrock principle of our Fourth Amendment jurisprudence, and even acknowledges that "Atwater's claim to live free of pointless indignity and confinement clearly outweighs anything the City can raise against it specific to her case." But instead of remedying this imbalance, the majority allows itself to be swayed by the worry that "every discretionary judgment in the field will be converted into an occasion for constitutional review." It therefore mints a new rule that "if an officer has probable cause to believe that an individual has committed even a very minor criminal offense in his presence, he may, without violating the Fourth Amendment, arrest the offender." This rule is not only unsupported by our precedent, but runs contrary to the principles that lie at the core of the Fourth Amendment.

As the majority tacitly acknowledges, we have never considered the precise question presented here, namely, the constitutionality of a warrantless arrest for an offense punishable only by fine. Indeed, on the rare occasions that Members of this Court have contemplated such an arrest, they have indicated disapproval.

A custodial arrest exacts an obvious toll on an individual's liberty and privacy, even when the period of custody is relatively brief. The arrestee is subject to a full search of her person and confiscation of her possessions. The arrestee may be detained for up to 48 hours without having a magistrate determine whether there in fact was probable cause for the arrest. Because people arrested for all types of violent and nonviolent offenses may be housed together awaiting such review, this detention period is potentially dangerous. And once the period of custody is over, the fact of the arrest is a permanent part of the public record.

We have said that "the penalty that may attach to any particular offense seems to provide the clearest and most consistent indication of the State's interest in arresting individuals suspected of committing that offense." If the State has decided that a fine, and not imprisonment, is the appropriate punishment for an offense, the State's interest in taking a person suspected of committing that offense into custody is surely limited, at best. This is not to say that the State will never have such an interest. A full custodial arrest may on occasion vindicate legitimate state interests, even if the crime is punishable only by fine. Arrest is the surest way to abate criminal conduct. It may also allow the police to verify the offender's identity and, if the offender poses a flight risk, to ensure her appearance at trial. But when such considerations are not present, a citation or summons may serve the State's remaining law enforcement interests every bit as effectively as an arrest.

Because a full custodial arrest is such a severe intrusion on an individual's liberty, its reasonableness hinges on the degree to which it is needed for the promotion of legitimate governmental interests. In light of the availability of citations to promote a State's interests when a fine-only offense has been committed, I cannot concur in a rule which deems a full custodial arrest to be reasonable in every circumstance. Giving police officers constitutional *carte blanche* to effect an arrest whenever there is probable cause to believe a fine-only misdemeanor has been committed is irreconcilable with the Fourth Amendment's command that seizures be reasonable. Instead, I would require that when there is probable cause to believe that a fine-only offense has been committed, the police officer should issue a citation unless the officer is able to point to specific and articulable facts which, taken together with rational inferences from those facts, reasonably warrant the additional intrusion of a full custodial arrest.

The record in this case makes it abundantly clear that Ms. Atwater's arrest was constitutionally unreasonable. Atwater readily admits—as she did when Officer Turek pulled her over—that she violated Texas' seatbelt law. While Turek was justified in stopping Atwater, neither law nor reason supports his decision to arrest her instead of simply giving her a citation. The officer's actions cannot sensibly be viewed as a permissible means of balancing Atwater's Fourth Amendment interests with the State's own legitimate interests.

There is no question that Officer Turek's actions severely infringed Atwater's liberty and privacy. Turek was loud and accusatory from the moment he approached Atwater's car. Atwater's young children were terrified and hysterical. Yet when Atwater asked Turek to lower his voice because he was scaring the children, he responded by jabbing his finger in Atwater's face and saying, "You're going to jail." Having made the decision to arrest, Turek did not inform Atwater of her right to remain silent. He instead asked for her license and insurance information.

Atwater asked if she could at least take her children to a friend's house down the street before going to the police station. But Turek—who had just castigated Atwater for not caring for her children—refused and said he would take the children into custody as well. Only the intervention of neighborhood children who had witnessed the scene and summoned one of Atwater's friends saved the children from being hauled to jail with their mother.

With the children gone, Officer Turek handcuffed Ms. Atwater with her hands behind her back, placed her in the police car, and drove her to the police station. Ironically, Turek did not secure Atwater in a seatbelt for the drive. At the station, Atwater was forced to remove her shoes, relinquish her possessions, and wait in a holding cell for about an hour. A judge finally informed Atwater of her rights and the charges against her, and released her when she posted bond. Atwater returned to the scene of the arrest, only to find that her car had been towed.

Ms. Atwater ultimately pleaded no contest to violating the seatbelt law and was fined $50. Even though that fine was the maximum penalty for her crime, and even though Officer Turek has never articulated any justification for his actions, the city contends that arresting Atwater was constitutionally reasonable because it advanced two legitimate interests: the enforcement of child safety laws and encouraging Atwater to appear for trial. It is difficult to see how arresting Atwater served either of these goals any more effectively than the issuance of a citation.

The city's justifications fall far short of rationalizing the extraordinary intrusion on Gail Atwater and her children. Measuring the degree to which Atwater's custodial arrest was needed for the promotion of legitimate governmental interests against the degree to which it intruded upon her privacy, it can hardly be doubted that Turek's actions were disproportionate to Atwater's crime. The majority's assessment that "Atwater's claim to live free of pointless indignity and confinement clearly outweighs anything the City can raise against it specific to her case," is quite correct. In my view, the Fourth Amendment inquiry ends there.

The Court's error, however, does not merely affect the disposition of this case. The *per se* rule that the Court creates has potentially serious consequences for the everyday lives of Americans. A broad range of conduct falls into the category of fine-only misdemeanors. In Texas alone, for example, disobeying any sort of traffic warning sign is a misdemeanor punishable only by fine, as is failing to pay a highway toll, and driving with expired license plates. Nor are fine-only crimes limited to the traffic context. In several States, for example, littering is a criminal offense punishable only by fine.

To be sure, such laws are valid and wise exercises of the States' power to protect the public health and welfare. My concern lies not with the decision to enact or enforce these laws, but rather with the manner in which they may be enforced. Under today's holding, when a police officer has probable cause to believe that a fine-only misdemeanor offense has occurred, that officer may stop the suspect, issue a citation, and let the person continue on her way. Or, if a traffic violation, the officer may stop the car, arrest the driver, search the driver, and impound the car and inventory all of its contents. Although the Fourth Amendment expressly requires that the latter course be a reasonable and proportional response to the circumstances of the offense, the majority gives officers unfettered discretion to choose that course without articulating a single reason why such action is appropriate.

Such unbounded discretion carries with it grave potential for abuse. The majority takes comfort in the lack of evidence of "an epidemic of unnecessary minor-offense arrests." But the relatively small number of published cases dealing with such arrests proves little and should provide little solace. Indeed, as the recent debate over racial profiling demonstrates all too clearly, a relatively minor traffic infraction may often serve as an excuse for stopping and harassing an individual. After today, the arsenal available to any officer extends to a full arrest and the searches permissible concomitant to that arrest. An officer's subjective motivations for making a traffic stop are not relevant considerations in determining the reasonableness of the stop. But it is precisely because these motivations are beyond our purview that we must vigilantly ensure that officers' poststop actions—which are properly within our reach— comport with the Fourth Amendment's guarantee of reasonableness.

In *Virginia v. Moore*, the Supreme Court held that even when an arrest for a minor offense is improper under state law, there is no Fourth Amendment violation as long as the police had the requisite probable cause.

VIRGINIA V. MOORE
553 U.S. 164 (2008)

Police arrested David Lee Moore for the misdemeanor of driving with a suspended license. The police searched Moore incident to the arrest and found that he was carrying crack cocaine. Moore was charged with possessing cocaine with the intent to distribute it. Under Virginia state law, the officers should have issued Moore a summons instead of arresting him because driving on a suspended license is not ordinarily an arrestable offense. Accordingly, Moore moved to suppress the cocaine found during the search incident to his improper arrest.

Virginia law does not, as a general matter, require suppression of evidence obtained in violation of state law, so Moore argued that suppression was required by the Fourth Amendment. The Virginia Supreme Court reversed Moore's conviction, holding that because the arresting officers should have issued Moore a citation under state law— and because the Fourth Amendment does not permit a search incident to citation under *Knowles v. Iowa*, 525 U.S. 113 (1998)—the search incident to the arrest violated the Fourth Amendment.

The U.S. Supreme Court held that even though Moore's arrest was improper under state law, it did not violate the Fourth Amendment: "In a long line of cases, we have said that when an officer has probable cause to believe a person committed even a minor crime in his presence, the balancing of private and public interests is not in doubt. The arrest is constitutionally reasonable." The Court went on to note that while states remain free to impose more stringent limits on police conduct than those required by the federal Constitution, "state law [does] not alter the content of the Fourth Amendment." To hold otherwise and incorporate state law arrest limitations into the Constitution "would produce a constitutional regime no less vague and unpredictable" than the one rejected in *Atwater v. City of Lago Vista*, 532 U.S. 318 (2001), since the "constitutional standard would only be as easy to apply as the underlying state law, and state law can be complicated indeed." Moreover, "linking Fourth Amendment protections to state law would cause them to vary from place to place and time to time."

In rejecting Moore's constitutional challenge, the Supreme Court summarized its holding as follows:

> We conclude that warrantless arrests for crimes committed in the presence of an arresting officer are reasonable under the Constitution, and that while States are free to regulate such arrests however they desire, state restrictions do not alter the Fourth Amendment's protections.

For What Crimes May a Person Be Arrested?

1.   If an officer has probable cause to believe that an individual has committed even a very minor criminal offense in his presence, the officer may, without violating the Fourth Amendment, arrest the offender. The Supreme Court has not decided whether the Fourth Amendment permits an officer to make a warrantless arrest in public for a minor offense that did not occur in the officer's presence.

2.   Even when an arrest for a minor offense is improper under state law, there is no Fourth Amendment violation as long as the arrest was based on probable cause.

CHAPTER 7

THE FOURTH AMENDMENT IN SPECIAL CONTEXTS

■ ■ ■

The Supreme Court often confronts Fourth Amendment issues in contexts beyond the ordinary criminal investigations that have produced many of the core doctrines in Investigative Criminal Procedure. These special contexts are sometimes classified, doctrinally, as additional exceptions to the warrant requirement. Alternatively, these special contexts are sometimes described as "special needs" situations in which strong government health, safety, and security considerations, balanced against limited privacy interests, justify dispensing with the traditional Fourth Amendment requirements of probable cause and a warrant.

Although the situations in which these Fourth Amendment problems arise are sometimes defined as "special," they are by no means uncommon. Indeed, virtually all children and adults will encounter many of these situations—safety inspections of homes and businesses, searches at or near the border, vehicle checkpoints, airport passenger screening, searches of students in public schools, and drug testing programs—at some point in their lives.

As you consider each of the special contexts surveyed in this Chapter, consider whether you believe the Supreme Court has struck an appropriate balance between the privacy rights of individuals and the safety and security concerns of law enforcement.

A. ADMINISTRATIVE SEARCHES

Local governments across the country have a variety of programs in place that permit or require routine inspections of homes, businesses, and buildings for compliance with health and safety regulations. The government inspectors who perform these "administrative searches" are not usually police officers, but their actions can be every bit as intrusive and intimidating, and their investigations can expose occupants of the property to civil and criminal liability.

Most administrative searches proceed without any difficulty, based upon the consent of the property owner. But what happens when a property owner refuses to permit the inspection? Can the property owner be arrested? Must the inspector secure a search warrant?

In *Camara v. Municipal Court*, the Supreme Court held that administrative searches are subject to the Fourth Amendment, but the probable cause and warrant requirements are somewhat different—and less stringent—than those imposed in criminal investigations.

CAMARA V. MUNICIPAL COURT OF THE CITY AND COUNTY OF SAN FRANCISCO

387 U.S. 523 (1967)

JUSTICE WHITE delivered the opinion of the Court.

In *Frank v. State of Maryland*, 359 U.S. 360 (1959), this Court upheld, by a five-to-four vote, a state court conviction of a homeowner who refused to permit a municipal health inspector to enter and inspect his premises without a search warrant. Since [that] closely divided decision, more intensive efforts at all levels of government to contain and eliminate urban blight have led to increasing use of such inspection techniques, while numerous decisions of this Court have more fully defined the Fourth Amendment's effect on state and municipal action. In view of the growing nationwide importance of the problem, we noted probable jurisdiction to re-examine whether administrative inspection programs, as presently authorized and conducted, violate Fourth Amendment rights as those rights are enforced against the States through the Fourteenth Amendment.

On November 6, 1963, an inspector of the Division of Housing Inspection of the San Francisco Department of Public Health entered an apartment building to make a routine annual inspection for possible violations of the city's Housing Code. The building's manager informed the inspector that appellant, lessee of the ground floor, was using the rear of his leasehold as a personal residence. Claiming that the building's occupancy permit did not allow residential use of the ground floor, the inspector confronted appellant and demanded that he permit an inspection of the premises. Appellant refused to allow the inspection because the inspector lacked a search warrant.

The inspector returned on November 8, again without a warrant, and appellant again refused to allow an inspection. A citation was then mailed ordering appellant to appear at the district attorney's office. When appellant failed to appear, two inspectors returned to his apartment on November 22. They informed appellant that he was required by law to permit an inspection under the Housing Code. Appellant nevertheless refused the inspectors access to his apartment without a search warrant. Thereafter, a complaint was filed charging him with refusing to permit a lawful inspection. Appellant was arrested on December 2 and released on bail.

I

The basic purpose of [the Fourth] Amendment, as recognized in countless decisions of this Court, is to safeguard the privacy and security of individuals against arbitrary invasions by governmental officials. Though there has been general agreement as to the fundamental purpose of the Fourth Amendment, translation of the abstract prohibition against "unreasonable searches and seizures" into workable guidelines for the decision of particular cases is a difficult task which has for many years divided the members of this Court. Nevertheless, one governing principle, justified by history and by current experience, has consistently been followed: except in certain carefully defined classes of cases, a search of private property without proper consent is "unreasonable" unless it has been authorized by a valid search warrant.

We may agree that a routine inspection of the physical condition of private property is a less hostile intrusion than the typical policeman's search for the fruits and instrumentalities of crime. But we cannot agree that the Fourth Amendment interests at stake in these inspection cases are merely peripheral. It is surely anomalous to say that the individual and his private property are fully protected by the Fourth Amendment only when the individual is suspected of criminal behavior. For instance, even the most law-abiding citizen has a very tangible interest in limiting the circumstances under which the sanctity of his home may be broken by official authority, for the possibility of criminal entry under the guise of official sanction is a serious threat to personal and family security. Inspections of the kind we are here considering do in fact jeopardize self-protection interests of the property owner. Like most regulatory laws, fire, health, and housing codes are enforced by criminal processes. In some cities, discovery of a violation by the inspector leads to a criminal complaint. Even in cities where discovery of a violation produces only an administrative compliance order, refusal to comply is a criminal offense, and the fact of compliance is verified by a second inspection, again without a warrant. Finally, as this case demonstrates, refusal to permit an inspection is itself a crime, punishable by fine or even by jail sentence.

Appellee asserts two other justifications for permitting administrative health and safety inspections without a warrant. First, it is argued that these inspections are designed to make the least possible demand on the individual occupant. The ordinances authorizing inspections are hedged with safeguards, and at any rate the inspector's particular decision to enter must comply with the constitutional standard of reasonableness even if he may enter without a warrant. In addition, the argument proceeds, the warrant process could not function effectively in this field. The decision to inspect an entire municipal area is based upon legislative or administrative assessment of broad factors such as the area's age and condition. Unless the magistrate is to review such policy matters, he must issue a "rubber stamp" warrant which provides no protection at all to the property owner.

In our opinion, these arguments unduly discount the purposes behind the warrant machinery contemplated by the Fourth Amendment. Under the present system, when the inspector demands entry, the occupant has no way of knowing whether enforcement of the municipal code involved requires inspection of his premises, no way of knowing the lawful limits of the inspector's power to search, and no way of knowing whether the inspector himself is acting under proper authorization. These are questions which may be reviewed by a neutral magistrate without any reassessment of the basic agency decision to canvass an area. Yet, only by refusing entry and risking a criminal conviction can the occupant at present challenge the inspector's decision to search. And even if the occupant possesses sufficient fortitude to take this risk, as appellant did here, he may never learn any more about the reason for the inspection than that the law generally allows housing inspectors to gain entry. The practical effect of this system is to leave the occupant subject to the discretion of the official in the field. This is precisely the discretion to invade private property which we have consistently circumscribed by a requirement that a disinterested party warrant the need to search. We simply cannot say that the protections provided by the warrant procedure are not needed in this context; broad statutory safeguards are no substitute for individualized review, particularly when those safeguards may only be invoked at the risk of a criminal penalty.

The final justification suggested for warrantless administrative searches is that the public interest demands such a rule: it is vigorously argued that the health and safety of entire urban populations is dependent upon enforcement of minimum fire, housing, and sanitation standards, and that the only effective means of enforcing such codes is by routine systematized inspection of all physical structures. But we think this argument misses the mark. The question is not, at this stage at least, whether these inspections may be made, but whether they may be made without a warrant. For example, to say that gambling raids may not be made at the discretion of the police without a warrant is not necessarily to say that gambling raids may never be made. In assessing whether the public interest demands creation of a general exception to the Fourth Amendment's warrant requirement, the question is not whether the public interest justifies the type of search in question, but whether the authority to search should be evidenced by a warrant, which in turn depends in part upon whether the burden of obtaining a warrant is likely to frustrate the governmental purpose behind the search. It has nowhere been urged that fire, health, and housing code inspection programs could not achieve their goals within the confines of a reasonable search warrant requirement. Thus, we do not find the public need argument dispositive.

In summary, we hold that administrative searches of the kind at issue here are significant intrusions upon the interests protected by the Fourth Amendment, that such searches when authorized and conducted without a warrant procedure lack the traditional safeguards which the Fourth Amendment guarantees to the individual, and that the reasons put forth for upholding these warrantless searches are insufficient to justify so substantial a weakening of the Fourth Amendment's protections. Because of the nature of the municipal programs under consideration, however, these conclusions must be the beginning, not the end, of our inquiry.

II

Borrowing from more typical Fourth Amendment cases, appellant argues not only that code enforcement inspection programs must be circumscribed by a warrant procedure, but also that warrants should issue only when the inspector possesses probable cause to believe that a particular dwelling contains violations of the minimum standards prescribed by the code being enforced. We disagree.

In cases in which the Fourth Amendment requires that a warrant to search be obtained, "probable cause" is the standard by which a particular decision to search is tested against the constitutional mandate of reasonableness. To apply this standard, it is obviously necessary first to focus upon the governmental interest which allegedly justifies official intrusion upon the constitutionally protected interests of the private citizen. For example, in a criminal investigation, the police may undertake to recover specific stolen or contraband goods. But that public interest would hardly justify a sweeping search of an entire city conducted in the hope that these goods might be found. Consequently, a search for these goods, even with a warrant, is "reasonable" only when there is "probable cause" to believe that they will be uncovered in a particular dwelling.

Unlike the search pursuant to a criminal investigation, the inspection programs at issue here are aimed at securing city-wide compliance with minimum physical standards for private property. The primary governmental interest at stake is to prevent even the unintentional development of conditions which are hazardous to public health and safety. Because fires and epidemics may ravage large urban areas, because unsightly conditions adversely affect the economic values of neighboring structures, numerous courts have upheld the police power of municipalities to impose and enforce such minimum standards even upon existing structures. In determining whether a particular inspection is reasonable—and thus in determining whether there is probable cause to issue a warrant for that inspection—the need for the inspection must be weighed in terms of these reasonable goals of code enforcement.

There is unanimous agreement among those most familiar with this field that the only effective way to seek universal compliance with the minimum standards required by municipal codes is through routine periodic inspections of all structures. It is here that the probable cause debate is focused, for the agency's decision to conduct an area inspection is unavoidably based on its appraisal of conditions in the area as a whole, not on its knowledge of conditions in each particular building. Appellee contends that, if the probable cause standard urged by appellant is adopted, the area inspection will be eliminated as a means of seeking compliance with code standards and the reasonable goals of code enforcement will be dealt a crushing blow.

In meeting this contention, appellant argues first, that his probable cause standard would not jeopardize area inspection programs because only a minute portion of the population will refuse to consent to such inspections, and second, that individual privacy in any event should be given preference to the public interest in conducting such inspections. The first argument, even if true, is irrelevant to the question whether the area inspection is reasonable within the meaning of the Fourth Amendment. The second argument is in effect an assertion that the area inspection is an unreasonable search. Unfortunately, there can be no ready test for determining reasonableness other than by balancing the need to search against the invasion which the search entails. But we think that a number of persuasive factors combine to support the reasonableness of area code-enforcement inspections. First, such programs have a long history of judicial and public acceptance. Second, the public interest demands that all dangerous conditions be prevented or abated, yet it is doubtful that any other canvassing technique would achieve acceptable results. Many such conditions—faulty wiring is an obvious example—are not observable from outside the building and indeed may not be apparent to the inexpert occupant himself. Finally, because the inspections are neither personal in nature nor aimed at the discovery of evidence of crime, they involve a relatively limited invasion of the urban citizen's privacy.

Having concluded that the area inspection is a "reasonable" search of private property within the meaning of the Fourth Amendment, it is obvious that "probable cause" to issue a warrant to inspect must exist if reasonable legislative or administrative standards for conducting an area inspection are satisfied with respect to a particular dwelling. Such standards, which will vary with the municipal program being enforced, may be based upon the passage of time, the nature of the building (e.g., a multifamily apartment house), or the condition of the entire area, but they will not necessarily depend upon specific knowledge of the condition of the particular dwelling. It has been suggested that so to vary the probable cause test from the standard applied in criminal cases would be to authorize a "synthetic search warrant" and thereby to lessen the overall protections of the Fourth Amendment. But we do not agree. The warrant procedure is designed to guarantee that a decision to search private property is justified by a reasonable governmental interest. But reasonableness is still the ultimate standard. If a valid public interest justifies the intrusion contemplated, then there is probable cause to issue a suitably restricted search warrant. Such an approach neither endangers time-honored doctrines applicable to criminal investigations nor makes a nullity of the probable cause requirement in this area. It merely gives full recognition to the competing public and private interests here at stake and, in so doing, best fulfills the historic purpose behind the constitutional right to be free from unreasonable government invasions of privacy.

III

Since our holding emphasizes the controlling standard of reasonableness, nothing we say today is intended to foreclose prompt inspections, even without a warrant, that the law has traditionally upheld in emergency situations. On the other hand, in the case of most routine area inspections, there is no compelling urgency to inspect at a particular time or on a particular day. Moreover, most citizens allow inspections of their property without a warrant. Thus, as a practical matter and in light of the Fourth Amendment's requirement that a warrant specify the property to be searched, it seems likely that warrants should normally be sought only after entry is refused unless there has been a citizen complaint or there is other satisfactory reason for securing immediate entry. Similarly, the requirement of a warrant procedure does not suggest any change in what seems to be the prevailing local policy, in most situations, of authorizing entry, but not entry by force, to inspect.

IV

In this case, appellant has been charged with a crime for his refusal to permit housing inspectors to enter his leasehold without a warrant. There was no emergency demanding immediate access; in fact, the inspectors made three trips to the building in an attempt to obtain appellant's consent to search. Yet no warrant was obtained and thus appellant was unable to verify either the need for or the appropriate limits of the inspection. No doubt, the inspectors entered the public portion of the building with the consent of the landlord, through the building's manager, but appellee does not contend that such consent was sufficient to authorize inspection of appellant's premises. Assuming the facts to be as the parties have alleged, we therefore conclude that appellant had a constitutional right to insist that the inspectors obtain a warrant to search and that appellant may not constitutionally be convicted for refusing to consent to the inspection.

In *See v. City of Seattle*, a companion case to *Camara*, the Supreme Court held that the Fourth Amendment also protects commercial property against warrantless administrative intrusions. Consistent with its longstanding interpretation of the Fourth Amendment, the Court did note, however, that commercial property may be inspected in many more situations than private homes.

SEE V. CITY OF SEATTLE
387 U.S. 541 (1967)

Norman See was convicted for refusing to permit a representative of the Seattle Fire Department to enter and inspect his locked commercial warehouse without a warrant and without probable cause to believe that there was a violation of any municipal ordinance. The inspection was conducted as part of a routine, periodic city-wide canvass to ensure compliance with the local fire code.

Relying heavily on its decision in *Camara v. Municipal Court*, the Supreme Court concluded that administrative searches of commercial property—like administrative searches of residential property—can only be enforced through an appropriate warrant procedure:

> We conclude that administrative entry, without consent, upon the portions of commercial premises which are not open to the public may only be compelled through prosecution or physical force within the framework of a warrant procedure. We do not in any way imply that business premises may not reasonably be inspected in many more situations than private homes, nor do we question such accepted regulatory techniques as licensing programs which require inspections prior to operating a business or marketing a product. Any constitutional challenge to such programs can only be resolved, as many have been in the past, on a case-by-case basis under the general Fourth Amendment standard of reasonableness. We hold only that the basic component of a reasonable search under the Fourth Amendment—that it not be enforced without a suitable warrant procedure—is applicable in this context, as in others, to business as well as to residential premises. Therefore, appellant may not be prosecuted for exercising his constitutional right to insist that the fire inspector obtain a warrant authorizing entry upon appellant's locked warehouse.

In *New York v. Burger*, the Supreme Court upheld a warrantless administrative search of an automobile junkyard. Although the search was performed by police officers and exposed the owner to both administrative and criminal penalties, the Court concluded that the

Fourth Amendment permits warrantless administrative searches of commercial property in "closely regulated" industries.

NEW YORK V. BURGER
482 U.S. 691 (1987)

JUSTICE BLACKMUN delivered the opinion of the Court.

This case presents the question whether the warrantless search of an automobile junkyard, conducted pursuant to a statute authorizing such a search, falls within the exception to the warrant requirement for administrative inspections of pervasively regulated industries. The case also presents the question whether an otherwise proper administrative inspection is unconstitutional because the ultimate purpose of the regulatory statute pursuant to which the search is done—the deterrence of criminal behavior—is the same as that of penal laws, with the result that the inspection may disclose violations not only of the regulatory statute but also of the penal statutes.

I

Respondent Joseph Burger is the owner of a junkyard in Brooklyn, N.Y. His business consists, in part, of the dismantling of automobiles and the selling of their parts. His junkyard is an open lot with no buildings. A high metal fence surrounds it, wherein are located, among other things, vehicles and parts of vehicles. At approximately noon on November 17, 1982, Officer Joseph Vega and four other plainclothes officers, all members of the Auto Crimes Division of the New York City Police Department, entered respondent's junkyard to conduct an inspection pursuant to [New York law]. On any given day, the Division conducts from 5 to 10 inspections of vehicle dismantlers, automobile junkyards, and related businesses.

Upon entering the junkyard, the officers asked to see Burger's license and his "police book"—the record of the automobiles and parts in his possession. Burger replied that he had neither a license nor a police book. The officers then announced their intention to conduct an inspection. Burger did not object. In accordance with their practice, the officers copied down the Vehicle Identification Numbers (VINs) of several vehicles and parts of vehicles that were in the junkyard. After checking these numbers against a police computer, the officers determined that respondent was in possession of stolen vehicles and parts. Accordingly, Burger was arrested and charged with five counts of possession of stolen property and one count of unregistered operation as a vehicle dismantler.

II

The Court long has recognized that the Fourth Amendment's prohibition on unreasonable searches and seizures is applicable to commercial premises, as well as to private homes. *See v. City of Seattle*, 387 U.S. 541 (1967). An owner or operator of a business thus has an expectation of privacy in commercial property, which society is prepared to consider to be reasonable. This expectation exists not only with respect to traditional police searches conducted for the gathering of criminal evidence but also with respect to administrative inspections designed to enforce regulatory statutes. An expectation of privacy in commercial premises, however, is different from, and indeed less than, a similar expectation in an individual's home. This expectation is particularly attenuated in commercial property employed in "closely regulated" industries. Certain industries have such a history of government oversight that no reasonable expectation of privacy could exist for a proprietor over the stock of such an enterprise.

The Court first examined the problem of inspections of "closely regulated" businesses in two enterprises that had a long tradition of close government supervision. In *Colonnade Corp. v. U.S.*, 397 U.S. 72 (1970), it considered a warrantless search of a catering business pursuant to several federal revenue statutes authorizing the inspection of the premises of liquor dealers. Although the Court disapproved the search because the statute provided that a sanction be imposed when entry was refused, and because it did not authorize entry without a warrant as an alternative in this situation, it recognized that "the liquor industry [was] long subject to close supervision and inspection." We returned to this issue in *U.S. v. Biswell*, 406 U.S. 311 (1972), which involved a warrantless inspection of the premises of a pawnshop operator, who was federally licensed to sell sporting weapons pursuant to the Gun Control Act of 1968. While noting that "[f]ederal regulation of the interstate traffic in firearms is not as deeply rooted in history as is governmental control of the liquor industry," we nonetheless concluded that the warrantless inspections authorized by the Gun Control Act would "pose only limited threats to the dealer's justifiable expectations of privacy." We observed: "When a dealer chooses to engage in this pervasively regulated business and to accept a federal license, he does so with the knowledge that his business records, firearms, and ammunition will be subject to effective inspection."

Because the owner or operator of commercial premises in a "closely regulated" industry has a reduced expectation of privacy, the warrant and probable-cause requirements, which fulfill the traditional Fourth Amendment standard of reasonableness for a government search, have lessened application in this context. Rather, we conclude that, as in other situations of "special need," where the privacy interests of the owner are weakened and the government interests in regulating particular businesses are concomitantly heightened, a warrantless inspection of commercial premises may well be reasonable within the meaning of the Fourth Amendment.

This warrantless inspection, however, even in the context of a pervasively regulated business, will be deemed to be reasonable only so long as three criteria are met. First, there must be a substantial government interest that informs the regulatory scheme pursuant to which the inspection is made. Second, the warrantless inspections must be necessary to further the regulatory scheme. Finally, the statute's inspection program, in terms of the certainty and regularity of its application, must provide a constitutionally adequate substitute for a warrant. In other words, the regulatory statute must perform the two basic functions of a warrant: it must advise the owner of the commercial premises that the search is being made pursuant to the law and has a properly defined scope, and it must limit the discretion of the inspecting officers. To perform this first function, the statute must be sufficiently comprehensive and defined that the owner of commercial property cannot help but be aware that his property will be subject to periodic inspections undertaken for specific purposes. In addition, in defining how a statute limits the discretion of the inspectors, it must be carefully limited in time, place, and scope.

III

Searches made pursuant to [the New York law], in our view, clearly fall within this established exception to the warrant requirement for administrative inspections in "closely regulated" businesses. First, the nature of the regulatory statute reveals that the operation of a junkyard, part of which is devoted to vehicle dismantling, is a "closely regulated" business in the State of New York. The provisions regulating the activity of vehicle dismantling are extensive. An operator cannot engage in this industry without first obtaining a license, which means that he must meet the registration requirements and must pay a fee. The operator must maintain a police book recording the acquisition and disposition of motor vehicles and vehicle parts, and make such records and inventory available for inspection by the police or any agent of the Department of Motor Vehicles. The operator also must display his registration number prominently at his place of business, on business documentation, and on vehicles and parts that pass through his business. Moreover, the person engaged in this activity is subject to criminal penalties, as well as to loss of license or civil fines, for failure to comply with these provisions. That other States besides New York have imposed similarly extensive regulations on automobile junkyards further supports the "closely regulated" status of this industry.

Accordingly, in light of the regulatory framework governing his business and the history of regulation of related industries, an operator of a junkyard engaging in vehicle dismantling has a reduced expectation of privacy in this "closely regulated" business.

The New York regulatory scheme satisfies the three criteria necessary to make reasonable warrantless inspections. First, the State has a substantial interest in regulating the vehicle-dismantling and automobile-junkyard industry because motor vehicle theft has increased in the State and because the problem of theft is associated with this industry. In this day, automobile theft has become a significant social problem, placing enormous economic and personal burdens upon the citizens of different States.

Second, regulation of the vehicle-dismantling industry reasonably serves the State's substantial interest in eradicating automobile theft. It is well established that the theft problem can be addressed effectively by controlling the receiver of, or market in, stolen property. Automobile junkyards and vehicle dismantlers provide the major market for stolen vehicles and vehicle parts. Thus, the State rationally may believe that it will reduce car theft by regulations that prevent automobile junkyards from becoming markets for stolen vehicles and that help trace the origin and destination of vehicle parts. Moreover, the warrantless administrative inspections are necessary to further the regulatory scheme. In the present case, a warrant requirement would interfere with the statute's purpose of deterring automobile theft accomplished by identifying vehicles and parts as stolen and shutting down the market in such items. Because stolen cars and parts often pass quickly through an automobile junkyard, frequent and unannounced inspections are necessary in order to detect them. In sum, surprise is crucial if the regulatory scheme aimed at remedying this major social problem is to function at all.

Third, [the New York statute] provides a constitutionally adequate substitute for a warrant. The statute informs the operator of a vehicle dismantling business that inspections will be made on a regular basis. Thus, the vehicle dismantler knows that the inspections to which he is subject do not constitute discretionary acts by a government official but are conducted pursuant to statute. [The law] also sets forth the scope of the inspection and, accordingly, places the operator on notice as to how to comply with the statute. In addition, it notifies the operator as to who is authorized to conduct an inspection.

Finally, the time, place, and scope of the inspection is limited, to place appropriate restraints upon the discretion of the inspecting officers. The officers are allowed to conduct an inspection only during regular and usual business hours. The inspections can be made only of vehicle-dismantling and related industries. And the permissible scope of these searches is narrowly defined: the inspectors may examine the records, as well as "any vehicles or parts of vehicles which are subject to the record keeping requirements of this section and which are on the premises."

IV

A search conducted pursuant to [the New York law], therefore, clearly falls within the well-established exception to the warrant requirement for administrative inspections of "closely regulated" businesses. The [New York] Court of Appeals, nevertheless, struck down the statute as violative of the Fourth Amendment because, in its view, the statute had no truly administrative purpose but was "designed simply to give the police an expedient means of enforcing penal sanctions for possession of stolen property." The court rested its conclusion that the administrative goal of the statute was pretextual and that [it] really "authorize[d] searches undertaken solely to uncover evidence of criminality" particularly on the fact that, even if an operator failed to produce his police book, the inspecting officers could continue their inspection for stolen vehicles and parts. The court also suggested that the identity of the inspectors—police officers—was significant in revealing the true nature of the statutory scheme.

In arriving at this conclusion, the Court of Appeals failed to recognize that a State can address a major social problem *both* by way of an administrative scheme *and* through penal sanctions. Administrative statutes and penal laws may have the same *ultimate* purpose of remedying the social problem, but they have different subsidiary purposes and prescribe different methods of addressing the problem. An administrative statute establishes how a particular business in a "closely regulated" industry should be operated, setting forth rules to guide an operator's conduct of the business and allowing government officials to ensure that those rules are followed. Such a regulatory approach contrasts with that of the penal laws, a major emphasis of which is the punishment of individuals for specific acts of behavior.

This case reveals that an administrative scheme may have the same ultimate purpose as penal laws, even if its regulatory goals are narrower. As we have explained above, New York, like many States, faces a serious social problem in automobile theft and has a substantial interest in regulating the vehicle-dismantling industry because of this problem. The New York penal laws address automobile theft by punishing it or the possession of stolen property, including possession by individuals in the business of buying and selling property. In accordance with its interest in regulating the automobile-junkyard industry, the State also has devised a regulatory manner of dealing with this problem. [The statute,] as a whole, serves the regulatory goals of seeking to ensure that vehicle dismantlers are legitimate businesspersons and that stolen vehicles and vehicle parts passing through automobile junkyards can be identified.

Nor do we think that this administrative scheme is unconstitutional simply because, in the course of enforcing it, an inspecting officer may discover evidence of crimes, besides violations of the scheme itself. The discovery of evidence of crimes in the course of an otherwise proper administrative inspection does not render that search illegal or the administrative scheme suspect.

Finally, we fail to see any constitutional significance in the fact that police officers, rather than "administrative" agents, are permitted to conduct the inspection. The significance respondent alleges lies in the role of police officers as enforcers of the penal laws and in the officers' power to arrest for offenses other than violations of the administrative scheme. It is, however, important to note that state police officers, like those in New York, have numerous duties in addition to those associated with traditional police work. As a practical matter, many States do not have the resources to assign the enforcement of a particular administrative scheme to a specialized agency. So long as a regulatory scheme is properly administrative, it is not rendered illegal by the fact that the inspecting officer has the power to arrest individuals for violations other than those created by the scheme itself. In sum, we decline to impose upon the States the burden of requiring the enforcement of their regulatory statutes to be carried out by specialized agents.

JUSTICE BRENNAN, with whom JUSTICE MARSHALL and JUSTICE O'CONNOR join, dissenting.

Warrantless inspections of pervasively regulated businesses are valid if necessary to further an urgent state interest, and if authorized by a statute that carefully limits their time, place, and scope. I have no objection to this general rule. Today, however, the Court finds pervasive regulation in the barest of administrative schemes. Burger's vehicle-dismantling business is not closely regulated (unless most New York City businesses are), and an administrative warrant therefore was required to search it. The Court also perceives careful guidance and control of police discretion in a statute that is patently insufficient to eliminate the need for a warrant. Finally, the Court characterizes as administrative a search for evidence of only criminal wrongdoing. As a result, the Court renders virtually meaningless the general rule that a warrant is required for administrative searches of commercial property.

In *See v. City of Seattle*, 387 U.S. 541 (1967), we held that an administrative search of commercial property generally must be supported by a warrant. We make an exception to this rule, and dispense with the warrant requirement, in cases involving "closely regulated" industries, where we believe that the commercial operator's privacy interest is adequately protected by detailed regulatory schemes authorizing warrantless inspections.[2] The Court has previously made

---

[2] In only three industries have we invoked this exception. See *Colonnade Catering Corp. v. U.S.*, 397 U.S. 72 (1970) (liquor industry); *U.S. v. Biswell*, 406 U.S. 311 (1972) (firearm and ammunitions sales); *Donovan v. Dewey*, 452 U.S. 594 (1981) (coal mining).

clear that "the closely regulated industry is the exception." Unfortunately, today's holding makes it the rule.

The provisions governing vehicle dismantling in New York simply are not extensive. A vehicle dismantler must register and pay a fee, display the registration in various circumstances, maintain a police book, and allow inspections. Of course, the inspections themselves cannot be cited as proof of pervasive regulation justifying elimination of the warrant requirement; that would be obvious bootstrapping. Nor can registration and recordkeeping requirements be characterized as close regulation. New York City, like many States and municipalities, imposes similar, and often more stringent licensing, recordkeeping, and other regulatory requirements on a myriad of trades and businesses. Few substantive qualifications are required of an aspiring vehicle dismantler; no regulation governs the condition of the premises, the method of operation, the hours of operation, the equipment utilized, etc. In sum, if New York City's administrative scheme renders the vehicle-dismantling business closely regulated, few businesses will escape such a finding. Under these circumstances, the warrant requirement is the exception, not the rule, and *See* has been constructively overruled.

Even if vehicle dismantling were a closely regulated industry, I would nonetheless conclude that this search violated the Fourth Amendment. The warrant requirement protects the owner of a business from the unbridled discretion of executive and administrative officers by ensuring that reasonable legislative or administrative standards for conducting an inspection are satisfied with respect to a particular business. In order to serve as the equivalent of a warrant, an administrative statute must create a predictable and guided governmental presence. [The New York statute] does not approach the level of certainty and regularity of application necessary to provide a constitutionally adequate substitute for a warrant.

The statute does not inform the operator of a vehicle-dismantling business that inspections will be made on a regular basis; in fact, there is *no* assurance that any inspections at all will occur. There is neither an upper nor a lower limit on the number of searches that may be conducted at any given operator's establishment in any given time period. Neither the statute, nor any regulations, nor any regulatory body, provides limits or guidance on the selection of vehicle dismantlers for inspection. In fact, the State could not explain why Burger's operation was selected for inspection.

The implications of the Court's opinion, if realized, will virtually eliminate Fourth Amendment protection of commercial entities in the context of administrative searches. No State may require, as a condition of doing business, a blanket submission to warrantless searches for any purpose. I respectfully dissent.

Administrative Searches

1.   Most administrative searches and inspections of residential property proceed without any difficulty, based on the consent of the property owner or an occupant. But if the owner or occupant refuses to permit an administrative search, and there is no emergency justifying a warrantless entry, the inspector must secure a warrant based upon probable cause. Probable cause to issue an inspection warrant exists if reasonable legislative or administrative standards for conducting an area inspection are satisfied with respect to a particular dwelling. Such standards may be based upon the passage of time, the nature of the building (a multifamily apartment house, for example), or the condition of the entire area, but they will not necessarily depend upon specific knowledge of the condition of the particular dwelling.

2.   Business premises may reasonably be inspected in many more situations than private homes, and most administrative searches and inspections of commercial property also proceed without any difficulty, based upon the consent of the owner or an occupant. But if the owner or occupant refuses entry, the inspector must secure a warrant based upon probable cause in order to inspect those portions of the commercial property that are not open to the public.

3.   Warrantless administrative inspections in "closely regulated" industries will be deemed reasonable under the Fourth Amendment provided three criteria are met:

   a.   There must be a substantial government interest that informs the regulatory scheme pursuant to which the inspection is made.

   b.   The warrantless inspections must be necessary to further the regulatory scheme.

   c.   The statutory inspection program, in terms of the certainty and regularity of its application, must provide a constitutionally adequate substitute for a warrant.

      i.   The statute must be sufficiently comprehensive and defined that the owner of commercial property cannot help but be aware that his property will be subject to periodic inspections undertaken for specific purposes.

      ii.   The statute must limit the discretion of the inspectors with restrictions on time, place, and scope.

4.   An administrative inspection program is not unconstitutional because it is carried out by police officers or because an inspecting officer may discover evidence of crimes other than violations of the inspection program itself.

B.   STOPS AND SEARCHES AT AND
NEAR THE BORDER

The Supreme Court has given the government broad authority to police our nation's borders through routine warrantless stops and searches of people, vehicles, and mail entering the United States. The Court has been somewhat less deferential, however, with respect to stops and searches that are discretionary, or highly invasive, or that occur some distance from the border. These non-routine stops and searches may still generally proceed without a warrant, but they must often be justified by reasonable suspicion.

The government's authority to stop and search is at its zenith at the border itself or at its functional equivalent—for example, the airport where an international flight lands in the U.S., or the location where a ship docks in the U.S. after arriving from foreign waters. The government's authority to stop and search *near* the border—to identify and apprehend illegal aliens, to intercept illegal drugs, or for some other purpose—is more limited.

1.   STOPS AND SEARCHES AT THE BORDER OR ITS FUNCTIONAL EQUIVALENT

In *U.S. v. Ramsey*, the Supreme Court held that mail entering the U.S. may be inspected without a warrant and without probable cause. The statute authorizing the inspection did, however, require officials to have "reasonable cause to suspect" a violation of the customs laws.

U.S. V. RAMSEY
431 U.S. 606 (1977)

JUSTICE REHNQUIST delivered the opinion of the Court.

Charles W. Ramsey and James W. Kelly jointly commenced a heroin-by-mail enterprise in the Washington, D.C., area. The process involved their procuring of heroin, which was mailed in letters from Bangkok, Thailand, and sent to various locations in the District of Columbia area for collection. Two of their suppliers, Sylvia Bailey and William Ward, who were located in West Germany, were engaged in international narcotics trafficking during the latter part of 1973 and the early part of 1974. West German agents, pursuant to court-authorized electronic surveillance, intercepted several trans-Atlantic conversations between Bailey and Ramsey during which their narcotics operation was discussed. By late January 1974, Bailey and Ward had gone to Thailand. Thai officials, alerted to their presence by West German authorities, placed them under surveillance. Ward was observed mailing letter-sized envelopes in six different mail boxes; five of these envelopes were recovered; and one of the addresses in Washington, D.C., was later linked to respondents. Bailey and Ward were arrested by Thai officials on February 2, 1974; among the items seized were eleven heroin-filed envelopes addressed to the Washington, D.C., area, and later connected with respondents.

Two days after this arrest of Bailey and Ward, Inspector George Kallnischkies, a United States customs officer in New York City, without any knowledge of the foregoing events, inspecting a sack of incoming international mail from Thailand, spotted eight envelopes that were bulky and which he believed might contain merchandise. The envelopes, all of which appeared to him to have been typed on the same typewriter, were addressed to four different locations in the Washington, D.C., area. Inspector Kallnischkies, based on the fact that the letters were from Thailand, a known source of narcotics, and were "rather bulky," suspected that the envelopes might contain merchandise or contraband rather than correspondence. He took the letters to an examining area in the post office, and felt one of the letters: It "felt like there was something in there, in the envelope. It was not just plain paper that the envelope is supposed to contain." He weighed one of the envelopes, and found it weighed 42 grams, some three to six times the normal weight of an airmail letter. Inspector Kallnischkies then opened that envelope: "In there I saw some cardboard and between the cardboard, if I recall, there was a plastic bag containing a white powdered substance, which, based on experience, I knew from Thailand would be heroin. I went ahead and removed a sample. Gave it a field test, a Marquis Reagent field test, and I had a positive reaction for heroin."

He proceeded to open the other seven envelopes which "in a lot of ways were identical"; examination revealed that at least the contents were in fact identical: each contained heroin.

The envelopes were then sent to Washington in a locked pouch where agents of the Drug Enforcement Administration, after obtaining a search warrant, opened the envelopes again and removed most of the heroin. The envelopes were then resealed, and six of them were delivered under surveillance. After Kelly collected the envelopes from the three different addressees, rendezvoused with Ramsey, and gave Ramsey a brown paper bag, federal agents arrested both of them. The bag contained the six envelopes with heroin, $1,100 in cash, and "cutting" material for the heroin.

Congress and the applicable postal regulations authorized the actions undertaken in this case. Title 19 U.S.C. § 482 explicitly deals with the search of an "envelope": "Any of the officers or persons authorized to board or search vessels may . . . search any trunk or envelope, wherever found, in which he may have a reasonable cause to suspect there is merchandise which was imported contrary to law." This provision authorizes customs officials to inspect, under the circumstances therein stated, incoming international mail. The "reasonable cause to suspect" test adopted by the statute is, we think, a practical test which imposes a less stringent requirement than that of "probable cause" imposed by the Fourth Amendment as a requirement for the issuance of warrants. Inspector Kallnischkies, at the time he opened the letters, knew that they were from Thailand, were bulky, were many times the weight of a normal airmail letter, and "felt like there was something in there." Under these circumstances, we have no doubt that he had reasonable "cause to suspect" that there was merchandise or contraband in the envelopes. The search, therefore, was plainly authorized by the statute.

Since the search in this case was authorized by statute, we are left simply with the question of whether the search nevertheless violated the Constitution. That searches made at the border, pursuant to the long-standing right of the sovereign to protect itself by stopping and examining persons and property crossing into this country, are reasonable simply by virtue of the fact that they occur at the border, should, by now, require no extended demonstration. The Congress which proposed the Bill of Rights, including the Fourth Amendment, to the state legislatures had, some two months prior to that proposal, enacted the first customs statute. Section 24 of this statute granted customs officials "full power and authority" to enter and search "any ship or vessel, in which they shall have reason to suspect any goods, wares or merchandise subject to duty shall be concealed." This acknowledgement of plenary customs power was differentiated from the more limited power to enter and search "any particular dwelling-house, store, building, or other place" where a warrant upon "cause to suspect" was required. The historical importance of the enactment of this customs statute by the same Congress which proposed the Fourth Amendment is, we think, manifest.

Border searches, then, from before the adoption of the Fourth Amendment, have been considered to be "reasonable" by the single fact that the person or item in question had entered into our country from outside. There has never been any additional requirement that the reasonableness of a border search depended on the existence of probable cause. This longstanding recognition that searches at our borders without probable cause and without a warrant are nonetheless "reasonable" has a history as old as the Fourth Amendment itself. We reaffirm it now.

Respondents urge upon us, however, the position that mailed letters are somehow different, and, whatever may be the normal rule with respect to border searches, different considerations, requiring the full panoply of Fourth Amendment protections, apply to international mail. The Court of Appeals agreed, and felt that whatever the rule may be with respect to travelers, their baggage, and even mailed packages, it would not "extend" the border-search exception to include mailed letter-size envelopes. We do not agree that this inclusion of letters within the border-search exception represents any "extension" of that exception.

The border-search exception is grounded in the recognized right of the sovereign to control, subject to substantive limitations imposed by the Constitution, who and what may enter the country. It is clear that there is nothing in the rationale behind the border-search exception which suggests that the mode of entry will be critical. It was conceded at oral argument that customs officials could search, without probable cause and without a warrant, envelopes carried by an entering traveler, whether in his luggage or on his person. Surely no different constitutional standard should apply simply because the envelopes were mailed, not carried. The critical fact is that the envelopes cross the border and enter this country, not that they are brought in by one mode of transportation rather than another. It is their entry into this country from without it that makes a resulting search "reasonable."

We therefore conclude that the Fourth Amendment does not interdict the actions taken by Inspector Kallnischkies in opening and searching the eight envelopes.

JUSTICE STEVENS, with whom JUSTICE BRENNAN and JUSTICE MARSHALL join, dissenting.

The decisive question in this case is whether Congress has granted customs officials the authority to open and inspect personal letters entering the United States from abroad without the knowledge or consent of the sender or the addressee, and without probable cause to believe the mail contains contraband or dutiable merchandise. I am convinced that Congress did not authorize the kind of secret searches of private mail that the Executive here conducted.

If the Government is allowed to exercise the power it claims, the door will be open to the wholesale, secret examination of all incoming international letter mail. No notice would be necessary either before or after the search. Until Congress has made an unambiguous policy decision that such an unprecedented intrusion upon a vital method of personal communication is in the Nation's interest, this Court should not address the serious constitutional question it decides today.

––––––––––––––––

In *U.S. v. Flores-Montano*, the Supreme Court held that border officials may detain a vehicle and disassemble the gas tank without a warrant, probable cause, or even reasonable suspicion. The Court regarded the length and scope of the intrusion as relatively minor compared to the government's important interest in preventing drugs from entering the country.

U.S. v. FLORES-MONTANO

541 U.S. 149 (2004)

CHIEF JUSTICE REHNQUIST delivered the opinion of the Court.

Customs officials seized 37 kilograms—a little more than 81 pounds—of marijuana from respondent Manuel Flores-Montano's gas tank at the international border. The Court of Appeals for the Ninth Circuit held that the Fourth Amendment forbade the fuel tank search absent reasonable suspicion. We hold that the search in question did not require reasonable suspicion.

Respondent, driving a 1987 Ford Taurus station wagon, attempted to enter the United States at the Otay Mesa Port of Entry in southern California. A customs inspector conducted an inspection of the station wagon, and requested respondent to leave the vehicle. The vehicle was then taken to a secondary inspection station.

At the secondary station, a second customs inspector inspected the gas tank by tapping it, and noted that the tank sounded solid. Subsequently, the inspector requested a mechanic under contract with Customs to come to the border station to remove the tank. Within 20 to 30 minutes, the mechanic arrived. He raised the car on a hydraulic lift, loosened the straps and unscrewed the bolts holding the gas tank to the undercarriage of the vehicle, and then disconnected some hoses and electrical connections. After the gas tank was removed, the inspector hammered off bondo (a putty-like hardening substance that is used to seal openings) from the top of the gas tank. The inspector opened an access plate underneath the bondo and found 37 kilograms of marijuana bricks. The process took 15 to 25 minutes.

A grand jury for the Southern District of California indicted respondent on one count of unlawfully importing marijuana and one count of possession of marijuana with intent to distribute. Respondent filed a motion to suppress the marijuana recovered from the gas tank.

The Government advised the District Court that it was not relying on reasonable suspicion as a basis for denying respondent's suppression motion. The District Court held that reasonable suspicion was required to justify the search and, accordingly, granted respondent's motion to suppress. The Court of Appeals summarily affirmed the District Court's judgment. We granted certiorari, and now reverse.

The Court of Appeals seized on language from our opinion in *U.S. v. Montoya de Hernandez*, 473 U.S. 531 (1985), in which we used the word "routine" as a descriptive term in discussing border searches ("Routine searches of the persons and effects of entrants are not subject to any requirement of reasonable suspicion, probable cause, or warrant"); ("Because the issues are not presented today we suggest no view on what level of suspicion, if any, is required for nonroutine border searches such as strip, body-cavity, or involuntary x-ray searches"). The Court of Appeals took the term "routine," fashioned a new balancing test, and extended it to searches of vehicles. But the reasons that might support a requirement of some level of suspicion in the case of highly intrusive searches of the person—dignity and privacy interests of the person being searched—simply do not carry over to vehicles. Complex balancing tests to determine what is a "routine" search of a vehicle, as opposed to a more "intrusive" search of a person, have no place in border searches of vehicles.

The Government's interest in preventing the entry of unwanted persons and effects is at its zenith at the international border. Time and again, we have stated that "searches made at the border, pursuant to the longstanding right of the sovereign to protect itself by stopping and examining persons and property crossing into this country, are reasonable simply by virtue of the fact that they occur at the border." *U.S. v. Ramsey*, 431 U.S. 606, 616 (1977). Congress, since the beginning of our Government, has granted the Executive plenary authority to conduct routine searches and seizures at the border, without probable cause or a warrant, in order to regulate the collection of duties and to prevent the introduction of contraband into this country. The modern statute that authorized the search in this case derived from a statute passed by the First Congress, and reflects the impressive historical pedigree of the Government's power and interest. It is axiomatic that the United States, as sovereign, has the inherent authority to protect, and a paramount interest in protecting, its territorial integrity.

That interest in protecting the borders is illustrated in this case by the evidence that smugglers frequently attempt to penetrate our borders with contraband secreted in their automobiles' fuel tank. Over the past 5 1/2 fiscal years, there have been 18,788 vehicle drug seizures at the southern California ports of entry. Of those 18,788, gas tank drug seizures have accounted for 4,619 of the vehicle drug seizures, or approximately 25%. In addition, instances of persons smuggled in and around gas tank compartments are discovered at the ports of entry of San Ysidro and Otay Mesa at a rate averaging 1 approximately every 10 days.

Respondent asserts two main arguments with respect to his Fourth Amendment interests. First, he urges that he has a privacy interest in his fuel tank, and that the suspicionless disassembly of his tank is an invasion of his privacy. But on many occasions, we have noted that the expectation of privacy is less at the border than it is in the interior. We have long recognized that automobiles seeking entry into this country may be searched. It is difficult to imagine how the search of a gas tank, which should be solely a repository for fuel, could be more of an invasion of privacy than the search of the automobile's passenger compartment.

Second, respondent argues that the Fourth Amendment protects property as well as privacy, and that the disassembly and reassembly of his gas tank is a significant deprivation of his property interest because it may damage the vehicle. He does not, and on the record cannot, truly contend that the procedure of removal, disassembly, and reassembly of the fuel tank in this case or any other has resulted in serious damage to, or destruction of, the property. According to the Government, for example, in fiscal year 2003, 348 gas tank searches conducted along the southern border were negative (*i.e.*, no contraband was found), the gas tanks were reassembled, and the vehicles continued their entry into the United States without incident.

Respondent cites not a single accident involving the vehicle or motorist in the many thousands of gas tank disassemblies that have occurred at the border. A gas tank search involves a brief procedure that can be reversed without damaging the safety or operation of the vehicle. If damage to a vehicle were to occur, the motorist might be entitled to recovery. While the interference with a motorist's possessory interest is not insignificant when the Government removes, disassembles, and reassembles his gas tank, it nevertheless is justified by the Government's paramount interest in protecting the border.[3]

For the reasons stated, we conclude that the Government's authority to conduct suspicionless inspections at the border includes the authority to remove, disassemble, and reassemble a vehicle's fuel tank. While it may be true that some searches of property are so destructive as to require a different result, this was not one of them.

———————

While border authorities may briefly stop and question travelers and search vehicles and property without a warrant and without any suspicion of wrongdoing, the Supreme Court has required reasonable suspicion for more intrusive searches or prolonged detentions. In *U.S. v. Montoya de Hernandez*, the Court upheld an extended detention of a traveler based on reasonable suspicion that she was smuggling drugs in her alimentary canal.

---

[3] Respondent also argued that he has some sort of Fourth Amendment right not to be subject to delay at the international border and that the need for the use of specialized labor, as well as the hour actual delay here and the potential for even greater delay for reassembly are an invasion of that right. Respondent points to no cases indicating the Fourth Amendment shields entrants from inconvenience or delay at the international border. The procedure in this case took about an hour (including the wait for the mechanic). At oral argument, the Government advised us that, depending on the type of car, a search involving the disassembly and reassembly of a gas tank may take one to two hours. We think it clear that delays of one to two hours at international borders are to be expected.

U.S. v. MONTOYA DE HERNANDEZ

473 U.S. 531 (1985)

JUSTICE REHNQUIST delivered the opinion of the Court.

Respondent Rosa Elvira Montoya de Hernandez was detained by customs officials upon her arrival at the Los Angeles Airport on a flight from Bogota, Colombia. She was found to be smuggling 88 cocaine-filled balloons in her alimentary canal, and was convicted after a bench trial of various federal narcotics offenses. A divided panel of the United States Court of Appeals for the Ninth Circuit reversed her convictions, holding that her detention violated the Fourth Amendment to the United States Constitution because the customs inspectors did not have a "clear indication" of alimentary canal smuggling at the time she was detained. Because of a conflict in the decisions of the Courts of Appeals on this question and the importance of its resolution to the enforcement of customs laws, we granted certiorari. We now reverse.

Respondent arrived at Los Angeles International Airport shortly after midnight, March 5, 1983, on Avianca Flight 080, a direct 10-hour flight from Bogota, Colombia. Her visa was in order so she was passed through Immigration and proceeded to the customs desk. At the customs desk she encountered Customs Inspector Talamantes, who reviewed her documents and noticed from her passport that she had made at least eight recent trips to either Miami or Los Angeles. Talamantes referred respondent to a secondary customs desk for further questioning. At this desk Talamantes and another inspector asked respondent general questions concerning herself and the purpose of her trip. Respondent revealed that she spoke no English and had no family or friends in the United States. She explained in Spanish that she had come to the United States to purchase goods for her husband's store in Bogota. The customs inspectors recognized Bogota as a "source city" for narcotics. Respondent possessed $5,000 in cash, mostly $50 bills, but had no billfold. She indicated to the inspectors that she had no appointments with merchandise vendors, but planned to ride around Los Angeles in taxicabs visiting retail stores such as J.C. Penney and K-Mart in order to buy goods for her husband's store with the $5,000.

Respondent admitted that she had no hotel reservations, but stated that she planned to stay at a Holiday Inn. Respondent could not recall how her airline ticket was purchased. When the inspectors opened respondent's one small valise they found about four changes of "cold weather" clothing. Respondent had no shoes other than the high-heeled pair she was wearing. Although respondent possessed no checks, waybills, credit cards, or letters of credit, she did produce a Colombian business card and a number of old receipts, waybills, and fabric swatches displayed in a photo album.

At this point Talamantes and the other inspector suspected that respondent was a "balloon swallower," one who attempts to smuggle narcotics into this country hidden in her alimentary canal. Over the years Inspector Talamantes had apprehended dozens of alimentary canal smugglers arriving on Avianca Flight 080.

The inspectors requested a female customs inspector to take respondent to a private area and conduct a patdown and strip search. During the search the female inspector felt respondent's abdomen area and noticed a firm fullness, as if respondent were wearing a girdle. The search revealed no contraband, but the inspector noticed that respondent was wearing two pairs of elastic underpants with a paper towel lining the crotch area.

When respondent returned to the customs area and the female inspector reported her discoveries, the inspector in charge told respondent that he suspected she was smuggling drugs in her alimentary canal. Respondent agreed to the inspector's request that she be x-rayed at a hospital but in answer to the inspector's query stated that she was pregnant. She agreed to a pregnancy test before the x-ray. Respondent withdrew the consent for an x-ray when she learned that she would have to be handcuffed en route to the hospital. The inspector then gave respondent the option of returning to Colombia on the next available flight, agreeing to an x-ray, or remaining in detention until she produced a monitored bowel movement that would confirm or rebut the inspectors' suspicions. Respondent chose the first option and was placed in a customs office under observation. She was told that if she went to the toilet she would have to use a wastebasket in the women's restroom, in order that female customs inspectors could inspect her stool for balloons or capsules carrying narcotics. The inspectors refused respondent's request to place a telephone call.

Respondent sat in the customs office, under observation, for the remainder of the night. During the night customs officials attempted to place respondent on a Mexican airline that was flying to Bogota via Mexico City in the morning. The airline refused to transport respondent because she lacked a Mexican visa necessary to land in Mexico City. Respondent was not permitted to leave, and was informed that she would be detained until she agreed to an x-ray or her bowels moved. She remained detained in the customs office under observation, for most of the time curled up in a chair leaning to one side. She refused all offers of food and drink, and refused to use the toilet facilities. The Court of Appeals noted that she exhibited symptoms of discomfort consistent with "heroic efforts to resist the usual calls of nature."

At the shift change at 4 o'clock the next afternoon, almost 16 hours after her flight had landed, respondent still had not defecated or urinated or partaken of food or drink. At that time customs officials sought a court order authorizing a pregnancy test, an x-ray, and a rectal examination. The Federal Magistrate issued an order just before midnight that evening, which authorized a rectal examination and involuntary x-ray, provided that the physician in charge considered respondent's claim of pregnancy. Respondent was taken to a hospital and given a pregnancy test, which later turned out to be negative. Before the results of the pregnancy test were known, a physician conducted a rectal examination and removed from respondent's rectum a balloon containing a foreign substance. Respondent was then placed formally under arrest. By 4:10 a.m. respondent had passed 6 similar balloons; over the next four days she passed 88 balloons containing a total of 528 grams of 80% pure cocaine hydrochloride.

After a suppression hearing the District Court admitted the cocaine in evidence against respondent. She was convicted of possession of cocaine with intent to distribute and unlawful importation of cocaine.

The Government contends that the customs inspectors reasonably suspected that respondent was an alimentary canal smuggler, and this suspicion was sufficient to justify the detention. In support of the judgment below respondent argues that reasonable suspicion would not support respondent's detention, and in any event the inspectors did not reasonably suspect that respondent was carrying narcotics internally.

The Fourth Amendment commands that searches and seizures be reasonable. What is reasonable depends upon all of the circumstances surrounding the search or seizure and the nature of the search or seizure itself. The permissibility of a particular law enforcement practice is judged by balancing its intrusion on the individual's Fourth Amendment interests against its promotion of legitimate governmental interests.

Here the seizure of respondent took place at the international border. Since the founding of our Republic, Congress has granted the Executive plenary authority to conduct routine searches and seizures at the border, without probable cause or a warrant, in order to regulate the collection of duties and to prevent the introduction of contraband into this country. This Court has long recognized Congress' power to police entrants at the border.

Consistently, therefore, with Congress' power to protect the Nation by stopping and examining persons entering this country, the Fourth Amendment's balance of reasonableness is qualitatively different at the international border than in the interior. Routine searches of the persons and effects of entrants are not subject to any requirement of reasonable suspicion, probable cause, or warrant, and first-class mail may be opened without a warrant on less than probable cause. Automotive travelers may be stopped at fixed checkpoints near the border without individualized suspicion even if the stop is based largely on ethnicity, and boats on inland waters with ready access to the sea may be hailed and boarded with no suspicion whatever.

Balanced against the sovereign's interests at the border are the Fourth Amendment rights of respondent. Having presented herself at the border for admission, and having subjected herself to the criminal enforcement powers of the Federal Government, respondent was entitled to be free from unreasonable search and seizure. But not only is the expectation of privacy less at the border than in the interior, the Fourth Amendment balance between the interests of the Government and the privacy right of the individual is also struck much more favorably to the Government at the border.

We have not previously decided what level of suspicion would justify a seizure of an incoming traveler for purposes other than a routine border search. The Court of Appeals held that the initial detention of respondent was permissible only if the inspectors possessed a "clear indication" of alimentary canal smuggling. The Court of Appeals viewed "clear indication" as an intermediate standard between "reasonable suspicion" and "probable cause."

We do not think that the Fourth Amendment's emphasis upon reasonableness is consistent with the creation of a third verbal standard in addition to "reasonable suspicion" and "probable cause"; we are dealing with a constitutional requirement of reasonableness, not *mens rea*, and subtle verbal gradations may obscure rather than elucidate the meaning of the provision in question.

We hold that the detention of a traveler at the border, beyond the scope of a routine customs search and inspection, is justified at its inception if customs agents, considering all the facts surrounding the traveler and her trip, reasonably suspect that the traveler is smuggling contraband in her alimentary canal.[4]

The "reasonable suspicion" standard has been applied in a number of contexts and effects a needed balance between private and public interests when law enforcement officials must make a limited intrusion on less than probable cause. It thus fits well into the situations involving alimentary canal smuggling at the border: this type of smuggling gives no external signs and inspectors will rarely possess probable cause to arrest or search, yet governmental interests in stopping smuggling at the border are high indeed. Under this standard officials at the border must have a "particularized and objective basis for suspecting the particular person" of alimentary canal smuggling.

---

[4]   It is also important to note what we do *not* hold. Because the issues are not presented today we suggest no view on what level of suspicion, if any, is required for nonroutine border searches such as strip, body cavity, or involuntary x-ray searches.

The facts, and their rational inferences, known to customs inspectors in this case clearly supported a reasonable suspicion that respondent was an alimentary canal smuggler. We need not belabor the facts, including respondent's implausible story, that supported this suspicion. The trained customs inspectors had encountered many alimentary canal smugglers and certainly had more than an "inchoate and unparticularized suspicion or hunch" that respondent was smuggling narcotics in her alimentary canal. The inspectors' suspicion was a "common-sense conclusion about human behavior" upon which "practical people," including government officials, are entitled to rely.

The final issue in this case is whether the detention of respondent was reasonably related in scope to the circumstances which justified it initially. In this regard we have cautioned that courts should not indulge in unrealistic second-guessing, and we have noted that "creative judges, engaged in *post hoc* evaluations of police conduct can almost always imagine some alternative means by which the objectives of the police might have been accomplished." But the fact that the protection of the public might, in the abstract, have been accomplished by "less intrusive" means does not, in itself, render the search unreasonable. Authorities must be allowed "to graduate their response to the demands of any particular situation." Here, respondent was detained incommunicado for almost 16 hours before inspectors sought a warrant; the warrant then took a number of hours to procure, through no apparent fault of the inspectors. This length of time undoubtedly exceeds any other detention we have approved under reasonable suspicion. But we have also consistently rejected hard-and-fast time limits. Instead, common sense and ordinary human experience must govern over rigid criteria.

The rudimentary knowledge of the human body which judges possess in common with the rest of humankind tells us that alimentary canal smuggling cannot be detected in the amount of time in which other illegal activity may be investigated through brief *Terry*-type stops. It presents few, if any external signs; a quick frisk will not do, nor will even a strip search. In the case of respondent the inspectors had available, as an alternative to simply awaiting her bowel movement, an x-ray. They offered her the alternative of submitting herself to that procedure. But when she refused that alternative, the customs inspectors were left with only two practical alternatives: detain her for such time as necessary to confirm their suspicions, a detention which would last much longer than the typical *Terry* stop, or turn her loose into the interior carrying the reasonably suspected contraband drugs.

The inspectors in this case followed this former procedure. They no doubt expected that respondent, having recently disembarked from a 10-hour direct flight with a full and stiff abdomen, would produce a bowel movement without extended delay. But her visible efforts to resist the call of nature, which the court below labeled "heroic," disappointed this expectation and in turn caused her humiliation and discomfort. Our prior cases have refused to charge police with delays in investigatory detention attributable to the suspect's evasive actions, and that principle applies here as well. Respondent alone was responsible for much of the duration and discomfort of the seizure.

Under these circumstances, we conclude that the detention in this case was not unreasonably long. It occurred at the international border, where the Fourth Amendment balance of interests leans heavily to the Government. At the border, customs officials have more than merely an investigative law enforcement role. They are also charged, along with immigration officials, with protecting this Nation from entrants who may bring anything harmful into this country, whether that be communicable diseases, narcotics, or explosives. In this regard the detention of a suspected alimentary canal smuggler at the border is analogous to the detention of a suspected tuberculosis carrier at the border: both are detained until their bodily processes dispel the suspicion that they will introduce a harmful agent into this country.

Respondent's detention was long, uncomfortable, indeed, humiliating; but both its length and its discomfort resulted solely from the method by which she chose to smuggle illicit drugs into this country. In the presence of articulable suspicion of smuggling in her alimentary canal, the customs officers were not required by the Fourth Amendment to pass respondent and her 88 cocaine-filled balloons into the interior. Her detention for the period of time necessary to either verify or dispel the suspicion was not unreasonable.

JUSTICE BRENNAN, with whom JUSTICE MARSHALL joins, dissenting.

We confront a disgusting and saddening episode at our Nation's border. Shortly after midnight on March 5, 1983, the respondent Rosa Elvira Montoya De Hernandez was detained by customs officers because she fit the profile of an "alimentary canal smuggler." This profile did not of course give the officers probable cause to believe that De Hernandez was smuggling drugs into the country, but at most a "reasonable suspicion" that she might be engaged in such an attempt. After a thorough strip search failed to uncover any contraband, De Hernandez agreed to go to a local hospital for an abdominal x-ray to resolve the matter. When the officers approached with handcuffs at the ready to lead her away, however, "she crossed her arms by her chest and began stepping backwards shaking her head negatively," protesting: "You are not going to put those on me. That is an insult to my character."

Stymied in their efforts, the officers decided on an alternative course: they would simply lock De Hernandez away in an adjacent manifest room "until her peristaltic functions produced a monitored bowel movement." The officers explained to De Hernandez that she could not leave until she had excreted by squatting over a wastebasket pursuant to the watchful eyes of two attending matrons. De Hernandez responded: "I will not submit to your degradation and I'd rather die." She was locked away with the matrons.

De Hernandez remained locked up in the room for almost *24 hours.* Three shifts of matrons came and went during this time. The room had no bed or couch on which she could lie, but only hard chairs and a table. The matrons told her that if she wished to sleep she could lie down on the hard, uncarpeted floor. De Hernandez instead "sat in her chair clutching her purse," "occasionally putting her head down on the table to nap." Most of the time she simply wept and pleaded "to go home." She repeatedly begged for permission "to call my husband and tell him what you are doing to me." Permission was denied. Sobbing, she insisted that she had to "make a phone call home so that she could talk to her children and to let them know that everything was all right." Permission again was denied. In fact, the matrons considered it highly "unusual" that "each time someone entered the search room, she would take out two small pictures of her children and show them to the person." De Hernandez also demanded that her attorney be contacted. Once again, permission was denied. As far as the outside world knew, Rosa De Hernandez had simply vanished. And although she already had been stripped and searched and probed, the customs officers decided about halfway through her ordeal to repeat that process—"to ensure the safety of the surveilling officers. The result was again negative."

After almost 24 hours had passed, someone finally had the presence of mind to consult a Magistrate and to obtain a court order for an x-ray and a body-cavity search. De Hernandez, "very agitated," was handcuffed and led away to the hospital. A rectal examination disclosed the presence of a cocaine-filled balloon. At approximately 3:15 on the morning of March 6, *almost 27 hours after her initial detention,* De Hernandez was formally placed under arrest and advised of her *Miranda* rights. Over the course of the next four days she excreted a total of 88 balloons.

The standards we fashion to govern the ferreting out of the guilty apply equally to the detention of the innocent, and may be exercised by the most unfit and ruthless officers as well as by the fit and responsible. Nor is the issue whether there is a "veritable national crisis in law enforcement caused by smuggling of illicit narcotics." There is, and "stern enforcement of the criminal law is the hallmark of a healthy and self-confident society."

The issue, instead, is simply this: Does the Fourth Amendment permit an international traveler, citizen or alien, to be subjected to the sort of treatment that occurred in this case without the sanction of a judicial officer and based on nothing more than the "reasonable suspicion" of low-ranking investigative officers that something might be amiss? The

Court today concludes that the Fourth Amendment grants such sweeping and unmonitored authority to customs officials.

I dissent. Indefinite involuntary incommunicado detentions "for investigation" are the hallmark of a police state, not a free society. In my opinion, Government officials may no more confine a person at the border under such circumstances for purposes of criminal investigation than they may within the interior of the country. The nature and duration of the detention here may well have been tolerable for spoiled meat or diseased animals, but not for human beings held on simple suspicion of criminal activity. I believe such indefinite detentions can be "reasonable" under the Fourth Amendment only with the approval of a magistrate. I also believe that such approval can be given only upon a showing of probable cause.

Travelers at the national border are routinely subjected to questioning, patdowns, and thorough searches of their belongings. These measures, which involve relatively limited invasions of privacy and which typically are conducted on all incoming travelers, do not violate the Fourth Amendment given the interests of "national self protection reasonably requiring one entering the country to identify himself as entitled to come in, and his belongings as effects which may be lawfully brought in." Individual travelers also may be singled out on "reasonable suspicion" and briefly held for further investigation. At some point, however, further investigation involves such severe intrusions on the values the Fourth Amendment protects that more stringent safeguards are required. For example, the length and nature of a detention may, at least when conducted for criminal-investigative purposes, ripen into something approximating a full-scale custodial arrest—indeed, the arrestee, unlike the detainee in cases such as this, is at least given such basic rights as a telephone call, *Miranda* warnings, a bed, a prompt hearing before the nearest federal magistrate, an appointed attorney, and consideration of bail. In addition, border detentions may involve the use of such highly intrusive investigative techniques as body-cavity searches, x-ray searches, and stomach-pumping.

I believe that detentions and searches falling into these more intrusive categories are presumptively "reasonable" within the meaning of the Fourth Amendment only if authorized by a judicial officer.

In my opinion, allowing the Government to hold someone in indefinite, involuntary, incommunicado isolation without probable cause and a judicial warrant violates our constitutional charter whether the purpose is to extract ransom or to investigate suspected criminal activity. Nothing in the Fourth Amendment permits an exception for such actions at the Nation's border.

Stops and Searches at the Border or Its Functional Equivalent

1.   Searches made at the border or its functional equivalent, pursuant to the long-standing right of the sovereign to protect itself by stopping and examining persons and property crossing into the U.S., are reasonable under the Fourth Amendment simply by virtue of the fact that they occur at the border or its functional equivalent. There is no additional requirement that such searches be supported by probable cause or a warrant.

2.   Under federal customs regulations, international mail entering the U.S. may be opened and searched without a warrant as long as authorities have "reasonable cause to suspect" a violation of the customs laws. The statutory "reasonable cause to suspect" standard is a practical test which imposes a less stringent requirement than the Fourth Amendment's requirement of probable cause.

3.   At the border or its functional equivalent, authorities may stop and search a vehicle—and even disassemble the gas tank—without a warrant, probable cause, or even reasonable suspicion.

4.   At the border or its functional equivalent, authorities may—without a warrant, probable cause, or even reasonable suspicion—briefly stop and question persons entering the country.

5.   A prolonged detention or an invasive search of a person at the border or its functional equivalent—beyond the scope of a routine customs search or inspection—is justified if authorities have reasonable suspicion of wrongdoing. The detention or search should be reasonably related in scope to the circumstances which justified it initially—the person should not be held longer or searched more invasively than necessary to verify or dispel the suspicion.

---

2.   STOPS AND SEARCHES NEAR THE BORDER

In *Almeida-Sanchez v. U.S.*, the Border Patrol had no warrant and no suspicion of wrongdoing when they stopped and searched the defendant's car 25 miles from the border with Mexico. The Supreme Court held that the stop and search violated the Fourth Amendment.

ALMEIDA-SANCHEZ V. U.S.

413 U.S. 266 (1973)

The defendant, a Mexican citizen holding a valid U.S. work permit, was stopped by the U.S. Border Patrol while driving on Highway 78 in California, about 25 miles north of the border with Mexico. A search of the car revealed a large quantity of marijuana. The Border Patrol had no search warrant, and there was no probable cause or even reasonable suspicion for the stop or search. The Border Patrol asserted that it had the authority to stop and search vehicles without a warrant and without probable cause under the federal Immigration and Nationality Act, which provided for warrantless searches of automobiles and other conveyances "within a reasonable distance from any external boundary of the United States." Regulations promulgated by the Attorney General defined "reasonable distance" as "within 100 air miles from any external boundary of the United States."

The Supreme Court confirmed the power of the federal government to conduct routine inspections and searches of individuals or conveyances entering the U.S. at the border or its functional equivalents:

> Whatever the permissible scope of intrusiveness of a routine border search might be, searches of this kind may in certain circumstances take place not only at the border itself, but at its functional equivalents as well. For example, searches at an established station near the border, at a point marking the confluence of two or more roads that extend from the border, might be functional equivalents of border searches. For another example, a search of the passengers and cargo of an airplane arriving at a St. Louis airport after a nonstop flight from Mexico City would clearly be the functional equivalent of a border search.

The Court noted, however, that the stop and search of the defendant's vehicle, on a California road more than 20 miles north of the Mexican border, "was of a wholly different sort." The Court held that in the absence of probable cause or consent, the search violated the defendant's Fourth Amendment right to be free of unreasonable searches and seizures.

In *U.S. v. Brignoni-Ponce*, the Supreme Court held that a roving stop near the border, like a traditional traffic stop, must be justified by reasonable suspicion of wrongdoing. The apparent Mexican ancestry of the occupants, while relevant, was insufficient to justify the stop.

U.S. v. BRIGNONI-PONCE
422 U.S. 873 (1975)

Border Patrol officers pursued and stopped the defendant's vehicle in an area near the border because the three occupants appeared to be of Mexican descent. The officers questioned the defendant and his two passengers about their citizenship, and learned that the passengers were aliens who had entered the country illegally. The defendant was charged with knowingly transporting illegal immigrants in violation of the federal

Immigration and Nationality Act. The defendant moved to suppress the testimony of and about the two passengers, claiming that the evidence was the fruit of an illegal seizure.

The Supreme Court held that the roving stop of the defendant's vehicle, like a traditional traffic stop, must be supported by reasonable suspicion:

> We hold that, when an officer's observations lead him reasonably to suspect that a particular vehicle may contain aliens who are illegally in the country, he may stop the car briefly and investigate the circumstances that provoke suspicion. The officer may question the driver and passengers about their citizenship and immigration status, and he may ask them to explain suspicious circumstances, but any further detention or search must be based on consent or probable cause.

The Court went on to describe a number of factors relevant to the reasonable suspicion inquiry:

> Any number of factors may be taken into account in deciding whether there is reasonable suspicion to stop a car in the border area. Officers may consider the characteristics of the area in which they encounter a vehicle. Its proximity to the border, the usual patterns of traffic on the particular road, and previous experience with alien traffic are all relevant. They also may consider information about recent illegal border crossings in the area. The driver's behavior may be relevant, as erratic driving or obvious attempts to evade officers can support a reasonable suspicion. Aspects of the vehicle itself may justify suspicion. For instance, officers say that certain station wagons, with large compartments for fold-down seats or spare tires, are frequently used for transporting concealed aliens. The vehicle may appear to be heavily loaded, it may have an extraordinary number of passengers, or the officers may observe persons trying to hide. The Government also points out that trained officers can recognize the characteristic appearance of persons who live in Mexico, relying on such factors as the mode of dress and haircut. In all situations, the officer is entitled to assess the facts in light of his experience in detecting illegal entry and smuggling.

The defendant's vehicle was stopped based solely on the apparent Mexican ancestry of the occupants. The Court held that this was relevant—but by itself was insufficient—to create the reasonable suspicion necessary to make a stop: "The likelihood that any given person of Mexican ancestry is an alien is high enough to make Mexican appearance a relevant factor, but, standing alone, it does not justify stopping all Mexican-Americans to ask if they are aliens."

In *U.S. v. Martinez-Fuerte*, the Supreme Court held that the government may maintain fixed immigration checkpoints, roughly 70 miles from the border with Mexico, to stop vehicles and question the occupants, even if there is no reason to believe that a particular vehicle contains illegal aliens.

U.S. V. MARTINEZ-FUERTE
428 U.S. 543 (1976)

In a consolidated appeal involving four separate prosecutions, the defendants challenged the constitutionality of their stops and arrests at two permanent immigration checkpoints, one located in San Clemente, California, and the other near Sarita, Texas. Both checkpoints are approximately 70 miles from the border with Mexico. The Supreme Court upheld the checkpoints and found that a brief stop of a vehicle, followed by questioning of the occupants, need not be authorized by a warrant or justified by reasonable suspicion:

> These cases involve criminal prosecutions for offenses relating to the transportation of illegal Mexican aliens. Each defendant was arrested at a permanent checkpoint operated by the Border Patrol away from the international border with Mexico, and each sought the exclusion of certain evidence on the ground that the operation of the checkpoint was incompatible with the Fourth Amendment. In each instance, whether the Fourth Amendment was violated turns primarily on whether a vehicle may be stopped at a fixed checkpoint for brief questioning of its occupants even though there is no reason to believe the particular vehicle contains illegal aliens. We hold today that such stops are consistent with the Fourth Amendment. We also hold that the operation of a fixed checkpoint need not be authorized in advance by a judicial warrant.

In *U.S. v. Ortiz*, the Supreme Court invalidated a suspicionless search at the fixed immigration checkpoint in San Clemente, California. A search, the Court held, must be supported by probable cause.

U.S. V. ORTIZ
422 U.S. 891 (1975)

Border Patrol officers stopped Luis Ortiz's car for a routine search at the fixed immigration checkpoint in San Clemente, California, approximately 60–70 miles from the border with Mexico. The officers found three aliens concealed in the trunk, and Ortiz was convicted on three counts of knowingly transporting aliens who were in the country illegally. Prior to the search, the officers had no special reason to suspect that Ortiz's car carried concealed aliens.

The Supreme Court was not persuaded that the checkpoint "limits to any meaningful extent the officer's discretion to select cars for search," since only 3% of the vehicles that passed through the checkpoint were stopped for questioning or a search. The Court also felt that a "search, even of an automobile, is a substantial invasion of privacy" that must be protected from "official arbitrariness." As a result, the Court held that probable cause or consent was required to perform a search: "We hold that at traffic checkpoints removed from the border and its functional equivalents, officers may not search private vehicles without consent or probable cause."

The Supreme Court went on to identify a number of factors relevant to the probable cause determination:

> The Government lists in its reply brief some of the factors on which officers have relied in deciding which cars to search. They include the number of persons in a vehicle, the appearance and behavior of the driver and passengers, their inability to speak English, the responses they give to officers' questions, the nature of the vehicle, and indications that it may be heavily loaded. All of these factors properly may be taken into account in deciding whether there is probable cause to search a particular vehicle. In addition, the officers are entitled to draw reasonable inferences from these facts in light of their knowledge of the area and their prior experience with aliens and smugglers.

The Supreme Court ultimately concluded that because the Border Patrol officers advanced "no special reasons for believing" that Ortiz's vehicle contained aliens, "the absence of probable cause makes the search invalid."

Stops and Searches Near the Border

1.   Immigration and law enforcement officials may establish fixed checkpoints near the border where, without a warrant or particularized suspicion, vehicles are briefly stopped and the occupants are questioned. In order to search a vehicle at a fixed checkpoint near the border, however, authorities must have consent or probable cause.

2.   Immigration and law enforcement officers may make a warrantless roving stop of a vehicle traveling near the border based on reasonable suspicion of wrongdoing. In order to search a vehicle following a roving stop, however, authorities must have consent or probable cause.

C. HIGHWAY CHECKPOINTS

In *U.S. v. Martinez-Fuerte*, 428 U.S. 543 (1976), presented above in connection with stops and searches near the border, the Supreme Court held that the Border Patrol could, without a warrant or reasonable suspicion, briefly stop and question motorists at permanent checkpoints near the border in order to ensure that all occupants were lawfully present in the United States. A few years later, in *Delaware v. Prouse*, 440 U.S. 648 (1979), excerpted in Chapter 6, the Supreme Court held that police must have reasonable suspicion of a traffic violation or some other violation of law in order to make a roving stop of a vehicle. The Court in *Prouse* was careful to note, however, that its decision did not preclude authorities from "developing methods for spot checks that involve less intrusion or that do not involve the unconstrained exercise of discretion," such as "questioning of all oncoming traffic at roadblock-type stops."

The decisions in *Martinez-Fuerte* and *Prouse*, coupled with growing concerns about the tragic consequences of drunk driving, led authorities in many states and localities to establish sobriety checkpoint programs with the aim of apprehending—or at least deterring—drivers under the influence of alcohol. Unlike the permanent immigration checkpoints in *Martinez-Fuerte*, most sobriety checkpoints are temporary. In fact, the location of a sobriety checkpoint might change from one day to the next, allowing authorities to target different areas of concern, while preventing motorists from developing alternate routes where their driving is less closely monitored.

In *Michigan Department of State Police v. Sitz*, the Supreme Court upheld a sobriety checkpoint program that allowed officers—without a warrant and without reasonable suspicion—to briefly stop, observe, and question drivers passing through the checkpoint.

MICHIGAN DEPARTMENT OF STATE POLICE V. SITZ
496 U.S. 444 (1990)

CHIEF JUSTICE REHNQUIST delivered the opinion of the Court.

This case poses the question whether a State's use of highway sobriety checkpoints violates the Fourth and Fourteenth Amendments to the United States Constitution. We hold that it does not and therefore reverse the contrary holding of the Court of Appeals of Michigan.

Petitioners, the Michigan Department of State Police and its director, established a sobriety checkpoint pilot program in early 1986. The director appointed a Sobriety Checkpoint Advisory Committee comprising representatives of the State Police force, local police forces, state prosecutors, and the University of Michigan Transportation Research Institute. Pursuant to its charge, the advisory committee created guidelines setting forth procedures governing checkpoint operations, site selection, and publicity.

Under the guidelines, checkpoints would be set up at selected sites along state roads. All vehicles passing through a checkpoint would be stopped and their drivers briefly examined for signs of intoxication. In cases where a checkpoint officer detected signs of intoxication, the motorist would be directed to a location out of the traffic flow where an officer would check the motorist's driver's license and car registration and, if warranted, conduct further sobriety tests. Should the field tests and the officer's observations suggest that the driver was intoxicated, an arrest would be made. All other drivers would be permitted to resume their journey immediately.

The first—and to date the only—sobriety checkpoint operated under the program was conducted in Saginaw County with the assistance of the Saginaw County Sheriff's Department. During the 75-minute duration of the checkpoint's operation, 126 vehicles passed through the checkpoint. The average delay for each vehicle was approximately 25 seconds. Two drivers were detained for field sobriety testing, and one of the two was arrested for driving under the influence of alcohol. A third driver who drove through without stopping was pulled over by an officer in an observation vehicle and arrested for driving under the influence.

On the day before the operation of the Saginaw County checkpoint, respondents filed a complaint in the Circuit Court of Wayne County seeking declaratory and injunctive relief from potential subjection to the checkpoints. Each of the respondents is a licensed driver in the State of Michigan who regularly travels throughout the State in his automobile. During pretrial proceedings, petitioners agreed to delay further implementation of the checkpoint program pending the outcome of this litigation.

After the trial, at which the court heard extensive testimony concerning the "effectiveness" of highway sobriety checkpoint programs, the court ruled that the Michigan program violated the Fourth Amendment. On appeal, the Michigan Court of Appeals affirmed the holding.

To decide this case the trial court performed a balancing test derived from our opinion in *Brown v. Texas*, 443 U.S. 47 (1979). As described by the Court of Appeals, the test involved "balancing the state's interest in preventing accidents caused by drunk drivers, the effectiveness of sobriety checkpoints in achieving that goal, and the level of intrusion on an individual's privacy caused by the checkpoints." The Court of Appeals agreed that "the *Brown* three-prong balancing test was the correct test to be used to determine the constitutionality of the sobriety checkpoint plan."

As characterized by the Court of Appeals, the trial court's findings with respect to the balancing factors were that the State has "a grave and legitimate" interest in curbing drunken driving; that sobriety checkpoint programs are generally "ineffective" and, therefore, do not significantly further that interest; and that the checkpoints' "subjective intrusion" on individual liberties is substantial. According to the court, the record disclosed no basis for disturbing the trial court's findings, which were made within the context of an analytical framework prescribed by this Court for determining the constitutionality of seizures less intrusive than traditional arrests.

Petitioners concede, correctly in our view, that a Fourth Amendment "seizure" occurs when a vehicle is stopped at a checkpoint. The question thus becomes whether such seizures are "reasonable" under the Fourth Amendment.

It is important to recognize what our inquiry is *not* about. No allegations are before us of unreasonable treatment of any person after an actual detention at a particular checkpoint. As pursued in the lower courts, the instant action challenges only the use of sobriety checkpoints generally. We address only the initial stop of each motorist passing through a checkpoint and the associated preliminary questioning and observation by checkpoint officers. Detention of particular motorists for more extensive field sobriety testing may require satisfaction of an individualized suspicion standard.

No one can seriously dispute the magnitude of the drunken driving problem or the States' interest in eradicating it. Media reports of alcohol-related death and mutilation on the Nation's roads are legion. The anecdotal is confirmed by the statistical. Drunk drivers cause an annual death toll of over 25,000 and in the same time span cause nearly one million personal injuries and more than five billion dollars in property damage.

Conversely, the weight bearing on the other scale—the measure of the intrusion on motorists stopped briefly at sobriety checkpoints—is slight. We reached a similar conclusion as to the intrusion on motorists subjected to a brief stop at a highway checkpoint for detecting illegal aliens. See *U.S. v. Martinez-Fuerte*, 428 U.S. 543 (1976). We see virtually no difference between the levels of intrusion on law-abiding motorists from the brief stops necessary to the effectuation of these two types of checkpoints, which to the average motorist would seem identical save for the nature of the questions the checkpoint officers might ask. The trial court and the Court of Appeals, thus, accurately gauged the "objective" intrusion, measured by the duration of the seizure and the intensity of the investigation, as minimal.

With respect to what it perceived to be the "subjective" intrusion on motorists, however, the Court of Appeals found such intrusion substantial. The court first affirmed the trial court's finding that the guidelines governing checkpoint operation minimize the discretion of the officers on the scene. But the court also agreed with the trial court's conclusion that the checkpoints have the potential to generate fear and surprise in motorists. This was so because the record failed to demonstrate that approaching motorists would be aware of their option to make U-turns or turnoffs to avoid the checkpoints. On that basis, the court deemed the subjective intrusion from the checkpoints unreasonable.

We believe the Michigan courts misread our cases concerning the degree of "subjective intrusion" and the potential for generating fear and surprise. The "fear and surprise" to be considered are not the natural fear of one who has been drinking over the prospect of being stopped at a sobriety checkpoint but, rather, the fear and surprise engendered in law-abiding motorists by the nature of the stop. This was made clear in *Martinez-Fuerte.* Comparing checkpoint stops to roving patrol stops considered in prior cases, we said:

> The circumstances surrounding a checkpoint stop and search are far less intrusive than those attending a roving-patrol stop. Roving patrols often operate at night on seldom-traveled roads, and their approach may frighten motorists. At traffic checkpoints the motorist can see that other vehicles are being stopped, he can see visible signs of the officers' authority, and he is much less likely to be frightened or annoyed by the intrusion.

Here, checkpoints are selected pursuant to the guidelines, and uniformed police officers stop every approaching vehicle. The intrusion resulting from the brief stop at the sobriety checkpoint is for constitutional purposes indistinguishable from the checkpoint stops we upheld in *Martinez-Fuerte.*

The Court of Appeals went on to consider as part of the balancing analysis the "effectiveness" of the proposed checkpoint program. Based on extensive testimony in the trial record, the court concluded that the checkpoint program failed the "effectiveness" part of the test, and that this failure materially discounted petitioners' strong interest in implementing the program. We think the Court of Appeals was wrong on this point as well.

The actual language from *Brown v. Texas,* upon which the Michigan courts based their evaluation of "effectiveness," describes the balancing factor as "the degree to which the seizure advances the public interest." This passage from *Brown* was not meant to transfer from politically accountable officials to the courts the decision as to which among reasonable alternative law enforcement techniques should be employed to deal with a serious public danger. Experts in police science might disagree over which of several methods of apprehending drunken drivers is preferable as an ideal. But for purposes of Fourth Amendment analysis, the choice among such reasonable alternatives remains with the governmental officials who have a unique understanding of, and a responsibility for, limited public resources, including a finite number of police officers.

In *Delaware v. Prouse*, 440 U.S. 648 (1979), we disapproved random stops made by Delaware Highway Patrol officers in an effort to apprehend unlicensed drivers and unsafe vehicles. We observed that *no* empirical evidence indicated that such stops would be an effective means of promoting roadway safety. Unlike *Prouse*, this case involves neither a complete absence of empirical data nor a challenge to random highway stops. During the operation of the Saginaw County checkpoint, the detention of the 126 vehicles that entered the checkpoint resulted in the arrest of two drunken drivers. Stated as a percentage, approximately 1.6 percent of the drivers passing through the checkpoint were arrested for alcohol impairment. In addition, an expert witness testified at the trial that experience in other States demonstrated that, on the whole, sobriety checkpoints resulted in drunken driving arrests of around 1 percent of all motorists stopped. By way of comparison, the record from one of the consolidated cases in *Martinez-Fuerte* showed that in the associated checkpoint, illegal aliens were found in only 0.12 percent of the vehicles passing through the checkpoint. The ratio of illegal aliens detected to vehicles stopped (considering that on occasion two or more illegal aliens were found in a single vehicle) was approximately 0.5 percent. We concluded that this "record provides a rather complete picture of the effectiveness of the San Clemente checkpoint," and we sustained its constitutionality. We see no justification for a different conclusion here.

In sum, the balance of the State's interest in preventing drunken driving, the extent to which this system can reasonably be said to advance that interest, and the degree of intrusion upon individual motorists who are briefly stopped, weighs in favor of the state program. We therefore hold that it is consistent with the Fourth Amendment.

JUSTICE BRENNAN, with whom JUSTICE MARSHALL joins, dissenting.

The Court ignores the fact that we have generally required the Government to prove that it had reasonable suspicion for a minimally intrusive seizure to be considered reasonable. See, *e.g.*, *Delaware v. Prouse*, 440 U.S. 648 (1979); *Terry v. Ohio*, 392 U.S. 1 (1968). Some level of individualized suspicion is a core component of the protection the Fourth Amendment provides against arbitrary government action. By holding that no level of suspicion is necessary before the police may stop a car for the purpose of preventing drunken driving, the Court potentially subjects the general public to arbitrary or harassing conduct by the police. I would have hoped that before taking such a step, the Court would carefully explain how such a plan fits within our constitutional framework.

JUSTICE STEVENS, with whom JUSTICE BRENNAN and JUSTICE MARSHALL join, dissenting.

A sobriety checkpoint is usually operated at night at an unannounced location. Surprise is crucial to its method. The test operation conducted by the Michigan State Police and the Saginaw County Sheriff's Department began shortly after midnight and lasted until about 1 a.m. During that period, the 19 officers participating in the operation made two arrests and stopped and questioned 124 other unsuspecting and innocent drivers. It is, of course, not known how many arrests would have been made during that period if those officers had been engaged in normal patrol activities. However, the findings of the trial court, based on an extensive record and affirmed by the Michigan Court of Appeals, indicate that the net effect of sobriety checkpoints on traffic safety is infinitesimal and possibly negative.

Indeed, the record in this case makes clear that a decision holding these suspicionless seizures unconstitutional would not impede the law enforcement community's remarkable progress in reducing the death toll on our highways. Because the Michigan program was patterned after an older program in Maryland, the trial judge gave special attention to that State's experience. Over a period of several years, Maryland operated 125 checkpoints; of the 41,000 motorists passing through those checkpoints, only 143 persons (0.3%) were arrested. The number of man-hours devoted to these operations is not in the record, but it seems inconceivable that a higher arrest rate could not have been achieved by more conventional means. Yet, even if the 143 checkpoint arrests were assumed to involve a net increase in the number of drunken driving arrests per year, the figure would still be insignificant by comparison to the 71,000 such arrests made by Michigan State Police without checkpoints in 1984 alone.

In light of these considerations, it seems evident that the Court today misapplies the balancing test announced in *Brown v. Texas*. The Court overvalues the law enforcement interest in using sobriety checkpoints, undervalues the citizen's interest in freedom from random, unannounced investigatory seizures, and mistakenly assumes that there is "virtually no difference" between a routine stop at a permanent, fixed checkpoint and a surprise stop at a sobriety checkpoint. I believe this case is controlled by our several precedents condemning suspicionless random stops of motorists for investigatory purposes.

––––––––––––

The Supreme Court's decisions in *Martinez-Fuerte* and *Sitz* seemed to suggest that authorities could establish highway checkpoints to prevent and deter a wide variety of illegal conduct. But in *City of Indianapolis v. Edmond*, the Supreme Court struck down a checkpoint program designed to discover and interdict illegal drugs. Are you persuaded by the majority's efforts to distinguish *Martinez-Fuerte* and *Sitz*?

CITY OF INDIANAPOLIS V. EDMOND
531 U.S. 32 (2000)

JUSTICE O'CONNOR delivered the opinion of the Court.

In *Michigan v. Sitz*, 496 U.S. 444 (1990), and *U.S. v. Martinez-Fuerte*, 428 U.S. 543 (1976), we held that brief, suspicionless seizures at highway checkpoints for the purposes of combating drunk driving and intercepting illegal immigrants were constitutional. We now consider the constitutionality of a highway checkpoint program whose primary purpose is the discovery and interdiction of illegal narcotics.

I

In August 1998, the city of Indianapolis began to operate vehicle checkpoints on Indianapolis roads in an effort to interdict unlawful drugs. The city conducted six such roadblocks between August and November that year, stopping 1,161 vehicles and arresting 104 motorists. Fifty-five arrests were for drug-related crimes, while 49 were for offenses unrelated to drugs. The overall "hit rate" of the program was thus approximately nine percent.

The parties stipulated to the facts concerning the operation of the checkpoints by the Indianapolis Police Department (IPD) for purposes of the preliminary injunction proceedings instituted below. At each checkpoint location, the police stop a predetermined number of vehicles. Approximately 30 officers are stationed at the checkpoint. Pursuant to written directives issued by the chief of police, at least one officer approaches the vehicle, advises the driver that he or she is being stopped briefly at a drug checkpoint, and asks the driver to produce a license and registration. The officer also looks for signs of impairment and conducts an open-view examination of the vehicle from the outside. A narcotics-detection dog walks around the outside of each stopped vehicle.

The directives instruct the officers that they may conduct a search only by consent or based on the appropriate quantum of particularized suspicion. The officers must conduct each stop in the same manner until particularized suspicion develops, and the officers have no discretion to stop any vehicle out of sequence. The city agreed in the stipulation to operate the checkpoints in such a way as to ensure that the total duration of each stop, absent reasonable suspicion or probable cause, would be five minutes or less.

Respondents James Edmond and Joell Palmer were each stopped at a narcotics checkpoint in late September 1998. Respondents then filed a lawsuit on behalf of themselves and the class of all motorists who had been stopped or were subject to being stopped in the future at the Indianapolis drug checkpoints. Respondents claimed that the roadblocks violated the Fourth Amendment of the United States Constitution and the search and seizure provision of the Indiana Constitution. Respondents requested declaratory and injunctive relief for the class, as well as damages and attorney's fees for themselves.

II

The Fourth Amendment requires that searches and seizures be reasonable. A search or seizure is ordinarily unreasonable in the absence of individualized suspicion of wrongdoing. We have recognized only limited circumstances in which the usual rule does not apply. For example, we have upheld certain regimes of suspicionless searches where the program was designed to serve "special needs, beyond the normal need for law enforcement." See, *e.g., Vernonia School District 47J v. Acton,* 515 U.S. 646 (1995) (random drug testing of student-athletes); *Treasury Employees v. Von Raab,* 489 U.S. 656 (1989) (drug tests for United States Customs Service employees seeking transfer or promotion to certain positions); *Skinner v. Railway Labor Executives' Association,* 489 U.S. 602 (1989) (drug and alcohol tests for railway employees involved in train accidents or found to be in violation of particular safety regulations). We have also allowed searches for certain administrative purposes without particularized suspicion of misconduct, provided that those searches are appropriately limited. See, *e.g., New York v. Burger,* 482 U.S. 691 (1987) (warrantless administrative inspection of premises of "closely regulated" business); *Michigan v. Tyler,* 436 U.S. 499 (1978) (administrative inspection of fire-damaged premises to determine cause of blaze); *Camara v. Municipal Court of City and County of San Francisco,* 387 U.S. 523 (1967) (administrative inspection to ensure compliance with city housing code).

We have also upheld brief, suspicionless seizures of motorists at a fixed Border Patrol checkpoint designed to intercept illegal aliens, *U.S. v. Martinez-Fuerte,* 428 U.S. 543 (1976), and at a sobriety checkpoint aimed at removing drunk drivers from the road, *Michigan Department of State Police v. Sitz,* 496 U.S. 444 (1990). In addition, in *Delaware v. Prouse,* 440 U.S. 648 (1979), we suggested that a similar type of roadblock with the purpose of verifying drivers' licenses and vehicle registrations would be permissible. In none of these cases, however, did we indicate approval of a checkpoint program whose primary purpose was to detect evidence of ordinary criminal wrongdoing.

Not only does the common thread of highway safety thus run through *Sitz* and *Prouse,* but *Prouse* itself reveals a difference in the Fourth Amendment significance of highway safety interests and the general interest in crime control.

III

It is well established that a vehicle stop at a highway checkpoint effectuates a seizure within the meaning of the Fourth Amendment. The fact that officers walk a narcotics-detection dog around the exterior of each car at the Indianapolis checkpoints does not transform the seizure into a search. Rather, what principally distinguishes these checkpoints from those we have previously approved is their primary purpose.

As petitioners concede, the Indianapolis checkpoint program unquestionably has the primary purpose of interdicting illegal narcotics. In their stipulation of facts, the parties repeatedly refer to the checkpoints as "drug checkpoints" and describe them as "being operated by the City of Indianapolis in an effort to interdict unlawful drugs in Indianapolis."

We have never approved a checkpoint program whose primary purpose was to detect evidence of ordinary criminal wrongdoing. Rather, our checkpoint cases have recognized only limited exceptions to the general rule that a seizure must be accompanied by some measure of individualized suspicion. We suggested in *Prouse* that we would not credit the "general interest in crime control" as justification for a regime of suspicionless stops. Consistent with this suggestion, each of the checkpoint programs that we have approved was designed primarily to serve purposes closely related to the problems of policing the border or the necessity of ensuring roadway safety. Because the primary purpose of the Indianapolis narcotics checkpoint program is to uncover evidence of ordinary criminal wrongdoing, the program contravenes the Fourth Amendment.

Petitioners propose several ways in which the narcotics-detection purpose of the instant checkpoint program may instead resemble the primary purposes of the checkpoints in *Sitz* and *Martinez-Fuerte*. Petitioners state that the checkpoints in those cases had the same ultimate purpose of arresting those suspected of committing crimes. Securing the border and apprehending drunk drivers are, of course, law enforcement activities, and law enforcement officers employ arrests and criminal prosecutions in pursuit of these goals. If we were to rest the case at this high level of generality, there would be little check on the ability of the authorities to construct roadblocks for almost any conceivable law enforcement purpose. Without drawing the line at roadblocks designed primarily to serve the general interest in crime control, the Fourth Amendment would do little to prevent such intrusions from becoming a routine part of American life.

Petitioners also emphasize the severe and intractable nature of the drug problem as justification for the checkpoint program. But the gravity of the threat alone cannot be dispositive of questions concerning what means law enforcement officers may employ to pursue a given purpose.

Rather, in determining whether individualized suspicion is required, we must consider the nature of the interests threatened and their connection to the particular law enforcement practices at issue. We are particularly reluctant to recognize exceptions to the general rule of individualized suspicion where governmental authorities primarily pursue their general crime control ends.

Nor can the narcotics-interdiction purpose of the checkpoints be rationalized in terms of a highway safety concern similar to that present in *Sitz*. The detection and punishment of almost any criminal offense serves broadly the safety of the community, and our streets would no doubt be safer but for the scourge of illegal drugs. Only with respect to a smaller class of offenses, however, is society confronted with the type of immediate, vehicle-bound threat to life and limb that the sobriety checkpoint in *Sitz* was designed to eliminate.

Petitioners also liken the anti-contraband agenda of the Indianapolis checkpoints to the anti-smuggling purpose of the checkpoints in *Martinez-Fuerte*. Petitioners cite this Court's conclusion in *Martinez-Fuerte* that the flow of traffic was too heavy to permit "particularized study of a given car that would enable it to be identified as a possible carrier of illegal aliens," and claim that this logic has even more force here. The problem with this argument is that the same logic prevails any time a vehicle is employed to conceal contraband or other evidence of a crime. This type of connection to the roadway is very different from the close connection to roadway safety that was present in *Sitz* and *Prouse*. Further, the Indianapolis checkpoints are far removed from the border context that was crucial in *Martinez-Fuerte*. While the difficulty of examining each passing car was an important factor in validating the law enforcement technique employed in *Martinez-Fuerte*, this factor alone cannot justify a regime of suspicionless searches or seizures. Rather, we must look more closely at the nature of the public interests that such a regime is designed principally to serve.

The primary purpose of the Indianapolis narcotics checkpoints is in the end to advance the general interest in crime control. We decline to suspend the usual requirement of individualized suspicion where the police seek to employ a checkpoint primarily for the ordinary enterprise of investigating crimes. We cannot sanction stops justified only by the generalized and ever-present possibility that interrogation and inspection may reveal that any given motorist has committed some crime.

Of course, there are circumstances that may justify a law enforcement checkpoint where the primary purpose would otherwise, but for some emergency, relate to ordinary crime control. For example, as the Court of Appeals noted, the Fourth Amendment would almost certainly permit an appropriately tailored roadblock set up to thwart an imminent terrorist attack or to catch a dangerous criminal who is likely to flee by way of a particular route. The exigencies created by these scenarios are far removed from the circumstances under which authorities might simply stop cars as a matter of course to see if there just happens to be a felon leaving the jurisdiction. While we do not limit the purposes that may justify a checkpoint program to any rigid set of categories, we decline to approve a program whose primary purpose is ultimately indistinguishable from the general interest in crime control.

Petitioners argue that the Indianapolis checkpoint program is justified by its lawful secondary purposes of keeping impaired motorists off the road and verifying licenses and registrations. If this were the case, however, law enforcement authorities would be able to establish checkpoints for virtually any purpose so long as they also included a license or sobriety check. For this reason, we examine the available evidence to determine the primary purpose of the checkpoint program. While we recognize the challenges inherent in a purpose inquiry, courts routinely engage in this enterprise in many areas of constitutional jurisprudence as a means of sifting abusive governmental conduct from that which is lawful. As a result, a program driven by an impermissible purpose may be proscribed while a program impelled by licit purposes is permitted, even though the challenged conduct may be outwardly similar. While reasonableness under the Fourth Amendment is predominantly an objective inquiry, our special needs and administrative search cases demonstrate that purpose is often relevant when suspicionless intrusions pursuant to a general scheme are at issue.[2]

It goes without saying that our holding today does nothing to alter the constitutional status of the sobriety and border checkpoints that we approved in *Sitz* and *Martinez-Fuerte*, or of the type of traffic checkpoint that we suggested would be lawful in *Prouse*. The constitutionality of such checkpoint programs still depends on a balancing of the competing interests at stake and the effectiveness of the program. When law enforcement authorities pursue primarily general crime control purposes at checkpoints such as here, however, stops can only be justified by some quantum of individualized suspicion.

Our holding also does not affect the validity of border searches or searches at places like airports and government buildings, where the need for such measures to ensure public safety can be particularly acute. Nor does our opinion speak to other intrusions aimed primarily at purposes beyond the general interest in crime control. Our holding also does not impair the ability of police officers to act appropriately upon

---

[2] Because petitioners concede that the primary purpose of the Indianapolis checkpoints is narcotics detection, we need not decide whether the State may establish a checkpoint program with the primary purpose of checking licenses or driver sobriety and a secondary purpose of interdicting narcotics. Specifically, we express no view on the question whether police may expand the scope of a license or sobriety checkpoint seizure in order to detect the presence of drugs in a stopped car.

information that they properly learn during a checkpoint stop justified by a lawful primary purpose, even where such action may result in the arrest of a motorist for an offense unrelated to that purpose. Finally, we caution that the purpose inquiry in this context is to be conducted only at the programmatic level and is not an invitation to probe the minds of individual officers acting at the scene.

Because the primary purpose of the Indianapolis checkpoint program is ultimately indistinguishable from the general interest in crime control, the checkpoints violate the Fourth Amendment.

CHIEF JUSTICE REHNQUIST, with whom JUSTICE THOMAS and JUSTICE SCALIA join, dissenting.

The State's use of a drug-sniffing dog, according to the Court's holding, annuls what is otherwise plainly constitutional under our Fourth Amendment jurisprudence: brief, standardized, discretionless, roadblock seizures of automobiles, seizures which effectively serve a weighty state interest with only minimal intrusion on the privacy of their occupants. Because these seizures serve the State's accepted and significant interests of preventing drunken driving and checking for driver's licenses and vehicle registrations, and because there is nothing in the record to indicate that the addition of the dog sniff lengthens these otherwise legitimate seizures, I dissent.

As it is nowhere to be found in the Court's opinion, I begin with blackletter roadblock seizure law. Roadblock seizures are consistent with the Fourth Amendment if they are carried out pursuant to a plan embodying explicit, neutral limitations on the conduct of individual officers. Specifically, the constitutionality of a seizure turns upon a weighing of the gravity of the public concerns served by the seizure, the degree to which the seizure advances the public interest, and the severity of the interference with individual liberty.

This case follows naturally from *Martinez-Fuerte* and *Sitz*. Petitioners acknowledge that the "primary purpose" of these roadblocks is to interdict illegal drugs, but this fact should not be controlling. The District Court found that another "purpose of the checkpoints is to check driver's licenses and vehicle registrations," and the written directives state that the police officers are to "[l]ook for signs of impairment." The use of roadblocks to look for signs of impairment was validated by *Sitz*, and the use of roadblocks to check for driver's licenses and vehicle registrations was expressly recognized in *Delaware v. Prouse*. That the roadblocks serve these legitimate state interests cannot be seriously disputed, as the 49 people arrested for offenses unrelated to drugs can attest. And it would be speculative to conclude—given the District Court's findings, the written directives, and the actual arrests—that petitioners would not have operated these roadblocks but for the State's interest in interdicting drugs.

Because of the valid reasons for conducting these roadblock seizures, it is constitutionally irrelevant that petitioners also hoped to interdict drugs. In *Whren v. U.S.*, 517 U.S. 806 (1996), we held that an officer's subjective intent would not invalidate an otherwise objectively justifiable stop of an automobile. The reasonableness of an officer's discretionary decision to stop an automobile, at issue in *Whren*, turns on whether there is probable cause to believe that a traffic violation has occurred. The reasonableness of highway checkpoints, at issue here, turns on whether they effectively serve a significant state interest with minimal intrusion on motorists. The stop in *Whren* was objectively reasonable because the police officers had witnessed traffic violations; so too the roadblocks here are objectively reasonable because they serve the substantial interests of preventing drunken driving and checking for driver's licenses and vehicle registrations with minimal intrusion on motorists.

Once the constitutional requirements for a particular seizure are satisfied, the subjective expectations of those responsible for it, be it police officers or members of a city council, are irrelevant. It is the objective effect of the State's actions on the privacy of the individual that animates the Fourth Amendment. Because the objective intrusion of a valid seizure does not turn upon anyone's subjective thoughts, neither should our constitutional analysis.

These stops effectively serve the State's legitimate interests; they are executed in a regularized and neutral manner; and they only minimally intrude upon the privacy of the motorists. They should therefore be constitutional.

———————————

In *Illinois v. Lidster*, the Supreme Court upheld a highway checkpoint designed to solicit the public's assistance in identifying the perpetrator in a recent hit-and-run accident. The Court felt that the checkpoint was more closely akin to those approved in *Martinez-Fuerte* and *Sitz* than to the one struck down in *Edmond*.

ILLINOIS V. LIDSTER

540 U.S. 419 (2004)

JUSTICE BREYER delivered the opinion of the Court.

This Fourth Amendment case focuses upon a highway checkpoint where police stopped motorists to ask them for information about a recent hit-and-run accident. We hold that the police stops were reasonable, hence, constitutional.

I

On Saturday, August 23, 1997, just after midnight, an unknown motorist traveling eastbound on a highway in Lombard, Illinois, struck and killed a 70-year-old bicyclist. The motorist drove off without identifying himself. About one week later at about the same time of night and at about the same place, local police set up a highway checkpoint designed to obtain more information about the accident from the motoring public.

Police cars with flashing lights partially blocked the eastbound lanes of the highway. The blockage forced traffic to slow down, leading to lines of up to 15 cars in each lane. As each vehicle drew up to the checkpoint, an officer would stop it for 10 to 15 seconds, ask the occupants whether they had seen anything happen there the previous weekend, and hand each driver a flyer. The flyer said "ALERT . . . FATAL HIT & RUN ACCIDENT" and requested "ASSISTANCE IN IDENTIFYING THE VEHICLE AND DRIVER INVOLVED IN THIS ACCIDENT WHICH KILLED A 70 YEAR OLD BICYCLIST."

Robert Lidster, the respondent, drove a minivan toward the checkpoint. As he approached the checkpoint, his van swerved, nearly hitting one of the officers. The officer smelled alcohol on Lidster's breath. He directed Lidster to a side street where another officer administered a sobriety test and then arrested Lidster. Lidster was tried and convicted in Illinois state court of driving under the influence of alcohol.

Lidster challenged the lawfulness of his arrest and conviction on the ground that the government had obtained much of the relevant evidence through use of a checkpoint stop that violated the Fourth Amendment. The trial court rejected that challenge. But an Illinois appellate court reached the opposite conclusion. The Illinois Supreme Court agreed with the appellate court. It held (by a vote of 4 to 3) that our decision in *Indianapolis v. Edmond*, 531 U.S. 32 (2000), required it to find the stop unconstitutional.

II

The Illinois Supreme Court basically held that our decision in *Edmond* governs the outcome of this case. We do not agree. *Edmond* involved a checkpoint at which police stopped vehicles to look for evidence of drug crimes committed by occupants of those vehicles. After stopping a vehicle at the checkpoint, police would examine (from outside the vehicle) the vehicle's interior; they would walk a drug-sniffing dog around the exterior; and, if they found sufficient evidence of drug (or other) crimes, they would arrest the vehicle's occupants. We found that police had set up this checkpoint primarily for general "crime control" purposes, *i.e.*, "to detect evidence of ordinary criminal wrongdoing." We noted that the stop was made without individualized suspicion. And we held that the Fourth Amendment forbids such a stop, in the absence of special circumstances.

The checkpoint stop here differs significantly from that in *Edmond*. The stop's primary law enforcement purpose was *not* to determine whether a vehicle's occupants were committing a crime, but to ask vehicle occupants, as members of the public, for their help in providing information about a crime in all likelihood committed by others. The police expected the information elicited to help them apprehend, not the vehicle's occupants, but other individuals.

Edmond's language, as well as its context, makes clear that the constitutionality of this latter, information-seeking kind of stop was not then before the Court. Neither do we believe, *Edmond* aside, that the Fourth Amendment would have us apply an *Edmond*-type rule of automatic unconstitutionality to brief, information-seeking highway stops of the kind now before us. For one thing, the fact that such stops normally lack individualized suspicion cannot by itself determine the constitutional outcome. As in *Edmond*, the stop here at issue involves a motorist. The Fourth Amendment does not treat a motorist's car as his castle. And special law enforcement concerns will sometimes justify highway stops without individualized suspicion. See *Michigan v. Sitz*, 496 U.S. 444 (1990) (sobriety checkpoint); *U.S. v. Martinez-Fuerte*, 428 U.S. 543 (1976) (Border Patrol checkpoint). Moreover, unlike *Edmond*, the context here (seeking information from the public) is one in which, by definition, the concept of individualized suspicion has little role to play. Like certain other forms of police activity, say, crowd control or public safety, an information-seeking stop is not the kind of event that involves suspicion, or lack of suspicion, of the relevant individual.

For another thing, information-seeking highway stops are less likely to provoke anxiety or to prove intrusive. The stops are likely brief. The police are not likely to ask questions designed to elicit self-incriminating information. And citizens will often react positively when police simply ask for their help as "responsible citizens" to give whatever information they may have to aid in law enforcement.

Further, the law ordinarily permits police to seek the voluntary cooperation of members of the public in the investigation of a crime. Law enforcement officers do not violate the Fourth Amendment by merely approaching an individual on the street or in another public place, by asking him if he is willing to answer some questions, or by putting questions to him if the person is willing to listen. That, in part, is because voluntary requests play a vital role in police investigatory work.

The importance of soliciting the public's assistance is offset to some degree by the need to stop a motorist to obtain that help—a need less likely present where a pedestrian, not a motorist, is involved. The difference is significant in light of our determinations that such an involuntary stop amounts to a "seizure" in Fourth Amendment terms. That difference, however, is not important enough to justify an *Edmond*-type rule here. After all, as we have said, the motorist stop will likely be brief. Any accompanying traffic delay should prove no more onerous than many that typically accompany normal traffic congestion. And the resulting voluntary questioning of a motorist is as likely to prove important for police investigation as is the questioning of a pedestrian. Given these considerations, it would seem anomalous were the law (1) ordinarily to allow police freely to seek the voluntary cooperation of pedestrians but (2) ordinarily to forbid police to seek similar voluntary cooperation from motorists.

Finally, we do not believe that an *Edmond*-type rule is needed to prevent an unreasonable proliferation of police checkpoints. Practical considerations—namely, limited police resources and community hostility to related traffic tieups—seem likely to inhibit any such proliferation. And, of course, the Fourth Amendment's normal insistence that the stop be reasonable in context will still provide an important legal limitation on police use of this kind of information-seeking checkpoint.

These considerations, taken together, convince us that an *Edmond*-type presumptive rule of unconstitutionality does not apply here. That does not mean the stop is automatically, or even presumptively, constitutional. It simply means that we must judge its reasonableness, hence, its constitutionality, on the basis of the individual circumstances. And as this Court said in *Brown v. Texas*, 443 U.S. 47, 51 (1979), in judging reasonableness, we look to "the gravity of the public concerns served by the seizure, the degree to which the seizure advances the public interest, and the severity of the interference with individual liberty."

III

We now consider the reasonableness of the checkpoint stop before us in light of the factors just mentioned. We hold that the stop was constitutional.

The relevant public concern was grave. Police were investigating a crime that had resulted in a human death. No one denies the police's need to obtain more information at that time. And the stop's objective was to help find the perpetrator of a specific and known crime, not of unknown crimes of a general sort.

The stop advanced this grave public concern to a significant degree. The police appropriately tailored their checkpoint stops to fit important criminal investigatory needs. The stops took place about one week after the hit-and-run accident, on the same highway near the location of the accident, and at about the same time of night. And police used the stops to obtain information from drivers, some of whom might well have been in the vicinity of the crime at the time it occurred.

Most importantly, the stops interfered only minimally with liberty of the sort the Fourth Amendment seeks to protect. Viewed objectively, each stop required only a brief wait in line—a very few minutes at most. Contact with the police lasted only a few seconds. Police contact consisted simply of a request for information and the distribution of a flyer. Viewed subjectively, the contact provided little reason for anxiety or alarm. The police stopped all vehicles systematically. And there is no allegation here that the police acted in a discriminatory or otherwise unlawful manner while questioning motorists during stops.

For these reasons we conclude that the checkpoint stop was constitutional.

Highway Checkpoints

1. A motorist who is briefly stopped at a checkpoint is "seized" under the Fourth Amendment, but the seizure need not be supported by a warrant, probable cause, or even reasonable suspicion of wrongdoing, as long as vehicles are stopped in a neutral fashion that limits the discretion of the police. In determining the constitutionality of a checkpoint seizure, a court should weigh the gravity of the public concerns served by the seizure, the degree to which the seizure advances the public interest, and the severity of the interference with individual liberty.

2. The Supreme Court has approved highway checkpoints to enforce immigration laws, to ensure roadway safety, and to seek the public's assistance in solving a crime. Authorities may not, however, establish a highway checkpoint program whose primary purpose is ordinary crime control or the discovery and interdiction of illegal drugs. The primary purpose inquiry is conducted at the programmatic level; a court should not probe the minds of individual officers acting at the scene. When authorities establish a checkpoint primarily for the ordinary investigation of crimes, a motorist may be stopped only if there is individualized suspicion.

3. An extended detention of a motorist—one who is singled out for additional investigation beyond the brief stop and questioning associated with the normal operation of the checkpoint—must be justified by reasonable suspicion of wrongdoing.

D. AIRPORT SEARCHES

In response to a dramatic increase in airplane hijacking in the late 1960s, the Federal Aviation Administration (FAA), in cooperation with commercial carriers, developed and implemented screening procedures designed to identify and apprehend potential hijackers. Only selected passengers—those who fit a "Hijacker Profile"—were subjected to these early screening procedures. In late 1972, the FAA ordered the airlines to screen *all* commercial passengers—utilizing a magnetometer (metal detector) to search their persons and an x-ray device or a manual inspection to search any carry-on luggage—for weapons that could be used in a hijacking. These searches, conducted without a warrant and without individualized suspicion, were the subject of numerous challenges in the lower federal courts. While sensitive to the general need for airport security and passenger screening, the lower courts often struggled to find a doctrinal basis under the Fourth Amendment to justify particular searches.[a]

In the aftermath of the airplane hijackings of September 11, 2001, a newly-created federal agency, the Transportation Security Administration (TSA), assumed responsibility for airport screening. Under the TSA, screening procedures have become more intrusive and intensive, as greater resources and more sophisticated technology allow for closer and more rigorous examination of passengers, carry-on bags, and checked luggage. Some of these new screening techniques and technologies have also been challenged in court, leading to modifications and refinements designed to protect passengers' privacy without sacrificing security. For example, in *Redfern v. Napolitano*, 727 F.3d 77 (1st Cir. 2013), the plaintiffs challenged the TSA's use of two types of Advanced Imaging Technology (AIT) body scanners that produced clear images of the nude body of anyone who was scanned. The U.S. Court of Appeals for the First Circuit ultimately dismissed the case as moot because the TSA had abandoned the use of one type of AIT scanner, and had developed privacy software for the other type that eliminated the nude images and instead displayed the location of potential threats on a generic human figure.

Somewhat surprisingly, the Supreme Court has never directly ruled on the constitutionality of any airport passenger screening procedures, although language in a number of opinions leaves little room for doubt as to the Court's predisposition. For example, in *City of Indianapolis v. Edmond*, 531 U.S. 32 (2000), presented above in connection with highway checkpoints, Justice O'Connor wrote for the majority:

> Our holding [invalidating a narcotics detection checkpoint] does not affect the validity of border searches or searches at places like airports and government buildings, where the need for such measures to ensure public safety can be particularly acute.

Similarly, Justice Stevens, dissenting in *Michigan Department of State Police v. Sitz*, 496 U.S. 444 (1990), was careful to explain that his

---

[a]   *See, e.g.,* *U.S. v. Skipwith*, 482 F.2d 1272 (5th Cir. 1973) (drawing an analogy between airport searches and border searches); *U.S. v. Edwards*, 498 F.2d 496 (2d Cir. 1974) (comparing airport searches to administrative searches); *U.S. v. Kroll*, 481 F.2d 884 (8th Cir. 1973) (noting that airport searches cannot be justified on the basis of free and voluntary consent when government conditions the right to travel on relinquishment of Fourth Amendment rights).

objections to sobriety checkpoints did not apply to airline passenger screening:

> My objections to random seizures or temporary checkpoints do not apply to a host of other investigatory procedures that do not depend upon surprise and are unquestionably permissible. These procedures have been used to address other threats to human life no less pressing than the threat posed by drunken drivers. It is, for example, common practice to require every prospective airline passenger, or every visitor to a public building, to pass through a metal detector that will reveal the presence of a firearm or an explosive. Permanent, nondiscretionary checkpoints could be used to control serious dangers at other publicly operated facilities.

Finally, in his dissent in *U.S. v. Drayton*, 536 U.S. 194 (2002), a case included in Chapter 6, Justice Souter—who was joined by Justices Stevens and Ginsburg—observed:

> Anyone who travels by air today submits to searches of the person and luggage as a condition of boarding the aircraft. It is universally accepted that such intrusions are necessary to hedge against risks that, nowadays, even small children understand.

Were the Supreme Court to accept a case involving airline passenger screening, the Court would presumably decide it based on factors similar to those used in the highway checkpoint cases, weighing the significant concerns served by the security measures, the degree to which the measures address those concerns, and the severity of the intrusion into individual privacy.

Airport Searches

While the Supreme Court has not definitively addressed the issue, lower courts have held that airline passengers, their luggage, and other belongings may be searched before being permitted on an airplane. Such searches—motivated by serious safety and security considerations rather than by an interest in ordinary crime control—may be conducted without a warrant and without individualized suspicion of wrongdoing.

E. SEARCHES OF PERSONS ON PROBATION OR PAROLE

Probation is a criminal sanction imposed by a court, generally as an alternative to incarceration, which places the offender under supervision within the community. Parole is the supervised early release of an offender before the end of his original prison sentence; the offender is permitted to serve the remaining portion of his sentence within the community. Those on probation or parole are often subject to a variety of conditions and restrictions designed to prevent recidivism and other problems. One such condition, commonly imposed as a matter of state law or through a court order, requires the probationer or parolee to agree to submit to a search or seizure by law enforcement without a warrant or even reasonable suspicion of wrongdoing.

In *U.S. v. Knights*, police searched a probationer's apartment without a warrant, but with reasonable suspicion of criminal activity. The Supreme Court held that the search was reasonable under the Fourth Amendment.

U.S. V. KNIGHTS
534 U.S. 112 (2001)

CHIEF JUSTICE REHNQUIST delivered the opinion of the Court.

A California court sentenced respondent Mark James Knights to summary probation for a drug offense. The probation order included the following condition: that Knights would "submit his . . . person, property, place of residence, vehicle, personal effects, to search at anytime, with or without a search warrant, warrant of arrest or reasonable cause by any probation officer or law enforcement officer." Knights signed the probation order, which stated immediately above his signature that "I HAVE RECEIVED A COPY, READ AND UNDERSTAND THE ABOVE TERMS AND CONDITIONS OF PROBATION AND AGREE TO ABIDE BY SAME." In this case, we decide whether a search pursuant to this probation condition, and supported by reasonable suspicion, satisfied the Fourth Amendment.

Three days after Knights was placed on probation, a Pacific Gas & Electric (PG & E) power transformer and adjacent Pacific Bell telecommunications vault near the Napa County Airport were pried open and set on fire, causing an estimated $1.5 million in damage. Brass padlocks had been removed and a gasoline accelerant had been used to ignite the fire. This incident was the latest in more than 30 recent acts of vandalism against PG & E facilities in Napa County. Suspicion for these acts had long focused on Knights and his friend, Steven Simoneau. The incidents began after PG & E had filed a theft-of-services complaint against Knights and discontinued his electrical service for failure to pay his bill. Detective Todd Hancock of the Napa County Sheriff's Department had noticed that the acts of vandalism coincided with Knights' court appearance dates concerning the theft of PG & E services. And just a week before the arson, a sheriff's deputy had stopped Knights and Simoneau near a PG & E gas line and observed pipes and gasoline in Simoneau's pickup truck.

After the PG & E arson, a sheriff's deputy drove by Knights' residence, where he saw Simoneau's truck parked in front. The deputy felt the hood of the truck. It was warm. Detective Hancock decided to set up surveillance of Knights' apartment. At about 3:10 the next morning, Simoneau exited the apartment carrying three cylindrical items. Detective Hancock believed the items were pipe bombs. Simoneau walked across the street to the bank of the Napa River, and Hancock heard three splashes. Simoneau returned without the cylinders and drove away in his truck. Simoneau then stopped in a driveway, parked, and left the area. Detective Hancock entered the driveway and observed a number of suspicious objects in the truck: a Molotov cocktail and explosive materials, a gasoline can, and two brass padlocks that fit the description of those removed from the PG & E transformer vault.

After viewing the objects in Simoneau's truck, Detective Hancock decided to conduct a search of Knights' apartment. Detective Hancock was aware of the search condition in Knights' probation order and thus believed that a warrant was not necessary. The search revealed a detonation cord, ammunition, liquid chemicals, instruction manuals on chemistry and electrical circuitry, bolt cutters, telephone pole-climbing spurs, drug paraphernalia, and a brass padlock stamped "PG & E."

Knights was arrested, and a federal grand jury subsequently indicted him for conspiracy to commit arson, for possession of an unregistered destructive device, and for being a felon in possession of ammunition. Knights moved to suppress the evidence obtained during the search of his apartment. The District Court held that Detective Hancock had "reasonable suspicion" to believe that Knights was involved with incendiary materials. The District Court nonetheless granted the motion to suppress on the ground that the search was for "investigatory" rather than "probationary" purposes. The Court of Appeals for the Ninth Circuit affirmed. The Court of Appeals relied on its earlier decisions holding that the search condition in Knights' probation order "must be seen as limited to probation searches, and must stop short of investigation searches."

The Supreme Court of California has rejected this distinction and upheld searches pursuant to the California probation condition "whether the purpose of the search is to monitor the probationer or to serve some other law enforcement purpose." We granted certiorari to assess the constitutionality of searches made pursuant to this common California probation condition.

Certainly nothing in the condition of probation suggests that it was confined to searches bearing upon probationary status and nothing more. The search condition provides that Knights will submit to a search "by any probation officer or law enforcement officer" and does not mention anything about purpose. The question then is whether the Fourth

Amendment limits searches pursuant to this probation condition to those with a "probationary" purpose.

In the Government's view, Knights' acceptance of the search condition was voluntary because he had the option of rejecting probation and going to prison instead, which the Government argues is analogous to the voluntary decision defendants often make to waive their right to a trial and accept a plea bargain.

We need not decide whether Knights' acceptance of the search condition constituted consent in the sense of a complete waiver of his Fourth Amendment rights, however, because we conclude that the search of Knights was reasonable under our general Fourth Amendment approach of examining the totality of the circumstances, with the probation search condition being a salient circumstance.

The touchstone of the Fourth Amendment is reasonableness, and the reasonableness of a search is determined by assessing, on the one hand, the degree to which it intrudes upon an individual's privacy and, on the other, the degree to which it is needed for the promotion of legitimate governmental interests. Knights' status as a probationer subject to a search condition informs both sides of that balance. Probation, like incarceration, is a form of criminal sanction imposed by a court upon an offender after verdict, finding, or plea of guilty. Probation is one point on a continuum of possible punishments ranging from solitary confinement in a maximum-security facility to a few hours of mandatory community service. Inherent in the very nature of probation is that probationers do not enjoy the absolute liberty to which every citizen is entitled. Just as other punishments for criminal convictions curtail an offender's freedoms, a court granting probation may impose reasonable conditions that deprive the offender of some freedoms enjoyed by law-abiding citizens.

The judge who sentenced Knights to probation determined that it was necessary to condition the probation on Knights' acceptance of the search provision. It was reasonable to conclude that the search condition would further the two primary goals of probation—rehabilitation and protecting society from future criminal violations. The probation order clearly expressed the search condition and Knights was unambiguously informed of it. The probation condition thus significantly diminished Knights' reasonable expectation of privacy.[6]

In assessing the governmental interest side of the balance, it must be remembered that the very assumption of the institution of probation is

---

[6] We do not decide whether the probation condition so diminished, or completely eliminated, Knights' reasonable expectation of privacy (or constituted consent) that a search by a law enforcement officer without any individualized suspicion would have satisfied the reasonableness requirement of the Fourth Amendment. The terms of the probation condition permit such a search, but we need not address the constitutionality of a suspicionless search because the search in this case was supported by reasonable suspicion.

that the probationer is more likely than the ordinary citizen to violate the law. The recidivism rate of probationers is significantly higher than the general crime rate. And probationers have even more of an incentive to conceal their criminal activities and quickly dispose of incriminating evidence than the ordinary criminal because probationers are aware that they may be subject to supervision and face revocation of probation, and possible incarceration, in proceedings in which the trial rights of a jury and proof beyond a reasonable doubt, among other things, do not apply.

The State has a dual concern with a probationer. On the one hand is the hope that he will successfully complete probation and be integrated back into the community. On the other is the concern, quite justified, that he will be more likely to engage in criminal conduct than an ordinary member of the community. The view of the Court of Appeals in this case would require the State to shut its eyes to the latter concern and concentrate only on the former. But we hold that the Fourth Amendment does not put the State to such a choice. Its interest in apprehending violators of the criminal law, thereby protecting potential victims of criminal enterprise, may therefore justifiably focus on probationers in a way that it does not on the ordinary citizen.

We hold that the balance of these considerations requires no more than reasonable suspicion to conduct a search of this probationer's house. The degree of individualized suspicion required of a search is a determination of when there is a sufficiently high probability that criminal conduct is occurring to make the intrusion on the individual's privacy interest reasonable. Although the Fourth Amendment ordinarily requires the degree of probability embodied in the term "probable cause," a lesser degree satisfies the Constitution when the balance of governmental and private interests makes such a standard reasonable. Those interests warrant a lesser than probable-cause standard here. When an officer has reasonable suspicion that a probationer subject to a search condition is engaged in criminal activity, there is enough likelihood that criminal conduct is occurring that an intrusion on the probationer's significantly diminished privacy interests is reasonable. The same circumstances that lead us to conclude that reasonable suspicion is constitutionally sufficient also render a warrant requirement unnecessary.

The District Court found, and Knights concedes, that the search in this case was supported by reasonable suspicion. We therefore hold that the warrantless search of Knights, supported by reasonable suspicion and authorized by a condition of probation, was reasonable within the meaning of the Fourth Amendment.

———————————

In *Knights*, the police had reasonable suspicion that the probationer was engaged in criminal activity; the Supreme Court declined to decide whether a suspicionless search would have been justified. In *Samson v. California*, however, the Supreme Court upheld a warrantless and suspicionless search of a parolee, finding that parolees have fewer expectations of privacy than those on probation.

SAMSON V. CALIFORNIA
547 U.S. 843 (2006)

JUSTICE THOMAS delivered the opinion of the Court.

California law provides that every prisoner eligible for release on state parole "shall agree in writing to be subject to search or seizure by a parole officer or other peace officer at any time of the day or night, with or without a search warrant and with or without cause." We granted certiorari to decide whether a suspicionless search, conducted under the authority of this statute, violates the Constitution. We hold that it does not.

In September 2002, petitioner Donald Curtis Samson was on state parole in California, following a conviction for being a felon in possession of a firearm. On September 6, 2002, Officer Alex Rohleder of the San Bruno Police Department observed petitioner walking down a street with a woman and a child. Based on a prior contact with petitioner, Officer Rohleder was aware that petitioner was on parole and believed that he was facing an at-large warrant. Accordingly, Officer Rohleder stopped petitioner and asked him whether he had an outstanding parole warrant. Petitioner responded that there was no outstanding warrant and that he "was in good standing with his parole agent." Officer Rohleder confirmed, by radio dispatch, that petitioner was on parole and that he did not have an outstanding warrant. Nevertheless, based solely on petitioner's status as a parolee, Officer Rohleder searched petitioner. During the search, Officer Rohleder found a cigarette box in petitioner's left breast pocket. Inside the box he found a plastic baggie containing methamphetamine.

The State charged petitioner with possession of methamphetamine. The trial court denied petitioner's motion to suppress the methamphetamine evidence. A jury convicted petitioner of the possession charge, and the trial court sentenced him to seven years' imprisonment.

We granted certiorari to answer a variation of the question this Court left open in *U.S. v. Knights*, 534 U.S. 112 (2001)—whether a condition of release can so diminish or eliminate a released prisoner's reasonable expectation of privacy that a suspicionless search by a law enforcement officer would not offend the Fourth Amendment. Answering that question in the affirmative today, we affirm the judgment of the California Court of Appeal.

Under our general Fourth Amendment approach we examine the totality of the circumstances to determine whether a search is reasonable within the meaning of the Fourth Amendment. Whether a search is reasonable is determined by assessing, on the one hand, the degree to which it intrudes upon an individual's privacy and, on the other, the degree to which it is needed for the promotion of legitimate governmental interests.

We recently applied this approach in *U.S. v. Knights*. In that case, California law required Knights, as a probationer, to "submit his . . . person, property, place of residence, vehicle, personal effects, to search at anytime, with or without a search warrant, warrant of arrest or reasonable cause by any probation officer or law enforcement officer." Several days after Knights had been placed on probation, police suspected that he had been involved in several incidents of arson and vandalism. Based upon that suspicion and pursuant to the search condition of his probation, a police officer conducted a warrantless search of Knights' apartment and found arson and drug paraphernalia.

Because the search at issue in *Knights* was predicated on both the probation search condition and reasonable suspicion, we did not reach the question whether the search would have been reasonable under the Fourth Amendment had it been solely predicated upon the condition of probation. Our attention is directed to that question today, albeit in the context of a parolee search.

As we noted in *Knights*, parolees are on the "continuum" of state-imposed punishments. On this continuum, parolees have fewer expectations of privacy than probationers, because parole is more akin to imprisonment than probation is to imprisonment. As this Court has pointed out, parole is an established variation on imprisonment of convicted criminals. The essence of parole is release from prison, before the completion of sentence, on the condition that the prisoner abide by certain rules during the balance of the sentence. In most cases, the State is willing to extend parole only because it is able to condition it upon compliance with certain requirements.

California's system of parole is consistent with these observations: A California inmate may serve his parole period either in physical custody, or elect to complete his sentence out of physical custody and subject to certain conditions. Under the latter option, an inmate-turned-parolee remains in the legal custody of the California Department of Corrections through the remainder of his term, and must comply with all of the terms and conditions of parole, including mandatory drug tests, restrictions on association with felons or gang members, and mandatory meetings with parole officers. General conditions of parole also require a parolee to report to his assigned parole officer immediately upon release, inform the parole officer within 72 hours of any change in employment status, request permission to travel a distance of more than 50 miles from the parolee's home, and refrain from criminal conduct and possession of firearms, specified weapons, or knives unrelated to employment. Parolees may also be subject to special conditions, including psychiatric treatment programs, mandatory abstinence from alcohol, residence approval, and any other condition deemed necessary by the Board of Parole Hearings or the Department of Corrections and Rehabilitation due to unusual circumstances. The extent and reach of these conditions clearly demonstrate that parolees like petitioner have severely diminished expectations of privacy by virtue of their status alone.

Additionally, as we found "salient" in *Knights* with respect to the probation search condition, the parole search condition under California law—requiring inmates who opt for parole to submit to suspicionless searches by a parole officer or other peace officer "at any time"—was clearly expressed to petitioner. He signed an order submitting to the condition and thus was unambiguously aware of it. In *Knights*, we found that acceptance of a clear and unambiguous search condition "significantly diminished Knights' reasonable expectation of privacy." Examining the totality of the circumstances pertaining to petitioner's status as a parolee, "an established variation on imprisonment," including the plain terms of the parole search condition, we conclude that petitioner did not have an expectation of privacy that society would recognize as legitimate.[3]

The State's interests, by contrast, are substantial. This Court has repeatedly acknowledged that a State has an "overwhelming interest" in supervising parolees because "parolees are more likely to commit future criminal offenses." Similarly, this Court has repeatedly acknowledged that a State's interests in reducing recidivism and thereby promoting reintegration and positive citizenship among probationers and parolees warrant privacy intrusions that would not otherwise be tolerated under the Fourth Amendment.

Contrary to petitioner's contention, California's ability to conduct suspicionless searches of parolees serves its interest in reducing recidivism, in a manner that aids, rather than hinders, the reintegration of parolees into productive society.

The concern that California's suspicionless search system gives officers unbridled discretion to conduct searches, thereby inflicting dignitary harms that arouse strong resentment in parolees and undermine their ability to reintegrate into productive society, is belied by California's prohibition on "arbitrary, capricious or harassing" searches. The dissent's claim that parolees under California law are subject to

---

[3]   Because we find that the search at issue here is reasonable under our general Fourth Amendment approach, we need not reach the issue whether acceptance of the search condition constituted consent in the sense of a complete waiver of his Fourth Amendment rights.

capricious searches conducted at the unchecked "whim" of law enforcement officers ignores this prohibition. Likewise, petitioner's concern that California's suspicionless search law frustrates reintegration efforts by permitting intrusions into the privacy interests of third parties is also unavailing because that concern would arise under a suspicion-based regime as well.

Thus, we conclude that the Fourth Amendment does not prohibit a police officer from conducting a suspicionless search of a parolee.

JUSTICE STEVENS, with whom JUSTICE SOUTER and JUSTICE BREYER join, dissenting.

Our prior cases have consistently assumed that the Fourth Amendment provides some degree of protection for probationers and parolees. The protection is not as robust as that afforded to ordinary citizens; we have held that probationers' lowered expectation of privacy may justify their warrantless search upon reasonable suspicion of wrongdoing. We have also recognized that the supervisory responsibilities of probation officers, who are required to provide "individualized counseling" and to monitor their charges' progress, and who are in a unique position to judge "how close a supervision the probationer requires," may give rise to special needs justifying departures from Fourth Amendment strictures. But [our prior cases do not] support a regime of suspicionless searches, conducted pursuant to a blanket grant of discretion untethered by any procedural safeguards, by law enforcement personnel who have no special interest in the welfare of the parolee or probationer.

What the Court sanctions today is an unprecedented curtailment of liberty. Combining faulty syllogism with circular reasoning, the Court concludes that parolees have no more legitimate an expectation of privacy in their persons than do prisoners. However superficially appealing that parity in treatment may seem, it runs roughshod over our precedent. It also rests on an intuition that fares poorly under scrutiny. And once one acknowledges that parolees do have legitimate expectations of privacy beyond those of prisoners, our Fourth Amendment jurisprudence does not permit the conclusion, reached by the Court here for the first time, that a search supported by neither individualized suspicion nor "special needs" is nonetheless "reasonable."

The suspicionless search is the very evil the Fourth Amendment was intended to stamp out. The pre-Revolutionary "writs of assistance," which permitted roving searches for contraband, were reviled precisely because they "placed the liberty of every man in the hands of every petty officer." While individualized suspicion is not an "irreducible" component of reasonableness under the Fourth Amendment, the requirement has been dispensed with only when programmatic searches were required to meet a "special need" divorced from the State's general interest in law enforcement.

Not surprisingly, the majority does not seek to justify the search of petitioner on "special needs" grounds. Although the Court has in the past relied on special needs to uphold warrantless searches of probationers, it has never gone so far as to hold that a probationer or parolee may be subjected to full search at the whim of any law enforcement officer he happens to encounter, whether or not the officer has reason to suspect him of wrongdoing.

Ignoring just how "closely guarded" is that "category of constitutionally permissible suspicionless searches," the Court for the first time upholds an entirely suspicionless search unsupported by any special need. And it goes further: In special needs cases we have at least insisted upon programmatic safeguards designed to ensure evenhandedness in application; if individualized suspicion is to be jettisoned, it must be replaced with measures to protect against the state actor's unfettered discretion. Here, by contrast, there are no policies in place—no standards, guidelines, or procedures—to rein in officers and furnish a bulwark against the arbitrary exercise of discretion that is the height of unreasonableness.

The Court seems to acknowledge that unreasonable searches "inflict dignitary harms that arouse strong resentment in parolees and undermine their ability to reintegrate into productive society." It is satisfied, however, that the California courts' prohibition against "arbitrary, capricious or harassing" searches suffices to avert those harms—which are of course counterproductive to the State's purported aim of rehabilitating former prisoners and reintegrating them into society. I am unpersuaded. The requirement of individualized suspicion, in all its iterations, is the shield the Framers selected to guard against the evils of arbitrary action, caprice, and harassment. To say that those evils may be averted without that shield is, I fear, to pay lipservice to the end while withdrawing the means.

Searches of Persons on Probation or Parole

1.   As a condition of probation, an officer may, without a warrant, search the person, property, or residence of a probationer based upon reasonable suspicion of criminal activity.

2.   As a condition of parole, an officer may, without a warrant and without any individualized suspicion of wrongdoing, search the person, property, or residence of a parolee. A released prisoner's status as a parolee, along with a parole search condition, can so diminish or eliminate the parolee's reasonable expectation of privacy that a suspicionless search by a law enforcement officer would not offend the Fourth Amendment.

> **Note:** Although the Supreme Court did not decide the issue, there are indications in *U.S. v. Knights* and *Samson v. California* that the Court would sustain a suspicionless search of a probationer if the probationer agreed to submit to such a search as a condition of probation.

F. SEARCHES IN PRISONS AND JAILS

The Supreme Court has given authorities wide latitude to establish policies designed to maintain safety and security in prisons and jails. In *Turner v. Safley*, 482 U.S. 78 (1987), the Court confirmed the importance of deference to correctional officials and explained that a regulation impinging on an inmate's constitutional rights must be upheld "if it is reasonably related to legitimate penological interests." As a consequence of the Court's deference to the judgment of correctional officials, prison and jail inmates have very limited privacy rights on their persons, in their cells, and in their communications, and authorities may generally perform highly intrusive searches without probable cause or a warrant.

In *Bell v. Wolfish*, 441 U.S. 520 (1979), the Supreme Court addressed a Fourth Amendment challenge to a rule requiring pretrial detainees—those who have been charged with a crime but not yet tried on the charge—to expose their body cavities for visual inspection as part of a strip search conducted after every contact visit with a person from outside the institution. The inmates at a federal correctional center in New York who were challenging the rule argued that there was no security justification for these searches, since guests were searched before they entered the visiting room, and the inmates were under constant surveillance during the visit. Moreover, there had been only one instance in which an inmate attempted to sneak contraband back into the facility. Despite these arguments, the Supreme Court upheld the search policy, deferring to the judgment of correctional officials that the inspections served not only to discover but also to deter the smuggling of weapons, drugs, and other prohibited items back into the institution.

More recently, in *Florence v. Board of Chosen Freeholders of County of Burlington*, 132 S.Ct. 1510 (2012), the Supreme Court addressed a Fourth Amendment challenge brought by Albert Florence, who was arrested for a minor offense, and then, as part of the routine intake process at jail, was forced to remove his clothing and expose his genitals to close visual inspection, all without any reasonable suspicion that he was concealing contraband. Noting that "[p]eople detained for minor offenses can turn out to be the most devious and dangerous criminals," and deferring to the judgment of correctional officials who warned that exemptions for certain detainees would prove unworkable and dangerous, the Supreme Court concluded that the intake search procedures "struck a reasonable balance between inmate privacy and the needs of the institutions."

In *Hudson v. Palmer*, 468 U.S. 517 (1984), a state prison inmate claimed that he was subjected to a "shakedown" search of his prison locker and cell for contraband. The inmate argued that the search was performed solely for purposes of harassment, that he had a limited right to privacy in his cell, and that searches of cells and personal effects should only be conducted pursuant to an established policy or upon reasonable suspicion. The Supreme Court rejected the inmate's claims, finding that prisoners have no reasonable expectation of privacy in their cells:

> Notwithstanding our caution in approaching claims that the Fourth Amendment is inapplicable in a given context, we hold that society is not prepared to recognize as legitimate any subjective expectation of privacy that a prisoner might have in his prison cell and that, accordingly, the Fourth Amendment proscription against unreasonable searches does not apply within the confines of the prison cell. The recognition of privacy rights for prisoners in their individual cells simply cannot be reconciled with the concept of incarceration and the needs and objectives of penal institutions.

Even verbal communications between prisoners and outsiders can be searched or monitored without the traditional Fourth Amendment protections of probable cause and a warrant. In an early pre-*Katz* decision, *Lanza v. New York*, 370 U.S. 139 (1962), Harry Lanza met with his brother, a jail inmate, in a room at the jail set aside for such visits. The conversation was electronically recorded and was used—not against the incarcerated brother, but against Harry Lanza himself—in an investigation of possible corruption in the state parole system. The Supreme Court concluded that although there was "no doubt" that surreptitious electronic eavesdropping may amount to an unreasonable search and seizure in certain circumstances, the conversation took place in an area that was not constitutionally protected:

> [W]ithout attempting either to define or to predict the ultimate scope of Fourth Amendment protection, it is obvious that a jail shares none of the attributes of privacy of a home, an automobile, an office, or a hotel room. In prison, official surveillance has traditionally been the order of the day.

Over the years, a number of lower courts have held that authorities may monitor and record inmate telephone conversations, except those that are protected by attorney-client privilege. These lower courts have generally reasoned that because inmates are warned ahead of time that their phone calls may be monitored and recorded, they should not expect their communications to remain private.[b]

---

[b] *See, e.g., U.S. v. Van Poyck*, 77 F.3d 285 (9th Cir. 1996); *U.S. v. Amen*, 831 F.2d 373 (2d Cir. 1987).

Searches in Prisons and Jails

1.   Deference should be given to the judgment of correctional officials in establishing policies designed to maintain safety and security in prisons and jails. Accordingly, a regulation impinging on an inmate's constitutional rights must be upheld if it is reasonably related to legitimate penological interests.

2.   Inmates in prisons and jails—including those who are convicted and serving a sentence, those who are pretrial detainees, and those who are merely arrestees being held for minor offenses—have very limited privacy rights in their persons, cells, and communications.

   a.   Authorities may subject inmates to invasive strip searches upon intake at a correctional facility or following contact with an outsider. Such searches may occur without individualized suspicion or a warrant.

   b.   Inmates are entitled to no expectation of privacy in their cells, which may be searched at any time without individualized suspicion or a warrant.

   c.   Authorities may monitor and record telephone calls and in-person conversations between inmates and outsiders, with the exception of those communications that are protected by attorney-client privilege. Such monitoring or recording may take place without individualized suspicion or a warrant.

G. SEARCHES IN SCHOOLS

As with most of the other special contexts presented in this Chapter, the Supreme Court has relaxed the traditional warrant and probable cause requirements for searches conducted by teachers and administrators in public schools. In *New Jersey v. T.L.O.*, the Court held that school officials could, without a warrant, search a student's purse based on reasonable suspicion that she was violating a school rule.

NEW JERSEY V. T.L.O.
469 U.S. 325 (1985)

JUSTICE WHITE delivered the opinion of the Court.

We here address the questions of the proper standard for assessing the legality of searches conducted by public school officials and the application of that standard to the facts of this case.

I

On March 7, 1980, a teacher at Piscataway High School in Middlesex County, N.J., discovered two girls smoking in a lavatory. One of the two girls was the respondent T.L.O., who at that time was a 14-year-old high school freshman. Because smoking in the lavatory was a violation of a school rule, the teacher took the two girls to the Principal's office, where they met with Assistant Vice Principal Theodore Choplick. In response to questioning by Mr. Choplick, T.L.O.'s companion admitted that she had violated the rule. T.L.O., however, denied that she had been smoking in the lavatory and claimed that she did not smoke at all.

Mr. Choplick asked T.L.O. to come into his private office and demanded to see her purse. Opening the purse, he found a pack of cigarettes, which he removed from the purse and held before T.L.O. as he accused her of having lied to him. As he reached into the purse for the cigarettes, Mr. Choplick also noticed a package of cigarette rolling papers. In his experience, possession of rolling papers by high school students was closely associated with the use of marihuana. Suspecting that a closer examination of the purse might yield further evidence of drug use, Mr. Choplick proceeded to search the purse thoroughly. The search revealed a small amount of marihuana, a pipe, a number of empty plastic bags, a substantial quantity of money in one-dollar bills, an index card that appeared to be a list of students who owed T.L.O. money, and two letters that implicated T.L.O. in marihuana dealing.

Mr. Choplick notified T.L.O.'s mother and the police, and turned the evidence of drug dealing over to the police. At the request of the police, T.L.O.'s mother took her daughter to police headquarters, where T.L.O. confessed that she had been selling marihuana at the high school. On the basis of the confession and the evidence seized by Mr. Choplick, the State brought delinquency charges against T.L.O. in the Juvenile and Domestic Relations Court of Middlesex County. Contending that Mr. Choplick's search of her purse violated the Fourth Amendment, T.L.O. moved to suppress the evidence found in her purse as well as her confession, which, she argued, was tainted by the allegedly unlawful search. The Juvenile Court denied the motion to suppress, found T.L.O. to be a delinquent and sentenced her to a year's probation.

II

In determining whether the search at issue in this case violated the Fourth Amendment, we are faced initially with the question whether that Amendment's prohibition on unreasonable searches and seizures applies to searches conducted by public school officials. We hold that it does.

It is now beyond dispute that the Federal Constitution, by virtue of the Fourteenth Amendment, prohibits unreasonable searches and seizures by state officers. Equally indisputable is the proposition that the Fourteenth Amendment protects the rights of students against encroachment by public school officials.

These two propositions—that the Fourth Amendment applies to the States through the Fourteenth Amendment, and that the actions of public school officials are subject to the limits placed on state action by the Fourteenth Amendment—might appear sufficient to answer the suggestion that the Fourth Amendment does not proscribe unreasonable searches by school officials. However, the State of New Jersey has argued that the history of the Fourth Amendment indicates that the Amendment was intended to regulate only searches and seizures carried out by law enforcement officers; accordingly, although public school officials are concededly state agents for purposes of the Fourteenth Amendment, the Fourth Amendment creates no rights enforceable against them.

It may well be true that the evil toward which the Fourth Amendment was primarily directed was the resurrection of the pre-Revolutionary practice of using general warrants or "writs of assistance" to authorize searches for contraband by officers of the Crown. But this Court has never limited the Amendment's prohibition on unreasonable searches and seizures to operations conducted by the police. Rather, the Court has long spoken of the Fourth Amendment's strictures as restraints imposed upon "governmental action"—that is, upon the activities of sovereign authority. Accordingly, we have held the Fourth Amendment applicable to the activities of civil as well as criminal authorities: building inspectors, Occupational Safety and Health Act inspectors, and even firemen entering privately owned premises to battle a fire are all subject to the restraints imposed by the Fourth Amendment.

Notwithstanding the general applicability of the Fourth Amendment to the activities of civil authorities, a few courts have concluded that school officials are exempt from the dictates of the Fourth Amendment by virtue of the special nature of their authority over schoolchildren. Teachers and school administrators, it is said, act *in loco parentis* in their dealings with students: their authority is that of the parent, not the State, and is therefore not subject to the limits of the Fourth Amendment.

Such reasoning is in tension with contemporary reality and the teachings of this Court. We have held school officials subject to the commands of the First Amendment and the Due Process Clause of the Fourteenth Amendment. If school authorities are state actors for purposes of the constitutional guarantees of freedom of expression and due process, it is difficult to understand why they should be deemed to be exercising parental rather than public authority when conducting searches of their students. Today's public school officials do not merely exercise authority voluntarily conferred on them by individual parents; rather, they act in furtherance of publicly mandated educational and disciplinary policies. In carrying out searches and other disciplinary functions pursuant to such policies, school officials act as representatives of the State, not merely as surrogates for the parents, and they cannot claim the parents' immunity from the strictures of the Fourth Amendment.

III

To hold that the Fourth Amendment applies to searches conducted by school authorities is only to begin the inquiry into the standards governing such searches. Although the underlying command of the Fourth Amendment is always that searches and seizures be reasonable, what is reasonable depends on the context within which a search takes place. The determination of the standard of reasonableness governing any specific class of searches requires balancing the need to search against the invasion which the search entails. On one side of the balance are arrayed the individual's legitimate expectations of privacy and personal security; on the other, the government's need for effective methods to deal with breaches of public order.

We have recognized that even a limited search of the person is a substantial invasion of privacy. We have also recognized that searches of closed items of personal luggage are intrusions on protected privacy interests, for the Fourth Amendment provides protection to the owner of every container that conceals its contents from plain view. A search of a child's person or of a closed purse or other bag carried on her person,[5] no less than a similar search carried out on an adult, is undoubtedly a severe violation of subjective expectations of privacy.

Of course, the Fourth Amendment does not protect subjective expectations of privacy that are unreasonable or otherwise "illegitimate." To receive the protection of the Fourth Amendment, an expectation of privacy must be one that society is prepared to recognize as legitimate. The State of New Jersey has argued that because of the pervasive supervision to which children in the schools are necessarily subject, a child has virtually no legitimate expectation of privacy in articles of personal property "unnecessarily" carried into a school. This argument has two factual premises: (1) the fundamental incompatibility of expectations of privacy with the maintenance of a sound educational environment; and (2) the minimal interest of the child in bringing any items of personal property into the school. Both premises are severely flawed.

Although this Court may take notice of the difficulty of maintaining discipline in the public schools today, the situation is not so dire that students in the schools may claim no legitimate expectations of privacy. We have recently recognized that the need to maintain order in a prison

---

[5]   We do not address the question, not presented by this case, whether a schoolchild has a legitimate expectation of privacy in lockers, desks, or other school property provided for the storage of school supplies. Nor do we express any opinion on the standards (if any) governing searches of such areas by school officials or by other public authorities acting at the request of school officials.

is such that prisoners retain no legitimate expectations of privacy in their cells, but it goes almost without saying that the prisoner and the schoolchild stand in wholly different circumstances, separated by the harsh facts of criminal conviction and incarceration. We are not yet ready to hold that the schools and the prisons need be equated for purposes of the Fourth Amendment.

Nor does the State's suggestion that children have no legitimate need to bring personal property into the schools seem well anchored in reality. Students at a minimum must bring to school not only the supplies needed for their studies, but also keys, money, and the necessaries of personal hygiene and grooming. In addition, students may carry on their persons or in purses or wallets such nondisruptive yet highly personal items as photographs, letters, and diaries. Finally, students may have perfectly legitimate reasons to carry with them articles of property needed in connection with extracurricular or recreational activities. In short, schoolchildren may find it necessary to carry with them a variety of legitimate, noncontraband items, and there is no reason to conclude that they have necessarily waived all rights to privacy in such items merely by bringing them onto school grounds.

Against the child's interest in privacy must be set the substantial interest of teachers and administrators in maintaining discipline in the classroom and on school grounds. Maintaining order in the classroom has never been easy, but in recent years, school disorder has often taken particularly ugly forms: drug use and violent crime in the schools have become major social problems. Even in schools that have been spared the most severe disciplinary problems, the preservation of order and a proper educational environment requires close supervision of schoolchildren, as well as the enforcement of rules against conduct that would be perfectly permissible if undertaken by an adult. Accordingly, we have recognized that maintaining security and order in the schools requires a certain degree of flexibility in school disciplinary procedures, and we have respected the value of preserving the informality of the student-teacher relationship.

How, then, should we strike the balance between the schoolchild's legitimate expectations of privacy and the school's equally legitimate need to maintain an environment in which learning can take place? It is evident that the school setting requires some easing of the restrictions to which searches by public authorities are ordinarily subject. The warrant requirement, in particular, is unsuited to the school environment: requiring a teacher to obtain a warrant before searching a child suspected of an infraction of school rules (or of the criminal law) would unduly interfere with the maintenance of the swift and informal disciplinary procedures needed in the schools. Just as we have in other cases dispensed with the warrant requirement when the burden of obtaining a warrant is likely to frustrate the governmental purpose behind the search, we hold today that school officials need not obtain a warrant before searching a student who is under their authority.

The school setting also requires some modification of the level of suspicion of illicit activity needed to justify a search. Ordinarily, a search—even one that may permissibly be carried out without a warrant—must be based upon "probable cause" to believe that a violation of the law has occurred. However, "probable cause" is not an irreducible requirement of a valid search. The fundamental command of the Fourth Amendment is that searches and seizures be reasonable, and although both the concept of probable cause and the requirement of a warrant bear on the reasonableness of a search, in certain limited circumstances neither is required. Where a careful balancing of governmental and private interests suggests that the public interest is best served by a Fourth Amendment standard of reasonableness that stops short of probable cause, we have not hesitated to adopt such a standard.

We join the majority of courts that have examined this issue in concluding that the accommodation of the privacy interests of schoolchildren with the substantial need of teachers and administrators for freedom to maintain order in the schools does not require strict adherence to the requirement that searches be based on probable cause to believe that the subject of the search has violated or is violating the law. Rather, the legality of a search of a student should depend simply on the reasonableness, under all the circumstances, of the search. Determining the reasonableness of any search involves a twofold inquiry: first, one must consider whether the action was justified at its inception; second, one must determine whether the search as actually conducted was reasonably related in scope to the circumstances which justified the interference in the first place. Under ordinary circumstances, a search of a student by a teacher or other school official[7] will be "justified at its inception" when there are reasonable grounds for suspecting that the search will turn up evidence that the student has violated or is violating either the law or the rules of the school. Such a search will be permissible in its scope when the measures adopted are reasonably related to the objectives of the search and not excessively intrusive in light of the age and sex of the student and the nature of the infraction.

This standard will, we trust, neither unduly burden the efforts of school authorities to maintain order in their schools nor authorize unrestrained intrusions upon the privacy of schoolchildren. By focusing attention on the question of reasonableness, the standard will spare teachers and school administrators the necessity of schooling themselves

---

[7] We here consider only searches carried out by school authorities acting alone and on their own authority. This case does not present the question of the appropriate standard for assessing the legality of searches conducted by school officials in conjunction with or at the behest of law enforcement agencies, and we express no opinion on that question.

in the niceties of probable cause and permit them to regulate their conduct according to the dictates of reason and common sense. At the same time, the reasonableness standard should ensure that the interests of students will be invaded no more than is necessary to achieve the legitimate end of preserving order in the schools.

IV

Our review of the facts surrounding the search leads us to conclude that the search was in no sense unreasonable for Fourth Amendment purposes.

The incident that gave rise to this case actually involved two separate searches, with the first—the search for cigarettes—providing the suspicion that gave rise to the second—the search for marihuana. Although it is the fruits of the second search that are at issue here, the validity of the search for marihuana must depend on the reasonableness of the initial search for cigarettes, as there would have been no reason to suspect that T.L.O. possessed marihuana had the first search not taken place. Accordingly, it is to the search for cigarettes that we first turn our attention.

The New Jersey Supreme Court pointed to two grounds for its holding that the search for cigarettes was unreasonable. First, the court observed that possession of cigarettes was not in itself illegal or a violation of school rules. Because the contents of T.L.O.'s purse would therefore have "no direct bearing on the infraction" of which she was accused (smoking in a lavatory where smoking was prohibited), there was no reason to search her purse. Second, even assuming that a search of T.L.O.'s purse might under some circumstances be reasonable in light of the accusation made against T.L.O., the New Jersey court concluded that Mr. Choplick in this particular case had no reasonable grounds to suspect that T.L.O. had cigarettes in her purse. At best, according to the court, Mr. Choplick had "a good hunch."

Both these conclusions are implausible. T.L.O. had been accused of smoking, and had denied the accusation in the strongest possible terms when she stated that she did not smoke at all. Surely it cannot be said that under these circumstances, T.L.O.'s possession of cigarettes would be irrelevant to the charges against her or to her response to those charges. T.L.O.'s possession of cigarettes, once it was discovered, would both corroborate the report that she had been smoking and undermine the credibility of her defense to the charge of smoking. To be sure, the discovery of the cigarettes would not prove that T.L.O. had been smoking in the lavatory; nor would it, strictly speaking, necessarily be inconsistent with her claim that she did not smoke at all. The relevance of T.L.O.'s possession of cigarettes to the question whether she had been smoking and to the credibility of her denial that she smoked supplied the necessary "nexus" between the item searched for and the infraction under investigation.

Of course, the New Jersey Supreme Court also held that Mr. Choplick had no reasonable suspicion that the purse would contain cigarettes. This conclusion is puzzling. A teacher had reported that T.L.O. was smoking in the lavatory. Certainly this report gave Mr. Choplick reason to suspect that T.L.O. was carrying cigarettes with her; and if she did have cigarettes, her purse was the obvious place in which to find them. Mr. Choplick's suspicion that there were cigarettes in the purse was not an inchoate and unparticularized suspicion or "hunch"; rather, it was the sort of common-sense conclusion about human behavior upon which practical people—including government officials—are entitled to rely. Of course, even if the teacher's report were true, T.L.O. *might* not have had a pack of cigarettes with her; she might have borrowed a cigarette from someone else or have been sharing a cigarette with another student. But the requirement of reasonable suspicion is not a requirement of absolute certainty. Because the hypothesis that T.L.O. was carrying cigarettes in her purse was itself not unreasonable, it is irrelevant that other hypotheses were also consistent with the teacher's accusation. Accordingly, it cannot be said that Mr. Choplick acted unreasonably when he examined T.L.O.'s purse to see if it contained cigarettes.

Our conclusion that Mr. Choplick's decision to open T.L.O.'s purse was reasonable brings us to the question of the further search for marihuana once the pack of cigarettes was located. The suspicion upon which the search for marihuana was founded was provided when Mr. Choplick observed a package of rolling papers in the purse as he removed the pack of cigarettes. Although T.L.O. does not dispute the reasonableness of Mr. Choplick's belief that the rolling papers indicated the presence of marihuana, she does contend that the scope of the search Mr. Choplick conducted exceeded permissible bounds when he seized and read certain letters that implicated T.L.O. in drug dealing. This argument, too, is unpersuasive. The discovery of the rolling papers concededly gave rise to a reasonable suspicion that T.L.O. was carrying marihuana as well as cigarettes in her purse. This suspicion justified further exploration of T.L.O.'s purse, which turned up more evidence of drug-related activities: a pipe, a number of plastic bags of the type commonly used to store marihuana, a small quantity of marihuana, and a fairly substantial amount of money. Under these circumstances, it was not unreasonable to extend the search to a separate zippered compartment of the purse; and when a search of that compartment revealed an index card containing a list of "people who owe me money" as well as two letters, the inference that T.L.O. was involved in marihuana trafficking was substantial enough to justify Mr. Choplick in examining the letters to determine whether they contained any further evidence. In short, we cannot conclude that the search for marihuana was unreasonable in any respect.

JUSTICE BRENNAN, with whom JUSTICE MARSHALL joins, concurring in part and dissenting in part.

I fully agree with Part II of the Court's opinion. Teachers, like all other government officials, must conform their conduct to the Fourth Amendment's protections of personal privacy and personal security.

I do not, however, otherwise join the Court's opinion. Today's decision sanctions school officials to conduct full-scale searches on a "reasonableness" standard whose only definite content is that it is *not* the same test as the "probable cause" standard found in the text of the Fourth Amendment. In adopting this unclear, unprecedented, and unnecessary departure from generally applicable Fourth Amendment standards, the Court carves out a broad exception to standards that this Court has developed over years of considering Fourth Amendment problems. Its decision is supported neither by precedent nor even by a fair application of the "balancing test" it proclaims in this very opinion.

I agree that schoolteachers or principals, when not acting as agents of law enforcement authorities, generally may conduct a search of their students' belongings without first obtaining a warrant. A teacher or principal could neither carry out essential teaching functions nor adequately protect students' safety if required to wait for a warrant before conducting a necessary search.

I emphatically disagree with the Court's decision to cast aside the constitutional probable-cause standard when assessing the constitutional validity of a schoolhouse search. The Court's decision jettisons the probable-cause standard—the only standard that finds support in the text of the Fourth Amendment—on the basis of its Rohrschach-like "balancing test." Use of such a "balancing test" to determine the standard for evaluating the validity of a full-scale search represents a sizable innovation in Fourth Amendment analysis. This innovation finds support neither in precedent nor policy and portends a dangerous weakening of the purpose of the Fourth Amendment to protect the privacy and security of our citizens.

––––––––––––

In *T.L.O.*, the Supreme Court held that a search of a student by a public school official is justified at its inception if the official has reasonable suspicion that the student has violated the law or a school rule. The Court went on to hold that the scope of the search must be reasonably related to its objectives and "not excessively intrusive in light of the age and sex of the student and the nature of the infraction." In *Safford Unified School District #1 v. Redding*, the Supreme Court held that a school's search of a student was, in fact, excessively intrusive when it included an inspection of the student's bra and underwear for Ibuprofen pills.

SAFFORD UNIFIED SCHOOL DISTRICT #1 V. REDDING
557 U.S. 364 (2009)

JUSTICE SOUTER delivered the opinion of the Court.

The issue here is whether a 13-year-old student's Fourth Amendment right was violated when she was subjected to a search of her bra and underpants by school officials acting on reasonable suspicion that she had brought forbidden prescription and over-the-counter drugs to school. Because there were no reasons to suspect the drugs presented a danger or were concealed in her underwear, we hold that the search did violate the Constitution, but because there is reason to question the clarity with which the right was established, the official who ordered the unconstitutional search is entitled to qualified immunity from liability.

I

The events immediately prior to the search in question began in 13-year-old Savana Redding's math class at Safford Middle School one October day in 2003. The assistant principal of the school, Kerry Wilson, came into the room and asked Savana to go to his office. There, he showed her a day planner, unzipped and open flat on his desk, in which there were several knives, lighters, a permanent marker, and a cigarette. Wilson asked Savana whether the planner was hers; she said it was, but that a few days before she had lent it to her friend, Marissa Glines. Savana stated that none of the items in the planner belonged to her.

Wilson then showed Savana four white prescription-strength ibuprofen 400-mg pills, and one over-the-counter blue naproxen 200-mg pill, all used for pain and inflammation but banned under school rules without advance permission. He asked Savana if she knew anything about the pills. Savana answered that she did not. Wilson then told Savana that he had received a report that she was giving these pills to fellow students; Savana denied it and agreed to let Wilson search her belongings. Helen Romero, an administrative assistant, came into the office, and together with Wilson they searched Savana's backpack, finding nothing.

At that point, Wilson instructed Romero to take Savana to the school nurse's office to search her clothes for pills. Romero and the nurse, Peggy Schwallier, asked Savana to remove her jacket, socks, and shoes, leaving her in stretch pants and a T-shirt (both without pockets), which she was then asked to remove. Finally, Savana was told to pull her bra out and to the side and shake it, and to pull out the elastic on her underpants, thus exposing her breasts and pelvic area to some degree. No pills were found.

Savana's mother filed suit against Safford Unified School District #1, Wilson, Romero, and Schwallier for conducting a strip search in violation of Savana's Fourth Amendment rights. The individuals (hereinafter petitioners) moved for summary judgment, raising a defense of qualified immunity.

II

The Fourth Amendment generally requires a law enforcement officer to have probable cause for conducting a search.

In *New Jersey v. T.L.O.*, 469 U.S. 325 (1985), we recognized that the school setting "requires some modification of the level of suspicion of illicit activity needed to justify a search," and held that for searches by school officials "a careful balancing of governmental and private interests suggests that the public interest is best served by a Fourth Amendment standard of reasonableness that stops short of probable cause." We have thus applied a standard of reasonable suspicion to determine the legality of a school administrator's search of a student, and have held that a school search "will be permissible in its scope when the measures adopted are reasonably related to the objectives of the search and not excessively intrusive in light of the age and sex of the student and the nature of the infraction."

A number of our cases on probable cause have an implicit bearing on the reliable knowledge element of reasonable suspicion, as we have attempted to flesh out the knowledge component by looking to the degree to which known facts imply prohibited conduct, the specificity of the information received, and the reliability of its source. At the end of the day, however, we have realized that these factors cannot rigidly control, and we have come back to saying that the standards are fluid concepts that take their substantive content from the particular contexts in which they are being assessed.

Perhaps the best that can be said generally about the required knowledge component of probable cause for a law enforcement officer's evidence search is that it raise a "fair probability," or a "substantial chance," of discovering evidence of criminal activity. The lesser standard for school searches could as readily be described as a moderate chance of finding evidence of wrongdoing.

III

In this case, the school's policies strictly prohibit the nonmedical use, possession, or sale of any drug on school grounds, including "[a]ny prescription or over-the-counter drug, except those for which permission to use in school has been granted pursuant to Board policy." A week before Savana was searched, another student, Jordan Romero (no relation of the school's administrative assistant), told the principal and Assistant Principal Wilson that "certain students were bringing drugs and weapons on campus," and that he had been sick after taking some pills that "he got from a classmate." On the morning of October 8, the same boy handed Wilson a white pill that he said Marissa Glines had given him. He told Wilson that students were planning to take the pills at lunch.

Wilson learned from Peggy Schwallier, the school nurse, that the pill was Ibuprofen 400 mg, available only by prescription. Wilson then called Marissa out of class. Outside the classroom, Marissa's teacher handed Wilson the day planner, found within Marissa's reach, containing various contraband items. Wilson escorted Marissa back to his office.

In the presence of Helen Romero, Wilson requested Marissa to turn out her pockets and open her wallet. Marissa produced a blue pill, several white ones, and a razor blade. Wilson asked where the blue pill came from, and Marissa answered, "I guess it slipped in when *she* gave me the IBU 400s." When Wilson asked whom she meant, Marissa replied, "Savana Redding." Wilson then enquired about the day planner and its contents; Marissa denied knowing anything about them. Wilson did not ask Marissa any followup questions to determine whether there was any likelihood that Savana presently had pills: neither asking when Marissa received the pills from Savana nor where Savana might be hiding them.

Schwallier did not immediately recognize the blue pill, but information provided through a poison control hotline indicated that the pill was a 200-mg dose of an anti-inflammatory drug, generically called naproxen, available over the counter. At Wilson's direction, Marissa was then subjected to a search of her bra and underpants by Romero and Schwallier, as Savana was later on. The search revealed no additional pills.

It was at this juncture that Wilson called Savana into his office and showed her the day planner. Their conversation established that Savana and Marissa were on friendly terms: while she denied knowledge of the contraband, Savana admitted that the day planner was hers and that she had lent it to Marissa. Wilson had other reports of their friendship from staff members, who had identified Savana and Marissa as part of an unusually rowdy group at the school's opening dance in August, during which alcohol and cigarettes were found in the girls' bathroom. Wilson had reason to connect the girls with this contraband, for Wilson knew that Jordan Romero had told the principal that before the dance, he had been at a party at Savana's house where alcohol was served. Marissa's statement that the pills came from Savana was thus sufficiently plausible to warrant suspicion that Savana was involved in pill distribution.

This suspicion of Wilson's was enough to justify a search of Savana's backpack and outer clothing. If a student is reasonably suspected of giving out contraband pills, she is reasonably suspected of carrying them on her person and in the carryall that has become an item of student uniform in most places today. If Wilson's reasonable suspicion of pill distribution were not understood to support searches of outer clothes and backpack, it would not justify any search worth making. And the look into Savana's bag, in her presence and in the relative privacy of Wilson's office, was not excessively intrusive, any more than Romero's subsequent search of her outer clothing.

Here it is that the parties part company, with Savana's claim that extending the search at Wilson's behest to the point of making her pull out her underwear was constitutionally unreasonable. The exact label for this final step in the intrusion is not important, though strip search is a fair way to speak of it. Romero and Schwallier directed Savana to remove her clothes down to her underwear, and then "pull out" her bra and the elastic band on her underpants. Although Romero and Schwallier stated that they did not see anything when Savana followed their instructions, we would not define strip search and its Fourth Amendment consequences in a way that would guarantee litigation about who was looking and how much was seen. The very fact of Savana's pulling her underwear away from her body in the presence of the two officials who were able to see her necessarily exposed her breasts and pelvic area to some degree, and both subjective and reasonable societal expectations of personal privacy support the treatment of such a search as categorically distinct, requiring distinct elements of justification on the part of school authorities for going beyond a search of outer clothing and belongings.

Savana's subjective expectation of privacy against such a search is inherent in her account of it as embarrassing, frightening, and humiliating. The reasonableness of her expectation (required by the Fourth Amendment standard) is indicated by the consistent experiences of other young people similarly searched, whose adolescent vulnerability intensifies the patent intrusiveness of the exposure. The common reaction of these adolescents simply registers the obviously different meaning of a search exposing the body from the experience of nakedness or near undress in other school circumstances. Changing for gym is getting ready for play; exposing for a search is responding to an accusation reserved for suspected wrongdoers and fairly understood as so degrading that a number of communities have decided that strip searches in schools are never reasonable and have banned them no matter what the facts may be.

The indignity of the search does not, of course, outlaw it, but it does implicate the rule of reasonableness as stated in *T.L.O.*, that "the search as actually conducted [be] reasonably related in scope to the circumstances which justified the interference in the first place." The scope will be permissible, that is, when it is "not excessively intrusive in light of the age and sex of the student and the nature of the infraction."

Here, the content of the suspicion failed to match the degree of intrusion. Wilson knew beforehand that the pills were prescription-strength ibuprofen and over-the-counter naproxen, common pain relievers equivalent to two Advil, or one Aleve. He must have been aware of the nature and limited threat of the specific drugs he was searching for, and while just about anything can be taken in quantities that will do real harm, Wilson had no reason to suspect that large amounts of the drugs were being passed around, or that individual students were receiving great numbers of pills.

Nor could Wilson have suspected that Savana was hiding common painkillers in her underwear. Petitioners suggest, as a truth universally acknowledged, that "students hide contraband in or under their clothing," and cite a smattering of cases of students with contraband in their underwear. But when the categorically extreme intrusiveness of a search down to the body of an adolescent requires some justification in suspected facts, general background possibilities fall short; a reasonable search that extensive calls for suspicion that it will pay off. But nondangerous school contraband does not raise the specter of stashes in intimate places, and there is no evidence in the record of any general practice among Safford Middle School students of hiding that sort of thing in underwear; neither Jordan nor Marissa suggested to Wilson that Savana was doing that, and the preceding search of Marissa that Wilson ordered yielded nothing. Wilson never even determined when Marissa had received the pills from Savana; if it had been a few days before, that would weigh heavily against any reasonable conclusion that Savana presently had the pills on her person, much less in her underwear.

In sum, what was missing from the suspected facts that pointed to Savana was any indication of danger to the students from the power of the drugs or their quantity, and any reason to suppose that Savana was carrying pills in her underwear. We think that the combination of these deficiencies was fatal to finding the search reasonable.

The *T.L.O.* concern to limit a school search to reasonable scope requires the support of reasonable suspicion of danger or of resort to underwear for hiding evidence of wrongdoing before a search can reasonably make the quantum leap from outer clothes and backpacks to exposure of intimate parts. The meaning of such a search, and the degradation its subject may reasonably feel, place a search that intrusive in a category of its own demanding its own specific suspicions.

IV

A school official searching a student is entitled to qualified immunity where clearly established law does not show that the search violated the Fourth Amendment.

The cases viewing school strip searches differently from the way we see them are numerous enough, with well-reasoned majority and dissenting opinions, to counsel doubt that we were sufficiently clear in the prior statement of law. We conclude that qualified immunity is warranted.

The strip search of Savana Redding was unreasonable and a violation of the Fourth Amendment, but petitioners Wilson, Romero, and Schwallier are nevertheless protected from liability through qualified immunity. Our conclusions here do not resolve, however, the question of the liability of petitioner Safford Unified School District #1, a claim the Ninth Circuit did not address. The judgment of the Ninth Circuit is therefore affirmed in part and reversed in part, and this case is remanded for consideration of [that] claim.

JUSTICE THOMAS, concurring in the judgment in part and dissenting in part.

I would hold that the search of Savana Redding did not violate the Fourth Amendment. The majority imposes a vague and amorphous standard on school administrators. It also grants judges sweeping authority to second-guess the measures that these officials take to maintain discipline in their schools and ensure the health and safety of the students in their charge. This deep intrusion into the administration of public schools exemplifies why the Court should return to the common-law doctrine of *in loco parentis* under which the judiciary was reluctant to interfere in the routine business of school administration, allowing schools and teachers to set and enforce rules and to maintain order.

In the majority's view, although the school officials had reasonable suspicion to believe that Redding had the pills on her person, they needed some greater level of particularized suspicion to conduct this "strip search." There is no support for this contortion of the Fourth Amendment.

The Court has generally held that the reasonableness of a search's scope depends only on whether it is limited to the area that is capable of concealing the object of the search. A search of a student therefore is permissible in scope under *T.L.O.* so long as it is objectively reasonable to believe that the area searched could conceal the contraband. The dissenting opinion below correctly captured this Fourth Amendment standard, noting that "if a student brought a baseball bat on campus in violation of school policy, a search of that student's shirt pocket would be patently unjustified."

The reasonable suspicion that Redding possessed the pills for distribution purposes did not dissipate simply because the search of her backpack turned up nothing. It was eminently reasonable to conclude that the backpack was empty because Redding was secreting the pills in a place she thought no one would look.

Had the suspected infraction involved a street drug, the majority implies that it would have approved the scope of the search. In effect, then, the majority has replaced a school rule that draws no distinction among drugs with a new one that does. As a result, a full search of a student's person for prohibited drugs will be permitted only if the Court agrees that the drug in question was sufficiently dangerous. Such a test is unworkable and unsound. School officials cannot be expected to halt searches based on the possibility that a court might later find that the particular infraction at issue is not severe enough to warrant an intrusive investigation.

In determining whether the search's scope was reasonable under the Fourth Amendment, it is therefore irrelevant whether officials suspected Redding of possessing prescription-strength Ibuprofen, nonprescription-strength Naproxen, or some harder street drug. Safford prohibited its possession on school property. Reasonable suspicion that Redding was in possession of drugs in violation of these policies, therefore, justified a search extending to any area where small pills could be concealed. The search did not violate the Fourth Amendment.

Searches in Schools

1.   The Fourth Amendment's prohibition on unreasonable searches and seizures applies to searches of students conducted by public school officials.

2.   A teacher or school official may, without a warrant or probable cause, search a child suspected of violating the law or the school's rules. The search must be justified at its inception and reasonably related in scope to the circumstances which justified the intrusion in the first place.

   a.   A search of a student by a teacher or school official is justified at its inception if there is reasonable suspicion that the search will turn up evidence that the student has violated or is violating the law or the school's rules.

   b.   A search of a student is permissible in scope when the measures adopted are reasonably related to the objectives of the search and not excessively intrusive in light of the age and sex of the student and the nature of the infraction.

3.   A highly intrusive search of a student—involving exposure of intimate parts—requires stronger suspicion of danger or suspicion that evidence of wrongdoing is hidden in the area to be searched than is required for a more limited search of a student's outer clothing, backpack, or other belongings.

H. DRUG TESTING

The Supreme Court has examined the constitutionality of mandatory drug testing programs adopted by public schools, government employers, and state-run hospitals. In all of these cases, the Court must balance the intrusion on individual privacy against the government's interests in health and safety.

1. DRUG TESTING IN SCHOOLS

In *Vernonia School District 47J v. Acton*, 515 U.S. 646 (1995), the Supreme Court upheld a school district's program that provided for random drug testing of students participating in interscholastic athletics. The district had strong evidence of a drug problem among its student athletes and pointed to the unique health and safety risks associated with the use of drugs by students competing in athletics. The Supreme Court concluded that the district's testing program was reasonable under the Fourth Amendment even though it was conducted without a warrant and without individualized suspicion of drug use.

In *Board of Education of Independent School District No. 92 of Pottawatomie County v. Earls*, the Supreme Court went even further, upholding the warrantless and suspicionless drug testing of all students participating in extracurricular activities, despite scant evidence of a drug problem in the district's schools.

BOARD OF EDUCATION OF INDEPENDENT SCHOOL DISTRICT NO. 92 OF POTTAWATOMIE COUNTY V. EARLS
536 U.S. 822 (2002)

JUSTICE THOMAS delivered the opinion of the Court.

The Student Activities Drug Testing Policy implemented by the Board of Education of Independent School District No. 92 of Pottawatomie County (School District) requires all students who participate in competitive extracurricular activities to submit to drug testing. Because this Policy reasonably serves the School District's important interest in detecting and preventing drug use among its students, we hold that it is constitutional.

I

The city of Tecumseh, Oklahoma, is a rural community located approximately 40 miles southeast of Oklahoma City. The School District administers all Tecumseh public schools. In the fall of 1998, the School District adopted the Student Activities Drug Testing Policy (Policy), which requires all middle and high school students to consent to drug testing in order to participate in any extracurricular activity. In practice, the Policy has been applied only to competitive extracurricular activities sanctioned by the Oklahoma Secondary Schools Activities Association, such as the Academic Team, Future Farmers of America, Future Homemakers of America, band, choir, pom-pom, cheerleading, and athletics. Under the Policy, students are required to take a drug test before participating in an extracurricular activity, must submit to random drug testing while participating in that activity, and must agree to be tested at any time upon reasonable suspicion. The urinalysis tests are designed to detect only the use of illegal drugs, including amphetamines, marijuana, cocaine, opiates, and barbituates, not medical conditions or the presence of authorized prescription medications.

At the time of their suit, both respondents attended Tecumseh High School. Respondent Lindsay Earls was a member of the show choir, the marching band, the Academic Team, and the National Honor Society. Respondent Daniel James sought to participate in the Academic Team. Together with their parents, Earls and James brought a Rev. Stat. § 1979, 42 U.S.C. § 1983 action against the School District, challenging the Policy both on its face and as applied to their participation in extracurricular activities. They alleged that the Policy violates the Fourth Amendment as incorporated by the Fourteenth Amendment and requested injunctive and declarative relief. They also argued that the School District failed to identify a special need for testing students who participate in extracurricular activities, and that the "Drug Testing Policy neither addresses a proven problem nor promises to bring any benefit to students or the school."

II

The Fourth Amendment to the United States Constitution protects "the right of the people to be secure in their persons, houses, papers, and effects, against unreasonable searches and seizures." Searches by public school officials, such as the collection of urine samples, implicate Fourth Amendment interests. We must therefore review the School District's Policy for "reasonableness," which is the touchstone of the constitutionality of a governmental search.

In the criminal context, reasonableness usually requires a showing of probable cause. The probable-cause standard, however, is peculiarly related to criminal investigations and may be unsuited to determining the reasonableness of administrative searches where the Government seeks to *prevent* the development of hazardous conditions. The Court has also held that a warrant and finding of probable cause are unnecessary in the public school context because such requirements would unduly interfere with the maintenance of the swift and informal disciplinary procedures that are needed.

Given that the School District's Policy is not in any way related to the conduct of criminal investigations, respondents do not contend that the School District requires probable cause before testing students for drug use. Respondents instead argue that drug testing must be based at least on some level of individualized suspicion. It is true that we generally determine the reasonableness of a search by balancing the nature of the intrusion on the individual's privacy against the promotion of legitimate governmental interests. But we have long held that the Fourth Amendment imposes no irreducible requirement of individualized suspicion. In certain limited circumstances, the Government's need to discover such latent or hidden conditions, or to prevent their development, is sufficiently compelling to justify the intrusion on privacy entailed by conducting such searches without any measure of individualized suspicion. Therefore, in the context of safety and administrative regulations, a search unsupported by probable cause may be reasonable when special needs, beyond the normal need for law enforcement, make the warrant and probable-cause requirement impracticable.

Significantly, this Court has previously held that "special needs" inhere in the public school context. See *Vernonia School District 47J v. Acton*, 515 U.S. 646, 653 (1995); *New Jersey v. T.L.O.*, 469 U.S. 325, 339–340 (1985). While schoolchildren do not shed their constitutional rights when they enter the schoolhouse, Fourth Amendment rights are different in public schools than elsewhere; the "reasonableness" inquiry cannot disregard the schools' custodial and tutelary responsibility for children. In particular, a finding of individualized suspicion may not be necessary when a school conducts drug testing.

In *Vernonia*, this Court held that the suspicionless drug testing of athletes was constitutional. The Court, however, did not simply authorize all school drug testing, but rather conducted a fact-specific balancing of the intrusion on the children's Fourth Amendment rights against the promotion of legitimate governmental interests. Applying the principles of *Vernonia* to the somewhat different facts of this case, we conclude that Tecumseh's Policy is also constitutional.

We first consider the nature of the privacy interest allegedly compromised by the drug testing. As in *Vernonia*, the context of the public school environment serves as the backdrop for the analysis of the privacy interest at stake and the reasonableness of the drug testing policy in general.

A student's privacy interest is limited in a public school environment where the State is responsible for maintaining discipline, health, and safety. Schoolchildren are routinely required to submit to physical examinations and vaccinations against disease. Securing order in the school environment sometimes requires that students be subjected to greater controls than those appropriate for adults.

Respondents argue that because children participating in nonathletic extracurricular activities are not subject to regular physicals and communal undress, they have a stronger expectation of privacy than the athletes tested in *Vernonia*. This distinction, however, was not essential to our decision in *Vernonia*, which depended primarily upon the school's custodial responsibility and authority.

In any event, students who participate in competitive extracurricular activities voluntarily subject themselves to many of the same intrusions on their privacy as do athletes. Some of these clubs and activities require occasional off-campus travel and communal undress. All of them have their own rules and requirements for participating students that do not apply to the student body as a whole. For example, each of the competitive extracurricular activities governed by the Policy must abide by the rules of the Oklahoma Secondary Schools Activities Association, and a faculty sponsor monitors the students for compliance with the various rules dictated by the clubs and activities. This regulation of extracurricular activities further diminishes the expectation of privacy among schoolchildren. We therefore conclude that the students affected by this Policy have a limited expectation of privacy.

Next, we consider the character of the intrusion imposed by the Policy. Urination is an excretory function traditionally shielded by great privacy. But the degree of intrusion on one's privacy caused by collecting a urine sample depends upon the manner in which production of the urine sample is monitored.

Under the Policy, a faculty monitor waits outside the closed restroom stall for the student to produce a sample and must "listen for the normal sounds of urination in order to guard against tampered specimens and to insure an accurate chain of custody." The monitor then pours the sample into two bottles that are sealed and placed into a mailing pouch along with a consent form signed by the student. This procedure is virtually identical to that reviewed in *Vernonia*, except that it additionally protects privacy by allowing male students to produce their samples behind a closed stall. Given that we considered the method of collection in *Vernonia* a "negligible" intrusion, the method here is even less problematic.

In addition, the Policy clearly requires that the test results be kept in confidential files separate from a student's other educational records and released to school personnel only on a "need to know" basis. Respondents nonetheless contend that the intrusion on students' privacy is significant because the Policy fails to protect effectively against the disclosure of confidential information and, specifically, that the school "has been careless in protecting that information: for example, the Choir teacher looked at students' prescription drug lists and left them where other students could see them." But the choir teacher is someone with a "need to know," because during off-campus trips she needs to know what medications are taken by her students. Even before the Policy was enacted the choir teacher had access to this information. In any event, there is no allegation that any other student did see such information.

This one example of alleged carelessness hardly increases the character of the intrusion.

Moreover, the test results are not turned over to any law enforcement authority. Nor do the test results here lead to the imposition of discipline or have any academic consequences. Rather, the only consequence of a failed drug test is to limit the student's privilege of participating in extracurricular activities. Indeed, a student may test positive for drugs twice and still be allowed to participate in extracurricular activities. After the first positive test, the school contacts the student's parent or guardian for a meeting. The student may continue to participate in the activity if within five days of the meeting the student shows proof of receiving drug counseling and submits to a second drug test in two weeks. For the second positive test, the student is suspended from participation in all extracurricular activities for 14 days, must complete four hours of substance abuse counseling, and must submit to monthly drug tests. Only after a third positive test will the student be suspended from participating in any extracurricular activity for the remainder of the school year, or 88 school days, whichever is longer.

Given the minimally intrusive nature of the sample collection and the limited uses to which the test results are put, we conclude that the invasion of students' privacy is not significant.

Finally, this Court must consider the nature and immediacy of the government's concerns and the efficacy of the Policy in meeting them. This Court has already articulated in detail the importance of the governmental concern in preventing drug use by schoolchildren. The drug abuse problem among our Nation's youth has hardly abated since *Vernonia* was decided in 1995. In fact, evidence suggests that it has only grown worse. Indeed, the nationwide drug epidemic makes the war against drugs a pressing concern in every school.

Additionally, the School District in this case has presented specific evidence of drug use at Tecumseh schools. Teachers testified that they had seen students who appeared to be under the influence of drugs and that they had heard students speaking openly about using drugs. A drug dog found marijuana cigarettes near the school parking lot. Police officers once found drugs or drug paraphernalia in a car driven by a Future Farmers of America member. We decline to second-guess the finding of the District Court that "viewing the evidence as a whole, it cannot be reasonably disputed that the School District was faced with a drug problem when it adopted the Policy."

Furthermore, this Court has not required a particularized or pervasive drug problem before allowing the government to conduct suspicionless drug testing. For instance, in *National Treasury Employees Union v. Von Raab*, 489 U.S. 656 (1989), the Court upheld the drug testing of customs officials on a purely preventive basis, without any documented history of drug use by such officials. Likewise, the need to prevent and deter the substantial harm of childhood drug use provides the necessary immediacy for a school testing policy. Indeed, it would make little sense to require a school district to wait for a substantial portion of its students to begin using drugs before it was allowed to institute a drug testing program designed to deter drug use.

Given the nationwide epidemic of drug use, and the evidence of increased drug use in Tecumseh schools, it was entirely reasonable for the School District to enact this particular drug testing policy. As we cannot articulate a threshold level of drug use that would suffice to justify a drug testing program for schoolchildren, we refuse to fashion what would in effect be a constitutional quantum of drug use necessary to show a "drug problem."

Respondents also argue that the testing of nonathletes does not implicate any safety concerns, and that safety is a "crucial factor" in applying the special needs framework. They contend that there must be "surpassing safety interests," or "extraordinary safety and national security hazards," in order to override the usual protections of the Fourth Amendment. Respondents are correct that safety factors into the special needs analysis, but the safety interest furthered by drug testing is undoubtedly substantial for all children, athletes and nonathletes alike. We know all too well that drug use carries a variety of health risks for children, including death from overdose.

We also reject respondents' argument that drug testing must presumptively be based upon an individualized reasonable suspicion of wrongdoing because such a testing regime would be less intrusive. In this context, the Fourth Amendment does not require a finding of individualized suspicion, and we decline to impose such a requirement on schools attempting to prevent and detect drug use by students. Moreover, we question whether testing based on individualized suspicion in fact would be less intrusive. Such a regime would place an additional burden on public school teachers who are already tasked with the difficult job of maintaining order and discipline. A program of individualized suspicion might unfairly target members of unpopular groups. The fear of lawsuits resulting from such targeted searches may chill enforcement of the program, rendering it ineffective in combating drug use. In any case, this Court has repeatedly stated that reasonableness under the Fourth Amendment does not require employing the least intrusive means, because the logic of such elaborate less-restrictive-alternative arguments could raise insuperable barriers to the exercise of virtually all search-and-seizure powers.

Finally, we find that testing students who participate in extracurricular activities is a reasonably effective means of addressing the School District's legitimate concerns in preventing, deterring, and detecting drug use. While in *Vernonia* there might have been a closer fit between the testing of athletes and the trial court's finding that the drug problem was fueled by the "role model" effect of athletes' drug use, such a finding was not essential to the holding. *Vernonia* did not require the school to test the group of students most likely to use drugs, but rather considered the constitutionality of the program in the context of the public school's custodial responsibilities. Evaluating the Policy in this context, we conclude that the drug testing of Tecumseh students who participate in extracurricular activities effectively serves the School District's interest in protecting the safety and health of its students.

III

Within the limits of the Fourth Amendment, local school boards must assess the desirability of drug testing schoolchildren. In upholding the constitutionality of the Policy, we express no opinion as to its wisdom. Rather, we hold only that Tecumseh's Policy is a reasonable means of furthering the School District's important interest in preventing and deterring drug use among its schoolchildren.

JUSTICE GINSBURG, with whom JUSTICE STEVENS, JUSTICE O'CONNOR, and JUSTICE SOUTER join, dissenting.

Seven years ago, in *Vernonia*, this Court determined that a school district's policy of randomly testing the urine of its student athletes for illicit drugs did not violate the Fourth Amendment. In so ruling, the Court emphasized that drug use "increased the risk of sports-related injury" and that Vernonia's athletes were the "leaders" of an aggressive local "drug culture" that had reached "epidemic proportions." Today, the Court relies upon *Vernonia* to permit a school district with a drug problem its superintendent repeatedly described as "not major" to test the urine of an academic team member solely by reason of her participation in a nonathletic, competitive extracurricular activity—participation associated with neither special dangers from, nor particular predilections for, drug use.

Although "special needs" inhere in the public school context, those needs are not so expansive or malleable as to render reasonable any program of student drug testing a school district elects to install. The particular testing program upheld today is not reasonable; it is capricious, even perverse: Petitioners' policy targets for testing a student population least likely to be at risk from illicit drugs and their damaging effects. I therefore dissent.

Nationwide, students who participate in extracurricular activities are significantly less likely to develop substance abuse problems than are their less-involved peers. Even if students might be deterred from drug use in order to preserve their extracurricular eligibility, it is at least as likely that other students might forgo their extracurricular involvement in order to avoid detection of their drug use. Tecumseh's policy thus falls short doubly if deterrence is its aim: It invades the privacy of students who need deterrence least, and risks steering students at greatest risk for substance abuse away from extracurricular involvement that potentially may palliate drug problems.

To summarize, this case resembles *Vernonia* only in that the School Districts in both cases conditioned engagement in activities outside the obligatory curriculum on random subjection to urinalysis. The defining characteristics of the two programs, however, are entirely dissimilar. The Vernonia district sought to test a subpopulation of students distinguished by their reduced expectation of privacy, their special susceptibility to drug-related injury, and their heavy involvement with drug use. The Tecumseh district seeks to test a much larger population associated with none of these factors. It does so, moreover, without carefully safeguarding student confidentiality and without regard to the program's untoward effects. A program so sweeping is not sheltered by *Vernonia*; its unreasonable reach renders it impermissible under the Fourth Amendment.

It is a sad irony that the petitioning School District seeks to justify its edict here by trumpeting "the schools' custodial and tutelary responsibility for children." In regulating an athletic program or endeavoring to combat an exploding drug epidemic, a school's custodial obligations may permit searches that would otherwise unacceptably abridge students' rights. When custodial duties are not ascendant, however, schools' tutelary obligations to their students require them to "teach by example" by avoiding symbolic measures that diminish constitutional protections.

Drug Testing in Schools

1.   As a condition of participation in athletics or other extracurricular activities, a school district may require its students to submit to a program of drug testing. A school district need not establish that it has a drug problem before adopting a testing program.

2.   In determining the constitutionality of a school district's drug testing program, a court should weigh the nature of the privacy interest allegedly compromised by the program, the character of the intrusion imposed by the testing, and the nature and immediacy of the district's concerns along with the efficacy of the drug testing program in meeting them. If, after consideration of these factors, the school district's interests outweigh the privacy interests of affected students, drug testing in schools may proceed without a warrant and without individualized suspicion of drug use.

---

2. DRUG TESTING IN THE WORKPLACE

In *Skinner v. Railway Labor Executives' Association*, the Supreme Court upheld federal regulations requiring alcohol and drug testing of railroad employees following an accident. The Court held that such testing could proceed without a warrant or individualized suspicion of alcohol or drug use.

SKINNER V. RAILWAY LABOR EXECUTIVES' ASSOCIATION
489 U.S. 602 (1989)

JUSTICE KENNEDY delivered the opinion of the Court.

The Federal Railroad Safety Act of 1970 authorizes the Secretary of Transportation to "prescribe, as necessary, appropriate rules, regulations, orders, and standards for all areas of railroad safety." Finding that alcohol and drug abuse by railroad employees poses a serious threat to safety, the Federal Railroad Administration (FRA) has promulgated regulations that mandate blood and urine tests of employees who are involved in certain train accidents. The FRA also has adopted regulations that do not require, but do authorize, railroads to administer breath and urine tests to employees who violate certain safety rules. The question presented by this case is whether these regulations violate the Fourth Amendment.

I

The problem of alcohol use on American railroads is as old as the industry itself, and efforts to deter it by carrier rules began at least a century ago. For many years, railroads have prohibited operating employees from possessing alcohol or being intoxicated while on duty and from consuming alcoholic beverages while subject to being called for duty. More recently, these proscriptions have been expanded to forbid possession or use of certain drugs.

To the extent pertinent here, two subparts of the regulations relate to testing. Subpart C, which is entitled "Post-Accident Toxicological Testing," is mandatory. It provides that railroads "shall take all practicable steps to assure that all covered employees of the railroad directly involved provide blood and urine samples for toxicological testing by FRA" upon the occurrence of certain specified events. Toxicological testing is required following a "major train accident," which is defined as any train accident that involves (i) a fatality, (ii) the release of hazardous material accompanied by an evacuation or a reportable injury, or (iii) damage to railroad property of $500,000 or more. The railroad has the further duty of collecting blood and urine samples for testing after an "impact accident," which is defined as a collision that results in a reportable injury, or in damage to railroad property of $50,000 or more.

Finally, the railroad is also obligated to test after "any train incident that involves a fatality to any on-duty railroad employee."

After occurrence of an event which activates its duty to test, the railroad must transport all crew members and other covered employees directly involved in the accident or incident to an independent medical facility, where both blood and urine samples must be obtained from each employee. After the samples have been collected, the railroad is required to ship them by prepaid air freight to the FRA laboratory for analysis. There, the samples are analyzed using "state-of-the-art equipment and techniques" to detect and measure alcohol and drugs. The FRA proposes to place primary reliance on analysis of blood samples, as blood is "the only available body fluid that can provide a clear indication not only of the presence of alcohol and drugs but also their current impairment effects." Urine samples are also necessary, however, because drug traces remain in the urine longer than in blood, and in some cases it will not be possible to transport employees to a medical facility before the time it takes for certain drugs to be eliminated from the bloodstream. In those instances, a "positive urine test, taken with specific information on the pattern of elimination for the particular drug and other information on the behavior of the employee and the circumstances of the accident, may be crucial to the determination of" the cause of an accident.

The regulations require that the FRA notify employees of the results of the tests and afford them an opportunity to respond in writing before preparation of any final investigative report. Employees who refuse to provide required blood or urine samples may not perform covered service for nine months, but they are entitled to a hearing concerning their refusal to take the test.

Subpart D of the regulations, which is entitled "Authorization to Test for Cause," is permissive. It authorizes railroads to require covered employees to submit to breath or urine tests in certain circumstances not addressed by Subpart C. Breath or urine tests, or both, may be ordered (1) after a reportable accident or incident, where a supervisor has a "reasonable suspicion" that an employee's acts or omissions contributed to the occurrence or severity of the accident or incident; or (2) in the event of certain specific rule violations, including noncompliance with a signal and excessive speeding. A railroad also may require breath tests where a supervisor has a "reasonable suspicion" that an employee is under the influence of alcohol, based upon specific, personal observations concerning the appearance, behavior, speech, or body odors of the employee. Where impairment is suspected, a railroad, in addition, may require urine tests, but only if two supervisors make the appropriate determination, and, where the supervisors suspect impairment due to a substance other than alcohol, at least one of those supervisors must have received specialized training in detecting the signs of drug intoxication.

Subpart D further provides that whenever the results of either breath or urine tests are intended for use in a disciplinary proceeding, the employee must be given the opportunity to provide a blood sample for analysis at an independent medical facility. If an employee declines to give a blood sample, the railroad may presume impairment, absent persuasive evidence to the contrary, from a positive showing of controlled substance residues in the urine. The railroad must, however, provide detailed notice of this presumption to its employees, and advise them of their right to provide a contemporaneous blood sample. As in the case of samples procured under Subpart C, the regulations set forth procedures for the collection of samples, and require that samples "be analyzed by a method that is reliable within known tolerances."

II

Because it is clear that the collection and testing of urine intrudes upon expectations of privacy that society has long recognized as reasonable, the Federal Courts of Appeals have concluded unanimously, and we agree, that these intrusions must be deemed searches under the Fourth Amendment.

In view of our conclusion that the collection and subsequent analysis of the requisite biological samples must be deemed Fourth Amendment searches, we need not characterize the employer's antecedent interference with the employee's freedom of movement as an independent Fourth Amendment seizure. As our precedents indicate, not every governmental interference with an individual's freedom of movement raises such constitutional concerns that there is a seizure of the person. For present purposes, it suffices to note that any limitation on an employee's freedom of movement that is necessary to obtain the blood, urine, or breath samples contemplated by the regulations must be considered in assessing the intrusiveness of the searches effected by the Government's testing program.

III

Except in certain well-defined circumstances, a search or seizure in such a case is not reasonable unless it is accomplished pursuant to a judicial warrant issued upon probable cause. We have recognized exceptions to this rule, however, when "special needs, beyond the normal need for law enforcement, make the warrant and probable-cause requirement impracticable." *New Jersey v. T.L.O.*, 469 U.S. 325, 351 (1985) (Blackmun, J., concurring in judgment). When faced with such special needs, we have not hesitated to balance the governmental and privacy interests to assess the practicality of the warrant and probable-cause requirements in the particular context.

The Government's interest in regulating the conduct of railroad employees to ensure safety, like its supervision of probationers or regulated industries, or its operation of a government office, school, or prison, likewise presents "special needs" beyond normal law enforcement that may justify departures from the usual warrant and probable-cause requirements.

The FRA has prescribed toxicological tests, not to assist in the prosecution of employees, but rather "to prevent accidents and casualties in railroad operations that result from impairment of employees by alcohol or drugs." This governmental interest in ensuring the safety of the traveling public and of the employees themselves plainly justifies prohibiting covered employees from using alcohol or drugs on duty, or while subject to being called for duty. This interest also requires and justifies the exercise of supervision to assure that the restrictions are in fact observed. The question that remains, then, is whether the Government's need to monitor compliance with these restrictions justifies the privacy intrusions at issue absent a warrant or individualized suspicion.

An essential purpose of a warrant requirement is to protect privacy interests by assuring citizens subject to a search or seizure that such intrusions are not the random or arbitrary acts of government agents. A warrant assures the citizen that the intrusion is authorized by law, and that it is narrowly limited in its objectives and scope. A warrant also provides the detached scrutiny of a neutral magistrate, and thus ensures an objective determination whether an intrusion is justified in any given case. In the present context, however, a warrant would do little to further these aims. Both the circumstances justifying toxicological testing and the permissible limits of such intrusions are defined narrowly and specifically in the regulations that authorize them, and doubtless are well known to covered employees. Indeed, in light of the standardized nature of the tests and the minimal discretion vested in those charged with administering the program, there are virtually no facts for a neutral magistrate to evaluate.

We have recognized, moreover, that the government's interest in dispensing with the warrant requirement is at its strongest when, as here, the burden of obtaining a warrant is likely to frustrate the governmental purpose behind the search. As the FRA recognized, alcohol and other drugs are eliminated from the bloodstream at a constant rate, and blood and breath samples taken to measure whether these substances were in the bloodstream when a triggering event occurred must be obtained as soon as possible. Although the metabolites of some drugs remain in the urine for longer periods of time and may enable the FRA to estimate whether the employee was impaired by those drugs at the time of a covered accident, incident, or rule violation, the delay necessary to procure a warrant nevertheless may result in the destruction of valuable evidence.

The Government's need to rely on private railroads to set the testing process in motion also indicates that insistence on a warrant requirement would impede the achievement of the Government's objective. Railroad supervisors, like school officials, and hospital administrators, are not in the business of investigating violations of the criminal laws or enforcing administrative codes, and otherwise have little occasion to become familiar with the intricacies of this Court's Fourth Amendment jurisprudence.

In sum, imposing a warrant requirement in the present context would add little to the assurances of certainty and regularity already afforded by the regulations, while significantly hindering, and in many cases frustrating, the objectives of the Government's testing program. We do not believe that a warrant is essential to render the intrusions here at issue reasonable under the Fourth Amendment.

Our cases indicate that even a search that may be performed without a warrant must be based, as a general matter, on probable cause to believe that the person to be searched has violated the law. When the balance of interests precludes insistence on a showing of probable cause, we have usually required some quantum of individualized suspicion before concluding that a search is reasonable. We made it clear, however, that a showing of individualized suspicion is not a constitutional floor, below which a search must be presumed unreasonable. In limited circumstances, where the privacy interests implicated by the search are minimal, and where an important governmental interest furthered by the intrusion would be placed in jeopardy by a requirement of individualized suspicion, a search may be reasonable despite the absence of such suspicion. We believe this is true of the intrusions in question here.

By and large, intrusions on privacy under the FRA regulations are limited. To the extent transportation and like restrictions are necessary to procure the requisite blood, breath, and urine samples for testing, this interference alone is minimal given the employment context in which it takes place.

More importantly, the expectations of privacy of covered employees are diminished by reason of their participation in an industry that is regulated pervasively to ensure safety, a goal dependent, in substantial part, on the health and fitness of covered employees.

We do not suggest, of course, that the interest in bodily security enjoyed by those employed in a regulated industry must always be considered minimal. Here, however, the covered employees have long been a principal focus of regulatory concern. Though some of the privacy interests implicated by the toxicological testing at issue reasonably might be viewed as significant in other contexts, logic and history show that a diminished expectation of privacy attaches to information relating to the physical condition of covered employees and to this reasonable means of procuring such information. We conclude, therefore, that the testing procedures contemplated by Subparts C and D pose only limited threats to the justifiable expectations of privacy of covered employees.

By contrast, the Government interest in testing without a showing of individualized suspicion is compelling. Employees subject to the tests discharge duties fraught with such risks of injury to others that even a momentary lapse of attention can have disastrous consequences.

While no procedure can identify all impaired employees with ease and perfect accuracy, the FRA regulations supply an effective means of deterring employees engaged in safety-sensitive tasks from using controlled substances or alcohol in the first place. By ensuring that employees in safety-sensitive positions know they will be tested upon the occurrence of a triggering event, the timing of which no employee can predict with certainty, the regulations significantly increase the deterrent effect of the administrative penalties associated with the prohibited conduct, concomitantly increasing the likelihood that employees will forgo using drugs or alcohol while subject to being called for duty.

The testing procedures contemplated by Subpart C also help railroads obtain invaluable information about the causes of major accidents, and to take appropriate measures to safeguard the general public. Positive test results would point toward drug or alcohol impairment on the part of members of the crew as a possible cause of an accident, and may help to establish whether a particular accident, otherwise not drug related, was made worse by the inability of impaired employees to respond appropriately. Negative test results would likewise furnish invaluable clues, for eliminating drug impairment as a potential cause or contributing factor would help establish the significance of equipment failure, inadequate training, or other potential causes, and suggest a more thorough examination of these alternatives.

A requirement of particularized suspicion of drug or alcohol use would seriously impede an employer's ability to obtain this information, despite its obvious importance. Experience confirms the FRA's judgment that the scene of a serious rail accident is chaotic. Investigators who arrive at the scene shortly after a major accident has occurred may find it difficult to determine which members of a train crew contributed to its occurrence. Obtaining evidence that might give rise to the suspicion that a particular employee is impaired, a difficult endeavor in the best of circumstances, is most impracticable in the aftermath of a serious accident. While events following the rule violations that activate the testing authority of Subpart D may be less chaotic, objective indicia of impairment are absent in these instances as well. Indeed, any attempt to gather evidence relating to the possible impairment of particular employees likely would result in the loss or deterioration of the evidence furnished by the tests. It would be unrealistic, and inimical to the

Government's goal of ensuring safety in rail transportation, to require a showing of individualized suspicion in these circumstances.

We conclude that the compelling Government interests served by the FRA's regulations would be significantly hindered if railroads were required to point to specific facts giving rise to a reasonable suspicion of impairment before testing a given employee. In view of our conclusion that, on the present record, the toxicological testing contemplated by the regulations is not an undue infringement on the justifiable expectations of privacy of covered employees, the Government's compelling interests outweigh privacy concerns.

IV

Because the testing procedures mandated or authorized by Subparts C and D effect searches of the person, they must meet the Fourth Amendment's reasonableness requirement. In light of the limited discretion exercised by the railroad employers under the regulations, the surpassing safety interests served by toxicological tests in this context, and the diminished expectation of privacy that attaches to information pertaining to the fitness of covered employees, we believe that it is reasonable to conduct such tests in the absence of a warrant or reasonable suspicion that any particular employee may be impaired. We hold that the alcohol and drug tests contemplated by Subparts C and D of the FRA's regulations are reasonable within the meaning of the Fourth Amendment.

JUSTICE MARSHALL, with whom JUSTICE BRENNAN joins, dissenting.

The issue in this case is not whether declaring a war on illegal drugs is good public policy. The importance of ridding our society of such drugs is, by now, apparent to all. Rather, the issue here is whether the Government's deployment in that war of a particularly Draconian weapon—the compulsory collection and chemical testing of railroad workers' blood and urine—comports with the Fourth Amendment. Precisely because the need for action against the drug scourge is manifest, the need for vigilance against unconstitutional excess is great.

The Court today takes its longest step yet toward reading the probable-cause requirement out of the Fourth Amendment. In widening the "special needs" exception to probable cause to authorize searches of the human body unsupported by *any* evidence of wrongdoing, the majority today completes the process begun in *New Jersey v. T.L.O.*, 469 U.S. 325 (1985), of eliminating altogether the probable-cause requirement for civil searches—those undertaken for reasons "beyond the normal need for law enforcement." In its place, the majority substitutes a manipulable balancing inquiry under which, upon the mere assertion of a "special need," even the deepest dignitary and privacy interests become vulnerable to governmental incursion. By its terms, however, the Fourth

Amendment—unlike the Fifth and Sixth—does not confine its protections to either criminal or civil actions. Instead, it protects generally "the right of the people to be secure."

The fact is that the malleable "special needs" balancing approach can be justified only on the basis of the policy results it allows the majority to reach. The majority's concern with the railroad safety problems caused by drug and alcohol abuse is laudable; its cavalier disregard for the text of the Constitution is not. There is no drug exception to the Constitution, any more than there is a communism exception or an exception for other real or imagined sources of domestic unrest. I reject the majority's "special needs" rationale as unprincipled and dangerous.

In *National Treasury Employees Union v. Von Raab*, a companion case to *Skinner*, the Supreme Court upheld a U.S. Customs Service program that required drug testing—without a warrant or individualized suspicion of drug use—of certain Customs Service employees.

NATIONAL TREASURY EMPLOYEES UNION V. VON RAAB
489 U.S. 656 (1989)

The federal Customs Service adopted a program that required drug testing of its employees upon their transfer or promotion to positions directly involved in drug interdiction, or to positions that required the employee to carry a firearm or handle classified material. The testing was performed without a warrant and without individualized suspicion of drug use. The test results could not be turned over to any other agency, including criminal prosecutors, without the employee's written consent. The Supreme Court upheld most aspects of the testing program:

> We hold that the suspicionless testing of employees who apply for promotion to positions directly involving the interdiction of illegal drugs, or to positions that require the incumbent to carry a firearm, is reasonable. The Government's compelling interests in preventing the promotion of drug users to positions where they might endanger the integrity of our Nation's borders or the life of the citizenry outweigh the privacy interests of those who seek promotion to these positions, who enjoy a diminished expectation of privacy by virtue of the special, and obvious, physical and ethical demands of those positions. We do not decide whether testing those who apply for promotion to positions where they would handle "classified" information is reasonable, because we find the record inadequate for this purpose.

In *Chandler v. Miller*, the Supreme Court struck down a Georgia law that required candidates for state office to submit to drug testing. The Court found no significant safety considerations comparable to those in *Skinner* and *Von Raab* that would justify the warrantless and suspicionless testing.

CHANDLER V. MILLER
520 U.S. 305 (1997)

In order to qualify for a place on the ballot, a Georgia statute required candidates for state office to present a certificate from a state-approved laboratory reporting that the candidate submitted to a urinalysis drug test within 30 days prior to qualifying for nomination or election and that the results were negative. The Supreme Court found that the state's interests were insufficient to sustain a regime of warrantless and suspicionless drug testing:

> By requiring candidates for public office to submit to drug testing, Georgia displays its commitment to the struggle against drug abuse. The suspicionless tests, according to respondents, signify that candidates, if elected, will be fit to serve their constituents free from the influence of illegal drugs. But Georgia asserts no evidence of a drug problem among the State's elected officials, those officials typically do not perform high-risk, safety-sensitive tasks, and the required certification immediately aids no interdiction effort. The need revealed, in short, is symbolic, not "special," as that term draws meaning from our case law.

Drug Testing in the Workplace

1. Government may require employees in high-risk, safety-sensitive positions—such as railroad workers and U.S. Customs Service employees responsible for drug interdiction or required to carry a firearm—to submit to drug testing. The government employer need not establish that it has a drug problem before adopting a testing program for high-risk, safety-sensitive positions.

2. In determining the constitutionality of a government employer's drug testing program, a court should weigh the government's safety interests against the intrusion into the privacy expectations of the affected employees. If the government's safety interests outweigh the privacy rights of the affected employees, drug testing in the workplace may proceed without a warrant and without individualized suspicion of drug use.

---

3. DRUG TESTING OF PATIENTS IN STATE-RUN HOSPITALS

In *Ferguson v. City of Charleston*, the Supreme Court invalidated a city policy that required drug testing of pregnant women at a state-run hospital. The Court was particularly troubled by the fact that positive test results were turned over to police, exposing the women to arrest and prosecution. The Court concluded that the purpose of the Charleston policy—like the purpose of the narcotics checkpoint policy in *City of Indianapolis v. Edmond*—was indistinguishable from the general interest in crime control. Accordingly, the Charleston policy did not fit within the "special needs" exception justifying a suspension of the Fourth Amendment's warrant and probable cause requirements.

FERGUSON V. CITY OF CHARLESTON
532 U.S. 67 (2001)

JUSTICE STEVENS delivered the opinion of the Court.

In this case, we must decide whether a state hospital's performance of a diagnostic test to obtain evidence of a patient's criminal conduct for law enforcement purposes is an unreasonable search if the patient has not consented to the procedure. More narrowly, the question is whether the interest in using the threat of criminal sanctions to deter pregnant women from using cocaine can justify a departure from the general rule that an official nonconsensual search is unconstitutional if not authorized by a valid warrant.

I

In the fall of 1988, staff members at the public hospital operated in the city of Charleston by the Medical University of South Carolina (MUSC) became concerned about an apparent increase in the use of cocaine by patients who were receiving prenatal treatment. In response to this perceived increase, as of April 1989, MUSC began to order drug screens to be performed on urine samples from maternity patients who were suspected of using cocaine. If a patient tested positive, she was then referred by MUSC staff to the county substance abuse commission for counseling and treatment. However, despite the referrals, the incidence of cocaine use among the patients at MUSC did not appear to change.

Some four months later, Nurse Shirley Brown, the case manager for the MUSC obstetrics department, heard a news broadcast reporting that the police in Greenville, South Carolina, were arresting pregnant users of cocaine on the theory that such use harmed the fetus and was therefore child abuse. Nurse Brown discussed the story with MUSC's general counsel, Joseph C. Good, Jr., who then contacted Charleston Solicitor

Charles Condon in order to offer MUSC's cooperation in prosecuting mothers whose children tested positive for drugs at birth.

After receiving Good's letter, Solicitor Condon took the first steps in developing the policy at issue in this case. The threat of law enforcement involvement was set forth in two protocols, the first dealing with the identification of drug use during pregnancy, and the second with identification of drug use after labor. Under the latter protocol, the police were to be notified without delay and the patient promptly arrested. Under the former, after the initial positive drug test, the police were to be notified (and the patient arrested) only if the patient tested positive for cocaine a second time or if she missed an appointment with a substance abuse counselor. In 1990, however, the policy was modified at the behest of the solicitor's office to give the patient who tested positive during labor, like the patient who tested positive during a prenatal care visit, an opportunity to avoid arrest by consenting to substance abuse treatment.

The last six pages of the policy contained forms for the patients to sign, as well as procedures for the police to follow when a patient was arrested. The policy also prescribed in detail the precise offenses with which a woman could be charged, depending on the stage of her pregnancy. If the pregnancy was 27 weeks or less, the patient was to be charged with simple possession. If it was 28 weeks or more, she was to be charged with possession and distribution to a person under the age of 18—in this case, the fetus. If she delivered "while testing positive for illegal drugs," she was also to be charged with unlawful neglect of a child. Under the policy, the police were instructed to interrogate the arrestee in order "to ascertain the identity of the subject who provided illegal drugs to the suspect." Other than the provisions describing the substance abuse treatment to be offered to women who tested positive, the policy made no mention of any change in the prenatal care of such patients, nor did it prescribe any special treatment for the newborns.

II

Petitioners are 10 women who received obstetrical care at MUSC and who were arrested after testing positive for cocaine. Four of them were arrested during the initial implementation of the policy; they were not offered the opportunity to receive drug treatment as an alternative to arrest. The others were arrested after the policy was modified in 1990; they either failed to comply with the terms of the drug treatment program or tested positive for a second time. Respondents include the city of Charleston, law enforcement officials who helped develop and enforce the policy, and representatives of MUSC.

Petitioners' complaint challenged the validity of the policy under various theories, including the claim that warrantless and nonconsensual drug tests conducted for criminal investigatory purposes were unconstitutional searches.

III

Because MUSC is a state hospital, the members of its staff are government actors, subject to the strictures of the Fourth Amendment. Moreover, the urine tests conducted by those staff members were indisputably searches within the meaning of the Fourth Amendment. Neither the District Court nor the Court of Appeals concluded that any of the nine criteria used to identify the women to be searched provided either probable cause to believe that they were using cocaine, or even the basis for a reasonable suspicion of such use. Rather, the District Court and the Court of Appeals viewed the case as one involving MUSC's right to conduct searches without warrants or probable cause. Furthermore, given the posture in which the case comes to us, we must assume for purposes of our decision that the tests were performed without the informed consent of the patients.

Because the hospital seeks to justify its authority to conduct drug tests and to turn the results over to law enforcement agents without the knowledge or consent of the patients, this case differs from the four previous cases in which we have considered whether comparable drug tests fit within the closely guarded category of constitutionally permissible suspicionless searches. In three of those cases, we sustained drug tests for railway employees involved in train accidents, *Skinner v. Railway Labor Executives' Association*, 489 U.S. 602 (1989), for United States Customs Service employees seeking promotion to certain sensitive positions, *National Treasury Employees Union v. Von Raab*, 489 U.S. 656 (1989), and for high school students participating in interscholastic sports, *Vernonia School District 47J v. Acton*, 515 U.S. 646 (1995). In the fourth case, we struck down such testing for candidates for designated state offices as unreasonable. *Chandler v. Miller*, 520 U.S. 305 (1997).

In each of those cases, we employed a balancing test that weighed the intrusion on the individual's interest in privacy against the "special needs" that supported the program. As an initial matter, we note that the invasion of privacy in this case is far more substantial than in those cases. In the previous four cases, there was no misunderstanding about the purpose of the test or the potential use of the test results, and there were protections against the dissemination of the results to third parties. The use of an adverse test result to disqualify one from eligibility for a particular benefit, such as a promotion or an opportunity to participate in an extracurricular activity, involves a less serious intrusion on privacy than the unauthorized dissemination of such results to third parties. The reasonable expectation of privacy enjoyed by the typical patient undergoing diagnostic tests in a hospital is that the results of those tests will not be shared with nonmedical personnel without her consent. In none of our prior cases was there any intrusion upon that kind of expectation.

The critical difference between those four drug-testing cases and this one, however, lies in the nature of the "special need" asserted as justification for the warrantless searches. In each of those earlier cases, the "special need" that was advanced as a justification for the absence of a warrant or individualized suspicion was one divorced from the State's general interest in law enforcement.[15] In this case, however, the central and indispensable feature of the policy from its inception was the use of law enforcement to coerce the patients into substance abuse treatment. This fact distinguishes this case from circumstances in which physicians or psychologists, in the course of ordinary medical procedures aimed at helping the patient herself, come across information that under rules of law or ethics is subject to reporting requirements, which no one has challenged here.

Respondents argue in essence that their ultimate purpose—namely, protecting the health of both mother and child—is a beneficent one. In this case, a review of the policy plainly reveals that the purpose actually served by the MUSC searches "is ultimately indistinguishable from the general interest in crime control." *Indianapolis v. Edmond*, 531 U.S. 32, 44 (2000).

In looking to the programmatic purpose, we consider all the available evidence in order to determine the relevant primary purpose. In this case, as Judge Blake put it in her dissent below, "it is clear from the record that an initial and continuing focus of the policy was on the arrest and prosecution of drug-abusing mothers." Tellingly, the document codifying the policy incorporates the police's operational guidelines. It devotes its attention to the chain of custody, the range of possible criminal charges, and the logistics of police notification and arrests. Nowhere, however, does the document discuss different courses of medical treatment for either mother or infant, aside from treatment for the mother's addiction.

Moreover, throughout the development and application of the policy, the Charleston prosecutors and police were extensively involved in the day-to-day administration of the policy. Police and prosecutors decided who would receive the reports of positive drug screens and what information would be included with those reports. Law enforcement officials also helped determine the procedures to be followed when performing the screens. In the course of the policy's administration, they had access to Nurse Brown's medical files on the women who tested positive, routinely attended the substance abuse team's meetings, and regularly received copies of team documents discussing the women's

---

[15] The "special needs" doctrine, which has been used to uphold certain suspicionless searches performed for reasons unrelated to law enforcement, is an exception to the general rule that a search must be based on individualized suspicion of wrongdoing. In special needs cases, we have tolerated suspension of the Fourth Amendment's warrant or probable-cause requirement in part because there was no law enforcement purpose behind the searches, and there was little, if any, entanglement with law enforcement.

progress. Police took pains to coordinate the timing and circumstances of the arrests with MUSC staff, and, in particular, Nurse Brown.

While the ultimate goal of the program may well have been to get the women in question into substance abuse treatment and off of drugs, the immediate objective of the searches was to generate evidence *for law enforcement purposes* in order to reach that goal. The threat of law enforcement may ultimately have been intended as a means to an end, but the direct and primary purpose of MUSC's policy was to ensure the use of those means. In our opinion, this distinction is critical. Because law enforcement involvement always serves some broader social purpose or objective, under respondents' view, virtually any nonconsensual suspicionless search could be immunized under the special needs doctrine by defining the search solely in terms of its ultimate, rather than immediate, purpose. Such an approach is inconsistent with the Fourth Amendment. Given the primary purpose of the Charleston program, which was to use the threat of arrest and prosecution in order to force women into treatment, and given the extensive involvement of law enforcement officials at every stage of the policy, this case simply does not fit within the closely guarded category of "special needs."

The fact that positive test results were turned over to the police does not merely provide a basis for distinguishing our prior cases applying the "special needs" balancing approach to the determination of drug use. It also provides an affirmative reason for enforcing the strictures of the Fourth Amendment. While state hospital employees, like other citizens, may have a duty to provide the police with evidence of criminal conduct that they inadvertently acquire in the course of routine treatment, when they undertake to obtain such evidence from their patients *for the specific purpose of incriminating those patients*, they have a special obligation to make sure that the patients are fully informed about their constitutional rights, as standards of knowing waiver require.

As respondents have repeatedly insisted, their motive was benign rather than punitive. Such a motive, however, cannot justify a departure from Fourth Amendment protections, given the pervasive involvement of law enforcement with the development and application of the MUSC policy. The stark and unique fact that characterizes this case is that [the policy] was designed to obtain evidence of criminal conduct by the tested patients that would be turned over to the police and that could be admissible in subsequent criminal prosecutions. While respondents are correct that drug abuse both was and is a serious problem, the gravity of the threat alone cannot be dispositive of questions concerning what means law enforcement officers may employ to pursue a given purpose. The Fourth Amendment's general prohibition against nonconsensual, warrantless, and suspicionless searches necessarily applies to such a policy.

JUSTICE SCALIA, with whom CHIEF JUSTICE REHNQUIST and JUSTICE THOMAS join, dissenting.

There is always an unappealing aspect to the use of doctors and nurses, ministers of mercy, to obtain incriminating evidence against the supposed objects of their ministration—although here, it is correctly pointed out, the doctors and nurses were ministering not just to the mothers but also to the children whom their cooperation with the police was meant to protect. But whatever may be the correct social judgment concerning the desirability of what occurred here, that is not the issue in the present case. The Constitution does not resolve all difficult social questions, but leaves the vast majority of them to resolution by debate and the democratic process—which would produce a decision by the citizens of Charleston, through their elected representatives, to forbid or permit the police action at issue here. The question before us is a narrower one: whether, whatever the desirability of this police conduct, it violates the Fourth Amendment's prohibition of unreasonable searches and seizures. In my view, it plainly does not.

The first step in Fourth Amendment analysis is to identify the search or seizure at issue. What petitioners, the Court, and to a lesser extent the concurrence really object to is not the urine testing, but the hospital's reporting of positive drug-test results to police. But the latter is obviously not a search. At most it may be a derivative use of the product of a past unlawful search, which, of course, works no new Fourth Amendment wrong and presents a question, not of rights, but of remedies. There is only one act that could conceivably be regarded as a search of petitioners in the present case: the *taking* of the urine sample. I suppose the *testing* of that urine for traces of unlawful drugs could be considered a search of sorts, but the Fourth Amendment protects only against searches of citizens' "persons, houses, papers, and effects"; and it is entirely unrealistic to regard urine as one of the "effects" (*i.e.*, part of the property) of the person who has passed and abandoned it. Some would argue, I suppose, that testing of the urine is prohibited by some generalized privacy right "emanating" from the "penumbras" of the Constitution (a question that is not before us); but it is not even arguable that the testing of urine that has been lawfully obtained is a Fourth Amendment search. (I may add that, even if it were, the factors legitimizing the taking of the sample, which I discuss below, would likewise legitimize the testing of it.)

It is rudimentary Fourth Amendment law that a search which has been consented to is not unreasonable. There is no contention in the present case that the urine samples were extracted forcibly. The only conceivable bases for saying that they were obtained without consent are the contentions (1) that the consent was coerced by the patients' need for medical treatment, (2) that the consent was uninformed because the patients were not told that the tests would include testing for drugs, and

(3) that the consent was uninformed because the patients were not told that the results of the tests would be provided to the police.

Until today, we have *never* held—or even suggested—that material which a person voluntarily entrusts to someone else cannot be given by that person to the police, and used for whatever evidence it may contain. Without so much as discussing the point, the Court today opens a hole in our Fourth Amendment jurisprudence, the size and shape of which is entirely indeterminate. I would adhere to our established law, which says that information obtained through violation of a relationship of trust is obtained consensually, and is hence not a search.

I think it clear, therefore, that there is no basis for saying that obtaining of the urine sample was unconstitutional. The special-needs doctrine is thus quite irrelevant, since it operates only to validate searches and seizures that are otherwise unlawful. In the ensuing discussion, however, I shall assume (contrary to legal precedent) that the taking of the urine sample was (either because of the patients' necessitous circumstances, or because of failure to disclose that the urine would be tested for drugs, or because of failure to disclose that the results of the test would be given to the police) coerced. Indeed, I shall even assume (contrary to common sense) that the testing of the urine constituted an unconsented search of the patients' effects. On those assumptions, the special-needs doctrine *would* become relevant; and, properly applied, would validate what was done here.

The conclusion of the Court that the special-needs doctrine is inapplicable rests upon its contention that respondents "undertook to obtain drug evidence from their patients" not for any medical purpose, but *"for the specific purpose of incriminating those patients."* In other words, the purported medical rationale was merely a pretext; there was no special need. This contention contradicts the District Court's finding of fact that the goal of the testing policy "was not to arrest patients but to facilitate their treatment and protect both the mother and unborn child." This finding is binding upon us unless clearly erroneous. Not only do I find it supportable; I think any other finding would have to be overturned.

In sum, there can be no basis for the Court's purported ability to "distinguish this case from circumstances in which physicians or psychologists, in the course of ordinary medical procedures aimed at helping the patient herself, come across information that is subject to reporting requirements," unless it is this: That the *addition* of a law-enforcement-related purpose *to* a legitimate medical purpose destroys applicability of the "special-needs" doctrine. But that is quite impossible, since the special-needs doctrine was developed, and is ordinarily employed, precisely to enable searches *by law enforcement officials* who, of course, ordinarily have a law enforcement objective.

As I indicated at the outset, it is not the function of this Court—at least not in Fourth Amendment cases—to weigh petitioners' privacy interest against the State's interest in meeting the crisis of "crack babies" that developed in the late 1980's. I cannot refrain from observing, however, that the outcome of a wise weighing of those interests is by no means clear. The initial goal of the doctors and nurses who conducted cocaine testing in this case was to refer pregnant drug addicts to treatment centers, and to prepare for necessary treatment of their possibly affected children. When the doctors and nurses agreed to the program providing test results to the police, they did so because (in addition to the fact that child abuse was required by law to be reported) they wanted to use the sanction of arrest as a strong incentive for their addicted patients to undertake drug-addiction treatment. And the police themselves used it for that benign purpose, as is shown by the fact that only 30 of 253 women testing positive for cocaine were ever arrested, and only 2 of those prosecuted. It would not be unreasonable to conclude that today's judgment, authorizing the assessment of damages against the county solicitor and individual doctors and nurses who participated in the program, proves once again that no good deed goes unpunished.

But as far as the Fourth Amendment is concerned: There was no unconsented search in this case. And if there was, it would have been validated by the special-needs doctrine. For these reasons, I respectfully dissent.

Drug Testing of Patients in State-Run Hospitals

1. The Fourth Amendment prohibits a state-run hospital from conducting drug tests and turning the results over to law enforcement without the knowledge or consent of patients, and without a warrant or individualized suspicion of drug use.

2. While state hospital employees may have a duty to provide the police with evidence of criminal conduct that they inadvertently acquire in the course of routine treatment, when they undertake to obtain such evidence from their patients for the specific purpose of incriminating those patients, they have a special obligation to make sure that the patients are fully informed about their constitutional rights.

I. WORKPLACE SEARCHES OF GOVERNMENT EMPLOYEES

Do government employees enjoy a right to privacy in their offices and desks? Must a government employer obtain a search warrant, based on probable cause, to enter an employee's office to look for an important file or to investigate allegations of misconduct? The Supreme Court addressed these questions in *O'Connor v. Ortega*, leading a plurality of the Court to adopt a standard similar to the one used by the Court to evaluate the reasonableness of searches of students in school.

O'CONNOR V. ORTEGA
480 U.S. 709 (1987)

Dr. Magno Ortega, a physician and psychiatrist, had primary responsibility for training young physicians in psychiatric residency programs at a California state hospital. In July 1981, hospital officials became concerned about possible improprieties in Dr. Ortega's management of the residency program. In particular, hospital officials were concerned about Dr. Ortega's acquisition of a computer for use in the residency program. The officials thought that Dr. Ortega may have financed the computer by the possibly coerced contributions of residents. Additionally, hospital officials were concerned about charges that Dr. Ortega had sexually harassed two female hospital employees, and had taken inappropriate disciplinary action against a resident. While Dr. Ortega was on vacation and administrative leave during the investigation of the charges, hospital personnel thoroughly searched Dr. Ortega's office, seizing a number of items from his desk and file cabinets, including a Valentine's Day card, a photograph, and a book of poetry all sent to Dr. Ortega by a former resident physician. These items were later used in a proceeding before a hearing officer of the California State Personnel Board to impeach the credibility of the former resident, who testified on Dr. Ortega's behalf. Dr. Ortega brought a federal civil rights suit under 42 U.S.C. § 1983, alleging that the search of his office violated the Fourth Amendment.

The Supreme Court had little difficulty concluding that "[s]earches and seizures by government employers or supervisors of the private property of their employees are subject to the restraints of the Fourth Amendment." Applying the *Katz* Test, the Court concluded that employees may "have a reasonable expectation of privacy in their place of work." The Court cautioned, however, that the "operational realities of the workplace may make *some* employees' expectations of privacy unreasonable when an intrusion is by a supervisor rather than a law enforcement official." As the Court explained:

> Public employees' expectations of privacy in their offices, desks, and file cabinets, like similar expectations of employees in the private sector, may be reduced by virtue of actual office practices and procedures, or by legitimate regulation. The employee's expectation of privacy must be assessed in the context of the employment relation. An office is seldom a private enclave free from entry by supervisors, other employees, and business and personal invitees. Instead, in many cases offices are continually entered by fellow employees and other visitors during the

workday for conferences, consultations, and other work-related visits. Simply put, it is the nature of government offices that others—such as fellow employees, supervisors, consensual visitors, and the general public—may have frequent access to an individual's office. Given the great variety of work environments in the public sector, the question whether an employee has a reasonable expectation of privacy must be addressed on a case-by-case basis.

The Court agreed that Dr. Ortega had a reasonable expectation of privacy in his office, particularly in his desk and file cabinets. The Court then proceeded to determine whether the search was reasonable under the Fourth Amendment by balancing "the invasion of the employee's legitimate expectations of privacy against the government's need for supervision, control, and the efficient operation of the workplace." Noting that an employer may need to enter an absent employee's office and desk to obtain correspondence or a file or certain records, the Court concluded that no search warrant was required for intrusions for "legitimate work-related reasons wholly unrelated to illegal conduct." Similarly, the Court found the traditional probable cause standard unsuited to the employment context. Instead, "public employer intrusions on the constitutionally protected privacy interests of government employees for noninvestigatory, work-related purposes, as well as for investigation of work-related misconduct, should be judged by the standard of reasonableness under all the circumstances."

Borrowing the basic standard used to evaluate the reasonableness of school searches in *New Jersey v. T.L.O.*, 469 U.S. 325 (1985), a plurality of four Justices explained that a public employer's intrusion into an employee's constitutionally protected privacy interests must be reasonable at inception and in scope:

> Ordinarily, a search of an employee's office by a supervisor will be justified at its inception when there are reasonable grounds for suspecting that the search will turn up evidence that the employee is guilty of work-related misconduct, or that the search is necessary for a noninvestigatory work-related purpose such as to retrieve a needed file. The search will be permissible in its scope when the measures adopted are reasonably related to the objectives of the search and not excessively intrusive in light of the nature of the misconduct.

The Supreme Court ultimately remanded the case to the trial court to determine the justification for the search and seizure of items in Dr. Ortega's office, and to evaluate the reasonableness of the search at both inception and in scope.

The Supreme Court applied the *O'Connor v. Ortega* standard in *City of Ontario v. Quon*, finding that a public employer did not violate the Fourth Amendment by reviewing an employee's text messages on an employer-provided pager.

CITY OF ONTARIO, CALIFORNIA V. QUON
560 U.S. 746 (2010)

The Ontario Police Department, under the direction of the city of Ontario, provided pagers capable of sending and receiving text messages to members of its SWAT team. The city made it clear to its employees, including Jeff Quon, a police sergeant and member of the SWAT team, that it reserved the right to monitor email, Internet use, and text messages, and that employees should not expect privacy or confidentiality when using the city-owned electronic devices. Over the next few months, Quon and other employees exceeded their monthly text message allotment, but were permitted to pay for the overages rather than have their messages audited. The police officer responsible for the city's contract with its wireless provider, Lieutenant Steven Duke, eventually grew tired of collecting the overage payments, and he decided to determine whether the text message limit was too low; he wanted to know whether officers were having to pay fees for work-related messages, or if the overages were for personal messages. Duke requested two months of transcripts of text messages sent by Quon and another officer who had exceeded the message allotment. Upon reviewing the transcripts, Duke discovered that many of the messages sent and received on Quon's pager were not work-related, and some were sexually explicit. Quon was then disciplined for pursuing personal matters while on duty. Quon brought a federal civil rights claim under 42 U.S.C. § 1983 alleging that the city had violated his Fourth Amendment rights by obtaining and reviewing the transcripts of his pager messages.

Applying the approach used in *O'Connor v. Ortega*, 480 U.S. 709 (1987), the Supreme Court held that the search was justified at its inception because there were "reasonable grounds for suspecting that the search was necessary for a noninvestigatory work-related purpose." In particular, the purpose of the search was to determine whether the text message limit was sufficient to meet the city's needs. The city and the Ontario Police Department "had a legitimate interest in ensuring that employees were not being forced to pay out of their own pockets for work-related expenses, or on the other hand that the city was not paying for extensive personal communications."

The Supreme Court also held that the scope of the search was reasonable, since reviewing the transcripts was "an efficient and expedient way to determine whether Quon's overages were the result of work-related messaging or personal use," and because the review was not "excessively intrusive."

Workplace Searches of Government Employees

1.   Searches and seizures by government employers or supervisors of the private property of their employees are subject to the restraints of the Fourth Amendment. But given the great variety of work environments in the public sector, the question whether an employee has a reasonable expectation of privacy in his office or workspace must be addressed on a case-by-case basis.

2.   A public employer needs neither a warrant nor probable cause to search an employee's office or workspace for legitimate work-related reasons wholly unrelated to illegal conduct. Instead, a public employer's intrusion on the constitutionally protected privacy interests of a government employee for noninvestigatory, work-related purposes, as well as for investigation of work-related misconduct, should be judged by the standard of reasonableness under all the circumstances. Such an intrusion must be reasonable in its inception and in its scope.

   a.   Ordinarily, a search of an employee's office by a supervisor will be justified at its inception when there are reasonable grounds for suspecting that the search will turn up evidence that the employee is guilty of work-related misconduct, or that the search is necessary for a noninvestigatory work-related purpose such as to retrieve a needed file.

   b.   The search will be permissible in its scope when the measures adopted are reasonably related to the objectives of the search and not excessively intrusive in light of the nature of the misconduct.

J. MEDICAL PROCEDURES

As several cases presented in Chapter 5 reveal, the Supreme Court has approved minor and relatively risk-free medical procedures and tests, even when the authorities lack a warrant and the individual subjected to the intrusion has refused to provide consent. For example, in *Schmerber v. California*, 384 U.S. 757 (1966), the Court held that the exigent circumstances exception to the warrant requirement allowed the police to obtain a blood sample from an individual suspected of drunk driving. Similarly, in *Cupp v. Murphy*, 412 U.S. 291 (1973), the Court permitted police—acting without a search warrant—to take fingernail scrapings from a man suspected of strangling his wife. More recently, in *Maryland v. King*, 133 S.Ct. 1958 (2013), the Supreme Court upheld a state law that permitted police—without a search warrant—to obtain a DNA sample from anyone arrested for a serious crime.

With respect to more invasive and risky medical procedures, however, the Supreme Court has been far more protective of individual privacy rights. In *Winston v. Lee*, the police had both probable cause and a court order—the functional equivalent of a warrant—authorizing surgery to remove a bullet from a man suspected of an attempted armed robbery. The Supreme Court unanimously rejected the state's effort to perform the surgery over the suspect's objections.

WINSTON V. LEE
470 U.S. 753 (1985)

JUSTICE BRENNAN delivered the opinion of the Court.

Schmerber v. California, 384 U.S. 757 (1966), held that a State may, over the suspect's protest, have a physician extract blood from a person suspected of drunken driving without violation of the suspect's right secured by the Fourth Amendment not to be subjected to unreasonable searches and seizures. However, *Schmerber* cautioned: "That we today hold that the Constitution does not forbid the States' minor intrusions into an individual's body under stringently limited conditions in no way indicates that it permits more substantial intrusions, or intrusions under other conditions." In this case, the Commonwealth of Virginia seeks to compel the respondent Rudolph Lee, who is suspected of attempting to commit armed robbery, to undergo a surgical procedure under a general anesthetic for removal of a bullet lodged in his chest. Petitioners allege that the bullet will provide evidence of respondent's guilt or innocence. We conclude that the procedure sought here is an example of the "more substantial intrusion" cautioned against in *Schmerber*, and hold that to permit the procedure would violate respondent's right to be secure in his person guaranteed by the Fourth Amendment.

I

At approximately 1 a.m. on July 18, 1982, Ralph E. Watkinson was closing his shop for the night. As he was locking the door, he observed someone armed with a gun coming toward him from across the street. Watkinson was also armed and when he drew his gun, the other person told him to freeze. Watkinson then fired at the other person, who returned his fire. Watkinson was hit in the legs, while the other individual, who appeared to be wounded in his left side, ran from the scene. The police arrived on the scene shortly thereafter, and Watkinson was taken by ambulance to the emergency room of the Medical College of Virginia (MCV) Hospital.

Approximately 20 minutes later, police officers responding to another call found respondent eight blocks from where the earlier shooting occurred. Respondent was suffering from a gunshot wound to his left chest area and told the police that he had been shot when two individuals attempted to rob him. An ambulance took respondent to the MCV Hospital. Watkinson was still in the MCV emergency room and, when respondent entered that room, said "that's the man that shot me." After an investigation, the police decided that respondent's story of having been himself the victim of a robbery was untrue and charged respondent with attempted robbery, malicious wounding, and two counts of using a firearm in the commission of a felony.

The Commonwealth shortly thereafter moved in state court for an order directing respondent to undergo surgery to remove an object thought to be a bullet lodged under his left collarbone. The court conducted several evidentiary hearings on the motion. At the first hearing, the Commonwealth's expert testified that the surgical procedure would take 45 minutes and would involve a three to four percent chance of temporary nerve damage, a one percent chance of permanent nerve damage, and a one-tenth of one percent chance of death. At the second hearing, the expert testified that on reexamination of respondent, he discovered that the bullet was not "back inside close to the nerves and arteries," as he originally had thought. Instead, he now believed the bullet to be located "just beneath the skin." He testified that the surgery would require an incision of only one and one-half centimeters (slightly more than one-half inch), could be performed under local anesthesia, and would result in "no danger on the basis that there's no general anesthesia employed." The state trial judge granted the motion to compel surgery.

On October 18, 1982, just before the surgery was scheduled, the surgeon ordered that X-rays be taken of respondent's chest. The X-rays revealed that the bullet was in fact lodged two and one-half to three centimeters (approximately one inch) deep in muscular tissue in respondent's chest, substantially deeper than had been thought when the state court granted the motion to compel surgery. The surgeon now believed that a general anesthetic would be desirable for medical reasons.

We granted certiorari to consider whether a State may consistently with the Fourth Amendment compel a suspect to undergo surgery of this kind in a search for evidence of a crime.

II

The Fourth Amendment protects "expectations of privacy"—the individual's legitimate expectations that in certain places and at certain times he has "the right to be let alone—the most comprehensive of rights and the right most valued by civilized men." *Olmstead v. U.S.*, 277 U.S. 438, 478 (1928) (Brandeis, J., dissenting). Putting to one side the procedural protections of the warrant requirement, the Fourth Amendment generally protects the "security" of "persons, houses, papers, and effects" against official intrusions up to the point where the community's need for evidence surmounts a specified standard, ordinarily "probable cause." Beyond this point, it is ordinarily justifiable for the community to demand that the individual give up some part of his interest in privacy and security to advance the community's vital interests in law enforcement; such a search is generally "reasonable" in the Amendment's terms.

A compelled surgical intrusion into an individual's body for evidence, however, implicates expectations of privacy and security of such magnitude that the intrusion may be "unreasonable" even if likely to produce evidence of a crime. In *Schmerber*, we addressed a claim that the State had breached the Fourth Amendment's protection of the right of the people to be secure in their *persons* against unreasonable searches and seizures when it compelled an individual suspected of drunken driving to undergo a blood test. Schmerber had been arrested at a hospital while receiving treatment for injuries suffered when the automobile he was driving struck a tree. Despite Schmerber's objection, a police officer at the hospital had directed a physician to take a blood sample from him. Schmerber subsequently objected to the introduction at trial of evidence obtained as a result of the blood test.

The authorities in *Schmerber* clearly had probable cause to believe that he had been driving while intoxicated, and to believe that a blood test would provide evidence that was exceptionally probative in confirming this belief. Because the case fell within the exigent-circumstances exception to the warrant requirement, no warrant was necessary. The search was not more intrusive than reasonably necessary to accomplish its goals. Nonetheless, Schmerber argued that the Fourth Amendment prohibited the authorities from intruding into his body to extract the blood that was needed as evidence.

The intrusion perhaps implicated Schmerber's most personal and deep-rooted expectations of privacy, and the Court recognized that Fourth Amendment analysis thus required a discerning inquiry into the facts and circumstances to determine whether the intrusion was justifiable.

The reasonableness of surgical intrusions beneath the skin depends on a case-by-case approach, in which the individual's interests in privacy and security are weighed against society's interests in conducting the procedure. In a given case, the question whether the community's need for evidence outweighs the substantial privacy interests at stake is a delicate one admitting of few categorical answers. We believe that *Schmerber*, however, provides the appropriate framework of analysis for such cases.

Schmerber recognized that the ordinary requirements of the Fourth Amendment would be the threshold requirements for conducting this kind of surgical search and seizure. We noted the importance of probable cause. And we pointed out: "Search warrants are ordinarily required for searches of dwellings, and, absent an emergency, no less could be required where intrusions into the human body are concerned. The importance of informed, detached and deliberate determinations of the issue whether or not to invade another's body in search of evidence of guilt is indisputable and great."

Beyond these standards, *Schmerber*'s inquiry considered a number of other factors in determining the "reasonableness" of the blood test. A crucial factor in analyzing the magnitude of the intrusion in *Schmerber* is the extent to which the procedure may threaten the safety or health of the individual. "For most people, a blood test involves virtually no risk, trauma, or pain." Moreover, all reasonable medical precautions were taken and no unusual or untested procedures were employed in *Schmerber*; the procedure was performed "by a physician in a hospital environment according to accepted medical practices." Notwithstanding the existence of probable cause, a search for evidence of a crime may be unjustifiable if it endangers the life or health of the suspect.

Another factor is the extent of intrusion upon the individual's dignitary interests in personal privacy and bodily integrity. Intruding into an individual's living room, eavesdropping upon an individual's telephone conversations, or forcing an individual to accompany police officers to the police station typically do not injure the physical person of the individual. Such intrusions do, however, damage the individual's sense of personal privacy and security and are thus subject to the Fourth Amendment's dictates. In noting that a blood test was "a commonplace in these days of periodic physical examinations," *Schmerber* recognized society's judgment that blood tests do not constitute an unduly extensive imposition on an individual's personal privacy and bodily integrity.

Weighed against these individual interests is the community's interest in fairly and accurately determining guilt or innocence. This interest is of course of great importance. We noted in *Schmerber* that a blood test is "a highly effective means of determining the degree to which a person is under the influence of alcohol." Moreover, there was "a clear indication that in fact desired evidence would be found" if the blood test were undertaken. Especially given the difficulty of proving drunkenness by other means, these considerations showed that results of the blood test were of vital importance if the State were to enforce its drunken driving laws. In *Schmerber*, we concluded that this state interest was sufficient to justify the intrusion, and the compelled blood test was thus "reasonable" for Fourth Amendment purposes.

III

Applying the *Schmerber* balancing test in this case, we believe that the Court of Appeals reached the correct result. The Commonwealth plainly had probable cause to conduct the search. In addition, all parties apparently agree that respondent has had a full measure of procedural protections and has been able fully to litigate the difficult medical and legal questions necessarily involved in analyzing the reasonableness of a surgical incision of this magnitude. Our inquiry therefore must focus on the extent of the intrusion on respondent's privacy interests and on the State's need for the evidence.

The threats to the health or safety of respondent posed by the surgery are the subject of sharp dispute between the parties. Before the new revelations of October 18, the District Court found that the procedure could be carried out "with virtually no risk to respondent." On rehearing, however, with new evidence before it, the District Court held that "the risks previously involved have increased in magnitude even as new risks are being added."

The Court of Appeals examined the medical evidence in the record and found that respondent would suffer some risks associated with the surgical procedure. One surgeon had testified that the difficulty of discovering the exact location of the bullet "could require extensive probing and retracting of the muscle tissue," carrying with it "the concomitant risks of injury to the muscle as well as injury to the nerves, blood vessels and other tissue in the chest and pleural cavity." The court further noted that "the greater intrusion and the larger incisions increase the risks of infection." Moreover, there was conflict in the testimony concerning the nature and the scope of the operation. One surgeon stated that it would take 15–20 minutes, while another predicted the procedure could take up to two and one-half hours. The court properly took the resulting uncertainty about the medical risks into account.

Both lower courts in this case believed that the proposed surgery, which for purely medical reasons required the use of a general anesthetic, would be an "extensive" intrusion on respondent's personal privacy and bodily integrity. When conducted with the consent of the patient, surgery requiring general anesthesia is not necessarily demeaning or intrusive. In such a case, the surgeon is carrying out the patient's own will concerning the patient's body and the patient's right to privacy is therefore preserved. In this case, however, the Court of Appeals noted that the Commonwealth proposes to take control of respondent's body, to "drug this citizen—not yet convicted of a criminal offense—with narcotics and barbiturates into a state of unconsciousness," and then to search beneath his skin for evidence of a crime. This kind of surgery involves a virtually total divestment of respondent's ordinary control over surgical probing beneath his skin.

The other part of the balance concerns the Commonwealth's need to intrude into respondent's body to retrieve the bullet. The Commonwealth claims to need the bullet to demonstrate that it was fired from Watkinson's gun, which in turn would show that respondent was the robber who confronted Watkinson. However, although we recognize the difficulty of making determinations in advance as to the strength of the case against respondent, petitioners' assertions of a compelling need for the bullet are hardly persuasive. The very circumstances relied on in this case to demonstrate probable cause to believe that evidence will be found tend to vitiate the Commonwealth's need to compel respondent to undergo surgery. The Commonwealth has available substantial additional evidence that respondent was the individual who accosted Watkinson on the night of the robbery. No party in this case suggests that Watkinson's entirely spontaneous identification of respondent at the hospital would be inadmissible. In addition, petitioners can no doubt prove that Watkinson was found a few blocks from Watkinson's store shortly after the incident took place. And petitioners can certainly show that the location of the bullet (under respondent's left collarbone) seems to correlate with Watkinson's report that the robber "jerked" to the left. The fact that the Commonwealth has available such substantial evidence of the origin of the bullet restricts the need for the Commonwealth to compel respondent to undergo the contemplated surgery.

In weighing the various factors in this case, we therefore reach the same conclusion as the courts below. The operation sought will intrude substantially on respondent's protected interests. The medical risks of the operation, although apparently not extremely severe, are a subject of considerable dispute; the very uncertainty militates against finding the operation to be "reasonable." In addition, the intrusion on respondent's privacy interests entailed by the operation can only be characterized as severe. On the other hand, although the bullet may turn out to be useful to the Commonwealth in prosecuting respondent, the Commonwealth has failed to demonstrate a compelling need for it. We believe that in these circumstances the Commonwealth has failed to demonstrate that it would be "reasonable" under the terms of the Fourth Amendment to search for evidence of this crime by means of the contemplated surgery.

Invasive Medical Procedures

The reasonableness of surgical intrusions beneath the skin for evidence of a crime depends on a case-by-case approach, in which the individual's interests in privacy and security are weighed against society's interests in conducting the procedure. Probable cause and a warrant are the threshold requirements for conducting this kind of surgical search and seizure. Other factors relevant to the reasonableness determination include:

    a.   The extent to which the procedure may threaten the safety or health of the individual. Notwithstanding the existence of probable cause, a search for evidence of a crime may be unjustifiable if it endangers the life or health of the suspect.

    b.   The extent of intrusion upon the individual's dignitary interests in personal privacy and bodily integrity.

c. The community's interest in fairly and accurately determining guilt or innocence. Is there a compelling need for the evidence that would be obtained in surgery, or is other evidence available through less invasive means?

CHAPTER 8

EXCEPTIONS TO THE EXCLUSIONARY RULE

■ ■ ■

The exclusionary rule is the basic remedy for violations of the Fourth Amendment. In fact, the exclusionary rule is one of the basic remedies in criminal cases for other constitutional violations as well. In *Mapp v. Ohio*, 367 U.S. 643 (1961), presented in Chapter 2, the Supreme Court articulated three justifications for the exclusionary rule: it deters police misconduct, it protects constitutional rights, and it safeguards judicial integrity. But the exclusionary rule also exacts a cost: the exclusion of important evidence necessary to convict and punish criminal offenders. Concerns about this cost have led the Supreme Court to create a number of exceptions to the exclusionary rule—situations in which the Court has declined to apply the rule despite a clear violation of the Fourth Amendment.

As you'll recall from the last part of Chapter 3, only those whose *own* Fourth Amendment rights have been violated have the requisite "standing" to challenge a search or seizure and invoke the exclusionary rule. But even in those cases where there has been a violation of the defendant's own constitutional rights—providing the defendant with the requisite standing to challenge a search or seizure—the illegally obtained evidence might still be admissible if the court finds that one or more exceptions to the exclusionary rule applies. This Chapter presents those exceptions. As you read the cases, consider your own views. Does the Supreme Court advance good reasons for the various exceptions, or do the exceptions undermine the basic purposes of the exclusionary rule?

A. INDEPENDENT SOURCE

Under the exclusionary rule, evidence that is unlawfully obtained by the police—sometimes described as "fruit of the poisonous tree"—is generally excluded from the defendant's trial and cannot be used to establish guilt. Under the independent source exception to the exclusionary rule, however, the evidence will still be admissible if it was also obtained through a source independent of the illegal actions of the police.

Suppose Carol Copper, a police officer, notices a car parked on the street belonging to Nick Narcotic, a notorious drug dealer. On a hunch,

Copper pries open the trunk, discovering a large quantity of drugs and several unregistered guns. Copper quickly closes the trunk and calls a judge to apply for a search warrant. The judge is confused and explains that she has already issued a warrant to search the particular car in question. While Copper continues talking on the phone with the judge, Ike Investigator, a police detective, arrives on the scene and opens the trunk. Unbeknownst to Carol Copper, Nick Narcotic had been under surveillance for the past month, and Ike Investigator had observed him placing drugs and guns in the trunk of the car. Investigator's observations established probable cause to search the car, and the judge issued the search warrant that Ike executed. Are the drugs and guns admissible against Nick Narcotic?

Nick Narcotic would argue that the drugs and guns are inadmissible because Carol Copper violated the Fourth Amendment in discovering them—she pried open the trunk without reasonable suspicion, probable cause, or a search warrant. In order to deter police misconduct of that sort, the exclusionary rule should be applied. While Nick Narcotic makes a compelling argument, the evidence would likely be admissible under the independent source exception to the exclusionary rule because the detective, Ike Investigator, discovered the evidence through lawful means independent of and untainted by Carol Copper's illegal actions.

In *Murray v. U.S.*, the Supreme Court explained the independent source exception and the requirements that must be satisfied in order for it to apply.

MURRAY V. U.S.
487 U.S. 533 (1988)

JUSTICE SCALIA delivered the opinion of the Court.

In *Segura v. U.S.*, 468 U.S. 796 (1984), we held that police officers' illegal entry upon private premises did not require suppression of evidence subsequently discovered at those premises when executing a search warrant obtained on the basis of information wholly unconnected with the initial entry. In these consolidated cases we are faced with the question whether, again assuming evidence obtained pursuant to an independently obtained search warrant, the portion of such evidence that had been observed in plain view at the time of a prior illegal entry must be suppressed.

I

Both cases arise out of the conviction of petitioner Michael F. Murray, petitioner James D. Carter, and others for conspiracy to possess and distribute illegal drugs. Insofar as relevant for our purposes, the facts are as follows: Based on information received from informants, federal law enforcement agents had been surveilling petitioner Murray and several of his co-conspirators. At about 1:45 p.m. on April 6, 1983, they observed Murray drive a truck and Carter drive a green camper, into a warehouse in South Boston. When the petitioners drove the vehicles out about 20 minutes later, the surveilling agents saw within the warehouse two individuals and a tractor-trailer rig bearing a long, dark container. Murray and Carter later turned over the truck and camper to other drivers, who were in turn followed and ultimately arrested, and the vehicles lawfully seized. Both vehicles were found to contain marijuana.

After receiving this information, several of the agents converged on the South Boston warehouse and forced entry. They found the warehouse unoccupied, but observed in plain view numerous burlap-wrapped bales that were later found to contain marijuana. They left without disturbing the bales, kept the warehouse under surveillance, and did not reenter it until they had a search warrant. In applying for the warrant, the agents did not mention the prior entry, and did not rely on any observations made during that entry. When the warrant was issued—at 10:40 p.m., approximately eight hours after the initial entry—the agents immediately reentered the warehouse and seized 270 bales of marijuana and notebooks listing customers for whom the bales were destined.

Before trial, petitioners moved to suppress the evidence found in the warehouse. The District Court denied the motion, rejecting petitioners' arguments that the warrant was invalid because the agents did not inform the Magistrate about their prior warrantless entry, and that the warrant was tainted by that entry. The First Circuit affirmed, assuming for purposes of its decision that the first entry into the warehouse was unlawful. Murray and Carter then separately filed petitions for certiorari, which we granted, and have consolidated here.

II

The exclusionary rule prohibits introduction into evidence of tangible materials seized during an unlawful search, and of testimony concerning knowledge acquired during an unlawful search. Beyond that, the exclusionary rule also prohibits the introduction of derivative evidence, both tangible and testimonial, that is the product of the primary evidence, or that is otherwise acquired as an indirect result of the unlawful search, up to the point at which the connection with the unlawful search becomes "so attenuated as to dissipate the taint." See *Wong Sun v. U.S.*, 371 U.S. 471, 484–485 (1963).

Almost simultaneously with our development of the exclusionary rule, in the first quarter of this century, we also announced what has come to be known as the "independent source" doctrine. See *Silverthorne Lumber Co. v. U.S.*, 251 U.S. 385 (1920). That doctrine, which has been applied to evidence acquired not only through Fourth Amendment violations but also through Fifth and Sixth Amendment violations, has recently been described [in *Nix v. Williams*, 467 U.S. 431 (1984)] as follows:

> The interest of society in deterring unlawful police conduct and the public interest in having juries receive all probative evidence of a crime are properly balanced by putting the police in the same, not a *worse*, position that they would have been in if no police error or misconduct had occurred. When the challenged evidence has an independent source, exclusion of such evidence would put the police in a worse position than they would have been in absent any error or violation.

The dispute here is over the scope of this doctrine. Petitioners contend that it applies only to evidence obtained for the first time during an independent lawful search. The Government argues that it applies also to evidence initially discovered during, or as a consequence of, an unlawful search, but later obtained independently from activities untainted by the initial illegality. We think the Government's view has better support in both precedent and policy.

Our cases have used the concept of "independent source" in a more general and a more specific sense. The more general sense identifies *all* evidence acquired in a fashion untainted by the illegal evidence-gathering activity. Thus, where an unlawful entry has given investigators knowledge of facts x and y, but fact z has been learned by other means, fact z can be said to be admissible because derived from an "independent source." This is how we used the term in *Segura*. In that case, agents unlawfully entered the defendant's apartment and remained there until a search warrant was obtained. The admissibility of what they discovered while waiting in the apartment was not before us, but we held that the evidence found for the first time during the execution of the valid and untainted search warrant was admissible because it was discovered pursuant to an "independent source."

The original use of the term, however, and its more important use for purposes of these cases, was more specific. It was originally applied in the exclusionary rule context, by Justice Holmes, with reference to that particular category of evidence acquired by an untainted search *which is identical to the evidence unlawfully acquired*—that is, in the example just given, to knowledge of facts x and y derived from an independent source:

> The essence of a provision forbidding the acquisition of evidence in a certain way is that not merely evidence so acquired shall not be used before the Court but that it shall not be used at all. Of course this does not mean that the facts thus obtained become sacred and inaccessible. If knowledge of them is gained from an independent source they may be proved like any others. *Silverthorne Lumber Co. v. U.S.*, 251 U.S. 385, 392 (1920).

Petitioners' asserted policy basis for excluding evidence which is initially discovered during an illegal search, but is subsequently acquired through an independent and lawful source, is that a contrary rule will remove all deterrence to, and indeed positively encourage, unlawful police searches. As petitioners see the incentives, law enforcement officers will routinely enter without a warrant to make sure that what they expect to be on the premises is in fact there. If it is not, they will have spared themselves the time and trouble of getting a warrant; if it is, they can get the warrant and use the evidence despite the unlawful entry. We see the incentives differently. An officer with probable cause sufficient to obtain a search warrant would be foolish to enter the premises first in an unlawful manner. By doing so, he would risk suppression of all evidence on the premises, both seen and unseen, since his action would add to the normal burden of convincing a magistrate that there is probable cause the much more onerous burden of convincing a trial court that no information gained from the illegal entry affected either the law enforcement officers' decision to seek a warrant or the magistrate's decision to grant it. Nor would the officer *without* sufficient probable cause to obtain a search warrant have any added incentive to conduct an unlawful entry, since whatever he finds cannot be used to establish probable cause before a magistrate.

III

To apply what we have said to the present cases: Knowledge that the marijuana was in the warehouse was assuredly acquired at the time of the unlawful entry. But it was also acquired at the time of entry pursuant to the warrant, and if that later acquisition was not the result of the earlier entry there is no reason why the independent source doctrine should not apply. Invoking the exclusionary rule would put the police (and society) not in the *same* position they would have occupied if no violation occurred, but in a *worse* one. We think this is also true with respect to the tangible evidence, the bales of marijuana.

The ultimate question, therefore, is whether the search pursuant to warrant was in fact a genuinely independent source of the information and tangible evidence at issue here. This would not have been the case if the agents' decision to seek the warrant was prompted by what they had seen during the initial entry, or if information obtained during that entry was presented to the Magistrate and affected his decision to issue the warrant. On this point the Court of Appeals said the following: "We can be absolutely certain that the warrantless entry in no way contributed in the slightest either to the issuance of a warrant or to the discovery of the evidence during the lawful search that occurred pursuant to the warrant."

Although these statements can be read to provide emphatic support for the Government's position, it is the function of the District Court rather than the Court of Appeals to determine the facts, and we do not think the Court of Appeals' conclusions are supported by adequate findings. The District Court found that the agents did not reveal their warrantless entry to the Magistrate, and that they did not include in their application for a warrant any recitation of their observations in the warehouse. It did not, however, explicitly find that the agents would have sought a warrant if they had not earlier entered the warehouse. The Government concedes this in its brief. To be sure, the District Court did determine that the purpose of the warrantless entry was in part "to guard against the destruction of possibly critical evidence," and one could perhaps infer from this that the agents who made the entry already planned to obtain that "critical evidence" through a warrant-authorized search. That inference is not, however, clear enough to justify the conclusion that the District Court's findings amounted to a determination of independent source.

Accordingly, we vacate the judgment and remand these cases to the Court of Appeals with instructions that it remand to the District Court for determination whether the warrant-authorized search of the warehouse was an independent source of the challenged evidence in the sense we have described.

JUSTICE MARSHALL, with whom JUSTICE STEVENS and JUSTICE O'CONNOR join, dissenting.

The Court today holds that the "independent source" exception to the exclusionary rule may justify admitting evidence discovered during an illegal warrantless search that is later "rediscovered" by the same team of investigators during a search pursuant to a warrant obtained immediately after the illegal search. I believe the Court's decision, by failing to provide sufficient guarantees that the subsequent search was, in fact, independent of the illegal search, emasculates the Warrant Clause and undermines the deterrence function of the exclusionary rule.

This Court has stated frequently that the exclusionary rule is principally designed to deter violations of the Fourth Amendment. The Court has crafted exceptions to the exclusionary rule when the purposes of the rule are not furthered by the exclusion. As the Court today recognizes, the independent source exception to the exclusionary rule "allows admission of evidence that has been discovered by means wholly independent of any constitutional violation." The independent source exception, like the inevitable discovery exception, is primarily based on a practical view that under certain circumstances the beneficial deterrent effect that exclusion will have on future constitutional violations is too slight to justify the social cost of excluding probative evidence from a criminal trial. When the seizure of the evidence at issue is "wholly independent of" the constitutional violation, then exclusion arguably will have no effect on a law enforcement officer's incentive to commit an unlawful search.

Under the circumstances of these cases, the admission of the evidence "reseized" during the second search severely undermines the deterrence function of the exclusionary rule. Indeed, admission in these cases affirmatively encourages illegal searches. The incentives for such illegal conduct are clear. Obtaining a warrant is inconvenient and time consuming. Even when officers have probable cause to support a warrant application, therefore, they have an incentive first to determine whether it is worthwhile to obtain a warrant. Probable cause is much less than certainty, and many "confirmatory" searches will result in the discovery that no evidence is present, thus saving the police the time and trouble of getting a warrant. If contraband is discovered, however, the officers may later seek a warrant to shield the evidence from the taint of the illegal search. The police thus know in advance that they have little to lose and much to gain by forgoing the bother of obtaining a warrant and undertaking an illegal search.

The Court, however, "sees the incentives differently." Under the Court's view, today's decision does not provide an incentive for unlawful searches, because the officer undertaking the search would know that "his action would add to the normal burden of convincing a magistrate that there is probable cause the much more onerous burden of convincing a trial court that no information gained from the illegal entry affected either the law enforcement officers' decision to seek a warrant or the magistrate's decision to grant it." The Court, however, provides no hint of why this risk would actually seem significant to the officers. Under the circumstances of these cases, the officers committing the illegal search have both knowledge and control of the factors central to the trial court's determination. First, it is a simple matter, as was done in these cases, to exclude from the warrant application any information gained from the initial entry so that the magistrate's determination of probable cause is not influenced by the prior illegal search. Second, today's decision makes the application of the independent source exception turn entirely on an evaluation of the officers' intent. It normally will be difficult for the trial court to verify, or the defendant to rebut, an assertion by officers that they always intended to obtain a warrant, regardless of the results of the illegal search. The testimony of the officers conducting the illegal search is the only direct evidence of intent, and the defendant will be relegated simply to arguing that the officers should not be believed. Under these circumstances, the litigation risk described by the Court seems hardly a risk at all; it does not significantly dampen the incentive to conduct the initial illegal search.

The strong Fourth Amendment interest in eliminating these incentives for illegal entry should cause this Court to scrutinize closely the application of the independent source exception to evidence obtained under the circumstances of the instant cases; respect for the constitutional guarantee requires a rule that does not undermine the deterrence function of the exclusionary rule. When, as here, the same team of investigators is involved in both the first and second search, there is a significant danger that the "independence" of the source will in fact be illusory, and that the initial search will have affected the decision to obtain a warrant notwithstanding the officers' subsequent assertions to the contrary. It is therefore crucial that the factual premise of the exception—complete independence—be clearly established before the exception can justify admission of the evidence. I believe the Court's reliance on the intent of the law enforcement officers who conducted the warrantless search provides insufficient guarantees that the subsequent legal search was unaffected by the prior illegal search.

To ensure that the source of the evidence is genuinely independent, the basis for a finding that a search was untainted by a prior illegal search must focus, as with the inevitable discovery doctrine, on "demonstrated historical facts capable of ready verification or impeachment." In the instant cases, there are no "demonstrated historical facts" capable of supporting a finding that the subsequent warrant search was wholly unaffected by the prior illegal search. The same team of investigators was involved in both searches. The warrant was obtained immediately after the illegal search, and no effort was made to obtain a warrant prior to the discovery of the marijuana during the illegal search. The only evidence available that the warrant search was wholly independent is the testimony of the agents who conducted the illegal search. Under these circumstances, the threat that the subsequent search was tainted by the illegal search is too great to allow for the application of the independent source exception. The Court's contrary holding lends itself to easy abuse, and offers an incentive to bypass the constitutional requirement that probable cause be assessed by a neutral and detached magistrate before the police invade an individual's privacy.

In sum, under circumstances as are presented in these cases, when the very law enforcement officers who participate in an illegal search immediately thereafter obtain a warrant to search the same premises, I believe the evidence discovered during the initial illegal entry must be suppressed. Any other result emasculates the Warrant Clause and provides an intolerable incentive for warrantless searches.

The Independent Source Exception to the Exclusionary Rule

The independent source exception to the exclusionary rule allows the admission of evidence that is discovered by lawful means wholly independent of and untainted by any constitutional violation. If information or evidence obtained during an unlawful search prompts the police to apply for a warrant or is used by the police to secure a warrant, the independent source exception does not apply.

B. INEVITABLE DISCOVERY

The inevitable discovery exception is a close cousin to the independent source exception. Even when evidence is unlawfully obtained, it may nevertheless be admissible if the police can show that they would have inevitably discovered the evidence through lawful means.

The hypothetical involving the discovery of drugs and guns in the trunk of Nick Narcotic's car, used in the preceding section to illustrate the independent source exception, can also be used to illustrate the inevitable discovery exception. When police officer Carol Copper illegally pried open the trunk of the car, Ike Investigator, the detective, was just moments away from executing a warrant to search the car. The drugs and guns would have inevitably been discovered through lawful means—during the search supported by the warrant—and they should therefore be admissible despite the illegal actions of Carol Copper.

In *Nix v. Williams*, the Supreme Court recognized the inevitable discovery exception and explained how it differs from the independent source exception. In the Court's view, the exclusion of illegally obtained evidence that would have inevitably been discovered by lawful means would not further the objectives of the exclusionary rule.

NIX V. WILLIAMS
467 U.S. 431 (1984)

CHIEF JUSTICE BURGER delivered the opinion of the Court.

We granted certiorari to consider whether, at respondent Williams' second murder trial in state court, evidence pertaining to the discovery and condition of the victim's body was properly admitted on the ground that it would ultimately or inevitably have been discovered even if no violation of any constitutional or statutory provision had taken place.

I

A

On December 24, 1968, 10-year-old Pamela Powers disappeared from a YMCA building in Des Moines, Iowa, where she had accompanied her parents to watch an athletic contest. Shortly after she disappeared, Williams was seen leaving the YMCA carrying a large bundle wrapped in a blanket; a 14-year-old boy who had helped Williams open his car door reported that he had seen "two legs in it and they were skinny and white."

Williams' car was found the next day 160 miles east of Des Moines in Davenport, Iowa. Later, several items of clothing belonging to the child, some of Williams' clothing, and an army blanket like the one used to wrap the bundle that Williams carried out of the YMCA were found at a rest stop on Interstate 80 near Grinnell, between Des Moines and Davenport. A warrant was issued for Williams' arrest.

Police surmised that Williams had left Pamela Powers or her body somewhere between Des Moines and the Grinnell rest stop where some of the young girl's clothing had been found. On December 26, the Iowa Bureau of Criminal Investigation initiated a large-scale search. Two hundred volunteers divided into teams began the search 21 miles east of Grinnell, covering an area several miles to the north and south of Interstate 80. They moved westward from Poweshiek County, in which Grinnell was located, into Jasper County. Searchers were instructed to check all roads, abandoned farm buildings, ditches, culverts, and any other place in which the body of a small child could be hidden.

Meanwhile, Williams surrendered to local police in Davenport, where he was promptly arraigned. Williams contacted a Des Moines attorney who arranged for an attorney in Davenport to meet Williams at the Davenport police station. Des Moines police informed counsel they would pick Williams up in Davenport and return him to Des Moines without questioning him. Two Des Moines detectives then drove to Davenport, took Williams into custody, and proceeded to drive him back to Des Moines.

During the return trip, one of the policemen, Detective Leaming, began a conversation with Williams, saying:

> I want to give you something to think about while we're traveling down the road. They are predicting several inches of snow for tonight, and I feel that you yourself are the only person that knows where this little girl's body is and if you get a snow on top of it you yourself may be unable to find it. And since we will be going right past the area [where the body is] on the way into Des Moines, I feel that we could stop and locate the body, that the parents of this little girl should be entitled to a Christian burial for the little girl who was snatched away from them on Christmas Eve and murdered. After a snow storm [we may not be] able to find it at all.

Leaming told Williams he knew the body was in the area of Mitchellville—a town they would be passing on the way to Des Moines. He concluded the conversation by saying "I do not want you to answer me. Just think about it."

Later, as the police car approached Grinnell, Williams asked Leaming whether the police had found the young girl's shoes. After Leaming replied that he was unsure, Williams directed the police to a point near a service station where he said he had left the shoes; they were not found. As they continued to drive to Des Moines, Williams asked whether the blanket had been found and then directed the officers to a rest area in Grinnell where he said he had disposed of the blanket; they did not find the blanket. At this point, Leaming and his party were joined by the officers in charge of the search. As they approached Mitchellville, Williams, without any further conversation, agreed to direct the officers to the child's body.

The officers directing the search had called off the search at 3 p.m., when they left the Grinnell Police Department to join Leaming at the rest area. At that time, one search team near the Jasper County-Polk County line was only two and one-half miles from where Williams soon guided Leaming and his party to the body. The child's body was found next to a culvert in a ditch beside a gravel road in Polk County, about two miles south of Interstate 80, and essentially within the area to be searched.

B
FIRST TRIAL

In February 1969 Williams was indicted for first-degree murder. Before trial in the Iowa court, his counsel moved to suppress evidence of the body and all related evidence including the condition of the body as shown by the autopsy. The ground for the motion was that such evidence was the "fruit" or product of Williams' statements made during the automobile ride from Davenport to Des Moines and prompted by Leaming's statements. The motion to suppress was denied.

The jury found Williams guilty of first-degree murder; the judgment of conviction was affirmed by the Iowa Supreme Court. Williams then sought release on habeas corpus in the United States District Court for the Southern District of Iowa. That court concluded that the evidence in question had been wrongly admitted at Williams' trial; a divided panel of the Court of Appeals for the Eighth Circuit agreed.

We granted certiorari, and a divided Court affirmed, holding that Detective Leaming had obtained incriminating statements from Williams by what was viewed as interrogation in violation of his right to counsel. *Brewer v. Williams*, 430 U.S. 387 (1977). This Court's opinion noted, however, that although Williams' incriminating statements could not be introduced into evidence at a second trial, evidence of the body's location and condition "might well be admissible on the theory that the body would have been discovered in any event, even had incriminating statements not been elicited from Williams."

C
SECOND TRIAL

At Williams' second trial in 1977 in the Iowa court, the prosecution did not offer Williams' statements into evidence, nor did it seek to show that Williams had directed the police to the child's body. However, evidence of the condition of her body as it was found, articles and photographs of her clothing, and the results of post mortem medical and chemical tests on the body were admitted. The trial court concluded that the State had proved by a preponderance of the evidence that, if the search had not been suspended and Williams had not led the police to the victim, her body would have been discovered "within a short time" in essentially the same condition as it was actually found. The trial court also ruled that if the police had not located the body, "the search would clearly have been taken up again where it left off, given the extreme circumstances of this case, and the body would [have] been found in short order."

In finding that the body would have been discovered in essentially the same condition as it was actually found, the court noted that freezing temperatures had prevailed and tissue deterioration would have been suspended. The challenged evidence was admitted and the jury again found Williams guilty of first-degree murder; he was sentenced to life in prison.

II

The Iowa Supreme Court correctly stated that the "vast majority" of all courts, both state and federal, recognize an inevitable discovery exception to the exclusionary rule. We are now urged to adopt and apply the so-called ultimate or inevitable discovery exception to the exclusionary rule.

Williams contends that evidence of the body's location and condition is "fruit of the poisonous tree," *i.e.*, the "fruit" or product of Detective Leaming's plea to help the child's parents give her "a Christian burial," which this Court had already held equated to interrogation. He contends that admitting the challenged evidence violated the Sixth Amendment whether it would have been inevitably discovered or not. Williams also contends that, if the inevitable discovery doctrine is constitutionally permissible, it must include a threshold showing of police good faith.

The doctrine requiring courts to suppress evidence as the tainted "fruit" of unlawful governmental conduct had its genesis in *Silverthorne Lumber Co. v. U.S.*, 251 U.S. 385 (1920); there, the Court held that the exclusionary rule applies not only to the illegally obtained evidence itself, but also to other incriminating evidence derived from the primary evidence.

Wong Sun v. U.S., 371 U.S. 471 (1963), extended the exclusionary rule to evidence that was the indirect product or "fruit" of unlawful police conduct, but there again the Court emphasized that evidence that has been illegally obtained need not always be suppressed.

Although *Silverthorne* and *Wong Sun* involved violations of the Fourth Amendment, the "fruit of the poisonous tree" doctrine has not been limited to cases in which there has been a Fourth Amendment violation. The Court has applied the doctrine where the violations were of the Sixth Amendment, as well as of the Fifth Amendment.

The core rationale consistently advanced by this Court for extending the exclusionary rule to evidence that is the fruit of unlawful police conduct has been that this admittedly drastic and socially costly course is needed to deter police from violations of constitutional and statutory protections. This Court has accepted the argument that the way to ensure such protections is to exclude evidence seized as a result of such violations notwithstanding the high social cost of letting persons obviously guilty go unpunished for their crimes. On this rationale, the prosecution is not to be put in a better position than it would have been in if no illegality had transpired.

By contrast, the derivative evidence analysis ensures that the prosecution is not put in a worse position simply because of some earlier police error or misconduct. The independent source doctrine allows admission of evidence that has been discovered by means wholly independent of any constitutional violation. That doctrine, although closely related to the inevitable discovery doctrine, does not apply here; Williams' statements to Leaming indeed led police to the child's body, but that is not the whole story. The independent source doctrine teaches us that the interest of society in deterring unlawful police conduct and the public interest in having juries receive all probative evidence of a crime are properly balanced by putting the police in the same, not a worse, position that they would have been in if no police error or misconduct had occurred. When the challenged evidence has an independent source, exclusion of such evidence would put the police in a worse position than they would have been in absent any error or violation. There is a functional similarity between these two doctrines in that exclusion of evidence that would inevitably have been discovered would also put the government in a worse position, because the police would have obtained that evidence if no misconduct had taken place. Thus, while the independent source exception would not justify admission of evidence in this case, its rationale is wholly consistent with and justifies our adoption of the ultimate or inevitable discovery exception to the exclusionary rule.

It is clear that the cases implementing the exclusionary rule begin with the premise that the challenged evidence is in some sense the product of illegal governmental activity. Of course, this does not end the inquiry. If the prosecution can establish by a preponderance of the evidence that the information ultimately or inevitably would have been discovered by lawful means—here the volunteers' search—then the deterrence rationale has so little basis that the evidence should be received. Anything less would reject logic, experience, and common sense.

The requirement that the prosecution must prove the absence of bad faith, imposed here by the Court of Appeals, would place courts in the position of withholding from juries relevant and undoubted truth that would have been available to police absent any unlawful police activity. Of course, that view would put the police in a worse position than they would have been in if no unlawful conduct had transpired. And, of equal importance, it wholly fails to take into account the enormous societal cost of excluding truth in the search for truth in the administration of justice. Nothing in this Court's prior holdings supports any such formalistic, pointless, and punitive approach.

The Court of Appeals concluded, without analysis, that if an absence-of-bad-faith requirement were not imposed, "the temptation to risk deliberate violations of the Sixth Amendment would be too great, and the deterrent effect of the Exclusionary Rule reduced too far." We reject that view. A police officer who is faced with the opportunity to obtain evidence illegally will rarely, if ever, be in a position to calculate whether the evidence sought would inevitably be discovered.

On the other hand, when an officer is aware that the evidence will inevitably be discovered, he will try to avoid engaging in any questionable practice. In that situation, there will be little to gain from taking any dubious "shortcuts" to obtain the evidence. Significant disincentives to obtaining evidence illegally—including the possibility of departmental discipline and civil liability—also lessen the likelihood that the ultimate or inevitable discovery exception will promote police misconduct. In these circumstances, the societal costs of the exclusionary rule far outweigh any possible benefits to deterrence that a good-faith requirement might produce.

Exclusion of physical evidence that would inevitably have been discovered adds nothing to either the integrity or fairness of a criminal trial. The Sixth Amendment right to counsel protects against unfairness by preserving the adversary process in which the reliability of proffered evidence may be tested in cross-examination. Here, however, Detective Leaming's conduct did nothing to impugn the reliability of the evidence in question—the body of the child and its condition as it was found, articles of clothing found on the body, and the autopsy. No one would seriously contend that the presence of counsel in the police car when Leaming appealed to Williams' decent human instincts would have had any bearing on the reliability of the body as evidence. Suppression, in these circumstances, would do nothing whatever to promote the integrity of the trial process, but would inflict a wholly unacceptable burden on the administration of criminal justice.

On this record it is clear that the search parties were approaching the actual location of the body, and we are satisfied, along with three courts earlier, that the volunteer search teams would have resumed the search had Williams not earlier led the police to the body, and the body inevitably would have been found.

JUSTICE BRENNAN, with whom JUSTICE MARSHALL joins, dissenting.

To the extent that today's decision adopts this "inevitable discovery" exception to the exclusionary rule, it simply acknowledges a doctrine that is akin to the "independent source" exception first recognized by the Court in *Silverthorne Lumber Co. v. U.S.* In particular, the Court concludes that unconstitutionally obtained evidence may be admitted at trial if it inevitably would have been discovered in the same condition by an independent line of investigation that was already being pursued when the constitutional violation occurred. As has every Federal Court of Appeals previously addressing this issue, I agree that in these circumstances the "inevitable discovery" exception to the exclusionary rule is consistent with the requirements of the Constitution.

In its zealous efforts to emasculate the exclusionary rule, however, the Court loses sight of the crucial difference between the "inevitable discovery" doctrine and the "independent source" exception from which it is derived. When properly applied, the "independent source" exception allows the prosecution to use evidence only if it was, in fact, obtained by fully lawful means. It therefore does no violence to the constitutional protections that the exclusionary rule is meant to enforce. The "inevitable discovery" exception is likewise compatible with the Constitution, though it differs in one key respect from its next of kin: specifically, the evidence sought to be introduced at trial has not actually been obtained from an independent source, but rather would have been discovered as a matter of course if independent investigations were allowed to proceed.

In my view, this distinction should require that the government satisfy a heightened burden of proof before it is allowed to use such evidence. The inevitable discovery exception necessarily implicates a hypothetical finding that differs in kind from the factual finding that precedes application of the independent source rule. To ensure that this hypothetical finding is narrowly confined to circumstances that are functionally equivalent to an independent source, and to protect fully the fundamental rights served by the exclusionary rule, I would require clear and convincing evidence before concluding that the government had met its burden of proof on this issue. Increasing the burden of proof serves to impress the factfinder with the importance of the decision and thereby reduces the risk that illegally obtained evidence will be admitted. Because the lower courts did not impose such a requirement, I would remand this case for application of this heightened burden of proof by the lower courts in the first instance. I am therefore unable to join either the Court's opinion or its judgment.

> **The Inevitable Discovery Exception to the Exclusionary Rule**
>
> The inevitable discovery exception to the exclusionary rule allows the admission of illegally obtained evidence if the prosecution can prove, by a preponderance of the evidence, that the illegally obtained evidence would have ultimately or inevitably been discovered by lawful means. The prosecution is not required to prove the absence of bad faith by police in order to invoke the inevitable discovery exception.

LEARN MORE WITH *LAW & ORDER*

In the following episode of *Law & Order* ("Virus," Season 3, Episode 19), the police are investigating a report of several recent deaths at a diabetes clinic. Detectives Briscoe and Logan discover that a computer virus infected the software on the blood analyzer at the clinic; as a result, a number of patients were given excessive amounts of insulin and died. The detectives trace the virus to a group of computer hackers known as Department of Doom (DOD), who meet on an electronic bulletin board. The detectives interview the system operator of DOD's electronic bulletin board, Kenny Rinker. As the detectives look on over his shoulder, Rinker accesses the bulletin board and determines that a hacker named "Striker One" was looking for information about the blood analyzer used at the clinic. With further encouragement from the detectives, Rinker is able to hack into Striker One's electronic mailbox. By reading Striker One's messages—and through further investigation—the detectives discover that Striker One is actually John Cook, a high school student. Armed with a search warrant, police visit Cook's apartment and find him in front of his computer. Police seize the computer as Cook attempts to delete some files. Technicians later discover fragments of the virus on the computer.

Cook's defense attorney moves to suppress the evidence of the computer virus, arguing that police had no warrant when they hacked into Cook's electronic mailbox, searched it, and discovered information that led to Cook's identity and the virus on his computer. Prosecutor Ben Stone points out that Kenny Rinker, a private citizen, actually hacked into the mailbox. The evidence should be admissible, Stone argues, because the Fourth Amendment only applies to searches conducted by police or the government. Cook's defense attorney notes that the detectives were looking over Rinker's shoulder and encouraging his actions; it was just as if they had asked Rinker to break into Cook's room because they couldn't get a warrant. The judge agrees that the evidence found on Cook's computer—along with any other evidence derived from it—was unlawfully obtained and inadmissible. Accordingly, the judge dismisses the charges against Cook.

With the critical evidence now inadmissible, the prosecutors resume the investigation and attempt to determine John Cook's motive. They eventually discover that John's father, Robert Cook, was a patient at the diabetes clinic. Robert lost his vision and was convinced that the clinic's doctors were responsible for ruining his life. Armed with this new information as to motive, Ben Stone returns to court and seeks to have the computer evidence declared admissible under the inevitable discovery exception to the exclusionary rule. In essence, Stone argues that the police, having lawfully determined John Cook's motive for the crime, would have inevitably obtained a warrant to search his computer, discovering the fragments of the virus.

The segments of the episode that depict the relevant Investigative Criminal Procedure issues appear at:

17:52 to 23:30; 25:46 to 31:18; 32:34 to 36:53

Law & Order **Episode**
"Virus," Season 3, Episode 19

This episode provides a great opportunity to review a number of important Fourth Amendment issues. First, the episode nicely depicts the government action requirement, previously discussed in Chapter 2. As you'll recall, the Fourth Amendment and other constitutional provisions in Investigative Criminal Procedure only provide protection against actions taken by government officials. Prosecutor Ben Stone argues that there was no illegal search because the police didn't hack into John Cook's electronic mailbox; instead, Kenny Rinker, a private citizen, did it. What Stone overlooks is that the government action requirement is also met if a private citizen acts as an agent or instrument of the government, or if the private citizen receives government assistance or encouragement. As the defense attorney points out, that's precisely what happened—Detectives Briscoe and Logan watched and encouraged Kenny Rinker as he hacked into John Cook's mailbox. Because there was government action, John Cook is entitled to the protections of the Fourth Amendment against unreasonable searches and seizures.

Second, did the act of hacking into John Cook's mailbox and reading his communications amount to a search under the Fourth Amendment? During the suppression hearing in the judge's office, the prosecutor, the defense attorney, and the judge all assume that there was a search. In fact, the defense attorney compares the computer hacking to breaking into John Cook's room without a warrant, an analogy that Ben Stone fails to answer. Does that analogy hold up under the relevant cases presented in Chapter 3? The two basic tests for determining whether a search has occurred are the *Jones* Physical Intrusion Test and the *Katz* Reasonable Expectations of Privacy Test. The Physical Intrusion Test isn't met, since Kenny Rinker (and the police) didn't *physically* intrude into John Cook's mailbox; they achieved the intrusion electronically. And under the *Katz* Test, Stone might have argued that John Cook lacked any reasonable expectation of privacy because he shared his electronic communications with others, including the phone company whose equipment transmitted those communications. To support this argument, Stone might have cited *Smith v. Maryland*, 442 U.S. 735 (1979), in which the Supreme Court held that the use of pen register did not amount to a search because "a person has no legitimate expectation of privacy in information he voluntarily turns over to third parties" like the telephone company. The problem with this line of argument is that *Smith* did not authorize the government to intercept the *content* of phone calls, and *Katz* itself expressly holds that listening to and recording an individual's phone calls amounts to a search requiring a warrant. More recently, in *Riley v. California*, 134 S.Ct. 2473 (2014), presented in Chapter 5, the Supreme Court recognized the importance of digital privacy and held that police must obtain a warrant to search the contents of an arrestee's cell phone. The Court's reasoning in *Riley* surely applies when police search electronic mail without a warrant—particularly when the owner isn't yet under arrest.

Third, the episode illustrates how even illegally obtained evidence might be declared admissible under the inevitable discovery exception to the exclusionary rule. After reopening the investigation and determining John Cook's motive for targeting the diabetes clinic, the prosecution argues that the previously excluded computer evidence should be admissible under the inevitable discovery exception recognized by the Supreme Court in *Nix v. Williams*, 467 U.S. 431 (1984). Ben Stone points out that an "independent investigation" yielded John Cook's identity and probable cause to search his apartment, where the police inevitably would have found the computer and the virus. The defense attorney points out that the prosecution's independent investigation led them to Robert Cook; there is no reason to believe the prosecution inevitably would have suspected his son, especially since John does not live with his father. Judge Henry Fillmore, noting that he doesn't see "clear and convincing evidence" that the police inevitably would have discovered John Cook's involvement and the evidence on his computer, declines to apply the inevitable discovery exception. Stone points out that the judge is applying an incorrect standard—*Nix v. Williams* only requires the prosecution to prove *by a preponderance of the evidence* that the illegally obtained evidence would have inevitably been discovered by lawful means. Judge Fillmore tells Stone he's "out of order," and the computer evidence remains inadmissible. (Trial judges do often apply the law incorrectly, forcing the appellate courts—including the U.S. Supreme Court—to clarify the relevant legal standards.)

Finally, the episode contains a good illustration of the "standing" requirement, previously discussed at the end of Chapter 3. As you'll recall, a defendant can challenge a search and invoke the exclusionary rule only if *his own* rights were violated. After Judge Fillmore declares the computer evidence inadmissible against John Cook, prosecutors Ben Stone and Paul Robinette have a conversation in which they discuss using the excluded evidence against Robert Cook, whose rights were never violated by the illegal search. Robert Cook, of course, had no legitimate expectation of privacy on his son's computer because he didn't live with his son and had no access at all to the computer. Using the computer evidence from John's computer and other lawfully gathered evidence, the prosecutors build a case against Robert Cook and ultimately put him on trial for conspiracy. Faced with the possibility that his father will be convicted of a crime he didn't commit, John Cook confesses.

C. INADEQUATE CAUSAL CONNECTION AND ATTENUATION OF THE TAINT

As you know, the exclusionary rule generally forbids the introduction of evidence that is illegally obtained by the police. But what happens when illegally obtained evidence leads police to other evidence that is obtained lawfully? Is the lawfully discovered evidence inadmissible too because it is derived from or linked to the illegally obtained evidence? The answer depends on the nature of the lawfully obtained evidence and how closely connected it is to the illegal conduct of the police.

To illustrate the point, let's return to the hypothetical we've used throughout this Chapter, but with a few additional facts. Suppose that Carol Copper—based only a hunch, and without reasonable suspicion, probable cause, or a warrant—pries open the trunk of Nick Narcotic's car. There is nothing inside the trunk except for a map of a rural area a few miles away. A large red "X" is in the center of the map, and written next to it: "N.N.'S STUFF BURIED HERE." Copper takes the map and drives to the area marked by the red "X" on the map. Just off a gravel road, she finds a patch of dirt that looks as if it has recently been disturbed. Copper begins to dig, and after a few minutes, she discovers a bloody knife with the initials "N.N." carved into the handle. Further digging leads to an even more gruesome discovery: the body of Marty Mobster, riddled with dozens of stab wounds.

When the crime scene unit arrives to process the scene, Copper drives a quarter mile down the gravel road, stopping at a secluded log cabin. Copper exits her vehicle and knocks on the front door. Olive Observant answers. Copper identifies herself and asks Olive if she's seen anything unusual recently. "About a week ago," Olive explains, "two men got out of a fancy car and had a terrible argument right in front of my home. One of the men eventually pulled out a knife, and told the other man to get back in the car. The other man did as he was ordered, and they drove off." Using her smartphone to access a police database, Carol Copper shows Olive pictures of Nick Narcotic, Marty Mobster, and Nick's car. "Yes, those are the men who were arguing, and that's the car they were traveling in," Olive confirms. Copper asks Olive if she'd be willing to testify in court about what she saw. "Yes," Olive answers, "it's part of my civic duty."

The crime scene unit finds Nick Narcotic's fingerprints on the bloody knife. Based on this evidence, the map with the red "X" identifying the location of "N.N.'S STUFF," and the statement from Olive Observant, Nick Narcotic is charged with the murder of Marty Mobster. At a suppression hearing shortly before the trial, the prosecutor acknowledges that Carol Copper illegally searched the trunk of Nick's car. Accordingly, the judge declares that the map is inadmissible. But the prosecutor insists that the bloody knife, pictures of Marty Mobster's dead body, and testimony from Olive Observant should all be admissible because Carol Copper did nothing illegal when she dug a hole on public land near the gravel road and discovered the buried evidence, nor was it improper for Copper to knock on Olive Observant's door and inquire whether she'd seen anything unusual. Nick Narcotic's defense attorney contends that the knife, pictures of the body, and Olive's testimony should all be inadmissible as well since they are all derived from or linked to the map that was obtained illegally from the trunk of Nick's car. Which items of evidence, if any, are admissible?

The answer to this difficult question begins with *Wong Sun v. U.S.*, in which the Supreme Court held that evidence derived from unlawful actions by the police may be admissible if the connection between the illegal actions of the police and the evidence is "so attenuated as to dissipate the taint."

WONG SUN V. U.S.
371 U.S. 471 (1963)

While investigating narcotics trafficking in San Francisco, federal agents broke into the laundry and adjacent apartment owned by James Wah Toy. Without probable cause or a warrant, the agents arrested Toy and handcuffed him, and he made incriminating statements about his involvement with heroin. Further investigation suggested that Toy had obtained heroin from Wong Sun. Again proceeding without probable cause or a warrant, the agents went to Wong Sun's home, where they handcuffed and arrested him. Although a search of the homes of both James Toy and Wong Sun revealed no heroin, each was charged with violations of the federal narcotics laws and released on his own recognizance. A few days later, a federal agent separately interrogated James Toy and Wong Sun after informing each of his rights to withhold incriminating information and to have the advice of counsel. Both James Toy and Wong Sun provided incriminating information that was recorded in written form by the federal agent, but neither would agree to sign the statement.

The Supreme Court found that the federal agents' "uninvited entry into Toy's living quarters was unlawful and that the bedroom arrest which followed was likewise unlawful." The Court held that Toy's incriminating statements in his bedroom were tainted by his illegal arrest, and were therefore inadmissible:

> The Government argues that Toy's statements to the officers in his bedroom, although closely consequent upon the invasion which we hold unlawful, were nevertheless admissible because they resulted from "an intervening independent act of a free will." This contention, however, takes insufficient account of the circumstances. Six or seven officers had broken the door and followed on Toy's heels into the bedroom where his wife and child were sleeping. He had been almost immediately handcuffed and arrested. Under such circumstances it is unreasonable to infer that Toy's response was sufficiently an act of free will to purge the primary taint of the unlawful invasion.

Although Wong Sun's arrest was similarly unlawful, the Supreme Court held that his unsigned statement—given several days after his illegal arrest—was admissible:

> [Wong Sun's] arrest, also, was without probable cause or reasonable grounds. At all events, no evidentiary consequences turn upon that question. For Wong Sun's unsigned confession was not the fruit of that arrest, and was therefore properly admitted at trial. On the evidence that Wong Sun had been released on his own recognizance after a lawful arraignment, and had returned voluntarily several days later to make the statement, we hold that the connection between the arrest and the statement had "become so attenuated as to dissipate the taint." The fact that the statement was unsigned, whatever bearing this may have upon its weight and credibility, does not render it inadmissible; Wong Sun understood and adopted its substance, though he could not comprehend the English words. The petitioner has never suggested any impropriety in the interrogation itself which would require the exclusion of this statement.

In *Brown v. Illinois*, the Supreme Court again considered whether statements given after an illegal arrest were nevertheless admissible. The prosecution claimed that the administration of *Miranda* warnings sufficiently dissipated the taint of the illegal arrest. Relying heavily on *Wong Sun*, the Supreme Court disagreed.

BROWN V. ILLINOIS
422 U.S. 590 (1975)

JUSTICE BLACKMUN delivered the opinion of the Court.

This case lies at the crossroads of the Fourth and the Fifth Amendments. Petitioner was arrested without probable cause and without a warrant. He was given, in full, the warnings prescribed by *Miranda v. Arizona*, 384 U.S. 436 (1966). Thereafter, while in custody, he made two inculpatory statements. The issue is whether evidence of those statements was properly admitted, or should have been excluded, in petitioner's subsequent trial for murder in state court. Expressed another way, the issue is whether the statements were to be excluded as the fruit of the illegal arrest, or were admissible because the giving of the *Miranda* warnings sufficiently attenuated the taint of the arrest. See *Wong Sun v. U.S.*, 371 U.S. 471 (1963).

I

As petitioner Richard Brown was climbing the last of the stairs leading to the rear entrance of his Chicago apartment in the early evening of May 13, 1968, he happened to glance at the window near the door. He saw, pointed at him through the window, a revolver held by a stranger who was inside the apartment. The man said: "Don't move, you are under arrest." Another man, also with a gun, came up behind Brown and repeated the statement that he was under arrest. It was about 7:45 p.m. The two men turned out to be Detectives William Nolan and William Lenz of the Chicago police force. It is not clear from the record exactly when they advised Brown of their identity, but it is not disputed that they broke into his apartment, searched it, and then arrested Brown, all without probable cause and without any warrant, when he arrived. They later testified that they made the arrest for the purpose of questioning Brown as part of their investigation of the murder of a man named Roger Corpus.

Corpus was murdered one week earlier, on May 6, with a .38-caliber revolver in his Chicago West Side second-floor apartment. Shortly thereafter, Detective Lenz obtained petitioner's name, among others, from Corpus' brother. Petitioner and the others were identified as acquaintances of the victim, not as suspects.

On the day of petitioner's arrest, Detectives Lenz and Nolan, armed with a photograph of Brown, and another officer arrived at petitioner's apartment about 5 p.m. While the third officer covered the front entrance downstairs, the two detectives broke into Brown's apartment and searched it. Lenz then positioned himself near the rear door and watched through the adjacent window which opened onto the back porch. Nolan sat near the front door.

As both officers held him at gunpoint, the three entered the apartment. Brown was ordered to stand against the wall and was searched. No weapon was found. He was asked his name. When he denied being Richard Brown, Detective Lenz showed him the photograph, informed him that he was under arrest for the murder of Roger Corpus, handcuffed him, and escorted him to the squad car.

The two detectives took petitioner to the Maxwell Street police station. During the 20-minute drive Nolan again asked Brown, who then was sitting with him in the back seat of the car, whether his name was Richard Brown and whether he owned a 1966 Oldsmobile. Brown alternately evaded these questions or answered them falsely. Upon arrival at the station house Brown was placed in the second-floor central interrogation room. The room was bare, except for a table and four chairs. He was left alone, apparently without handcuffs, for some minutes while the officers obtained the file on the Corpus homicide. They returned with the file, sat down at the table, one across from Brown and the other to his left, and spread the file on the table in front of him.

The officers warned Brown of his rights under *Miranda*. They then informed him that they knew of an incident that had occurred in a poolroom on May 5, when Brown, angry at having been cheated at dice, fired a shot from a revolver into the ceiling. Brown answered: "Oh, you know about that." Lenz informed him that a bullet had been obtained from the ceiling of the poolroom and had been taken to the crime laboratory to be compared with bullets taken from Corpus' body. Brown responded: "Oh, you know that, too." At this point—it was about 8:45 p.m.—Lenz asked Brown whether he wanted to talk about the Corpus homicide. Petitioner answered that he did. For the next 20 to 25 minutes Brown answered questions put to him by Nolan, as Lenz typed.

This questioning produced a two-page statement in which Brown acknowledged that he and a man named Jimmy Claggett visited Corpus on the evening of May 5; that the three for some time sat drinking and smoking marihuana; that Claggett ordered him at gunpoint to bind Corpus' hands and feet with cord from the headphone of a stereo set; and that Claggett, using a .38-caliber revolver sold to him by Brown, shot Corpus three times through a pillow. The statement was signed by Brown.

About 9:30 p.m. the two detectives and Brown left the station house to look for Claggett in an area of Chicago Brown knew him to frequent. They made a tour of that area but did not locate their quarry. They then went to police headquarters where they endeavored, without success, to obtain a photograph of Claggett. They resumed their search—it was now about 11 p.m.—and they finally observed Claggett crossing at an intersection. Lenz and Nolan arrested him. All four, the two detectives and the two arrested men, returned to the Maxwell Street station about 12:15 a.m.

Brown was again placed in the interrogation room. He was given coffee and was left alone, for the most part, until 2 a.m. when Assistant State's Attorney Crilly arrived.

Crilly, too, informed Brown of his *Miranda* rights. After a half hour's conversation, a court reporter appeared. Once again the *Miranda* warnings were given. Crilly told him that he "was sure he would be charged with murder." Brown gave a second statement, providing a factual account of the murder substantially in accord with his first statement, but containing factual inaccuracies with respect to his personal background. When the statement was completed, at about 3 a.m., Brown refused to sign it. An hour later he made a phone call to his mother. At 9:30 that morning, about 14 hours after his arrest, he was taken before a magistrate.

On June 20 Brown and Claggett were jointly indicted by a Cook County grand jury for Corpus' murder. Prior to trial, petitioner moved to suppress the two statements he had made. He alleged that his arrest and detention had been illegal and that the statements were taken from him in violation of his constitutional rights. After a hearing, the motion was denied.

The case proceeded to trial. The State introduced evidence of both statements. Detective Nolan testified as to the contents of the first, but the writing itself was not placed in evidence. The second statement was introduced and was read to the jury in full. The jury found petitioner guilty of murder.

On appeal, the Supreme Court of Illinois affirmed the judgment of conviction. The court refused to accept the State's argument that Brown's arrest was lawful. But it went on to hold in two significant and unembellished sentences:

> We conclude that the giving of the *Miranda* warnings, in the first instance by the police officer and in the second by the assistant State's Attorney, served to break the causal connection between the illegal arrest and the giving of the statements, and that defendant's act in making the statements was "sufficiently an act of free will to purge the primary taint of the unlawful invasion." We hold, therefore, that the circuit court did not err in admitting the statements into evidence.

Aside from its reliance upon the presence of the *Miranda* warnings, no specific aspect of the record or of the circumstances was cited by the court in support of its conclusion. The court, in other words, appears to have held that the *Miranda* warnings in and of themselves broke the causal chain so that any subsequent statement, even one induced by the continuing effects of unconstitutional custody, was admissible so long as, in the traditional sense, it was voluntary and not coerced in violation of the Fifth and Fourteenth Amendments.

II

In *Wong Sun*, the Court pronounced the principles to be applied where the issue is whether statements and other evidence obtained after an illegal arrest or search should be excluded. The Court said:

> We need not hold that all evidence is "fruit of the poisonous tree" simply because it would not have come to light but for the illegal actions of the police. Rather, the more apt question in such a case is "whether, granting establishment of the primary illegality, the evidence to which instant objection is made has been come at by exploitation of that illegality or instead by means sufficiently distinguishable to be purged of the primary taint."

The exclusionary rule thus was applied in *Wong Sun* primarily to protect Fourth Amendment rights. Protection of the Fifth Amendment right against self-incrimination was not the Court's paramount concern there. To the extent that the question whether Toy's statement was voluntary was considered, it was only to judge whether it "was sufficiently an act of free will to purge the primary taint of the unlawful invasion."

The Court in *Wong Sun*, as is customary, emphasized that application of the exclusionary rule on Toy's behalf protected Fourth Amendment guarantees in two respects: "in terms of deterring lawless conduct by federal officers," and by "closing the doors of the federal courts to any use of evidence unconstitutionally obtained." These considerations of deterrence and of judicial integrity, by now, have become rather commonplace in the Court's cases.

III

The Illinois courts refrained from resolving the question, as apt here as it was in *Wong Sun*, whether Brown's statements were obtained by exploitation of the illegality of his arrest. They assumed that the *Miranda* warnings, by themselves, assured that the statements (verbal acts, as contrasted with physical evidence) were of sufficient free will as to purge the primary taint of the unlawful arrest. *Wong Sun*, of course, preceded *Miranda*.

Although, almost 90 years ago, the Court observed that the Fifth Amendment is in "intimate relation" with the Fourth, the *Miranda* warnings thus far have not been regarded as a means either of remedying or deterring violations of Fourth Amendment rights. Frequently, as here, rights under the two Amendments may appear to coalesce since "the unreasonable searches and seizures condemned in the Fourth Amendment are almost always made for the purpose of compelling a man to give evidence against himself, which in criminal cases is condemned in the Fifth Amendment." The exclusionary rule, however, when utilized to effectuate the Fourth Amendment, serves interests and policies that are distinct from those it serves under the Fifth. It is directed at all unlawful searches and seizures, and not merely those that happen to produce incriminating material or testimony as fruits. In short, exclusion of a confession made without *Miranda* warnings might be regarded as necessary to effectuate the Fifth Amendment, but it would not be sufficient fully to protect the Fourth. *Miranda* warnings, and the exclusion of a confession made without them, do not alone sufficiently deter a Fourth Amendment violation.

Thus, even if the statements in this case were found to be voluntary under the Fifth Amendment, the Fourth Amendment issue remains. In order for the causal chain, between the illegal arrest and the statements made subsequent thereto, to be broken, *Wong Sun* requires not merely that the statement meet the Fifth Amendment standard of voluntariness but that it be "sufficiently an act of free will to purge the primary taint." *Wong Sun* thus mandates consideration of a statement's admissibility in light of the distinct policies and interests of the Fourth Amendment.

If *Miranda* warnings, by themselves, were held to attenuate the taint of an unconstitutional arrest, regardless of how wanton and purposeful the Fourth Amendment violation, the effect of the exclusionary rule would be substantially diluted. Arrests made without warrant or without probable cause, for questioning or "investigation," would be encouraged by the knowledge that evidence derived therefrom could well be made admissible at trial by the simple expedient of giving *Miranda* warnings. Any incentive to avoid Fourth Amendment violations would be eviscerated by making the warnings, in effect, a "cure-all," and the constitutional guarantee against unlawful searches and seizures could be said to be reduced to "a form of words."

It is entirely possible, of course, as the State here argues, that persons arrested illegally frequently may decide to confess, as an act of free will unaffected by the initial illegality. But the *Miranda* warnings, alone and *per se*, cannot always make the act sufficiently a product of free will to break, for Fourth Amendment purposes, the causal connection between the illegality and the confession. They cannot assure in every case that the Fourth Amendment violation has not been unduly exploited.

While we therefore reject the *per se* rule which the Illinois courts appear to have accepted, we also decline to adopt any alternative *per se* or "but for" rule. The petitioner himself professes not to demand so much. The question whether a confession is the product of a free will under *Wong Sun* must be answered on the facts of each case. No single fact is dispositive. The workings of the human mind are too complex, and the possibilities of misconduct too diverse, to permit protection of the Fourth Amendment to turn on such a talismanic test. The *Miranda* warnings are an important factor, to be sure, in determining whether the confession is obtained by exploitation of an illegal arrest. But they are not the only factor to be considered. The voluntariness of the statement is a threshold requirement. And the burden of showing admissibility rests, of course, on the prosecution.

IV

Although the Illinois courts failed to undertake the inquiry mandated by *Wong Sun* to evaluate the circumstances of this case in the light of the policy served by the exclusionary rule, the trial resulted in a record of amply sufficient detail and depth from which the determination may be made. We conclude that the State failed to sustain the burden of showing that the evidence in question was admissible under *Wong Sun*.

Brown's first statement was separated from his illegal arrest by less than two hours, and there was no intervening event of significance whatsoever. In its essentials, his situation is remarkably like that of James Wah Toy in *Wong Sun*.[11] We could hold Brown's first statement admissible only if we overrule *Wong Sun*. We decline to do so. And the second statement was clearly the result and the fruit of the first.

The illegality here, moreover, had a quality of purposefulness. The impropriety of the arrest was obvious; awareness of that fact was virtually conceded by the two detectives when they repeatedly acknowledged, in their testimony, that the purpose of their action was "for investigation" or for "questioning." The arrest, both in design and in execution, was investigatory. The detectives embarked upon this expedition for evidence in the hope that something might turn up. The manner in which Brown's arrest was affected gives the appearance of having been calculated to cause surprise, fright, and confusion.

We emphasize that our holding is a limited one. We decide only that the Illinois courts were in error in assuming that the *Miranda* warnings, by themselves, under *Wong Sun* always purge the taint of an illegal arrest.

---

[11] The situation here is thus in dramatic contrast to that of Wong Sun himself. Wong Sun's confession, which the Court held admissible, came several days after the illegality, and was preceded by a lawful arraignment and a release from custody on his own recognizance.

JUSTICE POWELL, with whom JUSTICE REHNQUIST joins, concurring in part.

I join the Court insofar as it holds that the *per se* rule adopted by the Illinois Supreme Court for determining the admissibility of petitioner's two statements inadequately accommodates the diverse interests underlying the Fourth Amendment exclusionary rule. I would, however, remand the case for reconsideration under the general standards articulated in the Court's opinion and elaborated herein.

On this record, I cannot conclude as readily as the Court that admission of the statements here at issue would constitute an effective overruling of *Wong Sun*. Although *Wong Sun* establishes the boundaries within which this case must be decided, the incompleteness of the record leaves me uncertain that it compels the exclusion of petitioner's statements. The statements at issue in *Wong Sun* were on the temporal extremes in relation to the illegal arrest. Toy's statement was obtained immediately after his pursuit and arrest by six agents. It appears to have been a spontaneous response to a question put to him in the frenzy of that event, and there is no indication that the agents made any attempt to inform him of his right to remain silent. Wong Sun's statement, by contrast, was not given until after he was arraigned and released on his own recognizance. Wong Sun voluntarily returned to the station a few days after the arrest for questioning. His statement was preceded by an official warning of his right to remain silent and to have counsel if he desired. The Court rejected the Government's assertion that Toy's statement resulted from an independent act of free will sufficient to purge the consequences of the illegal arrest. Wong Sun's statement, however, was deemed admissible. Given the circumstances in which Wong Sun's statement was obtained, the Court concluded that the connection between the arrest and the statement had "become so attenuated as to dissipate the taint."

The notion of the "dissipation of the taint" attempts to mark the point at which the detrimental consequences of illegal police action become so attenuated that the deterrent effect of the exclusionary rule no longer justifies its cost. Application of the *Wong Sun* doctrine will generate fact-specific cases bearing distinct differences as well as similarities, and the question of attenuation inevitably is largely a matter of degree. The Court today identifies the general factors that the trial court must consider in making this determination. I think it appropriate, however, to attempt to articulate the possible relationships to those factors in particular, broad categories of cases.

All Fourth Amendment violations are, by constitutional definition, "unreasonable." There are, however, significant practical differences that distinguish among violations, differences that measurably assist in identifying the kinds of cases in which disqualifying the evidence is likely to serve the deterrent purposes of the exclusionary rule. In my view, the point at which the taint can be said to have dissipated should be related, in the absence of other controlling circumstances, to the nature of that taint.

Bearing these considerations in mind, and recognizing that the deterrent value of the Fourth Amendment exclusionary rule is limited to certain kinds of police conduct, the following general categories can be identified. Those most readily identifiable are on the extremes: the flagrantly abusive violation of Fourth Amendment rights, on the one hand, and "technical" Fourth Amendment violations, on the other. In my view, these extremes call for significantly different judicial responses.

I would require the clearest indication of attenuation in cases in which official conduct was flagrantly abusive of Fourth Amendment rights. If, for example, the factors relied on by the police in determining to make the arrest were so lacking in indicia of probable cause as to render official belief in its existence entirely unreasonable, or if the evidence clearly suggested that the arrest was effectuated as a pretext for collateral objectives, or the physical circumstances of the arrest unnecessarily intrusive on personal privacy, I would consider the equalizing potential of *Miranda* warnings rarely sufficient to dissipate the taint. In such cases the deterrent value of the exclusionary rule is most likely to be effective, and the corresponding mandate to preserve judicial integrity most clearly demands that the fruits of official misconduct be denied. I thus would require some demonstrably effective break in the chain of events leading from the illegal arrest to the statement, such as actual consultation with counsel or the accused's presentation before a magistrate for a determination of probable cause, before the taint can be deemed removed.

At the opposite end of the spectrum lie "technical" violations of Fourth Amendment rights where, for example, officers in good faith arrest an individual in reliance on a warrant later invalidated or pursuant to a statute that subsequently is declared unconstitutional. Absent aggravating circumstances, I would consider a statement given at the station house after one has been advised of *Miranda* rights to be sufficiently removed from the immediate circumstances of the illegal arrest to justify its admission at trial.

Between these extremes lies a wide range of situations that defy ready categorization, and I will not attempt to embellish on the factors set forth in the Court's opinion other than to emphasize that the *Wong Sun* inquiry always should be conducted with the deterrent purpose of the Fourth Amendment exclusionary rule sharply in focus. And, in view of the inevitably fact-specific nature of the inquiry, we must place primary reliance on the learning, good sense, fairness and courage of judges who must make the determination in the first instance.

On the facts of record as I view them, it is possible that the police may have believed reasonably that there was probable cause for petitioner's arrest. I am not able to conclude on this record that the officers arrested petitioner solely for the purpose of questioning. To be sure, there is evidence suggesting, as the Court notes, an investigatory arrest. But the evidence is conflicting. I think it preferable to allow the state courts to reconsider the case under the general guidelines expressed in today's opinions. I therefore would remand for reconsideration[7] with directions to conduct such further factual inquiries as may be necessary to resolve the admissibility issue.

———————

In *New York v. Harris*, police arrested a suspect in his home without a warrant. Following administration of the *Miranda* warnings, the arrestee made incriminating statements inside his home; he later made additional incriminating statements at the police station. The Supreme Court held that the statements inside the home were inadmissible but the statements at the police station were admissible because they were not the fruit of the illegal arrest.

NEW YORK V. HARRIS
495 U.S. 14 (1990)

JUSTICE WHITE delivered the opinion of the Court.

On January 11, 1984, New York City police found the body of Ms. Thelma Staton murdered in her apartment. Various facts gave the officers probable cause to believe that the respondent in this case, Bernard Harris, had killed Ms. Staton. As a result, on January 16, 1984, three police officers went to Harris' apartment to take him into custody. They did not first obtain an arrest warrant.

When the police arrived, they knocked on the door, displaying their guns and badges. Harris let them enter. Once inside, the officers read Harris his rights under *Miranda v. Arizona*, 384 U.S. 436 (1966). Harris acknowledged that he understood the warnings, and agreed to answer the officers' questions. At that point, he reportedly admitted that he had killed Ms. Staton.

Harris was arrested, taken to the station house, and again informed of his *Miranda* rights. He then signed a written inculpatory statement.

———————

[7]   I also would leave the question of admissibility of [Brown's second] statement to the lower Illinois courts. Of course, if the first statement were ruled admissible under the general guidelines articulated in today's opinion, it would follow that the second statement also would be admissible. In any event, the question whether there was sufficient attenuation between the first and second statements to render the second admissible in spite of the inadmissibility of the first presents a factual issue which, like the factual issue underlying the possible admissibility of the first statement, has not been passed on by the state courts.

The police subsequently read Harris the *Miranda* warnings a third time and videotaped an incriminating interview between Harris and a district attorney, even though Harris had indicated that he wanted to end the interrogation.

The trial court suppressed Harris' first and third statements; the State does not challenge those rulings. The sole issue in this case is whether Harris' second statement—the written statement made at the station house—should have been suppressed because the police, by entering Harris' home without a warrant and without his consent, violated *Payton v. New York*, 445 U.S. 573 (1980), which held that the Fourth Amendment prohibits the police from effecting a warrantless and nonconsensual entry into a suspect's home in order to make a routine felony arrest. The New York trial court concluded that the statement was admissible. Following a bench trial, Harris was convicted of second-degree murder. The Appellate Division affirmed.

A divided New York Court of Appeals reversed. That court first accepted the trial court's finding that Harris did not consent to the police officers' entry into his home and that the warrantless arrest therefore violated *Payton* even though there was probable cause. Applying *Brown v. Illinois*, 422 U.S. 590 (1975), and its progeny, the court then determined that the station house statement must be deemed to be the inadmissible fruit of the illegal arrest because the connection between the statement and the arrest was not sufficiently attenuated.

For present purposes, we accept the finding below that Harris did not consent to the police officers' entry into his home and the conclusion that the police had probable cause to arrest him. It is also evident, in light of *Payton,* that arresting Harris in his home without an arrest warrant violated the Fourth Amendment. But, as emphasized in earlier cases, we have declined to adopt a *per se* or "but for" rule that would make inadmissible any evidence, whether tangible or live-witness testimony, which somehow came to light through a chain of causation that began with an illegal arrest. Rather, in this context, we have stated that the penalties visited upon the Government, and in turn upon the public, because its officers have violated the law must bear some relation to the purposes which the law is to serve. In light of these principles, we decline to apply the exclusionary rule in this context because the rule in *Payton* was designed to protect the physical integrity of the home; it was not intended to grant criminal suspects, like Harris, protection for statements made outside their premises where the police have probable cause to arrest the suspect for committing a crime.

Payton itself emphasized that our holding in that case stemmed from the "overriding respect for the sanctity of the home that has been embedded in our traditions since the origins of the Republic." Although it had long been settled that a warrantless arrest in a public place was permissible as long as the arresting officer had probable cause, *Payton* nevertheless drew a line at the entrance to the home. This special solicitude was necessary because "physical entry of the home is the chief evil against which the wording of the Fourth Amendment is directed." The arrest warrant was required to "interpose the magistrate's determination of probable cause" to arrest before the officers could enter a house to effect an arrest.

Nothing in the reasoning of that case suggests that an arrest in a home without a warrant but with probable cause somehow renders unlawful continued custody of the suspect once he is removed from the house. There could be no valid claim here that Harris was immune from prosecution because his person was the fruit of an illegal arrest. Nor is there any claim that the warrantless arrest required the police to release Harris or that Harris could not be immediately rearrested if momentarily released. Because the officers had probable cause to arrest Harris for a crime, Harris was not unlawfully in custody when he was removed to the station house, given *Miranda* warnings, and allowed to talk. For Fourth Amendment purposes, the legal issue is the same as it would be had the police arrested Harris on his doorstep, illegally entered his home to search for evidence, and later interrogated Harris at the station house. Similarly, if the police had made a warrantless entry into Harris' home, not found him there, but arrested him on the street when he returned, a later statement made by him after proper warnings would no doubt be admissible.

This case is therefore different from *Brown v. Illinois*, 422 U.S. 590 (1975), *Dunaway v. New York*, 442 U.S. 200 (1979), and *Taylor v. Alabama*, 457 U.S. 687 (1982). In each of those cases, evidence obtained from a criminal defendant following arrest was suppressed because the police lacked probable cause. The three cases stand for the familiar proposition that the indirect fruits of an illegal search or arrest should be suppressed when they bear a sufficiently close relationship to the underlying illegality. We have emphasized, however, that attenuation analysis is only appropriate where, as a threshold matter, courts determine that the challenged evidence is in some sense the product of illegal governmental activity. As Judge Titone, concurring in the judgment on the basis of New York State precedent, cogently argued below, "in cases such as *Brown v. Illinois* and its progeny, an affirmative answer to that preliminary question may be assumed, since the illegality is the absence of probable cause and the wrong consists of the police's having control of the defendant's person at the time he made the challenged statement. In these cases, the challenged evidence—*i.e.*, the post arrest confession—is unquestionably the product of the illegal governmental activity—*i.e.*, the wrongful detention."

Harris' statement taken at the police station was not the product of being in unlawful custody. Neither was it the fruit of having been arrested in the home rather than someplace else. Here, the police had a justification to question Harris prior to his arrest; therefore, his subsequent statement was not an exploitation of the illegal entry into Harris' home.

We do not hold, as the dissent suggests, that a statement taken by the police while a suspect is in custody is always admissible as long as the suspect is in legal custody. Statements taken during legal custody would of course be inadmissible, for example, if they were the product of coercion, if *Miranda* warnings were not given, or if there was a violation of the rule of *Edwards v. Arizona*, 451 U.S. 477 (1981). We do hold that the station house statement in this case was admissible because Harris was in legal custody, as the dissent concedes, and because the statement, while the product of an arrest and being in custody, was not the fruit of the fact that the arrest was made in the house rather than someplace else.

To put the matter another way, suppressing the statement taken outside the house would not serve the purpose of the rule that made Harris' in-house arrest illegal. The warrant requirement for an arrest in the home is imposed to protect the home, and anything incriminating the police gathered from arresting Harris in his home, rather than elsewhere, has been excluded, as it should have been; the purpose of the rule has thereby been vindicated. We are not required by the Constitution to go further and suppress statements later made by Harris in order to deter police from violating *Payton*. Even though we decline to suppress statements made outside the home following a *Payton* violation, the principal incentive to obey *Payton* still obtains: the police know that a warrantless entry will lead to the suppression of any evidence found, or statements taken, inside the home. If we did suppress statements like Harris', moreover, the incremental deterrent value would be minimal. Given that the police have probable cause to arrest a suspect in Harris' position, they need not violate *Payton* in order to interrogate the suspect. It is doubtful therefore that the desire to secure a statement from a criminal suspect would motivate the police to violate *Payton*. As a result, suppressing a station house statement obtained after a *Payton* violation will have little effect on the officers' actions, one way or another.

We hold that, where the police have probable cause to arrest a suspect, the exclusionary rule does not bar the State's use of a statement made by the defendant outside of his home, even though the statement is taken after an arrest made in the home in violation of *Payton*.

JUSTICE MARSHALL, with whom JUSTICE BRENNAN, JUSTICE BLACKMUN, and JUSTICE STEVENS join, dissenting.

When faced with a statement obtained after an illegal arrest, a court will have occasion to engage in the attenuation inquiry only if it first determines that the statement is "voluntary," for involuntary statements are suppressible in any event. Attenuation analysis *assumes* that the statement is "voluntary" and asks whether the connection between the illegal police conduct and the statement nevertheless requires suppression to deter Fourth Amendment violations. That question cannot be answered with a set of *per se* rules. An inquiry into whether a suspect's statement is properly treated as attributable to a Fourth Amendment violation or to the suspect's independent act of will has an irreducibly psychological aspect, and irrebuttable presumptions are peculiarly unhelpful in such a context. Accordingly, we have identified several factors as relevant to the issue of attenuation: the length of time between the arrest and the statement, the presence of intervening circumstances, and the "purpose and flagrancy" of the violation. See *Brown v. Illinois*, 422 U.S. 590, 603–604 (1975).

We have identified the last factor as "particularly" important. When a police officer intentionally violates what he knows to be a constitutional command, exclusion is essential to conform police behavior to the law. Such a "flagrant" violation is in marked contrast to a violation that is the product of a good-faith misunderstanding of the relevant constitutional requirements. This Court has suggested that excluding evidence that is the product of the latter variety of violation may result in deterrence of *legitimate* law enforcement efforts.

An application of the *Brown* factors to this case compels the conclusion that Harris' statement at the station house must be suppressed. About an hour elapsed between the illegal arrest and Harris' confession, without any intervening factor other than the warnings required by *Miranda*. This Court has held, however, that *Miranda* warnings, *alone* and *per se*, cannot assure in every case that the Fourth Amendment violation has not been unduly exploited. Indeed, in *Brown,* we held that a statement made almost *two* hours after an illegal arrest, and after *Miranda* warnings had been given, was not sufficiently removed from the violation so as to dissipate the taint.

As to the flagrancy of the violation, petitioner does not dispute that the officers were aware that the Fourth Amendment prohibited them from arresting Harris in his home without a warrant. The officers decided, apparently consistent with a "departmental policy," to violate Harris' Fourth Amendment rights so they could get evidence that they could not otherwise obtain. As the trial court held, "No more clear violation of *Payton*, in my view, could be established." Where, as here, there is a particularly flagrant constitutional violation and little in the way of elapsed time or intervening circumstances, the statement in the police station must be suppressed.

Had the Court analyzed this case as our precedents dictate that it should, I could end my discussion here—the dispute would reduce to an application of the *Brown* factors to the constitutional wrong and the inculpatory statement that followed. But the majority chooses no such unremarkable battleground. Instead, the Court redrafts our cases in the service of conclusions they straightforwardly and explicitly reject. Specifically, the Court finds suppression unwarranted on the authority of its newly fashioned *per se* rule. In the majority's view, when police officers make a warrantless home arrest in violation of *Payton,* their physical exit from the suspect's home *necessarily* breaks the causal chain between the illegality and any subsequent statement by the suspect, such that the statement is admissible regardless of the *Brown* factors.

The Court purports to defend its new rule on the basis of the self-evident proposition that the Fourth Amendment does not necessarily require the police to release or to forgo the prosecution of a suspect arrested in violation of *Payton.* To the Court, it follows as a matter of course from this proposition that a *Payton* violation cannot in any way be the "cause" of a statement obtained from the suspect after he has been forced from his home and is being lawfully detained. Because an attenuation inquiry presupposes *some* connection between the illegality and the statement, the Court concludes that no such inquiry is necessary here. Neither logic nor precedent supports that conclusion.

The majority's *per se* rule in this case fails to take account of our repeated holdings that violations of privacy in the home are especially invasive. Rather, its rule is necessarily premised on the proposition that the effect of a *Payton* violation magically vanishes once the suspect is dragged from his home. But the concerns that make a warrantless home arrest a violation of the Fourth Amendment are nothing so evanescent. A person who is forcibly separated from his family and home in the dark of night after uniformed officers have broken down his door, handcuffed him, and forced him at gunpoint to accompany them to a police station does not suddenly breathe a sigh of relief at the moment he is dragged across his doorstep. Rather, the suspect is likely to be so frightened and rattled that he will say something incriminating. These effects, of course, extend far beyond the moment the physical occupation of the home ends. The entire focus of the *Brown* factors is to fix the point at which those effects are sufficiently dissipated that deterrence is not meaningfully advanced by suppression. The majority's assertion, as though the proposition were axiomatic, that the effects of such an intrusion *must* end when the violation ends is both undefended and indefensible. The Court's saying it may make it law, but it does not make it true.

Perhaps the most alarming aspect of the Court's ruling is its practical consequences for the deterrence of *Payton* violations. Imagine a police officer who has probable cause to arrest a suspect but lacks a warrant. The officer knows if he were to break into the home to make the arrest without first securing a warrant, he would violate the Fourth Amendment and any evidence he finds in the house would be suppressed. Of course, if he does not enter the house, he will not be able to use any evidence inside the house either, for the simple reason that he will never see it. The officer also knows, though, that waiting for the suspect to leave his house before arresting him could entail a lot of waiting, and the time he would spend getting a warrant would be better spent arresting criminals. The officer could leave the scene to obtain a warrant, thus avoiding some of the delay, but that would entail giving the suspect an opportunity to flee.

More important, the officer knows that if he breaks into the house without a warrant and drags the suspect outside, the suspect, shaken by the enormous invasion of privacy he has just undergone, may say something incriminating. Before today's decision, the government would only be able to use that evidence if the Court found that the taint of the arrest had been attenuated; after the decision, the evidence will be admissible regardless of whether it was the product of the unconstitutional arrest. Thus, the officer envisions the following best-case scenario if he chooses to violate the Constitution: He avoids a major expenditure of time and effort, ensures that the suspect will not escape, and procures the most damaging evidence of all, a confession. His worst-case scenario is that he will avoid a major expenditure of effort, ensure that the suspect will not escape, and will see evidence in the house (which would have remained unknown absent the constitutional violation) that cannot be used in the prosecution's case in chief. The Court thus creates powerful incentives for police officers to violate the Fourth Amendment. In the context of our constitutional rights and the sanctity of our homes, we cannot afford to presume that officers will be entirely impervious to those incentives.

In *U.S. v. Ceccolini*, an illegal search led the police to a witness who ultimately provided testimony that incriminated the defendant. Focusing on the specific facts of the investigation, the Supreme Court held that the connection between the illegal search and the testimony of the witness was sufficiently attenuated to dissipate the taint.

U.S. v. Ceccolini
435 U.S. 268 (1978)

A police officer, Ronald Biro, was inside a flower shop chatting with Lois Hennessey, an employee of the shop. Biro noticed an envelope with money sticking out of it lying on the drawer of the cash register behind the counter. He picked up the envelope and, upon examining its contents, discovered that it contained not only money but "policy slips," evidence of an illegal gambling operation. Biro placed the envelope back on the register and, without telling Hennessey what he had seen, asked her who owned the envelope. Hennessey said the envelope belonged to Ralph Ceccolini, the owner of the flower shop, and that he had instructed her to give it to someone. The next day, Officer Biro mentioned his discovery to local detectives who in turn told an FBI agent. Four months later, the FBI agent interviewed Hennessey at her home, inquiring about Ceccolini's gambling activities in the flower shop. Hennessey said she was willing to help, then related the events that had occurred during her visit with Officer Biro four months earlier.

Ceccolini was summoned before a federal grand jury and testified that he had never taken bets at the flower shop. The next week, Hennessey testified to the contrary, and shortly thereafter, Ceccolini was indicted for perjury. At his perjury trial, Ceccolini moved to suppress evidence of the policy slips and the contents of the envelope, as well as Hennessey's testimony. The trial court excluded the envelope and its contents as the product of an illegal search; it also excluded Hennessey's testimony because she first came to the attention of the police as a result of the illegal search. The Court of Appeals affirmed, concluding that there was insufficient attenuation between Officer Biro's search and Hennessey's testimony.

The U.S. Supreme Court reversed. Citing *Wong Sun v. U.S.*, 371 U.S. 471 (1963), the Court noted that the constitutional question is whether "the connection between the lawless conduct of the police and the discovery of the challenged evidence has become so attenuated as to dissipate the taint." Applying this standard, the Court held that Hennessey's testimony was admissible:

> We hold that the Court of Appeals erred in holding that the degree of attenuation was not sufficient to dissipate the connection between the illegality and the testimony. The evidence indicates overwhelmingly that the testimony given by the witness was an act of her own free will in no way coerced or even induced by official authority as a result of Biro's discovery of the policy slips. Nor were the slips themselves used in questioning Hennessey. Substantial periods of time elapsed between the time of the illegal search and the initial contact with the witness, on the one hand, and between the latter and the

testimony at trial on the other. While the particular knowledge to which Hennessey testified at trial can be logically traced back to Biro's discovery of the policy slips, both the identity of Hennessey and her relationship with the respondent were well known to those investigating the case. There is, in addition, not the slightest evidence to suggest that Biro entered the shop or picked up the envelope with the intent of finding tangible evidence bearing on an illicit gambling operation, much less any suggestion that he entered the shop and searched with the intent of finding a willing and knowledgeable witness to testify against respondent. Application of the exclusionary rule in this situation could not have the slightest deterrent effect on the behavior of an officer such as Biro. The cost of permanently silencing Hennessey is too great for an evenhanded system of law enforcement to bear in order to secure such a speculative and very likely negligible deterrent effect.

The Supreme Court concluded by cautioning that the exclusionary rule "should be invoked with much greater reluctance where the claim is based on a causal relationship between a constitutional violation and the discovery of a live witness than when a similar claim is advanced to support suppression of an inanimate object."

Having reviewed *Wong Sun* and its progeny, let's return to the hypothetical at the beginning of this section involving Carol Copper's investigation of Nick Narcotic. There are four items of evidence at issue: (1) the map with the red "X" and the note "N.N.'S STUFF BURIED HERE," found in the trunk of Nick Narcotic's car; (2) the bloody knife with the initials "N.N." carved into the handle; (3) pictures of Marty Mobster's body, riddled with stab wounds; and (4) Olive Observant's testimony that she saw Nick Narcotic threatening Marty Mobster with a knife outside her home. The judge, as you may remember, has already ruled the map inadmissible because it was obtained when Carol Copper opened the car trunk on a "hunch," without reasonable suspicion, probable cause, or a warrant. But the knife, the pictures of Marty Mobster's body, and Olive Observant's testimony may still be admissible at Nick Narcotic's murder trial if the prosecution can establish that there is an inadequate causal connection between the illegal search of the trunk and the remaining items of evidence, or, phrased somewhat differently, if the link between the illegal search and the remaining items of evidence is sufficiently attenuated to dissipate the taint.

In *Brown v. Illinois*, the Supreme Court identified several factors relevant to determining whether the link between illegal police conduct and evidence is sufficiently attenuated to dissipate the taint, including the temporal proximity between the illegal police conduct and the evidence, the presence of intervening circumstances, and the purpose and flagrancy of the official misconduct. After illegally searching Nick Narcotic's car trunk and discovering the map, Carol Copper immediately drove to the marked location on the map—just "a few miles" away—and after "a few minutes" of digging, she unearthed the bloody knife and Marty Mobster's body. Thus, the temporal proximity between the illegal search of the trunk and the discovery of the knife and body was less than an hour, and there were no intervening circumstances that disrupted the direct link between the illegal search of the trunk and the discovery of the knife and body. Finally, Carol Copper's misconduct in searching the trunk was purposeful and flagrant—she pried open the trunk only because she had a "hunch" she might find something incriminating in a car belonging to a notorious drug dealer. There were no exigent circumstances or other reasons that might excuse Carol Copper's failure to obtain a warrant based upon probable cause. The link between the illegal search of the car trunk and the discovery of the knife and body is not at all distant or attenuated; accordingly, both the knife and the body (or pictures of the body) should be inadmissible.

The admissibility of Olive Observant's testimony turns on a close reading of *U.S. v. Ceccolini*. Olive's anticipated testimony at Nick Narcotic's murder trial, like Lois Hennessey's testimony in *Ceccolini*, is an act of her own free will and is not coerced or induced as a result of Copper's discovery of the map, the knife, or the body. Copper asked Olive only if she'd "seen anything unusual lately." Copper did not refer to any illegally obtained evidence—the map, the knife, or the body—in questioning Olive, just as Officer Biro in *Ceccolini* did not reference the illegally discovered policy slips when he asked Hennessey who owned the envelope. These similarities to *Ceccolini* suggest that Olive Observant's testimony should be admissible.

On the other hand, there also are some significant differences between the facts in our hypothetical and those in *Ceccolini*. Very little time passed—perhaps an hour or less—between Carol Copper's illegal conduct and her initial contact with Oliver Observant. In *Ceccolini*, by contrast, four months passed between Officer Biro's illegal search of the envelope and the FBI agent's interview with Hennessey as a potential witness. Moreover, Carol Copper drove to Olive Observant's home and spoke to her with the clear purpose of finding a witness or other evidence that would help solve Marty Mobster's murder. In *Ceccolini*, by contrast, the Supreme Court noted that there was no evidence "to suggest that Biro entered the shop or picked up the envelope with the intent of finding tangible evidence bearing on an illicit gambling operation, much less any suggestion that he entered the shop and searched with the intent of finding a willing and knowledgeable witness to testify against [Ceccolini]."

Given the Supreme Court's final caution in *Ceccolini* that the exclusionary rule should be invoked "with much greater reluctance" to exclude a live witness—as opposed to an inanimate object—discovered as a result of a constitutional violation, Olive Observant's testimony might ultimately be admissible despite the relatively close connection between her testimony and Carol Copper's illegal conduct. But the analogy to *Ceccolini* is far from perfect, and the admissibility of Olive Observant's testimony is one of those questions, like so many in the law, that could really go either way.

Inadequate Causal Connection and Attenuation of the Taint

1.   The exclusionary rule should not be applied if there is an inadequate causal connection between the illegal conduct of the police and the disputed evidence, or if the connection between the unlawful conduct of the police and the discovery of the challenged evidence has become so attenuated as to dissipate the taint. Factors relevant to this determination include:

    a.   The temporal proximity between the illegal police conduct and the evidence.

    b.   The presence of intervening circumstances.

    c.   The purpose and flagrancy of the official misconduct.

2.   *Miranda* warnings do not always, by themselves, purge the taint of an illegal arrest, rendering an arrestee's subsequent statement admissible. In order for the causal chain between the illegal arrest and the subsequent statement to be broken, the statement must not only meet the Fifth Amendment standard of voluntariness, but it must also be sufficiently an act of free will to purge the primary taint of the illegal arrest.

3.   When police make a warrantless arrest inside a suspect's home in violation of *Payton v. New York*, any evidence discovered or statements made by the suspect inside the home are inadmissible. But where the police have probable cause to arrest a suspect, the exclusionary rule does not bar the state's use of a statement made by the suspect outside of his home, even though the statement is taken after an arrest made in the home in violation of *Payton*.

4.   The exclusionary rule should be invoked with much greater reluctance to exclude a live witness—as opposed to an inanimate object—discovered as a result of a constitutional violation, particularly where the testimony by the witness is voluntarily given and is not coerced or induced by official authority.

D. GOOD FAITH AND NEGLIGENT MISTAKES

In *U.S. v. Leon*, the Supreme Court announced a "good faith" exception to the exclusionary rule, holding that the exclusionary rule does not bar the admission of evidence obtained by police who reasonably rely on a warrant that is later found to be unsupported by probable cause.

U.S. v. LEON
468 U.S. 897 (1984)

JUSTICE WHITE delivered the opinion of the Court.

This case presents the question whether the Fourth Amendment exclusionary rule should be modified so as not to bar the use in the prosecution's case in chief of evidence obtained by officers acting in reasonable reliance on a search warrant issued by a detached and neutral magistrate but ultimately found to be unsupported by probable cause. To resolve this question, we must consider once again the tension between the sometimes competing goals of, on the one hand, deterring official misconduct and removing inducements to unreasonable invasions of privacy and, on the other, establishing procedures under which criminal defendants are acquitted or convicted on the basis of all the evidence which exposes the truth.

I

In August 1981, a confidential informant of unproven reliability informed an officer of the Burbank Police Department that two persons known to him as "Armando" and "Patsy" were selling large quantities of cocaine and methaqualone from their residence at 620 Price Drive in Burbank, Cal. The informant also indicated that he had witnessed a sale of methaqualone by "Patsy" at the residence approximately five months earlier and had observed at that time a shoebox containing a large amount of cash that belonged to "Patsy." He further declared that "Armando" and "Patsy" generally kept only small quantities of drugs at their residence and stored the remainder at another location in Burbank.

On the basis of this information, the Burbank police initiated an extensive investigation focusing first on the Price Drive residence and later on two other residences as well. Cars parked at the Price Drive residence were determined to belong to respondents Armando Sanchez, who had previously been arrested for possession of marihuana, and Patsy Stewart, who had no criminal record. During the course of the investigation, officers observed an automobile belonging to respondent Ricardo Del Castillo, who had previously been arrested for possession of 50 pounds of marihuana, arrive at the Price Drive residence. The driver of that car entered the house, exited shortly thereafter carrying a small paper sack, and drove away. A check of Del Castillo's probation records led the officers to respondent Alberto Leon, whose telephone number Del Castillo had listed as his employer's. Leon had been arrested in 1980 on drug charges, and a companion had informed the police at that time that Leon was heavily involved in the importation of drugs into this country. Before the current investigation began, the Burbank officers had learned that an informant had told a Glendale police officer that Leon stored a large quantity of methaqualone at his residence in Glendale. During the course of this investigation, the Burbank officers learned that Leon was living at 716 South Sunset Canyon in Burbank.

Subsequently, the officers observed several persons, at least one of whom had prior drug involvement, arriving at the Price Drive residence and leaving with small packages; observed a variety of other material activity at the two residences as well as at a condominium at 7902 Via Magdalena; and witnessed a variety of relevant activity involving respondents' automobiles. The officers also observed respondents Sanchez and Stewart board separate flights for Miami. The pair later returned to Los Angeles together, consented to a search of their luggage that revealed only a small amount of marihuana, and left the airport. Based on these and other observations summarized in the affidavit, Officer Cyril Rombach of the Burbank Police Department, an experienced and well-trained narcotics investigator, prepared an application for a warrant to search 620 Price Drive, 716 South Sunset Canyon, 7902 Via Magdalena, and automobiles registered to each of the respondents for an extensive list of items believed to be related to respondents' drug-trafficking activities. Officer Rombach's extensive application was reviewed by several Deputy District Attorneys.

A facially valid search warrant was issued in September 1981 by a State Superior Court Judge. The ensuing searches produced large quantities of drugs at the Via Magdalena and Sunset Canyon addresses and a small quantity at the Price Drive residence. Other evidence was discovered at each of the residences and in Stewart's and Del Castillo's automobiles. Respondents were indicted by a grand jury in the District Court for the Central District of California and charged with conspiracy to possess and distribute cocaine and a variety of substantive counts.

The respondents then filed motions to suppress the evidence seized pursuant to the warrant. The District Court held an evidentiary hearing and, while recognizing that the case was a close one, granted the motions to suppress in part. It concluded that the affidavit was insufficient to establish probable cause, but did not suppress all of the evidence as to all of the respondents because none of the respondents had standing to challenge all of the searches. In response to a request from the Government, the court made clear that Officer Rombach had acted in good faith, but it rejected the Government's suggestion that the Fourth

Amendment exclusionary rule should not apply where evidence is seized in reasonable, good-faith reliance on a search warrant.

The Government's petition for certiorari expressly declined to seek review of the lower courts' determinations that the search warrant was unsupported by probable cause and presented only the question "whether the Fourth Amendment exclusionary rule should be modified so as not to bar the admission of evidence seized in reasonable, good-faith reliance on a search warrant that is subsequently held to be defective." We granted certiorari to consider the propriety of such a modification. We have concluded that, in the Fourth Amendment context, the exclusionary rule can be modified somewhat without jeopardizing its ability to perform its intended functions.

II

The Fourth Amendment contains no provision expressly precluding the use of evidence obtained in violation of its commands, and an examination of its origin and purposes makes clear that the use of fruits of a past unlawful search or seizure works no new Fourth Amendment wrong. The wrong condemned by the Amendment is fully accomplished by the unlawful search or seizure itself, and the exclusionary rule is neither intended nor able to cure the invasion of the defendant's rights which he has already suffered. The rule thus operates as a judicially created remedy designed to safeguard Fourth Amendment rights generally through its deterrent effect, rather than a personal constitutional right of the party aggrieved.

Whether the exclusionary sanction is appropriately imposed in a particular case, our decisions make clear, is an issue separate from the question whether the Fourth Amendment rights of the party seeking to invoke the rule were violated by police conduct. Only the former question is currently before us, and it must be resolved by weighing the costs and benefits of preventing the use in the prosecution's case in chief of inherently trustworthy tangible evidence obtained in reliance on a search warrant issued by a detached and neutral magistrate that ultimately is found to be defective.

The substantial social costs exacted by the exclusionary rule for the vindication of Fourth Amendment rights have long been a source of concern. Our cases have consistently recognized that unbending application of the exclusionary sanction to enforce ideals of governmental rectitude would impede unacceptably the truth-finding functions of judge and jury. An objectionable collateral consequence of this interference with the criminal justice system's truth-finding function is that some guilty defendants may go free or receive reduced sentences as a result of favorable plea bargains.[6] Particularly when law enforcement officers have acted in objective good faith or their transgressions have been minor, the magnitude of the benefit conferred on such guilty defendants offends basic concepts of the criminal justice system. Indiscriminate application of the exclusionary rule, therefore, may well generate disrespect for the law and administration of justice. Accordingly, as with any remedial device, the application of the rule has been restricted to those areas where its remedial objectives are thought most efficaciously served.

Close attention to those remedial objectives has characterized our recent decisions concerning the scope of the Fourth Amendment exclusionary rule. The Court has, to be sure, not seriously questioned, in the absence of a more efficacious sanction, the continued application of the rule to suppress evidence from the prosecution's case where a Fourth Amendment violation has been substantial and deliberate. Nevertheless, the balancing approach that has evolved in various contexts—including criminal trials—forcefully suggests that the exclusionary rule be more generally modified to permit the introduction of evidence obtained in the reasonable good-faith belief that a search or seizure was in accord with the Fourth Amendment.

As cases considering the use of unlawfully obtained evidence in criminal trials themselves make clear, it does not follow from the emphasis on the exclusionary rule's deterrent value that anything which deters illegal searches is thereby commanded by the Fourth Amendment. In determining whether persons aggrieved solely by the introduction of damaging evidence unlawfully obtained from their co-conspirators or co-defendants could seek suppression, for example, we found that the additional benefits of such an extension of the exclusionary rule would not outweigh its costs. Standing to invoke the rule has thus been limited to cases in which the prosecution seeks to use the fruits of an illegal search or seizure against the victim of police misconduct. *Rakas v. Illinois*, 439 U.S. 128 (1978); *Wong Sun v. U.S.*, 371 U.S. 471 (1963).

Even defendants with standing to challenge the introduction in their criminal trials of unlawfully obtained evidence cannot prevent every conceivable use of such evidence. Evidence obtained in violation of the Fourth Amendment and inadmissible in the prosecution's case in chief may be used to impeach a defendant's direct testimony. A similar assessment of the incremental furthering of the ends of the exclusionary

---

[6]   Researchers have only recently begun to study extensively the effects of the exclusionary rule on the disposition of felony arrests. One study suggests that the rule results in the nonprosecution or nonconviction of between 0.6% and 2.35% of individuals arrested for felonies. Davies, A Hard Look at What We Know (and Still Need to Learn) About the "Costs" of the Exclusionary Rule: The NIJ Study and Other Studies of "Lost" Arrests, 1983 *American Bar Foundation Research Journal* 611, 621. The estimates are higher for particular crimes the prosecution of which depends heavily on physical evidence. Thus, the cumulative loss due to nonprosecution or nonconviction of individuals arrested on felony drug charges is probably in the range of 2.8% to 7.1%.

rule led us to conclude that evidence inadmissible in the prosecution's case in chief or otherwise as substantive evidence of guilt may be used to impeach statements made by a defendant in response to proper cross-examination reasonably suggested by the defendant's direct examination.

When considering the use of evidence obtained in violation of the Fourth Amendment in the prosecution's case in chief, moreover, we have declined to adopt a *per se* or "but for" rule that would render inadmissible any evidence that came to light through a chain of causation that began with an illegal arrest. We also have held that a witness' testimony may be admitted even when his identity was discovered in an unconstitutional search. *U.S. v. Ceccolini*, 435 U.S. 268 (1978). The perception underlying these decisions—that the connection between police misconduct and evidence of crime may be sufficiently attenuated to permit the use of that evidence at trial—is a product of considerations relating to the exclusionary rule and the constitutional principles it is designed to protect. In short, the "dissipation of the taint" concept that the Court has applied in deciding whether exclusion is appropriate in a particular case attempts to mark the point at which the detrimental consequences of illegal police action become so attenuated that the deterrent effect of the exclusionary rule no longer justifies its cost. Not surprisingly in view of this purpose, an assessment of the flagrancy of the police misconduct constitutes an important step in the calculus.

As yet, we have not recognized any form of good-faith exception to the Fourth Amendment exclusionary rule. But the balancing approach that has evolved during the years of experience with the rule provides strong support for the modification currently urged upon us. As we discuss below, our evaluation of the costs and benefits of suppressing reliable physical evidence seized by officers reasonably relying on a warrant issued by a detached and neutral magistrate leads to the conclusion that such evidence should be admissible in the prosecution's case in chief.

III

Because a search warrant provides the detached scrutiny of a neutral magistrate, which is a more reliable safeguard against improper searches than the hurried judgment of a law enforcement officer engaged in the often competitive enterprise of ferreting out crime, we have expressed a strong preference for warrants and declared that in a doubtful or marginal case a search under a warrant may be sustainable where without one it would fall. Reasonable minds frequently may differ on the question whether a particular affidavit establishes probable cause, and we have thus concluded that the preference for warrants is most appropriately effectuated by according great deference to a magistrate's determination.

Deference to the magistrate, however, is not boundless. It is clear, first, that the deference accorded to a magistrate's finding of probable cause does not preclude inquiry into the knowing or reckless falsity of the affidavit on which that determination was based. *Franks v. Delaware*, 438 U.S. 154 (1978). Second, the courts must also insist that the magistrate purport to perform his neutral and detached function and not serve merely as a rubber stamp for the police. A magistrate failing to manifest that neutrality and detachment demanded of a judicial officer when presented with a warrant application and who acts instead as "an adjunct law enforcement officer" cannot provide valid authorization for an otherwise unconstitutional search.

Third, reviewing courts will not defer to a warrant based on an affidavit that does not provide the magistrate with a substantial basis for determining the existence of probable cause. Sufficient information must be presented to the magistrate to allow that official to determine probable cause; his action cannot be a mere ratification of the bare conclusions of others. Even if the warrant application was supported by more than a "bare bones" affidavit, a reviewing court may properly conclude that, notwithstanding the deference that magistrates deserve, the warrant was invalid because the magistrate's probable-cause determination reflected an improper analysis of the totality of the circumstances, or because the form of the warrant was improper in some respect.

Only in the first of these three situations, however, has the Court set forth a rationale for suppressing evidence obtained pursuant to a search warrant; in the other areas, it has simply excluded such evidence without considering whether Fourth Amendment interests will be advanced. To the extent that proponents of exclusion rely on its behavioral effects on judges and magistrates in these areas, their reliance is misplaced. First, the exclusionary rule is designed to deter police misconduct rather than to punish the errors of judges and magistrates. Second, there exists no evidence suggesting that judges and magistrates are inclined to ignore or subvert the Fourth Amendment or that lawlessness among these actors requires application of the extreme sanction of exclusion.

Third, and most important, we discern no basis, and are offered none, for believing that exclusion of evidence seized pursuant to a warrant will have a significant deterrent effect on the issuing judge or magistrate. Many of the factors that indicate that the exclusionary rule cannot provide an effective "special" or "general" deterrent for individual offending law enforcement officers apply as well to judges or magistrates. And, to the extent that the rule is thought to operate as a "systemic" deterrent on a wider audience, it clearly can have no such effect on individuals empowered to issue search warrants. Judges and magistrates are not adjuncts to the law enforcement team; as neutral judicial officers, they have no stake in the outcome of particular criminal prosecutions. The threat of exclusion thus cannot be expected significantly to deter them. Imposition of the exclusionary sanction is not necessary meaningfully to inform judicial officers of their errors, and we cannot conclude that admitting evidence obtained pursuant to a warrant while at the same time declaring that the warrant was somehow defective will in any way reduce judicial officers' professional incentives to comply with the Fourth Amendment, encourage them to repeat their mistakes, or lead to the granting of all colorable warrant requests.

If exclusion of evidence obtained pursuant to a subsequently invalidated warrant is to have any deterrent effect, therefore, it must alter the behavior of individual law enforcement officers or the policies of their departments. One could argue that applying the exclusionary rule in cases where the police failed to demonstrate probable cause in the warrant application deters future inadequate presentations or "magistrate shopping" and thus promotes the ends of the Fourth Amendment. Suppressing evidence obtained pursuant to a technically defective warrant supported by probable cause also might encourage officers to scrutinize more closely the form of the warrant and to point out suspected judicial errors. We find such arguments speculative and conclude that suppression of evidence obtained pursuant to a warrant should be ordered only on a case-by-case basis and only in those unusual cases in which exclusion will further the purposes of the exclusionary rule.

We have frequently questioned whether the exclusionary rule can have any deterrent effect when the offending officers acted in the objectively reasonable belief that their conduct did not violate the Fourth Amendment. But even assuming that the rule effectively deters some police misconduct and provides incentives for the law enforcement profession as a whole to conduct itself in accord with the Fourth Amendment, it cannot be expected, and should not be applied, to deter objectively reasonable law enforcement activity.[20] In short, where the officer's conduct is objectively reasonable, excluding the evidence will not further the ends of the exclusionary rule in any appreciable way; for it is painfully apparent that the officer is acting as a reasonable officer would and should act in similar circumstances.

This is particularly true, we believe, when an officer acting with objective good faith has obtained a search warrant from a judge or magistrate and acted within its scope. In most such cases, there is no police illegality and thus nothing to deter. It is the magistrate's responsibility to determine whether the officer's allegations establish probable cause and, if so, to issue a warrant comporting in form with the

---

[20] We emphasize that the standard of reasonableness we adopt is an objective one. Many objections to a good-faith exception assume that the exception will turn on the subjective good faith of individual officers. Grounding the modification in objective reasonableness, however, retains the value of the exclusionary rule as an incentive for the law enforcement profession as a whole to conduct themselves in accord with the Fourth Amendment. The objective standard we adopt, moreover, requires officers to have a reasonable knowledge of what the law prohibits.

requirements of the Fourth Amendment. In the ordinary case, an officer cannot be expected to question the magistrate's probable-cause determination or his judgment that the form of the warrant is technically sufficient. Once the warrant issues, there is literally nothing more the policeman can do in seeking to comply with the law. Penalizing the officer for the magistrate's error, rather than his own, cannot logically contribute to the deterrence of Fourth Amendment violations.

We conclude that the marginal or nonexistent benefits produced by suppressing evidence obtained in objectively reasonable reliance on a subsequently invalidated search warrant cannot justify the substantial costs of exclusion. We do not suggest, however, that exclusion is always inappropriate in cases where an officer has obtained a warrant and abided by its terms. The officer's reliance on the magistrate's probable-cause determination and on the technical sufficiency of the warrant he issues must be objectively reasonable, and it is clear that in some circumstances the officer[24] will have no reasonable grounds for believing that the warrant was properly issued.

Suppression therefore remains an appropriate remedy if the magistrate or judge in issuing a warrant was misled by information in an affidavit that the affiant knew was false or would have known was false except for his reckless disregard of the truth. *Franks v. Delaware*, 438 U.S. 154 (1978). The exception we recognize today will also not apply in cases where the issuing magistrate wholly abandoned his judicial role; in such circumstances, no reasonably well trained officer should rely on the warrant. Nor would an officer manifest objective good faith in relying on a warrant based on an affidavit so lacking in indicia of probable cause as to render official belief in its existence entirely unreasonable. Finally, depending on the circumstances of the particular case, a warrant may be so facially deficient—*i.e.*, in failing to particularize the place to be searched or the things to be seized—that the executing officers cannot reasonably presume it to be valid.

IV

Having determined that the warrant should not have issued, the Court of Appeals understandably declined to adopt a modification of the Fourth Amendment exclusionary rule that this Court had not previously sanctioned. Although the modification finds strong support in our previous cases, the Court of Appeals' commendable self-restraint is not to be criticized. We have now reexamined the purposes of the exclusionary

---

[24] References to "officer" throughout this opinion should not be read too narrowly. It is necessary to consider the objective reasonableness, not only of the officers who eventually executed a warrant, but also of the officers who originally obtained it or who provided information material to the probable-cause determination. Nothing in our opinion suggests, for example, that an officer could obtain a warrant on the basis of a "bare bones" affidavit and then rely on colleagues who are ignorant of the circumstances under which the warrant was obtained to conduct the search.

rule and the propriety of its application in cases where officers have relied on a subsequently invalidated search warrant. Our conclusion is that the rule's purposes will only rarely be served by applying it in such circumstances.

In the absence of an allegation that the magistrate abandoned his detached and neutral role, suppression is appropriate only if the officers were dishonest or reckless in preparing their affidavit or could not have harbored an objectively reasonable belief in the existence of probable cause. Only respondent Leon has contended that no reasonably well trained police officer could have believed that there existed probable cause to search his house; significantly, the other respondents advance no comparable argument. Officer Rombach's application for a warrant clearly was supported by much more than a "bare bones" affidavit. The affidavit related the results of an extensive investigation and, as the opinions of the divided panel of the Court of Appeals make clear, provided evidence sufficient to create disagreement among thoughtful and competent judges as to the existence of probable cause. Under these circumstances, the officers' reliance on the magistrate's determination of probable cause was objectively reasonable, and application of the extreme sanction of exclusion is inappropriate.

JUSTICE BRENNAN, with whom JUSTICE MARSHALL joins, dissenting.

In case after case, I have witnessed the Court's gradual but determined strangulation of the [exclusionary] rule. It now appears that the Court's victory over the Fourth Amendment is complete, for today the Court sanctions the use in the prosecution's case in chief of illegally obtained evidence against the individual whose rights have been violated—a result that had previously been thought to be foreclosed.

The Court seeks to justify this result on the ground that the "costs" of adhering to the exclusionary rule in cases like those before us exceed the "benefits." But the language of deterrence and of cost/benefit analysis, if used indiscriminately, can have a narcotic effect. It creates an illusion of technical precision and ineluctability. It suggests that not only constitutional principle but also empirical data support the majority's result. When the Court's analysis is examined carefully, however, it is clear that we have not been treated to an honest assessment of the merits of the exclusionary rule, but have instead been drawn into a curious world where the "costs" of excluding illegally obtained evidence loom to exaggerated heights and where the "benefits" of such exclusion are made to disappear with a mere wave of the hand.

The majority ignores the fundamental constitutional importance of what is at stake here. While the machinery of law enforcement and indeed the nature of crime itself have changed dramatically since the Fourth Amendment became part of the Nation's fundamental law in 1791, what the Framers understood then remains true today—that the task of combating crime and convicting the guilty will in every era seem of such critical and pressing concern that we may be lured by the temptations of expediency into forsaking our commitment to protecting individual liberty and privacy. It was for that very reason that the Framers of the Bill of Rights insisted that law enforcement efforts be permanently and unambiguously restricted in order to preserve personal freedoms. In the constitutional scheme they ordained, the sometimes unpopular task of ensuring that the government's enforcement efforts remain within the strict boundaries fixed by the Fourth Amendment was entrusted to the courts. If those independent tribunals lose their resolve, however, as the Court has done today, and give way to the seductive call of expediency, the vital guarantees of the Fourth Amendment are reduced to nothing more than a form of words.

A proper understanding of the broad purposes sought to be served by the Fourth Amendment demonstrates that the principles embodied in the exclusionary rule rest upon a far firmer constitutional foundation than the shifting sands of the Court's deterrence rationale. But even if I were to accept the Court's chosen method of analyzing the question posed by these cases, I would still conclude that the Court's decision cannot be justified.

I

At bottom, the Court's decision turns on the proposition that the exclusionary rule is merely a "judicially created remedy designed to safeguard Fourth Amendment rights generally through its deterrent effect, rather than a personal constitutional right." The germ of that idea is found in *Wolf v. Colorado*, 338 U.S. 25 (1949), and although I had thought that such a narrow conception of the rule had been forever put to rest by our decision in *Mapp v. Ohio*, 367 U.S. 643 (1961), it has been revived by the present Court and reaches full flower with today's decision. The essence of this view is that the sole "purpose of the Fourth Amendment is to prevent unreasonable governmental intrusions into the privacy of one's person, house, papers, or effects. The wrong condemned is the unjustified governmental invasion of these areas of an individual's life. That wrong is fully accomplished by the original search without probable cause." This reading of the Amendment implies that its proscriptions are directed solely at those government agents who may actually invade an individual's constitutionally protected privacy. The courts are not subject to any direct constitutional duty to exclude illegally obtained evidence, because the question of the admissibility of such evidence is not addressed by the Amendment. This view of the scope of the Amendment relegates the judiciary to the periphery. Because the only constitutionally cognizable injury has already been "fully accomplished" by the police by the time a case comes before the courts, the Constitution is not itself violated if the judge decides to admit the tainted evidence.

Indeed, the most the judge can do is wring his hands and hope that perhaps by excluding such evidence he can deter future transgressions by the police.

Such a reading appears plausible, because, as critics of the exclusionary rule never tire of repeating, the Fourth Amendment makes no express provision for the exclusion of evidence secured in violation of its commands. A short answer to this claim, of course, is that many of the Constitution's most vital imperatives are stated in general terms and the task of giving meaning to these precepts is therefore left to subsequent judicial decisionmaking in the context of concrete cases. A more direct answer may be supplied by recognizing that the Amendment, like other provisions of the Bill of Rights, restrains the power of the government as a whole; it does not specify only a particular agency and exempt all others. The judiciary is responsible, no less than the executive, for ensuring that constitutional rights are respected.

When that fact is kept in mind, the role of the courts and their possible involvement in the concerns of the Fourth Amendment comes into sharper focus. Because seizures are executed principally to secure evidence, and because such evidence generally has utility in our legal system only in the context of a trial supervised by a judge, it is apparent that the admission of illegally obtained evidence implicates the same constitutional concerns as the initial seizure of that evidence. Indeed, by admitting unlawfully seized evidence, the judiciary becomes a part of what is in fact a single governmental action prohibited by the terms of the Amendment. Once that connection between the evidence-gathering role of the police and the evidence-admitting function of the courts is acknowledged, the plausibility of the Court's interpretation becomes more suspect. Certainly nothing in the language or history of the Fourth Amendment suggests that a recognition of this evidentiary link between the police and the courts was meant to be foreclosed. It is difficult to give any meaning at all to the limitations imposed by the Amendment if they are read to proscribe only certain conduct by the police but to allow other agents of the same government to take advantage of evidence secured by the police in violation of its requirements. The Amendment therefore must be read to condemn not only the initial unconstitutional invasion of privacy—which is done, after all, for the purpose of securing evidence— but also the subsequent use of any evidence so obtained.

The Court evades this principle by drawing an artificial line between the constitutional rights and responsibilities that are engaged by actions of the police and those that are engaged when a defendant appears before the courts. According to the Court, the substantive protections of the Fourth Amendment are wholly exhausted at the moment when police unlawfully invade an individual's privacy and thus no substantive force remains to those protections at the time of trial when the government seeks to use evidence obtained by the police.

I submit that such a crabbed reading of the Fourth Amendment casts aside the teaching of those Justices who first formulated the exclusionary rule, and rests ultimately on an impoverished understanding of judicial responsibility in our constitutional scheme. For my part, "[t]he right of the people to be secure in their persons, houses, papers, and effects, against unreasonable searches and seizures" comprises a personal right to exclude all evidence secured by means of unreasonable searches and seizures. The right to be free from the initial invasion of privacy and the right of exclusion are coordinate components of the central embracing right to be free from unreasonable searches and seizures.

If the [Fourth] Amendment is to have any meaning, police and the courts cannot be regarded as constitutional strangers to each other; because the evidence-gathering role of the police is directly linked to the evidence-admitting function of the courts, an individual's Fourth Amendment rights may be undermined as completely by one as by the other.

From the foregoing, it is clear why the question whether the exclusion of evidence would deter future police misconduct was never considered a relevant concern in the early cases from *Weeks v. U.S.*, 232 U.S. 383 (1914), to *Olmstead v. U.S.*, 277 U.S. 438 (1928). In those formative decisions, the Court plainly understood that the exclusion of illegally obtained evidence was compelled not by judicially fashioned remedial purposes, but rather by a direct constitutional command.

Despite this clear pronouncement, however, the Court has gradually pressed the deterrence rationale for the rule back to center stage. The various arguments advanced by the Court in this campaign have only strengthened my conviction that the deterrence theory is both misguided and unworkable. First, the Court has frequently bewailed the "cost" of excluding reliable evidence. In large part, this criticism rests upon a refusal to acknowledge the function of the Fourth Amendment itself. If nothing else, the Amendment plainly operates to disable the government from gathering information and securing evidence in certain ways. In practical terms, of course, this restriction of official power means that some incriminating evidence inevitably will go undetected if the government obeys these constitutional restraints. It is the loss of that evidence that is the "price" our society pays for enjoying the freedom and privacy safeguarded by the Fourth Amendment. Thus, some criminals will go free not, in Justice (then Judge) Cardozo's misleading epigram, "because the constable has blundered," but rather because official compliance with Fourth Amendment requirements makes it more difficult to catch criminals. Understood in this way, the Amendment directly contemplates that some reliable and incriminating evidence will be lost to the government; therefore, it is not the exclusionary rule, but the Amendment itself that has imposed this cost.

In addition, the Court's decisions over the past decade have made plain that the entire enterprise of attempting to assess the benefits and costs of the exclusionary rule in various contexts is a virtually impossible task for the judiciary to perform honestly or accurately. Although the Court's language in those cases suggests that some specific empirical basis may support its analyses, the reality is that the Court's opinions represent inherently unstable compounds of intuition, hunches, and occasional pieces of partial and often inconclusive data. To the extent empirical data are available regarding the general costs and benefits of the exclusionary rule, such data have shown, on the one hand, as the Court acknowledges today, that the costs are not as substantial as critics have asserted in the past, and, on the other hand, that while the exclusionary rule may well have certain deterrent effects, it is extremely difficult to determine with any degree of precision whether the incidence of unlawful conduct by police is now lower than it was prior to *Mapp*. By remaining within its redoubt of empiricism and by basing the rule solely on the deterrence rationale, the Court has robbed the rule of legitimacy. A doctrine that is explained as if it were an empirical proposition but for which there is only limited empirical support is both inherently unstable and an easy mark for critics. The extent of this Court's fidelity to Fourth Amendment requirements, however, should not turn on such statistical uncertainties.

III

Even if I were to accept the Court's general approach to the exclusionary rule, I could not agree with today's result. At the outset, the Court suggests that society has been asked to pay a high price—in terms either of setting guilty persons free or of impeding the proper functioning of trials—as a result of excluding relevant physical evidence in cases where the police, in conducting searches and seizing evidence, have made only an "objectively reasonable" mistake concerning the constitutionality of their actions. But what evidence is there to support such a claim?

Significantly, the Court points to none, and, indeed, as the Court acknowledges, recent studies have demonstrated that the "costs" of the exclusionary rule—calculated in terms of dropped prosecutions and lost convictions—are quite low. Contrary to the claims of the rule's critics that exclusion leads to the release of countless guilty criminals, these studies have demonstrated that federal and state prosecutors very rarely drop cases because of potential search and seizure problems. For example, a 1979 study prepared at the request of Congress by the General Accounting Office reported that only 0.4% of all cases actually declined for prosecution by federal prosecutors were declined primarily because of illegal search problems. If the GAO data are restated as a percentage of all arrests, the study shows that only 0.2% of all felony arrests are declined for prosecution because of potential exclusionary rule problems. Of course, these data describe only the costs attributable to the exclusion of evidence in all cases; the costs due to the exclusion of evidence in the narrower category of cases where police have made objectively reasonable mistakes must necessarily be even smaller. The Court, however, ignores this distinction and mistakenly weighs the aggregated costs of exclusion in all cases, irrespective of the circumstances that led to exclusion, against the potential benefits associated with only those cases in which evidence is excluded because police reasonably but mistakenly believe that their conduct does not violate the Fourth Amendment. When such faulty scales are used, it is little wonder that the balance tips in favor of restricting the application of the rule.

What then supports the Court's insistence that this evidence be admitted? Apparently, the Court's only answer is that even though the costs of exclusion are not very substantial, the potential deterrent effect in these circumstances is so marginal that exclusion cannot be justified. The key to the Court's conclusion in this respect is its belief that the prospective deterrent effect of the exclusionary rule operates only in those situations in which police officers, when deciding whether to go forward with some particular search, have reason to know that their planned conduct will violate the requirements of the Fourth Amendment. If these officers in fact understand (or reasonably should understand because the law is well settled) that their proposed conduct will offend the Fourth Amendment and that, consequently, any evidence they seize will be suppressed in court, they will refrain from conducting the planned search. In those circumstances, the incentive system created by the exclusionary rule will have the hoped-for deterrent effect. But in situations where police officers reasonably (but mistakenly) believe that their planned conduct satisfies Fourth Amendment requirements—presumably either (a) because they are acting on the basis of an apparently valid warrant, or (b) because their conduct is only later determined to be invalid as a result of a subsequent change in the law or the resolution of an unsettled question of law—then such officers will have no reason to refrain from conducting the search and the exclusionary rule will have no effect.

At first blush, there is some logic to this position. Undoubtedly, in the situation hypothesized by the Court, the existence of the exclusionary rule cannot be expected to have any deterrent effect on the particular officers at the moment they are deciding whether to go forward with the search. Indeed, the subsequent exclusion of any evidence seized under such circumstances appears somehow "unfair" to the particular officers involved. As the Court suggests, these officers have acted in what they thought was an appropriate and constitutionally authorized manner, but then the fruit of their efforts is nullified by the application of the exclusionary rule.

The flaw in the Court's argument, however, is that its logic captures only one comparatively minor element of the generally acknowledged deterrent purposes of the exclusionary rule. To be sure, the rule operates to some extent to deter future misconduct by individual officers who have had evidence suppressed in their own cases. But what the Court overlooks is that the deterrence rationale for the rule is not designed to be, nor should it be thought of as, a form of "punishment" of individual police officers for their failures to obey the restraints imposed by the Fourth Amendment. Instead, the chief deterrent function of the rule is its tendency to promote institutional compliance with Fourth Amendment requirements on the part of law enforcement agencies generally. Thus, as the Court has previously recognized, "over the long term, [the] demonstration [provided by the exclusionary rule] that our society attaches serious consequences to violation of constitutional rights is thought to encourage those who formulate law enforcement policies, and the officers who implement them, to incorporate Fourth Amendment ideals into their value system." It is only through such an institutionwide mechanism that information concerning Fourth Amendment standards can be effectively communicated to rank-and-file officers.

If the overall educational effect of the exclusionary rule is considered, application of the rule to even those situations in which individual police officers have acted on the basis of a reasonable but mistaken belief that their conduct was authorized can still be expected to have a considerable long-term deterrent effect. If evidence is consistently excluded in these circumstances, police departments will surely be prompted to instruct their officers to devote greater care and attention to providing sufficient information to establish probable cause when applying for a warrant, and to review with some attention the form of the warrant that they have been issued, rather than automatically assuming that whatever document the magistrate has signed will necessarily comport with Fourth Amendment requirements.

After today's decisions, however, that institutional incentive will be lost. Indeed, the Court's "reasonable mistake" exception to the exclusionary rule will tend to put a premium on police ignorance of the law. Armed with the assurance provided by today's decisions that evidence will always be admissible whenever an officer has "reasonably" relied upon a warrant, police departments will be encouraged to train officers that if a warrant has simply been signed, it is reasonable, without more, to rely on it. Since in close cases there will no longer be any incentive to err on the side of constitutional behavior, police would have every reason to adopt a "let's-wait-until-it's-decided" approach in situations in which there is a question about a warrant's validity or the basis for its issuance.

Although the Court brushes these concerns aside, a host of grave consequences can be expected to result from its decision to carve this new exception out of the exclusionary rule. A chief consequence of today's decisions will be to convey a clear and unambiguous message to magistrates that their decisions to issue warrants are now insulated from subsequent judicial review. Creation of this new exception for good-faith reliance upon a warrant implicitly tells magistrates that they need not take much care in reviewing warrant applications, since their mistakes will from now on have virtually no consequence: If their decision to issue a warrant was correct, the evidence will be admitted; if their decision was incorrect but the police relied in good faith on the warrant, the evidence will also be admitted. Inevitably, the care and attention devoted to such an inconsequential chore will dwindle. Although the Court is correct to note that magistrates do not share the same stake in the outcome of a criminal case as the police, they nevertheless need to appreciate that their role is of some moment in order to continue performing the important task of carefully reviewing warrant applications. Today's decisions effectively remove that incentive.

Moreover, the good-faith exception will encourage police to provide only the bare minimum of information in future warrant applications. The police will now know that if they can secure a warrant, so long as the circumstances of its issuance are not "entirely unreasonable," all police conduct pursuant to that warrant will be protected from further judicial review. The clear incentive that operated in the past to establish probable cause adequately because reviewing courts would examine the magistrate's judgment carefully, has now been so completely vitiated that the police need only show that it was not "entirely unreasonable" under the circumstances of a particular case for them to believe that the warrant they were issued was valid. The long-run effect unquestionably will be to undermine the integrity of the warrant process.

In *Massachusetts v. Sheppard*, decided on the same day as *U.S. v. Leon*, the Supreme Court held that the newly-created good faith exception to the exclusionary rule permitted the introduction of evidence obtained by police who reasonably relied on a warrant that was later found to be technically defective.

MASSACHUSETTS V. SHEPPARD
468 U.S. 961 (1984)

In the course of a homicide investigation, a police detective prepared an affidavit in support of an application for a search warrant of Osborne Sheppard's residence. The affidavit was reviewed and approved by the District Attorney. Because it was Sunday, the local court was closed, and the detective couldn't find the correct warrant application form, so he used another form used to search for "controlled substances." The detective made some changes to the form and presented it and the affidavit to a judge, informing the judge that some further corrections to the warrant form might need to be made. The judge concluded that the affidavit established probable cause to search Sheppard's residence, and told the detective that he would make any further necessary changes to the warrant form. The judge made some changes, but did not change a provision that continued to authorize a search for controlled substances, nor did the judge alter the form to incorporate the detective's affidavit. The judge then signed the warrant and returned it and the affidavit to the detective, informing the detective that the warrant was sufficient in form and content to carry out the requested search. The ensuing search of Sheppard's residence was limited to the items listed in the affidavit, and several incriminating items of evidence were discovered.

At a pretrial suppression hearing, the trial judge ruled that the warrant was defective under the Fourth Amendment because it did not particularly describe the items to be seized, but the incriminating evidence was admissible because the police had acted in good faith in executing what they reasonably believed was a valid warrant. The U.S. Supreme Court agreed:

> The police conduct in this case clearly was objectively reasonable and largely error-free. An error of constitutional dimensions may have been committed with respect to the issuance of the warrant, but it was the judge, not the police officers, who made the critical mistake. Suppressing evidence because the judge failed to make all the necessary clerical corrections despite his assurances that such changes would be made will not serve the deterrent function that the exclusionary rule was designed to achieve. Accordingly, federal law does not require the exclusion of the disputed evidence in this case.

In *Herring v. U.S.*, the Supreme Court held that the exclusionary rule should be invoked only for deliberate, reckless, or grossly negligent conduct by the police. A recordkeeping mistake by the police, resulting from ordinary and isolated negligence, will not trigger the exclusionary rule.

HERRING v. U.S.
555 U.S. 135 (2009)

CHIEF JUSTICE ROBERTS delivered the opinion of the Court.

The Fourth Amendment forbids "unreasonable searches and seizures," and this usually requires the police to have probable cause or a warrant before making an arrest. What if an officer reasonably believes there is an outstanding arrest warrant, but that belief turns out to be wrong because of a negligent bookkeeping error by another police employee? The parties here agree that the ensuing arrest is still a violation of the Fourth Amendment, but dispute whether contraband found during a search incident to that arrest must be excluded in a later prosecution.

Our cases establish that such suppression is not an automatic consequence of a Fourth Amendment violation. Instead, the question turns on the culpability of the police and the potential of exclusion to deter wrongful police conduct. Here the error was the result of isolated negligence attenuated from the arrest. We hold that in these circumstances the jury should not be barred from considering all the evidence.

I

On July 7, 2004, Investigator Mark Anderson learned that Bennie Dean Herring had driven to the Coffee County Sheriff's Department to retrieve something from his impounded truck. Herring was no stranger to law enforcement, and Anderson asked the county's warrant clerk, Sandy Pope, to check for any outstanding warrants for Herring's arrest. When she found none, Anderson asked Pope to check with Sharon Morgan, her counterpart in neighboring Dale County. After checking Dale County's computer database, Morgan replied that there was an active arrest warrant for Herring's failure to appear on a felony charge. Pope relayed the information to Anderson and asked Morgan to fax over a copy of the warrant as confirmation. Anderson and a deputy followed Herring as he left the impound lot, pulled him over, and arrested him. A search incident to the arrest revealed methamphetamine in Herring's pocket, and a pistol (which as a felon he could not possess) in his vehicle.

There had, however, been a mistake about the warrant. The Dale County sheriff's computer records are supposed to correspond to actual arrest warrants, which the office also maintains. But when Morgan went to the files to retrieve the actual warrant to fax to Pope, Morgan was unable to find it. She called a court clerk and learned that the warrant had been recalled five months earlier. Normally when a warrant is recalled the court clerk's office or a judge's chambers calls Morgan, who enters the information in the sheriff's computer database and disposes of the physical copy. For whatever reason, the information about the recall of the warrant for Herring did not appear in the database. Morgan immediately called Pope to alert her to the mixup, and Pope contacted Anderson over a secure radio. This all unfolded in 10 to 15 minutes, but Herring had already been arrested and found with the gun and drugs, just a few hundred yards from the sheriff's office.

Herring was indicted in the District Court for the Middle District of Alabama for illegally possessing the gun and drugs. He moved to suppress the evidence on the ground that his initial arrest had been illegal because the warrant had been rescinded. The Magistrate Judge recommended denying the motion because the arresting officers had acted in a good-faith belief that the warrant was still outstanding. Thus, even if there were a Fourth Amendment violation, there was "no reason to believe that application of the exclusionary rule here would deter the occurrence of any future mistakes." The District Court adopted the Magistrate Judge's recommendation, and the Court of Appeals for the Eleventh Circuit affirmed. Because the error was merely negligent and attenuated from the arrest, the Eleventh Circuit concluded that the benefit of suppressing the evidence "would be marginal or nonexistent," and the evidence was therefore admissible under the good-faith rule of *U.S. v. Leon*, 468 U.S. 897 (1984).

II

The Fourth Amendment protects "the right of the people to be secure in their persons, houses, papers, and effects, against unreasonable searches and seizures," but contains no provision expressly precluding the use of evidence obtained in violation of its commands. Nonetheless, our decisions establish an exclusionary rule that, when applicable, forbids the use of improperly obtained evidence at trial. We have stated that this judicially created rule is designed to safeguard Fourth Amendment rights generally through its deterrent effect.

In analyzing the applicability of the rule, *Leon* admonished that we must consider the actions of all the police officers involved. The Coffee County officers did nothing improper. Indeed, the error was noticed so quickly because Coffee County requested a faxed confirmation of the warrant.

The Eleventh Circuit concluded, however, that somebody in Dale County should have updated the computer database to reflect the recall of the arrest warrant. The court also concluded that this error was negligent, but did not find it to be reckless or deliberate. That fact is crucial to our holding that this error is not enough by itself to require the extreme sanction of exclusion.

1.   The fact that a Fourth Amendment violation occurred—*i.e.*, that a search or arrest was unreasonable—does not necessarily mean that the exclusionary rule applies. Indeed, exclusion has always been our last

resort, not our first impulse, and our precedents establish important principles that constrain application of the exclusionary rule.

First, the exclusionary rule is not an individual right and applies only where it results in appreciable deterrence. We have repeatedly rejected the argument that exclusion is a necessary consequence of a Fourth Amendment violation. Instead we have focused on the efficacy of the rule in deterring Fourth Amendment violations in the future.

In addition, the benefits of deterrence must outweigh the costs. We have never suggested that the exclusionary rule must apply in every circumstance in which it might provide marginal deterrence. To the extent that application of the exclusionary rule could provide some incremental deterrent, that possible benefit must be weighed against its substantial social costs. The rule's costly toll upon truth-seeking and law enforcement objectives presents a high obstacle for those urging its application.

These principles are reflected in the holding of *Leon*: When police act under a warrant that is invalid for lack of probable cause, the exclusionary rule does not apply if the police acted "in objectively reasonable reliance" on the subsequently invalidated search warrant. We (perhaps confusingly) called this objectively reasonable reliance "good faith." In a companion case, *Massachusetts v. Sheppard*, 468 U.S. 981 (1984), we held that the exclusionary rule did not apply when a warrant was invalid because a judge forgot to make "clerical corrections" to it.

In *Arizona v. Evans*, 514 U.S. 1 (1995), we applied this good-faith rule to police who reasonably relied on mistaken information in a court's database that an arrest warrant was outstanding. We held that a mistake made by a judicial employee could not give rise to exclusion for three reasons: The exclusionary rule was crafted to curb police rather than judicial misconduct; court employees were unlikely to try to subvert the Fourth Amendment; and "most important, there was no basis for believing that application of the exclusionary rule in those circumstances" would have any significant effect in deterring the errors. *Evans* left unresolved "whether the evidence should be suppressed if police personnel were responsible for the error," an issue not argued by the State in that case, but one that we now confront.

2.   The extent to which the exclusionary rule is justified by these deterrence principles varies with the culpability of the law enforcement conduct. As we said in *Leon*, "an assessment of the flagrancy of the police misconduct constitutes an important step in the calculus" of applying the exclusionary rule.

Indeed, the abuses that gave rise to the exclusionary rule featured intentional conduct that was patently unconstitutional. In *Weeks v. U.S.*, 232 U.S. 383 (1914), a foundational exclusionary rule case, the officers had broken into the defendant's home (using a key shown to them by a neighbor), confiscated incriminating papers, then returned again with a U.S. Marshal to confiscate even more. Not only did they have no search warrant, which the Court held was required, but they could not have gotten one had they tried. They were so lacking in sworn and particularized information that "not even an order of court would have justified such procedure." *Silverthorne Lumber Co. v. U.S.*, 251 U.S. 385 (1920), on which petitioner repeatedly relies, was similar; federal officials "without a shadow of authority" went to the defendants' office and "made a clean sweep" of every paper they could find. Even the Government seemed to acknowledge that the "seizure was an outrage."

Equally flagrant conduct was at issue in *Mapp v. Ohio*, 367 U.S. 643 (1961), which overruled *Wolf v. Colorado*, 338 U.S. 25 (1949), and extended the exclusionary rule to the States. Officers forced open a door to Ms. Mapp's house, kept her lawyer from entering, brandished what the court concluded was a false warrant, then forced her into handcuffs and canvassed the house for obscenity. An error that arises from nonrecurring and attenuated negligence is thus far removed from the core concerns that led us to adopt the rule in the first place. And in fact since *Leon*, we have never applied the rule to exclude evidence obtained in violation of the Fourth Amendment, where the police conduct was no more intentional or culpable than this.

3.   To trigger the exclusionary rule, police conduct must be sufficiently deliberate that exclusion can meaningfully deter it, and sufficiently culpable that such deterrence is worth the price paid by the justice system. As laid out in our cases, the exclusionary rule serves to deter deliberate, reckless, or grossly negligent conduct, or in some circumstances recurring or systemic negligence. The error in this case does not rise to that level.

Our decision in *Franks v. Delaware*, 438 U.S. 154 (1978), provides an analogy. In *Franks*, we held that police negligence in obtaining a warrant did not even rise to the level of a Fourth Amendment violation, let alone meet the more stringent test for triggering the exclusionary rule. We held that the Constitution allowed defendants, in some circumstances, "to challenge the truthfulness of factual statements made in an affidavit supporting the warrant," even after the warrant had issued. If those false statements were necessary to the Magistrate Judge's probable-cause determination, the warrant would be "voided." But we did not find all false statements relevant: "There must be allegations of deliberate falsehood or of reckless disregard for the truth," and "allegations of negligence or innocent mistake are insufficient."

Both this case and *Franks* concern false information provided by police. Under *Franks*, negligent police miscommunications in the course of acquiring a warrant do not provide a basis to rescind a warrant and render a search or arrest invalid. Here, the miscommunications occurred in a different context—after the warrant had been issued and recalled—but that fact should not require excluding the evidence obtained.

The pertinent analysis of deterrence and culpability is objective, not an inquiry into the subjective awareness of arresting officers. We have already held that our good-faith inquiry is confined to the objectively ascertainable question whether a reasonably well trained officer would have known that the search was illegal in light of all of the circumstances. These circumstances frequently include a particular officer's knowledge and experience, but that does not make the test any more subjective than the one for probable cause, which looks to an officer's knowledge and experience, but not his subjective intent.

4.   We do not suggest that all recordkeeping errors by the police are immune from the exclusionary rule. In this case, however, the conduct at issue was not so objectively culpable as to require exclusion.

If the police have been shown to be reckless in maintaining a warrant system, or to have knowingly made false entries to lay the groundwork for future false arrests, exclusion would certainly be justified under our cases should such misconduct cause a Fourth Amendment violation. We said as much in *Leon*, explaining that an officer could not obtain a warrant on the basis of a "bare bones" affidavit and then rely on colleagues who are ignorant of the circumstances under which the warrant was obtained to conduct the search. Petitioner's fears that our decision will cause police departments to deliberately keep their officers ignorant are thus unfounded.

Justice Ginsburg's dissent also adverts to the possible unreliability of a number of databases not relevant to this case. In a case where systemic errors were demonstrated, it might be reckless for officers to rely on an unreliable warrant system. But there is no evidence that errors in Dale County's system are routine or widespread. Officer Anderson testified that he had never had reason to question information about a Dale County warrant, and both Sandy Pope and Sharon Morgan testified that they could remember no similar miscommunication ever happening on their watch. That is even less error than in the database at issue in *Evans*, where we also found reliance on the database to be objectively reasonable.

Petitioner's claim that police negligence automatically triggers suppression cannot be squared with the principles underlying the exclusionary rule, as they have been explained in our cases. In light of our repeated holdings that the deterrent effect of suppression must be substantial and outweigh any harm to the justice system, we conclude that when police mistakes are the result of negligence such as that described here, rather than systemic error or reckless disregard of constitutional requirements, any marginal deterrence does not pay its way. In such a case, the criminal should not "go free because the constable has blundered." *People v. Defore*, 242 N.Y. 13, 21 (1926) (opinion of the Court by Cardozo, J.).

JUSTICE GINSBURG, with whom JUSTICE STEVENS, JUSTICE SOUTER, and JUSTICE BREYER join, dissenting.

Beyond doubt, a main objective of the [exclusionary] rule is to deter—to compel respect for the constitutional guaranty in the only effectively available way—by removing the incentive to disregard it. But the rule also serves other important purposes: It enables the judiciary to avoid the taint of partnership in official lawlessness, and it assures the people—all potential victims of unlawful government conduct—that the government would not profit from its lawless behavior, thus minimizing the risk of seriously undermining popular trust in government.

The exclusionary rule, it bears emphasis, is often the only remedy effective to redress a Fourth Amendment violation. Civil liability will not lie for the vast majority of Fourth Amendment violations—the frequent infringements motivated by commendable zeal, not condemnable malice. Criminal prosecutions or administrative sanctions against the offending officers and injunctive relief against widespread violations are an even farther cry.

The Court maintains that Herring's case is one in which the exclusionary rule could have scant deterrent effect and therefore would not "pay its way." I disagree.

The exclusionary rule, the Court suggests, is capable of only marginal deterrence when the misconduct at issue is merely careless, not intentional or reckless. The suggestion runs counter to a foundational premise of tort law—that liability for negligence, *i.e.*, lack of due care, creates an incentive to act with greater care.

That the mistake here involved the failure to make a computer entry hardly means that application of the exclusionary rule would have minimal value. Just as the risk of *respondeat superior* liability encourages employers to supervise their employees' conduct more carefully, so the risk of exclusion of evidence encourages policymakers and systems managers to monitor the performance of the systems they install and the personnel employed to operate those systems.

Consider the potential impact of a decision applying the exclusionary rule in this case. As earlier observed, the record indicates that there is no electronic connection between the warrant database of the Dale County Sheriff's Department and that of the County Circuit Clerk's office, which is located in the basement of the same building. When a warrant is recalled, one of the many different people that have access to the warrants must find the hard copy of the warrant in the two or three different places where the Department houses warrants, return it to the

Clerk's office, and manually update the Department's database. The record reflects no routine practice of checking the database for accuracy, and the failure to remove the entry for Herring's warrant was not discovered until Investigator Anderson sought to pursue Herring five months later. Is it not altogether obvious that the Department could take further precautions to ensure the integrity of its database? The Sheriff's Department is in a position to remedy the situation and might well do so if the exclusionary rule is there to remove the incentive to do otherwise.

Is the potential deterrence here worth the costs it imposes? In light of the paramount importance of accurate recordkeeping in law enforcement, I would answer yes, and next explain why, as I see it, Herring's motion presents a particularly strong case for suppression.

Electronic databases form the nervous system of contemporary criminal justice operations. In recent years, their breadth and influence have dramatically expanded. Police today can access databases that include not only the updated National Crime Information Center (NCIC), but also terrorist watchlists, the Federal Government's employee eligibility system, and various commercial databases. Moreover, States are actively expanding information sharing between jurisdictions. As a result, law enforcement has an increasing supply of information within its easy electronic reach.

The risk of error stemming from these databases is not slim. Herring's *amici* warn that law enforcement databases are insufficiently monitored and often out of date. Government reports describe, for example, flaws in NCIC databases, terrorist watchlist databases, and databases associated with the Federal Government's employment eligibility verification system.

Inaccuracies in expansive, interconnected collections of electronic information raise grave concerns for individual liberty. The offense to the dignity of the citizen who is arrested, handcuffed, and searched on a public street simply because some bureaucrat has failed to maintain an accurate computer database is evocative of the use of general warrants that so outraged the authors of our Bill of Rights.

The Court assures that "exclusion would certainly be justified" if "the police have been shown to be reckless in maintaining a warrant system, or to have knowingly made false entries to lay the groundwork for future false arrests." This concession provides little comfort.

First, by restricting suppression to bookkeeping errors that are deliberate or reckless, the majority leaves Herring, and others like him, with no remedy for violations of their constitutional rights. There can be no serious assertion that relief is available under 42 U.S.C. § 1983. The arresting officer would be sheltered by qualified immunity, and the police department itself is not liable for the negligent acts of its employees.

Moreover, identifying the department employee who committed the error may be impossible.

Second, I doubt that police forces already possess sufficient incentives to maintain up-to-date records. The Government argues that police have no desire to send officers out on arrests unnecessarily, because arrests consume resources and place officers in danger. The facts of this case do not fit that description of police motivation. Here the officer wanted to arrest Herring and consulted the Department's records to legitimate his predisposition.

Third, even when deliberate or reckless conduct is afoot, the Court's assurance will often be an empty promise: How is an impecunious defendant to make the required showing? If the answer is that a defendant is entitled to discovery (and if necessary, an audit of police databases), then the Court has imposed a considerable administrative burden on courts and law enforcement.

Negligent recordkeeping errors by law enforcement threaten individual liberty, are susceptible to deterrence by the exclusionary rule, and cannot be remedied effectively through other means. Such errors present no occasion to further erode the exclusionary rule. The rule is needed to make the Fourth Amendment something real; a guarantee that does not carry with it the exclusion of evidence obtained by its violation is a chimera. In keeping with the rule's core concerns, suppression should have attended the unconstitutional search in this case.

In *Davis v. U.S.*, the Supreme Court held that evidence obtained during a search conducted in objectively reasonable reliance on binding judicial precedent is not subject to the exclusionary rule, even when the law is changed while the case is still pending on appeal.

DAVIS V. U.S.
131 S.Ct. 2419 (2011)

Police officers in Greenville, Alabama made a routine traffic stop that eventually led to the arrests of driver Stella Owens (for driving while intoxicated) and passenger Willie Davis (for giving a false name to police). The police handcuffed both Owens and Davis, then placed them in the back of separate patrol cars. The police then searched the passenger compartment of Owens' vehicle and found a revolver inside Davis' jacket pocket.

Davis was indicted on one count of possession of a firearm by a convicted felon. In his motion to suppress the revolver, Davis acknowledged that the search fully complied with the existing federal Eleventh Circuit precedent, but nevertheless challenged the search in order to preserve the issue for review on appeal. Like most courts, the Eleventh Circuit had long read the U.S. Supreme Court's decision in *New York v. Belton*, 453 U.S. 454 (1981), as establishing a bright-line rule authorizing substantially contemporaneous vehicle searches incident to arrests of recent occupants. (*Belton* is discussed briefly in Chapter 5.) The federal District Court, relying on the Eleventh Circuit's interpretation of *Belton*, denied Davis' motion to suppress the revolver, and Davis was convicted on the firearms charge.

While Davis' appeal was pending, the Supreme Court decided *Arizona v. Gant*, 556 U.S. 332 (2009), holding that an automobile search incident to a recent occupant's arrest is constitutional if the arrestee is within reaching distance of the vehicle during the search, or if the police have reason to believe that the vehicle contains evidence relevant to the crime of arrest. (*Gant* is presented in Chapter 5.) The Eleventh Circuit applied the new *Gant* rule in Davis' appeal and held that the vehicle search incident to Davis' arrest violated his Fourth Amendment rights. The Eleventh Circuit declined, however, to apply the exclusionary rule and suppress the revolver because it concluded that penalizing the arresting officer for following binding appellate precedent would not deter Fourth Amendment violations.

Relying heavily on its prior "good-faith" decisions—including *U.S. v. Leon*, 468 U.S. 897 (1984), and *Herring v. U.S.*, 555 U.S. 135 (2009)—the Supreme Court affirmed the Eleventh Circuit's decision upholding Davis' conviction:

> The question in this case is whether to apply the exclusionary rule when the police conduct a search in objectively reasonable reliance on binding judicial precedent. At the time of the search at issue here, we had not yet decided *Arizona v. Gant*, and the Eleventh Circuit had interpreted our decision in *New York v. Belton* to establish a bright-line rule authorizing the search of a vehicle's passenger compartment incident to a recent occupant's arrest. The search incident to Davis' arrest in this case followed the Eleventh Circuit's precedent to the letter. Although the search turned out to be unconstitutional under *Gant*, all agree that the officers' conduct was in strict compliance with then-binding Circuit law and was not culpable in any way.
>
> Under our exclusionary-rule precedents, this acknowledged absence of police culpability dooms Davis' claim. Police practices trigger the harsh sanction of exclusion only when they are deliberate enough to yield meaningful deterrence, and culpable enough to be worth the price paid by the justice system. The conduct of the officers here was neither of these things. The officers who conducted the search did not violate Davis' Fourth Amendment rights deliberately, recklessly, or with gross

negligence. Nor does this case involve any recurring or systemic negligence on the part of law enforcement. The police acted in strict compliance with binding precedent, and their behavior was not wrongful. Unless the exclusionary rule is to become a strict-liability regime, it can have no application in this case.

Indeed, in 27 years of practice under *Leon*'s good-faith exception, we have never applied the exclusionary rule to suppress evidence obtained as a result of nonculpable, innocent police conduct. If the police in this case had reasonably relied on a warrant in conducting their search (see *Leon*), or on an erroneous warrant record in a government database (see *Herring*), the exclusionary rule would not apply.

About all that exclusion would deter in this case is conscientious police work. That is not the kind of deterrence the exclusionary rule seeks to foster. We have stated before, and we reaffirm today, that the harsh sanction of exclusion should not be applied to deter objectively reasonable law enforcement activity. Evidence obtained during a search conducted in reasonable reliance on binding precedent is not subject to the exclusionary rule.

The Good Faith Exception to the Exclusionary Rule and Negligent Mistakes

1.   The exclusionary rule does not bar the admission of evidence obtained by police who, in good faith, reasonably rely on a warrant that is later found to be unsupported by probable cause or otherwise technically deficient. The officer's reliance on the magistrate's probable cause determination and on the technical sufficiency of the warrant must be objectively reasonable.

2.   The officer will have no reasonable grounds for believing that the warrant was properly issued and the good faith exception will not apply in any of the following circumstances:

a.   The magistrate or judge issuing the warrant was misled by information in an affidavit that the affiant knew was false or would have known was false except for his reckless disregard of the truth.

b.   The magistrate or judge issuing the warrant wholly abandoned his judicial role.

c.   The warrant is based on an affidavit so lacking in indicia of probable cause as to render official belief in its existence entirely unreasonable.

    d.   The warrant is so facially deficient—in failing to particularize the place to be searched or the things to be seized—that the executing officers cannot reasonably presume it to be valid.

3.   The exclusionary rule should be invoked only for deliberate, reckless, or grossly negligent conduct by the police. Minor mistakes resulting from ordinary and isolated negligence, including those made by police personnel, judges, or court employees, should not trigger the exclusionary rule.

4.   The exclusionary rule does not apply when the police conduct a search in objectively reasonable reliance on binding judicial precedent, even when the law is later changed while the case is pending on appeal.

E. THE "KNOCK AND ANNOUNCE" EXCEPTION

As noted in Chapter 4, in *Wilson v. Arkansas*, 514 U.S. 927 (1995), and in *Richards v. Wisconsin*, 520 U.S. 385 (1997), the Supreme Court held that in the absence of exigent circumstances, the police must knock and announce their presence before entering a residence to execute a search warrant. In *Hudson v. Michigan*, however, the Court held that the exclusionary rule does not apply to evidence discovered after the police violate the "knock and announce" requirement.

HUDSON V. MICHIGAN
547 U.S. 586 (2006)

JUSTICE SCALIA delivered the opinion of the Court.

We decide whether violation of the "knock-and-announce" rule requires the suppression of all evidence found in the search.

I

Police obtained a warrant authorizing a search for drugs and firearms at the home of petitioner Booker Hudson. They discovered both. Large quantities of drugs were found, including cocaine rocks in Hudson's pocket. A loaded gun was lodged between the cushion and armrest of the chair in which he was sitting. Hudson was charged under Michigan law with unlawful drug and firearm possession.

This case is before us only because of the method of entry into the house. When the police arrived to execute the warrant, they announced their presence, but waited only a short time—perhaps three to five seconds—before turning the knob of the unlocked front door and entering Hudson's home. Hudson moved to suppress all the inculpatory evidence, arguing that the premature entry violated his Fourth Amendment rights.

The Michigan trial court granted his motion. On interlocutory review, the Michigan Court of Appeals reversed, relying on Michigan

Supreme Court cases holding that suppression is inappropriate when entry is made pursuant to warrant but without proper "knock and announce." Hudson was convicted of drug possession.

II

The common-law principle that law enforcement officers must announce their presence and provide residents an opportunity to open the door is an ancient one. Since 1917, when Congress passed the Espionage Act, this traditional protection has been part of federal statutory law. Finally, in *Wilson v. Arkansas*, 514 U.S. 927 (1995), we were asked whether the rule was also a command of the Fourth Amendment. Tracing its origins in our English legal heritage, we concluded that it was.

We recognized that the new constitutional rule we had announced is not easily applied. *Wilson* and cases following it have noted the many situations in which it is not necessary to knock and announce. It is not necessary when "circumstances present a threat of physical violence," or if there is "reason to believe that evidence would likely be destroyed if advance notice were given," or if knocking and announcing would be "futile." *Richards v. Wisconsin*, 520 U.S. 385, 394 (1997). We require only that police "have a reasonable suspicion under the particular circumstances" that one of these grounds for failing to knock and announce exists, and we have acknowledged that "this showing is not high."

When the knock-and-announce rule does apply, it is not easy to determine precisely what officers must do. How many seconds' wait are too few? Our "reasonable wait time" standard is necessarily vague. *U.S. v. Banks*, 540 U.S. 31 (2003), (a drug case, like this one) held that the proper measure was not how long it would take the resident to reach the door, but how long it would take to dispose of the suspected drugs—but that such a time (15 to 20 seconds in that case) would necessarily be extended when, for instance, the suspected contraband was not easily concealed. If our *ex post* evaluation is subject to such calculations, it is unsurprising that, *ex ante*, police officers about to encounter someone who may try to harm them will be uncertain how long to wait.

Happily, these issues do not confront us here. From the trial level onward, Michigan has conceded that the entry was a knock-and-announce violation. The issue here is remedy. *Wilson* specifically declined to decide whether the exclusionary rule is appropriate for violation of the knock-and-announce requirement. That question is squarely before us now.

III

In *Weeks v. U.S.*, 232 U.S. 383 (1914), we adopted the federal exclusionary rule for evidence that was unlawfully seized from a home without a warrant in violation of the Fourth Amendment. We began applying the same rule to the States, through the Fourteenth Amendment, in *Mapp v. Ohio*, 367 U.S. 643 (1961).

Suppression of evidence, however, has always been our last resort, not our first impulse. The exclusionary rule generates substantial social costs, which sometimes include setting the guilty free and the dangerous at large. We have therefore been cautious against expanding it, and have repeatedly emphasized that the rule's costly toll upon truth-seeking and law enforcement objectives presents a high obstacle for those urging its application. We have rejected indiscriminate application of the rule, and have held it to be applicable only where its remedial objectives are thought most efficaciously served—that is, where its deterrence benefits outweigh its substantial social costs.

In other words, exclusion may not be premised on the mere fact that a constitutional violation was a "but-for" cause of obtaining evidence. Our cases show that but-for causality is only a necessary, not a sufficient, condition for suppression. In this case, of course, the constitutional violation of an illegal *manner* of entry was *not* a but-for cause of obtaining the evidence. Whether that preliminary misstep had occurred *or not,* the police would have executed the warrant they had obtained, and would have discovered the gun and drugs inside the house. But even if the illegal entry here could be characterized as a but-for cause of discovering what was inside, we have never held that evidence is "fruit of the poisonous tree" simply because it would not have come to light but for the illegal actions of the police. Rather, but-for cause, or causation in the logical sense alone, can be too attenuated to justify exclusion. Even in the early days of the exclusionary rule, we declined to hold that all evidence is "fruit of the poisonous tree" simply because it would not have come to light *but for* the illegal actions of the police. Rather, the more apt question in such a case is "whether, granting establishment of the primary illegality, the evidence to which instant objection is made has been come at by exploitation of that illegality or instead by means sufficiently distinguishable to be purged of the primary taint." *Wong Sun v. U.S.*, 371 U.S. 471, 487–488 (1963).

Attenuation can occur, of course, when the causal connection is remote. Attenuation also occurs when, even given a direct causal connection, the interest protected by the constitutional guarantee that has been violated would not be served by suppression of the evidence obtained.

For this reason, cases excluding the fruits of unlawful warrantless searches say nothing about the appropriateness of exclusion to vindicate the interests protected by the knock-and-announce requirement. Until a valid warrant has issued, citizens are entitled to shield "their persons, houses, papers, and effects" from the government's scrutiny. Exclusion of the evidence obtained by a warrantless search vindicates that entitlement. The interests protected by the knock-and-announce requirement are quite different—and do not include the shielding of potential evidence from the government's eyes.

One of those interests is the protection of human life and limb, because an unannounced entry may provoke violence in supposed self-defense by the surprised resident. Another interest is the protection of property. Breaking a house (as the old cases typically put it) absent an announcement would penalize someone who "did not know of the process, of which, if he had notice, it is to be presumed that he would obey it." The knock-and-announce rule gives individuals the opportunity to comply with the law and to avoid the destruction of property occasioned by a forcible entry. And thirdly, the knock-and-announce rule protects those elements of privacy and dignity that can be destroyed by a sudden entrance. It gives residents the opportunity to prepare themselves for the entry of the police. The brief interlude between announcement and entry with a warrant may be the opportunity that an individual has to pull on clothes or get out of bed. In other words, it assures the opportunity to collect oneself before answering the door.

What the knock-and-announce rule has never protected, however, is one's interest in preventing the government from seeing or taking evidence described in a warrant. Since the interests that *were* violated in this case have nothing to do with the seizure of the evidence, the exclusionary rule is inapplicable.

Quite apart from the requirement of unattenuated causation, the exclusionary rule has never been applied except where its deterrence benefits outweigh its substantial social costs. The costs here are considerable. In addition to the grave adverse consequence that exclusion of relevant incriminating evidence always entails (viz., the risk of releasing dangerous criminals into society), imposing that massive remedy for a knock-and-announce violation would generate a constant flood of alleged failures to observe the rule, and claims that any asserted *Richards* justification for a no-knock entry had inadequate support. The cost of entering this lottery would be small, but the jackpot enormous: suppression of all evidence, amounting in many cases to a get-out-of-jail-free card. Courts would experience as never before the reality that the exclusionary rule frequently requires extensive litigation to determine whether particular evidence must be excluded. Unlike the warrant or *Miranda* requirements, compliance with which is readily determined (either there was or was not a warrant; either the *Miranda* warning was given, or it was not), what constituted a "reasonable wait time" in a particular case (or, for that matter, how many seconds the police in fact waited), or whether there was "reasonable suspicion" of the sort that would invoke the *Richards* exceptions, is difficult for the trial court to determine and even more difficult for an appellate court to review.

Another consequence of the incongruent remedy Hudson proposes would be police officers' refraining from timely entry after knocking and announcing. As we have observed, the amount of time they must wait is necessarily uncertain. If the consequences of running afoul of the rule were so massive, officers would be inclined to wait longer than the law requires—producing preventable violence against officers in some cases, and the destruction of evidence in many others. We deemed these consequences severe enough to produce our unanimous agreement that a mere "reasonable suspicion" that knocking and announcing under the particular circumstances, would be dangerous or futile, or that it would inhibit the effective investigation of the crime, will cause the requirement to yield.

Next to these substantial social costs we must consider the deterrence benefits, existence of which is a necessary condition for exclusion. To begin with, the value of deterrence depends upon the strength of the incentive to commit the forbidden act. Viewed from this perspective, deterrence of knock-and-announce violations is not worth a lot. Violation of the warrant requirement sometimes produces incriminating evidence that could not otherwise be obtained. But ignoring knock-and-announce can realistically be expected to achieve absolutely nothing except the prevention of destruction of evidence and the avoidance of life-threatening resistance by occupants of the premises— dangers which, if there is even "reasonable suspicion" of their existence, *suspend the knock-and-announce requirement anyway*. Massive deterrence is hardly required.

It seems to us not even true, as Hudson contends, that without suppression there will be no deterrence of knock-and-announce violations at all. Of course even if this assertion were accurate, it would not necessarily justify suppression. Assuming (as the assertion must) that civil suit is not an effective deterrent, one can think of many forms of police misconduct that are similarly "undeterred." When, for example, a confessed suspect in the killing of a police officer, arrested (along with incriminating evidence) in a lawful warranted search, is subjected to physical abuse at the station house, would it seriously be suggested that the evidence must be excluded, since that is the only "effective deterrent"? And what, other than civil suit, is the "effective deterrent" of police violation of an already-confessed suspect's Sixth Amendment rights by denying him prompt access to counsel? Many would regard these violated rights as more significant than the right not to be intruded upon in one's nightclothes—and yet nothing but "ineffective" civil suit is available as a deterrent. And the police incentive for those violations is arguably greater than the incentive for disregarding the knock-and-announce rule.

Hudson points out that few published decisions to date announce huge awards for knock-and-announce violations. But this is an unhelpful statistic. Even if we thought that only large damages would deter police misconduct, we do not know how many claims have been settled, or indeed how many violations have occurred that produced anything more than nominal injury. It is clear, at least, that the lower courts are allowing colorable knock-and-announce suits to go forward, unimpeded by assertions of qualified immunity.

Another development over the past half-century that deters civil-rights violations is the increasing professionalism of police forces, including a new emphasis on internal police discipline. Numerous sources are now available to teach officers and their supervisors what is required of them under this Court's cases, how to respect constitutional guarantees in various situations, and how to craft an effective regime for internal discipline. Failure to teach and enforce constitutional requirements exposes municipalities to financial liability. Moreover, modern police forces are staffed with professionals; it is not credible to assert that internal discipline, which can limit successful careers, will not have a deterrent effect. There is also evidence that the increasing use of various forms of citizen review can enhance police accountability.

In sum, the social costs of applying the exclusionary rule to knock-and-announce violations are considerable; the incentive to such violations is minimal to begin with, and the extant deterrences against them are substantial—incomparably greater than the factors deterring warrantless entries when *Mapp* was decided. Resort to the massive remedy of suppressing evidence of guilt is unjustified.

JUSTICE BREYER, with whom JUSTICE STEVENS, JUSTICE SOUTER, and JUSTICE GINSBURG join, dissenting.

In *Wilson v. Arkansas*, 514 U.S. 927 (1995), a unanimous Court held that the Fourth Amendment normally requires law enforcement officers to knock and announce their presence before entering a dwelling. Today's opinion holds that evidence seized from a home following a violation of this requirement need not be suppressed

As a result, the Court destroys the strongest legal incentive to comply with the Constitution's knock-and-announce requirement. And the Court does so without significant support in precedent. At least I can find no such support in the many Fourth Amendment cases the Court has decided in the near century since it first set forth the exclusionary principle in *Weeks v. U.S.*, 232 U.S. 383 (1914).

Today's opinion is thus doubly troubling. It represents a significant departure from the Court's precedents. And it weakens, perhaps destroys, much of the practical value of the Constitution's knock-and-announce protection.

Why is application of the exclusionary rule any the less necessary here? Without such a rule, as in *Mapp*, police know that they can ignore the Constitution's requirements without risking suppression of evidence discovered after an unreasonable entry. As in *Mapp*, some government officers will find it easier, or believe it less risky, to proceed with what they consider a necessary search immediately and without the requisite constitutional (say, warrant or knock-and-announce) compliance.

Of course, the State or the Federal Government may provide alternative remedies for knock-and-announce violations. But that circumstance was true of *Mapp* as well. What reason is there to believe that those remedies (such as private damages actions), which the Court found inadequate in *Mapp*, can adequately deter unconstitutional police behavior here?

To argue, as the majority does, that new remedies, such as [federal civil rights actions under 42 U.S.C. § 1983] or better trained police, make suppression unnecessary is to argue that *Wolf*, not *Mapp*, is now the law. To argue that there may be few civil suits because violations may produce nothing "more than nominal injury" is to confirm, not to deny, the inability of civil suits to deter violations.

The majority's "substantial social costs" argument is an argument against the Fourth Amendment's exclusionary principle itself. And it is an argument that this Court, until now, has consistently rejected.

The "Knock and Announce" Exception to the Exclusionary Rule

In the absence of exigent circumstances, police must knock and announce their presence before entering a residence to execute a search warrant. Evidence discovered following a "knock and announce" violation will not, however, be suppressed under the exclusionary rule.

The cases in this Chapter describing various exceptions to the exclusionary rule mark a significant change from the Supreme Court's approach in *Mapp v. Ohio*, 367 U.S. 643 (1961). As explained in Chapter 2, the Court in *Mapp* established the exclusionary rule as the basic remedy for Fourth Amendment violations in order to deter police misconduct, protect the constitutional rights of criminal defendants, and safeguard judicial integrity. The majority opinions in most of the cases in this Chapter, by contrast, largely abandon any discussion of the rights of criminal defendants and the importance of judicial integrity and instead focus almost entirely on the deterrence rationale, asking whether the application of the exclusionary rule will deter police misconduct in particular circumstances, and whether that deterrence is worth the cost in terms of lost evidence and criminal convictions. Do you agree with this shift in emphasis? Do we reduce constitutional rights to mere words and undermine the integrity of the judiciary by admitting illegally obtained evidence in criminal trials, or are constitutional values and the integrity of the judiciary placed at risk when important evidence is suppressed and the guilty go free? Ultimately, there are no easy answers to these questions at the heart of the Fourth Amendment and Investigative Criminal Procedure.

PART III

LIMITS ON POLICE INTERROGATION AND THE PRIVILEGE AGAINST SELF-INCRIMINATION

▪ ▪ ▪

> **Amendment V:** No person shall be held to answer for a capital, or otherwise infamous crime, unless on a presentment or indictment of a Grand Jury, except in cases arising in the land or naval forces, or in the Militia, when in actual service in time of War or public danger; <u>nor shall any person</u> be subject for the same offence to be twice put in jeopardy of life or limb; nor shall <u>be compelled in any criminal case to be a witness against himself, nor be deprived of life, liberty, or property, without due process of law</u>; nor shall private property be taken for public use, without just compensation.
>
> **Amendment VI:** <u>In all criminal prosecutions, the accused shall enjoy the right</u> to a speedy and public trial, by an impartial jury of the State and district wherein the crime shall have been committed, which district shall have been previously ascertained by law, and to be informed of the nature and cause of the accusation; to be confronted with the witnesses against him; to have compulsory process for obtaining witnesses in his favor, and <u>to have the Assistance of Counsel for his defence</u>.
>
> **Amendment XIV, Section 1:** All persons born or naturalized in the United States, and subject to the jurisdiction thereof, are citizens of the United States and of the State wherein they reside. No State shall make or enforce any law which shall abridge the privileges or immunities of citizens of the United States; <u>nor shall any State deprive any person of life, liberty, or property, without due process of law</u>; nor deny to any person within its jurisdiction the equal protection of the laws.

Part II of this book, comprising Chapters 3 through 8, presented the rules and doctrines regulating searches and seizures, critical tools used by law enforcement to investigate crimes, gather evidence, and prosecute offenders. This Part addresses another investigatory technique often used by law enforcement—questioning or "interrogation" of suspects. In many cases, particularly those with scant physical evidence and no apparent witnesses, information elicited by police from potential suspects may prove critical in solving the crime and securing justice for the victims. While few would doubt the value of police questioning of suspects as an investigatory tool, it is—like searches and seizures—subject to certain limits. These limits are derived primarily from the Fifth Amendment's privilege against compulsory self-incrimination, from the Sixth Amendment's guarantee of assistance of counsel for criminal defendants, and from the due process clauses of the Fifth and Fourteenth Amendments.

The Supreme Court has developed an array of rules and doctrines to regulate the broad variety of circumstances in which police question or interrogate criminal suspects and obtain incriminating statements for later use at trial. The following four Chapters organize and discuss these rules and doctrines. Chapter 9 describes the requirement, as a matter of due process, that any statement introduced against a criminal defendant be one that was given "voluntarily." Chapter 10 examines the rules governing custodial interrogation developed in *Miranda v. Arizona*, 384 U.S. 436 (1966), and subsequent cases. Chapter 11 addresses some additional protections, rooted in the Sixth Amendment's right to counsel, against police efforts to elicit incriminating statements from a defendant after criminal charges have been filed. And Chapter 12 considers the Fifth Amendment's privilege against compulsory self-incrimination in situations that do not involve police interrogation.

As you read each of the following Chapters, consider the Supreme Court's views and your own views about the basic question at the heart of these materials: How do we protect the constitutional rights of individuals while preserving law enforcement's ability to investigate crimes and question criminal suspects?

CHAPTER 9

DUE PROCESS AND POLICE INTERROGATION

■ ■ ■

Long before *Miranda v. Arizona*, 384 U.S. 436 (1966), added a new layer of constitutional protection for those subjected to custodial interrogation by the police, the Supreme Court developed a significant body of law requiring proof that a confession was "voluntary" before it could be admitted into evidence against the accused. While the *Miranda* line of cases—presented in Chapter 10—provide specific protections for those interrogated while in police custody, the "voluntariness" requirement described in this Chapter protects those who make incriminating statements to police even when they are not in custody.

One important reason why a confession that is involuntary or the product of coercion is excluded is that it may be unreliable, resulting in a wrongful conviction. But even when a coerced confession is reliable— where, for example, there is strong corroborating evidence—exclusion may be the only effective way to deter abusive police practices and protect constitutional rights. The Supreme Court eloquently summarized these sentiments in *Jackson v. Denno*, 378 U.S. 368 (1964):

> It is now inescapably clear that the Fourteenth Amendment forbids the use of involuntary confessions not only because of the probable unreliability of confessions that are obtained in a manner deemed coercive, but also because of the strongly felt attitude of our society that important human values are sacrificed where an agency of the government, in the course of securing a conviction, wrings a confession out of an accused against his will, and because of the deep-rooted feeling that the police must obey the law while enforcing the law; that in the end life and liberty can be as much endangered from illegal methods used to convict those thought to be criminals as from the actual criminals themselves.

A. THE ORIGINS OF THE "VOLUNTARINESS" REQUIREMENT

In *Hopt v. People of the Territory of Utah*, 110 U.S. 574 (1884), the Supreme Court, relying heavily on English common law decisions, declared that a confession "should not go to the jury unless it appears to the court to have been voluntary"; if "freely and voluntarily made," however, a confession "is evidence of the most satisfactory character." Thirteen years later, in *Bram v. U.S.*, the Supreme Court held, for the first time, that the admission into evidence of an involuntary confession violated the Fifth Amendment's privilege against compulsory self-incrimination.

BRAM V. U.S.
168 U.S. 532 (1897)

A sailor accused Bram, the first officer of an American ship on the high seas, of murdering the captain. Bram was taken into custody, and when the ship reached the shore, a detective stripped him of his clothing and searched him. When the detective confronted Bram with the sailor's accusations, Bram denied any knowledge about the murder, but also said that the sailor could not have been in a position to observe him. At trial, the detective testified for the prosecution regarding Bram's statements. Bram was convicted and sentenced to death.

On appeal, the Supreme Court held that a confession must be voluntary under the Fifth Amendment:

> In criminal trials, in the courts of the United States, wherever a question arises whether a confession is incompetent because not voluntary, the issue is controlled by that portion of the Fifth Amendment to the Constitution of the United States commanding that no person "shall be compelled in any criminal case to be a witness against himself." The legal principle by which the admissibility of the confession of an accused person is to be determined is expressed as follows: "But a confession, in order to be admissible, must be free and voluntary; that is, must not be extracted by any sort of threats or violence, nor obtained by any direct or implied promises, however slight, nor by the exertion of any improper influence. A confession can never be received in evidence where the prisoner has been influenced by any threat or promise; for the law cannot measure the force of the influence used, or decide upon its effect upon the mind of the prisoner, and therefore excludes the declaration if any degree of influence has been exerted."

After careful examination of all of the facts and circumstances, the Court concluded that Bram's statement was involuntary:

> When all the surrounding circumstances are considered, not only is the claim that the statement was voluntary overthrown, but the impression is irresistibly produced that it must necessarily have been the result of either hope or fear, or both, operating on the mind. Bram had been brought from confinement to the office

of the detective, and there, when alone with him, while he was in the act of being stripped, or had been stripped, of his clothing, was interrogated by the officer, who was thus, while putting the questions and receiving answers thereto, exercising complete authority and control over the person he was interrogating. Although these facts may not, when isolated each from the other, be sufficient to warrant the inference that an influence compelling a statement had been exerted; yet, when taken as a whole, in conjunction with the nature of the communication made, they give room to the strongest inference that the statements of Bram were not made by one who, in law, could be considered a free agent.

The voluntariness requirement announced in *Bram*—rooted in the Fifth Amendment's privilege against self-incrimination—applied only to confessions introduced in federal courts. Nearly 40 years after *Bram*, in *Brown v. Mississippi*, the Supreme Court also barred involuntary confessions in state courts. When *Brown* was decided in 1936, the Supreme Court had not yet incorporated the Fifth Amendment's privilege against self-incrimination, making it applicable to the states. As a result, the Supreme Court's holding in *Brown v. Mississippi* was rooted in the Due Process Clause of the Fourteenth Amendment.

BROWN V. MISSISSIPPI
297 U.S. 278 (1936)

CHIEF JUSTICE HUGHES delivered the opinion of the Court.

The question in this case is whether convictions, which rest solely upon confessions shown to have been extorted by officers of the state by brutality and violence, are consistent with the due process of law required by the Fourteenth Amendment of the Constitution of the United States.

Petitioners were indicted for the murder of one Raymond Stewart, whose death occurred on March 30, 1934. They were indicted on April 4, 1934, and were then arraigned and pleaded not guilty. Counsel were appointed by the court to defend them. Trial was begun the next morning and was concluded on the following day, when they were found guilty and sentenced to death.

Aside from the confessions, there was no evidence sufficient to warrant the submission of the case to the jury. After a preliminary inquiry, testimony as to the confessions was received over the objection of defendants' counsel. Defendants then testified that the confessions were false and had been procured by physical torture.

There is no dispute as to the facts upon this point, and as they are clearly and adequately stated in the dissenting opinion of Judge Griffith (with whom Judge Anderson concurred)—showing both the extreme brutality of the measures to extort the confessions and the participation of the state authorities—we quote this part of his opinion in full, as follows:

The crime with which these defendants, all ignorant negroes, are charged, was discovered about 1 o'clock p.m. on Friday, March 30, 1934. On that night one Dial, a deputy sheriff, accompanied by others, came to the home of Ellington, one of the defendants, and requested him to accompany them to the house of the deceased, and there a number of white men were gathered, who began to accuse the defendant of the crime. Upon his denial they seized him, and with the participation of the deputy they hanged him by a rope to the limb of a tree, and, having let him down, they hung him again, and when he was let down the second time, and he still protested his innocence, he was tied to a tree and whipped, and, still declining to accede to the demands that he confess, he was finally released, and he returned with some difficulty to his home, suffering intense pain and agony. The record of the testimony shows that the signs of the rope on his neck were plainly visible during the so-called trial. A day or two thereafter the said deputy, accompanied by another, returned to the home of the said defendant and arrested him, and departed with the prisoner towards the jail in an adjoining county, but went by a route which led into the state of Alabama; and while on the way, in that state, the deputy stopped and again severely whipped the defendant, declaring that he would continue the whipping until he confessed, and the defendant then agreed to confess to such a statement as the deputy would dictate, and he did so, after which he was delivered to jail.

The other two defendants, Ed Brown and Henry Shields, were also arrested and taken to the same jail. On Sunday night, April 1, 1934, the same deputy, accompanied by a number of white men, one of whom was also an officer, and by the jailer, came to the jail, and the two last named defendants were made to strip and they were laid over chairs and their backs were cut to pieces with a leather strap with buckles on it, and they were likewise made by the said deputy definitely to understand that the whipping would be continued unless and until they confessed, and not only confessed, but confessed in every matter of detail as demanded by those present; and in this manner the defendants confessed the crime, and, as the whippings progressed and were repeated, they changed or adjusted their confession in all particulars of detail so as to conform to the demands of their torturers. When the confessions had been obtained in the exact form and contents as desired by the mob, they left with the parting admonition and warning that, if the defendants changed their story at any time in any respect from that last stated, the perpetrators of the outrage would administer the same or equally effective treatment.

All this having been accomplished, on the next day, that is, on Monday, April 2, when the defendants had been given time to recuperate somewhat from the tortures to which they had been subjected, the two sheriffs, one of the county where the crime was committed, and the other of the county of the jail in which the prisoners were confined, came to the jail, accompanied by eight other persons, some of them deputies, there to hear the free and voluntary confession of these miserable and abject defendants. The sheriff of the county of the crime admitted that he had heard of the whipping, but averred that he had no personal knowledge of it. He admitted that one of the defendants, when brought before him to confess, was limping and did not sit down, and that this particular defendant then and there stated that he had been strapped so severely that he could not sit down, and, as already stated, the signs of the rope on the neck of another of the defendants were plainly visible to all. Nevertheless the solemn farce of hearing the free and voluntary confessions was gone through with, and these two sheriffs and one other person then present were the three witnesses used in court to establish the so-called confessions, which were received by the court and admitted in evidence over the objections of the defendants duly entered of record as each of the said three witnesses delivered their alleged testimony.

The state is free to regulate the procedure of its courts in accordance with its own conceptions of policy, unless in so doing it offends some principle of justice so rooted in the traditions and conscience of our people as to be ranked as fundamental. But the freedom of the state in establishing its policy is the freedom of constitutional government and is limited by the requirement of due process of law. Because a state may dispense with a jury trial, it does not follow that it may substitute trial by ordeal. The rack and torture chamber may not be substituted for the witness stand. The state may not permit an accused to be hurried to conviction under mob domination—where the whole proceeding is but a mask—without supplying corrective process. The state may not deny to the accused the aid of counsel. Nor may a state, through the action of its officers, contrive a conviction through the pretense of a trial which in truth is but used as a means of depriving a defendant of liberty through a deliberate deception of court and jury by the presentation of testimony known to be perjured. And the trial equally is a mere pretense where the state authorities have contrived a conviction resting solely upon confessions obtained by violence. The due process clause requires that state action, whether through one agency or another, shall be consistent with the fundamental principles of liberty and justice which lie at the base of all our civil and political institutions. It would be difficult to conceive of methods more revolting to the sense of justice than those taken to procure the confessions of these petitioners, and the use of the confessions thus obtained as the basis for conviction and sentence was a clear denial of due process.

B. APPLICATION OF THE "VOLUNTARINESS" REQUIREMENT

In *Lego v. Twomey*, 404 U.S. 477 (1972), the Supreme Court held that before a defendant's confession can be introduced into evidence at trial, the prosecution must prove, by at least a preponderance of the evidence, that the confession was voluntary. Even if a confession is found to be voluntary and is admitted into evidence, however, the defendant may still present evidence that it was obtained in circumstances that make it unreliable. As the Supreme Court explained in *Crane v. Kentucky*, 476 U.S. 683 (1986):

> The circumstances surrounding the taking of a confession can be highly relevant to two separate inquiries, one legal and one factual. The manner in which a statement was extracted is, of course, relevant to the purely legal question of its voluntariness, a question most, but not all, States assign to the trial judge alone to resolve. But the physical and psychological environment that yielded the confession can also be of substantial relevance to the ultimate factual issue of the defendant's guilt or innocence. Confessions, even those that have been found to be voluntary, are not conclusive of guilt. And, as with any other part of the prosecutor's case, a confession may be shown to be insufficiently corroborated or otherwise unworthy of belief. Indeed, stripped of the power to describe to the jury the circumstances that prompted his confession, the defendant is effectively disabled from answering the one question every rational juror needs answered: If the defendant is innocent, why did he previously admit his guilt? Accordingly, regardless of whether the defendant marshaled the same evidence earlier in support of an unsuccessful motion to suppress, and entirely independent of any question of voluntariness, a defendant's case may stand or fall on his ability to convince the jury that the manner in which the confession was obtained casts doubt on its credibility.

In *Haynes v. Washington*, 373 U.S. 503 (1963), the Supreme Court noted that determining the voluntariness of a confession requires examination of the "totality of circumstances." In making the voluntariness determination, the Court has identified a number of relevant factors, including: the use of force or threats of force; the amount of time spent in police custody or under interrogation; deprivation of food, sleep, medical care, or other necessities; psychological ploys and police deception; and the age, education, and mental condition of the suspect. Many of these factors are often at work when the Supreme Court concludes that a confession is involuntary.

1.   USE OF FORCE OR THREATS OF FORCE

As *Brown v. Mississippi* powerfully demonstrates, a confession that is the product of physical abuse is not voluntary. But even mere threats of violence are sufficient to render a confession involuntary. *Payne v. Arkansas* is a good example.

PAYNE V. ARKANSAS
356 U.S. 560 (1958)

Frank Payne, a murder suspect, was held by police and repeatedly interrogated over a period of three days. On the third day, the local police chief told Payne that there was a mob of 30 to 40 people waiting to get him outside the jail. The chief said he would try to keep the mob away if Payne made a confession.

The Supreme Court noted that the absence of actual violence does not render a confession voluntary: "That petitioner was not physically tortured affords no answer to the question whether the confession was coerced, for there is torture of mind as well as body; the will is as much affected by fear as by force." Citing a number of factors, "particularly the culminating threat of mob violence," the Court concluded that Payne's confession was coerced and did not constitute an "expression of free choice."

In *Beecher v. Alabama*, police pointed their guns at the head of a suspect in order to extract a confession. Several days later, while in the hospital recovering from injuries, the suspect signed a written statement of the confession. The Supreme Court found that the confession was involuntary.

BEECHER V. ALABAMA
389 U.S. 35 (1967)

A day after Johnny Beecher escaped from a prison road gang, a woman's body was found about a mile from the prison camp. The next day, police saw Beecher as he fled into an open field and fired a bullet into his right leg. Beecher fell, and the local chief of police pressed a loaded gun to his face while another officer pointed a rifle against the side of his head. The police chief asked Beecher if he had raped and killed a white woman. Beecher said he had not. The police chief called him a liar and said, "If you don't tell the truth, I am going to kill you." The other officer then fired his rifle next to Beecher's ear, and Beecher immediately confessed. Five days later, while in the hospital, Beecher signed two written statements that were prepared for him. At the time, Beecher was feverish, in intense pain, and was regularly receiving morphine for the wound on his right leg. The confession at gunpoint was not introduced at Beecher's trial, but the written and signed statements were admitted over Beecher's objection.

Noting that "there was no break in the stream of events" from the initial confession at gunpoint to the signed statements five days later, the Supreme Court concluded that Beecher's statements were "the product of gross coercion" and involuntary.

In *Arizona v. Fulminante*, the Supreme Court found that the defendant's confession to a prison informant was made involuntarily, in response to threats of physical violence by other prisoners.

ARIZONA V. FULMINANTE
499 U.S. 279 (1991)

JUSTICE WHITE delivered the opinion of the Court.

The Arizona Supreme Court ruled in this case that respondent Oreste Fulminante's confession, received in evidence at his trial for murder, had been coerced and that its use against him was barred by the Fifth and Fourteenth Amendments to the United States Constitution. The court also held that the harmless-error rule could not be used to save the conviction. We affirm the judgment of the Arizona court, although for different reasons than those upon which that court relied.

I

Early in the morning of September 14, 1982, Fulminante called the Mesa, Arizona, Police Department to report that his 11-year-old stepdaughter, Jeneane Michelle Hunt, was missing. He had been caring for Jeneane while his wife, Jeneane's mother, was in the hospital. Two days later, Jeneane's body was found in the desert east of Mesa. She had been shot twice in the head at close range with a large caliber weapon, and a ligature was around her neck. Because of the decomposed condition of the body, it was impossible to tell whether she had been sexually assaulted.

Fulminante's statements to police concerning Jeneane's disappearance and his relationship with her contained a number of inconsistencies, and he became a suspect in her killing. When no charges were filed against him, Fulminante left Arizona for New Jersey. Fulminante was later convicted in New Jersey on federal charges of possession of a firearm by a felon.

Fulminante was incarcerated in the Ray Brook Federal Correctional Institution in New York. There he became friends with another inmate, Anthony Sarivola, then serving a 60-day sentence for extortion. The two men came to spend several hours a day together. Sarivola, a former police officer, had been involved in loansharking for organized crime but then became a paid informant for the Federal Bureau of Investigation. While at Ray Brook, he masqueraded as an organized crime figure. After becoming friends with Fulminante, Sarivola heard a rumor that Fulminante was suspected of killing a child in Arizona. Sarivola then raised the subject with Fulminante in several conversations, but Fulminante repeatedly denied any involvement in Jeneane's death. During one conversation, he told Sarivola that Jeneane had been killed by bikers looking for drugs; on another occasion, he said he did not know what had happened. Sarivola passed this information on to an agent of the Federal Bureau of Investigation, who instructed Sarivola to find out more.

Sarivola learned more one evening in October 1983, as he and Fulminante walked together around the prison track. Sarivola said that he knew Fulminante was "starting to get some tough treatment and whatnot" from other inmates because of the rumor. Sarivola offered to protect Fulminante from his fellow inmates, but told him, "You have to tell me about it, you know. I mean, in other words, for me to give you any help." Fulminante then admitted to Sarivola that he had driven Jeneane to the desert on his motorcycle, where he choked her, sexually assaulted her, and made her beg for her life, before shooting her twice in the head.

Sarivola was released from prison in November 1983. Fulminante was released the following May, only to be arrested the next month for another weapons violation. On September 4, 1984, Fulminante was indicted in Arizona for the first-degree murder of Jeneane.

Prior to trial, Fulminante moved to suppress the statement he had given Sarivola in prison, as well as a second confession he had given to Donna Sarivola, then Anthony Sarivola's fiancée and later his wife, following his May 1984 release from prison. He asserted that the confession to Sarivola was coerced, and that the second confession was the "fruit" of the first. Following the hearing, the trial court denied the motion to suppress, specifically finding that, based on the stipulated facts, the confessions were voluntary. The State introduced both confessions as evidence at trial, and on December 19, 1985, Fulminante was convicted of Jeneane's murder. He was subsequently sentenced to death.

Fulminante appealed, arguing, among other things, that his confession to Sarivola was the product of coercion and that its admission at trial violated his rights to due process under the Fifth and Fourteenth Amendments to the United States Constitution. After considering the evidence at trial as well as the stipulated facts before the trial court on the motion to suppress, the Arizona Supreme Court held that the confession was coerced, but initially determined that the admission of the confession at trial was harmless error, because of the overwhelming nature of the evidence against Fulminante. Upon Fulminante's motion for reconsideration, however, the court ruled that this Court's precedent precluded the use of the harmless-error analysis in the case of a coerced confession. The court therefore reversed the conviction and ordered that Fulminante be retried without the use of the confession to Sarivola.

II

We deal first with the State's contention that the court below erred in holding Fulminante's confession to have been coerced. In applying the totality of the circumstances test to determine that the confession to Sarivola was coerced, the Arizona Supreme Court focused on a number of relevant facts. First, the court noted that "because Fulminante was an alleged child murderer, he was in danger of physical harm at the hands of other inmates." In addition, Sarivola was aware that Fulminante had been receiving "rough treatment from the guys." Using his knowledge of these threats, Sarivola offered to protect Fulminante in exchange for a confession to Jeneane's murder, and "in response to Sarivola's offer of protection, Fulminante confessed." Agreeing with Fulminante that "Sarivola's promise was extremely coercive," the Arizona court declared: "The confession was obtained as a direct result of extreme coercion and was tendered in the belief that the defendant's life was in jeopardy if he did not confess. This is a true coerced confession in every sense of the word."[2]

We normally give great deference to the factual findings of the state court. Nevertheless, the ultimate issue of "voluntariness" is a legal question requiring independent federal determination. Although the

---

[2]   There are additional facts in the record, not relied upon by the Arizona Supreme Court, which also support a finding of coercion. Fulminante possesses low average to average intelligence; he dropped out of school in the fourth grade. He is short in stature and slight in build. Although he had been in prison before, he had not always adapted well to the stress of prison life. While incarcerated at the age of 26, he had "felt threatened by the prison population," and he therefore requested that he be placed in protective custody. Once there, however, he was unable to cope with the isolation and was admitted to a psychiatric hospital. The Court has previously recognized that factors such as these are relevant in determining whether a defendant's will has been overborne. In addition, we note that Sarivola's position as Fulminante's friend might well have made the latter particularly susceptible to the former's entreaties.

question is a close one, we agree with the Arizona Supreme Court's conclusion that Fulminante's confession was coerced. The Arizona Supreme Court found a credible threat of physical violence unless Fulminante confessed. Our cases have made clear that a finding of coercion need not depend upon actual violence by a government agent;[4] a credible threat is sufficient. As we have said, "coercion can be mental as well as physical, and the blood of the accused is not the only hallmark of an unconstitutional inquisition." As in *Payne v. Arkansas*, 356 U.S. 560 (1958), where the Court found that a confession was coerced because the interrogating police officer had promised that if the accused confessed, the officer would protect the accused from an angry mob outside the jailhouse door, so too here, the Arizona Supreme Court found that it was fear of physical violence, absent protection from his friend (and Government agent) Sarivola, which motivated Fulminante to confess. Accepting the Arizona court's finding, permissible on this record, that there was a credible threat of physical violence, we agree with its conclusion that Fulminante's will was overborne in such a way as to render his confession the product of coercion.

CHIEF JUSTICE REHNQUIST, with whom JUSTICE O'CONNOR, JUSTICE KENNEDY, and JUSTICE SOUTER join, dissenting.

The admissibility of a confession such as that made by respondent Fulminante depends upon whether it was voluntarily made. "The ultimate test remains that which has been the only clearly established test in Anglo-American courts for two hundred years: the test of voluntariness. Is the confession the product of an essentially free and unconstrained choice by its maker? If it is, if he has willed to confess, it may be used against him. If it is not, if his will has been overborne and his capacity for self-determination critically impaired, the use of his confession offends due process." *Culombe v. Connecticut*, 367 U.S. 568, 602 (1961).

Exercising our responsibility to make the independent examination of the record necessary to decide this federal question, I am at a loss to see how the Supreme Court of Arizona reached the conclusion that it did. Fulminante offered no evidence that he believed that his life was in danger or that he in fact confessed to Sarivola in order to obtain the proffered protection. Indeed, he had stipulated that "at no time did the defendant indicate he was in fear of other inmates nor did he ever seek Mr. Sarivola's protection." Sarivola's testimony that he told Fulminante that "if he would tell the truth, he could be protected," adds little if anything to the substance of the parties' stipulation. The decision of the Supreme Court of Arizona rests on an assumption that is squarely

---

[4]   The parties agree that Sarivola acted as an agent of the Government when he questioned Fulminante about the murder and elicited the confession.

contrary to this stipulation, and one that is not supported by any testimony of Fulminante.

The facts of record in the present case are quite different from those present in cases where we have found confessions to be coerced and involuntary. Since Fulminante was unaware that Sarivola was an FBI informant, there existed none of "the danger of coercion resulting from the interaction of custody and official interrogation." The fact that Sarivola was a Government informant does not by itself render Fulminante's confession involuntary, since we have consistently accepted the use of informants in the discovery of evidence of a crime as a legitimate investigatory procedure consistent with the Constitution. The conversations between Sarivola and Fulminante were not lengthy, and the defendant was free at all times to leave Sarivola's company. Sarivola at no time threatened him or demanded that he confess; he simply requested that he speak the truth about the matter. Fulminante was an experienced habitue of prisons, and presumably able to fend for himself. In concluding on these facts that Fulminante's confession was involuntary, the Court today embraces a more expansive definition of that term than is warranted by any of our decided cases.

2. THE AMOUNT OF TIME SPENT IN POLICE CUSTODY OR UNDER INTERROGATION

Because each case is decided on its own unique facts, the Supreme Court has not established a fixed period of time spent in police custody or under interrogation beyond which a suspect's confession becomes involuntary. The Court has often noted, however, that a confession that is the product of prolonged police custody and incommunicado interrogation is more likely to be deemed involuntary. In *Ashcraft v. Tennessee*, for example, the Court found that 36 hours of continuous interrogation rendered the suspect's confession involuntary.

ASHCRAFT V. TENNESSEE
322 U.S. 143 (1944)

Ashcraft was suspected of hiring another man to kill his wife. Police took him into custody and placed him in a room at the county jail. He was interrogated continuously by relays of officers over the next 36 hours without an opportunity to sleep or rest. Although Ashcraft claimed that he never actually confessed, the prosecutor was able to introduce an unsigned statement in which Ashcraft allegedly admitted to hiring his wife's killer.

Noting that Ashcraft was held "incommunicado, without sleep or rest," and that he was questioned "without respite" by "relays of officers, experienced investigators, and highly trained lawyers," the Supreme Court held that any confession Ashcraft made was involuntary:

> We think a situation such as that here shown is so inherently coercive that its very existence is irreconcilable with the possession of mental freedom by a lone suspect against whom its full coercive force is brought to bear. It is inconceivable that any court of justice in the land, conducted as our courts are, open to the public, would permit prosecutors serving in relays to keep a defendant witness under continuous cross-examination for thirty-six hours without rest or sleep in an effort to extract a "voluntary" confession. Nor can we, consistently with Constitutional due process of law, hold voluntary a confession where prosecutors do the same thing away from the restraining influences of a public trial in an open court room.

In *Watts v. Indiana*, the suspect was held in police custody and subjected to lengthy interrogations over a period of six days. The Supreme Court concluded that his confession was involuntary.

WATTS V. INDIANA
338 U.S. 49 (1949)

Robert Watts was arrested on suspicion of assault, and shortly thereafter, he became a suspect in a separate murder that occurred in the vicinity of the assault. He was held in police custody and interrogated by relays of officers—often in long overnight sessions—for six days until he made incriminating statements. Noting the coercive pressure of prolonged custody and interrogation, the Supreme Court concluded that the confession was involuntary:

> A statement, to be voluntary, of course need not be volunteered. But if it is the product of sustained pressure by the police, it does not issue from a free choice. When a suspect speaks because he is overborne, it is immaterial whether he has been subjected to a physical or a mental ordeal. Eventual yielding to questioning under such circumstances is plainly the product of the suction process of interrogation, and therefore the reverse of voluntary. We would have to shut our minds to the plain significance of what here transpired to deny that this was a calculated endeavor to secure a confession through the pressure of unrelenting interrogation. The very relentlessness of such interrogation implies that it is better for the prisoner to answer than to persist in the refusal of disclosure, which is his constitutional right. To turn the detention of an accused into a process of wrenching from him evidence which could not be extorted in open court,

with all its safeguards, is so grave an abuse of the power of arrest as to offend the procedural standards of due process.

———————

In *Davis v. North Carolina*, the suspect was held in police custody and interrogated over a period of 16 days before finally confessing. The Supreme Court found that the confession was involuntary.

DAVIS V. NORTH CAROLINA
384 U.S. 737 (1966)

Elmer Davis was taken into custody on suspicion of rape and murder. Police placed a note on his arrest sheet indicating that he was not permitted to have visitors. No one, other than police, spoke to Davis during 16 days of detention and interrogation that led to his confession. The Supreme Court held that the confession was involuntary:

> The facts established on the record demonstrate that Davis went through a prolonged period in which substantial coercive influences were brought to bear upon him to extort the confessions that marked the culmination of police efforts. Evidence of extended interrogation in such a coercive atmosphere has often resulted in a finding of involuntariness by this Court. We have never sustained the use of a confession obtained after such a lengthy period of detention and interrogation as was involved in this case. The fact that each individual interrogation session was of relatively short duration does not mitigate the substantial coercive effect created by repeated interrogation in these surroundings over 16 days. So far as Davis could have known, the interrogation in the overnight lockup might still be going on today had he not confessed.

3. DEPRIVATION OF FOOD, SLEEP, MEDICAL CARE, OR OTHER NECESSITIES

Even when the time spent in police custody or under interrogation is relatively short, a confession may be deemed involuntary if the suspect has been deprived of food, sleep, medical attention, or other basic necessities. In *Payne v. Arkansas*, 356 U.S. 560 (1958), excerpted above, in which the police chief elicited a confession by referring to an angry mob gathered outside the jail, one of the additional factors relevant to the Supreme Court's conclusion that the confession was involuntary was the fact that the suspect was denied food for 25 hours. *Greenwald v. Wisconsin* provides another example.

GREENWALD V. WISCONSIN
390 U.S. 519 (1968)

John Greenwald was arrested late in the evening on suspicion of burglary, more than six hours after he had last eaten and taken medication for high blood pressure. He was interrogated for over an hour that same night, then placed in a cell with a plank fastened to the wall that served as a bed, but he did not sleep. Early the next morning, police resumed the interrogation, and roughly 12 hours after he was initially arrested, Greenwald confessed. Throughout the morning, he was not offered food and did not have his medication. Citing a number of factors, including the "lack of food, sleep, and medication," the Supreme Court concluded that Greenwald's confession was involuntary.

4. PSYCHOLOGICAL PLOYS AND POLICE DECEPTION

Virtually all police interrogation techniques create psychological pressure that may ultimately lead a suspect to confess. The Supreme Court has not drawn a clear line between permissible psychological tactics and unconstitutional psychological coercion, but in a number of cases, the Court has found that confessions were involuntary due to improper psychological ploys or deception by the police. *Spano v. New York* is a leading example.

SPANO V. NEW YORK
360 U.S. 315 (1959)

CHIEF JUSTICE WARREN delivered the opinion of the Court.

This is another in the long line of cases presenting the question whether a confession was properly admitted into evidence under the Fourteenth Amendment. As in all such cases, we are forced to resolve a conflict between two fundamental interests of society; its interest in prompt and efficient law enforcement, and its interest in preventing the rights of its individual members from being abridged by unconstitutional methods of law enforcement. Because of the delicate nature of the constitutional determination which we must make, we cannot escape the responsibility of making our own examination of the record.

The State's evidence reveals the following: Petitioner Vincent Joseph Spano is a derivative citizen of this country, having been born in Messina, Italy. He was 25 years old at the time of the shooting in question and had graduated from junior high school. He had a record of regular employment. The shooting took place on January 22, 1957.

On that day, petitioner was drinking in a bar. The decedent, a former professional boxer weighing almost 200 pounds who had fought in Madison Square Garden, took some of petitioner's money from the bar.

Petitioner followed him out of the bar to recover it. A fight ensued, with the decedent knocking petitioner down and then kicking him in the head three or four times. Shock from the force of these blows caused petitioner to vomit. After the bartender applied some ice to his head, petitioner left the bar, walked to his apartment, secured a gun, and walked eight or nine blocks to a candy store where the decedent was frequently to be found. He entered the store in which decedent, three friends of decedent, at least two of whom were ex-convicts, and a boy who was supervising the store were present. He fired five shots, two of which entered the decedent's body, causing his death. The boy was the only eyewitness; the three friends of decedent did not see the person who fired the shot. Petitioner then disappeared for the next week or so.

On February 1, 1957, the Bronx County Grand Jury returned an indictment for first-degree murder against petitioner. Accordingly, a bench warrant was issued for his arrest, commanding that he be forthwith brought before the court to answer the indictment, or, if the court had adjourned for the term, that he be delivered into the custody of the Sheriff of Bronx County.

On February 3, 1957, petitioner called one Gaspar Bruno, a close friend of 8 or 10 years' standing who had attended school with him. Bruno was a fledgling police officer, having at that time not yet finished attending police academy. According to Bruno's testimony, petitioner told him "that he took a terrific beating, that the deceased hurt him real bad and he dropped him a couple of times and he was dazed; he didn't know what he was doing and that he went and shot at him." Petitioner told Bruno that he intended to get a lawyer and give himself up. Bruno relayed this information to his superiors.

The following day, February 4, at 7:10 p.m., petitioner, accompanied by counsel, surrendered himself to the authorities in front of the Bronx County Building, where both the office of the Assistant District Attorney who ultimately prosecuted his case and the courtroom in which he was ultimately tried were located. His attorney had cautioned him to answer no questions, and left him in the custody of the officers. He was promptly taken to the office of the Assistant District Attorney and at 7:15 p.m. the questioning began, being conducted by Assistant District Attorney Goldsmith, Lt. Gannon, Detectives Farrell, Lehrer and Motta, and Sgt. Clarke. The record reveals that the questioning was both persistent and continuous. Petitioner, in accordance with his attorney's instructions, steadfastly refused to answer. Detective Motta testified: "He refused to talk to me. He just looked up to the ceiling and refused to talk to me."

He asked one officer, Detective Ciccone, if he could speak to his attorney, but that request was denied. Detective Ciccone testified that he could not find the attorney's name in the telephone book. He was given two sandwiches, coffee and cake at 11 p.m.

At 12:15 a.m. on the morning of February 5, after five hours of questioning in which it became evident that petitioner was following his attorney's instructions, on the Assistant District Attorney's orders petitioner was transferred to the 46th Squad, Ryer Avenue Police Station. The Assistant District Attorney also went to the police station and to some extent continued to participate in the interrogation. Petitioner arrived at 12:30 and questioning was resumed at 12:40. But petitioner persisted in his refusal to answer, and again requested permission to see his attorney, this time from Detective Lehrer. His request was again denied.

It was then that those in charge of the investigation decided that petitioner's close friend, Bruno, could be of use. He had been called out on the case around 10 or 11 p.m., although he was not connected with the 46th Squad or Precinct in any way. Although, in fact, his job was in no way threatened, Bruno was told to tell petitioner that petitioner's telephone call had gotten him "in a lot of trouble," and that he should seek to extract sympathy from petitioner for Bruno's pregnant wife and three children. Bruno developed this theme with petitioner without success, and petitioner, also without success, again sought to see his attorney, a request which Bruno relayed unavailingly to his superiors. After this first session with petitioner, Bruno was again directed by Lt. Gannon to play on petitioner's sympathies, but again no confession was forthcoming. But the Lieutenant a third time ordered Bruno falsely to importune his friend to confess, but again petitioner clung to his attorney's advice. Inevitably, in the fourth such session directed by the Lieutenant, lasting a full hour, petitioner succumbed to his friend's prevarications and agreed to make a statement. Accordingly, at 3:25 a.m. the Assistant District Attorney, a stenographer, and several other law enforcement officials entered the room where petitioner was being questioned, and took his statement in question and answer form with the Assistant District Attorney asking the questions. The statement was completed at 4:05 a.m.

But this was not the end. At 4:30 a.m. three detectives took petitioner to Police Headquarters in Manhattan. On the way they attempted to find the bridge from which petitioner said he had thrown the murder weapon. They crossed the Triborough Bridge into Manhattan, arriving at Police Headquarters at 5 a.m., and left Manhattan for the Bronx at 5:40 a.m. via the Willis Avenue Bridge. When petitioner recognized neither bridge as the one from which he had thrown the weapon, they re-entered Manhattan via the Third Avenue Bridge, which petitioner stated was the right one, and then returned to the Bronx well after 6 a.m. During that trip the officers also elicited a statement from petitioner that the deceased was always "on (his) back," "always pushing" him and that he was "not sorry" he had shot the deceased. All three detectives testified to that statement at the trial. Court opened at 10 a.m. that morning, and petitioner was arraigned at 10:15.

At the trial, the confession was introduced in evidence over appropriate objections. The jury was instructed that it could rely on it only if it was found to be voluntary. The jury returned a guilty verdict and petitioner was sentenced to death. The New York Court of Appeals affirmed the conviction over three dissents, and we granted certiorari to resolve the serious problem presented under the Fourteenth Amendment.

We find use of the confession obtained here inconsistent with the Fourteenth Amendment under traditional principles. The abhorrence of society to the use of involuntary confessions does not turn alone on their inherent untrustworthiness. It also turns on the deep-rooted feeling that the police must obey the law while enforcing the law; that in the end life and liberty can be as much endangered from illegal methods used to convict those thought to be criminals as from the actual criminals themselves. Accordingly, the actions of police in obtaining confessions have come under scrutiny in a long series of cases. Those cases suggest that in recent years law enforcement officials have become increasingly aware of the burden which they share, along with our courts, in protecting fundamental rights of our citizenry, including that portion of our citizenry suspected of crime. The facts of no case recently in this Court have quite approached the brutal beatings in *Brown v. Mississippi*, 297 U.S. 278 (1936), or the 36 consecutive hours of questioning present in *Ashcraft v. Tennessee*, 322 U.S. 143 (1944). But as law enforcement officers become more responsible, and the methods used to extract confessions more sophisticated, our duty to enforce federal constitutional protections does not cease. It only becomes more difficult because of the more delicate judgments to be made. Our judgment here is that, on all the facts, this conviction cannot stand.

Petitioner was a foreign-born young man of 25 with no past history of law violation or of subjection to official interrogation, at least insofar as the record shows. He had progressed only one-half year into high school and the record indicates that he had a history of emotional instability. He did not make a narrative statement, but was subject to the leading questions of a skillful prosecutor in a question and answer confession. He was subjected to questioning not by a few men, but by many. They included Assistant District Attorney Goldsmith, one Hyland of the District Attorney's Office, Deputy Inspector Halks, Lieutenant Gannon, Detective Ciccone, Detective Motta, Detective Lehrer, Detective Marshal, Detective Farrell, Detective Leira, Detective Murphy, Detective Murtha, Sergeant Clarke, Patrolman Bruno and Stenographer Baldwin. All played some part, and the effect of such massive official interrogation must have been felt. Petitioner was questioned for virtually eight straight hours before he confessed, with his only respite being a transfer to an arena presumably considered more appropriate by the police for the task at hand. Nor was the questioning conducted during normal business hours, but began in early evening, continued into the night, and did not bear fruition until the not-too-early morning. The drama was not played out, with the final admissions obtained, until almost sunrise. In such circumstances slowly mounting fatigue does, and is calculated to, play its part. The questioners persisted in the face of his repeated refusals to answer on the advice of his attorney, and they ignored his reasonable requests to contact the local attorney whom he had already retained and who had personally delivered him into the custody of these officers in obedience to the bench warrant.

The use of Bruno, characterized in this Court by counsel for the State as a "childhood friend" of petitioner's, is another factor which deserves mention in the totality of the situation. Bruno's was the one face visible to petitioner in which he could put some trust. There was a bond of friendship between them going back a decade into adolescence. It was with this material that the officers felt that they could overcome petitioner's will. They instructed Bruno falsely to state that petitioner's telephone call had gotten him into trouble, that his job was in jeopardy, and that loss of his job would be disastrous to his three children, his wife and his unborn child. And Bruno played this part of a worried father, harried by his superiors, in not one, but four different acts, the final one lasting an hour. Petitioner was apparently unaware of John Gay's famous couplet: "An open foe may prove a curse, But a pretended friend is worse," and he yielded to his false friend's entreaties.

We conclude that petitioner's will was overborne by official pressure, fatigue and sympathy falsely aroused after considering all the facts in their post-indictment setting. Here a grand jury had already found sufficient cause to require petitioner to face trial on a charge of first-degree murder, and the police had an eyewitness to the shooting. The police were not therefore merely trying to solve a crime, or even to absolve a suspect. They were, rather, concerned primarily with securing a statement from defendant on which they could convict him. The undeviating intent of the officers to extract a confession from petitioner is therefore patent. When such an intent is shown, this Court has held that the confession obtained must be examined with the most careful scrutiny, and has reversed a conviction on facts less compelling than these. Accordingly, we hold that petitioner's conviction cannot stand under the Fourteenth Amendment.

In *Leyra v. Denno*, police subjected the suspect to hypnosis under the pretense of providing him with medical assistance for a sinus attack. The Supreme Court held that the defendant's eventual confession was coerced.

LEYRA V. DENNO
347 U.S. 556 (1954)

Camilo Leyra, suspected of murdering his parents, was questioned at length in the days following the discovery of their bodies, but he had not made a confession. After his parents' funeral, he was again brought in for questioning. At the time, Leyra was suffering from an "acutely painful attack of sinus," and a police captain promised to get a physician to help him. The captain introduced to Leyra to "Dr. Helfand," a psychiatrist with considerable knowledge of hypnosis. The Supreme Court explained what transpired:

> Petitioner was left with Dr. Helfand while Captain Meenahan joined the state District Attorney in the nearby listening room. Instead of giving petitioner the medical advice and treatment he expected, the psychiatrist by subtle and suggestive questions simply continued the police effort of the past days and nights to induce petitioner to admit his guilt. For an hour and a half or more the techniques of a highly trained psychiatrist were used to break petitioner's will in order to get him to say he had murdered his parents. Time and time and time again the psychiatrist told petitioner how much he wanted to and could help him, how bad it would be for petitioner if he did not confess, and how much better he would feel, and how much lighter and easier it would be on him if he would just unbosom himself to the doctor. Yet the doctor was at that very time the paid representative of the state whose prosecuting officials were listening in on every threat made and every promise of leniency given.

> A tape recording of the psychiatric examination was made and a transcription of the tape was read into the record of this case. The petitioner's answers indicate a mind dazed and bewildered. Time after time the petitioner complained about how tired and how sleepy he was and how he could not think. On occasion after occasion the doctor told petitioner either to open his eyes or to shut his eyes. Apparently many of petitioner's answers were barely audible. On occasions the doctor informed petitioner that his lips were moving but no sound could be heard. Many times petitioner was asked to speak louder. As time went on, the record indicates that petitioner began to accept suggestions of the psychiatrist. For instance, Dr. Helfand suggested that petitioner had hit his parents with a hammer and after some minutes petitioner agreed that must have been the weapon.

> Finally, after an hour and a half or longer, petitioner, encouraged by the doctor's assurances that he had done no moral

wrong and would be let off easily, called for Captain Meenahan. The captain immediately appeared. It was then that the confession was given to him which was admitted against petitioner in this trial.

Already "physically and emotionally exhausted" by the earlier questioning, his parents' funeral, and the sinus attack, the Supreme Court noted that Leyra's "ability to resist interrogation was broken to almost trance-like submission by use of the arts of a highly skilled psychiatrist." Concluding that the "undisputed facts in this case are irreconcilable with petitioner's mental freedom to confess or to deny a suspected participation in a crime," the Supreme Court held that the use of the confession at Leyra's trial violated due process.

In *Lynumn v. Illinois*, a suspect was falsely told she would not be prosecuted if she answered questions from the police, but would face an extended prison sentence and have her children taken away if she did not. The Supreme Court concluded that her confession was involuntary.

LYNUMN V. ILLINOIS
372 U.S. 528 (1963)

Beatrice Lynumn confessed that she had sold marijuana to a police informant. She later claimed that the confession was false, and was made only because three police officers in her apartment told her that unless she cooperated, she could get 10 years in jail, lose state financial assistance, and have her two children—aged three and four—taken away. The police also implied that Lynumn would not be prosecuted as long as she confessed. Noting that the State of Illinois had conceded that the totality of the circumstances "combined to produce an impellingly coercive effect" upon Lynumn, the Supreme Court held that the confession was "not voluntary, but coerced."

Although the Supreme Court has found that various psychological ploys are coercive, rendering the resulting confessions involuntary, the Court has given police some latitude in the use of deception. In *Frazier v. Cupp*, for example, the Supreme Court concluded that a suspect's confession was voluntary even though police misrepresented the strength of the state's case.

FRAZIER V. CUPP
394 U.S. 731 (1969)

Martin Frazier, a murder suspect, was questioned by police for roughly an hour. When asked where he was on the night of the murder, Frazier said he was with his cousin, Jerry Lee Rawls. Later, the officer questioning Frazier falsely told him that Rawls had been brought in for questioning and had confessed. Frazier was still reluctant to talk, so the officer sympathetically suggested that the victim had started a fight by making homosexual advances. At that point, Frazier began to convey his story, ultimately leading to a full confession. Citing a number of factors, the Supreme Court found that the confession was voluntary despite the misrepresentation:

> Before petitioner made any incriminating statements, he received partial warnings of his constitutional rights; this is, of course, a circumstance quite relevant to a finding of voluntariness. The questioning was of short duration, and petitioner was a mature individual of normal intelligence. The fact that the police misrepresented the statements that Rawls had made is, while relevant, insufficient in our view to make this otherwise voluntary confession inadmissible. These cases must be decided by viewing the "totality of the circumstances," and on the facts of this case we can find no error in the admission of petitioner's confession.

———————————

Is it possible to reconcile *Lynumn v. Illinois* and *Frazier v. Cupp*? Why were the threats about possible punishments and false police promises of leniency in exchange for cooperation sufficient to render the confession involuntary in *Lynumn*, while police misrepresentations about the evidence implicating the suspect in *Frazier* were insufficient to make his confession involuntary? One possible explanation is that the Supreme Court appears more tolerant of misrepresentations involving facts or evidence than misrepresentations involving the law, the suspect's constitutional rights, or the legal implications of a decision to confess.

5.   THE AGE, EDUCATION, AND MENTAL CONDITION OF THE SUSPECT

In many cases, the Supreme Court has considered the suspect's age, education, and mental condition as factors bearing upon the voluntariness of a confession. *Reck v. Pate* is a good example.

RECK V. PATE
367 U.S. 433 (1961)

Emil Reck, 19, was a suspect along with three other young men in the murder of a Chicago physician. Reck had been repeatedly classified as mentally retarded and deficient by psychologists and psychiatrists, and spent a year in an institution for the feebleminded. He dropped out of school at the age of 16, before completing the seventh grade, and was found to have the intelligence of a child between 10 and 11 years of age at the time of his trial.

For four days, he was held by police and subjected to six- or seven-hour stretches of incessant interrogation by groups of officers before finally confessing. While in custody, he became ill, vomited blood, and was hospitalized, all of which Reck claimed was the result of being beaten by the police. During the period preceding his confession, Reck was without adequate food, without counsel, physically weakened and in intense pain, and "for all practical purposes, held incommunicado."

Citing the "totality of coercive circumstances," and noting "Reck's youth, his subnormal intelligence, and his lack of previous experience with the police," the Supreme Court concluded that his confession was involuntary.

In *Culombe v. Connecticut*, decided just one week after *Reck v. Pate*, the Supreme Court again held that a confession was involuntary. The fact that the suspect was illiterate and of low intelligence weighed heavily in the Court's decision.

CULOMBE V. CONNECTICUT
367 U.S. 568 (1961)

Arthur Culombe and another man were suspects in a terrifying string of holdups and killings. Culombe was effectively in the control of the police for four nights and five days before he confessed. While detained by the police, Culombe was interrogated repeatedly—sometimes for long periods—but was not physically mistreated. At one point, Culombe said he wanted to see a lawyer. The police lieutenant who was questioning Culombe said he could have any lawyer he wanted if he would provide a name. The lieutenant knew that Culombe, an illiterate, was unable to use the telephone directory. Later, police brought Culombe's wife in to see him, and she urged him to confess to any crimes he committed.

After a careful review of all of the facts and the circumstances, the Supreme Court concluded that Columbe's confession was involuntary. In so holding, the Court emphasized Columbe's intellectual deficits:

The man who was thus cooperative with the police, Arthur Culombe, was a thirty-three-year-old mental defective of the moron class with an intelligence quotient of sixty-four and a mental age of nine to nine and a half years. He was wholly illiterate. Expert witnesses for the State, whose appraisal of Culombe's mental condition was the most favorable adduced at trial, classified him as a "high moron" and "a rather high grade mentally defective" and testified that his reactions would not be the same as those of the chronological nine-year-old because his greater physical maturity and fuller background of experience gave him a perspective that the nine-year-old would not possess. Culombe was, however, "handicapped."

Culombe had been in mental institutions for diagnosis and treatment. He had been in trouble with the law since he was an adolescent and had been in prison at least twice in Connecticut since his successful escape from a Massachusetts training school for mental defectives. During the three years immediately preceding his arrest he had held down, and adequately performed, a freight handler's job and had supported his wife and two young children. A psychiatrist testifying for the State said that, although he was not a fearful man, Culombe was suggestible and could be intimidated.

———————

Just as a lack of education or intellectual ability may make a suspect more susceptible to coercion, so too a strong educational background or a high level of intelligence may make it more likely that a suspect's confession is voluntary. In *Crooker v. California*, for example, the Supreme Court emphasized the defendant's intelligence and education in concluding that his confession was voluntary.

CROOKER V. CALIFORNIA
357 U.S. 433 (1958)

John Crooker, a college graduate who had attended one year of law school, was arrested for killing his lover after she terminated their relationship. After his arrest, Crooker was interrogated late into the night until he confessed the following morning, but he was given coffee and food and was permitted to smoke. During the interrogation, Crooker refused to take a lie detector test and said he wanted to call an attorney, but was not offered the use of a telephone.

Citing Crooker's intelligence, education, and knowledge of his right to remain silent, the Supreme Court concluded that the confession was voluntary:

Petitioner's claim of coercion, then, depends almost entirely on denial of his request to contact counsel. To be sure, coercion seems more likely to result from state denial of a specific request for opportunity to engage counsel than it does from state failure to appoint counsel immediately upon arrest. That greater possibility, however, is not decisive. It is negated here by petitioner's age, intelligence, and education. While in law school he had studied criminal law; indeed, when asked to take the lie detector test, he informed the operator that the results of such a test would not be admissible at trial absent a stipulation by the parties. Supplementing that background is the police statement to petitioner well before his confession that he did not have to answer questions. Moreover, the manner of his refusals to answer indicates full awareness of the right to be silent. On this record we are unable to say that petitioner's confession was anything other than voluntary.

In *Colorado v. Connelly*, the Supreme Court found that a confession was not involuntary simply because the suspect's mental condition compelled him to make it. The Court made it clear that coercive police action must be present in order for a confession to be deemed involuntary.

COLORADO V. CONNELLY

479 U.S. 157 (1986)

CHIEF JUSTICE REHNQUIST delivered the opinion of the Court.

In this case, the Supreme Court of Colorado held that the United States Constitution requires a court to suppress a confession when the mental state of the defendant, at the time he made the confession, interfered with his "rational intellect" and his "free will." We conclude that the admissibility of this kind of statement is governed by state rules of evidence, rather than by our previous decisions regarding coerced confessions and *Miranda* waivers. We therefore reverse.

I

On August 18, 1983, Officer Patrick Anderson of the Denver Police Department was in uniform, working in an off-duty capacity in downtown Denver. Respondent Francis Connelly approached Officer Anderson and, without any prompting, stated that he had murdered someone and wanted to talk about it. Anderson immediately advised respondent that he had the right to remain silent, that anything he said could be used against him in court, and that he had the right to an attorney prior to any police questioning. Respondent stated that he understood these rights but he still wanted to talk about the murder. Understandably bewildered by this confession, Officer Anderson asked respondent several questions. Connelly denied that he had been drinking, denied that he had been taking any drugs, and stated that, in the past, he had been a patient in several mental hospitals. Officer Anderson again told Connelly that he was under no obligation to say anything. Connelly replied that it was "all right," and that he would talk to Officer Anderson because his conscience had been bothering him. To Officer Anderson, respondent appeared to understand fully the nature of his acts.

Shortly thereafter, Homicide Detective Stephen Antuna arrived. Respondent was again advised of his rights, and Detective Antuna asked him "what he had on his mind." Respondent answered that he had come all the way from Boston to confess to the murder of Mary Ann Junta, a young girl whom he had killed in Denver sometime during November 1982. Respondent was taken to police headquarters, and a search of police records revealed that the body of an unidentified female had been found in April 1983. Respondent openly detailed his story to Detective Antuna and Sergeant Thomas Haney, and readily agreed to take the officers to the scene of the killing. Under Connelly's sole direction, the two officers and respondent proceeded in a police vehicle to the location of the crime. Respondent pointed out the exact location of the murder. Throughout this episode, Detective Antuna perceived no indication whatsoever that respondent was suffering from any kind of mental illness.

Respondent was held overnight. During an interview with the public defender's office the following morning, he became visibly disoriented. He began giving confused answers to questions, and for the first time, stated that "voices" had told him to come to Denver and that he had followed the directions of these voices in confessing. Respondent was sent to a state hospital for evaluation. He was initially found incompetent to assist in his own defense. By March 1984, however, the doctors evaluating respondent determined that he was competent to proceed to trial.

At a preliminary hearing, respondent moved to suppress all of his statements. Dr. Jeffrey Metzner, a psychiatrist employed by the state hospital, testified that respondent was suffering from chronic schizophrenia and was in a psychotic state at least as of August 17, 1983, the day before he confessed. Metzner's interviews with respondent revealed that respondent was following the "voice of God." This voice instructed respondent to withdraw money from the bank, to buy an airplane ticket, and to fly from Boston to Denver. When respondent arrived from Boston, God's voice became stronger and told respondent either to confess to the killing or to commit suicide. Reluctantly following the command of the voices, respondent approached Officer Anderson and confessed.

Dr. Metzner testified that, in his expert opinion, respondent was experiencing "command hallucinations." This condition interfered with respondent's "volitional abilities; that is, his ability to make free and rational choices." Dr. Metzner further testified that Connelly's illness did not significantly impair his cognitive abilities. Thus, respondent understood the rights he had when Officer Anderson and Detective Antuna advised him that he need not speak. Dr. Metzner admitted that the "voices" could in reality be Connelly's interpretation of his own guilt, but explained that in his opinion, Connelly's psychosis motivated his confession.

On the basis of this evidence the Colorado trial court decided that respondent's statements must be suppressed because they were "involuntary." The court ruled that a confession is admissible only if it is a product of the defendant's rational intellect and "free will." Although the court found that the police had done nothing wrong or coercive in securing respondent's confession, Connelly's illness destroyed his volition and compelled him to confess. The trial court also found that Connelly's mental state vitiated his attempted waiver of the right to counsel and the privilege against compulsory self-incrimination. Accordingly, respondent's initial statements and his custodial confession were suppressed.

The Colorado Supreme Court affirmed. In that court's view, the proper test for admissibility is whether the statements are "the product of a rational intellect and a free will." Indeed, "the absence of police coercion or duress does not foreclose a finding of involuntariness. One's capacity for rational judgment and free choice may be overborne as much by certain forms of severe mental illness as by external pressure." The court found that the very admission of the evidence in a court of law was sufficient state action to implicate the Due Process Clause of the Fourteenth Amendment to the United States Constitution. The evidence fully supported the conclusion that respondent's initial statement was not the product of a rational intellect and a free will. The court then considered respondent's attempted waiver of his constitutional rights and found that respondent's mental condition precluded his ability to make a valid waiver. The Colorado Supreme Court thus affirmed the trial court's decision to suppress all of Connelly's statements.

II

The Due Process Clause of the Fourteenth Amendment provides that no State shall "deprive any person of life, liberty, or property, without due process of law." By virtue of the Due Process Clause, "certain interrogation techniques, either in isolation or as applied to the unique characteristics of a particular suspect, are so offensive to a civilized system of justice that they must be condemned."

Indeed, coercive government misconduct was the catalyst for this Court's seminal confession case, *Brown v. Mississippi*, 297 U.S. 278 (1936). In that case, police officers extracted confessions from the accused through brutal torture. The Court had little difficulty concluding that even though the Fifth Amendment did not at that time apply to the States, the actions of the police were "revolting to the sense of justice." The Court has retained this due process focus, even after holding, in *Malloy v. Hogan*, 378 U.S. 1 (1964), that the Fifth Amendment privilege against compulsory self-incrimination applies to the States.

The cases considered by this Court over the 50 years since *Brown v. Mississippi* have focused upon the crucial element of police overreaching. While each confession case has turned on its own set of factors justifying the conclusion that police conduct was oppressive, all have contained a substantial element of coercive police conduct. Absent police conduct causally related to the confession, there is simply no basis for concluding that any state actor has deprived a criminal defendant of due process of law. Respondent correctly notes that as interrogators have turned to more subtle forms of psychological persuasion, courts have found the mental condition of the defendant a more significant factor in the "voluntariness" calculus. See *Spano v. New York*, 360 U.S. 315 (1959). But this fact does not justify a conclusion that a defendant's mental condition, by itself and apart from its relation to official coercion, should ever dispose of the inquiry into constitutional "voluntariness."

Respondent relies on *Blackburn v. Alabama*, 361 U.S. 199 (1960), and *Townsend v. Sain*, 372 U.S. 293 (1963), for the proposition that the "deficient mental condition of the defendants in those cases was sufficient to render their confessions involuntary." But respondent's reading of *Blackburn* and *Townsend* ignores the integral element of police overreaching present in both cases. In *Blackburn*, the Court found that the petitioner was probably insane at the time of his confession and the police learned during the interrogation that he had a history of mental problems. The police exploited this weakness with coercive tactics: "the eight- to nine-hour sustained interrogation in a tiny room which was upon occasion literally filled with police officers; the absence of Blackburn's friends, relatives, or legal counsel; [and] the composition of the confession by the Deputy Sheriff rather than by Blackburn." These tactics supported a finding that the confession was involuntary. Indeed, the Court specifically condemned police activity that "wrings a confession out of an accused against his will." *Townsend* presented a similar instance of police wrongdoing. In that case, a police physician had given Townsend a drug with truth-serum properties. The subsequent confession, obtained by officers who knew that Townsend had been given drugs, was held involuntary. These two cases demonstrate that while mental condition is surely relevant to an individual's susceptibility to police coercion, mere examination of the confessant's state of mind can never conclude the due process inquiry.

Our "involuntary confession" jurisprudence is entirely consistent with the settled law requiring some sort of "state action" to support a claim of violation of the Due Process Clause of the Fourteenth Amendment. The Colorado trial court, of course, found that the police committed no wrongful acts, and that finding has been neither challenged by respondent nor disturbed by the Supreme Court of Colorado. The latter court, however, concluded that sufficient state action was present by virtue of the admission of the confession into evidence in a court of the State.

The difficulty with the approach of the Supreme Court of Colorado is that it fails to recognize the essential link between coercive activity of the State, on the one hand, and a resulting confession by a defendant, on the other. The flaw in respondent's constitutional argument is that it would expand our previous line of "voluntariness" cases into a far-ranging requirement that courts must divine a defendant's motivation for speaking or acting as he did even though there be no claim that governmental conduct coerced his decision.

The most outrageous behavior by a private party seeking to secure evidence against a defendant does not make that evidence inadmissible under the Due Process Clause. Moreover, suppressing respondent's statements would serve absolutely no purpose in enforcing constitutional guarantees. The purpose of excluding evidence seized in violation of the Constitution is to substantially deter future violations of the Constitution. Only if we were to establish a brand new constitutional right—the right of a criminal defendant to confess to his crime only when totally rational and properly motivated—could respondent's present claim be sustained.

We have previously cautioned against expanding "currently applicable exclusionary rules by erecting additional barriers to placing truthful and probative evidence before state juries." We abide by that counsel now. The central purpose of a criminal trial is to decide the factual question of the defendant's guilt or innocence, and while we have previously held that exclusion of evidence may be necessary to protect constitutional guarantees, both the necessity for the collateral inquiry and the exclusion of evidence deflect a criminal trial from its basic purpose. Respondent would now have us require sweeping inquiries into the state of mind of a criminal defendant who has confessed, inquiries quite divorced from any coercion brought to bear on the defendant by the State. We think the Constitution rightly leaves this sort of inquiry to be resolved by state laws governing the admission of evidence and erects no standard of its own in this area. A statement rendered by one in the condition of respondent might be proved to be quite unreliable, but this is a matter to be governed by the evidentiary laws of the forum, and not by the Due Process Clause of the Fourteenth Amendment. "The aim of the requirement of due process is not to exclude presumptively false evidence, but to prevent fundamental unfairness in the use of evidence, whether true or false."

We hold that coercive police activity is a necessary predicate to the finding that a confession is not "voluntary" within the meaning of the Due Process Clause of the Fourteenth Amendment. We also conclude that the taking of respondent's statements, and their admission into evidence, constitute no violation of that Clause.

JUSTICE BRENNAN, with whom JUSTICE MARSHALL joins, dissenting.

Today the Court denies Mr. Connelly his fundamental right to make a vital choice with a sane mind, involving a determination that could allow the State to deprive him of liberty or even life. This holding is unprecedented: "Surely in the present stage of our civilization a most basic sense of justice is affronted by the spectacle of incarcerating a human being upon the basis of a statement he made while insane." *Blackburn v. Alabama*, 361 U.S. 199, 207 (1960). Because I believe that the use of a mentally ill person's involuntary confession is antithetical to the notion of fundamental fairness embodied in the Due Process Clause, I dissent.

The respondent's seriously impaired mental condition is clear on the record of this case. At the time of his confession, Mr. Connelly suffered from a "longstanding severe mental disorder," diagnosed as chronic paranoid schizophrenia. He had been hospitalized for psychiatric reasons five times prior to his confession; his longest hospitalization lasted for seven months. Mr. Connelly heard imaginary voices and saw nonexistent objects. He believed that his father was God, and that he was a reincarnation of Jesus.

At the time of his confession, Mr. Connelly's mental problems included "grandiose and delusional thinking." He had a known history of "thought withdrawal and insertion." Although physicians had treated Mr. Connelly "with a wide variety of medications in the past including antipsychotic medications," he had not taken any antipsychotic medications for at least six months prior to his confession. Following his arrest, Mr. Connelly initially was found incompetent to stand trial because the court-appointed psychiatrist, Dr. Metzner, "wasn't very confident that he could consistently relate accurate information." Dr. Metzner testified that Mr. Connelly was unable "to make free and rational choices" due to auditory hallucinations: "When he was read his *Miranda* rights, he probably had the capacity to know that he was being read his *Miranda* rights but he wasn't able to use that information because of the command hallucinations he had experienced." He achieved competency to stand trial only after six months of hospitalization and treatment with antipsychotic and sedative medications.

The state trial court found that the "overwhelming evidence presented by the Defense" indicated that the prosecution did not meet its burden of demonstrating by a preponderance of the evidence that the initial statement to Officer Anderson was voluntary. While the court found no police misconduct, it held: "There's no question that the Defendant did not exercise free will in choosing to talk to the police. He exercised a choice both *[sic]* of which were mandated by auditory hallucination, had no basis in reality, and were the product of a psychotic break with reality. The Defendant at the time of the confession had absolutely in the Court's estimation no volition or choice to make."

The absence of police wrongdoing should not, by itself, determine the voluntariness of a confession by a mentally ill person. The requirement that a confession be voluntary reflects a recognition of the importance of free will and of reliability in determining the admissibility of a confession, and thus demands an inquiry into the totality of the circumstances surrounding the confession.

Today's decision restricts the application of the term "involuntary" to those confessions obtained by police coercion. Confessions by mentally ill individuals or by persons coerced by parties other than police officers are now considered "voluntary." The Court's failure to recognize all forms of involuntariness or coercion as antithetical to due process reflects a refusal to acknowledge free will as a value of constitutional consequence. But due process derives much of its meaning from a conception of fundamental fairness that emphasizes the right to make vital choices voluntarily. This right requires vigilant protection if we are to safeguard the values of private conscience and human dignity.

This Court's assertion that we would be required "to establish a brand new constitutional right" to recognize the respondent's claim ignores 200 years of constitutional jurisprudence. A true commitment to fundamental fairness requires that the inquiry be "not whether the conduct of state officers in obtaining the confession is shocking, but whether the confession was free and voluntary." *Malloy v. Hogan*, 378 U.S. 1, 7 (1964).

We have never confined our focus to police coercion, because the value of freedom of will has demanded a broader inquiry. The confession cases decided by this Court over the 50 years since *Brown v. Mississippi* have focused upon both police overreaching and free will. While it is true that police overreaching has been an element of every confession case to date, it is also true that in every case the Court has made clear that ensuring that a confession is a product of free will is an independent concern. The fact that involuntary confessions have always been excluded in part because of police overreaching signifies only that this is a case of first impression. Until today, we have never upheld the admission of a confession that does not reflect the exercise of free will.

The Court's holding that involuntary confessions are only those procured through police misconduct is thus inconsistent with the Court's historical insistence that only confessions reflecting an exercise of free will be admitted into evidence.

Since the Court redefines voluntary confessions to include confessions by mentally ill individuals, the reliability of these confessions becomes a central concern. A concern for reliability is inherent in our criminal justice system, which relies upon accusatorial rather than inquisitorial practices. While an inquisitorial system prefers obtaining confessions from criminal defendants, an accusatorial system must place its faith in determinations of "guilt by evidence independently and freely secured."

Our distrust for reliance on confessions is due, in part, to their decisive impact upon the adversarial process. Triers of fact accord confessions such heavy weight in their determinations that "the introduction of a confession makes the other aspects of a trial in court superfluous, and the real trial, for all practical purposes, occurs when the confession is obtained." No other class of evidence is so profoundly prejudicial.

Because the admission of a confession so strongly tips the balance against the defendant in the adversarial process, we must be especially careful about a confession's reliability. We have to date not required a finding of reliability for involuntary confessions only because *all* such confessions have been excluded upon a finding of involuntariness, regardless of reliability. The Court's adoption today of a restrictive definition of an "involuntary" confession will require heightened scrutiny of a confession's reliability.

The instant case starkly highlights the danger of admitting a confession by a person with a severe mental illness. The trial court made no findings concerning the reliability of Mr. Connelly's involuntary confession, since it believed that the confession was excludable on the basis of involuntariness. However, the overwhelming evidence in the record points to the unreliability of Mr. Connelly's delusional mind. Mr. Connelly was found incompetent to stand trial because he was unable to relate accurate information, and the court-appointed psychiatrist indicated that Mr. Connelly was actively hallucinating and exhibited delusional thinking at the time of his confession. The Court, in fact, concedes that "a statement rendered by one in the condition of respondent might be proved to be quite unreliable."

Minimum standards of due process should require that the trial court find substantial indicia of reliability, on the basis of evidence extrinsic to the confession itself, before admitting the confession of a mentally ill person into evidence. I would require the trial court to make such a finding on remand. To hold otherwise allows the State to imprison and possibly to execute a mentally ill defendant based solely upon an inherently unreliable confession.

C. THE "VOLUNTARINESS" REQUIREMENT IN A NUTSHELL

The cases presented above yield a broad rule barring the admission into evidence of any involuntary statements obtained by authorities from the defendant. In applying the rule, a court must carefully examine all the facts and circumstances that led the defendant to make a confession.

The Voluntariness Requirement for Confessions

1. In order for a confession to be admitted into evidence against the accused, due process requires the prosecution to prove, by at least a preponderance of the evidence, that the confession was given voluntarily.

2. A court must examine the totality of the circumstances surrounding the confession to determine if it was voluntary or if the suspect's will was overborne. Coercive police activity must be present in order for a confession to be considered involuntary. Other factors bearing upon the voluntariness determination include: the use of force or threats of force; the amount of time spent in police custody or under interrogation; deprivation of food, sleep, medical care, or other necessities; psychological ploys and police deception; and the age, education, and mental condition of the suspect.

LEARN MORE WITH *LAW & ORDER*

In the following episode of *Law & Order* ("Thinking Makes It So," Season 16, Episode 18), police detectives are searching for a kidnapped girl. Detective Fontana eventually locates the kidnapper, Mitchell Lowell, hiding in his ex-wife's home. Lowell refuses to disclose the location of the girl until Fontana threatens him with a gun and shoves his head into a toilet. The police discover the girl, unharmed, on a boat.

Lowell's attorney, Randy Dworkin, moves to dismiss the charges against his client on the grounds that the location of the girl was coerced and all other evidence discovered thereafter was fruit of the involuntary confession. Assistant District Attorney Alexandra Borgia speaks to Detective Fontana, who says he did "the opposite" of everything Lowell alleges. The judge, citing Detective Fontana's credibility, rejects Lowell's claim of coercion and denies Dworkin's motion to dismiss.

At trial, the kidnapped girl testifies and implicates Lowell in her kidnapping. Detective Fontana then testifies and essentially admits that he physically threatened Lowell in order to obtain the location of the girl. Once again, Dworkin moves to dismiss all the charges, arguing that the confession was illegally obtained and the kidnapped girl's testimony was fruit of the poisonous tree. Before the judge can dismiss the case, however, Assistant District Attorney Borgia invokes the inevitable discovery exception to the exclusionary rule and argues that the location of the girl and other incriminating evidence would have been discovered even without the coerced confession.

The segments of the episode that depict the relevant Investigative Criminal Procedure issues appear at:

14:24 to 25:16; 29:07 to 30:47; 32:52 to 37:23

Law & Order **Episode**

"Thinking Makes It So," Season 16, Episode 18

The *Law & Order* episode nicely illustrates several important issues and raises a number of important questions. First, the central conflict in the episode revolves around the use of evidence obtained as a result of a confession coerced with force and threats of force. Should police be able to utilize these techniques when lives are at risk and time is of the essence? And even though we may abhor such brutal interrogation techniques, should the exclusionary rule bar the admission into evidence of a coerced confession that is demonstrably reliable?

Second, even when a confession is found to be voluntary and admissible, the defense is still permitted to argue, consistent with *Crane v. Kentucky*, 476 U.S. 683 (1986), that the confession was obtained under circumstances that make it unreliable. In the episode, defense attorney Randy Dworkin does just that, eliciting testimony from Detective Fontana about his use of force and threats of force to get Lowell to reveal the girl's location, even though the judge had previously ruled that Lowell's confession was voluntary and admissible.

Third, the episode provides an excellent illustration of the inevitable discovery exception to the exclusionary rule, presented in Chapter 8 in conjunction with *Nix v. Williams*, 467 U.S. 431 (1984). Based on Detective Fontana's testimony that he used force to extract the location of the girl from Lowell, the judge is poised to exclude much of the evidence and dismiss the case. At that point, Assistant District Attorney Borgia cites the inevitable discovery exception and notes that the harbormaster had told Lowell's ex-wife that Lowell was on her boat. Had Lowell refused to answer Detective Fontana's questions, Fontana would have interrogated the ex-wife, who would have disclosed what she had been told by the harbormaster, leading to the discovery of the girl on the boat. Because the girl's location would have inevitably been discovered by lawful means, her testimony against Lowell remains admissible despite the fact that Lowell's confession was coerced.

D. THE PROBLEM OF FALSE CONFESSIONS

As Justice Brennan noted in his *Colorado v. Connelly* dissent, a confession is often the most powerful evidence available in a criminal trial, and is typically accorded extraordinary weight by the judge or jury responsible for determining innocence or guilt. Precisely because evidence of a confession can be so damning, reliability is a major concern that is addressed, in part, by inquiring into whether it was made voluntarily. A finding that a confession was voluntary does little, however, to demonstrate its reliability, and many innocent people have been convicted on the basis of false confessions.[a]

One idea frequently advanced as a possible solution to the problem of coercive interrogation practices and false confessions is to require that all interrogations be videotaped, enabling judges and jurors to evaluate for themselves the conduct and words of the police and the suspect. Following the lead of a number of states and localities, U.S. Attorney General Eric Holder announced that the Justice Department will now require the FBI, the Drug Enforcement Administration, and other federal law enforcement agencies to record interrogations of criminal suspects held in custody.[b] The following link describes the new policy in greater detail.

**New Justice Department Policy Requiring
Recorded Interrogations**

http://www.justice.gov/opa/pr/2014/May/14–ag–548.html

While the trend toward more frequent recording of interrogations may help to curb police misconduct and reduce the incidence of false confessions, a recorded confession is not necessarily any more reliable than an unrecorded one. Indeed, a recorded false confession may be far more persuasive to a judge or jury than an unrecorded one, actually increasing the risk of a wrongful conviction. As Professor Jennifer Mnookin recently observed:

> The problem is that many of the red flags that frequently occur in false confessions—like unusually long interrogations, the inclusion of inaccurate details, or the police "feeding" some crime-related information to the suspect—can also occur in the confessions of the guilty. This means there's no surefire way to tell false confessions and true confessions apart by viewing a recording, except in extreme cases.

---

[a] *See* Jan Hoffman, *Police Refine Methods So Potent, Even the Innocent Have Confessed*, NEW YORK TIMES, March 30, 1998, available at http://www.nytimes.com/1998/03/30/nyregion/police-refine-methods-so-potent-even-the-innocent-have-confessed.html.

[b] *See* Michael S. Schmidt, *In Policy Change, Justice Dept. to Require Recording of Interrogations*, NEW YORK TIMES, May 22, 2014, available at http://www.nytimes.com/2014/05/23/us/politics/justice-dept-to-reverse-ban-on-recording-interrogations.html.

And yet by making confessions so vivid to juries, recording could paper over such complications, and sometimes even make the problem worse. The emotional impact of a suspect declaring his guilt out loud, on video, is powerful and hard to dislodge, even if the defense attorney points out reasons to doubt its accuracy.[c]

In recent years, there has been a great deal of research on false confessions in an effort to understand the scope of the problem, its causes, and possible solutions. The following websites summarize some of that research and are excellent resources for additional information.

Additional Resources on False Confessions

http://www.falseconfessions.org

http://www.innocenceproject.org/understand/False–Confessions.php

http://courses2.cit.cornell.edu/sociallaw/student_projects/
FalseConfessions.html

---

[c]   Jennifer L. Mnookin, *Can a Jury Believe What It Sees?*, NEW YORK TIMES, July 13, 2014, available at http://www.nytimes.com/2014/07/14/opinion/videotaped-confessions-can-be-mislead ing.html.

CHAPTER 10

THE FIFTH AMENDMENT AND POLICE INTERROGATION

■ ■ ■

While the voluntariness standard for confessions described in Chapter 9 provides an important measure of protection against coercive interrogation practices, it suffers from two principal deficiencies. First, it does not actually ensure that criminal suspects are apprised of their constitutional rights to remain silent or consult an attorney, rights that may be crucial in helping to relieve some of the coercive pressure associated with police interrogation. Second, because the application of the voluntariness standard depends on the particular facts and circumstances in each case, it provides little practical guidance to the police officers responsible for questioning criminal suspects.

In an effort to address these deficiencies, the Supreme Court in the 1960s announced additional constitutional protections for criminal suspects subjected to custodial interrogation by the police. The most important—and controversial—protections were established in the Court's landmark decision in *Miranda v. Arizona*, 384 U.S. 436 (1966). That decision—and subsequent cases interpreting and applying it—is the focus of this Chapter.

It's important to remember that *Miranda* does not supplant the voluntariness standard. Even when police properly administer the now-familiar *Miranda* warnings, the use of excessively coercive interrogation techniques may still render a confession involuntary. Thus, in evaluating the admissibility of a suspect's incriminating statement, a court must determine *both* whether it was given voluntarily *and* whether the police followed the requirements set forth in *Miranda* and its progeny. When the police do properly administer the *Miranda* warnings and follow the other requirements set forth in the decision, however, there is a presumption that any confession given by the suspect is voluntary and admissible.

A. FIFTH AMENDMENT LIMITATIONS ON CUSTODIAL INTERROGATION: *MIRANDA v. ARIZONA*

In *Escobedo v. Illinois*, 378 U.S. 478 (1964), the Supreme Court held that incriminating statements made by a murder suspect were inadmissible because they were obtained by police after denying the suspect's repeated requests to speak to an attorney. Two years later, in *Miranda v. Arizona*, the Supreme Court reviewed common police interrogation practices and found that they create a "compulsion to speak" that jeopardizes the Fifth Amendment privilege against self-incrimination. In order to counterbalance this coercive pressure, the Supreme Court held that prior to any custodial interrogation, a criminal suspect must be informed of certain constitutional rights, particularly the right to remain silent and the right to consult with an attorney.

MIRANDA V. ARIZONA
384 U.S. 436 (1966)

CHIEF JUSTICE WARREN delivered the opinion of the Court.

The cases before us raise questions which go to the roots of our concepts of American criminal jurisprudence: the restraints society must observe consistent with the Federal Constitution in prosecuting individuals for crime. More specifically, we deal with the admissibility of statements obtained from an individual who is subjected to custodial police interrogation and the necessity for procedures which assure that the individual is accorded his privilege under the Fifth Amendment to the Constitution not to be compelled to incriminate himself.

We dealt with certain phases of this problem recently in *Escobedo v. Illinois*, 378 U.S. 478 (1964). There, as in the four cases before us, law enforcement officials took the defendant into custody and interrogated him in a police station for the purpose of obtaining a confession. The police did not effectively advise him of his right to remain silent or of his right to consult with his attorney. Rather, they confronted him with an alleged accomplice who accused him of having perpetrated a murder. When the defendant denied the accusation and said "I didn't shoot Manuel, you did it," they handcuffed him and took him to an interrogation room. There, while handcuffed and standing, he was questioned for four hours until he confessed. During this interrogation, the police denied his request to speak to his attorney, and they prevented his retained attorney, who had come to the police station, from consulting with him. At his trial, the State, over his objection, introduced the confession against him. We held that the statements thus made were constitutionally inadmissible.

This case has been the subject of judicial interpretation and spirited legal debate since it was decided two years ago. We granted certiorari in these cases in order further to explore some facets of the problems, thus exposed, of applying the privilege against self-incrimination to in-custody interrogation, and to give concrete constitutional guidelines for law enforcement agencies and courts to follow.

We start here, as we did in *Escobedo*, with the premise that our holding is not an innovation in our jurisprudence, but is an application of principles long recognized and applied in other settings. We have undertaken a thorough re-examination of the *Escobedo* decision and the principles it announced, and we reaffirm it. That case was but an explication of basic rights that are enshrined in our Constitution—that "No person . . . shall be compelled in any criminal case to be a witness against himself," and that "the accused shall . . . have the Assistance of Counsel"—rights which were put in jeopardy in that case through official overbearing. These precious rights were fixed in our Constitution only after centuries of persecution and struggle.

Our holding will be spelled out with some specificity in the pages which follow but briefly stated it is this: the prosecution may not use statements, whether exculpatory or inculpatory, stemming from custodial interrogation of the defendant unless it demonstrates the use of procedural safeguards effective to secure the privilege against self-incrimination. By custodial interrogation, we mean questioning initiated by law enforcement officers after a person has been taken into custody or otherwise deprived of his freedom of action in any significant way. As for the procedural safeguards to be employed, unless other fully effective means are devised to inform accused persons of their right of silence and to assure a continuous opportunity to exercise it, the following measures are required. Prior to any questioning, the person must be warned that he has a right to remain silent, that any statement he does make may be used as evidence against him, and that he has a right to the presence of an attorney, either retained or appointed. The defendant may waive effectuation of these rights, provided the waiver is made voluntarily, knowingly and intelligently. If, however, he indicates in any manner and at any stage of the process that he wishes to consult with an attorney before speaking, there can be no questioning. Likewise, if the individual is alone and indicates in any manner that he does not wish to be interrogated, the police may not question him. The mere fact that he may have answered some questions or volunteered some statements on his own does not deprive him of the right to refrain from answering any further inquiries until he has consulted with an attorney and thereafter consents to be questioned.

I

The constitutional issue we decide in each of these cases is the admissibility of statements obtained from a defendant questioned while in custody or otherwise deprived of his freedom of action in any significant way. In each, the defendant was questioned by police officers, detectives, or a prosecuting attorney in a room in which he was cut off from the outside world. In none of these cases was the defendant given a full and effective warning of his rights at the outset of the interrogation process. In all the cases, the questioning elicited oral admissions, and in three of them, signed statements as well which were admitted at their trials. They all thus share salient features—incommunicado interrogation of individuals in a police-dominated atmosphere, resulting in self-incriminating statements without full warnings of constitutional rights.

An understanding of the nature and setting of this in-custody interrogation is essential to our decisions today. The difficulty in depicting what transpires at such interrogations stems from the fact that, in this country, they have largely taken place incommunicado. From extensive factual studies undertaken in the early 1930's, including the famous Wickersham Report to Congress by a Presidential Commission, it is clear that police violence and the "third degree" flourished at that time. In a series of cases decided by this Court long after these studies, the police resorted to physical brutality—beatings, hanging, whipping—and to sustained and protracted questioning incommunicado in order to extort confessions. The Commission on Civil Rights in 1961 found much evidence to indicate that "some policemen still resort to physical force to obtain confessions." The use of physical brutality and violence is not, unfortunately, relegated to the past or to any part of the country. Only recently in Kings County, New York, the police brutally beat, kicked and placed lighted cigarette butts on the back of a potential witness under interrogation for the purpose of securing a statement incriminating a third party.

The examples given above are undoubtedly the exception now, but they are sufficiently widespread to be the object of concern. Unless a proper limitation upon custodial interrogation is achieved—such as these decisions will advance—there can be no assurance that practices of this nature will be eradicated in the foreseeable future.

Again we stress that the modern practice of in-custody interrogation is psychologically, rather than physically, oriented. This Court has recognized that coercion can be mental as well as physical, and that the blood of the accused is not the only hallmark of an unconstitutional inquisition. Interrogation still takes place in privacy. Privacy results in secrecy and this in turn results in a gap in our knowledge as to what in fact goes on in the interrogation rooms. A valuable source of information about present police practices, however, may be found in various police manuals and texts which document procedures employed with success in the past, and which recommend various other effective tactics. These texts are used by law enforcement agencies themselves as guides. It should be noted that these texts professedly present the most enlightened and effective means presently used to obtain statements through custodial interrogation. By considering these texts and other data, it is possible to describe procedures observed and noted around the country.

The officers are told by the manuals that the "principal psychological factor contributing to a successful interrogation is privacy—being alone with the person under interrogation." To highlight the isolation and unfamiliar surroundings, the manuals instruct the police to display an air of confidence in the suspect's guilt and from outward appearance to maintain only an interest in confirming certain details. The guilt of the subject is to be posited as a fact. The interrogator should direct his comments toward the reasons why the subject committed the act, rather than court failure by asking the subject whether he did it. Like other men, perhaps the subject has had a bad family life, had an unhappy childhood, had too much to drink, had an unrequited desire for women. The officers are instructed to minimize the moral seriousness of the offense, to cast blame on the victim or on society. These tactics are designed to put the subject in a psychological state where his story is but an elaboration of what the police purport to know already—that he is guilty. Explanations to the contrary are dismissed and discouraged. The texts thus stress that the major qualities an interrogator should possess are patience and perseverance.

When the techniques described above prove unavailing, the texts recommend they be alternated with a show of some hostility. One ploy often used has been termed the "friendly-unfriendly" or the "Mutt and Jeff" act.

The interrogators sometimes are instructed to induce a confession out of trickery. The technique here is quite effective in crimes which require identification or which run in series. In the identification situation, the interrogator may take a break in his questioning to place the subject among a group of men in a line-up. "The witness or complainant (previously coached, if necessary) studies the line-up and confidently points out the subject as the guilty party." Then the questioning resumes "as though there were now no doubt about the guilt of the subject." A variation on this technique is called the "reverse line-up": "The accused is placed in a line-up, but this time he is identified by several fictitious witnesses or victims who associated him with different offenses. It is expected that the subject will become desperate and confess to the offense under investigation in order to escape from the false accusations."

The manuals also contain instructions for police on how to handle the individual who refuses to discuss the matter entirely, or who asks for an attorney or relatives. The examiner is to concede him the right to remain silent. "This usually has a very undermining effect. First of all, he is disappointed in his expectation of an unfavorable reaction on the part of the interrogator. Secondly, a concession of this right to remain silent impresses the subject with the apparent fairness of his interrogator."

After this psychological conditioning, however, the officer is told to point out the incriminating significance of the suspect's refusal to talk:

> Joe, you have a right to remain silent. That's your privilege and I'm the last person in the world who'll try to take it away from you. If that's the way you want to leave this, O.K. But let me ask you this. Suppose you were in my shoes and I were in yours and you called me in to ask me about this and I told you, "I don't want to answer any of your questions." You'd think I had something to hide, and you'd probably be right in thinking that. That's exactly what I'll have to think about you, and so will everybody else. So let's sit here and talk this whole thing over.

Few will persist in their initial refusal to talk, it is said, if this monologue is employed correctly. In the event that the subject wishes to speak to a relative or an attorney, the following advice is tendered:

> The interrogator should respond by suggesting that the subject first tell the truth to the interrogator himself rather than get anyone else involved in the matter. If the request is for an attorney, the interrogator may suggest that the subject save himself or his family the expense of any such professional service, particularly if he is innocent of the offense under investigation. The interrogator may also add, "Joe, I'm only looking for the truth, and if you're telling the truth, that's it. You can handle this by yourself."

From these representative samples of interrogation techniques, the setting prescribed by the manuals and observed in practice becomes clear. In essence, it is this: To be alone with the subject is essential to prevent distraction and to deprive him of any outside support. The aura of confidence in his guilt undermines his will to resist. He merely confirms the preconceived story the police seek to have him describe. Patience and persistence, at times relentless questioning, are employed. To obtain a confession, the interrogator must "patiently maneuver himself or his quarry into a position from which the desired objective may be attained." When normal procedures fail to produce the needed result, the police may resort to deceptive stratagems such as giving false legal advice. It is important to keep the subject off balance, for example, by trading on his insecurity about himself or his surroundings. The police then persuade, trick, or cajole him out of exercising his constitutional rights.

Even without employing brutality, the "third degree" or the specific stratagems described above, the very fact of custodial interrogation exacts a heavy toll on individual liberty and trades on the weakness of individuals.

In the cases before us today, given this background, we concern ourselves primarily with this interrogation atmosphere and the evils it can bring. In No. 759, *Miranda v. Arizona*, the police arrested the defendant and took him to a special interrogation room where they secured a confession. In No. 760, *Vignera v. New York*, the defendant made oral admissions to the police after interrogation in the afternoon, and then signed an inculpatory statement upon being questioned by an assistant district attorney later the same evening. In No. 761, *Westover v. U.S.*, the defendant was handed over to the Federal Bureau of Investigation by local authorities after they had detained and interrogated him for a lengthy period, both at night and the following morning. After some two hours of questioning, the federal officers had obtained signed statements from the defendant. Lastly, in No. 584, *California v. Stewart*, the local police held the defendant five days in the station and interrogated him on nine separate occasions before they secured his inculpatory statement.

In these cases, we might not find the defendants' statements to have been involuntary in traditional terms. Our concern for adequate safeguards to protect precious Fifth Amendment rights is, of course, not lessened in the slightest. In each of the cases, the defendant was thrust into an unfamiliar atmosphere and run through menacing police interrogation procedures. The potentiality for compulsion is forcefully apparent, for example, in *Miranda*, where the indigent Mexican defendant was a seriously disturbed individual with pronounced sexual fantasies, and in *Stewart*, in which the defendant was an indigent Los Angeles Negro who had dropped out of school in the sixth grade. To be sure, the records do not evince overt physical coercion or patent psychological ploys. The fact remains that in none of these cases did the officers undertake to afford appropriate safeguards at the outset of the interrogation to insure that the statements were truly the product of free choice.

It is obvious that such an interrogation environment is created for no purpose other than to subjugate the individual to the will of his examiner. This atmosphere carries its own badge of intimidation. To be sure, this is not physical intimidation, but it is equally destructive of human dignity. The current practice of incommunicado interrogation is at odds with one of our Nation's most cherished principles—that the individual may not be compelled to incriminate himself. Unless adequate protective devices are employed to dispel the compulsion inherent in custodial surroundings, no statement obtained from the defendant can truly be the product of his free choice.

II

We sometimes forget how long it has taken to establish the privilege against self-incrimination, the sources from which it came and the fervor with which it was defended. Its roots go back into ancient times.

We have recently noted that the privilege against self-incrimination—the essential mainstay of our adversary system—is founded on a complex of values. All these policies point to one overriding thought: the constitutional foundation underlying the privilege is the respect a government—state or federal—must accord to the dignity and integrity of its citizens. To respect the inviolability of the human personality, our accusatory system of criminal justice demands that the government seeking to punish an individual produce the evidence against him by its own independent labors, rather than by the cruel, simple expedient of compelling it from his own mouth. In sum, the privilege is fulfilled only when the person is guaranteed the right to remain silent unless he chooses to speak in the unfettered exercise of his own will.

The question in these cases is whether the privilege is fully applicable during a period of custodial interrogation. In this Court, the privilege has consistently been accorded a liberal construction. We are satisfied that all the principles embodied in the privilege apply to informal compulsion exerted by law-enforcement officers during in-custody questioning. An individual swept from familiar surroundings into police custody, surrounded by antagonistic forces, and subjected to the techniques of persuasion described above cannot be otherwise than under compulsion to speak. As a practical matter, the compulsion to speak in the isolated setting of the police station may well be greater than in courts or other official investigations, where there are often impartial observers to guard against intimidation or trickery.

III

Today, then, there can be no doubt that the Fifth Amendment privilege is available outside of criminal court proceedings and serves to protect persons in all settings in which their freedom of action is curtailed in any significant way from being compelled to incriminate themselves. We have concluded that, without proper safeguards, the process of in-custody interrogation of persons suspected or accused of crime contains inherently compelling pressures which work to undermine the individual's will to resist and to compel him to speak where he would not otherwise do so freely. In order to combat these pressures and to permit a full opportunity to exercise the privilege against self-incrimination, the accused must be adequately and effectively apprised of his rights and the exercise of those rights must be fully honored.

It is impossible for us to foresee the potential alternatives for protecting the privilege which might be devised by Congress or the States in the exercise of their creative rule-making capacities. Therefore we cannot say that the Constitution necessarily requires adherence to any particular solution for the inherent compulsions of the interrogation process as it is presently conducted. Our decision in no way creates a constitutional straitjacket which will handicap sound efforts at reform, nor is it intended to have this effect. We encourage Congress and the States to continue their laudable search for increasingly effective ways of protecting the rights of the individual while promoting efficient enforcement of our criminal laws. However, unless we are shown other procedures which are at least as effective in apprising accused persons of their right of silence and in assuring a continuous opportunity to exercise it, the following safeguards must be observed.

At the outset, if a person in custody is to be subjected to interrogation, he must first be informed in clear and unequivocal terms that he has the right to remain silent. For those unaware of the privilege, the warning is needed simply to make them aware of it—the threshold requirement for an intelligent decision as to its exercise. More important, such a warning is an absolute prerequisite in overcoming the inherent pressures of the interrogation atmosphere. It is not just the subnormal or woefully ignorant who succumb to an interrogator's imprecations, whether implied or expressly stated, that the interrogation will continue until a confession is obtained or that silence in the face of accusation is itself damning and will bode ill when presented to a jury.[37] Further, the warning will show the individual that his interrogators are prepared to recognize his privilege should he choose to exercise it.

The Fifth Amendment privilege is so fundamental to our system of constitutional rule, and the expedient of giving an adequate warning as to the availability of the privilege so simple, we will not pause to inquire in individual cases whether the defendant was aware of his rights without a warning being given. Assessments of the knowledge the defendant possessed, based on information as to his age, education, intelligence, or prior contact with authorities, can never be more than speculation; a warning is a clearcut fact. More important, whatever the background of the person interrogated, a warning at the time of the interrogation is indispensable to overcome its pressures and to insure that the individual knows he is free to exercise the privilege at that point in time.

The warning of the right to remain silent must be accompanied by the explanation that anything said can and will be used against the individual in court. This warning is needed in order to make him aware not only of the privilege, but also of the consequences of forgoing it. It is only through an awareness of these consequences that there can be any assurance of real understanding and intelligent exercise of the privilege. Moreover, this warning may serve to make the individual more acutely aware that he is faced with a phase of the adversary system—that he is not in the presence of persons acting solely in his interest.

---

[37] In accord with our decision today, it is impermissible to penalize an individual for exercising his Fifth Amendment privilege when he is under police custodial interrogation. The prosecution may not, therefore, use at trial the fact that he stood mute or claimed his privilege in the face of accusation.

The circumstances surrounding in-custody interrogation can operate very quickly to overbear the will of one merely made aware of his privilege by his interrogators. Therefore, the right to have counsel present at the interrogation is indispensable to the protection of the Fifth Amendment privilege under the system we delineate today. Our aim is to assure that the individual's right to choose between silence and speech remains unfettered throughout the interrogation process. A once-stated warning, delivered by those who will conduct the interrogation, cannot itself suffice to that end among those who most require knowledge of their rights. A mere warning given by the interrogators is not alone sufficient to accomplish that end. Thus, the need for counsel to protect the Fifth Amendment privilege comprehends not merely a right to consult with counsel prior to questioning, but also to have counsel present during any questioning if the defendant so desires.

The presence of counsel at the interrogation may serve several significant subsidiary functions as well. If the accused decides to talk to his interrogators, the assistance of counsel can mitigate the dangers of untrustworthiness. With a lawyer present the likelihood that the police will practice coercion is reduced, and if coercion is nevertheless exercised the lawyer can testify to it in court. The presence of a lawyer can also help to guarantee that the accused gives a fully accurate statement to the police, and that the statement is rightly reported by the prosecution at trial.

An individual need not make a pre-interrogation request for a lawyer. While such request affirmatively secures his right to have one, his failure to ask for a lawyer does not constitute a waiver. No effective waiver of the right to counsel during interrogation can be recognized unless specifically made after the warnings we here delineate have been given. The accused who does not know his rights and therefore does not make a request may be the person who most needs counsel.

Accordingly, we hold that an individual held for interrogation must be clearly informed that he has the right to consult with a lawyer and to have the lawyer with him during interrogation under the system for protecting the privilege we delineate today. As with the warnings of the right to remain silent and that anything stated can be used in evidence against him, this warning is an absolute prerequisite to interrogation. No amount of circumstantial evidence that the person may have been aware of this right will suffice to stand in its stead. Only through such a warning is there ascertainable assurance that the accused was aware of this right.

If an individual indicates that he wishes the assistance of counsel before any interrogation occurs, the authorities cannot rationally ignore or deny his request on the basis that the individual does not have or cannot afford a retained attorney. The financial ability of the individual has no relationship to the scope of the rights involved here. The privilege against self-incrimination secured by the Constitution applies to all individuals. The need for counsel in order to protect the privilege exists for the indigent as well as the affluent. In fact, were we to limit these constitutional rights to those who can retain an attorney, our decisions today would be of little significance. The cases before us, as well as the vast majority of confession cases with which we have dealt in the past, involve those unable to retain counsel. While authorities are not required to relieve the accused of his poverty, they have the obligation not to take advantage of indigence in the administration of justice. Denial of counsel to the indigent at the time of interrogation while allowing an attorney to those who can afford one would be no more supportable by reason or logic than the similar situation at trial and on appeal struck down in *Gideon v. Wainwright*, 372 U.S. 335 (1963), and *Douglas v. California*, 372 U.S. 353 (1963).

In order fully to apprise a person interrogated of the extent of his rights under this system, then, it is necessary to warn him not only that he has the right to consult with an attorney, but also that if he is indigent a lawyer will be appointed to represent him. Without this additional warning, the admonition of the right to consult with counsel would often be understood as meaning only that he can consult with a lawyer if he has one or has the funds to obtain one. The warning of a right to counsel would be hollow if not couched in terms that would convey to the indigent—the person most often subjected to interrogation—the knowledge that he too has a right to have counsel present. As with the warnings of the right to remain silent and of the general right to counsel, only by effective and express explanation to the indigent of this right can there be assurance that he was truly in a position to exercise it.

Once warnings have been given, the subsequent procedure is clear. If the individual indicates in any manner, at any time prior to or during questioning, that he wishes to remain silent, the interrogation must cease. At this point, he has shown that he intends to exercise his Fifth Amendment privilege; any statement taken after the person invokes his privilege cannot be other than the product of compulsion, subtle or otherwise. Without the right to cut off questioning, the setting of in-custody interrogation operates on the individual to overcome free choice in producing a statement after the privilege has been once invoked. If the individual states that he wants an attorney, the interrogation must cease until an attorney is present. At that time, the individual must have an opportunity to confer with the attorney and to have him present during any subsequent questioning. If the individual cannot obtain an attorney and he indicates that he wants one before speaking to police, they must respect his decision to remain silent.

This does not mean, as some have suggested, that each police station must have a "station house lawyer" present at all times to advise prisoners. It does mean, however, that if police propose to interrogate a person, they must make known to him that he is entitled to a lawyer and that, if he cannot afford one, a lawyer will be provided for him prior to any interrogation. If authorities conclude that they will not provide counsel during a reasonable period of time in which investigation in the field is carried out, they may refrain from doing so without violating the person's Fifth Amendment privilege so long as they do not question him during that time.

If the interrogation continues without the presence of an attorney and a statement is taken, a heavy burden rests on the government to demonstrate that the defendant knowingly and intelligently waived his privilege against self-incrimination and his right to retained or appointed counsel. This Court has always set high standards of proof for the waiver of constitutional rights, and we reassert these standards as applied to in-custody interrogation. Since the State is responsible for establishing the isolated circumstances under which the interrogation takes place, and has the only means of making available corroborated evidence of warnings given during incommunicado interrogation, the burden is rightly on its shoulders.

An express statement that the individual is willing to make a statement and does not want an attorney, followed closely by a statement, could constitute a waiver. But a valid waiver will not be presumed simply from the silence of the accused after warnings are given, or simply from the fact that a confession was, in fact, eventually obtained. Moreover, where in-custody interrogation is involved, there is no room for the contention that the privilege is waived if the individual answers some questions or gives some information on his own prior to invoking his right to remain silent when interrogated.

Whatever the testimony of the authorities as to waiver of rights by an accused, the fact of lengthy interrogation or incommunicado incarceration before a statement is made is strong evidence that the accused did not validly waive his rights. In these circumstances, the fact that the individual eventually made a statement is consistent with the conclusion that the compelling influence of the interrogation finally forced him to do so. It is inconsistent with any notion of a voluntary relinquishment of the privilege. Moreover, any evidence that the accused was threatened, tricked, or cajoled into a waiver will, of course, show that the defendant did not voluntarily waive his privilege. The requirement of warnings and waiver of rights is a fundamental with respect to the Fifth Amendment privilege, and not simply a preliminary ritual to existing methods of interrogation.

The warnings required and the waiver necessary in accordance with our opinion today are, in the absence of a fully effective equivalent, prerequisites to the admissibility of any statement made by a defendant. No distinction can be drawn between statements which are direct confessions and statements which amount to "admissions" of part or all of an offense. The privilege against self-incrimination protects the individual from being compelled to incriminate himself in any manner; it does not distinguish degrees of incrimination. Similarly, for precisely the same reason, no distinction may be drawn between inculpatory statements and statements alleged to be merely "exculpatory." If a statement made were in fact truly exculpatory it would, of course, never be used by the prosecution. In fact, statements merely intended to be exculpatory by the defendant are often used to impeach his testimony at trial or to demonstrate untruths in the statement given under interrogation, and thus to prove guilt by implication. These statements are incriminating in any meaningful sense of the word, and may not be used without the full warnings and effective waiver required for any other statement.

The principles announced today deal with the protection which must be given to the privilege against self-incrimination when the individual is first subjected to police interrogation while in custody at the station or otherwise deprived of his freedom of action in any significant way. It is at this point that our adversary system of criminal proceedings commences, distinguishing itself at the outset from the inquisitorial system recognized in some countries. Under the system of warnings we delineate today, or under any other system which may be devised and found effective, the safeguards to be erected about the privilege must come into play at this point.

Our decision is not intended to hamper the traditional function of police officers in investigating crime. When an individual is in custody on probable cause, the police may, of course, seek out evidence in the field to be used at trial against him. Such investigation may include inquiry of persons not under restraint. General on-the-scene questioning as to facts surrounding a crime or other general questioning of citizens in the fact-finding process is not affected by our holding. It is an act of responsible citizenship for individuals to give whatever information they may have to aid in law enforcement. In such situations, the compelling atmosphere inherent in the process of in-custody interrogation is not necessarily present.

In dealing with statements obtained through interrogation, we do not purport to find all confessions inadmissible. Confessions remain a proper element in law enforcement. Any statement given freely and voluntarily without any compelling influences is, of course, admissible in evidence. The fundamental import of the privilege while an individual is in custody is not whether he is allowed to talk to the police without the benefit of warnings and counsel, but whether he can be interrogated. There is no requirement that police stop a person who enters a police station and states that he wishes to confess to a crime, or a person who calls the police to offer a confession or any other statement he desires to make. Volunteered statements of any kind are not barred by the Fifth Amendment, and their admissibility is not affected by our holding today.

To summarize, we hold that, when an individual is taken into custody or otherwise deprived of his freedom by the authorities in any significant way and is subjected to questioning, the privilege against self-incrimination is jeopardized. Procedural safeguards must be employed to protect the privilege, and unless other fully effective means are adopted to notify the person of his right of silence and to assure that the exercise of the right will be scrupulously honored, the following measures are required. He must be warned prior to any questioning that he has the right to remain silent, that anything he says can be used against him in a court of law, that he has the right to the presence of an attorney, and that if he cannot afford an attorney one will be appointed for him prior to any questioning if he so desires. Opportunity to exercise these rights must be afforded to him throughout the interrogation. After such warnings have been given, and such opportunity afforded him, the individual may knowingly and intelligently waive these rights and agree to answer questions or make a statement. But unless and until such warnings and waiver are demonstrated by the prosecution at trial, no evidence obtained as a result of interrogation can be used against him.

IV

A recurrent argument made in these cases is that society's need for interrogation outweighs the privilege. This argument is not unfamiliar to this Court. The whole thrust of our foregoing discussion demonstrates that the Constitution has prescribed the rights of the individual when confronted with the power of government when it provided in the Fifth Amendment that an individual cannot be compelled to be a witness against himself. That right cannot be abridged.

If the individual desires to exercise his privilege, he has the right to do so. This is not for the authorities to decide. An attorney may advise his client not to talk to police until he has had an opportunity to investigate the case, or he may wish to be present with his client during any police questioning. In doing so an attorney is merely exercising the good professional judgment he has been taught. This is not cause for considering the attorney a menace to law enforcement. He is merely carrying out what he is sworn to do under his oath—to protect to the extent of his ability the rights of his client. In fulfilling this responsibility, the attorney plays a vital role in the administration of criminal justice under our Constitution.

In announcing these principles, we are not unmindful of the burdens which law enforcement officials must bear, often under trying circumstances. We also fully recognize the obligation of all citizens to aid in enforcing the criminal laws. This Court, while protecting individual rights, has always given ample latitude to law enforcement agencies in the legitimate exercise of their duties. The limits we have placed on the interrogation process should not constitute an undue interference with a proper system of law enforcement. As we have noted, our decision does not in any way preclude police from carrying out their traditional investigatory functions. Although confessions may play an important role in some convictions, the cases before us present graphic examples of the overstatement of the "need" for confessions. In each case, authorities conducted interrogations ranging up to five days in duration despite the presence, through standard investigating practices, of considerable evidence against each defendant. Further examples are chronicled in our prior cases.

Over the years the Federal Bureau of Investigation has compiled an exemplary record of effective law enforcement while advising any suspect or arrested person, at the outset of an interview, that he is not required to make a statement, that any statement may be used against him in court, that the individual may obtain the services of an attorney of his own choice and, more recently, that he has a right to free counsel if he is unable to pay. The practice of the FBI can readily be emulated by state and local enforcement agencies. The argument that the FBI deals with different crimes than are dealt with by state authorities does not mitigate the significance of the FBI experience.

It is also urged upon us that we withhold decision on this issue until state legislative bodies and advisory groups have had an opportunity to deal with these problems by rulemaking. We have already pointed out that the Constitution does not require any specific code of procedures for protecting the privilege against self-incrimination during custodial interrogation. Congress and the States are free to develop their own safeguards for the privilege, so long as they are fully as effective as those described above in informing accused persons of their right of silence and in affording a continuous opportunity to exercise it. In any event, however, the issues presented are of constitutional dimensions and must be determined by the courts. Where rights secured by the Constitution are involved, there can be no rulemaking or legislation which would abrogate them.

V

Because of the nature of the problem and because of its recurrent significance in numerous cases, we have to this point discussed the relationship of the Fifth Amendment privilege to police interrogation without specific concentration on the facts of the cases before us. We turn now to these facts to consider the application to these cases of the constitutional principles discussed above. In each instance, we have concluded that statements were obtained from the defendant under circumstances that did not meet constitutional standards for protection of the privilege.

On March 13, 1963, petitioner, Ernesto Miranda, was arrested at his home and taken in custody to a Phoenix police station. He was there identified by the complaining witness. The police then took him to "Interrogation Room No. 2" of the detective bureau. There he was questioned by two police officers. The officers admitted at trial that Miranda was not advised that he had a right to have an attorney present. Two hours later, the officers emerged from the interrogation room with a written confession signed by Miranda. At the top of the statement was a typed paragraph stating that the confession was made voluntarily, without threats or promises of immunity and "with full knowledge of my legal rights, understanding any statement I make may be used against me."[67]

At his trial before a jury, the written confession was admitted into evidence over the objection of defense counsel, and the officers testified to the prior oral confession made by Miranda during the interrogation. Miranda was found guilty of kidnapping and rape. He was sentenced to 20 to 30 years' imprisonment on each count, the sentences to run concurrently. On appeal, the Supreme Court of Arizona held that Miranda's constitutional rights were not violated in obtaining the confession, and affirmed the conviction. In reaching its decision, the court emphasized heavily the fact that Miranda did not specifically request counsel.

We reverse. From the testimony of the officers and by the admission of respondent, it is clear that Miranda was not in any way apprised of his right to consult with an attorney and to have one present during the interrogation, nor was his right not to be compelled to incriminate himself effectively protected in any other manner. Without these warnings, the statements were inadmissible. The mere fact that he signed a statement which contained a typed-in clause stating that he had "full knowledge" of his "legal rights" does not approach the knowing and intelligent waiver required to relinquish constitutional rights.

JUSTICE CLARK, dissenting.

It is with regret that I find it necessary to write in these cases. However, I am unable to join the majority because its opinion goes too far on too little, while my dissenting brethren do not go quite far enough. Nor can I join in the Court's criticism of the present practices of police and

---

[67] One of the officers testified that he read this paragraph to Miranda. Apparently, however, he did not do so until after Miranda had confessed orally.

investigatory agencies as to custodial interrogation. The materials it refers to as "police manuals" are, as I read them, merely writings in this field by professors and some police officers. Not one is shown by the record here to be the official manual of any police department, much less in universal use in crime detection. Moreover, the examples of police brutality mentioned by the Court are rare exceptions to the thousands of cases that appear every year in the law reports. The police agencies—all the way from municipal and state forces to the federal bureaus—are responsible for law enforcement and public safety in this country. I am proud of their efforts, which, in my view, are not fairly characterized by the Court's opinion.

The rule prior to today depended upon a totality of circumstances evidencing an involuntary admission of guilt. I would continue to follow that rule. Under the "totality of circumstances," I would consider in each case whether the police officer, prior to custodial interrogation, added the warning that the suspect might have counsel present at the interrogation, and, further, that a court would appoint one at his request if he was too poor to employ counsel. In the absence of warnings, the burden would be on the State to prove that counsel was knowingly and intelligently waived or that, in the totality of the circumstances, including the failure to give the necessary warnings, the confession was clearly voluntary.

Rather than employing the arbitrary Fifth Amendment rule which the Court lays down, I would follow the more pliable dictates of the Due Process Clauses of the Fifth and Fourteenth Amendments which we are accustomed to administering, and which we know from our cases are effective instruments in protecting persons in police custody. In this way, we would not be acting in the dark, nor, in one full sweep, changing the traditional rules of custodial interrogation which this Court has for so long recognized as a justifiable and proper tool in balancing individual rights against the rights of society. It will be soon enough to go further when we are able to appraise with somewhat better accuracy the effect of such a holding.

JUSTICE HARLAN, whom JUSTICE STEWART and JUSTICE WHITE join, dissenting.

I believe the decision of the Court represents poor constitutional law and entails harmful consequences for the country at large. How serious these consequences may prove to be, only time can tell. But the basic flaws in the Court's justification seem to me readily apparent now, once all sides of the problem are considered.

I.   INTRODUCTION

At the outset, it is well to note exactly what is required by the Court's new constitutional code of rules for confessions. The foremost requirement, upon which later admissibility of a confession depends, is that a fourfold warning be given to a person in custody before he is questioned, namely, that he has a right to remain silent, that anything he says may be used against him, that he has a right to have present an attorney during the questioning, and that, if indigent, he has a right to a lawyer without charge. To forgo these rights, some affirmative statement of rejection is seemingly required, and threats, tricks, or cajolings to obtain this waiver are forbidden. If before or during questioning the suspect seeks to invoke his right to remain silent, interrogation must be forgone or cease; a request for counsel brings about the same result until a lawyer is procured. Finally, there are a miscellany of minor directives, for example, the burden of proof of waiver is on the State, admissions and exculpatory statements are treated just like confessions, withdrawal of a waiver is always permitted, and so forth.

While the fine points of this scheme are far less clear than the Court admits, the tenor is quite apparent. The new rules are not designed to guard against police brutality or other unmistakably banned forms of coercion. Those who use third-degree tactics and deny them in court are equally able and destined to lie as skillfully about warnings and waivers. Rather, the thrust of the new rules is to negate all pressures, to reinforce the nervous or ignorant suspect, and ultimately to discourage any confession at all. The aim, in short, is toward "voluntariness" in a utopian sense, or to view it from a different angle, voluntariness with a vengeance.

To incorporate this notion into the Constitution requires a strained reading of history and precedent and a disregard of the very pragmatic concerns that alone may on occasion justify such strains. I believe that reasoned examination will show that the Due Process Clauses provide an adequate tool for coping with confessions, and that, even if the Fifth Amendment privilege against self-incrimination be invoked, its precedents taken as a whole do not sustain the present rules. Viewed as a choice based on pure policy, these new rules prove to be a highly debatable, if not one-sided, appraisal of the competing interests, imposed over widespread objection, at the very time when judicial restraint is most called for by the circumstances.

II. CONSTITUTIONAL PREMISES

It is most fitting to begin an inquiry into the constitutional precedents by surveying the limits on confessions the Court has evolved under the Due Process Clause of the Fourteenth Amendment. This is so because these cases show that there exists a workable and effective means of dealing with confessions in a judicial manner; because the cases are the baseline from which the Court now departs, and so serve to measure the actual, as opposed to the professed, distance it travels; and because examination of them helps reveal how the Court has coasted into its present position.

[Justice Harlan summarized earlier Supreme Court decisions holding that involuntary confessions are inadmissible as evidence under the Due Process Clause.]

Among the criteria often taken into account [in assessing the voluntariness and admissibility of a confession] were threats or imminent danger, physical deprivations such as lack of sleep or food, repeated or extended interrogation, limits on access to counsel or friends, length and illegality of detention under state law, and individual weakness or incapacities. Apart from direct physical coercion, however, no single default or fixed combination of defaults guaranteed exclusion, and synopses of the cases would serve little use because the overall gauge has been steadily changing, usually in the direction of restricting admissibility.

There are several relevant lessons to be drawn from this constitutional history. The first is that, with over 25 years of precedent, the Court has developed an elaborate, sophisticated, and sensitive approach to admissibility of confessions. It is "judicial" in its treatment of one case at a time, flexible in its ability to respond to the endless mutations of fact presented, and ever more familiar to the lower courts. Of course, strict certainty is not obtained in this developing process, but this is often so with constitutional principles, and disagreement is usually confined to that borderland of close cases where it matters least.

The second point is that, in practice and, from time to time, in principle, the Court has given ample recognition to society's interest in suspect questioning as an instrument of law enforcement. Cases countenancing quite significant pressures can be cited without difficulty, and the lower courts may often have been yet more tolerant. Of course, the limitations imposed today were rejected by necessary implication in case after case, the right to warnings having been explicitly rebuffed in this Court many years ago.

Finally, the cases disclose that the language in many of the opinions overstates the actual course of decision. It has been said, for example, that an admissible confession must be made by the suspect "in the unfettered exercise of his own will," and that "a prisoner is not to be made the deluded instrument of his own conviction." Though often repeated, such principles are rarely observed in full measure. Even the word "voluntary" may be deemed somewhat misleading, especially when one considers many of the confessions that have been brought under its umbrella. The tendency to overstate may be laid in part to the flagrant facts often before the Court; but, in any event, one must recognize how it has tempered attitudes and lent some color of authority to the approach now taken by the Court.

The Court's opinion, in my view, reveals no adequate basis for extending the Fifth Amendment's privilege against self-incrimination to the police station. Far more important, it fails to show that the Court's new rules are well supported, let alone compelled, by Fifth Amendment precedents. Instead, the new rules actually derive from quotation and analogy drawn from precedents under the Sixth Amendment, which should properly have no bearing on police interrogation.

The Court's opening contention, that the Fifth Amendment governs police station confessions, is perhaps not an impermissible extension of the law but it has little to commend itself in the present circumstances. Historically, the privilege against self-incrimination did not bear at all on the use of extra-legal confessions. Even those who would readily enlarge the privilege must concede some linguistic difficulties, since the Fifth Amendment in terms proscribes only compelling any person "in any criminal case to be a witness against himself."

Having decided that the Fifth Amendment privilege does apply in the police station, the Court reveals that the privilege imposes more exacting restrictions than does the Fourteenth Amendment's voluntariness test. It then emerges from a discussion of *Escobedo* that the Fifth Amendment requires, for an admissible confession, that it be given by one distinctly aware of his right not to speak and shielded from "the compelling atmosphere" of interrogation. From these key premises, the Court finally develops the safeguards of warning, counsel, and so forth. I do not believe these premises are sustained by precedents under the Fifth Amendment.

The more important premise is that pressure on the suspect must be eliminated, though it be only the subtle influence of the atmosphere and surroundings. The Fifth Amendment, however, has never been thought to forbid *all* pressure to incriminate one's self in the situations covered by it. This is not to say that, short of jail or torture, any sanction is permissible in any case; policy and history alike may impose sharp limits. However, the Court's unspoken assumption that *any* pressure violates the privilege is not supported by the precedents, and it has failed to show why the Fifth Amendment prohibits that relatively mild pressure the Due Process Clause permits.

The Court appears similarly wrong in thinking that precise knowledge of one's rights is a settled prerequisite under the Fifth Amendment to the loss of its protections. There might, of course, be reasons apart from Fifth Amendment precedent for requiring warning or any other safeguard on questioning, but that is a different matter entirely.

A closing word must be said about the Assistance of Counsel Clause of the Sixth Amendment, which is never expressly relied on by the Court, but whose judicial precedents turn out to be linchpins of the confession rules announced today. All these cases imparting glosses to the Sixth Amendment concerned counsel at trial or on appeal. While the Court finds no pertinent difference between judicial proceedings and police interrogation, I believe the differences are so vast as to disqualify wholly the Sixth Amendment precedents as suitable analogies in the present cases.

The only attempt in this Court to carry the right to counsel into the station house occurred in *Escobedo*, the Court repeating several times that that stage was no less "critical" than trial itself. This is hardly persuasive when we consider that a grand jury inquiry, the filing of a certiorari petition, and certainly the purchase of narcotics by an undercover agent from a prospective defendant may all be equally "critical," yet provision of counsel and advice on the score have never been thought compelled by the Constitution in such cases. The sound reason why this right is so freely extended for a criminal trial is the severe injustice risked by confronting an untrained defendant with a range of technical points of law, evidence, and tactics familiar to the prosecutor, but not to himself. This danger shrinks markedly in the police station, where, indeed, the lawyer, in fulfilling his professional responsibilities, of necessity may become an obstacle to truthfinding.

III. POLICY CONSIDERATIONS

Examined as an expression of public policy, the Court's new regime proves so dubious that there can be no due compensation for its weakness in constitutional law. The foregoing discussion has shown, I think, how mistaken is the Court in implying that the Constitution has struck the balance in favor of the approach the Court takes. Rather, precedent reveals that the Fourteenth Amendment in practice has been construed to strike a different balance, that the Fifth Amendment gives the Court little solid support in this context, and that the Sixth Amendment should have no bearing at all. Legal history has been stretched before to satisfy deep needs of society. In this instance, however, the Court has not and cannot make the powerful showing that its new rules are plainly desirable in the context of our society, something which is surely demanded before those rules are engrafted onto the Constitution and imposed on every State and county in the land.

Without at all subscribing to the generally black picture of police conduct painted by the Court, I think it must be frankly recognized at the outset that police questioning allowable under due process precedents may inherently entail some pressure on the suspect, and may seek advantage in his ignorance or weaknesses. The atmosphere and questioning techniques, proper and fair though they be, can, in themselves, exert a tug on the suspect to confess, and, in this light, to speak of any confessions of crime made after arrest as being "voluntary" or "uncoerced" is somewhat inaccurate, although traditional. A confession is wholly and incontestably voluntary only if a guilty person gives himself up to the law and becomes his own accuser. Until today, the role of the

Constitution has been only to sift out undue pressure, not to assure spontaneous confessions.

The Court's new rules aim to offset these minor pressures and disadvantages intrinsic to any kind of police interrogation. The rules do not serve due process interests in preventing blatant coercion since they do nothing to contain the policeman who is prepared to lie from the start. The rules work for reliability in confessions almost only in the Pickwickian sense that they can prevent some from being given at all. In short, the benefit of this new regime is simply to lessen or wipe out the inherent compulsion and inequalities to which the Court devotes some nine pages of description.

What the Court largely ignores is that its rules impair, if they will not eventually serve wholly to frustrate, an instrument of law enforcement that has long and quite reasonably been thought worth the price paid for it. There can be little doubt that the Court's new code would markedly decrease the number of confessions. To warn the suspect that he may remain silent and remind him that his confession may be used in court are minor obstructions. To require also an express waiver by the suspect and an end to questioning whenever he demurs must heavily handicap questioning. And to suggest or provide counsel for the suspect simply invites the end of the interrogation.

How much harm this decision will inflict on law enforcement cannot fairly be predicted with accuracy. We do know that some crimes cannot be solved without confessions, that ample expert testimony attests to their importance in crime control, and that the Court is taking a real risk with society's welfare in imposing its new regime on the country. The social costs of crime are too great to call the new rules anything but a hazardous experimentation.

While passing over the costs and risks of its experiment, the Court portrays the evils of normal police questioning in terms which I think are exaggerated. Albeit stringently confined by the due process standards, interrogation is no doubt often inconvenient and unpleasant for the suspect. However, it is no less so for a man to be arrested and jailed, to have his house searched, or to stand trial in court, yet all this may properly happen to the most innocent given probable cause, a warrant, or an indictment. Society has always paid a stiff price for law and order, and peaceful interrogation is not one of the dark moments of the law.

This brief statement of the competing considerations seems to me ample proof that the Court's preference is highly debatable, at best, and therefore not to be read into the Constitution. However, it may make the analysis more graphic to consider the actual facts of one of the four cases reversed by the Court. *Miranda v. Arizona* serves best, being neither the hardest nor easiest of the four under the Court's standards.

On March 3, 1963, an 18-year-old girl was kidnapped and forcibly raped near Phoenix, Arizona. Ten days later, on the morning of March 13, petitioner Miranda was arrested and taken to the police station. At this time Miranda was 23 years old, indigent, and educated to the extent of completing half the ninth grade. He had "an emotional illness" of the schizophrenic type, according to the doctor who eventually examined him; the doctor's report also stated that Miranda was "alert and oriented as to time, place, and person," intelligent within normal limits, competent to stand trial, and sane within the legal definition. At the police station, the victim picked Miranda out of a lineup, and two officers then took him into a separate room to interrogate him, starting about 11:30 a.m. Though at first denying his guilt, within a short time Miranda gave a detailed oral confession, and then wrote out in his own hand and signed a brief statement admitting and describing the crime. All this was accomplished in two hours or less, without any force, threats or promises and—I will assume this, though the record is uncertain—without any effective warnings at all.

Miranda's oral and written confessions are now held inadmissible under the Court's new rules. One is entitled to feel astonished that the Constitution can be read to produce this result. These confessions were obtained during brief, daytime questioning conducted by two officers and unmarked by any of the traditional indicia of coercion. They assured a conviction for a brutal and unsettling crime, for which the police had and quite possibly could obtain little evidence other than the victim's identifications, evidence which is frequently unreliable. There was, in sum, a legitimate purpose, no perceptible unfairness, and certainly little risk of injustice in the interrogation. Yet the resulting confessions, and the responsible course of police practice they represent, are to be sacrificed to the Court's own finespun conception of fairness, which I seriously doubt is shared by many thinking citizens in this country.

In conclusion: Nothing in the letter or the spirit of the Constitution or in the precedents squares with the heavy-handed and one-sided action that is so precipitously taken by the Court in the name of fulfilling its constitutional responsibilities. The foray which the Court makes today brings to mind the wise and farsighted words of Mr. Justice Jackson in *Douglas v. City of Jeannette*, 319 U.S. 157, 181 (1943): "This Court is forever adding new stories to the temples of constitutional law, and the temples have a way of collapsing when one story too many is added."

JUSTICE WHITE, with whom JUSTICE HARLAN and JUSTICE STEWART join, dissenting.

Although, in the Court's view, in-custody interrogation is inherently coercive, the Court says that the spontaneous product of the coercion of arrest and detention is still to be deemed voluntary. An accused, arrested on probable cause, may blurt out a confession which will be admissible despite the fact that he is alone and in custody, without any showing that he had any notion of his right to remain silent or of the consequences of his admission. Yet, under the Court's rule, if the police ask him a single question such as "Do you have anything to say?" or "Did you kill your wife?", his response, if there is one, has somehow been compelled, even if the accused has been clearly warned of his right to remain silent. Common sense informs us to the contrary. While one may say that the response was "involuntary" in the sense the question provoked or was the occasion for the response, and thus the defendant was induced to speak out when he might have remained silent if not arrested and not questioned, it is patently unsound to say the response is compelled.

If the rule announced today were truly based on a conclusion that all confessions resulting from custodial interrogation are coerced, then it would simply have no rational foundation. Even if one were to postulate that the Court's concern is not that all confessions induced by police interrogation are coerced, but rather that some such confessions are coerced and present judicial procedures are believed to be inadequate to identify the confessions that are coerced and those that are not, it would still not be essential to impose the rule that the Court has now fashioned. Transcripts or observers could be required, specific time limits, tailored to fit the cause, could be imposed, or other devices could be utilized to reduce the chances that otherwise indiscernible coercion will produce an inadmissible confession.

On the other hand, even if one assumed that there was an adequate factual basis for the conclusion that all confessions obtained during in-custody interrogation are the product of compulsion, the rule propounded by the Court will still be irrational, for, apparently, it is only if the accused is also warned of his right to counsel and waives both that right and the right against self-incrimination that the inherent compulsiveness of interrogation disappears. But if the defendant may not answer without a warning a question such as "Where were you last night?" without having his answer be a compelled one, how can the Court ever accept his negative answer to the question of whether he wants to consult his retained counsel or counsel whom the court will appoint? And why, if counsel is present and the accused nevertheless confesses, or counsel tells the accused to tell the truth, and that is what the accused does, is the situation any less coercive insofar as the accused is concerned? The Court apparently realizes its dilemma of foreclosing questioning without the necessary warnings but, at the same time, permitting the accused, sitting in the same chair in front of the same policemen, to waive his right to consult an attorney. It expects, however, that the accused will not often waive the right; and if it is claimed that he has, the State faces a severe, if not impossible burden of proof.

All of this makes very little sense in terms of the compulsion which the Fifth Amendment proscribes. That amendment deals with compelling the accused himself. It is his free will that is involved. Confessions and incriminating admissions, as such, are not forbidden evidence; only those which are compelled are banned. I doubt that the Court observes these distinctions today. By considering any answers to any interrogation to be compelled regardless of the content and course of examination, and by escalating the requirements to prove waiver, the Court not only prevents the use of compelled confessions, but, for all practical purposes, forbids interrogation except in the presence of counsel. That is, instead of confining itself to protection of the right against compelled self-incrimination, the Court has created a limited Fifth Amendment right to counsel—or, as the Court expresses it, a "need for counsel to protect the Fifth Amendment privilege." The focus then is not on the will of the accused, but on the will of counsel, and how much influence he can have on the accused. Obviously there is no warrant in the Fifth Amendment for thus installing counsel as the arbiter of the privilege.

The obvious underpinning of the Court's decision is a deep-seated distrust of all confessions. As the Court declares that the accused may not be interrogated without counsel present, absent a waiver of the right to counsel, and as the Court all but admonishes the lawyer to advise the accused to remain silent, the result adds up to a judicial judgment that evidence from the accused should not be used against him in any way, whether compelled or not. This is the not so subtle overtone of the opinion—that it is inherently wrong for the police to gather evidence from the accused himself. And this is precisely the nub of this dissent. I see nothing wrong or immoral, and certainly nothing unconstitutional, in the police's asking a suspect whom they have reasonable cause to arrest whether or not he killed his wife, or in confronting him with the evidence on which the arrest was based, at least where he has been plainly advised that he may remain completely silent. Particularly when corroborated, as where the police have confirmed the accused's disclosure of the hiding place of implements or fruits of the crime, such confessions have the highest reliability and significantly contribute to the certitude with which we may believe the accused is guilty. Moreover, it is by no means certain that the process of confessing is injurious to the accused. To the contrary, it may provide psychological relief and enhance the prospects for rehabilitation.

This is not to say that the value of respect for the inviolability of the accused's individual personality should be accorded no weight, or that all confessions should be indiscriminately admitted. This Court has long read the Constitution to proscribe compelled confessions, a salutary rule from which there should be no retreat. But I see no sound basis, factual or otherwise, and the Court gives none, for concluding that the present rule against the receipt of coerced confessions is inadequate for the task of sorting out inadmissible evidence, and must be replaced by the *per se* rule which is now imposed.

There is, in my view, every reason to believe that a good many criminal defendants who otherwise would have been convicted on what this Court has previously thought to be the most satisfactory kind of evidence will now, under this new version of the Fifth Amendment, either not be tried at all or will be acquitted if the State's evidence, minus the confession, is put to the test of litigation.

In some unknown number of cases, the Court's rule will return a killer, a rapist or other criminal to the streets and to the environment which produced him, to repeat his crime whenever it pleases him. As a consequence, there will not be a gain, but a loss, in human dignity.

Today's decision leaves open such questions as whether the accused was in custody, whether his statements were spontaneous or the product of interrogation, whether the accused has effectively waived his rights, and whether nontestimonial evidence introduced at trial is the fruit of statements made during a prohibited interrogation, all of which are certain to prove productive of uncertainty during investigation and litigation during prosecution. For all these reasons, if further restrictions on police interrogation are desirable at this time, a more flexible approach makes much more sense than the Court's constitutional straitjacket, which forecloses more discriminating treatment by legislative or rulemaking pronouncements.

Applying the traditional standards to the cases before the Court, I would hold these confessions voluntary.

Miranda was controversial when it was decided and remains so to this day. One major benefit of the decision was that it provided police and judges with greater clarity and guidance than the voluntariness standard by prescribing specific procedures to be followed prior to and during every custodial interrogation. But for many, this added clarity and guidance came with too high a cost. Critics of *Miranda*—including the four Justices who dissented—felt that the decision would unduly hamper law enforcement, reduce the number of confessions, and allow criminals to escape punishment. Numerous studies—some undertaken shortly after the decision, and others conducted decades later—have reached conflicting conclusions regarding the effect of *Miranda* on the behavior of police and criminal suspects, the extent to which the *Miranda* requirements have discouraged confessions or rendered them inadmissible, and the resulting impact on conviction rates and crime control.[a]

Beyond the debatable costs and benefits, the *Miranda* decision also contained a serious weakness highlighted in Justice White's dissent. The *Miranda* warnings serve to apprise a criminal suspect of constitutional rights that may be asserted prior to or during custodial interrogation— particularly the right to remain silent and right to consult with an attorney. These warnings, the *Miranda* majority notes, are necessary to offset the "inherently compelling pressures" associated with police interrogation. *Miranda* also permits a suspect to waive these rights "provided the waiver is made voluntarily, knowingly and intelligently." But how can a waiver be truly voluntary if it is given in a coercive police-dominated atmosphere that produces "inherently compelling pressures" to confess?

Congress responded to the controversy over *Miranda* by attempting to repeal it through legislation. Part of the Omnibus Crime Control and Safe Streets Act of 1968 (18 U.S.C. § 3501) provided that in the federal courts, a confession "shall be admissible in evidence if it is voluntarily given," regardless of whether *Miranda* warnings were properly administered. For more than 30 years, the Justice Department, operating under both Republican and Democratic Presidents, refused to invoke the statute because of a belief that it was unconstitutional. In *Dickerson v. U.S.*, the Supreme Court confirmed what the Justice Department had long suspected and held that *Miranda* is a constitutional rule that may not be abrogated by an Act of Congress.

DICKERSON V. U.S.

530 U.S. 428 (2000)

CHIEF JUSTICE REHNQUIST delivered the opinion of the Court.

In *Miranda v. Arizona*, 384 U.S. 436 (1966), we held that certain warnings must be given before a suspect's statement made during

---

[a] *See, e.g.,* Paul G. Cassell, *Miranda's Social Costs: An Empirical Reassessment*, 90 NORTHWESTERN UNIVERSITY LAW REVIEW 387 (1996) (a review of empirical research suggests that "*Miranda* has resulted in a lost confession in roughly one out of every six criminal cases and that confessions are needed to convict in one out of every four cases"; each year, *Miranda* results in "lost cases" against "roughly 28,000 serious violent offenders and 79,000 property offenders and produces plea bargains to reduced charges in almost the same number of cases"); Stephen J. Schulhofer, *Miranda's Practical Effect: Substantial Benefits and Vanishingly Small Social Costs*, 90 NORTHWESTERN UNIVERSITY LAW REVIEW 500 (1996) (noting that appropriate adjustments to data show that "*Miranda*'s empirically detectable harm to law enforcement shrinks virtually to zero"); Richard A. Leo, *The Impact of Miranda Revisited*, 86 JOURNAL OF CRIMINAL LAW AND CRIMINOLOGY 621 (1996) (summarizing older studies and his own recent research to evaluate the costs and benefits of *Miranda*); Paul G. Cassell, *Handcuffing the Cops: Miranda's Harmful Effects on Law Enforcement* (1998), available at http://www.ncpa.org/pub/st218 (estimating 3.8% fewer convictions every year as a result of *Miranda*, including 28,000 fewer convictions for violent crimes, 79,000 fewer convictions for property crimes, and 500,000 fewer convictions for other crimes).

custodial interrogation could be admitted in evidence. In the wake of that decision, Congress enacted 18 U.S.C. § 3501, which in essence laid down a rule that the admissibility of such statements should turn only on whether or not they were voluntarily made. We hold that *Miranda*, being a constitutional decision of this Court, may not be in effect overruled by an Act of Congress, and we decline to overrule *Miranda* ourselves. We therefore hold that *Miranda* and its progeny in this Court govern the admissibility of statements made during custodial interrogation in both state and federal courts.

Petitioner Dickerson was indicted for bank robbery, conspiracy to commit bank robbery, and using a firearm in the course of committing a crime of violence. Before trial, Dickerson moved to suppress a statement he had made at a Federal Bureau of Investigation field office, on the grounds that he had not received *Miranda* warnings before being interrogated. The District Court granted his motion to suppress, and the Government took an interlocutory appeal to the United States Court of Appeals for the Fourth Circuit. That court, by a divided vote, reversed the District Court's suppression order. It agreed with the District Court's conclusion that petitioner had not received *Miranda* warnings before making his statement. But it went on to hold that § 3501, which in effect makes the admissibility of statements such as Dickerson's turn solely on whether they were made voluntarily, was satisfied in this case. It then concluded that our decision in *Miranda* was not a constitutional holding, and that, therefore, Congress could by statute have the final say on the question of admissibility.

Because of the importance of the questions raised by the Court of Appeals' decision, we granted certiorari, and now reverse.

We begin with a brief historical account of the law governing the admission of confessions. Prior to *Miranda*, we evaluated the admissibility of a suspect's confession under a voluntariness test. The roots of this test developed in the common law, as the courts of England and then the United States recognized that coerced confessions are inherently untrustworthy. Over time, our cases recognized two constitutional bases for the requirement that a confession be voluntary to be admitted into evidence: the Fifth Amendment right against self-incrimination and the Due Process Clause of the Fourteenth Amendment. See, *e.g.*, *Bram v. U.S.*, 168 U.S. 532, 542 (1897) (stating that the voluntariness test "is controlled by that portion of the Fifth Amendment . . . commanding that no person shall be compelled in any criminal case to be a witness against himself"); *Brown v. Mississippi*, 297 U.S. 278 (1936) (reversing a criminal conviction under the Due Process Clause because it was based on a confession obtained by physical coercion).

While *Bram* was decided before *Brown* and its progeny, for the middle third of the 20th century our cases based the rule against admitting coerced confessions primarily, if not exclusively, on notions of due process. We applied the due process voluntariness test in some 30 different cases decided during the era that intervened between *Brown* and *Escobedo v. Illinois*, 378 U.S. 478 (1964). Those cases refined the test into an inquiry that examines whether a defendant's will was overborne by the circumstances surrounding the giving of a confession. The due process test takes into consideration the totality of all the surrounding circumstances—both the characteristics of the accused and the details of the interrogation.

We have never abandoned this due process jurisprudence, and thus continue to exclude confessions that were obtained involuntarily. But our decisions in *Malloy v. Hogan*, 378 U.S. 1 (1964), and *Miranda* changed the focus of much of the inquiry in determining the admissibility of suspects' incriminating statements. In *Malloy*, we held that the Fifth Amendment's Self-Incrimination Clause is incorporated in the Due Process Clause of the Fourteenth Amendment and thus applies to the States. We decided *Miranda* on the heels of *Malloy*.

Given § 3501's express designation of voluntariness as the touchstone of admissibility, its omission of any warning requirement, and the instruction for trial courts to consider a nonexclusive list of factors relevant to the circumstances of a confession, we agree with the Court of Appeals that Congress intended by its enactment to overrule *Miranda*. Because of the obvious conflict between our decision in *Miranda* and § 3501, we must address whether Congress has constitutional authority to thus supersede *Miranda*. If Congress has such authority, § 3501's totality-of-the-circumstances approach must prevail over *Miranda*'s requirement of warnings; if not, that section must yield to *Miranda*'s more specific requirements.

The law in this area is clear. This Court has supervisory authority over the federal courts, and we may use that authority to prescribe rules of evidence and procedure that are binding in those tribunals. However, the power to judicially create and enforce nonconstitutional "rules of procedure and evidence for the federal courts exists only in the absence of a relevant Act of Congress." Congress retains the ultimate authority to modify or set aside any judicially created rules of evidence and procedure that are not required by the Constitution.

But Congress may not legislatively supersede our decisions interpreting and applying the Constitution. This case therefore turns on whether the *Miranda* Court announced a constitutional rule or merely exercised its supervisory authority to regulate evidence in the absence of congressional direction. [T]he Court of Appeals concluded that the protections announced in *Miranda* are not constitutionally required.

We disagree with the Court of Appeals' conclusion, although we concede that there is language in some of our opinions that supports the view taken by that court. But first and foremost of the factors on the other side—that *Miranda* is a constitutional decision—is that both *Miranda* and two of its companion cases applied the rule to proceedings in state courts—to wit, Arizona, California, and New York. Since that time, we have consistently applied *Miranda*'s rule to prosecutions arising in state courts. It is beyond dispute that we do not hold a supervisory power over the courts of the several States. With respect to proceedings in state courts, our authority is limited to enforcing the commands of the United States Constitution.

The *Miranda* opinion itself begins by stating that the Court granted certiorari "to explore some facets of the problems . . . of applying the privilege against self-incrimination to in-custody interrogation, *and to give concrete constitutional guidelines for law enforcement agencies and courts to follow.*" In fact, the majority opinion is replete with statements indicating that the majority thought it was announcing a constitutional rule. Indeed, the Court's ultimate conclusion was that the unwarned confessions obtained in the four cases before the Court in *Miranda* "were obtained from the defendant under circumstances that did not meet constitutional standards for protection of the privilege."

Additional support for our conclusion that *Miranda* is constitutionally based is found in the *Miranda* Court's invitation for legislative action to protect the constitutional right against coerced self-incrimination. However, the Court emphasized that it could not foresee "the potential alternatives for protecting the privilege which might be devised by Congress or the States," and it accordingly opined that the Constitution would not preclude legislative solutions that differed from the prescribed *Miranda* warnings but which were "at least as effective in apprising accused persons of their right of silence and in assuring a continuous opportunity to exercise it."

Miranda requires procedures that will warn a suspect in custody of his right to remain silent and which will assure the suspect that the exercise of that right will be honored. As discussed above, § 3501 explicitly eschews a requirement of preinterrogation warnings in favor of an approach that looks to the administration of such warnings as only one factor in determining the voluntariness of a suspect's confession. The additional remedies cited by *amicus* do not, in our view, render them, together with § 3501, an adequate substitute for the warnings required by *Miranda*.

The dissent argues that it is judicial overreaching for this Court to hold § 3501 unconstitutional unless we hold that the *Miranda* warnings are required by the Constitution, in the sense that nothing else will suffice to satisfy constitutional requirements. But we need not go further than *Miranda* to decide this case. In *Miranda*, the Court noted that reliance on the traditional totality-of-the-circumstances test raised a risk of overlooking an involuntary custodial confession, a risk that the Court found unacceptably great when the confession is offered in the case in chief to prove guilt. The Court therefore concluded that something more than the totality test was necessary. As discussed above, § 3501 reinstates the totality test as sufficient. Section 3501 therefore cannot be sustained if *Miranda* is to remain the law.

Whether or not we would agree with *Miranda*'s reasoning and its resulting rule, were we addressing the issue in the first instance, the principles of *stare decisis* weigh heavily against overruling it now. While *stare decisis* is not an inexorable command, particularly when we are interpreting the Constitution, even in constitutional cases, the doctrine carries such persuasive force that we have always required a departure from precedent to be supported by some special justification.

We do not think there is such justification for overruling *Miranda*. *Miranda* has become embedded in routine police practice to the point where the warnings have become part of our national culture. While we have overruled our precedents when subsequent cases have undermined their doctrinal underpinnings, we do not believe that this has happened to the *Miranda* decision. If anything, our subsequent cases have reduced the impact of the *Miranda* rule on legitimate law enforcement while reaffirming the decision's core ruling that unwarned statements may not be used as evidence in the prosecution's case in chief.

The disadvantage of the *Miranda* rule is that statements which may be by no means involuntary, made by a defendant who is aware of his "rights," may nonetheless be excluded and a guilty defendant go free as a result. But experience suggests that the totality-of-the-circumstances test which § 3501 seeks to revive is more difficult than *Miranda* for law enforcement officers to conform to, and for courts to apply in a consistent manner. The requirement that *Miranda* warnings be given does not, of course, dispense with the voluntariness inquiry. But cases in which a defendant can make a colorable argument that a self-incriminating statement was "compelled" despite the fact that the law enforcement authorities adhered to the dictates of *Miranda* are rare.

In sum, we conclude that *Miranda* announced a constitutional rule that Congress may not supersede legislatively. Following the rule of *stare decisis,* we decline to overrule *Miranda* ourselves.

JUSTICE SCALIA, with whom JUSTICE THOMAS joins, dissenting.

Those to whom judicial decisions are an unconnected series of judgments that produce either favored or disfavored results will doubtless greet today's decision as a paragon of moderation, since it declines to overrule *Miranda v. Arizona*. Those who understand the judicial process will appreciate that today's decision is not a reaffirmation of *Miranda,* but a radical revision of the most significant element of *Miranda* (as of all cases): the rationale that gives it a permanent place in our jurisprudence.

Marbury v. Madison, 1 Cranch 137 (1803), held that an Act of Congress will not be enforced by the courts if what it prescribes violates the Constitution of the United States. That was the basis on which *Miranda* was decided. One will search today's opinion in vain, however, for a statement (surely simple enough to make) that what 18 U.S.C. § 3501 prescribes—the use at trial of a voluntary confession, even when a *Miranda* warning or its equivalent has failed to be given—violates the Constitution. The reason the statement does not appear is not only (and perhaps not so much) that it would be absurd, inasmuch as § 3501 excludes from trial precisely what the Constitution excludes from trial, viz., compelled confessions; but also that Justices whose votes are needed to compose today's majority are on record as believing that a violation of *Miranda* is *not* a violation of the Constitution. And so, to justify today's agreed-upon result, the Court must adopt a significant *new*, if not entirely comprehensible, principle of constitutional law. As the Court chooses to describe that principle, statutes of Congress can be disregarded, not only when what they prescribe violates the Constitution, but when what they prescribe contradicts a decision of this Court that "announced a constitutional rule." As I shall discuss in some detail, the only thing that can possibly mean in the context of this case is that this Court has the power, not merely to apply the Constitution but to expand it, imposing what it regards as useful "prophylactic" restrictions upon Congress and the States. That is an immense and frightening antidemocratic power, and it does not exist.

It takes only a small step to bring today's opinion out of the realm of power-judging and into the mainstream of legal reasoning: The Court need only go beyond its carefully couched iterations that "*Miranda* is a constitutional decision," that "*Miranda* is constitutionally based," that *Miranda* has "constitutional underpinnings," and come out and say quite clearly: "We reaffirm today that custodial interrogation that is not preceded by *Miranda* warnings or their equivalent violates the Constitution of the United States." It cannot say that, because a majority of the Court does not believe it. The Court therefore acts in plain violation of the Constitution when it denies effect to this Act of Congress.

Today's judgment converts *Miranda* from a milestone of judicial overreaching into the very Cheops' Pyramid (or perhaps the Sphinx would be a better analogue) of judicial arrogance. In imposing its Court-made code upon the States, the original opinion at least *asserted* that it was demanded by the Constitution. Today's decision does not pretend that it is—and yet *still* asserts the right to impose it against the will of the people's representatives in Congress. Far from believing that *stare decisis* compels this result, I believe we cannot allow to remain on the books even a celebrated decision—*especially* a celebrated decision—that has come to stand for the proposition that the Supreme Court has power to impose extraconstitutional constraints upon Congress and the States. This is not the system that was established by the Framers, or that would be established by any sane supporter of government by the people.

I dissent from today's decision, and, until § 3501 is repealed, will continue to apply it in all cases where there has been a sustainable finding that the defendant's confession was voluntary.

The *Miranda* Requirements

1.   When an individual is taken into custody or otherwise deprived of his freedom by the authorities in any significant way and is subjected to questioning, procedural safeguards must be employed to protect the privilege against self-incrimination. The individual must be warned prior to any questioning that he has the right to remain silent, that anything he says can be used against him in a court of law, that he has the right to the presence of an attorney, and that if he cannot afford an attorney, one will be appointed for him prior to any questioning if he so desires.

2.   Opportunity to exercise these rights must be afforded to the individual throughout the interrogation. After the individual has received the warnings and been given the opportunity to exercise his rights, he may knowingly and intelligently waive his rights and agree to answer questions or make a statement. But if the individual indicates in any manner, at any time prior to or during questioning, that he wishes to remain silent, the interrogation must cease. And if the individual states that he wants an attorney, the interrogation must cease until an attorney is present. At that time, the individual must have an opportunity to confer with the attorney and to have him present during any subsequent questioning. If the individual cannot obtain an attorney and indicates that he wants one before speaking to police, they must respect his decision to remain silent.

3.   No evidence obtained as a result of custodial interrogation can be used against the individual unless and until the prosecution demonstrates at trial that he received the required warnings and waived his rights.

B. CLARIFYING *MIRANDA*

The Supreme Court made it clear that the rules announced in *Miranda* apply to custodial interrogation. Less clear from the *Miranda* decision itself is what, precisely, constitutes "custodial interrogation," and what is required of the police when administering the *Miranda* warnings. In a number of important cases organized and excerpted below, the

Supreme Court has clarified the terms and requirements of its *Miranda* decision.

1. WHAT QUALIFIES AS "CUSTODY" UNDER *MIRANDA*?

The Supreme Court said in *Miranda* that the required warnings must be given "when the individual is first subjected to police interrogation while in custody at the station or otherwise deprived of his freedom of action in any significant way." The Court went on to note that its holding did not affect "[g]eneral on-the-scene questioning as to facts surrounding a crime or other general questioning of citizens in the fact-finding process" because in such situations "the compelling atmosphere inherent in the process of in-custody interrogation is not necessarily present." In a number of cases decided since *Miranda*, the Supreme Court has further refined the definition of custody for purposes of determining when the required warnings must be given.

In *Orozco v. Texas*, the police questioned a murder suspect in the familiar surroundings of his own bedroom. The Supreme Court nevertheless concluded that the suspect was in custody and his incriminating statements were inadmissible because police had failed to administer the *Miranda* warnings.

OROZCO V. TEXAS
394 U.S. 324 (1969)

JUSTICE BLACK delivered the opinion of the Court.

The petitioner, Reyes Arias Orozco, was convicted in the Criminal District Court of Dallas County, Texas, of murder without malice and was sentenced to serve in the state prison not less than two nor more than 10 years. The Court of Criminal Appeals of Texas affirmed the conviction, rejecting petitioner's contention that a material part of the evidence against him was obtained in violation of the provision of the Fifth Amendment to the United States Constitution, made applicable to the States by the Fourteenth Amendment, that: "No person . . . shall be compelled in any criminal case to be a witness against himself."

The evidence introduced at trial showed that petitioner and the deceased had quarreled outside the El Farleto Cafe in Dallas shortly before midnight on the date of the shooting. The deceased had apparently spoken to petitioner's female companion inside the restaurant. In the heat of the quarrel outside, the deceased is said to have beaten petitioner about the face and called him "Mexican Grease." A shot was fired killing the deceased. Petitioner left the scene and returned to his boardinghouse to sleep. At about 4 a.m. four police officers arrived at petitioner's boardinghouse, were admitted by an unidentified woman, and were told that petitioner was asleep in the bedroom. All four officers entered the bedroom and began to question petitioner. From the moment he gave his name, according to the testimony of one of the officers, petitioner was not free to go where he pleased but was "under arrest." The officers asked him if he had been to the El Farleto restaurant that night and when he answered "yes" he was asked if he owned a pistol. Petitioner admitted owning one. After being asked a second time where the pistol was located, he admitted that it was in the washing machine in a backroom of the boardinghouse. Ballistics tests indicated that the gun found in the washing machine was the gun that fired the fatal shot. At petitioner's trial, held after the effective date of this Court's decision in *Miranda v. Arizona*, 384 U.S. 436 (1966), the trial court allowed one of the officers, over the objection of petitioner's lawyer, to relate the statements made by petitioner concerning the gun and petitioner's presence at the scene of the shooting. The trial testimony clearly shows that the officers questioned petitioner about incriminating facts without first informing him of his right to remain silent, his right to have the advice of a lawyer before making any statement, and his right to have a lawyer appointed to assist him if he could not afford to hire one. The Texas Court of Criminal Appeals held, with one judge dissenting, that the admission of testimony concerning the statements petitioner had made without the above warnings was not precluded by *Miranda*. We disagree and hold that the use of these admissions obtained in the absence of the required warnings was a flat violation of the Self-Incrimination Clause of the Fifth Amendment as construed in *Miranda*.

The State has argued here that since petitioner was interrogated on his own bed, in familiar surroundings, our *Miranda* holding should not apply. It is true that the Court did say in *Miranda* that "compulsion to speak in the isolated setting of the police station may well be greater than in courts or other official investigations, where there are often impartial observers to guard against intimidation or trickery." But the opinion iterated and reiterated the absolute necessity for officers interrogating people "in custody" to give the described warnings. According to the officer's testimony, petitioner was under arrest and not free to leave when he was questioned in his bedroom in the early hours of the morning. The *Miranda* opinion declared that the warnings were required when the person being interrogated was "in custody at the station or otherwise deprived of his freedom of action in any significant way." The decision of this Court in *Miranda* was reached after careful consideration and lengthy opinions were announced by both the majority and dissenting Justices. There is no need to canvass those arguments again. We do not, as the dissent implies, expand or extend to the slightest extent our *Miranda* decision. We do adhere to our well-considered holding in that case and therefore reverse the conviction below.

JUSTICE WHITE, with whom JUSTICE STEWART joins, dissenting.

This decision carries the rule of *Miranda v. Arizona* to a new and unwarranted extreme. I continue to believe that the original rule amounted to a "constitutional straitjacket" on law enforcement which was justified neither by the words or history of the Constitution, nor by any reasonable view of the likely benefits of the rule as against its disadvantages. Even accepting *Miranda*, the Court extends the rule here and draws the straitjacket even tighter.

The opinion of the Court in *Miranda* was devoted in large part to an elaborate discussion of the subtle forms of psychological pressure which could be brought to bear when an accused person is interrogated at length in unfamiliar surroundings. The "salient features" of the cases decided in *Miranda* were "incommunicado interrogation of individuals in a police-dominated atmosphere." The danger was that in such circumstances the confidence of the prisoner could be eroded by techniques such as successive interrogations by police acting out friendly or unfriendly roles. These techniques are best developed in "isolation and unfamiliar surroundings." And they take time: "the major qualities an interrogator should possess are patience and perseverance." The techniques of an extended period of isolation, repeated interrogation, cajolery, and trickery often enough produced admissions which were actually coerced in the traditional sense so that new safeguards were deemed essential.

The Court now extends the same rules to all instances of in-custody questioning outside the station house. Once arrest occurs, the application of *Miranda* is automatic. The rule is simple but it ignores the purpose of *Miranda* to guard against what was thought to be the corrosive influence of practices which station house interrogation makes feasible. The Court wholly ignores the question whether similar hazards exist or even are possible when police arrest and interrogate on the spot, whether it be on the street corner or in the home, as in this case. No predicate is laid for believing that practices outside the station house are normally prolonged, carried out in isolation, or often productive of the physical or psychological coercion made so much of in *Miranda*. It is difficult to imagine the police duplicating in a person's home or on the street those conditions and practices which the Court found prevalent in the station house and which were thought so threatening to the right to silence. Without such a demonstration. *Miranda* hardly reaches this case or any cases similar to it.

Here, there was no prolonged interrogation, no unfamiliar surroundings, no opportunity for the police to invoke those procedures which moved the majority in *Miranda*. In fact, the conversation was by all accounts a very brief one. According to uncontradicted testimony, petitioner was awake when the officers entered his room, and they asked him four questions: his name, whether he had been at the El Farleto, whether he owned a pistol, and where it was. He gave his name, said he had been at the El Farleto, and admitted he owned a pistol without hesitation. He was slow in telling where the pistol was, and the question was repeated. He then took the police to the nearby washing machine where the gun was hidden.

It is unquestioned that this sequence of events in their totality would not constitute coercion in the traditional sense or lead any court to view the admissions as involuntary within the meaning of the rules by which we even now adjudicate claims of coercion relating to pre-*Miranda* trials. And, realistically, had Orozco refused to answer the questions asked of him, it seems most unlikely that prolonged interrogation would have followed in petitioner's own quarters; nothing similar to the station house model invoked by the court would have occurred here. The police had petitioner's name and description, had ample evidence that he had been at the night club and suspected that he had a gun. Surely had he refused to give his name or answer any other questions, they would have arrested him anyway, searched the house and found the gun, which would have been clearly admissible under all relevant authorities. But the Court insists that this case be reversed for failure to give *Miranda* warnings.

I cannot accept the dilution of the custody requirements of *Miranda* to this level, where the hazards to the right to silence are so equivocal and unsupported by experience in a recurring number of cases. Orozco was apprehended in the most familiar quarters, the questioning was brief, and no admissions were made which were not backed up by other evidence. This case does not involve the confession of an innocent man, or even of a guilty man from whom a confession has been wrung by physical abuse or the modern psychological methods discussed in *Miranda*. These are simply the terse remarks of a man who has been caught, almost in the act. Even if there were reason to encourage suspects to consult lawyers to tell them to be silent before quizzing at the station house, there is no reason why police in the field should have to preface every casual question of a suspect with the full panoply of *Miranda* warnings. The same danger of coercion is simply not present in such circumstances, and the answers to the questions may as often clear a suspect as help convict him. If the *Miranda* warnings have their intended effect, and the police are able to get no answers from suspects, innocent or guilty, without arresting them, then a great many more innocent men will be making unnecessary trips to the station house. Ultimately it may be necessary to arrest a man, bring him to the police station, and provide a lawyer, just to discover his name. Even if the man is innocent the process will be an unpleasant one.

Since the Court's extension of *Miranda*'s rule takes it into territory where even what rationale there originally was disappears, I dissent.

In *Beckwith v. U.S.*, the Supreme Court concluded that an individual who was questioned in connection with an IRS tax fraud investigation was not in custody and was not entitled to *Miranda* warnings prior to the interview.

BECKWITH V. U.S.
425 U.S. 341 (1976)

Two special agents of the Internal Revenue Service met with Alvin Beckwith at a private home where he occasionally stayed. The agents presented their credentials and explained that they were investigating the possibility of criminal tax fraud. Reading from a card, the senior agent advised Beckwith that he could not compel him to answer incriminating questions, that any statements or information he provided could be used against him, and that he could seek the assistance of an attorney before responding to their questions. The statements that were read to Beckwith did not constitute the full set of warnings required by *Miranda v. Arizona*, 384 U.S. 436 (1966). After Beckwith indicated that he understood his rights, the IRS agents proceeded to interview him for approximately three hours.

Before the end of the interview, the senior agent asked Beckwith to permit the agents to inspect certain records. Beckwith told the agents that the records were at his place of employment, and the agents asked if they could meet him there later. Beckwith agreed. About 45 minutes later, the agents met Beckwith at his place of employment. The senior agent informed Beckwith that he was not required to furnish any records, but Beckwith nevertheless handed them over.

Prior to trial, Beckwith moved to suppress all statements he made to the agents and evidence derived from those statements on the ground that he had not been given the warnings required by *Miranda*. Beckwith argued that because he was the "focus" of a criminal tax investigation when he was interviewed by the agents, he was under "psychological restraints" that are the functional and legal equivalent of custody.

The Supreme Court rejected Beckwith's argument, holding that he was not in custody and therefore not entitled to the *Miranda* warnings:

> An interview with Government agents in a situation such as the one shown by this record simply does not present the elements which the *Miranda* Court found so inherently coercive as to require its holding. Although the "focus" of an investigation may indeed have been on Beckwith at the time of the interview in the sense that it was his tax liability which was under scrutiny, he hardly found himself in the custodial situation described by the *Miranda* Court as the basis for its holding.

In *Oregon v. Mathiason*, a police officer investigating a burglary questioned the suspect, a parolee, in a closed room at the police station. Because the officer told the suspect that he was not under arrest, the Supreme Court concluded that he was not in custody for purposes of *Miranda*.

OREGON V. MATHIASON
429 U.S. 492 (1977)

PER CURIAM.

Respondent Carl Mathiason was convicted of first-degree burglary after a bench trial in which his confession was critical to the State's case. At trial he moved to suppress the confession as the fruit of questioning by the police not preceded by the warnings required in *Miranda v. Arizona*, 384 U.S. 436 (1966). The trial court refused to exclude the confession because it found that Mathiason was not in custody at the time of the confession.

The Oregon Court of Appeals affirmed respondent's conviction, but on his petition for review in the Supreme Court of Oregon, that court, by a divided vote, reversed the conviction. It found that although Mathiason had not been arrested or otherwise formally detained, the interrogation took place in a "coercive environment" of the sort to which *Miranda* was intended to apply. The State of Oregon has petitioned for certiorari to review the judgment of the Supreme Court of Oregon. We think that court has read *Miranda* too broadly, and we therefore reverse its judgment.

The Supreme Court of Oregon described the factual situation surrounding the confession as follows:

> An officer of the State Police investigated a theft at a residence near Pendleton. He asked the lady of the house which had been burglarized if she suspected anyone. She replied that the defendant was the only one she could think of. The defendant was a parolee and a "close associate" of her son. The officer tried to contact defendant on three or four occasions with no success. Finally, about 25 days after the burglary, the officer left his card at defendant's apartment with a note asking him to call because "I'd like to discuss something with you." The next afternoon, the defendant did call. The officer asked where it would be convenient to meet. The defendant had no preference, so the officer asked if the defendant could meet him at the state patrol office in about an hour and a half, about 5:00 p.m. The patrol office was about two blocks from defendant's apartment. The building housed several state agencies.

The officer met defendant in the hallway, shook hands and took him into an office. The defendant was told he was not under arrest. The door was closed. The two sat across a desk. The police radio in another room could be heard. The officer told defendant he wanted to talk to him about a burglary and that his truthfulness would possibly be considered by the district attorney or judge. The officer further advised that the police believed defendant was involved in the burglary and [falsely stated that] defendant's fingerprints were found at the scene. The defendant sat for a few minutes and then said he had taken the property. This occurred within five minutes after defendant had come to the office. The officer then advised defendant of his *Miranda* rights and took a taped confession.

At the end of the taped conversation the officer told defendant he was not arresting him at this time; he was released to go about his job and return to his family. The officer said he was referring the case to the district attorney for him to determine whether criminal charges would be brought. It was 5:30 p.m. when the defendant left the office.

The Supreme Court of Oregon reasoned from these facts that:

We hold the interrogation took place in a "coercive environment." The parties were in the offices of the State Police; they were alone behind closed doors; the officer informed the defendant he was a suspect in a theft and the authorities had evidence incriminating him in the crime; and the defendant was a parolee under supervision. We are of the opinion that this evidence is not overcome by the evidence that the defendant came to the office in response to a request and was told he was not under arrest.

Our decision in *Miranda* set forth rules of police procedure applicable to "custodial interrogation." [As we noted in *Miranda*:] "By custodial interrogation, we mean questioning initiated by law enforcement officers after a person has been taken into custody or otherwise deprived of his freedom of action in any significant way." Subsequently, we have found the *Miranda* principle applicable to questioning which takes place in a prison setting during a suspect's term of imprisonment on a separate offense, *Mathis v. U.S.*, 391 U.S. 1 (1968), and to questioning taking place in a suspect's home, after he has been arrested and is no longer free to go where he pleases, *Orozco v. Texas*, 394 U.S. 324 (1969).

In the present case, however, there is no indication that the questioning took place in a context where respondent's freedom to depart was restricted in any way. He came voluntarily to the police station, where he was immediately informed that he was not under arrest. At the close of a 1/2-hour interview respondent did in fact leave the police station without hindrance. It is clear from these facts that Mathiason was not in custody "or otherwise deprived of his freedom of action in any significant way."

Such a noncustodial situation is not converted to one in which *Miranda* applies simply because a reviewing court concludes that, even in the absence of any formal arrest or restraint on freedom of movement, the questioning took place in a "coercive environment." Any interview of one suspected of a crime by a police officer will have coercive aspects to it, simply by virtue of the fact that the police officer is part of a law enforcement system which may ultimately cause the suspect to be charged with a crime. But police officers are not required to administer *Miranda* warnings to everyone whom they question. Nor is the requirement of warnings to be imposed simply because the questioning takes place in the station house, or because the questioned person is one whom the police suspect. *Miranda* warnings are required only where there has been such a restriction on a person's freedom as to render him "in custody." It was that sort of coercive environment to which *Miranda* by its terms was made applicable, and to which it is limited.

The officer's false statement about having discovered Mathiason's fingerprints at the scene was found by the Supreme Court of Oregon to be another circumstance contributing to the coercive environment which makes the *Miranda* rationale applicable. Whatever relevance this fact may have to other issues in the case, it has nothing to do with whether respondent was in custody for purposes of the *Miranda* rule.

JUSTICE MARSHALL, dissenting.

The respondent in this case was interrogated behind closed doors at police headquarters in connection with a burglary investigation. He had been named by the victim of the burglary as a suspect, and was told by the police that they believed he was involved. He was falsely informed that his fingerprints had been found at the scene, and in effect was advised that by cooperating with the police he could help himself. Not until after he had confessed was he given the warnings set forth in *Miranda*.

The Court today holds that, for constitutional purposes, all this is irrelevant because respondent had not "been taken into custody or otherwise deprived of his freedom of action in any significant way." I do not believe that such a determination is possible on the record before us. It is true that respondent was not formally placed under arrest, but surely formalities alone cannot control. At the very least, if respondent entertained an objectively reasonable belief that he was not free to leave during the questioning, then he was "deprived of his freedom of action in a significant way." Plainly the respondent could have so believed, after being told by the police that they thought he was involved in a burglary and that his fingerprints had been found at the scene.

More fundamentally, however, I cannot agree with the Court's conclusion that if respondent were not in custody no warnings were required. I recognize that *Miranda* is limited to custodial interrogations, but that is because, as we noted last Term, the facts in the *Miranda* cases raised only this narrow issue. The rationale of *Miranda*, however, is not so easily cabined.

Miranda requires warnings to "combat" a situation in which there are "inherently compelling pressures which work to undermine the individual's will to resist and to compel him to speak where he would not otherwise do so freely." It is of course true, as the Court notes, that "any interview of one suspected of a crime by a police officer will have coercive aspects to it." But it does not follow that because police "are not required to administer *Miranda* warnings to everyone whom they question," that they need not administer warnings to anyone, unless the factual setting of the *Miranda* cases is replicated. Rather, faithfulness to *Miranda* requires us to distinguish situations that resemble the "coercive aspects" of custodial interrogation from those that more nearly resemble "general on-the-scene questioning . . . or other general questioning of citizens in the fact-finding process" which *Miranda* states usually can take place without warnings.

In my view, even if respondent were not in custody, the coercive elements in the instant case were so pervasive as to require *Miranda*-type warnings. Respondent was interrogated in "privacy" and in "unfamiliar surroundings," factors on which *Miranda* places great stress. The investigation had focused on respondent. And respondent was subjected to some of the "deceptive stratagems" which called forth the *Miranda* decision. I therefore agree with the Oregon Supreme Court that to excuse the absence of warnings given these facts is "contrary to the rationale expressed in *Miranda*."

JUSTICE STEVENS, dissenting.

In my opinion, the issues presented by this case are too important to be decided summarily. Of particular importance is the fact that the respondent was on parole at the time of his interrogation in the police station. This fact lends support to inconsistent conclusions.

On the one hand, the State surely has greater power to question a parolee about his activities than to question someone else. Moreover, as a practical matter, it seems unlikely that a *Miranda* warning would have much effect on a parolee's choice between silence and responding to police interrogation. Arguably, therefore, *Miranda* warnings are entirely inappropriate in the parole context.

On the other hand, a parolee is technically in legal custody continuously until his sentence has been served. Therefore, if a formalistic analysis of the custody question is to determine when the

Miranda warning is necessary, a parolee should always be warned. Moreover, *Miranda* teaches that even if a suspect is not in custody, warnings are necessary if he is "otherwise deprived of his freedom of action in any significant way." If a parolee being questioned in a police station is not described by that language, today's decision qualifies that part of *Miranda* to some extent. I believe we would have a better understanding of the extent of that qualification, and therefore of the situations in which warnings must be given to a suspect who is not technically in custody, if we had the benefit of full argument and plenary consideration.

In *Minnesota v. Murphy*, the Supreme Court addressed some of the questions raised by Justice Stevens in his *Oregon v. Mathiason* dissent and held that *Miranda* does not ordinarily apply to a probation interview because the probationer is not in custody.

MINNESOTA V. MURPHY
465 U.S. 420 (1984)

In 1980, in connection with a prosecution for criminal sexual conduct, Marshall Murphy pleaded guilty to a reduced charge of false imprisonment; his prison term of 16 months was suspended and he was placed on probation for three years. The terms of Murphy's probation required that he participate in a treatment program for sexual offenders, that he report to his probation officer as directed, and that he be truthful with the probation officer in all matters.

In 1981, while in the treatment program, Murphy admitted to a counselor that he had raped and murdered a teenage girl in 1974. The counselor reported the admission to Murphy's probation officer, who then asked Murphy to arrange a meeting with her. At the meeting, the probation officer explained what she had been told by the counselor. Murphy became angry at what he considered to be a breach of his confidences and stated that he "felt like calling a lawyer." As the meeting continued, Murphy denied the false imprisonment charge, admitted that he had committed the rape and murder, and attempted to persuade the probation officer that further treatment was unnecessary because several extenuating circumstances explained the prior crimes. At the conclusion of the meeting, the probation officer told Murphy that she had a duty to relay the information to authorities and encouraged him to turn himself in. Murphy then left the office. He was later arrested and charged with murder. At trial, Murphy sought to suppress testimony concerning his confession on the grounds that his probation officer had never administered the *Miranda* warnings prior to their meeting.

Although a person on probation is subject to a number of restrictions and is considered to be in custody for some purposes, the Supreme Court concluded that Murphy was not entitled to *Miranda* warnings because there was no "formal arrest or restraint on freedom of movement of the degree associated with a formal arrest." The Court proceeded to draw a number of distinctions between custodial interrogation requiring compliance with *Miranda* and the probation interview to which Murphy was subjected:

> Even a cursory comparison of custodial interrogation and probation interviews reveals the inaptness of the analogy to *Miranda*. Custodial arrest is said to convey to the suspect a message that he has no choice but to submit to the officers' will and to confess. It is unlikely that a probation interview, arranged by appointment at a mutually convenient time, would give rise to a similar impression. Moreover, custodial arrest thrusts an individual into an unfamiliar atmosphere or an interrogation environment created for no purpose other than to subjugate the individual to the will of his examiner. Many of the psychological ploys discussed in *Miranda* capitalize on the suspect's unfamiliarity with the officers and the environment. Murphy's regular meetings with his probation officer should have served to familiarize him with her and her office and to insulate him from psychological intimidation that might overbear his desire to claim the privilege [against self-incrimination]. Finally, the coercion inherent in custodial interrogation derives in large measure from an interrogator's insinuations that the interrogation will continue until a confession is obtained. Since Murphy was not physically restrained and could have left the office, any compulsion he might have felt from the possibility that terminating the meeting would have led to revocation of probation was not comparable to the pressure on a suspect who is painfully aware that he literally cannot escape a persistent custodial interrogator.

In *Berkemer v. McCarty*, the Supreme Court held that *Miranda* warnings should be administered to anyone subjected to custodial interrogation, even when the crime for which the suspect is being questioned is a misdemeanor. The Court went on to hold, however, that roadside questioning following a traffic stop does not constitute custodial interrogation for purposes of *Miranda*.

BERKEMER V. MCCARTY
468 U.S. 420 (1984)

JUSTICE MARSHALL delivered the opinion of the Court.

This case presents two related questions: First, does our decision in *Miranda v. Arizona*, 384 U.S. 436 (1966), govern the admissibility of statements made during custodial interrogation by a suspect accused of a misdemeanor traffic offense? Second, does the roadside questioning of a motorist detained pursuant to a traffic stop constitute custodial interrogation for the purposes of the doctrine enunciated in *Miranda*?

I

The parties have stipulated to the essential facts. On the evening of March 31, 1980, Trooper Williams of the Ohio State Highway Patrol observed respondent's car weaving in and out of a lane on Interstate Highway 270. After following the car for two miles, Williams forced respondent to stop and asked him to get out of the vehicle. When respondent complied, Williams noticed that he was having difficulty standing. At that point, Williams concluded that respondent would be charged with a traffic offense and, therefore, his freedom to leave the scene was terminated. However, respondent was not told that he would be taken into custody. Williams then asked respondent to perform a field sobriety test, commonly known as a "balancing test." Respondent could not do so without falling.

While still at the scene of the traffic stop, Williams asked respondent whether he had been using intoxicants. Respondent replied that "he had consumed two beers and had smoked several joints of marijuana a short time before." Respondent's speech was slurred, and Williams had difficulty understanding him. Williams thereupon formally placed respondent under arrest and transported him in the patrol car to the Franklin County Jail.

At the jail, respondent was given an intoxilyzer test to determine the concentration of alcohol in his blood. The test did not detect any alcohol whatsoever in respondent's system. Williams then resumed questioning respondent in order to obtain information for inclusion in the State Highway Patrol Alcohol Influence Report. Respondent answered affirmatively a question whether he had been drinking. When then asked if he was under the influence of alcohol, he said, "I guess, barely." Williams next asked respondent to indicate on the form whether the marihuana he had smoked had been treated with any chemicals. In the section of the report headed "Remarks," respondent wrote, "No angel dust or PCP in the pot. Rick McCarty."

At no point in this sequence of events did Williams or anyone else tell respondent that he had a right to remain silent, to consult with an attorney, and to have an attorney appointed for him if he could not afford one.

Respondent was charged with operating a motor vehicle while under the influence of alcohol and/or drugs. Under Ohio law, that offense is a first-degree misdemeanor and is punishable by fine or imprisonment for up to six months. Incarceration for a minimum of three days is mandatory.

Respondent moved to exclude the various incriminating statements he had made to Trooper Williams on the ground that introduction into evidence of those statements would violate the Fifth Amendment insofar as he had not been informed of his constitutional rights prior to his interrogation. When the trial court denied the motion, respondent pleaded "no contest" and was found guilty. He was sentenced to 90 days in jail, 80 of which were suspended, and was fined $300, $100 of which were suspended.

II

In the years since the decision in *Miranda*, we have frequently reaffirmed the central principle established by that case: if the police take a suspect into custody and then ask him questions without informing him of the rights enumerated above, his responses cannot be introduced into evidence to establish his guilt.

Petitioner asks us to carve an exception out of the foregoing principle. When the police arrest a person for allegedly committing a misdemeanor traffic offense and then ask him questions without telling him his constitutional rights, petitioner argues, his responses should be admissible against him. We cannot agree.

One of the principal advantages of the doctrine that suspects must be given warnings before being interrogated while in custody is the clarity of that rule. The exception to *Miranda* proposed by petitioner would substantially undermine this crucial advantage of the doctrine. The police often are unaware when they arrest a person whether he may have committed a misdemeanor or a felony. Consider, for example, the reasonably common situation in which the driver of a car involved in an accident is taken into custody. Under Ohio law, both driving while under the influence of intoxicants and negligent vehicular homicide are misdemeanors, while reckless vehicular homicide is a felony. When arresting a person for causing a collision, the police may not know which of these offenses he may have committed. Indeed, the nature of his offense may depend upon circumstances unknowable to the police, such as whether the suspect has previously committed a similar offense or has a criminal record of some other kind. It may even turn upon events yet to happen, such as whether a victim of the accident dies. It would be unreasonable to expect the police to make guesses as to the nature of the criminal conduct at issue before deciding how they may interrogate the suspect.

Equally importantly, the doctrinal complexities that would confront the courts if we accepted petitioner's proposal would be Byzantine. Difficult questions quickly spring to mind: For instance, investigations into seemingly minor offenses sometimes escalate gradually into investigations into more serious matters; at what point in the evolution of an affair of this sort would the police be obliged to give *Miranda* warnings to a suspect in custody? What evidence would be necessary to establish that an arrest for a misdemeanor offense was merely a pretext to enable the police to interrogate the suspect (in hopes of obtaining information about a felony) without providing him the safeguards prescribed by *Miranda*? The litigation necessary to resolve such matters would be time-consuming and disruptive of law enforcement. And the end result would be an elaborate set of rules, interlaced with exceptions and subtle distinctions, discriminating between different kinds of custodial interrogations. Neither the police nor criminal defendants would benefit from such a development.

Absent a compelling justification we surely would be unwilling so seriously to impair the simplicity and clarity of the holding of *Miranda*. Neither of the two arguments proffered by petitioner constitutes such a justification. Petitioner first contends that *Miranda* warnings are unnecessary when a suspect is questioned about a misdemeanor traffic offense, because the police have no reason to subject such a suspect to the sort of interrogation that most troubled the Court in *Miranda*. We cannot agree that the dangers of police abuse are so slight in this context. For example, the offense of driving while intoxicated is increasingly regarded in many jurisdictions as a very serious matter. Especially when the intoxicant at issue is a narcotic drug rather than alcohol, the police sometimes have difficulty obtaining evidence of this crime. Under such circumstances, the incentive for the police to try to induce the defendant to incriminate himself may well be substantial. Similar incentives are likely to be present when a person is arrested for a minor offense but the police suspect that a more serious crime may have been committed.

We do not suggest that there is any reason to think improper efforts were made in this case to induce respondent to make damaging admissions. More generally, we have no doubt that, in conducting most custodial interrogations of persons arrested for misdemeanor traffic offenses, the police behave responsibly and do not deliberately exert pressures upon the suspect to confess against his will. But the same might be said of custodial interrogations of persons arrested for felonies. The purposes of the safeguards prescribed by *Miranda* are to ensure that the police do not coerce or trick captive suspects into confessing, to relieve the "inherently compelling pressures" generated by the custodial setting itself, "which work to undermine the individual's will to resist," and as much as possible to free courts from the task of scrutinizing individual cases to try to determine, after the fact, whether particular confessions were voluntary. Those purposes are implicated as much by in-custody questioning of persons suspected of misdemeanors as they are by questioning of persons suspected of felonies.

Petitioner's second argument is that law enforcement would be more expeditious and effective in the absence of a requirement that persons arrested for traffic offenses be informed of their rights. Again, we are unpersuaded. The occasions on which the police arrest and then interrogate someone suspected only of a misdemeanor traffic offense are rare. The police are already well accustomed to giving *Miranda* warnings to persons taken into custody. Adherence to the principle that all suspects must be given such warnings will not significantly hamper the efforts of the police to investigate crimes.

We hold therefore that a person subjected to custodial interrogation is entitled to the benefit of the procedural safeguards enunciated in *Miranda*, regardless of the nature or severity of the offense of which he is suspected or for which he was arrested.

The implication of this holding is that the statements made by respondent at the County Jail were inadmissible. There can be no question that respondent was "in custody" at least as of the moment he was formally placed under arrest and instructed to get into the police car. Because he was not informed of his constitutional rights at that juncture, respondent's subsequent admissions should not have been used against him.

III

To assess the admissibility of the self-incriminating statements made by respondent prior to his formal arrest, we are obliged to address a second issue concerning the scope of our decision in *Miranda*: whether the roadside questioning of a motorist detained pursuant to a routine traffic stop should be considered "custodial interrogation." Respondent urges that it should, on the ground that *Miranda* by its terms applies whenever "a person has been taken into custody or otherwise deprived of his freedom of action in any significant way." Petitioner contends that a holding that every detained motorist must be advised of his rights before being questioned would constitute an unwarranted extension of the *Miranda* doctrine.

It must be acknowledged at the outset that a traffic stop significantly curtails the "freedom of action" of the driver and the passengers, if any, of the detained vehicle. Under the law of most States, it is a crime either to ignore a policeman's signal to stop one's car or, once having stopped, to drive away without permission. Certainly few motorists would feel free either to disobey a directive to pull over or to leave the scene of a traffic stop without being told they might do so. Partly for these reasons, we have long acknowledged that stopping an automobile and detaining its occupants constitute a "seizure" within the meaning of the Fourth Amendment, even though the purpose of the stop is limited and the resulting detention quite brief. *Delaware v. Prouse*, 440 U.S. 648 (1979).

However, we decline to accord talismanic power to the phrase in the *Miranda* opinion emphasized by respondent. Fidelity to the doctrine announced in *Miranda* requires that it be enforced strictly, but only in those types of situations in which the concerns that powered the decision are implicated. Thus, we must decide whether a traffic stop exerts upon a detained person pressures that sufficiently impair his free exercise of his privilege against self-incrimination to require that he be warned of his constitutional rights.

Two features of an ordinary traffic stop mitigate the danger that a person questioned will be induced "to speak where he would not otherwise do so freely." First, detention of a motorist pursuant to a traffic stop is presumptively temporary and brief. The vast majority of roadside detentions last only a few minutes. A motorist's expectations, when he sees a policeman's light flashing behind him, are that he will be obliged to spend a short period of time answering questions and waiting while the officer checks his license and registration, that he may then be given a citation, but that in the end he most likely will be allowed to continue on his way. In this respect, questioning incident to an ordinary traffic stop is quite different from stationhouse interrogation, which frequently is prolonged, and in which the detainee often is aware that questioning will continue until he provides his interrogators the answers they seek.

Second, circumstances associated with the typical traffic stop are not such that the motorist feels completely at the mercy of the police. To be sure, the aura of authority surrounding an armed, uniformed officer and the knowledge that the officer has some discretion in deciding whether to issue a citation, in combination, exert some pressure on the detainee to respond to questions. But other aspects of the situation substantially offset these forces. Perhaps most importantly, the typical traffic stop is public, at least to some degree. Passersby, on foot or in other cars, witness the interaction of officer and motorist. This exposure to public view both reduces the ability of an unscrupulous policeman to use illegitimate means to elicit self-incriminating statements and diminishes the motorist's fear that, if he does not cooperate, he will be subjected to abuse. The fact that the detained motorist typically is confronted by only one or at most two policemen further mutes his sense of vulnerability. In short, the atmosphere surrounding an ordinary traffic stop is substantially less "police dominated" than that surrounding the kinds of interrogation at issue in *Miranda* itself, and in the subsequent cases in which we have applied *Miranda*.

In both of these respects, the usual traffic stop is more analogous to a so-called "*Terry* stop," than to a formal arrest. [See *Terry v. Ohio*, 392 U.S. 1 (1968).] Under the Fourth Amendment, we have held, a policeman who lacks probable cause but whose observations lead him reasonably to suspect that a particular person has committed, is committing, or is about to commit a crime, may detain that person briefly in order to investigate the circumstances that provoke suspicion. The stop and inquiry must be reasonably related in scope to the justification for their initiation. Typically, this means that the officer may ask the detainee a moderate number of questions to determine his identity and to try to obtain information confirming or dispelling the officer's suspicions. But the detainee is not obliged to respond. And, unless the detainee's answers provide the officer with probable cause to arrest him, he must then be released. The comparatively nonthreatening character of detentions of this sort explains the absence of any suggestion in our opinions that *Terry* stops are subject to the dictates of *Miranda*. The similarly noncoercive aspect of ordinary traffic stops prompts us to hold that persons temporarily detained pursuant to such stops are not "in custody" for the purposes of *Miranda*.

Turning to the case before us, we find nothing in the record that indicates that respondent should have been given *Miranda* warnings at any point prior to the time Trooper Williams placed him under arrest. For the reasons indicated above, we reject the contention that the initial stop of respondent's car, by itself, rendered him "in custody." And respondent has failed to demonstrate that, at any time between the initial stop and the arrest, he was subjected to restraints comparable to those associated with a formal arrest. Only a short period of time elapsed between the stop and the arrest. At no point during that interval was respondent informed that his detention would not be temporary. Although Trooper Williams apparently decided as soon as respondent stepped out of his car that respondent would be taken into custody and charged with a traffic offense, Williams never communicated his intention to respondent. A policeman's unarticulated plan has no bearing on the question whether a suspect was "in custody" at a particular time; the only relevant inquiry is how a reasonable man in the suspect's position would have understood his situation. Nor do other aspects of the interaction of Williams and respondent support the contention that respondent was exposed to "custodial interrogation" at the scene of the stop. From aught that appears in the stipulation of facts, a single police officer asked respondent a modest number of questions and requested him to perform a simple balancing test at a location visible to passing motorists. Treatment of this sort cannot fairly be characterized as the functional equivalent of formal arrest.

We conclude, in short, that respondent was not taken into custody for the purposes of *Miranda* until Williams arrested him. Consequently, the statements respondent made prior to that point were admissible against him.

———————

Of particular importance in applying the custody test is whether the concerns underlying *Miranda* are present. When these concerns—coercive pressure on the suspect in a police-dominated atmosphere—are not present, the Supreme Court tends to view the situation as non-custodial, and no *Miranda* warnings are required. There was little evidence of coercive pressure in a police-dominated atmosphere during the home interview with the IRS agents in *Beckwith v. U.S.*, during the meeting at the probation office in *Minnesota v. Murphy*, and during the roadside questioning in *Berkemer v. McCarty*. Accordingly, the Supreme Court concluded in each of those cases that the person being questioned was not in custody, and no *Miranda* warnings were required.

In addition to analyzing whether the concerns motivating the decision in *Miranda* are present in a particular situation, the Supreme Court has also held that the custody determination is an objective one that focuses on how a reasonable person in the suspect's situation would perceive his circumstances; the subjective views of the interrogating officers and the person being questioned do *not* dictate whether a person is in custody. The proper inquiry, therefore, is whether a reasonable person in the suspect's circumstances would have felt free to terminate the interrogation and leave. As the sharply divided 5–4 vote in *Yarborough v. Alvarado* reveals, the same facts often yield conflicting interpretations as to whether the suspect was in custody.

YARBOROUGH V. ALVARADO

541 U.S. 652 (2004)

JUSTICE KENNEDY delivered the opinion of the Court.

I

Paul Soto and respondent Michael Alvarado attempted to steal a truck in the parking lot of a shopping mall in Santa Fe Springs, California. Soto and Alvarado were part of a larger group of teenagers at the mall that night. Soto decided to steal the truck, and Alvarado agreed to help. Soto pulled out a .357 Magnum and approached the driver, Francisco Castaneda, who was standing near the truck emptying trash into a dumpster. Soto demanded money and the ignition keys from Castaneda. Alvarado, then five months short of his 18th birthday, approached the passenger side door of the truck and crouched down.

When Castaneda refused to comply with Soto's demands, Soto shot Castaneda, killing him. Alvarado then helped hide Soto's gun.

Los Angeles County Sheriff's detective Cheryl Comstock led the investigation into the circumstances of Castaneda's death. About a month after the shooting, Comstock left word at Alvarado's house and also contacted Alvarado's mother at work with the message that she wished to speak with Alvarado. Alvarado's parents brought him to the Pico Rivera Sheriff's Station to be interviewed around lunchtime. They waited in the lobby while Alvarado went with Comstock to be interviewed. Alvarado contends that his parents asked to be present during the interview but were rebuffed.

Comstock brought Alvarado to a small interview room and began interviewing him at about 12:30 p.m. The interview lasted about two hours, and was recorded by Comstock with Alvarado's knowledge. Only Comstock and Alvarado were present. Alvarado was not given a warning under *Miranda v. Arizona*, 384 U.S. 436 (1966). Comstock began the interview by asking Alvarado to recount the events on the night of the shooting. On that night, Alvarado explained, he had been drinking alcohol at a friend's house with some other friends and acquaintances. After a few hours, part of the group went home and the rest walked to a nearby mall to use its public telephones. In Alvarado's initial telling, that was the end of it. The group went back to the friend's home and "just went to bed."

Unpersuaded, Comstock pressed on:

Q.   Okay. We did real good up until this point and everything you've said it's pretty accurate till this point, except for you left out the shooting.

A.   The shooting?

Q.   Uh huh, the shooting.

A.   Well I had never seen no shooting.

Q.   Well I'm afraid you did.

A.   I had never seen no shooting.

Q.   Well I beg to differ with you. I've been told quite the opposite and we have witnesses that are saying quite the opposite.

A.   That I had seen the shooting?

Q.   So why don't you take a deep breath, like I told you before, the very best thing is to be honest. . . . You can't have that many people get involved in a murder and expect that some of them aren't going to tell the truth, okay? Now granted if it was maybe one person, you might be able to keep your fingers crossed and say, god I hope he doesn't tell the truth, but the problem is is that they have to tell the truth, okay? Now all I'm simply doing is giving you the opportunity to tell the truth and when we got that many people telling a story and all of a sudden you tell something way far fetched different.

At this point, Alvarado slowly began to change his story. First he acknowledged being present when the carjacking occurred but claimed that he did not know what happened or who had a gun. When he hesitated to say more, Comstock tried to encourage Alvarado to discuss what happened by appealing to his sense of honesty and the need to bring the man who shot Castaneda to justice. Alvarado then admitted he had helped the other man try to steal the truck by standing near the passenger side door. Next he admitted that the other man was Paul Soto, that he knew Soto was armed, and that he had helped hide the gun after the murder. Alvarado explained that he had expected Soto to scare the driver with the gun, but that he did not expect Soto to kill anyone. Toward the end of the interview, Comstock twice asked Alvarado if he needed to take a break. Alvarado declined. When the interview was over, Comstock returned with Alvarado to the lobby of the sheriff's station where his parents were waiting. Alvarado's father drove him home.

A few months later, the State of California charged Soto and Alvarado with first-degree murder and attempted robbery. Citing *Miranda*, Alvarado moved to suppress his statements from the Comstock interview. The trial court denied the motion on the ground that the interview was noncustodial. Alvarado and Soto were tried together, and Alvarado testified in his own defense. He offered an innocent explanation for his conduct, testifying that he happened to be standing in the parking lot of the mall when a gun went off nearby. The government's cross-examination relied on Alvarado's statement to Comstock. Alvarado admitted having made some of the statements but denied others. When Alvarado denied particular statements, the prosecution countered by playing excerpts from the audio recording of the interview.

During cross-examination, Alvarado agreed that the interview with Comstock "was a pretty friendly conversation," that there was "sort of a free flow between [Alvarado] and Detective Comstock," and that Alvarado did not "feel coerced or threatened in any way" during the interview. The jury convicted Soto and Alvarado of first-degree murder and attempted robbery. The trial judge later reduced Alvarado's conviction to second-degree murder for his comparatively minor role in the offense. The judge sentenced Soto to life in prison and Alvarado to 15-years-to-life.

[Alvarado's conviction was affirmed by the California Court of Appeal, and his request for review by the California Supreme Court was denied. Alvarado then filed a habeas corpus petition in federal district court, but it was denied.] The Court of Appeals for the Ninth Circuit reversed. The Court of Appeals held that the state court erred in failing to account for Alvarado's youth and inexperience when evaluating whether a reasonable person in his position would have felt free to leave. It noted that this Court has considered a suspect's juvenile status when evaluating the voluntariness of confessions and the waiver of the privilege against self-incrimination. The Court of Appeals held that in light of these authorities, Alvarado's age and experience must be a factor in the *Miranda* custody inquiry. A minor with no criminal record would be more likely to feel coerced by police tactics and conclude he is under arrest than would an experienced adult, the Court of Appeals reasoned. According to the Court of Appeals, the effect of Alvarado's age and inexperience was so substantial that it turned the interview into a custodial interrogation.

II

Our more recent cases instruct that custody must be determined based on how a reasonable person in the suspect's situation would perceive his circumstances. In *Berkemer v. McCarty*, 468 U.S. 420 (1984), a police officer stopped a suspected drunk driver and asked him some questions. Although the officer reached the decision to arrest the driver at the beginning of the traffic stop, he did not do so until the driver failed a sobriety test and acknowledged that he had been drinking beer and smoking marijuana. The Court held the traffic stop noncustodial despite the officer's intent to arrest because he had not communicated that intent to the driver. A policeman's unarticulated plan has no bearing on the question whether a suspect was "in custody" at a particular time, the Court explained. "The only relevant inquiry is how a reasonable man in the suspect's position would have understood his situation." In a footnote, the Court cited a New York state case for the view that an objective test was preferable to a subjective test in part because it does not "place upon the police the burden of anticipating the frailties or idiosyncrasies of every person whom they question."

Stansbury v. California, 511 U.S. 318 (1994), confirmed this analytical framework. *Stansbury* explained that "the initial determination of custody depends on the objective circumstances of the interrogation, not on the subjective views harbored by either the interrogating officers or the person being questioned." Courts must examine "all of the circumstances surrounding the interrogation" and determine "how a reasonable person in the position of the individual being questioned would gauge the breadth of his or her freedom of action."

Finally, in *Thompson v. Keohane*, 516 U.S. 99 (1995), the Court offered the following description of the *Miranda* custody test:

> Two discrete inquiries are essential to the determination: first, what were the circumstances surrounding the interrogation; and second, given those circumstances, would a reasonable person

have felt he or she was not at liberty to terminate the interrogation and leave. Once the scene is set and the players' lines and actions are reconstructed, the court must apply an objective test to resolve the ultimate inquiry: was there a formal arrest or restraint on freedom of movement of the degree associated with a formal arrest.

Based on these principles, we conclude that the state court's application of our clearly established law was reasonable. It can be said that fairminded jurists could disagree over whether Alvarado was in custody. On one hand, certain facts weigh against a finding that Alvarado was in custody. The police did not transport Alvarado to the station or require him to appear at a particular time. They did not threaten him or suggest he would be placed under arrest. Alvarado's parents remained in the lobby during the interview, suggesting that the interview would be brief. In fact, according to trial counsel for Alvarado, he and his parents were told that the interview was "not going to be long." During the interview, Comstock focused on Soto's crimes rather than Alvarado's. Instead of pressuring Alvarado with the threat of arrest and prosecution, she appealed to his interest in telling the truth and being helpful to a police officer. In addition, Comstock twice asked Alvarado if he wanted to take a break. At the end of the interview, Alvarado went home. All of these objective facts are consistent with an interrogation environment in which a reasonable person would have felt free to terminate the interview and leave. Indeed, a number of the facts echo those of *Oregon v. Mathiason*, 429 U.S. 492 (1977), in which we found it "clear from these facts" that the suspect was not in custody.

Other facts point in the opposite direction. Comstock interviewed Alvarado at the police station. The interview lasted two hours, four times longer than the 30-minute interview in *Mathiason*. Unlike the officer in *Mathiason*, Comstock did not tell Alvarado that he was free to leave. Alvarado was brought to the police station by his legal guardians rather than arriving on his own accord, making the extent of his control over his presence unclear. Counsel for Alvarado alleges that Alvarado's parents asked to be present at the interview but were rebuffed, a fact that—if known to Alvarado—might reasonably have led someone in Alvarado's position to feel more restricted than otherwise. These facts weigh in favor of the view that Alvarado was in custody.

These differing indications lead us to hold that the state court's application of our custody standard was reasonable. The Court of Appeals was nowhere close to the mark when it concluded otherwise. The custody test is general, and the state court's application of our law fits within the matrix of our prior decisions.

III

The Court of Appeals reached the opposite result by placing considerable reliance on Alvarado's age and inexperience with law enforcement. Our Court has not stated that a suspect's age or experience is relevant to the *Miranda* custody analysis. According to the Court of Appeals, however, our Court's emphasis on juvenile status in other contexts demanded consideration of Alvarado's age and inexperience here.

Our opinions applying the *Miranda* custody test have not mentioned the suspect's age, much less mandated its consideration. The only indications in the Court's opinions relevant to a suspect's experience with law enforcement have rejected reliance on such factors.

There is an important conceptual difference between the *Miranda* custody test and the line of cases from other contexts considering age and experience. The *Miranda* custody inquiry is an objective test. To be sure, the line between permissible objective facts and impermissible subjective experiences can be indistinct in some cases. It is possible to subsume a subjective factor into an objective test by making the latter more specific in its formulation. Thus the Court of Appeals styled its inquiry as an objective test by considering what a "reasonable 17-year-old, with no prior history of arrest or police interviews," would perceive.

At the same time, the objective *Miranda* custody inquiry could reasonably be viewed as different from doctrinal tests that depend on the actual mindset of a particular suspect, where we do consider a suspect's age and experience. For example, the voluntariness of a statement is often said to depend on whether the defendant's will was overborne, a question that logically can depend on the characteristics of the accused. The characteristics of the accused can include the suspect's age, education, and intelligence, as well as a suspect's prior experience with law enforcement. In concluding that there was "no principled reason" why such factors should not also apply to the *Miranda* custody inquiry, the Court of Appeals ignored the argument that the custody inquiry states an objective rule designed to give clear guidance to the police, while consideration of a suspect's individual characteristics—including his age—could be viewed as creating a subjective inquiry. For these reasons, the state court's failure to consider Alvarado's age does not provide a proper basis for finding that the state court's decision was an unreasonable application of clearly established law.

Indeed, reliance on Alvarado's prior history with law enforcement was improper. In most cases, police officers will not know a suspect's interrogation history. Even if they do, the relationship between a suspect's past experiences and the likelihood a reasonable person with that experience would feel free to leave often will be speculative. True, suspects with prior law enforcement experience may understand police procedures and reasonably feel free to leave unless told otherwise. On the other hand, they may view past as prologue and expect another in a string of arrests. We do not ask police officers to consider these contingent psychological factors when deciding when suspects should be advised of their *Miranda* rights. The inquiry turns too much on the suspect's subjective state of mind and not enough on the objective circumstances of the interrogation.

JUSTICE O'CONNOR, concurring.

I join the opinion of the Court, but write separately to express an additional reason for reversal. There may be cases in which a suspect's age will be relevant to the "custody" inquiry under *Miranda*. In this case, however, Alvarado was almost 18 years old at the time of his interview. It is difficult to expect police to recognize that a suspect is a juvenile when he is so close to the age of majority. Even when police do know a suspect's age, it may be difficult for them to ascertain what bearing it has on the likelihood that the suspect would feel free to leave. That is especially true here; 17 1/2-year-olds vary widely in their reactions to police questioning, and many can be expected to behave as adults. Given these difficulties, I agree that the state court's decision in this case cannot be called an unreasonable application of federal law simply because it failed explicitly to mention Alvarado's age.

JUSTICE BREYER, with whom JUSTICE STEVENS, JUSTICE SOUTER, and JUSTICE GINSBURG join, dissenting.

In my view, Michael Alvarado clearly was "in custody" when the police questioned him (without *Miranda* warnings) about the murder of Francisco Castaneda. To put the question in terms of federal law's well-established legal standards: Would a "reasonable person" in Alvarado's "position" have felt he was "at liberty to terminate the interrogation and leave"? A court must answer this question in light of "all of the circumstances surrounding the interrogation." And the obvious answer here is "no."

The law in this case asks judges to apply, not arcane or complex legal directives, but ordinary common sense. Would a reasonable person in Alvarado's position have felt free simply to get up and walk out of the small room in the station house at will during his 2-hour police interrogation? I ask the reader to put himself, or herself, in Alvarado's circumstances and then answer that question: Alvarado hears from his parents that he is needed for police questioning. His parents take him to the station. On arrival, a police officer separates him from his parents. His parents ask to come along, but the officer says they may not. Another officer says, "What do we have here; we are going to question a suspect."

The police take Alvarado to a small interrogation room, away from the station's public area. A single officer begins to question him, making clear in the process that the police have evidence that he participated in an attempted carjacking connected with a murder. When he says that he never saw any shooting, the officer suggests that he is lying, while adding that she is "giving [him] the opportunity to tell the truth" and "take care of himself." Toward the end of the questioning, the officer gives him permission to take a bathroom or water break. After two hours, by which time he has admitted he was involved in the attempted theft, knew about the gun, and helped to hide it, the questioning ends.

What reasonable person in the circumstances—brought to a police station by his parents at police request, put in a small interrogation room, questioned for a solid two hours, and confronted with claims that there is strong evidence that he participated in a serious crime, could have thought to himself, "Well, anytime I want to leave I can just get up and walk out"? If the person harbored any doubts, would he still think he might be free to leave once he recalls that the police officer has just refused to let his parents remain with him during questioning? Would he still think that he, rather than the officer, controls the situation?

There is only one possible answer to these questions. A reasonable person would *not* have thought he was free simply to pick up and leave in the middle of the interrogation.

What about the Court's view that "fairminded jurists could disagree over whether Alvarado was in custody"? Consider each of the facts it says "weigh against a finding" of custody:

(1) *"The police did not transport Alvarado to the station or require him to appear at a particular time."* True. His parents brought him to the station at police request. But why does that matter? The relevant question is whether Alvarado came to the station of his own free will or submitted to questioning voluntarily. And the involvement of Alvarado's parents suggests *in*voluntary, not voluntary, behavior on Alvarado's part.

(2) *"Alvarado's parents remained in the lobby during the interview, suggesting that the interview would be brief. In fact, [Alvarado] and his parents were told that the interview was not going to be long."* Whatever was communicated to Alvarado *before* the questioning began, the fact is that the interview was not brief, nor, after the first half hour or so, would Alvarado have expected it to be brief. And those are the relevant considerations.

(3) *"At the end of the interview, Alvarado went home."* As the majority acknowledges, our recent case law makes clear that the relevant question is how a reasonable person would have gauged his freedom to leave *during*, not *after*, the interview.

(4) *"During the interview, Officer Comstock focused on Soto's crimes rather than Alvarado's."* In fact, the police officer characterized Soto as the ringleader, while making clear that she knew Alvarado had participated in the attempted carjacking during which Castaneda was

killed. Her questioning would have reinforced, not diminished, Alvarado's fear that he was not simply a witness, but also suspected of having been involved in a serious crime.

(5) *"The officer did not pressure Alvarado with the threat of arrest and prosecution but instead appealed to his interest in telling the truth and being helpful to a police officer."* This factor might be highly significant were the question one of "coercion." But it is not. The question is whether Alvarado would have felt free to terminate the interrogation and leave. In respect to that question, police politeness, while commendable, does not significantly help the majority.

(6) *"Comstock twice asked Alvarado if he wanted to take a break."* This circumstance, emphasizing the officer's control of Alvarado's movements, makes it *less* likely, not *more* likely, that Alvarado would have thought he was free to leave at will.

The facts to which the majority points make clear what the police did *not* do, for example, come to Alvarado's house, tell him he was under arrest, handcuff him, place him in a locked cell, threaten him, or tell him explicitly that he was not free to leave. But what is important here is what the police *did* do—namely, have Alvarado's parents bring him to the station, put him with a single officer in a small room, keep his parents out, let him know that he was a suspect, and question him for two hours. These latter facts compel a single conclusion: A reasonable person in Alvarado's circumstances would *not* have felt free to terminate the interrogation and leave.

What about Alvarado's youth? The fact that Alvarado was 17 helps to show that he was unlikely to have felt free to ignore his parents' request to come to the station. And a 17-year-old is more likely than, say, a 35-year-old, to take a police officer's assertion of authority to keep parents outside the room as an assertion of authority to keep their child inside as well.

The majority suggests that the law might *prevent* a judge from taking account of the fact that Alvarado was 17. I can find nothing in the law that supports that conclusion. Our cases do instruct lower courts to apply a "reasonable person" standard. But the "reasonable person" standard does not require a court to pretend that Alvarado was a 35-year-old with aging parents whose middle-aged children do what their parents ask only out of respect. Nor does it say that a court should pretend that Alvarado was the statistically determined "average person"—a working, married, 35-year-old white female with a high school degree.

Rather, the precise legal definition of "reasonable person" may, depending on legal context, appropriately account for certain personal characteristics. In negligence suits, for example, the question is what would a "reasonable person" do "under the same or similar circumstances." In answering that question, courts enjoy latitude and may make allowance not only for external facts, but sometimes for certain characteristics of the actor himself, including physical disability, youth, or advanced age.

In the present context, that of *Miranda*'s "in custody" inquiry, the law has introduced the concept of a "reasonable person" to avoid judicial inquiry into subjective states of mind, and to focus the inquiry instead upon objective circumstances that are known to both the officer and the suspect and that are likely relevant to the way a person would understand his situation. This focus helps to keep *Miranda* a workable rule.

In this case, Alvarado's youth is an objective circumstance that was known to the police. It is not a special quality, but rather a widely shared characteristic that generates commonsense conclusions about behavior and perception. To focus on the circumstance of age in a case like this does not complicate the "in custody" inquiry. And to say that courts should ignore widely shared, objective characteristics, like age, on the ground that only a (large) *minority* of the population possesses them would produce absurd results, the present instance being a case in point. I am not surprised that the majority points to no case suggesting any such limitation.

As I have said, the law in this case is clear. This Court's cases establish that, even if the police do not tell a suspect he is under arrest, do not handcuff him, do not lock him in a cell, and do not threaten him, he may nonetheless reasonably believe he is not free to leave the place of questioning—and thus be in custody for *Miranda* purposes.

Our cases also make clear that to determine how a suspect would have gauged his "freedom of movement," a court must carefully examine "all of the circumstances surrounding the interrogation," including, for example, how long the interrogation lasted (brief and routine or protracted?), how the suspect came to be questioned (voluntarily or against his will?), where the questioning took place (at a police station or in public?), and what the officer communicated to the individual during the interrogation (that he was a suspect? that he was under arrest? that he was free to leave at will?). In the present case, every one of these factors argues—and argues strongly—that Alvarado was in custody for *Miranda* purposes when the police questioned him.

Common sense, and an understanding of the law's basic purpose in this area, are enough to make clear that Alvarado's age—an objective, widely shared characteristic about which the police plainly knew—is also relevant to the inquiry. Unless one is prepared to pretend that Alvarado is someone he is not, a middle-aged gentleman, well versed in police practices, it seems to me clear that the California courts made a serious mistake.

The *Alvarado* majority suggested that a suspect's age or experience need not be taken into account as part of the objective custody determination under *Miranda*. As Justice O'Connor's concurring opinion pointed out, the majority's views may have been shaped, in part, by the fact that Alvarado was nearly 18 when he was questioned, and police cannot be expected "to recognize that a suspect is a juvenile when he is so close to the age of majority." More recently, in *J.D.B. v. North Carolina*, a 13-year-old seventh grader was removed from class by a uniformed officer, escorted to a closed-door conference room, and questioned by police for at least half an hour without administration of the *Miranda* warnings. The Supreme Court held that although the custody determination remains an objective one, a child's age, when known or apparent to police, is a relevant consideration that should be taken into account.

J.D.B. v. NORTH CAROLINA
131 S.Ct. 2394 (2011)

Police learned that a digital camera matching the description of one of the items stolen in two recent home break-ins had been found at J.D.B.'s middle school and seen in his possession. A police investigator went to the school to question J.D.B. A uniformed police officer (a "school resource officer") interrupted a social studies class, removed J.D.B. from the classroom, and escorted him to a school conference room. There, J.D.B. was met by the police investigator, the assistant principal, and an administrative intern. The door to the conference room was closed. With the two officers and two administrators present, J.D.B. was questioned, without *Miranda* warnings, for the next 30 to 45 minutes. J.D.B. was not given an opportunity to speak to his grandmother, his legal guardian, nor was he informed that he was free to leave the room. Under pressure from the assistant principal to "do the right thing," and upon learning from the investigator of the possibility of juvenile detention, J.D.B. admitted that he and a friend were responsible for the break-ins. The investigator then informed J.D.B. that he could refuse to answer his questions and that he was free to leave. Asked whether he understood, J.D.B. nodded and provided further detail, including the location of the stolen items. Eventually, at the investigator's request, J.D.B. wrote a statement. When the bell rang indicating the end of the school day, J.D.B. was allowed to leave to catch the bus home.

Two juvenile petitions were filed against J.D.B., each alleging one count of breaking and entering and one count of larceny. J.D.B.'s public defender moved to suppress his statements and the evidence derived therefrom, arguing that J.D.B. had been subjected to custodial interrogation without *Miranda* warnings, and that his statements were involuntary under the totality of the circumstances test. The trial court denied the motion, finding that J.D.B. was not in custody when interrogated at school and that his statements were voluntary. The North Carolina appellate courts affirmed.

Noting that it "is beyond dispute that children will often feel bound to submit to police questioning when an adult in the same circumstances would feel free to leave," the Supreme Court held that "a child's age properly informs the *Miranda* custody analysis." In fact, the Court continued, "in many cases involving juveniles, the custody analysis would be nonsensical absent some consideration of the suspect's age." Describing J.D.B.'s case as "a prime example," the Court explained:

> Were the court precluded from taking J.D.B.'s youth into account, it would be forced to evaluate the circumstances present here through the eyes of a reasonable person of average years. In other words, how would a reasonable adult understand his situation, after being removed from a seventh-grade social studies class by a uniformed school resource officer; being encouraged by his assistant principal to "do the right thing"; and being warned by a police investigator of the prospect of juvenile detention and separation from his guardian and primary caretaker? To describe such an inquiry is to demonstrate its absurdity. Neither officers nor courts can reasonably evaluate the effect of objective circumstances that, by their nature, are specific to children without accounting for the age of the child subjected to those circumstances.

In an effort to distinguish its earlier decision in *Yarborough v. Alvarado*, 541 U.S. 652 (2004), the Supreme Court made it clear that its holding was limited to those situations in which the child's age was already known or objectively apparent:

> [W]e hold that so long as the child's age was known to the officer at the time of police questioning, or would have been objectively apparent to a reasonable officer, its inclusion in the custody analysis is consistent with the objective nature of that test. This is not to say that a child's age will be a determinative, or even a significant, factor in every case. It is, however, a reality that courts cannot simply ignore.

The majority's decision in *J.D.B.* drew a strong dissent from Justice Alito, who was joined by Chief Justice Roberts, Justice Scalia, and Justice Thomas:

> Today's decision shifts the *Miranda* custody determination from a one-size-fits-all reasonable-person test into an inquiry that must account for at least one individualized characteristic— age—that is thought to correlate with susceptibility to coercive

pressures. Age, however, is in no way the only personal characteristic that may correlate with pliability, and in future cases the Court will be forced to choose between two unpalatable alternatives. It may choose to limit today's decision by arbitrarily distinguishing a suspect's age from other personal characteristics—such as intelligence, education, occupation, or prior experience with law enforcement—that may also correlate with susceptibility to coercive pressures. Or, if the Court is unwilling to draw these arbitrary lines, it will be forced to effect a fundamental transformation of the *Miranda* custody test— from a clear, easily applied prophylactic rule into a highly fact-intensive standard resembling the voluntariness test that the *Miranda* Court found to be unsatisfactory.

For at least three reasons, there is no need to go down this road. First, many minors subjected to police interrogation are near the age of majority, and for these suspects the one-size-fits-all *Miranda* custody rule may not be a bad fit. Second, many of the difficulties in applying the *Miranda* custody rule to minors arise because of the unique circumstances present when the police conduct interrogations at school. The *Miranda* custody rule has always taken into account the setting in which questioning occurs, and accounting for the school setting in such cases will address many of these problems. Third, in cases like the one now before us, where the suspect is especially young, courts applying the constitutional voluntariness standard can take special care to ensure that incriminating statements were not obtained through coercion.

In *Howes v. Fields*, the Supreme Court held that when police question a prisoner about events that occurred outside the prison, the inmate is not necessarily in custody for purposes of *Miranda*. In the course of its opinion, the Court reviewed its prior precedents and summarized the relevant factors in the custody determination.

HOWES V. FIELDS
132 S.Ct. 1181 (2012)

While serving a sentence in a Michigan jail, Randall Fields was escorted by corrections officers to a conference room where two sheriff's deputies questioned him about allegations that, before his imprisonment, he had engaged in sexual conduct with a 12-year-old boy. At the beginning of the interview and later, during the interview, Fields was told that he was free to leave and could return to his cell. The two deputies were armed during the interview, but Fields remained free of handcuffs and other restraints. The door to the conference room was sometimes open and sometimes shut. After five to seven hours of questioning, Fields confessed to engaging in sex acts with the boy. At no time was Fields given *Miranda* warnings or advised that he did not have to speak with the deputies.

In reversing the conclusion of the lower federal courts that Fields was subjected to custodial interrogation, the Supreme Court explained that "our decisions do not clearly establish that a prisoner is always in custody for purposes of *Miranda* whenever a prisoner is isolated from the general prison population and questioned about conduct outside the prison." On the contrary, the Supreme Court noted, "we have repeatedly declined to adopt any categorical rule with respect to whether the questioning of a prison inmate is custodial."

Relying heavily on its earlier decisions, the Court summarized the critical factors relevant to the custody inquiry under *Miranda*:

> As used in our *Miranda* case law, "custody" is a term of art that specifies circumstances that are thought generally to present a serious danger of coercion. In determining whether a person is in custody in this sense, the initial step is to ascertain whether, in light of the objective circumstances of the interrogation, a reasonable person would have felt he or she was not at liberty to terminate the interrogation and leave. And in order to determine how a suspect would have gauged his freedom of movement, courts must examine all of the circumstances surrounding the interrogation. Relevant factors include the location of the questioning, its duration, statements made during the interview, the presence or absence of physical restraints during the questioning, and the release of the interviewee at the end of the questioning.

> Determining whether an individual's freedom of movement was curtailed, however, is simply the first step in the analysis, not the last. Not all restraints on freedom of movement amount to custody for purposes of *Miranda*. We have declined to accord talismanic power to the freedom-of-movement inquiry, and have instead asked the additional question whether the relevant environment presents the same inherently coercive pressures as the type of station house questioning at issue in *Miranda*. Our cases make clear that the freedom-of-movement test identifies only a necessary and not a sufficient condition for *Miranda* custody.

The Supreme Court cited three reasons in support of its conclusion that "imprisonment alone is not enough to create a custodial situation" under *Miranda*:

First, questioning a person who is already serving a prison term does not generally involve the shock that very often accompanies arrest. In the paradigmatic *Miranda* situation—a person is arrested in his home or on the street and whisked to a police station for questioning—detention represents a sharp and ominous change, and the shock may give rise to coercive pressures. By contrast, when a person who is already serving a term of imprisonment is questioned, there is usually no such change. Second, a prisoner, unlike a person who has not been sentenced to a term of incarceration, is unlikely to be lured into speaking by a longing for prompt release. When a person is arrested and taken to a station house for interrogation, the person who is questioned may be pressured to speak by the hope that, after doing so, he will be allowed to leave and go home. On the other hand, when a prisoner is questioned, he knows that when the questioning ceases, he will remain under confinement. Third, a prisoner, unlike a person who has not been convicted and sentenced, knows that the law enforcement officers who question him probably lack the authority to affect the duration of his sentence.

After taking into account all of the circumstances under which Fields was questioned, "including especially the undisputed fact that [Fields] was told that he was free to end the questioning and to return to his cell," the Supreme Court held that he was not in custody within the meaning of *Miranda*.

The Meaning of "Custody" Under *Miranda*

1. *Miranda* warnings are required when an individual is subjected to police interrogation while in custody or otherwise deprived of his freedom of action in any significant way, regardless of the nature or severity of the offense of which he is suspected.

2. The custody determination focuses on the objective circumstances of the interrogation, not on the subjective views held by either the interrogating officers or the person being questioned. A court must examine all of the circumstances surrounding the interrogation and determine whether a reasonable person in the position of the individual being questioned would have felt free to terminate the interrogation and leave. Relevant factors include the location of the questioning, its duration, statements made during the interview, the presence or absence of physical restraints during the questioning, and the release of the interviewee at the end of the questioning. The ultimate inquiry is whether there was a formal arrest or restraint on freedom of movement of the degree associated with a formal arrest, coupled with consideration of whether the relevant environment presents the same

inherently coercive pressures as the type of stationhouse questioning at issue in *Miranda.*

3.   Although the custody determination is an objective one, a court may take a juvenile suspect's age into account when it is known to the officer—or would have been objectively apparent to a reasonable officer—at the time of police questioning.

4.   A person temporarily detained for roadside questioning during a routine traffic stop is not ordinarily "in custody" for purposes of *Miranda.*

5.   A probationer attending an interview at the request of his probation officer is not ordinarily "in custody" for purposes of *Miranda.*

6.   When a prisoner is isolated from the general prison population and questioned about conduct that occurred outside the prison, the inmate is not necessarily "in custody" for purposes of *Miranda.*

2.   WHAT COUNTS AS "INTERROGATION" UNDER *MIRANDA*?

In *Miranda*, the Supreme Court defined custodial interrogation as "questioning initiated by law enforcement officers after a person has been taken into custody or otherwise deprived of his freedom of action in any significant way." While direct questioning of a person in custody obviously qualifies as interrogation, the answer is not always so clear when the police use other techniques to elicit incriminating information from a suspect. *Brewer v. Williams* illustrates one such technique involving a direct appeal to the suspect's conscience.

BREWER V. WILLIAMS
430 U.S. 387 (1977)

Before transporting Robert Williams, a murder suspect, across Iowa in a police vehicle, Detective Cleatus Leaming promised Williams and his attorney that there would be no interrogation during the trip, but the detective would not permit the attorney to ride with Williams in the back of the vehicle. Detective Leaming knew that Williams was deeply religious, and during the car ride, he said the following:

> I want to give you something to think about while we're traveling down the road. . . . Number one, I want you to observe the weather conditions, it's raining, it's sleeting, it's freezing, driving is very treacherous, visibility is poor, it's going to be dark early this evening. They are predicting several inches of snow for tonight, and I feel that you yourself are the only person that knows where this little girl's body is, that you yourself have only been there once, and if you get a snow on top of it you yourself

may be unable to find it. And, since we will be going right past the area on the way into Des Moines, I feel that we could stop and locate the body, that the parents of this little girl should be entitled to a Christian burial for the little girl who was snatched away from them on Christmas Eve and murdered. And I feel we should stop and locate it on the way in rather than waiting until morning and trying to come back out after a snow storm and possibly not being able to find it at all.

Williams asked Detective Leaming why he thought their route to Des Moines would be taking them past the girl's body. Leaming responded that he knew the body was near Mitchellville, a town they would be passing on the way to Des Moines. Leaming then stated: "I do not want you to answer me. I don't want to discuss it any further. Just think about it as we're riding down the road." As the car approached Mitchellville, Williams said that he would show Leaming where the body of Pamela Powers was located. He then directed the police to the body.

The Supreme Court had little difficulty concluding that Detective Leaming's "Christian burial speech," directed at a suspect whom he knew to be deeply religious, resembled an interrogation:

> There can be no serious doubt that Detective Leaming deliberately and designedly set out to elicit information from Williams just as surely as—and perhaps more effectively than—if he had formally interrogated him. Detective Leaming was fully aware before departing for Des Moines that Williams was being represented in Davenport by [one attorney] and in Des Moines by [another attorney]. Yet he purposely sought during Williams' isolation from his lawyers to obtain as much incriminating information as possible. Indeed, Detective Leaming conceded as much when he testified at Williams' trial.

———————

Brewer v. Williams was ultimately decided on other grounds, and is excerpted more fully in Chapter 11 in connection with the Sixth Amendment right to counsel. Years later, the same case returned to the Supreme Court as *Nix v. Williams*, 467 U.S. 431 (1984), in which the Court found certain evidence admissible against Williams under the newly-created inevitable discovery exception to the exclusionary rule. You may recall the "Christian burial speech" reproduced above from your reading of *Nix v. Williams* in Chapter 8.

The Supreme Court clearly felt that the direct appeal to the suspect's conscience in *Brewer v. Williams* was tantamount to an interrogation. In *Rhode Island v. Innis*, police officers took a less direct approach when they had a conversation about a missing weapon within earshot of the suspect. The suspect interrupted and told the officers where the weapon was located. The Supreme Court provided a definition of interrogation and concluded that the suspect's remarks were admissible because he had not been interrogated under the Court's new standard.

RHODE ISLAND V. INNIS
446 U.S. 291 (1980)

JUSTICE STEWART delivered the opinion of the Court.

In *Miranda v. Arizona*, 384 U.S. 436 (1966), the Court held that, once a defendant in custody asks to speak with a lawyer, all interrogation must cease until a lawyer is present. The issue in this case is whether the respondent was "interrogated" in violation of the standards promulgated in the *Miranda* opinion.

I

On the night of January 12, 1975, John Mulvaney, a Providence, R.I., taxicab driver, disappeared after being dispatched to pick up a customer. His body was discovered four days later buried in a shallow grave in Coventry, R.I. He had died from a shotgun blast aimed at the back of his head.

On January 17, 1975, shortly after midnight, the Providence police received a telephone call from Gerald Aubin, also a taxicab driver, who reported that he had just been robbed by a man wielding a sawed-off shotgun. Aubin further reported that he had dropped off his assailant near Rhode Island College in a section of Providence known as Mount Pleasant. While at the Providence police station waiting to give a statement, Aubin noticed a picture of his assailant on a bulletin board. Aubin so informed one of the police officers present. The officer prepared a photo array, and again Aubin identified a picture of the same person. That person was the respondent. Shortly thereafter, the Providence police began a search of the Mount Pleasant area.

At approximately 4:30 a.m. on the same date, Patrolman Lovell, while cruising the streets of Mount Pleasant in a patrol car, spotted the respondent standing in the street facing him. When Patrolman Lovell stopped his car, the respondent walked towards it. Patrolman Lovell then arrested the respondent, who was unarmed, and advised him of his so-called *Miranda* rights. While the two men waited in the patrol car for other police officers to arrive, Patrolman Lovell did not converse with the respondent other than to respond to the latter's request for a cigarette.

Within minutes, Sergeant Sears arrived at the scene of the arrest, and he also gave the respondent the *Miranda* warnings. Immediately thereafter, Captain Leyden and other police officers arrived. Captain Leyden advised the respondent of his *Miranda* rights. The respondent stated that he understood those rights and wanted to speak with a lawyer. Captain Leyden then directed that the respondent be placed in a "caged wagon," a four-door police car with a wire screen mesh between the front and rear seats, and be driven to the central police station. Three officers, Patrolmen Gleckman, Williams, and McKenna, were assigned to accompany the respondent to the central station. They placed the respondent in the vehicle and shut the doors. Captain Leyden then instructed the officers not to question the respondent or intimidate or coerce him in any way. The three officers then entered the vehicle, and it departed.

While en route to the central station, Patrolman Gleckman initiated a conversation with Patrolman McKenna concerning the missing shotgun. As Patrolman Gleckman later testified:

> A. At this point, I was talking back and forth with Patrolman McKenna stating that I frequent this area while on patrol and [that because a school for handicapped children is located nearby,] there's a lot of handicapped children running around in this area, and God forbid one of them might find a weapon with shells and they might hurt themselves.

Patrolman McKenna apparently shared his fellow officer's concern:

> A. I more or less concurred with him [Gleckman] that it was a safety factor and that we should, you know, continue to search for the weapon and try to find it.

While Patrolman Williams said nothing, he overheard the conversation between the two officers:

> A. He [Gleckman] said it would be too bad if the little—I believe he said a girl—would pick up the gun, maybe kill herself.

The respondent then interrupted the conversation, stating that the officers should turn the car around so he could show them where the gun was located. At this point, Patrolman McKenna radioed back to Captain Leyden that they were returning to the scene of the arrest and that the respondent would inform them of the location of the gun. At the time the respondent indicated that the officers should turn back, they had traveled no more than a mile, a trip encompassing only a few minutes.

The police vehicle then returned to the scene of the arrest where a search for the shotgun was in progress. There, Captain Leyden again advised the respondent of his *Miranda* rights. The respondent replied that he understood those rights but that he "wanted to get the gun out of the way because of the kids in the area in the school." The respondent then led the police to a nearby field, where he pointed out the shotgun under some rocks by the side of the road.

On March 20, 1975, a grand jury returned an indictment charging the respondent with the kidnapping, robbery, and murder of John

Mulvaney. Before trial, the respondent moved to suppress the shotgun and the statements he had made to the police regarding it. After an evidentiary hearing at which the respondent elected not to testify, the trial judge found that the respondent had been "repeatedly and completely advised of his *Miranda* rights." He further found that it was "entirely understandable that [the officers in the police vehicle] would voice their concern [for the safety of the handicapped children] to each other." The judge then concluded that the respondent's decision to inform the police of the location of the shotgun was "a waiver, clearly, and on the basis of the evidence that I have heard, an intelligent waiver, of his [*Miranda*] right to remain silent." Thus, without passing on whether the police officers had in fact "interrogated" the respondent, the trial court sustained the admissibility of the shotgun and testimony related to its discovery. That evidence was later introduced at the respondent's trial, and the jury returned a verdict of guilty on all counts.

On appeal, the Rhode Island Supreme Court, in a 3–2 decision, set aside the respondent's conviction. The court concluded that the respondent had invoked his *Miranda* right to counsel and that, contrary to *Miranda*'s mandate that, in the absence of counsel, all custodial interrogation then cease, the police officers in the vehicle had "interrogated" the respondent without a valid waiver of his right to counsel. It was the view of the state appellate court that, even though the police officers may have been genuinely concerned about the public safety and even though the respondent had not been addressed personally by the police officers, the respondent nonetheless had been subjected to "subtle coercion" that was the equivalent of "interrogation" within the meaning of the *Miranda* opinion. Moreover, contrary to the holding of the trial court, the appellate court concluded that the evidence was insufficient to support a finding of waiver. Having concluded that both the shotgun and testimony relating to its discovery were obtained in violation of the *Miranda* standards and therefore should not have been admitted into evidence, the Rhode Island Supreme Court held that the respondent was entitled to a new trial.

We granted certiorari to address for the first time the meaning of "interrogation" under *Miranda v. Arizona.*

II

In the present case, the parties are in agreement that the respondent was fully informed of his *Miranda* rights and that he invoked his *Miranda* right to counsel when he told Captain Leyden that he wished to consult with a lawyer. It is also uncontested that the respondent was "in custody" while being transported to the police station.

The issue, therefore, is whether the respondent was "interrogated" by the police officers in violation of the respondent's undisputed right under *Miranda* to remain silent until he had consulted with a lawyer. In resolving this issue, we first define the term "interrogation" under *Miranda* before turning to a consideration of the facts of this case.

The starting point for defining "interrogation" in this context is, of course, the Court's *Miranda* opinion. There the Court observed that "by custodial interrogation, we mean *questioning* initiated by law enforcement officers after a person has been taken into custody or otherwise deprived of his freedom of action in any significant way." This passage and other references throughout the opinion to "questioning" might suggest that the *Miranda* rules were to apply only to those police interrogation practices that involve express questioning of a defendant while in custody.

We do not, however, construe the *Miranda* opinion so narrowly. The concern of the Court in *Miranda* was that the "interrogation environment" created by the interplay of interrogation and custody would "subjugate the individual to the will of his examiner" and thereby undermine the privilege against compulsory self-incrimination. The police practices that evoked this concern included several that did not involve express questioning. For example, one of the practices discussed in *Miranda* was the use of line-ups in which a coached witness would pick the defendant as the perpetrator. This was designed to establish that the defendant was in fact guilty as a predicate for further interrogation. A variation on this theme discussed in *Miranda* was the so-called "reverse line-up" in which a defendant would be identified by coached witnesses as the perpetrator of a fictitious crime, with the object of inducing him to confess to the actual crime of which he was suspected in order to escape the false prosecution. The Court in *Miranda* also included in its survey of interrogation practices the use of psychological ploys, such as to "posi[t]" "the guilt of the subject," to "minimize the moral seriousness of the offense," and "to cast blame on the victim or on society." It is clear that these techniques of persuasion, no less than express questioning, were thought, in a custodial setting, to amount to interrogation.

This is not to say, however, that all statements obtained by the police after a person has been taken into custody are to be considered the product of interrogation. As the Court in *Miranda* noted:

> Confessions remain a proper element in law enforcement. Any statement given freely and voluntarily without any compelling influences is, of course, admissible in evidence. The fundamental import of the privilege while an individual is in custody is not whether he is allowed to talk to the police without the benefit of warnings and counsel, but whether he can be interrogated. . . . Volunteered statements of any kind are not barred by the Fifth Amendment and their admissibility is not affected by our holding today.

It is clear therefore that the special procedural safeguards outlined in *Miranda* are required not where a suspect is simply taken into custody, but rather where a suspect in custody is subjected to interrogation. "Interrogation," as conceptualized in the *Miranda* opinion, must reflect a measure of compulsion above and beyond that inherent in custody itself.

We conclude that the *Miranda* safeguards come into play whenever a person in custody is subjected to either express questioning or its functional equivalent. That is to say, the term "interrogation" under *Miranda* refers not only to express questioning, but also to any words or actions on the part of the police (other than those normally attendant to arrest and custody) that the police should know are reasonably likely to elicit an incriminating response from the suspect. The latter portion of this definition focuses primarily upon the perceptions of the suspect, rather than the intent of the police. This focus reflects the fact that the *Miranda* safeguards were designed to vest a suspect in custody with an added measure of protection against coercive police practices, without regard to objective proof of the underlying intent of the police. A practice that the police should know is reasonably likely to evoke an incriminating response from a suspect thus amounts to interrogation.[7] But, since the police surely cannot be held accountable for the unforeseeable results of their words or actions, the definition of interrogation can extend only to words or actions on the part of police officers that they *should have known* were reasonably likely to elicit an incriminating response.[8]

Turning to the facts of the present case, we conclude that the respondent was not "interrogated" within the meaning of *Miranda*. It is undisputed that the first prong of the definition of "interrogation" was not satisfied, for the conversation between Patrolmen Gleckman and McKenna included no express questioning of the respondent. Rather, that conversation was, at least in form, nothing more than a dialogue between the two officers to which no response from the respondent was invited.

Moreover, it cannot be fairly concluded that the respondent was subjected to the "functional equivalent" of questioning. It cannot be said, in short, that Patrolmen Gleckman and McKenna should have known that their conversation was reasonably likely to elicit an incriminating response from the respondent. There is nothing in the record to suggest that the officers were aware that the respondent was peculiarly susceptible to an appeal to his conscience concerning the safety of

---

[7] This is not to say that the intent of the police is irrelevant, for it may well have a bearing on whether the police should have known that their words or actions were reasonably likely to evoke an incriminating response. In particular, where a police practice is designed to elicit an incriminating response from the accused, it is unlikely that the practice will not also be one which the police should have known was reasonably likely to have that effect.

[8] Any knowledge the police may have had concerning the unusual susceptibility of a defendant to a particular form of persuasion might be an important factor in determining whether the police should have known that their words or actions were reasonably likely to elicit an incriminating response from the suspect.

handicapped children. Nor is there anything in the record to suggest that the police knew that the respondent was unusually disoriented or upset at the time of his arrest.

The case thus boils down to whether, in the context of a brief conversation, the officers should have known that the respondent would suddenly be moved to make a self-incriminating response. Given the fact that the entire conversation appears to have consisted of no more than a few off hand remarks, we cannot say that the officers should have known that it was reasonably likely that Innis would so respond. This is not a case where the police carried on a lengthy harangue in the presence of the suspect. Nor does the record support the respondent's contention that, under the circumstances, the officers' comments were particularly "evocative." It is our view, therefore, that the respondent was not subjected by the police to words or actions that the police should have known were reasonably likely to elicit an incriminating response from him.

The Rhode Island Supreme Court erred, in short, in equating "subtle compulsion" with interrogation. That the officers' comments struck a responsive chord is readily apparent. Thus, it may be said, as the Rhode Island Supreme Court did say, that the respondent was subjected to "subtle compulsion." But that is not the end of the inquiry. It must also be established that a suspect's incriminating response was the product of words or actions on the part of the police that they should have known were reasonably likely to elicit an incriminating response. This was not established in the present case.

JUSTICE MARSHALL, with whom JUSTICE BRENNAN joins, dissenting.

I am substantially in agreement with the Court's definition of "interrogation" within the meaning of *Miranda v. Arizona*. In my view, the *Miranda* safeguards apply whenever police conduct is intended or likely to produce a response from a suspect in custody. As I read the Court's opinion, its definition of "interrogation" for *Miranda* purposes is equivalent, for practical purposes, to my formulation, since it contemplates that "where a police practice is designed to elicit an incriminating response from the accused, it is unlikely that the practice will not also be one which the police should have known was reasonably likely to have that effect." Thus, the Court requires an objective inquiry into the likely effect of police conduct on a typical individual, taking into account any special susceptibility of the suspect to certain kinds of pressure of which the police know or have reason to know.

I am utterly at a loss, however, to understand how this objective standard as applied to the facts before us can rationally lead to the conclusion that there was no interrogation. Innis was arrested at 4:30 a.m., handcuffed, searched, advised of his rights, and placed in the back seat of a patrol car. Within a short time he had been twice more advised of his rights and driven away in a four-door sedan with three police officers. Two officers sat in the front seat and one sat beside Innis in the back seat. Since the car traveled no more than a mile before Innis agreed to point out the location of the murder weapon, Officer Gleckman must have begun almost immediately to talk about the search for the shotgun.

The Court attempts to characterize Gleckman's statements as "no more than a few off hand remarks" which could not reasonably have been expected to elicit a response. If the statements had been addressed to respondent, it would be impossible to draw such a conclusion. The simple message of the "talking back and forth" between Gleckman and McKenna was that they had to find the shotgun to avert a child's death.

One can scarcely imagine a stronger appeal to the conscience of a suspect—*any* suspect—than the assertion that if the weapon is not found an innocent person will be hurt or killed. And not just any innocent person, but an innocent child—a little girl—a helpless, handicapped little girl on her way to school. The notion that such an appeal could not be expected to have any effect unless the suspect were known to have some special interest in handicapped children verges on the ludicrous. As a matter of fact, the appeal to a suspect to confess for the sake of others, to "display some evidence of decency and honor," is a classic interrogation technique.

Gleckman's remarks would obviously have constituted interrogation if they had been explicitly directed to respondent, and the result should not be different because they were nominally addressed to McKenna. This is not a case where police officers speaking among themselves are accidentally overheard by a suspect. These officers were "talking back and forth" in close quarters with the handcuffed suspect, traveling past the very place where they believed the weapon was located. They knew respondent would hear and attend to their conversation, and they are chargeable with knowledge of and responsibility for the pressures to speak which they created.

JUSTICE STEVENS, dissenting.

In my opinion the state court's conclusion that there was interrogation rests on a proper interpretation of both the facts and the law; thus, its determination that the products of the interrogation were inadmissible at trial should be affirmed.

In short, in order to give full protection to a suspect's right to be free from any interrogation at all, the definition of "interrogation" must include any police statement or conduct that has the same purpose or effect as a direct question. Statements that appear to call for a response from the suspect, as well as those that are designed to do so, should be considered interrogation. By prohibiting only those relatively few statements or actions that a police officer should know are likely to elicit an incriminating response, the Court today accords a suspect considerably less protection. Indeed, since I suppose most suspects are unlikely to incriminate themselves even when questioned directly, this new definition will almost certainly exclude every statement that is not punctuated with a question mark from the concept of "interrogation."

The difference between the approach required by a faithful adherence to *Miranda* and the stinted test applied by the Court today can be illustrated by comparing three different ways in which Officer Gleckman could have communicated his fears about the possible dangers posed by the shotgun to handicapped children. He could have: (1) Directly asked Innis: Will you please tell me where the shotgun is so we can protect handicapped school children from danger? (2) Announced to the other officers in the wagon: If the man sitting in the back seat with me should decide to tell us where the gun is, we can protect handicapped children from danger. Or (3) stated to the other officers: It would be too bad if a little handicapped girl would pick up the gun that this man left in the area and maybe kill herself.

In my opinion, all three of these statements should be considered interrogation because all three appear to be designed to elicit a response from anyone who in fact knew where the gun was located. Under the Court's test, on the other hand, the form of the statements would be critical. The third statement would not be interrogation because in the Court's view there was no reason for Officer Gleckman to believe that Innis was susceptible to this type of an implied appeal; therefore, the statement would not be reasonably likely to elicit an incriminating response. Assuming that this is true, then it seems to me that the first two statements, which would be just as unlikely to elicit such a response, should also not be considered interrogation. But, because the first statement is clearly an express question, it *would* be considered interrogation under the Court's test. The second statement, although just as clearly a deliberate appeal to Innis to reveal the location of the gun, would presumably not be interrogation because (a) it was not in form a direct question and (b) it does not fit within the "reasonably likely to elicit an incriminating response" category that applies to indirect interrogation.

As this example illustrates, the Court's test creates an incentive for police to ignore a suspect's invocation of his rights in order to make continued attempts to extract information from him. If a suspect does not appear to be susceptible to a particular type of psychological pressure, the police are apparently free to exert that pressure on him despite his request for counsel, so long as they are careful not to punctuate their statements with question marks. And if, contrary to all reasonable expectations, the suspect makes an incriminating statement, that statement can be used against him at trial. The Court thus turns

Miranda's unequivocal rule against any interrogation at all into a trap in which unwary suspects may be caught by police deception.

———————

In *Arizona v. Mauro*, the police allowed the suspect's wife to speak to him in the presence of an officer after the suspect had requested an attorney. While speaking to his wife, the suspect made statements that were later used against him at trial. The Supreme Court concluded that the statements were admissible because no interrogation had taken place.

ARIZONA V. MAURO
481 U.S. 520 (1987)

JUSTICE POWELL delivered the opinion of the Court.

While respondent in this case was in police custody, he indicated that he did not wish to answer any questions until a lawyer was present. The issue presented is whether, in the circumstances of this case, officers interrogated respondent in violation of the Fifth and Fourteenth Amendments when they allowed him to speak with his wife in the presence of a police officer.

On November 23, 1982, the Flagstaff Police Department received a telephone call from a local K Mart store. The caller stated that a man had entered the store claiming to have killed his son. When officers reached the store, respondent Mauro freely admitted that he had killed his son. He directed the officers to the child's body, and then was arrested and advised of his constitutional rights pursuant to *Miranda v. Arizona*, 384 U.S. 436 (1966). The officers then took Mauro to the police station, where he was advised of his *Miranda* rights again. At that point, Mauro told the officers that he did not wish to make any more statements without having a lawyer present. All questioning then ceased. As no secure detention area was available, Mauro was held in the office of the police captain.

At the same time, one of the officers, Detective Manson, was questioning Mauro's wife in another room. After she finished speaking with Manson, Mrs. Mauro asked if she could speak to her husband. Manson was reluctant to allow the meeting, but after Mrs. Mauro insisted, he discussed the request with his supervisor, Sergeant Allen. Allen testified that he "saw no harm in it and suggested to [Manson] that if she really sincerely wanted to talk to him to go ahead and allow it." Allen instructed Manson not to leave Mr. and Mrs. Mauro alone and suggested that Manson tape-record the conversation.

Manson then "told both Mr. and Mrs. Mauro that they could speak together only if an officer were present in the room to observe and hear what was going on." He brought Mrs. Mauro into the room and seated himself at a desk, placing a tape recorder in plain sight on the desk. He recorded their brief conversation, in which she expressed despair about their situation. During the conversation, Mauro told his wife not to answer questions until a lawyer was present.

Mauro's defense at trial was that he had been insane at the time of the crime. In rebuttal, the prosecution played the tape of the meeting between Mauro and his wife, arguing that it demonstrated that Mauro was sane on the day of the murder. Mauro sought suppression of the recording on the ground that it was a product of police interrogation in violation of his *Miranda* rights. The trial court refused to suppress the recording. Mauro was convicted of murder and child abuse, and sentenced to death.

The Arizona Supreme Court reversed. It found that by allowing Mauro to speak with his wife in the presence of a police officer, the detectives interrogated Mauro within the meaning of *Miranda*. This interrogation was impermissible, the court said, because Mauro previously had invoked the right to have counsel present before being questioned further. The court noted that both detectives had acknowledged in pretrial hearings that they knew it was "possible" that Mauro might make incriminating statements if he saw his wife. The court relied on our statement in *Rhode Island v. Innis*, 446 U.S. 291 (1980), that interrogation includes a "practice that the police should know is reasonably likely to evoke an incriminating response from a suspect." The court then concluded that the officers' testimony demonstrated that there had been interrogation, because "[t]hey both knew that if the conversation took place, incriminating statements were likely to be made." Therefore, it held that the tape recording was not properly admitted at Mauro's trial.

[T]he *Innis* Court concluded that the goals of the *Miranda* safeguards could be effectuated if those safeguards extended not only to express questioning, but also to "its functional equivalent." The Court explained the phrase "functional equivalent" of interrogation as including "any words or actions on the part of the police (other than those normally attendant to arrest and custody) that the police should know are reasonably likely to elicit an incriminating response from the suspect." Finally, it noted that "[t]he latter portion of this definition focuses primarily upon the perceptions of the suspect, rather than the intent of the police."

The officers gave Mauro the warnings required by *Miranda*. Mauro indicated that he did not wish to be questioned further without a lawyer present. Mauro never waived his right to have a lawyer present. The sole issue, then, is whether the officers' subsequent actions rose to the level of interrogation—that is, in the language of *Innis*, whether they were the "functional equivalent" of police interrogation. We think it is clear under both *Miranda* and *Innis* that Mauro was not interrogated. The tape recording of the conversation between Mauro and his wife shows that Detective Manson asked Mauro no questions about the crime or his conduct. Nor is it suggested—or supported by any evidence—that Sergeant Allen's decision to allow Mauro's wife to see him was the kind of psychological ploy that properly could be treated as the functional equivalent of interrogation.

There is no evidence that the officers sent Mrs. Mauro in to see her husband for the purpose of eliciting incriminating statements. As the trial court found, the officers tried to discourage her from talking to her husband, but finally "yielded to her insistent demands." Nor was Detective Manson's presence improper. His testimony, that the trial court found credible, indicated a number of legitimate reasons—not related to securing incriminating statements—for having a police officer present. Finally, the weakness of Mauro's claim that he was interrogated is underscored by examining the situation from his perspective. We doubt that a suspect, told by officers that his wife will be allowed to speak to him, would feel that he was being coerced to incriminate himself in any way.

The Arizona Supreme Court was correct to note that there was a "possibility" that Mauro would incriminate himself while talking to his wife. It also emphasized that the officers were aware of that possibility when they agreed to allow the Mauros to talk to each other. But the actions in this case were far less questionable than the "subtle compulsion" that we held *not* to be interrogation in *Innis*. Officers do not interrogate a suspect simply by hoping that he will incriminate himself. Mauro was not subjected to compelling influences, psychological ploys, or direct questioning. Thus, his volunteered statements cannot properly be considered the result of police interrogation.

In deciding whether particular police conduct is interrogation, we must remember the purpose behind our decision in *Miranda*: preventing government officials from using the coercive nature of confinement to extract confessions that would not be given in an unrestrained environment. The government actions in this case do not implicate this purpose in any way. Police departments need not adopt inflexible rules barring suspects from speaking with their spouses, nor must they ignore legitimate security concerns by allowing spouses to meet in private. In short, the officers in this case acted reasonably and lawfully by allowing Mrs. Mauro to speak with her husband. In this situation, the Federal Constitution does not forbid use of Mauro's subsequent statements at his criminal trial.

JUSTICE STEVENS, with whom JUSTICE BRENNAN, JUSTICE MARSHALL, and JUSTICE BLACKMUN join, dissenting.

The record indicates that the police employed a powerful psychological ploy; they failed to give respondent any advance warning that Mrs. Mauro was coming to talk to him, that a police officer would accompany her, or that their conversation would be recorded. As the transcript of the conversation reveals, respondent would not have freely chosen to speak with her. These facts compel the conclusion that the police took advantage of Mrs. Mauro's request to visit her husband, setting up a confrontation between them at a time when he manifestly desired to remain silent. Because they allowed respondent's conversation with his wife to commence at a time when they knew it was reasonably likely to produce an incriminating statement, the police interrogated him. The Court's opposite conclusion removes an important brick from the wall of protection against police overreaching that surrounds the Fifth Amendment rights of suspects in custody.

It is undisputed that a police decision to place two suspects in the same room and then to listen to or record their conversation may constitute a form of interrogation even if no questions are asked by any police officers. That is exactly what happened here. The police placed respondent and his wife, who was also in police custody, in the same small area. Mr. and Mrs. Mauro were both suspects in the murder of their son. Each of them had been interrogated separately before the officers decided to allow them to converse, an act that surely did not require a tape recorder or the presence of a police officer within hearing range. Under the circumstances, the police knew or should have known that Mrs. Mauro's encounter with respondent was reasonably likely to produce an incriminating response. Indeed, Officer Allen's supervisor testified that the police had a reasonable expectation that the spousal conversation would provide information on the murder investigation.

In my opinion, it was not only likely, but highly probable, that one of the suspects would make a statement that the prosecutor might seek to introduce at trial. It follows that the police conduct in this case was the "functional equivalent" of deliberate, direct interrogation.

The State should not be permitted to set aside this conclusion with testimony that merely indicates that the evidence-gathering purpose of the police was mixed with other motives. For example, it is irrelevant to the inquiry whether the police had legitimate security reasons for having an officer present that were "not related to securing incriminating statements." Nor does it matter that the officers lacked a precise expectation of how the statements Mauro would make might be incriminating; much interrogation is exploratory rather than directed at the admission of a fact whose incriminatory import is already known to the officers.

The Court's final proffered reason for disregarding the findings of the Supreme Court of Arizona is that the suspect may not have felt coerced to incriminate himself. The police did not compel or even encourage Mauro to speak with his wife. When they brought her into the room without warning Mauro in advance, however, they expected that the resulting conversation "could shed light on our case." Under the circumstances, the mere fact that respondent's wife made the initial request leading to the conversation does not alter the correctness of the Supreme Court of Arizona's analysis. The officers exercised exclusive control over whether and when the suspects spoke with each other; the police knew that whatever Mauro might wish to convey to his wife at that moment, he would have to say under the conditions unilaterally imposed by the officers. In brief, the police exploited the custodial situation and the understandable desire of Mrs. Mauro to speak with respondent to conduct an interrogation.

———————

In *Illinois v. Perkins*, police placed an undercover officer in jail with the suspect in an unsolved murder. For obvious reasons, the undercover officer never administered the *Miranda* warnings before conversing with the suspect, and the suspect eventually made incriminating statements. The Supreme Court concluded that the use of the undercover officer did not amount to interrogation under *Miranda*.

ILLINOIS V. PERKINS
496 U.S. 292 (1990)

JUSTICE KENNEDY delivered the opinion of the Court.

An undercover government agent was placed in the cell of respondent Perkins, who was incarcerated on charges unrelated to the subject of the agent's investigation. Respondent made statements that implicated him in the crime that the agent sought to solve. Respondent claims that the statements should be inadmissible because he had not been given *Miranda* warnings by the agent. We hold that the statements are admissible. *Miranda* warnings are not required when the suspect is unaware that he is speaking to a law enforcement officer and gives a voluntary statement.

I

In November 1984, Richard Stephenson was murdered in a suburb of East St. Louis, Illinois. The murder remained unsolved until March 1986, when one Donald Charlton told police that he had learned about a homicide from a fellow inmate at the Graham Correctional Facility, where Charlton had been serving a sentence for burglary. The fellow inmate was Lloyd Perkins, who is the respondent here. Charlton told police that, while at Graham, he had befriended respondent, who told him in detail about a murder that respondent had committed in East St. Louis. On hearing Charlton's account, the police recognized details of the

Stephenson murder that were not well known, and so they treated Charlton's story as a credible one.

By the time the police heard Charlton's account, respondent had been released from Graham, but police traced him to a jail in Montgomery County, Illinois, where he was being held pending trial on a charge of aggravated battery, unrelated to the Stephenson murder. The police wanted to investigate further respondent's connection to the Stephenson murder, but feared that the use of an eavesdropping device would prove impracticable and unsafe. They decided instead to place an undercover agent in the cellblock with respondent and Charlton. The plan was for Charlton and undercover agent John Parisi to pose as escapees from a work release program who had been arrested in the course of a burglary. Parisi and Charlton were instructed to engage respondent in casual conversation and report anything he said about the Stephenson murder.

Parisi, using the alias "Vito Bianco," and Charlton, both clothed in jail garb, were placed in the cellblock with respondent at the Montgomery County jail. The cellblock consisted of 12 separate cells that opened onto a common room. Respondent greeted Charlton who, after a brief conversation with respondent, introduced Parisi by his alias. Parisi told respondent that he "wasn't going to do any more time" and suggested that the three of them escape. Respondent replied that the Montgomery County jail was "rinky-dink" and that they could "break out." The trio met in respondent's cell later that evening, after the other inmates were asleep, to refine their plan. Respondent said that his girlfriend could smuggle in a pistol. Charlton said: "Hey, I'm not a murderer, I'm a burglar. That's your guys' profession." After telling Charlton that he would be responsible for any murder that occurred, Parisi asked respondent if he had ever "done" anybody. Respondent said that he had and proceeded to describe at length the events of the Stephenson murder. Parisi and respondent then engaged in some casual conversation before respondent went to sleep. Parisi did not give respondent *Miranda* warnings before the conversations.

Respondent was charged with the Stephenson murder. Before trial, he moved to suppress the statements made to Parisi in the jail. The trial court granted the motion to suppress, and the State appealed. The Appellate Court of Illinois affirmed, holding that *Miranda v. Arizona*, 384 U.S. 436 (1966), prohibits all undercover contacts with incarcerated suspects that are reasonably likely to elicit an incriminating response.

We granted certiorari to decide whether an undercover law enforcement officer must give *Miranda* warnings to an incarcerated suspect before asking him questions that may elicit an incriminating response. We now reverse.

II

In *Miranda v. Arizona*, the Court held that the Fifth Amendment privilege against self-incrimination prohibits admitting statements given by a suspect during "custodial interrogation" without a prior warning. Custodial interrogation means "questioning initiated by law enforcement officers after a person has been taken into custody." The warning mandated by *Miranda* was meant to preserve the privilege during "incommunicado interrogation of individuals in a police-dominated atmosphere." That atmosphere is said to generate "inherently compelling pressures which work to undermine the individual's will to resist and to compel him to speak where he would not otherwise do so freely." "Fidelity to the doctrine announced in *Miranda* requires that it be enforced strictly, but only in those types of situations in which the concerns that powered the decision are implicated." *Berkemer v. McCarty*, 468 U.S. 420, 437 (1984).

Conversations between suspects and undercover agents do not implicate the concerns underlying *Miranda*. The essential ingredients of a "police-dominated atmosphere" and compulsion are not present when an incarcerated person speaks freely to someone whom he believes to be a fellow inmate. Coercion is determined from the perspective of the suspect. When a suspect considers himself in the company of cellmates and not officers, the coercive atmosphere is lacking. There is no empirical basis for the assumption that a suspect speaking to those whom he assumes are not officers will feel compelled to speak by the fear of reprisal for remaining silent or in the hope of more lenient treatment should he confess.

It is the premise of *Miranda* that the danger of coercion results from the interaction of custody and official interrogation. We reject the argument that *Miranda* warnings are required whenever a suspect is in custody in a technical sense and converses with someone who happens to be a government agent. Questioning by captors, who appear to control the suspect's fate, may create mutually reinforcing pressures that the Court has assumed will weaken the suspect's will, but where a suspect does not know that he is conversing with a government agent, these pressures do not exist. The state court here mistakenly assumed that because the suspect was in custody, no undercover questioning could take place. When the suspect has no reason to think that the listeners have official power over him, it should not be assumed that his words are motivated by the reaction he expects from his listeners.

Miranda forbids coercion, not mere strategic deception by taking advantage of a suspect's misplaced trust in one he supposes to be a fellow prisoner. Ploys to mislead a suspect or lull him into a false sense of security that do not rise to the level of compulsion or coercion to speak are not within *Miranda*'s concerns.

Miranda was not meant to protect suspects from boasting about their criminal activities in front of persons whom they believe to be their cellmates. This case is illustrative. Respondent had no reason to feel that undercover agent Parisi had any legal authority to force him to answer questions or that Parisi could affect respondent's future treatment. Respondent viewed the cellmate-agent as an equal and showed no hint of being intimidated by the atmosphere of the jail. In recounting the details of the Stephenson murder, respondent was motivated solely by the desire to impress his fellow inmates. He spoke at his own peril.

This Court's Sixth Amendment decisions in *Massiah v. U.S.*, 377 U.S. 201 (1964), *U.S. v. Henry*, 447 U.S. 264 (1980), and *Maine v. Moulton*, 474 U.S. 159 (1985), also do not avail respondent. We held in those cases that the government may not use an undercover agent to circumvent the Sixth Amendment right to counsel once a suspect has been charged with the crime. After charges have been filed, the Sixth Amendment prevents the government from interfering with the accused's right to counsel. In the instant case no charges had been filed on the subject of the interrogation, and our Sixth Amendment precedents are not applicable.

Respondent can seek no help from his argument that a bright-line rule for the application of *Miranda* is desirable. Law enforcement officers will have little difficulty putting into practice our holding that undercover agents need not give *Miranda* warnings to incarcerated suspects. The use of undercover agents is a recognized law enforcement technique, often employed in the prison context to detect violence against correctional officials or inmates, as well as for the purposes served here. The interests protected by *Miranda* are not implicated in these cases, and the warnings are not required to safeguard the constitutional rights of inmates who make voluntary statements to undercover agents.

We hold that an undercover law enforcement officer posing as a fellow inmate need not give *Miranda* warnings to an incarcerated suspect before asking questions that may elicit an incriminating response. The statements at issue in this case were voluntary, and there is no federal obstacle to their admissibility at trial.

JUSTICE MARSHALL, dissenting.

The conditions that require the police to apprise a defendant of his constitutional rights—custodial interrogation conducted by an agent of the police—were present in this case. Because Lloyd Perkins received no *Miranda* warnings before he was subjected to custodial interrogation, his confession was not admissible.

The Court reaches the contrary conclusion by fashioning an exception to the *Miranda* rule that applies whenever "an undercover law enforcement officer posing as a fellow inmate . . . ask[s] questions that may elicit an incriminating response" from an incarcerated suspect. This exception is inconsistent with the rationale supporting *Miranda* and allows police officers intentionally to take advantage of suspects unaware of their constitutional rights. I therefore dissent.

The Court does not dispute that the police officer here conducted a custodial interrogation of a criminal suspect. Perkins was incarcerated in county jail during the questioning at issue here; under these circumstances, he was in custody as that term is defined in *Miranda*.

Although the Court does not dispute that Perkins was interrogated, it downplays the nature of the 35-minute questioning by disingenuously referring to it as a "conversation." The police officer ask[ed] a series of questions designed to elicit specific information about the victim, the crime scene, the weapon, Perkins' motive, and his actions during and after the shooting. This interaction was not a "conversation"; Perkins, the officer, and the informant were not equal participants in a free-ranging discussion, with each man offering his views on different topics. Rather, it was an interrogation: Perkins was subjected to express questioning likely to evoke an incriminating response.

Because Perkins was interrogated by police while he was in custody, *Miranda* required that the officer inform him of his rights. In rejecting that conclusion, the Court finds that "conversations" between undercover agents and suspects are devoid of the coercion inherent in station house interrogations conducted by law enforcement officials who openly represent the State. *Miranda* was not, however, concerned solely with police *coercion*. It dealt with *any* police tactics that may operate to compel a suspect in custody to make incriminating statements without full awareness of his constitutional rights. Thus, when a law enforcement agent structures a custodial interrogation so that a suspect feels compelled to reveal incriminating information, he must inform the suspect of his constitutional rights and give him an opportunity to decide whether or not to talk. The compulsion proscribed by *Miranda* includes deception by the police.

Custody works to the State's advantage in obtaining incriminating information. The psychological pressures inherent in confinement increase the suspect's anxiety, making him likely to seek relief by talking with others. The inmate is thus more susceptible to efforts by undercover agents to elicit information from him. Similarly, where the suspect is incarcerated, the constant threat of physical danger peculiar to the prison environment may make him demonstrate his toughness to other inmates by recounting or inventing past violent acts. In this case, the police deceptively took advantage of Perkins' psychological vulnerability by including him in a sham escape plot, a situation in which he would feel compelled to demonstrate his willingness to shoot a prison guard by revealing his past involvement in a murder.

Thus, the pressures unique to custody allow the police to use deceptive interrogation tactics to compel a suspect to make an incriminating statement. The compulsion is not eliminated by the suspect's ignorance of his interrogator's true identity. The Court therefore need not inquire past the bare facts of custody and interrogation to determine whether *Miranda* warnings are required.

The Court's holding today complicates a previously clear and straightforward doctrine. The Court opines that "law enforcement officers will have little difficulty putting into practice our holding that undercover agents need not give *Miranda* warnings to incarcerated suspects." Perhaps this prediction is true with respect to fact patterns virtually identical to the one before the Court today. But the outer boundaries of the exception created by the Court are by no means clear. Would *Miranda* be violated, for instance, if an undercover police officer beat a confession out of a suspect, but the suspect thought the officer was another prisoner who wanted the information for his own purposes?

Even if *Miranda,* as interpreted by the Court, would not permit such obviously compelled confessions, the ramifications of today's opinion are still disturbing. The exception carved out of the *Miranda* doctrine today may well result in a proliferation of departmental policies to encourage police officers to conduct interrogations of confined suspects through undercover agents, thereby circumventing the need to administer *Miranda* warnings. Indeed, if *Miranda* now requires a police officer to issue warnings only in those situations in which the suspect might feel compelled "to speak by the fear of reprisal for remaining silent or in the hope of more lenient treatment should he confess," presumably it allows custodial interrogation by an undercover officer posing as a member of the clergy or a suspect's defense attorney. Although such abhorrent tricks would play on a suspect's need to confide in a trusted adviser, neither would cause the suspect to "think that the listeners have official power over him." The Court's adoption of the "undercover agent" exception to the *Miranda* rule thus is necessarily also the adoption of a substantial loophole in our jurisprudence protecting suspects' Fifth Amendment rights.

———

Rhode Island v. Innis, *Arizona v. Mauro*, and *Illinois v. Perkins* collectively demonstrate that the concerns underlying *Miranda*—coercive pressure on the suspect in a police-dominated atmosphere—are relevant not only to the custody determination, but to the interrogation inquiry as well. When those concerns are not present, the Supreme Court is unlikely to find that a custodial interrogation took place, and the police are not required to adhere to the rules set forth in *Miranda*. Justice Kennedy captured this sentiment in his majority opinion in *Perkins*: "*Miranda* forbids coercion, not mere strategic deception by taking advantage of a suspect's misplaced trust[.] Ploys to mislead a suspect or lull him into a false sense of security that do not rise to the level of compulsion or coercion to speak are not within *Miranda*'s concerns."[b] Although the police used certain techniques in *Innis*, *Mauro*, and *Perkins* with the hope and intention of eliciting incriminating statements, the Supreme Court did not view them as forms of interrogation because the particular circumstances in which those techniques were employed seemed considerably less coercive than the conventional stationhouse interrogation at issue in *Miranda*. As a result, the definition of interrogation in *Innis* that initially seemed to encompass a broad variety of police methods designed to elicit incriminating information has actually been applied by the Supreme Court in a fairly narrow fashion, leaving the police with ample room to elicit incriminating statements from a suspect without resorting to the kind of formal interrogation governed by *Miranda*.

The Meaning of "Interrogation" Under *Miranda*

1.   The term "interrogation" under *Miranda* refers not only to express questioning, but also to any words or actions on the part of the police (other than those normally attendant to arrest and custody) that the police should know are reasonably likely to elicit an incriminating response from the suspect. The latter portion of this definition focuses primarily on the perceptions of the suspect, rather than the intent of the police.

     a.   Although the interrogation inquiry focuses primarily on the perceptions of the suspect rather than the intent of the police, when a police practice is designed to elicit an incriminating response from the accused, it is likely that the practice will also be one that the police should have known was reasonably likely to have that effect.

     b.   Any knowledge the police may have had concerning the unusual susceptibility of a defendant to a particular form of persuasion might be an important factor in determining whether the police should have known that their words or actions were reasonably likely to elicit an incriminating response from the suspect.

2.   An undercover law enforcement officer posing as a fellow inmate need not give *Miranda* warnings to an incarcerated suspect before asking questions that may elicit an incriminating response. Such questioning does not constitute "interrogation" for purposes of *Miranda*. The concerns underlying *Miranda*—the compulsion felt by

---

[b]   Justice Kennedy's majority opinion in *Perkins* was careful to note that the undercover officer had questioned Perkins about a crime with which he had not yet been formally charged. As Justice Kennedy explained, once a suspect is formally charged with a crime, the Sixth Amendment prevents the government or its agents from interfering with the accused's right to counsel. The cases that establish the contours of that rule are included in Chapter 11.

the suspect in a police-dominated atmosphere—are not present when an incarcerated person speaks freely to someone whom he believes to be a fellow inmate.

LEARN MORE WITH *LAW & ORDER*

The following episode of *Law & Order* ("Angel," Season 6, Episode 8) was inspired by the case of Susan Smith, a South Carolina mother who reported that her two young children were kidnapped in a carjacking in 1994. Over several days, Smith made dramatic pleas on television for the return of her children before ultimately confessing that she let her car roll into a nearby lake with her children strapped inside.

In the *Law & Order* episode, the police are searching for a missing baby who was apparently taken from her stroller while her mother, Leah Coleman, was in a church confessional. When the initial search and investigation turns up no sign of the baby, Detective Rey Curtis takes a walk with Leah to retrace her steps on the day the baby disappeared. Leah, who is separated from her husband, seems to bond with Curtis as they talk about their religious beliefs. Eventually, Curtis and Leah return to the church where the baby disappeared. Leah asks Curtis if he thinks her baby is dead, and Curtis replies that if she is, "she should have a Christian burial." Leah then asks Curtis to pray with her, and she confesses to smothering the baby with a pillow and placing it in an incinerator.

After Leah is charged with murder, her defense attorney, Ross Fineman, moves to exclude her confession on the grounds she was interrogated by Detective Curtis without the benefit of the *Miranda* warnings, creating an "irrebuttable presumption" that the confession was involuntary. Prosecutor Jack McCoy responds that *Miranda* applies only if the confession is the result of an interrogation, and explains that Detective Curtis never asked Leah if she had killed her child. Citing *Rhode Island v. Innis*, 446 U.S. 291 (1980), Fineman argues that interrogation includes not only direct questions, but also "any words or actions that the police should know are reasonably likely to elicit an incriminating response." Fineman contends that when Detective Curtis took Leah to her church and told her that her baby was entitled to a Christian burial, he intended to provoke an incriminating response. McCoy notes that because Leah confessed in her own church, she was not in custody because a reasonable person would have felt free to walk away.

At a subsequent hearing on the custody issue, Leah testifies that she did not feel free to leave Detective Curtis during the day they spent together. During cross-examination, however, Leah admits that Curtis wanted to leave, but she asked him to stay with her and pray. The judge ultimately rules that Leah Coleman's confession is admissible.

> **The segments of the episode that depict the relevant Investigative Criminal Procedure issues appear at:**
>
> 16:01 to 25:42

> ### *Law & Order* Episode
> ### "Angel," Season 6, Episode 8

This episode of *Law & Order* contains an excellent illustration of the custody and interrogation inquiries under *Miranda*, while also demonstrating the interplay between those two inquiries and the related voluntariness determination under the Due Process Clause of the Fourteenth Amendment. The prosecution and the defense agree that Leah Coleman never received *Miranda* warnings, which renders her confession involuntary and inadmissible if it was the product of custodial interrogation. The defense focuses initially on the interrogation inquiry, successfully demonstrating, under *Innis*, that even without direct questioning, police techniques designed to elicit an incriminating response may still amount to interrogation. In fact, Detective Curtis' statement to Leah that her child was entitled to a Christian burial is reminiscent of the famous "Christian burial speech" in *Brewer v. Williams*, 430 U.S. 387 (1977), that the Supreme Court found was designed to elicit information "just as surely and perhaps more effectively" than formal interrogation.

Perhaps sensing that the broad definition of interrogation under *Innis* makes it unlikely that he will prevail on that issue, prosecutor Jack McCoy shifts the discussion to the question of custody, noting that Leah confessed in her own church, a situation in which a reasonable person would have felt free to leave. Although Leah was not under arrest during the several hours she spent with Detective Curtis, her testimony reveals that she did not feel free to leave, either, since Curtis would not allow her husband to accompany them, and he insisted that they continue on when Leah wanted to return home. Ultimately, however, Leah's concession during cross-examination that she had stopped Curtis from leaving her in the church right before she confessed apparently convinces the judge that she was not in custody at that time. Because Leah was not subjected to *custodial* interrogation inside the church, *Miranda* warnings were not required and her confession is admissible.

3.   WHAT IS THE REQUIRED CONTENT OF THE *MIRANDA* WARNINGS?

In order to avoid significant deviations from the full set of warnings required by the *Miranda* decision, many police officers carry pre-printed

"*Miranda* cards" and, when appropriate, administer the warnings simply by reading from the card. But when reciting the warnings from memory or delivering them as part of a free-flowing conversation with a suspect, police do not always use the precise formulation prescribed by the Supreme Court. Do such deviations constitute a violation of *Miranda*?

In *California v. Prysock*, a suspect was not explicitly informed of his right to the services of a free attorney before and during interrogation. The Supreme Court concluded that the warnings he received adequately conveyed the substance of his rights under *Miranda*, rendering his incriminating statements admissible.

CALIFORNIA V. PRYSOCK
453 U.S. 355 (1981)

PER CURIAM.

This case presents the question whether the warnings given to respondent prior to a recorded conversation with a police officer satisfied the requirements of *Miranda v. Arizona*, 384 U.S. 436 (1966). Although ordinarily this Court would not be inclined to review a case involving application of that precedent to a particular set of facts, the opinion of the California Court of Appeal essentially laid down a flat rule requiring that the content of *Miranda* warnings be a virtual incantation of the precise language contained in the *Miranda* opinion. Because such a rigid rule was not mandated by *Miranda* or any other decision of this Court, and is not required to serve the purposes of *Miranda*, we reverse.

On January 30, 1978, Mrs. Donna Iris Erickson was brutally murdered. Later that evening, respondent and a codefendant were apprehended for commission of the offense. Respondent was brought to a substation of the Tulare County Sheriff's Department and advised of his *Miranda* rights. He declined to talk and, since he was a minor, his parents were notified. Respondent's parents arrived and, after meeting with them, respondent decided to answer police questions. An officer questioned respondent, on tape, with respondent's parents present. The tape reflects that the following warnings were given prior to any questioning:

> Sgt. Byrd: Mr. Randall James Prysock, earlier today I advised you of your legal rights and at that time you advised me you did not wish to talk to me, is that correct?
>
> Randall P.: Yeh.
>
> Sgt. Byrd: And, uh, during, at the first interview your folks were not present, they are now present. I want to go through your legal rights again with you and after each legal right I would like for you to answer whether you understand it or not. . . . Your

legal rights, Mr. Prysock, is [*sic*] follows: Number One, you have the right to remain silent. This means you don't have to talk to me at all unless you so desire. Do you understand this?

Randall P.: Yeh.

Sgt. Byrd: If you give up your right to remain silent, anything you say can and will be used as evidence against you in a court of law. Do you understand this?

Randall P.: Yes.

Sgt. Byrd: You have the right to talk to a lawyer before you are questioned, have him present with you while you are being questioned, and all during the questioning. Do you understand this?

Randall P.: Yes.

Sgt. Byrd: You also, being a juvenile, you have the right to have your parents present, which they are. Do you understand this?

Randall P.: Yes.

Sgt. Byrd: Even if they weren't here, you'd have this right. Do you understand this?

Randall P.: Yes.

Sgt. Byrd: You all, uh,—if,—you have the right to have a lawyer appointed to represent you at no cost to yourself. Do you understand this?

Randall P.: Yes.

Sgt. Byrd: Now, having all these legal rights in mind, do you wish to talk to me at this time?

Randall P.: Yes.

At this point, at the request of Mrs. Prysock, a conversation took place with the tape recorder turned off. According to Sgt. Byrd, Mrs. Prysock asked if respondent could still have an attorney at a later time if he gave a statement now without one. Sgt. Byrd assured Mrs. Prysock that respondent would have an attorney when he went to court and that "he could have one at this time if he wished one."

At trial in the Superior Court of Tulare County, the court denied respondent's motion to suppress the taped statement. Respondent was convicted by a jury of first-degree murder with two special circumstances—torture and robbery. He was also convicted of robbery with the use of a dangerous weapon, burglary with the use of a deadly weapon, automobile theft, escape from a youth facility, and destruction of evidence.

The Court of Appeal for the Fifth Appellate District reversed respondent's convictions and ordered a new trial because of what it thought to be error under *Miranda*. The Court of Appeal ruled that respondent's recorded incriminating statements, given with his parents present, had to be excluded from consideration by the jury because respondent was not properly advised of his right to the services of a free attorney before and during interrogation. Although respondent was indisputably informed that he had "the right to talk to a lawyer before you are questioned, have him present with you while you are being questioned, and all during the questioning," and further informed that he had "the right to have a lawyer appointed to represent you at no cost to yourself," the Court of Appeal ruled that these warnings were inadequate because respondent was not explicitly informed of his right to have an attorney appointed before further questioning. The Court of Appeal stated that "one of *Miranda*'s virtues is its precise requirements which are so easily met," and that "the rigidity of the *Miranda* rules and the way in which they are to be applied was conceived of and continues to be recognized as the decision's greatest strength."

This Court has never indicated that the "rigidity" of *Miranda* extends to the precise formulation of the warnings given a criminal defendant. This Court and others *have* stressed as one virtue of *Miranda* the fact that the giving of the warnings obviates the need for a case-by-case inquiry into the actual voluntariness of the admissions of the accused. Nothing in these observations suggests any desirable rigidity in the *form* of the required warnings.

Quite the contrary, *Miranda* itself indicated that no talismanic incantation was required to satisfy its strictures. The Court in that case stated that "the warnings required and the waiver necessary in accordance with our opinion today are, *in the absence of a fully effective equivalent*, prerequisites to the admissibility of any statement made by a defendant."

Nothing in the warnings given respondent suggested any limitation on the right to the presence of appointed counsel different from the clearly conveyed rights to a lawyer in general, including the right "to a lawyer before you are questioned, while you are being questioned, and all during the questioning."

It is clear that the police in this case fully conveyed to respondent his rights as required by *Miranda*. He was told of his right to have a lawyer present prior to and during interrogation, and his right to have a lawyer appointed at no cost if he could not afford one. These warnings conveyed to respondent his right to have a lawyer appointed if he could not afford one prior to and during interrogation. The Court of Appeal erred in holding that the warnings were inadequate simply because of the order in which they were given.

JUSTICE STEVENS, with whom JUSTICE BRENNAN and JUSTICE MARSHALL join, dissenting.

A juvenile informed by police that he has a right to counsel may understand that right to include one or more of three options: (1) that he has a right to have a lawyer represent him if he or his parents are able and willing to hire one; (2) that, if he cannot afford to hire an attorney, he has a right to have a lawyer represent him without charge *at trial*, even if his parents are unwilling to spend money on his behalf; or (3) that, if he is unable to afford an attorney, he has a right to consult a lawyer without charge before he decides whether to talk to the police, even if his parents decline to pay for such legal representation. All three of these options are encompassed within the right to counsel possessed by a juvenile charged with a crime. In this case, the first two options were explained to respondent, but the third was not.

The California Court of Appeal in this case analyzed the warning given respondent, and concluded that he had not been adequately informed of this crucial right. The police sergeant informed respondent that he had the right to have counsel present during questioning and, after a brief interlude, informed him that he had the right to appointed counsel. The Court of Appeal concluded that this warning was constitutionally inadequate, not because it deviated from the precise language of *Miranda*, but because "unfortunately, the minor was not given the crucial information that the services of the free attorney were available *prior to the impending questioning*."

There can be no question that *Miranda* requires, as a matter of federal constitutional law, that an accused effectively be provided with this "crucial information" in some form. The Court's demonstration that the Constitution does not require that the precise language of *Miranda* be recited to an accused simply fails to come to terms with the express finding of the California Court of Appeal that respondent was not given this information. The warning recited by the police sergeant is sufficiently ambiguous on its face to provide adequate support for the California court's finding. That court's conclusion is at least reasonable, and is clearly not so patently erroneous as to warrant summary reversal.

In *Duckworth v. Eagan*, the suspect received standard *Miranda* warnings and was also informed that if he could not afford a lawyer, one would be appointed for him "if and when you go to court." In a closely divided 5–4 decision, the Supreme Court held that the warnings were sufficient to satisfy *Miranda*.

DUCKWORTH V. EAGAN

492 U.S. 195 (1989)

CHIEF JUSTICE REHNQUIST delivered the opinion of the Court.

Respondent confessed to stabbing a woman nine times after she refused to have sexual relations with him, and he was convicted of attempted murder. Before confessing, respondent was given warnings by the police, which included the advice that a lawyer would be appointed "if and when you go to court." The United States Court of Appeals for the Seventh Circuit held that such advice did not comply with the requirements of *Miranda v. Arizona*, 384 U.S. 436 (1966). We disagree and reverse.

Late on May 16, 1982, respondent contacted a Chicago police officer he knew to report that he had seen the naked body of a dead woman lying on a Lake Michigan beach. Respondent denied any involvement in criminal activity. He then took several Chicago police officers to the beach, where the woman was crying for help. When she saw respondent, the woman exclaimed: "Why did you stab me? Why did you stab me?" Respondent told the officers that he had been with the woman earlier that night, but that they had been attacked by several men who abducted the woman in a van.

The next morning, after realizing that the crime had been committed in Indiana, the Chicago police turned the investigation over to the Hammond, Indiana, Police Department. Respondent repeated to the Hammond police officers his story that he had been attacked on the lakefront, and that the woman had been abducted by several men. After he filled out a battery complaint at a local police station, respondent agreed to go to the Hammond police headquarters for further questioning.

At about 11 a.m., the Hammond police questioned respondent. Before doing so, the police read to respondent a waiver form, entitled "Voluntary Appearance; Advice of Rights," and they asked him to sign it. The form provided:

> Before we ask you any questions, you must understand your rights. You have the right to remain silent. Anything you say can be used against you in court. You have a right to talk to a lawyer for advice before we ask you any questions, and to have him with you during questioning. You have this right to the advice and presence of a lawyer even if you cannot afford to hire one. We have no way of giving you a lawyer, but one will be appointed for you, if you wish, if and when you go to court. If you wish to answer questions now without a lawyer present, you have the right to stop answering questions at any time. You also have the right to stop answering at any time until you've talked to a lawyer.

Respondent signed the form and repeated his exculpatory explanation for his activities of the previous evening.

Respondent was then placed in the "lock up" at the Hammond police headquarters. Some 29 hours later, at about 4 p.m. on May 18, the police again interviewed respondent. Before this questioning, one of the officers read the following waiver form to respondent:

1.   Before making this statement, I was advised that I have the right to remain silent and that anything I might say may or will be used against me in a court of law.

2.   That I have the right to consult with an attorney of my own choice before saying anything, and that an attorney may be present while I am making any statement or throughout the course of any conversation with any police officer if I so choose.

3.   That I can stop and request an attorney at any time during the course of the taking of any statement or during the course of any such conversation.

4.   That in the course of any conversation I can refuse to answer any further questions and remain silent, thereby terminating the conversation.

5.   That if I do not hire an attorney, one will be provided for me.

Respondent read the form back to the officers and signed it. He proceeded to confess to stabbing the woman. The next morning, respondent led the officers to the Lake Michigan beach where they recovered the knife he had used in the stabbing and several items of clothing.

At trial, over respondent's objection, the state court admitted his confession, his first statement denying any involvement in the crime, the knife, and the clothing. The jury found respondent guilty of attempted murder, but acquitted him of rape. He was sentenced to 35 years' imprisonment. The conviction was upheld on appeal.

Respondent sought a writ of habeas corpus in the United States District Court for the Northern District of Indiana, claiming that his confession was inadmissible because the first waiver form did not comply with *Miranda*. The District Court denied the petition. A divided United States Court of Appeals for the Seventh Circuit reversed. The majority held that the advice that counsel would be appointed "if and when you go to court," which was included in the first warnings given to respondent, was "constitutionally defective because it denies an accused indigent a clear and unequivocal warning of the right to appointed counsel before any interrogation," and "links an indigent's right to counsel before interrogation with a future event."

We granted certiorari to resolve a conflict among the lower courts as to whether informing a suspect that an attorney would be appointed for him "if and when you go to court" renders *Miranda* warnings inadequate. We agree with the majority of the lower courts that it does not.

In *Miranda v. Arizona*, the Court established certain procedural safeguards that require police to advise criminal suspects of their rights under the Fifth and Fourteenth Amendments before commencing custodial interrogation. In now-familiar words, the Court said that the suspect must be told that "he has the right to remain silent, that anything he says can be used against him in a court of law, that he has the right to the presence of an attorney, and that if he cannot afford an attorney one will be appointed for him prior to any questioning if he so desires."

We have never insisted that *Miranda* warnings be given in the exact form described in that decision. In *Miranda* itself, the Court said that "the warnings required and the waiver necessary in accordance with our opinion today are, *in the absence of a fully effective equivalent*, prerequisites to the admissibility of any statement made by a defendant." Reviewing courts therefore need not examine *Miranda* warnings as if construing a will or defining the terms of an easement. The inquiry is simply whether the warnings reasonably "convey to a suspect his rights as required by *Miranda*."

We think the initial warnings given to respondent touched all of the bases required by *Miranda*. The police told respondent that he had the right to remain silent, that anything he said could be used against him in court, that he had the right to speak to an attorney before and during questioning, that he had "this right to the advice and presence of a lawyer even if he could not afford to hire one," and that he had the "right to stop answering at any time until he talked to a lawyer." As noted, the police also added that they could not provide respondent with a lawyer, but that one would be appointed "if and when you go to court." The Court of Appeals thought this "if and when you go to court" language suggested that "only those accused who can afford an attorney have the right to have one present before answering any questions," and "implied that if the accused does not go to court, *i.e.*, the government does not file charges, the accused is not entitled to counsel at all."

In our view, the Court of Appeals misapprehended the effect of the inclusion of "if and when you go to court" language in *Miranda* warnings. First, this instruction accurately described the procedure for the appointment of counsel in Indiana. Under Indiana law, counsel is appointed at the defendant's initial appearance in court, and formal charges must be filed at or before that hearing. We think it must be relatively commonplace for a suspect, after receiving *Miranda* warnings, to ask *when* he will obtain counsel. The "if and when you go to court" advice simply anticipates that question. Second, *Miranda* does not require that attorneys be producible on call, but only that the suspect be informed, as here, that he has the right to an attorney before and during questioning, and that an attorney would be appointed for him if he could not afford one. The Court in *Miranda* emphasized that it was not suggesting that "each police station must have a 'station house lawyer' present at all times to advise prisoners." If the police cannot provide appointed counsel, *Miranda* requires only that the police not question a suspect unless he waives his right to counsel. Here, respondent did just that.

We hold that the initial warnings given to respondent, in their totality, satisfied *Miranda*, and therefore that his first statement denying his involvement in the crime, as well as the knife and the clothing, was properly admitted into evidence.

JUSTICE MARSHALL, with whom JUSTICE BRENNAN, JUSTICE BLACKMUN, and JUSTICE STEVENS join, dissenting.

The majority holds today that a police warning advising a suspect that he is entitled to an appointed lawyer only "if and when he goes to court" satisfies the requirements of *Miranda v. Arizona*. The majority reaches this result by seriously mischaracterizing that decision. Under *Miranda*, a police warning must "clearly inform" a suspect taken into custody "that if he cannot afford an attorney one will be appointed for him *prior to any questioning* if he so desires." A warning qualified by an "if and when you go to court" caveat does nothing of the kind; instead, it leads the suspect to believe that a lawyer will not be provided until some indeterminate time in the future *after questioning*. I refuse to acquiesce in the continuing debasement of this historic precedent, and therefore dissent.

Miranda mandated no specific verbal formulation that police must use, but the Court, speaking through Chief Justice Warren, emphasized repeatedly that the offer of appointed counsel must be "effective and express." A clear and unequivocal offer to provide appointed counsel prior to questioning is, in short, an "absolute prerequisite to interrogation."

In concluding that the first warning given to respondent Eagan satisfies the dictates of *Miranda,* the majority makes a mockery of that decision. Eagan was initially advised that he had the right to the presence of counsel before and during questioning. But in the very next breath, the police informed Eagan that, if he could not afford a lawyer, one would be appointed to represent him only "if and when" he went to court. As the Court of Appeals found, Eagan could easily have concluded from the "if and when" caveat that only "those accused who can afford an attorney have the right to have one present before answering any questions; those who are not so fortunate must wait." Eagan was, after all, never told that questioning would be *delayed* until a lawyer was appointed "if and when" Eagan did, in fact, go to court. Thus, the "if and when" caveat may well have had the effect of negating the initial promise that counsel could be present. At best, a suspect like Eagan "would not know whether or not he had a right to the services of a lawyer."

In lawyerlike fashion, the Chief Justice parses the initial warnings given Eagan and finds that the most plausible interpretation is that Eagan would not be questioned until a lawyer was appointed when he later appeared in court. What goes wholly overlooked in the Chief Justice's analysis is that the recipients of police warnings are often frightened suspects unlettered in the law, not lawyers or judges or others schooled in interpreting legal or semantic nuance. Such suspects can hardly be expected to interpret, in as facile a manner as the Chief Justice, "the pretzel-like warnings here—intertwining, contradictory, and ambiguous as they are."

Even if the typical suspect could draw the inference the majority does—that questioning will not commence until a lawyer is provided at a later court appearance—a warning qualified by an "if and when" caveat still fails to give a suspect any indication of *when* he will be taken to court. Upon hearing the warnings given in this case, a suspect would likely conclude that no lawyer would be provided until trial. In common parlance, "going to court" is synonymous with "going to trial." Furthermore, the negative implication of the caveat is that, if the suspect is never taken to court, he "is not entitled to an attorney at all." An unwitting suspect harboring uncertainty on this score is precisely the sort of person who may feel compelled to talk "voluntarily" to the police, without the presence of counsel, in an effort to extricate himself from his predicament.

It poses no great burden on law enforcement officers to eradicate the confusion stemming from the "if and when" caveat. Deleting the sentence containing the offending language is all that needs to be done. Purged of this language, the warning tells the suspect in a straightforward fashion that he has the right to the presence of a lawyer before and during questioning, and that a lawyer will be appointed if he cannot afford one. The suspect is given no reason to believe that the appointment of an attorney may come after interrogation.

———————

In *Florida v. Powell*, the *Miranda* warnings given to a suspect were not entirely clear in describing his right to the presence of an attorney throughout the interrogation. The Supreme Court nevertheless held that the warnings adequately conveyed the suspect's rights under *Miranda*.

FLORIDA V. POWELL
559 U.S. 50 (2010)

After Kevin Powell was arrested and transported to the police station, officers provided *Miranda* warnings by reading from a standard form used by the Tampa Police Department. The form states:

> You have the right to remain silent. If you give up the right to remain silent, anything you say can be used against you in court. You have the right to talk to a lawyer before answering any of our questions. If you cannot afford to hire a lawyer, one will be appointed for you without cost and before any questioning. You have the right to use any of these rights at any time you want during this interview.

Acknowledging that he had been informed of his rights, that he understood them, and that he was willing to talk to the officers, Powell signed the form, then admitted that he owned the handgun found in the apartment where he was arrested. Powell knew he was prohibited from possessing a gun because he had previously been convicted of a felony, but said he had nevertheless purchased and carried the firearm for his protection.

Powell was charged in state court with possession of a weapon by a prohibited possessor, in violation of Florida law. Contending that the *Miranda* warnings were deficient because they did not adequately convey his right to the presence of an attorney during questioning, he moved to suppress his incriminating statements. The trial court denied the motion, concluding that the officers had properly notified Powell of his right to counsel, and a jury convicted Powell of the gun possession charge.

A Florida appellate court held that statements should have been suppressed because the *Miranda* warnings Powell received did not adequately inform him of his right to have an attorney present *throughout* the interrogation. The Florida Supreme Court agreed with the appellate court's reasoning.

Relying on *California v. Prysock*, 453 U.S. 355 (1981), and *Duckworth v. Eagan*, 492 U.S. 195 (1989), the U.S. Supreme Court reversed, holding that the warnings given to Powell reasonably conveyed his rights as required by *Miranda*:

> The Tampa officers did not entirely omit any information *Miranda* required them to impart. They informed Powell that he had "the right to talk to a lawyer before answering any of [their] questions" and "the right to use any of [his] rights at any time [he] want[ed] during th[e] interview." The first statement communicated that Powell could consult with a lawyer before answering any particular question, and the second statement confirmed that he could exercise that right while the

interrogation was underway. In combination, the two warnings reasonably conveyed Powell's right to have an attorney present, not only at the outset of interrogation, but at all times.

The Required Content of the *Miranda* Warnings

The police are not required to deliver the *Miranda* warnings in the precise formulation described by the Supreme Court's decision as long as the warnings are administered in a form that reasonably conveys to a suspect his rights as required by *Miranda*.

C. THE "FRUITS" OF A *MIRANDA* VIOLATION

As the *Miranda* decision itself makes clear, any statements made by a suspect during custodial interrogation are inadmissible if the prosecution cannot demonstrate that the suspect received and waived his rights under *Miranda*. But what happens when a statement obtained in violation of *Miranda* leads the police to other evidence that is obtained lawfully? Is the other evidence "tainted fruit" and inadmissible as well?

To bring the question into sharper focus, imagine that Chrissy Crooked has been arrested on suspicion of bank robbery. The arresting officers fail to administer the *Miranda* warnings, and during the ride to the police station, they begin questioning her. Chrissy denies any involvement and says that she was watching a movie with her boyfriend, Tom Truthy, when the bank was robbed. The officers drive directly to Tom's apartment. One officer stays in the car with Chrissy, while the other officer speaks to Tom. Inside his apartment, Tom tells the officer that on the day in question, Chrissy showed up at his apartment with a black duffel bag and seemed very nervous, then left a few minutes later after declining his offer to watch a movie. When the police officer returns to the car, he says to Chrissy: "Sorry, but Tom didn't corroborate your alibi. In fact, he says you were nervous and carrying a duffel bag when you showed up at his place."

Chrissy mulls things over for a few minutes before finally confessing to the bank robbery. One of the officers asks, "Where's the money?" Chrissy then admits that she buried it in the city park. The officers drive to the city park and Chrissy shows them the location of the buried money. The officers dig up a duffel bag—monogrammed with the initials "C.C." and filled with money—and put it in the trunk of their police car. Back at the police station, one of the officers finally administers the *Miranda* warnings, and Chrissy indicates that she understands her rights. Then the other officer says to Chrissy: "You've already done a good job telling us what we need to know, so why don't you just make it all official by writing it up in your own words and signing it." Chrissy thinks it over for a few moments, then writes out a confession and signs it.

Negotiations over the terms of a plea bargain break down, and Chrissy's case proceeds to trial. At a suppression hearing shortly before the trial, the prosecutor acknowledges that Chrissy's statements made before arriving at the police station are inadmissible because she was subjected to custodial interrogation without the benefit of *Miranda* warnings. But the prosecutor insists that Tom Truthy's testimony about Chrissy's appearance on the day of the bank robbery, the monogrammed duffel bag filled with money, and Chrissy's handwritten and signed confession should all be admissible. Chrissy's attorney contends that these items of evidence should be excluded as "tainted fruits" of the same *Miranda* violation that rendered Chrissy's statements outside the police station inadmissible. How should the judge rule?

The answer to this complex question begins with *Michigan v. Tucker*, in which the Supreme Court held that the testimony of a third-party witness was admissible even though his identity was discovered as a result of a *Miranda* violation.

MICHIGAN V. TUCKER
417 U.S. 433 (1974)

In April 1966—two months before *Miranda v. Arizona* was decided—Thomas Tucker, a suspect in a brutal rape, was arrested and brought to the police station for questioning. The police asked Tucker whether he knew the crime for which he had been arrested, whether he wanted an attorney, and whether he understood his constitutional rights. Tucker replied that he did understand the crime for which he was arrested, that he did not want an attorney, and that he understood his rights. The police further advised him that any statements he might make could be used against him at a later date in court. The police, however, did not advise Tucker that he would be furnished counsel free of charge if he could not pay for such services himself. The police questioned Tucker about his activities on the night of the rape, and he said that he had been with an acquaintance, Robert Henderson, and then later was home alone, asleep.

The police sought to confirm Tucker's story by contacting Henderson, but Henderson's story served to discredit rather than to bolster Tucker's account. Henderson acknowledged that Tucker had been with him on the night of the crime but said that he had left at a relatively early time. Furthermore, Henderson told police that he saw Tucker the following day and asked him about scratches on his face, wondering if he "got hold of a wild one or something." Tucker answered: "Something like that." Henderson then asked Tucker who it was, and Tucker said that it was a woman who lived the next block over.

One week after *Miranda v. Arizona* was decided, in *Johnson v. New Jersey*, 384 U.S. 719 (1966), the Supreme Court addressed the question of whether *Miranda* should be applied retroactively. The Court held that

Miranda applied only to cases in which the trial began after the date of the *Miranda* decision. Because Tucker's trial took place after *Miranda* was decided, *Miranda* was therefore applicable to the case even though the crime and Tucker's interrogation occurred before the *Miranda* decision. Accordingly, Tucker's appointed counsel made a motion before the trial to exclude Henderson's expected testimony because Tucker had revealed Henderson's identity without having received full *Miranda* warnings. Although Tucker's own statements taken during interrogation were excluded under the *Miranda* decision, the trial judge denied the motion to exclude Henderson's testimony. Henderson then testified at trial, and Tucker was convicted of rape and sentenced to 20 to 40 years in prison.

In determining whether Henderson's testimony was properly admitted, the Supreme Court began by considering the underlying purpose of the exclusionary rule:

> The deterrent purpose of the exclusionary rule necessarily assumes that the police have engaged in willful, or at the very least negligent, conduct which has deprived the defendant of some right. By refusing to admit evidence gained as a result of such conduct, the courts hope to instill in those particular investigating officers, or in their future counterparts, a greater degree of care toward the rights of an accused. Where the official action was pursued in complete good faith, however, the deterrence rationale loses much of its force.

Because Tucker was interrogated before *Miranda* was decided, the officers' failure to advise him of his right to appointed counsel was neither willful nor negligent, and the officers did ask Tucker if he wanted counsel, but he declined. Moreover, the Court found that despite the technical *Miranda* violation, Tucker's statements were not involuntary or the product of actual compulsion. After considering the various arguments, the Supreme Court ultimately concluded that the trial court was correct to admit Henderson's testimony:

> In summary, we do not think that any single reason supporting exclusion of [Henderson's] testimony, or all of them together, are very persuasive. By contrast, we find the arguments in favor of admitting the testimony quite strong. For, when balancing the interests involved, we must weigh the strong interest under any system of justice of making available to the trier of fact all concededly relevant and trustworthy evidence which either party seeks to adduce. In this particular case we also must consider society's interest in the effective prosecution of criminals in light of the protection our pre-*Miranda* standards afford criminal defendants. These interests may be outweighed by the need to provide an effective sanction to a constitutional right, but they

must in any event be valued. Here [Tucker's] own statement, which might have helped the prosecution show [his] guilty conscience at trial, had already been excised from the prosecution's case pursuant to this Court's decision [in *Johnson v. New Jersey*]. To extend the excision further under the circumstances of this case and exclude relevant testimony of a third-party witness would require far more persuasive arguments than those advanced.

In *Oregon v. Elstad*, police began questioning a suspect in his home without administering the *Miranda* warnings, and he admitted his involvement in a burglary. The suspect was then transported to the police station, and after receiving the *Miranda* warnings, he made a complete confession. The Supreme Court held that while the first statement in the suspect's home was properly excluded as the product of a *Miranda* violation, the police station confession was admissible because it was voluntarily given. In so holding, the Court rejected the argument that the police station confession was "tainted fruit" of the *Miranda* violation.

OREGON V. ELSTAD
470 U.S. 298 (1985)

JUSTICE O'CONNOR delivered the opinion of the Court.

This case requires us to decide whether an initial failure of law enforcement officers to administer the warnings required by *Miranda v. Arizona*, 384 U.S. 436 (1966), without more, "taints" subsequent admissions made after a suspect has been fully advised of and has waived his *Miranda* rights. Respondent, Michael James Elstad, was convicted of burglary by an Oregon trial court. The Oregon Court of Appeals reversed, holding that respondent's signed confession, although voluntary, was rendered inadmissible by a prior remark made in response to questioning without benefit of *Miranda* warnings. We now reverse.

I

In December 1981, the home of Mr. and Mrs. Gilbert Gross, in the town of Salem, Polk County, Ore., was burglarized. Missing were art objects and furnishings valued at $150,000. A witness to the burglary contacted the Polk County Sheriff's office, implicating respondent Michael Elstad, an 18-year-old neighbor and friend of the Grosses' teenage son. Thereupon, Officers Burke and McAllister went to the home of respondent Elstad, with a warrant for his arrest. Elstad's mother answered the door. She led the officers to her son's room where he lay on his bed, clad in shorts and listening to his stereo. The officers asked him to get dressed and to accompany them into the living room. Officer

McAllister asked respondent's mother to step into the kitchen, where he explained that they had a warrant for her son's arrest for the burglary of a neighbor's residence. Officer Burke remained with Elstad in the living room. He later testified:

> I sat down with Mr. Elstad and I asked him if he was aware of why Detective McAllister and myself were there to talk with him. He stated no, he had no idea why we were there. I then asked him if he knew a person by the name of Gross, and he said yes, he did, and also added that he heard that there was a robbery at the Gross house. And at that point I told Mr. Elstad that I felt he was involved in that, and he looked at me and stated, "Yes, I was there."

Elstad was transported to the Sheriff's headquarters and approximately one hour later, Officers Burke and McAllister joined him in McAllister's office. McAllister then advised respondent for the first time of his *Miranda* rights, reading from a standard card. Respondent indicated he understood his rights, and, having these rights in mind, wished to speak with the officers. Elstad gave a full statement, explaining that he had known that the Gross family was out of town and had been paid to lead several acquaintances to the Gross residence and show them how to gain entry through a defective sliding glass door. The statement was typed, reviewed by respondent, read back to him for correction, initialed and signed by Elstad and both officers. As an afterthought, Elstad added and initialed the sentence, "After leaving the house Robby & I went back to the van & Robby handed me a small bag of grass." Respondent concedes that the officers made no threats or promises either at his residence or at the Sheriff's office.

Respondent was charged with first-degree burglary. Respondent moved at once to suppress his oral statement and signed confession. He contended that the statement he made in response to questioning at his house "let the cat out of the bag," and tainted the subsequent confession as "fruit of the poisonous tree." The judge ruled that the statement, "I was there," had to be excluded because the defendant had not been advised of his *Miranda* rights. The written confession taken after Elstad's arrival at the Sheriff's office, however, was admitted in evidence.

II

The arguments advanced in favor of suppression of respondent's written confession rely heavily on metaphor. One metaphor, familiar from the Fourth Amendment context, would require that respondent's confession, regardless of its integrity, voluntariness, and probative value, be suppressed as the "tainted fruit of the poisonous tree" of the *Miranda* violation. A second metaphor questions whether a confession can be truly voluntary once the "cat is out of the bag." Taken out of context, each of these metaphors can be misleading. They should not be used to obscure fundamental differences between the role of the Fourth Amendment exclusionary rule and the function of *Miranda* in guarding against the prosecutorial use of compelled statements as prohibited by the Fifth Amendment. The Oregon court assumed and respondent here contends that a failure to administer *Miranda* warnings necessarily breeds the same consequences as police infringement of a constitutional right, so that evidence uncovered following an unwarned statement must be suppressed as "fruit of the poisonous tree." We believe this view misconstrues the nature of the protections afforded by *Miranda* warnings and therefore misreads the consequences of police failure to supply them.

A

Prior to *Miranda,* the admissibility of an accused's in-custody statements was judged solely by whether they were "voluntary" within the meaning of the Due Process Clause. If a suspect's statements had been obtained by "techniques and methods offensive to due process," or under circumstances in which the suspect clearly had no opportunity to exercise "a free and unconstrained will," the statements would not be admitted. The Court in *Miranda* required suppression of many statements that would have been admissible under traditional due process analysis by presuming that statements made while in custody and without adequate warnings were protected by the Fifth Amendment. The Fifth Amendment, of course, is not concerned with nontestimonial evidence. Nor is it concerned with moral and psychological pressures to confess emanating from sources other than official coercion. Voluntary statements remain a proper element in law enforcement.

Respondent's contention that his confession was tainted by the earlier failure of the police to provide *Miranda* warnings and must be excluded as "fruit of the poisonous tree" assumes the existence of a constitutional violation. This figure of speech is drawn from *Wong Sun v. U.S.,* 371 U.S. 471 (1963), in which the Court held that evidence and witnesses discovered as a result of a search in violation of the Fourth Amendment must be excluded from evidence. The *Wong Sun* doctrine applies as well when the fruit of the Fourth Amendment violation is a confession. It is settled law that "a confession obtained through custodial interrogation after an illegal arrest should be excluded unless intervening events break the causal connection between the illegal arrest and the confession so that the confession is sufficiently an act of free will to purge the primary taint."

But a procedural *Miranda* violation differs in significant respects from violations of the Fourth Amendment, which have traditionally mandated a broad application of the "fruits" doctrine. The purpose of the Fourth Amendment exclusionary rule is to deter unreasonable searches, no matter how probative their fruits. Where a Fourth Amendment violation "taints" the confession, a finding of voluntariness for the purposes of the Fifth Amendment is merely a threshold requirement in determining whether the confession may be admitted in evidence. Beyond this, the prosecution must show a sufficient break in events to undermine the inference that the confession was caused by the Fourth Amendment violation.

The *Miranda* exclusionary rule, however, serves the Fifth Amendment and sweeps more broadly than the Fifth Amendment itself. It may be triggered even in the absence of a Fifth Amendment violation. The Fifth Amendment prohibits use by the prosecution in its case in chief only of *compelled* testimony. Failure to administer *Miranda* warnings creates a presumption of compulsion. Consequently, unwarned statements that are otherwise voluntary within the meaning of the Fifth Amendment must nevertheless be excluded from evidence under *Miranda*. Thus, in the individual case, *Miranda*'s preventive medicine provides a remedy even to the defendant who has suffered no identifiable constitutional harm.

But the *Miranda* presumption, though irrebuttable for purposes of the prosecution's case in chief, does not require that the statements and their fruits be discarded as inherently tainted. Despite the fact that patently *voluntary* statements taken in violation of *Miranda* must be excluded from the prosecution's case, the presumption of coercion does not bar their use for impeachment purposes on cross-examination. *Harris v. New York*, 401 U.S. 222 (1971). Where an unwarned statement is preserved for use in situations that fall outside the sweep of the *Miranda* presumption, the primary criterion of admissibility remains the "old" due process voluntariness test.

In *Michigan v. Tucker*, 417 U.S. 433 (1974), the Court was asked to extend the *Wong Sun* fruits doctrine to suppress the testimony of a witness for the prosecution whose identity was discovered as the result of a statement taken from the accused without benefit of full *Miranda* warnings. As in respondent's case, the breach of the *Miranda* procedures in *Tucker* involved no actual compulsion. Since there was no actual infringement of the suspect's constitutional rights, the case was not controlled by the doctrine expressed in *Wong Sun* that fruits of a constitutional violation must be suppressed. In deciding "how sweeping the judicially imposed consequences" of a failure to administer *Miranda* warnings should be, the *Tucker* Court noted that neither the general goal of deterring improper police conduct nor the Fifth Amendment goal of assuring trustworthy evidence would be served by suppression of the witness' testimony. The unwarned confession must, of course, be suppressed, but the Court ruled that introduction of the third-party witness' testimony did not violate Tucker's Fifth Amendment rights.

We believe that this reasoning applies with equal force when the alleged "fruit" of a noncoercive *Miranda* violation is neither a witness nor an article of evidence but the accused's own voluntary testimony. As in *Tucker*, the absence of any coercion or improper tactics undercuts the twin rationales—trustworthiness and deterrence—for a broader rule. Once warned, the suspect is free to exercise his own volition in deciding whether or not to make a statement to the authorities.

Because *Miranda* warnings may inhibit persons from giving information, this Court has determined that they need be administered only after the person is taken into "custody" or his freedom has otherwise been significantly restrained. Unfortunately, the task of defining "custody" is a slippery one, and policemen investigating serious crimes cannot realistically be expected to make no errors whatsoever. If errors are made by law enforcement officers in administering the prophylactic *Miranda* procedures, they should not breed the same irremediable consequences as police infringement of the Fifth Amendment itself. It is an unwarranted extension of *Miranda* to hold that a simple failure to administer the warnings, unaccompanied by any actual coercion or other circumstances calculated to undermine the suspect's ability to exercise his free will, so taints the investigatory process that a subsequent voluntary and informed waiver is ineffective for some indeterminate period. Though *Miranda* requires that the unwarned admission must be suppressed, the admissibility of any subsequent statement should turn in these circumstances solely on whether it is knowingly and voluntarily made.

B

The Oregon court, however, believed that the unwarned remark compromised the voluntariness of respondent's later confession. It was the court's view that the prior *answer* and not the unwarned questioning impaired respondent's ability to give a valid waiver and that only lapse of time and change of place could dissipate what it termed the "coercive impact" of the inadmissible statement. When a prior statement is actually coerced, the time that passes between confessions, the change in place of interrogations, and the change in identity of the interrogators all bear on whether that coercion has carried over into the second confession. The failure of police to administer *Miranda* warnings does not mean that the statements received have actually been coerced, but only that courts will presume the privilege against compulsory self-incrimination has not been intelligently exercised.

The Oregon court nevertheless identified a subtle form of lingering compulsion, the psychological impact of the suspect's conviction that he has let the cat out of the bag and, in so doing, has sealed his own fate. But endowing the psychological effects of *voluntary* unwarned admissions with constitutional implications would, practically speaking, disable the police from obtaining the suspect's informed cooperation even when the official coercion proscribed by the Fifth Amendment played no part in either his warned or unwarned confessions.

This Court has never held that the psychological impact of voluntary disclosure of a guilty secret qualifies as state compulsion or compromises the voluntariness of a subsequent informed waiver. The Oregon court, by adopting this expansive view of Fifth Amendment compulsion, effectively immunizes a suspect who responds to pre-*Miranda* warning questions from the consequences of his subsequent informed waiver of the privilege of remaining silent. This immunity comes at a high cost to legitimate law enforcement activity, while adding little desirable protection to the individual's interest in not being *compelled* to testify against himself. When neither the initial nor the subsequent admission is coerced, little justification exists for permitting the highly probative evidence of a voluntary confession to be irretrievably lost to the factfinder.

There is a vast difference between the direct consequences flowing from coercion of a confession by physical violence or other deliberate means calculated to break the suspect's will and the uncertain consequences of disclosure of a "guilty secret" freely given in response to an unwarned but noncoercive question, as in this case. We must conclude that, absent deliberately coercive or improper tactics in obtaining the initial statement, the mere fact that a suspect has made an unwarned admission does not warrant a presumption of compulsion. A subsequent administration of *Miranda* warnings to a suspect who has given a voluntary but unwarned statement ordinarily should suffice to remove the conditions that precluded admission of the earlier statement. In such circumstances, the finder of fact may reasonably conclude that the suspect made a rational and intelligent choice whether to waive or invoke his rights.

III

Though belated, the reading of respondent's rights was undeniably complete. McAllister testified that he read the *Miranda* warnings aloud from a printed card and recorded Elstad's responses. There is no question that respondent knowingly and voluntarily waived his right to remain silent before he described his participation in the burglary. It is also beyond dispute that respondent's earlier remark was voluntary, within the meaning of the Fifth Amendment. Neither the environment nor the manner of either "interrogation" was coercive. The initial conversation took place at midday, in the living room area of respondent's own home, with his mother in the kitchen area, a few steps away. Although in retrospect the officers testified that respondent was then in custody, at the time he made his statement he had not been informed that he was under arrest. The arresting officers' testimony indicates that the brief stop in the living room before proceeding to the station house was not to interrogate the suspect but to notify his mother of the reason for his arrest.

Respondent has argued that he was unable to give a fully *informed* waiver of his rights because he was unaware that his prior statement could not be used against him. Respondent suggests that Officer McAllister, to cure this deficiency, should have added an additional warning to those given him at the Sheriff's office. Such a requirement is neither practicable nor constitutionally necessary. This Court has never embraced the theory that a defendant's ignorance of the full consequences of his decisions vitiates their voluntariness.

IV

When police ask questions of a suspect in custody without administering the required warnings, *Miranda* dictates that the answers received be presumed compelled and that they be excluded from evidence at trial in the State's case in chief. The Court today in no way retreats from the bright-line rule of *Miranda.* We do not imply that good faith excuses a failure to administer *Miranda* warnings; nor do we condone inherently coercive police tactics or methods offensive to due process that render the initial admission involuntary and undermine the suspect's will to invoke his rights once they are read to him. A handful of courts have, however, applied our precedents relating to confessions obtained under coercive circumstances to situations involving wholly voluntary admissions, requiring a passage of time or break in events before a second, fully warned statement can be deemed voluntary. Far from establishing a rigid rule, we direct courts to avoid one; there is no warrant for presuming coercive effect where the suspect's initial inculpatory statement, though technically in violation of *Miranda,* was voluntary. The relevant inquiry is whether, in fact, the second statement was also voluntarily made. As in any such inquiry, the finder of fact must examine the surrounding circumstances and the entire course of police conduct with respect to the suspect in evaluating the voluntariness of his statements. The fact that a suspect chooses to speak after being informed of his rights is, of course, highly probative. We find that the dictates of *Miranda* and the goals of the Fifth Amendment proscription against use of compelled testimony are fully satisfied in the circumstances of this case by barring use of the unwarned statement in the case in chief. No further purpose is served by imputing "taint" to subsequent statements obtained pursuant to a voluntary and knowing waiver. We hold today that a suspect who has once responded to unwarned yet uncoercive questioning is not thereby disabled from waiving his rights and confessing after he has been given the requisite *Miranda* warnings.

JUSTICE BRENNAN, with whom JUSTICE MARSHALL joins, dissenting.

The Court has engaged of late in a studied campaign to strip the *Miranda* decision piecemeal and to undermine the rights *Miranda* sought to secure. Today's decision not only extends this effort a further step, but delivers a potentially crippling blow to *Miranda* and the ability of courts to safeguard the rights of persons accused of crime. For at least with respect to successive confessions, the Court today appears to strip remedies for *Miranda* violations of the "fruit of the poisonous tree" doctrine prohibiting the use of evidence presumptively derived from official illegality.

Two major premises undergird the Court's decision. The Court rejects as nothing more than "speculative" the long-recognized presumption that an illegally extracted confession causes the accused to confess again out of the mistaken belief that he already has sealed his fate, and it condemns as "extravagant" the requirement that the prosecution affirmatively rebut the presumption before the subsequent confession may be admitted. The Court instead adopts a new rule that, so long as the accused is given the usual *Miranda* warnings before further interrogation, the taint of a previous confession obtained in violation of *Miranda* "ordinarily" must be viewed as *automatically* dissipated.

In the alternative, the Court asserts that neither the Fifth Amendment itself nor the judicial policy of deterring illegal police conduct requires the suppression of the "fruits" of a confession obtained in violation of *Miranda,* reasoning that to do otherwise would interfere with "legitimate law enforcement activity." If violations of constitutional rights may not be remedied through the well-established rules respecting derivative evidence, as the Court has held today, there is a critical danger that the rights will be rendered nothing more than a mere "form of words."

The threshold question is this: What effect should an admission or confession of guilt obtained in violation of an accused's *Miranda* rights be presumed to have upon the voluntariness of subsequent confessions that are preceded by *Miranda* warnings?

The correct approach, administered for almost 20 years by most courts with no untoward results, is to presume that an admission or confession obtained in violation of *Miranda* taints a subsequent confession unless the prosecution can show that the taint is so attenuated as to justify admission of the subsequent confession. Although the Court warns against the "irremediable consequences" of this presumption, it is obvious that a subsequent confession, just like any other evidence that follows upon illegal police action, does not become "sacred and inaccessible." As with any other evidence, the inquiry is whether the subsequent confession "has been come at by exploitation of the illegality or instead by means sufficiently distinguishable to be purged of the primary taint." *Wong Sun v. U.S.*, 371 U.S. 471, 488 (1963).

Until today the Court has recognized that the dissipation inquiry requires the prosecution to demonstrate that the official illegality did not taint the challenged confession, and we have rejected the simplistic view that abstract notions of "free will" are alone sufficient to dissipate the challenged taint.

The Supreme Court's decision in *Oregon v. Elstad* led various police organizations to adopt an interrogation protocol instructing officers to intentionally withhold *Miranda* warnings until the suspect makes incriminating statements. At that point, *Miranda* warnings would then be given, and the suspect would be asked to repeat his previous confession. This interrogation protocol, many police believed, was consistent with the holding of *Oregon v. Elstad* permitting the second confession to be introduced into evidence. The Supreme Court rejected the interrogation protocol in *Missouri v. Seibert*.

MISSOURI V. SEIBERT

542 U.S. 600 (2004)

JUSTICE SOUTER announced the judgment of the Court and delivered an opinion, in which JUSTICE STEVENS, JUSTICE GINSBURG, and JUSTICE BREYER join.

This case tests a police protocol for custodial interrogation that calls for giving no warnings of the rights to silence and counsel until interrogation has produced a confession. Although such a statement is generally inadmissible, since taken in violation of *Miranda v. Arizona*, 384 U.S. 436 (1966), the interrogating officer follows it with *Miranda* warnings and then leads the suspect to cover the same ground a second time. The question here is the admissibility of the repeated statement. Because this midstream recitation of warnings after interrogation and unwarned confession could not effectively comply with *Miranda*'s constitutional requirement, we hold that a statement repeated after a warning in such circumstances is inadmissible.

I

Respondent Patrice Seibert's 12-year-old son Jonathan had cerebral palsy, and when he died in his sleep she feared charges of neglect because of bedsores on his body. In her presence, two of her teenage sons and two of their friends devised a plan to conceal the facts surrounding Jonathan's death by incinerating his body in the course of burning the family's mobile home, in which they planned to leave Donald Rector, a mentally ill teenager living with the family, to avoid any appearance that Jonathan had been unattended. Seibert's son Darian and a friend set the fire, and Donald died.

Five days later, the police awakened Seibert at 3 a.m. at a hospital where Darian was being treated for burns. In arresting her, Officer Kevin

Clinton followed instructions from Rolla, Missouri, Officer Richard Hanrahan that he refrain from giving *Miranda* warnings. After Seibert had been taken to the police station and left alone in an interview room for 15 to 20 minutes, Officer Hanrahan questioned her without *Miranda* warnings for 30 to 40 minutes, squeezing her arm and repeating "Donald was also to die in his sleep." After Seibert finally admitted she knew Donald was meant to die in the fire, she was given a 20-minute coffee and cigarette break. Officer Hanrahan then turned on a tape recorder, gave Seibert the *Miranda* warnings, and obtained a signed waiver of rights from her. He resumed the questioning with "Ok, 'Trice, we've been talking for a little while about what happened on Wednesday the twelfth, haven't we?" and confronted her with her prewarning statements:

> Hanrahan: Now, in discussion you told us, you told us that there was an understanding about Donald.
>
> Seibert: Yes.
>
> Hanrahan: Did that take place earlier that morning?
>
> Seibert: Yes.
>
> Hanrahan: And what was the understanding about Donald?
>
> Seibert: If they could get him out of the trailer, to take him out of the trailer.
>
> Hanrahan: And if they couldn't?
>
> Seibert: I, I never even thought about it. I just figured they would.
>
> Hanrahan: 'Trice, didn't you tell me that he was supposed to die in his sleep?
>
> Seibert: If that would happen, 'cause he was on that new medicine, you know . . .
>
> Hanrahan: The Prozac? And it makes him sleepy. So he was supposed to die in his sleep?
>
> Seibert: Yes.

After being charged with first-degree murder for her role in Donald's death, Seibert sought to exclude both her prewarning and postwarning statements. At the suppression hearing, Officer Hanrahan testified that he made a "conscious decision" to withhold *Miranda* warnings, thus resorting to an interrogation technique he had been taught: question first, then give the warnings, and then repeat the question "until I get the answer that she's already provided once." He acknowledged that Seibert's ultimate statement was "largely a repeat of information obtained" prior to the warning.

The trial court suppressed the prewarning statement but admitted the responses given after the *Miranda* recitation. A jury convicted Seibert of second-degree murder. On appeal, the Missouri Court of Appeals affirmed, treating this case as indistinguishable from *Oregon v. Elstad*, 470 U.S. 298 (1985).

The Supreme Court of Missouri reversed, holding that "in the circumstances here, where the interrogation was nearly continuous, the second statement, clearly the product of the invalid first statement, should have been suppressed." The court distinguished *Elstad* on the ground that warnings had not intentionally been withheld there, and reasoned that "Officer Hanrahan's intentional omission of a *Miranda* warning was intended to deprive Seibert of the opportunity knowingly and intelligently to waive her *Miranda* rights." Since there were "no circumstances that would seem to dispel the effect of the *Miranda* violation," the court held that the postwarning confession was involuntary and therefore inadmissible. To allow the police to achieve an "end run" around *Miranda*, the court explained, would encourage *Miranda* violations and diminish *Miranda*'s role in protecting the privilege against self-incrimination.

III

The technique of interrogating in successive, unwarned and warned phases raises a new challenge to *Miranda*. Although we have no statistics on the frequency of this practice, it is not confined to Rolla, Missouri. An officer of that police department testified that the strategy of withholding *Miranda* warnings until after interrogating and drawing out a confession was promoted not only by his own department, but by a national police training organization and other departments in which he had worked. Consistently with the officer's testimony, the Police Law Institute, for example, instructs that "officers may conduct a two-stage interrogation. At any point during the pre-*Miranda* interrogation, usually after arrestees have confessed, officers may then read the *Miranda* warnings and ask for a waiver. If the arrestees waive their *Miranda* rights, officers will be able to repeat any *subsequent* incriminating statements later in court." The upshot of all this advice is a question-first practice of some popularity, as one can see from the reported cases describing its use, sometimes in obedience to departmental policy.

IV

The object of question-first is to render *Miranda* warnings ineffective by waiting for a particularly opportune time to give them, after the suspect has already confessed. The threshold issue when interrogators question first and warn later is thus whether it would be reasonable to find that in these circumstances the warnings could function "effectively" as *Miranda* requires. Could the warnings effectively advise the suspect that he had a real choice about giving an admissible statement at that juncture? Could they reasonably convey that he could choose to stop talking even if he had talked earlier? For unless the warnings could place a suspect who has just been interrogated in a position to make such an informed choice, there is no practical justification for accepting the formal warnings as compliance with *Miranda*, or for treating the second stage of interrogation as distinct from the first, unwarned and inadmissible segment.

There is no doubt about the answer that proponents of question-first give to this question about the effectiveness of warnings given only after successful interrogation, and we think their answer is correct. By any objective measure, applied to circumstances exemplified here, it is likely that if the interrogators employ the technique of withholding warnings until after interrogation succeeds in eliciting a confession, the warnings will be ineffective in preparing the suspect for successive interrogation, close in time and similar in content. After all, the reason that question-first is catching on is as obvious as its manifest purpose, which is to get a confession the suspect would not make if he understood his rights at the outset; the sensible underlying assumption is that with one confession in hand before the warnings, the interrogator can count on getting its duplicate, with trifling additional trouble. Upon hearing warnings only in the aftermath of interrogation and just after making a confession, a suspect would hardly think he had a genuine right to remain silent, let alone persist in so believing once the police began to lead him over the same ground again. A more likely reaction on a suspect's part would be perplexity about the reason for discussing rights at that point, bewilderment being an unpromising frame of mind for knowledgeable decision. What is worse, telling a suspect that "anything you say can and will be used against you," without expressly excepting the statement just given, could lead to an entirely reasonable inference that what he has just said will be used, with subsequent silence being of no avail. Thus, when *Miranda* warnings are inserted in the midst of coordinated and continuing interrogation, they are likely to mislead and deprive a defendant of knowledge essential to his ability to understand the nature of his rights and the consequences of abandoning them. By the same token, it would ordinarily be unrealistic to treat two spates of integrated and proximately conducted questioning as independent interrogations subject to independent evaluation simply because *Miranda* warnings formally punctuate them in the middle.

V

Missouri argues that a confession repeated at the end of an interrogation sequence envisioned in a question-first strategy is admissible on the authority of *Oregon v. Elstad*, 470 U.S. 298 (1985), but the argument disfigures that case. In *Elstad*, the police went to the young suspect's house to take him into custody on a charge of burglary. Before the arrest, one officer spoke with the suspect's mother, while the other one joined the suspect in a "brief stop in the living room," where the officer said he "felt" the young man was involved in a burglary. The suspect acknowledged he had been at the scene. This Court noted that the pause in the living room "was not to interrogate the suspect but to notify his mother of the reason for his arrest," and described the incident as having "none of the earmarks of coercion." The Court, indeed, took care to mention that the officer's initial failure to warn was an "oversight" that "may have been the result of confusion as to whether the brief exchange qualified as custodial interrogation or may simply have reflected reluctance to initiate an alarming police procedure before an officer had spoken with respondent's mother." At the outset of a later and systematic station house interrogation going well beyond the scope of the laconic prior admission, the suspect was given *Miranda* warnings and made a full confession. In holding the second statement admissible and voluntary, *Elstad* rejected the "cat out of the bag" theory that any short, earlier admission, obtained in arguably innocent neglect of *Miranda*, determined the character of the later, warned confession; on the facts of that case, the Court thought any causal connection between the first and second responses to the police was "speculative and attenuated." Although the *Elstad* Court expressed no explicit conclusion about either officer's state of mind, it is fair to read *Elstad* as treating the living room conversation as a good-faith *Miranda* mistake, not only open to correction by careful warnings before systematic questioning in that particular case, but posing no threat to warn-first practice generally.

The contrast between *Elstad* and this case reveals a series of relevant facts that bear on whether *Miranda* warnings delivered midstream could be effective enough to accomplish their object: the completeness and detail of the questions and answers in the first round of interrogation, the overlapping content of the two statements, the timing and setting of the first and the second, the continuity of police personnel, and the degree to which the interrogator's questions treated the second round as continuous with the first. In *Elstad*, it was not unreasonable to see the occasion for questioning at the station house as presenting a markedly different experience from the short conversation at home; since a reasonable person in the suspect's shoes could have seen the station house questioning as a new and distinct experience, the *Miranda* warnings could have made sense as presenting a genuine choice whether to follow up on the earlier admission.

At the opposite extreme are the facts here, which by any objective measure reveal a police strategy adapted to undermine the *Miranda* warnings. The unwarned interrogation was conducted in the station house, and the questioning was systematic, exhaustive, and managed with psychological skill. When the police were finished there was little, if anything, of incriminating potential left unsaid. The warned phase of questioning proceeded after a pause of only 15 to 20 minutes, in the same place as the unwarned segment. When the same officer who had conducted the first phase recited the *Miranda* warnings, he said nothing to counter the probable misimpression that the advice that anything Seibert said could be used against her also applied to the details of the inculpatory statement previously elicited. In particular, the police did not advise that her prior statement could not be used. Nothing was said or done to dispel the oddity of warning about legal rights to silence and counsel right after the police had led her through a systematic interrogation, and any uncertainty on her part about a right to stop talking about matters previously discussed would only have been aggravated by the way Officer Hanrahan set the scene by saying "we've been talking for a little while about what happened on Wednesday the twelfth, haven't we?" The impression that the further questioning was a mere continuation of the earlier questions and responses was fostered by references back to the confession already given. It would have been reasonable to regard the two sessions as parts of a continuum, in which it would have been unnatural to refuse to repeat at the second stage what had been said before. These circumstances must be seen as challenging the comprehensibility and efficacy of the *Miranda* warnings to the point that a reasonable person in the suspect's shoes would not have understood them to convey a message that she retained a choice about continuing to talk.

VI

Because the question-first tactic effectively threatens to thwart *Miranda*'s purpose of reducing the risk that a coerced confession would be admitted, and because the facts here do not reasonably support a conclusion that the warnings given could have served their purpose, Seibert's postwarning statements are inadmissible.

JUSTICE BREYER, concurring.

In my view, the following simple rule should apply to the two-stage interrogation technique: Courts should exclude the "fruits" of the initial unwarned questioning unless the failure to warn was in good faith. I believe this is a sound and workable approach to the problem this case presents. Prosecutors and judges have long understood how to apply the "fruits" approach, which they use in other areas of law. And in the workaday world of criminal law enforcement the administrative simplicity of the familiar has significant advantages over a more complex exclusionary rule.

I believe the plurality's approach in practice will function as a "fruits" test. The truly "effective" *Miranda* warnings on which the plurality insists will occur only when certain circumstances—a lapse in time, a change in location or interrogating officer, or a shift in the focus of the questioning—intervene between the unwarned questioning and any postwarning statement.

JUSTICE KENNEDY, concurring in the judgment.

The interrogation technique used in this case is designed to circumvent *Miranda v. Arizona*. It undermines the *Miranda* warning and obscures its meaning. The plurality opinion is correct to conclude that statements obtained through the use of this technique are inadmissible. Although I agree with much in the careful and convincing opinion for the plurality, my approach does differ in some respects, requiring this separate statement.

In my view, *Elstad* was correct in its reasoning and its result. *Elstad* reflects a balanced and pragmatic approach to enforcement of the *Miranda* warning. An officer may not realize that a suspect is in custody and warnings are required. The officer may not plan to question the suspect or may be waiting for a more appropriate time. Skilled investigators often interview suspects multiple times, and good police work may involve referring to prior statements to test their veracity or to refresh recollection. In light of these realities it would be extravagant to treat the presence of one statement that cannot be admitted under *Miranda* as sufficient reason to prohibit subsequent statements preceded by a proper warning.

This case presents different considerations. The police used a two-step questioning technique based on a deliberate violation of *Miranda*. The *Miranda* warning was withheld to obscure both the practical and legal significance of the admonition when finally given. The strategy is based on the assumption that *Miranda* warnings will tend to mean less when recited midinterrogation, after inculpatory statements have already been obtained. This tactic relies on an intentional misrepresentation of the protection that *Miranda* offers and does not serve any legitimate objectives that might otherwise justify its use.

Further, the interrogating officer here relied on the defendant's prewarning statement to obtain the postwarning statement used against her at trial. The postwarning interview resembled a cross-examination. The officer confronted the defendant with her inadmissible prewarning statements and pushed her to acknowledge them. This shows the temptations for abuse inherent in the two-step technique. Reference to the prewarning statement was an implicit suggestion that the mere repetition of the earlier statement was not independently incriminating. The implicit suggestion was false.

The technique used in this case distorts the meaning of *Miranda* and furthers no legitimate countervailing interest. The *Miranda* rule would be frustrated were we to allow police to undermine its meaning and effect. The technique simply creates too high a risk that postwarning statements will be obtained when a suspect was deprived of knowledge essential to his ability to understand the nature of his rights and the consequences of abandoning them. When an interrogator uses this deliberate, two-step strategy, predicated upon violating *Miranda* during an extended interview, postwarning statements that are related to the substance of prewarning statements must be excluded absent specific, curative steps.

The plurality concludes that whenever a two-stage interview occurs, admissibility of the postwarning statement should depend on "whether the *Miranda* warnings delivered midstream could have been effective enough to accomplish their object" given the specific facts of the case. This test envisions an objective inquiry from the perspective of the suspect, and applies in the case of both intentional and unintentional two-stage interrogations. In my view, this test cuts too broadly. *Miranda*'s clarity is one of its strengths, and a multifactor test that applies to every two-stage interrogation may serve to undermine that clarity. I would apply a narrower test applicable only in the infrequent case, such as we have here, in which the two-step interrogation technique was used in a calculated way to undermine the *Miranda* warning.

The admissibility of postwarning statements should continue to be governed by the principles of *Elstad* unless the deliberate two-step strategy was employed. If the deliberate two-step strategy has been used, postwarning statements that are related to the substance of prewarning statements must be excluded unless curative measures are taken before the postwarning statement is made. Curative measures should be designed to ensure that a reasonable person in the suspect's situation would understand the import and effect of the *Miranda* warning and of the *Miranda* waiver. For example, a substantial break in time and circumstances between the prewarning statement and the *Miranda* warning may suffice in most circumstances, as it allows the accused to distinguish the two contexts and appreciate that the interrogation has taken a new turn. Alternatively, an additional warning that explains the likely inadmissibility of the prewarning custodial statement may be sufficient. No curative steps were taken in this case, however, so the postwarning statements are inadmissible and the conviction cannot stand.

JUSTICE O'CONNOR, with whom CHIEF JUSTICE REHNQUIST, JUSTICE SCALIA, and JUSTICE THOMAS join, dissenting.

I believe that we are bound by *Elstad* to reach a different result, and I would vacate the judgment of the Supreme Court of Missouri.

I believe that the approach espoused by Justice Kennedy is ill advised. Justice Kennedy would extend *Miranda*'s exclusionary rule to any case in which the use of the "two-step interrogation technique" was "deliberate" or "calculated." This approach untethers the analysis from facts knowable to, and therefore having any potential directly to affect, the suspect. Far from promoting "clarity," the approach will add a third step to the suppression inquiry. In virtually every two-stage interrogation case, in addition to addressing the standard *Miranda* and voluntariness questions, courts will be forced to conduct the kind of difficult, state-of-mind inquiry that we normally take pains to avoid.

I would analyze the two-step interrogation procedure under the voluntariness standards central to the Fifth Amendment and reiterated in *Elstad*. *Elstad* commands that if Seibert's first statement is shown to have been involuntary, the court must examine whether the taint dissipated through the passing of time or a change in circumstances: "When a prior statement is actually coerced, the time that passes between confessions, the change in place of interrogations, and the change in identity of the interrogators all bear on whether that coercion has carried over into the second confession." In addition, Seibert's second statement should be suppressed if she showed that it was involuntary despite the *Miranda* warnings. Although I would leave this analysis for the Missouri courts to conduct on remand, I note that, unlike the officers in *Elstad*, Officer Hanrahan referred to Seibert's unwarned statement during the second part of the interrogation when she made a statement at odds with her unwarned confession. Such a tactic may bear on the voluntariness inquiry.

Because I believe that the plurality gives insufficient deference to *Elstad* and that Justice Kennedy places improper weight on subjective intent, I respectfully dissent.

Note that the decision in *Missouri v. Seibert* was narrowly split. Four Justices—Souter, Stevens, Ginsburg, and Breyer—concluded that Seibert's second confession was inadmissible because the strategic use of the question-first tactic rendered the mid-interrogation *Miranda* warnings confusing and ineffective. Four others—Chief Justice Rehnquist and Justices O'Connor, Scalia, and Thomas—felt that the case was governed by the rule in *Oregon v. Elstad*, and that Seibert's second statement was inadmissible only if it was given involuntarily. Justice Kennedy cast the deciding vote, holding that the "deliberate" use of the two-step interrogation technique rendered Seibert's second confession inadmissible because it was related to the substance of her pre-warning statement and the police failed to employ any "curative measures" to ensure that she understood the import and effect of the *Miranda* warning and waiver.

On the same day *Missouri v. Seibert* was decided, the Supreme Court announced its decision in another case that addressed the "fruits" of a *Miranda* violation. In *U.S. v. Patane*, another narrowly split decision with

Justice Kennedy casting the deciding vote, the Court held that physical evidence obtained as a result of a *Miranda* violation is admissible at trial.

U.S. v. PATANE

542 U.S. 630 (2004)

JUSTICE THOMAS announced the judgment of the Court and delivered an opinion, in which CHIEF JUSTICE REHNQUIST and JUSTICE SCALIA join.

In this case we must decide whether a failure to give a suspect the warnings prescribed by *Miranda v. Arizona*, 384 U.S. 436 (1966), requires suppression of the physical fruits of the suspect's unwarned but voluntary statements. Because the *Miranda* rule protects against violations of the Self-Incrimination Clause, which, in turn, is not implicated by the introduction at trial of physical evidence resulting from voluntary statements, we answer the question presented in the negative.

I

In June 2001, respondent, Samuel Francis Patane, was arrested for harassing his ex-girlfriend, Linda O'Donnell. He was released on bond, subject to a temporary restraining order that prohibited him from contacting O'Donnell. Respondent apparently violated the restraining order by attempting to telephone O'Donnell. On June 6, 2001, Officer Tracy Fox of the Colorado Springs Police Department began to investigate the matter. On the same day, a county probation officer informed an agent of the Bureau of Alcohol, Tobacco and Firearms (ATF), that respondent, a convicted felon, illegally possessed a .40 Glock pistol. The ATF relayed this information to Detective Josh Benner, who worked closely with the ATF. Together, Detective Benner and Officer Fox proceeded to respondent's residence.

After reaching the residence and inquiring into respondent's attempts to contact O'Donnell, Officer Fox arrested respondent for violating the restraining order. Detective Benner attempted to advise respondent of his *Miranda* rights but got no further than the right to remain silent. At that point, respondent interrupted, asserting that he knew his rights, and neither officer attempted to complete the warning.

Detective Benner then asked respondent about the Glock. Respondent was initially reluctant to discuss the matter, stating: "I am not sure I should tell you anything about the Glock because I don't want you to take it away from me." Detective Benner persisted, and respondent told him that the pistol was in his bedroom. Respondent then gave Detective Benner permission to retrieve the pistol. Detective Benner found the pistol and seized it.

A grand jury indicted respondent for possession of a firearm by a convicted felon. The District Court granted respondent's motion to suppress the firearm, reasoning that the officers lacked probable cause to arrest respondent for violating the restraining order. It therefore declined to rule on respondent's alternative argument that the gun should be suppressed as the fruit of an unwarned statement.

The Court of Appeals reversed the District Court's ruling with respect to probable cause but affirmed the suppression order on respondent's alternative theory.

As we explain below, the *Miranda* rule is a prophylactic employed to protect against violations of the Self-Incrimination Clause. The Self-Incrimination Clause, however, is not implicated by the admission into evidence of the physical fruit of a voluntary statement. Accordingly, there is no justification for extending the *Miranda* rule to this context. And just as the Self-Incrimination Clause primarily focuses on the criminal trial, so too does the *Miranda* rule. The *Miranda* rule is not a code of police conduct, and police do not violate the Constitution (or even the *Miranda* rule, for that matter) by mere failures to warn. For this reason, the exclusionary rule articulated in cases such as *Wong Sun v. U.S.*, 371 U.S. 471 (1963), does not apply. Accordingly, we reverse the judgment of the Court of Appeals and remand the case for further proceedings.

II

For present purposes, it suffices to note that the core protection afforded by the Self-Incrimination Clause is a prohibition on compelling a criminal defendant to testify against himself at trial. The Clause cannot be violated by the introduction of nontestimonial evidence obtained as a result of voluntary statements.

To be sure, the Court has recognized and applied several prophylactic rules designed to protect the core privilege against self-incrimination. For example, although the text of the Self-Incrimination Clause at least suggests that its coverage is limited to compelled testimony that is used against the defendant in the trial itself, potential suspects may, at times, assert the privilege in proceedings in which answers might be used to incriminate them in a subsequent criminal case. The natural concern which underlies these decisions is that an inability to protect the right at one stage of a proceeding may make its invocation useless at a later stage.

Similarly, in *Miranda*, the Court concluded that the possibility of coercion inherent in custodial interrogations unacceptably raises the risk that a suspect's privilege against self-incrimination might be violated. To protect against this danger, the *Miranda* rule creates a presumption of coercion, in the absence of specific warnings, that is generally irrebuttable for purposes of the prosecution's case in chief.

But because these prophylactic rules (including the *Miranda* rule) necessarily sweep beyond the actual protections of the Self-Incrimination Clause, any further extension of these rules must be justified by its necessity for the protection of the actual right against compelled self-incrimination.

It is for these reasons that statements taken without *Miranda* warnings (though not actually compelled) can be used to impeach a defendant's testimony at trial, though the fruits of actually compelled testimony cannot. More generally, the *Miranda* rule does not require that the statements taken without complying with the rule and their fruits be discarded as inherently tainted. Such a blanket suppression rule could not be justified by reference to the Fifth Amendment goal of assuring trustworthy evidence or by any deterrence rationale, and would therefore fail our close-fit requirement.

Furthermore, the Self-Incrimination Clause contains its own exclusionary rule. It provides that "no person . . . shall be compelled in any criminal case to be a witness against himself." Unlike the Fourth Amendment's bar on unreasonable searches, the Self-Incrimination Clause is self-executing. We have repeatedly explained that those subjected to coercive police interrogations have an *automatic* protection from the use of their involuntary statements (or evidence derived from their statements) in any subsequent criminal trial. This explicit textual protection supports a strong presumption against expanding the *Miranda* rule any further.

III

Our cases also make clear the related point that a mere failure to give *Miranda* warnings does not, by itself, violate a suspect's constitutional rights or even the *Miranda* rule. It follows that police do not violate a suspect's constitutional rights (or the *Miranda* rule) by negligent or even deliberate failures to provide the suspect with the full panoply of warnings prescribed by *Miranda*. Potential violations occur, if at all, only upon the admission of unwarned statements into evidence at trial. And, at that point, the exclusion of unwarned statements is a complete and sufficient remedy for any perceived *Miranda* violation.

Thus, unlike unreasonable searches under the Fourth Amendment or actual violations of the Due Process Clause or the Self-Incrimination Clause, there is, with respect to mere failures to warn, nothing to deter. There is therefore no reason to apply the "fruit of the poisonous tree" doctrine of *Wong Sun*. It is not for this Court to impose its preferred police practices on either federal law enforcement officials or their state counterparts.

IV

Introduction of the nontestimonial fruit of a voluntary statement, such as respondent's Glock, does not implicate the Self-Incrimination Clause. The admission of such fruit presents no risk that a defendant's coerced statements (however defined) will be used against him at a criminal trial. In any case, the exclusion of unwarned statements is a complete and sufficient remedy for any perceived *Miranda* violation. There is simply no need to extend (and therefore no justification for extending) the prophylactic rule of *Miranda* to this context.

Similarly, because police cannot violate the Self-Incrimination Clause by taking unwarned though voluntary statements, an exclusionary rule cannot be justified by reference to a deterrence effect on law enforcement, as the Court of Appeals believed. The Court of Appeals ascribed significance to the fact that, in this case, there might be "little practical difference between respondent's confessional statement" and the actual physical evidence. The distinction, the court said, "appears to make little sense as a matter of policy." But, putting policy aside, we have held that the word "witness" in the constitutional text limits the scope of the Self-Incrimination Clause to testimonial evidence. The Constitution itself makes the distinction. And although it is true that the Court requires the exclusion of the physical fruit of actually coerced statements, it must be remembered that statements taken without sufficient *Miranda* warnings are presumed to have been coerced only for certain purposes and then only when necessary to protect the privilege against self-incrimination. For the reasons discussed above, we decline to extend that presumption further.

JUSTICE KENNEDY, with whom JUSTICE O'CONNOR joins, concurring in the judgment.

In *Oregon v. Elstad*, 470 U.S. 298 (1985), *New York v. Quarles*, 467 U.S. 649 (1984), and *Harris v. New York,* 401 U.S. 222 (1971), evidence obtained following an unwarned interrogation was held admissible. This result was based in large part on our recognition that the concerns underlying the *Miranda* rule must be accommodated to other objectives of the criminal justice system. Here, it is sufficient to note that the Government presents an even stronger case for admitting the evidence obtained as the result of Patane's unwarned statement. Admission of nontestimonial physical fruits (the Glock in this case), even more so than the postwarning statements to the police in *Elstad*, does not run the risk of admitting into trial an accused's coerced incriminating statements against himself. In light of the important probative value of reliable physical evidence, it is doubtful that exclusion can be justified by a deterrence rationale sensitive to both law enforcement interests and a suspect's rights during an in-custody interrogation. Unlike the plurality, however, I find it unnecessary to decide whether the detective's failure to give Patane the full *Miranda* warnings should be characterized as a violation of the *Miranda* rule itself, or whether there is "anything to deter" so long as the unwarned statements are not later introduced at trial.

JUSTICE SOUTER, with whom JUSTICE STEVENS and JUSTICE GINSBURG join, dissenting.

The plurality repeatedly says that the Fifth Amendment does not address the admissibility of nontestimonial evidence, an overstatement that is beside the point. The issue actually presented today is whether courts should apply the fruit of the poisonous tree doctrine lest we create an incentive for the police to omit *Miranda* warnings before custodial interrogation. In closing their eyes to the consequences of giving an evidentiary advantage to those who ignore *Miranda*, the plurality adds an important inducement for interrogators to ignore the rule in that case.

Miranda rested on insight into the inherently coercive character of custodial interrogation and the inherently difficult exercise of assessing the voluntariness of any confession resulting from it. Unless the police give the prescribed warnings meant to counter the coercive atmosphere, a custodial confession is inadmissible, there being no need for the previous time-consuming and difficult enquiry into voluntariness. That inducement to forestall involuntary statements and troublesome issues of fact can only atrophy if we turn around and recognize an evidentiary benefit when an unwarned statement leads investigators to tangible evidence. There is, of course, a price for excluding evidence, but the Fifth Amendment is worth a price, and in the absence of a very good reason, the logic of *Miranda* should be followed: a *Miranda* violation raises a presumption of coercion, and the Fifth Amendment privilege against compelled self-incrimination extends to the exclusion of derivative evidence. That should be the end of this case.

There is no way to read this case except as an unjustifiable invitation to law enforcement officers to flout *Miranda* when there may be physical evidence to be gained. The incentive is an odd one, coming from the Court on the same day it decides *Missouri v. Seibert*, 542 U.S. 600 (2004).

JUSTICE BREYER, dissenting.

For reasons similar to those set forth in Justice Souter's dissent and in my concurring opinion in *Missouri v. Seibert*, I would extend to this context the "fruit of the poisonous tree" approach, which I believe the Court has come close to adopting in *Seibert*. Under that approach, courts would exclude physical evidence derived from unwarned questioning unless the failure to provide *Miranda* warnings was in good faith. Because the courts below made no explicit finding as to good or bad faith, I would remand for such a determination.

Having reviewed *Michigan v. Tucker*, *Oregon v. Elstad*, *Missouri v. Seibert*, and *U.S. v. Patane*, let's return to the hypothetical at the beginning of this section involving the statements and evidence obtained following Chrissy's Crooked's arrest. As you'll recall, the prosecutor concedes that the statements Chrissy made before arriving at the police station are inadmissible because she was subjected to custodial interrogation without the benefit of the *Miranda* warnings. But the prosecutor contends that other evidence derived from the *Miranda* violation remains admissible, including: (1) Tom Truthy's testimony about Chrissy's appearance on the day of the bank robbery; (2) the monogrammed duffel bag filled with money that was found buried in the city park; and (3) the handwritten and signed confession Chrissy provided after she received *Miranda* warnings at the police station.

Tom Truthy's testimony would likely be admissible under *Michigan v. Tucker*. In *Tucker*, police discovered the identity of a third-party witness, Henderson, when they questioned Tucker without first providing the complete set of warnings required by *Miranda*. The Supreme Court held that Henderson's testimony was admissible because the police did not willfully or negligently violate *Miranda* when they questioned Tucker, and because Tucker's revelation of Henderson's identity was not actually compelled. Similarly, in the hypothetical, police discovered Tom's identity when Chrissy mentioned him as a possible alibi witness while she was being questioned without the benefit of *Miranda* warnings in the back of the police car. When interviewed by the police, however, Tom provides information that suggests Chrissy's involvement in the bank robbery, much like Henderson, whose name Tucker mentioned as a possible alibi witness, wound up providing information that suggested Tucker was guilty of rape. In the absence of any evidence that the police willfully or negligently withheld *Miranda* warnings, or that Chrissy's comments were actually compelled when she was questioned in the back of the police car, Tom Truthy's testimony should be admissible.

The monogrammed duffel bag filled with money would likely be admissible under *U.S. v. Patane*. In *Patane*, police located a gun when they questioned Patane after failing to provide the full set of *Miranda* warnings. The Supreme Court held that physical evidence stemming from a voluntary statement given after a *Miranda* violation was not "tainted fruit" and remained admissible at trial. Similarly, in the hypothetical, the police discovered the duffel bag when Chrissy, prior to receiving the *Miranda* warnings, revealed its location during questioning in the police car. In the absence of any evidence that Chrissy's disclosure of the location of the duffel bag was actually coerced or involuntary, the duffel bag should be admissible.

The admissibility of Chrissy's handwritten and signed confession—provided in the police station *after* she received *Miranda* warnings—is a much closer call. The prosecutor would argue that the issue is governed by *Oregon v. Elstad*, in which the Court rejected the notion that Elstad's stationhouse confession was inadmissible "tainted fruit" of the unwarned statement made inside his home. The prosecution would contend that the failure to administer *Miranda* warnings prior to questioning Chrissy in the police car was an inadvertent oversight that was corrected by the full set of warnings given at the station; that the police employed no coercive or improper tactics in questioning Chrissy; and that Chrissy's willingness to provide a written confession after receiving *Miranda* warnings shows that the confession was made voluntarily.

Chrissy's defense attorney would argue that the admissibility of the stationhouse confession is governed by *Missouri v. Seibert*, in which the Court held that a confession was inadmissible—even though it was obtained following the administration of *Miranda* warnings—because the police rendered the warnings confusing and ineffective by withholding them until after Seibert had already made incriminating statements. Chrissy's attorney would maintain that the failure to administer *Miranda* warnings inside the police car was deliberate; that the stationhouse interrogation was essentially an extension of the police car interrogation; and the stationhouse administration of *Miranda* warnings was insufficient to cure the earlier *Miranda* violation because Chrissy was never told that her earlier statements were inadmissible.

The conflicting arguments of the prosecutor and defense attorney nicely frame two important questions that determine the admissibility of Chrissy's written confession. First, was the failure to administer *Miranda* warnings prior to the questioning inside the police car a simple mistake or oversight similar to the one in *Oregon v. Elstad*, or did the police deliberately withhold the *Miranda* warnings as an interrogation tactic similar to the one described in *Missouri v. Seibert*? And second, was the police station interrogation sufficiently distinct in time, place, and circumstance from the earlier questioning in the police car such that the stationhouse administration of *Miranda* warnings was sufficient to cure the earlier violation and render the warnings effective in informing Chrissy that she still had a choice about whether to confess?

The hypothetical itself doesn't really provide any facts that would help to answer the first question and determine whether the failure to administer *Miranda* warnings in the police car was a mistake or a calculated interrogation tactic. And with respect to the second question, the facts point in different directions. On the one hand, the stationhouse interrogation could be viewed as a mere extension of the police car questioning since the same two officers were involved, they alluded to Chrissy's previous remarks by praising her for a "telling us what we need to know," and they never sought to cure the original *Miranda* violation by explaining to Chrissy that her remarks in the police car were inadmissible. On the other hand, the stationhouse interrogation could be viewed as separate and distinct since it took place in a different location following administration of the *Miranda* warnings, Chrissy indicated that she understood her rights when she received the warnings, and the officer's suggestion that Chrissy "make it all official by writing it up" could be interpreted to mean that Chrissy's prior confession was unofficial, off-the-record, and inadmissible, curing the earlier *Miranda* violation.

The admissibility of Chrissy's written confession will ultimately depend on the judge's view of the critical facts. If the prosecutor can persuade the judge that the facts and circumstances are analogous to those in *Oregon v. Elstad*, the written confession would likely be admissible. But if the defense attorney can convince the judge that the facts and circumstances are more closely akin to *Missouri v. Seibert*, Chrissy's written confession would likely be deemed inadmissible.

The "Fruits" of a *Miranda* Violation

1.   Any statements made by a suspect during custodial interrogation are presumed compelled and are inadmissible if the prosecution fails to demonstrate that the suspect received and waived his rights under *Miranda*. But other evidence that is "fruit" of the *Miranda* violation may be admissible if the *Miranda* violation was not deliberate, and if the suspect's statement was voluntarily given and not actually compelled.

2.   Testimony from a third-party witness whose identity is discovered as a result of a *Miranda* violation is admissible if the police did not willfully or negligently violate *Miranda*, and if the suspect's disclosure of the witness' identity was voluntary and not actually compelled.

3.   Physical evidence discovered as a result of a suspect's voluntary statement following a *Miranda* violation is admissible. If the suspect's statement is actually coerced, however, any physical "fruit" of the statement will be inadmissible as well.

4.   When police obtain a confession following a *Miranda* violation and then obtain a second confession after administration of the *Miranda* warnings, the first confession is inadmissible, but the admissibility of the second confession depends on a number of factors.

   a.   Was either the first or second confession coerced, or were both given voluntarily?

   b.   Was the failure to administer *Miranda* warnings prior to the first confession a "good-faith" mistake or oversight, or was it a deliberate interrogation tactic designed to circumvent *Miranda*?

   c.   Taking into account any changes in time, place, circumstances, and the content of the communications between the suspect and the police during the first and second interrogations, would a reasonable person in the suspect's shoes perceive the second interrogation as a continuation of the first, or as a separate and distinct experience in which the *Miranda* warnings effectively informed him that he still had a choice about whether to confess?

d.   Did the police employ any curative measures before the second confession to ensure that a reasonable person in the suspect's situation would understand the import and effect of the *Miranda* warning and of the *Miranda* waiver? Such curative measures might include a substantial break in time and circumstances between the first confession and the *Miranda* warning, or an additional warning that explains the likely inadmissibility of the first confession.

D. EXCEPTIONS TO *MIRANDA*

There are certain circumstances in which a suspect's incriminating statements given during custodial interrogation may be introduced into evidence despite a failure on the part of the police to properly administer the *Miranda* warnings. These exceptions to *Miranda* fall into three categories: statements made during questioning designed to address a threat to public safety, answers provided in response to routine booking questions, and statements that are being used for purposes of impeachment.

1. THE PUBLIC SAFETY EXCEPTION

In *New York v. Quarles*, the Supreme Court created a public safety exception to *Miranda*, holding that a statement given by a suspect subjected to custodial interrogation prior to administration of the *Miranda* warnings could be admitted into evidence because the questioning was reasonably prompted by a concern for public safety.

NEW YORK V. QUARLES
467 U.S. 649 (1984)

JUSTICE REHNQUIST delivered the opinion of the Court.

Respondent Benjamin Quarles was charged in the New York trial court with criminal possession of a weapon. The trial court suppressed the gun in question, and a statement made by respondent, because the statement was obtained by police before they read respondent his "*Miranda* rights." That ruling was affirmed on appeal through the New York Court of Appeals. We granted certiorari, and we now reverse. We conclude that under the circumstances involved in this case, overriding considerations of public safety justify the officer's failure to provide *Miranda* warnings before he asked questions devoted to locating the abandoned weapon.

On September 11, 1980, at approximately 12:30 a.m., Officer Frank Kraft and Officer Sal Scarring were on road patrol in Queens, N.Y., when a young woman approached their car. She told them that she had just been raped by a black male, approximately six feet tall, who was wearing a black jacket with the name "Big Ben" printed in yellow letters on the back. She told the officers that the man had just entered an A & P supermarket located nearby and that the man was carrying a gun.

The officers drove the woman to the supermarket, and Officer Kraft entered the store while Officer Scarring radioed for assistance. Officer Kraft quickly spotted respondent, who matched the description given by the woman, approaching a checkout counter. Apparently upon seeing the officer, respondent turned and ran toward the rear of the store, and Officer Kraft pursued him with a drawn gun. When respondent turned the corner at the end of an aisle, Officer Kraft lost sight of him for several seconds, and upon regaining sight of respondent, ordered him to stop and put his hands over his head.

Although more than three other officers had arrived on the scene by that time, Officer Kraft was the first to reach respondent. He frisked him and discovered that he was wearing a shoulder holster which was then empty. After handcuffing him, Officer Kraft asked him where the gun was. Respondent nodded in the direction of some empty cartons and responded, "the gun is over there." Officer Kraft thereafter retrieved a loaded .38-caliber revolver from one of the cartons, formally placed respondent under arrest, and read him his *Miranda* rights from a printed card. Respondent indicated that he would be willing to answer questions without an attorney present. Officer Kraft then asked respondent if he owned the gun and where he had purchased it. Respondent answered that he did own it and that he had purchased it in Miami, Fla.

In the subsequent prosecution of respondent for criminal possession of a weapon, the judge excluded the statement, "the gun is over there," and the gun because the officer had not given respondent the warnings required by our decision in *Miranda v. Arizona*, 384 U.S. 436 (1966), before asking him where the gun was located. The judge excluded the other statements about respondent's ownership of the gun and the place of purchase, as evidence tainted by the prior *Miranda* violation.

The Court of Appeals granted leave to appeal and affirmed by a 4–3 vote. It concluded that respondent was in "custody" within the meaning of *Miranda* during all questioning and rejected the State's argument that the exigencies of the situation justified Officer Kraft's failure to read respondent his *Miranda* rights until after he had located the gun. The court declined to recognize an exigency exception to the usual requirements of *Miranda* because it found no indication from Officer Kraft's testimony at the suppression hearing that his subjective motivation in asking the question was to protect his own safety or the safety of the public. For the reasons which follow, we believe that this case presents a situation where concern for public safety must be paramount to adherence to the literal language of the prophylactic rules enunciated in *Miranda*.

In this case we have before us no claim that respondent's statements were actually compelled by police conduct which overcame his will to resist. Thus the only issue before us is whether Officer Kraft was justified in failing to make available to respondent the procedural safeguards associated with the privilege against compulsory self-incrimination since *Miranda*.[5]

The New York Court of Appeals was undoubtedly correct in deciding that the facts of this case come within the ambit of the *Miranda* decision as we have subsequently interpreted it. We agree that respondent was in police custody because we have noted that the ultimate inquiry is simply whether there is a "formal arrest or restraint on freedom of movement" of the degree associated with a formal arrest. Here Quarles was surrounded by at least four police officers and was handcuffed when the questioning at issue took place. As the New York Court of Appeals observed, there was nothing to suggest that any of the officers were any longer concerned for their own physical safety. The New York Court of Appeals' majority declined to express an opinion as to whether there might be an exception to the *Miranda* rule if the police had been acting to protect the public, because the lower courts in New York had made no factual determination that the police had acted with that motive.

We hold that on these facts there is a "public safety" exception to the requirement that *Miranda* warnings be given before a suspect's answers may be admitted into evidence, and that the availability of that exception does not depend upon the motivation of the individual officers involved. In a kaleidoscopic situation such as the one confronting these officers, where spontaneity rather than adherence to a police manual is necessarily the order of the day, the application of the exception which we recognize today should not be made to depend on *post hoc* findings at a suppression hearing concerning the subjective motivation of the arresting officer. Undoubtedly most police officers, if placed in Officer Kraft's position, would act out of a host of different, instinctive, and largely unverifiable motives—their own safety, the safety of others, and perhaps as well the desire to obtain incriminating evidence from the suspect.

---

[5] The dissent curiously takes us to task for "endors[ing] the introduction of coerced self-incriminating statements in criminal prosecutions," and for "sanction[ing] *sub silentio* criminal prosecutions based on compelled self-incriminating statements." Of course our decision today does nothing of the kind. As the *Miranda* Court itself recognized, the failure to provide *Miranda* warnings in and of itself does not render a confession involuntary, and respondent is certainly free on remand to argue that his statement was coerced under traditional due process standards. Today we merely reject the only argument that respondent has raised to support the exclusion of his statement, that the statement must be presumed compelled because of Officer Kraft's failure to read him his *Miranda* warnings.

Whatever the motivation of individual officers in such a situation, we do not believe that the doctrinal underpinnings of *Miranda* require that it be applied in all its rigor to a situation in which police officers ask questions reasonably prompted by a concern for the public safety. The *Miranda* decision was based in large part on this Court's view that the warnings which it required police to give to suspects in custody would reduce the likelihood that the suspects would fall victim to constitutionally impermissible practices of police interrogation in the presumptively coercive environment of the station house. The dissenters warned that the requirement of *Miranda* warnings would have the effect of decreasing the number of suspects who respond to police questioning. The *Miranda* majority, however, apparently felt that whatever the cost to society in terms of fewer convictions of guilty suspects, that cost would simply have to be borne in the interest of enlarged protection for the Fifth Amendment privilege.

The police in this case, in the very act of apprehending a suspect, were confronted with the immediate necessity of ascertaining the whereabouts of a gun which they had every reason to believe the suspect had just removed from his empty holster and discarded in the supermarket. So long as the gun was concealed somewhere in the supermarket, with its actual whereabouts unknown, it obviously posed more than one danger to the public safety: an accomplice might make use of it, a customer or employee might later come upon it.

In such a situation, if the police are required to recite the familiar *Miranda* warnings before asking the whereabouts of the gun, suspects in Quarles' position might well be deterred from responding. Procedural safeguards which deter a suspect from responding were deemed acceptable in *Miranda* in order to protect the Fifth Amendment privilege; when the primary social cost of those added protections is the possibility of fewer convictions, the *Miranda* majority was willing to bear that cost. Here, had *Miranda* warnings deterred Quarles from responding to Officer Kraft's question about the whereabouts of the gun, the cost would have been something more than merely the failure to obtain evidence useful in convicting Quarles. Officer Kraft needed an answer to his question not simply to make his case against Quarles but to insure that further danger to the public did not result from the concealment of the gun in a public area.

We conclude that the need for answers to questions in a situation posing a threat to the public safety outweighs the need for the prophylactic rule protecting the Fifth Amendment's privilege against self-incrimination. We decline to place officers such as Officer Kraft in the untenable position of having to consider, often in a matter of seconds, whether it best serves society for them to ask the necessary questions without the *Miranda* warnings and render whatever probative evidence they uncover inadmissible, or for them to give the warnings in order to preserve the admissibility of evidence they might uncover but possibly damage or destroy their ability to obtain that evidence and neutralize the volatile situation confronting them.[7]

In recognizing a narrow exception to the *Miranda* rule in this case, we acknowledge that to some degree we lessen the desirable clarity of that rule. At least in part in order to preserve its clarity, we have over the years refused to sanction attempts to expand our *Miranda* holding. But as we have pointed out, we believe that the exception which we recognize today lessens the necessity of that on-the-scene balancing process. The exception will not be difficult for police officers to apply because in each case it will be circumscribed by the exigency which justifies it. We think police officers can and will distinguish almost instinctively between questions necessary to secure their own safety or the safety of the public and questions designed solely to elicit testimonial evidence from a suspect.

The facts of this case clearly demonstrate that distinction and an officer's ability to recognize it. Officer Kraft asked only the question necessary to locate the missing gun before advising respondent of his rights. It was only after securing the loaded revolver and giving the warnings that he continued with investigatory questions about the ownership and place of purchase of the gun. The exception which we recognize today, far from complicating the thought processes and the on-the-scene judgments of police officers, will simply free them to follow their legitimate instincts when confronting situations presenting a danger to the public safety.

We hold that the Court of Appeals in this case erred in excluding the statement, "the gun is over there," and the gun because of the officer's failure to read respondent his *Miranda* rights before attempting to locate the weapon. Accordingly we hold that it also erred in excluding the subsequent statements as illegal fruits of a *Miranda* violation.

JUSTICE O'CONNOR, concurring in the judgment in part and dissenting in part.

Were the Court writing from a clean slate, I could agree with its holding. But *Miranda* is now the law and, in my view, the Court has not provided sufficient justification for departing from it or for blurring its now clear strictures. Accordingly, I would require suppression of the

---

[7]   The dissent argues that a public safety exception to *Miranda* is unnecessary because in every case an officer can simply ask the necessary questions to protect himself or the public, and then the prosecution can decline to introduce any incriminating responses at a subsequent trial. But absent actual coercion by the officer, there is no constitutional imperative requiring the exclusion of the evidence that results from police inquiry of this kind; and we do not believe that the doctrinal underpinnings of *Miranda* require us to exclude the evidence, thus penalizing officers for asking the very questions which are the most crucial to their efforts to protect themselves and the public.

initial statement taken from respondent in this case. On the other hand, nothing in *Miranda* or the privilege itself requires exclusion of nontestimonial evidence derived from informal custodial interrogation, and I therefore agree with the Court that admission of the gun in evidence is proper.

In my view, a "public safety" exception unnecessarily blurs the edges of the clear line heretofore established and makes *Miranda*'s requirements more difficult to understand. In some cases, police will benefit because a reviewing court will find that an exigency excused their failure to administer the required warnings. But in other cases, police will suffer because, though they thought an exigency excused their noncompliance, a reviewing court will view the "objective" circumstances differently and require exclusion of admissions thereby obtained. The end result will be a finespun new doctrine on public safety exigencies incident to custodial interrogation, complete with the hair-splitting distinctions that currently plague our Fourth Amendment jurisprudence.

The justification the Court provides for upsetting the equilibrium that has finally been achieved—that police cannot and should not balance considerations of public safety against the individual's interest in avoiding compulsory testimonial self-incrimination—really misses the critical question to be decided. *Miranda* has never been read to prohibit the police from asking questions to secure the public safety. Rather, the critical question *Miranda* addresses is who shall bear the cost of securing the public safety when such questions are asked and answered: the defendant or the State. *Miranda*, for better or worse, found the resolution of that question implicit in the prohibition against compulsory self-incrimination and placed the burden on the State. When police ask custodial questions without administering the required warnings, *Miranda* quite clearly requires that the answers received be presumed compelled and that they be excluded from evidence at trial.

The Court concedes, as it must, both that respondent was in "custody" and subject to "interrogation" and that his statement "the gun is over there" was compelled within the meaning of our precedent. In my view, since there is nothing about an exigency that makes custodial interrogation any less compelling, a principled application of *Miranda* requires that respondent's statement be suppressed.

The court below assumed, without discussion, that the privilege against self-incrimination required that the gun derived from respondent's statement also be suppressed, whether or not the State could independently link it to him. That conclusion was, in my view, incorrect.

The gun respondent was compelled to supply is clearly evidence of the "real or physical" sort. What makes the question of its admissibility difficult is the fact that, in asking respondent to produce the gun, the police also "compelled" him, in the *Miranda* sense, to create an incriminating testimonial response. In other words, the case is problematic because police compelled respondent not only to provide the gun but also to admit that he knew where it was and that it was his.

To be sure, admission of nontestimonial evidence secured through informal custodial interrogation will reduce the incentives to enforce the *Miranda* code. But that fact simply begs the question of how much enforcement is appropriate. There are some situations, as the Court's struggle to accommodate a "public safety" exception demonstrates, in which the societal cost of administering the *Miranda* warnings is very high indeed. The *Miranda* decision quite practically does not express any societal interest in having those warnings administered for their own sake. Rather, the warnings and waiver are only required to ensure that "testimony" used against the accused at trial is voluntarily given. Therefore, if the testimonial aspects of the accused's custodial communications are suppressed, the failure to administer the *Miranda* warnings should cease to be of concern.

JUSTICE MARSHALL, with whom JUSTICE BRENNAN and JUSTICE STEVENS join, dissenting.

The majority's entire analysis rests on the factual assumption that the public was at risk during Quarles' interrogation. This assumption is completely in conflict with the facts as found by New York's highest court. Before the interrogation began, Quarles had been "reduced to a condition of physical powerlessness." Contrary to the majority's speculations, Quarles was not believed to have, nor did he in fact have, an accomplice to come to his rescue. When the questioning began, the arresting officers were sufficiently confident of their safety to put away their guns. As Officer Kraft acknowledged at the suppression hearing, "the situation was under control." Based on Officer Kraft's own testimony, the New York Court of Appeals found: "Nothing suggests that any of the officers was by that time concerned for his own physical safety." The Court of Appeals also determined that there was no evidence that the interrogation was prompted by the arresting officers' concern for the public's safety.

The majority attempts to slip away from these unambiguous findings of New York's highest court by proposing that danger be measured by objective facts rather than the subjective intentions of arresting officers. Though clever, this ploy was anticipated by the New York Court of Appeals: "[T]here is no evidence in the record before us that there were exigent circumstances posing a risk to the public safety."

The New York court's conclusion that neither Quarles nor his missing gun posed a threat to the public's safety is amply supported by the evidence presented at the suppression hearing. Again contrary to the majority's intimations, no customers or employees were wandering about the store in danger of coming across Quarles' discarded weapon. Although the supermarket was open to the public, Quarles' arrest took place during the middle of the night when the store was apparently deserted except for the clerks at the checkout counter. The police could easily have cordoned off the store and searched for the missing gun. Had they done so, they would have found the gun forthwith. The police were well aware that Quarles had discarded his weapon somewhere near the scene of the arrest.

The majority contends that the law, as it currently stands, places police officers in a dilemma whenever they interrogate a suspect who appears to know of some threat to the public's safety. If the police interrogate the suspect without advising him of his rights, the suspect may reveal information that the authorities can use to defuse the threat, but the suspect's statements will be inadmissible at trial. If, on the other hand, the police advise the suspect of his rights, the suspect may be deterred from responding to the police's questions, and the risk to the public may continue unabated. According to the majority, the police must now choose between establishing the suspect's guilt and safeguarding the public from danger.

The majority proposes to eliminate this dilemma by creating an exception to *Miranda v. Arizona* for custodial interrogations concerning matters of public safety. Under the majority's exception, police would be permitted to interrogate suspects about such matters before the suspects have been advised of their constitutional rights. Without being "deterred" by the knowledge that they have a constitutional right not to respond, these suspects will be likely to answer the questions. Should the answers also be incriminating, the State would be free to introduce them as evidence in a criminal prosecution. I find in this reasoning an unwise and unprincipled departure from our Fifth Amendment precedents.

Before today's opinion, the procedures established in *Miranda v. Arizona* had the virtue of informing police and prosecutors with specificity as to what they may do in conducting custodial interrogation, and of informing courts under what circumstances statements obtained during such interrogation are not admissible. In a chimerical quest for public safety, the majority has abandoned the rule that brought 18 years of doctrinal tranquility to the field of custodial interrogations. As the majority candidly concedes, a public-safety exception destroys forever the clarity of *Miranda* for both law enforcement officers and members of the judiciary. The Court's candor cannot mask what a serious loss the administration of justice has incurred.

This case is illustrative of the chaos the "public-safety" exception will unleash. The circumstances of Quarles' arrest have never been in dispute. After the benefit of briefing and oral argument, the New York Court of Appeals, as previously noted, concluded that there was "no evidence in the record before us that there were exigent circumstances posing a risk to the public safety." Upon reviewing the same facts and hearing the same arguments, a majority of this Court has come to precisely the opposite conclusion: "So long as the gun was concealed somewhere in the supermarket, with its actual whereabouts unknown, it obviously posed more than one danger to the public safety."

If after plenary review two appellate courts so fundamentally differ over the threat to public safety presented by the simple and uncontested facts of this case, one must seriously question how law enforcement officers will respond to the majority's new rule in the confusion and haste of the real world.

Though unfortunate, the difficulty of administering the "public-safety" exception is not the most profound flaw in the majority's decision. The majority has lost sight of the fact that *Miranda v. Arizona* and our earlier custodial-interrogation cases all implemented a constitutional privilege against self-incrimination. The rules established in these cases were designed to protect criminal defendants against prosecutions based on coerced self-incriminating statements. The majority today turns its back on these constitutional considerations, and invites the government to prosecute through the use of what necessarily are coerced statements.

In its cost-benefit analysis, the Court's strongest argument in favor of a "public-safety" exception to *Miranda* is that the police would be better able to protect the public's safety if they were not always required to give suspects their *Miranda* warnings. The crux of this argument is that, by deliberately withholding *Miranda* warnings, the police can get information out of suspects who would refuse to respond to police questioning were they advised of their constitutional rights. The "public-safety" exception is efficacious precisely because it permits police officers to coerce criminal defendants into making involuntary statements.

Until today, coerced confessions were simply inadmissible in criminal prosecutions. The "public-safety" exception departs from this principle by expressly inviting police officers to coerce defendants into making incriminating statements, and then permitting prosecutors to introduce those statements at trial. Though the majority's opinion is cloaked in the beguiling language of utilitarianism, the Court has sanctioned *sub silentio* criminal prosecutions based on compelled self-incriminating statements. I find this result in direct conflict with the Fifth Amendment's dictate that "no person . . . shall be compelled in any criminal case to be a witness against himself."

The irony of the majority's decision is that the public's safety can be perfectly well protected without abridging the Fifth Amendment. If a bomb is about to explode or the public is otherwise imminently imperiled, the police are free to interrogate suspects without advising them of their constitutional rights. Such unconsented questioning may take place not only when police officers act on instinct but also when higher faculties lead them to believe that advising a suspect of his constitutional rights might decrease the likelihood that the suspect would reveal life-saving information. If trickery is necessary to protect the public, then the police may trick a suspect into confessing. While the Fourteenth Amendment sets limits on such behavior, nothing in the Fifth Amendment or our decision in *Miranda v. Arizona* proscribes this sort of emergency questioning. All the Fifth Amendment forbids is the introduction of coerced statements at trial.

To a limited degree, the majority is correct that there is a cost associated with the Fifth Amendment's ban on introducing coerced self-incriminating statements at trial. Without a "public-safety" exception, there would be occasions when a defendant incriminated himself by revealing a threat to the public, and the State was unable to prosecute because the defendant retracted his statement after consulting with counsel and the police cannot find independent proof of guilt. Such occasions would not, however, be common. The prosecution does not always lose the use of incriminating information revealed in these situations. After consulting with counsel, a suspect may well volunteer to repeat his statement in hopes of gaining a favorable plea bargain or more lenient sentence. The majority thus overstates its case when it suggests that a police officer must necessarily choose between public safety and admissibility. But however frequently or infrequently such cases arise, their regularity is irrelevant. The Fifth Amendment prohibits compelled self-incrimination.

Having determined that the Fifth Amendment renders inadmissible Quarles' response to Officer Kraft's questioning, I have no doubt that our precedents require that the gun discovered as a direct result of Quarles' statement must be presumed inadmissible as well. The gun was the direct product of a coercive custodial interrogation.

The U.S. Justice Department has invoked the public safety exception to justify the questioning of terrorism suspects prior to the administration of *Miranda* warnings. On December 25, 2009, a Nigerian named Umar Farouk Abdulmutallab tried to blow up a Detroit-bound airplane by detonating an explosive device hidden in his underwear. The plane landed safely, and Abdulmutallab was met by federal law enforcement officers and transported to a hospital for treatment of his burns. After Abdulmutallab was treated and received pain medication, an FBI agent questioned him for 50 minutes without first advising him of his *Miranda* rights. Each question posed by the FBI agent was designed to identify any other potential attackers and to prevent further attacks. Abdulmutallab answered the agent's questions, providing numerous incriminating statements that the government later sought to introduce against him at trial.

On September 16, 2011, in *U.S. v. Abdulmutallab*, 2011 WL 4345243, Judge Nancy G. Edmunds of the U.S. District Court for the Eastern District of Michigan denied Abdulmutallab's motion to suppress the statements made at the hospital. Judge Edmonds held that the statements were made voluntarily, and that the circumstances at the time of the questioning fell within the public safety exception to *Miranda* recognized in *New York v. Quarles*.

In the aftermath of Abdulmutallab's attempted attack, the FBI issued an internal memorandum instructing its agents to interrogate suspected terrorists about immediate threats to public safety without first advising them of their rights under *Miranda* to remain silent and to have an attorney present.[c] FBI agents later followed that directive in questioning Dzhokhar Tsarnaev, one of the two brothers suspected in the bombing of the Boston Marathon on April 15, 2013. When Tsarnaev awoke in the hospital two days after his capture, specially trained FBI agents questioned him without first providing *Miranda* warnings. Tsarnaev apparently admitted his and his brother's role in the bombing, explained their motivations, and said that they had acted alone and were not connected to a larger terrorist network.[d]

The Public Safety Exception to *Miranda*

1.   Statements made by a suspect during custodial interrogation before administration of the *Miranda* warnings are admissible if the statements were not actually compelled and the police questioning was reasonably prompted by a concern for public safety.

2.   The public safety exception is limited by the exigency that justifies it, and allows the introduction into evidence only of those statements made in response to questions posed for the safety of the public or other officers. The exception does not permit the introduction into evidence of statements made in response to questions unrelated to public safety or designed solely to elicit testimonial evidence from a suspect.

3.   The availability of the public safety exception does not depend on the subjective motivations of the individual officers involved.

---

   c   *See* Charlie Savage, *Delayed Miranda Warning Ordered for Terror Suspects*, NEW YORK TIMES, March 24, 2011, available at http://www.nytimes.com/2011/03/25/us/25miranda.html.

   d   *See* Charlie Savage, *Debate Over Delaying of Miranda Warning*, NEW YORK TIMES, April 20, 2013, available at http://www.nytimes.com/2013/04/21/us/a-debate-over-delaying-suspects-miranda-rights.html; Eric Schmitt, Mark Mazzetti, Michael S. Schmidt, and Scott Shane, *Boston Plotters Said to Initially Target July 4 for Attack*, NEW YORK TIMES, May 2, 2013, available at http://www.nytimes.com/2013/05/03/us/Boston-bombing-suspects-planned-july-fourth-attack.html.

2. THE ROUTINE BOOKING QUESTION EXCEPTION

In *Pennsylvania v. Muniz*, the Supreme Court held that incriminating statements given in response to routine booking questions at jail are admissible even if the police have not yet administered the *Miranda* warnings.

PENNSYLVANIA V. MUNIZ
496 U.S. 583 (1990)

Inocencio Muniz was arrested on suspicion of driving while intoxicated and was transported to a county booking center. At the booking center, Muniz was informed that his actions and voice were being recorded, but he was not advised of his *Miranda* rights. An officer asked Muniz his name, address, height, weight, eye color, date of birth, and current age. Muniz responded to each of these questions, stumbling over his address and age. Muniz's videotaped responses to the questions were admitted into evidence at his trial, and he was convicted of driving under the influence of alcohol.

The Supreme Court held that Muniz's videotaped answers were properly admitted into evidence, notwithstanding the lack of *Miranda* warnings, under a "routine booking question" exception to *Miranda*:

> We disagree with the Commonwealth's contention that [the officer's] first seven questions regarding Muniz's name, address, height, weight, eye color, date of birth, and current age do not qualify as custodial interrogation as we defined the term merely because the questions were not intended to elicit information for investigatory purposes. We agree with *amicus* United States, however, that Muniz's answers to these first seven questions are nonetheless admissible because the questions fall within a "routine booking question" exception which exempts from *Miranda*'s coverage questions to secure the "biographical data necessary to complete booking or pretrial services." The state court found that the first seven questions were "requested for record-keeping purposes only," and therefore the questions appear reasonably related to the police's administrative concerns. In this context, therefore, the first seven questions asked at the booking center fall outside the protections of *Miranda* and the answers thereto need not be suppressed.

In a footnote, the Supreme Court added that its recognition of a booking exception to *Miranda* does not mean "that any question asked during the booking process falls within that exception." The police "may not ask questions, even during booking, that are designed to elicit incriminatory admissions" without first "obtaining a waiver of the suspect's *Miranda* rights."

> ### The Routine Booking Question Exception to *Miranda*
>
> Statements made by a suspect in response to routine booking questions posed prior to the administration of *Miranda* warnings may be introduced into evidence as long as the questions are reasonably related to administrative concerns and are not designed to elicit incriminating admissions.

3. THE IMPEACHMENT EXCEPTION

In *Harris v. New York*, the Supreme Court held that although a statement taken in violation of *Miranda* may not be introduced by the prosecution to prove the defendant's guilt, the statement may be used to impeach the defendant's credibility if she takes the stand in her own defense and provides testimony inconsistent with the prior statement.

HARRIS V. NEW YORK
401 U.S. 222 (1971)

CHIEF JUSTICE BURGER delivered the opinion of the Court.

We granted the writ in this case to consider petitioner's claim that a statement made by him to police under circumstances rendering it inadmissible to establish the prosecution's case in chief under *Miranda v. Arizona*, 384 U.S. 436 (1966), may not be used to impeach his credibility.

The State of New York charged petitioner in a two-count indictment with twice selling heroin to an undercover police officer. At a subsequent jury trial the officer was the State's chief witness, and he testified as to details of the two sales. A second officer verified collateral details of the sales, and a third offered testimony about the chemical analysis of the heroin.

Petitioner took the stand in his own defense. He admitted knowing the undercover police officer but denied a sale on January 4, 1966. He admitted making a sale of contents of a glassine bag to the officer on January 6 but claimed it was baking powder and part of a scheme to defraud the purchaser.

On cross-examination petitioner was asked seriatim whether he had made specified statements to the police immediately following his arrest on January 7—statements that partially contradicted petitioner's direct testimony at trial. In response to the cross-examination, petitioner testified that he could not remember virtually any of the questions or answers recited by the prosecutor. At the request of petitioner's counsel, the written statement from which the prosecutor had read questions and answers in his impeaching process was placed in the record for possible use on appeal; the statement was not shown to the jury.

The trial judge instructed the jury that the statements attributed to petitioner by the prosecution could be considered only in passing on petitioner's credibility and not as evidence of guilt. In closing summations, both counsel argued the substance of the impeaching statements. The jury then found petitioner guilty on the second count of the indictment. The New York Court of Appeals affirmed.

At trial the prosecution made no effort in its case in chief to use the statements allegedly made by petitioner, conceding that they were inadmissible under *Miranda v. Arizona.* The transcript of the interrogation used in the impeachment, but not given to the jury, shows that no warning of a right to appointed counsel was given before questions were put to petitioner when he was taken into custody. Petitioner makes no claim that the statements made to the police were coerced or involuntary.

Some comments in the *Miranda* opinion can indeed be read as indicating a bar to use of an uncounseled statement for any purpose, but discussion of that issue was not at all necessary to the Court's holding and cannot be regarded as controlling. *Miranda* barred the prosecution from making its case with statements of an accused made while in custody prior to having or effectively waiving counsel. It does not follow from *Miranda* that evidence inadmissible against an accused in the prosecution's case in chief is barred for all purposes, provided of course that the trustworthiness of the evidence satisfies legal standards.

Petitioner's testimony in his own behalf concerning the events of January 7 contrasted sharply with what he told the police shortly after his arrest. The impeachment process here undoubtedly provided valuable aid to the jury in assessing petitioner's credibility, and the benefits of this process should not be lost, in our view, because of the speculative possibility that impermissible police conduct will be encouraged thereby. Assuming that the exclusionary rule has a deterrent effect on proscribed police conduct, sufficient deterrence flows when the evidence in question is made unavailable to the prosecution in its case in chief.

Every criminal defendant is privileged to testify in his own defense, or to refuse to do so. But that privilege cannot be construed to include the right to commit perjury. Having voluntarily taken the stand, petitioner was under an obligation to speak truthfully and accurately, and the prosecution here did no more than utilize the traditional truth-testing devices of the adversary process. Had inconsistent statements been made by the accused to some third person, it could hardly be contended that the conflict could not be laid before the jury by way of cross-examination and impeachment.

The shield provided by *Miranda* cannot be perverted into a license to use perjury by way of a defense, free from the risk of confrontation with prior inconsistent utterances. We hold, therefore, that petitioner's credibility was appropriately impeached by use of his earlier conflicting statements.

JUSTICE BRENNAN, with whom JUSTICE DOUGLAS and JUSTICE MARSHALL, join, dissenting.

The prosecution's use of the tainted statement cuts down on the privilege [against self-incrimination] by making its assertion costly. Thus, the accused is denied an unfettered choice when the decision whether to take the stand is burdened by the risk that an illegally obtained prior statement may be introduced to impeach his direct testimony denying complicity in the crime charged against him

To the extent that *Miranda* was aimed at deterring police practices in disregard of the Constitution, I fear that today's holding will seriously undermine the achievement of that objective. The Court today tells the police that they may freely interrogate an accused incommunicado and without counsel and know that although any statement they obtain in violation of *Miranda* cannot be used on the State's direct case, it may be introduced if the defendant has the temerity to testify in his own defense. This goes far toward undoing much of the progress made in conforming police methods to the Constitution.

As the majority opinion in *Harris v. New York* notes, when a statement is admitted for purposes of impeachment, the judge typically instructs the jury to consider the statement only in passing upon the defendant's credibility as a witness and not as evidence of guilt. Do you think most jurors are able to follow such an instruction? If the statement contradicts the defendant's testimony and makes her seem less credible as a witness, wouldn't *you* be more inclined to think that she's guilty of the crime with which she is charged?

The Impeachment Exception to *Miranda*

Although a statement taken in violation of *Miranda* may not be introduced in the prosecution's case in chief to prove the defendant's guilt, the statement—if voluntarily given and not actually compelled—may be used to impeach the defendant's credibility if she takes the stand in her own defense and provides testimony inconsistent with the prior statement.

E. WAIVER OF *MIRANDA* RIGHTS

While *Miranda* required police to inform a suspect, prior to any custodial interrogation, of his constitutional rights to remain silent and to consult an attorney, the Court also made it clear that an individual could waive those rights. Indeed, this has long been viewed as one of the major weaknesses of the *Miranda* decision: How can a waiver ever be valid if, as the *Miranda* majority notes, custodial interrogation is intimidating, psychologically coercive, and creates "inherently compelling pressures" to confess? *Miranda* answers this criticism by suggesting that the required warnings "dispel the compulsion inherent in custodial surroundings," providing some assurance that any statement obtained from a suspect is the "product of his free choice."

When *Miranda* was announced, critics feared that the required warnings would dramatically reduce the number of confessions and frustrate the efforts of law enforcement. While that may be true in some cases, several studies have shown that most criminal suspects subjected to custodial interrogation in the aftermath of *Miranda* do, in fact, waive their rights and speak to the police without an attorney.[e] This may be due, in part, to the variety of techniques police have developed to induce suspects to answer questions.[f]

In reviewing the Supreme Court's pronouncements with regard to waivers, be sure to take note of the general guidelines used to determine the validity of *Miranda* waivers, along with the specific rules governing the invocation and waiver of the right to remain silent and the right to counsel.

1.   GENERAL GUIDELINES FOR *MIRANDA* WAIVERS

The Supreme Court in *Miranda* recognized that an individual may waive the right to remain silent and the right to counsel "provided the waiver is made voluntarily, knowingly and intelligently." Later in its opinion, the Court noted that "a heavy burden rests on the government to demonstrate that the defendant knowingly and intelligently waived his privilege against self-incrimination and his right to retained or appointed counsel." This heavy burden was justified because the Court "has always set high standards of proof for the waiver of constitutional rights," and because "the State is responsible for establishing the isolated circumstances under which the interrogation takes place and has the only

---

[e] *See* Richard A. Leo, *Inside the Interrogation Room*, 86 JOURNAL OF CRIMINAL LAW AND CRIMINOLOGY 266, 276 (1996) (in a study of 175 interrogations where *Miranda* warnings were administered, over 78% ultimately waived their rights); Richard A. Leo, *The Impact of Miranda Revisited*, 86 JOURNAL OF CRIMINAL LAW AND CRIMINOLOGY 621, 631–632 (1996) (noting that the "general consensus" of the studies conducted in the immediate aftermath of *Miranda* was that "most criminal suspects routinely waive their constitutional rights" despite administration of the standard warnings).

[f] *See* Jan Hoffman, *Police Tactics Chipping Away at Suspects' Rights*, NEW YORK TIMES, March 29, 1998, available at http://www.nytimes.com/1998/03/29/nyregion/police-tactics-chipping-away-at-suspects-rights.html (describing techniques used by police to secure waivers of *Miranda* rights); Richard A. Leo, *The Impact of Miranda Revisited*, 86 JOURNAL OF CRIMINAL LAW AND CRIMINOLOGY 621, 660–665 (1996) (describing psychological strategies used by police to obtain waivers of *Miranda* rights); Richard A. Leo, *Inside the Interrogation Room*, 86 JOURNAL OF CRIMINAL LAW AND CRIMINOLOGY 266, 292–298 (1996) (describing various interrogation tactics and their effectiveness in producing incriminating statements).

means of making available corroborated evidence of warnings given during incommunicado interrogation."

In *Colorado v. Connelly*, 479 U.S. 157 (1986), the Supreme Court held that the government's "heavy burden" of demonstrating a waiver may be satisfied by a preponderance of the evidence: "Whenever the State bears the burden of proof in a motion to suppress a statement that the defendant claims was obtained in violation of our *Miranda* doctrine, the State need prove waiver only by a preponderance of the evidence."

In determining whether an individual has validly waived his *Miranda* rights, the Supreme Court has instructed the lower courts to examine the totality of the circumstances. In *Fare v. Michael C.*, 442 U.S. 707 (1979), a case involving interrogation of a juvenile suspect, the Court explained:

> [T]he determination whether statements obtained during custodial interrogation are admissible against the accused is to be made upon an inquiry into the totality of the circumstances surrounding the interrogation, to ascertain whether the accused in fact knowingly and voluntarily decided to forgo his rights to remain silent and to have the assistance of counsel. This totality-of-the-circumstances approach is adequate to determine whether there has been a waiver even where interrogation of juveniles is involved. The totality approach permits—indeed, it mandates— inquiry into all the circumstances surrounding the interrogation. This includes evaluation of the juvenile's age, experience, education, background, and intelligence, and into whether he has the capacity to understand the warnings given him, the nature of his Fifth Amendment rights, and the consequences of waiving those rights.

The factors cited by the Court in *Fare v. Michael C.* are relevant only to the extent they bear upon conduct by the police in eliciting incriminating statements. As you may recall from your reading in Chapter 9 of *Colorado v. Connelly*, 479 U.S. 157 (1986), the Supreme Court rejected the argument that the defendant's waiver of *Miranda* rights was invalid because he was suffering from a psychosis that interfered with his ability to make free and voluntary choices:

> The sole concern of the Fifth Amendment, on which *Miranda* was based, is governmental coercion. The voluntariness of a waiver of [the Fifth Amendment] privilege has always depended on the absence of police overreaching, not on "free choice" in any broader sense of the word.

Can a *Miranda* waiver still be regarded as voluntary, knowing, and intelligent if the police withhold certain information from the suspect? In *Moran v. Burbine*, the sister of a murder suspect hired an attorney to represent her brother, and the attorney received assurances from the police that no interrogation would occur until the following day. Without relaying any of this information to the suspect, police proceeded with the interrogation and obtained a *Miranda* waiver and a confession. Although critical of the conduct of the police, the Supreme Court found that there was no constitutional violation and concluded that the waiver was valid.

MORAN V. BURBINE
475 U.S. 412 (1986)

JUSTICE O'CONNOR delivered the opinion of the Court.

After being informed of his rights pursuant to *Miranda v. Arizona*, 384 U.S. 436 (1966), and after executing a series of written waivers, respondent confessed to the murder of a young woman. At no point during the course of the interrogation, which occurred prior to arraignment, did he request an attorney. While he was in police custody, his sister attempted to retain a lawyer to represent him. The attorney telephoned the police station and received assurances that respondent would not be questioned further until the next day. In fact, the interrogation session that yielded the inculpatory statements began later that evening. The question presented is whether either the conduct of the police or respondent's ignorance of the attorney's efforts to reach him taints the validity of the waivers and therefore requires exclusion of the confessions.

I

On the morning of March 3, 1977, Mary Jo Hickey was found unconscious in a factory parking lot in Providence, Rhode Island. Suffering from injuries to her skull apparently inflicted by a metal pipe found at the scene, she was rushed to a nearby hospital. Three weeks later, she died from her wounds.

Several months after her death, the Cranston, Rhode Island, police arrested respondent and two others in connection with a local burglary. Shortly before the arrest, Detective Ferranti of the Cranston police force had learned from a confidential informant that the man responsible for Ms. Hickey's death lived at a certain address and went by the name of "Butch." Upon discovering that respondent lived at that address and was known by that name, Detective Ferranti informed respondent of his *Miranda* rights. When respondent refused to execute a written waiver, Detective Ferranti spoke separately with the two other suspects arrested on the breaking and entering charge and obtained statements further implicating respondent in Ms. Hickey's murder. At approximately 6 p.m., Detective Ferranti telephoned the police in Providence to convey the information he had uncovered. An hour later, three officers from that department arrived at the Cranston headquarters for the purpose of questioning respondent about the murder.

That same evening, at about 7:45 p.m., respondent's sister telephoned the Public Defender's Office to obtain legal assistance for her brother. Her sole concern was the breaking and entering charge, as she was unaware that respondent was then under suspicion for murder. She asked for Richard Casparian who had been scheduled to meet with respondent earlier that afternoon to discuss another charge unrelated to either the break-in or the murder. As soon as the conversation ended, the attorney who took the call attempted to reach Mr. Casparian. When those efforts were unsuccessful, she telephoned Allegra Munson, another Assistant Public Defender, and told her about respondent's arrest and his sister's subsequent request that the office represent him.

At 8:15 p.m., Ms. Munson telephoned the Cranston police station and asked that her call be transferred to the detective division. In the words of the Supreme Court of Rhode Island, whose factual findings we treat as presumptively correct, the conversation proceeded as follows:

> A male voice responded with the word "Detectives." Ms. Munson identified herself and asked if Brian Burbine was being held; the person responded affirmatively. Ms. Munson explained to the person that Burbine was represented by attorney Casparian who was not available; she further stated that she would act as Burbine's legal counsel in the event that the police intended to place him in a lineup or question him. The unidentified person told Ms. Munson that the police would not be questioning Burbine or putting him in a lineup and that they were through with him for the night. Ms. Munson was not informed that the Providence Police were at the Cranston police station or that Burbine was a suspect in Mary's murder.

At all relevant times, respondent was unaware of his sister's efforts to retain counsel and of the fact and contents of Ms. Munson's telephone conversation.

Less than an hour later, the police brought respondent to an interrogation room and conducted the first of a series of interviews concerning the murder. Prior to each session, respondent was informed of his *Miranda* rights, and on three separate occasions he signed a written form acknowledging that he understood his right to the presence of an attorney and explicitly indicating that he "did not want an attorney called or appointed for him" before he gave a statement. Uncontradicted evidence at the suppression hearing indicated that at least twice during the course of the evening, respondent was left in a room where he had access to a telephone, which he apparently declined to use. Eventually, respondent signed three written statements fully admitting to the murder.

Prior to trial, respondent moved to suppress the statements. The court denied the motion, finding that respondent had received the

Miranda warnings and had "knowingly, intelligently, and voluntarily waived his privilege against self-incrimination and his right to counsel." Rejecting the contrary testimony of the police, the court found that Ms. Munson did telephone the detective bureau on the evening in question, but concluded that "there was no conspiracy or collusion on the part of the Cranston Police Department to secrete this defendant from his attorney." In any event, the court held, the constitutional right to request the presence of an attorney belongs solely to the defendant and may not be asserted by his lawyer. Because the evidence was clear that respondent never asked for the services of an attorney, the telephone call had no relevance to the validity of the waiver or the admissibility of the statements.

The jury found respondent guilty of murder in the first degree, and he appealed to the Supreme Court of Rhode Island. A divided court rejected his contention that the Fifth and Fourteenth Amendments to the Constitution required the suppression of the inculpatory statements and affirmed the conviction. Failure to inform respondent of Ms. Munson's efforts to represent him, the court held, did not undermine the validity of the waivers. We granted certiorari to decide whether a prearraignment confession preceded by an otherwise valid waiver must be suppressed either because the police misinformed an inquiring attorney about their plans concerning the suspect or because they failed to inform the suspect of the attorney's efforts to reach him.

II

In *Miranda v. Arizona*, the Court recognized that custodial interrogations, by their very nature, generate "compelling pressures which work to undermine the individual's will to resist and to compel him to speak where he would not otherwise do so freely." To combat this inherent compulsion, and thereby protect the Fifth Amendment privilege against self-incrimination, *Miranda* imposed on the police an obligation to follow certain procedures in their dealings with the accused.

Respondent does not dispute that the Providence police followed these procedures with precision. The record amply supports the state-court findings that the police administered the required warnings, sought to assure that respondent understood his rights, and obtained an express written waiver prior to eliciting each of the three statements. Nor does respondent contest the Rhode Island courts' determination that he at no point requested the presence of a lawyer. He contends instead that the confessions must be suppressed because the police's failure to inform him of the attorney's telephone call deprived him of information essential to his ability to knowingly waive his Fifth Amendment rights. In the alternative, he suggests that to fully protect the Fifth Amendment values served by *Miranda*, we should extend that decision to condemn the conduct of the Providence police. We address each contention in turn.

A

Echoing the standard first articulated in *Johnson v. Zerbst*, 304 U.S. 458 (1938), *Miranda* holds that "the defendant may waive effectuation" of the rights conveyed in the warnings "provided the waiver is made voluntarily, knowingly and intelligently." The inquiry has two distinct dimensions. First, the relinquishment of the right must have been voluntary in the sense that it was the product of a free and deliberate choice rather than intimidation, coercion, or deception. Second, the waiver must have been made with a full awareness of both the nature of the right being abandoned and the consequences of the decision to abandon it. Only if the "totality of the circumstances surrounding the interrogation" reveal both an uncoerced choice and the requisite level of comprehension may a court properly conclude that the *Miranda* rights have been waived.

Under this standard, we have no doubt that respondent validly waived his right to remain silent and to the presence of counsel. The voluntariness of the waiver is not at issue. As the Court of Appeals correctly acknowledged, the record is devoid of any suggestion that police resorted to physical or psychological pressure to elicit the statements. Indeed it appears that it was respondent, and not the police, who spontaneously initiated the conversation that led to the first and most damaging confession. Nor is there any question about respondent's comprehension of the full panoply of rights set out in the *Miranda* warnings and of the potential consequences of a decision to relinquish them. Nonetheless, the Court of Appeals believed that the "deliberate or reckless" conduct of the police, in particular their failure to inform respondent of the telephone call, fatally undermined the validity of the otherwise proper waiver. We find this conclusion untenable as a matter of both logic and precedent.

Events occurring outside of the presence of the suspect and entirely unknown to him surely can have no bearing on the capacity to comprehend and knowingly relinquish a constitutional right. Under the analysis of the Court of Appeals, the same defendant, armed with the same information and confronted with precisely the same police conduct, would have knowingly waived his *Miranda* rights had a lawyer not telephoned the police station to inquire about his status. Nothing in any of our waiver decisions or in our understanding of the essential components of a valid waiver requires so incongruous a result. No doubt the additional information would have been useful to respondent; perhaps even it might have affected his decision to confess. But we have never read the Constitution to require that the police supply a suspect with a flow of information to help him calibrate his self-interest in deciding whether to speak or stand by his rights. Once it is determined that a suspect's decision not to rely on his rights was uncoerced, that he at all times knew he could stand mute and request a lawyer, and that he was aware of the State's intention to use his statements to secure a conviction, the analysis is complete and the waiver is valid as a matter of law. The Court of Appeals' conclusion to the contrary was in error.

Nor do we believe that the level of the police's culpability in failing to inform respondent of the telephone call has any bearing on the validity of the waivers. In light of the state-court findings that there was no "conspiracy or collusion" on the part of the police, we have serious doubts about whether the Court of Appeals was free to conclude that their conduct constituted "deliberate or reckless irresponsibility." But whether intentional or inadvertent, the state of mind of the police is irrelevant to the question of the intelligence and voluntariness of respondent's election to abandon his rights. Although highly inappropriate, even deliberate deception of an attorney could not possibly affect a suspect's decision to waive his *Miranda* rights unless he were at least aware of the incident. Nor was the failure to inform respondent of the telephone call the kind of "trickery" that can vitiate the validity of a waiver. Granting that the "deliberate or reckless" withholding of information is objectionable as a matter of ethics, such conduct is only relevant to the constitutional validity of a waiver if it deprives a defendant of knowledge essential to his ability to understand the nature of his rights and the consequences of abandoning them. Because respondent's voluntary decision to speak was made with full awareness and comprehension of all the information *Miranda* requires the police to convey, the waivers were valid.

B

At oral argument respondent acknowledged that a constitutional rule requiring the police to inform a suspect of an attorney's efforts to reach him would represent a significant extension of our precedents. He contends, however, that the conduct of the Providence police was so inimical to the Fifth Amendment values *Miranda* seeks to protect that we should read that decision to condemn their behavior. Regardless of any issue of waiver, he urges, the Fifth Amendment requires the reversal of a conviction if the police are less than forthright in their dealings with an attorney or if they fail to tell a suspect of a lawyer's unilateral efforts to contact him. Because the proposed modification ignores the underlying purposes of the *Miranda* rules and because we think that the decision as written strikes the proper balance between society's legitimate law enforcement interests and the protection of the defendant's Fifth Amendment rights, we decline the invitation to further extend *Miranda*'s reach.

At the outset, while we share respondent's distaste for the deliberate misleading of an officer of the court, reading *Miranda* to forbid police deception of an *attorney* would cut the decision completely loose from its own explicitly stated rationale. As is now well established, the *Miranda* warnings are not themselves rights protected by the Constitution but are instead measures to insure that the suspect's right against compulsory self-incrimination is protected. Their objective is not to mold police conduct for its own sake. Nothing in the Constitution vests in us the authority to mandate a code of behavior for state officials wholly unconnected to any federal right or privilege. The purpose of the *Miranda* warnings instead is to dissipate the compulsion inherent in custodial interrogation and, in so doing, guard against abridgment of the suspect's Fifth Amendment rights. Clearly, a rule that focuses on how the police treat an attorney—conduct that has no relevance at all to the degree of compulsion experienced by the defendant during interrogation—would ignore both *Miranda*'s mission and its only source of legitimacy.

Nor are we prepared to adopt a rule requiring that the police inform a suspect of an attorney's efforts to reach him. While such a rule might add marginally to *Miranda*'s goal of dispelling the compulsion inherent in custodial interrogation, overriding practical considerations counsel against its adoption. As we have stressed on numerous occasions, one of the principal advantages of *Miranda* is the ease and clarity of its application. We have little doubt that the approach urged by respondent and endorsed by the Court of Appeals would have the inevitable consequence of muddying *Miranda*'s otherwise relatively clear waters. The legal questions it would spawn are legion: To what extent should the police be held accountable for knowing that the accused has counsel? Is it enough that someone in the station house knows, or must the interrogating officer himself know of counsel's efforts to contact the suspect? Do counsel's efforts to talk to the suspect concerning one criminal investigation trigger the obligation to inform the defendant before interrogation may proceed on a wholly separate matter? We are unwilling to modify *Miranda* in a manner that would so clearly undermine the decision's central virtue of informing police and prosecutors with specificity what they may do in conducting a custodial interrogation, and of informing courts under what circumstances statements obtained during such interrogation are not admissible.

Moreover, problems of clarity to one side, reading *Miranda* to require the police in each instance to inform a suspect of an attorney's efforts to reach him would work a substantial and, we think, inappropriate shift in the subtle balance struck in that decision. Custodial interrogations implicate two competing concerns. On the one hand, the need for police questioning as a tool for effective enforcement of criminal laws cannot be doubted. Admissions of guilt are more than merely desirable, they are essential to society's compelling interest in finding, convicting, and punishing those who violate the law. On the other hand, the Court has recognized that the interrogation process is "inherently coercive" and that, as a consequence, there exists a substantial risk that the police will inadvertently traverse the fine line between legitimate efforts to elicit admissions and constitutionally impermissible compulsion. *Miranda* attempted to reconcile these opposing concerns by giving the *defendant* the power to exert some control over the course of the interrogation. Declining to adopt the more extreme position that the actual presence of a lawyer was necessary to dispel the coercion inherent in custodial interrogation, the Court found that the suspect's Fifth Amendment rights could be adequately protected by less intrusive means. Police questioning, often an essential part of the investigatory process, could continue in its traditional form, the Court held, but only if the suspect clearly understood that, at any time, he could bring the proceeding to a halt or, short of that, call in an attorney to give advice and monitor the conduct of his interrogators.

The position urged by respondent would upset this carefully drawn approach in a manner that is both unnecessary for the protection of the Fifth Amendment privilege and injurious to legitimate law enforcement. Because, as *Miranda* holds, full comprehension of the rights to remain silent and request an attorney are sufficient to dispel whatever coercion is inherent in the interrogation process, a rule requiring the police to inform the suspect of an attorney's efforts to contact him would contribute to the protection of the Fifth Amendment privilege only incidentally, if at all. This minimal benefit, however, would come at a substantial cost to society's legitimate and substantial interest in securing admissions of guilt. Indeed, the very premise of the Court of Appeals was not that awareness of Ms. Munson's phone call would have dissipated the coercion of the interrogation room, but that it might have convinced respondent not to speak at all. Because neither the letter nor purposes of *Miranda* require this additional handicap on otherwise permissible investigatory efforts, we are unwilling to expand the *Miranda* rules to require the police to keep the suspect abreast of the status of his legal representation.

We acknowledge that a number of state courts have reached a contrary conclusion. We recognize also that our interpretation of the Federal Constitution, if given the dissent's expansive gloss, is at odds with the policy recommendations embodied in the American Bar Association Standards of Criminal Justice. Notwithstanding the dissent's protestations, however, our interpretive duties go well beyond deferring to the numerical preponderance of lower court decisions or to the subconstitutional recommendations of even so esteemed a body as the American Bar Association. Nothing we say today disables the States from adopting different requirements for the conduct of its employees and officials as a matter of state law. We hold only that the Court of Appeals erred in construing the Fifth Amendment to the Federal Constitution to require the exclusion of respondent's three confessions.

JUSTICE STEVENS, with whom JUSTICE BRENNAN and JUSTICE MARSHALL join, dissenting.

The Court concludes that the police may deceive an attorney by giving her false information about whether her client will be questioned, and that the police may deceive a suspect by failing to inform him of his attorney's communications and efforts to represent him. For the majority, this conclusion, though "distasteful," is not even debatable. The deception of the attorney is irrelevant because the attorney has no right to information, accuracy, honesty, or fairness in the police response to her questions about her client. The deception of the client is acceptable, because, although the information would affect the client's assertion of his rights, the client's actions in ignorance of the availability of his attorney are voluntary, knowing, and intelligent; additionally, society's interest in apprehending, prosecuting, and punishing criminals outweighs the suspect's interest in information regarding his attorney's efforts to communicate with him. Finally, even mendacious police interference in the communications between a suspect and his lawyer does not violate any notion of fundamental fairness because it does not shock the conscience of the majority.

The Court's holding focuses on the period after a suspect has been taken into custody and before he has been charged with an offense. The core of the Court's holding is that police interference with an attorney's access to her client during that period is not unconstitutional. The Court reasons that a State has a compelling interest, not simply in custodial interrogation, but in lawyer-free, incommunicado custodial interrogation. Such incommunicado interrogation is so important that a lawyer may be given false information that prevents her presence and representation; it is so important that police may refuse to inform a suspect of his attorney's communications and immediate availability. This conclusion flies in the face of this Court's repeated expressions of deep concern about incommunicado questioning. Until today, incommunicado questioning has been viewed with the strictest scrutiny by this Court; today, incommunicado questioning is embraced as a societal goal of the highest order that justifies police deception of the shabbiest kind.

It is not only the Court's ultimate conclusion that is deeply disturbing; it is also its manner of reaching that conclusion. The Court completely rejects an entire body of law on the subject—the many carefully reasoned state decisions that have come to precisely the opposite conclusion. The Court similarly dismisses the fact that the police deception which it sanctions quite clearly violates the American Bar Association's Standards for Criminal Justice—Standards which [Chief Justice Warren Burger] has described as "the single most comprehensive and probably the most monumental undertaking in the field of criminal justice ever attempted by the American legal profession in our national history," and which this Court frequently finds helpful. And, of course, the Court dismisses the fact that the American Bar Association has emphatically endorsed the prevailing state-court position and expressed its serious concern about the effect that a contrary view—a view, such as the Court's, that exalts incommunicado interrogation, sanctions police deception, and demeans the right to consult with an attorney—will have in police stations and courtrooms throughout this Nation. Of greatest importance, the Court misapprehends or rejects the central principles that have, for several decades, animated this Court's decisions concerning incommunicado interrogation.

Well-settled principles of law lead inexorably to the conclusion that the failure to inform Burbine of the call from his attorney makes the subsequent waiver of his constitutional rights invalid. Analysis should begin with an acknowledgment that the burden of proving the validity of a waiver of constitutional rights is always on the *government*. When such a waiver occurs in a custodial setting, that burden is an especially heavy one because custodial interrogation is inherently coercive, because disinterested witnesses are seldom available to describe what actually happened, and because history has taught us that the danger of overreaching during incommunicado interrogation is so real.

Like the failure to give warnings and like police initiation of interrogation after a request for counsel, police deception of a suspect through omission of information regarding attorney communications greatly exacerbates the inherent problems of incommunicado interrogation and requires a clear principle to safeguard the presumption against the waiver of constitutional rights. As in those situations, the police deception should render a subsequent waiver invalid.

In this case it would be perfectly clear that Burbine's waiver was invalid if, for example, Detective Ferranti had threatened, tricked, or cajoled Burbine in their private preconfession meeting—perhaps by misdescribing the statements obtained from DiOrio and Sparks [the two other men arrested with Burbine in connection with the burglary]—even though, under the Court's truncated analysis of the issue, Burbine fully understood his rights. For *Miranda* clearly condemns threats or trickery that cause a suspect to make an unwise waiver of his rights even though he fully understands those rights. In my opinion there can be no constitutional distinction between a deceptive misstatement and the concealment by the police of the critical fact that an attorney retained by the accused or his family has offered assistance, either by telephone or in person.

In *Spring v. Colorado*, police did not inform a suspect about one of the crimes for which they wanted to question him. The Supreme Court held that this did not affect the validity of the defendant's *Miranda* waiver.

SPRING V. COLORADO
479 U.S. 564 (1987)

An informant told agents for the Bureau of Alcohol, Tobacco, and Firearms (ATF) that John Leroy Spring was engaged in the interstate transportation of stolen firearms. The informant also told the agents that Spring had discussed his participation in a killing in Colorado. On March 30, 1979, ATF agents set up an undercover operation to purchase firearms from Spring, and he was arrested during the transaction. ATF agents informed Spring of his *Miranda* rights upon arrest and provided them a second time after he was transported to the ATF office in Kansas City, Missouri. Spring then signed a written form stating that he understood and waived his rights, and that he was willing to make a statement and answer questions.

The ATF agents first questioned Spring about the firearms transactions that led to his arrest, then asked Spring if he had a criminal record. Spring admitted that he had a juvenile record for shooting his aunt when he was 10 years old. The agents asked if Spring had ever shot anyone else. Spring ducked his head and mumbled, "I shot another guy once." In response to additional questions, Spring denied any involvement in the Colorado killing.

Two months later, on May 26, 1979, Colorado law enforcement officials visited Spring while he was in jail in Kansas City for his arrest on the firearms offenses. The officers gave Spring the *Miranda* warnings, and he again signed a written form indicating that he understood his rights and was willing to waive them. The officers informed Spring that they wanted to question him about the Colorado homicide. Spring indicated that he "wanted to get it off his chest," and in an interview that lasted approximately 90 minutes, Spring confessed to the murder.

Spring sought to suppress the March 30 and May 26 statements, claiming that his waiver of *Miranda* rights prior to the first interrogation was invalid because he was not informed that he would be questioned about the Colorado murder. The Supreme Court rejected Spring's argument:

> This Court's holding in *Miranda* specifically required that the police inform a criminal suspect that he has the right to remain silent and that *anything* he says may be used against him. There is no qualification of this broad and explicit warning. The warning, as formulated in *Miranda*, conveys to a suspect the nature of his constitutional privilege and the consequences of abandoning it. Accordingly, we hold that a suspect's awareness

of all the possible subjects of questioning in advance of interrogation is not relevant to determining whether the suspect voluntarily, knowingly, and intelligently waived his Fifth Amendment privilege.

In *North Carolina v. Butler*, the Supreme Court held that a *Miranda* waiver need not be express, but can be inferred from the suspect's words and actions.

NORTH CAROLINA V. BUTLER
441 U.S. 369 (1979)

JUSTICE STEWART delivered the opinion of the Court.

In evident conflict with the present view of every other court that has considered the issue, the North Carolina Supreme Court has held that *Miranda v. Arizona*, 384 U.S. 436 (1966), requires that no statement of a person under custodial interrogation may be admitted in evidence against him unless, at the time the statement was made, he explicitly waived the right to the presence of a lawyer. We granted certiorari to consider whether this *per se* rule reflects a proper understanding of the *Miranda* decision.

The respondent was convicted in a North Carolina trial court of kidnapping, armed robbery, and felonious assault. The evidence at his trial showed that he and a man named Elmer Lee had robbed a gas station in Goldsboro, N.C., in December 1976, and had shot the station attendant as he was attempting to escape. The attendant was paralyzed, but survived to testify against the respondent.

The prosecution also produced evidence of incriminating statements made by the respondent shortly after his arrest by Federal Bureau of Investigation agents in the Bronx, N.Y., on the basis of a North Carolina fugitive warrant. Outside the presence of the jury, FBI Agent Martinez testified that at the time of the arrest he fully advised the respondent of the rights delineated in the *Miranda* case. According to the uncontroverted testimony of Martinez, the agents then took the respondent to the FBI office in nearby New Rochelle, N.Y. There, after the agents determined that the respondent had an 11th grade education and was literate, he was given the Bureau's "Advice of Rights" form which he read. When asked if he understood his rights, he replied that he did. The respondent refused to sign the waiver at the bottom of the form. He was told that he need neither speak nor sign the form, but that the agents would like him to talk to them. The respondent replied: "I will talk to you but I am not signing any form." He then made inculpatory statements. Agent Martinez testified that the respondent said nothing when advised of his right to the assistance of a lawyer. At no time did the respondent request counsel or attempt to terminate the agents' questioning.

At the conclusion of this testimony the respondent moved to suppress the evidence of his incriminating statements on the ground that he had not waived his right to the assistance of counsel at the time the statements were made. The court denied the motion. The respondent's statements were then admitted into evidence, and the jury ultimately found the respondent guilty of each offense charged.

On appeal, the North Carolina Supreme Court reversed the convictions and ordered a new trial. It found that the statements had been admitted in violation of the requirements of the *Miranda* decision, noting that the respondent had refused to waive in writing his right to have counsel present and that there had not been a *specific* oral waiver. As it had in at least two earlier cases, the court read the *Miranda* opinion as "providing in plain language that waiver of the right to counsel during interrogation will not be recognized unless such waiver is specifically made after the *Miranda* warnings have been given."

We conclude that the North Carolina Supreme Court erred in its reading of the *Miranda* opinion. There, this Court said: "If the interrogation continues without the presence of an attorney and a statement is taken, a heavy burden rests on the government to demonstrate that the defendant knowingly and intelligently waived his privilege against self-incrimination and his right to retained or appointed counsel." The Court's opinion went on to say: "An express statement that the individual is willing to make a statement and does not want an attorney followed closely by a statement could constitute a waiver. But a valid waiver will not be presumed simply from the silence of the accused after warnings are given or simply from the fact that a confession was in fact eventually obtained."

Thus, the Court held that an express statement can constitute a waiver, and that silence alone after such warnings cannot do so. But the Court did not hold that such an express statement is indispensable to a finding of waiver.

An express written or oral statement of waiver of the right to remain silent or of the right to counsel is usually strong proof of the validity of that waiver, but is not inevitably either necessary or sufficient to establish waiver. The question is not one of form, but rather whether the defendant in fact knowingly and voluntarily waived the rights delineated in the *Miranda* case. As was unequivocally said in *Miranda*, mere silence is not enough. That does not mean that the defendant's silence, coupled with an understanding of his rights and a course of conduct indicating waiver, may never support a conclusion that a defendant has waived his rights. The courts must presume that a defendant did not waive his rights; the prosecution's burden is great; but in at least some cases, waiver can be clearly inferred from the actions and words of the person interrogated.

There is no doubt that this respondent was adequately and effectively apprised of his rights. The only question is whether he waived the exercise of one of those rights, the right to the presence of a lawyer. Neither the state court nor the respondent has offered any reason why there must be a negative answer to that question in the absence of an *express* waiver. This is not the first criminal case to question whether a defendant waived his constitutional rights. It is an issue with which courts must repeatedly deal. Even when a right so fundamental as that to counsel at trial is involved, the question of waiver must be determined on the particular facts and circumstances surrounding that case, including the background, experience, and conduct of the accused.

We see no reason to discard that standard and replace it with an inflexible *per se* rule in a case such as this. As stated at the outset of this opinion, it appears that every court that has considered this question has now reached the same conclusion. Ten of the eleven United States Courts of Appeals and the courts of at least 17 States have held that an explicit statement of waiver is not invariably necessary to support a finding that the defendant waived the right to remain silent or the right to counsel guaranteed by the *Miranda* case. By creating an inflexible rule that no implicit waiver can ever suffice, the North Carolina Supreme Court has gone beyond the requirements of federal organic law. It follows that its judgment cannot stand, since a state court can neither add to nor subtract from the mandates of the United States Constitution.

JUSTICE BRENNAN, with whom JUSTICE MARSHALL and JUSTICE STEVENS join, dissenting.

Miranda v. Arizona, 384 U.S. 436 (1966), held that "no effective waiver of the right to counsel during interrogation can be recognized unless *specifically* made after the warnings we here delineate have been given."

There is no allegation of an affirmative waiver in this case. As the Court concedes, the respondent here refused to sign the waiver form, and "said nothing when advised of his right to the assistance of a lawyer." In the absence of an "affirmative waiver" in the form of an express written or oral statement, the Supreme Court of North Carolina correctly granted a new trial. I would, therefore, affirm its decision.

The rule announced by the Court today allows a finding of waiver based upon "inference from the actions and words of the person interrogated." The Court thus shrouds in half-light the question of waiver, allowing courts to construct inferences from ambiguous words and gestures. But the very premise of *Miranda* requires that ambiguity be interpreted against the interrogator. That premise is the recognition of the "compulsion inherent in custodial" interrogation, and of its purpose "to subjugate the individual to the will of his examiner." Under such conditions, only the most explicit waivers of rights can be considered knowingly and freely given.

Faced with "actions and words" of uncertain meaning, some judges may find waivers where none occurred. Others may fail to find them where they did. In the former case, the defendant's rights will have been violated; in the latter, society's interest in effective law enforcement will have been frustrated. A simple prophylactic rule requiring the police to obtain an express waiver of the right to counsel before proceeding with interrogation eliminates these difficulties. And since the Court agrees that *Miranda* requires the police to obtain some kind of waiver—whether express or implied—the requirement of an express waiver would impose no burden on the police not imposed by the Court's interpretation. It would merely make that burden explicit. Had Agent Martinez simply elicited a clear answer from Willie Butler to the question, "Do you waive your right to a lawyer?" this journey through three courts would not have been necessary.

General Guidelines for *Miranda* Waivers

1. An individual may expressly or implicitly waive the right to remain silent and the right to counsel provided the waiver is made voluntarily, knowingly, and intelligently. The inquiry has two distinct dimensions:

   a. The relinquishment of the right must have been voluntary in the sense that it was the product of a free and deliberate choice rather than intimidation, coercion, or deception.

   b. The waiver must have been made with a full awareness of both the nature of the right being abandoned and the consequences of the decision to abandon it.

2. A court must examine the totality of the circumstances surrounding the interrogation to determine whether an individual has validly waived his *Miranda* rights. Relevant factors include the suspect's age, experience, education, background, and whether he has the capacity to understand the *Miranda* warnings given to him, the nature of his Fifth Amendment rights, and the consequences of waiving those rights.

3. A suspect's mental illness or similar condition does not render a waiver involuntary so long as there is no coercion or police overreaching in obtaining any incriminating statements.

4. The failure of the police to notify a suspect that an attorney has been retained for him or is attempting to reach him does not render a

Miranda waiver invalid since events occurring outside the presence of the suspect and entirely unknown to him have no bearing on his capacity to comprehend and knowingly relinquish a constitutional right.

5.   The failure of police to notify a suspect in advance about the subject matter of the intended questioning does not render a *Miranda* waiver invalid.

6.   The prosecution has the burden of proving a *Miranda* waiver by a preponderance of the evidence.

2.   INVOCATION AND WAIVER OF *MIRANDA*'S RIGHT TO REMAIN SILENT

In addition to the general guidelines for *Miranda* waivers set forth above, the Supreme Court has established a number of specific rules regarding the invocation and waiver of *Miranda*'s right to remain silent. Many of these rules come directly from the *Miranda* decision itself. First and foremost, *Miranda* notes, "[i]f the individual indicates in any manner, at any time prior to or during questioning, that he wishes to remain silent, the interrogation must cease." The right to remain silent can, however, be waived, and an "express statement that the individual is willing to make a statement and does not want an attorney followed closely by a statement could constitute a waiver." But, the *Miranda* Court cautioned, "a valid waiver will not be presumed simply from the silence of the accused after warnings are given or simply from the fact that a confession was in fact eventually obtained." And, the Court added, "there is no room for the contention that the privilege is waived if the individual answers some questions or gives some information on his own prior to invoking his right to remain silent when interrogated." Finally, *Miranda* expressed deep skepticism about the validity of any waiver preceded by lengthy incommunicado interrogation:

> Whatever the testimony of the authorities as to waiver of rights by an accused, the fact of lengthy interrogation or incommunicado incarceration before a statement is made is strong evidence that the accused did not validly waive his rights. In these circumstances the fact that the individual eventually made a statement is consistent with the conclusion that the compelling influence of the interrogation finally forced him to do so. It is inconsistent with any notion of a voluntary relinquishment of the privilege.

In *Berghuis v. Thompkins*, the Supreme Court revisited the rules established by *Miranda* for the invocation and waiver of the right to remain silent. When Thompkins, a murder suspect, was arrested, he received *Miranda* warnings but refused to sign a form demonstrating that he understood his rights. Police began their interrogation, and although Thompkins never said he wanted to remain silent or wanted an attorney, he remained largely silent for nearly three hours until finally making an incriminating admission. In a sharply divided 5–4 decision, the Supreme Court held that Thompkins never invoked his right to remain silent and, in fact, had implicitly waived it by making a voluntary statement after he received and understood his rights under *Miranda*.

BERGHUIS V. THOMPKINS
560 U.S. 370 (2010)

JUSTICE KENNEDY delivered the opinion of the Court.

I

On January 10, 2000, a shooting occurred outside a mall in Southfield, Michigan. Among the victims was Samuel Morris, who died from multiple gunshot wounds. The other victim, Frederick France, recovered from his injuries and later testified. Thompkins, who was a suspect, fled. About one year later he was found in Ohio and arrested there.

Two Southfield police officers traveled to Ohio to interrogate Thompkins, then awaiting transfer to Michigan. The interrogation began around 1:30 p.m. and lasted about three hours. The interrogation was conducted in a room that was 8 by 10 feet, and Thompkins sat in a chair that resembled a school desk (it had an arm on it that swings around to provide a surface to write on). At the beginning of the interrogation, one of the officers, Detective Helgert, presented Thompkins with a form derived from the *Miranda* rule. It stated:

NOTIFICATION OF CONSTITUTIONAL
RIGHTS AND STATEMENT

1.   You have the right to remain silent.

2.   Anything you say can and will be used against you in a court of law.

3.   You have a right to talk to a lawyer before answering any questions and you have the right to have a lawyer present with you while you are answering any questions.

4.   If you cannot afford to hire a lawyer, one will be appointed to represent you before any questioning, if you wish one.

5.   You have the right to decide at any time before or during questioning to use your right to remain silent and your right to talk with a lawyer while you are being questioned.

Helgert asked Thompkins to read the fifth warning out loud. Thompkins complied. Helgert later said this was to ensure that

Thompkins could read, and Helgert concluded that Thompkins understood English. Helgert then read the other four *Miranda* warnings out loud and asked Thompkins to sign the form to demonstrate that he understood his rights. Thompkins declined to sign the form. The record contains conflicting evidence about whether Thompkins then verbally confirmed that he understood the rights listed on the form.

Officers began an interrogation. At no point during the interrogation did Thompkins say that he wanted to remain silent, that he did not want to talk with the police, or that he wanted an attorney. Thompkins was largely silent during the interrogation, which lasted about three hours. He did give a few limited verbal responses, however, such as "yeah," "no," or "I don't know." And on occasion he communicated by nodding his head. Thompkins also said that he "didn't want a peppermint" that was offered to him by the police and that the chair he was "sitting in was hard."

About 2 hours and 45 minutes into the interrogation, Helgert asked Thompkins, "Do you believe in God?" Thompkins made eye contact with Helgert and said "Yes," as his eyes "welled up with tears." Helgert asked, "Do you pray to God?" Thompkins said "Yes." Helgert asked, "Do you pray to God to forgive you for shooting that boy down?" Thompkins answered "Yes" and looked away. Thompkins refused to make a written confession, and the interrogation ended about 15 minutes later.

Thompkins was charged with first-degree murder, assault with intent to commit murder, and certain firearms-related offenses. He moved to suppress the statements made during the interrogation. He argued that he had invoked his Fifth Amendment right to remain silent, requiring police to end the interrogation at once, that he had not waived his right to remain silent, and that his inculpatory statements were involuntary. The trial court denied the motion. The jury found Thompkins guilty on all counts. He was sentenced to life in prison without parole.

III

The *Miranda* Court formulated a warning that must be given to suspects before they can be subjected to custodial interrogation. The substance of the warning still must be given to suspects today. All concede that the warning given in this case was in full compliance with these requirements. The dispute centers on the response—or nonresponse—from the suspect.

A

Thompkins makes various arguments that his answers to questions from the detectives were inadmissible. He first contends that he invoked his privilege to remain silent by not saying anything for a sufficient period of time, so the interrogation should have ceased before he made his inculpatory statements.

This argument is unpersuasive. In the context of invoking the *Miranda* right to counsel, the Court in *Davis v. U.S.*, 512 U.S. 452 (1994), held that a suspect must do so "unambiguously." If an accused makes a statement concerning the right to counsel "that is ambiguous or equivocal" or makes no statement, the police are not required to end the interrogation, or ask questions to clarify whether the accused wants to invoke his or her *Miranda* rights.

The Court has not yet stated whether an invocation of the right to remain silent can be ambiguous or equivocal, but there is no principled reason to adopt different standards for determining when an accused has invoked the *Miranda* right to remain silent and the *Miranda* right to counsel at issue in *Davis*. Both protect the privilege against compulsory self-incrimination by requiring an interrogation to cease when either right is invoked.

There is good reason to require an accused who wants to invoke his or her right to remain silent to do so unambiguously. A requirement of an unambiguous invocation of *Miranda* rights results in an objective inquiry that avoids difficulties of proof and provides guidance to officers on how to proceed in the face of ambiguity. If an ambiguous act, omission, or statement could require police to end the interrogation, police would be required to make difficult decisions about an accused's unclear intent and face the consequence of suppression if they guess wrong. Suppression of a voluntary confession in these circumstances would place a significant burden on society's interest in prosecuting criminal activity. Treating an ambiguous or equivocal act, omission, or statement as an invocation of *Miranda* rights might add marginally to *Miranda*'s goal of dispelling the compulsion inherent in custodial interrogation. But as *Miranda* holds, full comprehension of the rights to remain silent and request an attorney are sufficient to dispel whatever coercion is inherent in the interrogation process.

Thompkins did not say that he wanted to remain silent or that he did not want to talk with the police. Had he made either of these simple, unambiguous statements, he would have invoked his right to cut off questioning. Here he did neither, so he did not invoke his right to remain silent.

B

We next consider whether Thompkins waived his right to remain silent. Even absent the accused's invocation of the right to remain silent, the accused's statement during a custodial interrogation is inadmissible at trial unless the prosecution can establish that the accused in fact knowingly and voluntarily waived *Miranda* rights when making the statement. The waiver inquiry has two distinct dimensions: waiver must be voluntary in the sense that it was the product of a free and deliberate choice rather than intimidation, coercion, or deception, and made with a full awareness of both the nature of the right being abandoned and the consequences of the decision to abandon it.

Some language in *Miranda* could be read to indicate that waivers are difficult to establish absent an explicit written waiver or a formal, express oral statement. *Miranda* said "a valid waiver will not be presumed simply from the silence of the accused after warnings are given or simply from the fact that a confession was in fact eventually obtained." In addition, the *Miranda* Court stated that "a heavy burden rests on the government to demonstrate that the defendant knowingly and intelligently waived his privilege against self-incrimination and his right to retained or appointed counsel."

The course of decisions since *Miranda*, informed by the application of *Miranda* warnings in the whole course of law enforcement, demonstrates that waivers can be established even absent formal or express statements of waiver that would be expected in, say, a judicial hearing to determine if a guilty plea has been properly entered. The main purpose of *Miranda* is to ensure that an accused is advised of and understands the right to remain silent and the right to counsel.

One of the first cases to decide the meaning and import of *Miranda* with respect to the question of waiver was *North Carolina v. Butler*, 441 U.S. 369 (1979). The *Butler* Court, after discussing some of the problems created by the language in *Miranda*, established certain important propositions. *Butler* interpreted the *Miranda* language concerning the "heavy burden" to show waiver in accord with usual principles of determining waiver, which can include waiver implied from all the circumstances. And in a later case, the Court stated that this "heavy burden" is not more than the burden to establish waiver by a preponderance of the evidence.

The prosecution therefore does not need to show that a waiver of *Miranda* rights was express. An "implicit waiver" of the "right to remain silent" is sufficient to admit a suspect's statement into evidence. *Butler* made clear that a waiver of *Miranda* rights may be implied through "the defendant's silence, coupled with an understanding of his rights and a course of conduct indicating waiver." The Court in *Butler* therefore "retreated" from the "language and tenor of the *Miranda* opinion," which "suggested that the Court would require that a waiver be specifically made."

If the State establishes that a *Miranda* warning was given and the accused made an uncoerced statement, this showing, standing alone, is insufficient to demonstrate a valid waiver of *Miranda* rights. The prosecution must make the additional showing that the accused understood these rights. Where the prosecution shows that a *Miranda* warning was given and that it was understood by the accused, an accused's uncoerced statement establishes an implied waiver of the right to remain silent.

Although *Miranda* imposes on the police a rule that is both formalistic and practical when it prevents them from interrogating suspects without first providing them with a *Miranda* warning, it does not impose a formalistic waiver procedure that a suspect must follow to relinquish those rights. As a general proposition, the law can presume that an individual who, with a full understanding of his or her rights, acts in a manner inconsistent with their exercise has made a deliberate choice to relinquish the protection those rights afford. As *Butler* recognized, *Miranda* rights can therefore be waived through means less formal than a typical waiver on the record in a courtroom, given the practical constraints and necessities of interrogation and the fact that *Miranda*'s main protection lies in advising defendants of their rights.

The record in this case shows that Thompkins waived his right to remain silent. There is no basis in this case to conclude that he did not understand his rights; and on these facts it follows that he chose not to invoke or rely on those rights when he did speak. First, there is no contention that Thompkins did not understand his rights; and from this it follows that he knew what he gave up when he spoke. There was more than enough evidence in the record to conclude that Thompkins understood his *Miranda* rights. Thompkins received a written copy of the *Miranda* warnings; Detective Helgert determined that Thompkins could read and understand English; and Thompkins was given time to read the warnings. Thompkins, furthermore, read aloud the fifth warning, which stated that "you have the right to decide at any time before or during questioning to use your right to remain silent and your right to talk with a lawyer while you are being questioned." He was thus aware that his right to remain silent would not dissipate after a certain amount of time and that police would have to honor his right to be silent and his right to counsel during the whole course of interrogation. Those rights, the warning made clear, could be asserted at any time. Helgert, moreover, read the warnings aloud.

Second, Thompkins' answer to Detective Helgert's question about whether Thompkins prayed to God for forgiveness for shooting the victim is a "course of conduct indicating waiver" of the right to remain silent. If Thompkins wanted to remain silent, he could have said nothing in response to Helgert's questions, or he could have unambiguously invoked his *Miranda* rights and ended the interrogation. The fact that Thompkins made a statement about three hours after receiving a *Miranda* warning does not overcome the fact that he engaged in a course of conduct indicating waiver. Police are not required to rewarn suspects from time to time. Thompkins' answer to Helgert's question about praying to God for forgiveness for shooting the victim was sufficient to show a course of conduct indicating waiver. This is confirmed by the fact that before then Thompkins had given sporadic answers to questions throughout the interrogation.

Third, there is no evidence that Thompkins' statement was coerced. Thompkins does not claim that police threatened or injured him during the interrogation or that he was in any way fearful. The interrogation was conducted in a standard-sized room in the middle of the afternoon. It is true that apparently he was in a straight-backed chair for three hours, but there is no authority for the proposition that an interrogation of this length is inherently coercive. Indeed, even where interrogations of greater duration were held to be improper, they were accompanied, as this one was not, by other facts indicating coercion, such as an incapacitated and sedated suspect, sleep and food deprivation, and threats. The fact that Helgert's question referred to Thompkins' religious beliefs also did not render Thompkins' statement involuntary. The Fifth Amendment privilege is not concerned with moral and psychological pressures to confess emanating from sources other than official coercion. In these circumstances, Thompkins knowingly and voluntarily made a statement to police, so he waived his right to remain silent.

C

Thompkins next argues that, even if his answer to Detective Helgert could constitute a waiver of his right to remain silent, the police were not allowed to question him until they obtained a waiver first. *Butler* forecloses this argument. The *Butler* Court held that courts can infer a waiver of *Miranda* rights "from the actions and words of the person interrogated." This principle would be inconsistent with a rule that requires a waiver at the outset. The *Butler* Court thus rejected the rule proposed by the *Butler* dissent, which would have required the police to obtain an express waiver of *Miranda* rights before proceeding with interrogation. This holding also makes sense given that the primary protection afforded suspects subjected to custodial interrogation is the *Miranda* warnings themselves. The *Miranda* rule and its requirements are met if a suspect receives adequate *Miranda* warnings, understands them, and has an opportunity to invoke the rights before giving any answers or admissions. Any waiver, express or implied, may be contradicted by an invocation at any time. If the right to counsel or the right to remain silent is invoked at any point during questioning, further interrogation must cease.

Interrogation provides the suspect with additional information that can put his or her decision to waive, or not to invoke, into perspective. As questioning commences and then continues, the suspect has the opportunity to consider the choices he or she faces and to make a more informed decision, either to insist on silence or to cooperate. When the suspect knows that *Miranda* rights can be invoked at any time, he or she has the opportunity to reassess his or her immediate and long-term interests. Cooperation with the police may result in more favorable treatment for the suspect; the apprehension of accomplices; the prevention of continuing injury and fear; beginning steps towards relief or solace for the victims; and the beginning of the suspect's own return to the law and the social order it seeks to protect.

In order for an accused's statement to be admissible at trial, police must have given the accused a *Miranda* warning. If that condition is established, the court can proceed to consider whether there has been an express or implied waiver of *Miranda* rights. In making its ruling on the admissibility of a statement made during custodial questioning, the trial court, of course, considers whether there is evidence to support the conclusion that, from the whole course of questioning, an express or implied waiver has been established. Thus, after giving a *Miranda* warning, police may interrogate a suspect who has neither invoked nor waived his or her *Miranda* rights. On these premises, it follows the police were not required to obtain a waiver of Thompkins' *Miranda* rights before commencing the interrogation.

D

In sum, a suspect who has received and understood the *Miranda* warnings, and has not invoked his *Miranda* rights, waives the right to remain silent by making an uncoerced statement to the police. Thompkins did not invoke his right to remain silent and stop the questioning. Understanding his rights in full, he waived his right to remain silent by making a voluntary statement to the police. The police, moreover, were not required to obtain a waiver of Thompkins' right to remain silent before interrogating him.

JUSTICE SOTOMAYOR, with whom JUSTICE STEVENS, JUSTICE GINSBURG, and JUSTICE BREYER join, dissenting.

The Court concludes today that a criminal suspect waives his right to remain silent if, after sitting tacit and uncommunicative through nearly three hours of police interrogation, he utters a few one-word responses. The Court also concludes that a suspect who wishes to guard his right to remain silent against such a finding of "waiver" must, counterintuitively, speak—and must do so with sufficient precision to satisfy a clear-statement rule that construes ambiguity in favor of the police. Both propositions mark a substantial retreat from the protection against compelled self-incrimination that *Miranda v. Arizona* has long provided during custodial interrogation.

I

The strength of Thompkins' *Miranda* claims depends in large part on the circumstances of the 3-hour interrogation, at the end of which he made inculpatory statements later introduced at trial. The Court's opinion downplays record evidence that Thompkins remained almost completely silent and unresponsive throughout that session. One of the interrogating officers, Detective Helgert, testified that although Thompkins was administered *Miranda* warnings, the last of which he read aloud, Thompkins expressly declined to sign a written acknowledgment that he had been advised of and understood his rights. There is conflicting evidence in the record about whether Thompkins ever verbally confirmed understanding his rights. The record contains no indication that the officers sought or obtained an express waiver.

As to the interrogation itself, Helgert candidly characterized it as "very, very one-sided" and "nearly a monologue." Thompkins was "peculiar," "sullen," and "generally quiet." Helgert and his partner "did most of the talking," as Thompkins was "not verbally communicative" and "largely" remained silent. To the extent Thompkins gave any response, his answers consisted of "a word or two. A 'yeah,' or a 'no,' or 'I don't know.' And sometimes he simply sat down with his head in his hands looking down. Sometimes he would look up and make eye-contact would be the only response." After proceeding in this fashion for approximately 2 hours and 45 minutes, Helgert asked Thompkins three questions relating to his faith in God. The prosecution relied at trial on Thompkins' one-word answers of "yes."

Thompkins' nonresponsiveness is particularly striking in the context of the officers' interview strategy, later explained as conveying to Thompkins that "this was his opportunity to explain his side" of the story because "everybody else, including his co-defendants, had given their version," and asking him "who is going to speak up for you if you don't speak up for yourself?" Yet, Helgert confirmed that the "only thing Thompkins said relative to his involvement in the shooting" occurred near the end of the interview—*i.e.*, in response to the questions about God. The only other responses Helgert could remember Thompkins giving were that "he didn't want a peppermint" and "the chair that he was sitting in was hard." Nevertheless, the Michigan court concluded on this record that Thompkins had not invoked his right to remain silent because "he continued to talk with the officer, albeit sporadically," and that he voluntarily waived that right.

Even when warnings have been administered and a suspect has not affirmatively invoked his rights, statements made in custodial interrogation may not be admitted as part of the prosecution's case in chief unless and until the prosecution demonstrates that an individual knowingly and intelligently waived his rights. A heavy burden rests on the government to demonstrate that the defendant knowingly and intelligently waived his privilege against self-incrimination and his right to retained or appointed counsel.

The question whether a suspect has validly waived his right is entirely distinct as a matter of law from whether he invoked that right. The questions are related, however, in terms of the practical effect on the exercise of a suspect's rights. A suspect may at any time revoke his prior waiver of rights—or, closer to the facts of this case, guard against the possibility of a future finding that he implicitly waived his rights—by invoking the rights and thereby requiring the police to cease questioning.

II

This Court's decisions subsequent to *Miranda* have emphasized the prosecution's "heavy burden" in proving waiver. We have also reaffirmed that a court may not presume waiver from a suspect's silence or from the mere fact that a confession was eventually obtained.

Rarely do this Court's precedents provide clearly established law so closely on point with the facts of a particular case. Together, *Miranda* and *Butler* establish that a court "must presume that a defendant did not waive his rights"; the prosecution bears a "heavy burden" in attempting to demonstrate waiver; the fact of a "lengthy interrogation" prior to obtaining statements is "strong evidence" against a finding of valid waiver; "mere silence" in response to questioning is "not enough"; and waiver may not be presumed "simply from the fact that a confession was in fact eventually obtained."

It is undisputed here that Thompkins never expressly waived his right to remain silent. His refusal to sign even an acknowledgment that he understood his *Miranda* rights evinces, if anything, an intent not to waive those rights. That Thompkins did not make the inculpatory statements at issue until after approximately 2 hours and 45 minutes of interrogation serves as strong evidence against waiver. *Miranda* and *Butler* expressly preclude the possibility that the inculpatory statements themselves are sufficient to establish waiver.

In these circumstances, Thompkins' "actions and words" preceding the inculpatory statements simply do not evidence a "course of conduct indicating waiver" sufficient to carry the prosecution's burden. Although the Michigan court stated that Thompkins "sporadically" participated in the interview, that court's opinion and the record before us are silent as to the subject matter or context of even a single question to which Thompkins purportedly responded, other than the exchange about God and the statements respecting the peppermint and the chair. Unlike in *Butler*, Thompkins made no initial declaration akin to "I will talk to you." Indeed, Michigan and the United States concede that no waiver occurred in this case until Thompkins responded "yes" to the questions about God. I believe it is objectively unreasonable under our clearly established precedents to conclude the prosecution met its "heavy burden" of proof on a record consisting of three one-word answers, following 2 hours and 45 minutes of silence punctuated by a few largely nonverbal responses to unidentified questions.

The Court concludes that when *Miranda* warnings have been given and understood, "an accused's uncoerced statement establishes an implied waiver of the right to remain silent." More broadly still, the Court states that, "as a general proposition, the law can presume that an individual who, with a full understanding of his or her rights, acts in a manner inconsistent with their exercise has made a deliberate choice to relinquish the protection those rights afford."

These principles flatly contradict our longstanding views that a valid waiver will not be presumed simply from the fact that a confession was in fact eventually obtained, and that the courts must presume that a defendant did not waive his rights. At best, the Court today creates an unworkable and conflicting set of presumptions that will undermine *Miranda*'s goal of providing concrete constitutional guidelines for law enforcement agencies and courts to follow. At worst, it overrules *sub silentio* an essential aspect of the protections *Miranda* has long provided for the constitutional guarantee against self-incrimination.

The Court's conclusion that Thompkins' inculpatory statements were sufficient to establish an implied waiver finds no support in *Butler*. *Butler* itself distinguished between a sufficient "course of conduct" and inculpatory statements, reiterating *Miranda*'s admonition that "a valid waiver will not be presumed simply from the fact that a confession was in fact eventually obtained." Michigan suggests Butler's silence when advised of his right to the assistance of a lawyer, combined with our remand for the state court to apply the implied-waiver standard, shows that silence followed by statements can be a "course of conduct." But the evidence of implied waiver in *Butler* was worlds apart from the evidence in this case, because Butler unequivocally said "I will talk to you" after having been read *Miranda* warnings. Thompkins, of course, made no such statement.

Today's dilution of the prosecution's burden of proof to the bare fact that a suspect made inculpatory statements after *Miranda* warnings were given and understood takes an unprecedented step away from the "high standards of proof for the waiver of constitutional rights" this Court has long demanded. When waiver is to be inferred during a custodial interrogation, there are sound reasons to require evidence beyond inculpatory statements themselves. *Miranda* and our subsequent cases are premised on the idea that custodial interrogation is inherently coercive. Requiring proof of a course of conduct beyond the inculpatory statements themselves is critical to ensuring that those statements are voluntary admissions and not the dubious product of an overborne will.

III

I cannot agree with the Court's much broader ruling that a suspect must clearly invoke his right to silence by speaking. Taken together with the Court's reformulation of the prosecution's burden of proof as to waiver, today's novel clear-statement rule for invocation invites police to question a suspect at length—notwithstanding his persistent refusal to answer questions—in the hope of eventually obtaining a single inculpatory response which will suffice to prove waiver of rights.

The Court holds that police may continue questioning a suspect until he unambiguously invokes his right to remain silent. Because Thompkins neither said "he wanted to remain silent" nor said "he did not want to talk with the police," the Court concludes, he did not clearly invoke his right to silence.

In my mind, a more appropriate standard for addressing a suspect's ambiguous invocation of the right to remain silent is the constraint *Michigan v. Mosley*, 423 U.S. 96 (1975), places on questioning a suspect who has invoked that right: The suspect's "right to cut off questioning" must be "scrupulously honored." Such a standard is necessarily precautionary and fact specific. The rule would acknowledge that some statements or conduct are so equivocal that police may scrupulously honor a suspect's rights without terminating questioning—for instance, if a suspect's actions are reasonably understood to indicate a willingness to listen before deciding whether to respond. But other statements or actions—in particular, when a suspect sits silent throughout prolonged interrogation, long past the point when he could be deciding whether to respond—cannot reasonably be understood other than as an invocation of the right to remain silent. Under such circumstances, "scrupulous" respect for the suspect's rights will require police to terminate questioning under *Mosley*.

Today's decision turns *Miranda* upside down. Criminal suspects must now unambiguously invoke their right to remain silent—which, counterintuitively, requires them to speak. At the same time, suspects will be legally presumed to have waived their rights even if they have given no clear expression of their intent to do so. Those results, in my view, find no basis in *Miranda* or our subsequent cases and are inconsistent with the fair-trial principles on which those precedents are grounded.

———————

In *Berghuis v. Thompkins*, the Supreme Court concluded that Thompkins had never actually invoked his right to remain silent under *Miranda*. In *Michigan v. Mosley*, by contrast, Richard Mosley, a robbery suspect, received *Miranda* warnings, then he clearly invoked his right to remain silent and the interrogation ended. Two hours later, another detective provided a second set of *Miranda* warnings, then questioned Mosley about an unrelated murder. Mosley made an incriminating statement about the murder but later claimed it should be suppressed because police were not permitted to question him and seek a waiver of his *Miranda* rights *after* he had already invoked his right to remain silent. The Supreme Court rejected this argument and found that Mosley had waived his right to remain silent.

MICHIGAN V. MOSLEY

423 U.S. 96 (1975)

JUSTICE STEWART delivered the opinion of the Court.

The respondent, Richard Bert Mosley, was arrested in Detroit, Mich., in the early afternoon of April 8, 1971, in connection with robberies that had recently occurred at the Blue Goose Bar and the White Tower Restaurant on that city's lower east side. The arresting officer, Detective James Cowie of the Armed Robbery Section of the Detroit Police Department, was acting on a tip implicating Mosley and three other men in the robberies. After effecting the arrest, Detective Cowie brought Mosley to the Robbery, Breaking and Entering Bureau of the Police Department, located on the fourth floor of the departmental headquarters building. The officer advised Mosley of his rights under this Court's decision in *Miranda v. Arizona*, 384 U.S. 436 (1966), and had him read and sign the department's constitutional rights notification certificate. After filling out the necessary arrest papers, Cowie began questioning Mosley about the robbery of the White Tower Restaurant. When Mosley said he did not want to answer any questions about the robberies, Cowie promptly ceased the interrogation. The completion of the arrest papers and the questioning of Mosley together took approximately 20 minutes. At no time during the questioning did Mosley indicate a desire to consult with a lawyer, and there is no claim that the procedures followed to this point did not fully comply with the strictures of the *Miranda* opinion. Mosley was then taken to a ninth-floor cell block.

Shortly after 6 p.m., Detective Hill of the Detroit Police Department Homicide Bureau brought Mosley from the cell block to the fifth-floor office of the Homicide Bureau for questioning about the fatal shooting of a man named Leroy Williams. Williams had been killed on January 9, 1971, during a holdup attempt outside the 101 Ranch Bar in Detroit. Mosley had not been arrested on this charge or interrogated about it by Detective Cowie. Before questioning Mosley about this homicide, Detective Hill carefully advised him of his "*Miranda* rights." Mosley read the notification form both silently and aloud, and Detective Hill then read and explained the warnings to him and had him sign the form. Mosley at first denied any involvement in the Williams murder, but after the officer told him that Anthony Smith had confessed to participating in the slaying and had named him as the "shooter," Mosley made a statement implicating himself in the homicide. The interrogation by Detective Hill lasted approximately 15 minutes, and at no time during its course did Mosley ask to consult with a lawyer or indicate that he did not want to discuss the homicide. In short, there is no claim that the procedures followed during Detective Hill's interrogation of Mosley, standing alone, did not fully comply with the strictures of the *Miranda* opinion.

Mosley was subsequently charged in a one-count information with first-degree murder. Before the trial he moved to suppress his incriminating statement on a number of grounds, among them the claim that under the doctrine of the *Miranda* case it was constitutionally impermissible for Detective Hill to question him about the Williams murder after he had told Detective Cowie that he did not want to answer any questions about the robberies. The trial court denied the motion to suppress after an evidentiary hearing, and the incriminating statement was subsequently introduced in evidence against Mosley at his trial. The jury convicted Mosley of first-degree murder, and the court imposed a mandatory sentence of life imprisonment.

Neither party in the present case challenges the continuing validity of the *Miranda* decision, or of any of the so-called guidelines it established to protect what the Court there said was a person's constitutional privilege against compulsory self-incrimination. The issue in this case, rather, is whether the conduct of the Detroit police that led to Mosley's incriminating statement did in fact violate the *Miranda* "guidelines," so as to render the statement inadmissible in evidence against Mosley at his trial. Resolution of the question turns almost entirely on the interpretation of a single passage in the *Miranda* opinion, upon which the Michigan appellate court relied in finding a *per se* violation of *Miranda*:

> Once warnings have been given, the subsequent procedure is clear. If the individual indicates in any manner, at any time prior to or during questioning, that he wishes to remain silent, the interrogation must cease. At this point he has shown that he intends to exercise his Fifth Amendment privilege; any statement taken after the person invokes his privilege cannot be other than the product of compulsion, subtle or otherwise. Without the right to cut off questioning, the setting of in-custody interrogation operates on the individual to overcome free choice in producing a statement after the privilege has been once invoked.

This passage states that "the interrogation must cease" when the person in custody indicates that "he wishes to remain silent." It does not state under what circumstances, if any, a resumption of questioning is permissible. The passage could be literally read to mean that a person who has invoked his "right to silence" can never again be subjected to custodial interrogation by any police officer at any time or place on any subject. Another possible construction of the passage would characterize "any statement taken after the person invokes his privilege" as "the product of compulsion" and would therefore mandate its exclusion from evidence, even if it were volunteered by the person in custody without any further interrogation whatever. Or the passage could be interpreted to require only the immediate cessation of questioning, and to permit a resumption of interrogation after a momentary respite.

It is evident that any of these possible literal interpretations would lead to absurd and unintended results. To permit the continuation of custodial interrogation after a momentary cessation would clearly frustrate the purposes of *Miranda* by allowing repeated rounds of questioning to undermine the will of the person being questioned. At the other extreme, a blanket prohibition against the taking of voluntary statements or a permanent immunity from further interrogation, regardless of the circumstances, would transform the *Miranda* safeguards into wholly irrational obstacles to legitimate police investigative activity, and deprive suspects of an opportunity to make informed and intelligent assessments of their interests. Clearly, therefore, neither this passage nor any other passage in the *Miranda* opinion can sensibly be read to create a *per se* proscription of indefinite duration upon any further questioning by any police officer on any subject, once the person in custody has indicated a desire to remain silent.

A reasonable and faithful interpretation of the *Miranda* opinion must rest on the intention of the Court in that case to adopt "fully effective means to notify the person of his right of silence and to assure that the exercise of the right will be scrupulously honored." The critical safeguard identified in the passage at issue is a person's "right to cut off questioning." Through the exercise of his option to terminate questioning he can control the time at which questioning occurs, the subjects discussed, and the duration of the interrogation. The requirement that law enforcement authorities must respect a person's exercise of that option counteracts the coercive pressures of the custodial setting. We therefore conclude that the admissibility of statements obtained after the person in custody has decided to remain silent depends under *Miranda* on whether his "right to cut off questioning" was "scrupulously honored."

A review of the circumstances leading to Mosley's confession reveals that his "right to cut off questioning" was fully respected in this case. Before his initial interrogation, Mosley was carefully advised that he was under no obligation to answer any questions and could remain silent if he wished. He orally acknowledged that he understood the *Miranda* warnings and then signed a printed notification-of-rights form. When Mosley stated that he did not want to discuss the robberies, Detective Cowie immediately ceased the interrogation and did not try either to resume the questioning or in any way to persuade Mosley to reconsider his position. After an interval of more than two hours, Mosley was questioned by another police officer at another location about an unrelated holdup murder. He was given full and complete *Miranda* warnings at the outset of the second interrogation. He was thus reminded again that he could remain silent and could consult with a lawyer, and was carefully given a full and fair opportunity to exercise these options. The subsequent questioning did not undercut Mosley's previous decision not to answer Detective Cowie's inquiries. Detective Hill did not resume the interrogation about the White Tower Restaurant robbery or inquire about the Blue Goose Bar robbery, but instead focused exclusively on the Leroy Williams homicide, a crime different in nature and in time and place of occurrence from the robberies for which Mosley had been arrested and interrogated by Detective Cowie. Although it is not clear from the record how much Detective Hill knew about the earlier interrogation, his questioning of Mosley about an unrelated homicide was quite consistent with a reasonable interpretation of Mosley's earlier refusal to answer any questions about the robberies.

This is not a case, therefore, where the police failed to honor a decision of a person in custody to cut off questioning, either by refusing to discontinue the interrogation upon request or by persisting in repeated efforts to wear down his resistance and make him change his mind. In contrast to such practices, the police here immediately ceased the interrogation, resumed questioning only after the passage of a significant period of time and the provision of a fresh set of warnings, and restricted the second interrogation to a crime that had not been a subject of the earlier interrogation.

For these reasons, we conclude that the admission in evidence of Mosley's incriminating statement did not violate the principles of *Miranda v. Arizona.*

JUSTICE BRENNAN, with whom JUSTICE MARSHALL joins, dissenting.

In formulating its procedural safeguard, the Court skirts the problem of compulsion and thereby fails to join issue with the dictates of *Miranda.* The language which the Court finds controlling in this case teaches that renewed questioning itself is part of the process which invariably operates to overcome the will of a suspect. That teaching is embodied in the form of a proscription on any further questioning once the suspect has exercised his right to remain silent. Today's decision uncritically abandons that teaching. The Court assumes, contrary to the controlling language, that "scrupulously honoring" an initial exercise of the right to remain silent preserves the efficaciousness of initial and future warnings despite the fact that the suspect has once been subjected to interrogation and then has been detained for a lengthy period of time.

Observing that the suspect can control the circumstances of interrogation "through the exercise of his option to terminate questioning," the Court concludes that the admissibility of statements obtained after the person in custody has decided to remain silent depends on whether his "right to cut off questioning" was "scrupulously honored." But scrupulously honoring exercises of the right to cut off questioning is only meaningful insofar as the suspect's will to exercise that right remains wholly unfettered. The Court's formulation thus assumes the very matter at issue here: whether renewed questioning following a lengthy period of detention acts to overbear the suspect's will, irrespective of giving the *Miranda* warnings a second time (and scrupulously honoring them), thereby rendering inconsequential any failure to exercise the right to remain silent. For the Court it is enough conclusorily to assert that "the subsequent questioning did not undercut Mosley's previous decision not to answer Detective Cowie's inquiries." Under *Miranda*, however, Mosley's failure to exercise the right upon renewed questioning is presumptively the consequence of an overbearing in which detention and that subsequent questioning played central roles.

I agree that *Miranda* is not to be read, on the one hand, to impose an absolute ban on resumption of questioning "at any time or place on any subject," or on the other hand, "to permit a resumption of interrogation after a momentary respite." But this surely cannot justify adoption of a vague and ineffective procedural standard that falls somewhere between those absurd extremes, for *Miranda* in flat and unambiguous terms requires that questioning "cease" when a suspect exercises the right to remain silent. *Miranda*'s terms, however, are not so uncompromising as to preclude the fashioning of guidelines to govern this case.

The fashioning of guidelines for this case is an easy task. Adequate procedures are readily available. Michigan law requires that the suspect be arraigned before a judicial officer "without unnecessary delay," certainly not a burdensome requirement. Alternatively, a requirement that resumption of questioning should await appointment and arrival of counsel for the suspect would be an acceptable and readily satisfied precondition to resumption.

These procedures would be wholly consistent with the Court's rejection of a "*per se* proscription of indefinite duration," a rejection to which I fully subscribe. Today's decision, however, virtually empties *Miranda* of principle, for plainly the decision encourages police asked to cease interrogation to continue the suspect's detention until the police station's coercive atmosphere does its work and the suspect responds to resumed questioning.

Invocation and Waiver of *Miranda*'s Right to Remain Silent

1.   A suspect who wishes to invoke her right to remain silent under *Miranda* must do so unambiguously by, for example, stating that she wishes to remain silent or does not want to talk to the police. If the suspect invokes her right to remain silent at any time prior to or during questioning, the interrogation must cease.

2.   Where the prosecution shows that a *Miranda* warning was given and that it was understood by the suspect, the suspect's uncoerced statement establishes an implied waiver of the right to remain silent.

3.   The admissibility of statements obtained after a suspect in custody has invoked her right to remain silent depends on whether her right to cut off questioning was scrupulously honored. This standard is satisfied and the suspect's statements are admissible if, for example, the police immediately cease the interrogation when the suspect invokes her right to remain silent, resume questioning only after passage of a significant period of time and the provision of a fresh set of *Miranda* warnings, and restrict the second interrogation to a crime that had not been a subject of the earlier interrogation.

Note: The "General Guidelines for *Miranda* Waivers" set forth above are also applicable to the specific question of whether a suspect has invoked or waived the right to remain silent during custodial interrogation.

---

3.   INVOCATION AND WAIVER OF *MIRANDA*'S RIGHT TO AN ATTORNEY

Beyond the general guidelines for *Miranda* waivers set forth above, the Supreme Court has created a number of specific rules regarding invocation and waiver of *Miranda*'s right to an attorney during custodial interrogation. These rules differ in some important respects from the rules governing invocation and waiver of the right to remain silent. Once again, the starting point for these rules is the *Miranda* decision itself, in which Chief Justice Warren wrote for the Court:

> If the individual states that he wants an attorney, the interrogation must cease until an attorney is present. At that time, the individual must have an opportunity to confer with the attorney and to have him present during any subsequent questioning. If the individual cannot obtain an attorney and he indicates that he wants one before speaking to police, they must respect his decision to remain silent.

The *Miranda* Court went on to note that police need not have a "station house lawyer" present to advise criminal suspects. But if the authorities "conclude that they will not provide counsel during a reasonable period of time" while pursuing investigation in the field, they must not question the suspect during that time. And if police continue the interrogation "without the presence of an attorney and a statement is taken, a heavy burden rests on the government to demonstrate that the defendant knowingly and intelligently waived his privilege against self-incrimination and his right to retained or appointed counsel."

In *Michigan v. Mosley*, 423 U.S. 96 (1975), presented above, the Supreme Court noted that when an individual invokes the right to remain silent, police must stop the interrogation, but they can reapproach a few hours later, offer a fresh set of *Miranda* warnings, and inquire about other crimes that were not previously discussed. Any statements the individual makes at that point will be admissible—by speaking to the police, the individual effectively waives the right to remain silent even though he previously asserted it.

The right to an attorney during custodial interrogation operates somewhat differently. Once invoked, police must stop the interrogation and they cannot seek to resume questioning later unless counsel is actually present or the suspect himself initiates further communication with the police. If the police fail to follow these procedures, any statement made by the suspect will be inadmissible—the suspect's previous invocation of the right to counsel is *not* waived by responding to further police-initiated interrogation. The Supreme Court first articulated these principles in *Edwards v. Arizona*.

EDWARDS V. ARIZONA
451 U.S. 477 (1981)

JUSTICE WHITE delivered the opinion of the Court.

I

On January 19, 1976, a sworn complaint was filed against Edwards in Arizona state court charging him with robbery, burglary, and first-degree murder. An arrest warrant was issued pursuant to the complaint, and Edwards was arrested at his home later that same day. At the police station, he was informed of his rights as required by *Miranda v. Arizona*, 384 U.S. 436 (1966). Petitioner stated that he understood his rights, and was willing to submit to questioning. After being told that another suspect already in custody had implicated him in the crime, Edwards denied involvement and gave a taped statement presenting an alibi defense. He then sought to "make a deal." The interrogating officer told him that he wanted a statement, but that he did not have the authority to negotiate a deal. The officer provided Edwards with the telephone number of a county attorney. Petitioner made the call, but hung up after a few moments. Edwards then said: "I want an attorney before making a deal." At that point, questioning ceased and Edwards was taken to county jail.

At 9:15 the next morning, two detectives, colleagues of the officer who had interrogated Edwards the previous night, came to the jail and asked to see Edwards. When the detention officer informed Edwards that the detectives wished to speak with him, he replied that he did not want to talk to anyone. The guard told him that "he had" to talk and then took him to meet with the detectives. The officers identified themselves, stated they wanted to talk to him, and informed him of his *Miranda* rights. Edwards was willing to talk, but he first wanted to hear the taped statement of the alleged accomplice who had implicated him. After listening to the tape for several minutes, petitioner said that he would make a statement so long as it was not tape-recorded. The detectives informed him that the recording was irrelevant since they could testify in court concerning whatever he said. Edwards replied: "I'll tell you anything you want to know, but I don't want it on tape." He thereupon implicated himself in the crime.

Prior to trial, Edwards moved to suppress his confession on the ground that his *Miranda* rights had been violated when the officers returned to question him after he had invoked his right to counsel.

II

In *Miranda v. Arizona*, the Court determined that the Fifth and Fourteenth Amendments' prohibition against compelled self-incrimination required that custodial interrogation be preceded by advice to the putative defendant that he has the right to remain silent and also the right to the presence of an attorney. The Court also indicated the procedures to be followed subsequent to the warnings. If the accused indicates that he wishes to remain silent, "the interrogation must cease." If he requests counsel, "the interrogation must cease until an attorney is present."

Miranda thus declared that an accused has a Fifth and Fourteenth Amendment right to have counsel present during custodial interrogation. Here, the critical facts as found by the Arizona Supreme Court are that Edwards asserted his right to counsel and his right to remain silent on January 19, but that the police, without furnishing him counsel, returned the next morning to confront him and as a result of the meeting secured incriminating oral admissions. Contrary to the holdings of the state courts, Edwards insists that having exercised his right on the 19th to have counsel present during interrogation, he did not validly waive that right on the 20th. For the following reasons, we agree.

First, the Arizona Supreme Court applied an erroneous standard for determining waiver where the accused has specifically invoked his right to counsel. It is reasonably clear under our cases that waivers of counsel must not only be voluntary, but must also constitute a knowing and intelligent relinquishment or abandonment of a known right or privilege, a matter which depends in each case upon the particular facts and circumstances surrounding that case, including the background, experience, and conduct of the accused.

Considering the proceedings in the state courts in the light of this standard, we note that in denying petitioner's motion to suppress, the trial court found the admission to have been "voluntary," without separately focusing on whether Edwards had knowingly and intelligently relinquished his right to counsel. Here, however sound the conclusion of the state courts as to the voluntariness of Edwards' admission may be, neither the trial court nor the Arizona Supreme Court undertook to focus on whether Edwards understood his right to counsel and intelligently and knowingly relinquished it. It is thus apparent that the decision below misunderstood the requirement for finding a valid waiver of the right to counsel, once invoked.

Second, although we have held that after initially being advised of his *Miranda* rights, the accused may himself validly waive his rights and respond to interrogation, the Court has strongly indicated that additional safeguards are necessary when the accused asks for counsel; and we now hold that when an accused has invoked his right to have counsel present during custodial interrogation, a valid waiver of that right cannot be established by showing only that he responded to further police-initiated custodial interrogation even if he has been advised of his rights. We further hold that an accused, such as Edwards, having expressed his desire to deal with the police only through counsel, is not subject to further interrogation by the authorities until counsel has been made available to him, unless the accused himself initiates further communication, exchanges, or conversations with the police.

Miranda itself indicated that the assertion of the right to counsel was a significant event and that once exercised by the accused, the interrogation must cease until an attorney is present. Our later cases have not abandoned that view. We emphasize that it is inconsistent with *Miranda* and its progeny for the authorities, at their instance, to reinterrogate an accused in custody if he has clearly asserted his right to counsel.

In concluding that the fruits of the interrogation initiated by the police on January 20 could not be used against Edwards, we do not hold or imply that Edwards was powerless to countermand his election or that the authorities could in no event use any incriminating statements made by Edwards prior to his having access to counsel. Had Edwards initiated the meeting on January 20, nothing in the Fifth and Fourteenth Amendments would prohibit the police from merely listening to his voluntary, volunteered statements and using them against him at the trial. The Fifth Amendment right identified in *Miranda* is the right to have counsel present at any custodial interrogation. Absent such interrogation, there would have been no infringement of the right that Edwards invoked and there would be no occasion to determine whether there had been a valid waiver.

But this is not what the facts of this case show. Here, the officers conducting the interrogation on the evening of January 19 ceased interrogation when Edwards requested counsel as he had been advised he had the right to do. The Arizona Supreme Court was of the opinion that this was a sufficient invocation of his *Miranda* rights, and we are in accord. It is also clear that without making counsel available to Edwards, the police returned to him the next day. This was not at his suggestion or request. Indeed, Edwards informed the detention officer that he did not want to talk to anyone. At the meeting, the detectives told Edwards that they wanted to talk to him and again advised him of his *Miranda* rights. Edwards stated that he would talk, but what prompted this action does not appear. He listened at his own request to part of the taped statement made by one of his alleged accomplices and then made an incriminating statement, which was used against him at his trial. We think it is clear that Edwards was subjected to custodial interrogation on January 20 within the meaning of *Rhode Island v. Innis*, 446 U.S. 291 (1980), and that this occurred at the instance of the authorities. His statement, made without having had access to counsel, did not amount to a valid waiver and hence was inadmissible.

In *Davis v. U.S.*, the Supreme Court held that the *Edwards* rule—prohibiting police from reinitiating custodial interrogation once a suspect asks for an attorney—is triggered only if the suspect *unambiguously* requests counsel.

DAVIS V. U.S.
512 U.S. 452 (1994)

JUSTICE O'CONNOR delivered the opinion of the Court.

In *Edwards v. Arizona*, 451 U.S. 477 (1981), we held that law enforcement officers must immediately cease questioning a suspect who has clearly asserted his right to have counsel present during custodial interrogation. In this case we decide how law enforcement officers should respond when a suspect makes a reference to counsel that is insufficiently clear to invoke the *Edwards* prohibition on further questioning.

I

Pool brought trouble—not to River City, but to the Charleston Naval Base. Petitioner, a member of the United States Navy, spent the evening of October 2, 1988, shooting pool at a club on the base. Another sailor, Keith Shackleton, lost a game and a $30 wager to petitioner, but Shackleton refused to pay. After the club closed, Shackleton was beaten to death with a pool cue on a loading dock behind the commissary. The body was found early the next morning.

The investigation by the Naval Investigative Service (NIS) gradually focused on petitioner. Investigative agents determined that petitioner was at the club that evening, and that he was absent without authorization from his duty station the next morning. The agents also learned that only privately owned pool cues could be removed from the club premises, and that petitioner owned two cues—one of which had a bloodstain on it. The agents were told by various people that petitioner either had admitted committing the crime or had recounted details that clearly indicated his involvement in the killing.

On November 4, 1988, petitioner was interviewed at the NIS office. As required by military law, the agents advised petitioner that he was a suspect in the killing, that he was not required to make a statement, that any statement could be used against him at a trial by court-martial, and that he was entitled to speak with an attorney and have an attorney present during questioning. Petitioner waived his rights to remain silent and to counsel, both orally and in writing.

About an hour and a half into the interview, petitioner said, "Maybe I should talk to a lawyer." According to the uncontradicted testimony of one of the interviewing agents, the interview then proceeded as follows:

> We made it very clear that we're not here to violate his rights, that if he wants a lawyer, then we will stop any kind of questioning with him, that we weren't going to pursue the matter unless we have it clarified is he asking for a lawyer or is he just making a comment about a lawyer, and he said, "No, I'm not asking for a lawyer," and then he continued on, and said, "No, I don't want a lawyer."

After a short break, the agents reminded petitioner of his rights to remain silent and to counsel. The interview then continued for another hour, until petitioner said, "I think I want a lawyer before I say anything else." At that point, questioning ceased.

At his general court-martial, petitioner moved to suppress statements made during the November 4 interview. The Military Judge denied the motion, holding that "the mention of a lawyer by petitioner during the course of the interrogation was not in the form of a request for counsel and the agents properly determined that petitioner was not indicating a desire for or invoking his right to counsel." Petitioner was convicted on one specification of unpremeditated murder. He was sentenced to confinement for life, a dishonorable discharge, forfeiture of all pay and allowances, and a reduction to the lowest pay grade.

Although we have twice previously noted the varying approaches the lower courts have adopted with respect to ambiguous or equivocal references to counsel during custodial interrogation, we have not addressed the issue on the merits. We granted certiorari to do so.

II

The Sixth Amendment right to counsel attaches only at the initiation of adversary criminal proceedings, and before proceedings are initiated a suspect in a criminal investigation has no constitutional right to the assistance of counsel. Nevertheless, we held in *Miranda v. Arizona*, 384 U.S. 436 (1966), that a suspect subject to custodial interrogation has the right to consult with an attorney and to have counsel present during questioning, and that the police must explain this right to him before questioning begins. The right to counsel established in *Miranda* was one of a series of recommended "procedural safeguards" that were not themselves rights protected by the Constitution but were instead measures to insure that the right against compulsory self-incrimination was protected.

The right to counsel recognized in *Miranda* is sufficiently important to suspects in criminal investigations, we have held, that it requires the special protection of the knowing and intelligent waiver standard. If the suspect effectively waives his right to counsel after receiving the *Miranda* warnings, law enforcement officers are free to question him. But if a suspect requests counsel at any time during the interview, he is not subject to further questioning until a lawyer has been made available or the suspect himself reinitiates conversation. This second layer of prophylaxis for the *Miranda* right to counsel is designed to prevent police from badgering a defendant into waiving his previously asserted *Miranda* rights. To that end, we have held that a suspect who has invoked the right to counsel cannot be questioned regarding any offense unless an attorney is actually present.

The applicability of the "rigid prophylactic rule" of *Edwards* requires courts to determine whether the accused *actually invoked* his right to counsel. To avoid difficulties of proof and to provide guidance to officers conducting interrogations, this is an objective inquiry. Invocation of the *Miranda* right to counsel requires, at a minimum, some statement that can reasonably be construed to be an expression of a desire for the assistance of an attorney. But if a suspect makes a reference to an attorney that is ambiguous or equivocal in that a reasonable officer in light of the circumstances would have understood only that the suspect *might* be invoking the right to counsel, our precedents do not require the cessation of questioning.

Rather, the suspect must unambiguously request counsel. As we have observed, "a statement either is such an assertion of the right to counsel or it is not." Although a suspect need not "speak with the discrimination of an Oxford don," he must articulate his desire to have counsel present sufficiently clearly that a reasonable police officer in the circumstances would understand the statement to be a request for an attorney. If the statement fails to meet the requisite level of clarity, *Edwards* does not require that the officers stop questioning the suspect.

We decline petitioner's invitation to extend *Edwards* and require law enforcement officers to cease questioning immediately upon the making of an ambiguous or equivocal reference to an attorney. The rationale underlying *Edwards* is that the police must respect a suspect's wishes regarding his right to have an attorney present during custodial interrogation. But when the officers conducting the questioning reasonably do not know whether or not the suspect wants a lawyer, a rule requiring the immediate cessation of questioning would transform the *Miranda* safeguards into wholly irrational obstacles to legitimate police investigative activity because it would needlessly prevent the police from questioning a suspect in the absence of counsel even if the suspect did not wish to have a lawyer present. Nothing in *Edwards* requires the provision of counsel to a suspect who consents to answer questions without the assistance of a lawyer. In *Miranda* itself, we expressly rejected the suggestion that each police station must have a "station house lawyer" present at all times to advise prisoners, and held instead that a suspect must be told of his right to have an attorney present and that he may not be questioned after invoking his right to counsel. We also noted that if a suspect is "indecisive in his request for counsel," the officers need not always cease questioning.

We recognize that requiring a clear assertion of the right to counsel might disadvantage some suspects who—because of fear, intimidation, lack of linguistic skills, or a variety of other reasons—will not clearly articulate their right to counsel although they actually want to have a lawyer present. But the primary protection afforded suspects subject to custodial interrogation is the *Miranda* warnings themselves. A suspect who knowingly and voluntarily waives his right to counsel after having that right explained to him has indicated his willingness to deal with the police unassisted. Although *Edwards* provides an additional protection— if a suspect subsequently requests an attorney, questioning must cease— it is one that must be affirmatively invoked by the suspect.

In considering how a suspect must invoke the right to counsel, we must consider the other side of the *Miranda* equation: the need for effective law enforcement. Although the courts ensure compliance with the *Miranda* requirements through the exclusionary rule, it is police officers who must actually decide whether or not they can question a suspect. The *Edwards* rule—questioning must cease if the suspect asks for a lawyer—provides a bright line that can be applied by officers in the real world of investigation and interrogation without unduly hampering the gathering of information. But if we were to require questioning to cease if a suspect makes a statement that *might* be a request for an attorney, this clarity and ease of application would be lost. Police officers would be forced to make difficult judgment calls about whether the suspect in fact wants a lawyer even though he has not said so, with the threat of suppression if they guess wrong. We therefore hold that, after a knowing and voluntary waiver of the *Miranda* rights, law enforcement officers may continue questioning until and unless the suspect clearly requests an attorney.

Of course, when a suspect makes an ambiguous or equivocal statement it will often be good police practice for the interviewing officers to clarify whether or not he actually wants an attorney. That was the procedure followed by the NIS agents in this case. Clarifying questions help protect the rights of the suspect by ensuring that he gets an attorney if he wants one, and will minimize the chance of a confession being suppressed due to subsequent judicial second-guessing as to the meaning of the suspect's statement regarding counsel. But we decline to adopt a rule requiring officers to ask clarifying questions. If the suspect's statement is not an unambiguous or unequivocal request for counsel, the officers have no obligation to stop questioning him.

To recapitulate: We held in *Miranda* that a suspect is entitled to the assistance of counsel during custodial interrogation even though the Constitution does not provide for such assistance. We held in *Edwards* that if the suspect invokes the right to counsel at any time, the police must immediately cease questioning him until an attorney is present. But we are unwilling to create a third layer of prophylaxis to prevent police questioning when the suspect *might* want a lawyer. Unless the suspect actually requests an attorney, questioning may continue.

The courts below found that petitioner's remark to the NIS agents— "Maybe I should talk to a lawyer"—was not a request for counsel, and we see no reason to disturb that conclusion. The NIS agents therefore were not required to stop questioning petitioner, though it was entirely proper for them to clarify whether petitioner in fact wanted a lawyer.

JUSTICE SOUTER, with whom JUSTICE BLACKMUN, JUSTICE STEVENS, and JUSTICE GINSBURG join, concurring in the judgment.

I agree with the majority that the Constitution does not forbid law enforcement officers to pose questions (like those directed at Davis) aimed solely at clarifying whether a suspect's ambiguous reference to counsel was meant to assert his Fifth Amendment right. Accordingly I concur in the judgment affirming Davis' conviction, resting partly on evidence of statements given after agents ascertained that he did not wish to deal with them through counsel. I cannot, however, join in my colleagues' further conclusion that if the investigators here had been so inclined, they were at liberty to disregard Davis' reference to a lawyer entirely, in accordance with a general rule that interrogators have no legal obligation to discover what a custodial subject meant by an ambiguous statement that could reasonably be understood to express a desire to consult a lawyer.

Our own precedent, the reasonable judgments of the majority of the many courts already to have addressed the issue before us, and the advocacy of a considerable body of law enforcement officials are to the contrary. All argue against the Court's approach today, which draws a sharp line between interrogated suspects who "clearly" assert their right to counsel, and those who say something that may, but may not, express a desire for counsel's presence, the former suspects being assured that questioning will not resume without counsel present, the latter being left to fend for themselves. The concerns of fairness and practicality that have long anchored our *Miranda* case law point to a different response: when law enforcement officials "reasonably do not know whether or not the suspect wants a lawyer," they should stop their interrogation and ask him to make his choice clear.

———

Consistent with the holding in *Davis v. U.S.* that a suspect must request an attorney unambiguously to bring an end to custodial interrogation, the Supreme Court held, in *Fare v. Michael C.*, 442 U.S. 707 (1979), that a juvenile's request to have his probation officer with him during custodial interrogation was not the same as a request for an attorney. Thus, as a matter of federal constitutional law, *Miranda* rights are not invoked—and the protections of *Edwards* do not apply—when a suspect asks for his probation officer, a religious adviser, or a friend. Such requests may, however, be considered as part of the "totality of the circumstances" determination of the voluntariness of any subsequent waiver of *Miranda* rights.

In sharp contrast to *Michigan v. Mosley*, in which the Supreme Court permitted the police to interrogate Mosley about a murder two hours after he asserted his right to remain silent when questioned about two robberies, the *Edwards* rule prohibiting further police-initiated interrogation after a suspect has invoked his right to counsel applies even when the police seek to question the suspect about a different crime. The Supreme Court explained the reasons for this rule in *Arizona v. Roberson*.

ARIZONA V. ROBERSON
486 U.S. 675 (1988)

JUSTICE STEVENS delivered the opinion of the Court.

In *Edwards v. Arizona*, 451 U.S. 477 (1981), we held that a suspect who has "expressed his desire to deal with the police only through counsel is not subject to further interrogation by the authorities until counsel has been made available to him, unless the accused himself initiates further communication, exchanges, or conversations with the police." In this case Arizona asks us to craft an exception to that rule for cases in which the police want to interrogate a suspect about an offense that is unrelated to the subject of their initial interrogation.

On April 16, 1985, respondent was arrested at the scene of a just-completed burglary. The arresting officer advised him that he had a constitutional right to remain silent and also the right to have an attorney present during any interrogation. Respondent replied that he "wanted a lawyer before answering any questions." This fact was duly recorded in the officer's written report of the incident. In due course, respondent was convicted of the April 16, 1985, burglary.

On April 19, 1985, while respondent was still in custody pursuant to the arrest three days earlier, a different officer interrogated him about a different burglary that had occurred on April 15. That officer was not aware of the fact that respondent had requested the assistance of counsel three days earlier. After advising respondent of his rights, the officer obtained an incriminating statement concerning the April 15 burglary. In the prosecution for that offense, the trial court suppressed that statement. The Arizona Court of Appeals affirmed the suppression order in a brief opinion, and the Arizona Supreme Court denied a petition for review. We granted certiorari to resolve a conflict with certain other state court decisions. We now affirm.

In *Edwards,* we emphasized that it is inconsistent with *Miranda* and its progeny for the authorities, at their instance, to reinterrogate an accused in custody if he has clearly asserted his right to counsel. We concluded that reinterrogation may only occur if "the accused himself initiates further communication, exchanges, or conversations with the police." Thus, the prophylactic protections that the *Miranda* warnings provide to counteract the "inherently compelling pressures" of custodial interrogation and to "permit a full opportunity to exercise the privilege against self-incrimination" are implemented by the application of the *Edwards* corollary that if a suspect believes that he is not capable of undergoing such questioning without advice of counsel, then it is presumed that any subsequent waiver that has come at the authorities' behest, and not at the suspect's own instigation, is itself the product of the "inherently compelling pressures" and not the purely voluntary choice of the suspect.

The *Edwards* rule serves the purpose of providing clear and unequivocal guidelines to the law enforcement profession. Surely there is nothing ambiguous about the requirement that after a person in custody has expressed his desire to deal with the police only through counsel, he "is not subject to further interrogation by the authorities until counsel has been made available to him, unless the accused himself initiates further communication, exchanges, or conversations with the police."

Petitioner contends that the bright-line, prophylactic *Edwards* rule should not apply when the police-initiated interrogation following a suspect's request for counsel occurs in the context of a separate investigation. According to petitioner, both our cases and the nature of the factual setting compel this distinction. We are unpersuaded.

Petitioner points to our holding in *Michigan v. Mosley*, 423 U.S. 96 (1975), that when a suspect asserts his right to cut off questioning, the police may "scrupulously honor" that right by "immediately ceas[ing] the interrogation, resum[ing] questioning only after the passage of a significant period of time and the provision of a fresh set of warnings, and restrict[ing] the second interrogation to a crime that had not been a subject of the earlier interrogation." The police in this case followed precisely that course, claims the State. However, as *Mosley* made clear, a suspect's decision to cut off questioning, unlike his request for counsel, does not raise the presumption that he is unable to proceed without a lawyer's advice.

Roberson's unwillingness to answer any questions without the advice of counsel indicated that he did not feel sufficiently comfortable with the pressures of custodial interrogation to answer questions without an attorney. This discomfort is precisely the state of mind that *Edwards* presumes to persist unless the suspect himself initiates further conversation about the investigation; unless he otherwise states, there is no reason to assume that a suspect's state of mind is in any way investigation-specific. Further, to a suspect who has indicated his inability to cope with the pressures of custodial interrogation by requesting counsel, any further interrogation without counsel having been provided will surely exacerbate whatever compulsion to speak the suspect may be feeling. Thus, we also disagree with petitioner's contention that fresh sets of *Miranda* warnings will "reassure" a suspect who has been denied the counsel he has clearly requested that his rights have remained untrammeled. Especially in a case such as this, in which a period of three days elapsed between the unsatisfied request for counsel and the interrogation about a second offense, there is a serious risk that the mere repetition of the *Miranda* warnings would not overcome the presumption of coercion that is created by prolonged police custody.

The United States, as *amicus curiae* supporting petitioner, suggests that a suspect in custody might have "good reasons for wanting to speak with the police about the offenses involved in the new investigation, or at least to learn from the police what the new investigation is about so that he can decide whether it is in his interest to make a statement about that matter without the assistance of counsel." The simple answer is that the suspect, having requested counsel, can determine how to deal with the separate investigations with counsel's advice. Further, even if the police have decided temporarily not to provide counsel, they are free to inform the suspect of the facts of the second investigation as long as such communication does not constitute interrogation [under] *Rhode Island v. Innis*, 446 U.S. 291 (1980). As we have made clear, any "further communication, exchanges, or conversations with the police" that the suspect himself initiates are perfectly valid.

Finally, we attach no significance to the fact that the officer who conducted the second interrogation did not know that respondent had made a request for counsel. In addition to the fact that *Edwards* focuses on the state of mind of the suspect and not of the police, custodial interrogation must be conducted pursuant to established procedures, and those procedures in turn must enable an officer who proposes to initiate an interrogation to determine whether the suspect has previously requested counsel. In this case, respondent's request had been properly memorialized in a written report but the officer who conducted the interrogation simply failed to examine that report. Whether a contemplated reinterrogation concerns the same or a different offense, or whether the same or different law enforcement authorities are involved in the second investigation, the same need to determine whether the suspect has requested counsel exists. The police department's failure to honor that request cannot be justified by the lack of diligence of a particular officer.

JUSTICE KENNEDY, with whom CHIEF JUSTICE REHNQUIST joins, dissenting.

The majority's rule is not necessary to protect the rights of suspects, and it will in many instances deprive our nationwide law enforcement network of a legitimate investigative technique now routinely used to resolve major crimes.

When a suspect is in custody for even the most minor offense, his name and fingerprints are checked against master files. It is a frequent occurrence that the suspect is wanted for questioning with respect to crimes unrelated to the one for which he has been apprehended. The rule announced today will bar law enforcement officials, even those from some other city or other jurisdiction, from questioning a suspect about an unrelated matter if he is in custody and has requested counsel to assist in answering questions put to him about the crime for which he was arrested.

The rule in *Edwards* was in effect a prophylactic rule, designed to protect an accused in police custody from being badgered by police officers in the manner in which the defendant in *Edwards* was. Where the subsequent questioning is confined to an entirely independent investigation, there is little risk that the suspect will be badgered into submission.

Unless there are so many separate investigations that fresh teams of police are regularly turning up to question the suspect, the danger of badgering is minimal, and insufficient to justify a rigid *per se* rule. Whatever their eagerness, the police in a separate investigation may not commence any questioning unless the suspect is readvised of his *Miranda* rights and consents to the interrogation, and they are required by *Edwards* to cease questioning him if he invokes his right to counsel. Consequently, the legitimate interest of the suspect in not being subjected to coercive badgering is already protected. The reason for the *Edwards* rule is not that confessions are disfavored but that coercion is feared. The rule announced today, however, prohibits the police from resuming questions, after a second *Miranda* warning, when there is no more likelihood of coercion than when the first interrogation began.

The Court suggests that the suspect may believe his rights are fictitious if he must assert them a second time, but the support for this suggestion is weak. The suspect, having observed that his earlier invocation of rights was effective in terminating questioning and having been advised that further questioning may not relate to that crime, would understand that he may invoke his rights again with respect to the new investigation, and so terminate questioning regarding that investigation as well. Indeed, the new warnings and explanations will reinforce his comprehension of a suspect's rights.

Allowing authorities who conduct a separate investigation to read the suspect his *Miranda* rights and ask him whether he wishes to invoke them strikes an appropriate balance, which protects the suspect's freedom from coercion without unnecessarily disrupting legitimate law enforcement efforts.

In *Minnick v. Mississippi*, the Supreme Court reaffirmed the *Edwards* rule and made it clear that once a suspect requests counsel, police may not reinitiate interrogation unless counsel is actually present.

MINNICK V. MISSISSIPPI
498 U.S. 146 (1990)

JUSTICE KENNEDY delivered the opinion of the Court.

To protect the privilege against self-incrimination guaranteed by the Fifth Amendment, we have held that the police must terminate interrogation of an accused in custody if the accused requests the assistance of counsel. *Miranda v. Arizona*, 384 U.S. 436 (1966). We reinforced the protections of *Miranda* in *Edwards v. Arizona*, 451 U.S. 477 (1981), which held that once the accused requests counsel, officials may not reinitiate questioning "until counsel has been made available" to him. The issue in the case before us is whether *Edwards*' protection ceases once the suspect has consulted with an attorney.

Petitioner Robert Minnick and fellow prisoner James Dyess escaped from a county jail in Mississippi and, a day later, broke into a mobile home in search of weapons. In the course of the burglary they were interrupted by the arrival of the trailer's owner, Ellis Thomas, accompanied by Lamar Lafferty and Lafferty's infant son. Dyess and Minnick used the stolen weapons to kill Thomas and the senior Lafferty. Minnick's story is that Dyess murdered one victim and forced Minnick to shoot the other. Before the escapees could get away, two young women arrived at the mobile home. They were held at gunpoint, then bound hand and foot. Dyess and Minnick fled in Thomas' truck, abandoning the vehicle in New Orleans. The fugitives continued to Mexico, where they fought, and Minnick then proceeded alone to California. Minnick was arrested in Lemon Grove, California, on a Mississippi warrant, some four months after the murders.

The confession at issue here resulted from the last interrogation of Minnick while he was held in the San Diego jail, but we first recount the events which preceded it. Minnick was arrested on Friday, August 22, 1986. Petitioner testified that he was mistreated by local police during and after the arrest. The day following the arrest, Saturday, two Federal Bureau of Investigation (FBI) agents came to the jail to interview him. Petitioner testified that he refused to go to the interview, but was told he would "have to go down or else." The FBI report indicates that the agents read petitioner his *Miranda* warnings, and that he acknowledged he understood his rights. He refused to sign a rights waiver form, however, and said he would not answer "very many" questions. Minnick told the agents about the jailbreak and the flight, and described how Dyess threatened and beat him. Early in the interview, he sobbed "it was my life or theirs," but otherwise he hesitated to tell what happened at the trailer. The agents reminded him he did not have to answer questions without a lawyer present. According to the report, Minnick stated "Come back Monday when I have a lawyer," and stated that he would make a more complete statement then with his lawyer present. The FBI interview ended.

After the FBI interview, an appointed attorney met with petitioner. Petitioner spoke with the lawyer on two or three occasions, though it is not clear from the record whether all of these conferences were in person.

On Monday, August 25, Deputy Sheriff J.C. Denham of Clarke County, Mississippi, came to the San Diego jail to question Minnick. Minnick testified that his jailers again told him he would "have to talk" to Denham and that he "could not refuse." Denham advised petitioner of his rights, and petitioner again declined to sign a rights waiver form. Petitioner told Denham about the escape and then proceeded to describe the events at the mobile home. According to petitioner, Dyess jumped out of the mobile home and shot the first of the two victims, once in the back with a shotgun and once in the head with a pistol. Dyess then handed the pistol to petitioner and ordered him to shoot the other victim, holding the shotgun on petitioner until he did so. Petitioner also said that when the two girls arrived, he talked Dyess out of raping or otherwise hurting them.

Minnick was tried for murder in Mississippi. He moved to suppress all statements given to the FBI or other police officers, including Denham. The trial court denied the motion with respect to petitioner's statements to Denham, but suppressed his other statements. Petitioner was convicted on two counts of capital murder and sentenced to death.

On appeal, petitioner argued that the confession to Denham was taken in violation of his rights to counsel under the Fifth and Sixth Amendments. The Mississippi Supreme Court rejected the claims. With respect to the Fifth Amendment aspect of the case, the court found "the *Edwards* bright-line rule as to initiation" inapplicable. Relying on language in *Edwards* indicating that the bar on interrogating the accused after a request for counsel applies "until counsel has been made available to him," the court concluded that "since counsel was made available to Minnick, his Fifth Amendment right to counsel was satisfied." The court also rejected the Sixth Amendment claim, finding that petitioner waived his Sixth Amendment right to counsel when he spoke with Denham. We granted certiorari, and, without reaching any Sixth Amendment implications in the case, we decide that the Fifth Amendment protection of *Edwards* is not terminated or suspended by consultation with counsel.

Edwards is designed to prevent police from badgering a defendant into waiving his previously asserted *Miranda* rights. The rule ensures that any statement made in subsequent interrogation is not the result of coercive pressures. *Edwards* conserves judicial resources which would otherwise be expended in making difficult determinations of voluntariness, and implements the protections of *Miranda* in practical and straightforward terms.

The Mississippi Supreme Court relied on our statement in *Edwards* that an accused who invokes his right to counsel "is not subject to further interrogation by the authorities until counsel has been made available to him." We do not interpret this language to mean, as the Mississippi court thought, that the protection of *Edwards* terminates once counsel has consulted with the suspect. In context, the requirement that counsel be "made available" to the accused refers to more than an opportunity to consult with an attorney outside the interrogation room.

In our view, a fair reading of *Edwards* and subsequent cases demonstrates that we have interpreted the rule to bar police-initiated interrogation unless the accused has counsel with him at the time of questioning. Whatever the ambiguities of our earlier cases on this point, we now hold that when counsel is requested, interrogation must cease, and officials may not reinitiate interrogation without counsel present, whether or not the accused has consulted with his attorney.

We consider our ruling to be an appropriate and necessary application of the *Edwards* rule. A single consultation with an attorney does not remove the suspect from persistent attempts by officials to persuade him to waive his rights, or from the coercive pressures that accompany custody and that may increase as custody is prolonged. The case before us well illustrates the pressures, and abuses, that may be concomitants of custody. Petitioner testified that though he resisted, he was required to submit to both the FBI and the Denham interviews. In the latter instance, the compulsion to submit to interrogation followed petitioner's unequivocal request during the FBI interview that questioning cease until counsel was present. The case illustrates also that consultation is not always effective in instructing the suspect of his rights. One plausible interpretation of the record is that petitioner thought he could keep his admissions out of evidence by refusing to sign a formal waiver of rights. If the authorities had complied with Minnick's request to have counsel present during interrogation, the attorney could have corrected Minnick's misunderstanding, or indeed counseled him that he need not make a statement at all. We decline to remove protection from police-initiated questioning based on isolated consultations with counsel who is absent when the interrogation resumes.

Edwards does not foreclose finding a waiver of Fifth Amendment protections after counsel has been requested, provided the accused has initiated the conversation or discussions with the authorities; but that is not the case before us. There can be no doubt that the interrogation in question was initiated by the police; it was a formal interview which petitioner was compelled to attend. Since petitioner made a specific request for counsel before the interview, the police-initiated interrogation was impermissible. Petitioner's statement to Denham was not admissible at trial.

JUSTICE SCALIA, with whom CHIEF JUSTICE REHNQUIST joins, dissenting.

The Court today establishes an irrebuttable presumption that a criminal suspect, after invoking his *Miranda* right to counsel, can *never* validly waive that right during any police-initiated encounter, even after the suspect has been provided multiple *Miranda* warnings and has actually consulted his attorney. Because I see no justification for applying the *Edwards* irrebuttable presumption when a criminal suspect has actually consulted with his attorney, I respectfully dissent.

In this case, of course, we have not been called upon to reconsider *Edwards*, but simply to determine whether its irrebuttable presumption should continue after a suspect has actually consulted with his attorney. Whatever justifications might support *Edwards* are even less convincing in this context.

Most of the Court's discussion of *Edwards*—which stresses repeatedly, in various formulations, the case's emphasis upon the "right to have counsel *present* during custodial interrogation"—is beside the point. The existence and the importance of the *Miranda*-created right "to have counsel *present*" are unquestioned here. What *is* questioned is why a State should not be given the opportunity to prove that the right was *voluntarily waived* by a suspect who, after having been read his *Miranda* rights twice and having consulted with counsel at least twice, chose to speak to a police officer (and to admit his involvement in two murders) without counsel present.

Edwards did not assert the principle that no waiver of the *Miranda* right "to have counsel *present*" is possible. It simply adopted the presumption that no waiver is *voluntary* in certain circumstances, and the issue before us today is how broadly those circumstances are to be defined. They should not, in my view, extend beyond the circumstances present in *Edwards* itself—where the suspect in custody asked to consult an attorney and was interrogated before that attorney had ever been provided. In those circumstances, the *Edwards* rule rests upon an assumption similar to that of *Miranda* itself: that when a suspect in police custody is first questioned he is likely to be ignorant of his rights and to feel isolated in a hostile environment. This likelihood is thought to justify special protection against unknowing or coerced waiver of rights. After a suspect has seen his request for an attorney honored, however, and has actually spoken with that attorney, the probabilities change. The suspect then knows that he has an advocate on his side, and that the police will permit him to consult that advocate. He almost certainly also has a heightened awareness (above what the *Miranda* warning itself will provide) of his right to remain silent—since at the earliest opportunity "any lawyer worth his salt will tell the suspect in no uncertain terms to make no statement to the police under any circumstances."

Under these circumstances, an irrebuttable presumption that any police-prompted confession is the result of ignorance of rights, or of coercion, has no genuine basis in fact. After the first consultation, therefore, the *Edwards* exclusionary rule should cease to apply. Does this mean, as the Court implies, that the police will thereafter have license to "badger" the suspect? Only if all one means by "badger" is asking, without such insistence or frequency as would constitute coercion, whether he would like to reconsider his decision not to confess. Nothing in the Constitution (the only basis for our intervention here) prohibits such inquiry, which may often produce the desirable result of a voluntary confession.

One should not underestimate the extent to which the Court's expansion of *Edwards* constricts law enforcement. Today's ruling, that the invocation of a right to counsel permanently prevents a police-initiated waiver, makes it largely impossible for the police to urge a prisoner who has initially declined to confess to change his mind—or indeed, even to ask whether he has changed his mind. Many persons in custody will invoke the *Miranda* right to counsel during the first interrogation, so that the permanent prohibition will attach at once. Those who do not do so will almost certainly request or obtain counsel at arraignment.

It seems obvious to me that, even in *Edwards* itself but surely in today's decision, we have gone far beyond any genuine concern about suspects who do not *know* their right to remain silent, or who have been *coerced* to abandon it. Both holdings are explicable, in my view, only as an effort to protect suspects against what is regarded as their own folly. The sharp-witted criminal would know better than to confess; why should the dull-witted suffer for his lack of mental endowment? Providing him an attorney at every stage where he might be induced or persuaded (though not coerced) to incriminate himself will even the odds. Apart from the fact that this protective enterprise is beyond our authority under the Fifth Amendment or any other provision of the Constitution, it is unwise. The procedural protections of the Constitution protect the guilty as well as the innocent, but it is not their objective to set the guilty free. That some clever criminals may employ those protections to their advantage is poor reason to allow criminals who have not done so to escape justice.

Thus, even if I were to concede that an honest confession is a foolish mistake, I would welcome rather than reject it; a rule that foolish mistakes do not count would leave most offenders not only unconvicted but undetected. We should, then, rejoice at an honest confession, rather than pity the "poor fool" who has made it; and we should regret the attempted retraction of that good act, rather than seek to facilitate and encourage it. To design our laws on premises contrary to these is to abandon belief in either personal responsibility or the moral claim of just government to obedience.

Edwards, in effect, creates a presumption of involuntariness regarding any waiver of rights following police-initiated interrogation after a suspect invokes his *Miranda* right to counsel. But how long does this presumption last? If a suspect requests counsel during custodial interrogation and triggers the *Edwards* presumption, are the police barred from *ever* reapproaching him, outside the presence of counsel, to inquire whether he's willing to answer questions? What if, after the suspect requests counsel, the investigation fails to yield enough evidence to file charges and he is released from police custody, only to be arrested again six months later when new evidence emerges? If, at that later juncture, the police reinitiate questioning and the suspect confesses, does the *Edwards* rule render the waiver invalid and the confession inadmissible? The Supreme Court addressed these questions in *Maryland v. Shatzer* and adopted a "break in custody" limitation on the *Edwards* presumption that allows police to reinitiate contact with a suspect after his invocation of the right to counsel if there has been a break in *Miranda* custody of at least 14 days before the renewed attempt at interrogation.

MARYLAND V. SHATZER
559 U.S. 98 (2010)

JUSTICE SCALIA delivered the opinion of the Court.

We consider whether a break in custody ends the presumption of involuntariness established in *Edwards v. Arizona*, 451 U.S. 477 (1981).

I

In August 2003, a social worker assigned to the Child Advocacy Center in the Criminal Investigation Division of the Hagerstown Police Department referred to the department allegations that respondent Michael Shatzer, Sr., had sexually abused his 3-year-old son. At that time, Shatzer was incarcerated at the Maryland Correctional Institution-Hagerstown, serving a sentence for an unrelated child-sexual-abuse offense. Detective Shane Blankenship was assigned to the investigation and interviewed Shatzer at the correctional institution on August 7, 2003. Before asking any questions, Blankenship reviewed Shatzer's *Miranda* rights with him, and obtained a written waiver of those rights. When Blankenship explained that he was there to question Shatzer about sexually abusing his son, Shatzer expressed confusion—he had thought Blankenship was an attorney there to discuss the prior crime for which he was incarcerated. Blankenship clarified the purpose of his visit, and Shatzer declined to speak without an attorney. Accordingly, Blankenship ended the interview, and Shatzer was released back into the general prison population. Shortly thereafter, Blankenship closed the investigation.

Two years and six months later, the same social worker referred more specific allegations to the department about the same incident involving Shatzer. Detective Paul Hoover, from the same division, was assigned to the investigation. He and the social worker interviewed the victim, then eight years old, who described the incident in more detail. With this new information in hand, on March 2, 2006, they went to the Roxbury Correctional Institute, to which Shatzer had since been transferred, and interviewed Shatzer in a maintenance room outfitted with a desk and three chairs. Hoover explained that he wanted to ask Shatzer about the alleged incident involving Shatzer's son. Shatzer was surprised because he thought that the investigation had been closed, but Hoover explained they had opened a new file. Hoover then read Shatzer his *Miranda* rights and obtained a written waiver on a standard department form.

Hoover interrogated Shatzer about the incident for approximately 30 minutes. Shatzer denied ordering his son to perform fellatio on him, but admitted to masturbating in front of his son from a distance of less than three feet. Before the interview ended, Shatzer agreed to Hoover's request that he submit to a polygraph examination. At no point during the interrogation did Shatzer request to speak with an attorney or refer to his prior refusal to answer questions without one.

Five days later, on March 7, 2006, Hoover and another detective met with Shatzer at the correctional facility to administer the polygraph examination. After reading Shatzer his *Miranda* rights and obtaining a written waiver, the other detective administered the test and concluded that Shatzer had failed. When the detectives then questioned Shatzer, he became upset, started to cry, and incriminated himself by saying, "I didn't force him. I didn't force him." After making this inculpatory statement, Shatzer requested an attorney, and Hoover promptly ended the interrogation.

The State's Attorney for Washington County charged Shatzer with second-degree sexual offense, sexual child abuse, second-degree assault, and contributing to conditions rendering a child in need of assistance. Shatzer moved to suppress his March 2006 statements pursuant to *Edwards*. The trial court held a suppression hearing and later denied Shatzer's motion. The *Edwards* protections did not apply, it reasoned, because Shatzer had experienced a break in custody for *Miranda* purposes between the 2003 and 2006 interrogations. Shatzer pleaded not guilty, waived his right to a jury trial, and proceeded to a bench trial based on an agreed statement of facts. In accordance with the agreement, the State described the interview with the victim and Shatzer's 2006 statements to the detectives. Based on the proffered testimony of the victim and the "admission of the defendant as to the act of masturbation," the trial court found Shatzer guilty of sexual child abuse of his son.

Over the dissent of two judges, the Court of Appeals of Maryland reversed and remanded. The court held that "the passage of time *alone* is insufficient to end the protections afforded by *Edwards*," and that, assuming, *arguendo*, a break-in-custody exception to *Edwards* existed, Shatzer's release back into the general prison population between interrogations did not constitute a break in custody.

II

In *Miranda v. Arizona*, 384 U.S. 436 (1966), the Court adopted a set of prophylactic measures to protect a suspect's Fifth Amendment right from the "inherently compelling pressures" of custodial interrogation. To counteract the coercive pressure, *Miranda* announced that police officers must warn a suspect prior to questioning that he has a right to remain silent, and a right to the presence of an attorney. After the warnings are given, if the suspect indicates that he wishes to remain silent, the interrogation must cease. Similarly, if the suspect states that he wants an attorney, the interrogation must cease until an attorney is present. Critically, however, a suspect can waive these rights. To establish a valid waiver, the State must show that the waiver was knowing, intelligent, and voluntary under the high standard of proof for the waiver of constitutional rights set forth in *Johnson v. Zerbst*, 304 U.S. 458 (1938).

In *Edwards*, the Court determined that *Zerbst*'s traditional standard for waiver was not sufficient to protect a suspect's right to have counsel present at a subsequent interrogation if he had previously requested counsel; "additional safeguards" were necessary. The Court therefore superimposed a "second layer of prophylaxis." *Edwards* held:

> When an accused has invoked his right to have counsel present during custodial interrogation, a valid waiver of that right cannot be established by showing only that he responded to further police-initiated custodial interrogation even if he has been advised of his rights. He is not subject to further interrogation by the authorities until counsel has been made available to him, unless the accused himself initiates further communication, exchanges, or conversations with the police.

The rationale of *Edwards* is that once a suspect indicates that he is not capable of undergoing custodial questioning without advice of counsel, any subsequent waiver that has come at the authorities' behest, and not at the suspect's own instigation, is itself the product of the "inherently compelling pressures" and not the purely voluntary choice of the suspect. Under this rule, a voluntary *Miranda* waiver is sufficient at the time of an initial attempted interrogation to protect a suspect's right to have counsel present, but it is not sufficient at the time of subsequent attempts if the suspect initially requested the presence of counsel. The implicit assumption, of course, is that the subsequent requests for interrogation pose a significantly greater risk of coercion. That increased risk results not only from the police's persistence in trying to get the suspect to talk, but also from the continued pressure that begins when the individual is taken into custody as a suspect and sought to be interrogated—pressure likely to increase as custody is prolonged. The *Edwards* presumption of involuntariness ensures that police will not take advantage of the mounting coercive pressures of prolonged police custody by repeatedly attempting to question a suspect who previously requested counsel until the suspect is "badgered into submission."

We have frequently emphasized that the *Edwards* rule is not a constitutional mandate, but judicially prescribed prophylaxis. Lower courts have uniformly held that a break in custody ends the *Edwards* presumption, but we have previously addressed the issue only in dicta.

A judicially crafted rule is justified only by reference to its prophylactic purpose, and applies only where its benefits outweigh its costs. We begin with the benefits. *Edwards'* presumption of involuntariness has the incidental effect of conserving judicial resources which would otherwise be expended in making difficult determinations of voluntariness. Its fundamental purpose, however, is to preserve the integrity of an accused's choice to communicate with police only through counsel, by preventing police from badgering a defendant into waiving his previously asserted *Miranda* rights. Thus, the benefits of the rule are measured by the number of coerced confessions it suppresses that otherwise would have been admitted.

It is easy to believe that a suspect may be coerced or badgered into abandoning his earlier refusal to be questioned without counsel in the paradigm *Edwards* case. That is a case in which the suspect has been arrested for a particular crime and is held in uninterrupted pretrial custody while that crime is being actively investigated. After the initial interrogation, and up to and including the second one, he remains cut off from his normal life and companions, thrust into and isolated in an unfamiliar, police-dominated atmosphere, where his captors appear to control his fate.

When a suspect has been released from his pretrial custody and has returned to his normal life for some time before the later attempted interrogation, there is little reason to think that his change of heart regarding interrogation without counsel has been coerced. He has no longer been isolated. He has likely been able to seek advice from an attorney, family members, and friends. And he knows from his earlier experience that he need only demand counsel to bring the interrogation to a halt; and that investigative custody does not last indefinitely. In these circumstances, it is far fetched to think that a police officer's asking the suspect whether he would like to waive his *Miranda* rights will any more "wear down the accused" than did the first such request at the original attempted interrogation—which is of course not deemed coercive. His change of heart is less likely attributable to "badgering" than it is to the fact that further deliberation in familiar surroundings has caused him to believe (rightly or wrongly) that cooperating with the investigation is in his interest. Uncritical extension of *Edwards* to this situation would not significantly increase the number of genuinely coerced confessions excluded.

At the same time that extending the *Edwards* rule yields diminished benefits, extending the rule also increases its costs: the in-fact voluntary confessions it excludes from trial, and the voluntary confessions it deters law enforcement officers from even trying to obtain. Voluntary confessions are not merely a proper element in law enforcement, they are an unmitigated good, essential to society's compelling interest in finding, convicting, and punishing those who violate the law.

The only logical endpoint of *Edwards* disability is termination of *Miranda* custody and any of its lingering effects. Without that limitation—and barring some purely arbitrary time-limit—every *Edwards* prohibition of custodial interrogation of a particular suspect would be eternal. The prohibition applies, of course, when the subsequent interrogation pertains to a different crime, when it is conducted by a different law enforcement authority, and even when the suspect has met with an attorney after the first interrogation. And it not only prevents questioning *ex ante*; it would render invalid *ex post* confessions invited and obtained from suspects who (unbeknownst to the interrogators) have acquired *Edwards* immunity previously in connection with any offense in any jurisdiction. In a country that harbors a large number of repeat offenders, this consequence is disastrous.

We conclude that such an extension of *Edwards* is not justified. The protections offered by *Miranda*, which we have deemed sufficient to ensure that the police respect the suspect's desire to have an attorney present the first time police interrogate him, adequately ensure that result when a suspect who initially requested counsel is reinterrogated after a break in custody that is of sufficient duration to dissipate its coercive effects.

If Shatzer's return to the general prison population qualified as a break in custody (a question we address in Part III), there is no doubt that it lasted long enough (2 1/2 years) to meet that durational requirement. But what about a break that has lasted only one year? Or only one week? It is impractical to leave the answer to that question for clarification in future case-by-case adjudication; law enforcement officers need to know, with certainty and beforehand, when renewed interrogation is lawful. And while it is certainly unusual for this Court to set forth precise time limits governing police action, it is not unheard-of. It seems to us that period is 14 days. That provides plenty of time for the suspect to get reacclimated to his normal life, to consult with friends and counsel, and to shake off any residual coercive effects of his prior custody.

The 14-day limitation meets Shatzer's concern that a break-in-custody rule lends itself to police abuse. He envisions that once a suspect invokes his *Miranda* right to counsel, the police will release the suspect briefly (to end the *Edwards* presumption) and then promptly bring him back into custody for reinterrogation. But once the suspect has been out of custody long enough (14 days) to eliminate its coercive effect, there will be nothing to gain by such gamesmanship—nothing, that is, except the entirely appropriate gain of being able to interrogate a suspect who has made a valid waiver of his *Miranda* rights.[7]

Shatzer argues that ending the *Edwards* protections at a break in custody will undermine *Edwards'* purpose to conserve judicial resources. To be sure, we have said that the merit of the *Edwards* decision lies in the clarity of its command and the certainty of its application. But clarity and certainty are not goals in themselves. They are valuable only when they reasonably further the achievement of some substantive end—here, the exclusion of compelled confessions. Confessions obtained after a 2-week break in custody and a waiver of *Miranda* rights are most unlikely to be compelled, and hence are unreasonably excluded. In any case, a break-in-custody exception will dim only marginally, if at all, the bright-line nature of *Edwards*. In every case involving *Edwards*, the courts must determine whether the suspect was in custody when he requested counsel and when he later made the statements he seeks to suppress. Now, in cases where there is an alleged break in custody, they simply have to repeat the inquiry for the time between the initial invocation and reinterrogation. In most cases that determination will be easy. And when it is determined that the defendant pleading *Edwards* has been out of custody for two weeks before the contested interrogation, the court is spared the fact-intensive inquiry into whether he ever, anywhere, asserted his *Miranda* right to counsel.

III

The facts of this case present an additional issue. No one questions that Shatzer was in custody for *Miranda* purposes during the interviews with Detective Blankenship in 2003 and Detective Hoover in 2006. Likewise, no one questions that Shatzer triggered the *Edwards* protections when, according to Detective Blankenship's notes of the 2003

---

[7] A defendant who experiences a 14-day break in custody after invoking the *Miranda* right to counsel is not left without protection. *Edwards* establishes a *presumption* that a suspect's waiver of *Miranda* rights is involuntary. Even without this "second layer of prophylaxis," a defendant is still free to claim the prophylactic protection of *Miranda*—arguing that his waiver of *Miranda* rights was in fact involuntary under *Johnson v. Zerbst*.

interview, he stated that "he would not talk about this case without having an attorney present." After the 2003 interview, Shatzer was released back into the general prison population where he was serving an unrelated sentence. The issue is whether that constitutes a break in *Miranda* custody.

We have never decided whether incarceration constitutes custody for *Miranda* purposes, and have indeed explicitly declined to address the issue. Whether it does depends upon whether it exerts the coercive pressure that *Miranda* was designed to guard against—the danger of coercion that results from the *interaction* of custody and official interrogation. To determine whether a suspect was in *Miranda* custody we have asked whether there is a formal arrest or restraint on freedom of movement of the degree associated with a formal arrest. This test, no doubt, is satisfied by all forms of incarceration. Our cases make clear, however, that the freedom-of-movement test identifies only a necessary and not a sufficient condition for *Miranda* custody. We have declined to accord it talismanic power, because *Miranda* is to be enforced only in those types of situations in which the concerns that powered the decision are implicated. Thus, the temporary and relatively nonthreatening detention involved in a traffic stop or *Terry* stop does not constitute *Miranda* custody.

Here, we are addressing the interim period during which a suspect was not interrogated, but was subject to a baseline set of restraints imposed pursuant to a prior conviction. Without minimizing the harsh realities of incarceration, we think lawful imprisonment imposed upon conviction of a crime does not create the coercive pressures identified in *Miranda*.

Interrogated suspects who have previously been convicted of crime live in prison. When they are released back into the general prison population, they return to their accustomed surroundings and daily routine—they regain the degree of control they had over their lives prior to the interrogation. Sentenced prisoners, in contrast to the *Miranda* paradigm, are not isolated with their accusers. They live among other inmates, guards, and workers, and often can receive visitors and communicate with people on the outside by mail or telephone.

Their detention, moreover, is relatively disconnected from their prior unwillingness to cooperate in an investigation. The former interrogator has no power to increase the duration of incarceration, which was determined at sentencing.[8] And even where the possibility of parole

---

[8]   We distinguish the duration of incarceration from the duration of what might be termed interrogative custody. When a prisoner is removed from the general prison population and taken to a separate location for questioning, the duration of *that separation* is assuredly dependent upon his interrogators. For which reason once he has asserted a refusal to speak without assistance of counsel *Edwards* prevents any efforts to get him to change his mind during that interrogative custody.

exists, the former interrogator has no apparent power to decrease the time served.

Shatzer's experience illustrates the vast differences between *Miranda* custody and incarceration pursuant to conviction. At the time of the 2003 attempted interrogation, Shatzer was already serving a sentence for a prior conviction. After that, he returned to the general prison population in the Maryland Correctional Institution-Hagerstown and was later transferred, for unrelated reasons, down the street to the Roxbury Correctional Institute. Both are medium-security state correctional facilities. Inmates in these facilities generally can visit the library each week, have regular exercise and recreation periods, can participate in basic adult education and occupational training, are able to send and receive mail, and are allowed to receive visitors twice a week. His continued detention after the 2003 interrogation did not depend on what he said (or did not say) to Detective Blankenship, and he has not alleged that he was placed in a higher level of security or faced any continuing restraints as a result of the 2003 interrogation. The "inherently compelling pressures" of custodial interrogation ended when he returned to his normal life.

Because Shatzer experienced a break in *Miranda* custody lasting more than two weeks between the first and second attempts at interrogation, *Edwards* does not mandate suppression of his March 2006 statements.

Invocation and Waiver of *Miranda*'s Right to an Attorney

1.   A suspect who wishes to invoke her right to an attorney under *Miranda* must do so unambiguously. This is an objective standard that requires the suspect to articulate her desire to have counsel present sufficiently clearly that a reasonable police officer in the circumstances would understand the statement to be a request for an attorney. If the suspect invokes her right to an attorney at any time prior to or during custodial interrogation, the interrogation must cease.

   a.   If a suspect makes an ambiguous or equivocal reference to an attorney, it will often be good police practice for the interviewing officers to clarify whether she actually wants an attorney, but the officers are not required to ask clarifying questions. If the suspect's statement is not an unambiguous or unequivocal request for counsel, the officers have no obligation to stop questioning her.

   b.   A suspect's request to have a probation officer, a relative, a friend, or a religious adviser with her during custodial interrogation is not the same as a request for an attorney, and police are not obliged to end the interrogation to honor such requests. Such requests may, however, be considered as part of the "totality of the circumstances" determination of the voluntariness of any subsequent waiver of *Miranda* rights.

2.   A suspect who has received *Miranda* warnings may validly waive the right to an attorney during custodial interrogation so long as the relinquishment of the right is voluntary, knowing, and intelligent. The validity of a waiver depends in each case upon the particular facts and circumstances, including the background, experience, and conduct of the suspect.

3.   If a suspect invokes her right to an attorney during custodial interrogation, a valid waiver of that right cannot be established by showing only that she responded to further police-initiated custodial interrogation, even if she has been given a fresh set of *Miranda* warnings. Having expressed her desire to deal with the police only through counsel, the suspect is not subject to further interrogation by police until counsel is actually present, unless the suspect herself initiates further communication, exchanges, or conversations with the police. A statement obtained by police following a violation of this rule is presumed to be the product of an involuntary waiver and is inadmissible.

4.   The prohibition on police-initiated custodial interrogation after a suspect requests an attorney applies even if different officers, unaware of suspect's previous invocation of the right to counsel, seek to question the suspect about a crime that is unrelated to the subject of the first interrogation.

5.   Police may reinitiate contact with a suspect after her invocation of the right to counsel if there has been a break in *Miranda* custody of at least 14 days before the renewed attempt at interrogation.

Note: The "General Guidelines for *Miranda* Waivers" set forth above are also applicable to the specific question of whether a suspect has invoked or waived the right to an attorney during custodial interrogation.

CHAPTER 11

THE SIXTH AMENDMENT RIGHT TO COUNSEL AND "DELIBERATE ELICITATION"

■ ■ ■

The Sixth Amendment provides that "in all criminal prosecutions, the accused shall enjoy the right . . . to have the Assistance of Counsel for his defence." At its core, this provision guarantees to a criminal defendant facing possible imprisonment the opportunity to consult with an attorney who can prepare and present a defense at trial. But beyond protecting the right to an attorney at *trial* and in certain appeals, the Sixth Amendment right to counsel also protects the defendant's right to have counsel present at various "critical" *pretrial* stages that could affect the outcome of the trial. As the Supreme Court explained in *Maine v. Moulton*, 474 U.S. 159 (1985):

> The assistance of counsel cannot be limited to participation in a trial; to deprive a person of counsel during the period prior to trial may be more damaging than denial of counsel during the trial itself. Recognizing that the right to the assistance of counsel is shaped by the need for the assistance of counsel, we have found that the right attaches at earlier, "critical" stages in the criminal justice process where the results might well settle the accused's fate and reduce the trial itself to a mere formality. And, whatever else it may mean, the right to counsel granted by the Sixth and Fourteenth Amendments means at least that a person is entitled to the help of a lawyer at or after the time that judicial proceedings have been initiated against him. This is because, after the initiation of adversary criminal proceedings, the government has committed itself to prosecute, and the adverse positions of government and defendant have solidified. It is then that a defendant finds himself faced with the prosecutorial forces of organized society, and immersed in the intricacies of substantive and procedural criminal law.

One such "critical" stage during which the Sixth Amendment provides protection occurs when law enforcement officers or their agents question a suspect or otherwise attempt to elicit incriminating statements *after* charges have been filed and adversary judicial criminal proceedings have begun. While police can and often do continue their investigation after criminal charges are filed, they must not do so in a way that circumvents the defendant's right to the presence of counsel.

The Sixth Amendment prohibition on "deliberate elicitation" of incriminating statements is similar in some respects to the constitutional rules discussed in Chapters 9 and 10 that are designed to prevent coerced confessions. There are, however, some significant differences as well, and it's important to understand the circumstances under which each of the various constitutional protections come into play. As explained in Chapter 9, due process requires the prosecution to prove that a confession was voluntarily given before it can be admitted into evidence. The voluntariness requirement is designed to prevent police from coercing a confession, and it applies both before and after criminal charges have been filed and regardless of whether the suspect is in "custody" or subjected to "interrogation," as those terms are defined in *Miranda* and subsequent cases.

The *Miranda* requirements described in Chapter 10—including the requirement that questioning cease if the suspect requests an attorney— likewise serve to guard against coerced confessions while protecting the Fifth Amendment privilege against self-incrimination. *Miranda* applies both before and after criminal charges have been filed, but only when the suspect is subjected to "custodial interrogation."

By its terms, the Sixth Amendment provides for the assistance of counsel only in "criminal prosecutions." Accordingly, the prohibition on deliberate elicitation of incriminating statements that is the focus of this Chapter applies only after the Sixth Amendment right to counsel "attaches" with the commencement of a *prosecution*—when adversary judicial criminal proceedings are initiated and the defendant is charged with a crime. And like the voluntariness requirement, the prohibition on deliberate elicitation applies regardless of whether the defendant is in "custody" or is subjected to "interrogation," as those terms are defined in *Miranda* and its progeny.

A. *MASSIAH v. U.S.* AND THE PROHIBITION ON "DELIBERATE ELICITATION"

In *Massiah v. U.S.*, a government informant obtained incriminating statements from Massiah after he had been charged with a crime and was represented by an attorney. The Supreme Court held that the statements were inadmissible because they were "deliberately elicited" in violation of the Sixth Amendment right to counsel.

MASSIAH V. U.S.

377 U.S. 201 (1964)

JUSTICE STEWART delivered the opinion of the Court.

The petitioner was indicted for violating the federal narcotics laws. He retained a lawyer, pleaded not guilty, and was released on bail. While he was free on bail, a federal agent succeeded by surreptitious means in listening to incriminating statements made by him. Evidence of these statements was introduced against the petitioner at his trial over his objection. He was convicted, and the Court of Appeals affirmed. We granted certiorari to consider whether, under the circumstances here presented, the prosecution's use at the trial of evidence of the petitioner's own incriminating statements deprived him of any right secured to him under the Federal Constitution.

The petitioner, a merchant seaman, was in 1958 a member of the crew of the S.S. *Santa Maria*. In April of that year, federal customs officials in New York received information that he was going to transport a quantity of narcotics aboard that ship from South America to the United States. As a result of this and other information, the agents searched the *Santa Maria* upon its arrival in New York and found in the afterpeak of the vessel five packages containing about three and a half pounds of cocaine. They also learned of circumstances, not here relevant, tending to connect the petitioner with the cocaine. He was arrested, promptly arraigned, and subsequently indicted for possession of narcotics aboard a United States vessel. In July, a superseding indictment was returned, charging the petitioner and a man named Colson with the same substantive offense, and in separate counts charging the petitioner, Colson, and others with having conspired to possess narcotics aboard a United States vessel, and to import, conceal, and facilitate the sale of narcotics. The petitioner, who had retained a lawyer, pleaded not guilty and was released on bail, along with Colson.

A few days later, and quite without the petitioner's knowledge, Colson decided to cooperate with the government agents in their continuing investigation of the narcotics activities in which the petitioner, Colson, and others had allegedly been engaged. Colson permitted an agent named Murphy to install a Schmidt radio transmitter under the front seat of Colson's automobile, by means of which Murphy, equipped with an appropriate receiving device, could overhear from some distance away conversations carried on in Colson's car.

On the evening of November 19, 1959, Colson and the petitioner held a lengthy conversation while sitting in Colson's automobile, parked on a New York street. By prearrangement with Colson, and totally unbeknown to the petitioner, the agent Murphy sat in a car parked out of sight down the street and listened over the radio to the entire conversation. The petitioner made several incriminating statements during the course of this conversation. At the petitioner's trial, these incriminating statements were brought before the jury through Murphy's testimony, despite the insistent objection of defense counsel. The jury convicted the petitioner of several related narcotics offenses, and the convictions were affirmed by the Court of Appeals.

The petitioner argues that it was an error of constitutional dimensions to permit the agent Murphy at the trial to testify to the petitioner's incriminating statements which Murphy had overheard under the circumstances disclosed by this record. It is said that the petitioner's Fifth and Sixth Amendment rights were violated by the use in evidence against him of incriminating statements which government agents had deliberately elicited from him after he had been indicted and in the absence of his retained counsel.

In *Spano v. New York*, 360 U.S. 315 (1959), this Court reversed a state criminal conviction because a confession had been wrongly admitted into evidence against the defendant at his trial. In that case, the defendant had already been indicted for first-degree murder at the time he confessed. The Court held that the defendant's conviction could not stand under the Fourteenth Amendment. While the Court's opinion relied upon the totality of the circumstances under which the confession had been obtained, four concurring Justices pointed out that the Constitution required reversal of the conviction upon the sole and specific ground that the confession had been deliberately elicited by the police after the defendant had been indicted, and therefore at a time when he was clearly entitled to a lawyer's help. It was pointed out that, under our system of justice, the most elemental concepts of due process of law contemplate that an indictment be followed by a trial, "in an orderly courtroom, presided over by a judge, open to the public, and protected by all the procedural safeguards of the law." It was said that a Constitution which guarantees a defendant the aid of counsel at such a trial could surely vouchsafe no less to an indicted defendant under interrogation by the police in a completely extrajudicial proceeding. Anything less, it was said, might deny a defendant "effective representation by counsel at the only stage when legal aid and advice would help him."

This view no more than reflects a constitutional principle established as long ago as *Powell v. Alabama*, 287 U.S. 45 (1933), where the Court noted that "during perhaps the most critical period of the proceedings, from the time of their arraignment until the beginning of their trial, when consultation, thorough-going investigation and preparation are vitally important, the defendants are as much entitled to such aid of counsel during that period as at the trial itself." And, since the *Spano* decision, the same basic constitutional principle has been broadly reaffirmed by this Court.

Here we deal not with a state court conviction, but with a federal case, where the specific guarantee of the Sixth Amendment directly applies. We hold that the petitioner was denied the basic protections of that guarantee when there was used against him at his trial evidence of his own incriminating words, which federal agents had deliberately elicited from him after he had been indicted and in the absence of his counsel. It is true that, in the *Spano* case, the defendant was interrogated in a police station, while here the damaging testimony was elicited from the defendant without his knowledge while he was free on bail. But, as Judge Hays pointed out in his dissent in the Court of Appeals, "if such a rule is to have any efficacy, it must apply to indirect and surreptitious interrogations as well as those conducted in the jailhouse. In this case, Massiah was more seriously imposed upon because he did not even know that he was under interrogation by a government agent."

The Solicitor General, in his brief and oral argument, has strenuously contended that the federal law enforcement agents had the right, if not indeed the duty, to continue their investigation of the petitioner and his alleged criminal associates even though the petitioner had been indicted. He points out that the Government was continuing its investigation in order to uncover not only the source of narcotics found on the S.S. *Santa Maria*, but also their intended buyer. He says that the quantity of narcotics involved was such as to suggest that the petitioner was part of a large and well-organized ring, and indeed that the continuing investigation confirmed this suspicion, since it resulted in criminal charges against many defendants. Under these circumstances, the Solicitor General concludes that the Government agents were completely "justified in making use of Colson's cooperation by having Colson continue his normal associations and by surveilling them."

We do not question that in this case, as in many cases, it was entirely proper to continue an investigation of the suspected criminal activities of the defendant and his alleged confederates, even though the defendant had already been indicted. All that we hold is that the defendant's own incriminating statements, obtained by federal agents under the circumstances here disclosed, could not constitutionally be used by the prosecution as evidence against him at his trial.

JUSTICE WHITE, with whom JUSTICE CLARK and JUSTICE HARLAN join, dissenting.

I am unable to see how this case presents an unconstitutional interference with Massiah's right to counsel. Massiah was not prevented from consulting with counsel as often as he wished. No meetings with counsel were disturbed or spied upon. Preparation for trial was in no way obstructed. It is only a sterile syllogism—an unsound one, besides—to say that because Massiah had a right to counsel's aid before and during the trial, his out-of-court conversations and admissions must be excluded if obtained without counsel's consent or presence. The right to counsel has never meant as much before, and its extension in this case requires some further explanation, so far unarticulated by the Court.

At the time of the conversation in question, petitioner was not in custody but free on bail. He was not questioned in what anyone could call an atmosphere of official coercion. What he said was said to his partner in crime who had also been indicted. There was no suggestion or any possibility of coercion. What petitioner did not know was that Colson had decided to report the conversation to the police. Had there been no prior arrangements between Colson and the police, had Colson simply gone to the police after the conversation had occurred, his testimony relating Massiah's statements would be readily admissible at the trial, as would a recording which he might have made of the conversation. In such event, it would simply be said that Massiah risked talking to a friend who decided to disclose what he knew of Massiah's criminal activities. But, if, as occurred here, Colson had been cooperating with the police prior to his meeting with Massiah, both his evidence and the recorded conversation are somehow transformed into inadmissible evidence despite the fact that the hazard to Massiah remains precisely the same—the defection of a confederate in crime.

Reporting criminal behavior is expected or even demanded of the ordinary citizen. Friends may be subpoenaed to testify about friends, relatives about relatives and partners about partners. I therefore question the soundness of insulating Massiah from the apostasy of his partner in crime and of furnishing constitutional sanction for the strict secrecy and discipline of criminal organizations. Neither the ordinary citizen nor the confessed criminal should be discouraged from reporting what he knows to the authorities and from lending his aid to secure evidence of crime. Certainly, after this case, the Colsons will be few and far between; and the Massiahs can breathe much more easily, secure in the knowledge that the Constitution furnishes an important measure of protection against faithless compatriots and guarantees sporting treatment for sporting peddlers of narcotics.

Meanwhile, of course, the public will again be the loser and law enforcement will be presented with another serious dilemma. The general issue lurking in the background of the Court's opinion is the legitimacy of penetrating or obtaining confederates in criminal organizations. For the law enforcement agency, the answer for the time being can only be in the form of a prediction about the future application of today's new constitutional doctrine. More narrowly, and posed by the precise situation involved here, the question is this: when the police have arrested and released on bail one member of a criminal ring and another member, a confederate, is cooperating with the police, can the confederate be allowed to continue his association with the ring or must he somehow be withdrawn to avoid challenge to trial evidence on the ground that it was acquired after, rather than before, the arrest, after, rather than before, the indictment?

Massiah and those like him receive ample protection from the long line of precedents in this Court holding that confessions may not be introduced unless they are voluntary. In making these determinations, the courts must consider the absence of counsel as one of several factors by which voluntariness is to be judged. This is a wiser rule than the automatic rule announced by the Court, which requires courts and juries to disregard voluntary admissions which they might well find to be the best possible evidence in discharging their responsibility for ascertaining truth.

When challenged on other constitutional grounds, the Supreme Court has upheld the investigative technique employed in *Massiah*—the use of an informant to extract incriminating statements—as long as the suspect has not yet been charged with the crime. In *U.S. v. White*, 401 U.S. 745 (1971), presented in Chapter 3, the Court held that the use of a "wired" informant was not a search under the Fourth Amendment, making a search warrant unnecessary. And in *Illinois v. Perkins*, 496 U.S. 292 (1990), presented in Chapter 10, the Court held that the use of an undercover police officer to elicit incriminating statements from a suspect in jail did not qualify as a custodial interrogation to which the *Miranda* protections would apply. Citing the *Massiah* line of cases, the Court in *Perkins* was careful to note, however, that "the government may not use an undercover agent to circumvent the Sixth Amendment right to counsel once a suspect has been charged with the crime."

When the Supreme Court decided *Miranda* in 1966, it was unclear what effect, if any, it would have on *Massiah*, which was decided just two years earlier. The fact that *Miranda* announced a right to the presence of counsel during custodial interrogation, but never even mentioned *Massiah*, only added to the confusion. While the Supreme Court was busy clarifying the *Miranda* requirements in the decade after it was decided, *Massiah* remained largely "dormant" until the Court breathed new life into the rule in *Brewer v. Williams*.

BREWER v. WILLIAMS
430 U.S. 387 (1977)

JUSTICE STEWART delivered the opinion of the Court.

I

On the afternoon of December 24, 1968, a 10-year-old girl named Pamela Powers went with her family to the YMCA in Des Moines, Iowa, to watch a wrestling tournament in which her brother was participating. When she failed to return from a trip to the washroom, a search for her began. The search was unsuccessful.

Robert Williams, who had recently escaped from a mental hospital, was a resident of the YMCA. Soon after the girl's disappearance, Williams was seen in the YMCA lobby carrying some clothing and a large bundle wrapped in a blanket. He obtained help from a 14-year-old boy in opening the street door of the YMCA and the door to his automobile parked outside. When Williams placed the bundle in the front seat of his car, the boy "saw two legs in it and they were skinny and white." Before anyone could see what was in the bundle, Williams drove away. His abandoned car was found the following day in Davenport, Iowa, roughly 160 miles east of Des Moines. A warrant was then issued in Des Moines for his arrest on a charge of abduction.

On the morning of December 26, a Des Moines lawyer named Henry McKnight went to the Des Moines police station and informed the officers present that he had just received a long-distance call from Williams, and that he had advised Williams to turn himself in to the Davenport police. Williams did surrender that morning to the police in Davenport, and they booked him on the charge specified in the arrest warrant and gave him the warnings required by *Miranda v. Arizona*, 384 U.S. 436 (1966). The Davenport police then telephoned their counterparts in Des Moines to inform them that Williams had surrendered. McKnight, the lawyer, was still at the Des Moines police headquarters, and Williams conversed with McKnight on the telephone. In the presence of the Des Moines chief of police and a police detective named Leaming, McKnight advised Williams that Des Moines police officers would be driving to Davenport to pick him up, that the officers would not interrogate him or mistreat him, and that Williams was not to talk to the officers about Pamela Powers until after consulting with McKnight upon his return to Des Moines. As a result of these conversations, it was agreed between McKnight and the Des Moines police officials that Detective Leaming and a fellow officer would drive to Davenport to pick up Williams, that they would bring him directly back to Des Moines, and that they would not question him during the trip.

In the meantime, Williams was arraigned before a judge in Davenport on the outstanding arrest warrant. The judge advised him of his *Miranda* rights and committed him to jail. Before leaving the courtroom, Williams conferred with a lawyer named Kelly, who advised him not to make any statements until consulting with McKnight back in Des Moines.

Detective Leaming and his fellow officer arrived in Davenport about noon to pick up Williams and return him to Des Moines. Soon after their arrival they met with Williams and Kelly, who, they understood, was acting as Williams' lawyer. Detective Leaming repeated the *Miranda* warnings.

Williams then conferred again with Kelly alone, and after this conference Kelly reiterated to Detective Leaming that Williams was not to be questioned about the disappearance of Pamela Powers until after he had consulted with McKnight back in Des Moines. When Leaming expressed some reservations, Kelly firmly stated that the agreement with McKnight was to be carried out—that there was to be no interrogation of Williams during the automobile journey to Des Moines. Kelly was denied permission to ride in the police car back to Des Moines with Williams and the two officers.

The two detectives, with Williams in their charge, then set out on the 160-mile drive. At no time during the trip did Williams express a willingness to be interrogated in the absence of an attorney. Instead, he stated several times that "when I get to Des Moines and see Mr. McKnight, I am going to tell you the whole story." Detective Leaming knew that Williams was a former mental patient, and knew also that he was deeply religious.

The detective and his prisoner soon embarked on a wide-ranging conversation covering a variety of topics, including the subject of religion. Then, not long after leaving Davenport and reaching the interstate highway, Detective Leaming delivered what has been referred to in the briefs and oral arguments as the "Christian burial speech." Addressing Williams as "Reverend," the detective said:

> I want to give you something to think about while we're traveling down the road. . . . Number one, I want you to observe the weather conditions, it's raining, it's sleeting, it's freezing, driving is very treacherous, visibility is poor, it's going to be dark early this evening. They are predicting several inches of snow for tonight, and I feel that you yourself are the only person that knows where this little girl's body is, that you yourself have only been there once, and if you get a snow on top of it you yourself may be unable to find it. And, since we will be going right past the area on the way into Des Moines, I feel that we could stop and locate the body, that the parents of this little girl should be entitled to a Christian burial for the little girl who was snatched away from them on Christmas Eve and murdered. And I feel we should stop and locate it on the way in rather than waiting until morning and trying to come back out after a snow storm and possibly not being able to find it at all.

Williams asked Detective Leaming why he thought their route to Des Moines would be taking them past the girl's body, and Leaming responded that he knew the body was in the area of Mitchellville—a town they would be passing on the way to Des Moines. Leaming then stated: "I do not want you to answer me. I don't want to discuss it any further. Just think about it as we're riding down the road."

As the car approached Grinnell, a town approximately 100 miles west of Davenport, Williams asked whether the police had found the victim's shoes. When Detective Leaming replied that he was unsure, Williams directed the officers to a service station where he said he had left the shoes; a search for them proved unsuccessful. As they continued towards Des Moines, Williams asked whether the police had found the blanket, and directed the officers to a rest area where he said he had disposed of the blanket. Nothing was found. The car continued towards Des Moines, and as it approached Mitchellville, Williams said that he would show the officers where the body was. He then directed the police to the body of Pamela Powers.

Williams was indicted for first-degree murder. Before trial, his counsel moved to suppress all evidence relating to or resulting from any statements Williams had made during the automobile ride from Davenport to Des Moines. After an evidentiary hearing, the trial judge denied the motion. He found that "an agreement was made between defense counsel and the police officials to the effect that the Defendant was not to be questioned on the return trip to Des Moines," and that the evidence in question had been elicited from Williams during "a critical stage in the proceedings requiring the presence of counsel on his request." The judge ruled, however, that Williams had "waived his right to have an attorney present during the giving of such information."

The evidence in question was introduced over counsel's continuing objection at the subsequent trial. The jury found Williams guilty of murder, and the judgment of conviction was affirmed by the Iowa Supreme Court, a bare majority of whose members agreed with the trial court that Williams had "waived his right to the presence of his counsel" on the automobile ride from Davenport to Des Moines. The four dissenting justices expressed the view that "when counsel and police have agreed defendant is not to be questioned until counsel is present and defendant has been advised not to talk and repeatedly has stated he will tell the whole story after he talks with counsel, the state should be required to make a stronger showing of intentional voluntary waiver than was made here."

II

It is clear that Williams was deprived of the right to the assistance of counsel. This right, guaranteed by the Sixth and Fourteenth Amendments, is indispensable to the fair administration of our adversary system of criminal justice.

There has occasionally been a difference of opinion within the Court as to the peripheral scope of this constitutional right. But its basic contours, which are identical in state and federal contexts, are too well established to require extensive elaboration here. Whatever else it may mean, the right to counsel granted by the Sixth and Fourteenth Amendments means at least that a person is entitled to the help of a lawyer at or after the time that judicial proceedings have been initiated against him—whether by way of formal charge, preliminary hearing, indictment, information, or arraignment.

There can be no doubt in the present case that judicial proceedings had been initiated against Williams before the start of the automobile ride from Davenport to Des Moines. A warrant had been issued for his arrest, he had been arraigned on that warrant before a judge in a Davenport courtroom, and he had been committed by the court to confinement in jail. The State does not contend otherwise.

There can be no serious doubt, either, that Detective Leaming deliberately and designedly set out to elicit information from Williams just as surely as—and perhaps more effectively than—if he had formally interrogated him. Detective Leaming was fully aware before departing for Des Moines that Williams was being represented in Davenport by Kelly and in Des Moines by McKnight. Yet he purposely sought during Williams' isolation from his lawyers to obtain as much incriminating information as possible. Indeed, Detective Leaming conceded as much when he testified at Williams' trial.

The state courts clearly proceeded upon the hypothesis that Detective Leaming's "Christian burial speech" had been tantamount to interrogation. Both courts recognized that Williams had been entitled to the assistance of counsel at the time he made the incriminating statements. Yet no such constitutional protection would have come into play if there had been no interrogation.

The circumstances of this case are thus constitutionally indistinguishable from those presented in *Massiah v. U.S.*, 377 U.S. 201 (1964). That the incriminating statements were elicited surreptitiously in the *Massiah* case, and otherwise here, is constitutionally irrelevant. Rather, the clear rule of *Massiah* is that once adversary proceedings have commenced against an individual, he has a right to legal representation when the government interrogates him. It thus requires no wooden or technical application of the *Massiah* doctrine to conclude that Williams was entitled to the assistance of counsel guaranteed to him by the Sixth and Fourteenth Amendments.

III

The Iowa courts recognized that Williams had been denied the constitutional right to the assistance of counsel. They held, however, that he had waived that right during the course of the automobile trip from Davenport to Des Moines.

In determining the question of waiver as a matter of federal constitutional law, it was incumbent upon the State to prove "an intentional relinquishment or abandonment of a known right or privilege." That standard has been reiterated in many cases. We have said that the right to counsel does not depend upon a request by the defendant, and that courts indulge in every reasonable presumption against waiver. This strict standard applies equally to an alleged waiver of the right to counsel whether at trial or at a critical stage of pretrial proceedings.

Judged by these standards, the record in this case falls far short of sustaining petitioner's burden. It is true that Williams had been informed of and appeared to understand his right to counsel. But waiver requires not merely comprehension, but relinquishment, and Williams' consistent reliance upon the advice of counsel in dealing with the authorities refutes any suggestion that he waived that right. He consulted McKnight by long-distance telephone before turning himself in. He spoke with McKnight by telephone again shortly after being booked. After he was arraigned, Williams sought out and obtained legal advice from Kelly. Williams again consulted with Kelly after Detective Leaming and his fellow officer arrived in Davenport. Throughout, Williams was advised not to make any statements before seeing McKnight in Des Moines, and was assured that the police had agreed not to question him. His statements while in the car that he would tell the whole story after seeing McKnight in Des Moines were the clearest expressions by Williams himself that he desired the presence of an attorney before any interrogation took place. But even before making these statements, Williams had effectively asserted his right to counsel by having secured attorneys at both ends of the automobile trip, both of whom, acting as his agents, had made clear to the police that no interrogation was to occur during the journey. Williams knew of that agreement and, particularly in view of his consistent reliance on counsel, there is no basis for concluding that he disavowed it.

Despite Williams' express and implicit assertions of his right to counsel, Detective Leaming proceeded to elicit incriminating statements from Williams. Leaming did not preface this effort by telling Williams that he had a right to the presence of a lawyer, and made no effort at all to ascertain whether Williams wished to relinquish that right. The circumstances of record in this case thus provide no reasonable basis for finding that Williams waived his right to the assistance of counsel.

The crime of which Williams was convicted was senseless and brutal, calling for swift and energetic action by the police to apprehend the perpetrator and gather evidence with which he could be convicted. No mission of law enforcement officials is more important. Although we do not lightly affirm the issuance of a writ of habeas corpus in this case, so clear a violation of the Sixth and Fourteenth Amendments as here occurred cannot be condoned. The pressures on state executive and judicial officers charged with the administration of the criminal law are great, especially when the crime is murder and the victim a small child. But it is precisely the predictability of those pressures that makes imperative a resolute loyalty to the guarantees that the Constitution extends to us all.

CHIEF JUSTICE BURGER, dissenting.

The result in this case ought to be intolerable in any society which purports to call itself an organized society. It continues the Court—by the narrowest margin—on the much-criticized course of punishing the public for the mistakes and misdeeds of law enforcement officers, instead of punishing the officer directly, if in fact he is guilty of wrongdoing. It mechanically and blindly keeps reliable evidence from juries whether the claimed constitutional violation involves gross police misconduct or honest human error.

Williams is guilty of the savage murder of a small child; no member of the Court contends he is not. While in custody, and after no fewer than five warnings of his rights to silence and to counsel, he led police to the concealed body of his victim. The Court concedes Williams was not threatened or coerced, and that he spoke and acted voluntarily and with full awareness of his constitutional rights. In the face of all this, the Court now holds that, because Williams was prompted by the detective's statement—not interrogation, but a statement—the jury must not be told how the police found the body.

I categorically reject the remarkable notion that the police in this case were guilty of unconstitutional misconduct, or any conduct justifying the bizarre result reached by the Court.

The evidence is uncontradicted that Williams had abundant knowledge of his right to have counsel present and of his right to silence. Since the Court does not question his mental competence, it boggles the mind to suggest that Williams could not understand that leading police to the child's body would have other than the most serious consequences. All of the elements necessary to make out a valid waiver are shown by the record and acknowledged by the Court; we thus are left to guess how the Court reached its holding.

JUSTICE WHITE, with whom JUSTICE BLACKMUN and JUSTICE REHNQUIST join, dissenting.

The strictest test of waiver which might be applied to this case is that set forth in *Johnson v. Zerbst*, 304 U.S. 458 (1938), and quoted by the majority. In order to show that a right has been waived under this test, the State must prove "an intentional relinquishment or abandonment of a known right or privilege." The majority creates no new rule preventing an accused who has retained a lawyer from waiving his right to the lawyer's presence during questioning. The majority simply finds that no waiver was proved in this case. I disagree. That respondent knew of his right not to say anything to the officers without advice and presence of counsel is established on this record to a moral certainty. He was advised of the right by three officials of the State—telling at least one that he understood the right—and by two lawyers. Finally, he further demonstrated his knowledge of the right by informing the police that he would tell them the story in the presence of McKnight when they arrived in Des Moines. The issue in this case, then, is whether respondent relinquished that right intentionally.

Respondent relinquished his right not to talk to the police about his crime when the car approached the place where he had hidden the victim's clothes. Men usually intend to do what they do, and there is nothing in the record to support the proposition that respondent's decision to talk was anything but an exercise of his own free will. Apparently, without any prodding from the officers, respondent—who had earlier said that he would tell the whole story when he arrived in Des Moines—spontaneously changed his mind about the timing of his disclosures when the car approached the places where he had hidden the evidence. However, even if his statements were influenced by Detective Leaming's above-quoted statement, respondent's decision to talk in the absence of counsel can hardly be viewed as the product of an overborne will. The statement by Leaming was not coercive; it was accompanied by a request that respondent not respond to it; and it was delivered hours before respondent decided to make any statement. Respondent's waiver was thus knowing and intentional.

The majority's contrary conclusion seems to rest on the fact that respondent "asserted" his right to counsel by retaining and consulting with one lawyer and by consulting with another. How this supports the conclusion that respondent's later relinquishment of his right not to talk in the absence of counsel was unintentional is a mystery. The fact that respondent consulted with counsel on the question whether he should talk to the police in counsel's absence makes his later decision to talk in counsel's absence better informed and, if anything, more intelligent.

The majority recognizes that even after this "assertion" of his right to counsel, it would have found that respondent waived his right not to talk in counsel's absence if his waiver had been express—i.e., if the officers had asked him in the car whether he would be willing to answer questions in counsel's absence and if he had answered "yes." But waiver is not a formalistic concept. Waiver is shown whenever the facts establish that an accused knew of a right and intended to relinquish it. Such waiver, even if not express, was plainly shown here. The only other conceivable basis for the majority's holding is the implicit suggestion that the right involved in *Massiah*, as distinguished from the right involved in

Miranda, is a right not to be asked any questions in counsel's absence rather than a right not to answer any questions in counsel's absence, and that the right not to be asked questions must be waived before the questions are asked. Such wafer-thin distinctions cannot determine whether a guilty murderer should go free.

Brewer v. Williams should be familiar because we've encountered the basic facts and the underlying crime twice before. Chapter 8 presented a related Supreme Court case, *Nix v. Williams*, 467 U.S. 431 (1984), which recognized the inevitable discovery exception to the exclusionary rule and allowed the admission of evidence related to the location and condition of the victim's body even though the defendant's own statements were excluded by the decision in *Brewer v. Williams*. Chapter 10 also included a brief summary of *Brewer v. Williams*, along with Detective Leaming's "Christian burial speech," to illustrate how a direct appeal to a suspect's conscience might be regarded as a form of interrogation for purposes of *Miranda*.

Brewer v. Williams is useful in clarifying that the Sixth Amendment right to counsel and the prohibition on deliberate elicitation announced in *Massiah* attach "at or after judicial proceedings have been initiated against [the accused]—whether by way of formal charge, preliminary hearing, indictment, information, or arraignment." But for many, including the dissenting Supreme Court Justices, the result in *Brewer* represented an inappropriate and unjustified extension of the *Massiah* rule. First, the police in *Brewer* didn't trick or surreptitiously question the defendant, as they had in *Massiah*. Williams was riding in a police car and knew that the two men who were transporting him were police detectives whose interests were adverse to his own. Second, although Williams was obviously in police custody, there was little evidence of coercion or actual interrogation. Detective Leaming certainly hoped that the "Christian burial speech" would move Williams to disclose the location of the body, but he didn't directly question Williams; in fact, Leaming actually told Williams not to answer, but rather to "just think about it as we're riding down the road." Third, even if the majority is correct in its view that Leaming deliberately elicited a statement from Williams in the absence of his lawyer, why did the Court reject the argument that Williams had waived his right to counsel by speaking to the detectives and directing them to the body? How should Williams' actions be characterized if not as a voluntary and intelligent waiver of a right he knew he had—the right to consult with his attorney before speaking with the police?

Although both *Massiah v. U.S.* and *Brewer v. Williams* excluded incriminating statements that had been obtained in violation of the Sixth Amendment right to counsel, neither decision was entirely clear regarding the government conduct necessary to a finding of deliberate elicitation. In *U.S. v. Henry*, the Supreme Court more clearly defined some of the factors relevant to its deliberate elicitation determination. In so doing, the Court held that the authorities violated the Sixth Amendment right to counsel even though they instructed their jailhouse informant not to question or initiate conversations with the accused.

U.S. v. HENRY
447 U.S. 264 (1980)

CHIEF JUSTICE BURGER delivered the opinion of the Court.

We granted certiorari to consider whether respondent's Sixth Amendment right to the assistance of counsel was violated by the admission at trial of incriminating statements made by respondent to his cellmate, an undisclosed Government informant, after indictment and while in custody.

I

The Janaf Branch of the United Virginia Bank/Seaboard National in Norfolk, Va., was robbed in August 1972. Witnesses saw two men wearing masks and carrying guns enter the bank while a third man waited in the car. No witnesses were able to identify respondent Henry as one of the participants. About an hour after the robbery, the getaway car was discovered. Inside was found a rent receipt signed by one "Allen R. Norris" and a lease, also signed by Norris, for a house in Norfolk. Two men, who were subsequently convicted of participating in the robbery, were arrested at the rented house. Discovered with them were the proceeds of the robbery and the guns and masks used by the gunman.

Government agents traced the rent receipt to Henry; on the basis of this information, Henry was arrested in Atlanta, Ga., in November 1972. Two weeks later, he was indicted for armed robbery. He was held pending trial in the Norfolk city jail. Counsel was appointed on November 27.

On November 21, 1972, shortly after Henry was incarcerated, Government agents working on the Janaf robbery contacted one Nichols, an inmate at the Norfolk city jail, who for some time prior to this meeting had been engaged to provide confidential information to the Federal Bureau of Investigation as a paid informant. Nichols was then serving a sentence on local forgery charges. The record does not disclose whether the agent contacted Nichols specifically to acquire information about Henry or the Janaf robbery.[1]

---

[1] The record does disclose that on November 21, 1972, the same day the agent contacted Nichols, the agent's supervisor interrogated Henry at the jail. After denying participation in the robbery, Henry exercised his right to terminate the interview.

Nichols informed the agent that he was housed in the same cellblock with several federal prisoners awaiting trial, including Henry. The agent told him to be alert to any statements made by the federal prisoners, but not to initiate any conversation with or question Henry regarding the bank robbery. In early December, after Nichols had been released from jail, the agent again contacted Nichols, who reported that he and Henry had engaged in conversation, and that Henry had told him about the robbery of the Janaf bank. Nichols was paid for furnishing the information.

When Henry was tried in March 1973, an agent of the Federal Bureau of Investigation testified concerning the events surrounding the discovery of the rental slip and the evidence uncovered at the rented house. Other witnesses also connected Henry to the rented house, including the rental agent who positively identified Henry as the "Allen R. Norris" who had rented the house and had taken the rental receipt described earlier. A neighbor testified that, prior to the robbery, she saw Henry at the rented house with John Luck, one of the two men who had by the time of Henry's trial been convicted for the robbery. In addition, palm prints found on the lease agreement matched those of Henry.

Nichols testified at trial that he had "an opportunity to have some conversations with Mr. Henry while he was in the jail," and that Henry told him that on several occasions he had gone to the Janaf Branch to see which employees opened the vault. Nichols also testified that Henry described to him the details of the robbery and stated that the only evidence connecting him to the robbery was the rental receipt. The jury was not informed that Nichols was a paid Government informant.

On the basis of this testimony, Henry was convicted of bank robbery and sentenced to a term of imprisonment of 25 years. On August 28, 1975, Henry moved to vacate his sentence. At this stage, he stated that he had just learned that Nichols was a paid Government informant and alleged that he had been intentionally placed in the same cell with Nichols so that Nichols could secure information about the robbery. Thus, Henry contended that the introduction of Nichols' testimony violated his Sixth Amendment right to the assistance of counsel. The District Court denied the motion without a hearing.

The Court of Appeals reversed and remanded, holding that the actions of the Government impaired the Sixth Amendment rights of the defendant under *Massiah v. U.S.*, 377 U.S. 201 (1964). The court noted that Nichols had engaged in conversation with Henry and concluded that, if by association, by general conversation, or both, Nichols had developed a relationship of trust and confidence with Henry such that Henry revealed incriminating information, this constituted interference with the right to the assistance of counsel under the Sixth Amendment.

II

This Court has scrutinized postindictment confrontations between Government agents and the accused to determine whether they are "critical stages" of the prosecution at which the Sixth Amendment right to the assistance of counsel attaches. The present case involves incriminating statements made by the accused to an undisclosed and undercover Government informant while in custody and after indictment. The Government characterizes Henry's incriminating statements as voluntary, and not the result of any affirmative conduct on the part of Government agents to elicit evidence. From this, the Government argues that Henry's rights were not violated, even assuming the Sixth Amendment applies to such surreptitious confrontations; in short, it is contended that the Government has not interfered with Henry's right to counsel.

The question here is whether, under the facts of this case, a Government agent "deliberately elicited" incriminating statements from Henry within the meaning of *Massiah*. Three factors are important. First, Nichols was acting under instructions as a paid informant for the Government; second, Nichols was ostensibly no more than a fellow inmate of Henry; and third, Henry was in custody and under indictment at the time he was engaged in conversation by Nichols.

The Court of Appeals viewed the record as showing that Nichols deliberately used his position to secure incriminating information from Henry when counsel was not present, and held that conduct attributable to the Government. Nichols had been a paid Government informant for more than a year; moreover, the FBI agent was aware that Nichols had access to Henry and would be able to engage him in conversations without arousing Henry's suspicion. The arrangement between Nichols and the agent was on a contingent-fee basis; Nichols was to be paid only if he produced useful information. This combination of circumstances is sufficient to support the Court of Appeals' determination. Even if the agent's statement that he did not intend that Nichols would take affirmative steps to secure incriminating information is accepted, he must have known that such propinquity likely would lead to that result.

The Government argues that the federal agents instructed Nichols not to question Henry about the robbery. Yet according to his own testimony, Nichols was not a passive listener; rather, he had "some conversations with Mr. Henry" while he was in jail and Henry's incriminatory statements were "the product of this conversation." While affirmative interrogation, absent waiver, would certainly satisfy *Massiah*, we are not persuaded, as the Government contends, that *Brewer v. Williams*, 430 U.S. 387 (1977), modified *Massiah*'s "deliberately elicited" test.[9] In *Massiah*, no inquiry was made as to whether Massiah or his codefendant first raised the subject of the crime under investigation.

It is undisputed that Henry was unaware of Nichols' role as a Government informant. The government argues that this Court should apply a less rigorous standard under the Sixth Amendment where the accused is prompted by an undisclosed undercover informant than where the accused is speaking in the hearing of persons he knows to be Government officers. That line of argument, however, seeks to infuse Fifth Amendment concerns against compelled self-incrimination into the Sixth Amendment protection of the right to the assistance of counsel. An accused speaking to a known Government agent is typically aware that his statements may be used against him. The adversary positions at that stage are well established; the parties are then "arms' length" adversaries.

When the accused is in the company of a fellow inmate who is acting by prearrangement as a Government agent, the same cannot be said. Conversation stimulated in such circumstances may elicit information that an accused would not intentionally reveal to persons known to be Government agents. Indeed, the *Massiah* Court noted that if the Sixth Amendment "is to have any efficacy it must apply to indirect and surreptitious interrogations as well as those conducted in the jailhouse." The Court pointedly observed that Massiah was more seriously imposed upon because he did not know that his codefendant was a Government agent.

Moreover, the concept of a knowing and voluntary waiver of Sixth Amendment rights does not apply in the context of communications with an undisclosed undercover informant acting for the Government. In that setting, Henry, being unaware that Nichols was a Government agent expressly commissioned to secure evidence, cannot be held to have waived his right to the assistance of counsel.

Finally, Henry's incarceration at the time he was engaged in conversation by Nichols is also a relevant factor. As a ground for imposing the prophylactic requirements in *Miranda v. Arizona*, 384 U.S. 436 (1966), this Court noted the powerful psychological inducements to reach for aid when a person is in confinement. While the concern in *Miranda* was limited to custodial police interrogation, the mere fact of custody imposes pressures on the accused; confinement may bring into play subtle influences that will make him particularly susceptible to the ploys of undercover Government agents. The Court of Appeals determined that, on this record, the incriminating conversations between Henry and

---

[9] The situation where the "listening post" is an inanimate electronic device differs; such a device has no capability of leading the conversation into any particular subject or prompting any particular replies. However, that situation is not presented in this case, and there is no occasion to treat it; nor are we called upon to pass on the situation where an informant is placed in close proximity but makes no effort to stimulate conversations about the crime charged.

Nichols were facilitated by Nichols' conduct and apparent status as a person sharing a common plight. That Nichols had managed to gain the confidence of Henry, as the Court of Appeals determined, is confirmed by Henry's request that Nichols assist him in his escape plans when Nichols was released from confinement.

Under the strictures of the Court's holdings on the exclusion of evidence, we conclude that the Court of Appeals did not err in holding that Henry's statements to Nichols should not have been admitted at trial. By intentionally creating a situation likely to induce Henry to make incriminating statements without the assistance of counsel, the Government violated Henry's Sixth Amendment right to counsel.

JUSTICE BLACKMUN, with whom JUSTICE WHITE joins, dissenting.

Massiah mandates exclusion only if a federal agent "deliberately elicited" statements from the accused in the absence of counsel. The word "deliberately" denotes intent. *Massiah* ties this intent to the act of elicitation, that is, to conduct that draws forth a response. Thus *Massiah*, by its own terms, covers only action undertaken with the specific intent to evoke an inculpatory disclosure.

Faced with Agent Coughlin's unequivocal expression of an intent *not* to elicit statements from respondent Henry, but merely passively to receive them, the Court has no choice but to depart from the natural meaning of the *Massiah* formulation. The Court deems it critical that informant Nichols had been a paid informant; that Agent Coughlin was aware that Nichols "had access" to Henry and "would be able to engage him in conversations without arousing Henry's suspicion"; and that payment to Nichols was on a contingent-fee basis. Thus, it is said, even if Coughlin's "statement is accepted . . . he must have known that such propinquity likely would lead to that result" (that is, that Nichols would take "affirmative steps to secure incriminating information"). Later, the Court goes even further, characterizing this as a case of "intentionally creating a situation *likely to induce* Henry to make incriminating statements." This determination, coupled with the statement that Nichols "prompted" respondent Henry's remarks, leads the Court to find a *Massiah* violation.

Thus, while claiming to retain the "deliberately elicited" test, the Court really forges a new test that saps the word "deliberately" of all significance. The Court's extension of *Massiah* would cover even a "negligent" triggering of events resulting in reception of disclosures. This approach, in my view, is unsupported and unwise.

————————

In *Kuhlman v. Wilson*, authorities instructed a jailhouse informant to "keep his ears open," but not to question the accused. Although the informant at one point told the accused that his explanation of the crime—in which the accused claimed to be only a witness and not a participant—was not persuasive, the Supreme Court concluded that the accused's later incriminating statements had not been deliberately elicited in violation of the Sixth Amendment right to counsel.

KUHLMAN V. WILSON
477 U.S. 436 (1986)

JUSTICE POWELL delivered the opinion of the Court.

In the early morning of July 4, 1970, respondent and two confederates robbed the Star Taxicab Garage in the Bronx, New York, and fatally shot the night dispatcher. Shortly before, employees of the garage had observed respondent, a former employee there, on the premises conversing with two other men. They also witnessed respondent fleeing after the robbery, carrying loose money in his arms. After eluding the police for four days, respondent turned himself in. Respondent admitted that he had been present when the crimes took place, claimed that he had witnessed the robbery, gave the police a description of the robbers, but denied knowing them. Respondent also denied any involvement in the robbery or murder, claiming that he had fled because he was afraid of being blamed for the crimes.

After his arraignment, respondent was confined in the Bronx House of Detention, where he was placed in a cell with a prisoner named Benny Lee. Unknown to respondent, Lee had agreed to act as a police informant. Respondent made incriminating statements that Lee reported to the police. Prior to trial, respondent moved to suppress the statements on the ground that they were obtained in violation of his right to counsel. The trial court held an evidentiary hearing on the suppression motion, which revealed that the statements were made under the following circumstances.

Before respondent arrived in the jail, Lee had entered into an arrangement with Detective Cullen, according to which Lee agreed to listen to respondent's conversations and report his remarks to Cullen. Since the police had positive evidence of respondent's participation, the purpose of placing Lee in the cell was to determine the identities of respondent's confederates. Cullen instructed Lee not to ask respondent any questions, but simply to "keep his ears open" for the names of the other perpetrators. Respondent first spoke to Lee about the crimes after he looked out the cellblock window at the Star Taxicab Garage, where the crimes had occurred. Respondent said, "someone's messing with me," and began talking to Lee about the robbery, narrating the same story that he had given the police at the time of his arrest. Lee advised respondent that this explanation "didn't sound too good," but respondent did not alter his story. Over the next few days, however, respondent changed details of his original account. Respondent then received a visit from his brother, who mentioned that members of his family were upset because they believed that respondent had murdered the dispatcher. After the visit, respondent again described the crimes to Lee. Respondent now admitted that he and two other men, whom he never identified, had planned and carried out the robbery, and had murdered the dispatcher. Lee informed Cullen of respondent's statements and furnished Cullen with notes that he had written surreptitiously while sharing the cell with respondent.

After hearing the testimony of Cullen and Lee, the trial court found that Cullen had instructed Lee "to ask no questions of respondent about the crime but merely to listen as to what respondent might say in his presence." The court determined that Lee obeyed these instructions, that he "at no time asked any questions with respect to the crime," and that he "only listened to respondent and made notes regarding what respondent had to say." The trial court also found that respondent's statements to Lee were "spontaneous" and "unsolicited." Under state precedent, a defendant's volunteered statements to a police agent were admissible in evidence because the police were not required to prevent talkative defendants from making incriminating statements. The trial court accordingly denied the suppression motion.

The jury convicted respondent of common-law murder and felonious possession of a weapon. On May 18, 1972, the trial court sentenced him to a term of 20 years to life on the murder count and to a concurrent term of up to 7 years on the weapons count.

Following this Court's decision in *U.S. v. Henry*, 447 U.S. 264 (1980), which applied the *Massiah* test to suppress statements made to a paid jailhouse informant, respondent decided to relitigate his Sixth Amendment claim.

Henry left open the question whether the Sixth Amendment forbids admission in evidence of an accused's statements to a jailhouse informant who was "placed in close proximity but made no effort to stimulate conversations about the crime charged." Our review of the line of cases beginning with *Massiah v. U.S.*, 377 U.S. 201 (1964), shows that this question must be answered negatively.

The primary concern of the *Massiah* line of decisions is secret interrogation by investigatory techniques that are the equivalent of direct police interrogation. Since the Sixth Amendment is not violated whenever—by luck or happenstance—the State obtains incriminating statements from the accused after the right to counsel has attached, a defendant does not make out a violation of that right simply by showing that an informant, either through prior arrangement or voluntarily, reported his incriminating statements to the police. Rather, the defendant must demonstrate that the police and their informant took some action, beyond merely listening, that was designed deliberately to elicit incriminating remarks.

The state court found that Officer Cullen had instructed Lee only to listen to respondent for the purpose of determining the identities of the other participants in the robbery and murder. The police already had solid evidence of respondent's participation. The court further found that Lee followed those instructions, that he "at no time asked any questions" of respondent concerning the pending charges, and that he "only listened" to respondent's "spontaneous" and "unsolicited" statements. The only remark made by Lee that has any support in this record was his comment that respondent's initial version of his participation in the crimes "didn't sound too good." The Court of Appeals focused on that one remark and gave a description of Lee's interaction with respondent that is completely at odds with the facts found by the trial court. In the Court of Appeals' view, "subtly and slowly, but surely, Lee's ongoing verbal intercourse with respondent served to exacerbate respondent's already troubled state of mind." After thus revising some of the trial court's findings, and ignoring other more relevant findings, the Court of Appeals concluded that the police "deliberately elicited" respondent's incriminating statements. This conclusion conflicts with the decision of every other state and federal judge who reviewed this record, and is clear error.

CHIEF JUSTICE BURGER, concurring.

I agree fully with the Court's opinion and judgment. This case is clearly distinguishable from *U.S. v. Henry*, 447 U.S. 264 (1980). There is a vast difference between placing an "ear" in the suspect's cell and placing a voice in the cell to encourage conversation for the "ear" to record.

JUSTICE BRENNAN, with whom JUSTICE MARSHALL joins, dissenting.

I disagree with the Court that the instant case presents the "listening post" question. The Court of Appeals did not disregard the state court's finding that Lee asked respondent no direct questions regarding the crime. Rather, the Court of Appeals *expressly accepted* that finding, but concluded that, as a matter of law, the deliberate elicitation standard of *Henry* and *Massiah* encompasses other, more subtle forms of stimulating incriminating admissions than overt questioning. The court suggested that the police deliberately placed respondent in a cell that overlooked the scene of the crime, hoping that the view would trigger an inculpatory comment to respondent's cellmate. The court also observed that, while Lee asked respondent no questions, Lee nonetheless stimulated conversation concerning respondents' role in the Star Taxicab Garage robbery and murder by remarking that respondent's exculpatory story did not "sound too good" and that he had better come up with a better one. Thus, the Court of Appeals concluded that respondent's case did not present the situation reserved in *Henry*, where an accused makes an incriminating remark within the hearing of a jailhouse informant, who "makes no effort to stimulate conversations about the crime charged." Instead, the court determined this case to be virtually indistinguishable from *Henry*.

The Sixth Amendment guarantees an accused, at least after the initiation of formal charges, the right to rely on counsel as the "medium" between himself and the State. To be sure, the Sixth Amendment is not violated whenever, "by luck or happenstance," the State obtains incriminating statements from the accused after the right to counsel has attached. It is violated, however, when "the State obtains incriminating statements by knowingly circumventing the accused's right to have counsel present in a confrontation between the accused and a state agent." As we explained in *Henry*, where the accused has not waived his right to counsel, the government knowingly circumvents the defendant's right to counsel where it "deliberately elicits" inculpatory admissions, that is, "intentionally creates a situation likely to induce the accused to make incriminating statements without the assistance of counsel."

In the instant case, as in *Henry*, the accused was incarcerated and therefore was "susceptible to the ploys of undercover Government agents." Like Nichols, Lee was a secret informant, usually received consideration for the services he rendered the police, and therefore had an incentive to produce the information which he knew the police hoped to obtain. Just as Nichols had done, Lee obeyed instructions not to question respondent and to report to the police any statements made by the respondent in Lee's presence about the crime in question. And, like Nichols, Lee encouraged respondent to talk about his crime by conversing with him on the subject over the course of several days and by telling respondent that his exculpatory story would not convince anyone without more work. However, unlike the situation in *Henry*, a disturbing visit from respondent's brother, rather than a conversation with the informant, seems to have been the immediate catalyst for respondent's confession to Lee. While it might appear from this sequence of events that Lee's comment regarding respondent's story and his general willingness to converse with respondent about the crime were not the *immediate* causes of respondent's admission, I think that the deliberate-elicitation standard requires consideration of the entire course of government behavior.

The State intentionally created a situation in which it was foreseeable that respondent would make incriminating statements without the assistance of counsel—it assigned respondent to a cell overlooking the scene of the crime and designated a secret informant to be respondent's cellmate. The informant, while avoiding direct questions, nonetheless developed a relationship of cellmate camaraderie with respondent and encouraged him to talk about his crime. While the *coup de grace* was delivered by respondent's brother, the groundwork for respondent's confession was laid by the State. Clearly the State's actions had a sufficient nexus with respondent's admission of guilt to constitute deliberate elicitation within the meaning of *Henry*.

Can *U.S. v. Henry* and *Kuhlman v. Wilson* be reconciled? In both cases, the government placed an informant in close proximity to the defendant with instructions to take note of the defendant's remarks but not to ask any questions; the informant then participated in conversations over a period of days during which the defendant ultimately made incriminating statements. *Henry* held that the government violated the prohibition on deliberate elicitation, while *Kuhlman* found no constitutional violation despite the factual similarities.

One explanation for the different outcomes may relate to the timing and causes of the defendant's incriminating statements. In *Henry*, the incriminating statements followed closely on the heels of the informant's conversations with the defendant; in *Kuhlman*, the incriminating statements came shortly after the defendant received a visit from his brother, who mentioned that family members were upset because they believed he was guilty of murder. Another explanation for the different results may relate to the behavior of each informant. The Supreme Court suggests that the informant in *Henry* assumed a more active role in the conversations than the informant in *Kuhlman*, who is portrayed as a passive listener. The informant in *Kuhlman* was quite active, however, in one important respect when he encouraged the defendant to rethink his story by remarking that the given explanation "didn't sound too good." The many similarities and subtle differences in *Henry* and *Kuhlman* make it difficult to draw a clear line between permissible passive listening and prohibited deliberate elicitation.

All of the cases presented thus far in this Chapter—*Massiah v. U.S.*, *Brewer v. Williams*, *U.S. v. Henry*, and *Kuhlman v. Wilson*—focus on the government's knowledge or intent in determining whether deliberate elicitation took place. In each of those cases, it was police or their informants who instigated or arranged the meeting with the accused, and in *Massiah*, *Brewer*, and *Henry*, the Supreme Court concluded that the government knew—or as *Henry* put it, "must have known"—that its officers or agents were likely to obtain incriminating statements from the accused in the absence of counsel. In *Maine v. Moulton*, however, the Supreme Court held that deliberate elicitation can occur even when the accused initiates conversations or meetings with an informant.

MAINE V. MOULTON
474 U.S. 159 (1985)

In April 1981, Perley Moulton and Gary Colson were indicted for stealing several vehicles and assorted automotive parts. In November 1982, as the trial date neared, Colson and his attorney met with police. Colson admitted that he and Moulton committed the charged offenses along with various other crimes. The police offered Colson a deal in which no further charges would be brought against him if he agreed to testify against Moulton and otherwise cooperate in the prosecution of Moulton on the pending charges. Colson agreed to cooperate.

Police placed a recording device on Colson's telephone, and over the next month, he and Moulton spoke three times. In the phone calls, Moulton did not make any incriminating statements, but he asked to meet with Colson so that they could plan their defense. Colson and Moulton met on December 26, 1982, and Colson wore a wire transmitter to record the conversation. During the meeting, Colson discussed the pending charges with Moulton, repeatedly asked Moulton to remind him of the details of the charged crime, and encouraged Moulton to describe an inchoate plan for killing witnesses. Throughout the December 26 meeting, Moulton made several incriminating statements about the stolen vehicles for which he was indicted, and these statements were admitted into evidence at his trial. Moulton was convicted, but the Supreme Judicial Court of Maine ordered a new trial because the admission of the statements made to Colson violated Moulton's Sixth Amendment right to counsel.

On appeal to the U.S. Supreme Court, the State contended that there was no deliberate elicitation because it was Moulton, rather than the police, who had initiated the telephone calls and the meeting with Colson. After noting that "the identity of the party who instigated the meeting at which the Government obtained incriminating statements was not decisive or even important to our decisions in *Massiah* or *Henry*," the Supreme Court rejected the State's argument:

> The Sixth Amendment guarantees the accused, at least after the initiation of formal charges, the right to rely on counsel as a "medium" between him and the State. This guarantee includes the State's affirmative obligation not to act in a manner that circumvents the protections accorded the accused by invoking this right. The determination whether particular action by state agents violates the accused's right to the assistance of counsel must be made in light of this obligation. Thus, the Sixth Amendment is not violated whenever—by luck or happenstance—the State obtains incriminating statements from the accused after the right to counsel has attached. However, knowing exploitation by the State of an opportunity to confront

the accused without counsel being present is as much a breach of the State's obligation not to circumvent the right to the assistance of counsel as is the intentional creation of such an opportunity. Accordingly, the Sixth Amendment is violated when the State obtains incriminating statements by knowingly circumventing the accused's right to have counsel present in a confrontation between the accused and a state agent.

The Supreme Court concluded that the investigatory techniques employed by the police constituted deliberate elicitation, denying Moulton his Sixth Amendment right to counsel on the pending charges:

> Because Moulton thought of Colson only as his codefendant, Colson's engaging Moulton in active conversation about their upcoming trial was certain to elicit statements that Moulton would not intentionally reveal—and had a constitutional right not to reveal—to persons known to be police agents. Under these circumstances, Colson's merely participating in this conversation was the functional equivalent of interrogation. In addition, Colson frequently pressed Moulton for details of various thefts and in so doing elicited much incriminating information that the State later used at trial.

As the Supreme Court noted in *Kuhlman*, "the primary concern of the *Massiah* line of decisions is secret interrogation by investigatory techniques that are the equivalent of direct police interrogation." But the Court has also held, most notably in *Fellers v. U.S.*, that deliberate elicitation can occur even in the absence of "interrogation" as defined by *Miranda*.

FELLERS V. U.S.
540 U.S. 519 (2004)

After a grand jury indicted Fellers, police officers went to his home to arrest him. When Fellers answered the door, the officers identified themselves and asked if they could come inside. Fellers invited the officers into his living room. The officers told Fellers they had come to discuss his involvement in methamphetamine distribution. They informed him that they had a federal warrant for his arrest and that a grand jury had indicted him for conspiracy to distribute methamphetamine. The officers told Fellers that the indictment referred to his involvement with certain individuals, four of whom they named. Fellers then told the officers that he knew the four people and had used methamphetamine during his association with them.

Fellers argued that his incriminating statement should be suppressed because the officers failed to administer the *Miranda* warnings and deliberately elicited the statement inside his home in violation of the Sixth Amendment right to counsel. While the trial and appellate courts suppressed the statement due to the *Miranda* violation, the appellate court noted that the Sixth Amendment was not applicable because Fellers was not interrogated inside his home.

The Supreme Court held a defendant need not show that he was interrogated in order to establish a deliberate elicitation claim:

> We have consistently applied the deliberate-elicitation standard in Sixth Amendment cases, and we have expressly distinguished this standard from the Fifth Amendment custodial-interrogation standard.

> The Court of Appeals erred in holding that the absence of an "interrogation" foreclosed petitioner's claim that [his] statements should have been suppressed. First, there is no question that the officers in this case "deliberately elicited" information from petitioner. Indeed, the officers, upon arriving at petitioner's house, informed him that their purpose in coming was to discuss his involvement in the distribution of methamphetamine and his association with certain charged co-conspirators. Because the ensuing discussion took place after petitioner had been indicted, outside the presence of counsel, and in the absence of any waiver of petitioner's Sixth Amendment rights, the Court of Appeals erred in holding that the officers' actions did not violate the Sixth Amendment standards established in *Massiah* and its progeny.

The Sixth Amendment Right to Counsel and the Prohibition on Deliberate Elicitation

1.   The Sixth Amendment right to counsel attaches at or after the initiation of adversary judicial criminal proceedings, whether by way of formal charge, preliminary hearing, indictment, information, or arraignment.

2.   Once the Sixth Amendment right to counsel has attached, police cannot deliberately elicit incriminating statements from the accused outside the presence of counsel.

a.   Deliberate elicitation occurs when the government or its agents knowingly exploit the opportunity to confront the accused without counsel being present, or when the government or its agents intentionally create a situation likely to induce the accused to make incriminating statements without the assistance of counsel.

b. In order to prove deliberate elicitation, the defendant must demonstrate that the police or their agents or informants took some action, beyond merely listening, that was designed deliberately to elicit incriminating remarks. The fact that an informant, either through prior arrangement or voluntarily, reported the defendant's incriminating statements to the police is insufficient to establish a violation of the right to counsel.

c. The fact that the accused initiates conversations or meetings with government agents or informants does not preclude a finding of deliberate elicitation.

d. Deliberate elicitation can occur even in the absence of "custodial interrogation" as defined by *Miranda* and its progeny.

3. Statements taken in violation of the Sixth Amendment prohibition on deliberate elicitation cannot be introduced at trial as evidence of the defendant's guilt.

LEARN MORE WITH *LAW & ORDER*

In the following episode of *Law & Order* ("Blood is Thicker," Season 2, Episode 14), Lois Ryder is discovered dead in an alley, apparently the victim of a violent mugging. Jonathan Ryder, the victim's husband, is eventually charged with the murder, but is released on bail. Later, however, he is taken into custody because he temporarily left the country, violating one the conditions of his bail. The prosecuting attorney, Ben Stone, places an informant—an armed robber named Morgan—in Ryder's jail cell, but instructs Morgan not to ask Ryder any questions. Ryder eventually makes incriminating statements—including references to the guilt he feels over having to face his daughter, Alison—and Morgan reports these statements to Ben Stone.

Stone arranges a hearing so that the Morgan can tell the judge what Ryder said. At the hearing, however, Morgan claims that he fabricated Ryder's confession. The prosecutors inform the judge that they believe that Ryder's wealthy and powerful mother, Barbara, engaged in witness tampering to alter Morgan's testimony. The judge says she wouldn't have admitted Morgan's testimony anyway, since jailhouse informants always claim they don't say anything to the accused when, in fact, they actually do try to elicit incriminating statements.

Since Morgan is not permitted to testify at the trial, Ben Stone asks the judge for an order to examine Alison Ryder as a potential witness. The defense attorney argues that Alison Ryder is "fruit of the poisonous tree," since the prosecution learned about her through the inadmissible statements that Ryder made in jail to Morgan. The judge scoffs at this argument, noting that there is no "poisonous tree"—or constitutional violation—since Morgan changed his story and claimed Ryder made no confession. Stone then interjects and argues that even if there was a constitutional violation, he should be permitted to examine Alison under the authority of *U.S. v. Ceccolini*, 435 U.S. 268 (1978)—presented in Chapter 8—in which the Supreme Court refused to exclude the testimony of a live witness even though police discovered her as a result of an illegal search. The judge permits Stone to obtain a psychiatric examination of Alison Ryder, and during the exam, she reveals the existence of a family secret—one that leads the prosecution to additional evidence necessary to convict her father.

The segments of the episode that depict the relevant Investigative Criminal Procedure issues appear at:

29:00 to 30:34; 38:10 to 41:00

***Law & Order* Episode**
"Blood is Thicker," Season 2, Episode 14

The *Law & Order* episode includes a useful illustration of some of the practical and legal difficulties associated with the use of a jailhouse informant, particularly after a suspect has been charged with a crime. Once Jonathan Ryder was charged with the murder of his wife, his Sixth Amendment right to counsel attached. At that point, police may not "deliberately elicit" incriminating statements from the defendant outside the presence of counsel. In *Massiah v. U.S.*, 377 U.S. 201 (1977), *U.S. v. Henry*, 447 U.S. 264 (1980), and *Maine v. Moulton*, 474 U.S. 159 (1985), prosecutors used an informant to obtain incriminating statements from a charged defendant, and in each case, the Supreme Court held that the statements were inadmissible because they had been deliberately elicited in violation of the defendant's Sixth Amendment right to counsel. In *Kuhlman v. Wilson*, 477 U.S. 436 (1986), however, the Supreme Court held that incriminating statements made by a charged defendant to an informant were admissible, largely because the informant was essentially a passive listener and asked no questions of the defendant.

With these Supreme Court precedents in mind, Ben Stone clearly instructs his informant, Morgan, not to ask Ryder any questions and Morgan apparently follows this instruction by placing a magazine in his mouth when Ryder starts to confess. If Morgan was truly a passive listener and did not elicit incriminating statements, his testimony about Ryder's confession should be admissible under *Kuhlman v. Wilson*. Morgan's testimony becomes useless, however, when he explains at a hearing (not seen in the episode) that he fabricated Ryder's confession.

The trial judge, almost as an afterthought, says she wouldn't have admitted Morgan's account of Ryder's confession anyway, since she believes jailhouse informants engage in deliberate elicitation even when they claim otherwise. In *U.S. v. Henry*, the Supreme Court expressed similar skepticism about the use of jailhouse informants after the Sixth Amendment right to counsel has attached, finding that the government violated the prohibition on deliberate elicitation even though the informant was instructed not to initiate any conversations or ask any questions of the defendant.

Although Morgan's account of Ryder's confession is inadmissible, Ben Stone cites *U.S. v. Ceccolini* and successfully argues that he should be permitted to examine Ryder's daughter, Alison, even though the prosecution learned about her possible relevance to the case through the inadmissible statements that Ryder purportedly made to Morgan. The reference to *Ceccolini* presents a good opportunity to review the "fruits doctrine" and the extent to which evidence linked to or derived from illegally obtained evidence may nevertheless be admissible.

B. THE SIXTH AMENDMENT RIGHT TO COUNSEL IS "OFFENSE SPECIFIC"

As you'll recall from Chapter 10, *Miranda* and the prophylactic rule in *Edwards v. Arizona*, 451 U.S. 477 (1981), require the police to stop questioning—and refrain from reinitiating questioning—after a suspect has invoked his Fifth Amendment right to counsel. In fact, *Arizona v. Roberson*, 486 U.S. 675 (1988), held that once a suspect invokes his *Miranda* right to counsel, the police cannot reinitiate questioning even to discuss an entirely different crime unrelated to the subject of the first interrogation.

The Sixth Amendment right to counsel operates in a different manner because it is "offense specific." Once the Sixth Amendment right to counsel attaches, police must not question the accused about the specific crimes with which he has been charged. The police remain free, however, to ask questions about other crimes—including factually related crimes—for which charges have not yet been brought. If the suspect is in custody when questioned, he can still, of course, exercise his *Miranda* rights by declining to answer or requesting an attorney. But the suspect cannot seek protection under the umbrella of the Sixth Amendment right to counsel when the police pose questions about uncharged offenses. *McNeil v. Wisconsin* explains the law enforcement considerations that led the Supreme Court to conclude that the Sixth Amendment right to counsel is offense specific.

MCNEIL V. WISCONSIN
501 U.S. 171 (1991)

Paul McNeil was charged with an armed robbery that had occurred in a suburb of Milwaukee, and was represented by a public defender during his initial appearance in court. Later that evening, detectives visited McNeil in jail, advised him of his *Miranda* rights, and after McNeil signed a *Miranda* waiver form, they questioned him about a separate crime involving armed burglary, attempted murder, and murder that took place in the town of Caledonia, Wisconsin. McNeil did not deny knowledge of the Caledonia crimes, but said that he was not involved. In two subsequent meetings with detectives, McNeil again received and waived his *Miranda* rights, then made incriminating statements admitting his involvement in the Caledonia crimes.

McNeil argued that his incriminating statements about the Caledonia crimes should be suppressed because once his right to counsel had attached for the armed robbery in the Milwaukee suburb, police were prohibited from questioning him about other offenses. The Supreme Court rejected McNeil's argument, holding that the Sixth Amendment right to counsel is offense specific:

> The Sixth Amendment right is offense specific. It cannot be invoked once for all future prosecutions, for it does not attach until a prosecution is commenced, that is, at or after the initiation of adversary judicial criminal proceedings—whether by way of formal charge, preliminary hearing, indictment, information, or arraignment.

The Supreme Court went on to note that McNeil's proposed rule would frustrate effective law enforcement:

> If we were to adopt petitioner's rule, most persons in pretrial custody for serious offenses would be *unapproachable* by police officers suspecting them of involvement in other crimes, *even though they have never expressed any unwillingness to be questioned.* Since the ready ability to obtain uncoerced confessions is not an evil but an unmitigated good, society would be the loser.

In *Texas v. Cobb*, the Supreme Court reaffirmed its conclusion in *McNeil* that the Sixth Amendment right to counsel is offense specific. The Court went on to adopt a narrow definition of the term "offense" that permits police to question a suspect about factually related but uncharged offenses without violating the right to counsel.

TEXAS V. COBB

532 U.S. 162 (2001)

CHIEF JUSTICE REHNQUIST delivered the opinion of the Court.

The Texas Court of Criminal Appeals held that a criminal defendant's Sixth Amendment right to counsel attaches not only to the offense with which he is charged, but to other offenses "closely related factually" to the charged offense. We hold that our decision in *McNeil v. Wisconsin*, 501 U.S. 171 (1991), meant what it said, and that the Sixth Amendment right is "offense specific."

In December 1993, Lindsey Owings reported to the Walker County, Texas, Sheriff's Office that the home he shared with his wife, Margaret, and their 16-month-old daughter, Kori Rae, had been burglarized. He also informed police that his wife and daughter were missing. Respondent Raymond Levi Cobb lived across the street from the Owings. Acting on an anonymous tip that respondent was involved in the burglary, Walker County investigators questioned him about the events. He denied involvement. In July 1994, while under arrest for an unrelated offense, respondent was again questioned about the incident. Respondent then gave a written statement confessing to the burglary, but he denied knowledge relating to the disappearances. Respondent was subsequently indicted for the burglary, and Hal Ridley was appointed in August 1994 to represent respondent on that charge.

Shortly after Ridley's appointment, investigators asked and received his permission to question respondent about the disappearances. Respondent continued to deny involvement. Investigators repeated this process in September 1995, again with Ridley's permission and again with the same result.

In November 1995, respondent, free on bond in the burglary case, was living with his father in Odessa, Texas. At that time, respondent's father contacted the Walker County Sheriff's Office to report that respondent had confessed to him that he killed Margaret Owings in the course of the burglary. Walker County investigators directed respondent's father to the Odessa police station, where he gave a statement. Odessa police then faxed the statement to Walker County, where investigators secured a warrant for respondent's arrest and faxed it back to Odessa. Shortly thereafter, Odessa police took respondent into custody and administered warnings pursuant to *Miranda v. Arizona*, 384 U.S. 436 (1966). Respondent waived these rights.

After a short time, respondent confessed to murdering both Margaret and Kori Rae. Respondent explained that when Margaret confronted him as he was attempting to remove the Owings' stereo, he stabbed her in the stomach with a knife he was carrying. Respondent told police that he dragged her body to a wooded area a few hundred yards from the house.

[Cobb then told police that he returned to the house, found the baby sleeping on its bed, took it to the wooded area, and placed it on the ground a few feet from its mother. Cobb then dug a hole. When the baby awoke and started crawling toward its mother, it fell into the hole. Then Cobb placed the mother's body in the hole and covered both her and the baby with dirt.] Respondent later led police to the location where he had buried the victims' bodies.

Respondent was convicted of capital murder for murdering more than one person in the course of a single criminal transaction. He was sentenced to death. On appeal to the Court of Criminal Appeals of Texas, respondent argued that his confession should have been suppressed because it was obtained in violation of his Sixth Amendment right to counsel. Respondent contended that his right to counsel had attached when Ridley was appointed in the burglary case and that Odessa police were therefore required to secure Ridley's permission before proceeding with the interrogation.

The Court of Criminal Appeals reversed respondent's conviction by a divided vote and remanded for a new trial. The court held that "once the right to counsel attaches to the offense charged, it also attaches to any other offense that is very closely related factually to the offense charged." Finding the capital murder charge to be "factually interwoven with the burglary," the court concluded that respondent's Sixth Amendment right to counsel had attached on the capital murder charge even though respondent had not yet been charged with that offense. The court further found that respondent had asserted that right by accepting Ridley's appointment in the burglary case. Accordingly, it deemed the confession inadmissible and found that its introduction had not been harmless error.

The State sought review in this Court, and we granted certiorari to consider first whether the Sixth Amendment right to counsel extends to crimes that are "factually related" to those that have actually been charged, and second whether respondent made a valid unilateral waiver of that right in this case. Because we answer the first question in the negative, we do not reach the second.

The Sixth Amendment provides that "in all criminal prosecutions, the accused shall enjoy the right . . . to have the Assistance of Counsel for his defence." In *McNeil v. Wisconsin*, we explained when this right arises: "The Sixth Amendment right to counsel is offense specific. It cannot be invoked once for all future prosecutions, for it does not attach until a prosecution is commenced, that is, at or after the initiation of adversary judicial criminal proceedings—whether by way of formal charge, preliminary hearing, indictment, information, or arraignment." Accordingly, we held that a defendant's statements regarding offenses for which he had not been charged were admissible notwithstanding the attachment of his Sixth Amendment right to counsel on other charged offenses.

Some state courts and Federal Courts of Appeals, however, have read into *McNeil's* offense-specific definition an exception for crimes that are "factually related" to a charged offense. We decline to do so.

Respondent predicts that the offense-specific rule will prove "disastrous" to suspects' constitutional rights and will "permit law enforcement officers almost complete and total license to conduct unwanted and uncounseled interrogations." Besides offering no evidence that such a parade of horribles has occurred in those jurisdictions that have not enlarged upon *McNeil*, he fails to appreciate the significance of two critical considerations. First, there can be no doubt that a suspect must be apprised of his rights against compulsory self-incrimination and to consult with an attorney before authorities may conduct custodial interrogation. In the present case, police scrupulously followed *Miranda's* dictates when questioning respondent.[2] Second, it is critical to recognize that the Constitution does not negate society's interest in the ability of police to talk to witnesses and suspects, even those who have been charged with other offenses.

Although it is clear that the Sixth Amendment right to counsel attaches only to charged offenses, we have recognized in other contexts that the definition of an "offense" is not necessarily limited to the four corners of a charging instrument. In *Blockburger v. U.S.*, 284 U.S. 299 (1932), we explained that "where the same act or transaction constitutes a violation of two distinct statutory provisions, the test to be applied to determine whether there are two offenses or only one, is whether each provision requires proof of a fact which the other does not." We have since applied the *Blockburger* test to delineate the scope of the Fifth Amendment's Double Jeopardy Clause, which prevents multiple or successive prosecutions for the "same offence." We see no constitutional difference between the meaning of the term "offense" in the contexts of double jeopardy and of the right to counsel. Accordingly, we hold that when the Sixth Amendment right to counsel attaches, it does encompass offenses that, even if not formally charged, would be considered the same offense under the *Blockburger* test.

---

[2] Curiously, while predicting disastrous consequences for the core values underlying the Sixth Amendment, the dissenters give short shrift to the Fifth Amendment's role in protecting a defendant's right to consult with counsel before talking to police. Even though the Sixth Amendment right to counsel has not attached to uncharged offenses, defendants retain the ability under *Miranda* to refuse any police questioning, and, indeed, charged defendants presumably have met with counsel and have had the opportunity to discuss whether it is advisable to invoke those Fifth Amendment rights. Thus, in all but the rarest of cases, the Court's decision today will have no impact whatsoever upon a defendant's ability to protect his Sixth Amendment right. It is also worth noting that, contrary to the dissent's suggestion, there is no "background principle" of our Sixth Amendment jurisprudence establishing that there may be no contact between a defendant and police without counsel present.

It remains only to apply these principles to the facts at hand. At the time he confessed to Odessa police, respondent had been indicted for burglary of the Owings residence, but he had not been charged in the murders of Margaret and Kori Rae. As defined by Texas law, burglary and capital murder are not the same offense under *Blockburger*. Accordingly, the Sixth Amendment right to counsel did not bar police from interrogating respondent regarding the murders, and respondent's confession was therefore admissible.

JUSTICE BREYER, with whom JUSTICE STEVENS, JUSTICE SOUTER, and JUSTICE GINSBURG join, dissenting.

This case focuses upon the meaning of a single word, "offense," when it arises in the context of the Sixth Amendment. Several basic background principles define that context.

First, the Sixth Amendment right to counsel plays a central role in ensuring the fairness of criminal proceedings in our system of justice. Second, the right attaches when adversary proceedings, triggered by the government's formal accusation of a crime, begin. Third, once this right attaches, law enforcement officials are required, in most circumstances, to deal with the defendant through counsel rather than directly, even if the defendant has waived his Fifth Amendment rights. Fourth, the particular aspect of the right here at issue—the rule that the police ordinarily must communicate with the defendant through counsel—has important limits. In particular, recognizing the need for law enforcement officials to investigate new or additional crimes not the subject of current proceedings, this Court has made clear that the right to counsel does not attach to any and every crime that an accused may commit or have committed. The right cannot be invoked once for all future prosecutions, and it does not forbid interrogation unrelated to the charge. In a word, as this Court previously noted, the right is "offense specific."

This case focuses upon the last-mentioned principle, in particular upon the meaning of the words "offense specific." These words appear in this Court's Sixth Amendment case law, not in the Sixth Amendment's text. The definition of these words is not self-evident. Sometimes the term "offense" may refer to words that are written in a criminal statute; sometimes it may refer generally to a course of conduct in the world, aspects of which constitute the elements of one or more crimes; and sometimes it may refer, narrowly and technically, just to the conceptually severable aspects of the latter. This case requires us to determine whether an "offense"—for Sixth Amendment purposes—includes factually related aspects of a single course of conduct other than those few acts that make up the essential elements of the crime charged.

We should answer this question in light of the Sixth Amendment's basic objectives as set forth in this Court's case law. At the very least, we should answer it in a way that does not undermine those objectives. But the Court today decides that "offense" means the crime set forth within "the four corners of a charging instrument," along with other crimes that "would be considered the same offense" under the test established by *Blockburger*. In my view, this unnecessarily technical definition undermines Sixth Amendment protections while doing nothing to further effective law enforcement.

For one thing, the majority's rule, while leaving the Fifth Amendment's protections in place, threatens to diminish severely the additional protection that, under this Court's rulings, the Sixth Amendment provides when it grants the right to counsel to defendants who have been charged with a crime and insists that law enforcement officers thereafter communicate with them through that counsel. The police may not force a suspect who has asked for legal counsel to make a critical legal choice without the legal assistance that he has requested and that the Constitution guarantees.

For these reasons, the Sixth Amendment right at issue is independent of the Fifth Amendment's protections; and the importance of this Sixth Amendment right has been repeatedly recognized in our cases. The majority's rule permits law enforcement officials to question those charged with a crime without first approaching counsel, through the simple device of asking questions about any other related crime not actually charged in the indictment. Thus, the police could ask the individual charged with robbery about, say, the assault of the cashier not yet charged, or about any other uncharged offense (unless under *Blockburger*'s definition it counts as the "same crime"), all *without notifying counsel*. Indeed, the majority's rule would permit law enforcement officials to question anyone charged with any crime in any one of the examples just given about his or her conduct on the single relevant occasion without notifying counsel unless the prosecutor has charged every possible crime arising out of that same brief course of conduct. What Sixth Amendment sense—what common sense—does such a rule make? What is left of the "communicate through counsel" rule? The majority's approach is inconsistent with any common understanding of the scope of counsel's representation. It will undermine the lawyer's role as "medium" between the defendant and the government. And it will, on a random basis, remove a significant portion of the protection that this Court has found inherent in the Sixth Amendment.

The simple-sounding *Blockburger* test has proved extraordinarily difficult to administer in practice. Judges, lawyers, and law professors often disagree about how to apply it. Yet the Court now asks, not the lawyers and judges who ordinarily work with double jeopardy law, but police officers in the field, to navigate *Blockburger* when they question suspects.

There is, of course, an alternative. We can, and should, define "offense" in terms of the conduct that constitutes the crime that the offender committed on a particular occasion, including criminal acts that are "closely related to" or "inextricably intertwined with" the particular crime set forth in the charging instrument. This alternative is not perfect. The language used lacks the precision for which police officers may hope; and it requires lower courts to specify its meaning further as they apply it in individual cases. Yet virtually every lower court in the United States to consider the issue has defined "offense" in the Sixth Amendment context to encompass such closely related acts.

One cannot say in favor of this commonly followed approach that it is perfectly clear—only that, because it comports with common sense, it is far easier to apply than that of the majority. And, most importantly, the "closely related" test furthers, rather than undermines, the Sixth Amendment's "right to counsel," a right so necessary to the realization in practice of that most noble ideal, a fair trial.

The Texas Court of Criminal Appeals, following this commonly accepted approach, found that the charged burglary and the uncharged murders were "closely related." All occurred during a short period of time on the same day in the same basic location. The victims of the murders were also victims of the burglary. Cobb committed one of the murders in furtherance of the robbery, the other to cover up the crimes. The police, when questioning Cobb, knew that he already had a lawyer representing him on the burglary charges and had demonstrated their belief that this lawyer also represented Cobb in respect to the murders by asking his permission to question Cobb about the murders on previous occasions. The relatedness of the crimes is well illustrated by the impossibility of questioning Cobb about the murders without eliciting admissions about the burglary. Nor, in my view, did Cobb waive his right to counsel. These considerations are sufficient. The police officers ought to have spoken to Cobb's counsel before questioning Cobb.

The Sixth Amendment Right to Counsel Is Offense Specific

1.   The Sixth Amendment right to counsel is offense specific—it attaches only for those crimes with which the defendant has been charged—leaving the police free to question a defendant about factually related but uncharged offenses without violating the right to counsel.

2.   The definition of "offense" is not limited to the four corners of a charging instrument. Where the same act or transaction constitutes a violation of two distinct statutory provisions, the test to be applied to determine whether there are two offenses or only one is whether each provision requires proof of a fact which the other does not.

C. THE IMPEACHMENT EXCEPTION

In *Harris v. New York*, 401 U.S. 222 (1971), presented in Chapter 10, the Supreme Court held that although a statement taken in violation of *Miranda* may not be introduced by the prosecution to prove the defendant's guilt, the statement may be used to impeach the defendant's credibility if he takes the stand in his own defense and provides testimony inconsistent with the earlier statement. Similarly, in *Kansas v. Ventris*, the Supreme Court held that although a deliberately elicited statement taken in violation of the Sixth Amendment right to counsel may not be introduced by the prosecution to prove the defendant's guilt, the statement may be used to impeach the defendant's credibility if he takes the stand in his own defense and gives testimony inconsistent with his prior elicited statement.

KANSAS V. VENTRIS
556 U.S. 586 (2009)

JUSTICE SCALIA delivered the opinion of the Court.

We address in this case the question whether a defendant's incriminating statement to a jailhouse informant, concededly elicited in violation of Sixth Amendment strictures, is admissible at trial to impeach the defendant's conflicting statement.

I

In the early hours of January 7, 2004, after two days of no sleep and some drug use, Rhonda Theel and respondent Donnie Ray Ventris reached an ill-conceived agreement to confront Ernest Hicks in his home. The couple testified that the aim of the visit was simply to investigate rumors that Hicks abused children, but the couple may have been inspired by the potential for financial gain: Theel had recently learned that Hicks carried large amounts of cash.

The encounter did not end well. One or both of the pair shot and killed Hicks with shots from a .38-caliber revolver, and the companions drove off in Hicks' truck with approximately $300 of his money and his cell phone. On receiving a tip from two friends of the couple who had helped transport them to Hicks' home, officers arrested Ventris and Theel and charged them with various crimes, chief among them murder and aggravated robbery. The State dropped the murder charge against Theel in exchange for her guilty plea to the robbery charge and her testimony identifying Ventris as the shooter.

Prior to trial, officers planted an informant in Ventris' holding cell, instructing him to "keep his ear open and listen" for incriminating statements. According to the informant, in response to his statement that Ventris appeared to have "something more serious weighing in on his mind," Ventris divulged that "he'd shot this man in his head and in his chest" and taken "his keys, his wallet, about $350.00, and a vehicle."

At trial, Ventris took the stand and blamed the robbery and shooting entirely on Theel. The government sought to call the informant, to testify to Ventris' prior contradictory statement; Ventris objected. The State conceded that there was "probably a violation" of Ventris' Sixth Amendment right to counsel but nonetheless argued that the statement was admissible for impeachment purposes because the violation "doesn't give the Defendant a license to just get on the stand and lie." The trial court agreed and allowed the informant's testimony, but instructed the jury to "consider with caution" all testimony given in exchange for benefits from the State. The jury ultimately acquitted Ventris of felony murder and misdemeanor theft but returned a guilty verdict on the aggravated burglary and aggravated robbery counts.

The Kansas Supreme Court reversed the conviction, holding that "once a criminal prosecution has commenced, the defendant's statements made to an undercover informant surreptitiously acting as an agent for the State are not admissible at trial for any reason, including the impeachment of the defendant's testimony."

II

The Sixth Amendment, applied to the States through the Fourteenth Amendment, guarantees that "in all criminal prosecutions, the accused shall . . . have the Assistance of Counsel for his defence." The core of this right has historically been, and remains today, the opportunity for a defendant to consult with an attorney and to have him investigate the case and prepare a defense for trial. We have held, however, that the right extends to having counsel present at various pretrial "critical" interactions between the defendant and the State, including the deliberate elicitation by law enforcement officers (and their agents) of statements pertaining to the charge, *Massiah v. U.S.*, 377 U.S. 201 (1964). The State has conceded throughout these proceedings that Ventris' confession was taken in violation of *Massiah*'s dictates and was therefore not admissible in the prosecution's case in chief. Without affirming that this concession was necessary, we accept it as the law of the case. The only question we answer today is whether the State must bear the additional consequence of inability to counter Ventris' contradictory testimony by placing the informant on the stand.

Whether otherwise excluded evidence can be admitted for purposes of impeachment depends upon the nature of the constitutional guarantee that is violated. Sometimes that explicitly mandates exclusion from trial, and sometimes it does not. The Fifth Amendment guarantees that no person shall be compelled to give evidence against himself, and so is violated whenever a truly coerced confession is introduced at trial, whether by way of impeachment or otherwise. The Fourth Amendment, on the other hand, guarantees that no person shall be subjected to unreasonable searches or seizures, and says nothing about excluding their fruits from evidence; exclusion comes by way of deterrent sanction rather than to avoid violation of the substantive guarantee. Inadmissibility has not been automatic, therefore, but we have instead applied an exclusionary-rule balancing test. The same is true for violations of the Fifth and Sixth Amendment prophylactic rules forbidding certain pretrial police conduct.

Respondent argues that the Sixth Amendment's right to counsel is a "right an accused is to enjoy at trial." The core of the right to counsel is indeed a trial right, ensuring that the prosecution's case is subjected to the crucible of meaningful adversarial testing. But our opinions under the Sixth Amendment, as under the Fifth, have held that the right covers pretrial interrogations to ensure that police manipulation does not render counsel entirely impotent—depriving the defendant of effective representation by counsel at the only stage when legal aid and advice would help him.

Our opinion in *Massiah*, to be sure, was equivocal on what precisely constituted the violation. It quoted various authorities indicating that the violation occurred at the moment of the postindictment interrogation because such questioning "contravenes the basic dictates of fairness in the conduct of criminal causes." But the opinion later suggested that the violation occurred only when the improperly obtained evidence was "used against the defendant at his trial." That question was irrelevant to the decision in *Massiah* in any event. Now that we are confronted with the question, we conclude that the *Massiah* right is a right to be free of uncounseled interrogation, and is infringed at the time of the interrogation. That, we think, is when the "Assistance of Counsel" is denied.

It is illogical to say that the right is not violated until trial counsel's task of opposing conviction has been undermined by the statement's admission into evidence. A defendant is not denied counsel merely because the prosecution has been permitted to introduce evidence of guilt—even evidence so overwhelming that the attorney's job of gaining an acquittal is rendered impossible. In such circumstances the accused continues to enjoy the assistance of counsel; the assistance is simply not worth much. The assistance of counsel has been denied, however, at the prior critical stage which produced the inculpatory evidence. Our cases acknowledge that reality in holding that the stringency of the warnings necessary for a waiver of the assistance of counsel varies according to the usefulness of counsel to the accused at the particular pretrial proceeding. It is *that* deprivation which demands a remedy.

The United States insists that "post-charge deliberate elicitation of statements without the defendant's counsel or a valid waiver of counsel is not intrinsically unlawful." That is true when the questioning is unrelated to charged crimes—the Sixth Amendment right is "offense specific." We have never said, however, that officers may badger counseled defendants about charged crimes so long as they do not use information they gain. The constitutional violation occurs when the uncounseled interrogation is conducted.

This case does not involve, therefore, the prevention of a constitutional violation, but rather the scope of the remedy for a violation that has already occurred. Our precedents make clear that the game of excluding tainted evidence for impeachment purposes is not worth the candle. The interests safeguarded by such exclusion are outweighed by the need to prevent perjury and to assure the integrity of the trial process. It is one thing to say that the Government cannot make an affirmative use of evidence unlawfully obtained. It is quite another to say that the defendant can provide himself with a shield against contradiction of his untruths. Once the defendant testifies in a way that contradicts prior statements, denying the prosecution use of the traditional truth-testing devices of the adversary process is a high price to pay for vindication of the right to counsel at the prior stage.

On the other side of the scale, preventing impeachment use of statements taken in violation of *Massiah* would add little appreciable deterrence. Officers have significant incentive to ensure that they and their informants comply with the Constitution's demands, since statements lawfully obtained can be used for all purposes rather than simply for impeachment. And the *ex ante* probability that evidence gained in violation of *Massiah* would be of use for impeachment is exceedingly small. An investigator would have to anticipate both that the defendant would choose to testify at trial (an unusual occurrence to begin with) *and* that he would testify inconsistently despite the admissibility of his prior statement for impeachment. Not likely to happen—or at least not likely enough to risk squandering the opportunity of using a properly obtained statement for the prosecution's case in chief.

In any event, even if the officer may be said to have little to lose and perhaps something to gain by way of possibly uncovering impeachment material, we have multiple times rejected the argument that this speculative possibility can trump the costs of allowing perjurious statements to go unchallenged. We have held in every other context that tainted evidence—evidence whose very introduction does not constitute the constitutional violation, but whose obtaining was constitutionally invalid—is admissible for impeachment. See *Harris v. New York*, 401 U.S. 222 (1971). We see no distinction that would alter the balance here.

We hold that the informant's testimony, concededly elicited in violation of the Sixth Amendment, was admissible to challenge Ventris' inconsistent testimony at trial.

**The Impeachment Exception
for Deliberately Elicited Statements**

Although a statement deliberately elicited in violation of the Sixth Amendment right to counsel may not be introduced in the prosecution's case in chief to prove the defendant's guilt, the statement may be used to impeach the defendant's credibility if he takes the stand in his own defense and gives testimony inconsistent with his prior elicited statement.

D. WAIVER OF THE SIXTH AMENDMENT RIGHT TO COUNSEL

Just as *Miranda*'s right to have an attorney present during custodial interrogation may be waived, so too an individual, after having been charged with a crime, may waive her Sixth Amendment right to counsel and agree to speak to the police without her attorney—provided the waiver is voluntary, knowing, and intelligent. In *Patterson v. Illinois*, the Supreme Court held that the administration of *Miranda* warnings, followed by execution of a standard waiver, is ordinarily sufficient to constitute a valid waiver the Sixth Amendment right to counsel. The police do not need to provide any special language, beyond the standard *Miranda* warnings, that explains the difference between *Miranda*'s right to have an attorney present during custodial interrogation and the Sixth Amendment's right to counsel during post-indictment questioning.

PATTERSON V. ILLINOIS
487 U.S. 285 (1988)

JUSTICE WHITE delivered the opinion of the Court.

In this case, we are called on to determine whether the interrogation of petitioner after his indictment violated his Sixth Amendment right to counsel.

I

Before dawn on August 21, 1983, petitioner and other members of the "Vice Lords" street gang became involved in a fight with members of a rival gang, the "Black Mobsters." Some time after the fight, a former member of the Black Mobsters, James Jackson, went to the home where the Vice Lords had fled. A second fight broke out there, with petitioner and three other Vice Lords beating Jackson severely. The Vice Lords then put Jackson into a car, drove to the end of a nearby street, and left him face down in a puddle of water. Later that morning, police discovered Jackson, dead, where he had been left.

That afternoon, local police officers obtained warrants for the arrest of the Vice Lords, on charges of battery and mob action, in connection with the first fight. One of the gang members who was arrested gave the police a statement concerning the first fight; the statement also implicated several of the Vice Lords (including petitioner) in Jackson's murder. A few hours later, petitioner was apprehended. Petitioner was informed of his rights under *Miranda v. Arizona*, 384 U.S. 436 (1966), and volunteered to answer questions put to him by the police. Petitioner gave a statement concerning the initial fight between the rival gangs, but denied knowing anything about Jackson's death. Petitioner was held in custody the following day, August 22, as law enforcement authorities completed their investigation of the Jackson murder.

On August 23, a Cook County grand jury indicted petitioner and two other gang members for the murder of James Jackson. Police Officer Michael Gresham, who had questioned petitioner earlier, removed him from the lockup where he was being held, and told petitioner that because he had been indicted he was being transferred to the Cook County jail. Petitioner asked Gresham which of the gang members had been charged with Jackson's murder, and upon learning that one particular Vice Lord had been omitted from the indictments, asked: "Why wasn't he indicted, he did everything." Petitioner also began to explain that there was a witness who would support his account of the crime.

At this point, Gresham interrupted petitioner, and handed him a *Miranda* waiver form. The form contained five specific warnings, as suggested by this Court's *Miranda* decision, to make petitioner aware of his right to counsel and of the consequences of any statement he might make to police. Gresham read the warnings aloud, as petitioner read along with him. Petitioner initialed each of the five warnings, and signed the waiver form. Petitioner then gave a lengthy statement to police officers concerning the Jackson murder; petitioner's statement described in detail the role of each of the Vice Lords—including himself—in the murder of James Jackson.

Later that day, petitioner confessed involvement in the murder for a second time. This confession came in an interview with Assistant State's Attorney (ASA) George Smith. At the outset of the interview, Smith reviewed with petitioner the *Miranda* waiver he had previously signed, and petitioner confirmed that he had signed the waiver and understood his rights. Smith went through the waiver procedure once again: reading petitioner his rights, having petitioner initial each one, and sign a waiver form. In addition, Smith informed petitioner that he was a lawyer working with the police investigating the Jackson case. Petitioner then gave another inculpatory statement concerning the crime.

Before trial, petitioner moved to suppress his statements, arguing that they were obtained in a manner at odds with various constitutional guarantees. The trial court denied these motions, and the statements were used against petitioner at his trial. The jury found petitioner guilty of murder, and petitioner was sentenced to a 24-year prison term.

On appeal, petitioner argued that he had not "knowingly and intelligently" waived his Sixth Amendment right to counsel before he gave his uncounseled postindictment confessions. Petitioner contended that the warnings he received, while adequate for the purposes of protecting his *Fifth* Amendment rights as guaranteed by *Miranda,* did not adequately inform him of his *Sixth* Amendment right to counsel. The Illinois Supreme Court, however, rejected this theory.

II

There can be no doubt that petitioner had the right to have the assistance of counsel at his postindictment interviews with law enforcement authorities. Our cases make it plain that the Sixth Amendment guarantees this right to criminal defendants.

Petitioner's principal claim is that questioning him without counsel present violated the Sixth Amendment because he did not validly waive his right to have counsel present during the interviews. Since it is clear that after the *Miranda* warnings were given to petitioner, he not only voluntarily answered questions without claiming his right to silence or his right to have a lawyer present to advise him but also executed a written waiver of his right to counsel during questioning, the specific issue posed here is whether this waiver was a "knowing and intelligent" waiver of his Sixth Amendment right.[4]

In the past, this Court has held that a waiver of the Sixth Amendment right to counsel is valid only when it reflects "an intentional relinquishment or abandonment of a known right or privilege." In other words, the accused must "know what he is doing" so that "his choice is made with eyes open." In a case arising under the Fifth Amendment, we described this requirement as "a full awareness of both the nature of the right being abandoned and the consequences of the decision to abandon it." *Moran v. Burbine,* 475 U.S. 412, 421 (1986). Whichever of these formulations is used, the key inquiry in a case such as this one must be: Was the accused, who waived his Sixth Amendment rights during postindictment questioning, made sufficiently aware of his right to have counsel present during the questioning, and of the possible consequences of a decision to forgo the aid of counsel? In this case, we are convinced that by admonishing petitioner with the *Miranda* warnings, respondent

---

[4] Of course, we also require that any such waiver must be voluntary. Petitioner contested the voluntariness of his confession in the trial court and in the intermediate appellate courts, which rejected petitioner's claim that his confessions were coerced. Petitioner does not press this argument here. Thus, the "voluntariness" of petitioner's confessions is not before us.

has met this burden and that petitioner's waiver of his right to counsel at the questioning was valid.[5]

First, the *Miranda* warnings given petitioner made him aware of his right to have counsel present during the questioning. By telling petitioner that he had a right to consult with an attorney, to have a lawyer present while he was questioned, and even to have a lawyer appointed for him if he could not afford to retain one on his own, Officer Gresham and ASA Smith conveyed to petitioner the sum and substance of the rights that the Sixth Amendment provided him. Indeed, it seems self-evident that one who is told he has such rights to counsel is in a curious posture to later complain that his waiver of these rights was unknowing. There is little more petitioner could have possibly been told in an effort to satisfy this portion of the waiver inquiry.

Second, the *Miranda* warnings also served to make petitioner aware of the consequences of a decision by him to waive his Sixth Amendment rights during postindictment questioning. Petitioner knew that any statement that he made could be used against him in subsequent criminal proceedings. This is the ultimate adverse consequence petitioner could have suffered by virtue of his choice to make uncounseled admissions to the authorities. This warning also sufficed to let petitioner know what a lawyer could "do for him" during the postindictment questioning: namely, advise petitioner to refrain from making any such statements. By knowing what could be done with any statements he might make, and therefore, what benefit could be obtained by having the aid of counsel while making such statements, petitioner was essentially informed of the possible consequences of going without counsel during questioning. If petitioner nonetheless lacked a full and complete appreciation of all of the consequences flowing from his waiver, it does not defeat the State's showing that the information it provided to him satisfied the constitutional minimum.

Our conclusion is supported by petitioner's inability, in the proceedings before this Court, to articulate with precision what additional information should have been provided to him before he would have been competent to waive his right to counsel. All that petitioner's brief and reply brief suggest is petitioner should have been made aware of his "right under the Sixth Amendment to the broad protection of counsel"—a rather nebulous suggestion—and the "gravity of [his] situation." But surely this latter "requirement" (if it is one) was met when Officer Gresham informed petitioner that he had been formally charged with the murder of James Jackson. Under close questioning on this same point at argument, petitioner likewise failed to suggest any meaningful additional

---

[5] Petitioner's waiver was binding on him *only* so long as he wished it to be. Under this Court's precedents, at any time during the questioning petitioner could have changed his mind, elected to have the assistance of counsel, and immediately dissolve the effectiveness of his waiver with respect to any subsequent statements. Our decision today does nothing to change this rule.

information that he should have been, but was not, provided in advance of his decision to waive his right to counsel.

As a general matter, then, an accused who is admonished with the warnings prescribed by this Court in *Miranda* has been sufficiently apprised of the nature of his Sixth Amendment rights, and of the consequences of abandoning those rights, so that his waiver on this basis will be considered a knowing and intelligent one.[9] We feel that our conclusion in a recent Fifth Amendment case is equally apposite here: "Once it is determined that a suspect's decision not to rely on his rights was uncoerced, that he at all times knew he could stand mute and request a lawyer, and that he was aware of the State's intention to use his statements to secure a conviction, the analysis is complete and the waiver is valid as a matter of law." See *Moran v. Burbine*, 475 U.S. 412, 422–423 (1986).

We consequently reject petitioner's argument, which has some acceptance from courts and commentators, that since "the sixth amendment right [to counsel] is far superior to that of the fifth amendment right" and since "[t]he greater the right the greater the loss from a waiver of that right," waiver of an accused's Sixth Amendment right to counsel should be "more difficult" to effectuate than waiver of a suspect's Fifth Amendment rights. While our cases have recognized a "difference" between the Fifth Amendment and Sixth Amendment rights to counsel, and the "policies" behind these constitutional guarantees, we have never suggested that one right is "superior" or "greater" than the other, nor is there any support in our cases for the notion that because a Sixth Amendment right may be involved, it is more difficult to waive than the Fifth Amendment counterpart.

Instead, we have taken a more pragmatic approach to the waiver question—asking what purposes a lawyer can serve at the particular stage of the proceedings in question, and what assistance he could provide to an accused at that stage—to determine the scope of the Sixth Amendment right to counsel, and the type of warnings and procedures that should be required before a waiver of that right will be recognized.

---

[9] This does not mean, of course, that all Sixth Amendment challenges to the conduct of postindictment questioning will fail whenever the challenged practice would pass constitutional muster under *Miranda*. For example, [in *Moran v. Burbine*,] we permitted a *Miranda* waiver to stand where a suspect was not told that his lawyer was trying to reach him during questioning; in the Sixth Amendment context, this waiver would not be valid. Likewise a surreptitious conversation between an undercover police officer and an unindicted suspect would not give rise to any *Miranda* violation as long as the "interrogation" was not in a custodial setting; however, once the accused is indicted, such questioning would be prohibited. See *U.S. v. Henry*, 447 U.S. 264 (1980).

Thus, because the Sixth Amendment's protection of the attorney-client relationship—the right to rely on counsel as a "medium" between the accused and the State—extends beyond *Miranda*'s protection of the Fifth Amendment right to counsel, there will be cases where a waiver which would be valid under *Miranda* will not suffice for Sixth Amendment purposes.

At one end of the spectrum, we have concluded there is no Sixth Amendment right to counsel whatsoever at a postindictment photographic display identification, because this procedure is not one at which the accused requires aid in coping with legal problems or assistance in meeting his adversary. At the other extreme, recognizing the enormous importance and role that an attorney plays at a criminal trial, we have imposed the most rigorous restrictions on the information that must be conveyed to a defendant, and the procedures that must be observed, before permitting him to waive his right to counsel at trial. In these extreme cases, and in others that fall between these two poles, we have defined the scope of the right to counsel by a pragmatic assessment of the usefulness of counsel to the accused at the particular proceeding, and the dangers to the accused of proceeding without counsel. An accused's waiver of his right to counsel is "knowing" when he is made aware of these basic facts.

Applying this approach, it is our view that whatever warnings suffice for *Miranda*'s purposes will also be sufficient in the context of postindictment questioning. The State's decision to take an additional step and commence formal adversarial proceedings against the accused does not substantially increase the value of counsel to the accused at questioning, or expand the limited purpose that an attorney serves when the accused is questioned by authorities. With respect to this inquiry, we do not discern a substantial difference between the usefulness of a lawyer to a suspect during custodial interrogation, and his value to an accused at postindictment questioning.

Thus, we require a more searching or formal inquiry before permitting an accused to waive his right to counsel at trial than we require for a Sixth Amendment waiver during postindictment questioning—*not* because postindictment questioning is "less important" than a trial (the analysis that petitioner's "hierarchical" approach would suggest)—but because the full dangers and disadvantages of self-representation during questioning are less substantial and more obvious to an accused than they are at trial. Because the role of counsel at questioning is relatively simple and limited, we see no problem in having a waiver procedure at that stage which is likewise simple and limited. So long as the accused is made aware of the dangers and disadvantages of self-representation during postindictment questioning, by use of the *Miranda* warnings, his waiver of his Sixth Amendment right to counsel at such questioning is "knowing and intelligent."

III

Before confessing to the murder of James Jackson, petitioner was meticulously informed by authorities of his right to counsel, and of the consequences of any choice not to exercise that right. On two separate occasions, petitioner elected to forgo the assistance of counsel, and speak directly to officials concerning his role in the murder. Because we believe that petitioner's waiver of his Sixth Amendment rights was "knowing and intelligent," we find no error in the decision of the trial court to permit petitioner's confessions to be used against him.

JUSTICE STEVENS, with whom JUSTICE BRENNAN and JUSTICE MARSHALL join, dissenting.

The Court should not condone unethical forms of trial preparation by prosecutors or their investigators. In civil litigation it is improper for a lawyer to communicate with his or her adversary's client without either notice to opposing counsel or the permission of the court. An attempt to obtain evidence for use at trial by going behind the back of one's adversary would be not only a serious breach of professional ethics but also a manifestly unfair form of trial practice. In the criminal context, the same ethical rules apply and, in my opinion, notions of fairness that are at least as demanding should also be enforced.

After a jury has been empaneled and a criminal trial is in progress, it would obviously be improper for the prosecutor to conduct a private interview with the defendant for the purpose of obtaining evidence to be used against him at trial. By "private interview" I mean, of course, an interview initiated by the prosecutor, or his or her agents, without notice to the defendant's lawyer and without the permission of the court. Even if such an interview were to be commenced by giving the defendant the five items of legal advice that are mandated by *Miranda*, I have no doubt that this Court would promptly and unanimously condemn such a shabby practice.

The question that this case raises, therefore, is at what point in the adversary process does it become impermissible for the prosecutor, or his or her agents, to conduct such private interviews with the opposing party? Several alternatives are conceivable: when the trial commences, when the defendant has actually met and accepted representation by his or her appointed counsel, when counsel is appointed, or when the adversary process commences. In my opinion, the Sixth Amendment right to counsel demands that a firm and unequivocal line be drawn at the point at which adversary proceedings commence.

Today, in reaching a decision similarly favorable to the interest in law enforcement unfettered by process concerns, the Court backs away from the significance previously attributed to the initiation of formal proceedings. In the majority's view, the purported waiver of counsel in this case is properly equated with that of an unindicted suspect. Yet important differences separate the two. The return of an indictment, or like instrument, substantially alters the relationship between the state and the accused. Only after a formal accusation has the government committed itself to prosecute, and only then have the adverse positions of government and defendant solidified. Moreover, the return of an indictment also presumably signals the government's conclusion that it has sufficient evidence to establish a prima facie case. As a result, any further interrogation can only be designed to buttress the government's case; authorities are no longer simply attempting "to solve a crime." Given the significance of the initiation of formal proceedings and the concomitant shift in the relationship between the state and the accused, I think it quite wrong to suggest that *Miranda* warnings—or for that matter, any warnings offered by an adverse party—provide a sufficient basis for permitting the undoubtedly prejudicial—and, in my view, unfair—practice of permitting trained law enforcement personnel and prosecuting attorneys to communicate with as-of-yet unrepresented criminal defendants.

The majority premises its conclusion that *Miranda* warnings lay a sufficient basis for accepting a waiver of the right to counsel on the assumption that those warnings make clear to an accused what a lawyer could "do for him" during the postindictment questioning: namely, advise him to refrain from making any incriminating statements. Yet, this is surely a gross understatement of the disadvantage of proceeding without a lawyer and an understatement of what a defendant must understand to make a knowing waiver. The *Miranda* warnings do not, for example, inform the accused that a lawyer might examine the indictment for legal sufficiency before submitting his or her client to interrogation or that a lawyer is likely to be considerably more skillful at negotiating a plea bargain and that such negotiations may be most fruitful if initiated prior to any interrogation. Rather, the warnings do not even go so far as to explain to the accused the nature of the charges pending against him— advice that a court would insist upon before allowing a defendant to enter a guilty plea with or without the presence of an attorney. Without defining precisely the nature of the inquiry required to establish a valid waiver of the Sixth Amendment right to counsel, it must be conceded that at least minimal advice is necessary—the accused must be told of the dangers and disadvantages of self-representation.

In sum, without a careful discussion of the pitfalls of proceeding without counsel, the Sixth Amendment right cannot properly be waived. An adversary party, moreover, cannot adequately provide such advice. As a result, once the right to counsel attaches and the adversary relationship between the state and the accused solidifies, a prosecutor cannot conduct a private interview with an accused party without diluting the protection afforded by the right to counsel.

———————————

In *Edwards v. Arizona*, 451 U.S. 477 (1981), presented in Chapter 10, the Supreme Court held that once a suspect invokes her *Miranda* right to an attorney during custodial interrogation, the interrogation must end and police may not initiate further questioning until counsel is present.

Edwards also held that a suspect's earlier invocation of the right to an attorney is not waived by responding to further police-initiated interrogation, even if she has been advised of her *Miranda* rights. In *Michigan v. Jackson*, 475 U.S. 625 (1986), the Supreme Court borrowed heavily from *Edwards* in holding that once a defendant has invoked her Sixth Amendment right to counsel at an arraignment or similar proceeding, any waiver of that right in response to police-initiated interrogation is invalid. In *Montejo v. Louisiana*, however, the Supreme Court reconsidered and ultimately overruled *Michigan v. Jackson*, finding that the *Edwards* protections are sufficient to prevent police from badgering a defendant into waiving her Sixth Amendment right to counsel. As a result, a defendant in custody whose Sixth Amendment right to counsel has attached *can* waive that right in response to police-initiated questions, provided the police administer the *Miranda* warnings.

MONTEJO V. LOUISIANA
556 U.S. 778 (2009)

JUSTICE SCALIA delivered the opinion of the Court.

We consider in this case the scope and continued viability of the rule announced by this Court in *Michigan v. Jackson*, 475 U.S. 625 (1986), forbidding police to initiate interrogation of a criminal defendant once he has requested counsel at an arraignment or similar proceeding.

I

Petitioner Jesse Montejo was arrested on September 6, 2002, in connection with the robbery and murder of Lewis Ferrari, who had been found dead in his own home one day earlier. Suspicion quickly focused on Jerry Moore, a disgruntled former employee of Ferrari's dry cleaning business. Police sought to question Montejo, who was a known associate of Moore.

Montejo waived his rights under *Miranda v. Arizona*, 384 U.S. 436 (1966), and was interrogated at the sheriff's office by police detectives through the late afternoon and evening of September 6 and the early morning of September 7. During the interrogation, Montejo repeatedly changed his account of the crime, at first claiming that he had only driven Moore to the victim's home, and ultimately admitting that he had shot and killed Ferrari in the course of a botched burglary. These police interrogations were videotaped.

On September 10, Montejo was brought before a judge for what is known in Louisiana as a "72-hour hearing"—a preliminary hearing required under state law. Although the proceedings were not transcribed, the minute record indicates what transpired: "The defendant being charged with First Degree Murder, Court ordered N[o] Bond set in this matter. Further, Court ordered the Office of Indigent Defender be appointed to represent the defendant."

Later that same day, two police detectives visited Montejo back at the prison and requested that he accompany them on an excursion to locate the murder weapon (which Montejo had earlier indicated he had thrown into a lake). After some back-and-forth, the substance of which remains in dispute, Montejo was again read his *Miranda* rights and agreed to go along; during the excursion, he wrote an inculpatory letter of apology to the victim's widow. Only upon their return did Montejo finally meet his court-appointed attorney, who was quite upset that the detectives had interrogated his client in his absence.

At trial, the letter of apology was admitted over defense objection. The jury convicted Montejo of first-degree murder, and he was sentenced to death. The Louisiana Supreme Court affirmed the conviction and sentence. As relevant here, the court rejected Montejo's argument that under the rule of *Michigan v. Jackson* the letter should have been suppressed. *Jackson* held that "if police initiate interrogation after a defendant's assertion, at an arraignment or similar proceeding, of his right to counsel, any waiver of the defendant's right to counsel for that police-initiated interrogation is invalid."

The Louisiana Supreme Court reasoned that the prophylactic protection of *Jackson* is not triggered unless and until the defendant has actually requested a lawyer or has otherwise asserted his Sixth Amendment right to counsel. Because Montejo simply stood mute at his 72-hour hearing while the judge ordered the appointment of counsel, he had made no such request or assertion. So the proper inquiry, the court ruled, was only whether he had knowingly, intelligently, and voluntarily waived his right to have counsel present during the interaction with the police. And because Montejo had been read his *Miranda* rights and agreed to waive them, the Court answered that question in the affirmative and upheld the conviction.

II

Montejo and his *amici* raise a number of pragmatic objections to the Louisiana Supreme Court's interpretation of *Jackson*. We agree that the approach taken below would lead either to an unworkable standard, or to arbitrary and anomalous distinctions between defendants in different States. Neither would be acceptable.

Under the rule adopted by the Louisiana Supreme Court, a criminal defendant must request counsel, or otherwise "assert" his Sixth Amendment right at the preliminary hearing, before the *Jackson* protections are triggered. If he does so, the police may not initiate further interrogation in the absence of counsel. But if the court on its own appoints counsel, with the defendant taking no affirmative action to invoke his right to counsel, then police are free to initiate further interrogations provided that they first obtain an otherwise valid waiver by the defendant of his right to have counsel present.

This rule would apply well enough in States that require the indigent defendant formally to request counsel before any appointment is made, which usually occurs after the court has informed him that he will receive counsel if he asks for it. That is how the system works in Michigan, for example, whose scheme produced the factual background for this Court's decision in *Michigan v. Jackson*. Jackson, like all other represented indigent defendants in the State, had requested counsel in accordance with the applicable state law.

But many States follow other practices. In some two dozen, the appointment of counsel is automatic upon a finding of indigency; and in a number of others, appointment can be made either upon the defendant's request or *sua sponte* by the court. Nothing in our *Jackson* opinion indicates whether we were then aware that not all States require that a defendant affirmatively request counsel before one is appointed; and of course we had no occasion there to decide how the rule we announced would apply to these other States.

The Louisiana Supreme Court's answer to that unresolved question is troublesome. The central distinction it draws—between defendants who "assert" their right to counsel and those who do not—is exceedingly hazy when applied to States that appoint counsel absent request from the defendant. How to categorize a defendant who merely asks, prior to appointment, whether he will be appointed counsel? Or who inquires, after the fact, whether he has been? What treatment for one who thanks the court after the appointment is made? And if the court asks a defendant whether he would object to appointment, will a quick shake of his head count as an assertion of his right?

To the extent that the Louisiana Supreme Court's rule also permits a defendant to trigger *Jackson* through the "acceptance" of counsel, that notion is even more mysterious: How does one affirmatively accept counsel appointed by court order? An indigent defendant has no right to choose his counsel, so it is hard to imagine what his "acceptance" would look like, beyond the passive silence that Montejo exhibited.

In practice, judicial application of the Louisiana rule in States that do not require a defendant to make a request for counsel could take either of two paths. Courts might ask on a case-by-case basis whether a defendant has somehow invoked his right to counsel, looking to his conduct at the preliminary hearing—his statements and gestures—and the totality of the circumstances. Or, courts might simply determine as a categorical matter that defendants in these States—over half of those in the Union—simply have no opportunity to assert their right to counsel at the hearing and are therefore out of luck.

Neither approach is desirable. The former would be particularly impractical in light of the fact that, as *amici* describe, preliminary hearings are often rushed, and are frequently not recorded or transcribed. The sheer volume of indigent defendants would render the monitoring of each particular defendant's reaction to the appointment of counsel almost impossible. And sometimes the defendant is not even present. Police who did not attend the hearing would have no way to know whether they could approach a particular defendant; and for a court to adjudicate that question *ex post* would be a fact-intensive and burdensome task, even if monitoring were possible and transcription available. Because clarity of command and certainty of application are crucial in rules that govern law enforcement, this would be an unfortunate way to proceed.

The second possible course fares no better, for it would achieve clarity and certainty only at the expense of introducing arbitrary distinctions: Defendants in States that automatically appoint counsel would have no opportunity to invoke their rights and trigger *Jackson* while those in other States, effectively instructed by the court to request counsel, would be lucky winners. That sort of hollow formalism is out of place in a doctrine that purports to serve as a practical safeguard for defendants' rights.

III

But if the Louisiana Supreme Court's application of *Jackson* is unsound as a practical matter, then Montejo's solution is untenable as a theoretical and doctrinal matter. Under his approach, once a defendant is *represented* by counsel, police may not initiate any further interrogation. Such a rule would be entirely untethered from the original rationale of *Jackson*.

It is worth emphasizing first what is *not* in dispute or at stake here. Under our precedents, once the adversary judicial process has been initiated, the Sixth Amendment guarantees a defendant the right to have counsel present at all "critical" stages of the criminal proceedings. Interrogation by the State is such a stage. *Massiah v. U.S.*, 377 U.S. 201 (1964).

Our precedents also place beyond doubt that the Sixth Amendment right to counsel may be waived by a defendant, so long as relinquishment of the right is voluntary, knowing, and intelligent. The defendant may waive the right whether or not he is already represented by counsel; the decision to waive need not itself be counseled. And when a defendant is read his *Miranda* rights (which include the right to have counsel present during interrogation) and agrees to waive those rights, that typically does the trick, even though the *Miranda* rights purportedly have their source in the *Fifth* Amendment.

The *only* question raised by this case, and the only one addressed by the *Jackson* rule, is whether courts must *presume* that such a waiver is invalid under certain circumstances. We created such a presumption in *Jackson* by analogy to a similar prophylactic rule established to protect the Fifth Amendment based *Miranda* right to have counsel present at any custodial interrogation. *Edwards v. Arizona*, 451 U.S. 477 (1981), decided that once "an accused has invoked his right to have counsel present during custodial interrogation . . . [he] is not subject to further interrogation by the authorities until counsel has been made available," unless he initiates the contact.

The *Edwards* rule is designed to prevent police from badgering a defendant into waiving his previously asserted *Miranda* rights. It does this by presuming his postassertion statements to be involuntary, even where the suspect executes a waiver and his statements would be considered voluntary under traditional standards. This prophylactic rule thus protects a suspect's voluntary choice not to speak outside his lawyer's presence.

Jackson represented a wholesale importation of the *Edwards* rule into the Sixth Amendment. The *Jackson* Court decided that a request for counsel at an arraignment should be treated as an invocation of the Sixth Amendment right to counsel "at every critical stage of the prosecution," despite doubt that defendants "actually intend their request for counsel to encompass representation during any further questioning," because doubts must be "resolved in favor of protecting the constitutional claim." Citing *Edwards*, the Court held that any subsequent waiver would thus be "insufficient to justify police-initiated interrogation." In other words, we presume such waivers involuntary based on the supposition that suspects who assert their right to counsel are unlikely to waive that right voluntarily in subsequent interactions with police.

The dissent claims that the [*Jackson*] decision actually established "a rule designed to safeguard a defendant's right to rely on the assistance of counsel," not one "designed to prevent police badgering." To safeguard the right to assistance of counsel from *what*? From a knowing and voluntary waiver by the defendant himself? Unless the dissent seeks to prevent a defendant altogether from waiving his Sixth Amendment rights, the answer must be: from police pressure, *i.e.*, badgering. The antibadgering rationale is the only way to make sense of *Jackson*'s repeated citations of *Edwards*, and the only way to reconcile the opinion with our waiver jurisprudence.[2]

---

[2]   The dissent responds that *Jackson* also ensures that the defendant's counsel receives notice of any interrogation. But notice to what end? Surely not in order to protect some constitutional right to receive counsel's advice regarding waiver of the right to have counsel present. Contrary to the dissent's intimations, neither the advice nor the presence of counsel is needed in order to effectuate a knowing waiver of the Sixth Amendment right. Our cases make

With this understanding of what *Jackson* stands for and whence it came, it should be clear that Montejo's interpretation of that decision—that no *represented* defendant can ever be approached by the State and asked to consent to interrogation—is off the mark. When a court appoints counsel for an indigent defendant in the absence of any request on his part, there is no basis for a presumption that any subsequent waiver of the right to counsel will be involuntary. There is no *"initial* election" to exercise the right that must be preserved through a prophylactic rule against later waivers. No reason exists to assume that a defendant like Montejo, who has done *nothing at all* to express his intentions with respect to his Sixth Amendment rights, would not be perfectly amenable to speaking with the police without having counsel present. And no reason exists to prohibit the police from inquiring. *Edwards* and *Jackson* are meant to prevent police from badgering defendants into changing their minds about their rights, but a defendant who never asked for counsel has not yet made up his mind in the first instance.

The dissent's argument to the contrary rests on a flawed *a fortiori*: "If a defendant is entitled to protection from police-initiated interrogation under the Sixth Amendment when he merely *requests* a lawyer, he is even more obviously entitled to such protection when he has *secured* a lawyer." The question in *Jackson*, however, was not whether respondents were entitled to counsel (they unquestionably were), but "whether respondents validly waived their right to counsel"; and even if it is reasonable to presume from a defendant's *request* for counsel that any subsequent waiver of the right was coerced, no such presumption can seriously be entertained when a lawyer was merely "secured" on the defendant's behalf, by the State itself, as a matter of course. Of course, reading the dissent's analysis, one would have no idea that Montejo executed any waiver at all.

In practice, Montejo's rule would prevent police-initiated interrogation entirely once the Sixth Amendment right attaches, at least in those States that appoint counsel promptly without request from the defendant. Montejo's rule appears to have its theoretical roots in codes of legal ethics, not the Sixth Amendment. The American Bar Association's Model Rules of Professional Conduct (which nearly all States have adopted into law in whole or in part) mandate that "a lawyer shall not communicate about the subject of [a] representation with a party the lawyer knows to be represented by another lawyer in the matter, unless the lawyer has the consent of the other lawyer or is authorized to do so by law or a court order." Model Rule 4.2 (2008). But the Constitution does not codify the ABA's Model Rules, and does not make investigating police officers lawyers.

---

clear that the *Miranda* waivers typically suffice; indeed, even an *unrepresented* defendant can waive his right to counsel.

The upshot is that even on *Jackson*'s own terms, it would be completely unjustified to presume that a defendant's consent to police-initiated interrogation was involuntary or coerced simply because he had previously been appointed a lawyer.

IV

So on the one hand, requiring an initial "invocation" of the right to counsel in order to trigger the *Jackson* presumption is consistent with the theory of that decision, but would be unworkable in more than half the States of the Union. On the other hand, eliminating the invocation requirement would render the rule easy to apply but depart fundamentally from the *Jackson* rationale.

We do not think that *stare decisis* requires us to expand significantly the holding of a prior decision—fundamentally revising its theoretical basis in the process—in order to cure its practical deficiencies. To the contrary, the fact that a decision has proved "unworkable" is a traditional ground for overruling it. Accordingly, we called for supplemental briefing addressed to the question whether *Michigan v. Jackson* should be overruled.

What does the *Jackson* rule actually achieve by way of preventing unconstitutional conduct? Recall that the purpose of the rule is to preclude the State from badgering defendants into waiving their previously asserted rights. The effect of this badgering might be to coerce a waiver, which would render the subsequent interrogation a violation of the Sixth Amendment. Even though involuntary waivers are invalid even apart from *Jackson*, mistakes are of course possible when courts conduct case-by-case voluntariness review. A bright-line rule like that adopted in *Jackson* ensures that no fruits of interrogations made possible by badgering-induced involuntary waivers are ever erroneously admitted at trial.

But without *Jackson*, how many would be? The answer is few if any. The principal reason is that the Court has already taken substantial other, overlapping measures toward the same end. Under *Miranda*'s prophylactic protection of the right against compelled self-incrimination, any suspect subject to custodial interrogation has the right to have a lawyer present if he so requests, and to be advised of that right. Under *Edwards*' prophylactic protection of the *Miranda* right, once such a defendant has invoked his right to have counsel present, interrogation must stop. And under *Minnick*'s [*Minnick v. Mississippi*, 498 U.S. 146 (1990)] prophylactic protection of the *Edwards* right, no subsequent interrogation may take place until counsel is present, whether or not the accused has consulted with his attorney.

These three layers of prophylaxis are sufficient. Under the *Miranda-Edwards-Minnick* line of cases (which is not in doubt), a defendant who does not want to speak to the police without counsel present need only say as much when he is first approached and given the *Miranda* warnings. At that point, not only must the immediate contact end, but "badgering" by later requests is prohibited. If that regime suffices to protect the integrity of a suspect's voluntary choice not to speak outside his lawyer's presence before his arraignment, it is hard to see why it would not also suffice to protect that same choice after arraignment, when Sixth Amendment rights have attached. And if so, then *Jackson* is simply superfluous.

It is true, as Montejo points out, that the doctrine established by *Miranda* and *Edwards* is designed to protect Fifth Amendment, not Sixth Amendment, rights. But that is irrelevant. What matters is that these cases, like *Jackson*, protect the right to have counsel during custodial interrogation—which right happens to be guaranteed (once the adversary judicial process has begun) by *two* sources of law. Since the right under both sources is waived using the same procedure, doctrines ensuring voluntariness of the Fifth Amendment waiver simultaneously ensure the voluntariness of the Sixth Amendment waiver.

Montejo also correctly observes that the *Miranda-Edwards* regime is narrower than *Jackson* in one respect: The former applies only in the context of custodial interrogation. If the defendant is not in custody then those decisions do not apply; nor do they govern other, noninterrogative types of interactions between the defendant and the State (like pretrial lineups). However, those uncovered situations are the *least* likely to pose a risk of coerced waivers. When a defendant is not in custody, he is in control, and need only shut his door or walk away to avoid police badgering. And noninterrogative interactions with the State do not involve the inherently compelling pressures that one might reasonably fear could lead to involuntary waivers.

Jackson was policy driven, and if that policy is being adequately served through other means, there is no reason to retain its rule.

On the other side of the equation are the costs of adding the bright-line *Jackson* rule on top of *Edwards* and other extant protections. The principal cost of applying any exclusionary rule is, of course, letting guilty and possibly dangerous criminals go free. *Jackson* not only operates to invalidate a confession given by the free choice of suspects who have received proper advice of their *Miranda* rights but waived them nonetheless, but also deters law enforcement officers from even trying to obtain voluntary confessions. The ready ability to obtain uncoerced confessions is not an evil but an unmitigated good. Without these confessions, crimes go unsolved and criminals unpunished. These are not negligible costs, and in our view the *Jackson* Court gave them too short shrift.

In sum, when the marginal benefits of the *Jackson* rule are weighed against its substantial costs to the truth-seeking process and the criminal justice system, we readily conclude that the rule does not pay its way. *Michigan v. Jackson* should be and now is overruled.

V

Although our holding means that the Louisiana Supreme Court correctly rejected Montejo's claim under *Jackson*, we think that Montejo should be given an opportunity to contend that his letter of apology should still have been suppressed under the rule of *Edwards*. If Montejo made a clear assertion of the right to counsel when the officers approached him about accompanying them on the excursion for the murder weapon, then no interrogation should have taken place unless Montejo initiated it. Even if Montejo subsequently agreed to waive his rights, that waiver would have been invalid had it followed an unequivocal election of the right.

Montejo understandably did not pursue an *Edwards* objection, because *Jackson* served as the Sixth Amendment analogy to *Edwards* and offered broader protections. Our decision today, overruling *Jackson*, changes the legal landscape and does so in part based on the protections already provided by *Edwards*. Thus we think that a remand is appropriate so that Montejo can pursue this alternative avenue for relief. Montejo may also seek on remand to press any claim he might have that his Sixth Amendment waiver was not knowing and voluntary, *e.g.*, his argument that the waiver was invalid because it was based on misrepresentations by police as to whether he had been appointed a lawyer. These matters have heightened importance in light of our opinion today.

We do not venture to resolve these issues ourselves, not only because we are a court of final review, but also because the relevant facts remain unclear. Montejo and the police gave inconsistent testimony about exactly what took place on the afternoon of September 10, 2002, and the Louisiana Supreme Court did not make an explicit credibility determination. Moreover, Montejo's testimony came not at the suppression hearing, but rather only at trial, and we are unsure whether under state law that testimony came too late to affect the propriety of the admission of the evidence. These matters are best left for resolution on remand.

We do reject, however, the dissent's revisionist legal analysis of the "knowing and voluntary" issue. In determining whether a Sixth Amendment waiver was knowing and voluntary, there is no reason categorically to distinguish an unrepresented defendant from a represented one. It is equally true for each that, as we held in *Patterson v. Illinois*, 487 U.S. 285 (1988), the *Miranda* warnings adequately inform him "of his right to have counsel present during the questioning," and make him "aware of the consequences of a decision by him to waive his Sixth Amendment rights." Somewhat surprisingly for an opinion that extols the virtues of *stare decisis*, the dissent complains that our "treatment of the waiver question rests entirely on the dubious decision in *Patterson*." The Court in *Patterson* did not consider the result dubious, nor does the Court today.

JUSTICE STEVENS, with whom JUSTICE SOUTER, JUSTICE GINSBURG, and JUSTICE BREYER join, dissenting.

Today the Court properly concludes that the Louisiana Supreme Court's parsimonious reading of our decision in *Michigan v. Jackson*, 475 U.S. 625 (1986), is indefensible. Yet the Court does not reverse. Rather, on its own initiative and without any evidence that the longstanding Sixth Amendment protections established in *Jackson* have caused any harm to the workings of the criminal justice system, the Court rejects *Jackson* outright on the ground that it is "untenable as a theoretical and doctrinal matter." That conclusion rests on a misinterpretation of *Jackson*'s rationale and a gross undervaluation of the rule of *stare decisis*. The police interrogation in this case clearly violated petitioner's Sixth Amendment right to counsel.

The majority's decision to overrule *Jackson* rests on its assumption that *Jackson*'s protective rule was intended to "prevent police from badgering defendants into changing their minds about their rights," just as the rule adopted in *Edwards v. Arizona*, 451 U.S. 477 (1981), was designed to prevent police from coercing unindicted suspects into revoking their requests for counsel at interrogation. Operating on that limited understanding of the purpose behind *Jackson*'s protective rule, the Court concludes that *Jackson* provides no safeguard not already secured by this Court's Fifth Amendment jurisprudence.

The majority's analysis flagrantly misrepresents *Jackson*'s underlying rationale and the constitutional interests the decision sought to protect. While it is true that the rule adopted in *Jackson* was patterned after the rule in *Edwards*, the *Jackson* opinion does not even mention the anti-badgering considerations that provide the basis for the Court's decision today. Instead, *Jackson* relied primarily on cases discussing the broad protections guaranteed by the Sixth Amendment right to counsel— not its Fifth Amendment counterpart. *Jackson* emphasized that the purpose of the Sixth Amendment is to "protect the unaided layman at critical confrontations with his adversary" by giving him "the right to rely on counsel as a 'medium' between himself and the State." Underscoring that the commencement of criminal proceedings is a decisive event that transforms a suspect into an accused within the meaning of the Sixth Amendment, we concluded that arraigned defendants are entitled to "at least as much protection" during interrogation as the Fifth Amendment affords unindicted suspects. Thus, although the rules adopted in *Edwards* and *Jackson* are similar, *Jackson* did not rely on the reasoning of *Edwards* but remained firmly rooted in the unique protections afforded to the attorney-client relationship by the Sixth Amendment.[2]

Even if *Jackson* had never been decided, it would be clear that Montejo's Sixth Amendment rights were violated. Today's decision eliminates the rule that any waiver of Sixth Amendment rights given in a discussion initiated by police is presumed invalid once a defendant has invoked his right to counsel. Nevertheless, under the undisputed facts of this case, there is no sound basis for concluding that Montejo made a knowing and valid waiver of his Sixth Amendment right to counsel before acquiescing in police interrogation following his 72-hour hearing. Because police questioned Montejo without notice to, and outside the presence of, his lawyer, the interrogation violated Montejo's right to counsel even under pre-*Jackson* precedent.

Our pre-*Jackson* case law makes clear that "the Sixth Amendment is violated when the State obtains incriminating statements by knowingly circumventing the accused's right to have counsel present in a confrontation between the accused and a state agent." *Maine v. Moulton*, 474 U.S. 159, 176 (1985). The Sixth Amendment entitles indicted defendants to have counsel notified of and present during critical confrontations with the state throughout the pretrial process. Given the realities of modern criminal prosecution, the critical proceedings at which counsel's assistance is required more and more often occur outside the courtroom in pretrial proceedings where the results might well settle the accused's fate and reduce the trial itself to a mere formality.

The Court avoids confronting the serious Sixth Amendment concerns raised by the police interrogation in this case by assuming that Montejo validly waived his Sixth Amendment rights before submitting to interrogation. It does so by summarily concluding that "doctrines ensuring voluntariness of the Fifth Amendment waiver simultaneously ensure the voluntariness of the Sixth Amendment waiver"; thus, because Montejo was given *Miranda* warnings prior to interrogation, his waiver was presumptively valid.

---

[2] The majority insists that protection from police badgering is the only purpose the *Jackson* rule can plausibly serve. After all, it asks, from what other evil would the rule guard? There are two obvious answers. First, most narrowly, it protects the defendant from any police-initiated interrogation without notice to his counsel, not just from "badgering" which is not necessarily a part of police questioning. Second, and of prime importance, it assures that any waiver of counsel will be valid. The assistance offered by counsel protects a defendant from surrendering his rights with an insufficient appreciation of what those rights are and how the decision to respond to interrogation might advance or compromise his exercise of those rights throughout the course of criminal proceedings. A lawyer can provide her client with advice regarding the legal and practical options available to him; the potential consequences, both good and bad, of choosing to discuss his case with police; the likely effect of such a conversation on the resolution of the charges against him; and an informed assessment of the best course of action under the circumstances. Such assistance goes far beyond mere protection against police badgering.

The majority's cursory treatment of the waiver question rests entirely on the dubious decision in *Patterson v. Illinois*, 487 U.S. 285 (1988), in which we addressed whether, by providing *Miranda* warnings, police had adequately advised an indicted but unrepresented defendant of his Sixth Amendment right to counsel. The majority held that "as a general matter, an accused who is admonished with the warnings prescribed in *Miranda* has been sufficiently apprised of the nature of his Sixth Amendment rights, and of the consequences of abandoning those rights." The Court recognized, however, that "because the Sixth Amendment's protection of the attorney-client relationship extends beyond *Miranda*'s protection of the Fifth Amendment right to counsel, there will be cases where a waiver which would be valid under *Miranda* will not suffice for Sixth Amendment purposes." This is such a case.

As I observed in *Patterson*, the conclusion that *Miranda* warnings ordinarily provide a sufficient basis for a knowing waiver of the right to counsel rests on the questionable assumption that those warnings make clear to defendants the assistance a lawyer can render during post-indictment interrogation. Because *Miranda* warnings do not hint at the ways in which a lawyer might assist her client during conversations with the police, I remain convinced that the warnings prescribed in *Miranda*, while sufficient to apprise a defendant of his Fifth Amendment right to remain silent, are inadequate to inform an unrepresented, indicted defendant of his Sixth Amendment right to have a lawyer present at all critical stages of a criminal prosecution. The inadequacy of those warnings is even more obvious in the case of a *represented* defendant. While it can be argued that informing an indicted but unrepresented defendant of his right to counsel at least alerts him to the fact that he is entitled to obtain something he does not already possess, providing that same warning to a defendant who has *already* secured counsel is more likely to confound than enlighten. By glibly assuming that the *Miranda* warnings given in this case were sufficient to ensure Montejo's waiver was both knowing and voluntary, the Court conveniently avoids any comment on the actual advice Montejo received, which did not adequately inform him of his relevant Sixth Amendment rights or alert him to the possible consequences of waiving those rights.

A defendant's decision to forgo counsel's assistance and speak openly with police is a momentous one. Given the high stakes of making such a choice and the potential value of counsel's advice and mediation at that critical stage of the criminal proceedings, it is imperative that a defendant possess a full awareness of both the nature of the right being abandoned and the consequences of the decision to abandon it before his waiver is deemed valid. Because the administration of *Miranda* warnings was insufficient to ensure Montejo understood the Sixth Amendment right he was being asked to surrender, the record in this case provides no basis for concluding that Montejo validly waived his right to counsel, even in the absence of *Jackson*'s enhanced protections.

———————

Who gets the better of the debate between the majority and dissent in *Montejo*? Did the *Jackson* rule play an important role in protecting against police efforts to extract incriminating statements while safeguarding the defendant's Sixth Amendment right to counsel, or are those interests already sufficiently protected by the administration of *Miranda* warnings and the *Edwards* rule that bars further police-initiated interrogation once a suspect asks for an attorney?

Waiver of the Sixth Amendment Right to Counsel

1.   An individual who has been charged with a crime may waive her Sixth Amendment right to counsel and agree to speak with the police without an attorney. In order to be valid, the waiver must be voluntary, knowing, and intelligent. The critical inquiry focuses on whether the accused was made sufficiently aware of her right to have counsel present during the questioning, and of the possible consequences of a decision to forgo the aid of counsel.

2.   *Miranda* warnings are ordinarily sufficient to apprise the accused of the nature of her Sixth Amendment right to counsel, and of the consequences of abandoning it, so that her waiver on this basis will be considered a knowing and intelligent one. A waiver that would be valid under *Miranda* will not, however, always suffice for Sixth Amendment purposes. For example, a *Miranda* waiver obtained by police who fail to inform a charged defendant that her attorney was trying to reach her would not constitute a valid waiver of the Sixth Amendment right to counsel. Similarly, a charged defendant has not validly waived her Sixth Amendment right to counsel when incriminating statements are deliberately elicited from her by an undercover police officer.

3.   A defendant in custody whose Sixth Amendment right to counsel has attached *can* waive that right in response to police-initiated questions, provided the police administer the *Miranda* warnings. If, however, the defendant has previously requested an attorney during custodial interrogation, any waiver obtained as a result of further police-initiated custodial interrogation is invalid under *Edwards v. Arizona*.

CHAPTER 12

THE FIFTH AMENDMENT PRIVILEGE AGAINST SELF-INCRIMINATION IN OTHER CONTEXTS

∎ ∎ ∎

While Fifth Amendment issues in Investigative Criminal Procedure arise most frequently in connection with custodial interrogation, there are a number of other contexts in which the privilege against self-incrimination can be invoked. In fact, an individual can assert the privilege against self-incrimination not just in criminal proceedings, but in civil or administrative proceedings as well.

Each of the three previous Chapters addressed various protections—rooted in due process, the Fifth Amendment privilege against self-incrimination, and the Sixth Amendment right to counsel—against police efforts to obtain and use a suspect's own statements against him. But what happens when police seek to use as evidence something else belonging to the suspect, such as a document, a DNA or blood sample, fingerprints, a voice or handwriting sample, or even the suspect's own face through compulsory participation in a lineup? Or suppose the prosecution seeks critical testimony from the suspect's business partner, who refuses to testify on the grounds that she herself might face criminal charges. Can the police force the business partner to testify through a grant of immunity? This Chapter answers these important questions and others in exploring the contours of the privilege against self-incrimination in contexts that do not involve custodial interrogation.

A. REQUIREMENTS FOR INVOKING THE PRIVILEGE AGAINST SELF-INCRIMINATION

There are four basic requirements that must be met in order for the privilege against self-incrimination to apply. First, an individual—and not an entity—must assert the privilege. Second, the evidence sought must be testimonial—rather than physical—in nature. Third, there must be compulsion. And fourth, there must be a possibility of incrimination. Each of these requirements is addressed in turn.

1. ONLY INDIVIDUALS MAY INVOKE THE PRIVILEGE

The text of the Fifth Amendment states that "No *person* . . . shall be compelled in any criminal case to be a witness against *himself*," and the

Supreme Court has long held that the privilege against self-incrimination may be invoked only by individuals, and not by legal entities such as corporations, labor unions, and partnerships. In *U.S. v. White*, 322 U.S. 694 (1944)—not to be confused with the 1971 case of the same name, presented in Chapter 3, involving the use of a "wired" informant—the Supreme Court explained the personal nature of the privilege against self-incrimination and held that it may not be asserted by an organization or by an individual acting on behalf of an organization:

> The constitutional privilege against self-incrimination is essentially a personal one, applying only to natural individuals. It grows out of the high sentiment and regard of our jurisprudence for conducting criminal trials and investigatory proceedings upon a plane of dignity, humanity and impartiality. It is designed to prevent the use of legal process to force from the lips of the accused individual the evidence necessary to convict him or to force him to produce and authenticate any personal documents or effects that might incriminate him. Physical torture and other less violent but equally reprehensible modes of compelling the production of incriminating evidence are thereby avoided.

> Since the privilege against self-incrimination is a purely personal one, it cannot be utilized by or on behalf of any organization, such as a corporation. Moreover, the papers and effects which the privilege protects must be the private property of the person claiming the privilege, or at least in his possession in a purely personal capacity. But individuals, when acting as representatives of a collective group, cannot be said to be exercising their personal rights and duties, nor to be entitled to their purely personal privileges. Rather, they assume the rights, duties and privileges of the artificial entity or association of which they are agents or officers, and they are bound by its obligations. In their official capacity, therefore, they have no privilege against self-incrimination. And the official records and documents of the organization that are held by them in a representative, rather than in a personal, capacity cannot be the subject of the personal privilege against self-incrimination, even though production of the papers might tend to incriminate them personally.

Extension of the privilege against self-incrimination to organizations, the Court in *White* continued, would frustrate effective law enforcement:

> The reason underlying the restriction of this constitutional privilege to natural individuals acting in their own private capacity is clear. The scope and nature of the economic activities of incorporated and unincorporated organizations and their

representatives demand that the constitutional power of the federal and state governments to regulate those activities be correspondingly effective. The greater portion of evidence of wrongdoing by an organization or its representatives is usually to be found in the official records and documents of that organization. Were the cloak of the privilege to be thrown around these impersonal records and documents, effective enforcement of many federal and state laws would be impossible.

The Privilege Against Self-Incrimination Is Available Only to Individuals

1.   Only individuals—and not legal entities or organizations such as corporations, labor unions, or partnerships—may successfully invoke the privilege against self-incrimination.

2.   The privilege against self-incrimination does not shield official records and documents belonging to an organization that are held by an individual in her personal—rather than representative—capacity, even though production of the documents might tend to incriminate the individual personally.

---

2.   THE PRIVILEGE SHIELDS ONLY TESTIMONIAL EVIDENCE

The Fifth Amendment privilege against self-incrimination applies only if the evidence sought is "testimonial" in nature. This requirement stems from the language of the Fifth Amendment, which protects the right of an individual not to be a *"witness* against himself." The word "witness," the Supreme Court has reasoned, means that the privilege against self-incrimination is implicated only when the individual is compelled to provide testimony against himself. As the Supreme Court explained in *Doe v. U.S.*, 487 U.S. 201 (1988): "In order to be testimonial, an accused's communication must itself, explicitly or implicitly, relate a factual assertion or disclose information. Only then is a person compelled to be a 'witness' against himself."

Because the privilege against self-incrimination shields only testimonial communications, it does not prevent the government from compelling the accused to provide *physical evidence* that may be incriminating. For example, in *Schmerber v. California*, police required the defendant to submit to a blood test because he was suspected of driving while intoxicated. The defendant argued that the use of the test results against him violated his privilege against self-incrimination. The Supreme Court rejected this claim, holding that the blood evidence was physical—rather than testimonial—in nature.

SCHMERBER V. CALIFORNIA
384 U.S. 757 (1966)

JUSTICE BRENNAN delivered the opinion of the Court.

Petitioner was convicted in Los Angeles Municipal Court of the criminal offense of driving an automobile while under the influence of intoxicating liquor. He had been arrested at a hospital while receiving treatment for injuries suffered in an accident involving the automobile that he had apparently been driving. At the direction of a police officer, a blood sample was then withdrawn from petitioner's body by a physician at the hospital. The chemical analysis of this sample revealed a percent by weight of alcohol in his blood at the time of the offense which indicated intoxication, and the report of this analysis was admitted in evidence at the trial. Petitioner objected to receipt of this evidence of the analysis on the ground that the blood had been withdrawn despite his refusal, on the advice of his counsel, to consent to the test. He contended that, in that circumstance, the withdrawal of the blood and the admission of the analysis in evidence [violated various constitutional rights, including] his privilege against self-incrimination under the Fifth Amendment.

We hold that the privilege protects an accused only from being compelled to testify against himself, or otherwise provide the State with evidence of a testimonial or communicative nature, and that the withdrawal of blood and use of the analysis in question in this case did not involve compulsion to these ends.

It could not be denied that, in requiring petitioner to submit to the withdrawal and chemical analysis of his blood, the State compelled him to submit to an attempt to discover evidence that might be used to prosecute him for a criminal offense. He submitted only after the police officer rejected his objection and directed the physician to proceed. The officer's direction to the physician to administer the test over petitioner's objection constituted compulsion for the purposes of the privilege. The critical question, then, is whether petitioner was thus compelled "to be a witness against himself."

If the scope of the privilege coincided with the complex of values it helps to protect, we might be obliged to conclude that the privilege was violated. In *Miranda v. Arizona*, 384 U.S. 436, 460 (1966), the Court said of the interests protected by the privilege: "All these policies point to one overriding thought: the constitutional foundation underlying the privilege is the respect a government—state or federal—must accord to the dignity and integrity of its citizens. To maintain a fair state-individual balance, to require the government to shoulder the entire load, to respect the inviolability of the human personality, our accusatory system of criminal justice demands that the government seeking to punish an individual produce the evidence against him by its own independent labors, rather than by the cruel, simple expedient of compelling it from his own mouth." The withdrawal of blood necessarily involves puncturing the skin for extraction, and the percent by weight of alcohol in that blood, as established by chemical analysis, is evidence of criminal guilt. Compelled submission fails on one view to respect the "inviolability of the human personality." Moreover, since it enables the State to rely on evidence forced from the accused, the compulsion violates at least one meaning of the requirement that the State procure the evidence against an accused "by its own independent labors."

As the passage in *Miranda* implicitly recognizes, however, the privilege has never been given the full scope which the values it helps to protect suggest. History and a long line of authorities in lower courts have consistently limited its protection to situations in which the State seeks to submerge those values by obtaining the evidence against an accused through the cruel, simple expedient of compelling it from his own mouth. In sum, the privilege is fulfilled only when the person is guaranteed the right to remain silent unless he chooses to speak in the unfettered exercise of his own will. The leading case in this Court is *Holt v. U.S.*, 218 U.S. 245 (1910). There the question was whether evidence was admissible that the accused, prior to trial and over his protest, put on a blouse that fitted him. It was contended that compelling the accused to submit to the demand that he model the blouse violated the privilege. Mr. Justice Holmes, speaking for the Court, rejected the argument as "based upon an extravagant extension of the Fifth Amendment," and went on to say: "The prohibition of compelling a man in a criminal court to be witness against himself is a prohibition of the use of physical or moral compulsion to extort communications from him, not an exclusion of his body as evidence when it may be material. The objection in principle would forbid a jury to look at a prisoner and compare his features with a photograph in proof."

Both federal and state courts have usually held that [the privilege against self-incrimination] offers no protection against compulsion to submit to fingerprinting, photographing, or measurements, to write or speak for identification, to appear in court, to stand, to assume a stance, to walk, or to make a particular gesture. The distinction which has emerged, often expressed in different ways, is that the privilege is a bar against compelling "communications" or "testimony," but that compulsion which makes a suspect or accused the source of "real or physical evidence" does not violate it.

Although we agree that this distinction is a helpful framework for analysis, we are not to be understood to agree with past applications in all instances. There will be many cases in which such a distinction is not readily drawn. Some tests seemingly directed to obtain "physical evidence," for example, lie detector tests measuring changes in body function during interrogation, may actually be directed to eliciting responses which are essentially testimonial. To compel a person to submit to testing in which an effort will be made to determine his guilt or innocence on the basis of physiological responses, whether willed or not, is to evoke the spirit and history of the Fifth Amendment. Such situations call to mind the principle that the protection of the privilege "is as broad as the mischief against which it seeks to guard."

In the present case, however, no such problem of application is presented. Not even a shadow of testimonial compulsion upon or enforced communication by the accused was involved either in the extraction or in the chemical analysis. Petitioner's testimonial capacities were in no way implicated; indeed, his participation, except as a donor, was irrelevant to the results of the test, which depend on chemical analysis and on that alone.[9] Since the blood test evidence, although an incriminating product of compulsion, was neither petitioner's testimony nor evidence relating to some communicative act or writing by the petitioner, it was not inadmissible on privilege grounds.

JUSTICE BLACK with whom JUSTICE DOUGLAS joins, dissenting.

I disagree with the Court's holding that California did not violate petitioner's constitutional right against self-incrimination when it compelled him, against his will, to allow a doctor to puncture his blood vessels in order to extract a sample of blood and analyze it for alcoholic content, and then used that analysis as evidence to convict petitioner of a crime.

To reach the conclusion that compelling a person to give his blood to help the State convict him is not equivalent to compelling him to be a witness against himself strikes me as quite an extraordinary feat. The Court, however, overcomes what had seemed to me to be an insuperable obstacle to its conclusion by holding that "the privilege protects an accused only from being compelled to testify against himself, or otherwise provide the State with evidence of a testimonial or communicative nature, and that the withdrawal of blood and use of the analysis in question in this case did not involve compulsion to these ends."

I cannot agree that this distinction and reasoning of the Court justify denying petitioner his Bill of Rights' guarantee that he must not be compelled to be a witness against himself.

---

[9] This conclusion would not necessarily govern had the State tried to show that the accused had incriminated himself when told that he would have to be tested. Such incriminating evidence may be an unavoidable by-product of the compulsion to take the test, especially for an individual who fears the extraction or opposes it on religious grounds. If it wishes to compel persons to submit to such attempts to discover evidence, the State may have to forgo the advantage of any testimonial products of administering the test—products which would fall within the privilege. Indeed, there may be circumstances in which the pain, danger, or severity of an operation would almost inevitably cause a person to prefer confession to undergoing the "search," and nothing we say today should be taken as establishing the permissibility of compulsion in that case. But no such situation is presented in this case.

In the first place it seems to me that the compulsory extraction of petitioner's blood for analysis so that the person who analyzed it could give evidence to convict him had both a "testimonial" and a "communicative nature." The sole purpose of this project, which proved to be successful, was to obtain "testimony" from some person to prove that petitioner had alcohol in his blood at the time he was arrested. And the purpose of the project was certainly "communicative" in that the analysis of the blood was to supply information to enable a witness to communicate to the court and jury that petitioner was more or less drunk.

I think it unfortunate that the Court rests so heavily for its very restrictive reading of the Fifth Amendment's privilege against self-incrimination on the words "testimonial" and "communicative." These words are not models of clarity and precision, as the Court's rather labored explication shows. Nor can the Court, so far as I know, find precedent in the former opinions of this Court for using these particular words to limit the scope of the Fifth Amendment's protection.

How can it reasonably be doubted that the blood test evidence was not in all respects the actual equivalent of "testimony" taken from petitioner when the result of the test was offered as testimony, was considered by the jury as testimony, and the jury's verdict of guilt rests in part on that testimony? The refined, subtle reasoning and balancing process used here to narrow the scope of the Bill of Rights' safeguard against self-incrimination provides a handy instrument for further narrowing of that constitutional protection, as well as others, in the future. Believing with the Framers that these constitutional safeguards broadly construed by independent tribunals of justice provide our best hope for keeping our people free from governmental oppression, I deeply regret the Court's holding.

The Supreme Court has reaffirmed the distinction between "physical" and "testimonial" evidence in other contexts where the evidence can be produced only through some volitional act on the part of the suspect. In *U.S. v. Wade*, 388 U.S. 218 (1967), the Court held that a suspect could be compelled to participate in a lineup and to repeat a phrase provided by the police so that witnesses could view him and listen to his voice. The suspect's presence and speech at a lineup reflected "compulsion of the accused to exhibit his physical characteristics, not compulsion to disclose any knowledge he might have." Similarly, in *Gilbert v. California*, 388 U.S. 263 (1967), the Court held that a suspect could be compelled to provide a handwriting sample; the Court explained that handwriting, "in contrast to the content of what is written, like the voice or body itself, is an identifying physical characteristic outside the privilege's protection." And in *U.S. v. Dionisio*, 410 U.S. 1 (1973), the Court held that suspects could be compelled to read a transcript in order to provide voice exemplars because the "voice recordings were to be used solely to measure the physical properties of the witnesses' voices, not for the testimonial or communicative content of what was to be said."

It's important to remember that although the Fifth Amendment privilege against self-incrimination does not protect physical evidence, there are other constitutional provisions that do, including the Fourth Amendment's prohibition on unreasonable searches and seizures. As you may recall from the discussion of *Schmerber v. California* in Chapter 5, the defendant also objected to the use of the blood test evidence because it had been extracted from him without a warrant and without his consent. This, he asserted, violated the Fourth Amendment prohibition on unreasonable searches and seizures. The Supreme Court rejected this claim, holding that the exigent circumstances exception—the loss of evidence associated with the body's elimination of alcohol from the system—permitted the blood draw without a warrant. The Court suggested, however, that the result might have been different if the blood test was not performed by medical personnel, or involved serious risk, trauma, or pain.

**The Privilege Against Self-Incrimination Protects
Only Testimonial Evidence**

1.   The privilege against self-incrimination protects only testimonial evidence. In order to be testimonial, an accused's communication must itself, explicitly or implicitly, relate a factual assertion or disclose information.

2.   The privilege against self-incrimination does not prevent the compulsion of physical evidence, and as a consequence, the privilege is not violated when the defendant is compelled to stand in a lineup, to provide fingerprints, or to produce a sample of his blood, voice, handwriting, or other physical features.

---

3.   THE PRIVILEGE APPLIES ONLY IF
THERE IS COMPULSION

The privilege against self-incrimination applies only if there is compulsion—if an individual is forced or coerced into making incriminating statements when he would otherwise prefer to remain silent. The compulsion requirement comes directly from the language of the Fifth Amendment: "No person . . . shall be *compelled* in any criminal case to be a witness against himself."

Voluntary statements do not violate the privilege against self-incrimination. But where is the line drawn between statements that are voluntary and those that are compelled? When police, prosecutors, or other government authorities ask for information, anyone would naturally feel some pressure to speak. Under what circumstances does that pressure rise to the level of an unconstitutional compulsion to testify against oneself? In *McKune v. Lile*, 536 U.S. 24 (2002), the Supreme Court attempted to offer some guidance:

> Determining what constitutes unconstitutional compulsion involves a question of judgment: Courts must determine whether the consequences of [a] choice to remain silent are closer to the physical torture against which the Constitution protects or the *de minimis* harms which it does not.

We've already encountered one situation—custodial interrogation— in which compulsion is present. In fact, the Supreme Court presumes that any statements made by a suspect during custodial interrogation are the product of compulsion unless he received and waived his *Miranda* rights.

Compulsion can also occur when a court permits comments to be made or adverse inferences to be drawn at a criminal trial or sentencing hearing based on the defendant's refusal to testify, effectively penalizing the decision to remain silent. In *Griffin v. California*, 380 U.S. 609 (1965), the judge in a murder trial instructed the jury that it could draw unfavorable inferences from the defendant's failure to testify on his own behalf. The judge also allowed the prosecutor to comment to the jury on the defendant's failure to take the stand to deny or explain the evidence that was presented against him. The Supreme Court held that the judge's and the prosecutor's comments violated the Fifth Amendment:

> [C]omment on the refusal to testify is a remnant of the inquisitorial system of criminal justice, which the Fifth Amendment outlaws. It is a penalty imposed by courts for exercising a constitutional privilege. It cuts down on the privilege by making its assertion costly. It is said, however, that the inference of guilt for failure to testify as to facts peculiarly within the accused's knowledge is in any event natural and irresistible, and that comment on the failure does not magnify that inference into a penalty for asserting a constitutional privilege. What the jury may infer, given no help from the court, is one thing. What it may infer when the court solemnizes the silence of the accused into evidence against him is quite another.

In *Mitchell v. U.S.*, 526 U.S. 314 (1999), the Supreme Court extended its holding in *Griffin* to prohibit adverse comments or inferences based on a defendant's failure to testify at sentencing:

> The concerns which mandate the rule against negative inferences at a criminal trial apply with equal force at sentencing. Without question, the stakes are high: Here, the inference drawn by the District Court from petitioner's silence

may have resulted in decades of added imprisonment. The Government often has a motive to demand a severe sentence, so the central purpose of the privilege—to protect a defendant from being the unwilling instrument of his or her own condemnation—remains of vital importance.

The Supreme Court has also found unconstitutional compulsion in situations where government penalizes an individual's decision not to testify by inflicting serious economic harm. In *Garrity v. New Jersey*, 385 U.S. 493 (1967), for example, New Jersey police officers were questioned during a state investigation into alleged "fixing" of traffic tickets. The officers were told that they could refuse to answer if the disclosures would be incriminating, but such refusal would result in termination of their employment. The Supreme Court held that New Jersey had compelled the officers' testimony in violation of the Fifth Amendment: "The choice given petitioners was either to forfeit their jobs or to incriminate themselves. The option to lose their means of livelihood or to pay the penalty of self-incrimination is the antithesis of free choice to speak out or to remain silent."

The Supreme Court reached a similar conclusion in *Spevack v. Klein*, 385 U.S. 511 (1967), decided on the same day as *Garrity*. In *Spevack*, a New York attorney was disbarred for refusing to produce records and testify at a judicial hearing. The attorney refused to cooperate on Fifth Amendment grounds, claiming that the records and testimony would tend to incriminate him. The Supreme Court overturned the disbarment order, finding that New York had attempted to compel the attorney's testimony in violation of the Fifth Amendment:

> The threat of disbarment and the loss of professional standing, professional reputation, and of livelihood are powerful forms of compulsion to make a lawyer relinquish the privilege. That threat is indeed as powerful an instrument of compulsion as the use of legal process to force from the lips of the accused individual the evidence necessary to convict him.

While compulsion has been found in a variety of settings, the Supreme Court has been reluctant to find it in prison hearings or similar proceedings where the inmate may be asked to take responsibility for his crimes in order to receive more favorable consideration for clemency or other benefits. Although these situations may present hard choices, they do not rise to the level of compulsion in violation of the privilege against self-incrimination. In *Ohio Adult Parole Authority v. Woodard*, for example, the Supreme Court found that there was no compulsion when a parole board was permitted to draw adverse inferences from an inmate's refusal to testify at a clemency hearing.

OHIO ADULT PAROLE AUTHORITY V. WOODARD
523 U.S. 272 (1998)

Eugene Woodard, a death row inmate, was given the opportunity to participate in a clemency hearing before the scheduled date of execution, but the board conducting the hearing offered no guarantees that his statements or his silence would not be used against him. The Supreme Court found that although Woodard confronted a difficult choice similar those faced by criminal defendants at trial, there was no compulsion to testify in violation of the Fifth Amendment:

> Assuming that the [Parole] Authority will draw adverse inferences from respondent's refusal to answer questions, we do not think that respondent's testimony at a clemency interview would be "compelled" within the meaning of the Fifth Amendment. It is difficult to see how a voluntary interview could "compel" respondent to speak. He merely faces a choice quite similar to the sorts of choices that a criminal defendant must make in the course of criminal proceedings, none of which has ever been held to violate the Fifth Amendment.

> Long ago we held that a defendant who took the stand in his own defense could not claim the privilege against self-incrimination when the prosecution sought to cross-examine him. A defendant who takes the stand in his own behalf may be impeached by proof of prior convictions without violation of the Fifth Amendment privilege. A defendant whose motion for acquittal at the close of the government's case is denied must then elect whether to stand on his motion or to put on a defense, with the accompanying risk that in doing so he will augment the government's case against him. In each of these situations, there are undoubted pressures—generated by the strength of the government's case against him—pushing the criminal defendant to testify. But it has never been suggested that such pressures constitute "compulsion" for Fifth Amendment purposes.

> Here, respondent has the same choice of providing information to the Authority—at the risk of damaging his case for clemency or for postconviction relief—or of remaining silent. But this pressure to speak in the hope of improving his chance of being granted clemency does not make the interview compelled.

In *McKune v. Lile*, the Supreme Court found no compulsion when prison officials transferred a convicted sex offender to a higher-security housing unit after he refused to accept responsibility for his crime and disclose all prior sexual activities, including those that involved uncharged criminal offenses.

McKUNE V. LILE
536 U.S. 24 (2002)

Prison officials ordered Robert Lile, a convicted sex offender, to participate in a Sexual Abuse Treatment Program (SATP) a few years before his release. As part of the rehabilitation program, Lile was asked to complete and sign a form accepting responsibility for his crime and to describe all prior sexual activities, even if such activities included uncharged criminal offenses. The state left open the possibility that new evidence disclosed by Lile might be used in future criminal proceedings. Lile refused to participate, claiming the required disclosures would violate his Fifth Amendment privilege against self-incrimination. As a consequence, he was told that he would be transferred to a higher-security housing unit and would lose various prison privileges.

Citing the state's strong interests in the rehabilitation program, and noting that the Fifth Amendment is designed to protect against significant compulsion akin to "physical torture" rather than "*de minimis* harms," the Supreme Court rejected Lile's self-incrimination claim:

> The SATP does not compel prisoners to incriminate themselves in violation of the Constitution. The consequences in question here—a transfer to another prison where television sets are not placed in each inmate's cell, where exercise facilities are not readily available, and where work and wage opportunities are more limited—are not ones that compel a prisoner to speak about his past crimes despite a desire to remain silent. The fact that these consequences are imposed on prisoners, rather than ordinary citizens, moreover, is important in weighing respondent's constitutional claim.

The Supreme Court went on to note that Lile faced a "choice," rather than unconstitutional compulsion:

> Prison context or not, respondent's choice is marked less by compulsion than by choices the Court has held give no rise to a self-incrimination claim. The criminal process, like the rest of the legal system, is replete with situations requiring the making of difficult judgments as to which course to follow. Although a defendant may have a right, even of constitutional dimensions, to follow whichever course he chooses, the Constitution does not by that token always forbid requiring him to choose. It is well settled that the government need not make the exercise of the Fifth Amendment privilege cost free.

> ### The Privilege Against Self-Incrimination Applies
> ### Only if There Is Compulsion
>
> 1.   The privilege against self-incrimination applies only when an individual is compelled to provide statements or testimony against himself. Determining what constitutes unconstitutional compulsion involves a question of judgment in which a court must decide whether the consequences of a choice to remain silent are closer to the physical torture against which the Constitution protects or the *de minimis* harms which it does not.
>
> 2.   Statements or testimony may be considered compelled in a variety of situations, including:
>
>   a.   When police subject an individual to custodial interrogation without first providing *Miranda* warnings.
>
>   b.   When a court permits comments to be made or adverse inferences to be drawn at a criminal trial or sentencing hearing based on the defendant's refusal to testify.
>
>   c.   When government inflicts serious economic harm—such as loss of employment—as a consequence of an individual's decision not to testify.
>
> 3.   The inherent psychological pressure to respond to unfavorable evidence at a criminal trial or in a post-conviction prison hearing requires that an individual make a difficult choice about whether to testify, but the psychological pressure and the related difficult choice do not rise to the level of unconstitutional compulsion in violation of the privilege against self-incrimination.

4.   THE PRIVILEGE APPLIES ONLY IF THERE IS A POSSIBILITY OF SELF-INCRIMINATION

The privilege against self-incrimination applies only if the solicited statements or information could expose a person to *criminal* liability. The privilege does not guard against revelations that may be embarrassing, create social stigma, or even expose a person to civil liability. As the Supreme Court noted in *Hale v. Henkel*, 201 U.S. 43 (1906), the privilege against self-incrimination does not prevent an individual from being "compelled to testify to facts which may impair his reputation for probity, or even tend to disgrace him, but the line is drawn at testimony which may expose him to prosecution." The Court in *Hale* went on to explain that the Fifth Amendment "operates only where a witness is asked to incriminate himself—in other words, to give testimony which may possibly expose him to a criminal charge."

There must be a genuine threat of criminal liability in order to invoke the privilege against self-incrimination. As the Supreme Court put it in *Brown v. Walker*, 161 U.S. 591 (1896), the danger of criminal prosecution must be "real and appreciable," not "imaginary and unsubstantial," or so "remote and naked" that "no reasonable man would be affected by" it. While a court must ultimately decide whether an assertion of the privilege against self-incrimination is justified, the court must give the individual the benefit of the doubt, shielding against any disclosure that would itself be incriminating along with disclosures that might lead to other evidence necessary to prosecute. As the Supreme Court explained in *Hoffman v. U.S.*, 341 U.S. 479 (1951):

> [The Fifth Amendment privilege against self-incrimination] must be accorded liberal construction in favor of the right it was intended to secure. The privilege afforded not only extends to answers that would in themselves support a conviction under a criminal statute, but likewise embraces those which would furnish a link in the chain of evidence needed to prosecute the claimant for a crime. But this protection must be confined to instances where the witness has reasonable cause to apprehend danger from a direct answer. The witness is not exonerated from answering merely because he declares that, in so doing, he would incriminate himself—his say-so does not of itself establish the hazard of incrimination. It is for the court to say whether his silence is justified, and to require him to answer if it clearly appears to the court that he is mistaken. To sustain the privilege, it need only be evident from the implications of the question, in the setting in which it is asked, that a responsive answer to the question or an explanation of why it cannot be answered might be dangerous because injurious disclosure could result.

The Supreme Court applied these principles in *Hiibel v. Sixth Judicial District Court of Nevada*—previously presented in Chapter 6 in connection with the Fourth Amendment "*Terry* stop" issues—and held that a state law requiring an individual to identify himself when lawfully stopped by police did not violate the Fifth Amendment because the possibility of incrimination was remote.

HIIBEL V. SIXTH JUDICIAL DISTRICT COURT OF NEVADA
542 U.S. 177 (2004)

Police received an anonymous telephone call reporting an assault that apparently occurred in a truck on a local road. When an officer arrived at the scene, he found the truck parked on the side of the road with a young woman inside and man standing nearby. The officer explained that he was investigating a report of a fight and asked the man,

Larry Hiibel, for some form of identification. Hiibel refused repeated requests by the officer to provide identification and was arrested for violating a Nevada statute that allows a police officer to detain a person "to ascertain his identity and the suspicious circumstances surrounding his presence abroad." The statute also provides: "Any person so detained shall identify himself, but may not be compelled to answer any other inquiry of any peace officer." Hiibel was convicted of obstructing a police investigation and fined $250.

On appeal, the Supreme Court rejected Hiibel's claim that the Nevada statute violated the Fourth and Fifth Amendments. With respect to the Fifth Amendment claim, the Court found no significant risk that the disclosure required of Hiibel would result in self-incrimination:

> The Fifth Amendment privilege against compulsory self-incrimination protects against any disclosures that the witness reasonably believes could be used in a criminal prosecution or could lead to other evidence that might be so used.

> In this case petitioner's refusal to disclose his name was not based on any articulated real and appreciable fear that his name would be used to incriminate him, or that it would furnish a link in the chain of evidence needed to prosecute him. As best we can tell, petitioner refused to identify himself only because he thought his name was none of the officer's business. Even today, petitioner does not explain how the disclosure of his name could have been used against him in a criminal case. While we recognize petitioner's strong belief that he should not have to disclose his identity, the Fifth Amendment does not override the Nevada Legislature's judgment to the contrary absent a reasonable belief that the disclosure would tend to incriminate him.

> The narrow scope of the disclosure requirement is also important. One's identity is, by definition, unique; yet it is, in another sense, a universal characteristic. Answering a request to disclose a name is likely to be so insignificant in the scheme of things as to be incriminating only in unusual circumstances. In every criminal case, it is known and must be known who has been arrested and who is being tried. Even witnesses who plan to invoke the Fifth Amendment privilege answer when their names are called to take the stand. Still, a case may arise where there is a substantial allegation that furnishing identity at the time of a stop would have given the police a link in the chain of evidence needed to convict the individual of a separate offense. In that case, the court can then consider whether the privilege applies, and, if the Fifth Amendment has been violated, what remedy must follow. We need not resolve those questions here.

Justice Stevens, in dissent, disagreed with the majority regarding the likelihood of incrimination as a result of disclosing one's name:

> Given a proper understanding of the category of "incriminating" communications that fall within the Fifth Amendment privilege, it is clear that the disclosure of petitioner's identity is protected. The Court reasons that we should not assume that the disclosure of petitioner's "name would be used to incriminate him, or that it would furnish a link in [a] chain of evidence needed to prosecute him." But why else would an officer ask for it? And why else would the Nevada Legislature require its disclosure only when circumstances "reasonably indicate that the person has committed, is committing or is about to commit a crime"? Indeed, if we accept the predicate for the Court's holding, the statute requires nothing more than a useless invasion of privacy. I think that, on the contrary, the Nevada Legislature intended to provide its police officers with a useful law enforcement tool, and that the very existence of the statute demonstrates the value of the information it demands.

> A person's identity obviously bears informational and incriminating worth, even if the name itself is not inculpatory. A name can provide the key to a broad array of information about the person, particularly in the hands of a police officer with access to a range of law enforcement databases. And that information, in turn, can be tremendously useful in a criminal prosecution. It is therefore quite wrong to suggest that a person's identity provides a link in the chain to incriminating evidence "only in unusual circumstances."

The Privilege Against Self-Incrimination Applies Only if There Is a Possibility of Criminal Liability

1. The privilege against self-incrimination applies only if the disclosures could expose a person to *criminal* liability. The privilege does not guard against revelations that may be embarrassing, create social stigma, or even expose a person to civil liability.

2. In order to successfully invoke the privilege against self-incrimination, the danger of criminal prosecution must be "real and appreciable," not "imaginary and unsubstantial."

3. The privilege against self-incrimination should be given a liberal construction, protecting not only those answers that would in themselves support a conviction under a criminal statute, but also those answers that would furnish a link in the chain of evidence needed to prosecute the claimant for a crime.

4. Disclosure of one's name is likely to be incriminating only in unusual circumstances.

LEARN MORE WITH *LAW & ORDER*

In the following episode of *Law & Order* ("Night and Fog," Season 3, Episode 13), police are investigating the death of Ursula Steinmetz, an elderly woman with multiple sclerosis. Ursula's husband, David Steinmetz, confesses that he killed his wife by filling a prescription and helping her to take an overdose of pills. Prosecutors charge Steinmetz with manslaughter for assisting his wife's suicide. The defense moves to suppress Steinmetz's confession because, during questioning, he asked to see his daughter, a social worker. This request, the defense claims, was tantamount to a request for counsel that the police ignored. The trial judge accepts the defense's argument and suppresses Steinmetz's confession.

With the confession inadmissible, the police continue to investigate the circumstances of Ursula's death. They learn that both Ursula and David Steinmetz survived the Holocaust after spending time in concentration camps. They also learn that Ursula and David were arguing about the Holocaust in the weeks before Ursula's death. Further investigation suggests that David Steinmetz is actually Jakub Skulman, who is wanted for war crimes in Poland. The police and prosecutors believe that Ursula Steinmetz discovered her husband's secret, confronted him about it, and then he killed her and tried to make it look like a suicide.

The prosecutors locate a record of Jakub Skulman's concentration camp tattoo, and they ask David Steinmetz to help establish his innocence by allowing them to examine the numbers tattooed on his arm. Steinmetz and his attorney refuse to cooperate, citing the privilege against self-incrimination. Although troubled by the prosecution's request to delve into sensitive history, the trial judge rejects Steinmetz's self-incrimination claim because compulsory disclosure of the tattoo is not testimonial—it is analogous to being compelled to provide fingerprints or exhibit one's face in a lineup.

The segments of the episode that depict the relevant Investigative Criminal Procedure issues appear at:

4:30 to 6:22; 9:28 to 11:24; 20:31 to 27:55

Law & Order Episode
"Night and Fog," Season 3, Episode 13

The *Law & Order* episode nicely illustrates two issues. First, it presents an opportunity to review the rules governing a request for counsel during custodial interrogation, previously described in Chapter 10. Early in the episode, during interrogation by police, Steinmetz asks to see his daughter, but the police don't terminate the interrogation, nor do they honor his request. Steinmetz's attorney later argues that the request to see his daughter—who is a social worker—was essentially a request for counsel, requiring the police to end the interrogation and refrain from reinitiating it until counsel is present. (Although the defense attorney does not cite them, the rules are rooted in the *Miranda* decision itself and in *Edwards v. Arizona*, 451 U.S. 477 (1981), both of which are presented in Chapter 10.) In support of his argument, the defense attorney cites the California Supreme Court's decision in *Fare v. Michael C.*, which concluded that a suspect's request to see his probation officer during custodial interrogation had the same effect as a request for an attorney. Ben Stone, the prosecutor, points out that the U.S. Supreme Court reversed the California Supreme Court's decision in *Fare v. Michael C.*, 442 U.S. 707 (1979), and held that a request to see a probation officer is not the same as a request for an attorney; accordingly, police are not required to terminate an interrogation when a suspect asks for a probation officer, a religious adviser, or a friend. (Chapter 10 also contains a brief discussion of *Fare v. Michael C.*) Steinmetz's defense attorney then notes that states are free, as a matter of state law, to define the right to counsel more broadly than the U.S. Supreme Court did, as a matter of federal law, in *Fare v. Michael C.* The trial judge is persuaded by this argument, and she declares Steinmetz's confession to be inadmissible under New York state law because his request to see his daughter/social worker was the functional equivalent of asking for an attorney.

Second, the episode illustrates one of the key concepts from this Chapter—the Fifth Amendment privilege against self-incrimination protects only those disclosures that are *testimonial*. The numbers tattooed on David Steinmetz's arm may indeed incriminate him by proving that he is Jakub Skulman, but revealing his arm to the prosecutors is not a testimonial act because Steinmetz is not being compelled to *communicate* anything; he is only being compelled to display a physical characteristic. In a series of cases cited in this Chapter—including *Schmerber v. California*, 384 U.S. 757 (1966), *U.S. v. Wade*, 388 U.S. 218 (1967), *Gilbert v. California*, 388 U.S. 263 (1967), and *U.S. v. Dionisio*, 410 U.S. 1 (1973)—the Supreme Court has repeatedly held that the Fifth Amendment does not prevent the compulsion of physical evidence such as a blood, voice, fingerprint, or handwriting sample. If Steinmetz can be made to stand in a lineup and exhibit his face under *U.S. v. Wade* because that is not a testimonial act protected by the privilege against self-incrimination, he can similarly be compelled to exhibit his arm (and the tattoo) even if it stirs up painful memories and makes it easier for the prosecution to convict him by establishing the real motive for killing his wife.

B. COMPELLED PRODUCTION OF DOCUMENTS AND OTHER THINGS

Just as the government may not compel an individual to make incriminating oral statements, so too the government cannot compel an individual to make incriminating written statements. The privilege against self-incrimination protects not just oral communications, but written ones as well, provided the basic requirements for application of the privilege are met.

Most incriminating writings or documents that the government might wish to use as evidence are obviously testimonial because they implicitly or explicitly relate a factual assertion or disclose information. But not all incriminating writings or documents are "compelled" within the meaning of the Fifth Amendment because the government did not require the *original* creation or production of the items. Thus, incriminating information that an individual voluntarily commits to writing—before the government asks for it—cannot be shielded under the umbrella of the Fifth Amendment as long as the physical act of handing over the document to the government (the "act of production") is not itself incriminating.

Put somewhat differently, the *contents* of a document that was voluntarily created cannot be shielded by the privilege against self-incrimination because the compulsion requirement is not met—the government did not compel the author of the document to make or create the incriminating statements. The physical act of handing over the document to the government—known as the "act of production"—may, however, be protected by the privilege against self-incrimination when there are components of that physical act that are both testimonial and incriminating.

Accordingly, when government seeks writings or documents for use in a criminal trial, it must do so in a manner that does not require the individual from whom the items are sought to incriminate herself. A search warrant authorizing police to look for and seize incriminating documents or other items does not require the person against whom the search is directed to communicate anything; she must merely step aside while the police conduct the search. But when the government demands documents through a *subpoena duces tecum*—a summons to produce documents or other tangible evidence—the individual's act of compliance not only demonstrates her possession of the items, but may also serve to authenticate them. In some cases, this creates a real possibility of self-incrimination. As the Supreme Court explained in *Fisher v. U.S.*, 425 U.S. 291 (1976):

> The act of producing evidence in response to a subpoena has communicative aspects of its own, wholly aside from the contents of the papers produced. Compliance with the subpoena tacitly concedes the existence of the papers demanded and their possession or control by the [individual]. It also would indicate the [individual's] belief that the papers are those described in the subpoena. The elements of compulsion are clearly present, but the more difficult issues are whether the tacit averments of the [individual] are both "testimonial" and "incriminating" for purposes of applying the Fifth Amendment. These questions perhaps do not lend themselves to categorical answers; their resolution may instead depend on the facts and circumstances of particular cases or classes thereof.

A simple example may prove helpful here. Suppose a priceless Picasso painting was recently stolen from the home of its owner. Police suspect that Frankie Fence was involved and may be helping to arrange the sale of the painting on the black market. Accordingly, authorities serve Frankie with a subpoena requiring him to produce all paintings in his possession or control. If Frankie does indeed have the Picasso, the compelled act of handing it over to the government in response to the subpoena is potentially incriminating since it demonstrates his possession of stolen property. Accordingly, Frankie may be able to resist the subpoena by asserting the privilege against self-incrimination. If police recover the painting under the authority of a valid search warrant, however, the privilege against self-incrimination offers no help to Frankie. Indeed, search warrants would be utterly useless if criminal suspects could challenge them simply by asserting that the evidence discovered during the search might prove incriminating!

The Supreme Court reviewed and explained the key principles governing compelled production of documents and other things in *Andresen v. Maryland*.

ANDRESEN V. MARYLAND
427 U.S. 463 (1976)

JUSTICE BLACKMUN delivered the opinion of the Court.

[Under the authority of a search warrant, state investigators seized numerous documents from the defendant's office that demonstrated his involvement in a fraudulent real estate scheme. Several of the documents were then used at trial, and the defendant was found guilty of five counts of false pretenses and three counts of fraudulent misappropriation by a fiduciary. The Supreme Court's full summary of the facts is included in Chapter 4, where other excerpts of this case were presented in connection with the Fourth Amendment's "particularly" requirement for search warrants.]

The Fifth Amendment, made applicable to the States by the Fourteenth Amendment, provides that "no person . . . shall be compelled in any criminal case to be a witness against himself." As the Court often has noted, the development of this protection was in part a response to certain historical practices, such as ecclesiastical inquisitions and the proceedings of the Star Chamber, which placed a premium on compelling subjects of the investigation to admit guilt from their own lips. The historic function of the privilege has been to protect a natural individual from compulsory incrimination through his own testimony or personal records.

There is no question that the records seized from petitioner's offices and introduced against him were incriminating. Moreover, it is undisputed that some of these business records contain statements made by petitioner. The question, therefore, is whether the seizure of these business records, and their admission into evidence at his trial, compelled petitioner to testify against himself in violation of the Fifth Amendment.

Petitioner contends that "the Fifth Amendment prohibition against compulsory self-incrimination applies as well to personal business papers seized from his offices as it does to the same papers being required to be produced under a subpoena." He bases his argument, naturally, on dicta in a number of cases which imply, or state, that the search for and seizure of a person's private papers violate the privilege against self-incrimination.

We do not agree, however, that these broad statements compel suppression of this petitioner's business records as a violation of the Fifth Amendment. In the very recent case of *Fisher v. U.S.*, 425 U.S. 391 (1976), the Court held that an attorney's production, pursuant to a lawful summons, of his client's tax records in his hands did not violate the Fifth Amendment privilege of the taxpayer "because enforcement against a taxpayer's lawyer would not compel the taxpayer to do anything and certainly would not compel him to be a witness against himself." Compulsion of the accused was also absent in *Couch v. U.S.*, 409 U.S. 322 (1973), where the Court held that a summons served on a taxpayer's accountant requiring him to produce the taxpayer's personal business records in his possession did not violate the taxpayer's Fifth Amendment rights.

Similarly, in this case, petitioner was not asked to say or to do anything. The records seized contained statements that petitioner had voluntarily committed to writing. The search for and seizure of these records were conducted by law enforcement personnel. Finally, when these records were introduced at trial, they were authenticated by a handwriting expert, not by petitioner. Any compulsion of petitioner to speak, other than the inherent psychological pressure to respond at trial to unfavorable evidence, was not present.

This case thus falls within the principle stated by Mr. Justice Holmes: "A party is privileged from producing the evidence but not from its production." This principle recognizes that the protection afforded by the Self-Incrimination Clause of the Fifth Amendment adheres basically to the person, not to information that may incriminate him. Thus, although the Fifth Amendment may protect an individual from complying with a subpoena for the production of his personal records in his possession because the very act of production may constitute a compulsory authentication of incriminating information, a seizure of the same materials by law enforcement officers differs in a crucial respect— the individual against whom the search is directed is not required to aid in the discovery, production, or authentication of incriminating evidence.

A contrary determination would prohibit the admission of evidence traditionally used in criminal cases and traditionally admissible despite the Fifth Amendment. For example, it would bar the admission of an accused's gambling records in a prosecution for gambling; a note given temporarily to a bank teller during a robbery and subsequently seized in the accused's automobile or home in a prosecution for bank robbery; and incriminating notes prepared, but not sent, by an accused in a kidnaping or blackmail prosecution.

We find a useful analogy to the Fifth Amendment question in those cases that deal with the "seizure" of oral communications. As the Court has explained, "the constitutional privilege against self-incrimination is designed to prevent the use of legal process to force from the lips of the accused individual the evidence necessary to convict him or to force him to produce and authenticate any personal documents or effects that might incriminate him." The significant aspect of this principle was apparent and applied in *Hoffa v. U.S.*, 385 U.S. 293 (1966), where the Court rejected the contention that an informant's "seizure" of the accused's conversation with him, and his subsequent testimony at trial concerning that conversation, violated the Fifth Amendment. The rationale was that, although the accused's statements may have been elicited by the informant for the purpose of gathering evidence against him, they were made voluntarily. We see no reasoned distinction to be made between the compulsion upon the accused in that case and the compulsion in this one. In each, the communication, whether oral or written, was made voluntarily. The fact that seizure was contemporaneous with the communication in Hoffa but subsequent to the communication here does not affect the question whether the accused was compelled to speak.

Finally, we do not believe that permitting the introduction into evidence of a person's business records seized during an otherwise lawful search would offend or undermine any of the policies undergirding the privilege. In this case, petitioner, at the time he recorded his communication, at the time of the search, and at the time the records were admitted at trial, was not subjected to "the cruel trilemma of self-accusation, perjury or contempt." Indeed, he was never required to say or to do anything under penalty of sanction. Similarly, permitting the admission of the records in question does not convert our accusatorial system of justice into an inquisitorial system. In this case, the statements seized were voluntarily committed to paper before the police arrived to search for them, and petitioner was not treated discourteously during the search. Also, the "good cause" to "disturb" petitioner was independently determined by the judge who issued the warrants; and the State bore the burden of executing them. Finally, there is no chance in this case of petitioner's statements being self-deprecatory and untrustworthy because they were extracted from him—they were already in existence and had been made voluntarily.

We recognize, of course, that the Fifth Amendment protects privacy to some extent. However, the Court has never suggested that every invasion of privacy violates the privilege. Indeed, we recently held that unless incriminating testimony is "compelled," any invasion of privacy is outside the scope of the Fifth Amendment's protection, saying that "the Fifth Amendment protects against compelled self-incrimination, not the disclosure of private information." Here, as we have already noted, petitioner was not compelled to testify in any manner.

Accordingly, we hold that the search of an individual's office for business records, their seizure, and subsequent introduction into evidence do not offend the Fifth Amendment's proscription that "no person . . . shall be compelled in any criminal case to be a witness against himself."

JUSTICE BRENNAN, dissenting.

In a concurring opinion earlier this Term in *Fisher v. U.S.*, 425 U.S. 391 (1976), I stated my view that the Fifth Amendment protects an individual citizen against the compelled production of testimonial matter that might tend to incriminate him, provided it is matter that comes within the zone of privacy recognized by the Amendment to secure to the individual "a private inner sanctum of individual feeling and thought." *Couch v. U.S.*, 409 U.S. 322, 327 (1973). Accordingly, the production of testimonial material falling within this zone of privacy may not be compelled by subpoena. The Court holds today that the search and seizure, pursuant to a valid warrant, of business records in petitioner's possession and containing statements made by the petitioner does not violate the Fifth Amendment. I can perceive no distinction of meaningful substance between compelling the production of such records through subpoena and seizing such records against the will of the petitioner.

———————

In *Baltimore Department of Social Services v. Bouknight*, the Supreme Court held that a parent could not invoke the privilege against self-incrimination to resist a court order to produce a child entrusted to her custody, even when the act of production might be incriminating.

BALTIMORE DEPARTMENT OF SOCIAL SERVICES V. BOUKNIGHT
493 U.S. 549 (1990)

Based on evidence that Jacqueline Bouknight had abused her infant son, Maurice, the Baltimore City Department of Social Services (BCDSS) secured a juvenile court order removing him from her control. That order was subsequently modified to return custody to Bouknight pursuant to extensive conditions and subject to further court order. After Bouknight violated those conditions—and fearing that Maurice was endangered or perhaps dead—the court granted a BCDSS petition to remove Maurice from Bouknight's control and held her in civil contempt when she failed to produce the child as ordered. Citing the Fifth Amendment privilege against self-incrimination, Bouknight resisted the court's order to produce Maurice, claiming that the act of production would amount to testimony regarding her control over, and possession of, her son—facts that might aid the state in prosecuting her for child abuse or even homicide.

The Supreme Court rejected Bouknight's attempt to invoke the privilege against self-incrimination because she had assumed the obligation to produce her son under state laws governing the custody and care of children:

> The possibility that a production order will compel testimonial assertions that may prove incriminating does not, in all contexts, justify invoking the privilege to resist production. Even assuming that this limited testimonial assertion is sufficiently incriminating and sufficiently testimonial for purposes of the privilege, Bouknight may not invoke the privilege to resist the production order because she has assumed custodial duties related to production and because production is required as part of a noncriminal regulatory regime.

The Court concluded that Bouknight's concerns about self-incrimination were insufficient to overcome the state's compelling interests in Maurice's welfare:

Even when criminal conduct may exist, the court may properly request production and return of the child, and enforce that request through exercise of the contempt power, for reasons related entirely to the child's well-being and through measures unrelated to criminal law enforcement or investigation. This case provides an illustration: concern for the child's safety underlay the efforts to gain access to and then compel production of Maurice. Finally, production in the vast majority of cases will embody no incriminating testimony, even if in particular cases the act of production may incriminate the custodian through an assertion of possession or the existence, or the identity, of the child. These orders to produce children cannot be characterized as efforts to gain some testimonial component of the act of production. The government demands production of the very public charge entrusted to a custodian, and makes the demand for compelling reasons unrelated to criminal law enforcement and as part of a broadly applied regulatory regime. In these circumstances, Bouknight cannot invoke the privilege to resist the order to produce Maurice.

Despite the Supreme Court's decision, Jacqueline Bouknight never did produce Maurice or otherwise reveal what had happened to him. She spent seven years in jail for contempt of court—for refusing to disclose her son's whereabouts—and was finally freed in 1995.[a]

Compelled Production of Documents and Other Things

1. The contents of an incriminating document or writing that was voluntarily created before the government asked for or discovered it cannot be shielded by the privilege against self-incrimination because there was no compulsion associated with its original creation.

2. The "act of production"—the physical act of handing over a document, writing, or other tangible item to the government pursuant to a subpoena or court order—may be protected by the privilege against self-incrimination when there are components of the physical act that are both testimonial and incriminating. For example, an individual's compliance with a subpoena may tacitly concede the existence, possession, and control of the items demanded; in some instances, compliance with a subpoena may serve to authenticate the items demanded as well.

---

[a] *See Mother Ends 7-Year Jail Stay, Still Silent About Missing Child*, NEW YORK TIMES, November 2, 1995, available at http://www.nytimes.com/1995/11/02/us/mother-ends-7-year-jail-stay-still-silent-about-missing-child.html.

3. The privilege against self-incrimination may not be invoked to resist compliance with a regulatory regime—such as the one governing the care and custody of children—constructed to effect the government's public purposes unrelated to the enforcement of its criminal laws.

C. OVERCOMING THE PRIVILEGE AGAINST SELF-INCRIMINATION: IMMUNITY

What happens when the government needs testimony from a witness to successfully prosecute, but the witness refuses to testify, citing the privilege against self-incrimination? Suppose, for example, the government wishes to prosecute Don Devious, the criminal mastermind behind a recent electronic theft of nearly $1,000,000 from a local bank. Lisa Loyal, Don's accountant, helped to launder the money, but she refuses to testify because her testimony would obviously expose her to criminal liability. Lisa is also reluctant to "make a deal" with the government for a lighter sentence in exchange for her testimony because she is a single parent and has no one available to care for her child if she's in prison. The government fears that without Lisa's testimony, it will not have enough other evidence to convict Don. What can the government do?

As noted earlier, the privilege against self-incrimination can be successfully invoked only if there is a real possibility of criminal liability. If the government removes that possibility through a grant of immunity—a promise not to use a person's incriminating testimony against her in a criminal prosecution—it may overcome the privilege against self-incrimination and compel a reluctant witness to testify.

There are two types of immunity. The broader of the two is "transactional immunity," a promise that the reluctant witness will not be prosecuted for offenses related to her compelled testimony. More narrow and more commonly used is "use and derivative use immunity," a promise that the government will not use any statements made by the reluctant witness under a grant of immunity—or anything derived from those statements—to criminally prosecute her. (There is one important exception to the general rule prohibiting the use or derivative use of testimony compelled under a grant of immunity: If the witness testifies falsely, her testimony may be used in a prosecution for perjury.) Thus, transactional immunity prevents the government from prosecuting the reluctant witness for the underlying offenses to which her testimony relates. With use and derivative use immunity, prosecution for the underlying offenses is still a possibility as long as the government proves that its evidence was obtained from a legitimate source wholly independent of the compelled testimony.

In *Kastigar v. U.S.*, the Supreme Court held that the government may, consistent with the Fifth Amendment, compel testimony through a grant of use and derivative use immunity. The Court also explained the government's evidentiary burden in the event it decides to prosecute the reluctant witness after a grant of use and derivative use immunity.

KASTIGAR V. U.S.
406 U.S. 441 (1972)

JUSTICE POWELL delivered the opinion of the Court.

This case presents the question whether the United States Government may compel testimony from an unwilling witness, who invokes the Fifth Amendment privilege against compulsory self-incrimination, by conferring on the witness immunity from use of the compelled testimony in subsequent criminal proceedings, as well as immunity from use of evidence derived from the testimony.

Petitioners were subpoenaed to appear before a United States grand jury in the Central District of California on February 4, 1971. The Government believed that petitioners were likely to assert their Fifth Amendment privilege. Prior to the scheduled appearances, the Government applied to the District Court for an order directing petitioners to answer questions and produce evidence before the grand jury under a grant of immunity conferred pursuant to 18 U.S.C. §§ 6002, 6003. Petitioners opposed issuance of the order, contending primarily that the scope of the immunity provided by the statute was not coextensive with the scope of the privilege against self-incrimination, and therefore was not sufficient to supplant the privilege and compel their testimony. The District Court rejected this contention, and ordered petitioners to appear before the grand jury and answer its questions under the grant of immunity.

Petitioners appeared but refused to answer questions, asserting their privilege against compulsory self-incrimination. They were brought before the District Court, and each persisted in his refusal to answer the grand jury's questions, notwithstanding the grant of immunity. The court found both in contempt, and committed them to the custody of the Attorney General until either they answered the grand jury's questions or the term of the grand jury expired. The Court of Appeals for the Ninth Circuit affirmed. This Court granted certiorari to resolve the important question whether testimony may be compelled by granting immunity from the use of compelled testimony and evidence derived therefrom ("use and derivative use" immunity), or whether it is necessary to grant immunity from prosecution for offenses to which compelled testimony relates ("transactional" immunity).

I

The power of government to compel persons to testify in court or before grand juries and other governmental agencies is firmly established in Anglo-American jurisprudence. But the power to compel testimony is not absolute. There are a number of exemptions from the testimonial duty, the most important of which is the Fifth Amendment privilege against compulsory self-incrimination. The privilege reflects a complex of our fundamental values and aspirations, and marks an important advance in the development of our liberty. It can be asserted in any proceeding, civil or criminal, administrative or judicial, investigatory or adjudicatory; and it protects against any disclosures which the witness reasonably believes could be used in a criminal prosecution or could lead to other evidence that might be so used. This Court has been zealous to safeguard the values which underlie the privilege.

Immunity statutes, which have historical roots deep in Anglo-American jurisprudence, are not incompatible with these values. Rather, they seek a rational accommodation between the imperatives of the privilege and the legitimate demands of government to compel citizens to testify. The existence of these statutes reflects the importance of testimony, and the fact that many offenses are of such a character that the only persons capable of giving useful testimony are those implicated in the crime. Indeed, their origins were in the context of such offenses, and their primary use has been to investigate such offenses. Congress included immunity statutes in many of the regulatory measures adopted in the first half of this century. Indeed, prior to the enactment of the statute under consideration in this case, there were in force over 50 federal immunity statutes. In addition, every State in the Union, as well as the District of Columbia and Puerto Rico, has one or more such statutes. The commentators, and this Court on several occasions, have characterized immunity statutes as essential to the effective enforcement of various criminal statutes.

II

Petitioners contend, first, that the Fifth Amendment's privilege against compulsory self-incrimination deprives Congress of power to enact laws that compel self-incrimination, even if complete immunity from prosecution is granted prior to the compulsion of the incriminatory testimony. In other words, petitioners assert that no immunity statute, however drawn, can afford a lawful basis for compelling incriminatory testimony. They ask us to reconsider and overrule *Brown v. Walker*, 161 U.S. 591 (1896), and *Ullmann v. U.S.*, 350 U.S. 422 (1956), decisions that uphold the constitutionality of immunity statutes. We find no merit to this contention and reaffirm the decisions in *Brown* and *Ullmann*.

III

Petitioners' second contention is that the scope of immunity provided by the federal witness immunity statute, 18 U.S.C. § 6002, is not coextensive with the scope of the Fifth Amendment privilege against compulsory self-incrimination, and therefore is not sufficient to supplant the privilege and compel testimony over a claim of the privilege. The statute provides that when a witness is compelled by district court order to testify over a claim of the privilege:

> [T]he witness may not refuse to comply with the order on the basis of his privilege against self-incrimination; but no testimony or other information compelled under the order (or any information directly or indirectly derived from such testimony or other information) may be used against the witness in any criminal case, except a prosecution for perjury, giving a false statement, or otherwise failing to comply with the order.

The constitutional inquiry, rooted in logic and history, as well as in the decisions of this Court, is whether the immunity granted under this statute is coextensive with the scope of the privilege. If so, petitioners' refusals to answer based on the privilege were unjustified, and the judgments of contempt were proper, for the grant of immunity has removed the dangers against which the privilege protects. If, on the other hand, the immunity granted is not as comprehensive as the protection afforded by the privilege, petitioners were justified in refusing to answer, and the judgments of contempt must be vacated.

Petitioners draw a distinction between statutes that provide transactional immunity and those that provide, as does the statute before us, immunity from use and derivative use. They contend that a statute must, at a minimum, grant full transactional immunity in order to be coextensive with the scope of the privilege.

The [federal witness immunity] statute's explicit proscription of the use in any criminal case of "testimony or other information compelled under the order (or any information directly or indirectly derived from such testimony or other information)" is consonant with Fifth Amendment standards. We hold that such immunity from use and derivative use is coextensive with the scope of the privilege against self-incrimination, and therefore is sufficient to compel testimony over a claim of the privilege. While a grant of immunity must afford protection commensurate with that afforded by the privilege, it need not be broader. Transactional immunity, which accords full immunity from prosecution for the offense to which the compelled testimony relates, affords the witness considerably broader protection than does the Fifth Amendment privilege. The privilege has never been construed to mean that one who invokes it cannot subsequently be prosecuted. Its sole concern is to afford protection against being "forced to give testimony leading to the infliction of penalties affixed to criminal acts." Immunity from the use of compelled testimony, as well as evidence derived directly and indirectly therefrom, affords this protection. It prohibits the prosecutorial authorities from using the compelled testimony in any respect, and it therefore insures that the testimony cannot lead to the infliction of criminal penalties on the witness.

IV

Petitioners argue that use and derivative-use immunity will not adequately protect a witness from various possible incriminating uses of the compelled testimony: for example, the prosecutor or other law enforcement officials may obtain leads, names of witnesses, or other information not otherwise available that might result in a prosecution. It will be difficult and perhaps impossible, the argument goes, to identify, by testimony or cross-examination, the subtle ways in which the compelled testimony may disadvantage a witness, especially in the jurisdiction granting the immunity.

This argument presupposes that the statute's prohibition will prove impossible to enforce. The statute provides a sweeping proscription of any use, direct or indirect, of the compelled testimony and any information derived therefrom: "[N]o testimony or other information compelled under the order (or any information directly or indirectly derived from such testimony or other information) may be used against the witness in any criminal case."

This total prohibition on use provides a comprehensive safeguard, barring the use of compelled testimony as an "investigatory lead," and also barring the use of any evidence obtained by focusing investigation on a witness as a result of his compelled disclosures.

A person accorded this immunity under 18 U.S.C. § 6002, and subsequently prosecuted, is not dependent for the preservation of his rights upon the integrity and good faith of the prosecuting authorities. As stated in *Murphy v. Waterfront Commission*, 378 U.S. 52, 79 n.18 (1964):

> Once a defendant demonstrates that he has testified, under a state grant of immunity, to matters related to the federal prosecution, the federal authorities have the burden of showing that their evidence is not tainted by establishing that they had an independent, legitimate source for the disputed evidence.

This burden of proof, which we reaffirm as appropriate, is not limited to a negation of taint; rather, it imposes on the prosecution the affirmative duty to prove that the evidence it proposes to use is derived from a legitimate source wholly independent of the compelled testimony.

This is very substantial protection, commensurate with that resulting from invoking the privilege itself. The privilege assures that a citizen is not compelled to incriminate himself by his own testimony. It usually operates to allow a citizen to remain silent when asked a question requiring an incriminatory answer. This statute, which operates after a witness has given incriminatory testimony, affords the same protection by assuring that the compelled testimony can in no way lead to the infliction of criminal penalties. The statute, like the Fifth Amendment, grants neither pardon nor amnesty. Both the statute and the Fifth Amendment allow the government to prosecute using evidence from legitimate independent sources.

The statutory proscription is analogous to the Fifth Amendment requirement in cases of coerced confessions. A coerced confession, as revealing of leads as testimony given in exchange for immunity, is inadmissible in a criminal trial, but it does not bar prosecution. Moreover, a defendant against whom incriminating evidence has been obtained through a grant of immunity may be in a stronger position at trial than a defendant who asserts a Fifth Amendment coerced-confession claim. One raising a claim under this statute need only show that he testified under a grant of immunity in order to shift to the government the heavy burden of proving that all of the evidence it proposes to use was derived from legitimate independent sources. On the other hand, a defendant raising a coerced-confession claim under the Fifth Amendment must first prevail in a voluntariness hearing before his confession and evidence derived from it become inadmissible. There can be no justification in reason or policy for holding that the Constitution requires an amnesty grant where, acting pursuant to statute and accompanying safeguards, testimony is compelled in exchange for immunity from use and derivative use when no such amnesty is required where the government, acting without colorable right, coerces a defendant into incriminating himself.

We conclude that the immunity provided by 18 U.S.C. § 6002 leaves the witness and the prosecutorial authorities in substantially the same position as if the witness had claimed the Fifth Amendment privilege. The immunity therefore is coextensive with the privilege and suffices to supplant it.

JUSTICE MARSHALL, dissenting.

Today the Court holds that the United States may compel a witness to give incriminating testimony, and subsequently prosecute him for crimes to which that testimony relates. I cannot believe the Fifth Amendment permits that result.

The Fifth Amendment gives a witness an absolute right to resist interrogation, if the testimony sought would tend to incriminate him. A grant of immunity may strip the witness of the right to refuse to testify, but only if it is broad enough to eliminate all possibility that the testimony will in fact operate to incriminate him. It must put him in precisely the same position, *vis-a-vis* the government that has compelled his testimony, as he would have been in had he remained silent in reliance on the privilege.

The Court recognizes that an immunity statute must be tested by that standard, that the relevant inquiry is whether it "leaves the witness and the prosecutorial authorities in substantially the same position as if the witness had claimed the Fifth Amendment privilege." I assume, moreover, that in theory that test would be met by a complete ban on the use of the compelled testimony, including all derivative use, however remote and indirect. But I cannot agree that a ban on use will in practice be total, if it remains open for the government to convict the witness on the basis of evidence derived from a legitimate independent source. The Court asserts that the witness is adequately protected by a rule imposing on the government a heavy burden of proof if it would establish the independent character of evidence to be used against the witness. But in light of the inevitable uncertainties of the fact-finding process, a greater margin of protection is required in order to provide a reliable guarantee that the witness is in exactly the same position as if he had not testified. That margin can be provided only by immunity from prosecution for the offenses to which the testimony relates, *i.e.*, transactional immunity.

Kastigar makes it clear that in the hypothetical above, the government can compel Lisa Loyal to testify against Don Devious through a grant of use and derivative use testimony. After she testifies, the government can still prosecute Lisa for her role in the electronic theft and money laundering, but the government must prove that its evidence against Lisa was obtained from legitimate sources wholly independent of her compelled testimony. The government can, if it wishes, give Lisa transactional immunity and promise not to prosecute her for her criminal activities with Don, but it is not constitutionally obliged to do so.

What happens if a reluctant witness still refuses to testify, even after a grant of immunity? Suppose, for example, that Lisa's real worry is not the possibility of criminal prosecution or jail time, but instead she fears that Don will kill her if she testifies against him. If Lisa still refuses to testify after a grant of immunity, she can be held in contempt of court—and subjected to fines and jail time—until she agrees to testify. A day or two in jail is usually enough to persuade a reluctant witness to testify—but not always, as the *Bouknight* case, excerpted above, illustrates. The Supreme Court concluded that Jacqueline Bouknight could not invoke the privilege against self-incrimination to resist the Maryland court's order to produce her son, Maurice. When Bouknight still refused to produce her son, the Maryland court presiding over her case held her in contempt of court—and ordered her jailed—until she complied with the court's order. She remained in jail for seven years—all the while still refusing to produce her son—until she was finally released in 1995. In a 2004 interview, Bouknight claimed that her son was alive and well, but the interviewer was skeptical.[b]

In *U.S. v. Hubbell*, the government used a subpoena in an effort to obtain thousands of pages of documents from Webster Hubbell, the Associate Attorney General in the Clinton Administration, as part of a wide-ranging investigation into Hubbell's activities at his former law firm. Hubbell refused to produce the documents, citing his privilege against self-incrimination, and he was given use and derivative use immunity. Hubbell then produced the documents sought by the government. Despite the grant of immunity, Hubbell was later prosecuted for various crimes. The Supreme Court held that the government violated the grant of immunity by making derivative use of the documents that Hubbell produced.

U.S. v. HUBBELL
530 U.S. 27 (2000)

JUSTICE STEVENS delivered the opinion of the Court.

The two questions presented concern the scope of a witness' protection against compelled self-incrimination: (1) whether the Fifth Amendment privilege protects a witness from being compelled to disclose the existence of incriminating documents that the Government is unable to describe with reasonable particularity; and (2) if the witness produces such documents pursuant to a grant of immunity, whether 18 U.S.C. § 6002 prevents the Government from using them to prepare criminal charges against him.

I

This proceeding arises out of the second prosecution of respondent, Webster Hubbell, commenced by the Independent Counsel appointed in August 1994 to investigate possible violations of federal law relating to the Whitewater Development Corporation. The first prosecution was terminated pursuant to a plea bargain. In December 1994, respondent pleaded guilty to charges of mail fraud and tax evasion arising out of his billing practices as a member of an Arkansas law firm from 1989 to 1992, and was sentenced to 21 months in prison. In the plea agreement, respondent promised to provide the Independent Counsel with "full, complete, accurate, and truthful information" about matters relating to the Whitewater investigation.

The second prosecution resulted from the Independent Counsel's attempt to determine whether respondent had violated that promise. In October 1996, while respondent was incarcerated, the Independent

---

[b] *See* Ann Lolordo, *Where's Maurice?*, BALTIMORE SUN, February 28, 2004, available at http://articles.baltimoresun.com/2004-02-28/news/0402280178_1_bouknight-child-welfare-ciara.

Counsel served him with a subpoena *duces tecum* calling for the production of 11 categories of documents before a grand jury sitting in Little Rock, Arkansas. On November 19, he appeared before the grand jury and invoked his Fifth Amendment privilege against self-incrimination. In response to questioning by the prosecutor, respondent initially refused "to state whether there are documents within my possession, custody, or control responsive to the Subpoena." Thereafter, the prosecutor produced an order, which had previously been obtained from the District Court pursuant to 18 U.S.C. § 6003(a), directing him to respond to the subpoena and granting him immunity "to the extent allowed by law." Respondent then produced 13,120 pages of documents and records and responded to a series of questions that established that those were all of the documents in his custody or control that were responsive to the commands in the subpoena, with the exception of a few documents he claimed were shielded by the attorney-client and attorney work-product privileges.

The contents of the documents produced by respondent provided the Independent Counsel with the information that led to this second prosecution. On April 30, 1998, a grand jury in the District of Columbia returned a 10-count indictment charging respondent with various tax-related crimes and mail and wire fraud. The District Court dismissed the indictment relying, in part, on the ground that the Independent Counsel's use of the subpoenaed documents violated § 6002 because all of the evidence he would offer against respondent at trial derived either directly or indirectly from the testimonial aspects of respondent's immunized act of producing those documents. The Court of Appeals vacated the judgment and remanded for further proceedings. We granted the Independent Counsel's petition for a writ of certiorari in order to determine the precise scope of a grant of immunity with respect to the production of documents in response to a subpoena.

II

A person may be required to produce specific documents even though they contain incriminating assertions of fact or belief because the creation of those documents was not "compelled" within the meaning of the privilege. Our decision in *Fisher v. U.S.*, 425 U.S. 391 (1976), dealt with summonses issued by the Internal Revenue Service (IRS) seeking working papers used in the preparation of tax returns. Because the papers had been voluntarily prepared prior to the issuance of the summonses, they could not be "said to contain compelled testimonial evidence, either of the taxpayers or of anyone else." Accordingly, the taxpayer could not "avoid compliance with the subpoena merely by asserting that the item of evidence which he is required to produce contains incriminating writing, whether his own or that of someone else." It is clear, therefore, that respondent Hubbell could not avoid compliance with the subpoena served on him merely because the demanded documents contained incriminating evidence, whether written by others or voluntarily prepared by himself.

On the other hand, we have also made it clear that the act of producing documents in response to a subpoena may have a compelled testimonial aspect. We have held that "the act of production" itself may implicitly communicate "statements of fact." By producing documents in compliance with a subpoena, the witness would admit that the papers existed, were in his possession or control, and were authentic. Moreover, as was true in this case, when the custodian of documents responds to a subpoena, he may be compelled to take the witness stand and answer questions designed to determine whether he has produced everything demanded by the subpoena. The answers to those questions, as well as the act of production itself, may certainly communicate information about the existence, custody, and authenticity of the documents. Whether the constitutional privilege protects the answers to such questions, or protects the act of production itself, is a question that is distinct from the question whether the unprotected contents of the documents themselves are incriminating.

Finally, the phrase "in any criminal case" in the text of the Fifth Amendment might have been read to limit its coverage to compelled testimony that is used against the defendant in the trial itself. It has, however, long been settled that its protection encompasses compelled statements that lead to the discovery of incriminating evidence even though the statements themselves are not incriminating and are not introduced into evidence.

Compelled testimony that communicates information that may "lead to incriminating evidence" is privileged even if the information itself is not inculpatory. It is the Fifth Amendment's protection against the prosecutor's use of incriminating information derived directly or indirectly from the compelled testimony of the respondent that is of primary relevance in this case.

III

Acting pursuant to 18 U.S.C. § 6002, the District Court entered an order compelling respondent to produce "any and all documents" described in the grand jury subpoena and granting him "immunity to the extent allowed by law."

The "compelled testimony" that is relevant in this case is not to be found in the contents of the documents produced in response to the subpoena. It is, rather, the testimony inherent in the act of producing those documents. The disagreement between the parties focuses entirely on the significance of that testimonial aspect.

IV

The Government correctly emphasizes that the testimonial aspect of a response to a subpoena *duces tecum* does nothing more than establish the existence, authenticity, and custody of items that are produced. We assume that the Government is also entirely correct in its submission that it would not have to advert to respondent's act of production in order to prove the existence, authenticity, or custody of any documents that it might offer in evidence at a criminal trial; indeed, the Government disclaims any need to introduce any of the documents produced by respondent into evidence in order to prove the charges against him. It follows, according to the Government, that it has no intention of making improper "use" of respondent's compelled testimony.

The question, however, is not whether the response to the subpoena may be introduced into evidence at his criminal trial. That would surely be a prohibited "use" of the immunized act of production. But the fact that the Government intends no such use of the act of production leaves open the separate question whether it has already made "derivative use" of the testimonial aspect of that act in obtaining the indictment against respondent and in preparing its case for trial. It clearly has.

It is apparent from the text of the subpoena itself that the prosecutor needed respondent's assistance both to identify potential sources of information and to produce those sources. Given the breadth of the description of the 11 categories of documents called for by the subpoena, the collection and production of the materials demanded was tantamount to answering a series of interrogatories asking a witness to disclose the existence and location of particular documents fitting certain broad descriptions. The assembly of literally hundreds of pages of material in response to a request for "any and all documents reflecting, referring, or relating to any direct or indirect sources of money or other things of value received by or provided to" an individual or members of his family during a 3-year period is the functional equivalent of the preparation of an answer to either a detailed written interrogatory or a series of oral questions at a discovery deposition. Entirely apart from the contents of the 13,120 pages of materials that respondent produced in this case, it is undeniable that providing a catalog of existing documents fitting within any of the 11 broadly worded subpoena categories could provide a prosecutor with a "lead to incriminating evidence," or "a link in the chain of evidence needed to prosecute."

Indeed, the record makes it clear that that is what happened in this case. The documents were produced before a grand jury sitting in the Eastern District of Arkansas in aid of the Independent Counsel's attempt to determine whether respondent had violated a commitment in his first plea agreement. The use of those sources of information eventually led to the return of an indictment by a grand jury sitting in the District of

Columbia for offenses that apparently are unrelated to that plea agreement. What the District Court characterized as a "fishing expedition" did produce a fish, but not the one that the Independent Counsel expected to hook. It is abundantly clear that the testimonial aspect of respondent's act of producing subpoenaed documents was the first step in a chain of evidence that led to this prosecution. The documents did not magically appear in the prosecutor's office like "manna from heaven." They arrived there only after respondent asserted his constitutional privilege, received a grant of immunity, and—under the compulsion of the District Court's order—took the mental and physical steps necessary to provide the prosecutor with an accurate inventory of the many sources of potentially incriminating evidence sought by the subpoena. It was only through respondent's truthful reply to the subpoena that the Government received the incriminating documents of which it made substantial use in the investigation that led to the indictment.

For these reasons, we cannot accept the Government's submission that respondent's immunity did not preclude its derivative use of the produced documents because its "possession of the documents [was] the fruit *only* of a simple physical act—the act of producing the documents." It was unquestionably necessary for respondent to make extensive use of "the contents of his own mind" in identifying the hundreds of documents responsive to the requests in the subpoena. The assembly of those documents was like telling an inquisitor the combination to a wall safe, not like being forced to surrender the key to a strongbox. The Government's anemic view of respondent's act of production as a mere physical act that is principally nontestimonial in character and can be entirely divorced from its "implicit" testimonial aspect so as to constitute a "legitimate, wholly independent source" (as required by *Kastigar*) for the documents produced simply fails to account for these realities.

In sum, we have no doubt that the constitutional privilege against self-incrimination protects the target of a grand jury investigation from being compelled to answer questions designed to elicit information about the existence of sources of potentially incriminating evidence. That constitutional privilege has the same application to the testimonial aspect of a response to a subpoena seeking discovery of those sources.

Given our conclusion that respondent's act of production had a testimonial aspect, at least with respect to the existence and location of the documents sought by the Government's subpoena, respondent could not be compelled to produce those documents without first receiving a grant of immunity under § 6003. As we construed § 6002 in *Kastigar*, such immunity is coextensive with the constitutional privilege. *Kastigar* requires that respondent's motion to dismiss the indictment on immunity grounds be granted unless the Government proves that the evidence it used in obtaining the indictment and proposed to use at trial was derived from legitimate sources "wholly independent" of the testimonial aspect of respondent's immunized conduct in assembling and producing the documents described in the subpoena. The Government, however, does not claim that it could make such a showing. Rather, it contends that its prosecution of respondent must be considered proper unless someone—presumably respondent—shows that "there is some substantial relation between the compelled testimonial communications implicit in the act of production (as opposed to the act of production standing alone) and some aspect of the information used in the investigation or the evidence presented at trial." We could not accept this submission without repudiating the basis for our conclusion in *Kastigar* that the statutory guarantee of use and derivative-use immunity is as broad as the constitutional privilege itself. This we are not prepared to do.

Accordingly, the indictment against respondent must be dismissed.

JUSTICE THOMAS, with whom JUSTICE SCALIA joins, concurring.

Our decision today involves the application of the act-of-production doctrine, which provides that persons compelled to turn over incriminating papers or other physical evidence pursuant to a subpoena *duces tecum* or a summons may invoke the Fifth Amendment privilege against self-incrimination as a bar to production only where the act of producing the evidence would contain "testimonial" features. I join the opinion of the Court because it properly applies this doctrine, but I write separately to note that this doctrine may be inconsistent with the original meaning of the Fifth Amendment's Self-Incrimination Clause. A substantial body of evidence suggests that the Fifth Amendment privilege protects against the compelled production not just of incriminating testimony, but of any incriminating evidence. In a future case, I would be willing to reconsider the scope and meaning of the Self-Incrimination Clause.

The Fifth Amendment provides that "[n]o person . . . shall be compelled in any criminal case to be a witness against himself." The key word at issue in this case is "witness." The Court's opinion, relying on prior cases, essentially defines "witness" as a person who provides testimony, and thus restricts the Fifth Amendment's ban to only those communications that are "testimonial" in character. None of this Court's cases, however, has undertaken an analysis of the meaning of the term at the time of the founding. A review of that period reveals substantial support for the view that the term "witness" meant a person who gives or furnishes evidence, a broader meaning than that which our case law currently ascribes to the term. If this is so, a person who responds to a subpoena *duces tecum* [a summons to produce documents or other tangible evicence] would be just as much a "witness" as a person who responds to a subpoena *ad testificandum* [a summons to give oral testimony].

Immunity and the Privilege Against Self-Incrimination

1. The government may overcome the privilege against self-incrimination and compel testimony from an unwilling witness through a grant of immunity.

    a. In order to compel testimony through a grant of immunity, the government must, at a minimum, provide "use and derivative use" immunity—immunity from use of the compelled testimony in subsequent criminal proceedings, as well as immunity from use of evidence derived from the testimony.

    b. The government can also compel testimony by providing "transactional" immunity—immunity from prosecution for offenses related to the compelled testimony. The government is not obligated to provide transactional immunity in order to compel testimony; use and derivative use immunity is constitutionally sufficient.

2. If an individual is prosecuted following a grant of use and derivative use immunity, the prosecution has an affirmative duty to prove that the evidence it proposes to use is derived from a legitimate source wholly independent of the compelled testimony.

PART IV

POLICE IDENTIFICATION
PROCEDURES

■ ■ ■

Amendment V: <u>No person shall</u> be held to answer for a capital, or otherwise infamous crime, unless on a presentment or indictment of a Grand Jury, except in cases arising in the land or naval forces, or in the Militia, when in actual service in time of War or public danger; nor shall any person be subject for the same offence to be twice put in jeopardy of life or limb; nor shall be compelled in any criminal case to be a witness against himself, nor <u>be deprived of life, liberty, or property, without due process of law</u>; nor shall private property be taken for public use, without just compensation.

Amendment VI: <u>In all criminal prosecutions, the accused shall enjoy the right</u> to a speedy and public trial, by an impartial jury of the State and district wherein the crime shall have been committed, which district shall have been previously ascertained by law, and to be informed of the nature and cause of the accusation; to be confronted with the witnesses against him; to have compulsory process for obtaining witnesses in his favor, and <u>to have the Assistance of Counsel for his defence</u>.

Amendment XIV, Section 1: All persons born or naturalized in the United States, and subject to the jurisdiction thereof, are citizens of the United States and of the State wherein they reside. No State shall make or enforce any law which shall abridge the privileges or immunities of citizens of the United States; <u>nor shall any State deprive any person of life, liberty, or property, without due process of law</u>; nor deny to any person within its jurisdiction the equal protection of the laws.

Parts II and III of this book each addressed investigatory techniques—searches and seizures, and questioning or interrogation of suspects—used by law enforcement to gather evidence of crimes and prosecute the responsible offenders. This Part addresses a third investigatory technique often used by law enforcement: procedures that allow an eyewitness to a crime to identify the suspected perpetrator.

Eyewitness testimony and other identification evidence can be extremely powerful, and is often viewed by judges and jurors as compelling evidence of guilt. At the same time, decades of research has revealed a broad range of physical and psychological factors that can cause eyewitnesses to make serious mistakes. Police suggestion and manipulation—whether intentional or unintentional—can likewise corrupt the accuracy and reliability of many identification procedures. The stakes couldn't be higher: A mistaken identification can send an innocent person to prison or even to death.

The Supreme Court has used two constitutional provisions to regulate identification procedures and reduce the possibility of improper police suggestion. First, the Court has held that there is a Sixth Amendment right to the presence of counsel for certain identification procedures that take place after the defendant has been charged with a crime. And second, the Court has held that unnecessarily suggestive identification procedures violate due process. (Unnecessarily suggestive identification procedures used by federal law enforcement authorities can be challenged under the Due Process Clause of the Fifth Amendment; state and local identification procedures that are unnecessarily suggestive can be challenged under the Fourteenth Amendment's Due Process Clause.)

As you read the material in Chapter 13, consider whether you believe the Supreme Court has done enough to regulate identification procedures, reduce mistakes, and ensure that innocent people are not convicted.

CHAPTER 13

CONSTITUTIONAL LIMITS ON IDENTIFICATION PROCEDURES

■ ■ ■

While there are, broadly speaking, many techniques that can aid in the identification of a suspect—such as DNA testing, or analysis of fingerprints, hair, or handwriting—there are three identification procedures commonly used by police that have received the special attention of the Supreme Court. In a *lineup*, police ask the witness whether she can identify the person who committed the crime from a group of individuals of relatively similar build and appearance. (A less common variant is a "voice lineup," in which the witness is asked if she can identify the perpetrator's voice from samples provided by different individuals.) In a *showup*, police arrange for the witness to be in close proximity to just one possible suspect, and then ask the witness whether she can make an identification. And in a *photo array*, police ask the witness whether she can identify the person who committed the crime from a group of photographs of individuals of relatively similar appearance.

An initial identification through one of the described methods—often coupled with a subsequent in-court identification—can serve as powerful evidence of guilt. Indeed, there is seldom any evidence that is more compelling than a witness who takes the stand, points at the defendant, and testifies, "That's the person I saw commit the crime." The problem is that there is a large body of scientific research showing that eyewitnesses are often mistaken. These mistakes can be the result of many factors, including faulty memory, selective perception, personal biases, the stress associated with observing a crime, the fleeting nature of the observation, the tendency to "see" what one expects to see, police suggestion or manipulation, and countless others. Many of the factors that contribute to mistaken identifications are physical or psychological and cannot be controlled because they are part of human nature. One factor that can be controlled, however, is police suggestion during the construction and administration of the identification procedure.

Although police identification procedures and related testimony are among the most important parts of many criminal investigations and trials, there are surprisingly few constitutional limits on those procedures and the powerful testimony they help to generate. As Chapter 12 made clear, the Fifth Amendment privilege against self-incrimination provides no protection to a suspect who hopes to avoid identification by refusing to consent to a blood test, fingerprinting, participation in a lineup, or any other display of his physical characteristics.

The Supreme Court has, however, developed two constitutional doctrines to curb police suggestion and minimize the possibility of mistaken identification. First, the Court has held that there is a right to counsel under the Sixth Amendment for a lineup or showup that occurs after the defendant has been charged with a crime. While a lawyer cannot tell the police how to conduct a fair identification procedure, her presence may reduce the likelihood that police will do or say anything to influence the outcome. Second, the Court has held that unnecessarily suggestive identification procedures violate due process, providing a separate avenue to challenge an identification even if the suspect has not yet been charged with a crime and the Sixth Amendment right to counsel does not apply.

Many criminal cases actually involve two separate identifications. The first typically involves the victim or an eyewitness identifying the perpetrator in a police-arranged lineup, showup, or photo array. The second usually occurs during the actual trial, when the victim or eyewitness is testifying and is asked to identify the defendant—usually seated nearby in the courtroom—as the perpetrator of the crime. While on the witness stand, the victim or eyewitness might also be asked questions about the earlier out-of-court identification in the lineup, showup, or photo array. In reviewing the cases in this Chapter, be sure to understand the rules governing the admissibility of both the in-court and out-of-court identifications. In particular, if the earlier identification in a lineup, showup, or photo array is inadmissible because the defendant's counsel was not present or the identification procedure was unnecessarily suggestive, what must the prosecutor prove in order to enable the victim or eyewitness to make an in-court identification?

A. EYEWITNESS TESTIMONY AND THE DANGER OF MISTAKEN IDENTIFICATION

There is a tremendous body of research—far too extensive to properly summarize here—demonstrating the countless variables that can diminish the accuracy and reliability of eyewitness identifications. To begin with, human memory is not particularly good, it is easily manipulated, and it often changes or fades as a result of time, stress, and other factors. The possibility of mistake is compounded by the fact that many people look or dress similarly. How many times have you waved excitedly at someone you recognize before realizing, upon closer inspection, that he or she is a complete stranger? Sometimes we truly believe we see something that isn't really there as a result of the "expectancy effect," the brain's tendency to add missing details based on pre-existing biases or expectations. For example, if a witness sees hair protruding from underneath a perpetrator's hat, he may assume or expect that the perpetrator has a full head of hair, rather than being completely bald on the part of the head covered by the hat. The stress associated with witnessing or being victimized by a crime—especially when a weapon is involved—often inhibits accurate identifications. Researchers have documented a "weapon focus effect," the tendency of a witness to focus his attention on the weapon, rather than on the perpetrator or the circumstances of the crime. Racial stereotypes and prejudices can lead to mistaken identifications, and witnesses asked to make cross-racial identifications are especially prone to error. And, of course, the manner in which an identification procedure is constructed or administered by the police can affect the result, even when there is no desire or intent to influence the witness or otherwise taint the process.

There are many thoughtful articles and books describing all of these phenomena—and many others—that plague eyewitness testimony and create real dangers of mistaken identifications.[a] There are also a number of websites and videos that are excellent resources for additional information. Go ahead and take a look—some of resources below even offer interactive opportunities to test your own skills as an eyewitness!

**Additional Resources on Eyewitness Testimony
and Mistaken Identification**

http://www.innocenceproject.org/understand/Eyewitness–
Misidentification.php

http://courses2.cit.cornell.edu/sociallaw/topics/Eyewitness
Identification.html

http://eyewitness.utep.edu/

http://public.psych.iastate.edu/glwells/

http://www.eyeid.org/

Elizabeth Loftus TED Talk: The Fiction of Memory

http://www.youtube.com/watch?v=gCswq5JDTaw

60 Minutes Report on Eyewitness Testimony, Part 1

http://www.youtube.com/watch?v=u-SBTRLoPuo

---

[a]   *See, e.g.*, Elizabeth F. Loftus, EYEWITNESS TESTIMONY (1996); Robert Buckhout, *Eyewitness Testimony*, SCIENTIFIC AMERICAN, December 1974, pp. 23–31; Nancy Mehrkens Steblay, *A Meta-Analytic Review of the Weapon Focus Effect*, 16 LAW AND HUMAN BEHAVIOR 413 (1992), available at http://web.augsburg.edu/~steblay/weaponfocusmetaanalysis.pdf; Sheri Lynn Johnson, *Cross-Racial Identification Errors in Criminal Cases*, 69 CORNELL LAW REVIEW 934 (1984).

B. THE RIGHT TO COUNSEL DURING POLICE IDENTIFICATION PROCEDURES

The Supreme Court has held that once adversary judicial criminal proceedings are initiated, the Sixth Amendment guarantees a defendant the right to have counsel present at lineups and showups. The Court has made it clear, however, that the right to counsel is not available at all for photo arrays, nor is it available for lineups and showups that take place before adversary judicial criminal proceedings begin.

1. LINEUPS

In *U.S. v. Wade*, the Supreme Court held that an identification lineup that takes place after the defendant has been charged with a crime is a "critical" stage of the prosecution during which the defendant is entitled to the assistance of counsel under the Sixth Amendment. Because the lineup in *Wade* was conducted outside the presence of defense counsel, and because the subsequent in-court identifications may have been tainted by the illegal lineup, the Supreme Court vacated the defendant's conviction and remanded the case to the lower courts for appropriate further action.

U.S. V. WADE
388 U.S. 218 (1967)

JUSTICE BRENNAN delivered the opinion of the Court.

The question here is whether courtroom identifications of an accused at trial are to be excluded from evidence because the accused was exhibited to the witnesses before trial at a post-indictment lineup conducted for identification purposes without notice to, and in the absence of, the accused's appointed counsel.

The federally insured bank in Eustace, Texas, was robbed on September 21, 1964. A man with a small strip of tape on each side of his face entered the bank, pointed a pistol at the female cashier and the vice president, the only persons in the bank at the time, and forced them to fill a pillowcase with the bank's money. The man then drove away with an accomplice who had been waiting in a stolen car outside the bank. On March 23, 1965, an indictment was returned against respondent, Wade, and two others for conspiring to rob the bank, and against Wade and the accomplice for the robbery itself. Wade was arrested on April 2, and counsel was appointed to represent him on April 26. Fifteen days later, an FBI agent, without notice to Wade's lawyer, arranged to have the two bank employees observe a lineup made up of Wade and five or six other prisoners and conducted in a courtroom of the local county courthouse. Each person in the line wore strips of tape such as allegedly worn by the robber. And, upon direction, each said something like "put the money in the bag," the words allegedly uttered by the robber. Both bank employees identified Wade in the lineup as the bank robber.

At trial, the two employees, when asked on direct examination if the robber was in the courtroom, pointed to Wade. The prior lineup identification was then elicited from both employees on cross-examination. At the close of testimony, Wade's counsel moved for a judgment of acquittal or, alternatively, to strike the bank officials' courtroom identifications on the ground that conduct of the lineup, without notice to and in the absence of his appointed counsel, violated his Fifth Amendment privilege against self-incrimination and his Sixth Amendment right to the assistance of counsel. The motion was denied, and Wade was convicted.

I

Neither the lineup itself nor anything shown by this record that Wade was required to do in the lineup violated his privilege against self-incrimination. We have only recently reaffirmed that the privilege "protects an accused only from being compelled to testify against himself, or otherwise provide the State with evidence of a testimonial or communicative nature." *Schmerber v. California*, 384 U.S. 757, 761 (1966). We there held that compelling a suspect to submit to a withdrawal of a sample of his blood for analysis for alcohol content and the admission in evidence of the analysis report were not compulsion to those ends.

We have no doubt that compelling the accused merely to exhibit his person for observation by a prosecution witness prior to trial involves no compulsion of the accused to give evidence having testimonial significance. It is compulsion of the accused to exhibit his physical characteristics, not compulsion to disclose any knowledge he might have. It is no different from compelling Schmerber to provide a blood sample, and is not within the cover of the privilege. Similarly, compelling Wade to speak within hearing distance of the witnesses, even to utter words purportedly uttered by the robber, was not compulsion to utter statements of a "testimonial" nature; he was required to use his voice as an identifying physical characteristic, not to speak his guilt.

II

The fact that the lineup involved no violation of Wade's privilege against self-incrimination does not, however, dispose of his contention that the courtroom identifications should have been excluded because the lineup was conducted without notice to, and in the absence of, his counsel. It is urged that the assistance of counsel at the lineup was indispensable to protect Wade's most basic right as a criminal defendant—his right to a fair trial at which the witnesses against him might be meaningfully cross-examined.

The Framers of the Bill of Rights envisaged a broader role for counsel than under the practice then prevailing in England of merely advising his client in "matters of law," and eschewing any responsibility for "matters of fact." The constitutions in at least 11 of the 13 States expressly or impliedly abolished this distinction. This background is reflected in the scope given by our decisions to the Sixth Amendment's guarantee to an accused of the assistance of counsel for his defense. When the Bill of Rights was adopted, there were no organized police forces as we know them today. The accused confronted the prosecutor and the witnesses against him, and the evidence was marshalled, largely at the trial itself. In contrast, today's law enforcement machinery involves critical confrontations of the accused by the prosecution at pretrial proceedings where the results might well settle the accused's fate and reduce the trial itself to a mere formality. In recognition of these realities of modern criminal prosecution, our cases have construed the Sixth Amendment guarantee to apply to "critical" stages of the proceedings. The guarantee reads: "In all criminal prosecutions, the accused shall enjoy the right . . . to have the Assistance of Counsel for his defence." The plain wording of this guarantee thus encompasses counsel's assistance whenever necessary to assure a meaningful "defence."

As early as *Powell v. Alabama*, 287 U.S. 45 (1932), we recognized that the period from arraignment to trial was "perhaps the most critical period of the proceedings," during which the accused "requires the guiding hand of counsel" if the guarantee is not to prove an empty right. That principle has since been applied to require the assistance of counsel at the type of arraignment—for example, that provided by Alabama— where certain rights might be sacrificed or lost: "What happens there may affect the whole trial. Available defenses may be irretrievably lost, if not then and there asserted."

It is central to that principle that, in addition to counsel's presence at trial, the accused is guaranteed that he need not stand alone against the State at any stage of the prosecution, formal or informal, in court or out, where counsel's absence might derogate from the accused's right to a fair trial. The security of that right is as much the aim of the right to counsel as it is of the other guarantees of the Sixth Amendment—the right of the accused to a speedy and public trial by an impartial jury, his right to be informed of the nature and cause of the accusation, and his right to be confronted with the witnesses against him and to have compulsory process for obtaining witnesses in his favor. The presence of counsel at such critical confrontations, as at the trial itself, operates to assure that the accused's interests will be protected consistently with our adversary theory of criminal prosecution.

In sum, the principle of *Powell v. Alabama* and succeeding cases requires that we scrutinize any pretrial confrontation of the accused to determine whether the presence of his counsel is necessary to preserve the defendant's basic right to a fair trial as affected by his right meaningfully to cross-examine the witnesses against him and to have effective assistance of counsel at the trial itself. It calls upon us to analyze whether potential substantial prejudice to defendant's rights inheres in the particular confrontation and the ability of counsel to help avoid that prejudice.

III

The Government characterizes the lineup as a mere preparatory step in the gathering of the prosecution's evidence, not different—for Sixth Amendment purposes—from various other preparatory steps, such as systematized or scientific analyzing of the accused's fingerprints, blood sample, clothing, hair, and the like. We think there are differences which preclude such stages being characterized as critical stages at which the accused has the right to the presence of his counsel. Knowledge of the techniques of science and technology is sufficiently available, and the variables in techniques few enough, that the accused has the opportunity for a meaningful confrontation of the Government's case at trial through the ordinary processes of cross-examination of the Government's expert witnesses and the presentation of the evidence of his own experts. The denial of a right to have his counsel present at such analyses does not therefore violate the Sixth Amendment; they are not critical stages since there is minimal risk that his counsel's absence at such stages might derogate from his right to a fair trial.

IV

But the confrontation compelled by the State between the accused and the victim or witnesses to a crime to elicit identification evidence is peculiarly riddled with innumerable dangers and variable factors which might seriously, even crucially, derogate from a fair trial. The vagaries of eyewitness identification are well-known; the annals of criminal law are rife with instances of mistaken identification. A major factor contributing to the high incidence of miscarriage of justice from mistaken identification has been the degree of suggestion inherent in the manner in which the prosecution presents the suspect to witnesses for pretrial identification. A commentator has observed that "the influence of improper suggestion upon identifying witnesses probably accounts for more miscarriages of justice than any other single factor—perhaps it is responsible for more such errors than all other factors combined." Suggestion can be created intentionally or unintentionally in many subtle ways. And the dangers for the suspect are particularly grave when the witness' opportunity for observation was insubstantial, and thus his susceptibility to suggestion the greatest.

Moreover, it is a matter of common experience that, once a witness has picked out the accused at the line-up, he is not likely to go back on his word later on, so that, in practice, the issue of identity may (in the absence of other relevant evidence) for all practical purposes be determined there and then, before the trial.

The pretrial confrontation for purpose of identification may take the form of a lineup, also known as an "identification parade" or "showup," as in the present case, or presentation of the suspect alone to the witness, as in *Stovall v. Denno*, 388 U.S. 293 (1967). It is obvious that risks of suggestion attend either form of confrontation and increase the dangers inhering in eyewitness identification. But as is the case with secret interrogations, there is serious difficulty in depicting what transpires at lineups and other forms of identification confrontations. "Privacy results in secrecy and this in turn results in a gap in our knowledge as to what in fact goes on." *Miranda v. Arizona*, 384 U.S. 436, 448 (1966). For the same reasons, the defense can seldom reconstruct the manner and mode of lineup identification for judge or jury at trial. Those participating in a lineup with the accused may often be police officers; in any event, the participants' names are rarely recorded or divulged at trial. The impediments to an objective observation are increased when the victim is the witness. Lineups are prevalent in rape and robbery prosecutions, and present a particular hazard that a victim's understandable outrage may excite vengeful or spiteful motives. In any event, neither witnesses nor lineup participants are apt to be alert for conditions prejudicial to the suspect. And if they were, it would likely be of scant benefit to the suspect, since neither witnesses nor lineup participants are likely to be schooled in the detection of suggestive influences. Improper influences may go undetected by a suspect, guilty or not, who experiences the emotional tension which we might expect in one being confronted with potential accusers. Even when he does observe abuse, if he has a criminal record, he may be reluctant to take the stand and open up the admission of prior convictions. Moreover, any protestations by the suspect of the fairness of the lineup made at trial are likely to be in vain; the jury's choice is between the accused's unsupported version and that of the police officers present. In short, the accused's inability effectively to reconstruct at trial any unfairness that occurred at the lineup may deprive him of his only opportunity meaningfully to attack the credibility of the witness' courtroom identification.

State reports, in the course of describing prior identifications admitted as evidence of guilt, reveal numerous instances of suggestive procedures, for example, that all in the lineup but the suspect were known to the identifying witness, that the other participants in a lineup were grossly dissimilar in appearance to the suspect, that only the suspect was required to wear distinctive clothing which the culprit allegedly wore, that the witness is told by the police that they have caught the culprit after which the defendant is brought before the witness alone or is viewed in jail, that the suspect is pointed out before or during a lineup, and that the participants in the lineup are asked to try on an article of clothing which fits only the suspect.

The potential for improper influence is illustrated by the circumstances, insofar as they appear, surrounding the prior identifications in the three cases we decide today. In the present case, the testimony of the identifying witnesses elicited on cross-examination revealed that those witnesses were taken to the courthouse and seated in the courtroom to await assembly of the lineup. The courtroom faced on a hallway observable to the witnesses through an open door. The cashier testified that she saw Wade "standing in the hall" within sight of an FBI agent. Five or six other prisoners later appeared in the hall. The vice president testified that he saw a person in the hall in the custody of the agent who "resembled the person that we identified as the one that had entered the bank."

The lineup in *Gilbert v. California*, 388 U.S. 263 (1967), was conducted in an auditorium in which some 100 witnesses to several alleged state and federal robberies charged to Gilbert made wholesale identifications of Gilbert as the robber in each other's presence, a procedure said to be fraught with dangers of suggestion. And the vice of suggestion created by the identification in *Stovall* was the presentation to the witness of the suspect alone handcuffed to police officers. It is hard to imagine a situation more clearly conveying the suggestion to the witness that the one presented is believed guilty by the police.

The few cases that have surfaced therefore reveal the existence of a process attended with hazards of serious unfairness to the criminal accused, and strongly suggest the plight of the more numerous defendants who are unable to ferret out suggestive influences in the secrecy of the confrontation. We do not assume that these risks are the result of police procedures intentionally designed to prejudice an accused. Rather, we assume they derive from the dangers inherent in eyewitness identification and the suggestibility inherent in the context of the pretrial identification.

Insofar as the accused's conviction may rest on a courtroom identification, in fact, the fruit of a suspect pretrial identification which the accused is helpless to subject to effective scrutiny at trial, the accused is deprived of that right of cross-examination which is an essential safeguard to his right to confront the witnesses against him. And even though cross-examination is a precious safeguard to a fair trial, it cannot be viewed as an absolute assurance of accuracy and reliability. Thus, in the present context, where so many variables and pitfalls exist, the first line of defense must be the prevention of unfairness and the lessening of the hazards of eyewitness identification at the lineup itself. The trial which might determine the accused's fate may well not be that in the courtroom but that at the pretrial confrontation, with the State aligned against the accused, the witness the sole jury, and the accused unprotected against the overreaching, intentional or unintentional, and with little or no effective appeal from the judgment there rendered by the witness—"that's the man."

Since it appears that there is grave potential for prejudice, intentional or not, in the pretrial lineup, which may not be capable of reconstruction at trial, and since presence of counsel itself can often avert prejudice and assure a meaningful confrontation at trial, there can be little doubt that, for Wade, the postindictment lineup was a critical stage of the prosecution at which he was as much entitled to aid of counsel as at the trial itself. Thus, both Wade and his counsel should have been notified of the impending lineup, and counsel's presence should have been a requisite to conduct of the lineup, absent an "intelligent waiver." No substantial countervailing policy considerations have been advanced against the requirement of the presence of counsel. Concern is expressed that the requirement will forestall prompt identifications and result in obstruction of the confrontations. As for the first, we note that in the two cases in which the right to counsel is today held to apply, counsel had already been appointed and no argument is made in either case that notice to counsel would have prejudicially delayed the confrontations. Moreover, we leave open the question whether the presence of substitute counsel might not suffice where notification and presence of the suspect's own counsel would result in prejudicial delay. And to refuse to recognize the right to counsel for fear that counsel will obstruct the course of justice is contrary to the basic assumptions upon which this Court has operated in Sixth Amendment cases. We rejected similar logic in *Miranda v. Arizona*, concerning presence of counsel during custodial interrogation.

In our view, counsel can hardly impede legitimate law enforcement; on the contrary, for the reasons expressed, law enforcement may be assisted by preventing the infiltration of taint in the prosecution's identification evidence. That result cannot help the guilty avoid conviction, but can only help assure that the right man has been brought to justice.

V

We come now to the question whether the denial of Wade's motion to strike the courtroom identification by the bank witnesses at trial because of the absence of his counsel at the lineup required, as the Court of Appeals held, the grant of a new trial at which such evidence is to be excluded. We do not think this disposition can be justified without first giving the Government the opportunity to establish by clear and convincing evidence that the in-court identifications were based upon observations of the suspect other than the lineup identification. Where, as here, the admissibility of evidence of the lineup identification itself is not involved, a *per se* rule of exclusion of courtroom identification would be unjustified. A rule limited solely to the exclusion of testimony concerning identification at the lineup itself, without regard to admissibility of the courtroom identification, would render the right to counsel an empty one. The lineup is most often used, as in the present case, to crystallize the witnesses' identification of the defendant for future reference. We have already noted that the lineup identification will have that effect. The State may then rest upon the witnesses' unequivocal courtroom identifications, and not mention the pretrial identification as part of the State's case at trial. Counsel is then in the predicament in which Wade's counsel found himself—realizing that possible unfairness at the lineup may be the sole means of attack upon the unequivocal courtroom identification, and having to probe in the dark in an attempt to discover and reveal unfairness, while bolstering the government witness' courtroom identification by bringing out and dwelling upon his prior identification. Since counsel's presence at the lineup would equip him to attack not only the lineup identification, but the courtroom identification as well, limiting the impact of violation of the right to counsel to exclusion of evidence only of identification at the lineup itself disregards a critical element of that right.

We think it follows that the proper test to be applied in these situations is that quoted in *Wong Sun v. U.S.*, 371 U.S. 471, 488 (1963): "Whether, granting establishment of the primary illegality, the evidence to which instant objection is made has been come at by exploitation of that illegality or instead by means sufficiently distinguishable to be purged of the primary taint." Application of this test in the present context requires consideration of various factors; for example, the prior opportunity to observe the alleged criminal act, the existence of any discrepancy between any pre-lineup description and the defendant's actual description, any identification prior to lineup of another person, the identification by picture of the defendant prior to the lineup, failure to identify the defendant on a prior occasion, and the lapse of time between the alleged act and the lineup identification. It is also relevant to consider those facts which, despite the absence of counsel, are disclosed concerning the conduct of the lineup.

On the record now before us, we cannot make the determination whether the in-court identifications had an independent origin. This was not an issue at trial, although there is some evidence relevant to a determination. That inquiry is most properly made in the District Court. We therefore think the appropriate procedure to be followed is to vacate the conviction pending a hearing to determine whether the in-court identifications had an independent source, or whether, in any event, the introduction of the evidence was harmless error, and for the District Court to reinstate the conviction or order a new trial, as may be proper.

JUSTICE WHITE, whom JUSTICE HARLAN and JUSTICE STEWART join, dissenting in part and concurring in part.

The Court has again propounded a broad constitutional rule barring the use of a wide spectrum of relevant and probative evidence, solely because a step in its ascertainment or discovery occurs outside the presence of defense counsel. This was the approach of the Court in *Miranda v. Arizona.* I objected then to what I thought was an uncritical and doctrinaire approach without satisfactory factual foundation. I have much the same view of the present ruling, and therefore dissent from the judgment and from Parts II, IV, and V of the Court's opinion.

The Court's opinion is far-reaching. It proceeds first by creating a new *per se* rule of constitutional law: a criminal suspect cannot be subjected to a pretrial identification process in the absence of his counsel without violating the Sixth Amendment. If he is, the State may not buttress a later courtroom identification of the witness by any reference to the previous identification. Furthermore, the courtroom identification is not admissible at all unless the State can establish by clear and convincing proof that the testimony is not the fruit of the earlier identification made in the absence of defendant's counsel—admittedly a heavy burden for the State and probably an impossible one. To all intents and purposes, courtroom identifications are barred if pretrial identifications have occurred without counsel being present.

The rule applies to any lineup, to any other techniques employed to produce an identification, and *a fortiori* to a face-to-face encounter between the witness and the suspect alone, regardless of when the identification occurs in time or place, and whether before or after indictment or information. It matters not how well the witness knows the suspect, whether the witness is the suspect's mother, brother, or long-time associate, and no matter how long or well the witness observed the perpetrator at the scene of the crime. The kidnap victim who has lived for days with his abductor is in the same category as the witness who has had only a fleeting glimpse of the criminal. Neither may identify the suspect without defendant's counsel being present. The same strictures apply regardless of the number of other witnesses who positively identify the defendant, and regardless of the corroborative evidence showing that it was the defendant who had committed the crime.

The premise for the Court's rule is not the general unreliability of eyewitness identifications, nor the difficulties inherent in observation, recall, and recognition. The Court assumes a narrower evil as the basis for its rule—improper police suggestion which contributes to erroneous identifications. The Court apparently believes that improper police procedures are so widespread that a broad prophylactic rule must be laid down, requiring the presence of counsel at all pretrial identifications, in order to detect recurring instances of police misconduct. I do not share this pervasive distrust of all official investigations. None of the materials the Court relies upon supports it. Certainly, I would bow to solid fact, but the Court quite obviously does not have before it any reliable, comprehensive survey of current police practices on which to base its new rule. Until it does, the Court should avoid excluding relevant evidence from state criminal trials.

The Court goes beyond assuming that a great majority of the country's police departments are following improper practices at pretrial identifications. To find the lineup a "critical" stage of the proceeding and to exclude identifications made in the absence of counsel, the Court must also assume that police "suggestion," if it occurs at all, leads to erroneous, rather than accurate, identifications, and that reprehensible police conduct will have an unavoidable and largely undiscoverable impact on the trial. This, in turn, assumes that there is now no adequate source from which defense counsel can learn about the circumstances of the pretrial identification in order to place before the jury all of the considerations which should enter into an appraisal of courtroom identification evidence. But these are treacherous and unsupported assumptions, resting as they do on the notion that the defendant will not be aware, that the police and the witnesses will forget or prevaricate, that defense counsel will be unable to bring out the truth, and that neither jury, judge, nor appellate court is a sufficient safeguard against unacceptable police conduct occurring at a pretrial identification procedure. I am unable to share the Court's view of the willingness of the police and the ordinary citizen-witness to dissemble, either with respect to the identification of the defendant or with respect to the circumstances surrounding a pretrial identification.

There are several striking aspects to the Court's holding. First, the rule does not bar courtroom identifications where there have been no previous identifications in the presence of the police, although when identified in the courtroom, the defendant is known to be in custody and charged with the commission of a crime. Second, the Court seems to say that, if suitable legislative standards were adopted for the conduct of pretrial identifications, thereby lessening the hazards in such confrontations, it would not insist on the presence of counsel. But if this is true, why does not the Court simply fashion what it deems to be constitutionally acceptable procedures for the authorities to follow? Certainly the Court is correct in suggesting that the new rule will be wholly inapplicable where police departments themselves have established suitable safeguards.

Third, courtroom identification may be barred, absent counsel at a prior identification, regardless of the extent of counsel's information concerning the circumstances of the previous confrontation between witness and defendant—apparently even if there were recordings or sound-movies of the events as they occurred. But if the rule is premised on the defendant's right to have his counsel know, there seems little basis for not accepting other means to inform. A disinterested observer, recordings, photographs—any one of them would seem adequate to furnish the basis for a meaningful cross-examination of the eyewitness who identifies the defendant in the courtroom.

I share the Court's view that the criminal trial, at the very least, should aim at truthful factfinding, including accurate eyewitness identifications. I doubt, however, on the basis of our present information, that the tragic mistakes which have occurred in criminal trials are as much the product of improper police conduct as they are the consequence of the difficulties inherent in eyewitness testimony and in resolving evidentiary conflicts by court or jury. I doubt that the Court's new rule will obviate these difficulties, or that the situation will be measurably improved by inserting defense counsel into the investigative processes of police departments everywhere.

But, it may be asked, what possible state interest militates against requiring the presence of defense counsel at lineups? After all, the argument goes, he may do some good, he may upgrade the quality of identification evidence in state courts, and he can scarcely do any harm. Even if true, this is a feeble foundation for fastening an ironclad constitutional rule upon state criminal procedures. Absent some reliably established constitutional violation, the processes by which the States enforce their criminal laws are their own prerogative. The States do have an interest in conducting their own affairs, an interest which cannot be displaced simply by saying that there are no valid arguments with respect to the merits of a federal rule emanating from this Court.

Beyond this, however, requiring counsel at pretrial identifications as an invariable rule trenches on other valid state interests. One of them is its concern with the prompt and efficient enforcement of its criminal laws. Identifications frequently take place after arrest, but before an indictment is returned or an information is filed. The police may have arrested a suspect on probable cause, but may still have the wrong man. Both the suspect and the State have every interest in a prompt identification at that stage, the suspect in order to secure his immediate release and the State because prompt and early identification enhances accurate identification and because it must know whether it is on the right investigative track. Unavoidably, however, the absolute rule requiring the presence of counsel will cause significant delay and it may very well result in no pretrial identification at all. Counsel must be appointed and a time arranged convenient for him and the witnesses. Meanwhile, it may be necessary to file charges against the suspect who may then be released on bail, in the federal system very often on his own recognizance, with neither the State nor the defendant having the benefit of a properly conducted identification procedure.

Nor do I think the witnesses themselves can be ignored. They will now be required to be present at the convenience of counsel rather than their own. Many may be much less willing to participate if the identification stage is transformed into an adversary proceeding not under the control of a judge. Others may fear for their own safety if their identity is known at an early date, especially when there is no way of knowing until the lineup occurs whether or not the police really have the right man.

Finally, I think the Court's new rule is vulnerable in terms of its own unimpeachable purpose of increasing the reliability of identification testimony.

Law enforcement officers have the obligation to convict the guilty and to make sure they do not convict the innocent. They must be dedicated to making the criminal trial a procedure for the ascertainment of the true facts surrounding the commission of the crime. To this extent, our so-called adversary system is not adversary at all; nor should it be. But defense counsel has no comparable obligation to ascertain or present the truth. Our system assigns him a different mission. He must be and is interested in preventing the conviction of the innocent, but, absent a voluntary plea of guilty, we also insist that he defend his client whether he is innocent or guilty. The State has the obligation to present the evidence. Defense counsel need present nothing, even if he knows what the truth is. He need not furnish any witnesses to the police, or reveal any confidences of his client, or furnish any other information to help the prosecution's case. If he can confuse a witness, even a truthful one, or make him appear at a disadvantage, unsure or indecisive, that will be his normal course. Our interest in not convicting the innocent permits counsel to put the State to its proof, to put the State's case in the worst possible light, regardless of what he thinks or knows to be the truth. Undoubtedly there are some limits which defense counsel must observe, but more often than not, defense counsel will cross-examine a prosecution witness, and impeach him if he can, even if he thinks the witness is telling the truth, just as he will attempt to destroy a witness who he thinks is lying. In this respect, as part of our modified adversary system and as part of the duty imposed on the most honorable defense counsel, we countenance or require conduct which, in many instances, has little, if any, relation to the search for truth.

I would not extend this system, at least as it presently operates, to police investigations, and would not require counsel's presence at pretrial identification procedures. Counsel's interest is in not having his client placed at the scene of the crime, regardless of his whereabouts. Some counsel may advise their clients to refuse to make any movements or to speak any words in a lineup or even to appear in one. To that extent, the impact on truthful factfinding is quite obvious. Others will not only observe what occurs and develop possibility for later cross-examination, but will hover over witnesses and begin their cross-examination then, menacing truthful factfinding as thoroughly as the Court fears the police now do. Certainly there is an implicit invitation to counsel to suggest rules for the lineup and to manage and produce it as best he can. I therefore doubt that the Court's new rule, at least absent some clearly defined limits on counsel's role, will measurably contribute to more reliable pretrial identifications. My fears are that it will have precisely the opposite result. It may well produce fewer convictions, but that is hardly a proper measure of its long-run acceptability. In my view, the State is entitled to investigate and develop its case outside the presence of defense counsel. This includes the right to have private conversations with identification witnesses, just as defense counsel may have his own consultations with these and other witnesses without having the prosecutor present.

In *Wade*, the witness identified the defendant in court, but the prosecution did not try to introduce into evidence the identification from the earlier lineup. By contrast, in *Gilbert v. California*, decided the same day as *Wade*, witnesses identified the defendant in court and the prosecution also introduced evidence of the earlier lineup identification that was conducted without the defendant's counsel. Citing *Wade*, the Supreme Court held that evidence related to the lineup identification was inadmissible because the defendant's counsel was not present. The Court then returned the case to the lower courts to determine whether the in-court identifications had an independent source or if they were tainted by the illegal lineup.

GILBERT V. CALIFORNIA
388 U.S. 263 (1967)

Jesse James Gilbert was indicted for armed robbery of four banks and for the murder of a police officer that occurred in connection with one of the robberies. After the indictment and after Gilbert was represented by counsel, police conducted a lineup outside the presence of counsel. At the lineup, a number of witnesses from the various robberies identified Gilbert. Later, at the guilt and penalty phases of Gilbert's trial, several of those same witnesses made in-court identifications of Gilbert and also offered testimony about their prior identifications of Gilbert at the lineup.

Relying on *U.S. v. Wade*, 388 U.S. 218 (1967), the Supreme Court held that all evidence and testimony related to the lineup identifications was inadmissible because the lineup had been conducted outside the presence of defense counsel after Gilbert was indicted, in violation of the Sixth Amendment right to counsel. The Court also held that the in-court identifications were admissible only if they were untainted by the illegal lineup:

> The admission of the in-court identifications without first determining that they were not tainted by the illegal lineup but were of independent origin was constitutional error [under *U.S. v. Wade*]. We there held that a post-indictment pretrial lineup at which the accused is exhibited to identifying witnesses is a critical stage of the criminal prosecution; that police conduct of such a lineup without notice to and in the absence of his counsel denies the accused his Sixth Amendment right to counsel and calls in question the admissibility at trial of the in-court identifications of the accused by witnesses who attended the lineup. However, as in *Wade*, the record does not permit an informed judgment whether the in-court identifications at the two stages of the trial had an independent source. Gilbert is therefore entitled only to a vacation of his conviction pending the holding of such proceedings as the California Supreme Court may deem appropriate to afford the State the opportunity to establish that the in-court identifications had an independent source, or that their introduction in evidence was in any event harmless error.

> Quite different considerations are involved as to the admission of the testimony of the manager of the apartment house at the guilt phase and of the eight witnesses at the penalty stage that they identified Gilbert at the lineup. That testimony is the direct result of the illegal lineup "come at by exploitation of (the primary) illegality." *Wong Sun v. U.S.*, 371 U.S. 471, 488 (1963). The State is therefore not entitled to an opportunity to show that that testimony had an independent source. Only a *per se* exclusionary rule as to such testimony can be an effective sanction to assure that law enforcement authorities will respect the accused's constitutional right to the presence of his counsel at the critical lineup. In the absence of legislative regulations adequate to avoid the hazards to a fair trial which inhere in lineups as presently conducted, the desirability of deterring the constitutionally objectionable practice must prevail over the undesirability of excluding relevant evidence. That conclusion is buttressed by the consideration that the witness' testimony of his lineup identification will enhance the impact of his in-court identification on the jury and seriously aggravate whatever derogation exists of the accused's right to a fair trial. Therefore, unless the California Supreme Court is able to declare a belief that it was harmless beyond a reasonable doubt, Gilbert will be

entitled on remand to a new trial or, if no prejudicial error is found on the guilt stage but only in the penalty stage, to whatever relief California law affords where the penalty stage must be set aside.

As *Gilbert* makes clear, if evidence of an earlier lineup identification is inadmissible, the prosecutor may still ask the witness to make an in-court identification, but only if the prosecutor can show that the in-court identification has an independent source and is untainted by the illegal lineup. In many cases, the prosecutor will attempt to meet this burden through careful questioning of the witness in an effort to show that the in-court identification stems from the witness' recollection of the actual crime, rather than from events at the tainted lineup.

The Right to Counsel: Lineups

1. Once adversary judicial criminal proceedings have commenced—whether by way of formal charge, preliminary hearing, indictment, information, or arraignment—the defendant is entitled, under the Sixth Amendment, to have counsel present at any lineup identification. Any evidence or testimony regarding a lineup identification conducted in violation of the defendant's right to counsel is inadmissible.

2. If testimony or other evidence regarding a lineup identification is inadmissible because the lineup took place after the initiation of adversary judicial criminal proceedings and the defendant's counsel was not present, the prosecution may still attempt to elicit an in-court identification from the witness, provided the prosecution proves, by clear and convincing evidence, that the in-court identification is based upon observations of the suspect other than the lineup identification. Put somewhat differently, the prosecution must show, by clear and convincing evidence, that the in-court identification has an independent origin untainted by the illegal lineup. Application of this test requires consideration of various factors, such as the prior opportunity to observe the alleged criminal act, the existence of any discrepancy between any pre-lineup description and the defendant's actual description, any identification prior to the lineup of another person, the identification by picture of the defendant prior to the lineup, failure to identify the defendant on a prior occasion, the lapse of time between the alleged act and the lineup identification, and any facts disclosed concerning the conduct of the lineup.

2. SHOWUPS

The dissenting Justices in *Wade* feared that the majority's rule requiring that defense counsel be notified or present at any lineup would apply as well to other identification procedures, including those conducted before the suspect was indicted or otherwise charged with a crime. The Supreme Court quickly put to rest those fears in *Illinois v. Kirby*, holding that the defendant was not entitled to the presence of counsel at a pre-indictment showup.

KIRBY V. ILLINOIS
406 U.S. 682 (1972)

JUSTICE STEWART announced the judgment of the Court and an opinion in which CHIEF JUSTICE BURGER, JUSTICE BLACKMUN, and JUSTICE REHNQUIST join.

In *U.S. v. Wade*, 388 U.S. 218 (1967), and *Gilbert v. California*, 388 U.S. 263 (1967), this Court held that a post-indictment pretrial lineup at which the accused is exhibited to identifying witnesses is a critical stage of the criminal prosecution; that police conduct of such a lineup without notice to and in the absence of his counsel denies the accused his Sixth (and Fourteenth) Amendment right to counsel and calls in question the admissibility at trial of the in-court identifications of the accused by witnesses who attended the lineup. Those cases further held that no "in-court identifications" are admissible in evidence if their "source" is a lineup conducted in violation of this constitutional standard. "Only a *per se* exclusionary rule as to such testimony can be an effective sanction," the Court said, "to assure that law enforcement authorities will respect the accused's constitutional right to the presence of his counsel at the critical lineup." In the present case, we are asked to extend the *Wade-Gilbert per se* exclusionary rule to identification testimony based upon a police station showup that took place before the defendant had been indicted or otherwise formally charged with any criminal offense.

On February 21, 1968, a man named Willie Shard reported to the Chicago police that the previous day two men had robbed him on a Chicago street of a wallet containing, among other things, traveler's checks and a Social Security card. On February 22, two police officers stopped the petitioner and a companion, Ralph Bean, on West Madison Street in Chicago. When asked for identification, the petitioner produced a wallet that contained three traveler's checks and a Social Security card, all bearing the name of Willie Shard. Papers with Shard's name on them were also found in Bean's possession. When asked to explain his possession of Shard's property, the petitioner first said that the traveler's checks were "play money," and then told the officers that he had won them in a crap game. The officers then arrested the petitioner and Bean and took them to a police station.

Only after arriving at the police station, and checking the records there, did the arresting officers learn of the Shard robbery. A police car was then dispatched to Shard's place of employment, where it picked up Shard and brought him to the police station. Immediately upon entering the room in the police station where the petitioner and Bean were seated at a table, Shard positively identified them as the men who had robbed him two days earlier. No lawyer was present in the room, and neither the petitioner nor Bean had asked for legal assistance, or been advised of any right to the presence of counsel.

More than six weeks later, the petitioner and Bean were indicted for the robbery of Willie Shard. Upon arraignment, counsel was appointed to represent them, and they pleaded not guilty. A pretrial motion to suppress Shard's identification testimony was denied, and at the trial Shard testified as a witness for the prosecution. In his testimony, he described his identification of the two men at the police station on February 22, and identified them again in the courtroom as the men who had robbed him on February 20. He was cross-examined at length regarding the circumstances of his identification of the two defendants. The jury found both defendants guilty, and the petitioner's conviction was affirmed on appeal.

In a line of constitutional cases in this Court stemming back to the Court's landmark opinion in *Powell v. Alabama*, 287 U.S. 45 (1932), it has been firmly established that a person's Sixth and Fourteenth Amendment right to counsel attaches only at or after the time that adversary judicial proceedings have been initiated against him.

This is not to say that a defendant in a criminal case has a constitutional right to counsel only at the trial itself. The *Powell* case makes clear that the right attaches at the time of arraignment, and the Court has recently held that it exists also at the time of a preliminary hearing. But the point is that, while members of the Court have differed as to existence of the right to counsel in the contexts of some of the above cases, all of those cases have involved points of time at or after the initiation of adversary judicial criminal proceedings—whether by way of formal charge, preliminary hearing, indictment, information, or arraignment.

The initiation of judicial criminal proceedings is far from a mere formalism. It is the starting point of our whole system of adversary criminal justice. For it is only then that the government has committed itself to prosecute, and only then that the adverse positions of government and defendant have solidified. It is then that a defendant finds himself faced with the prosecutorial forces of organized society, and immersed in the intricacies of substantive and procedural criminal law. It is this point, therefore, that marks the commencement of the "criminal prosecutions" to which alone the explicit guarantees of the Sixth Amendment are applicable.

In this case, we are asked to import into a routine police investigation an absolute constitutional guarantee historically and rationally applicable only after the onset of formal prosecutorial proceedings. We decline to [impose] a *per se* exclusionary rule upon testimony concerning an identification that took place long before the commencement of any prosecution whatever.

What has been said is not to suggest that there may not be occasions during the course of a criminal investigation when the police do abuse identification procedures. Such abuses are not beyond the reach of the Constitution. The Due Process Clause of the Fifth and Fourteenth Amendments forbids a lineup that is unnecessarily suggestive and conducive to irreparable mistaken identification.

JUSTICE BRENNAN, with whom JUSTICE DOUGLAS and JUSTICE MARSHALL join, dissenting.

While it should go without saying, it appears necessary, in view of the plurality opinion today, to re-emphasize that *U.S. v. Wade* did not require the presence of counsel at pretrial confrontations for identification purposes simply on the basis of an abstract consideration of the words "criminal prosecutions" in the Sixth Amendment. Counsel is required at those confrontations because "the dangers inherent in eyewitness identification and the suggestibility inherent in the context of the pretrial identification" mean that protection must be afforded to the "most basic right of a criminal defendant—his right to a fair trial at which the witnesses against him might be meaningfully cross-examined." Hence, "the initiation of adversary judicial criminal proceedings" is completely irrelevant to whether counsel is necessary at a pretrial confrontation for identification in order to safeguard the accused's constitutional rights to confrontation and the effective assistance of counsel at his trial.

In view of *Wade*, it is plain, and the plurality today does not attempt to dispute it, that there inhere in a confrontation for identification conducted after arrest the identical hazards to a fair trial that inhere in such a confrontation conducted "after the onset of formal prosecutorial proceedings." The plurality apparently considers an arrest, which for present purposes we must assume to be based upon probable cause, to be nothing more than part of "a routine police investigation," and thus not "the starting point of our whole system of adversary criminal justice." An arrest, according to the plurality, does not face the accused "with the prosecutorial forces of organized society," nor immerse him "in the intricacies of substantive and procedural criminal law." Those consequences ensue, says the plurality, only with "the initiation of judicial criminal proceedings," for "it is only then that the government has committed itself to prosecute, and only then that the adverse positions of government and defendant have solidified." If these propositions do not amount to "mere formalism," it is difficult to know how to characterize them. An arrest evidences the belief of the police that the perpetrator of a crime has been caught. A post-arrest confrontation for identification is not "a mere preparatory step in the gathering of the prosecution's evidence." A primary, and frequently sole, purpose of the confrontation for identification at that stage is to accumulate proof to buttress the conclusion of the police that they have the offender in hand. The plurality offers no reason, and I can think of none, for concluding that a post-arrest confrontation for identification, unlike a post-charge confrontation, is not among those "critical confrontations of the accused by the prosecution at pretrial proceedings where the results might well settle the accused's fate and reduce the trial itself to a mere formality."

The highly suggestive form of confrontation employed in this case underscores the point. This showup was particularly fraught with the peril of mistaken identification. In the setting of a police station squad room where all present except petitioner and Bean were police officers, the danger was quite real that Shard's understandable resentment might lead him too readily to agree with the police that the pair under arrest, and the only persons exhibited to him, were indeed the robbers. It is hard to imagine a situation more clearly conveying the suggestion to the witness that the one presented is believed guilty by the police. The State had no case without Shard's identification testimony, and safeguards against that consequence were therefore of critical importance. Shard's testimony itself demonstrates the necessity for such safeguards. On direct examination, Shard identified petitioner and Bean not as the alleged robbers on trial in the courtroom, but as the pair he saw at the police station. His testimony thus lends strong support to the observation, quoted by the Court in *Wade*, that "it is a matter of common experience that, once a witness has picked out the accused at the line-up, he is not likely to go back on his word later on, so that in practice the issue of identity may (in the absence of other relevant evidence) for all practical purposes be determined there and then, before the trial."

Wade and *Gilbert*, of course, happened to involve post-indictment confrontations. Yet even a cursory perusal of the opinions in those cases reveals that nothing at all turned upon that particular circumstance. For my part, I do not agree that we "extend" *Wade* and *Gilbert* by holding that the principles of those cases apply to confrontations for identification conducted after arrest.

———

When a showup is conducted before charges are filed, *Kirby* governs and the suspect is not entitled to have counsel present. Under *Moore v. Illinois*, however, if the showup takes place at a preliminary hearing or after adversary judicial criminal proceedings have begun, the suspect is entitled to have counsel present.

MOORE V. ILLINOIS
434 U.S. 220 (1977)

A rape victim identified her attacker in a photo array. Based on that identification and other evidence, police arrested James Moore and held him in jail overnight pending a preliminary hearing to determine whether he should be bound over to the grand jury and to set bail. The next morning, a policeman accompanied the victim to the court for the hearing. The policeman told her she was going to view a suspect and should identify him if she could. He also had her sign a complaint that named Moore as her assailant. At the hearing, Moore's name was called and he was led before the bench. The judge told Moore that he was charged with rape and deviate sexual behavior. The judge then called the victim, who had been in the courtroom waiting for the case to be called, to come before the bench. The State's Attorney stated that police had found evidence linking Moore with the offenses charged. He asked the victim whether she saw her assailant in the courtroom, and she pointed at Moore. Moore was not represented by counsel at the hearing, and the court did not offer to appoint counsel.

At trial, the victim testified on direct examination that she had identified Moore as her assailant at the preliminary hearing. She also testified that the defendant on trial was the man who had raped her. The jury found petitioner guilty on all counts, and the trial court sentenced him to 30 to 50 years in prison.

Relying on *Kirby*, the Supreme Court initially held that the preliminary hearing marked the beginning of adversary judicial criminal proceedings against Moore, meaning that his right to counsel under the Sixth Amendment had attached. The Court then rejected the contention that *Wade* and *Gilbert* did not apply because the identification at the preliminary hearing was not a lineup:

> The Court of Appeals suggested that *Wade* and *Gilbert* did not apply here because the "in-court identification could hardly be considered a line-up." The meaning of this statement is not entirely clear. If the court meant that a one-on-one identification procedure, as distinguished from a lineup, is not subject to the counsel requirement, it was mistaken. Although *Wade* and *Gilbert* both involved lineups, *Wade* clearly contemplated that counsel would be required in both situations: "The pretrial confrontation for purpose of identification may take the form of a lineup . . . or presentation of the suspect alone to the witness. . . . It is obvious that risks of suggestion attend either form of confrontation." Indeed, a one-on-one confrontation generally is

thought to present greater risks of mistaken identification than a lineup. There is no reason, then, to hold that a one-on-one identification procedure is not subject to the same requirements as a lineup.

The Supreme Court went on to hold that the victim's testimony regarding her identification of Moore at the preliminary hearing was inadmissible because the defendant was entitled to have counsel present during the identification:

> The reasons supporting *Wade*'s holding that a corporeal identification is a critical stage of a criminal prosecution for Sixth Amendment purposes apply with equal force to this identification. It is difficult to imagine a more suggestive manner in which to present a suspect to a witness for their critical first confrontation than was employed in this case. The victim, who had seen her assailant for only 10 to 15 seconds, was asked to make her identification after she was told that she was going to view a suspect, after she was told his name and heard it called as he was led before the bench, and after she heard the prosecutor recite the evidence believed to implicate petitioner. Had petitioner been represented by counsel, some or all of this suggestiveness could have been avoided.

The Right to Counsel: Showups

1.   A suspect is not entitled to have counsel present at a showup identification that takes place before adversary judicial criminal proceedings have commenced. But once such proceedings have begun— whether by way of formal charge, preliminary hearing, indictment, information, or arraignment—the defendant is entitled, under the Sixth Amendment, to have counsel present at any showup identification. Any evidence or testimony regarding a showup identification conducted in violation of the defendant's right to counsel is inadmissible.

2.   If testimony or other evidence regarding a showup identification is inadmissible because the showup took place after the initiation of adversary judicial criminal proceedings and the defendant's counsel was not present, the prosecution may still attempt to elicit an in-court identification from the witness, provided the prosecution proves, by clear and convincing evidence, that the in-court identification has an independent origin untainted by the illegal showup. Application of this test requires consideration of various factors, such as the prior opportunity to observe the alleged criminal act, the existence of any discrepancy between any pre-showup description and the defendant's actual description, any identification prior to the showup of another

person, the identification by picture of the defendant prior to the showup, failure to identify the defendant on a prior occasion, the lapse of time between the alleged act and the showup identification, and any facts disclosed concerning the conduct of the showup.

3. PHOTO ARRAYS

In the Supreme Court's view, a photo array presents far fewer opportunities for police suggestion or manipulation than does a lineup or showup. A photo array can also be reproduced at trial more easily than a lineup or showup. Accordingly, the Court held in *U.S. v. Ash* that a suspect is not entitled to have counsel present at a photographic identification, even one that takes place after criminal charges have been filed.

U.S. v. ASH

413 U.S. 300 (1973)

JUSTICE BLACKMUN delivered the opinion of the Court.

In this case, the Court is called upon to decide whether the Sixth Amendment grants an accused the right to have counsel present whenever the Government conducts a post-indictment photographic display, containing a picture of the accused, for the purpose of allowing a witness to attempt an identification of the offender.

I

On the morning of August 26, 1965, a man with a stocking mask entered a bank in Washington, D.C., and began waving a pistol. He ordered an employee to hang up the telephone and instructed all others present not to move. Seconds later, a second man, also wearing a stocking mask, entered the bank, scooped up money from tellers' drawers into a bag, and left. The gunman followed, and both men escaped through an alley. The robbery lasted three or four minutes.

A Government informer, Clarence McFarland, told authorities that he had discussed the robbery with Charles J. Ash, Jr., the respondent here. Acting on this information, an FBI agent, in February 1966, showed five black-and-white mug shots of Negro males of generally the same age, height, and weight, one of which was of Ash, to four witnesses. All four made uncertain identifications of Ash's picture. At this time, Ash was not in custody and had not been charged. On April 1, 1966, an indictment was returned charging Ash and a codefendant, John L. Bailey, in five counts related to this bank robbery.

Trial was finally set for May 1968, almost three years after the crime. In preparing for trial, the prosecutor decided to use a photographic display to determine whether the witnesses he planned to call would be able to make in-court identifications. Shortly before the trial, an FBI agent and the prosecutor showed five color photographs to the four witnesses who previously had tentatively identified the black-and-white photograph of Ash. Three of the witnesses selected the picture of Ash, but one was unable to make any selection. None of the witnesses selected the picture of Bailey which was in the group. This post-indictment identification provides the basis for respondent Ash's claim that he was denied the right to counsel at a "critical stage" of the prosecution.

II

The core purpose of the counsel guarantee was to assure "Assistance" at trial, when the accused was confronted with both the intricacies of the law and the advocacy of the public prosecutor. Later developments have led this Court to recognize that "Assistance" would be less than meaningful if it were limited to the formal trial itself.

This extension of the right to counsel to events before trial has resulted from changing patterns of criminal procedure and investigation that have tended to generate pretrial events that might appropriately be considered to be parts of the trial itself. At these newly emerging and significant events, the accused was confronted, just as at trial, by the procedural system, or by his expert adversary, or by both. In *U.S. v. Wade*, 388 U.S. 218, 224 (1967), the Court explained the process of expanding the counsel guarantee to these confrontations:

> When the Bill of Rights was adopted, there were no organized police forces as we know them today. The accused confronted the prosecutor and the witnesses against him, and the evidence was marshalled, largely at the trial itself. In contrast, today's law enforcement machinery involves critical confrontations of the accused by the prosecution at pretrial proceedings where the results might well settle the accused's fate and reduce the trial itself to a mere formality. In recognition of these realities of modern criminal prosecution, our cases have construed the Sixth Amendment guarantee to apply to "critical" stages of the proceedings.

The Court consistently has applied a historical interpretation of the guarantee, and has expanded the constitutional right to counsel only when new contexts appear presenting the same dangers that gave birth initially to the right itself.

Throughout this expansion of the counsel guarantee to trial-like confrontations, the function of the lawyer has remained essentially the same as his function at trial. In all cases considered by the Court, counsel has continued to act as a spokesman for, or advisor to, the accused. The accused's right to the "Assistance of Counsel" has meant just that, namely, the right of the accused to have counsel acting as his assistant.

The function of counsel in rendering "Assistance" continued at the lineup under consideration in *Wade* and its companion cases. Although the accused was not confronted there with legal questions, the lineup offered opportunities for prosecuting authorities to take advantage of the accused. Counsel was seen by the Court as being more sensitive to, and aware of, suggestive influences than the accused himself, and as better able to reconstruct the events at trial. Counsel present at lineup would be able to remove disabilities of the accused in precisely the same fashion that counsel compensated for the disabilities of the layman at trial. Thus, the Court mentioned that the accused's memory might be dimmed by "emotional tension," that the accused's credibility at trial would be diminished by his status as defendant, and that the accused might be unable to present his version effectively without giving up his privilege against compulsory self-incrimination. It was in order to compensate for these deficiencies that the Court found the need for the assistance of counsel.

This review of the history and expansion of the Sixth Amendment counsel guarantee demonstrates that the test utilized by the Court has called for examination of the event in order to determine whether the accused required aid in coping with legal problems or assistance in meeting his adversary.

III

After the Court in *Wade* held that a lineup constituted a trial-like confrontation requiring counsel, a more difficult issue remained in the case for consideration. The same changes in law enforcement that led to lineups and pretrial hearings also generated other events at which the accused was confronted by the prosecution. The Government had argued in *Wade* that if counsel was required at a lineup, the same forceful considerations would mandate counsel at other preparatory steps in the gathering of the prosecution's evidence, such as the taking of fingerprints or blood samples.

The Court concluded that there were differences. Rather than distinguishing these situations from the lineup in terms of the need for counsel to assure an equal confrontation at the time, the Court recognized that there were times when the subsequent trial would cure a one-sided confrontation between prosecuting authorities and the uncounseled defendant. In other words, such stages were not "critical." Referring to fingerprints, hair, clothing, and other blood samples, the Court explained:

> Knowledge of the techniques of science and technology is sufficiently available, and the variables in techniques few enough, that the accused has the opportunity for a meaningful confrontation of the Government's case at trial through the ordinary processes of cross-examination of the Government's

expert witnesses and the presentation of the evidence of his own experts.

The structure of *Wade*, viewed in light of the careful limitation of the Court's language to "confrontations," makes it clear that lack of scientific precision and inability to reconstruct an event are not the tests for requiring counsel in the first instance. These are, instead, the tests to determine whether confrontation with counsel at trial can serve as a substitute for counsel at the pretrial confrontation. If accurate reconstruction is possible, the risks inherent in any confrontation still remain, but the opportunity to cure defects at trial causes the confrontation to cease to be "critical."

IV

A substantial departure from the historical test would be necessary if the Sixth Amendment were interpreted to give Ash a right to counsel at the photographic identification in this case. Since the accused himself is not present at the time of the photographic display, and asserts no right to be present, no possibility arises that the accused might be misled by his lack of familiarity with the law or overpowered by his professional adversary. Similarly, the counsel guarantee would not be used to produce equality in a trial-like adversary confrontation. Rather, the guarantee was used by the Court of Appeals to produce confrontation at an event that previously was not analogous to an adversary trial.

Even if we were willing to view the counsel guarantee in broad terms as a generalized protection of the adversary process, we would be unwilling to go so far as to extend the right to a portion of the prosecutor's trial-preparation interviews with witnesses. Although photography is relatively new, the interviewing of witnesses before trial is a procedure that predates the Sixth Amendment. The traditional counterbalance in the American adversary system for these interviews arises from the equal ability of defense counsel to seek and interview witnesses himself.

That adversary mechanism remains as effective for a photographic display as for other parts of pretrial interviews. No greater limitations are placed on defense counsel in constructing displays, seeking witnesses, and conducting photographic identifications than those applicable to the prosecution. Selection of the picture of a person other than the accused, or the inability of a witness to make any selection, will be useful to the defense in precisely the same manner that the selection of a picture of the defendant would be useful to the prosecution. In this very case, for example, the initial tender of the photographic display was by Bailey's counsel, who sought to demonstrate that the witness had failed to make a photographic identification. Although we do not suggest that equality of access to photographs removes all potential for abuse, it does remove any inequality in the adversary process itself and thereby fully satisfies the historical spirit of the Sixth Amendment's counsel guarantee.

The argument has been advanced that requiring counsel might compel the police to observe more scientific procedures or might encourage them to utilize corporeal rather than photographic displays. This Court has recognized that improved procedures can minimize the dangers of suggestion.

Pretrial photographic identifications, however, are hardly unique in offering possibilities for the actions of the prosecutor unfairly to prejudice the accused. Evidence favorable to the accused may be withheld; testimony of witnesses may be manipulated; the results of laboratory tests may be contrived. In many ways, the prosecutor, by accident or by design, may improperly subvert the trial. The primary safeguard against abuses of this kind is the ethical responsibility of the prosecutor, who, as so often has been said, may "strike hard blows" but not "foul ones." If that safeguard fails, review remains available under due process standards. These same safeguards apply to misuse of photographs.

We are not persuaded that the risks inherent in the use of photographic displays are so pernicious that an extraordinary system of safeguards is required. We hold, then, that the Sixth Amendment does not grant the right to counsel at photographic displays conducted by the Government for the purpose of allowing a witness to attempt an identification of the offender.

JUSTICE STEWART, concurring in the judgment.

A photographic identification is quite different from a lineup, for there are substantially fewer possibilities of impermissible suggestion when photographs are used, and those unfair influences can be readily reconstructed at trial. It is true that the defendant's photograph may be markedly different from the others displayed, but this unfairness can be demonstrated at trial from an actual comparison of the photographs used or from the witness' description of the display. Similarly, it is possible that the photographs could be arranged in a suggestive manner, or that by comment or gesture the prosecuting authorities might single out the defendant's picture. But these are the kinds of overt influence that a witness can easily recount and that would serve to impeach the identification testimony. In short, there are few possibilities for unfair suggestiveness—and those rather blatant and easily reconstructed. Accordingly, an accused would not be foreclosed from an effective cross-examination of an identification witness simply because his counsel was not present at the photographic display. For this reason, a photographic display cannot fairly be considered a "critical stage" of the prosecution.

JUSTICE BRENNAN, with whom JUSTICE DOUGLAS and JUSTICE MARSHALL join, dissenting.

The Court holds today that a pretrial display of photographs to the witnesses of a crime for the purpose of identifying the accused, unlike a lineup, does not constitute a "critical stage" of the prosecution at which the accused is constitutionally entitled to the presence of counsel. In my view, today's decision is wholly unsupportable in terms of such considerations as logic, consistency, and, indeed, fairness. As a result, I must reluctantly conclude that today's decision marks simply another step towards the complete evisceration of the fundamental constitutional principles established by this Court, only six years ago, in *U.S. v. Wade*, 388 U.S. 218 (1967), *Gilbert v. California*, 388 U.S. 263 (1967), and *Stovall v. Denno*, 388 U.S. 293 (1967).

In essence, those decisions held (1) that a pretrial lineup is a "critical stage" in the criminal process at which the accused is constitutionally entitled to the presence of counsel; (2) that evidence of an identification of the accused at such an uncounseled lineup is *per se* inadmissible; and (3) that evidence of a subsequent in-court identification of the accused is likewise inadmissible unless the Government can demonstrate by clear and convincing evidence that the in-court identification was based upon observations of the accused independent of the prior uncounseled lineup identification. The considerations relied upon by the Court in reaching these conclusions are clearly applicable to photographic as well as corporeal identifications.

As the Court of Appeals recognized, "the dangers of mistaken identification set forth in *Wade* are applicable in large measure to photographic as well as corporeal identifications." To the extent that misidentification may be attributable to a witness' faulty memory or perception, or inadequate opportunity for detailed observation during the crime, the risks are obviously as great at a photographic display as at a lineup.

Moreover, as in the lineup situation, the possibilities for impermissible suggestion in the context of a photographic display are manifold. Such suggestion, intentional or unintentional, may derive from three possible sources. First, the photographs themselves might tend to suggest which of the pictures is that of the suspect. For example, differences in age, pose, or other physical characteristics of the persons represented, and variations in the mounting, background, lighting, or markings of the photographs all might have the effect of singling out the accused.

Second, impermissible suggestion may inhere in the manner in which the photographs are displayed to the witness. The danger of misidentification is, of course, increased if the police display to the witness the pictures of several persons among which the photograph of a single such individual recurs or is in some way emphasized. And, if the photographs are arranged in an asymmetrical pattern, or if they are displayed in a time sequence that tends to emphasize a particular photograph, any identification of the photograph which stands out from the rest is no more reliable than an identification of a single photograph, exhibited alone.

Third, gestures or comments of the prosecutor at the time of the display may lead an otherwise uncertain witness to select the "correct" photograph. For example, the prosecutor might indicate to the witness that he has other evidence that one of the persons pictured committed the crime, and might even point to a particular photograph and ask whether the person pictured looks familiar. More subtly, the prosecutor's inflection, facial expressions, physical motions, and myriad other almost imperceptible means of communication might tend, intentionally or unintentionally, to compromise the witness' objectivity. Thus, as is the case with lineups, improper photographic identification procedures, by exerting a suggestive influence upon the witnesses, can often lead to an erroneous identification. And regardless of how the initial misidentification comes about, the witness thereafter is apt to retain in his memory the image of the photograph rather than of the person actually seen. As a result, the issue of identity may (in the absence of other relevant evidence) for all practical purposes be determined there and then, before the trial.

Moreover, as with lineups, the defense can seldom reconstruct at trial the mode and manner of photographic identification. It is true, of course, that the photographs used at the pretrial display might be preserved for examination at trial. In reality, preservation of the photographs affords little protection to the unrepresented accused. For, although retention of the photographs may mitigate the dangers of misidentification due to the suggestiveness of the photographs themselves, it cannot in any sense reveal to defense counsel the more subtle, and therefore more dangerous, suggestiveness that might derive from the manner in which the photographs were displayed or any accompanying comments or gestures. Moreover, the accused cannot rely upon the witnesses themselves to expose these latter sources of suggestion, for the witnesses are not apt to be alert for conditions prejudicial to the suspect. And if they were, it would likely be of scant benefit to the suspect since the witnesses are hardly likely to be schooled in the detection of suggestive influences.

Finally, and unlike the lineup situation, the accused himself is not even present at the photographic identification, thereby reducing the likelihood that irregularities in the procedures will ever come to light. Thus, the difficulties of reconstructing at trial an uncounseled photographic display are at least equal to, and possibly greater than, those involved in reconstructing an uncounseled lineup.

Ironically, the Court does not seriously challenge the proposition that presence of counsel at a pretrial photographic display is essential to preserve the accused's right to a fair trial on the issue of identification.

Rather, in what I can only characterize as a triumph of form over substance, the Court seeks to justify its result by engrafting a wholly unprecedented—and wholly unsupportable—limitation on the Sixth Amendment right of the accused "to have the Assistance of Counsel for his defence." Although apparently conceding that the right to counsel attaches, not only at the trial itself, but at all "critical stages" of the prosecution, the Court holds today that, in order to be deemed "critical," the particular stage of the prosecution under consideration must, at the very least, involve the physical "presence of the accused," at a "trial-like confrontation" with the Government, at which the accused requires the "guiding hand of counsel." According to the Court, a pretrial photographic identification does not, of course, meet these criteria.

The fundamental premise underlying all of this Court's decisions holding the right to counsel applicable at "critical" pretrial proceedings, is that a "stage" of the prosecution must be deemed "critical" for the purposes of the Sixth Amendment if it is one at which the presence of counsel is necessary to protect the fairness of the trial itself. This established conception of the Sixth Amendment guarantee is, of course, in no sense dependent upon the physical "presence of the accused," at a "trial-like confrontation" with the Government, at which the accused requires the "guiding hand of counsel."

There is something ironic about the Court's conclusion today that a pretrial lineup identification is a "critical stage" of the prosecution because counsel's presence can help to compensate for the accused's deficiencies as an observer, but that a pretrial photographic identification is not a "critical stage" of the prosecution because the accused is not able to observe at all. In my view, there simply is no meaningful difference, in terms of the need for attendance of counsel, between corporeal and photographic identifications. And applying established and well-reasoned Sixth Amendment principles, I can only conclude that a pretrial photographic display, like a pretrial lineup, is a "critical stage" of the prosecution at which the accused is constitutionally entitled to the presence of counsel.

The Right to Counsel: Photo Arrays

A suspect is not entitled to have counsel present at a pretrial photographic identification, regardless of whether adversary judicial criminal proceedings have commenced.

C. DUE PROCESS PROTECTION DURING POLICE IDENTIFICATION PROCEDURES

Even if a suspect does not have a Sixth Amendment right to have counsel present at a pretrial identification procedure, he may still be able to successfully challenge the identification as unnecessarily suggestive, in violation of due process. The Supreme Court opened the door to such challenges in *Stovall v. Denno*, a case decided on the same day as *U.S. v. Wade* and *Gilbert v. California*.

STOVALL V. DENNO
388 U.S. 293 (1967)

Dr. Paul Behrendt was stabbed to death in the kitchen of his home. Dr. Behrendt's wife, also a physician, had followed her husband into the kitchen and jumped at the assailant. She was knocked to the floor and stabbed 11 times. Police found a shirt on the kitchen floor and keys in a pocket that they traced to Theodore Stovall. Police arrested him and an arraignment was promptly held, but was postponed until Stovall could retain counsel.

Mrs. Behrendt was hospitalized for major surgery to save her life. The police, without affording Stovall time to retain counsel, arranged with her surgeon to permit them to bring Stovall to her hospital room the day after the surgery. Stovall was handcuffed to one of five police officers who, with two members of the staff of the District Attorney, brought him to the hospital room. Stovall was the only African-American in the room. Mrs. Behrendt identified him from her hospital bed after being asked by an officer whether he "was the man" and after Stovall repeated at the direction of an officer a few words for voice identification. Mrs. Behrendt and the officers testified at the trial regarding her identification of Stovall in the hospital room, and she also made an in-court identification of Stovall. Stovall was convicted and sentenced to death.

On appeal, Stovall challenged the hospital room identification under the Sixth Amendment, claiming he was deprived of counsel during the confrontation. The Supreme Court held that its decisions in *U.S. v. Wade*, 388 U.S. 218 (1967), and *Gilbert v. California*, 388 U.S. 263 (1967), did not apply retroactively: "We hold that *Wade* and *Gilbert* affect only those cases and all future cases which involve confrontations for identification purposes conducted in the absence of counsel after this date. The rulings of *Wade* and *Gilbert* are therefore inapplicable in the present case."

The Supreme Court recognized, however, that Stovall could still challenge the hospital room identification if he could show, independent of his right to counsel claim, that the identification was "so unnecessarily suggestive and conducive to irreparable mistaken identification that he was denied due process of law." The Court noted that the "practice of showing suspects singly to persons for the purpose of identification, and not as part of a lineup, has been widely condemned." After considering the totality of the circumstances surrounding the identification, the Court concluded that although it was suggestive, it was also "imperative."

Quoting from the opinion of the lower court, the Supreme Court explained the necessity of using the suggestive hospital room showup:

> Here was the only person in the world who could possibly exonerate Stovall. [Mrs. Behrendt's] words, and only her words, "He is not the man," could have resulted in freedom for Stovall. The hospital was not far distant from the courthouse and jail. No one knew how long Mrs. Behrendt might live. Faced with the responsibility of identifying the attacker, with the need for immediate action and with the knowledge that Mrs. Behrendt could not visit the jail, the police followed the only feasible procedure and took Stovall to the hospital room. Under these circumstances, the usual police station line-up, which Stovall now argues he should have had, was out of the question.

Two years after *Stovall* was decided, in *Foster v. California*, the Supreme Court set aside a conviction because, under the totality of the circumstances, the lineup identification procedures were "so unnecessarily suggestive and conducive to irreparable mistaken identification" as to constitute a denial of due process.

FOSTER V. CALIFORNIA
394 U.S. 440 (1969)

JUSTICE FORTAS delivered the opinion of the Court.

Petitioner was charged by information with the armed robbery of a Western Union office. The day after the robbery, one of the robbers, Clay, surrendered to the police and implicated Foster and Grice. Allegedly, Foster and Clay had entered the office while Grice waited in a car. Foster and Grice were tried together. Grice was acquitted. Foster was convicted. We granted certiorari, limited to the question whether the conduct of the police lineup resulted in a violation of petitioner's constitutional rights.

Except for the robbers themselves, the only witness to the crime was Joseph David, the late-night manager of the Western Union office. After Foster had been arrested, David was called to the police station to view a lineup. There were three men in the lineup. One was petitioner. He is a tall man—close to six feet in height. The other two men were short—five feet, five or six inches. Petitioner wore a leather jacket which David said was similar to the one he had seen underneath the coveralls worn by the robber. After seeing this lineup, David could not positively identify petitioner as the robber. He "thought" he was the man, but he was not sure. David then asked to speak to petitioner, and petitioner was brought into an office and sat across from David at a table. Except for prosecuting officials there was no one else in the room. Even after this one-to-one confrontation, David still was uncertain whether petitioner was one of the robbers: "truthfully—I was not sure," he testified at trial. A week or 10 days later, the police arranged for David to view a second lineup. There were five men in that lineup. Petitioner was the only person in the second lineup who had appeared in the first lineup. This time David was "convinced" petitioner was the man.

At trial, David testified to his identification of petitioner in the lineups, as summarized above. He also repeated his identification of petitioner in the courtroom. The only other evidence against petitioner which concerned the particular robbery with which he was charged was the testimony of the alleged accomplice Clay.[1]

In *U.S. v. Wade*, 388 U.S. 218 (1967), and *Gilbert v. California*, 388 U.S. 263 (1967), this Court held that because of the possibility of unfairness to the accused in the way a lineup is conducted, a lineup is a "critical stage" in the prosecution, at which the accused must be given the opportunity to be represented by counsel. That holding does not, however, apply to petitioner's case, for the lineups in which he appeared occurred before June 12, 1967. *Stovall v. Denno*, 388 U.S. 293 (1967). But in declaring the rule of *Wade* and *Gilbert* to be applicable only to lineups conducted after those cases were decided, we recognized that, judged by the "totality of the circumstances," the conduct of identification procedures may be "so unnecessarily suggestive and conducive to irreparable mistaken identification" as to be a denial of due process of law.

Judged by that standard, this case presents a compelling example of unfair lineup procedures. In the first lineup arranged by the police, petitioner stood out from the other two men by the contrast of his height and by the fact that he was wearing a leather jacket similar to that worn by the robber. When this did not lead to positive identification, the police permitted a one-to-one confrontation between petitioner and the witness. This Court pointed out in *Stovall* that "the practice of showing suspects singly to persons for the purpose of identification, and not as part of a lineup, has been widely condemned." Even after this, the witness' identification of petitioner was tentative. So, some days later, another lineup was arranged. Petitioner was the only person in this lineup who had also participated in the first lineup. This finally produced a definite identification.

The suggestive elements in this identification procedure made it all but inevitable that David would identify petitioner whether or not he was, in fact, "the man." In effect, the police repeatedly said to the witness, "This is the man." This procedure so undermined the reliability of the eyewitness identification as to violate due process.

---

[1] California law requires that an accomplice's testimony be corroborated. There was also evidence that Foster had been convicted for a similar robbery committed six years before.

JUSTICE BLACK, dissenting.

The Court here directs the California courts to set aside petitioner Foster's conviction for armed robbery of the Western Union Telegraph Co. at Fresno, California. The night manager of the telegraph company testified before the court and jury that two men came into the office just after midnight, January 25, 1966, wrote a note telling him it was a holdup, put it under his face, and demanded money, flashed guns, took $531 and fled. The night manager identified Foster in the courtroom as one of the men, and he also related his identification of Foster in a lineup a week or so after the crime. The manager's evidence, which no witness disputed, was corroborated by the testimony of a man named Clay, who was Foster's accomplice in the robbery and who testified for the State. The testimony of these two eyewitnesses was also corroborated by proof that Foster and another person had committed a prior armed robbery of a Western Union office in another city six years before, when they appeared at the company's office, presented a note to an employee announcing their holdup, flashed a gun, and fled with company money. In this case, Foster's attorney admitted conviction for the prior Western Union armed robbery. The circumstances of the two robberies appear to have been practically indistinguishable. Such evidence that a particular person committed a prior crime has been almost universally accepted as relevant and admissible to prove that the same person was responsible for a later crime of the same nature. A narration of these facts, falling from the lips of eyewitnesses, and not denied by other eyewitnesses, would be enough, I am convinced, to persuade nearly all lawyers and judges, unhesitatingly to say, "There was clearly enough evidence of guilt here for a jury to convict the defendant since, according to practice, and indeed constitutional command, the weight of evidence is for a jury, and not for judges." Nevertheless the Court in this case looks behind the evidence given by witnesses on the stand and decides that, because of the circumstances under which one witness first identified the defendant as the criminal, the United States Constitution requires that the conviction be reversed. The Court, however, fails to spell out exactly what should happen to this defendant if there must be a retrial, and thus avoids the apparently distasteful task of specifying whether (1) at the new trial the jury would again be permitted to hear the eyewitness' testimony and the in-court identification, so long as he does not refer to the previous lineups, or (2) the eyewitness' "tainted" identification testimony must be entirely excluded, thus compelling Foster's acquittal. Objection to this ambiguity is the first of my reasons for dissent.

Far more fundamental, however, is my objection to the Court's basic holding that evidence can be ruled constitutionally inadmissible whenever it results from identification procedures that the Court considers to be "unnecessarily suggestive and conducive to irreparable mistaken identification." One of the proudest achievements of this country's Founders was that they had eternally guaranteed a trial by jury in criminal cases, at least until the Constitution they wrote had been amended in the manner they prescribed. Of course, it is an incontestable fact in our judicial history that the jury is the sole tribunal to weigh and determine facts. That means that the jury must, if we keep faith with the Constitution, be allowed to hear eyewitnesses and decide for itself whether it can recognize the truth and whether they are telling the truth. It means that the jury must be allowed to decide for itself whether the darkness of the night, the weakness of a witness' eyesight, or any other factor impaired the witness' ability to make an accurate identification. To take that power away from the jury is to rob it of the responsibility to perform the precise functions the Founders most wanted it to perform. And certainly a Constitution written to preserve this indispensable, unerodible core of our system for trying criminal cases would not have included, hidden among its provisions, a slumbering sleeper granting the judges license to destroy trial by jury in whole or in part.

Foster v. California marked the one and only time that the Supreme Court has overturned a conviction based on a due process challenge to an unnecessarily suggestive identification procedure. In other cases, the Court has clarified the requirements necessary to make out a due process challenge, and has consistently found that one or more of the requirements is lacking.

Collectively, the Supreme Court's decisions in this area make it clear that the inquiry into whether a pretrial identification procedure was "unnecessarily suggestive and conducive to irreparable mistaken identification" actually comprises four distinct elements. First, a criminal defendant must show that the identification procedure was suggestive. Second, the defendant must show that the suggestive aspects of the identification were arranged by law enforcement. Third, the defendant must show that the identification procedure was unnecessary. Finally, even if the first three elements have been proven, suppression of the identification is warranted only if the identification procedure created a substantial likelihood of misidentification, rendering the identification unreliable. The Supreme Court recently reviewed these requirements in *Perry v. New Hampshire*.

PERRY V. NEW HAMPSHIRE
132 S.Ct. 716 (2012)

The Nashua, New Hampshire Police Department received a call at around 3 a.m. reporting that a male African-American was trying to break into cars parked in the lot of the caller's apartment building. When an officer responding to the call asked eyewitness Nubia Blandon to describe the man, Blandon pointed to her kitchen window and said the man she saw breaking into the car was standing in the parking lot, next to another police officer. Barion Perry's arrest followed this identification. About one month later, the police showed Blandon a photographic array that included a picture of Perry and asked her to point out the man who had broken into the car. Blandon was unable to identify Perry.

Before trial, Perry moved to suppress Blandon's identification, claiming that its admission into evidence would violate due process. Perry argued that Blandon witnessed what amounted to a suggestive one-person showup in the parking lot, which all but guaranteed that she would identify him as the culprit.

In evaluating Perry's appeal, the Supreme Court explained the approach it uses to determine whether due process requires the suppression of an eyewitness identification tainted by police arrangement:

> [D]ue process concerns arise only when law enforcement officers use an identification procedure that is both suggestive and unnecessary. Even when the police use such a procedure, suppression of the resulting identification is not the inevitable consequence. A rule requiring automatic exclusion would go too far, for it would keep evidence from the jury that is reliable and relevant, and may result, on occasion, in the guilty going free. Instead of mandating a *per se* exclusionary rule, the Due Process Clause requires courts to assess, on a case-by-case basis, whether improper police conduct created a substantial likelihood of misidentification. Reliability of the eyewitness identification is the linchpin of that evaluation. Where the indicators of a witness' ability to make an accurate identification are outweighed by the corrupting effect of law enforcement suggestion, the identification should be suppressed. Otherwise, the evidence (if admissible in all other respects) should be submitted to the jury.

In a footnote, the Court listed the factors to be considered in evaluating a witness' ability to make an accurate identification:

> [T]he opportunity of the witness to view the criminal at the time of the crime, the witness' degree of attention, the accuracy of his prior description of the criminal, the level of certainty demonstrated at the confrontation, and the time between the crime and the confrontation.

In his motion to suppress, Perry had asked the trial court to prescreen Blandon's identification for reliability, applying the factors above. The Supreme Court held that the trial court was correct in declining to do so because Perry had failed to show that the police had done anything improper to rig the identification procedure:

> We have not extended pretrial screening for reliability to cases in which the suggestive circumstances were not arranged by law enforcement officers. Petitioner requests that we do so because of the grave risk that mistaken identification will yield a miscarriage of justice. Our decisions, however, turn on the presence of state action and aim to deter police from rigging identification procedures, for example, at a lineup, showup, or photograph array. When no improper law enforcement activity is involved, we hold, it suffices to test reliability through the rights and opportunities generally designed for that purpose, notably, the presence of counsel at postindictment lineups, vigorous cross-examination, protective rules of evidence, and jury instructions on both the fallibility of eyewitness identification and the requirement that guilt be proved beyond a reasonable doubt.

In *Simmons v. U.S.*, the Supreme Court concluded that although a photographic identification was suggestive, it was necessary and did not likely result in a misidentification. Accordingly, the Court rejected the defendant's due process challenge.

SIMMONS V. U.S.
390 U.S. 377 (1968)

JUSTICE HARLAN delivered the opinion of the Court.

This case presents issues arising out of the petitioners' trial and conviction in the United States District Court for the Northern District of Illinois for the armed robbery of a federally insured savings and loan association.

The evidence at trial showed that at about 1:45 p.m. on February 27, 1964, two men entered a Chicago savings and loan association. One of them pointed a gun at a teller and ordered her to put money into a sack which the gunman supplied. The men remained in the bank about five minutes. After they left, a bank employee rushed to the street and saw one of the men sitting on the passenger side of a departing white 1960 Thunderbird automobile with a large scrape on the right door. Within an hour, police located in the vicinity a car matching this description. They discovered that it belonged to a Mrs. Rey, sister-in-law of petitioner Simmons. She told the police that she had loaned the car for the afternoon to her brother, William Andrews.

At about 5:15 p.m. the same day, two FBI agents came to the house of Mrs. Mahon, Andrews' mother, about half a block from the place where the car was then parked. The agents had no warrant, and at trial it was disputed whether Mrs. Mahon gave them permission to search the house. They did search, and in the basement they found two suitcases, of which Mrs. Mahon disclaimed any knowledge. One suitcase contained, among other items, a gun holster, a sack similar to the one used in the robbery, and several coin cards and bill wrappers from the bank which had been robbed.

The following morning, the FBI obtained from another of Andrews' sisters some snapshots of Andrews and of petitioner Simmons, who was said by the sister to have been with Andrews the previous afternoon. These snapshots were shown to the five bank employees who had witnessed the robbery. Each witness identified pictures of Simmons as representing one of the robbers. A week or two later, three of these employees identified photographs of petitioner Garrett as depicting the other robber, the other two witnesses stating that they did not have a clear view of the second robber.

The petitioners, together with William Andrews, subsequently were indicted and tried for the robbery, as indicated. During the trial, all five bank employee witnesses identified Simmons as one of the robbers. Three of them identified Garrett as the second robber, the other two testifying that they did not get a good look at the second robber. The jury found Simmons and Garrett, as well as Andrews, guilty as charged.

The facts as to the identification claim are these. As has been noted previously, FBI agents on the day following the robbery obtained from Andrews' sister a number of snapshots of Andrews and Simmons. There seem to have been at least six of these pictures, consisting mostly of group photographs of Andrews, Simmons, and others. Later the same day, these were shown to the five bank employees who had witnessed the robbery at their place of work, the photographs being exhibited to each employee separately. Each of the five employees identified Simmons from the photographs. At later dates, some of these witnesses were again interviewed by the FBI and shown indeterminate numbers of pictures. Again, all identified Simmons. At trial, the Government did not introduce any of the photographs, but relied upon in-court identification by the five eyewitnesses, each of whom swore that Simmons was one of the robbers.

In support of his argument, Simmons looks to last Term's "lineup" decisions—*U.S. v. Wade*, 388 U.S. 218 (1967), and *Gilbert v. California*, 388 U.S. 263 (1967)—in which this Court first departed from the rule that the manner of an extra-judicial identification affects only the weight, not the admissibility, of identification testimony at trial. The rationale of those cases was that an accused is entitled to counsel at any "critical stage of the prosecution," and that a post-indictment lineup is such a "critical stage." Simmons, however, does not contend that he was entitled to counsel at the time the pictures were shown to the witnesses. Rather, he asserts simply that, in the circumstances, the identification procedure was so unduly prejudicial as fatally to taint his conviction. This is a claim which must be evaluated in light of the totality of surrounding circumstances. Viewed in that context, we find the claim untenable.

It must be recognized that improper employment of photographs by police may sometimes cause witnesses to err in identifying criminals. A witness may have obtained only a brief glimpse of a criminal, or may have seen him under poor conditions. Even if the police subsequently follow the most correct photographic identification procedures and show him the pictures of a number of individuals without indicating whom they suspect, there is some danger that the witness may make an incorrect identification. This danger will be increased if the police display to the witness only the picture of a single individual who generally resembles the person he saw, or if they show him the pictures of several persons among which the photograph of a single such individual recurs or is in some way emphasized. The chance of misidentification is also heightened if the police indicate to the witness that they have other evidence that one of the persons pictured committed the crime. Regardless of how the initial misidentification comes about, the witness thereafter is apt to retain in his memory the image of the photograph rather than of the person actually seen, reducing the trustworthiness of subsequent lineup or courtroom identification.

Despite the hazards of initial identification by photograph, this procedure has been used widely and effectively in criminal law enforcement, from the standpoint both of apprehending offenders and of sparing innocent suspects the ignominy of arrest by allowing eyewitnesses to exonerate them through scrutiny of photographs. The danger that use of the technique may result in convictions based on misidentification may be substantially lessened by a course of cross-examination at trial which exposes to the jury the method's potential for error. We are unwilling to prohibit its employment, either in the exercise of our supervisory power or, still less, as a matter of constitutional requirement. Instead, we hold that each case must be considered on its own facts, and that convictions based on eyewitness identification at trial following a pretrial identification by photograph will be set aside on that ground only if the photographic identification procedure was so impermissibly suggestive as to give rise to a very substantial likelihood of irreparable misidentification.

Applying the standard to this case, we conclude that petitioner Simmons' claim on this score must fail. In the first place, it is not suggested that it was unnecessary for the FBI to resort to photographic identification in this instance. A serious felony had been committed. The perpetrators were still at large. The inconclusive clues which law enforcement officials possessed led to Andrews and Simmons. It was essential for the FBI agents swiftly to determine whether they were on the right track, so that they could properly deploy their forces in Chicago and, if necessary, alert officials in other cities. The justification for this method of procedure was hardly less compelling than that which we found to justify the "one-man lineup" in *Stovall v. Denno*, 388 U.S. 293 (1967).

In the second place, there was in the circumstances of this case little chance that the procedure utilized led to misidentification of Simmons. The robbery took place in the afternoon in a well-lighted bank. The robbers wore no masks. Five bank employees had been able to see the robber later identified as Simmons for periods ranging up to five minutes. Those witnesses were shown the photographs only a day later, while their memories were still fresh. At least six photographs were displayed to each witness. Apparently, these consisted primarily of group photographs, with Simmons and Andrews each appearing several times in the series. Each witness was alone when he or she saw the photographs. There is no evidence to indicate that the witnesses were told anything about the progress of the investigation, or that the FBI agents in any other way suggested which persons in the pictures were under suspicion.

Under these conditions, all five eyewitnesses identified Simmons as one of the robbers. None identified Andrews, who apparently was as prominent in the photographs as Simmons. These initial identifications were confirmed by all five witnesses in subsequent viewings of photographs and at trial, where each witness identified Simmons in person. Notwithstanding cross-examination, none of the witnesses displayed any doubt about their respective identifications of Simmons. Taken together, these circumstances leave little room for doubt that the identification of Simmons was correct, even though the identification procedure employed may have in some respects fallen short of the ideal. We hold that, in the factual surroundings of this case, the identification procedure used was not such as to deny Simmons due process of law or to call for reversal under our supervisory authority.

In *Neil v. Biggers*, the Supreme Court examined a number of factors—the opportunity of the witness to view the criminal at the time of the crime, the witness' degree of attention, the accuracy of the witness' prior description of the criminal, the level of certainty demonstrated by the witness at the confrontation, and the length of time between the crime and the confrontation—and concluded that the identification was reliable even though the police-arranged showup was suggestive.

NEIL v. BIGGERS

409 U.S. 188 (1972)

JUSTICE POWELL delivered the opinion of the Court.

In 1965, after a jury trial in a Tennessee court, respondent was convicted of rape and was sentenced to 20 years' imprisonment. The State's evidence consisted in part of testimony concerning a station-house identification of respondent by the victim. We granted certiorari to decide whether the identification procedure violated due process.

The victim testified at trial that on the evening of January 22, 1965, a youth with a butcher knife grabbed her in the doorway to her kitchen:

A. He grabbed me from behind, and grappled-twisted me on the floor. Threw me down on the floor.

Q. And there was no light in that kitchen?

A. Not in the kitchen.

Q. So you couldn't have seen him then?

A. Yet, I could see him, when I looked up in his face.

Q. In the dark?

A. He was right in the doorway—it was enough light from the bedroom shining through. Yes, I could see who he was.

Q. You could see? No light? And you could see him and know him then?

A. Yes.

When the victim screamed, her 12-year-old daughter came out of her bedroom and also began to scream. The assailant directed the victim to "tell her (the daughter) to shut up, or I'll kill you both." She did so, and was then walked at knifepoint about two blocks along a railroad track, taken into a woods, and raped there. She testified that "the moon was shining brightly, full moon." After the rape, the assailant ran off, and she returned home, the whole incident having taken between 15 minutes and half an hour.

She then gave the police what the Federal District Court characterized as "only a very general description," describing him as "being fat and flabby with smooth skin, bushy hair and a youthful voice." Additionally, though not mentioned by the District Court, she testified at the habeas corpus hearing that she had described her assailant as being between 16 and 18 years old and between five feet ten inches and six feet tall, as weighing between 180 and 200 pounds, and as having a dark brown complexion. This testimony was substantially corroborated by that of a police officer who was testifying from his notes.

On several occasions over the course of the next seven months, she viewed suspects in her home or at the police station, some in lineups and others in showups, and was shown between 30 and 40 photographs. She told the police that a man pictured in one of the photographs had features similar to those of her assailant, but identified none of the suspects. On August 17, the police called her to the station to view respondent, who was being detained on another charge. In an effort to construct a suitable lineup, the police checked the city jail and the city juvenile home. Finding no one at either place fitting respondent's unusual physical description, they conducted a showup instead.

The showup itself consisted of two detectives walking respondent past the victim. At the victim's request, the police directed respondent to say "shut up or I'll kill you." The testimony at trial was not altogether clear as to whether the victim first identified him and then asked that he repeat the words or made her identification after he had spoken. In any event, the victim testified that she had "no doubt" about her identification. At the habeas corpus hearing, she elaborated in response to questioning.

A.   That I have no doubt, I mean that I am sure that when I— see, when I first laid eyes on him, I knew that it was the individual, because his face—well, there was just something that I don't think I could ever forget. I believe—

Q.   You say when you first laid eyes on him, which time are you referring to?

A.   When I identified him—when I seen him in the courthouse when I was took up to view the suspect.

We must decide whether, as the courts below held, this identification and the circumstances surrounding it failed to comport with due process requirements. Some general guidelines emerge from [our prior] cases as to the relationship between suggestiveness and misidentification. It is, first of all, apparent that the primary evil to be avoided is "a very substantial likelihood of irreparable misidentification." While the phrase was coined as a standard for determining whether an in-court identification would be admissible in the wake of a suggestive out-of-court identification, with the deletion of "irreparable" it serves equally well as a standard for the admissibility of testimony concerning the out-of-court identification itself. It is the likelihood of misidentification which violates a defendant's right to due process. Suggestive confrontations are disapproved because they increase the likelihood of misidentification, and unnecessarily suggestive ones are condemned for the further reason that the increased chance of misidentification is gratuitous.

What is less clear from our cases is whether unnecessary suggestiveness alone requires the exclusion of evidence. While we are inclined to agree with the courts below that the police did not exhaust all possibilities in seeking persons physically comparable to respondent, we do not think that the evidence must therefore be excluded. The purpose of a strict rule barring evidence of unnecessarily suggestive confrontations would be to deter the police from using a less reliable procedure where a more reliable one may be available, and would not be based on the assumption that in every instance the admission of evidence of such a confrontation offends due process.

We turn, then, to the central question, whether under the "totality of the circumstances" the identification was reliable even though the confrontation procedure was suggestive. As indicated by our cases, the factors to be considered in evaluating the likelihood of misidentification include the opportunity of the witness to view the criminal at the time of the crime, the witness' degree of attention, the accuracy of the witness' prior description of the criminal, the level of certainty demonstrated by the witness at the confrontation, and the length of time between the crime and the confrontation.

We find that the District Court's conclusions on the critical facts are unsupported by the record and clearly erroneous. The victim spent a considerable period of time with her assailant, up to half an hour. She was with him under adequate artificial light in her house and under a full moon outdoors, and at least twice, once in the house and later in the woods, faced him directly and intimately. She was no casual observer, but rather the victim of one of the most personally humiliating of all crimes. Her description to the police, which included the assailant's approximate age, height, weight, complexion, skin texture, build, and voice, was more than ordinarily thorough. She had "no doubt" that respondent was the person who raped her. In the nature of the crime, there are rarely witnesses to a rape other than the victim, who often has a limited opportunity of observation. The victim here, a practical nurse by profession, had an unusual opportunity to observe and identify her assailant. She testified at the habeas corpus hearing that there was something about his face "I don't think I could ever forget."

There was, to be sure, a lapse of seven months between the rape and the confrontation. This would be a seriously negative factor in most cases. Here, however, the testimony is undisputed that the victim made no previous identification at any of the showups, lineups, or photographic showings. Her record for reliability was thus a good one, as she had previously resisted whatever suggestiveness inheres in a showup. Weighing all the factors, we find no substantial likelihood of misidentification. The evidence was properly allowed to go to the jury.

JUSTICE BRENNAN, with whom JUSTICE DOUGLAS and JUSTICE MARSHALL join, dissenting in part.

As the Court recognizes, a pre-*Stovall* identification obtained as a result of an unnecessarily suggestive showup may still be introduced in evidence if, under the "totality of the circumstances," the identification retains strong indicia of reliability. After an extensive hearing and careful review of the state court record, however, the District Court found that, under the circumstances of this case, there existed an intolerable risk of misidentification. Moreover, in making this determination, the court specifically found that "the complaining witness did not get an opportunity to obtain a good view of the suspect during the commission of the crime," "the show-up confrontation was not conducted near the time of the alleged crime, but, rather, some seven months after its commission," and the complaining witness was unable to give "a good physical description of her assailant" to the police. The Court of Appeals, which conducted its own review of the record, upheld the District Court's findings in their entirety.

Even a cursory examination of the Court's opinion reveals that its concern is not limited solely to the proper application of legal principles but, rather, extends to an essentially *de novo* inquiry into such "elemental facts" as the nature of the victim's opportunity to observe the assailant and the type of description the victim gave the police at the time of the crime. And although we might reasonably disagree with the lower courts' findings as to such matters, [we should not be] cavalierly substituting our own view of the facts simply because we might adopt a different construction of the evidence or resolve the ambiguities differently.

In *Manson v. Brathwaite*, a photographic identification was both suggestive and unnecessary. The Supreme Court concluded, however, that the identification did not need to be suppressed because it was reliable despite the suggestive influences.

MANSON V. BRATHWAITE
432 U.S. 98 (1977)

JUSTICE BLACKMUN delivered the opinion of the Court.

This case presents the issue as to whether the Due Process Clause of the Fourteenth Amendment compels the exclusion, in a state criminal trial, apart from any consideration of reliability, of pretrial identification evidence obtained by a police procedure that was both suggestive and unnecessary.

I

Jimmy D. Glover, a full-time trooper of the Connecticut State Police, in 1970 was assigned to the Narcotics Division in an undercover capacity. On May 5 of that year, about 7:45 p.m., and while there was still daylight, Glover and Henry Alton Brown, an informant, went to an apartment building at 201 Westland, in Hartford, for the purpose of purchasing narcotics from "Dickie Boy" Cicero, a known narcotics dealer. Cicero, it was thought, lived on the third floor of that apartment building. Glover and Brown entered the building, observed by back-up Officers D'Onofrio and Gaffey, and proceeded by stairs to the third floor. Glover knocked at the door of one of the two apartments served by the stairway. The area was illuminated by natural light from a window in the third floor hallway. The door was opened 12 to 18 inches in response to the knock. Glover observed a man standing at the door and, behind him, a woman. Brown identified himself. Glover then asked for "two things" of narcotics. The man at the door held out his hand, and Glover gave him two $10 bills. The door closed. Soon the man returned and handed Glover two glassine bags. While the door was open, Glover stood within two feet of the person from whom he made the purchase and observed his face. Five to seven minutes elapsed from the time the door first opened until it closed the second time.

Glover and Brown then left the building. This was about eight minutes after their arrival. Glover drove to headquarters where he described the seller to D'Onofrio and Gaffey. Glover at that time did not know the identity of the seller. He described him as being "a colored man, approximately five feet eleven inches tall, dark complexion, black hair, short Afro style, and having high cheekbones, and of heavy build. He was wearing at the time blue pants and a plaid shirt." D'Onofrio, suspecting from this description that respondent might be the seller, obtained a photograph of respondent from the Records Division of the Hartford Police Department. He left it at Glover's office. D'Onofrio was not acquainted with respondent personally but did know him by sight and had seen him "several times" prior to May 5. Glover, when alone, viewed the photograph for the first time upon his return to headquarters on May 7; he identified the person shown as the one from whom he had purchased the narcotics.

The toxicological report on the contents of the glassine bags revealed the presence of heroin. The report was dated July 16, 1970.

Respondent was arrested on July 27 while visiting at the apartment of a Mrs. Ramsey on the third floor of 201 Westland. This was the apartment at which the narcotics sale had taken place on May 5.

Respondent was charged, in a two-count information, with possession and sale of heroin. At his trial in January 1971, the photograph from which Glover had identified respondent was received in evidence without objection on the part of the defense. Glover also testified that, although he had not seen respondent in the eight months that had elapsed since the sale, "there was no doubt whatsoever" in his mind that the person shown on the photograph was respondent. Glover also made a positive in-court identification without objection. No explanation was offered by the prosecution for the failure to utilize a photographic array or to conduct a lineup.

Respondent, who took the stand in his own defense, testified that on May 5, the day in question, he had been ill at his Albany Avenue apartment and that at no time on that particular day had he been at 201 Westland. His wife testified that she recalled, after her husband had refreshed her memory, that he was home all day on May 5.

The jury found respondent guilty on both counts of the information. He received a sentence of not less than six nor more than nine years.

III

In the present case the District Court observed that the "sole evidence tying Brathwaite to the possession and sale of the heroin consisted in his identifications by the police undercover agent, Jimmy Glover." On the constitutional issue, the court stated that the first inquiry was whether the police used an impermissibly suggestive procedure in obtaining the out-of-court identification. If so, the second inquiry is whether, under all the circumstances, that suggestive procedure gave rise to a substantial likelihood of irreparable misidentification.

IV

Petitioner at the outset acknowledges that "the procedure in the instant case was suggestive (because only one photograph was used) and unnecessary" (because there was no emergency or exigent circumstance). The respondent, in agreement with the Court of Appeals, proposes a *per se* rule of exclusion that he claims is dictated by the demands of the Fourteenth Amendment's guarantee of due process.

Since the decision in *Neil v. Biggers*, 409 U.S. 188 (1972), the Courts of Appeals appear to have developed at least two approaches to [identification] evidence. The first, or *per se* approach, employed by the Second Circuit in the present case, focuses on the procedures employed and requires exclusion of the out-of-court identification evidence, without regard to reliability, whenever it has been obtained through unnecessarily suggested confrontation procedures. The justifications advanced are the elimination of evidence of uncertain reliability, deterrence of the police and prosecutors, and the stated "fair assurance against the awful risks of misidentification."

The second, or more lenient, approach is one that continues to rely on the totality of the circumstances. It permits the admission of the confrontation evidence if, despite the suggestive aspect, the out-of-court identification possesses certain features of reliability.

The respondent here stresses the need for deterrence of improper identification practice, a factor he regards as pre-eminent. Photographic identification, it is said, continues to be needlessly employed. He argues that a totality rule cannot be expected to have a significant deterrent impact; only a strict rule of exclusion will have direct and immediate impact on law enforcement agents. Identification evidence is so convincing to the jury that sweeping exclusionary rules are required. Fairness of the trial is threatened by suggestive confrontation evidence, and thus, it is said, an exclusionary rule has an established constitutional predicate.

The driving force behind *U.S. v. Wade*, 388 U.S. 218 (1967), *Gilbert v. California*, 388 U.S. 263 (1967), and *Stovall v. Denno*, 388 U.S. 293 (1967), all decided on the same day, was the Court's concern with the problems of eyewitness identification. Usually the witness must testify about an encounter with a total stranger under circumstances of emergency or emotional stress. The witness' recollection of the stranger can be distorted easily by the circumstances or by later actions of the police. Thus, *Wade* and its companion cases reflect the concern that the jury not hear eyewitness testimony unless that evidence has aspects of reliability. The *per se* rule, however, goes too far, since its application automatically and peremptorily, and without consideration of alleviating factors, keeps evidence from the jury that is reliable and relevant.

The second factor is deterrence. Although the *per se* approach has the more significant deterrent effect, the totality approach also has an influence on police behavior. The police will guard against unnecessarily suggestive procedures under the totality rule, as well as the *per se* one, for fear that their actions will lead to the exclusion of identifications as unreliable.

The third factor is the effect on the administration of justice. Here, the *per se* approach suffers serious drawbacks. Since it denies the trier reliable evidence, it may result, on occasion, in the guilty going free. Also, because of its rigidity, the *per se* approach may make error by the trial judge more likely than the totality approach. And in those cases in which the admission of identification evidence is error under the *per se* approach but not under the totality approach—cases in which the identification is reliable despite an unnecessarily suggestive identification procedure— reversal is a Draconian sanction.

The standard, after all, is that of fairness as required by the Due Process Clause of the Fourteenth Amendment. *Stovall*, with its reference to "the totality of the circumstances," and *Biggers*, with its continuing stress on the same totality, did not, singly or together, establish a strict exclusionary rule or new standard of due process.

We therefore conclude that reliability is the linchpin in determining the admissibility of identification testimony. The factors to be considered are set out in *Biggers*. These include the opportunity of the witness to view the criminal at the time of the crime, the witness' degree of attention, the accuracy of his prior description of the criminal, the level of certainty demonstrated at the confrontation, and the time between the crime and the confrontation. Against these factors is to be weighed the corrupting effect of the suggestive identification itself.

V

We turn, then, to the facts of this case and apply the analysis:

1. The opportunity to view. Glover testified that for two to three minutes he stood at the apartment door, within two feet of the respondent. The door opened twice, and each time the man stood at the door. The moments passed, the conversation took place, and payment was made. Glover looked directly at his vendor. It was near sunset, to be sure, but the sun had not yet set, so it was not dark or even dusk or twilight. Natural light from outside entered the hallway through a window. There was natural light, as well, from inside the apartment.

2. The degree of attention. Glover was not a casual or passing observer, as is so often the case with eyewitness identification. Trooper Glover was a trained police officer on duty—and specialized and dangerous duty—when he called at the third floor of 201 Westland in Hartford on May 5, 1970. Glover himself was a Negro and unlikely to perceive only general features of "hundreds of Hartford black males," as the Court of Appeals stated. It is true that Glover's duty was that of ferreting out narcotics offenders and that he would be expected in his work to produce results. But it is also true that, as a specially trained, assigned, and experienced officer, he could be expected to pay scrupulous attention to detail, for he knew that subsequently he would have to find and arrest his vendor. In addition, he knew that his claimed observations would be subject later to close scrutiny and examination at any trial.

3. The accuracy of the description. Glover's description was given to D'Onofrio within minutes after the transaction. It included the vendor's race, his height, his build, the color and style of his hair, and the high cheekbone facial feature. It also included clothing the vendor wore. No claim has been made that respondent did not possess the physical characteristics so described. D'Onofrio reacted positively at once. Two days later, when Glover was alone, he viewed the photograph D'Onofrio produced and identified its subject as the narcotics seller.

4. The witness' level of certainty. There is no dispute that the photograph in question was that of respondent. Glover, in response to a question whether the photograph was that of the person from whom he made the purchase, testified: "There is no question whatsoever." This positive assurance was repeated.

5. The time between the crime and the confrontation. Glover's description of his vendor was given to D'Onofrio within minutes of the crime. The photographic identification took place only two days later. We

do not have here the passage of weeks or months between the crime and the viewing of the photograph.

These indicators of Glover's ability to make an accurate identification are hardly outweighed by the corrupting effect of the challenged identification itself. Although identifications arising from single-photograph displays may be viewed in general with suspicion, we find in the instant case little pressure on the witness to acquiesce in the suggestion that such a display entails. D'Onofrio had left the photograph at Glover's office and was not present when Glover first viewed it two days after the event. There thus was little urgency and Glover could view the photograph at his leisure. And since Glover examined the photograph alone, there was no coercive pressure to make an identification arising from the presence of another. The identification was made in circumstances allowing care and reflection.

Although it plays no part in our analysis, all this assurance as to the reliability of the identification is hardly undermined by the facts that respondent was arrested in the very apartment where the sale had taken place, and that he acknowledged his frequent visits to that apartment.

Surely, we cannot say that under all the circumstances of this case there is "a very substantial likelihood of irreparable misidentification." Short of that point, such evidence is for the jury to weigh. We are content to rely upon the good sense and judgment of American juries, for evidence with some element of untrustworthiness is customary grist for the jury mill. Juries are not so susceptible that they cannot measure intelligently the weight of identification testimony that has some questionable feature.

Of course, it would have been better had D'Onofrio presented Glover with a photographic array including a reasonable number of persons. The use of that procedure would have enhanced the force of the identification at trial and would have avoided the risk that the evidence would be excluded as unreliable. But we are not disposed to view D'Onofrio's failure as one of constitutional dimension to be enforced by a rigorous and unbending exclusionary rule. The defect, if there be one, goes to weight and not to substance.

JUSTICE MARSHALL, with whom JUSTICE BRENNAN joins, dissenting.

Today's decision can come as no surprise to those who have been watching the Court dismantle the protections against mistaken eyewitness testimony erected a decade ago in *Wade*, *Gilbert*, and *Stovall*. But it is still distressing to see the Court virtually ignore the teaching of experience embodied in those decisions and blindly uphold the conviction of a defendant who may well be innocent.

The Court weighs three factors in deciding that the totality approach, which is essentially the test used in *Biggers*, should be applied. In my view, the Court wrongly evaluates the impact of these factors.

First, the Court acknowledges that one of the factors, deterrence of police use of unnecessarily suggestive identification procedures, favors the *per se* rule. Indeed, it does so heavily, for such a rule would make it unquestionably clear to the police they must never use a suggestive procedure when a fairer alternative is available. I have no doubt that conduct would quickly conform to the rule.

Second, the Court gives passing consideration to the dangers of eyewitness identification recognized in the *Wade* trilogy. It concludes, however, that the grave risk of error does not justify adoption of the *per se* approach because that would too often result in exclusion of relevant evidence. In my view, this conclusion totally ignores the lessons of *Wade*. The dangers of mistaken identification are simply too great to permit unnecessarily suggestive identifications. Neither *Biggers* nor the Court's opinion today points to any contrary empirical evidence. Studies since *Wade* have only reinforced the validity of its assessment of the dangers of identification testimony. While the Court is "content to rely on the good sense and judgment of American juries," the impetus for *Stovall* and *Wade* was repeated miscarriages of justice resulting from juries' willingness to credit inaccurate eyewitness testimony.

Finally, the Court errs in its assessment of the relative impact of the two approaches on the administration of justice. The Court relies most heavily on this factor, finding that "reversal is a Draconian sanction" in cases where the identification is reliable despite an unnecessarily suggestive procedure used to obtain it. Relying on little more than a strong distaste for "inflexible rules of exclusion," the Court rejects the *per se* test. In so doing, the Court disregards two significant distinctions between the *per se* rule advocated in this case and the exclusionary remedies for certain other constitutional violations.

First, the *per se* rule here is not "inflexible." Where evidence is suppressed, for example, as the fruit of an unlawful search, it may well be forever lost to the prosecution. Identification evidence, however, can by its very nature be readily and effectively reproduced. The in-court identification, permitted under *Wade* and *Simmons* if it has a source independent of an uncounseled or suggestive procedure, is one example. Similarly, when a prosecuting attorney learns that there has been a suggestive confrontation, he can easily arrange another lineup conducted under scrupulously fair conditions. Since the same factors are evaluated in applying both the Court's totality test and the *Wade-Simmons* independent-source inquiry, any identification which is "reliable" under the Court's test will support admission of evidence concerning such a fairly conducted lineup. The evidence of an additional, properly conducted confrontation will be more persuasive to a jury, thereby increasing the chance of a justified conviction where a reliable identification was tainted by a suggestive confrontation. At the same time, however, the effect of an unnecessarily suggestive identification which has no value whatsoever in the law enforcement process will be completely eliminated.

Second, other exclusionary rules have been criticized for preventing jury consideration of relevant and usually reliable evidence in order to serve interests unrelated to guilt or innocence, such as discouraging illegal searches or denial of counsel. Suggestively obtained eyewitness testimony is excluded, in contrast, precisely because of its unreliability and concomitant irrelevance. Its exclusion both protects the integrity of the truth-seeking function of the trial and discourages police use of needlessly inaccurate and ineffective investigatory methods.

Indeed, impermissibly suggestive identifications are not merely worthless law enforcement tools. They pose a grave threat to society at large in a more direct way than most governmental disobedience of the law. For if the police and the public erroneously conclude, on the basis of an unnecessarily suggestive confrontation, that the right man has been caught and convicted, the real outlaw must still remain at large. Law enforcement has failed in its primary function and has left society unprotected from the depredations of an active criminal.

For these reasons, I conclude that adoption of the *per se* rule would enhance, rather than detract from, the effective administration of justice. In my view, the Court's totality test will allow seriously unreliable and misleading evidence to be put before juries. Equally important, it will allow dangerous criminals to remain on the streets while citizens assume that police action has given them protection. According to my calculus, all three of the factors upon which the Court relies point to acceptance of the *per se* approach.

Even more disturbing than the Court's reliance on the totality test, however, is the analysis it uses, which suggests a reinterpretation of the concept of due process of law in criminal cases. The decision suggests that due process violations in identification procedures may not be measured by whether the government employed procedures violating standards of fundamental fairness. By relying on the probable accuracy of a challenged identification, instead of the necessity for its use, the Court seems to be ascertaining whether the defendant was probably guilty. Until today, I had though that "Equal justice under law" meant that the existence of constitutional violations did not depend on the race, sex, religion, nationality, or likely guilt of the accused. The Due Process Clause requires adherence to the same high standard of fundamental fairness in dealing with every criminal defendant, whatever his personal characteristics and irrespective of the strength of the State's case against him. Strong evidence that the defendant is guilty should be relevant only to the determination whether an error of constitutional magnitude was nevertheless harmless beyond a reasonable doubt. By importing the question of guilt into the initial determination of whether there was a constitutional violation, the apparent effect of the Court's decision is to undermine the protection afforded by the Due Process Clause.

By displaying a single photograph of respondent to the witness Glover under the circumstances in this record, almost everything that could have been done wrong was done wrong. In the first place, there was no need to use a photograph at all. Because photos are static, two-dimensional, and often outdated, they are clearly inferior in reliability to corporeal procedures. While the use of photographs is justifiable and often essential where the police have no knowledge of an offender's identity, the poor reliability of photos makes their use inexcusable where any other means of identification is available. Here, since Detective D'Onofrio believed that he knew the seller's identity, further investigation without resort to a photographic showup was easily possible. With little inconvenience, a corporeal lineup including Brathwaite might have been arranged. Properly conducted, such a procedure would have gone far to remove any doubt about the fairness and accuracy of the identification.

Worse still than the failure to use an easily available corporeal identification was the display to Glover of only a single picture, rather than a photo array. With good reason, such single-suspect procedures have been widely condemned. They give no assurance that the witness can identify the criminal from among a number of persons of similar appearance, surely the strongest evidence that there was no misidentification.

The use of a single picture (or the display of a single live suspect, for that matter) is a grave error, of course, because it dramatically suggests to the witness that the person shown must be the culprit. Why else would the police choose the person? And it is deeply ingrained in human nature to agree with the expressed opinions of others—particularly others who should be more knowledgeable—when making a difficult decision. In this case, moreover, the pressure was not limited to that inherent in the display of a single photograph. Glover, the identifying witness, was a state police officer on special assignment. He knew that D'Onofrio, an experienced Hartford narcotics detective, presumably familiar with local drug operations, believed respondent to be the seller. There was at work, then, both loyalty to another police officer and deference to a better-informed colleague. Finally, of course, there was Glover's knowledge that without an identification and arrest, government funds used to buy heroin had been wasted.

The Court discounts this overwhelming evidence of suggestiveness, however. It reasons that because D'Onofrio was not present when Glover viewed the photograph, there was "little pressure on the witness to acquiesce in the suggestion." That conclusion blinks psychological reality. There is no doubt in my mind that even in D'Onofrio's absence, a clear and powerful message was telegraphed to Glover as he looked at respondent's photograph. He was emphatically told that "this is the man," and he responded by identifying respondent then and at trial whether or not he was in fact "the man."

I must conclude that this record presents compelling evidence that there was "a very substantial likelihood of misidentification" of respondent Brathwaite. The suggestive display of respondent's photograph to the witness Glover likely erased any independent memory that Glover had retained of the seller from his barely adequate opportunity to observe the criminal.

The cases excerpted above illustrate the various grounds upon which the Supreme Court has generally rejected due process challenges to identification procedures. The Court has been willing to acknowledge that there are suggestive elements in virtually all identification procedures, and with the exception of those rare situations like that in *Perry v. New Hampshire*, the police are usually responsible for any suggestive influences. (In *Perry*, as you'll recall, the perpetrator just happened to be standing near a police officer when a witness peered out the window and made the identification.) Accordingly, most defendants have little difficulty meeting the first two requirements for a successful due process challenge—proving that there was a suggestive identification procedure, and that it was arranged by the police.

The other two requirements—showing that the identification procedure was unnecessary and was so unreliable that it likely led to a misidentification—have been far more difficult to satisfy. In *Stovall v. Denno* and in *U.S. v. Simmons*, for example, the Supreme Court found that the identification procedures were necessary despite their suggestive features. In *Stovall*, the witness was severely injured and there was really no alternative to the hospital room showup arranged by police. And in *Simmons*, the perpetrators of a serious felony were still at large, and the FBI needed to know quickly if they were on the right track; there was no alternative means of identification other than the available photographs.

Even if a defendant satisfies the first three requirements for a due process challenge by proving that the police arranged a suggestive and unnecessary identification procedure, suppression of the identification is appropriate only if there was such a substantial likelihood of misidentification that the identification should be deemed unreliable. The due process challenges in *Simmons v. U.S.*, *Neil v. Biggers*, and *Manson v. Brathwaite* ultimately failed because the Court concluded, under the totality of the circumstances, that the identifications were reliable even though the procedures were suggestive.[b]

Due Process Challenges to Police Identification Procedures

1.   A defendant may challenge a police identification procedure by showing that it was so unnecessarily suggestive and conducive to irreparable mistaken identification as to constitute a denial of due process of law. In order to satisfy this burden, the defendant must show all of the following:

    a.   The identification procedure was suggestive.

    b.   The suggestive aspects of the identification were arranged by law enforcement.

    c.   The identification procedure was unnecessary.

    d.   The identification procedure created a substantial likelihood of misidentification, rendering the identification unreliable.

2.   In determining whether the identification procedure created a substantial likelihood of misidentification, the court must decide whether there are indicators of a witness' ability to make an accurate identification that outweigh the corrupting effect of law enforcement suggestion. Among the factors to be considered are:

    a.   The opportunity of the witness to view the criminal at the time of the crime.

    b.   The witness' degree of attention.

    c.   The accuracy of the witness' prior description of the criminal.

    d.   The level of certainty demonstrated at the confrontation.

    e.   The time between the crime and the confrontation.

3.   Where the indicators of a witness' ability to make an accurate identification are outweighed by the corrupting effect of law enforcement suggestion, the identification should be suppressed. But where the indicators show that the identification is reliable despite law enforcement's suggestive influences, the identification evidence is admissible and should be evaluated by the jury.

---

[b]   For an assessment and critique of the Supreme Court's approach to identification evidence in light of recent science in the field, *see* Gary L. Wells and Deah S. Quinlivan, *Suggestive Eyewitness Identification Procedures and the Supreme Court's Reliability Test in Light of Eyewitness Science: 30 Years Later*, 33 LAW AND HUMAN BEHAVIOR 1 (2009), available at http://public.psych.iastate.edu/glwells/Wells%20pdfs/2000-009/Wells_Quinlivan_2009_LHB.pdf.

D. ADDITIONAL SAFEGUARDS AGAINST MISIDENTIFICATION

Although a great deal of sophisticated research into the factors that can undermine the accuracy and reliability of human memory, identification procedures, and eyewitness testimony has been published in recent years, the Supreme Court's approach to the problem of misidentification has remained essentially static since the basic constitutional rules were first announced almost half a century ago in *U.S. v. Wade*, *Gilbert v. California*, and *Stovall v. Denno*.

Perry v. New Hampshire, 132 S.Ct. 716 (2012), excerpted above, was the Supreme Court's first significant eyewitness identification case in 35 years. In the months before the decision was released, there was some speculation that the Court might use the case to modify its approach and announce new guidelines that would require judges to more carefully screen identification evidence for reliability before allowing its use at trial. While the Court's decision in *Perry* was mindful of the most current research on eyewitness identifications, it did not, in the end, adopt any new rules to help ensure the reliability of identification evidence. Instead, the Court noted, there are a multitude of "other safeguards built into our adversary system that caution juries against placing undue weight on eyewitness testimony of questionable reliability." The Court summarized these safeguards as follows:

> [The] protections include the defendant's Sixth Amendment right to confront the eyewitness. Another is the defendant's right to the effective assistance of an attorney, who can expose the flaws in the eyewitness' testimony during cross-examination and focus the jury's attention on the fallibility of such testimony during opening and closing arguments. Eyewitness-specific jury instructions, which many federal and state courts have adopted, likewise warn the jury to take care in appraising identification evidence. The constitutional requirement that the government prove the defendant's guilt beyond a reasonable doubt also impedes convictions based on dubious identification evidence. State and federal rules of evidence, moreover, permit trial judges to exclude relevant evidence if its probative value is substantially outweighed by its prejudicial impact or potential for misleading the jury. In appropriate cases, some States also permit defendants to present expert testimony on the hazards of eyewitness identification evidence.

While the lower federal courts are constrained by the Supreme Court's pronouncements, state courts and legislatures have considerably more leeway to formulate new rules governing the admissibility of identification evidence in trials that occur within their respective state court systems. For example, in *State v. Henderson*, 208 N.J. 208 (2011), the New Jersey Supreme Court, acknowledging a "troubling lack of reliability in eyewitness identifications," and noting that "eyewitness misidentification is the leading cause of wrongful convictions across the country," announced sweeping new rules that make it easier for defendants to challenge identification evidence in criminal cases.[c] A year later, the New Jersey Supreme Court codified its decision in *Henderson* by releasing expanded jury instructions, a new court rule, and a revised court rule relating to eyewitness identifications in criminal cases. The following links describe in greater detail the recent changes in New Jersey's approach.

Recent Changes in New Jersey's Rules Governing Eyewitness Identification

New Jersey Supreme Court Press Release
http://www.judiciary.state.nj.us/pressrel/2012/pr120719a.htm

Expanded Jury Instructions
http://www.judiciary.state.nj.us/pressrel/2012/jury_instruction.pdf

New Court Rule
http://www.judiciary.state.nj.us/pressrel/2012/new_rule.pdf

Revised Court Rule
http://www.judiciary.state.nj.us/pressrel/2012/rev_rule.pdf

In addition to the traditional safeguards against unreliable identification evidence that are already part of the adversary system, and the dramatic new safeguards adopted in states like New Jersey, the use of expert testimony is an increasingly common means of challenging eyewitness identifications in criminal cases. These expert witnesses—often psychologists and scholars who are widely published in the complexities of memory and eyewitness identification—can provide compelling testimony on behalf of a defendant, helping the jury to understand how an apparently certain eyewitness identification might actually be the result of a lapse of memory, a mistake, or police suggestion. As a general rule, however, federal and state trial judges have a great deal of discretion in deciding whether to permit expert testimony of this sort, and because qualified experts typically charge for their services, they may be unaffordable for many criminal defendants.

In an effort to respond to the risks of misidentification, some law enforcement agencies have taken a proactive approach, relying on expert

---

[c] *See* Benjamin Weiser, *In New Jersey, Rules Are Changed on Witness IDs*, NEW YORK TIMES, August 24, 2011, available at http://www.nytimes.com/2011/08/25/nyregion/in-new-jersey-rules-changed-on-witness-ids.html.

recommendations to develop specific rules governing identification procedures in an effort to ensure greater accuracy and reduce the possibility of police suggestion. One technique that can improve accuracy and reduce the possibility of police suggestion is simply to tell the witness that the actual perpetrator may—or may not—be present in the lineup or photo array. If the witness knows there is a "none of the above" option, she may feel less pressure to make an uncertain identification. Another technique that can reduce the possibility of even unintentional police suggestion is blind administration, in which the identification procedure is conducted by an officer who is not involved in the investigation and who does not know the identity of the suspect. There are many other modest changes in the way identifications are conducted that can improve accuracy and reduce the possibility of police suggestion; some of these changes have already been adopted by police departments around the country.[d]

LEARN MORE WITH *LAW & ORDER*

In the following episode of *Law & Order* ("Acid," Season 16, Episode 10), police are investigating the apparent suicide of a young woman, Emily Newton, whose face was badly burned and permanently scarred by drain cleaner. As it turns out, police Lieutenant Anita Van Buren knows Emily's mother, Christine Hill, because they attended John Jay College together. The police learn that an angry ex-boyfriend, Jason Corley, was responsible for Emily's disfigurement. Police arrange a photo array, but Christine fails to identify Corley. Later, Christine does successfully identify Corley in a lineup, but shortly thereafter, while speaking privately with Van Buren, she recants because she fears for the safety of her remaining daughter, Callie. Van Buren doesn't disclose Christine's remarks, and the prosecution against Corley proceeds.

Corley's attorney asks for a *"Wade* hearing"—named after *U.S. v. Wade*, 388 U.S. 218 (1967)—in an effort to suppress the lineup identification. Van Buren testifies at the hearing, and admits that Christine failed to identify Corley in the photo array. The defense then exposes Van Buren's friendship with Emily Newton and her mother, Christine, and suggests that the close personal relationship may have tainted the lineup. During her testimony, Van Buren fails to disclose that Christine recanted her lineup identification.

---

[d] *See* Erica Goode and John Schwartz, *Police Lineups Start to Face Fact: Eyes Can Lie*, NEW YORK TIMES, August 28, 2011, available at http://www.nytimes.com/2011/08/29/us/29witness.html; *5 Suggested Techniques to Aid in Identifying Suspects*, NEW YORK TIMES, August 28, 2011, available at http://www.nytimes.com/2011/08/29/us/29witnessbox.html; Gary L. Wells, Amina Memon, and Steven D. Penrod, *Eyewitness Evidence: Improving Its Probative Value*, 7 PSYCHOLOGICAL SCIENCE IN THE PUBLIC INTEREST 45 (2006), available at https://www.psychologicalscience.org/journals/pspi/pspi_7_2_article.pdf

The *Wade* hearing stretches into a second day, and Van Buren does finally admit that Christine disavowed the lineup identification, but maintains that this was a result of intimidation by Corley rather than the product of police suggestion or a mistake. The judge ultimately suppresses the lineup identification due to Van Buren's near-perjury. With the identification inadmissible, the case against Corley collapses, and the police are compelled to develop other evidence to bring him to justice.

The segments of the episode that depict the relevant Investigative Criminal Procedure issues appear at:

13:48 to 15:06; 18:00 to 21:16; 23:14 to 35:03

Law & Order Episode
"Acid," Season 16, Episode 10

The *Law & Order* episode demonstrates two of the identification techniques—a photo array and a lineup—commonly used by police. Because both the photo array and the lineup took place before Corley was formally charged with the assault on Emily Newton, there was no violation of Corley's Sixth Amendment right to counsel. (In *U.S. v. Ash*, 413 U.S. 300 (1973), the Supreme Court held that a suspect is not entitled to have counsel present at *any* photo array, even one that takes place after criminal charges have been filed.) Accordingly, Corley's defense attorney is left only with a due process challenge to the lineup identification.

At the "*Wade* hearing," the defense attorney elicits from Van Buren that Christine failed to identify Corley in the photo array. Van Buren attempts to explain this away by noting that it was an old DMV photo. But the use of Corley's image in the photo array makes the subsequent lineup more suggestive, since Corley was the only person to appear in both the photo array and the lineup. In *Foster v. California*, 394 U.S. 440 (1969), for example, the witness failed to make an identification in the first lineup, but did make an identification in a second lineup a week later. In finding the identification suggestive and inadmissible, the Supreme Court noted that the suspect was the only person to appear in both lineups.

Corley's defense attorney also elicits testimony from Van Buren regarding her personal relationship with the crime victim and her mother. This, the defense attorney explains, may have resulted in "subtle pressures" during the lineup, and he asks the judge to order the other detectives present at the lineup to testify. When Van Buren admits, the following day, that Christine recanted shortly after the lineup, this casts further doubt on the accuracy of the initial identification.

The judge ultimately suppresses the lineup identification because there are a number of reasons to believe it may be mistaken or the product of improper suggestion: the witness failed to identify Corley at the photo array; Corley was the only person to appear in both the photo array and the lineup; Van Buren, present at the lineup, had a personal relationship with both the crime victim and the identifying witness; the witness recanted her identification shortly after the lineup; and Van Buren nearly committed perjury in failing to disclose the recantation.

Even when a defense attorney fails to obtain suppression of an identification, any suspicious facts and circumstances revealed at a *"Wade hearing"* can be brought out at trial through vigorous cross-examination of the witness and others present at the identification procedure. The jury would then be left to weigh the facts and determine what weight—if any—to give to the identification as evidence of the defendant's guilt.

INDEX

References are to Pages